THE DECLINE AND FALL
OF THE ROMAN EMPIRE

VOLUME I

THE
DECLINE AND FALL
OF THE
ROMAN EMPIRE

VOLUME I

EDWARD GIBBON

INTRODUCTION BY DANIEL J. BOORSTIN
A NOTE ON PIRANESI BY PAUL McPHARLIN

ILLUSTRATED FROM THE ETCHINGS BY GIAN BATTISTA PIRANESI

THE MODERN LIBRARY
NEW YORK

LIBRARY OF CONGRESS CATALOGING-IN-PUBLICATION DATA
Gibbon, Edward, 1737-1794.
[History of the decline and fall of the Roman Empire]
The decline and fall of the Roman Empire/Edward Gibbon; the text edited
by J. B. Bury, with the notes by Mr. Gibbon, the introduction and the index as
prepared by professor Bury; with an introduction by Daniel J. Boorstin; illustrated
from the etchings by Gian Battista Piranesi.
p.   cm.
Contents: v. 1. The history of the Empire from A.D. 98 to A.D. 395—
v. 2. The history of the Empire from A.D. 395 to A.D. 1185—
v. 3. The history of the Empire from A.D. 695 to A.D. 1430
ISBN 0-679-60148-1 (v. 1).—ISBN 0-679-60149-X (v. 2).—
ISBN 0-679-60150-3 (v. 3)
1. Rome—History—Empire, 30 B.C.-476 A.D.   2. Byzantine Empire—History.
I. Bury, J. B. (John Bagnell), 1861–1927.   II. Title.
DG311.G5   1995
937'.06—dc20   94-27080

INTRODUCTION
by Daniel J. Boorstin

HERE ARE MANY REASONS to admire Edward Gibbon's *History of the Decline and Fall of the Roman Empire*. Since it was first published in several volumes between 1776 and 1788, few books of history have been so widely or so indiscriminately praised. His twentieth-century editor, historian J. B. Bury, calls him "one of those few writers who hold as high a place in the history of literature as in the roll of great historians." Most students of history and of literature would agree.

Praise of Gibbon (1737–1794) has become especially fashionable with the rise of liberal and Marxist prejudices against religion. And, as pessimism has become increasingly fashionable about the future of our Western civilization, the *Decline and Fall of the Roman Empire* has become a handy guide to the sources of decay in other empires and civilizations. I will not enter the debate over the adequacy of Gibbon's explanations of the fall of Rome. Nor will I explore the easy—or uneasy—analogies between the career of the ancient Roman Empire and that of our modern Western civilization.

My interest in Gibbon's work is quite different. I will not assess it as a "great" book. Rather I will consider it as an "intimate" book. By this I mean a book that has something personal to say to us today. I am aware that it may seem odd to characterize a man of Gibbon's grandiloquence of phrase and a multivolume work on such a grandiose subject as "intimate."

For me personally Gibbon's book has an especially intimate significance. It was the first extensive work of English literature (or of history) which I read and reread. It occupied much of my thought during my university years as an undergraduate. And the engraving of Gibbon's rotund face, made by Chapman in 1807, a dozen years after his death, hangs on the wall of my study. Gibbon's face has been with me ever since I first made his acquaintance.

Gibbon's work can have an intimate, personal significance for all history readers and history writers in our age. He may help us discover some of the peculiar weaknesses and strengths of our way of looking at the past. To discover this intimacy we must try to see Gibbon not simply as a spokesman for the Enlightenment, nor his work as an effort to perfect one genre in the social sciences. Rather, let us think of him as an original, giving his own form to a large chunk of the past.

Toward this end it will help us at the outset to recognize a distinctive, if not entirely unique, feature of his place in the roll of great Western historians. Despite the wide popularity and continuity of Gibbon's audience, he seems not to have founded a "Gibbonian" school of historical interpretation. For example, the authoritative *International Encyclopedia of the Social Sciences,* which includes extensive articles on such lesser figures as Bryce, Burckhardt, Huizinga, Maitland, Ranke, Savigny, and Spengler, gives no such attention to Gibbon. Serious scholars do not doubt the originality or the significance of Gibbon's work. Still, he has not become the founder of a "school." He has not taken a place as the originator of any large new conceptual framework, or any novel way of pigeonholing the human past. I will suggest that this is a clue to the intimacy of his message about that past, and what he can tell each of us about the role of people in the grand chronicle of empires and civilizations.

The historical profession, with all its paraphernalia of learned societies and prestigious academic specialties, has grown up only since Gibbon's day. Not until the early nineteenth century did professional historians reach beyond the techniques of classical scholarship and textual criticism, to draw on the new disciplines of archaeology and philology, anthropology, sociology, and economics, to create new vocations of searchers for facts and movements and forces.

It is doubtful if there is another example in the social sciences of a work of similar longevity, respectability, and popularity, which has had so small a dogmatic or doctrinaire ingredient. The comprehensive historical works of recent years—those which are taken seriously by students of the social sciences—are heavily laced with dogma. I am thinking of the potent works, for example, of Macaulay, Carlyle, Marx, Pareto, Tawney, and Toynbee. These seem to owe much of their fame and their influence to the special charm of some new formulas to explain or contain historical experience.

How, then, can we explain the power and longevity and appeal of Gibbon, despite his lack of substantial original conceptual content?

In the first place, we must remember that Gibbon had the advantage of being an amateur. Unlike some other great interpreters of the past, many of whom were also amateurs, he was not enticed or driven to his subject by the urgencies of his time, or by a revolutionary, a religious, or a patriotic passion. In the original sense of the word "amateur," he was simply a lover of his subject. And in a famous passage in his memoirs he recalls the precise moment when, as he sat in the Colosseum in Rome, he first felt that passion. In another, less famous passage, he recalled his mixed emotions as that exacting love affair came to an end:

> It was on the night of June 27, 1787, between the hours of eleven and twelve, that I wrote the last lines of the last page, in a Summerhouse garden. . . . I will not dissemble the first emotions of joy on the recovery of my freedom, and perhaps, the establishment of my fame. But my pride was soon humbled, and a sober melancholy was spread over my mind, by the idea that I had taken an everlasting leave of an old and agreeable companion, and that whatsoever might be the future date of my History, the life of the historian must be short and precarious.

Like other great amateurs—and other lovers—he had taken his plunge without really being ready for it. He was not equipped by formal training for his work as a historian of the Roman Empire. His fourteen "unprofitable months" at Magdalen College, in an Oxford which, according to him, was "steeped in port and prejudice," did not give him the academic tools he needed. He lamented that his desultory training in Greek left him without the "scrupulous ear of the well-flogged critic." His work as an ancient historian was never part of the perfunctory duties of an academic post.

Except for this one passion, he was not a man of passionate commitment. At the age of sixteen he did commit himself to the Roman Catholic Church, but when he was sent to Lausanne by his father, his tutor there quickly brought him back to Protestantism. Despite his skepticism of established Christianity, he found it natural to be a Tory. He had the advantage of some political experience—as a member of Parliament and a commissioner of trade and plantations. His politics were prudent and pragmatic. He was a friend and admirer of Lord North, for whom he wrote a state paper against France in the years before the Revolution. When the American colonies protested the power of Parliament and began a civil war to break away, he believed that they were wrong. But, after the Battle of Saratoga made it plain that the ocean and independent enthusiasms had already separated the American colonies, he confessed that Lord North's costly efforts to subject the Americans were hopeless.

In an age that was filled with sycophants and that rewarded sycophancy, he did not dedicate his work to anyone—a fact for which he has not received the credit that is his due. He helps us understand why, and incidentally helps us share his vision of the significance of *people* in the vicissitudes of empire. He wrote these words in the preface to his fourth and final volume, published soon after Lord North had fallen from power:

Were I ambitious of any other Patron than the Public, I would inscribe this work to a Statesman, who in a long, a stormy, and at length an unfortunate administration, had many political opponents, almost without a personal enemy: who has retained, in his fall from power, many faithful and disinterested friends; and who, under the pressure of severe infirmity, enjoys the lively vigour of his mind, and the felicity of his incomparable temper. Lord North will permit me to express the feelings of friendship in the language of truth: but even truth and friendship should be silent, if he still dispensed the favours of the crown.

Gibbon remained uncommitted to any but his own opinions. The shrewd observer Horace Walpole, as he greeted the first volume of Gibbon's history with surprise as "a truly classic work," also noted that in Parliament Gibbon had been called "a whimsical because he votes variously as his opinion leads him. I . . . never suspected the extent of his talents, he is perfectly modest."

Gibbon's amorous commitments also were dominated by prudence and propriety. As a young man of twenty in Lausanne (1757) he became infatuated by the beautiful and witty Suzanne Curchod (1739–1794), then only eighteen. But when Gibbon's father objected, he broke off the engagement. Later she married Jacques Necker, the French financier and statesman, and established one of the celebrated salons of modern Paris. (*Their* daughter, incidentally, was the saloniste and prolific author, Madame de Staël!) Gibbon's broken engagement took place seven years before he conceived the *Decline and Fall.* What might Gibbon have done with his talents if, instead of listening to his father, he had shared his life with the charming Suzanne?

Gibbon once modestly declared that "diligence and accuracy are the only merits which an historical writer may ascribe to himself; if any merit indeed can be assumed from the performance of an indispensable duty." Yet the product of his twenty years' passion showed that a historical masterpiece required much more. Not least was his inexhaustible sense of wonder and his tolerant curiosity about the foibles of the human race. The cast of an eye, the excess of an appetite, the perversity of tastes, the beauty or deformity of stature—he witnessed all these with delight.

He managed with deceptive ease to translate the catastrophes of nature into parables of human nature. The earthquakes which shook the eastern Mediterranean on A.D. July 21, 365, led him to observe:

> . . . their affrighted imagination enlarged the real extent of a momentary evil. . . . And their fearful vanity was disposed to confound the symptoms of a declining empire and a sinking world. It was the fashion of the times to attribute every remarkable event to the particular will of the Deity; the alterations of nature were connected, by an invisible

chain, with the moral and metaphysical opinions of the human mind; and the most sagacious divines could distinguish, according to the colour of their respective prejudices, that the establishment of heresy tended to produce an earthquake, or that a deluge was the inevitable consequence of the progress of sin and error. Without presuming to discuss the truth or propriety of these lofty speculations, the historian may content himself with the observation, which seems to be justified by experience, that man has much more to fear from the passions of his fellow-creatures than from the convulsions of the elements.

The daily habits of remote and unfamiliar peoples help us understand their life-and-death commitments. Of the Scythians or Tartars he noted "with some reluctance" that "the pastoral manners which have been adorned with the fairest attributes of peace and innocence are much better adapted to the fierce and cruel habits of a military life." Their diet (not corn, but freshly slaughtered meat) and their light and easily moved tents both help us grasp that it was easy for them to behave as they did. "The exploits of the hunters of Scythia are not confined to the destruction of timid or innoxious beasts; they boldly encounter the angry wild boar, when he turns against his pursuers, excite the sluggish courage of the bear, and provoke the fury of the tiger, as he slumbers in the thicket." And so the nuances of human nature are newly revealed to us "on the immense plains of Scythia or Tartary."

Gibbon was fortunate to be born into an age when men of letters were expected to provide "amusement and instruction." The world of science—despite our clichés of an Age of Reason—was newly liberated from the medieval demand for meaning. In the Royal Society and other "invisible colleges" scientists, virtuosi, and amateurs were expanding the world with tiny increments of knowledge. Of course there were a few dazzlers, like Sir Isaac Newton. But the most important shift in attitude toward knowledge was from the interest in the cosmos to the interest in facts. Now it seemed possible for every man to become his own scientist. The telescope, the "flea glass" (microscope), the thermometer, and scores of other measuring devices were transforming experience into experiment. This new incremental approach to the physical world—spawning a wonderful newgrown wilderness of facts and contraptions—was also Gibbon's approach to the world of human nature. The time had not yet come when scientific quest for meaning threatened to transform the social world into another cosmos of dogmatic simplicities. Gibbon gives us incremental history on a grand scale.

For Gibbon, while human nature is anything but unintelligible, it remains only partly explicable. For him the menace to understanding was not so much ignorance as the illusion of knowledge. His explanations of rise and fall, of prosperity and decline are always *lists*. What he recounts is "the triumph of barbarism *and* religion." He recounts the quirks and quibbles of theologians, the rivalries of Eastern monarchs, their wives and mistresses and sons and daughters, not simply because they are amusing, but also because they are instructive. Without such trivia we cannot understand what the Eastern Empire was or what it became.

It is more accurate to insist that for Gibbon there are no trivia. Human habits, utterances, exclamations, and emotions are the very essence of his history—not mere raw material for distilling "forces" and "movements." The more vividly we see them, the better we know our subject. Inevitably, then, he must remain a skeptic about our capacity finally to grasp the whole story.

But despite—perhaps because of—this recognition, he is not a pessimist. The spectacle which he has unfolded of "the greatest, perhaps, and the most awful scene in the history of mankind" rewards us. He sees the whole planet as a stage for more grand spectacles, which will also be a stage for renewal. "If a savage conqueror should issue from the deserts of Tartary, he must repeatedly vanquish the robust peasants of Russia, the numerous armies of Germany, the gallant nobles of France, and the intrepid freemen of Britain; who, perhaps, might confederate for their common defence. Should the victorious Barbarians carry slavery and desolation as far as the Atlantic Ocean, ten thousand vessels would transport beyond their pursuit the remains of civilized society; and Europe would revive and flourish in the American world which is already filled with her colonies and institutions."

In his optimism Gibbon seems a spokesman for the Age of the Enlightenment. He seems, sometimes, to speak for a faith, burgeoning in his lifetime, that man's uninhibited critical faculties can grasp the world. I once thought of Gibbon in precisely that way. He spoke to me from and for a *period* of history. But in the years since Gibbon first spoke to me, he has come to say something more. He has become a more personal historian and hence more intimate, both in what he said and in what I hear.

Some eloquent outspoken prophets of the Age of Reason make it easy for historians to confine the epoch in that epithet. Among historians the great systematizers include such authors as Montesquieu (1689–1755) and Vico (1668–1744) and Voltaire (1694–1778). Of course these men—who are copiously treated in encyclopedias of the social sciences—still interest their fellow systematizers. Among the writers of narrative history in his epoch, Voltaire still speaks vividly to some of us. But his most popular contemporary competitors in narrative history—David Hume and William Robertson—have become historiographical antiques. Gibbon still can and does speak to all of us.

What he saw and what he accomplished was possible, he gladly acknowledged, only because of the peculiar opportunities of his place and time. "I shall ever glory in the name and character of an Englishman," he observed gratefully at the conclusion of his work, "I am proud of my birth in a free and enlightened country; and the approbation of that country is the best and most honourable reward for my labours." If he had not exploited the new opportunities and shared the new vistas of his age, he could not have given us his history. Yet his greatness, the intimate ingredient in his work, is his peculiar talent at transcending the characteristic enthusiasms of his age. Nowadays John Dryden and Alexander Pope and Jonathan Swift, and even Laurence Sterne and Henry Fielding, seem to have a certain quaintness. It is doubly remarkable that Edward Gibbon, whose style was at least as idiosyncratic as theirs, somehow manages to talk to us in our own idiom.

This is what I mean by the intimacy of Gibbon's *Decline and Fall.* Gibbon succeeds in this intimacy precisely because he does not offer us obsolescing parables of science or the social sciences. Nor is he stultified by the etiquette of a particular genre of literature. The chronological lopsidedness of his work—which gives more space to the first few centuries than to the last millennium of his thirteen-century tale—is itself a witness to his determination to shape the story, not by the a priori dimensions of centuries, but by his own concerns. He has the courage to juxtapose his lists of large causes with the minutiae of persons and places. He reminds us of our ties to the cosmos without pretending to unlock its secrets. He remains a modest man, refusing to carve neat channels where the course of history must flow. He lacks the conceit of the system builder, whose naïveté is revealed only with the centuries.

No historian has seen more vividly how nettlesome is the texture of the human past. Yet few have been bolder or more successful at grasping the nettle. He helps us share his pleasure at touching the random prickliness of experience. All this he does because he does not overestimate the dogmatic capacities of his own "enlightened age" nor does he underestimate the mystery of what remains untold and untellable.

At the end of his twenty years' voyage into the Roman Empire, he asks himself whether he should try another such voyage. With characteristic prudence he concludes that "in the repetition of similar attempts a successful Author has much more to lose, than he can hope to gain." Yet he insists that "the annals of ancient and modern times may afford many rich and interesting subjects. . . . To an active mind, indolence is more painful than labor." So he cheers us on, both readers and writers of history. For he, as much as any other writer in our language, reminds us that, even across the centuries and the oceans, people can talk to people about people. Just as Gibbon was not imprisoned in the jargon and special conceits of his age, so perhaps we need not be imprisoned in ours.

This essay appeared as "The Intimacy of Gibbon's *Decline and Fall*" in *Hidden History,* 1987.

A NOTE ON PIRANESI

When Gibbon was in Rome as a young man in 1764–1765, he may have visited a shop which was noted in the address book of many of his well-to-do countrymen. It was that of Giovanni Battista Piranesi in the Palazzo Tomati, where antique sculptures (expertly restored) were to be bought, and an excellent series of prints of the Roman landmarks could be purchased for so little as two and a half paoli apiece—about half a crown—say, a dollar today. Gibbon may not have laid out any money on these impressive etchings, inexpensive as they were, for he was doing the grand tour economically, on an allowance of £100 a year, which had to cover his own expenses and those of his tutor–traveling companion. But he must have lingered wishfully over the portfolios.

There is no record that he acquired any of these Roman views in later years when he was more affluent. He was not the sort to dress up his house for show or to stock his library with ornamental accessories. His snug workroom in Bentinck Street, London, eschewing the usual mahogany, had shelves painted blue and white, which probably took most of the wall space. He could not have framed and hung a series of Piranesi views, as Sir Walter Scott was presently to do in his dining room at Abbotsford. Nor was Gibbon's next library, in his house "La Grotte" at Lausanne, adapted for prints on the wall. In commenting on this room, or series of rooms, when he was making an addition to it, he wrote, "not forgetting the water closet, few authors of six Volumes in quarto will be more agreeably lodged than myself." He was apparently content without the mementos and pictures which seem appropriate for the professional writer's study, for his bookcases lined the walls, having solid wooden doors so that they could be locked like boxes. The southern windows overlooking Lake Geneva were the only pictures necessary.

(We know about "La Grotte" because it was still intact in the 1880's. The Geneva post office now occupies its site, and there is a balcony toward the lake over approximately the spot where Gibbon put the final touch to the *Decline and Fall* in his summerhouse one evening as the moon was rising. William Beckford, author of *Vathek* and caliph of Fonthill, to whom Piranesi dedicated a plate of an antique vase, had purchased the place, thousands of books and all, after Gibbon's death, "to have something to read," he remarked, "when I passed through Lausanne.")

A record exists of about four-fifths of the books that Gibbon possessed. He himself kept catalogues of them; that of the library at "La Grotte" is a card index, written on the backs of playing cards. Among these there were no bound volumes of Piranesi such as an English gentleman might have cherished as a souvenir of Rome. Gibbon was no sentimental collector. He bought only what he could use; once he had decided upon the subject that was to occupy most of his writing life, it was reference material. He had seen Rome. Why, therefore, squander money on views of it?

He had, in fact, seen more of the antique Rome than exists today. While there have been new excavations and clearances of Renaissance structures from old remains since his time, many ruins have also dwindled and vanished. Piranesi too saw Rome as it stood in the eighteenth century, columns deep in the rubbish of centuries, greenery sprouting from the architraves, and goats grazing where senators had paced. This Rome in its twilight, with the barefoot friars of St. Francis in the Temple of Jupiter, had wrought a strong spell on young Gibbon. "It was among the ruins of the Capitol that I first conceived the idea of a work which has amused and exercised near twenty years of my life."

At the period of Gibbon's grand tour Piranesi had reached the peak of his career. He had been elected a fellow of the British Society of Antiquarians in 1757. He was a good friend of the British architect Robert Adam, who caused nymphs of Herculaneum to appear on the mantlepieces of far-away Bath, and even those of Boston and Salem in New England. He dedicated many of his plates to the Englishmen and Scotchmen who found their way to his shop. He was shortly to be knighted by the pope, who had subsidized the series of Roman views and made gifts of it to visiting dignitaries. He was a scholarly artist, but he had a lively imagination, bringing the dry ruins that he loved to dramatic animation in his etchings.

Born in Venice 4 October 1720, the son of a stone-mason, he was educated as an architect, but found his medium of expression in images on paper, unhampered by the restrictions of actual building. Under Giuseppe Vasi, who had engraved a colossal view of Rome, he studied etching. He is supposed to have worked in the shop of the theatrical scene-painter Ferdinando Bibiena, whose palaces transcended stone. He may have been for a while in the studio of Tiepolo. All these influences he fused in his characteristic work.

Among his earliest etchings is a set of imaginary prisons, vast operatic backdrops of dungeons with heavy arches, endless flights of steps, ponderous chains, and murky instruments of torture. Coleridge and De Quincey were haunted with their opium-dream quality. Pure architectural inventions, they disclosed Piranesi's forte. He could imbue a stone structure with drama, to play upon the emotions. These fabulous edifices have not lost their power to this day; one finds echoes of them in a T. M. Cleland automobile advertisement, a Chirico painting, a Moscow subway station.

In 1748 Piranesi published a series of small prints, *Antichità Romane de' Tempi della Repubblica e de' primi Imperatori,* which included views of the forum, triumphal arches, the Coliseum, and temples. These were followed shortly by *Varie Vedute di Roma Antica e Moderna,* a series of larger size to which additions were made until it included 137 subjects. Some of these plates are over 18 by 28 inches, and their monumental scale of drawing makes the most of it. It is from among these two series that most of the illustrations in this edition of Gibbon have been selected. Additions have been made from other series, such as that of antique vases and candelabri, of fragments discovered in excavations, and from the maps which articulate the whole Roman scene as Piranesi knew it. He was vastly prolific of etchings, making about a thousand.

The views of Rome proved to be the most popular things that he ever did. Every tourist wanted a selection of them. Impression after impression was pulled from the etched plates. After Piranesi's death in 1778, two years after the publication of the first volume of the *Decline and Fall,* the plates, beginning to show signs of wear, were somewhat reworked with the graver and again bitten with acid to strengthen their lines; this was done by his sons Francesco and Pietro and his daughter Laura, who had helped in his shop, and who took the plates to Paris, transferring the family business there about 1800.

The prints here reproduced are from a fine set, bound up in calf gilt, with the label of Tessier, Rue de la Harpe, "Relieur et Doreur de la Trésorerie nationale, du Bureau de la Guerre, et de la Calcographie Piranesi à Paris." This would date them between 1800 and 1807. While they are not the very first impressions, they still have the lucidity that Piranesi would have wanted. There are impressions from plates so worn and so often re-etched as to be ruins themselves, so recent as Italy's entrance into the recent war. The plates are again in Rome, deposited in the Regia Calcografia. Modern impressions are mere ghosts, murky and sad.

When Piranesi drew a building he presented it as he felt it ought to look. He was not untruthful; like a portrait painter, he altered details in the interest of artistry while preserving the likeness. Every shrub in his forum may not be placed just where it grew, but the buildings are in their proper relationship and pretty much in their proper proportion. If they look gargantuan, it is because he shrank the human figures he placed in such thespian postures about them—an old trick still favoured by factory owners who show their plant on a letterhead. Piranesi did not hesitate to apply imagination when a decorative detail in the original had disappeared. But he was so conversant with ancient Rome that his friezes and rosettes were almost as good as the originals. In his shop he restored actual stonework. His customers preferred things whole.

Whether or not they met or knew each other's work, Gibbon and Piranesi are kindred artists, each giving pulsing life to his record. From a fragment of a palace or an anecdote of an emperor we are permitted to see the past in the bright definition of morning light. Both the historian and the etcher have the same knack of shifting time backwards and forwards, so that morning fades to sunset, sharp images waver and go out of focus, and one sees in successive moments, as in a dissolving view on a screen, Rome in pristine splendor and decrepit age. There is a note of doom in this magic lantern show. One sees the universality of decline and fall. But this is not mere brooding over death; the hope of rebirth is implicit.

Curiously enough, Piranesi was a romantic and Gibbon was a realist; of the two, Gibbon belonged more to the eighteenth century; Piranesi anticipated dream worlds which were alien to the Age of Reason. Yet both reshaped their material as they felt it ought to look; for a realist can skirt reality as gingerly as a romantic. However they modeled their forms, they arrived at the same heroic end. Curiously, again, they have had to wait a century and a half to share the same volumes.

Analysis of Piranesi's work has attracted several scholars. As authority for the present note, Arthur M. Hind's *Critical Study* of Piranesi is cited. Therein the Roman views are numbered and described, and his productions are considered in detail.

Research has found that the eighteenth century misidentified some of the Roman remains. Piranesi naturally titled his subjects according to the knowledge of his day; Gibbon knew the monuments by the same misnomers. The Temple of Vespasian was thought to be that of Jupiter Tonans; the Basilica of Constantine, the Temple of Peace; the Baths of Trajan, the Baths of Titus; and so on. For the plates of this edition the correct names are given, sometimes in juxtaposition with Piranesi's variants.

The greatest problem of translation lay in the names of monuments on the

map of the Fora. While Piranesi showed with reasonable accuracy the buildings still existing in his day, he indulged in broad flights of fancy when he
plotted the sites of those which were buried or gone. He made wonderfully-
patterned plans, but they are only that. His numbers have been assigned to
sites as we know them; and of course correct names are substituted for incorrect. This chore was undertaken by Francis W. Robinson, Curator of
European Art at the Detroit Institute of Arts, long a resident in Rome and
student of its antiquities. He has also helped with translating Piranesi's titles
and captions.

Many of the monuments depicted by Piranesi may be located on this map.
Some of them fall outside the region of the Fora, and some are of course outside Rome. If one were to take a tourist's walk he might begin with the
Roman Forum, as we do in the order of pictures in this first volume, and
proceed from the Capitol to the Coliseum. Then he would visit the adjoining
imperial Fora, the Cattle Market, the Palatine Hill, and finally get out to the
gates of the ancient city, with the aqueducts, roads, and tombs beyond. If
he had a chariot he might drive on to see the bridges, Tivoli with its falls, the
Villa of Maecenas and the Villa of Hadrian, and finally, with changes of
horses, Cori and Beneventum.

PAUL McPHARLIN

INTRODUCTION

Edward gibbon is one of those few who hold as high a place in the history of literature as in the roll of great historians. He concerns us here as an historian; our business is to consider how far the view which he has presented of the decline and fall of the Roman Empire can be accepted as faithful to the facts, and in what respects it needs correction in the light of discoveries which have been made since he wrote. But the fact that his work, composed more than a hundred years ago, is still successful with the general circle of educated people, and has not gone the way of Hume and Robertson, whom we laud as "classics" and leave on the cold shelves, is due to the singularly happy union of the historian and the man of letters. Gibbon thus ranks with Thucydides and Tacitus, and is perhaps the clearest example that brilliance of style and accuracy of statement—in Livy's case conspicuously divorced—are perfectly compatible in an historian.

His position among men of letters depends both on the fact that he was an exponent of important ideas and on his style. The appreciation of his style devolves upon the history of literature; but it may be interesting to illustrate how much attention he paid to it, by alterations which he made in his text. The first volume was published, in quarto form, in 1776, and the second quarto edition of this volume, which appeared in 1782, exhibits a considerable number of variants. Having carefully collated the two editions throughout the first fourteen chapters, I have observed that, in most cases, the changes were made for the sake not of correcting mis-statements of fact, but of improving the turn of a sentence, rearranging the dactyls and cretics, or securing greater accuracy of expression.

But Gibbon has his place in literature not only as the stylist, who never lays aside his toga when he takes up his pen, but as the expounder of a large and striking idea in a sphere of intense interest to mankind, and as a powerful representative of certain tendencies of his age. The guiding idea or "moral" of his history is briefly stated in his epigram: "I have described the triumph of barbarism and religion." In other words, the historical development of human societies, since the second century after Christ, was a retrogression (according to ordinary views of "progress"), for which Christianity was mainly to blame. This conclusion of Gibbon tended in the same direction as the theories of Rousseau; only, while Rousseau dated the decline from the day when men left Arcadia, Gibbon's era was the death of Marcus Aurelius.

We are thus taken into a region of speculation where every traveler must make his own chart. But to attempt to deny a general truth in Gibbon's point of view is vain; and it is feeble to deprecate his sneer. We may spare more sympathy than he for the warriors and the churchmen; but all that has since been added to his knowledge of facts has neither reversed nor blunted the point of the "Decline and Fall". Optimism of temperament may shut the eyes; faith, wedded to some "one increasing purpose" which it shrinks from grasping, may divert from the path of facts. But for an inquirer not blinded by religious prepossessions, or misled by comfortable sophistries, Gibbon really expounded one of the chief data with which the philosophy of history has to reckon. How are we to define progress? how recognize retrogression? What is the end in relation to which such words have their meaning, and is there a law which will explain "the triumph of barbarism and religion" as a necessary moment in a reasonable process towards that end, whatever it may be? Answers have been given since Gibbon's day, engaging to the intellect, but always making some demand on the faith—answers for which he would have the same smile as for Leo's Dogmatic Epistle. There is certainly some reason for thinking these questions insoluble. We may say at least that the meaning of the philosophy of history is misapprehended until it is recognized that its function is not to solve problems but to transform them.

But, though the moral of Gibbon's work has not lost its meaning yet, it is otherwise with the particular treatment of Christian theology and Christian institutions. Our point of view has altered, and, if Gibbon were writing now, the tone of his "candid and rational inquiry" would certainly be different. His manner would not be that of sometimes open, sometimes transparently veiled, dislike; he would rather assume an attitude of detachment. He would be affected by that merely historical point of view, which is a note of the present century and its larger tolerances; and more than half disarmed by that wide diffusion of unobtrusive scepticism among educated people, which seems to render offensive warfare superfluous. The man of letters admires the fine edge of subtle sarcasm, wielded by Gibbon with such skill and effect; while the historian is interested in an historical standpoint of the last century. Neither the historian nor the man of letters will any longer subscribe, without a thousand reserves, to the theological chapters of the "Decline and Fall," and no discreet inquirer would go there for his ecclesiastical history. Yet we need not hide the fact that Gibbon's success has in a large measure been due to his scorn for the Church; which, most emphatically expressed in the theological chapters, has, as one might say, spiced his book. The attack of a man, equipped with erudition, and of perfectly sober judgment, on cherished beliefs and revered institutions, must always excite the interest, by irritating the passions, of men. Gibbon's classical moderation of judgment, his temperate mood, was responsible, as well as foreign education and the influence of French thought, for his attitude to Christianity and to Mahometanism. He hated excess, and the immoderation of the multitude. He could suffer the tolerant piety of a learned abbé or "the fat slumbers of the Church"; but with the religious faith of a fanatical populace or the ardour of its demagogues his reason was unable to sympathize. In the spirit of Cicero or Tacitus he despised the superstitions of the vulgar, and regarded the unmeasured enthusiasm of the early Christians as many sober Churchmen regard the fanaticism of Islam. He dealt out the same measure to the opposite enthusiasm of Julian the Apostate. His work was all the more effective, because he was never dogmatic himself. His irony should not be construed as insincerity, but rather as showing that he was profoundly—one might say, constitutionally—convinced of the truth of that sceptical conclusion which has been, in a different spirit, formulated precisely by the Bishop of Oxford; "there is no room for sweeping denunciations or trenchant criticisms in the dealings of a world whose falsehoods and veracities are separated by so very thin a barrier".

Thus Gibbon's attitude to religion, while it was conditioned by the intellectual atmosphere of Europe in that age, was also the expression of the man. When Dean Milman spoke of his "bold and disingenuous attack on Christianity," he made one of those futile charges which it would be impossible to prove and impossible to disprove; such imputations as are characteristic of theologians in the heat of controversy and may be condoned to politicians in the heat of electioneering, but in an historical critic are merely an impertinence.

It has sometimes been remarked that those histories are most readable which are written to prove a thesis. The indictment of the Empire by Tacitus, the defence of Cæsarianism by Mommsen, Grote's vindication of democracy, Droysen's advocacy of monarchy, might be cited as examples. All these writers intended to present the facts as they took place, but all wrote with prepossessions and opinions, in the light of which they interpreted the events of history. Arnold deliberately advocated such partiality on the ground that "the past is reflected to us by the present and the party-man feels the present most." Another Oxford Regius Professor remarked that "without some infusion of spite it seems as if history could not be written." On the other side stands the formula of Ranke as to the true task of the historian: "Ich will bloss sagen wie es eigentlich gewesen ist." The *Greek History* of Bishop Thirlwall, the *English Constitutional History* of Bishop Stubbs himself, were written in this spirit. But the most striking instances perhaps, because they tread with such light feet on the treacherous ashes of more recent history, are Ranke and Bishop Creighton. Thucydides is the most ancient example of this historical reserve. It cannot be said that Gibbon sat down to write with any ulterior purpose, but, as we have seen, he allowed his temperament to colour his history, and used it to prove a congenial thesis. But, while he put things in the light demanded by this thesis, he related his facts accurately. If we take into account the vast range of his work, his accuracy is amazing. He laboured under some disadvantages, which are set forth in his own Memoirs. He had not enjoyed that school and university training in the languages and literatures of Greece and Rome which is probably the best preparation for historical research. His knowledge of Greek was imperfect; he was very far from having the "scrupulous ear of the well-flogged critic". He has committed errors of translation, and was capable of writing "Gregory of Nazianzen". But such slips are singularly few. Nor is he accustomed to take lightly quotations at second hand; like that famous passage of Eligius of Noyon—held up by Arnold as a warning—

which Robertson and Hallam successively copied from Mosheim, where it had appeared in a garbled form, to prove exactly the opposite of its true meaning.

From one curious inaccuracy, which neither critics nor editors seem to have observed, he must, I think, be acquitted. In his account of the disturbances in Africa and Egypt in the reign of Diocletian, we meet the following passage:—

> "Julian had assumed the purple at Carthage. Achilleus at Alexandria, and even the Blemmyes, renewed, or rather continued, their incursions into the Upper Egypt."

Achilleus arose at this time (295-6 A.D.) as a tyrant at Alexandria; but that he made either at this date or at any previous date an incursion into the Upper Egypt, there is not a trace of evidence in our authorities. I am convinced, however, that this error was not originally due to the author, but merely a treacherous misprint, which was overlooked by him in correcting the proof sheets, and which has also escaped the notice of his editors. By a slight change in punctuation we obtain a perfectly correct statement of the situation:—

> "Julian had assumed the purple at Carthage, Achilleus at Alexandria; and even the Blemmyes renewed, or rather continued, their incursions into the Upper Egypt."

I have no doubts that this was the sentence originally meant and probably written by Gibbon, and have felt no scruple in extirpating the inveterate error from the text.

Gibbon's diligent accuracy in the use of his materials cannot be over-praised, and it will not be diminished by giving the due credit to his French predecessor Tillemont. The *Histoire des Empereurs* and the *Mémoires ecclésiastiques,* laborious and exhaustive collections of material, were addressed to the special student and not to the general reader, but scholars may still consult them with profit. It is interesting to find Mommsen in his later years retracting one of his earlier judgments and reverting to a conclusion of Tillemont. In his recent edition of the Laterculus of Polemius Silvius, he writes thus:—

> "L'auteur de la Notice—peritissimi Tillemontii verba sunt (hist. 5, 699)—vivoit en Occident et ne savoit pas trop l'état où estoit l'Orient; *ei iuvenis contradixi hodie subscribo.*"

It is one of Gibbon's merits that he made full use of Tillemont, "whose inimitable accuracy almost assumes the character of genius," as far as Tillemont guided him, up to the reign of Anastasius I.; and it is only just to the mighty work of the Frenchman to impute to him a large share in the accuracy which the English-man achieved. From the historical, though not from the literary, point of view, Gibbon, deserted by Tillemont, distinctly declines, though he is well sustained through the wars of Justinian by the clear narrative of Procopius.

Recognizing that Gibbon was accurate, we do not acknowledge by implication that he was always right; for accuracy is relative to opportunities. The discovery of new materials, the researches of numerous scholars, in the course of a hundred years, have not only added to our knowledge of facts, but have modified and upset conclusions which Gibbon with his materials was justified in drawing. Compare a chapter or two of Mr. Hodgkin's *Italy and her Invaders* with the corresponding episode in Gibbon, and many minor points will appear in which correction has been needful. If Gibbon were alive and writing now, his history would be very different. Affected by the intellectual experiences of the past century he could not adopt quite the same historical attitude; and we should consequently lose the colouring of his brilliant attack on Christianity. Again, he would have found it an absolute necessity to learn what he insolently called that "barbarous idiom," the German language; and this might have affected his style as it would certainly have affected his matter. We dare not deplore Gibbon's limitations, for they were the conditions of his great achievement.

Not the least important aspect of the *Decline and Fall* is its lesson in the unity of history, the favourite theme of Mr. Freeman. The title displays the cardinal fact that the Empire founded by Augustus fell in 1461; that all the changes which transformed the Europe of Marcus Aurelius into the Europe of Erasmus had not abolished the name and memory of the Empire. And whatever names of contempt—in harmony with his thesis—Gibbon might apply to the institution in the period of its later decline, such as the "Lower Empire," or "Greek Empire," his title rectified any false impressions that such language might cause. On the continuity of the Roman Empire depended the unity of his work. By the emphasis laid on this fact he did the same kind of service to the study of history in England, that Mr. Bryce has done in his *Holy Roman Empire* by tracing the thread which connects the Europe of Francis the Second with the Europe of Charles the Great.

Gibbon read widely, and had a large general knowledge of history, which supplied him with many happy illustrations. It is worth pointing out that the gap in his knowledge of ancient history was the period of the Diadochi and Epigoni. If he had been familiar with that period, he would not have said that Diocletian was the first to give to the world the example of a resignation of sovereignty. He would have referred to the conspicuous case of Ptolemy Soter; Mr. Freeman would have added Lydiadas, the tyrant of Megalopolis. Of the earlier example of Asarhaddon Gibbon could not have known.

To pass from scope and spirit to method, Gibbon's historical sense kept him constantly right in dealing with his sources, but he can hardly be said to have treated them methodically. The growth of German erudition is one of the leading features of the intellectual history of the nineteenth century; and one of its most important contributions to historical method lies in the investigation of sources. German scholars have indeed pressed this "Quellenkunde" further than it can safely be pressed. A philologist, writing his doctoral dissertation, will bring plausible reasons to prove where exactly Diodorus ceased to "write out" Ephorus, whose work we do not possess, and began to write out somebody else, whose work is also lost to us. But, though the method lends itself to the multiplication of vain subtleties, it is absolutely indispensable for scientific historiography. It is in fact part of the science of evidence. The distinction of primary and derivative authorities might be used as a test. The untrained historian fails to recognize that nothing is added to the value of a statement of Widukind by its repetition by Thietmar or Ekkehard, and that a record in the Continuation of Theophanes gains no further credibility from the fact that it likewise occurs in Cedrenus, Zonaras or Glycas.

While evidence is more systematically arranged, greater care is bestowed on sifting and probing what our authorities say, and in distinguishing contemporary from later witnesses. Not a few important results have been derived from such methods; they enable us to trace the growth of stories. The evidence against Faustina shrinks into nothing; the existence of Pope Joan is exploded. It is irrelevant to condemn a statement of Zonaras as made by a "modern Greek". The question is, where did he get it?

The difficult questions connected with the authorship and compilation of the *Historia Augusta* have produced a chestful of German pamphlets, but they did not trouble Gibbon. The relationships of the later Greek chronicles and histories are more difficult and intricate even than the questions raised by the *Historia Augusta,* but he did not even formulate a prudent interrogation. Fer-

dinand Hirsch, twenty years ago, cleared new roads through this
forest, in which George the Monk and the Logothete who continued him, Leo Grammaticus and Simeon Magister, John Scylitzes, George Cedrenus and Zonaras lived in promiscuous obscurity. Büttner-Wobst on one side, C. de Boor on the other, have been
working effectually on the same lines, clearing up the haze which
surrounds George the Monk—the time has gone by for calling him
George Hamartolus. Another formidable problem, that of John
Malalas—with his namesake John of Antioch, so hard to catch,—
having been grappled with by Jeep, Sotiriadês and others, is now
being more effectively treated by Patzig.

Criticism, too, has rejected some sources from which Gibbon
drew without suspicion. In the interest of literature we may perhaps be glad that like Ockley he used with confidence the now dis-
credited Al Wakidi. Before such maintained perfection of manner, to choose is hard; but the chapters on the origin of Mahometanism and its first triumphs against the Empire would alone be
enough to win perpetual literary fame. Without Al Wakidi's romance they would not have been written; and the historian, compelled to regard Gibbon's description as he would a Life of Charles
the Great based on the monk of St. Gall, must refer the inquirer
after facts to Sprenger's *Life of Mahomet* and Weil's *History of the
Caliphs.*

In connexion with the use of materials, reference may be made
to a mode of proceeding which Gibbon has sometimes adopted
and which modern method condemns. It is not legitimate to blend
the evidence of two different periods in order to paint a complete
picture of an institution. Great caution, for example, is needed in
using the Greek epics, of which the earliest and latest parts differ
by a long interval, for the purpose of portraying a so-called Hom-
eric or heroic age. A notice of Fredegarius will not be necessarily
applicable to the age of the sons and grandsons of Chlodwig, and
a custom which was familiar to Gregory or Venantius may have
become obsolete before the days of the last Merwings. It is instructive to compare Gibbon's description of the social and political institutions of our Teutonic forefathers with that of Bishop Stubbs.
Gibbon blends together with dexterity the evidence of Cæsar and
Tacitus, between whom a century had elapsed, and composes a
single picture; whereas Bishop Stubbs keeps the statements of the
two Romans carefully apart, and by comparing them is able to
show that in certain respects the Germans had developed in the

interval. Gibbon's account of the military establishment of the Empire, in the first chapter of his work, is open to a like objection. He has blended, without due criticism, the evidence of Vegetius with that of earlier writers.

In the study of sources, then, our advance has been great, while the labours of an historian have become more arduous. It leads us to another advance of the highest importance. To use historical documents with confidence, an assurance that the words of the writer have been correctly transmitted is manifestly indispensable. It generally happens that our texts have come down in several MSS., of different ages, and there are often various discrepancies. We have then to determine the relations of the MSS. to each other and their comparative values. To the pure philologist this is part of the alphabet of his profession; but the pure historian takes time to realize it, and it was not realized in the age of Gibbon as it is to-day. Nothing forces upon the historian the necessity of having a sound text so impressively as the process of comparing different documents in order to determine whether one was dependent on another,—the process of investigating sources. In this respect we have now to be thankful for many blessings denied to Gibbon and —so recent is our progress—denied to Milman and Finlay. We have Mommsen's editions of Jordanes and the *Variae* of Cassiodorius, his *Chronica Minora* (still incomplete), including, for instance, Idatius, the Prospers, Count Marcellinus; we have Peter's *Historia Augusta,* Gardthausen's *Ammianus,* Luetjohann's *Sidonius Apollinaris;* Du Chesne's *Liber Pontificalis;* and a large number of critical texts of ecclesiastical writers might be mentioned. The Greek historians have been less fortunate. The Bonn edition of the *Byzantine Writers,* issued under the auspices of Niebuhr and Bekker in the early part of this century, was the most lamentably feeble production ever given to the world by German scholars of great reputation. It marked no advance on the older folio edition, except that it was cheaper, and that one or two new documents were included. But there is now a reasonable prospect that we shall by degrees have a complete series of trustworthy texts. De Boor showed the way by his spendid edition of Theophanes and his smaller texts of Theophylactus Simocatta and the Patriarch Nicephorus. Mendelssohn's Zosimus, and Reifferscheid's Anna Comnena stand beside them. Haury promises a Procopius, and we are expecting from Seger a long desired John Scylitzes, the greater part of whose text, though existing in a MS. at Paris, has never been printed and can only be inferred by a comparison of the Latin translation of Gabius with the chronicle of Cedrenus, who copied him with faithful servility.

The legends of the Saints, though properly outside the domain of the historian proper, often supply him with valuable help. For "Culturgeschichte" they are a direct source. Finlay observed that the *Acta Sanctorum* contain an unexplored mine for the social life of the Eastern Empire. But before they can be confidently dealt with, trained criticism must do its will on the texts; the relations between the various versions of each legend must be defined and the tradition in each case made clear. The task is huge; the libraries of Europe and Hither Asia are full of these holy tales. But Usener has made a good beginning and Krumbacher has rendered the immense service of pointing out precisely what the problems are.

Besides improved methods of dealing with the old material, much new material of various kinds has been discovered, since the work of Gibbon. To take one department, our coins have increased in number. It seems a pity that he who worked at his Spanheim with such diligence was not able to make use of Eckhel's great work on Imperial coinage which began to appear in 1792 and was completed in 1798. Since then we have had Cohen, and the special works of Saulcy and Sabatier. M. Schlumberger's splendid study of Byzantine sigillography must be mentioned in the same connexion.

The constitution and history of the Principate, and the provincial government of the early Emperors, have been placed on an entirely new basis by Mommsen and his school. The *Römisches Staatsrecht* is a fabric for whose rearing was needed not only improved scholarship but an extensive collection of epigraphic material. The Corpus of Latin Inscriptions is the keystone of the work.

Hence Gibbon's first chapters are somewhat "out of date." But on the other hand his admirable description of the change from the Principate to absolute Monarchy, and the system of Diocletian and Constantine, is still most valuable. Here inscriptions are less illustrative, and he disposed of much the same material as we, especially the *Codex Theodosianus*. New light is badly wanted, and has not been to any extent forthcoming, on the respective contributions of Diocletian and Constantine to the organization of the new monarchy. As to the arrangement of the provinces we have indeed a precious document in the Verona List (published by Mommsen), which, dating from 297 A.D., shows Diocletian's reorganization.

The modifications which were made between this year and the beginning of the fifth century when the Notitia Dignitatum was drawn up, can be largely determined not only by lists in Rufus and Ammianus, but, as far as the eastern provinces are concerned, by the Laterculus of Polemius Silvius. Thus, partly by critical method applied to Polemius, partly by the discovery of a new document, we are enabled to rectify the list of Gibbon, who adopted the simple plan of ascribing to Diocletian and Constantine the detailed organization of the Notitia. Otherwise our knowledge of the changes of Diocletian has not been greatly augmented; but our clearer conception of the Principate and its steady development towards pure monarchy has reflected light on Diocletian's system; and the tendencies of the third century, though still obscure at many points, have been made more distinct. The year of the Gordians is still as great a puzzle as ever; but the dates of Alexandrine coins with the tribunician years give us here, as elsewhere, limits of which Gibbon was ignorant. While speaking of the third century, I may add that Calpurnius Siculus, whom Gibbon claimed as a contemporary of Carinus, has been restored by modern criticism to the reign of Nero, and this error has vitiated some of Gibbon's pages.

The constitutional history of the Empire from Diocletian forward has still to be written systematically. Some noteworthy contributions to this subject have been made by Russian scholars.

Gibbon's forty-first chapter is still not only famous, but admired by jurists as a brief and brilliant exposition of the principles of Roman law. To say that it is worthy of the subject is the best tribute that can be paid to it. A series of foreign scholars of acute legal ability has elaborated the study of the science in the present century; I need only refer to such names as Savigny and Jhering. A critical edition of the Corpus juris Romani by Mommsen himself has been one of the chief contributions. The manuscript of Gaius is the new discovery to be recorded; and we can imagine with what interest Gibbon, were he restored to earth, would compare in Gneist's parallel columns the Institutions with the elder treatise.

But whoever takes up Gibbon's theme now will not be content with an exposition of the Justinianean Law. He must go on to its later development in the subsequent centuries, in the company of Zachariä von Lingenthal and Heimbach. Such a study has been made possible and comparatively easy by the magnificent works of Zachariä; among whose achievements I may single out the restoration of the Ecloga, which used to be ascribed to Leo VI., to its true author Leo III.; a discovery which illuminated in a most welcome manner the Isaurian reformation. It is interesting to observe that the last work which engaged him even on his death-bed was an attempt to prove exactly the same thing for the military treatise known as the Tactics of Leo VI. Here too Zachariä thinks that Leo was the Isaurian, while the received view is that he was the "Philosopher."

Having illustrated by examples the advantages open to an historian of the present day, which were not open to Gibbon, for dealing with Gibbon's theme,—improved and refined methods, a closer union of philology with history, and ampler material—we may go on to consider a general defect in his treatment of the Later Empire, and here to exhibit, by a few instances, progress made in particular departments.

Gibbon ended the first half of his work with the so-called fall of the Western Empire in 476 A.D.—a date which has been fixed out of regard for Italy and Rome, and should strictly be 480 A.D. in consideration of Julius Nepos. Thus the same space is devoted to the first three hundred years which is allowed to the remaining nine hundred and eighty. Nor does the inequality end here. More than a quarter of the second half of the work deals with the first two of these ten centuries. The mere statement of the fact shows that the history of the Empire from Heraclius to the last Grand Comnenus of Trebizond is merely a sketch with certain episodes more fully treated. The personal history and domestic policy of all the Emperors, from the son of Heraclius to Isaac Angelus, are compressed into one chapter. This mode of dealing with the subject is in harmony with the author's contemptuous attitude to the "Byzantine" or "Lower" Empire.

But Gibbon's account of the internal history of the Empire after Heraclius is not only superficial; it gives an entirely false impression of the facts. If the materials had been then as well sifted and studied as they are even to-day, he could not have failed to see that beneath the intrigues and crimes of the Palace there were deeper causes at work, and beyond the revolutions of the Capital City wider issues implied. The cause for which the Iconoclasts contended involved far more than an ecclesiastical rule or usage; it meant, and they realized it, the regeneration of the Empire. Or, to take another instance: the key to the history of the tenth and eleventh centuries is the struggle between the Imperial throne and the great landed interests of Asia Minor; the accession of Alexius Commenus marked the final victory of the latter. Nor had Gibbon any conception of the great ability of most of the Emperors from Leo the Isaurian to Basil II., or, we might say, to Constantine the conqueror of Armenia. The designation of the story of the later Empire as a "uniform tale of weakness and misery" is one of the most untrue, and most effective, judgments ever uttered by a thoughtful historian. Before the outrage of 1204, the Empire was the bulwark of the West.

Against Gibbon's point of view there has been a gradual reaction which may be said to have culminated within the last ten years of the nineteenth century. It was begun by Finlay, whose unprosperous speculations in Greece after the Revolution prompted him to seek for the causes of the insecurity of investments in land, and, leading him back to the year 146 B.C., involved him in a history of the "Byzantine Empire" which embedded a history of Greece. The great value of Finlay's work lies not only in its impartiality and in his trained discernment of the commercial and financial facts underlying the superficial history of the chronicles, but in its full and trustworthy narration of the events. By the time that Mr. Tozer's edition appeared in 1876, it was being recognized that Gibbon's word on the later Empire was not the last. Meanwhile Hertzberg was going over the ground in Germany, and Gfrörer, whose ecclesiastical studies had taken him into those regions, had written a good deal of various value. Hirsch's *Byzantinische Studien* had just appeared, and Rambaud's *l'Empire grec au xme siècle*. M. Sathas was bringing out his *Bibliotheca Græca medii aevi*—including two volumes of Psellus—and was beginning his *Documents inédits*. Professor Lambros was working at his *Athens in the Twelfth Century* and preparing his editio princeps of the great Archbishop Akominatos. Hopf had collected a mass of new materials from the archives of southern cities. In England, Freeman was pointing out the true position of New Rome and her Emperors in the history of Europe.

These tendencies increased in volume and velocity within the last twenty years of the nineteenth century. They may be said to have reached their culminating point in the publication of Professor Krumbacher's *History of Byzantine Literature*. The importance of this work, of vast scope and extraordinary accuracy, can only be fully understood by the specialist. It has promoted and facilitated the progress of the study in an incalculable measure;

xxxi

and it was followed by the inauguration of a journal, entirely devoted to works on "Byzantine" subjects, by the same scholar. The *Byzantinische Zeitschrift* would have been impossible at an earlier period, and nothing shows more surely the turn of the tide. Professor Krumbacher's work formed as important an epoch as that of Ducange.

Meanwhile in a part of Europe which deems itself to have received the torch from the Emperors as it has received their torch from the Patriarchs, and which has always had a special regard for the city of Constantine, some excellent work was being done. In Russia, Muralt edited the chronicle of George the monk and his Continuers, and compiled Byzantine Fasti. The Journal of the Ministry of Public Instruction is the storehouse of a long series of most valuable articles dealing, from various sides, with the history of the later Empire, by those indefatigable workers Uspenski and Vasilievski. At length, in 1894, Krumbacher's lead has been followed, and the *Vizantiski Vremennik,* a Russian counterpart of the *Byzantinische Zeitschrift,* has been started under the joint editorship of Vasilievski and Regel, and is clearly destined, with the help of Veselovski, Kondakov, Bieliaiev and the rest of a goodly fellowship, to make its mark.

After this general sketch of the new prospects of later Imperial history, it will be useful to show by some examples what sort of progress is being made, and what kind of work has to be done. I will first take some special points of interest connected with Justinian. My second example shall be the topography of Constantinople; and my third the large field of literature composed in colloquial Greek. Lastly, the capital defect of the second half of Gibbon's work, his inadequate treatment, or rather his neglect, of the Slavs, will serve to illustrate our historical progress.

New light has been cast, from more than one side, on the reign of Justinian, where there are so many uncertain and interesting places. The first step that methodical history had to take was a thoroughgoing criticism of Procopius, and this was more than half done by Dahn in his elaborate monograph. The double problem of the *Secret History* has stimulated the curiosity of the historian and the critic. Was Procopius the author? and in any case, are the statements credible? Gibbon has inserted in his notes the worst bits of the scandals which far outdid the convivium quinquaginta meretricum described by Burchard, or the feast of Sophonius Tigellinus; and he did not hesitate to believe them. Their credibility is now generally questioned, but the historian of Cæsarea is a much more interesting figure if it can be shown that he was the author. From a careful comparison of the *Secret History* with the works of Procopian authorship, in point of style, Dahn concluded that Procopius wrote it. Ranke argued against this view and maintained that it was the work of a malcontent who had obtained possession of a private diary of Procopius, on which framework he constructed the scandalous chronicle, imitating successfully the Procopian style.

The question has been placed on a new footing by Haury; and it is very interesting to find that the solution depends on the right determination of certain dates. The result is briefly as follows:—

Procopius was a malcontent who hated Justinian and all his works. He set himself the task of writing a history of his time, which, as the secretary of Belisarius, he had good opportunities of observing. He composed a narrative of the military events, in which he abstained from committing himself, so that it could be safely published in his own lifetime. Even here his critical attitude to the government is sometimes clear. He allows it to be read between the lines that he regarded the reconquest of Africa and Italy as calamities for those countries; which thus came under an oppressor, to be stripped by his governors and tax gatherers. But the domestic administration was more dangerous ground, on which Procopius could not tread without raising a voice of bitter indignation and hatred. So he dealt with this in a book which was to be kept secret during his own life, and bequeathed to friends who might be trusted to give it to the world at a suitable time. The greater part of the *Military History,* which treated in seven Books the Persian, Vandalic, and Gothic wars, was finished in 545 A.D., and perhaps read to a select circle of friends; at a later time some additions were made, but no changes in what had been already written. The *Secret History,* as Haury has proved from internal evidence, was written in 550. About three years later the *Military History* received an eighth Book, bringing the story down to the end of the Gothic war. Then the work came under the notice of Justinian, who saw that a great historian had arisen; and Procopius, who had certainly not described the wars for the purpose of pleasing the Emperor, but had sailed as close to the wind as he dared, was called upon to undertake the disagreeable task of lauding the oppressor. An Im-

perial command was clearly the origin of the *De Aedificiis* (560
A.D.), in which the reluctant writer adopted the plan of making
adulation so fulsome, that, except to Justinian's vanity, he might
appear to be laughing in his sleeve. At the very beginning of the
treatise he has a sly allusion to the explosives which were lying in
his desk, unknown to the Imperial spies.

Such is the outline of the literary motives of Procopius as we
must conceive them, now that we have a practical certainty that
he, and no other, wrote the *Secret History*. For Haury's dates enable us, as he points out, to argue as follows: If Procopius did not
write the book, it was obviously written by a forger, who wished
it to pass as a Procopian work. But in 550 no forger could have had
the close acquaintance with the *Military History* which is exhibited
by the author of the Anecdota. And moreover the identity of the
introduction of the eighth Book of the *Military History* with that
of the *Secret History,* which was urged by Ranke as an objection
to the genuineness of the latter work, now tells decisively in favor
of it. For if Procopius composed it in 553, how could a forger, writing in 550, have anticipated it? And if the forger composed it in
550, how are we to explain its appearances in a later work of Procopius himself? These considerations put it beyond all reasonable
doubt that Procopius was the author of the *Secret History;* for this
assumption is the only one which supplies an intelligible explanation of the facts.

Another puzzle in connexion with Justinian lay in certain biographical details relating to that emperor and his family, which
Alemanni, in his commentary on the *Secret History,* quoted on
the authority of a Life of Justinian by a certain Abbot Theophilus,
said to have been the Emperor's preceptor. Of these biographical
notices, and of Justinian's preceptor Theophilus, we otherwise
knew nothing; nor had any one, since Alemanni, seen the Biography. Gibbon and other historians accepted without question the
statements quoted by Alemanni; though it would have been wiser
to treat them with more reserve, until some data for criticizing
them were discovered. The puzzle of Alemanni's source, the Life
of Theophilus, was solved by Mr. Bryce, who discovered in the library of the Barbarini palace at Rome the original text from which
Alemanni drew his information. It professes to be an extract from
a Slavonic work, containing the Life of Justinian up to the thirtieth year of his reign, composed by Bogomil, abbot of the monastery of St. Alexander in Dardania. This extract was translated by

Marnavich, Canon of Sebenico (afterwards Bishop of Bosnia, 1631-1639), a friend of Alemanni, and some notes were appended by the same scholar. *Bogomil* is the Slavonic equivalent of the Greek *Theophilus,* which was accordingly adopted by Alemanni in his references. Mr. Bryce has shown clearly that this document, interesting as it is in illustrating how Slavonic legends had grown up round the name of Justinian, is worthless as history, and that there is no reason to suppose that such a person as the Dardanian Bogomil ever existed. We are indeed met by a new problem, which, however, is of no serious concern to the practical purposes of history. How did Marnavich obtain a copy of the original Life, from which he made the extract, and which he declares to be preserved in the library of the monks who profess the rule of St. Basil on Mount Athos? Does the original still exist, on Mount Athos or elsewhere? or did it ever exist?

The wars of Justinian in the west have been fully and admirably related by Mr. Hodgkin, with the exception of the obscure conquest of Spain, on which there is too little to be said and nothing further seems likely to come to light. In regard to the ecclesiastical policy of Justinian there is still a field for research.

As for the study of the great work of Anthemius, which brings us to the general subject of Byzantine art, much has been done within the last half century. Gibbon had nothing to help him for the buildings of Constantinople that could compare with Adam's splendid work which he consulted for the buildings of Spalato. We have now Salzenberg's luxurious work, *Alt-christliche Baudenkmale von Constantinopel,* published just fifty years ago by the Prussian government, with plates which enable us to make a full study of the architecture of St. Sophia. A few months ago a complete and scholarly English study of this church by Messrs. Lethaby and Swainson appeared. Other churches, too, especially those at Ravenna, have received careful attention; De Voguë's admirable work on the architecture of Syria is well known; but Strzygovski has only too good reason for complaining that the study of Byzantine architecture, as a whole, has not yet properly begun. A large work on the churches of Greece, by two English scholars, did much to further the cause which Strzygovski had at heart, and to which he made valuable contributions himself. More progress is perhaps being made in the study of miniature painting and iconography; and in this field the work of the Russian student Kondakov is the most noteworthy.

The study of works of architecture in ancient cities, like Athens, Rome, or Constantinople, naturally entails a study of the topography of the town; and in the case of Constantinople this study is equally important for the historian. Little progress of a satisfactory kind can be made until either Constantinople passes under a European government, or a complete change comes over the spirit of Turkish administration. The region of the Imperial Palace and the ground between the Hippodrome and St. Sophia must be excavated before certainty on the main points can be attained. Labarte's *a priori* reconstruction of the plan of the palace, on the basis of the Cerimonies of Constantine Porphyrogennetos and scattered notices in other Greek writers, was wonderfully ingenious and a certain part of it is manifestly right, though there is much which is not borne out by a more careful examination of the sources. The next step was taken by a Russian scholar, Bieliaiev, who published a most valuable study on the Cerimonies, in which he has tested the reconstruction of Labarte and shown us exactly where we are, —what we know, and what with our present materials we cannot possibly know. Between Labarte and Bieliaiev the whole problem was obscured by the unscholarly work of Paspatês, the Greek antiquarian; whose sole merit was that he kept the subject before the world. As the acropolis is the scene of so many great events in the history which Gibbon recorded, it is well to warn the reader that our sources make it absolutely certain that the Hippodrome adjoined the Palace; there was no public space between them. The Augusteum did not lie, as Paspatês asserted, between the Palace and the Hippodrome, but between the north side of the Hippodrome and St. Sophia.

On the trades and industries of the Imperial City, on the trade corporations and the minute control exercised over them by the government, new light has been thrown by M. Nicole's discovery and publication of the Prefect's Book, a code of regulations drawn up by Leo VI. The *demes* of Constantinople are a subject which need investigation. They are certainly not to be regarded as Gibbon and his successors have regarded them, as mere circus parties. They must represent, as Uspenski points out in the opening number of the new *Vizantiski Vremennik,* organized divisions of the population.

A field in which the historian must wander to breathe the spirit and learn the manner of the mediæval Greek world is that of the romance, both prose and verse, written in the vulgar tongue. This field was closed to Gibbon, but the labours of many scholars, above all Legrand, have rendered it now easily accessible. Out of a large number of interesting things I may refer especially to two. One is the epic of Digenes Akritas, the Roland or Cid of the Later Empire, a poem of the tenth century, which illustrates the life of Armatoli and the border warfare against the Saracens in the Cilician mountains. The other is the *Book of the Conquest of the Morea,* a mixture of fiction and fact, but invaluable for realizing the fascinating though complicated history of the "Latin" settlements in Greece. That history was set aside by Gibbon, with the phrase, "I shall not pursue the obscure and various dynasties that rose and fell on the continent or in the isles," though he deigns to give a page or two to Athens. But it is a subject with unusual possibilities for picturesque treatment, and out of which Gibbon, if he had apprehended the opportunity and had possessed the materials, would have made a brilliant chapter. Since Finlay, who entered into this episode of Greek history with great fulness, the material has been largely increased by the researches of Hopf.

As I have already observed, it is perhaps on the Slavonic side of the history of the Empire that Gibbon is most conspicuously inadequate. Since he wrote, various causes have combined to increase our knowledge of Slavonic antiquity. The Slavs themselves have engaged in methodical investigation of their own past; and, since the entire or partial emancipations of the southern Slavs from Asiatic rule, a general interest in Slavonic things has grown up throughout Europe. Gibbon dismissed the history of the First Bulgarian Kingdom, from its foundation in the reign of Constantine Pogonatus to its overthrow by the second Basil, in two pages. To-day the author of a history of the Empire on the same scale would find two hundred a strict limit. Gibbon tells us nothing of the Slavonic missionaries, Cyril and Methodius, round whose names an extensive literature has been formed. It is only in recent years that the geography of the Illyrian peninsula has become an accessible subject of study.

The investigation of the history of the northern peoples who came under the influence of the Empire has been stimulated by controversy, and controversy has been animated and even embittered by national pride. The question of Slavonic settlements in Greece has been thoroughly ventilated, because Fallmerayer excited the scholarship of Hellenes and Philhellenes to refute what they regarded as an insulting paradox. So, too, the pride of the

Roumanians was irritated by Roesler, who denied that they were descended from the inhabitants of Trajan's Dacia and described them as later immigrants of the thirteenth century. Pic arose against him; then Hermuzaki argued for an intermediate date. The best Hungarian scholar of the day joined the fray, on the other side; and the contention became bitter between Vlach and Magyar, the Roumanian pretensions to Siebenbürgen—"Dacia irredenta"—sharpening the lances of the foes. The Roumanians have not come out of their "question" as well as the Hellenes. Hungary too has its own question. Are the Magyars to be ethnically associated with the Finns or given over to the family of the Turks, whom as champions of Christendom they had opposed at Mahácz and Varna? It was a matter of pride for the Hungarian to detach himself from the Turk; and the evidence is certainly on his side. Hunfalvy's conclusions have successfully defied the assaults of Vámbéry. Again in Russia there has been a long and vigorous contest,—the so-called Norman or Varangian question. No doubt is felt now by the impartial judge as to the Scandinavian origin of the princes of Kiev, and that the making of Russia was due to Northmen or Varangians. Kunik and Pogodin were reinforced by Thomsen of Denmark; and the pure Slavism of Ilovaiski and Gedeonov, though its champions were certainly able, is a lost cause.

From such collisions sparks have flown and illuminated dark corners. For the Slavs the road was first cleared by Safarik. The development of the comparative philology of the Indo-Germanic tongues has had its effect; the Slavonic languages have been brought into line, chiefly by the lifework of Miklosich; and the science is being developed by such scholars as Jagic and Leskien. The several countries of the Balkan lands have their archæologists and archæological journals; and the difficulty which now meets the historian is not the absence, but the plenitude, of philological and historical literature.

A word may be added about the Hungarians, who have not been so successful with their early history as the Slavs. Until the appearance of Hunfalvy, their methods were antediluvian, and their temper credulous. The special work of Jászay, and the first chapters of Szalay's great History of Hungary, showed no advance on Katóna and Pray, who were consulted by Gibbon. All believed in the Anonymous Scribe of King Béla; Jászay simply transcribed him. Then Roesler came and dispelled the illusion. Our main sources now are Constantine Porphyrogennetos, and the earlier

Asiatic traveller Ibn Dasta, who has been rendered accessible by
Chwolson. The linguistic researches of Ahlquist, Hunfalvy and
others into Vogul, Ostjak and the rest of the Ugro-Finnic kindred, The Editor's
must be taken into account by the critic who is dealing with those Introduction
main sources. The Chazars, to whom the Hungarians were once
subject, the Patzinaks, who drove the Magyars from "Lebedia" to
"Atelkuzu" and from "Atelkuzu" to Pannonia, and other peoples
of the same kind, have profited by these investigations.

The foregoing instances will serve to give a general idea of the
respects in which Gibbon's history might be described as behind
date. To follow out all the highways and byways of progress
would mean the usurpation of at least a volume by the editor. What
more has to be said, must be said briefly in notes and appendices.
That Gibbon is behind date in many details, and in some departments of importance, simply signifies that we and our fathers have
not lived in an absolutely incompetent world. But in the main
things he is still our master, above and beyond "date." It is needless to dwell on the obvious qualities which secure to him immunity from the common lot of historical writers,—such as the bold
and certain measure of his progress through the ages; his accurate
vision, and his tact in managing perspective; his discreet reserves
of judgment and timely scepticism; the immortal affectation of
his unique manner. By virtue of these superiorities he can defy the
danger with which the activity of successors must always threaten
the worthies of the past. But there is another point which was
touched on in an earlier page and to which here, in a different connexion, we may briefly revert. It is well to realize that the greatest
history of modern times was written by one in whom a distrust of
enthusiasm was deeply rooted. This cynicism was not inconsistent
with partiality, with definite prepossessions, with a certain spite.
In fact, it supplied the antipathy which the artist infused when he
mixed his most effective colours. The conviction that enthusiasm
is inconsistent with intellectual balance was engrained in his mental constitution, and confirmed by study and experience. It might
be reasonably maintained that zeal for men or causes is an historian's marring, and that "reserve sympathy"—the principle of
Thucydides—is the first lesson he has to learn. But without venturing on any generalization, we must consider Gibbon's zealous distrust of zeal as an essential and most suggestive characteristic of the
"Decline and Fall".

J. B. BURY

CONTENTS

"Cast your eyes on the Palatine hill and seek, among the shapeless and enormous fragments, the marble theatre, the obelisks, the colossal statues, the porticoes of Nero's palace; survey the other hills of the city; the vacant space is interrupted only by ruins and gardens."

"*Cast your eyes on the Palatine hill and seek, among the shapeless and enormous fragments, the marble theatre, the obelisks, the colossal statues, the porticoes of Nero's palace; survey the other hills of the city; the vacant space is interrupted only by ruins and gardens.*"

A LIST OF ILLUSTRATIONS

It is not my intention to detain the reader by expatiating on the variety, or the importance of the subject, which I have undertaken to treat; since the merit of the choice would serve to render the weakness of the execution still more apparent, and still less excusable. But, as I have presumed to lay before the Public a *first* volume only of the History of the Decline and Fall of the Roman Empire, it will perhaps be expected that I should explain, in a few words, the nature and limits of my general plan.

The memorable series of revolutions, which, in the course of about thirteen centuries, gradually undermined, and at length destroyed, the solid fabric of human greatness, may, with some propriety, be divided into the three following periods:

I. The first of these periods may be traced from the age of Trajan and the Antonines, when the Roman monarchy, having attained its full strength and maturity, began to verge towards its decline; and will extend to the subversion of the Western Empire, by the barbarians of Germany and Scythia, the rude ancestors of the most polished nations of modern Europe. This extraordinary revolution, which subjected Rome to the power of a Gothic conqueror, was completed about the beginning of the sixth century.

II. The second period of the Decline and Fall of Rome, may be supposed to commence with the reign of Justinian, who by his laws, as well as by his victories, restored a transient splendour to the Eastern Empire. It will comprehend the invasion of Italy by the Lombards; the conquest of the Asiatic and African provinces by the Arabs, who embraced the religion of Mahomet; the revolt of the Roman people against the feeble princes of Constantinople; and the elevation of Charlemagne, who, in the year 800, established the second, or German, Empire of the West.

III. The last and longest of these periods includes about six centuries and a half; from the revival of the Western Empire till the taking of Constantinople by the Turks and the extinction of a degenerate race of princes, who continued to assume the titles of Cæsar and Augustus, after their dominions were contracted to the limits of a single city; in which the language, as well as manners, of the ancient Romans had been long since forgotten. The writer who should undertake to relate the events of this period would find himself obliged to enter into the general history of the Crusades, as far as they contributed to the ruin of the Greek Empire; and he would scarcely be able to restrain his curiosity from making some enquiry into the state of the city of Rome during the darkness and confusion of the middle ages.

As I have ventured, perhaps too hastily, to commit to the press a work, which, in every sense of the word, deserves the epithet of imperfect, I consider myself as contracting an engagement to finish, most probably in a second volume, the first of these memorable periods; and to deliver to the Public the complete History of the Decline and Fall of Rome, from the age of the Antonines to the subversion of the Western Empire. With regard to the subsequent periods, though I may entertain some hopes, I dare not presume to give any assurances. The execution of the extensive plan which I have described would connect the ancient and modern history of the World; but it would require many years of health, of leisure, and of perseverance.

BENTINCK STREET,
 February 1, 1776.

P.S.—The entire History, which is now published, of the Decline and Fall of the Roman Empire in the West abundantly discharges my engagements with the Public. Perhaps their favourable opinion may encourage me to prosecute a work, which, however laborious it may seem, is the most agreeable occupation of my leisure hours.

BENTINCK STREET,
 March 1, 1781.

An Author easily persuades himself that the public opinion is still favourable to his labours; and I have now embraced the serious resolution of proceeding to the last period of my original design, and of the Roman Empire, the taking of Constantinople by the Turks, in the year one thousand four hundred and fifty-three. The most patient reader, who computes that three ponderous volumes have been already employed on the events of four centuries, may, perhaps, be alarmed at the long prospect of nine hundred years. But it is not my intention to expatiate with the same minuteness on the whole series of the Byzantine history. At our entrance into this period, the reign of Justinian and the conquests of the Mahometans will deserve and detain our attention, and the last age of Constantinople (the Crusades and the Turks) is connected with the revolutions of Modern Europe. From the seventh to the eleventh century, the obscure interval will be supplied by a concise narrative of such facts as may still appear either interesting or important.

BENTINCK STREET,
March 1, 1782.

HIBERNIA

BRITANNIA

GERMANIA

Colonia Agrippina

Belgica

Moguntiacum

Treveri

Celtica

GALLIA

RÆTIA

NORICUM

Aquitania

Lugdunum

PANNONIA

Aginnum

Mediolanum

Aquileia

Tolosa

Massilia

ITALIA

Ravenna

Tarraconensis

Narbo

ILLY

Salon

HISPANIA

CORSICA

ROMA

Lusitania

Bœtica

Gades

Carthago Nova

SARDINIA

Baleares

MAURETANIA

NUMIDIA

SICILIA

Syracusæ

AFRICA

I: THE ROMAN EMPIRE

AT THE DEATH OF AUGUSTUS

A.D. 13

I

THE EXTENT AND MILITARY FORCE OF THE EMPIRE IN THE AGE
OF THE ANTONINES WHICH WAS IN THE YEARS 98–180 A.D.

IN THE second century of the
Christian æra, the empire of Rome comprehended the fairest part
of the earth, and the most civilized portion of mankind. The frontiers of that extensive monarchy were guarded by ancient renown
and disciplined valour. The gentle, but powerful, influence of laws
and manners had gradually cemented the union of the provinces.
Their peaceful inhabitants enjoyed and abused the advantages of
wealth and luxury. The image of a free constitution was preserved
with decent reverence. The Roman senate appeared to possess the
sovereign authority, and devolved on the emperors all the executive powers of government. During a happy period of more than
fourscore years, the public administration was conducted by the
virtue and abilities of Nerva, Trajan, Hadrian, and the two Antonines. It is the design of this and of the two succeeding chapters,
to describe the prosperous condition of their empire; and afterwards, from the death of Marcus Antoninus, to deduce the most
important circumstances of its decline and fall: a revolution which
will ever be remembered, and is still felt by the nations of the earth.

The principal conquests of the Romans were achieved under the
republic; and the emperors, for the most part, were satisfied with
preserving those dominions which had been acquired by the policy
of the senate, the active emulation of the consuls, and the martial
enthusiasm of the people. The seven first centuries were filled with
a rapid succession of triumphs; but it was reserved for Augustus to
relinquish the ambitious design of subduing the whole earth, and to
introduce a spirit of moderation into the public councils. Inclined
to peace by his temper and situation, it was easy for him to discover
that Rome, in her present exalted situation, had much less to hope
than to fear from the chance of arms; and that, in the prosecution
of remote wars, the undertaking became every day more difficult,

the event more doubtful, and the possession more precarious and less beneficial. The experience of Augustus added weight to these salutary reflections, and effectually convinced him that, by the prudent vigour of his counsels, it would be easy to secure every concession which the safety or the dignity of Rome might require from the most formidable barbarians. Instead of exposing his person and his legions to the arrows of the Parthians, he obtained, by an honourable treaty, the restitution of the standards and prisoners which had been taken in the defeat of Crassus.

His generals, in the early part of his reign, attempted the reduction of Æthiopia and Arabia Felix. They marched near a thousand miles to the south of the tropic; but the heat of the climate soon repelled the invaders and protected the unwarlike natives of those sequestered regions.[1] The northern countries of Europe scarcely deserved the expense and labour of conquest. The forests and morasses of Germany were filled with a hardy race of barbarians, who despised life when it was separated from freedom; and though, on the first attack, they seemed to yield to the weight of the Roman power, they soon, by a signal act of despair, regained their independence, and reminded Augustus of the vicissitude of fortune.[2] On the death of that emperor his testament was publicly read in the senate. He bequeathed, as a valuable legacy to his successors, the advice of confining the empire within those limits which nature seemed to have placed as its permanent bulwarks and boundaries; on the west the Atlantic Ocean; the Rhine and Danube on the north; the Euphrates on the east; and towards the south the sandy deserts of Arabia and Africa.

Happily for the repose of mankind, the moderate system recommended by the wisdom of Augustus was adopted by the fears and vices of his immediate successors. Engaged in the pursuit of pleasure or in the exercise of tyranny, the first Cæsars seldom showed themselves to the armies, or to the provinces; nor were they disposed to suffer that those triumphs which *their* indolence neglected should be usurped by the conduct and valour of their lieutenants. The military fame of a subject was considered as an insolent invasion of the Imperial prerogative; and it became the duty, as well as interest, of every Roman general, to guard the frontiers intrusted to his care, without aspiring to conquests which might have proved no less fatal to himself than to the vanquished barbarians.[3]

The only accession which the Roman empire received during the first century of the Christian æra was the province of Britain. In this

[1] *Strabo, Pliny the elder and Dion Cassius have left us very curious details concerning these wars. The Romans made themselves masters of Mariaba, or Merab, a city of Arabia Felix. They were arrived within three days' journey of the Spice country, the rich object of their invasion.*

[2] *By the slaughter of Varus and his three legions. Augustus did not receive the melancholy news with all the temper and firmness that might have been expected from his character.*

[3] *Germanicus, Suetonius Paulinus, and Agricola were checked and recalled in the course of their victories. Corbulo was put to death. Military merit, as it is admirably expressed by Tacitus, was, in the strictest sense of the word,* imperatoria virtus.

single instance the successors of Cæsar and Augustus were persuaded to follow the example of the former, rather than the precept of the latter. The proximity of its situation to the coast of Gaul seemed to invite their arms; the pleasing, though doubtful, intelligence of a pearl fishery attracted their avarice;[4] and as Britain was viewed in the light of a distinct and insulated world, the conquest scarcely formed any exception to the general system of continental measures. After a war of about forty years, undertaken by the most stupid,[5] maintained by the most dissolute, and terminated by the most timid of all the emperors, the far greater part of the island submitted to the Roman yoke. The various tribes of Britons possessed valour without conduct, and the love of freedom without the spirit of union. They took up arms with savage fierceness, they laid them down, or turned them against each other with wild inconstancy; and while they fought singly, they were successively subdued. Neither the fortitude of Caractacus, nor the despair of Boadicea, nor the fanaticism of the Druids, could avert the slavery of their country, or resist the steady progress of the Imperial generals, who maintained the national glory, when the throne was disgraced by the weakest or the most vicious of mankind. At the very time when Domitian, confined to his palace, felt the terrors which he inspired, his legions, under the command of the virtuous Agricola, defeated the collected force of the Caledonians at the foot of the Grampian hills; and his fleets, venturing to explore an unknown and dangerous navigation, displayed the Roman arms round every part of the island. The conquest of Britain was considered as already achieved; and it was the design of Agricola to complete and ensure his success by the easy reduction of Ireland, for which, in his opinion, one legion and a few auxiliaries were sufficient.[6] The western isle might be improved into a valuable possession, and the Britons would wear their chains with the less reluctance, if the prospect and example of freedom was on every side removed from before their eyes.

But the superior merit of Agricola soon occasioned his removal from the government of Britain; and for ever disappointed this rational, though extensive, scheme of conquest. Before his departure the prudent general had provided for security as well as for dominion. He had observed that the island is almost divided into two unequal parts by the opposite gulfs or, as they are now called, the Friths of Scotland. Across the narrow interval of about forty miles he had drawn a line of military stations, which was afterwards fortified, in the reign of Antoninus Pius, by a turf rampart, erected on

[4] *Cæsar himself conceals that ignoble motive; but it is mentioned by Suetonius. The British pearls proved, however, of little value, on account of their dark and livid colour.*

[5] *Claudius, Nero and Domitian. A hope is expressed by Pomponius Mela (he wrote under Claudius), that, by the success of the Roman arms, the island and its savage inhabitants would soon be better known. It is amusing enough to peruse such passages in the midst of London.*

[6] *The Irish writers, jealous of their national honour, are extremely provoked on this occasion, both with Tacitus and with Agricola.*

foundations of stone. This wall of Antoninus, at a small distance beyond the modern cities of Edinburgh and Glasgow, was fixed as the limit of the Roman province. The native Caledonians preserved, in the northern extremity of the island, their wild independence, for which they were not less indebted to their poverty than to their valour. Their incursions were frequently repelled and chastised; but their country was never subdued. The masters of the fairest and most wealthy climates of the globe turned with contempt from gloomy hills assailed by the winter tempest, from lakes concealed in a blue mist, and from cold and lonely heaths, over which the deer of the forest were chased by a troop of naked barbarians.

Such was the state of the Roman frontiers, and such the maxims of Imperial policy, from the death of Augustus to the accession of Trajan. That virtuous and active prince had received the education of a soldier, and possessed the talents of a general. The peaceful system of his predecessors was interrupted by scenes of war and conquest; and the legions, after a long interval, beheld a military emperor at their head. The first exploits of Trajan were against the Dacians, the most warlike of men, who dwelt beyond the Danube, and who, during the reign of Domitian, had insulted, with impunity, the majesty of Rome. To the strength and fierceness of barbarians they added a contempt for life, which was derived from a warm persuasion of the immortality and transmigration of the soul. Decebalus, the Dacian king, approved himself a rival not unworthy of Trajan; nor did he despair of his own and the public fortune, till, by the confession of his enemies, he had exhausted every resource both of valour and policy. This memorable war, with a very short suspension of hostilities, lasted five years; and as the emperor could exert, without control, the whole force of the state, it was terminated by the absolute submission of the barbarians. The new province of Dacia, which formed a second exception to the precept of Augustus, was about thirteen hundred miles in circumference. Its natural boundaries were the Dniester, the Theiss, or Tibiscus, the Lower Danube, and the Euxine Sea. The vestiges of a military road may still be traced from the banks of the Danube to the neighbourhood of Bender, a place famous in modern history, and the actual frontier of the Turkish and Russian empires.

Trajan was ambitious of fame; and as long as mankind shall continue to bestow more liberal applause on their destroyers than on their benefactors, the thirst of military glory will ever be the vice of the most exalted characters. The praises of Alexander, transmitted by a succession of poets and historians, had kindled a dangerous emulation in the mind of Trajan. Like him, the Roman emperor undertook an expedition against the nations of the east, but he lamented with a sigh that his advanced age scarcely left him any hopes of equalling the renown of the son of Philip. Yet the success of Trajan, however transient, was rapid and specious. The degenerate Parthians, broken by intestine discord, fled before his arms. He descended the river Tigris in triumph, from the mountains of Armenia to the Persian Gulf. He enjoyed the honour of being the first, as he was the last, of the Roman generals, who ever navigated that remote sea. His fleets ravished the coasts of Arabia; and Trajan vainly flattered himself that he was approaching towards the confines of India. Every day the astonished senate received the intelligence of new names and new nations that acknowledged his sway. They were informed that the kings of Bosphorus, Colchos, Iberia, Albania, Osrhoene, and even the Parthian monarch himself, had accepted their diadems from the hands of the emperor; that the independent tribes of the Median and Carduchian hills had implored his protection; and that the rich countries of Armenia, Mesopotamia, and Assyria, were reduced into the state of provinces. But the death of Trajan soon clouded the splendid prospect; and it was justly to be dreaded that so many distant nations would throw off the unaccustomed yoke, when they were no longer restrained by the powerful hand which had imposed it.

It was an ancient tradition that, when the Capitol was founded by one of the Roman kings, the god Terminus (who presided over boundaries, and was represented according to the fashion of that age by a large stone) alone, among all the inferior deities, refused to yield his place to Jupiter himself. A favourable inference was drawn from his obstinacy, which was interpreted by the augurs as a sure presage that the boundaries of the Roman power would never recede. During many ages, the prediction, as it is usual, contributed to its own accomplishment. But though Terminus had resisted the majesty of Jupiter, he submitted to the authority of the emperor Hadrian. The resignation of all the eastern conquests of Trajan was the first measure of his reign. He restored to the Parthians the election of an independent sovereign; withdrew the Roman garrisons from the provinces of Armenia, Mesopotamia, and Assyria; and, in compliance with the precepts of Augustus, once more established the Euphrates as the frontier of the empire. Censure, which arraigns the public actions and the private motives of princes, has ascribed to envy a conduct which might be attributed to the prudence and moderation of Hadrian. The various character of that emperor, capable, by turns, of the meanest and the most generous sentiments, may afford some colour to the suspicion. It was, however, scarcely in his power to place the superiority of his predecessor in a more conspicuous light, than by thus confessing himself unequal to the task of defending the conquests of Trajan.

The martial and ambitious spirit of Trajan formed a very singular contrast with the moderation of his successor. The restless activity of Hadrian was not less remarkable when compared with the gentle repose of Antoninus Pius. The life of the former was almost a perpetual journey; and as he possessed the various talents of the soldier, the statesman, and the scholar, he gratified his curiosity in the discharge of his duty. Careless of the difference of seasons and of climates, he marched on foot, and bareheaded, over the snows of Caledonia, and the sultry plains of the Upper Egypt; nor was there a province of the empire which, in the course of his reign, was not honoured with the presence of the monarch.[7] But the tranquil life of Antoninus Pius was spent in the bosom of Italy; and, during the twenty-three years that he directed the public administration, the longest journeys of that amiable prince extended no farther than from his palace in Rome to the retirement of his Lanuvian villa.

Notwithstanding this difference in their personal conduct, the general system of Augustus was equally adopted and uniformly pursued by Hadrian and by the two Antonines. They persisted in the design of maintaining the dignity of the empire, without attempting to enlarge its limits. By every honourable expedient they invited the friendship of the barbarians; and endeavoured to convince mankind that the Roman power, raised above the temptation of conquest, was actuated only by the love of order and justice. During a long period of forty-three years their virtuous labours were crowned with success; and, if we except a few slight hostilities that served to exercise the legions of the frontier, the reigns of Hadrian and Antoninus Pius offer the fair prospect of universal peace.[8] The Roman name was revered among the most remote nations of the earth. The fiercest barbarians frequently submitted their differences to the arbitration of the emperor; and we are informed by a contemporary historian that he had seen ambassadors who were refused the honour which they came to solicit, of being admitted into the rank of subjects.

The terror of the Roman arms added weight and dignity to the

[7] If all our historians were lost, medals, inscriptions, and other monuments would be sufficient to record the travels of Hadrian.

[8] We must, however, remember that, in the time of Hadrian, a rebellion of the Jews raged with religious fury, though only in a single province. Pausanias mentions two necessary and successful wars, conducted by the generals of Pius. 1st, Against the wandering Moors, who were driven into the solitudes of Atlas. 2nd, Against the Brigantes of Britain, who had invaded the Roman province. Both these wars (with several other hostilities) are mentioned in the Augustan History.

moderation of the emperors. They preserved peace by a constant preparation for war; and while justice regulated their conduct, they announced to the nations on their confines that they were as little disposed to endure as to offer an injury. The military strength, which it had been sufficient for Hadrian and the elder Antoninus to display, was exerted against the Parthians and the Germans by the emperor Marcus. The hostilities of the barbarians provoked the resentment of that philosophic monarch, and, in the prosecution of a just defence, Marcus and his generals obtained many signal victories, both on the Euphrates and on the Danube. The military establishment of the Roman empire, which thus assured either its tranquillity or success, will now become the proper and important object of our attention.

In the purer ages of the commonwealth, the use of arms was reserved for those ranks of citizens who had a country to love, a property to defend, and some share in enacting those laws which it was their interest, as well as duty, to maintain. But in proportion as the public freedom was lost in extent of conquest, war was gradually improved into an art, and degraded into a trade.[9] The legions themselves, even at the time when they were recruited in the most distant provinces, were supposed to consist of Roman citizens. That distinction was generally considered either as a legal qualification or as a proper recompense for the soldier; but a more serious regard was paid to the essential merit of age, strength, and military stature.[10] In all levies, a just preference was given to the climates of the north over those of the south; the race of men born to the exercise of arms was sought for in the country rather than in cities, and it was very reasonably presumed that the hardy occupations of smiths, carpenters, and huntsmen would supply more vigour and resolution than the sedentary trades which are employed in the service of luxury. After every qualification of property had been laid aside, the armies of the Roman emperors were still commanded, for the most part, by officers of a liberal birth and education; but the common soldiers, like the mercenary troops of modern Europe, were drawn from the meanest, and very frequently from the most profligate, of mankind.

That public virtue, which among the ancients was denominated patriotism, is derived from a strong sense of our own interest in the preservation and prosperity of the free government of which we are members. Such a sentiment, which had rendered the legions of the republic almost invincible, could make but a very feeble impression on the mercenary servants of a despotic prince; and it became neces-

[9] *The poorest rank of soldiers possessed above forty pounds sterling, a very high qualification, at a time when money was so scarce, that an ounce of silver was equivalent to seventy pound weight of brass. The populace, excluded by the ancient constitution, were indiscriminately admitted by Marius.*

[10] *Cæsar formed his legion Alauda of Gauls and strangers; but it was during the licence of civil war; and after the victory he gave them the freedom of the city, for their reward.*

sary to supply that defect by other motives, of a different, but not less forcible nature,—honour and religion. The peasant, or mechanic, imbibed the useful prejudice that he was advanced to the more dignified profession of arms, in which his rank and reputation would depend on his own valour; and that, although the prowess of a private soldier must often escape the notice of fame, his own behaviour might sometimes confer glory or disgrace on the company, the legion, or even the army, to whose honours he was associated. On his first entrance into the service, an oath was administered to him with every circumstance of solemnity. He promised never to desert his standard, to submit his own will to the commands of his leaders, and to sacrifice his life for the safety of the emperor and the empire.[11] The attachment of the Roman troops to their standards was inspired by the united influence of religion and of honour. The golden eagle, which glittered in the front of the legion, was the object of their fondest devotion; nor was it esteemed less impious than it was ignominious, to abandon that sacred ensign in the hour of danger.[12] These motives, which derived their strength from the imagination, were enforced by fears and hopes of a more substantial kind. Regular pay, occasional donatives, and a stated recompense, after the appointed term of service, alleviated the hardships of the military life,[13] whilst, on the other hand, it was impossible for cowardice or disobedience to escape the severest punishment. The centurions were authorized to chastise with blows, the generals had a right to punish with death; and it was an inflexible maxim of Roman discipline, that a good soldier should dread his officers far more than the enemy. From such laudable arts did the valour of the Imperial troops receive a degree of firmness and docility, unattainable by the impetuous and irregular passions of barbarians.

And yet so sensible were the Romans of the imperfection of valour without skill and practice, that, in their language, the name of an army was borrowed from the word which signified exercise. Military exercises were the important and unremitted object of their discipline. The recruits and young soldiers were constantly trained, both in the morning and in the evening, nor was age or knowledge allowed to excuse the veterans from the daily repetition of what they had completely learnt. Large sheds were erected in the winter-quarters of the troops, that their useful labours might not receive any interruption from the most tempestuous weather; and it was carefully observed, that the arms destined to this imitation of war should be of double the weight which was required in real action.

[11] *The oath of service and fidelity to the emperor was annually renewed by the troops, on the first of January.*

[12] *Tacitus calls the Roman Eagles, Bellorum Deos. They were placed in a chapel in the camp, and with the other deities received the religious worship of the troops.*

[13] *The emperor Domitian raised the annual stipend of the legionaries to twelve pieces of gold, which, in his time, was equivalent to about ten of our guineas. This pay, somewhat higher than our own, had been, and was afterwards, gradually increased, according to the progress of wealth and military government. After twenty years' service, the veteran received three thousand denarii (about one hundred pounds sterling), or a proportionable allowance of land. The pay and advantages of the guards were, in general, about double those of the legions.*

It is not the purpose of this work to enter into any minute description of the Roman exercises. We shall only remark that they comprehended whatever could add strength to the body, activity to the limbs, or grace to the motions. The soldiers were diligently instructed to march, to run, to leap, to swim, to carry heavy burdens, to handle every species of arms that was used either for offence or for defence, either in distant engagement or in a closer onset; to form a variety of evolutions; and to move to the sound of flutes in the Pyrrhic or martial dance. In the midst of peace, the Roman troops familiarised themselves with the practice of war; and it is prettily remarked by an ancient historian who had fought against them, that the effusion of blood was the only circumstance which distinguished a field of battle from a field of exercise. It was the policy of the ablest generals, and even of the emperors themselves, to encourage these military studies by their presence and example; and we are informed that Hadrian, as well as Trajan, frequently condescended to instruct the inexperienced soldiers, to reward the diligent, and sometimes to dispute with them the prize of superior strength or dexterity. Under the reigns of those princes, the science of tactics was cultivated with success; and as long as the empire retained any vigour, their military instructions were respected as the most perfect model of Roman discipline.

Nine centuries of war had gradually introduced into the service many alterations and improvements. The legions, as they are described by Polybius, in the time of the Punic wars, differed very materially from those which achieved the victories of Cæsar, or defended the monarchy of Hadrian and the Antonines. The constitution of the Imperial legion may be described in a few words. The heavy armed infantry, which composed its principal strength, was divided into ten cohorts, and fifty-five companies, under the orders of a correspondent number of tribunes and centurions. The first cohort, which always claimed the post of honour and the custody of the eagle, was formed of eleven hundred and five soldiers, the most approved for valour and fidelity. The remaining nine cohorts consisted each of five hundred and fifty-five; and the whole body of legionary infantry amounted to six thousand one hundred men. Their arms were uniform, and admirably adapted to the nature of their service: an open helmet, with a lofty crest; a breast-plate, or coat of mail; greaves on their legs, and an ample buckler on their left arm. The buckler was of an oblong and concave figure, four feet in length, and two and a half in breadth, framed of a light wood, covered with a bull's hide, and strongly guarded with plates of brass. Besides a lighter spear, the legionary soldier grasped in his right hand the formidable *pilum,* a ponderous javelin, whose utmost length was about six feet, and which was terminated by a massy triangular point of steel of eighteen inches. This instrument was indeed much inferior to our modern fire-arms; since it was exhausted by a single discharge, at the distance of only ten or twelve paces. Yet, when it was launched by a firm and skilful hand, there was not any cavalry that durst venture within its reach, nor any shield or corslet that could sustain the impetuosity of its weight. As soon as the Roman had darted his *pilum,* he drew his sword, and rushed forwards to close with the enemy. It was a short well-tempered Spanish blade, that carried a double edge, and was alike suited to the purpose of striking or of pushing; but the soldier was always instructed to prefer the latter use of his weapon, as his own body remained less exposed, whilst he inflicted a more dangerous wound on his adversary. The legion was usually drawn up eight deep; and the regular distance of three feet was left between the files as well as ranks. A body of troops, habituated to preserve this open order, in a long front and a rapid charge, found themselves prepared to execute every disposition which the circumstances of war, or the skill of their leader, might suggest. The soldier possessed a free space for his arms and motions, and sufficient intervals were allowed, through which seasonable reinforcements might be introduced to the relief of the exhausted combatants. The tactics of the Greeks and Macedonians were formed on very different principles. The strength of the phalanx depended on sixteen ranks of long pikes, wedged together in the closest array. But it was soon discovered, by reflection as well as by the event, that the strength of the phalanx was unable to contend with the activity of the legion.

The cavalry, without which the force of the legion would have remained imperfect, was divided into ten troops or squadrons; the first, as the companion of the first cohort, consisted of an hundred and thirty-two men; whilst each of the other nine amounted only to sixty-six. The entire establishment formed a regiment, if we may use the modern expression, of seven hundred and twenty-six horse, naturally connected with its respective legion, but occasionally separated to act in the line, and to compose a part of the wings of the army. The cavalry of the emperors was no longer composed, like that of the ancient republic, of the noblest youths of Rome and Italy, who, by performing their military service on horseback, prepared themselves for the offices of senator and consul; and solicited, by deeds of valour, the future suffrages of their countrymen. Since the alteration of manners and government, the most wealthy of the equestrian order were engaged in the administration of justice, and of the revenue; and whenever they embraced the profession of arms, they were immediately intrusted with a troop of horse, or a cohort of foot.[14] Trajan and Hadrian formed their cavalry from the same provinces, and the same class of their subjects, which recruited the ranks of the legion. The horses were bred, for the most part, in Spain or Cappadocia. The Roman troopers despised the complete armour with which the cavalry of the East was encumbered. *Their* more useful arms consisted in a helmet, an oblong shield, light boots, and a coat of mail. A javelin, and a long broad sword, were their principal weapons of offence. The use of lances and of iron maces they seemed to have borrowed from the barbarians.

The safety and honour of the empire was principally intrusted to the legions, but the policy of Rome condescended to adopt every useful instrument of war. Considerable levies were regularly made among the provincials, who had not yet deserved the honourable distinction of Romans. Many dependent princes and communities, dispersed round the frontiers, were permitted, for a while, to hold their freedom and security by the tenure of military service. Even select troops of hostile barbarians were frequently compelled or persuaded to consume their dangerous valour in remote climates, and for the benefit of the state.[15] All these were included under the general name of auxiliaries; and howsoever they might vary according to the difference of times and circumstances, their numbers were seldom much inferior to those of the legions themselves. Among the auxiliaries, the bravest and most faithful bands were placed under the command of præfects and centurions, and severely trained in the arts of Roman discipline; but the far greater part retained those arms, to which the nature of their country, or their early habits of life, more peculiarly adapted them. By this institution, each legion, to whom a certain proportion of auxiliaries was allotted, contained within itself every species of lighter troops, and of missile weapons; and was capable of encountering every nation with the advantages of its respective arms and discipline. Nor was the legion destitute of what, in modern language, would be styled a train of artillery. It consisted in ten military engines of the largest, and fifty-five of a smaller size; but all of which, either in an oblique or horizontal manner, discharged stones and darts with irresistible violence.[16]

[14] *As in the instance of Horace and Agricola. This appears to have been a defect in the Roman discipline; which Hadrian endeavoured to remedy by ascertaining the legal age of a tribune.*

[15] *Marcus Antoninus obliged the vanquished Quadi and Marcomanni to supply him with a large body of troops, which he immediately sent into Britain.*

[16] *The subject of the ancient machines is treated with great knowledge and ingenuity by the Chevalier Folard. He prefers them in many respects to our modern cannon and mortars. We may observe that the use of them in the field gradually became more prevalent, in proportion as personal valour and military skill declined with the Roman empire. When men were no longer found, their place was supplied by machines.*

The camp of a Roman legion presented the appearance of a fortified city. As soon as the space was marked out, the pioneers carefully levelled the ground, and removed every impediment that might interrupt its perfect regularity. Its form was an exact quadrangle; and we may calculate, that a square of about seven hundred yards was sufficient for the encampment of twenty thousand Romans; though a similar number of our own troops would expose to the enemy a front of more than treble that extent. In the midst of the camp, the prætorium, or general's quarters, rose above the others; the cavalry, the infantry, and the auxiliaries occupied their respective stations; the streets were broad and perfectly straight, and a vacant space of two hundred feet was left on all sides, between the tents and the rampart. The rampart itself was usually twelve feet high, armed with a line of strong and intricate palisades, and defended by a ditch of twelve feet in depth as well as in breadth. This important labour was performed by the hands of the legionaries themselves; to whom the use of the spade and the pick-axe was no less familiar than that of the sword or *pilum*. Active valour may often be the present of nature; but such patient diligence can be the fruit only of habit and discipline.

Whenever the trumpet gave the signal of departure, the camp was almost instantly broken up, and the troops fell into their ranks without delay or confusion. Besides their arms, which the legionaries scarcely considered as an encumbrance, they were laden with their kitchen furniture, the instruments of fortification, and the provision of many days. Under this weight, which would oppress the delicacy of a modern soldier, they were trained by a regular step to advance, in about six hours, near twenty miles. On the appearance of an enemy, they threw aside their baggage, and, by easy and rapid evolutions, converted the column of march into an order of battle. The slingers and archers skirmished in the front; the auxiliaries formed the first line, and were seconded or sustained by the strength of the legions; the cavalry covered the flanks, and the military engines were placed in the rear.

Such were the arts of war, by which the Roman emperors defended their extensive conquests, and preserved a military spirit, at a time when every other virtue was oppressed by luxury and despotism. If, in the consideration of their armies, we pass from their discipline to their numbers, we shall not find it easy to define them with any tolerable accuracy. We may compute, however, that the legion, which was itself a body of six thousand eight hundred and thirty-one Romans, might, with its attendant auxiliaries, amount to about twelve thousand five hundred men. The peace establishment of Hadrian and his successors was composed of no less than thirty of these formidable brigades; and most probably formed a standing force of three hundred and seventy-five thousand men. Instead of being confined within the walls of fortified cities, which the Romans considered as the refuge of weakness or pusillanimity, the legions were encamped on the banks of the great rivers, and along the frontiers of the barbarians. As their stations, for the most part, remained fixed and permanent, we may venture to describe the distribution of the troops. Three legions were sufficient for Britain. The principal strength lay upon the Rhine and Danube, and consisted of sixteen legions, in the following proportions; two in the Lower, and three in the Upper Germany; one in Rhætia, one in Noricum, four in Pannonia, three in Mæsia, and two in Dacia. The defence of the Euphrates was intrusted to eight legions, six of whom were planted in Syria, and the other two in Cappadocia. With regard to Egypt, Africa and Spain, as they were far removed from any important scene of war, a single legion maintained the domestic tranquillity of each of those great provinces. Even Italy was not left destitute of a military force. Above twenty thousand chosen soldiers, distinguished by the titles of City Cohorts and Prætorian Guards, watched over the safety of the monarch and the capital. As the authors of almost every revolution that distracted the empire, the Prætorians will very soon and very loudly demand our attention; but, in their arms and institutions, we cannot find any circumstance which discriminated them from the legions, unless it were a more splendid appearance, and a less rigid discipline.

The navy maintained by the emperors might seem inadequate to their greatness; but it was fully sufficient for every useful purpose of government. The ambition of the Romans was confined to the land; nor was that warlike people ever actuated by the enterprising spirit which had prompted the navigators of Tyre, of Carthage, and even of Marseilles, to enlarge the bounds of the world, and to explore the most remote coasts of the ocean. To the Romans the ocean remained an object of terror rather than of curiosity; the whole extent of the Mediterranean, after the destruction of Carthage and the extirpation of the pirates, was included within their provinces. The policy of the emperors was directed only to preserve the peaceful dominion of that sea, and to protect the commerce of their subjects. With these moderate views, Augustus stationed two permanent fleets in the most convenient ports of Italy, the one at Ravenna, on the Adriatic, the other at Misenum, in the bay of Naples. Experience seems at length to have convinced the ancients that, as soon as their galleys exceeded two, or at the most three ranks of oars, they were suited rather for vain pomp than for real service. Augustus himself, in the victory of Actium, had seen the superiority of his own light frigates (they were called Liburnians) over the lofty but unwieldy castles of his rival.[17] Of these Liburnians he composed the two fleets of Ravenna and Misenum, destined to command, the one the eastern, the other the western division of the Mediterranean; and to each of the squadrons he attached a body of several thousand marines. Besides these two ports, which may be considered as the principal seats of the Roman navy, a very considerable force was stationed at Frejus, on the coast of Provence, and the Euxine was guarded by forty ships, and three thousand soldiers. To all these we add the fleet which preserved the communication between Gaul and Britain, and a great number of vessels constantly maintained on the Rhine and Danube, to harass the country, or to intercept the passage of the barbarians. If we review this general state of the Imperial forces, of the cavalry as well as infantry, of the legions, the auxiliaries, the guards, and the navy, the most liberal computation will not allow us to fix the entire establishment by sea and by land at more than four hundred and fifty thousand men: a military power which, however formidable it may seem, was equalled by a monarch of the last century, whose kingdom was confined within a single province of the Roman empire.[18]

We have attempted to explain the spirit which moderated, and the strength which supported, the power of Hadrian and the Antonines. We shall now endeavour, with clearness and precision, to describe the provinces once united under their sway, but, at present, divided into so many independent and hostile states.

Spain, the western extremity of the empire, of Europe, and of the ancient world, has, in every age, invariably preserved the same natural limits; the Pyrenean mountains, the Mediterranean, and the Atlantic Ocean. That great peninsula, at present so unequally divided between two sovereigns, was distributed by Augustus into three provinces, Lusitania, Bætica, and Tarraconensis. The kingdom of Portugal now fills the place of the warlike country of the Lusitanians; and the loss sustained by the former, on the side of the East, is compensated by an accession of territory towards the North. The confines of Grenada and Andalusia correspond with those of

---

[17] *And yet if we may credit Orosius, these monstrous castles were no more than ten feet above the water.*

[18] *It must, however, be remembered, that France still feels that extraordinary effort.*

ancient Bætica. The remainder of Spain—Gallicia, and the Asturias, Biscay, and Navarre, Leon, and the two Castilles, Murcia, Valencia, Catalonia, and Arragon,—all contributed to form the third and most considerable of the Roman governments, which, from the name of its capital, was styled the province of Tarragona. Of the native barbarians, the Celtiberians were the most powerful, as the Cantabrians and Asturians proved the most obstinate. Confident in the strength of their mountains, they were the last who submitted to the arms of Rome, and the first who threw off the yoke of the Arabs.

Ancient Gaul, as it contained the whole country between the Pyrenees, the Alps, the Rhine, and the Ocean, was of greater extent than modern France. To the dominions of that powerful monarchy, with its recent acquisitions of Alsace and Lorraine, we must add the duchy of Savoy, the cantons of Switzerland, the four electorates of the Rhine, and the territories of Liege, Luxemburg, Hainault, Flanders and Brabant. When Augustus gave laws to the conquests of his father, he introduced a division of Gaul equally adapted to the progress of the legions, to the course of the rivers, and to the principal national distinctions, which had comprehended above an hundred independent states. The sea-coast of the Mediterranean, Languedoc, Provence, and Dauphiné, received their provincial appellation from the colony of Narbonne. The government of Aquitaine was extended from the Pyrenees to the Loire. The country between the Loire and the Seine was styled the Celtic Gaul, and soon borrowed a new denomination from the celebrated colony of Lugdunum, or Lyons. The Belgic lay beyond the Seine, and in more ancient times had been bounded only by the Rhine; but a little before the age of Cæsar, the Germans, abusing their superiority of valour, had occupied a considerable portion of the Belgic territory. The Roman conquerors very eagerly embraced so flattering a circumstance, and the Gallic frontier of the Rhine, from Basil to Leyden, received the pompous names of the Upper and the Lower Germany. Such, under the reign of the Antonines, were the six provinces of Gaul; the Narbonnese, Aquitaine, the Celtic, or Lyonnese, the Belgic, and the two Germanies.

We have already had occasion to mention the conquest of Britain, and to fix the boundary of the Roman province in this island. It comprehended all England, Wales, and the Lowlands of Scotland, as far as the Friths of Dumbarton and Edinburgh. Before Britain lost her freedom, the country was irregularly divided between thirty tribes of barbarians, of whom the most considerable were the Belgæ in the West, the Brigantes in the North, the Silures in South Wales, and the Iceni in Norfolk and Suffolk. As far as we can either trace or credit the resemblance of manners and language, Spain, Gaul and Britain were peopled by the same hardy race of savages. Before they yielded to the Roman arms, they often disputed the field, and often renewed the contest. After their submission they constituted the western division of the European provinces, which extended from the columns of Hercules to the wall of Antoninus, and from the mouth of the Tagus to the sources of the Rhine and Danube.

Before the Roman conquest, the country which is now called Lombardy was not considered as a part of Italy. It had been occupied by a powerful colony of Gauls, who, settling themselves along the banks of the Po, from Piedmont to Romagna, carried their arms and diffused their name from the Alps to the Apennine. The Ligurians dwelt on the rocky coast, which now forms the republic of Genoa. Venice was yet unborn; but the territories of that state, which lie to the east of the Adige, were inhabited by the Venetians.[19] The middle part of the peninsula, that now composes the duchy of Tuscany and the ecclesiastical state, was the ancient seat of the Etruscans and Umbrians; to the former of whom Italy was indebted for the first rudiments of a civilized life. The Tiber rolled at the foot of the seven hills of Rome, and the country of the Sabines, the Latins, and the Volsci, from that river to the frontiers of Naples, was the theatre of her infant victories. On that celebrated ground the first consuls deserved triumphs, their successors adorned villas, and *their* posterity have erected convents.[20] Capua and Campania possessed the immediate territory of Naples; the rest of the kingdom was inhabited by many warlike nations, the Marsi, the Samnites, the Apulians, and the Lucanians; and the sea-coasts had been covered by the flourishing colonies of the Greeks. We may remark, that when Augustus divided Italy into eleven regions, the little province of Istria was annexed to that seat of Roman sovereignty.

The European provinces of Rome were protected by the course of the Rhine and the Danube. The latter of those mighty streams, which rises at the distance of only thirty miles from the former, flows above thirteen hundred miles, for the most part to the southeast, collects the tribute of sixty navigable rivers, and is, at length, through six months, received into the Euxine, which appears scarcely equal to such an accession of waters. The provinces of the Danube soon acquired the general appellation of Illyricum, or the

[19] *The Italian Veneti, though often confounded with the Gauls, were more probably of Illyrian origin.*

[20] *The first contrast was observed by the ancients. The second must strike every modern traveller.*

Illyrian frontier,[21] and were esteemed the most warlike of the empire; but they deserve to be more particularly considered under the names of Rhætia, Noricum, Pannonia, Dalmatia, Dacia, Mæsia, Thrace, Macedonia, and Greece.

The province of Rhætia, which soon extinguished the name of the Vindelicians, extended from the summit of the Alps to the banks of the Danube; from its source, as far as its conflux with the Inn. The greatest part of the flat country is subject to the elector of Bavaria; the city of Augsburg is protected by the constitution of the German empire; the Grisons are safe in their mountains; and the country of Tyrol is ranked among the numerous provinces of the house of Austria.

The wide extent of territory which is included between the Inn, the Danube, and the Save,—Austria, Styria, Carinthia, Carniola, the Lower Hungary and Sclavonia,—was known to the ancients under the names of Noricum and Pannonia. In their original state of independence their fierce inhabitants were intimately connected. Under the Roman government they were frequently united, and they still remain the patrimony of a single family. They now contain the residence of a German prince, who styles himself Emperor of the Romans, and form the centre, as well as strength, of the Austrian power. It may not be improper to observe, that, if we except Bohemia, Moravia, the northern skirts of Austria, and a part of Hungary, between the Theiss and the Danube, all the other dominions of the house of Austria were comprised within the limits of the Roman empire.

Dalmatia, to which the name of Illyricum more properly belonged, was a long, but narrow tract, between the Save and the Adriatic. The best part of the sea-coast, which still retains its ancient appellation, is a province of the Venetian state, and the seat of the little republic of Ragusa. The inland parts have assumed the Sclavonian names of Croatia and Bosnia; the former obeys an Austrian governor, the latter a Turkish pasha; but the whole country is still infested by tribes of barbarians, whose savage independence marks the doubtful limit of the Christian and Mahometan power.

After the Danube had received the waters of the Theiss and the Save, it acquired, at least among the Greeks, the name of Ister.[22] It formerly divided Mæsia and Dacia, the latter of which, as we have already seen, was a conquest of Trajan, and the only province beyond the river. If we inquire into the present state of those countries, we shall find that, on the left hand of the Danube, Temeswar

[21] *The name of Illyricum originally belonged to the sea-coast of the Adriatic, and was gradually extended by the Romans from the Alps to the Euxine Sea.*

[22] *The Save rises near the confines of* Istria, *and was considered by the more early Greeks as the principal stream of the Danube.*

and Transylvania have been annexed, after many revolutions, to the crown of Hungary; whilst the principalities of Moldavia and Wallachia acknowledge the supremacy of the Ottoman Porte. On the right hand of the Danube, Mæsia, which during the middle ages was broken into the barbarian kingdoms of Servia and Bulgaria, is again united in Turkish slavery.

The appellation of Roumelia, which is still bestowed by the Turks on the extensive countries of Thrace, Macedonia, and Greece, preserves the memory of their ancient state under the Roman empire. In the time of the Antonines, the martial regions of Thrace, from the mountains of Hæmus and Rhodope to the Bosphorus and the Hellespont, had assumed the form of a province. Notwithstanding the change of masters and of religion, the new city of Rome, founded by Constantine on the banks of the Bosphorus, has ever since remained the capital of a great monarchy. The kingdom of Macedonia, which, under the reign of Alexander, gave laws to Asia, derived more solid advantages from the policy of the two Philips; and, with its dependencies of Epirus and Thessaly, extended from the Ægean to the Ionian sea. When we reflect on the fame of Thebes and Argos, of Sparta and Athens, we can scarcely persuade ourselves that so many immortal republics of ancient Greece were lost in a single province of the Roman empire, which, from the superior influence of the Achæan league, was usually denominated the province of Achaia.

Such was the state of Europe under the Roman emperors. The provinces of Asia, without excepting the transient conquests of Trajan, are all comprehended within the limits of the Turkish power. But instead of following the arbitrary divisions of despotism and ignorance, it will be safer for us, as well as more agreeable, to observe the indelible characters of nature. The name of Asia Minor is attributed, with some propriety, to the peninsula which, confined between the Euxine and the Mediterranean, advances from the Euphrates towards Europe. The most extensive and flourishing district westward of Mount Taurus and the river Halys, was dignified by the Romans with the exclusive title of Asia. The jurisdiction of that province extended over the ancient monarchies of Troy, Lydia, and Phrygia, the maritime countries of the Pamphylians, Lycians, and Carians, and the Grecian colonies of Ionia, which equalled in arts, though not in arms, the glory of their parent. The kingdoms of Bithynia and Pontus possessed the northern side of the peninsula from Constantinople to Trebizond. On the opposite side the province of Cilicia was terminated by the mountains of Syria: the inland country, separated from the Roman Asia by the river Halys, and from Armenia by the Euphrates, had once formed the independent kingdom of Cappadocia. In this place we may observe that the northern shores of the Euxine, beyond Trebizond in Asia and beyond the Danube in Europe, acknowledged the sovereignty of the emperors, and received at their hands either tributary princes or Roman garrisons. Budzak, Crim Tartary, Circassia, and Mingrelia, are the modern appellations of those savage countries.

Under the successors of Alexander, Syria was the seat of the Seleucidæ, who reigned over Upper Asia, till the successful revolt of the Parthians confined their dominions between the Euphrates and the Mediterranean. When Syria became subject to the Romans, it formed the eastern frontier of their empire; nor did that province, in its utmost latitude, know any other bounds than the mountains of Cappadocia to the north, and, towards the south, the confines of Egypt and the Red Sea. Phœnicia and Palestine were sometimes annexed to, and sometimes separated from, the jurisdiction of Syria. The former of these was a narrow and rocky coast; the latter was a territory scarcely superior to Wales, either in fertility or extent. Yet Phœnicia and Palestine will for ever live in the memory of mankind; since America, as well as Europe, has received letters from the one, and religion from the other.[23] A sandy desert, alike destitute of wood and water, skirts along the doubtful confine of Syria, from the Euphrates to the Red Sea. The wandering life of the Arabs was inseparably connected with their independence, and wherever, on some spots less barren than the rest, they ventured to form any settled habitations, they soon became subjects to the Roman empire.

The geographers of antiquity have frequently hesitated to what portion of the globe they should ascribe Egypt.[24] By its situation that celebrated kingdom is included within the immense peninsula of Africa; but it is accessible only on the side of Asia, whose revolutions, in almost every period of history, Egypt has humbly obeyed. A Roman præfect was seated on the splendid throne of the Ptolemies; and the iron sceptre of the Mamalukes is now in the hands of a Turkish pasha. The Nile flows down the country, above five hundred miles from the tropic of Cancer to the Mediterranean, and marks, on either side, the extent of fertility by the measure of its inundations. Cyrene, situated towards the west and along the seacoast, was first a Greek colony, afterwards a province of Egypt, and is now lost in the desert of Barca.

[23] *The progress of religion is well known. The use of letters was introduced among the savages of Europe about fifteen hundred years before Christ; and the Europeans carried them to America, about fifteen centuries after the Christian æra. But in a period of three thousand years, the Phœnician alphabet received considerable alterations as it passed through the hands of the Greeks and Romans.*

[24] *Ptolemy and Strabo, with the modern geographers, fix the Isthmus of Suez as the boundary of Asia and Africa. Dionysius, Mela, Pliny, Sallust, Hirtius, and Solinus, have preferred for that purpose the western branch of the Nile, or even the great Catabathmus, or descent, which last would assign to Asia not only Egypt, but part of Libya.*

From Cyrene to the ocean, the coast of Africa extends above fifteen hundred miles; yet so closely is it pressed between the Mediterranean and the Sahara, or sandy desert, that its breadth seldom exceeds fourscore or an hundred miles. The eastern division was considered by the Romans as the more peculiar and proper province of Africa. Till the arrival of the Phœnician colonies, that fertile country was inhabited by the Libyans, the most savage of mankind. Under the immediate jurisdiction of Carthage it became the centre of commerce and empire; but the republic of Carthage is now degenerated into the feeble and disorderly states of Tripoli and Tunis. The military government of Algiers oppresses the wide extent of Numidia, as it was once united under Massinissa and Jugurtha: but in the time of Augustus the limits of Numidia were contracted; and at least two-thirds of the country acquiesced in the name of Mauritania, with the epithet of Cæsariensis. The genuine Mauritania, or country of the Moors, which, from the ancient city of Tingi, or Tangier, was distinguished by the appellation of Tingitana, is represented by the modern kingdom of Fez. Sallè, on the Ocean, so infamous at present for its piratical depredations, was noticed by the Romans, as the extreme object of their power, and almost of their geography. A city of their foundation may still be discovered near Mequinez, the residence of the barbarian whom we condescend to style the Emperor of Morocco; but it does not appear that his more southern dominions, Morocco itself, and Segelmessa, were ever comprehended within the Roman province. The western parts of Africa are intersected by the branches of Mount Atlas, a name so idly celebrated by the fancy of poets;[25] but which is now diffused over the immense ocean that rolls between the ancient and the new continent.[26]

Having now finished the circuit of the Roman empire, we may observe that Africa is divided from Spain by a narrow strait of about twelve miles, through which the Atlantic flows into the Mediterranean. The columns of Hercules, so famous among the ancients, were two mountains which seemed to have been torn asunder by some convulsion of the elements; and at the foot of the European mountain the fortress of Gibraltar is now seated. The whole extent of the Mediterranean Sea, its coasts and its islands, were comprised within the Roman dominion. Of the larger islands, the two Baleares, which derive their names of Majorca and Minorca from their respective size, are subject at present, the former to Spain, the latter to Great Britain. It is easier to deplore the fate than to describe the

[25] The long range, moderate height, and gentle declivity of Mount Atlas are very unlike a solitary mountain which rears its head into the clouds, and seems to support the heavens. The peak of Teneriff, on the contrary, rises a league and a half above the surface of the sea, and, as it was frequently visited by the Phœnicians, might engage the notice of the Greek poets.

[26] M. de Voltaire, unsupported by either fact or probability, has generously bestowed the Canary Islands on the Roman empire.

actual condition of Corsica. Two Italian sovereigns assume a regal title from Sardinia and Sicily. Crete, or Candia, with Cyprus, and most of the smaller islands of Greece and Asia, have been subdued by the Turkish arms; whilst the little rock of Malta defies their power, and has emerged, under the government of its military Order, into fame and opulence.

This long enumeration of provinces, whose broken fragments have formed so many powerful kingdoms, might almost induce us to forgive the vanity or ignorance of the ancients. Dazzled with the extensive sway, the irresistible strength, and the real or affected moderation of the emperors, they permitted themselves to despise, and sometimes to forget, the outlying countries which had been left in the enjoyment of a barbarous independence; and they gradually assumed the licence of confounding the Roman monarchy with the globe of the earth. But the temper, as well as knowledge, of a modern historian require a more sober and accurate language. He may impress a juster image of the greatness of Rome by observing that the empire was above two thousand miles in breadth, from the wall of Antoninus and the northern limits of Dacia to Mount Atlas and the tropic of Cancer; that it extended in length more than three thousand miles, from the Western Ocean to the Euphrates; that it was situated in the finest part of the Temperate Zone, between the twenty-fourth and fifty-sixth degrees of northern latitude; and that it was supposed to contain above sixteen hundred thousand square miles, for the most part of fertile and well-cultivated land.

II

OF THE UNION AND INTERNAL PROSPERITY OF THE ROMAN
EMPIRE IN THE AGE OF THE ANTONINES · ART · CHARACTER

I T I S not alone by the rapidity or
extent of conquest that we should estimate the greatness of Rome.
The sovereign of the Russian deserts commands a larger portion of
the globe. In the seventh summer after his passage of the Hellespont, Alexander erected the Macedonian trophies on the banks of
the Hyphasis.[1] Within less than a century, the irresistible Zingis, and
the Mogul princes of his race, spread their cruel devastations and
transient empire from the sea of China to the confines of Egypt
and Germany. But the firm edifice of Roman power was raised and
preserved by the wisdom of ages. The obedient provinces of Trajan
and the Antonines were united by laws and adorned by arts. They
might occasionally suffer from the partial abuse of delegated authority; but the general principle of government was wise, simple,
and beneficent. They enjoyed the religion of their ancestors, whilst
in civil honours and advantages they were exalted, by just degrees,
to an equality with their conquerors.

I. The policy of the emperors and the senate, as far as it concerned religion, was happily seconded by the reflections of the enlightened, and by the habits of the superstitious, part of their subjects. The various modes of worship which prevailed in the Roman
world were all considered by the people as equally true; by the philosopher as equally false; and by the magistrate as equally useful.
And thus toleration produced not only mutual indulgence, but even
religious concord.

The superstition of the people was not embittered by any mixture
of theological rancour; nor was it confined by the chains of any
speculative system. The devout polytheist, though fondly attached
to his national rites, admitted with implicit faith the different religions of the earth.[2] Fear, gratitude, and curiosity, a dream or an
omen, a singular disorder, or a distant journey, perpetually disposed

[1] *They were erected
about the midway be-
tween Lahor and Delhi.
The conquests of Alex-
ander in Hindostan were
confined to the Punjab, a
country watered by the
five great streams of the
Indus.*

[2] *Some obscure traces of
an intolerant spirit ap-
pear in the conduct of
the Egyptians; and the
Christians as well as
Jews, who lived under
the Roman empire,
formed a very important
exception: so important
indeed, that the discus-
sion will require a dis-
tinct chapter of this
work.*

him to multiply the articles of his belief, and to enlarge the list of his protectors. The thin texture of the pagan mythology was interwoven with various but not discordant materials. As soon as it was allowed that sages and heroes, who had lived or who had died for the benefit of their country, were exalted to a state of power and immortality, it was universally confessed that they deserved, if not the adoration, at least the reverence of all mankind. The deities of a thousand groves and a thousand streams possessed in peace their local and respective influence; nor could the Roman who deprecated the wrath of the Tiber deride the Egyptian who presented his offering to the beneficent genius of the Nile. The visible powers of Nature, the planets, and the elements, were the same throughout the universe. The invisible governors of the moral world were inevitably cast in a similar mould of fiction and allegory. Every virtue, and even vice, acquired its divine representative; every art and profession its patron, whose attributes in the most distant ages and countries were uniformly derived from the character of their peculiar votaries. A republic of gods of such opposite tempers and interests required, in every system, the moderating hand of a supreme magistrate, who, by the progress of knowledge and of flattery, was gradually invested with the sublime perfections of an Eternal Parent and an Omnipotent Monarch.[3] Such was the mild spirit of antiquity, that the nations were less attentive to the difference than to the resemblance of their religious worship. The Greek, the Roman, and the Barbarian, as they met before their respective altars, easily persuaded themselves that, under various names and with various ceremonies, they adored the same deities. The elegant mythology of Homer gave a beautiful and almost a regular form to the polytheism of the ancient world.[4]

The philosophers of Greece deduced their morals from the nature of man rather than from that of God. They meditated, however, on the Divine Nature as a very curious and important speculation, and in the profound inquiry they displayed the strength and weakness of the human understanding.[5] Of the four most celebrated schools, the Stoics and the Platonists endeavoured to reconcile the jarring interests of reason and piety. They have left us the most sublime proofs of the existence and perfections of the first cause; but, as it was impossible for them to conceive the creation of matter, the workman in the Stoic philosophy was not sufficiently distinguished from the work; whilst, on the contrary, the spiritual God of Plato and his disciples resembled an idea rather than a substance. The

[3] *The rights, power, and pretensions of the sovereign of Olympus are very clearly described in the fifteenth book of the Iliad: in the Greek original, I mean; for Mr. Pope, without perceiving it, has improved the theology of Homer.*

[4] *Within a century or two the Gauls themselves applied to their gods the names of Mercury, Mars, Apollo, &c.*

[5] *The admirable work of Cicero de Naturâ Deorum, is the best clue we have to guide us through the dark and profound abyss. He represents with candour, and confutes with subtlety, the opinions of the philosophers.*

opinions of the Academics and Epicureans were of a less religious cast; but, whilst the modest science of the former induced them to doubt, the positive ignorance of the latter urged them to deny, the providence of a Supreme Ruler. The spirit of inquiry, prompted by emulation and supported by freedom, had divided the public teachers of philosophy into a variety of contending sects; but the ingenuous youth, who from every part resorted to Athens and the other seats of learning in the Roman empire, were alike instructed in every school to reject and to despise the religion of the multitude. How, indeed, was it possible that a philosopher should accept as divine truths the idle tales of the poets, and the incoherent traditions of antiquity; or that he should adore, as gods, those imperfect beings whom he must have despised, as men! Against such unworthy adversaries, Cicero condescended to employ the arms of reason and eloquence; but the satire of Lucian was a much more adequate as well as more efficacious weapon. We may be well assured that a writer conversant with the world would never have ventured to expose the gods of his country to public ridicule, had they not already been the objects of secret contempt among the polished and enlightened orders of society.[6]

Notwithstanding the fashionable irreligion which prevailed in the age of the Antonines, both the interests of the priests and the credulity of the people were sufficiently respected. In their writings and conversation the philosophers of antiquity asserted the independent dignity of reason; but they resigned their actions to the commands of law and of custom. Viewing with a smile of pity and indulgence the various errors of the vulgar, they diligently practised the ceremonies of their fathers, devoutly frequented the temples of the gods; and, sometimes condescending to act a part on the theatre of superstition, they concealed the sentiments of an Atheist under the sacerdotal robes. Reasoners of such a temper were scarcely inclined to wrangle about their respective modes of faith or of worship. It was indifferent to them what shape the folly of the multitude might choose to assume; and they approached, with the same inward contempt and the same external reverence, the altars of the Libyan, the Olympian, or the Capitoline Jupiter.[7]

It is not easy to conceive from what motives a spirit of persecution could introduce itself into the Roman councils. The magistrates could not be actuated by a blind though honest bigotry, since the magistrates were themselves philosophers; and the schools of Athens had given laws to the senate. They could not be impelled by

[6] *I do not pretend to assert that, in this irreligious age, the natural terrors of superstition, dreams, omens, apparitions, &c., had lost their efficacy.*

[7] *Socrates, Epicurus, Cicero, and Plutarch, always inculcated a decent reverence for the religion of their own country, and of mankind. The devotion of Epicurus was assiduous and exemplary.*

"*There existed* five *principal* Fora; *but, as they were all contiguous and adjacent, in the plain which is surrounded by the Capitoline, the Quirinal, the Esquiline, and the Palatine hills, they might fairly be considered as* one."

"*Whatever fancy may conceive, the severe compass of the geographer defines the circumference of Rome within a line of twelve miles and three hundred and forty-five paces; and that circumference, except in the Vatican, has invariably been the same from the triumph of Aurelian to the peaceful but obscure reign of the modern popes. But in the day of her greatness, the space within her walls was crowded with habitations and inhabitants; and the populous suburbs, that stretched along the public roads, were darted like so many rays from one centre. Adversity swept away these extraneous ornaments, and left naked and desolate a considerable part even of the seven hills.*"

A MAP WITH THE HILLS AND ANCIENT MONUMENTS OF ROME
AND FRAGMENTS OF AN EARLY-THIRD-CENTURY MARBLE MAP

The seven hills of ancient Rome were the Palatine, Capitoline, Quirinal, Viminal, Esquiline, Cælean, and Aventine. Other hills were the Janiculum, Pincian, Appean, and Vatican. The fragments of the early-third-century marble map of the city of Rome were part of a map originally on the exterior wall of the Temple of the Sacred City in the Forum of Peace. They were reassembled in the Conservatori Museum on the Capitoline.

ambition or avarice, as the temporal and ecclesiastical powers were united in the same hands. The pontiffs were chosen among the most illustrious of the senators; and the office of Supreme Pontiff was constantly exercised by the emperors themselves. They knew and valued the advantages of religion, as it is connected with civil government. They encouraged the public festivals which humanize the manners of the people. They managed the arts of divination as a convenient instrument of policy; and they respected, as the firmest bond of society, the useful persuasion that, either in this or in a future life, the crime of perjury is most assuredly punished by the avenging gods.[8] But, whilst they acknowledged the general advantages of religion, they were convinced that the various modes of worship contributed alike to the same salutary purposes; and that, in every country, the form of superstition which had received the sanction of time and experience was the best adapted to the climate and to its inhabitants. Avarice and taste very frequently despoiled the vanquished nations of the elegant statues of their gods and the rich ornaments of their temples; but, in the exercise of the religion which they derived from their ancestors, they uniformly experienced the indulgence, and even protection, of the Roman conquerors. The province of Gaul seems, and indeed only seems, an exception to this universal toleration. Under the specious pretext of abolishing human sacrifices, the emperors Tiberius and Claudius suppressed the dangerous power of the Druids; but the priests themselves, their gods, and their altars, subsisted in peaceful obscurity till the final destruction of Paganism.

Rome, the capital of a great monarchy, was incessantly filled with subjects and strangers from every part of the world, who all introduced and enjoyed the favourite superstitions of their native country. Every city in the empire was justified in maintaining the purity of its ancient ceremonies; and the Roman senate, using the common privilege, sometimes interposed to check this inundation of foreign rites. The Egyptian superstition, of all the most contemptible and abject, was frequently prohibited; the temples of Serapis and Isis demolished, and their worshippers banished from Rome and Italy.[9] But the zeal of fanaticism prevailed over the cold and feeble efforts of policy. The exiles returned, the proselytes multiplied, the temples were restored with increasing splendour, and Isis and Serapis at length assumed their place among the Roman deities.[10] Nor was this indulgence a departure from the old maxims of government. In the purest ages of the commonwealth, Cybele and Æsculapius had

[8] *Juvenal laments that in his time this apprehension had lost much of its effect.*

[9] *In the year of Rome 701, the temple of Isis and Serapis was demolished by the order of the senate, and even by the hands of the consul. After the death of Cæsar, it was restored at the public expense. When Augustus was in Egypt, he revered the majesty of Serapis; but in the Pomœrium of Rome, and a mile round it, he prohibited the worship of the Egyptian gods. They remained, however, very fashionable under his reign and that of his successor, till the justice of Tiberius was provoked to some acts of severity.*

[10] *I am inclined to attribute their establishment to the devotion of the Flavian family.*

been invited by solemn embassies; and it was customary to tempt the protectors of besieged cities by the promise of more distinguished honours than they possessed in their native country. Rome gradually became the common temple of her subjects; and the freedom of the city was bestowed on all the gods of mankind.

II. The narrow policy of preserving without any foreign mixture the pure blood of the ancient citizens, had checked the fortune, and hastened the ruin, of Athens and Sparta. The aspiring genius of Rome sacrificed vanity to ambition, and deemed it more prudent, as well as honourable, to adopt virtue and merit for her own wheresoever they were found, among slaves or strangers, enemies or barbarians. During the most flourishing æra of the Athenian commonwealth the number of citizens gradually decreased from about thirty to twenty-one thousand. If, on the contrary, we study the growth of the Roman republic, we may discover that, notwithstanding the incessant demands of wars and colonies, the citizens, who, in the first census of Servius Tullius, amounted to no more than eighty-three thousand, were multiplied, before the commencement of the social war, to the number of four hundred and sixty-three thousand men able to bear arms in the service of their country. When the allies of Rome claimed an equal share of honours and privileges, the senate indeed preferred the chance of arms to an ignominious concession. The Samnites and the Lucanians paid the severe penalty of their rashness; but the rest of the Italian states, as they successively returned to their duty, were admitted into the bosom of the republic, and soon contributed to the ruin of public freedom. Under a democratical government the citizens exercise the powers of sovereignty; and those powers will be first abused, and afterwards lost, if they are committed to an unwieldy multitude. But, when the popular assemblies had been suppressed by the administration of the emperors, the conquerors were distinguished from the vanquished nations only as the first and most honourable order of subjects; and their increase, however rapid, was no longer exposed to the same dangers. Yet the wisest princes who adopted the maxims of Augustus guarded with the strictest care the dignity of the Roman name, and diffused the freedom of the city with a prudent liberality.[11]

Till the privileges of Romans had been progressively extended to all the inhabitants of the empire, an important distinction was preserved between Italy and the provinces. The former was esteemed the centre of public unity, and the firm basis of the constitution.

[11] *Mæcenas had advised him to declare, by one edict, all his subjects citizens. But we may justly suspect that the Historian Dion was the author of a counsel, so much adapted to the practice of his own age, and so little to that of Augustus.*

Italy claimed the birth, or at least the residence, of the emperors and the senate.[12] The estates of the Italians were exempt from taxes, their persons from the arbitary jurisdiction of governors. Their municipal corporations, formed after the perfect model of the capital, were intrusted, under the immediate eye of the supreme power, with the execution of the laws. From the foot of the Alps to the extremity of Calabria, all the natives of Italy were born citizens of Rome. Their partial distinctions were obliterated, and they insensibly coalesced into one great nation, united by language, manners, and civil institutions, and equal to the weight of a powerful empire. The republic gloried in her generous policy, and was frequently rewarded by the merit and services of her adopted sons. Had she always confined the distinction of Romans to the ancient families within the walls of the city, that immortal name would have been deprived of some of its noblest ornaments. Virgil was a native of Mantua; Horace was inclined to doubt whether he should call himself an Apulian or a Lucanian; it was in Padua that an historian was found worthy to record the majestic series of Roman victories. The patriot family of the Catos emerged from Tusculum; and the little town of Arpinum claimed the double honour of producing Marius and Cicero, the former of whom deserved, after Romulus and Camillus, to be styled the Third Founder of Rome; and the latter, after saving his country from the designs of Catiline, enabled her to contend with Athens for the palm of eloquence.

The provinces of the empire (as they have been described in the preceding chapter) were destitute of any public force or constitutional freedom. In Etruria, in Greece,[13] and in Gaul, it was the first care of the senate to dissolve those dangerous confederacies which taught mankind that, as the Roman arms prevailed by division, they might be resisted by union. Those princes whom the ostentation of gratitude or generosity permitted for a while to hold a precarious sceptre were dismissed from their thrones, as soon as they had performed their appointed task of fashioning to the yoke the vanquished nations. The free states and cities which had embraced the cause of Rome were rewarded with a nominal alliance, and insensibly sunk into real servitude. The public authority was everywhere exercised by the ministers of the senate and of the emperors, and that authority was absolute and without control. But the same salutary maxims of government, which had secured the peace and obedience of Italy, were extended to the most distant conquests. A nation of Romans was gradually formed in the provinces, by the

[12] *The senators were obliged to have one-third of their own landed property in Italy. The qualification was reduced by Marcus to one-fourth. Since the reign of Trajan, Italy had sunk nearer to the level of the provinces.*

[13] *The Romans condescended to restore the names of those assemblies, when they could no longer be dangerous.*

27

double expedient of introducing colonies, and of admitting the most faithful and deserving of the provincials to the freedom of Rome.

"Wheresoever the Roman conquers, he inhabits," is a very just observation of Seneca, confirmed by history and experience. The natives of Italy, allured by pleasure or by interest, hastened to enjoy the advantages of victory; and we may remark that, about forty years after the reduction of Asia, eighty thousand Romans were massacred in one day by the cruel orders of Mithridates.[14] These voluntary exiles were engaged for the most part in the occupations of commerce, agriculture, and the farm of the revenue. But after the legions were rendered permanent by the emperors, the provinces were peopled by a race of soldiers; and the veterans, whether they received the reward of their service in land or in money, usually settled with their families in the country where they had honourably spent their youth. Throughout the empire, but more particularly in the western parts, the most fertile districts and the most convenient situations were reserved for the establishment of colonies; some of which were of a civil and others of a military nature. In their manners and internal policy, the colonies formed a perfect representation of their great parent; and [as] they were soon endeared to the natives by the ties of friendship and alliance, they effectually diffused a reverence for the Roman name, and a desire which was seldom disappointed of sharing, in due time, its honours and advantages.[15] The municipal cities insensibly equalled the rank and splendour of the colonies; and in the reign of Hadrian it was disputed which was the preferable condition, of those societies which had issued from, or those which had been received into, the bosom of Rome.[16] The right of Latium, as it was called, conferred on the cities to which it had been granted a more partial favour. The magistrates only, at the expiration of their office, assumed the quality of Roman citizens; but as those offices were annual, in a few years they circulated round the principal families. Those of the provincials who were permitted to bear arms in the legions; those who exercised any civil employment; all, in a word, who performed any public service, or displayed any personal talents, were rewarded with a present, whose value was continually diminished by the increasing liberality of the emperors. Yet even in the age of the Antonines, when the freedom of the city had been bestowed on the greater number of their subjects, it was still accompanied with very solid advantages. The bulk of the people acquired, with that title, the benefit of the

[14] *Plutarch and Dion Cassius swell the massacre to 150,000 citizens; but I should esteem the smaller number to be more than sufficient.*

[15] *Twenty-five colonies were settled in Spain; and nine in Britain, of which London, Colchester, Lincoln, Chester, Gloucester, and Bath, still remain considerable cities.*

[16] *The Emperor Hadrian expressed his surprise that the cities of Utica, Gades, and Italica, which already enjoyed the rights of* Municipia, *should solicit the title of colonies. Their example, however, became fashionable, and the empire was filled with honorary colonies.*

Roman laws, particularly in the interesting articles of marriage, testaments, and inheritances; and the road of fortune was open to those whose pretensions were seconded by favour or merit. The grandsons of the Gauls who had besieged Julius Cæsar in Alesia commanded legions, governed provinces, and were admitted into the senate of Rome. Their ambition, instead of disturbing the tranquillity of the state, was intimately connected with its safety and greatness.

So sensible were the Romans of the influence of language over national manners, that it was their most serious care to extend, with the progress of their arms, the use of the Latin tongue. The ancient dialects of Italy, the Sabine, the Etruscan, and the Venetian, sunk into oblivion; but in the provinces, the east was less docile than the west to the voice of its victorious preceptors. This obvious difference marked the two portions of the empire with a distinction of colours, which, though it was in some degree concealed during the meridian splendour of prosperity, became gradually more visible as the shades of night descended upon the Roman world. The western countries were civilized by the same hands which subdued them. As soon as the barbarians were reconciled to obedience, their minds were opened to any new impressions of knowledge and politeness. The language of Virgil and Cicero, though with some inevitable mixture of corruption, was so universally adopted in Africa, Spain, Gaul, Britain, and Pannonia, that the faint traces of the Punic or Celtic idioms were preserved only in the mountains, or among the peasants.[17] Education and study insensibly inspired the natives of those countries with the sentiments of Romans; and Italy gave fashions, as well as laws, to her Latin provincials. They solicited with more ardour, and obtained with more facility, the freedom and honours of the state; supported the national dignity in letters[18] and in arms; and, at length, in the person of Trajan, produced an emperor whom the Scipios would not have disowned for their countryman. The situation of the Greeks was very different from that of the barbarians. The former had been long since civilized and corrupted. They had too much taste to relinquish their language, and too much vanity to adopt any foreign institutions. Still preserving the prejudices, after they had lost the virtues, of their ancestors, they affected to despise the unpolished manners of the Roman conquerors, whilst they were compelled to respect their superior wisdom and power.[19] Nor was the influence of the Grecian language and sentiments confined to the narrow limits of that once celebrated country. Their

[17] *The Celtic was preserved in the mountains of Wales, Cornwall, and Armorica. We may observe that Apuleius reproaches an African youth, who lived among the populace, with the use of the Punic; whilst he had almost forgot Greek, and neither could nor would speak Latin. The greater part of St. Austin's congregations were strangers to the Punic.*

[18] *Spain alone produced Columella, the Senecas, Lucan, Martial, and Quintilian.*

[19] *There is not, I believe, from Dionysius to Libanius, a single Greek critic who mentions Virgil or Horace. They seem ignorant that the Romans had any good writers.*

empire, by the progress of colonies and conquest, had been diffused from the Hadriatic to the Euphrates and the Nile. Asia was covered with Greek cities, and the long reign of the Macedonian kings had introduced a silent revolution into Syria and Egypt. In their pompous courts those princes united the elegance of Athens with the luxury of the East, and the example of the court was imitated, at an humble distance, by the higher ranks of their subjects. Such was the general division of the Roman empire into the Latin and Greek languages. To these we may add a third distinction for the body of the natives in Syria, and especially in Egypt. The use of their ancient dialects, by secluding them from the commerce of mankind, checked the improvements of those barbarians. The slothful effeminacy of the former exposed them to the contempt, the sullen ferociousness of the latter excited the aversion, of the conquerors. Those nations had submitted to the Roman power, but they seldom desired or deserved the freedom of the city; and it was remarked that more than two hundred and thirty years elapsed after the ruin of the Ptolemies, before an Egyptian was admitted into the senate of Rome.[20]

It is a just though trite observation, that victorious Rome was herself subdued by the arts of Greece. Those immortal writers who still command the admiration of modern Europe soon became the favourite object of study and imitation in Italy and the western provinces. But the elegant amusements of the Romans were not suffered to interfere with their sound maxims of policy. Whilst they acknowledged the charms of the Greek, they asserted the dignity of the Latin, tongue, and the exclusive use of the latter was inflexibly maintained in the administration of civil as well as military government.[21] The two languages exercised at the same time their separate jurisdiction throughout the empire: the former, as the natural idiom of science; the latter, as the legal dialect of public transactions. Those who united letters with business were equally conversant with both; and it was almost impossible, in any province, to find a Roman subject, of a liberal education, who was at once a stranger to the Greek and to the Latin language.

It was by such institutions that the nations of the empire insensibly melted away into the Roman name and people. But there still remained, in the centre of every province and of every family, an unhappy condition of men who endured the weight, without sharing the benefits, of society. In the free states of antiquity the domestic slaves were exposed to the wanton rigour of despotism. The

[20] *The first instance happened under the reign of Septimius Severus.*

[21] *The Emperor Claudius disfranchised an eminent Grecian for not understanding Latin. He was probably in some public office.*

perfect settlement of the Roman empire was preceded by ages of violence and rapine. The slaves consisted, for the most part, of barbarian captives, taken in thousands by the chance of war, purchased at a vile price,[22] accustomed to a life of independence, and impatient to break and to revenge their fetters. Against such internal enemies, whose desperate insurrections had more than once reduced the republic to the brink of destruction, the most severe regulations and the most cruel treatment seemed almost justified by the great law of self-preservation. But when the principal nations of Europe, Asia, and Africa were united under the laws of one sovereign, the source of foreign supplies flowed with much less abundance, and the Romans were reduced to the milder but more tedious method of propagation. In their numerous families, and particularly in their country estates, they encouraged the marriage of their slaves. The sentiments of nature, the habits of education, and the possession of a dependent species of property, contributed to alleviate the hardships of servitude. The existence of a slave became an object of greater value, and though his happiness still depended on the temper and circumstances of the master, the humanity of the latter, instead of being restrained by fear, was encouraged by the sense of his own interest. The progress of manners was accelerated by the virtue or policy of the emperors; and by the edicts of Hadrian and the Antonines the protection of the laws was extended to the most abject part of mankind. The jurisdiction of life and death over the slaves, a power long exercised and often abused, was taken out of private hands, and reserved to the magistrates alone. The subterraneous prisons were abolished; and, upon a just complaint of intolerable treatment, the injured slave obtained either his deliverance or a less cruel master.

Hope, the best comfort of our imperfect condition, was not denied to the Roman slave; and, if he had any opportunity of making himself either useful or agreeable, he might very naturally expect that the diligence and fidelity of a few years would be rewarded with the inestimable gift of freedom. The benevolence of the master was so frequently prompted by the meaner suggestions of vanity and avarice, that the laws found it more necessary to restrain than to encourage a profuse and undistinguishing liberality, which might degenerate into a very dangerous abuse. It was a maxim of ancient jurisprudence, that a slave had not any country of his own; he acquired with his liberty an admission into the political society of which his patron was a member. The consequences of this maxim would have prostituted the privileges of the Roman city to a mean

[22] *In the camp of Lucullus, an ox sold for a drachma, and a slave for four drachmæ, or about three shillings.*

and promiscuous multitude. Some seasonable exceptions were therefore provided; and the honourable distinction was confined to such slaves only as, for just causes, and with the approbation of the magistrate, should receive a solemn and legal manumission. Even these chosen freedmen obtained no more than the private rights of citizens, and were rigorously excluded from civil or military honours. Whatever might be the merit or fortune of their sons, *they* likewise were esteemed unworthy of a seat in the senate; nor were the traces of a servile origin allowed to be completely obliterated till the third or fourth generation. Without destroying the distinction of ranks, a distant prospect of freedom and honours was presented, even to those whom pride and prejudice almost disdained to number among the human species.

It was once proposed to discriminate the slaves by a peculiar habit, but it was justly apprehended that there might be some danger in acquainting them with their own numbers. Without interpreting, in their utmost strictness, the liberal appellations of legions and myriads, we may venture to pronounce that the proportion of slaves, who were valued as property, was more considerable than that of servants, who can be computed only as an expense.[23] The youths of a promising genius were instructed in the arts and sciences, and their price was ascertained by the degree of their skill and talents.[24] Almost every profession, either liberal[25] or mechanical, might be found in the household of an opulent senator. The ministers of pomp and sensuality were multiplied beyond the conception of modern luxury. It was more for the interest of the merchant or manufacturer to purchase than to hire his workmen; and in the country slaves were employed as the cheapest and most laborious instruments of agriculture. To confirm the general observation, and to display the multitude of slaves, we might allege a variety of particular instances. It was discovered, on a very melancholy occasion, that four hundred slaves were maintained in a single palace of Rome.[26] The same number of four hundred belonged to an estate, which an African widow, of a very private condition, resigned to her son, whilst she reserved for herself a much larger share of her property. A freedman, under the reign of Augustus, though his fortune had suffered great losses in the civil wars, left behind him three thousand six hundred yoke of oxen, two hundred and fifty thousand head of smaller cattle, and, what was almost included in the description of cattle, four thousand one hundred and sixteen slaves.

The number of subjects who acknowledged the laws of Rome, of

[23] *In Paris there are not more than 43,700 domestics of every sort, and not a twelfth part of the inhabitants.*

[24] *A learned slave sold for many hundred pounds sterling; Atticus always bred and taught them himself.*

[25] *Many of the Roman physicians were slaves.*

[26] *They all were executed for not preventing their master's murder.*

citizens, of provincials, and of slaves, cannot now be fixed with such a degree of accuracy as the importance of the object would deserve. We are informed that, when the emperor Claudius exercised the office of censor, he took an account of six million nine hundred and forty-five thousand Roman citizens, who, with the proportion of women and children, must have amounted to about twenty millions of souls. The multitude of subjects of an inferior rank was uncertain and fluctuating. But, after weighing with attention every circumstance which could influence the balance, it seems probable that there existed, in the time of Claudius, about twice as many provincials as there were citizens, of either sex and of every age; and that the slaves were at least equal in number to the free inhabitants of the Roman world. The total amount of this imperfect calculation would rise to about one hundred and twenty millions of persons: a degree of population which possibly exceeds that of modern Europe,[27] and forms the most numerous society that has ever been united under the same system of government.

Domestic peace and union were the natural consequences of the moderate and comprehensive policy embraced by the Romans. If we turn our eyes towards the monarchies of Asia, we shall behold despotism in the centre and weakness in the extremities; the collection of the revenue, or the administration of justice, enforced by the presence of an army; hostile barbarians, established in the heart of the country, hereditary satraps usurping the dominion of the provinces and subjects, inclined to rebellion, though incapable of freedom. But the obedience of the Roman world was uniform, voluntary, and permanent. The vanquished nations, blended into one great people, resigned the hope, nay even the wish, of resuming their independence, and scarcely considered their own existence as distinct from the existence of Rome. The established authority of the emperors pervaded without an effort the wide extent of their dominions, and was exercised with the same facility on the banks of the Thames, or of the Nile, as on those of the Tiber. The legions were destined to serve against the public enemy, and the civil magistrate seldom required the aid of a military force. In this state of general security, the leisure as well as opulence both of the prince and people were devoted to improve and to adorn the Roman empire.

Among the innumerable monuments of architecture constructed by the Romans, how many have escaped the notice of history, how few have resisted the ravages of time and barbarism! And yet even the majestic ruins that are still scattered over Italy and the provinces

[27] *Compute twenty millions in France, twenty-two in Germany, four in Hungary, ten in Italy with its islands, eight in Great Britain and Ireland, eight in Spain and Portugal, ten or twelve in the European Russia, six in Poland, six in Greece and Turkey, four in Sweden, three in Denmark and Norway, four in the Low Countries. The whole would amount to one hundred and five, or one hundred and seven millions.* [*Gibbon's estimate of the collective subjects of the Roman Empire is probably more correct than many calculations that have been made; yet he seems to have rated them too high; and he is undoubtedly wrong when he adds that they were more numerous than the whole present (1779) population of Europe, the total of which would seem to have been something like one hundred and twenty-five millions.*]

would be sufficient to prove that those countries were once the seat of a polite and powerful empire. Their greatness alone, or their beauty, might deserve our attention; but they are rendered more interesting by two important circumstances, which connect the agreeable history of the arts with the more useful history of human manners. Many of those works were erected at private expense, and almost all were intended for public benefit.

It is natural to suppose that the greatest number, as well as the most considerable of the Roman edifices, were raised by the emperors, who possessed so unbounded a command both of men and money. Augustus was accustomed to boast that he had found his capital of brick, and that he had left it of marble.[28] The strict economy of Vespasian was the source of his magnificence. The works of Trajan bear the stamp of his genius. The public monuments with which Hadrian adorned every province of the empire were executed not only by his orders, but under his immediate inspection. He was himself an artist; and he loved the arts, as they conduced to the glory of the monarch. They were encouraged by the Antonines, as they contributed to the happiness of the people. But if the emperors were the first, they were not the only architects of their dominions. Their example was universally imitated by their principal subjects, who were not afraid of declaring that they had spirit to conceive, and wealth to accomplish, the noblest undertakings. Scarcely had the proud structure of the Coliseum been dedicated at Rome, before the edifices of a smaller scale indeed, but of the same design and materials, were erected for the use, and at the expense, of the cities of Capua and Verona. The inscription of the stupendous bridge of Alcantara attests that it was thrown over the Tagus by the contribution of a few Lusitanian communities. When Pliny was intrusted with the government of Bithynia and Pontus, provinces by no means the richest or most considerable of the empire, he found the cities within his jurisdiction striving with each other in every useful and ornamental work that might deserve the curiosity of strangers or the gratitude of their citizens. It was the duty of the Proconsul to supply their deficiencies, to direct their taste, and sometimes to moderate their emulation.[29] The opulent senators of Rome and the provinces esteemed it an honour, and almost an obligation, to adorn the splendour of their age and country; and the influence of fashion very frequently supplied the want of taste or generosity. Among a crowd of these private benefactors, we may select Herodes Atticus, an Athenian citizen, who lived in the age of the Antonines. What-

[28] *Augustus built in Rome the temple and forum of Mars the Avenger; the Temple of Jupiter Tonans in the capitol; that of Apollo Palatine, with public libraries; the portico and basilica of Caius and Lucius; the porticoes of Livia and Octavia, and the theatre of Marcellus. The example of the sovereign was imitated by his ministers and generals; and his friend Agrippa left behind him the immortal monument of the Pantheon.*

[29] *Pliny mentions the following works, carried on at the expense of the cities. At Nicomedia, a new forum, an aqueduct, and a canal, left unfinished by a king; at Nice, a Gymnasium and a theatre, which had already cost near ninety thousand pounds; baths at Prusa and Claudiopolis; and an aqueduct of sixteen miles in length for the use of Sinope.*

ever might be the motive of his conduct, his magnificence would have been worthy of the greatest kings.

The family of Herod, at least after it had been favoured by fortune, was lineally descended from Cimon and Miltiades, Theseus and Cecrops, Æacus and Jupiter. But the posterity of so many gods and heroes was fallen into the most abject state. His grandfather had suffered by the hands of justice, and Julius Atticus, his father, must have ended his life in poverty and contempt, had he not discovered an immense treasure buried under an old house, the last remains of his patrimony. According to the rigour of law, the emperor might have asserted his claim; and the prudent Atticus prevented, by a frank confession, the officiousness of informers. But the equitable Nerva, who then filled the throne, refused to accept any part of it, and commanded him to use, without scruple, the present of fortune. The cautious Athenian still insisted that the treasure was too considerable for a subject, and that he knew not how to *use it*. *Abuse it then,* replied the monarch, with a good-natured peevishness; for it is your own.[30] Many will be of opinion that Atticus literally obeyed the emperor's last instructions, since he expended the greatest part of his fortune, which was much increased by an advantageous marriage, in the service of the Public. He had obtained for his son Herod the prefecture of the free cities of Asia; and the young magistrate, observing that the town of Troas was indifferently supplied with water, obtained from the munificence of Hadrian three hundred myriads of drachms (about a hundred thousand pounds) for the construction of a new aqueduct. But in the execution of the work the charge amounted to more than double the estimate, and the officers of the revenue began to murmur, till the generous Atticus silenced their complaints by requesting that he might be permitted to take upon himself the whole additional expense.

The ablest preceptors of Greece and Asia had been invited by liberal rewards to direct the education of young Herod. Their pupil soon became a celebrated orator in the useless rhetoric of that age, which, confining itself to the schools, disdained to visit either the Forum or the Senate. He was honoured with the consulship at Rome; but the greatest part of his life was spent in a philosophic retirement at Athens, and his adjacent villas; perpetually surrounded by sophists, who acknowledged, without reluctance, the superiority of a rich and generous rival. The monuments of his genius have perished; some remains still preserve the fame of his taste and munificence: modern travellers have measured the re-

[30] *Hadrian afterwards made a very equitable regulation, which divided all treasure trove between the right of property and that of discovery.*

mains of the stadium which he constructed at Athens. It was six hundred feet in length, built entirely of white marble, capable of admitting the whole body of the people, and finished in four years, whilst Herod was president of the Athenian games. To the memory of his wife Regilla he dedicated a theatre, scarcely to be paralleled in the empire: no wood except cedar very curiously carved, was employed in any part of the building. The Odeum, designed by Pericles for musical performances and the rehearsal of new tragedies, had been a trophy of the victory of the arts over Barbaric greatness; as the timbers employed in the construction consisted chiefly of the masts of the Persian vessels. Notwithstanding the repairs bestowed on that ancient edifice by a king of Cappadocia, it was again fallen to decay. Herod restored its ancient beauty and magnificence. Nor was the liberality of that illustrious citizen confined to the walls of Athens. The most splendid ornaments bestowed on the temple of Neptune in the Isthmus, a theatre at Corinth, a stadium at Delphi, a bath at Thermopylæ, and an aqueduct at Canusium in Italy, were insufficient to exhaust his treasures. The people of Epirus, Thessaly, Eubœa, Bœotia, and Peloponnesus, experienced his favours; and many inscriptions of the cities of Greece and Asia gratefully style Herodes Atticus their patron and benefactor.

In the commonwealths of Athens and Rome, the modest simplicity of private houses announced the equal condition of freedom; whilst the sovereignty of the people was represented in the majestic edifices destined to the public use: nor was this republican spirit totally extinguished by the introduction of wealth and monarchy. It was in works of national honour and benefit that the most virtuous of the emperors affected to display their magnificence. The golden palace of Nero excited a just indignation, but the vast extent of ground which had been usurped by his selfish luxury was more nobly filled under the succeeding reigns by the Coliseum, the baths of Titus, the Claudian portico, and the temples dedicated to the goddess of Peace and to the genius of Rome.[31] These monuments of architecture, the property of the Roman people, were adorned with the most beautiful productions of Grecian painting and sculpture; and in the temple of Peace a very curious library was open to the curiosity of the learned. At a small distance from thence was situated the Forum of Trajan. It was surrounded with a lofty portico in the form of a quadrangle, into which four triumphal arches opened a noble and spacious entrance: in the centre arose a column of marble, whose height of one hundred and ten feet denoted the

[31] *Two celebrated pictures of Timanthes and of Protogenes are mentioned by Pliny as in the Temple of Peace; and the Laocoon was found in the baths of Titus.*

36

elevation of the hill that had been cut away. This column, which still subsists in its ancient beauty, exhibited an exact representation of the Dacian victories of its founder. The veteran soldier contemplated the story of his own campaigns, and, by an easy illusion of national vanity, the peaceful citizen associated himself to the honours of the triumph. All the other quarters of the capital, and all the provinces of the empire, were embellished by the same liberal spirit of public magnificence, and were filled with amphitheatres, theatres, temples, porticos, triumphal arches, baths and aqueducts, all variously conducive to the health, the devotion, and the pleasures of the meanest citizen. The last mentioned of those edifices deserve our peculiar attention. The boldness of the enterprise, the solidity of the execution, and the uses to which they were subservient, rank the aqueducts among the noblest monuments of Roman genius and power. The aqueducts of the capital claim a just pre-eminence; but the curious traveller, who, without the light of history, should examine those of Spoleto, of Metz, or of Segovia, would very naturally conclude that those provincial towns had formerly been the residence of some potent monarch. The solitudes of Asia and Africa were once covered with flourishing cities, whose populousness, and even whose existence, was derived from such artificial supplies of a perennial stream of fresh water.

We have computed the inhabitants, and contemplated the public works, of the Roman empire. The observation of the number and greatness of its cities will serve to confirm the former and to multiply the latter. It may not be unpleasing to collect a few scattered instances relative to that subject, without forgetting, however, that, from the vanity of nations and the poverty of language, the vague appellation of city has been indifferently bestowed on Rome and upon Laurentum. I. *Ancient* Italy is said to have contained eleven hundred and ninety-seven cities; and, for whatsoever æra of antiquity the expression might be intended, there is not any reason to believe the country less populous in the age of the Antonines, than in that of Romulus. The petty states of Latium were contained within the metropolis of the empire, by whose superior influence they had been attracted. Those parts of Italy which have so long languished under the lazy tyranny of priests and viceroys had been afflicted only by the more tolerable calamities of war; and the first symptoms of decay which *they* experienced were amply compensated by the rapid improvements of the Cisalpine Gaul. The splendour of Verona may be traced in its remains: yet Verona was less

[32] *The list seems authentic and accurate: the division of the provinces and the different condition of the cities are minutely distinguished.*

[33] *I have taken some pains in consulting and comparing modern travellers, with regard to the fate of those eleven cities of Asia; seven or eight are totally destroyed, Hypæpe, Tralles, Laodicea, Ilium, Halicarnassus, Miletus, Ephesus, and we may add Sardis. Of the remaining three, Pergamus is a straggling village of two or three thousand inhabitants; Magnesia, under the name of Guzel-hissar, a town of some consequence; and Smyrna, a great city, peopled by a hundred thousand souls. But even at Smyrna, while the Franks have maintained commerce, the Turks have ruined the arts.*

[34] *Aristides pronounced an oration which is still extant, to recommend concord to the rival cities.*

[35] *The inhabitants of Egypt, exclusive of Alexandria, amounted to seven millions and a half. Under the military government of the Mamalukes, Syria was supposed to contain sixty thousand villages.*

celebrated than Aquileia or Padua, Milan or Ravenna. II. The spirit of improvement had passed the Alps, and been felt even in the woods of Britain, which were gradually cleared away to open a free space for convenient and elegant habitations. York was the seat of government; London was already enriched by commerce; and Bath was celebrated for the salutary effects of its medicinal waters. Gaul could boast of her twelve hundred cities; and, though, in the northern parts, many of them, without excepting Paris itself, were little more than the rude and imperfect townships of a rising people, the southern provinces imitated the wealth and elegance of Italy. Many were the cities of Gaul, Marseilles, Arles, Nismes, Narbonne, Toulouse, Bordeaux, Autun, Vienne, Lyons, Langres, and Treves, whose ancient condition might sustain an equal, and perhaps advantageous, comparison with their present state. With regard to Spain, that country flourished as a province, and has declined as a kingdom. Exhausted by the abuse of her strength, by America, and by superstition, her pride might possibly be confounded, if we required such a list of three hundred and sixty cities as Pliny has exhibited under the reign of Vespasian.[32] III. Three hundred African cities had once acknowledged the authority of Carthage, nor is it likely that their numbers diminished under the administration of the emperors: Carthage itself rose with new splendour from its ashes; and that capital, as well as Capua and Corinth, soon recovered all the advantages which can be separated from independent sovereignty. IV. The provinces of the east present the contrast of Roman magnificence with Turkish barbarism. The ruins of antiquity, scattered over uncultivated fields, and ascribed by ignorance to the power of magic, scarcely afford a shelter to the oppressed peasant or wandering Arab. Under the reign of the Cæsars, the proper Asia alone contained five hundred populous cities, enriched with all the gifts of nature, and adorned with all the refinements of art. Eleven cities of Asia had once disputed the honour of dedicating a temple to Tiberius, and their respective merits were examined by the senate.[33] Four of them were immediately rejected as unequal to the burden; and among these was Laodicea, whose splendour is still displayed in its ruins. Laodicea collected a very considerable revenue from its flocks of sheep, celebrated for the fineness of their wool, and had received, a little before the contest, a legacy of above four hundred thousand pounds by the testament of a generous citizen. If such was the poverty of Laodicea, what must have been the wealth of those cities, whose claim appeared preferable, and particularly of Pergamus, of

Smyrna, and of Ephesus, who so long disputed with each other the titular primacy of Asia?[34] The capitals of Syria and Egypt held a still superior rank in the empire: Antioch and Alexandria looked down with disdain on a crowd of dependent cities,[35] and yielded with reluctance to the majesty of Rome itself.

All these cities were connected with each other, and with the capital, by the public highways, which, issuing from the Forum of Rome, traversed Italy, pervaded the provinces, and were terminated only by the frontiers of the empire. If we carefully trace the distance from the wall of Antoninus to Rome, and from thence to Jerusalem, it will be found that the great chain of communication, from the north-west to the south-east point of the empire, was drawn out to the length of four thousand and eighty Roman miles.[36] The public roads were accurately divided by milestones, and ran in a direct line from one city to another, with very little respect for the obstacles either of nature or private property. Mountains were perforated, and bold arches thrown over the broadest and most rapid streams. The middle part of the road was raised into a terrace which commanded the adjacent country, consisted of several strata of sand, gravel, and cement and was paved with large stones, or, in some places near the capital, with granite. Such was the solid construction of the Roman highways, whose firmness has not entirely yielded to the effort of fifteen centuries. They united the subjects of the most distant provinces by an easy and familiar intercourse; but their primary object had been to facilitate the marches of the legions; nor was any country considered as completely subdued, till it had been rendered, in all its parts, pervious to the arms and authority of the conqueror. The advantage of receiving the earliest intelligence, and of conveying their orders with celerity, induced the emperors to establish, throughout their extensive dominions, the regular institution of posts. Houses were everywhere erected at the distance only of five or six miles; each of them was constantly provided with forty horses, and, by the help of these relays, it was easy to travel an hundred miles in a day along the Roman roads.[37] The use of the posts was allowed to those who claimed it by an Imperial mandate; but, though originally intended for the public service, it was sometimes indulged to the business or conveniency of private citizens.[38] Nor was the communication of the Roman empire less free and open by sea than it was by land. The provinces surrounded and enclosed the Mediterranean; and Italy, in the shape of an immense promontory, advanced into the midst of that great

[36] *The following Itinerary may serve to convey some idea of the direction of the road, and of the distance between the principal towns. I. From the wall of Antoninus to York, 222 Roman miles. II. London 227. III. Rhutupiæ or Sandwich 67. IV. The navigation to Boulogne 45. V. Rheims 174. VI. Lyons 330. VII. Milan 324. VIII. Rome 426. IX. Brundusium 360. X. The navigation to Dyrrachium 40. XI. Byzantium 711. XII. Ancyra 283. XIII. Tarsus 301. XIV. Antioch 141. XV. Tyre 252. XVI. Jerusalem 168. In all 4080 Roman, or 3740 English miles.*

[37] *In the time of Theodosius, Cæsarius, a magistrate of high rank, went post from Antioch to Constantinople. He began his journey at night, was in Cappadocia (165 miles from Antioch) the ensuing evening, and arrived at Constantinople the sixth day about noon. The whole distance was 725 Roman, or 665 English miles.*

[38] *Pliny, though a favourite and a minister, made an apology for granting post horses to his wife on the most urgent business.*

lake. The coasts of Italy are, in general, destitute of safe harbours; but human industry had corrected the deficiencies of nature; and the artificial port of Ostia, in particular, situate at the mouth of the Tiber, and formed by the Emperor Claudius, was an useful monument of Roman greatness. From this port, which was only sixteen miles from the capital, a favourable breeze frequently carried vessels in seven days to the columns of Hercules, and in nine or ten to Alexandria in Egypt.

Whatever evils either reason or declamation have imputed to extensive empire, the power of Rome was attended with some beneficial consequences to mankind; and the same freedom of intercourse which extended the vices, diffused likewise the improvements, of social life. In the more remote ages of antiquity, the world was unequally divided. The east was in the immemorial possession of arts and luxury; whilst the west was inhabited by rude and warlike barbarians, who either disdained agriculture, or to whom it was totally unknown. Under the protection of an established government, the productions of happier climates and the industry of more civilized nations were gradually introduced into the western countries of Europe; and the natives were encouraged, by an open and profitable commerce, to multiply the former as well as to improve the latter. It would be almost impossible to enumerate all the articles, either of the animal or the vegetable reign, which were successively imported into Europe from Asia and Egypt;[39] but it will not be unworthy of the dignity, and much less of the utility, of an historical work, slightly to touch on a few of the principal heads. 1. Almost all the flowers, the herbs, and the fruits that grow in our European gardens are of foreign extraction, which, in many cases, is betrayed even by their names: the apple was a native of Italy, and, when the Romans had tasted the richer flavour of the apricot, the peach, the pomegranate, the citron, and the orange, they contented themselves with applying to all these new fruits the common denomination of apple, discriminating them from each other by the additional epithet of their country. 2. In the time of Homer, the vine grew wild in the island of Sicily and most probably in the adjacent continent; but it was not improved by the skill, nor did it afford a liquor grateful to the taste, of the savage inhabitants. A thousand years afterwards, Italy could boast that, of the fourscore most generous and celebrated wines, more than two-thirds were produced from her soil. The blessing was soon communicated to the Narbonnese province of Gaul; but so intense was the cold to the

[39] *It is not improbable that the Greeks and Phœnicians introduced some new arts and productions into the neighbourhood of Marseilles and Gades.*

north of the Cevennes, that, in the time of Strabo, it was thought impossible to ripen the grapes in those parts of Gaul.[40] This difficulty, however, was gradually vanquished; and there is some reason to believe that the vineyards of Burgundy are as old as the age of the Antonines.[41] 3. The olive, in the western world, followed the progress of peace, of which it was considered as the symbol. Two centuries after the foundation of Rome, both Italy and Africa were strangers to that useful plant; it was naturalized in those countries; and at length carried into the heart of Spain and Gaul. The timid errors of the ancients, that it required a certain degree of heat, and could only flourish in the neighbourhood of the sea, were insensibly exploded by industry and experience. 4. The cultivation of flax was transported from Egypt to Gaul, and enriched the whole country, however it might impoverish the particular lands on which it was sown. 5. The use of artificial grasses became familiar to the farmers both of Italy and the provinces, particularly the Lucerne, which derived its name and origin from Media. The assured supply of wholesome and plentiful food for the cattle during winter multiplied the number of the flocks and herds, which in their turn contributed to the fertility of the soil. To all these improvements may be added an assiduous attention to mines and fisheries, which, by employing a multitude of laborious hands, serve to increase the pleasures of the rich and the subsistence of the poor. The elegant treatise of Columella describes the advanced state of the Spanish husbandry, under the reign of Tiberius; and it may be observed that those famines which so frequently afflicted the infant republic were seldom or never experienced by the extensive empire of Rome. The accidental scarcity, in any single province, was immediately relieved by the plenty of its more fortunate neighbours.

Agriculture is the foundation of manufactures; since the productions of nature are the materials of art. Under the Roman empire, the labour of an industrious and ingenious people was variously, but incessantly, employed in the service of the rich. In their dress, their table, their houses, and their furniture, the favourites of fortune united every refinement of conveniency, of elegance, and of splendour, whatever could soothe their pride or gratify their sensuality. Such refinements, under the odious name of luxury, have been severely arraigned by the moralists of every age; and it might perhaps be more conducive to the virtue, as well as happiness, of mankind, if all possessed the necessaries, and none the superfluities, of life. But in the present imperfect condition of society, luxury,

[40] *The intense cold of a Gallic winter was almost proverbial among the ancients.*

[41] *In the beginning of the fourth century, the orator Eumenius speaks of the vines in the territory of Autun, which were decayed through age, and the first plantation of which was totally unknown. The Pagus Arebrignus is supposed by M. d'Anville to be the district of Beaune, celebrated, even at present, for one of the first growths of Burgundy.*

though it may proceed from vice or folly, seems to be the only means that can correct the unequal distribution of property. The diligent mechanic, and the skilful artist, who have obtained no share in the division of the earth, receive a voluntary tax from the possessors of land; and the latter are prompted, by a sense of interest, to improve those estates, with whose produce they may purchase additional pleasures. This operation, the particular effects of which are felt in every society, acted with much more diffusive energy in the Roman world. The provinces would soon have been exhausted of their wealth, if the manufactures and commerce of luxury had not insensibly restored to the industrious subjects the sums which were exacted from them by the arms and authority of Rome. As long as the circulation was confined within the bounds of the empire, it impressed the political machine with a new degree of activity, and its consequences, sometimes beneficial, could never become pernicious.

But it is no easy task to confine luxury within the limits of an empire. The most remote countries of the ancient world were ransacked to supply the pomp and delicacy of Rome. The forest of Scythia afforded some valuable furs. Amber was brought over land from the shores of the Baltic to the Danube; and the barbarians were astonished at the price which they received in exchange for so useless a commodity.[42] There was a considerable demand for Babylonian carpets, and other manufactures of the East; but the most important and unpopular branch of foreign trade was carried on with Arabia and India. Every year, about the time of the summer solstice, a fleet of an hundred and twenty vessels sailed from Myoshormos, a port of Egypt, on the Red Sea. By the periodical assistance of the monsoons, they traversed the ocean in about forty days. The coast of Malabar, or the island of Ceylon,[43] was the usual term of their navigation, and it was in those markets that the merchants from the more remote countries of Asia expected their arrival. The return of the fleet of Egypt was fixed to the months of December or January; and as soon as their rich cargo had been transported on the backs of camels from the Red Sea to the Nile, and had descended that river as far as Alexandria, it was poured, without delay, into the capital of the empire. The objects of oriental traffic were splendid and trifling: silk, a pound of which was esteemed not inferior in value to a pound of gold;[44] precious stones, among which the pearl claimed the first rank after the diamond;[45] and a variety of aromatics, that were consumed in religious worship and the pomp

[42] *Pliny observes, with some humour, that even fashion had not yet found out the use of amber. Nero sent a Roman knight to purchase great quantities on the spot where it was produced; the coast of modern Prussia.*

[43] *Called Taprobana by the Romans, and Screndib by the Arabs. It was discovered under the reign of Claudius, and gradually became the principal mart of the East.*

[44] *A silk garment was considered as an ornament to a woman, but as a disgrace to a man.*

[45] *The two great pearl fisheries were the same as at present, Ormuz and Cape Comorin. As well as we can compare ancient with modern geography, Rome was supplied with diamonds from the mine of Sumelpur, in Bengal.*

of funerals. The labour and risk of the voyage was rewarded with almost incredible profit; but the profit was made upon Roman subjects, and a few individuals were enriched at the expense of the Public. As the natives of Arabia and India were contented with the productions and manufactures of their own country, silver, on the side of the Romans, was the principal, if not the only, instrument of commerce. It was a complaint worthy of the gravity of the senate, that, in the purchase of female ornaments, the wealth of the state was irrecoverably given away to foreign and hostile nations. The annual loss is computed, by a writer of an inquisitive but censorious temper, at upwards of eight hundred thousand pounds sterling. Such was the style of discontent, brooding over the dark prospect of approaching poverty. And yet, if we compare the proportion between gold and silver, as it stood in the time of Pliny, and as it was fixed in the reign of Constantine, we shall discover within that period a very considerable increase.[46] There is not the least reason to suppose that gold was become more scarce; it is therefore evident that silver was grown more common; that whatever might be the amount of the Indian and Arabian exports, they were far from exhausting the wealth of the Roman world; and that the produce of the mines abundantly supplied the demands of commerce.

Notwithstanding the propensity of mankind to exalt the past, and to depreciate the present, the tranquil and prosperous state of the empire was warmly felt, and honestly confessed, by the provincials as well as Romans. "They acknowledged that the true principles of social life, laws, agriculture, and science, which had been first invented by the wisdom of Athens, were now firmly established by the power of Rome, under whose auspicious influence the fiercest barbarians were united by an equal government and common language. They affirm that, with the improvement of arts, the human species was visibly multiplied. They celebrate the increasing splendour of the cities, the beautiful face of the country, cultivated and adorned like an immense garden; and the long festival of peace, which was enjoyed by so many nations, forgetful of their ancient animosities, and delivered from the apprehension of future danger." Whatever suspicions may be suggested by the air of rhetoric and declamation which seems to prevail in these passages, the substance of them is perfectly agreeable to historic truth.

It was scarcely possible that the eyes of contemporaries should discover in the public felicity the latent causes of decay and corruption. This long peace, and the uniform government of the Romans,

[46] *The proportion, which was 1 to 10, and 12½, rose to 14⅖, the legal regulation of Constantine.*

introduced a slow and secret poison into the vitals of the empire. The minds of men were gradually reduced to the same level, the fire of genius was extinguished, and even the military spirit evaporated. The natives of Europe were brave and robust. Spain, Gaul, Britain, and Illyricum supplied the legions with excellent soldiers, and constituted the real strength of the monarchy. Their personal valour remained, but they no longer possessed that public courage which is nourished by the love of independence, the sense of national honour, the presence of danger, and the habit of command. They received laws and governors from the will of their sovereign, and trusted for their defence to a mercenary army. The posterity of their boldest leaders was contented with the rank of citizens and subjects. The most aspiring spirits resorted to the court or standard of the emperors; and the deserted provinces, deprived of political strength or union, insensibly sunk into the languid indifference of private life.

The love of letters, almost inseparable from peace and refinement, was fashionable among the subjects of Hadrian and the Antonines, who were themselves men of learning and curiosity. It was diffused over the whole extent of their empire; the most northern tribes of Britons had acquired a taste for rhetoric; Homer as well as Virgil were transcribed and studied on the banks of the Rhine and Danube; and the most liberal rewards sought out the faintest glimmerings of literary merit.[47] The sciences of physic and astronomy were successfully cultivated by the Greeks; the observations of Ptolemy and the writings of Galen are studied by those who have improved their discoveries and corrected their errors; but, if we except the inimitable Lucian, this age of indolence passed away without having produced a single writer of original genius or who excelled in the arts of elegant composition. The authority of Plato and Aristotle, of Zeno and Epicurus, still reigned in the schools, and their systems, transmitted with blind deference from one generation of disciples to another, precluded every generous attempt to exercise the powers, or enlarge the limits, of the human mind. The beauties of the poets and orators, instead of kindling a fire like their own, inspired only cold and servile imitations: or, if any ventured to deviate from those models, they deviated at the same time from good sense and propriety. On the revival of letters, the youthful vigour of the imagination after a long repose, national emulation, a new religion, new languages, and a new world, called forth the genius of Europe. But the provincials of Rome, trained by a uni-

[47] *Herodes Atticus gave the sophist Polemo above eight thousand pounds for three declamations. The Antonines founded a school at Athens, in which professors of grammar, rhetoric, politics, and the four great sects of philosophy, were maintained at the public expense for the instruction of youth. The salary of a philosopher was ten thousand drachmæ, between three and four hundred pounds a year. Similar establishments were formed in the other great cities of the empire.*

form artificial foreign education, were engaged in a very unequal competition with those bold ancients, who, by expressing their genuine feelings in their native tongue, had already occupied every place of honour. The name of Poet was almost forgotten; that of Orator was usurped by the sophists. A cloud of critics, of compilers, of commentators, darkened the face of learning, and the decline of genius was soon followed by the corruption of taste.

The sublime Longinus, who in somewhat a later period, and in the court of a Syrian queen, preserved the spirit of ancient Athens, observes and laments this degeneracy of his contemporaries, which debased their sentiments, enervated their courage, and depressed their talents. "In the same manner," says he, "as some children always remain pigmies, whose infant limbs have been too closely confined; thus our tender minds, fettered by the prejudices and habits of a just servitude, are unable to expand themselves, or to attain that well-proportioned greatness which we admire in the ancients, who, living under a popular government, wrote with the same freedom as they acted." [48] This diminutive stature of mankind, if we pursue the metaphor, was daily sinking below the old standard, and the Roman world was indeed peopled by a race of pigmies, when the fierce giants of the north broke in and mended the puny breed. They restored a manly spirit of freedom; and, after the revolution of ten centuries, freedom became the happy parent of taste and science.

[48] *Here too we may say of Longinus, "his own example strengthens all his laws." Instead of proposing his sentiments with a manly boldness, he insinuates them with the most guarded caution, puts them into the mouth of a friend, and, as far as we can collect from a corrupted text, makes a show of refuting them himself.*

III

THE obvious definition of a monarchy seems to be that of a state, in which a single person, by whatsoever name he may be distinguished, is intrusted with the execution of the laws, the management of the revenue, and the command of the army. But unless public liberty is protected by intrepid and vigilant guardians, the authority of so formidable a magistrate will soon degenerate into despotism. The influence of the clergy, in an age of superstition, might be usefully employed to assert the rights of mankind; but so intimate is the connexion between the throne and the altar, that the banner of the church has very seldom been seen on the side of the people. A martial nobility and stubborn commons, possessed of arms, tenacious of property, and collected into constitutional assemblies, form the only balance capable of preserving a free constitution against enterprises of an aspiring prince.

Every barrier of the Roman constitution had been levelled by the vast ambition of the dictator; every fence had been extirpated by the cruel hand of the triumvir. After the victory of Actium, the fate of the Roman world depended on the will of Octavianus, surnamed Cæsar by his uncle's adoption, and afterwards Augustus, by the flattery of the senate. The conqueror was at the head of forty-four veteran legions, conscious of their own strength and of the weakness of the constitution, habituated during twenty years' civil war to every act of blood and violence, and passionately devoted to the house of Cæsar, from whence alone they had received and expected the most lavish rewards. The provinces long oppressed by the ministers of the republic, sighed for the government of a single person, who would be the master, not the accomplice, of those petty tyrants. The people of Rome, viewing with a secret pleasure the humiliation of the aristocracy, demanded only bread and public shows, and were supplied with both by the liberal hand of Augustus. The rich and

polite Italians, who had almost universally embraced the philosophy of Epicurus, enjoyed the present blessings of ease and tranquillity, and suffered not the pleasing dream to be interrupted by
the memory of their old tumultuous freedom. With its power, the
senate had lost its dignity; many of the most noble families were
extinct. The republicans of spirit and ability had perished in the
field of battle, or in the proscription. The door of the assembly had
been designedly left open for a mixed multitude of more than a
thousand persons, who reflected disgrace upon their rank, instead
of deriving honour from it.[1]

The reformation of the senate, was one of the first steps in which
Augustus laid aside the tyrant, and professed himself the father of
his country. He was elected censor; and, in concert with his faithful
Agrippa, he examined the list of the senators, expelled a few members, whose vices or whose obstinacy required a public example,
persuaded near two hundred to prevent the shame of an expulsion
by a voluntary retreat, raised the qualification of a senator to about
ten thousand pounds, created a sufficient number of patrician families, and accepted for himself the honourable title of Prince of the
Senate, which had always been bestowed by the censors on the citizen the most eminent for his honours and services. But, whilst he
thus restored the dignity, he destroyed the independence of the senate. The principles of a free constitution are irrecoverably lost, when
the legislative power is nominated by the executive.

Before an assembly thus modelled and prepared, Augustus pronounced a studied oration, which displayed his patriotism, and disguised his ambition. "He lamented, yet excused, his past conduct.
Filial piety had required at his hands the revenge of his father's
murder; the humanity of his own nature had sometimes given way
to the stern laws of necessity, and to a forced connexion with two
unworthy colleagues: as long as Antony lived, the republic forbad
him to abandon her to a degenerate Roman and a barbarian queen.
He was now at liberty to satisfy his duty and his inclination. He solemnly restored the senate and people to all their ancient rights; and
wished only to mingle with the crowd of his fellow-citizens, and to
share the blessings which he had obtained for his country."[2]

It would require the pen of Tacitus (if Tacitus had assisted at this
assembly) to describe the various emotions of the senate; those that
were suppressed, and those that were affected. It was dangerous to
trust the sincerity of Augustus; to seem to distrust it was still more
dangerous. The respective advantages of monarchy and a republic

[1] *Julius Cæsar intro-
duced soldiers, stran-
gers and half-barbarians,
into the senate. The
abuse became still more
scandalous after his
death.*

[2] *Dion gives us a prolix
and bombastic speech on
this great occasion. I
have borrowed from
Suetonius and Tacitus
the general language of
Augustus.*

have often divided speculative inquirers; the present greatness of the Roman state, the corruption of manners, and the licence of the soldiers, supplied new arguments to the advocates of monarchy; and these general views of government were again warped by the hopes and fears of each individual. Amidst this confusion of sentiments, the answer of the senate was unanimous and decisive. They refused to accept the resignation of Augustus; they conjured him not to desert the republic which he had saved. After a decent resistance the crafty tyrant submitted to the orders of the senate; and consented to receive the government of the provinces, and the general command of the Roman armies, under the well-known names of PROCONSUL and IMPERATOR.[3] But he would receive them only for ten years. Even before the expiration of that period, he hoped that the wounds of civil discord would be completely healed, and that the republic, restored to its pristine health and vigour, would no longer require the dangerous interposition of so extraordinary a magistrate. The memory of this comedy, repeated several times during the life of Augustus, was preserved to the last ages of the empire by the peculiar pomp with which the perpetual monarchs of Rome always solemnized the tenth years of their reign.

Without any violation of the principles of the constitution, the general of the Roman armies might receive and exercise an authority almost despotic over the soldiers, the enemies, and the subjects of the republic. With regard to the soldiers, the jealousy of freedom had, even from the earliest ages of Rome, given way to the hopes of conquest, and a just sense of military discipline. The dictator, or consul, had a right to command the service of the Roman youth, and to punish an obstinate or cowardly disobedience by the most severe and ignominious penalties, by striking the offender out of the list of citizens, by confiscating his property, and by selling his person into slavery. The most sacred rights of freedom, confirmed by the Porcian and Sempronian laws, were suspended by the military engagement. In his camp the general exercised an absolute power of life and death; his jurisdiction was not confined by any forms of trial or rules of proceeding, and the execution of the sentence was immediate and without appeal.[4] The choice of the enemies of Rome was regularly decided by the legislative authority. The most important resolutions of peace and war were seriously debated in the senate, and solemnly ratified by the people. But when the arms of the legions were carried to a great distance from Italy, the generals assumed the liberty of directing them against whatever

[3] Imperator *(from which we have derived emperor) signified under the republic no more than* general, *and was emphatically bestowed by the soldiers, when on the field of battle they proclaimed their victorious leader worthy of that title. When the Roman* emperors *assumed it in that sense, they placed it after their name, and marked how often they had taken it.*

[4] *See in the eighth book of Livy, the conduct of Manlius Torquatus and Papirius Cursor. They violated the laws of nature and humanity, but they asserted those of military discipline; and the people, who abhorred the action, were obliged to respect the principle.*

48

people, and in whatever manner, they judged most advantageous for the public service. It was from the success, not from the justice, of their enterprises, that they expected the honours of a triumph. In the use of victory, especially after they were no longer controlled by the commissioners of the senate, they exercised the most unbounded despotism. When Pompey commanded in the East, he rewarded his soldiers and allies, dethroned princes, divided kingdoms, founded colonies, and distributed the treasures of Mithridates. On his return to Rome he obtained, by a single act of the senate and people, the universal ratification of all his proceedings.[5] Such was the power over the soldiers, and over the enemies of Rome, which was either granted to, or assumed by, the generals of the republic. They were, at the same time, the governors, or rather monarchs, of the conquered provinces, united the civil with the military character, administered justice as well as the finances, and exercised both the executive and legislative power of the state.

From what has been already observed in the first chapter of this work, some notion may be formed of the armies and provinces thus intrusted to the ruling hand of Augustus. But, as it was impossible that he could personally command the legions of so many distant frontiers, he was indulged by the senate, as Pompey had already been, in the permission of devolving the execution of his great office on a sufficient number of lieutenants. In rank and authority these officers seemed not inferior to the ancient proconsuls; but their station was dependent and precarious. They received and held their commissions at the will of a superior, to whose *auspicious* influence the merit of their action was legally attributed.[6] They were the representatives of the emperor. The emperor alone was the general of the republic, and his jurisdiction, civil as well as military, extended over all the conquests of Rome. It was some satisfaction, however, to the senate that he always delegated his power to the members of their body. The imperial lieutenants were of consular or prætorian dignity; the legions were commanded by senators, and the præfecture of Egypt was the only important trust committed to a Roman knight.

Within six days after Augustus had been compelled to accept so very liberal a grant, he resolved to gratify the pride of the senate by an easy sacrifice. He represented to them that they had enlarged his powers, even beyond that degree which might be required by the melancholy condition of the times. They had not permitted him to refuse the laborious command of the armies and the frontiers; but

[5] *By the lavish but unconstrained suffrages of the people, Pompey had obtained a military command scarcely inferior to that of Augustus. Among the extraordinary acts of power executed by the former, we may remark the foundation of twenty-nine cities, and the distribution of three or four millions sterling to his troops. The ratification of his acts met with some opposition and delays in the senate.*

[6] *Under the commonwealth, a triumph could only be claimed by the general, who was authorized to take the Auspices in the name of the people. By an exact consequence, drawn from this principle of policy and religion, the triumph was reserved to the emperor, and his most successful lieutenants were satisfied with some marks of distinction, which, under the name of triumphal honours, were invented in their favour.*

he must insist on being allowed to restore the more peaceful and secure provinces to the mild administration of the civil magistrate. In the division of the provinces Augustus provided for his own power and for the dignity of the republic. The proconsuls of the senate, particularly those of Asia, Greece, and Africa, enjoyed a more honourable character than the lieutenants of the emperor, who commanded in Gaul or Syria. The former were attended by lictors, the latter by soldiers. A law was passed that, wherever the emperor was present, his extraordinary commission should supersede the ordinary jurisdiction of the governor; a custom was introduced, that the new conquests belonged to the imperial portion; and it was soon discovered that the authority of the *Prince,* the favourite epithet of Augustus, was the same in every part of the empire.

In return for this imaginary concession, Augustus obtained an important privilege, which rendered him master of Rome and Italy. By a dangerous exception to the ancient maxims, he was authorized to preserve his military command, supported by a numerous body of guards, even in time of peace, and in the heart of the capital. His command, indeed, was confined to those citizens who were engaged in the service by the military oath; but such was the propensity of the Romans to servitude, that the oath was voluntarily taken by the magistrates, the senators, and the equestrian order, till the homage of flattery was insensibly converted into an annual and solemn protestation of fidelity.

Although Augustus considered a military force as the firmest foundation, he wisely rejected it as a very odious instrument, of government. It was more agreeable to his temper, as well as to his policy, to reign under the venerable names of ancient magistracy, and artfully to collect in his own person all the scattered rays of civil jurisdiction. With this view, he permitted the senate to confer upon him, for his life, the powers of the consular [7] and tribunitian offices,[8] which were, in the same manner, continued to all his successors. The consuls had succeeded to the kings of Rome, and represented the dignity of the state. They superintended the ceremonies of religion, levied and commanded the legions, gave audience to foreign ambassadors, and presided in the assemblies both of the senate and people. The general control of the finances was intrusted to their care and, though they seldom had leisure to administer justice in person, they were considered as the supreme guardians of law, equity, and the public peace. Such was their ordinary jurisdiction;

[7] *Cicero gives the consular office the name* Regia potestas; *and Polybius observes three powers in the Roman constitution. The monarchical was represented and exercised by the consuls.*

[8] *As the tribunitian power (distinct from the annual office) was first invented for the dictator Cæsar, we may easily conceive, that it was given as a reward for having so nobly asserted, by arms, the sacred rights of the tribunes and people.*

but whenever the senate empowered the first magistrate to consult the safety of the commonwealth, he was raised by that degree above the laws, and exercised, in the defence of liberty, a temporary despotism.[9] The character of the tribunes was, in every respect, different from that of the consuls. The appearance of the former was modest and humble; but their persons were sacred and inviolable. Their force was suited rather for opposition than for action. They were instituted to defend the oppressed, to pardon offences, to arraign the enemies of the people, and, when they judged it necessary, to stop, by a single word, the whole machine of government. As long as the republic subsisted, the dangerous influence which either the consul or the tribune might derive from their respective jurisdiction was diminished by several important restrictions. Their authority expired with the year in which they were elected; the former office was divided between two, the latter among ten persons; and, as both in their private and public interest they were adverse to each other, their mutual conflicts contributed, for the most part, to strengthen rather than to destroy the balance of the constitution. But when the consular and tribunitian powers were united, when they were vested for life in a single person, when the general of the army was, at the same time, the minister of the senate and the representative of the Roman people, it was impossible to resist the exercise, nor was it easy to define the limits, of his imperial prerogative.

To these accumulated honours the policy of Augustus soon added the splendid as well as important dignities of supreme pontiff, and of censor. By the former he acquired the management of the religion, and by the latter a legal inspection over the manners and fortunes, of the Roman people. If so many distinct and independent powers did not exactly unite with each other, the complaisance of the senate was prepared to supply every deficiency by the most ample and extraordinary concessions. The emperors, as the first ministers of the republic, were exempted from the obligation and penalty of many inconvenient laws: they were authorized to convoke the senate, to make several motions in the same day, to recommend candidates for the honours of the state, to enlarge the bounds of the city, to employ the revenue at their discretion, to declare peace and war, to ratify treaties; and by a most comprehensive clause, they were empowered to execute whatsoever they should judge advantageous to the empire, and agreeable to the majesty of things private or public, human or divine.[10]

When all the various powers of executive government were com-

[9] Augustus exercised nine annual consulships without interruption. He then most artfully refused that magistracy as well as the dictatorship, absented himself from Rome, and waited till the fatal effects of tumult and faction forced the senate to invest him with a perpetual consulship. Augustus, as well as his successors, affected, however, to conceal so invidious a title.

[10] See a fragment of a Decree of the Senate, conferring on the Emperor Vespasian all the powers granted to his predecessors, Augustus, Tiberius, and Claudius.

mitted to the *Imperial magistrate,* the ordinary magistrates of the commonwealth languished in obscurity, without vigour, and almost without business. The names and forms of the ancient administration were preserved by Augustus with the most anxious care. The usual number of consuls, prætors, and tribunes [11] were annually invested with their respective ensigns of office, and continued to discharge some of their least important functions. Those honours still attracted the vain ambition of the Romans; and the emperors themselves, though invested for life with the powers of the consulship, frequently aspired to the title of that annual dignity, which they condescended to share with the most illustrious of their fellow-citizens.[12] In the election of these magistrates, the people, during the reign of Augustus, were permitted to expose all the inconveniences of a wild democracy. That artful prince, instead of discovering the least symptom of impatience, humbly solicited their suffrages for himself or his friends, and scrupulously practised all the duties of an ordinary candidate. But we may venture to ascribe to his councils the first measure of the succeeding reign, by which the elections were transferred to the senate. The assemblies of the people were for ever abolished, and the emperors were delivered from a dangerous multitude, who, without restoring liberty, might have disturbed, and perhaps endangered, the established government.

By declaring themselves the protectors of the people, Marius and Cæsar had subverted the constitution of their country. But as soon as the senate had been humbled and disarmed, such an assembly, consisting of five or six hundred persons, was found a much more tractable and useful instrument of dominion. It was on the dignity of the senate that Augustus and his successors founded their new empire; and they affected, on every occasion, to adopt the language and principles of Patricians. In the administration of their own powers, they frequently consulted the great national council, and *seemed* to refer to its decision the most important concerns of peace and war. Rome, Italy, and the internal provinces were subject to the immediate jurisdiction of the senate. With regard to civil objects, it was the supreme court of appeal; with regard to criminal matters, a tribunal, constituted for the trial of all offences that were committed by men in any public station, or that affected the peace and majesty of the Roman people. The exercise of the judicial power became the most frequent and serious occupation of the senate; and the important causes that were pleaded before them afforded a last refuge to the spirit of ancient eloquence. As a council of state, and

[11] *Two consuls were created on the Calends of January; but in the course of the year others were substituted in their places, till the annual number seems to have amounted to no less than twelve. The prætors were usually sixteen or eighteen. I have not mentioned the Ædiles or Quæstors. Officers of the police or revenue easily adapt themselves to any form of government. In the time of Nero the tribunes legally possessed the right of intercession, though it might be dangerous to exercise it. In the time of Trajan, it was doubtful whether the tribuneship was an office or a name.*

[12] *The tyrants themselves were ambitious of the consulship. The virtuous princes were moderate in the pursuit, and exact in the discharge, of it. Trajan revived the ancient oath, and swore before the consul's tribunal that he would observe the laws.*

as a court of justice, the senate possessed very considerable prerogatives; but in its legislative capacity, in which it was supposed virtually to represent the people, the rights of sovereignty were acknowledged to reside in that assembly. Every power was derived from their authority, every law was ratified by their sanction. Their regular meetings were held on three stated days in every month, the Calends, the Nones, and the Ides. The debates were conducted with decent freedom; and the emperors themselves, who gloried in the name of senators, sat, voted, and divided with their equals.

To resume, in a few words, the system of the Imperial government, as it was instituted by Augustus, and maintained by those princes who understood their own interest and that of the people, it may be defined an absolute monarchy disguised by the forms of a commonwealth. The masters of the Roman world surrounded their throne with darkness, concealed their irresistible strength, and humbly professed themselves the accountable ministers of the senate, whose supreme decrees they dictated and obeyed.

The face of the court corresponded with the forms of the administration. The emperors, if we except those tyrants whose capricious folly violated every law of nature and decency, disdained that pomp and ceremony which might offend their countrymen, but could add nothing to their real power. In all the offices of life, they affected to confound themselves with their subjects, and maintained with them an equal intercourse of visits and entertainments. Their habit, their palace, their table, were suited only to the rank of an opulent senator. Their family, however numerous or splendid, was composed entirely of their domestic slaves and freedmen.[13] Augustus or Trajan would have blushed at employing the meanest of the Romans in those menial offices which, in the household and bedchamber of a limited monarch, are so eagerly solicited by the proudest nobles of Britain.

The deification of the emperors is the only instance in which they departed from their accustomed prudence and modesty. The Asiatic Greeks were the first inventors, the successors of Alexander the first objects, of this servile and impious mode of adulation. It was easily transferred from the kings to the governors of Asia; and the Roman magistrates very frequently were adored as provincial deities, with the pomp of altars and temples, of festivals and sacrifices. It was natural that the emperors should not refuse what the proconsuls had accepted; and the divine honours which both the one and the other received from the provinces attested rather the despotism than

[13] *A weak prince will always be governed by his domestics. The power of slaves aggravated the shame of the Romans; and the senate paid court to a Pallas or a Narcissus. There is a chance that a modern favourite may be a gentleman.*

the servitude of Rome. But the conquerors soon imitated the vanquished nations in the arts of flattery; and the imperious spirit of the first Cæsar too easily consented to assume, during his life time, a place among the tutelar deities of Rome. The milder temper of his successor declined so dangerous an ambition, which was never afterwards revived, except by the madness of Caligula and Domitian. Augustus permitted indeed some of the provincial cities to erect temples to his honour, on condition that they should associate the worship of Rome with that of the sovereign; he tolerated private superstition, of which he might be the object;[14] but he contented himself with being revered by the senate and people in his human character, and wisely left to his successor the care of his public deification. A regular custom was introduced, that, on the decease of every emperor who had neither lived nor died like a tyrant, the senate by a solemn decree should place him in the number of the gods: and the ceremonies of his apotheosis were blended with those of his funeral. This legal, and, as it should seem, injudicious profanation, so abhorrent to our stricter principles, was received with a very faint murmur[15] by the easy nature of Polytheism; but it was received as an institution, not of religion, but of policy. We should disgrace the virtues of the Antonines by comparing them with the vices of Hercules or Jupiter. Even the characters of Cæsar or Augustus were far superior to those of the popular deities. But it was the misfortune of the former to live in an enlightened age, and their actions were too faithfully recorded to admit of such a mixture of fable and mystery as the devotion of the vulgar requires. As soon as their divinity was established by law, it sunk into oblivion, without contributing either to their own fame or to the dignity of succeeding princes.

In the consideration of the Imperial government, we have frequently mentioned the artful founder, under his well-known title of Augustus, which was not however conferred upon him till the edifice was almost completed. The obscure name of Octavianus he derived from a mean family in the little town of Aricia. It was stained with the blood of the proscriptions; and he was desirous, had it been possible, to erase all memory of his former life. The illustrious surname of Cæsar he had assumed, as the adopted son of the dictator; but he had too much good sense either to hope to be confounded, or to wish to be compared, with that extraordinary man. It was proposed in the senate to dignify their minister with a new appellation; and after a very serious discussion, that of Augustus was chosen, among several others, as being the most expressive of

[14] *Jurandasque tuum per nomen ponimus aras,* says Horace to the emperor himself, and Horace was well acquainted with the court of Augustus.

[15] *Julian in Cæsaribus, Inque Deûm templis jurabit Roma per umbras,* is the indignant expression of Lucan; but it is a patriotic rather than a devout indignation.

the character of peace and sanctity which he uniformly affected. *Augustus* was therefore a personal, *Cæsar* a family distinction. The former should naturally have expired with the prince on whom it was bestowed; and however the latter was diffused by adoption and female alliance, Nero was the last prince who could allege any hereditary claim to the honours of the Julian line. But, at the time of his death, the practice of a century had inseparably connected those appellations with the Imperial dignity, and they have been preserved by a long succession of emperors,—Romans, Greeks, Franks, and Germans,—from the fall of the republic to the present time. A distinction was, however, soon introduced. The sacred title of Augustus was always reserved for the monarch, whilst the name of Cæsar was more freely communicated to his relations; and, from the reign of Hadrian at least, was appropriated to the second person in the state, who was considered as the presumptive heir of the empire.

The tender respect of Augustus for a free constitution which he had destroyed can only be explained by an attentive consideration of the character of that subtle tyrant. A cool head, an unfeeling heart, and a cowardly disposition, prompted him at the age of nineteen to assume the mask of hypocrisy, which he never afterwards laid aside. With the same hand, and probably with the same temper, he signed the proscription of Cicero and the pardon of Cinna. His virtues, and even his vices, were artificial; and according to the various dictates of his interest, he was at first the enemy, and at last the father, of the Roman world.[16] When he framed the artful system of the Imperial authority, his moderation was inspired by his fears. He wished to deceive the people by an image of civil liberty, and the armies by an image of civil government.

I. The death of Cæsar was ever before his eyes. He had lavished wealth and honours on his adherents; but the most favoured friends of his uncle were in the number of the conspirators. The fidelity of the legions might defend his authority against open rebellion, but their vigilance could not secure his person from the dagger of a determined republican; and the Romans, who revered the memory of Brutus,[17] would applaud the imitation of his virtue, Cæsar had provoked his fate as much by the ostentation of his power as by his power itself. The consul or the tribune might have reigned in peace. The title of king had armed the Romans against his life. Augustus was sensible that mankind is governed by names; nor was he deceived in his expectation that the senate and people would submit

[16] *As Octavianus advanced to the banquet of the Cæsars, his colour changed like that of the chameleon; pale at first, then red, afterwards black, he at last assumed the mild livery of Venus and the Graces. This image, employed by Julian in his ingenious fiction, is just and elegant; but, when he considers this change of character as real, and ascribes it to the power of philosophy, he does too much honour to philosophy and to Octavianus.*

[17] *Two centuries after the establishment of monarchy, the emperor Marcus Antoninus recommends the character of Brutus as a perfect model of Roman virtue.*

to slavery, provided they were respectfully assured that they still enjoyed their ancient freedom. A feeble senate and enervated people cheerfully acquiesced in the pleasing illusion, as long as it was supported by the virtue, or by even the prudence, of the successors of Augustus. It was a motive of self-preservation, not a principle of liberty, that animated the conspirators against Caligula, Nero, and Domitian. They attacked the person of the tyrant, without aiming their blow at the authority of the emperor.

There appears, indeed, *one* memorable occasion, in which the senate, after seventy years of patience, made an ineffectual attempt to reassume its long-forgotten rights. When the throne was vacant by the murder of Caligula, the consuls convoked that assembly in the Capitol, condemned the memory of the Cæsars, gave the watchword *liberty* to the few cohorts who faintly adhered to their standard, and during eight and forty hours, acted as the independent chiefs of a free commonwealth. But while they deliberated, the prætorian guards had resolved. The stupid Claudius, brother of Germanicus, was already in their camp, invested with the Imperial purple, and prepared to support his election by arms. The dream of liberty was at an end; and the senate awoke to all the horrors of inevitable servitude. Deserted by the people, and threatened by a military force, that feeble assembly was compelled to ratify the choice of the prætorians, and to embrace the benefit of an amnesty, which Claudius had the prudence to offer, and the generosity to observe.[18]

II. The insolence of the armies inspired Augustus with fears of a still more alarming nature. The despair of the citizens could only attempt what the power of the soldiers was, at any time, able to execute. How precarious was his own authority over men whom he had taught to violate every social duty! He had heard their seditious clamours; he dreaded their calmer moments of reflection. One revolution had been purchased by immense rewards; but a second revolution might double those rewards. The troops professed the fondest attachment to the house of Cæsar; but the attachments of the multitude are capricious and inconstant. Augustus summoned to his aid whatever remained in those fierce minds of Roman prejudices; enforced the rigour of discipline by the sanction of law; and, interposing the majesty of the senate between the emperor and the army, boldly claimed their allegiance as the first magistrate of the republic.[19]

During a long period of two hundred and twenty years, from the

[18] *It is much to be regretted that we have lost the part of Tacitus which treated of that transaction. We are forced to content ourselves with the popular rumours of Josephus, and the imperfect hints of Dion and Suetonius.*

[19] *Augustus restored the ancient severity of discipline. After the civil wars, he dropped the endearing name of Fellow-Soldiers, and called them only Soldiers.*

"*The greatest number, as well as the most considerable of the Roman edifices, were raised by the
emperors, who possessed so unbounded a command both of men and money. Augustus was accustomed to boast that he had found his capital of
brick, and that he had left it of marble.*"

"*The map, the description, the monuments of
ancient Rome have been elucidated by the diligence of the antiquarian and the student; and the
footsteps of heroes, the relics, not of superstition,
but of empire, are devoutly visited by a new race
of pilgrims from the remote, and once savage,
countries of the North.*"

Monuments existing in Piranesi's day are shown in heavy line; lighter lines indicate his conjectural reconstructions. Modern identifications are given, not necessarily Piranesi's.

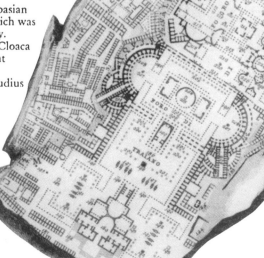

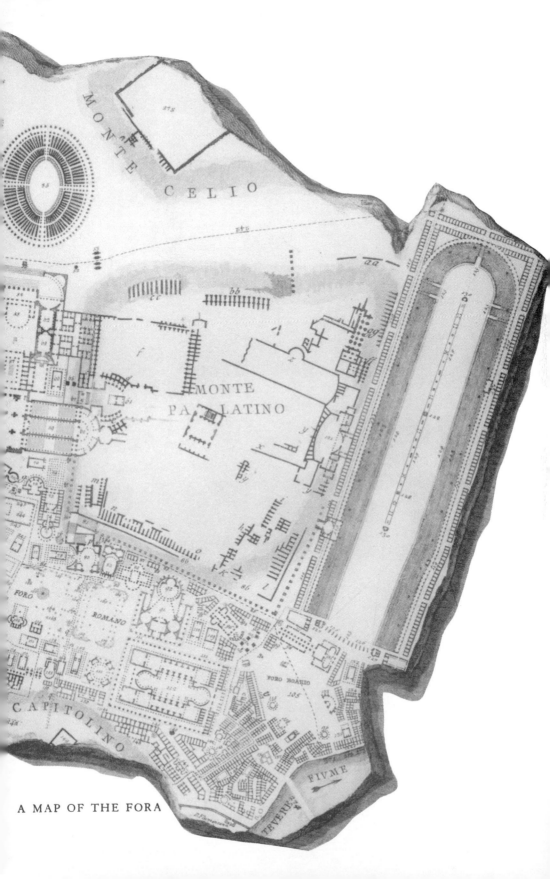

MONTE

CELIO

MONTE
PALATINO

FORO

ROMANO

CAPITOLINO

FORO BOARIO

FIVME

TEVERE

A MAP OF THE FORA

establishment of this artful system to the death of Commodus, the dangers inherent to a military government were, in a great measure, suspended. The soldiers were seldom roused to that fatal sense of their own strength, and of the weakness of the civil authority, which was, before and afterwards, productive of such dreadful calamities. Caligula and Domitian were assassinated in their palace by their own domestics: the convulsions which agitated Rome on the death of the former were confined to the walls of the city. But Nero involved the whole empire in his ruin. In the space of eighteen months four princes perished by the sword; and the Roman world was shaken by the fury of the contending armies. Excepting only this short, though violent, eruption of military licence, the two centuries from Augustus to Commodus passed away, unstained with civil blood, and undisturbed by revolutions. The emperor was elected by the *authority of the senate and the consent of the soldiers*.[20] The legions respected their oath of fidelity; and it requires a minute inspection of the Roman annals to discover three inconsiderable rebellions, which were all suppressed in a few months, and without even the hazard of a battle.[21]

In elective monarchies, the vacancy of the throne is a moment big with danger and mischief. The Roman emperors, desirous to spare the legions that interval of suspense, and the temptation of an irregular choice, invested their designed successor with so large a share of present power, as should enable him, after their decease, to assume the remainder without suffering the empire to perceive the change of masters. Thus Augustus, after all his fairer prospects had been snatched from him by untimely deaths, rested his last hopes on Tiberius, obtained for his adopted son the censorial and tribunitian powers, and dictated a law, by which the future prince was invested with an authority equal to his own over the provinces and the armies. Thus Vespasian subdued the generous mind of his eldest son. Titus was adored by the eastern legions, which, under his command, had recently achieved the conquest of Judea. His power was dreaded, and, as his virtues were clouded by the intemperance of youth, his designs were suspected. Instead of listening to such unworthy suspicions, the prudent monarch associated Titus to the full powers of the Imperial dignity; and the grateful son ever approved himself the humble and faithful minister of so indulgent a father.

The good sense of Vespasian engaged him indeed to embrace every measure that might confirm his recent and precarious elevation. The military oath, and the fidelity of the troops, had been con-

[20] *These words seem to have been the constitutional language.*

[21] *The first was Camillus Scribonianus, who took up arms in Dalmatia against Claudius, and was deserted by his own troops in five days; the second, L. Antonius, in Germany, who rebelled against Domitian; and the third, Avidius Cassius, in the reign of M. Antoninus. The two last reigned but a few months and were cut off by their own adherents. We may observe, that both Camillus and Cassius coloured their ambition with the design of restoring the republic, a task, said Cassius, peculiarly reserved for his name and family.*

secrated, by the habits of an hundred years, to the name and family of the Cæsars; and, although that family had been continued only by the fictitious rite of adoption, the Romans still revered, in the person of Nero, the grandson of Germanicus, and the lineal successor of Augustus. It was not without reluctance and remorse that the prætorian guards had been persuaded to abandon the cause of the tyrant.[22] The rapid downfall of Galba, Otho, and Vitellius, taught the armies to consider the emperors as the creatures of *their* will, and the instruments of *their* licence. The birth of Vespasian was mean; his grandfather had been a private soldier, his father a petty officer of the revenue,[23] his own merit had raised him, in an advanced age, to the empire; but his merit was rather useful than shining, and his virtues were disgraced by a strict and even sordid parsimony. Such a prince consulted his true interest by the association of a son whose more splendid and amiable character might turn the public attention from the obscure origin to the future glories of the Flavian house. Under the mild administration of Titus, the Roman world enjoyed a transient felicity, and his beloved memory served to protect, above fifteen years, the vices of his brother Domitian.

Nerva had scarcely accepted the purple from the assassins of Domitian before he discovered that his feeble age was unable to stem the torrent of public disorders which had multiplied under the long tyranny of his predecessor. His mild disposition was respected by the good; but the degenerate Romans required a more vigorous character, whose justice should strike terror into the guilty. Though he had several relations, he fixed his choice on a stranger. He adopted Trajan, then about forty years of age, and who commanded a powerful army in the Lower Germany; and immediately, by a decree of the senate, declared him his colleague and successor in the empire. It is sincerely to be lamented, that, whilst we are fatigued with the disgustful relation of Nero's crimes and follies, we are reduced to collect the actions of Trajan from the glimmerings of an abridgment, or the doubtful light of a panegyric. There remains, however, one panegyric far removed beyond the suspicion of flattery. Above two hundred and fifty years after the death of Trajan, the senate, in pouring out the customary acclamations on the accession of a new emperor, wished that he might surpass the felicity of Augustus, and the virtue of Trajan.[24]

We may readily believe that the father of his country hesitated whether he ought to intrust the various and doubtful character of his kinsman Hadrian with sovereign power. In his last moments,

[22] *This idea is frequently and strongly inculcated by Tacitus.*

[23] *The emperor Vespasian, with his usual good sense, laughed at the Genealogists, who deduced his family from Flavius, the founder of Reate (his native country), and one of the companions of Hercules.*

[24] *Felicior Augusto,* MELIOR TRAJANO.

the arts of the empress Plotina either fixed the irresolution of Trajan, or boldly supposed a fictitious adoption,[25] the truth of which could not be safely disputed; and Hadrian was peaceably acknowledged as his lawful successor. Under his reign, as has been already mentioned, the empire flourished in peace and prosperity. He encouraged the arts, reformed the laws, asserted military discipline, and visited all his provinces in person. His vast and active genius was equally suited to the most enlarged views and the minute details of civil policy. But the ruling passions of his soul were curiosity and vanity. As they prevailed, and as they were attracted by different objects, Hadrian was, by turns, an excellent prince, a ridiculous sophist, and a jealous tyrant. The general tenor of his conduct deserved praise for its equity and moderation. Yet, in the first days of his reign, he put to death four consular senators, his personal enemies, and men who had been judged worthy of empire; and the tediousness of a painful illness rendered him, at last, peevish and cruel. The senate doubted whether they should pronounce him a god or a tyrant; and the honours decreed to his memory were granted to the prayers of the pious Antoninus.

The caprice of Hadrian influenced his choice of a successor. After revolving in his mind several men of distinguished merit, whom he esteemed and hated, he adopted Ælius Verus, a gay and voluptuous nobleman, recommended by uncommon beauty to the lover of Antinous.[26] But while Hadrian was delighting himself with his own applause, and the acclamations of the soldiers, whose consent had been secured by an immense donative, the new Cæsar was ravished from his embraces by an untimely death. He left only one son. Hadrian commended the boy to the gratitude of the Antonines. He was adopted by Pius; and, on the accession of Marcus, was invested with an equal share of sovereign power. Among the many vices of this younger Verus, he possessed one virtue—a dutiful reverence for his wiser colleague, to whom he willingly abandoned the ruder cares of empire. The philosophic emperor dissembled his follies, lamented his early death, and cast a decent veil over his memory.

As soon as Hadrian's passion was either gratified or disappointed, he resolved to deserve the thanks of posterity by placing the most exalted merit on the Roman throne. His discerning eye easily discovered a senator about fifty years of age, blameless in all the offices of life; and a youth of about seventeen, whose riper years opened the fair prospect of every virtue: the elder of these was declared the son and successor of Hadrian, on condition, however, that he himself

[25] *Dion affirms the whole to have been a fiction, on the authority of his father, who being governor of the province where Trajan died, had very good opportunities of sifting this mysterious transaction. Yet Dodwell has maintained, that Hadrian was called to the certain hope of the empire during the lifetime of Trajan.*

[26] *The deification of Antinous, his medals, statues, temples, city, oracles, and constellation, are well known, and still dishonour the memory of Hadrian. Yet we may remark, that of the first fifteen emperors Claudius was the only one whose taste in love was entirely correct.*

should immediately adopt the younger. The two Antonines (for it is of them that we are now speaking) governed the Roman world forty-two years with the same invariable spirit of wisdom and virtue. Although Pius had two sons,[27] he preferred the welfare of Rome to the interest of his family, gave his daughter Faustina in marriage to young Marcus, obtained from the senate the tribunitian and proconsular powers, and, with a noble disdain, or rather ignorance, of jealousy, associated him to all the labours of government. Marcus, on the other hand, revered the character of his benefactor, loved him as a parent, obeyed him as his sovereign,[28] and, after he was no more, regulated his own administration by the example and maxims of his predecessor. Their united reigns are possibly the only period of history in which the happiness of a great people was the sole object of government.

Titus Antoninus Pius had been justly denominated a second Numa. The same love of religion, justice, and peace, was the distinguishing characteristic of both princes. But the situation of the latter opened a much larger field for the exercise of those virtues. Numa could only prevent a few neighbouring villages from plundering each other's harvests. Antoninus diffused order and tranquillity over the greatest part of the earth. His reign is marked by the rare advantage of furnishing very few materials for history; which is, indeed, little more than the register of the crimes, follies, and misfortunes of mankind. In private life he was an amiable as well as a good man. The native simplicity of his virtue was a stranger to vanity or affectation. He enjoyed with moderation the conveniences of his fortune, and the innocent pleasures of society;[29] and the benevolence of his soul displayed itself in a cheerful serenity of temper.

The virtue of Marcus Aurelius Antoninus was of a severer and more laborious kind.[30] It was the well-earned harvest of many a learned conference, of many a patient lecture, and many a midnight lucubration. At the age of twelve years he embraced the rigid system of the Stoics, which taught him to submit his body to his mind, his passions to his reason; to consider virtue as the only good, vice as the only evil, all things external as things indifferent. His Meditations, composed in the tumult of a camp, are still extant; and he even condescended to give lessons on philosophy, in a more public manner than was perhaps consistent with the modesty of a sage or the dignity of an emperor.[31] But his life was the noblest commentary on the precepts of Zeno. He was severe to himself, indulgent to the imper-

[27] *Without the help of medals and inscriptions, we should be ignorant of this fact, so honourable to the memory of Pius.*

[28] *During the twenty-three years of Pius's reign, Marcus was only two nights absent from the palace, and even those were at different times.*

[29] *He was fond of the theatre and not insensible to the charms of the fair sex.*

[30] *The enemies of Marcus charged him with hypocrisy and with a want of that simplicity which distinguished Pius and even Verus. This suspicion, unjust as it was, may serve to account for the superior applause bestowed upon personal qualifications, in preference to the social virtues. Even Marcus Antoninus has been called a hypocrite; but the wildest scepticism never insinuated that Cæsar might possibly be a coward, or Tully a fool. Wit and valour are qualifications more easily ascertained than humanity or the love of justice.*

fection of others, just and beneficent to all mankind. He regretted that Avidius Cassius, who excited a rebellion in Syria, had disappointed him, by a voluntary death, of the pleasure of converting an enemy into a friend; and he justified the sincerity of that sentiment, by moderating the zeal of the senate against the adherents of the traitor. War he detested, as the disgrace and calamity of human nature; but when the necessity of a just defence called upon him to take up arms, he readily exposed his person to eight winter campaigns on the frozen banks of the Danube, the severity of which was at last fatal to the weakness of his constitution. His memory was revered by a grateful posterity, and above a century after his death many persons preserved the image of Marcus Antoninus among those of their household gods.

[31] *Before he went on the second expedition against the Germans, he read lectures of philosophy to the Roman people, during three days. He had already done the same in the cities of Greece and Asia.*

If a man were called to fix the period in the history of the world during which the condition of the human race was most happy and prosperous, he would, without hesitation, name that which elapsed from the death of Domitian to the accession of Commodus. The vast extent of the Roman empire was governed by absolute power, under the guidance of virtue and wisdom. The armies were restrained by the firm but gentle hand of four successive emperors, whose characters and authority commanded involuntary respect. The forms of the civil administration were carefully preserved by Nerva, Trajan, Hadrian, and the Antonines, who delighted in the image of liberty, and were pleased with considering themselves as the accountable ministers of the laws. Such princes deserved the honour of restoring the republic, had the Romans of their days been capable of enjoying a rational freedom.

The labours of these monarchs were over-paid by the immense reward that inseparably waited on their success; by the honest pride of virtue, and by the exquisite delight of beholding the general happiness of which they were the authors. A just but melancholy reflection embittered, however, the noblest of human enjoyments. They must often have recollected the instability of a happiness which depended on the character of a single man. The fatal moment was perhaps approaching, when some licentious youth, or some jealous tyrant, would abuse, to the destruction, that absolute power which they had exerted for the benefit of their people. The ideal restraints of the senate and the laws might serve to display the virtues, but could never correct the vices, of the emperor. The military force was a blind and irresistible instrument of oppression; and the corruption of Roman manners would always supply flatterers eager to applaud, and ministers prepared to serve, the fear or the avarice, the lust or the cruelty, of their masters.

These gloomy apprehensions had been already justified by the experience of the Romans. The annals of the emperors exhibit a strong and various picture of human nature, which we should vainly seek among the mixed and doubtful characters of modern history. In the conduct of those monarchs we may trace the utmost lines of vice and virtue; the most exalted perfection and the meanest degeneracy of our own species. The golden age of Trajan and the Antonines had been preceded by an age of iron. It is almost superfluous to enumerate the unworthy successors of Augustus. Their unparalleled vices, and the splendid theatre on which they were acted, have saved them from oblivion. The dark unrelenting Tiberius, the furious Caligula, the stupid Claudius, the profligate and cruel Nero, the beastly Vitellius,[32] and the timid inhuman Domitian, are condemned to everlasting infamy. During fourscore years (excepting only the short and doubtful respite of Vespasian's reign),[33] Rome groaned beneath an unremitting tyranny, which exterminated the ancient families of the republic, and was fatal to almost every virtue and every talent that arose in that unhappy period.

Under the reign of these monsters the slavery of the Romans was accompanied with two peculiar circumstances, the one occasioned by their former liberty, the other by their extensive conquests, which rendered their condition more wretched than that of the victims of tyranny in any other age or country. From these causes were derived, 1. The exquisite sensibility of the sufferers; and 2. The impossibility of escaping from the hand of the oppressor.

I. When Persia was governed by the descendants of Sefi, a race of princes whose wanton cruelty often stained their divan, their table, and their bed with the blood of their favourites, there is a saying recorded of a young nobleman, That he never departed from the sultan's presence without satisfying himself whether his head was still on his shoulders. The experience of every day might almost justify the scepticism of Rustan. Yet the fatal sword, suspended above him by a single thread, seems not to have disturbed the slumbers, or interrupted the tranquillity, of the Persian. The monarch's frown, he well knew, could level him with the dust; but the stroke of lightning or apoplexy might be equally fatal; and it was the part of a wise man to forget the inevitable calamities of human life in the enjoyment of the fleeting hour. He was dignified with the appellation of the king's slave;[34] had, perhaps, been purchased **from**

[32] *Vitellius consumed in mere eating at least six millions of our money, in about seven months. It is not easy to express his vices with dignity, or even decency. Tacitus fairly calls him a hog; but it is by substituting for a coarse word a very fine image.*

[33] *The execution of Helvidius Priscus and of the virtuous Eponina disgraced the reign of Vespasian.*

[34] *The practice of raising slaves to the great offices of state is still more common among the Turks than among the Persians. The miserable countries of Georgia and Circassia supply rulers to the greatest part of the East.*

obscure parents, in a country which he had never known; and was trained up from his infancy in the severe discipline of the seraglio. His name, his wealth, his honours, were the gift of a master, who might, without injustice, resume what he had bestowed. Rustan's knowledge, if he possessed any, could only serve to confirm his habits by prejudices. His language afforded not words for any form of government, except absolute monarchy. The history of the East informed him that such had ever been the condition of mankind.[35] The Koran, and the interpreters of that divine book, inculcated to him that the sultan was the descendant of the prophet, and the vicegerent of heaven; that patience was the first virtue of a Mussulman, and unlimited obedience the great duty of a subject.

The minds of the Romans were very differently prepared for slavery. Oppressed beneath the weight of their own corruption and of military violence, they for a long while preserved the sentiments, or at least the ideas, of their freeborn ancestors. The education of Helvidius and Thrasea, of Tacitus and Pliny, was the same as that of Cato and Cicero. From Grecian philosophy they had imbibed the justest and most liberal notions of the dignity of human nature and the origin of civil society. The history of their own country had taught them to revere a free, a virtuous, and a victorious commonwealth; to abhor the successful crimes of Cæsar and Augustus; and inwardly to despise those tyrants whom they adored with the most abject flattery. As magistrates and senators, they were admitted into the great council which had once dictated laws to the earth, whose name gave still a sanction to the acts of the monarch, and whose authority was so often prostituted to the vilest purposes of tyranny. Tiberius, and those emperors who adopted his maxims, attempted to disguise their murders by the formalities of justice, and perhaps enjoyed a secret pleasure in rendering the senate their accomplice as well as their victim. By this assembly the last of the Romans were condemned for imaginary crimes and real virtues. Their infamous accusers assumed the language of independent patriots, who arraigned a dangerous citizen before the tribunal of his country; and the public service was rewarded by riches and honours.[36] The servile judges professed to assert the majesty of the commonwealth, violated in the person of its first magistrate,[37] whose clemency they most applauded when they trembled the most at his inexorable and impending cruelty.[38] The tyrant beheld their baseness with just contempt, and encountered their secret sentiments of detestation with sincere and avowed hatred for the whole body of the senate.

[35] Chardin says that European travellers have diffused among the Persians some ideas of the freedom and mildness of our governments. They have done them a very ill office.

[36] They alleged the example of Scipio and Cato. Marcellus Eprius and Crispius Vibius had acquired two millions and a half under Nero. Their wealth, which aggravated their crimes, protected them under Vespasian. For one accusation, Regulus, the just object of Pliny's satire, received from the senate the consular ornaments, and a present of sixty thousand pounds.

[37] The crime of majesty was formerly a treasonable offence against the Roman people. As tribunes of the people, Augustus and Tiberius applied it to their own persons, and extended it to an infinite latitude.

[38] After the virtuous and unfortunate widow of Germanicus had been put to death, Tiberius received the thanks of the senate for his clemency. She had not been publicly strangled; nor was the body drawn with a hook to the Gemoniæ, where those of common malefactors were exposed.

II. The division of Europe into a number of independent states, connected, however, with each other, by the general resemblance of religion, language and manners, is productive of the most beneficial consequences to the liberty of mankind. A modern tyrant, who should find no resistance either in his own breast or in his people, would soon experience a gentle restraint from the example of his equals, the dread of present censure, the advice of his allies, and the apprehension of his enemies. The object of his displeasure, escaping from the narrow limits of his dominions, would easily obtain, in a happier climate, a secure refuge, a new fortune adequate to his merit, the freedom of complaint, and perhaps the means of revenge. But the empire of the Romans filled the world, and, when that empire fell into the hands of a single person, the world became a safe and dreary prison for his enemies. The slave of Imperial despotism, whether he was condemned to drag his gilded chain in Rome and the senate, or to wear out a life of exile on the barren rock of Seriphus, or the frozen banks of the Danube, expected his fate in silent despair.[39] To resist was fatal, and it was impossible to fly. On every side he was encompassed with a vast extent of sea and land, which he could never hope to traverse without being discovered, seized, and restored to his irritated master. Beyond the frontiers, his anxious view could discover nothing, except the ocean, inhospitable deserts, hostile tribes of barbarians, of fierce manners and unknown language, or dependent kings, who would gladly purchase the emperor's protection by the sacrifice of an obnoxious fugitive.[40] "Wherever you are," said Cicero to the exiled Marcellus, "remember that you are equally within the power of the conqueror."

[39] Seriphus was a small rocky island in the Ægean Sea, the inhabitants of which were despised for their ignorance and obscurity. The place of Ovid's exile is well known by his just but unmanly lamentations. It should seem that he only received an order to leave Rome in so many days, and to transport himself to Tomi. Guards and gaolers were unnecessary.

[40] Under Tiberius, a Roman knight attempted to fly to the Parthians. He was stopt in the straits of Sicily; but so little danger did there appear in the example, that the most jealous of tyrants disdained to punish it.

IV

THE CRUELTY, FOLLIES, AND MURDER OF COMMODUS · ELEC-
TION OF PERTINAX · HIS ATTEMPTS TO REFORM THE STATE ·
HIS ASSASSINATION BY PRÆTORIAN GUARDS · INDIGNATION

THE mildness of Marcus, which the rigid discipline of the Stoics was unable to eradicate, formed, at the same time, the most amiable, and the only defective, part of his character. His excellent understanding was often deceived by the unsuspecting goodness of his heart. Artful men, who study the passions of princes and conceal their own, approached his person in the disguise of philosophic sanctity, and acquired riches and honours by affecting to despise them.[1] His excessive indulgence to his brother, his wife, and his son, exceeded the bounds of private virtue, and became a public injury, by the example and consequences of their vices.

Faustina, the daughter of Pius and the wife of Marcus, has been as much celebrated for her gallantries as for her beauty. The grave simplicity of the philosopher was ill calculated to engage her wanton levity, or to fix that unbounded passion for variety which often discovered personal merit in the meanest of mankind. The Cupid of the ancients was, in general, a very sensual deity; and the amours of an empress, as they exact on her side the plainest advances, are seldom susceptible of much sentimental delicacy. Marcus was the only man in the empire who seemed ignorant or insensible of the irregularities of Faustina; which, according to the prejudices of every age, reflected some disgrace on the injured husband. He promoted several of her lovers to posts of honour and profit, and, during a connexion of thirty years, invariably gave her proofs of the most tender confidence, and of a respect which ended not with her life. In his Meditations he thanks the gods, who had bestowed on him a wife so faithful, so gentle, and of such a wonderful simplicity of manners.[2] The obsequious senate, at his earnest request, declared her a goddess. She was represented in her temples, with the attributes of

[1] *See the complaints of Avidius Cassius. These are, it is true, the complaints of faction; but even faction exaggerates, rather than invents.*

[2] *The world has laughed at the credulity of Marcus; but Madame Dacier assures us (and we may credit a lady) that the husband will always be deceived, if the wife condescends to dissemble.*

Juno, Venus, and Ceres; and it was decreed that, on the day of their nuptials, the youth of either sex should pay their vows before the altar of their chaste patroness.[3]

The monstrous vices of the son have cast a shade on the purity of the father's virtues. It has been objected to Marcus, that he sacrificed the happiness of millions to a fond partiality for a worthless boy; and that he chose a successor in his own family rather than in the republic. Nothing, however, was neglected by the anxious father, and by the men of virtue and learning whom he summoned to his assistance, to expand the narrow mind of young Commodus, to correct his growing vices, and to render him worthy of the throne for which he was designed. But the power of instruction is seldom of much efficacy, except in those happy dispositions where it is almost superfluous. The distasteful lesson of a grave philosopher was, in a moment, obliterated by the whisper of a profligate favourite; and Marcus himself blasted the fruits of this laboured education, by admitting his son, at the age of fourteen or fifteen, to a full participation of the Imperial power. He lived but four years afterwards; but he lived long enough to repent a rash measure, which raised the impetuous youth above the restraint of reason and authority.

Most of the crimes which disturb the internal peace of society are produced by the restraint which the necessary, but unequal, laws of property have imposed on the appetites of mankind, by confining to a few the possession of those objects that are coveted by many. Of all our passions and appetites, the love of power is of the most imperious and unsociable nature, since the pride of one man requires the submission of the multitude. In the tumult of civil discord the laws of society lose their force, and their place is seldom supplied by those of humanity. The ardour of contention, the pride of victory, the despair of success, the memory of past injuries, and the fear of future dangers, all contribute to inflame the mind, and to silence the voice of pity. From such motives almost every page of history has been stained with civil blood; but these motives will not account for the unprovoked cruelties of Commodus, who had nothing to wish, and everything to enjoy. The beloved son of Marcus succeeded to his father, amidst the acclamations of the senate and armies;[4] and when he ascended the throne, the happy youth saw round him neither competitor to remove, nor enemies to punish. In this calm elevated station it was surely natural that he should prefer the love of mankind to their detestation, the mild glories of his five predecessors to the ignominious fate of Nero and Domitian.

[3] *The deification of Faustina is the only defect which Julian's criticism is able to discover in the all-accomplished character of Marcus.*

[4] *Commodus was the first* Porphyrogenitus *(born since his father's accession to the throne). By a new strain of flattery, the Egyptian medals date by the years of his life; as if they were synonymous to those of his reign.*

Yet Commodus was not, as he has been represented, a tiger born with an insatiate thirst of human blood, and capable, from his infancy, of the most inhuman actions. Nature had formed him of a weak, rather than a wicked, disposition. His simplicity and timidity rendered him the slave of his attendants, who gradually corrupted his mind. His cruelty, which at first obeyed the dictates of others, degenerated into habit, and at length became the ruling passion of his soul.

Upon the death of his father Commodus found himself embarrassed with the command of a great army, and the conduct of a difficult war against the Quadi and Marcomanni.[5] The servile and profligate youths whom Marcus had banished soon regained their station and influence about the new emperor. They exaggerated the hardships and dangers of a campaign in the wild countries beyond the Danube; and they assured the indolent prince that the terror of his name and the arms of his lieutenants would be sufficient to complete the conquest of the dismayed barbarians, or to impose such conditions as were more advantageous than any conquest. By a dexterous application to his sensual appetites, they compared the tranquillity, the splendour, the refined pleasures of Rome with the tumult of a Pannonian camp, which afforded neither leisure nor materials for luxury. Commodus listened to the pleasing advice; but whilst he hesitated between his own inclination and the awe which he still retained for his father's counsellors, the summer insensibly elapsed, and his triumphal entry into the capital was deferred till the autumn. His graceful person, popular address, and imagined virtues attracted the public favour; the honourable peace which he had recently granted to the barbarians diffused an universal joy;[6] his impatience to revisit Rome was fondly ascribed to the love of his country; and his dissolute course of amusements was faintly condemned in a prince of nineteen years of age.

During the three first years of his reign, the forms, and even the spirit, of the old administration were maintained by those faithful counsellors, to whom Marcus had recommended his son, and for whose wisdom and integrity Commodus still entertained a reluctant esteem. The young prince and his profligate favourites revelled in all the licence of sovereign power; but his hands were yet unstained with blood; and he had even displayed a generosity of sentiment, which might perhaps have ripened into solid virtue.[7] A fatal incident decided his fluctuating character.

One evening, as the emperor was returning to the palace through

[5] According to Tertullian he died at Sirmium. But the situation of Vindobona, or Vienna, where both the Victors place his death, is better adapted to the operations of the war against the Marcomanni and Quadi.

[6] This universal joy is well described from the medals as well as historians.

[7] Manilius, the confidential secretary of Avidius Cassius, was discovered after he had lain concealed for several years. The emperor nobly relieved the public anxiety by refusing to see him, and burning his papers without opening them.

a dark and narrow portico in the amphitheatre, an assassin, who waited his passage, rushed upon him with a drawn sword, loudly exclaiming, *The senate sends you this.* The menace prevented the deed; the assassin was seized by the guards, and immediately revealed the authors of the conspiracy. It had been formed, not in the state, but within the walls of the palace. Lucilla, the emperor's sister, and widow of Lucius Verus, impatient of the second rank, and jealous of the reigning empress, had armed the murderer against her brother's life. She had not ventured to communicate the black design to her second husband, Claudius Pompeianus, a senator of distinguished merit and unshaken loyalty; but among the crowd of her lovers (for she imitated the manners of Faustina) she found men of desperate fortunes and wild ambition, who were prepared to serve her more violent as well as her tender passions. The conspirators experienced the rigour of justice, and the abandoned princess was punished, first with exile, and afterwards with death.

But the words of the assassin sunk deep into the mind of Commodus, and left an indelible impression of fear and hatred against the whole body of the senate. Those whom he had dreaded as importunate ministers, he now suspected as secret enemies. The Delators, a race of men discouraged, and almost extinguished, under the former reigns, again became formidable as soon as they discovered that the emperor was desirous of finding disaffection and treason in the senate. That assembly, whom Marcus had ever considered as the great council of the nation, was composed of the most distinguished of the Romans; and distinction of every kind soon became criminal. The possession of wealth stimulated the diligence of the informers; rigid virtue implied a tacit censure of the irregularities of Commodus; important services implied a dangerous superiority of merit, and the friendship of the father always insured the aversion of the son. Suspicion was equivalent to proof; trial to condemnation. The execution of a considerable senator was attended with the death of all who might lament or revenge his fate; and when Commodus had once tasted human blood, he became incapable of pity or remorse.

Of these innocent victims of tyranny, none died more lamented than the two brothers of the Quintilian family, Maximus and Condianus, whose fraternal love has saved their names from oblivion, and endeared their memory to posterity. Their studies and their occupations, their pursuits and their pleasures, were still the same. In the enjoyment of a great estate, they never admitted the idea of a separate interest: some fragments are now extant of a treatise which they composed in common; and in every action of life it was observed that their two bodies were animated by one soul. The Antonines, who valued their virtues and delighted in their union, raised them, in the same year, to the consulship; and Marcus afterwards intrusted to their joint care the civil administration of Greece, and a great military command, in which they obtained a signal victory over the Germans. The kind cruelty of Commodus united them in death.

The tyrant's rage, after having shed the noblest blood of the senate, at length recoiled on the principal instrument of his cruelty. Whilst Commodus was immersed in blood and luxury, he devolved the detail of the public business on Perennis; a servile and ambitious minister, who had obtained his post by the murder of his predecessor, but who possessed a considerable share of vigour and ability. By acts of extortion, and the forfeited estates of the nobles sacrificed to his avarice, he had accumulated an immense treasure. The Prætorian guards were under his immediate command; and his son, who already discovered a military genius, was at the head of the Illyrian legions. Perennis aspired to the empire; or what, in the eyes of Commodus, amounted to the same crime, he was capable of aspiring to it, had he not been prevented, surprised, and put to death. The fall of a minister is a very trifling incident in the general history of the empire; but it was hastened by an extraordinary circumstance, which proved how much the nerves of discipline were already relaxed. The legions of Britain, discontented with the administration of Perennis, formed a deputation of fifteen hundred select men, with instructions to march to Rome, and lay their complaints before the emperor. These military petitioners, by their own determined behaviour, by inflaming the divisions of the guards, by exaggerating the strength of the British army, and by alarming the fears of Commodus, exacted and obtained the minister's death, as the only redress of their grievances.[8] This presumption of a distant army, and their discovery of the weakness of government, was a sure presage of the most dreadful convulsions.

The negligence of the public administration was betrayed soon afterwards by a new disorder, which arose from the smallest beginnings. A spirit of desertion began to prevail among the troops, and the deserters, instead of seeking their safety in flight or concealment, infested the highways. Maternus, a private soldier, of a daring boldness above his station, collected these bands of robbers into a

[8] *Dion gives a much less odious character of Perennis than the other historians. His moderation is almost a pledge of his veracity.*

little army, set open the prisons, invited the slaves to assert their freedom, and plundered with impunity the rich and defenceless cities of Gaul and Spain. The governors of the provinces, who had long been the spectators, and perhaps the partners, of his depredations, were, at length, roused from their supine indolence by the threatening commands of the emperor. Maternus found that he was encompassed, and foresaw that he must be overpowered. A great effort of despair was his last resource. He ordered his followers to disperse, to pass the Alps in small parties and various disguises, and to assemble at Rome, during the licentious tumult of the festival of Cybele.[9] To murder Commodus, and to ascend the vacant throne, was the ambition of no vulgar robber. His measures were so ably concerted that his concealed troops already filled the streets of Rome. The envy of an accomplice discovered and ruined this singular enterprise in the moment when it was ripe for execution.

Suspicious princes often promote the last of mankind, from a vain persuasion that those who have no dependence except on their favour will have no attachment except to the person of their benefactor. Cleander, the successor of Perennis, was a Phrygian by birth; of a nation, over whose stubborn but servile temper blows only could prevail. He had been sent from his native country to Rome, in the capacity of a slave. As a slave he entered the imperial palace, rendered himself useful to his master's passions, and rapidly ascended to the most exalted station which a subject could enjoy. His influence over the mind of Commodus was much greater than that of his predecessor; for Cleander was devoid of any ability or virtue which could inspire the emperor with envy or distrust. Avarice was the reigning passion of his soul, and the great principle of his administration. The rank of consul, of Patrician, of senator, was exposed to public sale; and it would have been considered as disaffection if any one had refused to purchase these empty and disgraceful honours with the greatest part of his fortune.[10] In the lucrative provincial employments the minister shared with the governor the spoils of the people. The execution of the laws was venal and arbitrary. A wealthy criminal might obtain not only the reversal of the sentence by which he was justly condemned; but might likewise inflict whatever punishment he pleased on the accuser, the witnesses, and the judge.

By these means Cleander, in the space of three years, had accumulated more wealth than had ever yet been possessed by any freedman.[11] Commodus was perfectly satisfied with the magnificent pres-

[9] *During the second Punic war, the Romans imported from Asia the worship of the mother of the gods. Her festival, the* Megalesia, *began on the fourth of April, and lasted six days. The streets were crowded with mad processions, the theatres with spectators, and the public tables with unbidden guests. Order and police were suspended, and pleasure was the only serious business of the city.*

[10] *One of these dear-bought promotions occasioned a current bon mot, that Julius Solon was* banished *into the senate.*

[11] *Dion observes that no freedman had possessed riches equal to those of Cleander. The fortune of Pallas amounted, however, to upwards of five and twenty hundred thousand pounds—*ter millies.

ents which the artful courtier laid at his feet in the most seasonable moments. To divert the public envy, Cleander, under the emperor's name, erected baths, porticos, and places of exercise, for the use of the people.[12] He flattered himself that the Romans, dazzled and amused by this apparent liberality, would be less affected by the bloody scenes which were daily exhibited; that they would forget the death of Byrrhus, a senator to whose superior merit the late emperor had granted one of his daughters; and that they would forgive the execution of Arrius Antoninus, the last representative of the name and virtues of the Antonines. The former, with more integrity than prudence, had attempted to disclose to his brother-in-law the true character of Cleander. An equitable sentence pronounced by the latter, when proconsul of Asia, against a worthless creature of the favourite, proved fatal to him. After the fall of Perennis the terrors of Commodus had, for a short time, assumed the appearance of a return to virtue. He repealed the most odious of his acts, loaded his memory with the public execration, and ascribed to the pernicious counsels of that wicked minister all the errors of his inexperienced youth. But his repentance lasted only thirty days; and, under Cleander's tyranny, the administration of Perennis was often regretted.

Pestilence and famine contributed to fill up the measure of the calamities of Rome.[13] The first could only be imputed to the just indignation of the gods; but a monopoly of corn, supported by the riches and power of the minister, was considered as the immediate cause of the second. The popular discontent, after it had long circulated in whispers, broke out in the assembled circus. The people quitted their favourite amusements for the more delicious pleasure of revenge, rushed in crowds towards a palace in the suburbs, one of the emperor's retirements, and demanded, with angry clamours, the head of the public enemy. Cleander, who commanded the Prætorian guards,[14] ordered a body of cavalry to sally forth and disperse the seditious multitude. The multitude fled with precipitation towards the city; several were slain, and many more were trampled to death; but, when the cavalry entered the streets their pursuit was checked by a shower of stones and darts from the roofs and windows of the houses. The foot guards,[15] who had been long jealous of the prerogatives and insolence of the Prætorian cavalry, embraced the party of the people. The tumult became a regular engagement, and threatened a general massacre. The Prætorians at length gave way, oppressed with numbers; and the tide of popular fury returned

[12] *These baths were situated near the* Porta Capena.

[13] *Dion says that two thousand persons died every day at Rome, during a considerable length of time.*

[14] *From some remains of modesty, Cleander declined the title, whilst he assumed the powers, of Prætorian Præfect. As the other freedmen were styled, from their several departments, a* rationibus, ab epistolis; *Cleander called himself* a pugione, *as intrusted with the defence of his master's person.*

[15] *It is doubtful whether Herodian means the Prætorian infantry, or the cohortes urbanæ, a body of six thousand men, but whose rank and discipline were not equal to their numbers.*

with redoubled violence against the gates of the palace, where Commodus lay dissolved in luxury, and alone unconscious of the civil war. It was death to approach his person with the unwelcome news. He would have perished in this supine security had not two women, his eldest sister Fadilla, and Marcia the most favoured of his concubines, ventured to break into his presence. Bathed in tears, and with dishevelled hair they threw themselves at his feet, and, with all the pressing eloquence of fear, discovered to the affrighted emperor the crimes of the minister, the rage of the people, and the impending ruin which in a few minutes would burst over his palace and person. Commodus started from his dream of pleasure, and commanded that the head of Cleander should be thrown out to the people. The desired spectacle instantly appeased the tumult; and the son of Marcus might even yet have regained the affection and confidence of his subjects.

But every sentiment of virtue and humanity was extinct in the mind of Commodus. Whilst he thus abandoned the reins of empire to these unworthy favourites, he valued nothing in sovereign power except the unbounded licence of indulging his sensual appetites. His hours were spent in a seraglio of three hundred beautiful women and as many boys, of every rank and of every province; and, wherever the arts of seduction proved ineffectual, the brutal lover had recourse to violence. The ancient historians have expatiated on these abandoned scenes of prostitution, which scorned every restraint of nature or modesty; but it would not be easy to translate their too faithful descriptions into the decency of modern language. The intervals of lust were filled up with the basest amusements. The influence of a polite age and the labour of an attentive education had never been able to infuse into his rude and brutish mind the least tincture of learning; and he was the first of the Roman emperors totally devoid of taste for the pleasures of the understanding. Nero himself excelled, or affected to excel, in the elegant arts of music and poetry; nor should we despise his pursuits, had he not converted the pleasing relaxation of a leisure hour into the serious business and ambition of his life. But Commodus, from his earliest infancy, discovered an aversion to whatever was rational or liberal, and a fond attachment to the amusements of the populace,—the sports of the circus and amphitheatre, the combats of gladiators, and the hunting of wild beasts. The masters in every branch of learning, whom Marcus provided for his son, were heard with inattention and disgust; whilst the Moors and Parthians, who taught him to dart the javelin and to shoot with the bow, found a disciple who delighted in his application, and soon equalled the most skilful of his instructors in the steadiness of the eye and the dexterity of the hand.

The servile crowd, whose fortune depended on their master's vices, applauded these ignoble pursuits. The perfidious voice of flattery reminded him that, by exploits of the same nature, by the defeat of the Nemean lion, and the slaughter of the wild boar of Erymanthus, the Grecian Hercules had acquired a place among the gods, and an immortal memory among men. They only forgot to observe that, in the first ages of society, when the fiercer animals often dispute with man the possession of an unsettled country, a successful war against those savages is one of the most innocent and beneficial labours of heroism. In the civilized state of the Roman empire the wild beasts had long since retired from the face of man and the neighbourhood of populous cities. To surprise them in their solitary haunts, and to transport them to Rome, that they might be slain in pomp by the hand of an emperor, was an enterprise equally ridiculous for the prince and oppressive for the people.[16] Ignorant of these distinctions, Commodus eagerly embraced the glorious resemblance, and styled himself (as we still read on his medals) the *Roman Hercules*. The club and the lion's hide were placed by the side of the throne amongst the ensigns of sovereignty; and statues were erected, in which Commodus was represented in the character and with the attributes of the God whose valour and dexterity he endeavoured to emulate in the daily course of his ferocious amusements.

Elated with these praises, which gradually extinguished the innate sense of shame, Commodus resolved to exhibit, before the eyes of the Roman people, those exercises which till then he had decently confined within the walls of his palace and to the presence of a few favourites. On the appointed day the various motives of flattery, fear, and curiosity, attracted to the amphitheatre an innumerable multitude of spectators; and some degree of applause was deservedly bestowed on the uncommon skill of the Imperial performer. Whether he aimed at the head or heart of the animal, the wound was alike certain and mortal. With arrows, whose point was shaped into the form of a crescent, Commodus often intercepted the rapid career and cut asunder the long bony neck of the ostrich.[17] A panther was let loose; and the archer waited till he had leaped upon a trembling malefactor. In the same instant the shaft flew, the beast dropt

[16] *The African lions, when pressed by hunger, infested the open villages and cultivated country; and they infested them with impunity. The royal beast was reserved for the pleasures of the emperor and the capital; and the unfortunate peasant, who killed one of them, though in his own defence, incurred a very heavy penalty. This extraordinary game law was mitigated by Honorius, and finally repealed by Justinian.*

[17] *The ostrich's neck is three feet long, and composed of seventeen vertebræ.*

[18] *Commodus killed a camelopardalis or giraffe, the tallest, the most gentle, and the most useless of the large quadrupeds. This singular animal, a native only of the interior parts of Africa, has not been seen in Europe since the revival of letters, and though M. de Buffon has endeavoured to describe, he has not ventured to delineate, the giraffe.*

[19] *The virtuous, and even the wise, princes forbade the senators and knights to embrace this scandalous profession, under pain of infamy, or what was more dreaded by those profligate wretches, of exile. The tyrants allured them to dishonour by threats and rewards. Nero once produced, in the arena, forty senators and sixty knights.*

[20] *Juvenal in the eighth satire gives a picturesque description of this combat.*

[21] *He received, for each time, decies, about £8,000 sterling.*

[22] *Victor tells us that Commodus only allowed his antagonists a leaden weapon, dreading most probably the consequences of their despair.*

[23] *They were obliged to repeat six hundred and*

dead, and the man remained unhurt. The dens of the amphitheatre disgorged at once a hundred lions; a hundred darts from the unerring hand of Commodus laid them dead as they ran raging round the *Arena.* Neither the huge bulk of the elephant nor the scaly hide of the rhinoceros could defend them from his stroke. Æthiopia and India yielded their most extraordinary productions; and several animals were slain in the amphitheatre which had been seen only in the representations of art, or perhaps of fancy.[18] In all these exhibitions, the surest precautions were used to protect the person of the Roman Hercules from the desperate spring of any savage who might possibly disregard the dignity of the emperor and the sanctity of the god.

But the meanest of the populace were affected with shame and indignation, when they beheld their sovereign enter the lists as a gladiator, and glory in a profession which the laws and manners of the Romans had branded with the justest note of infamy.[19] He chose the habit and arms of the *Secutor,* whose combat with the *Retiarius* formed one of the most lively scenes in the bloody sports of the amphitheatre. The *Secutor* was armed with an helmet, sword, and buckler; his naked antagonist had only a large net and a trident; with the one he endeavoured to entangle, with the other to dispatch, his enemy. If he missed the first throw he was obliged to fly from the pursuit of the *Secutor* till he had prepared his net for a second cast.[20] The emperor fought in this character seven hundred and thirty-five several times. These glorious achievements were carefully recorded in the public acts of the empire; and, that he might omit no circumstance of infamy, he received from the common fund of gladiators a stipend so exorbitant that it became a new and most ignominious tax upon the Roman people.[21] It may be easily supposed that in these engagements the master of the world was always successful: in the amphitheatre his victories were not often sanguinary; but when he exercised his skill in the school of gladiators, or his own palace, his wretched antagonists were frequently honoured with a mortal wound from the hand of Commodus, and obliged to seal their flattery with their blood.[22] He now disdained the appellation of Hercules. The name of Paulus, a celebrated Secutor, was the only one which delighted his ear. It was inscribed on his colossal statues, and repeated in the redoubled acclamations [23] of the mournful and applauding senate. Claudius Pompeianus, the virtuous husband of Lucilla, was the only senator who asserted the honour of his rank. As a father he permitted his sons to consult their safety by attending the amphitheatre. As a Roman he declared that his own life was in the emperor's hands, but that he would never behold the son of Marcus prostituting his person and dignity. Notwithstanding his manly resolution, Pompeianus escaped the resentment of the tyrant, and, with his honour, had the good fortune to preserve his life.[24]

Commodus had now attained the summit of vice and infamy. Amidst the acclamations of a flattering court, he was unable to disguise from himself that he had deserved the contempt and hatred of every man of sense and virtue in his empire. His ferocious spirit was irritated by the consciousness of that hatred, by the envy of every kind of merit, by the just apprehension of danger, and by the habit of slaughter which he contracted in his daily amusements. History has preserved a long list of consular senators sacrificed to his wanton suspicion, which sought out, with peculiar anxiety, those unfortunate persons connected, however remotely, with the family of the Antonines, without sparing even the ministers of his crimes or pleasures.[25] His cruelty proved at last fatal to himself. He had shed with impunity the noblest blood of Rome: he perished as soon as he was dreaded by his own domestics. Marcia, his favourite concubine, Eclectus, his chamberlain, and Lætus, his Prætorian præfect, alarmed by the fate of their companions and predecessors, resolved to prevent the destruction which every hour hung over their heads, either from the mad caprice of the tyrant, or the sudden indignation of the people. Marcia seized the occasion of presenting a draught of wine to her lover, after he had fatigued himself with hunting some wild beasts. Commodus retired to sleep; but whilst he was labouring with the effects of poison and drunkenness, a robust youth, by profession a wrestler, entered his chamber, and strangled him without resistance. The body was secretly conveyed out of the palace, before the least suspicion was entertained in the city, or even in the court, of the emperor's death. Such was the fate of the son of Marcus, and so easy was it to destroy a hated tyrant, who, by the artificial powers of government, had oppressed, during thirteen years, so many millions of subjects, every one of whom was equal to their master in personal strength and personal abilities.

The measures of the conspirators were conducted with the deliberate coolness and celerity which the greatness of the occasion required. They resolved instantly to fill the vacant throne with an emperor whose character would justify and maintain the action that had been committed. They fixed on Pertinax,[26] præfect of the

twenty-six times, Paulus, first of the Secutors, &c.

[24] *He mixed however some prudence with his courage, and passed the greatest part of his time in a country retirement; alleging his advanced age, and the weakness of his eyes. "I never saw him in the senate," says Dion, "except during the short reign of Pertinax." All his infirmities had suddenly left him, and they returned as suddenly upon the murder of that excellent prince.*

[25] *The præfects were changed almost hourly or daily; and the caprice of Commodus was often fatal to his most favoured chamberlains.*

[26] *Pertinax was a native of Alba Pompeia, in Piedmont, and son of a timber merchant. The order of his employments (it is marked by Capitolinus) well deserves to be set down as expressive of the form of government and manners of the age. 1. He was a centurion.*

2. Præfect of a cohort
in Syria in the Parthian
war, and in Britain.
3. He obtained an Ala,
or squadron of horse, in
in Mæsia. 4. He was
commissary of provi-
sions on the Æmilian
way. 5. He commanded
the fleet upon the Rhine.
6. He was procurator of
Dacia, with a salary of
about £1600 a year.
7. He commanded the
Veterans of a legion.
8. He obtained the rank
of senator. 9. Of prætor.
10. With the command
of the first legion in
Rhætia and Noricum.
11. He was consul about
the year 175. 12. He at-
tended Marcus into the
East. 13. He commanded
an army on the Danube.
14. He was consular
legate of Mæsia. 15. Of
Dacia. 16. Of Syria.
17. Of Britain. 18. He
had the care of the
public provisions at
Rome. 19. He was pro-
consul of Africa. 20. Præfect of the city. Herodian
does justice to his dis-
interested spirit; but
Capitolinus, who col-
lected every popular
rumour, charges him
with a great fortune ac-
quired by bribery and
corruption.

²⁷ Julian, in the Cæsars,
taxes him with being
accessory to the death of
Commodus.

city, an ancient senator of consular rank, whose conspicuous merit had broke through the obscurity of his birth, and raised him to the first honours of the state. He had successively governed most of the provinces of the empire; and in all his great employments, military as well as civil, he had uniformly distinguished himself, by the firmness, the prudence, and the integrity of his conduct. He now remained almost alone of the friends and ministers of Marcus; and, when, at a late hour of the night, he was awakened with the news that the chamberlain and the præfect were at his door, he received them with intrepid resignation, and desired they would execute their master's orders. Instead of death, they offered him the throne of the Roman world. During some moments he distrusted their intentions and assurances. Convinced at length of the death of Commodus, he accepted the purple with a sincere reluctance, the natural effect of his knowledge both of the duties and of the dangers of the supreme rank.²⁷

Lætus conducted without delay his new emperor to the camp of the Prætorians, diffusing at the same time through the city a seasonable report that Commodus died suddenly of an apoplexy; and that the virtuous Pertinax had *already* succeeded to the throne. The guards were rather surprised than pleased with the suspicious death of a prince whose indulgence and liberality they alone had experienced; but the emergency of the occasion, the authority of their præfect, the reputation of Pertinax, and the clamours of the people, obliged them to stifle their secret discontents, to except the donative promised by the new emperor, to swear allegiance to him, and, with joyful acclamations and laurels in their hands, to conduct him to the senate-house, that the military consent might be ratified by the civil authority.

This important night was now far spent; with the dawn of day, and the commencement of the new year, the senators expected a summons to attend an ignominious ceremony. In spite of all remonstrances, even of those of his creatures who yet preserved any regard for prudence or decency, Commodus had resolved to pass the night in the gladiators' school, and from thence to take possession of the consulship, in the habit and with the attendance of that infamous crew. On a sudden, before the break of day, the senate was called together in the temple of Concord, to meet the guards, and to ratify the election of a new emperor. For a few minutes they sat in silent suspense, doubtful of their unexpected deliverance, and suspicious of the cruel artifices of Commodus: but, when at length they were assured that the tyrant was no more, they resigned themselves to all the transports of joy and indignation. Pertinax, who modestly represented the meanness of his extraction, and pointed out several noble senators more deserving than himself of the empire, was constrained by their dutiful violence to ascend the throne, and received all the titles of Imperial power, confirmed by the most sincere vows of fidelity. The memory of Commodus was branded with eternal infamy. The names of tyrant, of gladiator, of public enemy, resounded in every corner of the house. They decreed in tumultuous votes, that his honours should be reversed, his titles erased from the public monuments, his statues thrown down, his body dragged with a hook into the stripping-room of the gladiators, to satiate the public fury; and they expressed some indignation against those officious servants who had already presumed to screen his remains from the justice of the senate. But Pertinax could not refuse those last rites to the memory of Marcus and the tears of his first protector Claudius Pompeianus, who lamented the cruel fate of his brother-in-law, and lamented still more that he had deserved it.[28]

These effusions of impotent rage against a dead emperor, whom the senate had flattered when alive with the most abject servility, betrayed a just but ungenerous spirit of revenge. The legality of these decrees was, however, supported by the principles of the Imperial constitution. To censure, to depose, or to punish with death, the first magistrate of the republic who had abused his delegated trust, was the ancient and undoubted prerogative of the Roman senate;[29] but that feeble assembly was obliged to content itself with inflicting on a fallen tyrant that public justice from which, during his life and reign, he had been shielded by the strong arm of military despotism.

Pertinax found a nobler way of condemning his predecessor's memory,—by the contrast of his own virtues with the vices of Commodus. On the day of his accession he resigned over to his wife and son his whole private fortune; that they might have no pretence to solicit favours at the expense of the state. He refused to flatter the vanity of the former with the title of Augusta, or to corrupt the inexperienced youth of the latter by the rank of Cæsar. Accurately distinguishing between the duties of a parent and those of a sovereign, he educated his son with a severe simplicity, which, while it gave him no assured prospect of the throne, might in time have rendered him worthy of it. In public the behaviour of Pertinax was grave and affable. He lived with the virtuous part of the senate (and, in

[28] *Capitolinus gives us the particulars of these tumultuary votes, which were moved by one senator, and repeated, or rather chaunted, by the whole body.*

[29] *The senate condemned Nero to be put to death* more majorum.

a private station, he had been acquainted with the true character of each individual), without either pride or jealousy; considered them as friends and companions, with whom he had shared the dangers of the tyranny, and with whom he wished to enjoy the security of the present time. He very frequently invited them to familiar entertainments, the frugality of which was ridiculed by those who remembered and regretted the luxurious prodigality of Commodus.[30]

To heal, as far as it was possible, the wounds inflicted by the hand of tyranny, was the pleasing, but melancholy, task of Pertinax. The innocent victims who yet survived were recalled from exile, released from prison, and restored to the full possession of their honours and fortunes. The unburied bodies of murdered senators (for the cruelty of Commodus endeavoured to extend itself beyond death) were deposited in the sepulchres of their ancestors; their memory was justified; and every consolation was bestowed on their ruined and afflicted families. Among these consolations, one of the most grateful was the punishment of the Delators, the common enemies of their master, of virtue, and of their country. Yet, even in the inquisition of these legal assassins, Pertinax proceeded with a steady temper, which gave everything to justice, and nothing to popular prejudice and resentment.

The finances of the state demanded the most vigilant care of the emperor. Though every measure of injustice and extortion had been adopted which could collect the property of the subject into the coffers of the prince, the rapaciousness of Commodus had been so very inadequate to his extravagance that, upon his death, no more than eight thousand pounds were found in the exhausted treasury,[31] to defray the current expenses of government, and to discharge the pressing demand of a liberal donative, which the new emperor had been obliged to promise to the Prætorian guards. Yet, under these distressed circumstances, Pertinax had the generous firmness to remit all the oppressive taxes invented by Commodus, and to cancel all the unjust claims of the treasury; declaring, in a decree of the senate, "that he was better satisfied to administer a poor republic with innocence, than to acquire riches by the ways of tyranny and dishonour." Economy and industry he considered as the pure and genuine sources of wealth; and from them he soon derived a copious supply for the public necessities. The expense of the household was immediately reduced to one half. All the instruments of luxury Pertinax exposed to public auction,[32] gold and silver plate, chariots of a singular construction, a superfluous wardrobe of silk and em-

[30] Dion speaks of these entertainments, as a senator who had supped with the emperor; Capitolinus like a slave who had received his intelligence from one of the scullions.

[31] Decies. The blameless economy of Pius left his successors a treasure of vicies septies millies, above two and twenty millions sterling.

[32] Besides the design of converting these useless ornaments into money, Dion assigns two secret motives of Pertinax. He wished to expose the vices of Commodus, and to discover by the purchasers those who most resembled him.

broidery, and a great number of beautiful slaves of both sexes; excepting only, with attentive humanity, those who were born in a state of freedom, and had been ravished from the arms of their weeping parents. At the same time that he obliged the worthless favourites of the tyrant to resign a part of their ill-gotten wealth, he satisfied the just creditors of the state, and unexpectedly discharged the long arrears of honest services. He removed the oppressive restrictions which had been laid upon commerce, and granted all the uncultivated lands in Italy and the provinces to those who would improve them; with an exemption from tribute during the term of ten years.[33]

Such an uniform conduct had already secured to Pertinax the noblest reward of a sovereign, the love and esteem of his people. Those who remembered the virtues of Marcus were happy to contemplate in their new emperor the features of that bright original, and flattered themselves that they should long enjoy the benign influence of his administration. A hasty zeal to reform the corrupted state, accompanied with less prudence than might have been expected from the years and experience of Pertinax, proved fatal to himself and to his country. His honest indiscretion united against him the servile crowd, who found their private benefit in the public disorders, and who preferred the favour of a tyrant to the inexorable equality of the laws.

Amidst the general joy the sullen and angry countenance of the Prætorian guards betrayed their inward dissatisfaction. They had reluctantly submitted to Pertinax; they dreaded the strictness of the ancient discipline, which he was preparing to restore; and they regretted the licence of the former reign. Their discontents were secretly fomented by Lætus, their præfect, who found, when it was too late, that his new emperor would reward a servant, but would not be ruled by a favourite. On the third day of his reign, the soldiers seized on a noble senator, with a design to carry him to the camp, and to invest him with the imperial purple. Instead of being dazzled by the dangerous honour, the affrighted victim escaped from their violence, and took refuge at the feet of Pertinax. A short time afterwards Sosius Falco, one of the consuls of the year, a rash youth,[34] but of an ancient and opulent family, listened to the voice of ambition; and a conspiracy was formed during a short absence of Pertinax, which was crushed by his sudden return to Rome and his resolute behaviour. Falco was on the point of being justly condemned to death as a public enemy, had he not been saved by the earnest and

[33] Though Capitolinus has picked up many idle tales of the private life of Pertinax, he joins with Dion and Herodian in admiring his public conduct.

[34] If we credit Capitolinus (which is rather difficult) Falco behaved with the most petulant indecency to Pertinax on the day of his accession. The wise emperor only admonished him of his youth and inexperience.

sincere entreaties of the injured emperor; who conjured the senate that the purity of his reign might not be stained by the blood even of a guilty senator.

These disappointments served only to irritate the rage of the Prætorian guards. On the twenty-eight of March, eighty-six days only after the death of Commodus, a general sedition broke out in the camp, which the officers wanted either power or inclination to suppress. Two or three hundred of the most desperate soldiers marched at noon-day, with arms in their hands and fury in their looks, towards the Imperial palace. The gates were thrown open by their companions upon guard; and by the domestics of the old court, who had already formed a secret conspiracy against the life of the too virtuous emperor. On the news of their approach, Pertinax, disdaining either flight or concealment, advanced to meet his assassins; and recalled to their minds his own innocence, and the sanctity of their recent oath. For a few moments they stood in silent suspense, ashamed of their atrocious design, and awed by the venerable aspect and majestic firmness of their sovereign, till at length, the despair of pardon reviving their fury, a barbarian of the country of Tongres [35] levelled the first blow against Pertinax, who was instantly dispatched with a multitude of wounds. His head, separated from his body, and placed on a lance, was carried in triumph to the Prætorian camp, in the sight of a mournful and indignant people, who lamented the unworthy fate of that excellent prince, and the transient blessings of a reign, the memory of which could serve only to aggravate their approaching misfortunes.

[35] *The modern bishopric of Liege. This soldier probably belonged to the Batavian horse-guards, who were mostly raised in the Duchy of Gueldres and the neighbourhood, and were distinguished by their valour, and by the boldness with which they swam their horses across the broadest and most rapid rivers.*

V

PUBLIC SALE OF THE EMPIRE TO DIDIUS JULIANUS BY THE
PRÆTORIAN GUARDS · CLODIUS ALBINUS IN BRITAIN, PESCEN-
NIUS NIGER IN SYRIA, AND SEPTIMIUS SEVERUS IN PANNONIA,
DECLARE AGAINST THE MURDERERS OF PERTINAX · CIVIL
WARS, AND VICTORY OF SEVERUS OVER HIS THREE RIVALS ·
RELAXATION OF DISCIPLINE · NEW MAXIMS OF GOVERNMENT

THE power of the sword is more sensibly felt in an extensive monarchy than in a small community. It has been calculated by the ablest politicians that no state, without being soon exhausted, can maintain above the hundredth part of its members in arms and idleness. But, although this relative proportion may be uniform, its influence over the rest of the society will vary according to the degree of its positive strength. The advantages of military science and discipline cannot be exerted, unless a proper number of soldiers are united into one body, and actuated by one soul. With a handful of men, such an union would be ineffectual; with an unwieldy host, it would be impracticable; and the powers of the machine would be alike destroyed by the extreme minuteness, or the excessive weight, of its springs. To illustrate this observation we need only reflect that there is no superiority of natural strength, artificial weapons, or acquired skill, which could enable one man to keep in constant subjection one hundred of his fellow-creatures: the tyrant of a single town, or a small district, would soon discover that an hundred armed followers were a weak defence against ten thousand peasants or citizens; but an hundred thousand well-disciplined soldiers will command, with despotic sway, ten millions of subjects; and a body of ten or fifteen thousand guards will strike terror into the most numerous populace that ever crowded the streets of an immense capital.

The Prætorian bands, whose licentious fury was the first symptom and cause of the decline of the Roman empire, scarcely amounted to

[1] *They were originally nine or ten thousand men (for Tacitus and Dion are not agreed upon the subject), divided into as many cohorts. Vitellius increased them to sixteen thousand, and, as far as we can learn from inscriptions, they never afterwards sunk much below that number.*

[2] *In the civil war between Vitellius and Vespasian, the Prætorian camp was attacked and defended with all the machines used in the siege of the best fortified cities.*

[3] *Close to the walls of the city, on the broad summit of the Quirinal and Viminal hills.*

[4] *Claudius, raised by the soldiers to the empire, was the first who gave a donative. He gave* quina dena, £120: *when Marcus, with his colleague Lucius Verus, took quiet possession of the throne, he gave* vicena, £160, *to each of the guards. We may form some idea of the amount of these sums, by Hadrian's complaint, that the promotion of a Cæsar had cost him* ter millies, *two millions and a half sterling.*

[5] *The first book of Livy, and the second of Dionysius of Halicarnassus, show the au-*

the last mentioned number.[1] They derived their institution from Augustus. That crafty tyrant, sensible that laws might colour, but that arms alone could maintain, his usurped dominion, had gradually formed this powerful body of guards, in constant readiness to protect his person, to awe the senate, and either to prevent or to crush the first motions of rebellion. He distinguished these favoured troops by a double pay, and superior privileges; but, as their formidable aspect would at once have alarmed and irritated the Roman people, three cohorts only were stationed in the capital; whilst the remainder was dispersed in the adjacent towns of Italy. But after fifty years of peace and servitude, Tiberius ventured on a decisive measure, which for ever riveted the fetters of his country. Under the fair pretences of relieving Italy from the heavy burden of military quarters, and of introducing a stricter discipline among the guards, he assembled them at Rome, in a permanent camp, which was fortified with skilful care,[2] and placed on a commanding situation.[3]

Such formidable servants are always necessary, but often fatal, to the throne of despotism. By thus introducing the Prætorian guards, as it were, into the palace and the senate, the emperors taught them to perceive their own strength, and the weakness of the civil government; to view the vices of their masters with familiar contempt, and to lay aside that reverential awe which distance only, and mystery, can preserve towards an imaginary power. In the luxurious idleness of an opulent city, their pride was nourished by the sense of their irresistible weight; nor was it possible to conceal from them that the person of the sovereign, the authority of the senate, the public treasure, and the seat of empire, were all in their hands. To divert the Prætorian bands from these dangerous reflections the firmest and best established princes were obliged to mix blandishments with commands, rewards with punishments, to flatter their pride, indulge their pleasures, connive at their irregularities, and to purchase their precarious faith by a liberal donative; which, since the elevation of Claudius, was exacted as a legal claim on the accession of every new emperor.[4]

The advocates of the guards endeavoured to justify by arguments the power which they asserted by arms; and to maintain that, according to the purest principles of the constitution, *their* consent was essentially necessary in the appointment of an emperor. The election of consuls, of generals, and of magistrates, however it had been recently usurped by the senate, was the ancient and undoubted right of the Roman people.[5] But where was the Roman people to be found? Not surely amongst the mixed multitude of slaves and strangers that filled the streets of Rome; a servile populace, as devoid of spirit as destitute of property. The defenders of the state, selected from the flower of Italian youth,[6] and trained in the exercise of arms and virtue, were the genuine representatives of the people, and the best entitled to elect the military chief of the republic. These assertions, however defective in reason, became unanswerable, when the fierce Prætorians increased their weight, by throwing, like the barbarian conqueror of Rome, their swords into the scale.[7]

The Prætorians had violated the sanctity of the throne, by the atrocious murder of Pertinax; they dishonoured the majesty of it, by their subsequent conduct. The camp was without a leader, for even the præfect Lætus, who had excited the tempest, prudently declined the public indignation. Amidst the wild disorder, Sulpicianus, the emperor's father-in-law, and governor of the city, who had been sent to the camp on the first alarm of mutiny, was endeavouring to calm the fury of the multitude, when he was silenced by the clamorous return of the murderers, bearing on a lance the head of Pertinax. Though history has accustomed us to observe every principle and every passion yielding to the imperious dictates of ambition, it is scarcely credible that, in these moments of horror, Sulpicianus should have aspired to ascend a throne polluted with the recent blood of so near a relation, and so excellent a prince. He had already begun to use the only effectual argument, and to treat for the Imperial dignity; but the more prudent of the Prætorians, apprehensive that, in this private contract, they should not obtain a just price for so valuable a commodity, ran out upon the ramparts; and, with a loud voice, proclaimed that the Roman world was to be disposed of to the best bidder by public auction.[8]

This infamous offer, the most insolent excess of military licence, diffused an universal grief, shame, and indignation throughout the city. It reached at length the ears of Didius Julianus, a wealthy senator, who, regardless of the public calamities, was indulging himself in the luxury of the table.[9] His wife and his daughter, his freedmen and his parasites, easily convinced him that he deserved the throne, and earnestly conjured him to embrace so fortunate an opportunity. The vain old man hastened to the Prætorian camp, where Sulpicianus was still in treaty with the guards; and began to bid against him from the foot of the rampart. The unworthy negotiation was transacted by faithful emissaries, who passed alternately from one candidate to the other, and acquainted each of them with the offers

thority of the people, even in the election of the kings.

[6] *They were originally recruited in Latium, Etruria, and the old colonies. The emperor Otho compliments their vanity, with the flattering titles of Italiæ Alumni, Romana vere juventus.*

[7] *In the siege of Rome by the Gauls.*

[8] *Though three historians agree that it was in fact an auction, Herodian alone affirms that it was proclaimed as such by the soldiers.*

[9] *Spartianus softens the most odious parts of the character and elevation of Julian.*

of his rival. Sulpicianus had already promised a donative of five thousand drachms (above one hundred and sixty pounds) to each soldier; when Julian, eager for the prize, rose at once to the sum of six thousand two hundred and fifty drachms, or upwards of two hundred pounds sterling. The gates of the camp were instantly thrown open to the purchaser; he was declared emperor, and received an oath of allegiance from the soldiers, who retained humanity enough to stipulate that he should pardon and forget the competition of Sulpicianus.

It was now incumbent on the Prætorians to fulfil the conditions of the sale. They placed their new sovereign, whom they served and despised, in the centre of their ranks, surrounded him on every side with their shields, and conducted him in close order of battle through the deserted streets of the city. The senate was commanded to assemble, and those who had been the distinguished friends of Pertinax, or the personal enemies of Julian, found it necessary to affect a more than common share of satisfaction at this happy revolution.[10] After Julian had filled the senate-house with armed soldiers, he expatiated on the freedom of his election, his own eminent virtues, and his full assurance of the affections of the senate. The obsequious assembly congratulated their own and the public felicity; engaged their allegiance, and conferred on him all the several branches of the Imperial power.[11] From the senate Julian was conducted by the same military procession, to take possession of the palace. The first objects which struck his eyes were the abandoned trunk of Pertinax, and the frugal entertainment prepared for his supper. The one he viewed with indifference; the other with contempt. A magnificent feast was prepared by his order, and he amused himself till a very late hour, with dice, and the performances of Pylades, a celebrated dancer. Yet it was observed that, after the crowd of flatterers dispersed, and left him to darkness, solitude, and terrible reflection, he passed a sleepless night; revolving most probably in his mind his own rash folly, the fate of his virtuous predecessor, and the doubtful and dangerous tenure of an empire, which had not been acquired by merit, but purchased by money.

He had reason to tremble. On the throne of the world he found himself without a friend, and even without an adherent. The guards themselves were ashamed of the prince whom their avarice had persuaded them to accept; nor was there a citizen who did not consider his elevation with horror, as the last insult on the Roman name. The nobility, whose conspicuous station and ample possessions exacted

[10] *Dion Cassius, at that time prætor, had been a personal enemy to Julian.*

[11] *We learn from thence one curious circumstance, that the new emperor, whatever had been his birth, was immediately aggregated to the number of Patrician families.*

the strictest caution, dissembled their sentiments, and met the affected civility of the emperor with smiles of complacency and professions of duty. But the people, secure in their numbers and obscurity, gave a free vent to their passions. The streets and public places of Rome resounded with clamours and imprecations. The enraged multitude affronted the person of Julian, rejected his liberality, and, conscious of the impotence of their own resentment, they called aloud on the legions of the frontiers to assert the violated majesty of the Roman empire.

The public discontent was soon diffused from the centre to the frontiers of the empire. The armies of Britain, of Syria, and of Illyricum, lamented the death of Pertinax, in whose company, or under whose command, they had so often fought and conquered. They received with surprise, with indignation, and perhaps with envy, the extraordinary intelligence that the Prætorians had disposed of the empire by public auction; and they sternly refused to ratify the ignominious bargain. Their immediate and unanimous revolt was fatal to Julian, but it was fatal at the same time to the public peace; as the generals of the respective armies, Clodius Albinus, Pescennius Niger, and Septimius Severus, were still more anxious to succeed than to revenge the murdered Pertinax. Their forces were exactly balanced. Each of them was at the head of three legions, with a numerous train of auxiliaries; and, however different in their characters, they were all soldiers of experience and capacity.

Clodius Albinus, governor of Britain, surpassed both his competitors in the nobility of his extraction, which he derived from some of the most illustrious names of the old republic.[12] But the branch, from whence he claimed his descent, was sunk into mean circumstances, and transplanted into a remote province. It is difficult to form a just idea of his true character. Under the philosophic cloak of austerity, he stands accused of concealing most of the vices which degrade human nature.[13] But his accusers are those venal writers who adored the fortune of Severus, and trampled on the ashes of an unsuccessful rival. Virtue, or the appearance of virtue, recommended Albinus to the confidence and good opinion of Marcus; and his preserving with the son the same interest which he had acquired with the father is a proof at least that he was possessed of a very flexible disposition. The favour of a tyrant does not always suppose a want of merit in the object of it; he may, without intending it, reward a man of worth and ability, or he may find such a man useful to his own service. It does not appear that Albinus

[12] *The Postumian and the Cejonian; the former of whom was raised to the consulship in the fifth year after its institution.*

[13] *Spartianus in his undigested collection, mixes up all the virtues and all the vices that enter into the human composition, and bestows them on the same object. Such, indeed, are many of the characters in the Augustan history.*

served the son of Marcus, either as the minister of his cruelties, or even as the associate of his pleasures. He was employed in a distant honourable command, when he received a confidential letter from the emperor, acquainting him of the treasonable designs of some discontented generals, and authorizing him to declare himself the guardian and successor of the throne, by assuming the title and ensigns of Cæsar. The governor of Britain wisely declined the dangerous honour, which would have marked him for the jealousy, or involved him in the approaching ruin, of Commodus. He courted power by nobler, or, at least, by more specious, arts. On a premature report of the death of the emperor, he assembled his troops; and, in an eloquent discourse, deplored the inevitable mischiefs of despotism, described the happiness and glory which their ancestors had enjoyed under the consular government, and declared his firm resolution to reinstate the senate and people in their legal authority. This popular harangue was answered by the loud acclamations of the British legions, and received at Rome with a secret murmur of applause. Safe in the possession of his little world, and in the command of an army less distinguished indeed for discipline than for numbers and valour,[14] Albinus braved the menaces of Commodus, maintained towards Pertinax a stately ambiguous reserve, and instantly declared against the usurpation of Julian. The convulsions of the capital added new weight to his sentiments, or rather to his professions, of patriotism. A regard to decency induced him to decline the lofty titles of Augustus and Emperor, and he imitated perhaps the example of Galba, who, on a similar occasion, had styled himself the Lieutenant of the senate and people.

Personal merit alone had raised Pescennius Niger from an obscure birth and station to the government of Syria; a lucrative and important command, which in times of civil confusion gave him a near prospect of the throne. Yet his parts seem to have been better suited to the second than to the first rank; he was an unequal rival, though he might have approved himself an excellent lieutenant, to Severus, who afterwards displayed the greatness of his mind by adopting several useful institutions from a vanquished enemy. In his government, Niger acquired the esteem of the soldiers and the love of the provincials. His rigid discipline fortified the valour and confirmed the obedience of the former, whilst the voluptuous Syrians were less delighted with the mild firmness of his administration than with the affability of his manners and the apparent pleasure with which he attended their frequent and pompous festivals.[15] As

[14] *Pertinax, who governed Britain a few years before, had been left for dead in a mutiny of the soldiers. Yet they loved and regretted him; admirantibus eam virtutem cui irascebantur.*

[15] *The Chronicle of John Malala, of Antioch, shows the zealous attachment of his countrymen to these festivals, which at once gratified their superstition, and their love of pleasure.*

soon as the intelligence of the atrocious murder of Pertinax had reached Antioch, the wishes of Asia invited Niger to assume the Imperial purple and revenge his death. The legions of the eastern frontier embraced his cause; the opulent but unarmed provinces, from the frontiers of Æthiopia [16] to the Hadriatic, cheerfully submitted to his power; and the kings beyond the Tigris and the Euphrates congratulated his election, and offered him their homage and services. The mind of Niger was not capable of receiving this sudden tide of fortune; he flattered himself that his accession would be undisturbed by competition, and unstained by civil blood; and whilst he enjoyed the vain pomp of triumph, he neglected to secure the means of victory. Instead of entering into an effectual negotiation with the powerful armies of the West, whose resolution might decide, or at least must balance, the mighty contest; instead of advancing without delay towards Rome and Italy, where his presence was impatiently expected,[17] Niger trifled away in the luxury of Antioch those irretrievable moments which were diligently improved by the decisive activity of Severus.

The country of Pannonia and Dalmatia, which occupied the space between the Danube and the Hadriatic, was one of the last and most difficult conquests of the Romans. In the defence of national freedom, two hundred thousand of these barbarians had once appeared in the field, alarmed the declining age of Augustus, and exercised the vigilant prudence of Tiberius at the head of the collected force of the empire. The Pannonians yielded at length to the arms and institutions of Rome. Their recent subjection, however, the neighbourhood, and even the mixture of the unconquered tribes, and perhaps the climate, adapted, as it has been observed, to the production of great bodies and slow minds,[18] all contributed to preserve some remains of their original ferocity, and, under the tame resemblance of Roman provincials, the hardy features of the natives were still to be discerned. Their warlike youth afforded an inexhaustible supply of recruits to the legions stationed on the banks of the Danube, and which, from a perpetual warfare against the Germans and Sarmatians, were deservedly esteemed the best troops in the service.

The Pannonian army was at this time commanded by Septimius Severus, a native of Africa, who, in the gradual ascent of private honours, had concealed his daring ambition, which was never diverted from its steady course by the allurements of pleasure, the apprehension of danger, or the feelings of humanity.[19] On the first news of the murder of Pertinax, he assembled his troops, painted in

[16] *A king of Thebes, in Egypt, is mentioned in the Augustan History, as an ally, and, indeed, as a personal friend of Niger. If Spartianus is not, as I strongly suspect, mistaken, he has brought to light a dynasty of tributary princes totally unknown to history.*

[17] *A verse in every one's mouth at that time, seems to express the general opinion of the three rivals; Optimus est Niger, bonus Afer, pessimus Albus.*

[18] *Such is the reflection of Herodian. Will the modern Austrians allow the influence?*

[19] *In the letter to Albinus, already mentioned, Commodus accuses Severus as one of the ambitious generals who censured his conduct, and wished to occupy his place.*

the most lively colours the crime, the insolence, and the weakness of the Prætorian guards, and animated the legions to arms and to revenge. He concluded (and the peroration was thought extremely eloquent) with promising every soldier about four hundred pounds; an honourable donative, double in value to the infamous bribe with which Julian had purchased the empire.[20] The acclamations of the army immediately saluted Severus with the names of Augustus, Pertinax, and Emperor; and he thus attained the lofty station to which he was invited by conscious merit and a long train of dreams and omens, the fruitful offspring of his superstition or policy.[21]

The new candidate for empire saw and improved the peculiar advantage of his situation. His province extended to the Julian Alps, which gave an easy access into Italy; and he remembered the saying of Augustus, That a Pannonian army might in ten days appear in sight of Rome.[22] By a celerity proportioned to the greatness of the occasion, he might reasonably hope to revenge Pertinax, punish Julian, and receive the homage of the senate and people, as their lawful emperor, before his competitors, separated from Italy by an immense tract of sea and land, were apprized of his success, or even of his election. During the whole expedition, he scarcely allowed himself any moments for sleep or food; marching on foot, and in complete armour, at the head of his columns, he insinuated himself into the confidence and affection of his troops, pressed their diligence, revived their spirits, animated their hopes, and was well satisfied to share the hardships of the meanest soldier, whilst he kept in view the infinite superiority of his reward.

The wretched Julian had expected, and thought himself prepared, to dispute the empire with the governor of Syria; but in the invincible and rapid approach of the Pannonian legions, he saw his inevitable ruin. The hasty arrival of every messenger increased his just apprehensions. He was successively informed that Severus had passed the Alps; that the Italian cities, unwilling or unable to oppose his progress, had received him with the warmest professions of joy and duty; that the important place of Ravenna had surrendered without resistance, and that the Hadriatic fleet was in the hands of the conqueror. The enemy was now within two hundred and fifty miles of Rome; and every moment diminished the narrow span of life and empire allotted to Julian.

He attempted, however, to prevent, or at least to protract, his ruin. He implored the venal faith of the Prætorians, filled the city with unavailing preparations for war, drew lines round the suburbs, and

[20] *Pannonia was too poor to supply such a sum. It was probably promised in the camp, and paid at Rome, after the victory.*

[21] *Severus was declared emperor on the banks of the Danube, either at Carnuntum, according to Spartianus, or else at Sabaria, according to Victor. Mr. Hume, in supposing that the birth and dignity of Severus were too much inferior to the Imperial crown, and that he marched into Italy as general only, has not considered this transaction with his usual accuracy.*

[22] *We must reckon the march from the nearest verge of Pannonia, and extend the sight of the city, as far as two hundred miles.*

"The emperor Vespasian, with his usual good sense, laughed at the genealogists, who deduced his family from Flavius, the founder of Reate (his native country), and one of the companions of Hercules."

"The accumulation of rubbish and the earth that had been washed down from the hills is supposed to have elevated the plain of Rome fourteen or fifteen feet, perhaps, above the ancient level."

THE TEMPLE OF VESPASIAN

Right, the modern Capitoline palace built on the foundations of the ancient Tabularium.

even strengthened the fortifications of the palace; as if those last intrenchments could be defended, without hope of relief, against a victorious invader. Fear and shame prevented the guards from deserting his standard; but they trembled at the name of the Pannonian legions, commanded by an experienced general, and accustomed to vanquish the barbarians on the frozen Danube.[23] They quitted, with a sigh, the pleasures of the baths and theatres, to put on arms, whose use they had almost forgotten, and beneath the weight of which they were oppressed. The unpractised elephants, whose uncouth appearance, it was hoped, would strike terror into the army of the north, threw their unskilful riders; and the awkward evolutions of the marines, drawn from the fleet of Misenum, were an object of ridicule to the populace; whilst the senate enjoyed, with secret pleasure, the distress and weakness of the usurper.[24]

Every motion of Julian betrayed his trembling perplexity. He insisted that Severus should be declared a public enemy by the senate. He entreated that the Pannonian general might be associated to the empire. He sent public ambassadors of consular rank to negotiate with his rival; he dispatched private assassins to take away his life. He designed that the Vestal virgins, and all the colleges of priests, in their sacerdotal habits, and bearing before them the sacred pledges of the Roman religion, should advance, in solemn procession, to meet the Pannonian legions; and, at the same time, he vainly tried to interrogate, or to appease, the fates, by magic ceremonies, and unlawful sacrifices.

Severus, who dreaded neither his arms nor his enchantments, guarded himself from the only danger of secret conspiracy by the faithful attendance of six hundred chosen men, who never quitted his person or their cuirasses, either by night or by day, during the whole march. Advancing with a steady and rapid course, he passed, without difficulty, the defiles of the Apennine, received into his party the troops and ambassadors sent to retard his progress, and made a short halt at Interamna, about seventy miles from Rome. His victory was already secure; but the despair of the Prætorians might have rendered it bloody; and Severus had the laudable ambition of ascending the throne without drawing the sword.[25] His emissaries, dispersed in the capital, assured the guards that, provided they would abandon their worthless prince, and the perpetrators of the murder of Pertinax, to the justice of the conqueror, he would no longer consider that melancholy event as the act of the whole body. The faithless Prætorians, whose resistance was supported only by

[23] *This is not a puerile figure of rhetoric, but an allusion to a real fact recorded by Dion. It probably happened more than once.*

[24] *There is no surer proof of the military skill of the Romans, than their first surmounting the idle terror, and afterwards disdaining the dangerous use, of elephants in war.*

[25] *Victor and Eutropius mention a combat near the Milvian Bridge, the Ponte Molle, unknown to the better and more ancient writers.*

sullen obstinacy, gladly complied with the easy conditions, seized the greatest part of the assassins, and signified to the senate that they no longer defended the cause of Julian. That assembly, convoked by the consul, unanimously acknowledged Severus as lawful emperor, decreed divine honours to Pertinax, and pronounced a sentence of deposition and death against his unfortunate successor. Julian was conducted into a private apartment of the baths of the palace, and beheaded as a common criminal, after having purchased, with an immense treasure, an anxious and precarious reign of only sixty-six days. The almost incredible expedition of Severus, who, in so short a space of time, conducted a numerous army from the banks of the Danube to those of the Tiber, proves at once the plenty of provisions produced by agriculture and commerce, the goodness of the roads, the discipline of the legions, and the indolent subdued temper of the provinces.[26]

The first cares of Severus were bestowed on two measures, the one dictated by policy, the other by decency; the revenge, and the honours due to the memory of Pertinax. Before the new emperor entered Rome, he issued his commands to the Prætorian guards, directing them to wait his arrival on a large plain near the city, without arms, but in the habits of ceremony in which they were accustomed to attend their sovereign. He was obeyed by those haughty troops, whose contrition was the effect of their just terrors. A chosen part of the Illyrian army encompassed them with levelled spears. Incapable of flight or resistance, they expected their fate in silent consternation. Severus mounted the tribunal, sternly reproached them with perfidy and cowardice, dismissed them with ignominy from the trust which they had betrayed, despoiled them of their splendid ornaments, and banished them, on pain of death, to the distance of an hundred miles from the capital. During the transaction, another detachment had been sent to seize their arms, occupy their camp, and prevent the hasty consequences of their despair.

The funeral and consecration of Pertinax was next solemnized with every circumstance of sad magnificence.[27] The senate, with a melancholy pleasure, performed the last rites to that excellent prince, whom they had loved and still regretted. The concern of his successor was probably less sincere. He esteemed the virtues of Pertinax, but those virtues would for ever have confined his ambition to a private station. Severus pronounced his funeral oration with studied eloquence, inward satisfaction, and well-acted sorrow; and by this pious regard to his memory, convinced the credulous mul-

[26] *From these sixty-six days, we must first deduct sixteen, as Pertinax was murdered on the 28th of March, and Severus most probably elected on the 13th of April. We cannot allow less than ten days after his election, to put a numerous army in motion. Forty days remain for this rapid march, and, as we may compute about eight hundred miles from Rome to the neighbourhood of Vienna, the army of Severus marched twenty miles every day, without halt or intermission.*

[27] *Dion, who assisted at the ceremony as a senator, gives a most pompous description of it.*

titude that *he alone* was worthy to supply his place. Sensible, however, that arms, not ceremonies, must assert his claim to the empire, he left Rome at the end of thirty days, and, without suffering himself to be elated by this easy victory, prepared to encounter his more formidable rivals.

The uncommon abilities and fortune of Severus have induced an elegant historian to compare him with the first and greatest of the Cæsars. The parallel is, at least, imperfect. Where shall we find, in the character of Severus, the commanding superiority of soul, the generous clemency, and the various genius, which could reconcile and unite the love of pleasure, the thirst of knowledge, and the fire of ambition? [28] In one instance only, they may be compared, with some degree of propriety, in the celerity of their motion, and their civil victories. In less than four years,[29] Severus subdued the riches of the east, and the valour of the west. He vanquished two competitors of reputation and ability, and defeated numerous armies, provided with weapons and discipline equal to his own. In that age, the art of fortification and the principles of tactics, were well understood by all the Roman generals; and the constant superiority of Severus was that of an artist, who uses the same instruments with more skill and industry than his rivals. I shall not, however, enter into a minute narrative of these military operations; but as the two civil wars against Niger and against Albinus, were almost the same in their conduct, event, and consequences, I shall collect into one point of view the most striking circumstances, tending to develop the character of the conqueror, and the state of the empire.

Falsehood and insincerity, unsuitable as they seem to the dignity of public transactions, offend us with a less degrading idea of meanness than when they are found in the intercourse of private life. In the latter, they discover a want of courage; in the other, only a defect of power; and, as it is impossible for the most able statesmen to subdue millions of followers and enemies by their own personal strength, the world, under the name of policy, seems to have granted them a very liberal indulgence of craft and dissimulation. Yet the arts of Severus cannot be justified by the most ample privileges of state-reason. He promised only to betray, he flattered only to ruin; and however he might occasionally bind himself by oaths and treaties, his conscience, obsequious to his interest, always released him from the inconvenient obligation.

If his two competitors, reconciled by their common danger, had advanced upon him without delay, perhaps Severus would have

[28] *Though it is not, most assuredly, the intention of Lucan to exalt the character of Cæsar, yet the idea he gives of that hero, in the tenth book of the Pharsalia, where he describes him, at the same time, making love to Cleopatra, sustaining a siege against the power of Egypt, and conversing with the sages of the country, is, in reality, the noblest panegyric.*

[29] *Reckoning from his election, April 13, 193, to the death of Albinus, February 19, 197.*

sunk under their united effort. Had they even attacked him at the same time, with separate views and separate armies, the contest might have been long and doubtful. But they fell, singly and successively, an easy prey to the arts as well as arms of their subtle enemy, lulled into security by the moderation of his professions, and overwhelmed by the rapidity of his action. He first marched against Niger, whose reputation and power he the most dreaded: but he declined any hostile declarations, suppressed the name of his antagonist, and only signified to the senate and people his intention of regulating the eastern provinces. In private he spoke of Niger, his old friend and intended successor,[30] with the most affectionate regard, and highly applauded his generous design of revenging the murder of Pertinax. To punish the vile usurper of the throne was the duty of every Roman general. To persevere in arms, and to resist a lawful emperor, acknowledged by the senate, would alone render him criminal. The sons of Niger had fallen into his hands among the children of the provincial governors, detained at Rome as pledges for the loyalty of their parents.[31] As long as the power of Niger inspired terror, or even respect, they were educated with the most tender care, with the children of Severus himself; but they were soon involved in their father's ruin, and removed, first by exile, and afterwards by death, from the eye of public compassion.

Whilst Severus was engaged in his eastern war, he had reason to apprehend that the governor of Britain might pass the sea and the Alps, occupy the vacant seat of empire, and oppose his return with the authority of the senate and the forces of the West. The ambiguous conduct of Albinus, in not assuming the Imperial title, left room for negotiation. Forgetting at once his professions of patriotism and the jealousy of sovereign power, he accepted the precarious rank of Cæsar, as a reward for his fatal neutrality. Till the first contest was decided, Severus treated the man whom he had doomed to destruction with every mark of esteem and regard. Even in the letter in which he announced his victory over Niger he styles Albinus the brother of his soul and empire, sends him the affectionate salutations of his wife Julia, and his young family, and entreats him to preserve the armies and the republic faithful to their common interest. The messengers charged with this letter were instructed to accost the Cæsar with respect, to desire a private audience, and to plunge their daggers into his heart.[32] The conspiracy was discovered, and the too credulous Albinus at length passed over to the continent, and prepared for an unequal contest with his rival,

[30] *Whilst Severus was very dangerously ill, it was industriously given out that he intended to appoint Niger and Albinus his successors. As he could not be sincere with respect to both, he might not be so with regard to either. Yet Severus carried his hypocrisy so far as to profess that intention in the memoirs of his own life.*

[31] *This practice, invented by Commodus, proved very useful to Severus. He found, at Rome, the children of many of the principal adherents of his rivals; and he employed them more than once to intimidate, or seduce, the parents.*

[32] *Spartianus has inserted this curious letter at full length.*

who rushed upon him at the head of a veteran and victorious army.

The military labours of Severus seem inadequate to the importance of his conquests. Two engagements, the one near the Hellespont, the other in the narrow defiles of Cilicia, decided the fate of his Syrian competitor; and the troops of Europe asserted their usual ascendant over the effeminate natives of Asia. The battle of Lyons, where one hundred and fifty thousand Romans were engaged, was equally fatal to Albinus. The valour of the British army maintained, indeed, a sharp and doubtful contest with the hardy discipline of the Illyrian legions. The fame and person of Severus appeared, during a few moments, irrecoverably lost, till that warlike prince rallied his fainting troops, and led them on to a decisive victory.[33] The war was finished by that memorable day.

The civil wars of modern Europe have been distinguished, not only by the fierce animosity, but likewise by the obstinate perseverance, of the contending factions. They have generally been justified by some principle, or, at least, coloured by some pretext, of religion, freedom, or loyalty. The leaders were nobles of independent property and hereditary influence. The troops fought like men interested in the decision of the quarrel; and as military spirit and party zeal were strongly diffused throughout the whole community, a vanquished chief was immediately supplied with new adherents, eager to shed their blood in the same cause. But the Romans, after the fall of the republic, combated only for the choice of masters. Under the standard of a popular candidate for empire, a few enlisted from affection, some from fear, many from interest, none from principle. The legions, uninflamed by party zeal, were allured into civil war by liberal donatives, and still more liberal promises. A defeat, by disabling the chief from the performance of his engagements, dissolved the mercenary allegiance of his followers, and left them to consult their own safety by a timely desertion of an unsuccessful cause. It was of little moment to the provinces under whose name they were oppressed or governed; they were driven by the impulsion of the present power, and as soon as that power yielded to a superior force, they hastened to implore the clemency of the conqueror, who, as he had an immense debt to discharge, was obliged to sacrifice the most guilty countries to the avarice of his soldiers. In the vast extent of the Roman empire there were few fortified cities capable of protecting a routed army; nor was there any person, or family, or order of men, whose natural interest, unsupported by the powers of government, was capable of restoring a sinking party.

[33] *The battle was fought in the plain of Trevoux, three or four leagues from Lyons.*

Yet, in the contest between Niger and Severus, a single city deserves an honourable exception. As Byzantium was one of the greatest passages from Europe into Asia, it had been provided with a strong garrison, and a fleet of five hundred vessels was anchored in the harbour.[34] The impetuosity of Severus disappointed this prudent scheme of defence; he left to his generals the siege of Byzantium, forced the less guarded passage of the Hellespont, and, impatient of a meaner enemy, pressed forward to encounter his rival. Byzantium, attacked by a numerous and increasing army, and afterwards by the whole naval power of the empire, sustained a siege of three years, and remained faithful to the name and memory of Niger. The citizens and soldiers (we know not from what cause) were animated with equal fury; several of the principal officers of Niger, who despaired of, or who disdained a pardon, had thrown themselves into this last refuge; the fortifications were esteemed impregnable, and, in the defence of the place, a celebrated engineer displayed all the mechanic powers known to the ancients.[35] Byzantium, at length, surrendered to famine. The magistrates and soldiers were put to the sword, the walls demolished, the privileges suppressed, and the destined capital of the East subsisted only as an open village, subject to the insulting jurisdiction of Perinthus. The historian Dion, who had admired the flourishing, and lamented the desolate, state of Byzantium, accused the revenge of Severus for depriving the Roman people of the strongest bulwark against the barbarians of Pontus and Asia.[36] The truth of this observation was but too well justified in the succeeding age, when the Gothic fleets covered the Euxine, and passed through the undefended Bosphorus into the centre of the Mediterranean.

Both Niger and Albinus were discovered and put to death in their flight from the field of battle. Their fate excited neither surprise nor compassion. They had staked their lives against the chance of empire, and suffered what they would have inflicted; nor did Severus claim the arrogant superiority of suffering his rivals to live in a private station. But his unforgiving temper, stimulated by avarice, indulged a spirit of revenge, where there was no room for apprehension. The most considerable of the provincials, who, without any dislike to the fortunate candidate, had obeyed the governor under whose authority they were accidentally placed, were punished by death, exile, and especially by the confiscation of their estates. Many cities of the East were stript of their ancient honours, and obliged to pay, into the treasury of Severus, four times the amount of the

[34] Most of these, as may be supposed, were small open vessels; some, however, were galleys of two, and a few of three, ranks of oars.

[35] The engineer's name was Priscus. His skill saved his life, and he was taken into the service of the conqueror.

[36] Notwithstanding the authority of Spartianus and some modern Greeks, we may be assured, from Dion and Herodian, that Byzantium, many years after the death of Severus, lay in ruins.

sums which had been contributed by them for the service of Niger.

Till the final decision of the war, the cruelty of Severus was, in some measure, restrained by the uncertainty of the event and his pretended reverence for the senate. The head of Albinus, accompanied with a menacing letter, announced to the Romans that he was resolved to spare none of the adherents of his unfortunate competitors. He was irritated by the just suspicion that he had never possessed the affections of the senate, and he concealed his old malevolence under the recent discovery of some treasonable correspondencies. Thirty-five senators, however, accused of having favoured the party of Albinus, he freely pardoned; and, by his subsequent behaviour, endeavoured to convince them that he had forgotten, as well as forgiven, their supposed offences. But, at the same time, he condemned forty-one[37] other senators, whose names history has recorded; their wives, children, and clients, attended them in death, and the noblest provincials of Spain and Gaul were involved in the same ruin. Such rigid justice, for so he termed it, was, in the opinion of Severus, the only conduct capable of ensuring peace to the people, or stability to the prince; and he condescended slightly to lament that, to be mild, it was necessary that he should first be cruel.

The true interest of an absolute monarch generally coincides with that of his people. Their numbers, their wealth, their order, and their security, are the best and only foundations of his real greatness; and, were he totally devoid of virtue, prudence might supply its place, and would dictate the same rule of conduct. Severus considered the Roman empire as his property, and had no sooner secured the possession, than he bestowed his care on the cultivation and improvement of so valuable an acquisition. Salutary laws, executed with inflexible firmness, soon corrected most of the abuses with which, since the death of Marcus, every part of the government had been infected. In the administration of justice, the judgments of the emperor were characterized by attention, discernment, and impartiality; and, whenever he deviated from the strict line of equity, it was generally in favour of the poor and oppressed; not so much indeed from any sense of humanity, as from the natural propensity of a despot to humble the pride of greatness, and to sink all his subjects to the same common level of absolute dependence. His expensive taste for building, magnificent shows, and, above all, a constant and liberal distribution of corn and provisions, were the surest means of captivating the affection of the Roman people.[38] The misfortunes of civil discord were obliterated. The calm of peace

[37] *Only twenty-nine senators are mentioned by Dion, but forty-one are named in the Augustan History, among whom were six of the name of Pescennius. Herodian speaks in general of the cruelties of Severus.*

[38] *Severus celebrated the secular games with extraordinary magnificence, and he left in the public granaries a provision of corn for seven years, at the rate of 75,000 modii, or about 2500 quarters per day. I am persuaded that the granaries of Severus were supplied for a long term, but I am not less persuaded that policy on one hand, and admiration on the other, magnified the hoard far beyond its true contents.*

and prosperity was once more experienced in the provinces, and many cities, restored by the munificence of Severus, assumed the title of his colonies, and attested by public monuments their gratitude and felicity.[39] The fame of the Roman arms was revived by that warlike and successful emperor,[40] and he boasted, with a just pride, that, having received the empire oppressed with foreign and domestic wars, he left it established in profound, universal and honourable peace.[41]

Although the wounds of civil war appeared completely healed, its mortal poison still lurked in the vitals of the constitution. Severus possessed a considerable share of vigour and ability; but the daring soul of the first Cæsar, or the deep policy of Augustus, were scarcely equal to the task of curbing the insolence of the victorious legions. By gratitude, by misguided policy, by seeming necessity, Severus was induced to relax the nerves of discipline. The vanity of his soldiers was flattered with the honour of wearing gold rings; their ease was indulged in the permission of living with their wives in the idleness of quarters. He increased their pay beyond the example of former times, and taught them to expect, and soon to claim, extraordinary donatives on every public occasion of danger or festivity. Elated by success, enervated by luxury, and raised above the level of subjects by their dangerous privileges,[42] they soon became incapable of military fatigue, oppressive to the country, and impatient of a just subordination. Their officers asserted the superiority of rank by a more profuse and elegant luxury. There is still extant a letter of Severus, lamenting the licentious state of the army, and exhorting one of his generals to begin the necessary reformation from the tribunes themselves; since, as he justly observes, the officer who has forfeited the esteem, will never command the obedience, of his soldiers. Had the emperor pursued the train of reflection, he would have discovered that the primary cause of this general corruption might be ascribed, not indeed to the example, but to the pernicious indulgence, however, of the commander-in-chief.

The Prætorians, who murdered their emperor and sold the empire, had received the just punishment of their treason; but the necessary, though dangerous, institution of guards was soon restored on a new model by Severus, and increased to four times the ancient number. Formerly these troops had been recruited in Italy; and, as the adjacent provinces gradually imbibed the softer manners of Rome, the levies were extended to Macedonia, Noricum and Spain. In the room of these elegant troops, better adapted to the pomp of

[39] *Our learned travellers Spon and Wheeler, Shaw, Pocock, &c., in Africa, Greece, and Asia, have found more monuments of Severus than of any other Roman emperor whatsoever.*

[40] *He carried his victorious arms to Seleucia and Ctesiphon, the capitals of the Parthian monarchy. I shall have occasion to mention this war in its proper place.*

[41] *Etiam in Britannis, was his own just and emphatic expression.*

[42] *Upon the insolence and privileges of the soldiers [Prætorian guards], the 16th satire, falsely ascribed to Juvenal, may be consulted; the style and circumstances of it would induce me to believe that it was composed under the reign of Severus or that of his son.*

courts than to the uses of war, it was established by Severus, that, from all the legions of the frontiers, the soldiers most distinguished for strength, valour, and fidelity, should be occasionally draughted, and promoted, as an honour and reward, into the more eligible service of the guards. By this new institution, the Italian youth were diverted from the exercise of arms, and the capital was terrified by the strange aspect and manners of a multitude of barbarians. But Severus flattered himself that the legions would consider these chosen Prætorians as the representatives of the whole military order; and that the present aid of fifty thousand men, superior in arms and appointments to any force that could be brought into the field against them, would for ever crush the hopes of rebellion, and secure the empire to himself and his posterity.

The command of these favoured and formidable troops soon became the first office of the empire. As the government degenerated into military despotism, the Prætorian præfect, who in his origin had been a simple captain of the guards, was placed, not only at the head of the army, but of the finances, and even of the law. In every department of administration, he represented the person, and exercised the authority, of the emperor. The first præfect who enjoyed and abused this immense power was Plautianus, the favourite minister of Severus. His reign lasted above ten years, till the marriage of his daughter with the eldest son of the emperor, which seemed to assure his fortune, proved the occasion of his ruin. The animosities of the palace, by irritating the ambition and alarming the fears of Plautianus, threatened to produce a revolution, and obliged the emperor, who still loved him, to consent with reluctance to his death. After the fall of Plautianus, an eminent lawyer, the celebrated Papinian, was appointed to execute the motley office of Prætorian præfect.

Till the reign of Severus, the virtue, and even the good sense of the emperors had been distinguished by their zeal or affected reverence for the senate, and by a tender regard to the nice frame of civil policy instituted by Augustus. But the youth of Severus had been trained in the implicit obedience of camps, and his riper years spent in the despotism of military command. His haughty and inflexible spirit could not discover, or would not acknowledge, the advantage of preserving an intermediate power, however imaginary, between the emperor and the army. He disdained to profess himself the servant of an assembly that detested his person and trembled at his frown; he issued his commands, where his request would have proved as effectual; assumed the conduct and style of a sovereign and a conqueror, and exercised, without disguise, the whole legislative as well as the executive power.

The victory over the senate was easy and inglorious. Every eye and every passion were directed to the supreme magistrate, who possessed the arms and treasure of the state; whilst the senate, neither elected by the people, nor guarded by the military force, nor animated by public spirit, rested its declining authority on the frail and crumbling basis of ancient opinion. The fine theory of a republic insensibly vanished, and made way for the more natural and substantial feelings of monarchy. As the freedom and honours of Rome were successfully communicated to the provinces, in which the old government had been either unknown, or was remembered with abhorrence, the tradition of republican maxims was gradually obliterated. The Greek historians of the age of the Antonines observe, with a malicious pleasure, that, although the sovereign of Rome, in compliance with an obsolete prejudice, abstained from the name of king, he possessed the full measure of regal power. In the reign of Severus, the senate was filled with polished and eloquent slaves from the eastern provinces, who justified personal flattery by speculative principles of servitude. These new advocates of prerogative were heard with pleasure by the court, and with patience by the people, when they inculcated the duty of passive obedience, and descanted on the inevitable mischiefs of freedom. The lawyers and the historians concurred in teaching that the Imperial authority was held, not by the delegated commission, but by the irrevocable resignation, of the senate; that the emperor was freed from the restraint of civil laws, could command by his arbitrary will the lives and fortunes of his subjects, and might dispose of the empire as of his private patrimony. The most eminent of the civil lawyers, and particularly Papinian, Paulus, and Ulpian, flourished under the house of Severus; and the Roman jurisprudence, having closely united itself with the system of monarchy, was supposed to have attained its full maturity and perfection.

The contemporaries of Severus, in the enjoyment of the peace and glory of his reign, forgave the cruelties by which it had been introduced. Posterity, who experienced the fatal effect of his maxims and example, justly considered him as the principal author of the decline of the Roman empire.

VI

THE DEATH OF SEVERUS · TYRANNY OF CARACALLA · USUR-
PATION OF MACRINUS · FOLLIES OF ELAGABALUS · VIRTUES
OF ALEXANDER SEVERUS · LICENTIOUSNESS OF THE ARMY ·
GENERAL STATE OF THE ROMAN FINANCES · TAX & TRIBUTE

T H E ascent to greatness, however steep and dangerous, may entertain an active spirit with the consciousness and exercise of its own powers: but the possession of a throne could never yet afford a lasting satisfaction to an ambitious mind. This melancholy truth was felt and acknowledged by Severus. Fortune and merit had, from an humble station, elevated him to the first place among mankind. He had been "all things," as he said himself, "and all was of little value." Distracted with the care, not of acquiring, but of preserving, an empire, oppressed with age and infirmities, careless of fame, and satiated with power, all his prospects of life were closed. The desire of perpetuating the greatness of his family was the only remaining wish of his ambition and paternal tenderness.

Like most of the Africans, Severus was passionately addicted to the vain studies of magic and divination, deeply versed in the interpretation of dreams and omens, and perfectly acquainted with the science of judicial astrology; which, in almost every age except the present, has maintained its dominion over the mind of man. He had lost his first wife whilst he was governor of the Lyonnese Gaul.[1] In the choice of a second, he sought only to connect himself with some favourite of fortune; and, as soon as he had discovered that a young lady of Emesa in Syria had *a royal nativity*, he solicited and obtained her hand. Julia Domna (for that was her name) deserved all that the stars could promise her. She possessed, even in an advanced age, the attractions of beauty, and united to a lively imagination a firmness of mind, and strength of judgment, seldom bestowed on her sex. Her amiable qualities never made any deep

[1] *About the year 186. M. de Tillemont is miserably embarrassed with a passage of Dion, in which the Empress Faustina, who died in the year 175, is introduced as having contributed to the marriage of Severus and Julia. The learned compiler forgot that Dion is relating, not a real fact, but a dream of Severus; and dreams are circumscribed to no limits of time or space.*

99

impression on the dark and jealous temper of her husband; but, in her son's reign, she administered the principal affairs of the empire with a prudence that supported his authority; and with a moderation that sometimes corrected his wild extravagancies. Julia applied herself to letters and philosophy with some success, and with the most splendid reputation. She was the patroness of every art, and the friend of every man of genius. The grateful flattery of the learned has celebrated her virtues; but, if we may credit the scandal of ancient history, chastity was very far from being the most conspicuous virtue of the Empress Julia.

Two sons, Caracalla [2] and Geta, were the fruit of this marriage, and the destined heirs of the empire. The fond hopes of the father, and of the Roman world, were soon disappointed by these vain youths, who displayed the indolent security of hereditary princes, and a presumption that fortune would supply the place of merit and application. Without any emulation of virtue or talents, they discovered, almost from their infancy, a fixed and implacable antipathy for each other.

Their aversion, confirmed by years, and fomented by the arts of their interested favourites, broke out in childish, and gradually in more serious, competitions; and at length divided the theatre, the circus, and the court, into two factions, actuated by the hopes and fears of their respective leaders. The prudent emperor endeavoured, by every expedient of advice and authority, to allay this growing animosity. The unhappy discord of his sons clouded all his prospects, and threatened to overturn a throne raised with so much labour, cemented with so much blood, and guarded with every defence of arms and treasure. With an impartial hand he maintained between them an exact balance of favour, conferred on both the rank of Augustus, with the revered name of Antoninus; and for the first time the Roman world beheld three emperors. [3] Yet even this equal conduct served only to inflame the contest, whilst the fierce Caracalla asserted the right of primogeniture, and the milder Geta courted the affections of the people and the soldiers. In the anguish of a disappointed father, Severus foretold that the weaker of his sons would fall a sacrifice to the stronger; who, in his turn, would be ruined by his own vices.

In these circumstances the intelligence of a war in Britain, and of an invasion of the province by the barbarians of the North, was received with pleasure by Severus. Though the vigilance of his lieutenants might have been sufficient to repel the distant enemy, he

[2] *Bassianus was his first name, as it had been that of his maternal grandfather. During his reign he assumed the appellation of Antoninus, which is employed by lawyers and ancient historians. After his death, the public indignation loaded him with the nicknames of Tarantus and Caracalla. The first was borrowed from a celebrated Gladiator, the second from a long Gallic gown which he distributed to the people of Rome.*

[3] *The elevation of Caracalla is fixed by the accurate M. de Tillemont to the year 198; the association of Geta, to the year 208.*

resolved to embrace the honourable pretext of withdrawing his sons from the luxury of Rome, which enervated their minds and irritated their passions, and of inuring their youth to the toils of war and government. Notwithstanding his advanced age (for he was above threescore), and his gout, which obliged him to be carried in a litter, he transported himself in person into that remote island, attended by his two sons, his whole court, and a formidable army. He immediately passed the walls of Hadrian and Antoninus, and entered the enemy's country, with the design of completing the long-attempted conquest of Britain. He penetrated to the northern extremity of the island without meeting an enemy. But the concealed ambuscades of the Caledonians, who hung unseen on the rear and flanks of his army, the coldness of the climate, and the severity of a winter march across the hills and morasses of Scotland, are reported to have cost the Romans above fifty thousand men. The Caledonians at length yielded to the powerful and obstinate attack, sued for peace, and surrendered a part of their arms, and a large tract of territory. But their apparent submission lasted no longer than the present terror. As soon as the Roman legions had retired, they resumed their hostile independence. Their restless spirit provoked Severus to send a new army into Caledonia, with the most bloody orders, not to subdue, but to extirpate the natives. They were saved by the death of their haughty enemy.

This Caledonian war, neither marked by decisive events, nor attended with any important consequences, would ill deserve our attention; but it is supposed, not without a considerable degree of probability, that the invasion of Severus is connected with the most shining period of the British history or fable. Fingal, whose fame, with that of his heroes and bards, has been revived in our language by a recent publication, is said to have commanded the Caledonians in that memorable juncture, to have eluded the power of Severus, and to have obtained a signal victory on the banks of the Carun, in which the son of *the King of the World,* Caracul, fled from his arms along the fields of his pride. Something of a doubtful mist still hangs over these Highland traditions; nor can it be entirely dispelled by the most ingenious researches of modern criticism:[4] but if we could, with safety, indulge the pleasing supposition that Fingal lived, and that Ossian sung, the striking contrast of the situation and manners of the contending nations might amuse a philosophic mind. The parallel would be little to the advantage of the more civilized people, if we compared the unrelenting revenge of Severus

[4] *That the Caracul of Ossian is the Caracalla of the Roman history, is, perhaps, the only point of British antiquity in which Mr. Macpherson and Mr. Whitaker are of the same opinion; and yet the opinion is not without difficulty. In the Caledonian war, the son of Severus was known only by the appellation of Antoninus; and it may seem strange that the Highland bard should describe him by a nickname, invented four years afterwards, scarcely used by the Romans till after the death of that emperor, and seldom employed by the most ancient historians.*

with the generous clemency of Fingal; the timid and brutal cruelty of Caracalla, with the bravery, the tenderness, the elegant genius of Ossian; the mercenary chiefs who, from motives of fear or interest, served under the Imperial standard, with the freeborn warriors who started to arms at the voice of the King of Morven; if, in a word, we contemplated the untutored Caledonians, glowing with the warm virtues of nature, and the degenerate Romans, polluted with the mean vices of wealth and slavery.

The declining health and last illness of Severus inflamed the wild ambition and black passions of Caracalla's soul. Impatient of any delay or division of empire, he attempted, more than once, to shorten the small remainder of his father's days, and endeavoured, but without success, to excite a mutiny among the troops. The old emperor had often censured the misguided lenity of Marcus, who, by a single act of justice, might have saved the Romans from the tyranny of his worthless son. Placed in the same situation, he experienced how easily the rigour of a judge dissolves away in the tenderness of a parent. He deliberated, he threatened, but he could not punish; and this last and only instance of mercy was more fatal to the empire than a long series of cruelty. The disorder of his mind irritated the pains of his body; he wished impatiently for death, and hastened the instant of it by his impatience. He expired at York in the sixty-fifth year of his life, and in the eighteenth of a glorious and successful reign. In his last moments he recommended concord to his sons, and his sons to the army. The salutary advice never reached the heart, or even the understanding, of the impetuous youths; but the more obedient troops, mindful of their oath of allegiance, and of the authority of their deceased master, resisted the solicitations of Caracalla, and proclaimed both brothers emperors of Rome. The new princes soon left the Caledonians in peace, returned to the capital, celebrated their father's funeral with divine honours, and were cheerfully acknowledged as lawful sovereigns by the senate, the people, and the provinces. Some pre-eminence of rank seems to have been allowed to the elder brother; but they both administered the empire with equal and independent power.

Such a divided form of government would have proved a source of discord between the most affectionate brothers. It was impossible that it could long subsist between two implacable enemies, who neither desired nor could trust a reconciliation. It was visible that one only could reign, and that the other must fall; and each of them, judging of his rival's designs by his own, guarded his life with the most jealous vigilance from the repeated attacks of poison or the sword. Their rapid journey through Gaul and Italy, during which they never ate at the same table, or slept in the same house, displayed to the provinces the odious spectacle of fraternal discord. On their arrival at Rome, they immediately divided the vast extent of the Imperial palace.[5] No communication was allowed between their apartments; the doors and passages were diligently fortified, and guards posted and relieved with the same strictness as in a besieged place. The emperors met only in public, in the presence of their afflicted mother; and each surrounded by a numerous train of armed followers. Even on these occasions of ceremony, the dissimulation of courts could ill disguise the rancour of their hearts.

This latent civil war already distracted the whole government, when a scheme was suggested that seemed of mutual benefit to the hostile brothers. It was proposed, that, since it was impossible to reconcile their minds, they should separate their interest, and divide the empire between them. The conditions of the treaty were already drawn with some accuracy. It was agreed, that Caracalla, as the elder brother, should remain in possession of Europe and the western Africa; and that he should relinquish the sovereignty of Asia and Egypt to Geta, who might fix his residence at Alexandria or Antioch, cities little inferior to Rome itself in wealth and greatness; that numerous armies should be constantly encamped on either side of the Thracian Bosphorus, to guard the frontiers of the rival monarchies; and that the senators of European extraction should acknowledge the sovereign of Rome, whilst the natives of Asia followed the emperor of the East. The tears of the empress Julia interrupted the negotiation, the first idea of which had filled every Roman breast with surprise and indignation. The mighty mass of conquest was so intimately connected by the hand of time and policy, that it required the most forcible violence to rend it asunder. The Romans had reason to dread that the disjointed members would soon be reduced by a civil war under the dominion of one master; but, if the separation was permanent, the division of the provinces must terminate in the dissolution of an empire whose unity had hitherto remained inviolate.

Had the treaty been carried into execution, the sovereign of Europe might soon have been the conqueror of Asia; but Caracalla obtained an easier though a more guilty victory. He artfully listened to his mother's entreaties, and consented to meet his brother in her apartment, on terms of peace and reconciliation. In the midst

[5] Mr. Hume is justly surprised at a passage of Herodian, who, on this occasion, represents the Imperial palace as equal in extent to the rest of Rome. The whole region of the Palatine Mount on which it was built occupied, at most, a circumference of eleven or twelve thousand feet. But we should recollect that the opulent senators had almost surrounded the city with their extensive gardens and suburb palaces, the greatest part of which had been gradually confiscated by the emperors. If Geta resided in the gardens that bore his name on the Janiculum, and if Caracalla inhabited the gardens of Mæcenas on the Esquiline, the rival brothers were separated from each other by the distance of several miles; and yet the intermediate space was filled by the Imperial gardens of Sallust, of Lucullus, of Agrippa, of Domitian, of Caius, &c., all skirting round the city, and all connected with each other, and with the palace, by bridges thrown over the Tiber and the streets. But this explanation of Herodian would require, though it ill deserves, a particular dissertation, illustrated by a map of ancient Rome.

of their conversation, some centurions, who had contrived to conceal themselves, rushed with drawn swords upon the unfortunate Geta. His distracted mother strove to protect him in her arms; but in the unavailing struggle, she was wounded in the hand, and covered with the blood of her younger son, while she saw the elder animating and assisting [6] the fury of the assassins. As soon as the deed was perpetrated, Caracalla, with hasty steps and horror in his countenance, ran towards the Prætorian camp, as his only refuge, and threw himself on the ground before the statues of the tutelar deities.[7] The soldiers attempted to raise and comfort him. In broken and disordered words he informed them of his imminent danger and fortunate escape: insinuating that he had prevented the designs of his enemy, and declared his resolution to live and die with his faithful troops. Geta had been the favourite of the soldiers; but complaint was useless, revenge was dangerous, and they still reverenced the son of Severus. Their discontent died away in idle murmurs, and Caracalla soon convinced them of the justice of his cause, by distributing in one lavish donative the accumulated treasures of his father's reign. The real *sentiments* of the soldiers alone were of importance to his power or safety. Their declaration in his favour commanded the dutiful *professions* of the senate. The obsequious assembly was always prepared to ratify the decision of fortune; but as Caracalla wished to assuage the first emotions of public indignation, the name of Geta was mentioned with decency, and he received the funeral honours of a Roman emperor.[8] Posterity, in pity to his misfortune, has cast a veil over his vices. We consider that young prince as the innocent victim of his brother's ambition, without recollecting that he himself wanted power, rather than inclination, to consummate the same attempts of revenge and murder.

The crime went not unpunished. Neither business, nor pleasure, nor flattery, could defend Caracalla from the stings of a guilty conscience; and he confessed, in the anguish of a tortured mind, that his disordered fancy often beheld the angry forms of his father and his brother rising into life, to threaten and upbraid him. The consciousness of his crime should have induced him to convince mankind, by the virtues of his reign, that the bloody deed had been the involuntary effect of fatal necessity. But the repentance of Caracalla only prompted him to remove from the world whatever could remind him of his guilt, or recall the memory of his murdered brother. On his return from the senate to the palace, he found his mother in the company of several noble matrons, weeping over the

[6] *Caracalla consecrated, in the temple of Serapis, the sword with which, as he boasted, he had slain his brother Geta.*

[7] *In every Roman camp there was a small chapel near the headquarters, in which the statues of the tutelar deities were preserved and adored; and we may remark that the eagles, and other military ensigns, were in the first rank of these deities; an excellent institution, which confirmed discipline by the sanction of religion.*

[8] *Geta was placed among the gods. Sit* divus, *dum non sit* vivus, *said his brother. Some marks of Geta's consecration are still found upon medals.*

untimely fate of her younger son. The jealous emperor threatened them with instant death: the sentence was executed against Fadilla, the last remaining daughter of the Emperor Marcus; and even the afflicted Julia was obliged to silence her lamentations, to suppress her sighs, and to receive the assassin with smiles of joy and approbation. It was computed that, under the vague appellation of the friends of Geta, above twenty thousand persons of both sexes suffered death. His guards and freedmen, the ministers of his serious business, and the companions of his looser hours, those who by his interest had been promoted to any commands in the army or provinces, with the long connected chain of their dependants, were included in the proscription; which endeavoured to reach every one who had maintained the smallest correspondence with Geta, who lamented his death, or who even mentioned his name.[9] Helvius Pertinax, son to the prince of that name, lost his life by an unseasonable witticism.[10] It was a sufficient crime of Thrasea Priscus to be descended from a family in which the love of liberty seemed an hereditary quality.[11] The particular causes of calumny and suspicion were at length exhausted; and when a senator was accused of being a secret enemy to the government, the emperor was satisfied with the general proof that he was a man of property and virtue. From this well-grounded principle, he frequently drew the most bloody inferences.

The execution of so many innocent citizens was bewailed by the secret tears of their friends and families. The death of Papinian, the Prætorian præfect, was lamented as a public calamity. During the last seven years of Severus, he had exercised the most important offices of the state, and, by his salutary influence, guided the emperor's steps in the paths of justice and moderation. In full assurance of his virtue and abilities, Severus, on his deathbed, had conjured him to watch over the prosperity and union of the Imperial family.[12] The honest labours of Papinian served only to inflame the hatred which Caracalla had already conceived against his father's minister. After the murder of Geta, the præfect was commanded to exert the powers of his skill and eloquence in a studied apology for that atrocious deed. The philosophic Seneca had condescended to compose a similar epistle to the senate, in the name of the son and assassin of Agrippina. "That it was easier to commit than to justify a parricide," was the glorious reply of Papinian, who did not hesitate between the loss of life and that of honour. Such intrepid virtue, which had escaped pure and unsullied from the intrigues of courts, the

[9] *Dion says that the comic poets no longer durst employ the name of Geta in their plays, and that the estates of those who mentioned it in their testaments were confiscated.*

[10] *Caracalla had assumed the names of several conquered nations; Pertinax observed, that the name of* Geticus *(he had obtained some advantage over the Goths or Getæ) would be a proper addition to* Parthicus, Alemannicus, &c.

[11] *He was probably descended from Helvidius Priscus, and Thrasea Pætus, those patriots whose firm, but useless and unseasonable, virtue has been immortalized by Tacitus.*

[12] *It is said that Papinian was himself a relation of the Empress Julia.*

habits of business, and the arts of his profession, reflects more lustre on the memory of Papinian than all his great employments, his numerous writings, and the superior reputation as a lawyer, which he has preserved through every age of the Roman jurisprudence.

It had hitherto been the peculiar felicity of the Romans, and in the worst of times their consolation, that the virtue of the emperors was active, and their vice indolent. Augustus, Trajan, Hadrian, and Marcus, visited their extensive dominions in person, and their progress was marked by acts of wisdom and beneficence. The tyranny of Tiberius, Nero, and Domitian, who resided almost constantly at Rome, or in the adjacent villas, was confined to the senatorial and equestrian orders.[13] But Caracalla was the common enemy of mankind. He left the capital (and he never returned to it) about a year after the murder of Geta. The rest of his reign was spent in the several provinces of the empire, particularly those of the East, and every province was, by turns, the scene of his rapine and cruelty. The senators, compelled by fear to attend his capricious motions, were obliged to provide daily entertainments at an immense expense, which he abandoned with contempt to his guards; and to erect, in every city, magnificent palaces and theatres, which he either disdained to visit, or ordered to be immediately thrown down. The most wealthy families were ruined by partial fines and confiscations, and the great body of his subjects oppressed by ingenious and aggravated taxes. In the midst of peace, and upon the slightest provocation, he issued his commands, at Alexandria in Egypt, for a general massacre. From a secure post in the temple of Serapis, he viewed and directed the slaughter of many thousand citizens, as well as strangers, without distinguishing either the number or the crime of the sufferers; since, as he coolly informed the senate, *all* the Alexandrians, those who had perished and those who had escaped, were alike guilty.[14]

The wise instructions of Severus never made any lasting impression on the mind of his son, who, although not destitute of imagination and eloquence, was equally devoid of judgment and humanity. One dangerous maxim, worthy of a tyrant, was remembered and abused by Caracalla, "To secure the affections of the army, and to esteem the rest of his subjects as of little moment."[15] But the liberality of the father had been restrained by prudence, and his indulgence to the troops was tempered by firmness and authority. The careless profusion of the son was the policy of one reign, and the inevitable ruin both of the army and of the empire. The vigour of

[13] *Tiberius and Domitian never moved from the neighbourhood of Rome. Nero made a short journey into Greece.*

[14] *Dion represents it as a cruel massacre, Herodian as a perfidious one too. It seems probable that the Alexandrians had irritated the tyrant by their railleries, and perhaps by their tumults.*

[15] *M. Wotton suspects that this maxim was invented by Caracalla himself and attributed to his father.*

the soldiers, instead of being confirmed by the severe discipline of camps, melted away in the luxury of cities. The excessive increase of their pay and donatives [16] exhausted the state to enrich the military order, whose modesty in peace, and service in war, is best secured by an honourable poverty. The demeanour of Caracalla was haughty and full of pride; but with the troops he forgot even the proper dignity of his rank, encouraged their insolent familiarity, and, neglecting the essential duties of a general, affected to imitate the dress and manners of a common soldier.

It was impossible that such a character and such a conduct as that of Caracalla could inspire either love or esteem; but, as long as his vices were beneficial to the armies, he was secure from the danger of rebellion. A secret conspiracy, provoked by his own jealousy, was fatal to the tyrant. The Prætorian præfecture was divided between two ministers. The military department was intrusted to Adventus, an experienced rather than an able soldier; and the civil affairs were transacted by Opilius Macrinus, who, by his dexterity in business, had raised himself, with a fair character, to that high office. But his favour varied with the caprice of the emperor, and his life might depend on the slightest suspicion, or the most casual circumstance. Malice or fanaticism had suggested to an African, deeply skilled in the knowledge of futurity, a very dangerous prediction, that Macrinus and his son were destined to reign over the empire. The report was soon diffused through the province; and, when the man was sent in chains to Rome, he still asserted, in the presence of the præfect of the city, the faith of his prophecy. That magistrate, who had received the most pressing instructions to inform himself of the *successors* of Caracalla, immediately communicated the examination of the African to the Imperial court, which at that time resided in Syria. But notwithstanding the diligence of the public messengers, a friend of Macrinus found means to apprize him of the approaching danger. The emperor received the letters from Rome; and, as he was then engaged in the conduct of a chariot race, he delivered them unopened to the Prætorian præfect, directing him to dispatch the ordinary affairs, and to report the more important business that might be contained in them. Macrinus read his fate and resolved to prevent it. He inflamed the discontents of some inferior officers, and employed the hand of Martialis, a desperate soldier, who had been refused the rank of centurion. The devotion of Caracalla had prompted him to make a pilgrimage from Edessa to the celebrated temple of the Moon at Carrhæ. He was attended by

[16] *Dion informs us that the extraordinary gifts of Caracalla to the army amounted annually to seventy millions of drachmæ (about two millions three hundred and fifty thousand pounds). There is another passage in Dion, concerning the military pay, infinitely curious; were it not obscure, imperfect, and probably corrupt. The best sense seems to be, that the Prætorian guards received twelve hundred and fifty drachmæ (forty pounds) a year. Under the reign of Augustus, they were paid at the rate of two drachmæ, or denarii, per day, 720 a year. Domitian, who increased the soldiers' pay one-fourth, must have raised the Prætorians' to 960 drachmæ. These successive augmentations ruined the empire, for, with the soldiers' pay, their numbers too were increased. We have seen the Prætorians alone increased from 10,000 to 50,000 men.*

a body of cavalry; but having stopped on the road for some necessary occasion, his guards preserved a respectful distance, and Martialis, approaching his person under a pretence of duty, stabbed him with a dagger. The bold assassin was instantly killed by a Scythian archer of the Imperial guard. Such was the end of a monster whose life disgraced human nature, and whose reign accused the patience of the Romans. The grateful soldiers forgot his vices, remembered only his partial liberality, and obliged the senate to prostitute their own dignity and that of religion by granting him a place among the gods. Whilst he was upon earth, Alexander the Great was the only hero whom this god deemed worthy his admiration. He assumed the name and ensigns of Alexander, formed a Macedonian phalanx of guards, persecuted the disciples of Aristotle, and displayed with a puerile enthusiasm the only sentiment by which he discovered any regard for virtue or glory. We can easily conceive that, after the battle of Narva and the conquest of Poland, Charles the Twelfth (though he still wanted the more elegant accomplishments of the son of Philip) might boast of having rivalled his valour and magnanimity; but in no one action of his life did Caracalla express the faintest resemblance of the Macedonian hero, except in the murder of a great number of his own and of his father's friends.[17]

[17] *The fondness of Caracalla for the name and ensigns of Alexander, is still preserved on the medals of that emperor. Herodian had seen very ridiculous pictures, in which a figure was drawn with one side of the face like Alexander, and the other like Caracalla.*

After the extinction of the house of Severus, the Roman world remained three days without a master. The choice of the army (for the authority of a distant and feeble senate was little regarded) hung in anxious suspense; as no candidate presented himself whose distinguished birth and merit could engage their attachment and unite their suffrages. The decisive weight of the Prætorian guards elevated the hopes of their præfects, and these powerful ministers began to assert their *legal* claim to fill the vacancy of the Imperial throne. Adventus, however, the senior præfect, conscious of his age and infirmities, of his small reputation and his smaller abilities, resigned the dangerous honour to the crafty ambition of his colleague Macrinus, whose well dissembled grief removed all suspicion of his being accessory to his master's death. The troops neither loved nor esteemed his character. They cast their eyes around in search of a competitor, and at last yielded with reluctance to his promises of unbounded liberality and indulgence. A short time after his accession he conferred on his son Diadumenianus, at the age of only ten years, the Imperial title and the popular name of Antoninus. The beautiful figure of the youth, assisted by an additional donative, for which the ceremony furnished a pretext, might attract, it was hoped, the favour of the army, and secure the doubtful throne of Macrinus.

The authority of the new sovereign had been ratified by the cheerful submission of the senate and provinces. They exulted in their unexpected deliverance from a hated tyrant, and it seemed of little consequence to examine into the virtues of the successor of Caracalla. But as soon as the first transports of joy and surprise had subsided, they began to scrutinize the merits of Macrinus with a critical severity, and to arraign the hasty choice of the army. It had hitherto been considered as a fundamental maxim of the constitution that the emperor must always be chosen in the senate, and the sovereign power, no longer exercised by the whole body, was always delegated to one of its members. But Macrinus was not a senator.[18] The sudden elevation of the Prætorian præfects betrayed the meanness of their origin; and the equestrian order was still in possession of that great office, which commanded with arbitrary sway the lives and fortunes of the senate. A murmur of indignation was heard, that a man, whose obscure [19] extraction had never been illustrated by any signal service, should dare to invest himself with the purple, instead of bestowing it on some distinguished senator, equal in birth and dignity to the splendour of the Imperial station. As soon as the character of Macrinus was surveyed by the sharp eye of discontent, some vices, and many defects, were easily discovered. The choice of his ministers was in several instances justly censured, and the dissatisfied people, with their usual candour, accused at once his indolent tameness and his excessive severity.[20]

His rash ambition had climbed a height where it was difficult to stand with firmness, and impossible to fall without instant destruction. Trained in the arts of courts and the forms of civil business, he trembled in the presence of the fierce and undisciplined multitude, over whom he had assumed the command: his military talents were despised, and his personal courage suspected: a whisper that circulated in the camp, disclosed the fatal secret of the conspiracy against the late emperor, aggravated the guilt of murder by the baseness of hypocrisy, and heightened contempt by detestation. To alienate the soldiers, and to provoke inevitable ruin, the character of a reformer was only wanting; and such was the peculiar hardship of his fate, that Macrinus was compelled to exercise that invidious office. The prodigality of Caracalla had left behind it a long train of ruin and disorder: and, if that worthless tyrant had been capable of reflecting on the sure consequences of his own con-

[18] *Elagabalus reproached his predecessor, with daring to seat himself on the throne; though, as Prætorian præfect, he could not have been admitted into the senate after the voice of the crier had cleared the house. The personal favour of Plautianus and Sejanus had broke through the established rule. They rose indeed from the equestrian order; but they preserved the præfecture with the rank of senator, and even with the consulship.*

[19] *He was a native of Cæsarea, in Numidia, and began his fortune by serving in the household of Plautian, from whose ruin he narrowly escaped. His enemies asserted that he was born a slave, and had exercised, among other infamous professions, that of Gladiator. The fashion of aspersing the birth and condition of an adversary seems to have lasted from the time of the Greek orators to the learned grammarians of the last age.*

[20] *Both Dion and Herodian speak of the virtues and vices of Macrinus with candour and impartiality; but the author of his Life, in the Augustan History, seems to have implicitly copied some of the venal writers*

employed by Elagabalus
to blacken the memory
of his predecessor.

duct, he would perhaps have enjoyed the dark prospect of the distress and calamities which he bequeathed to his successors.

In the management of this necessary reformation, Macrinus proceeded with a cautious prudence which would have restored health
and vigour to the Roman army in an easy and almost imperceptible manner. To the soldiers already engaged in the service, he was
constrained to leave the dangerous privileges and extravagant pay
given by Caracalla; but the new recruits were received on the more
moderate, though liberal, establishment of Severus, and gradually
formed to modesty and obedience. One fatal error destroyed the
salutary effects of this judicious plan. The numerous army, assembled in the East by the late emperor, instead of being immediately
dispersed by Macrinus through the several provinces, was suffered
to remain united in Syria during the winter that followed his elevation. In the luxurious idleness of their quarters, the troops viewed
their strength and numbers, communicated their complaints, and
revolved in their minds the advantages of another revolution. The
veterans, instead of being flattered by the advantageous distinction,
were alarmed by the first steps of the emperor, which they considered as the presage of his future intentions. The recruits, with sullen reluctance, entered on a service, whose labours were increased
while its rewards were diminished by a covetous and unwarlike
sovereign. The murmurs of the army swelled with impunity into
seditious clamours; and the partial mutinies betrayed a spirit of
discontent and disaffection, that waited only for the slightest occasion to break out on every side into a general rebellion. To minds
thus disposed the occasion soon presented itself.

The Empress Julia had experienced all the vicissitudes of fortune.
From an humble station, she had been raised to greatness, only to
taste the superior bitterness of an exalted rank. She was doomed to
weep over the death of one of her sons, and over the life of the
other. The cruel fate of Caracalla, though her good sense must have
long taught her to expect it, awakened the feelings of a mother and
of an empress. Notwithstanding the respectful civility expressed
by the usurper towards the widow of Severus, she descended with
a painful struggle into the condition of a subject, and soon withdrew herself by a voluntary death from the anxious and humiliating dependence. Julia Mæsa, her sister, was ordered to leave the
court and Antioch. She retired to Emesa with an immense fortune,
the fruit of twenty years' favour, accompanied by her two daughters, Soæmias and Mamæa, each of whom was a widow, and each

had an only son. Bassianus, for that was the name of the son of Soæmias, was consecrated to the honourable ministry of high priest of the Sun; and this holy vocation, embraced either from prudence or superstition, contributed to raise the Syrian youth to the empire of Rome. A numerous body of troops were stationed at Emesa; and, as the severe discipline of Macrinus had constrained them to pass the winter encamped, they were eager to revenge the cruelty of such unaccustomed hardships. The soldiers, who resorted in crowds to the temple of the Sun, beheld with veneration and delight the elegant dress and figure of the young pontiff: they recognized, or thought that they recognized, the features of Caracalla, whose memory they now adored. The artful Mæsa saw and cherished their rising partiality, and, readily sacrificing her daughter's reputation to the fortune of her grandson, she insinuated that Bassianus was the natural son of their murdered sovereign. The sums distributed by her emissaries with a lavish hand silenced every objection, and the profusion sufficiently proved the affinity, or at least the resemblance, of Bassianus with the great original. The young Antoninus (for he had assumed and polluted that respectable name) was declared emperor by the troops of Emesa, asserted his hereditary right, and called aloud on the armies to follow the standard of a young and liberal prince, who had taken up arms to revenge his father's death and the oppression of the military order.[21]

Whilst a conspiracy of women and eunuchs was concerted with prudence, and conducted with rapid vigour, Macrinus, who by a decisive motion might have crushed his infant enemy, floated between the opposite extremes of terror and security, which alike fixed him inactive at Antioch. A spirit of rebellion diffused itself through all the camps and garrisons of Syria, successive detachments murdered their officers,[22] and joined the party of the rebels; and the tardy restitution of military pay and privileges was imputed to the acknowledged weakness of Macrinus. At length he marched out of Antioch, to meet the increasing and zealous army of the young pretender. His own troops seemed to take the field with faintness and reluctance; but, in the heat of battle,[23] the Prætorian guards, almost by an involuntary impulse, asserted the superiority of their valour and discipline. The rebel ranks were broken; when the mother and grandmother of the Syrian prince, who, according to their eastern custom, had attended the army, threw themselves from their covered chariots, and, by exciting the compassion of the soldiers, endeavoured to animate their drooping courage. Anto-

[21] *According to Lampridius, Alexander Severus lived twenty-nine years, three months, and seven days. As he was killed March 19, 235, he was born December 12, 205, and was consequently about this time thirteen years old, as his elder cousin might be about seventeen. This computation suits much better the history of the young princes than that of Herodian, who represents them as three years younger; whilst, by an opposite error of chronology, he lengthens the reign of Elagabalus two years beyond its real duration.*

[22] *By a most dangerous proclamation of the pretended Antoninus, every soldier who brought in his officer's head became entitled to his private estate, as well as to his military commission.*

[23] *The battle was fought near the village of Immæ, about two-and-twenty miles from Antioch.*

ninus himself, who in the rest of his life never acted like a man, in this important crisis of his fate approved himself a hero, mounted his horse, and, at the head of his rallied troops, charged sword in hand among the thickest of the enemy; whilst the eunuch Gannys, whose occupation had been confined to female cares and the soft luxury of Asia, displayed the talents of an able and experienced general. The battle still raged with doubtful violence, and Macrinus might have obtained the victory, had he not betrayed his own cause by a shameful and precipitate flight. His cowardice served only to protract his life a few days, and to stamp deserved ignominy on his misfortunes. It is scarcely necessary to add that his son Diadumenianus was involved in the same fate. As soon as the stubborn Prætorians could be convinced that they fought for a prince who had basely deserted them, they surrendered to the conqueror; the contending parties of the Roman army, mingling tears of joy and tenderness, united under the banners of the imagined son of Caracalla, and the East acknowledged with pleasure the first emperor of Asiatic extraction.

The letters of Macrinus had condescended to inform the senate of the slight disturbance occasioned by an impostor in Syria, and a decree immediately passed, declaring the rebel and his family public enemies; with a promise of pardon, however, to such of his deluded adherents as should merit it by an immediate return to their duty. During the twenty days that elapsed from the declaration to the victory of Antoninus (for in so short an interval was the fate of the Roman world decided), the capital and the provinces, more especially those of the East, were distracted with hopes and fears, agitated with tumult, and stained with a useless effusion of civil blood, since whosoever of the rivals prevailed in Syria must reign over the empire. The specious letters in which the young conqueror announced his victory to the obedient senate were filled with professions of virtue and moderation; the shining examples of Marcus and Augustus he should ever consider as the great rule of his administration; and he affected to dwell with pride on the striking resemblance of his own age and fortunes with those of Augustus, who in the earliest youth had revenged by a successful war the murder of his father. By adopting the style of Marcus Aurelius Antoninus, son of Antoninus, and grandson of Severus, he tacitly asserted his hereditary claim to empire; but, by assuming the tribunitian and proconsular powers before they had been conferred on him by a decree of the senate, he offended the delicacy of Roman prejudice. This new and injudicious violation of the constitution was probably dictated either by the ignorance of his Syrian courtiers, or the fierce disdain of his military followers.

As the attention of the new emperor was diverted by the most trifling amusements, he wasted many months in his luxurious progress from Syria to Italy, passed at Nicomedia the first winter after his victory, and deferred till the ensuing summer his triumphal entry into the capital. A faithful picture, however, which preceded his arrival, and was placed by his immediate order over the altar of Victory in the senate-house, conveyed to the Romans the just but unworthy resemblance of his person and manners. He was drawn in his sacerdotal robes of silk and gold, after the loose flowing fashion of the Medes and Phœnicians; his head was covered with a lofty tiara, his numerous collars and bracelets were adorned with gems of an inestimable value. His eye-brows were tinged with black, and his cheeks painted with an artificial red and white. The grave senators confessed with a sigh, that, after having long experienced the stern tyranny of their own countrymen, Rome was at length humbled beneath the effeminate luxury of Oriental despotism.

The sun was worshipped at Emesa under the name of Elagabalus,[24] and under the form of a black conical stone, which, as it was universally believed, had fallen from heaven on that sacred place. To this protecting deity, Antoninus, not without some reason, ascribed his elevation to the throne. The display of superstitious gratitude was the only serious business of his reign. The triumph of the god of Emesa over all the religions of the earth, was the great object of his zeal and vanity; and the appellation of Elagabalus (for he presumed as pontiff and favourite to adopt that sacred name) was dearer to him than all the titles of Imperial greatness. In a solemn procession through the streets of Rome, the way was strewed with gold dust; the black stone, set in precious gems, was placed on a chariot drawn by six milk-white horses richly caparisoned. The pious emperor held the reins, and, supported by his ministers, moved slowly backwards, that he might perpetually enjoy the felicity of the divine presence. In a magnificent temple raised on the Palatine Mount, the sacrifices of the god Elagabalus were celebrated with every circumstance of cost and solemnity. The richest wines, the most extraordinary victims, and the rarest aromatics, were profusely consumed on his altar. Around the altar a chorus of Syrian damsels performed their lascivious dances to the sound of barbarian music, whilst the gravest personages of the state and army, clothed

[24] *This name is derived by the learned, from two Syriac words, Ela, a god, and Gabal, to form, the forming, or plastic God; a proper, and even happy epithet for the Sun.*

in long Phœnician tunics, officiated in the meanest functions, with affected zeal and secret indignation.

To this temple, as to the common centre of religious worship, the Imperial fanatic attempted to remove the Ancilia, the Palladium,[25] and all the sacred pledges of the faith of Numa. A crowd of inferior deities attended in various stations the majesty of the god of Emesa; but his court was still imperfect, till a female of distinguished rank was admitted to his bed. Pallas had been first chosen for his consort; but, as it was dreaded that her warlike terrors might affright the soft delicacy of a Syrian deity, the Moon, adored by the Africans under the name of Astarte, was deemed a more suitable companion for the Sun. Her image, with the rich offerings of her temple as a marriage portion, was transported with solemn pomp from Carthage to Rome, and the day of these mystic nuptials was a general festival in the capital and throughout the empire.[26]

A rational voluptuary adheres with invariable respect to the temperate dictates of nature, and improves the gratifications of sense by social intercourse, endearing connexions, and the soft colouring of taste and imagination. But Elagabalus (I speak of the emperor of that name), corrupted by his youth, his country, and his fortune, abandoned himself to the grossest pleasures with ungoverned fury, and soon found disgust and satiety in the midst of his enjoyments. The inflammatory powers of art were summoned to his aid: the confused multitude of women, of wines, and of dishes, and the studied variety of attitudes and sauces, served to revive his languid appetites. New terms and new inventions in these sciences, the only ones cultivated and patronized by the monarch,[27] signalized his reign, and transmitted his infamy to succeeding times. A capricious prodigality supplied the want of taste and elegance; and, whilst Elagabalus lavished away the treasures of his people in the wildest extravagance, his own voice and that of his flatterers applauded a spirit and magnificence unknown to the tameness of his predecessors. To confound the order of seasons and climates,[28] to sport with the passions and prejudices of his subjects, and to subvert every law of nature and decency, were in the number of his most delicious amusements. A long train of concubines, and a rapid succession of wives, among whom was a Vestal virgin, ravished by force from her sacred asylum, were insufficient to satisfy the impotence of his passions. The master of the Roman world affected to copy the dress and manners of the female sex, preferred the distaff to the sceptre, and dishonoured the principal dignities of the empire by distribut-

---

[25] He broke into the sanctuary of Vesta, and carried away a statue, which he supposed to be the Palladium; but the Vestals boasted that, by a pious fraud, they had imposed a counterfeit image on the profane intruder.

[26] The subjects of the empire were obliged to make liberal presents to the new-married couple; and whatever they had promised during the life of Elagabalus was carefully exacted under the administration of Mamæa.

[27] The invention of a new sauce was liberally rewarded: but if it was not relished, the inventor was confined to eat of nothing else, till he had discovered another more agreeable to the Imperial palate.

[28] He never would eat sea-fish except at a great distance from the sea; he then would distribute vast quantities of the rarest sorts, brought at an immense expense, to the peasants of the inland country.

ing them among his numerous lovers; one of whom was publicly invested with the title and authority of the emperor's, or, as he more properly styled himself, of the empress's husband.[29]

It may seem probable the vices and follies of Elagabalus have been adorned by fancy and blackened by prejudice.[30] Yet, confining ourselves to the public scenes displayed before the Roman people, and attested by grave and contemporary historians, their inexpressible infamy surpasses that of any other age or country. The licence of an eastern monarch is secluded from the eye of curiosity by the inaccessible walls of the seraglio. The sentiments of honour and gallantry have introduced a refinement of pleasure, a regard for decency, and a respect for the public opinion, into the modern courts of Europe; but the corrupt and opulent nobles of Rome gratified every vice that could be collected from the mighty conflux of nations and manners. Secure of impunity, careless of censure, they lived without restraint in the patient and humble society of their slaves and parasites. The emperor, in his turn, viewing every rank of his subjects with the same contemptuous indifference, asserted without control his sovereign privilege of lust and luxury.

The most worthless of mankind are not afraid to condemn in others the same disorders which they allow in themselves; and can readily discover some nice difference of age, character, or station, to justify the partial distinction. The licentious soldiers, who had raised to the throne the dissolute son of Caracalla, blushed at their ignominious choice, and turned with disgust from that monster, to contemplate with pleasure the opening virtues of his cousin Alexander, the son of Mamæa. The crafty Mæsa, sensible that her grandson Elagabalus must inevitably destroy himself by his own vices, had provided another and surer support of her family. Embracing a favourable moment of fondness and devotion, she had persuaded the young emperor to adopt Alexander, and to invest him with the title of Cæsar, that his own divine occupations might be no longer interrupted by the care of the earth. In the second rank, that amiable prince soon acquired the affections of the public, and excited the tyrant's jealousy, who resolved to terminate the dangerous competition either by corrupting the manners, or by taking away the life, of his rival. His arts proved unsuccessful; his vain designs were constantly discovered by his own loquacious folly, and disappointed by those virtuous and faithful servants whom the prudence of Mamæa had placed about the person of her son. In a hasty sally of passion, Elagabalus resolved to execute by force what he had

[29] *Hierocles enjoyed that honour; but he would have been supplanted by one Zoticus, had he not contrived, by a potion, to enervate the powers of his rival, who, being found on trial unequal to his reputation, was driven with ignominy from the palace. A dancer was made præfect of the city, a charioteer præfect of the watch, a barber præfect of the provisions. These three ministers, with many inferior officers, were all recommended enormitate membrorum.*

[30] *Even the credulous compiler of his Life, in the Augustan History, is inclined to suspect that his vices may have been exaggerated.*

been unable to compass by fraud, and by a despotic sentence degraded his cousin from the rank and honours of Cæsar. The message was received in the senate with silence, and in the camp with fury. The Prætorian guards swore to protect Alexander, and to revenge the dishonoured majesty of the throne. The tears and promises of the trembling Elagabalus, who only begged them to spare his life, and to leave him in the possession of his beloved Hierocles, diverted their just indignation; and they contented themselves with empowering their præfects to watch over the safety of Alexander and the conduct of the emperor.

It was impossible that such a reconciliation should last, or that even the mean soul of Elagabalus could hold an empire on such humiliating terms of dependence. He soon attempted, by a dangerous experiment, to try the temper of the soldiers. The report of the death of Alexander, and the natural suspicion that he had been murdered, inflamed their passions into fury, and the tempest of the camp could only be appeased by the presence and authority of the popular youth. Provoked at this new instance of their affection for his cousin, and their contempt for his person, the emperor ventured to punish some of the leaders of the mutiny. His unseasonable severity proved instantly fatal to his minions, his mother, and himself. Elagabalus was massacred by the indignant Prætorians, his mutilated corpse dragged through the streets of the city, and thrown into the Tiber. His memory was branded with eternal infamy by the senate; the justice of whose decree has been ratified by posterity.[31]

In the room of Elagabalus, his cousin Alexander was raised to the throne by the Prætorian guards. His relation to the family of Severus, whose name he assumed, was the same as that of his predecessor; his virtue and his danger had already endeared him to the Romans, and the eager liberality of the senate conferred upon him, in one day, the various titles and powers of the Imperial dignity.[32] But, as Alexander was a modest and dutiful youth of only seventeen years of age, the reins of government were in the hands of two women, of his mother Mamæa, and of Mæsa, his grandmother. After the death of the latter, who survived but a short time the elevation of Alexander, Mamæa remained the sole regent of her son and of the empire.

In every age and country, the wiser, or at least the stronger, of the two sexes, has usurped the powers of the state, and confined the other to the cares and pleasures of domestic life. In hereditary mon-

[31] Elagabalus reigned three years, nine months, and four days, from his victory over Macrinus, and was killed March 10, 222. But what shall we reply to the medals, undoubtedly genuine, which reckon the fifth year of his tribunitian power? We shall reply, with the learned Valsecchi, that the usurpation of Macrinus was annihilated, and that the son of Caracalla dated his reign from his father's death.

[32] By this unusual precipitation, the senate meant to confound the hopes of pretenders, and prevent the factions of the armies.

archies, however, and especially in those of modern Europe, the gallant spirit of chivalry, and the law of succession, have accustomed us to allow a singular exception; and a woman is often acknowledged the absolute sovereign of a great kingdom, in which she would be deemed incapable of exercising the smallest employment, civil or military. But as the Roman emperors were still considered as the generals and magistrates of the republic, their wives and mothers, although distinguished by the name of Augusta, were never associated to their personal honours; and a female reign would have appeared an inexpiable prodigy in the eyes of those primitive Romans, who married without love, or loved without delicacy and respect.[33] The haughty Agrippina aspired, indeed, to share the honours of the empire, which she had conferred on her son; but her mad ambition, detested by every citizen who felt for the dignity of Rome, was disappointed by the artful firmness of Seneca and Burrhus. The good sense, or the indifference, of succeeding princes, restrained them from offending the prejudices of their subjects; and it was reserved for the profligate Elagabalus to disgrace the acts of the senate with the name of his mother Soæmias, who was placed by the side of the consuls, and subscribed, as a regular member, the decrees of the legislative assembly. Her more prudent sister, Mamæa, declined the useless and odious prerogative, and a solemn law was enacted, excluding women for ever from the senate, and devoting to the infernal gods the head of the wretch by whom this sanction should be violated. The substance, not the pageantry, of power was the object of Mamæa's manly ambition. She maintained an absolute and lasting empire over the mind of her son, and in his affection the mother could not brook a rival. Alexander, with her consent, married the daughter of a patrician; but his respect for his father-in-law, and love for the empress, were inconsistent with the tenderness or interest of Mamæa. The patrician was executed on the ready accusation of treason, and the wife of Alexander driven with ignominy from the palace, and banished into Africa.[34]

Notwithstanding this act of jealous cruelty, as well as some instances of avarice, with which Mamæa is charged, the general tenor of her administration was equally for the benefit of her son and of the empire. With the approbation of the senate, she chose sixteen of the wisest and most virtuous senators, as a perpetual council of state, before whom every public business of moment was debated and determined. The celebrated Ulpian, equally distinguished by

[33] *Metellus Numidicus, the censor, acknowledged to the Roman people, in a public oration, that, had kind Nature allowed us to exist without the help of woman, we should be delivered from a very troublesome companion; and he could recommend matrimony only as the sacrifice of private pleasure to public duty.*

[34] *Herodian represents the patrician as innocent. The Augustan History, on the authority of Dexippus, condemns him as guilty of a conspiracy against the life of Alexander. It is impossible to pronounce between them: but Dion is an irreproachable witness of the jealousy and cruelty of Mamæa towards the young empress, whose hard fate Alexander lamented, but durst not oppose.*

his knowledge of, and his respect for, the laws of Rome, was at their head; and the prudent firmness of this aristocracy restored order and authority to the government. As soon as they had purged the city from foreign superstition and luxury, the remains of the capricious tyranny of Elagabalus, they applied themselves to remove his worthless creatures from every department of public administration, and to supply their places with men of virtue and ability. Learning, and the love of justice, became the only recommendations for civil offices; valour, and the love of discipline, the only qualifications for military employments.[35]

[35] *The Augustan History insinuates that, when any law was to be passed, the council was assisted by a number of able lawyers and experienced senators, whose opinions were separately given and taken down in writing.*

But the most important care of Mamæa and her wise counsellors was to form the character of the young emperor, on whose personal qualities the happiness or misery of the Roman world must ultimately depend. The fortunate soil assisted, and even prevented, the hand of cultivation. An excellent understanding soon convinced Alexander of the advantages of virtue, the pleasure of knowledge, and the necessity of labour. A natural mildness and moderation of temper preserved him from the assaults of passion and the allurements of vice. His unalterable regard for his mother, and his esteem for the wise Ulpian, guarded his unexperienced youth from the poison of flattery.

The simple journal of his ordinary occupations exhibits a pleasing picture of an accomplished emperor, and, with some allowance for the difference of manners, might well deserve the imitation of modern princes. Alexander rose early; the first moments of the day were consecrated to private devotion, and his domestic chapel was filled with the images of those heroes who, by improving or reforming human life, had deserved the grateful reverence of posterity. But, as he deemed the service of mankind the most acceptable worship of the gods, the greatest part of his morning hours was employed in his council, where he discussed public affairs, and determined private causes, with a patience and discretion above his years. The dryness of business was relieved by the charms of literature; and a portion of time was always set apart for his favourite studies of poetry, history, and philosophy. The works of Virgil and Horace, the republics of Plato and Cicero, formed his taste, enlarged his understanding, and gave him the noblest ideas of man and government. The exercises of the body succeeded to those of the mind; and Alexander, who was tall, active, and robust, surpassed most of his equals in the gymnastic arts. Refreshed by the use of the bath and a slight dinner, he resumed, with new vigour, the business of the day, and, till the hour of supper, the principal meal of the Romans, he was attended by his secretaries, with whom he read and answered the multitude of letters, memorials, and petitions, that must have been addressed to the master of the greatest part of the world. His table was served with the most frugal simplicity; and, whenever he was at liberty to consult his own inclination, the company consisted of a few select friends, men of learning and virtue, amongst whom Ulpian was constantly invited. Their conversation was familiar and instructive; and the pauses were occasionally enlivened by the recital of some pleasing composition, which supplied the place of the dancers, comedians, and even gladiators, so frequently summoned to the tables of the rich and luxurious Romans. The dress of Alexander was plain and modest, his demeanour courteous and affable: at the proper hours his palace was open to all his subjects, but the voice of a crier was heard, as in the Eleusinian mysteries, pronouncing the same salutary admonition: "Let none enter these holy walls, unless he is conscious of a pure and innocent mind."

Such an uniform tenor of life, which left not a moment for vice or folly, is a better proof of the wisdom and justice of Alexander's government than all the trifling details preserved in the compilation of Lampridius. Since the accession of Commodus the Roman world had experienced, during a term of forty years, the successive and various vices of four tyrants. From the death of Elagabalus it enjoyed an auspicious calm of thirteen years. The provinces, relieved from the oppressive taxes invented by Caracalla and his pretended son, flourished in peace and prosperity under the administration of magistrates, who were convinced by experience that to deserve the love of the subjects was their best and only method of obtaining the favour of their sovereign. While some gentle restraints were imposed on the innocent luxury of the Roman people, the price of provisions and the interest of money were reduced by the paternal care of Alexander, whose prudent liberality, without distressing the industrious, supplied the wants and amusements of the populace. The dignity, the freedom, the authority of the senate was restored; and every virtuous senator might approach the person of the emperor without a fear and without a blush.

The name of Antoninus, ennobled by the virtues of Pius and Marcus, had been communicated by adoption to the dissolute Verus, and by descent to the cruel Commodus. It became the honourable appellation of the sons of Severus, was bestowed on young

Diadumenianus, and at length prostituted to the infamy of the high priest of Emesa. Alexander, though pressed by the studied, and perhaps sincere, importunity of the senate, nobly refused the borrowed lustre of a name; whilst in his whole conduct he laboured to restore the glories and felicity of the age of the genuine Antonines.[36]

In the civil administration of Alexander, wisdom was enforced by power, and the people, sensible of the public felicity, repaid their benefactor with their love and gratitude. There still remained a greater, a more necessary, but a more difficult enterprise: the reformation of the military order, whose interest and temper, confirmed by long impunity, rendered them impatient of the restraints of discipline, and careless of the blessings of public tranquillity. In the execution of his design the emperor affected to display his love, and to conceal his fear, of the army. The most rigid economy in every other branch of the administration supplied a fund of gold and silver for the ordinary pay and the extraordinary rewards of the troops. In their marches he relaxed the severe obligation of carrying seventeen days' provision on their shoulders. Ample magazines were formed along the public roads, and as soon as they entered the enemy's country, a numerous train of mules and camels waited on their haughty laziness. As Alexander despaired of correcting the luxury of his soldiers, he attempted, at least, to direct it to objects of martial pomp and ornament, fine horses, splendid armour, and shields enriched with silver and gold. He shared whatever fatigues he was obliged to impose, visited, in person, the sick and wounded, preserved an exact register of their services and his own gratitude, and expressed, on every occasion, the warmest regard for a body of men, whose welfare, as he affected to declare, was so closely connected with that of the state.[37] By the most gentle arts he laboured to inspire the fierce multitude with a sense of duty, and to restore at least a faint image of that discipline to which the Romans owed their empire over so many other nations, as warlike and more powerful than themselves. But his prudence was vain, his courage fatal, and the attempt towards a reformation served only to inflame the ills it was meant to cure.

The Prætorian guards were attached to the youth of Alexander. They loved him as a tender pupil, whom they had saved from a tyrant's fury, and placed on the Imperial throne. That amiable prince was sensible of the obligation; but, as his gratitude was restrained within the limits of reason and justice, they soon were more dissatisfied with the virtues of Alexander than they had ever

[36] See in the Hist. August. the whole contest between Alexander and the senate, extracted from the journals of that assembly. It happened on the sixth of March, probably of the year 223, when the Romans had enjoyed, almost a twelvemonth, the blessings of his reign. Before the appellation of Antoninus was offered him as a title of honour, the senate waited to see whether Alexander would not assume it as a family name.

[37] It was a favourite saying of the emperor's, Se milites magis servare, quam seipsum; quod salus publica in his esset.

been with the vices of Elagabalus. Their præfect, the wise Ulpian, was the friend of the laws and of the people; he was considered as the enemy of the soldiers, and to his pernicious counsels every scheme of reformation was imputed. Some trifling accident blew up their discontent into a furious mutiny; and a civil war raged, during three days, in Rome, whilst the life of that excellent minister was defended by the grateful people. Terrified, at length, by the sight of some houses in flames, and by the threats of a general conflagration, the people yielded with a sigh, and left the virtuous but unfortunate Ulpian to his fate. He was pursued into the Imperial palace, and massacred at the feet of his master, who vainly strove to cover him with the purple, and to obtain his pardon from the inexorable soldiers. Such was the deplorable weakness of government that the emperor was unable to revenge his murdered friend and his insulted dignity, without stooping to the arts of patience and dissimulation. Epagathus, the principal leader of the mutiny, was removed from Rome, by the honourable employment of præfect of Egypt; from that high rank he was gently degraded to the government of Crete; and when, at length, his popularity among the guards was effaced by time and absence, Alexander ventured to inflict the tardy, but deserved, punishment of his crimes. Under the reign of a just and virtuous prince, the tyranny of the army threatened with instant death his most faithful ministers, who were suspected of an intention to correct their intolerable disorders. The historian Dion Cassius had commanded the Pannonian legions with the spirit of ancient discipline. Their brethren of Rome, embracing the common cause of military licence, demanded the head of the reformer. Alexander, however, instead of yielding to their seditious clamours, showed a just sense of his merit and services, by appointing him his colleague in the consulship, and defraying from his own treasury the expense of that vain dignity; but, as it was justly apprehended that if the soldiers beheld him with the ensigns of his office they would revenge the insult in his blood, the nominal first magistrate of the states retired, by the emperor's advice, from the city, and spent the greatest part of his consulship at his villas in Campania.

The lenity of the emperor confirmed the insolence of the troops; the legions imitated the example of the guards, and defended their prerogative of licentiousness with the same furious obstinacy. The administration of Alexander was an unavailing struggle against the corruption of his age. In Illyricum, in Mauritania, in Armenia, in

Mesopotamia, in Germany, fresh mutinies perpetually broke out; his officers were murdered, his authority was insulted, and his life at last sacrificed to the fierce discontents of the army. One particular fact well deserves to be recorded, as it illustrates the manners of the troops, and exhibits a singular instance of their return to a sense of duty and obedience. Whilst the emperor lay at Antioch, in his Persian expedition, the particulars of which we shall hereafter relate, the punishment of some soldiers, who had been discovered in the baths of women, excited a sedition in the legion to which they belonged. Alexander ascended his tribunal, and with a modest firmness represented to the armed multitude the absolute necessity, as well as his inflexible resolution, of correcting the vices introduced by his impure predecessor, and of maintaining the discipline, which could not be relaxed without the ruin of the Roman name and empire. Their clamours interrupted his mild expostulation. "Reserve your shouts," said the undaunted emperor, "till you take the field against the Persians, the Germans, and the Sarmatians. Be silent in the presence of your sovereign and benefactor, who bestows upon you the corn, the clothing, and the money of the provinces. Be silent, or I shall no longer style you soldiers, but *citizens*,[38] if those indeed who disclaim the laws of Rome deserve to be ranked among the meanest of the people." His menaces inflamed the fury of the legion, and their brandished arms already threatened his person. "Your courage," resumed the intrepid Alexander, "would be more nobly displayed in the field of battle; *me* you may destroy, you cannot intimidate; and the severe justice of the republic would punish your crime and revenge my death." The legion still persisted in clamorous sedition, when the emperor pronounced, with a loud voice, the decisive sentence, "Citizens! lay down your arms, and depart in peace to your respective habitations." The tempest was instantly appeased; the soldiers, filled with grief and shame, silently confessed the justice of their punishment and the power of discipline, yielded up their arms and military ensigns, and retired in confusion, not to their camp, but to the several inns of the city. Alexander enjoyed, during thirty days, the edifying spectacle of their repentance; nor did he restore them to their former rank in the army, till he had punished with death those tribunes whose connivance had occasioned the mutiny. The grateful legion served the emperor whilst living, and revenged him when dead.

The resolutions of the multitude generally depend on a moment; and the caprice of passion might equally determine the seditious

[38] *Julius Cæsar had appeased a sedition with the same word,* Quirites: *which, thus opposed to* Soldiers, *was used in a sense of contempt, and reduced the offenders to the less honourable condition of mere citizens.*

legion to lay down their arms at the emperor's feet, or to plunge them into his breast. Perhaps, if the singular transaction had been investigated by the penetration of a philosopher, we should discover the secret causes which on that occasion authorized the boldness of the prince and commanded the obedience of the troops; and perhaps, if it had been related by a judicious historian, we should find this action, worthy of Cæsar himself, reduced nearer to the level of probability and the common standard of the character of Alexander Severus. The abilities of that amiable prince seem to have been inadequate to the difficulties of his situation, the firmness of his conduct inferior to the purity of his intentions. His virtues, as well as the vices of Elagabalus, contracted a tincture of weakness and effeminacy from the soft climate of Syria, of which he was a native; though he blushed at his foreign origin, and listened with a vain complacency to the flattering genealogists, who derived his race from the ancient stock of Roman nobility.[39] The pride and avarice of his mother cast a shade on the glories of his reign; and by exacting from his riper years the same dutiful obedience which she had justly claimed from his unexperienced youth, Mamæa exposed to public ridicule both her son's character and her own. The fatigues of the Persian war irritated the military discontent; the unsuccessful event degraded the reputation of the emperor as a general, and even as a soldier. Every cause prepared, and every circumstance hastened, a revolution, which distracted the Roman empire with a long series of intestine calamities.

[39] *From the Metelli. The choice was judicious. In one short period of twelve years, the Metelli could reckon seven consulships, and five triumphs.*

The dissolute tyranny of Commodus, the civil wars occasioned by his death, and the new maxims of policy introduced by the house of Severus, had all contributed to increase the dangerous power of the army, and to obliterate the faint image of laws and liberty that was still impressed on the minds of the Romans. This internal change, which undermined the foundations of the empire, we have endeavoured to explain with some degree of order and perspicuity. The personal characters of the emperors, their victories, laws, follies and fortunes, can interest us no further than as they are connected with the general history of the Decline and Fall of the monarchy. Our constant attention to that great object will not suffer us to overlook a most important edict of Antoninus Caracalla, which communicated to all the free inhabitants of the empire the name and privileges of Roman citizens. His unbounded liberality flowed not, however, from the sentiments of a generous mind; it was the sordid result of avarice, and will naturally be illustrated by some observations on the finances of that state, from the victorious ages of the commonwealth to the reign of Alexander Severus.

The siege of Veii in Tuscany, the first considerable enterprise of the Romans, was protracted to the tenth year, much less by the strength of the place than by the unskilfulness of the besiegers. The unaccustomed hardships of so many winter campaigns, at the distance of near twenty miles from home,[40] required more than common encouragements; and the senate wisely prevented the clamours of the people, by the institution of a regular pay for the soldiers, which was levied by a general tribute, assessed according to an equitable proportion on the property of the citizens.[41] During more than two hundred years after the conquest of Veii, the victories of the republic added less to the wealth than to the power of Rome. The states of Italy paid their tribute in military service only, and the vast force, both by sea and land, which was exerted in the Punic wars, was maintained at the expense of the Romans themselves. That high-spirited people (such is often the generous enthusiasm of freedom) cheerfully submitted to the most excessive but voluntary burdens, in the just confidence that they should speedily enjoy the rich harvest of their labours. Their expectations were not disappointed. In the course of a few years, the riches of Syracuse, of Carthage, of Macedonia, and of Asia, were brought in triumph to Rome. The treasures of Perseus alone amounted to near two millions sterling, and the Roman people, the sovereign of so many nations, was for ever delivered from the weight of taxes. The increasing revenue of the provinces was found sufficient to defray the ordinary establishment of war and government, and the superfluous mass of gold and silver was deposited in the temple of Saturn, and reserved for any unforeseen emergency of the state.

History has never perhaps suffered a greater or more irreparable injury than in the loss of that curious register bequeathed by Augustus to the senate, in which that experienced prince so accurately balanced the revenues and expenses of the Roman empire.[42] Deprived of this clear and comprehensive estimate, we are reduced to collect a few imperfect hints from such of the ancients as have accidently turned aside from the splendid to the more useful parts of history. We are informed that, by the conquests of Pompey, the tributes of Asia were raised from fifty to one hundred and thirty-five millions of drachms, or about four millions and a half sterling. Under the last and most indolent of the Ptolemies, the revenue of Egypt is said to have amounted to twelve thousand five hundred talents; a

[40] According to the more accurate Dionysius, the city itself was only an hundred stadia, or twelve miles and a half from Rome; though some outposts might be advanced farther on the side of Etruria. Nardini, in a professed treatise, has combated the popular opinion and the authority of two popes, and has removed Veii from Civitá Castellana, to a little spot called Isola, in the midway between Rome and the lake Bracciano.

[41] In the Roman census, property, power, and taxation, were commensurate with each other.

[42] It seems to have existed in the time of Appian.

sum equivalent to more than two millions and a half of our money, but which was afterwards considerably improved by the more exact economy of the Romans, and the increase of the trade of Æthiopia and India. Gaul was enriched by rapine, as Egypt was by commerce, and the tributes of those two great provinces have been compared as nearly equal to each other in value. The ten thousand Euboic or Phœnician talents, about four millions sterling,[43] which vanquished Carthage was condemned to pay within the term of fifty years, were a slight acknowledgment of the superiority of Rome, and cannot bear the least proportion with the taxes afterwards raised both on the lands and on the persons of the inhabitants, when the fertile coast of Africa was reduced into a province.

Spain, by a very singular fatality, was the Peru and Mexico of the old world. The discovery of the rich western continent by the Phœnicians, and the oppression of the simple natives, who were compelled to labour in their own mines for the benefit of strangers, form an exact type of the more recent history of Spanish America.[44] The Phœnicians were acquainted only with the sea-coast of Spain; avarice as well as ambition carried the arms of Rome and Carthage into the heart of the country, and almost every part of the soil was found pregnant with copper, silver, and gold. Mention is made of a mine near Carthagena which yielded every day twenty-five thousand drachms of silver, or about three hundred thousand pounds a year. Twenty thousand pounds weight of gold was annually received from the provinces of Asturia, Gallicia, and Lusitania.[45]

We want both leisure and materials to pursue this curious inquiry through the many potent states that were annihilated in the Roman empire. Some notion, however, may be formed of the revenue of the provinces where considerable wealth had been deposited by nature, or collected by man, if we observe the severe attention that was directed to the abodes of solitude and sterility. Augustus once received a petition from the inhabitants of Gyarus, humbly praying that they might be relieved from one third of their excessive impositions. Their whole tax amounted indeed to no more than one hundred and fifty drachms, or about five pounds; but Gyarus was a little island, or rather a rock, of the Ægean Sea, destitute of fresh water and every necessary of life, and inhabited only by a few wretched fishermen.

From the faint glimmerings of such doubtful and scattered lights, we should be inclined to believe, 1st, That (with every fair allowance for the difference of times and circumstances) the general in-

[43] *The Euboic, the Phœnician, and Alexandrian talents, were double in weight to the Attic. It is very probable that the same talent was carried from Tyre to Carthage.*

[44] *Cadiz was built by the Phœnicians a little more than a thousand years before Christ.*

[45] *Pliny mentions likewise a silver mine in Dalmatia, that yielded every day fifty pounds to the state.*

come of the Roman provinces could seldom amount to less than fifteen or twenty millions of our money;⁴⁶ and, 2ndly, That so ample a revenue must have been fully adequate to all the expenses of the moderate government instituted by Augustus, whose court was the modest family of a private senator, and whose military establishment was calculated for the defence of the frontiers, without any aspiring views of conquest, or any serious apprehension of a foreign invasion.

Notwithstanding the seeming probability of both these conclusions, the latter of them at least is positively disowned by the language and conduct of Augustus. It is not easy to determine whether, on this occasion, he acted as the common father of the Roman world, or as the oppressor of liberty; whether he wished to relieve the provinces, or to impoverish the senate and the equestrian order. But no sooner had he assumed the reins of government than he frequently intimated the insufficiency of the tributes, and the necessity of throwing an equitable proportion of the public burden upon Rome and Italy. In the prosecution of this unpopular design, he advanced, however, by cautious and well-weighed steps. The introduction of customs was followed by the establishment of an excise, and the scheme of taxation was completed by an artful assessment on the real and personal property of the Roman citizens, who had been exempted from any kind of contribution above a century and a half.

I. In a great empire like that of Rome, a natural balance of money must have gradually established itself. It has been already observed that, as the wealth of the provinces was attracted to the capital by the strong hand of conquest and power, so a considerable part of it was restored to the industrious provinces by the gentle influence of commerce and arts. In the reign of Augustus and his successors, duties were imposed on every kind of merchandise, which through a thousand channels flowed to the great centre of opulence and luxury; and in whatsoever manner the law was expressed, it was the Roman purchaser, and not the provincial merchant, who paid the tax. The rate of the customs varied from the eighth to the fortieth part of the value of the commodity; and we have a right to suppose that the variation was directed by the unalterable maxims of policy: that a higher duty was fixed on the articles of luxury than on those of necessity, and that the productions raised or manufactured by the labour of the subjects of the empire were treated with more indulgence than was shown to the pernicious, or at least the unpopular, commerce of Arabia and India.[47] There is still extant a long but imperfect catalogue of eastern commodities, which about the time of Alexander Severus were subject to the payment of duties: cinnamon, myrrh, pepper, ginger, and the whole tribe of aromatics; a great variety of precious stones, among which the diamond was the most remarkable for its price, and the emerald for its beauty:[48] Parthian and Babylonian leather, cottons, silks, both raw and manufactured, ebony, ivory, and eunuchs. We may observe that the use and value of those effeminate slaves gradually rose with the decline of the empire.

II. The excise, introduced by Augustus after the civil wars, was extremely moderate, but it was general. It seldom exceeded one *per cent.;* but it comprehended whatever was sold in the markets or by public auction, from the most considerable purchases of land and houses to those minute objects which can only derive a value from their infinite multitude and daily consumption. Such a tax, as it affects the body of the people, has ever been the occasion of clamour and discontent. An emperor well acquainted with the wants and resources of the state was obliged to declare, by a public edict, that the support of the army depended in a great measure on the produce of the excise.[49]

III. When Augustus resolved to establish a permanent military force for the defence of his government against foreign and domestic enemies, he instituted a peculiar treasury for the pay of the soldiers, the rewards of the veterans, and the extraordinary expenses of war. The ample revenue of the excise, though peculiarly appropriated to those uses, was found inadequate. To supply the deficiency, the emperor suggested a new tax of five *per cent.* on all legacies and inheritances. But the nobles of Rome were more tenacious of property than of freedom. Their indignant murmurs were received by Augustus with his usual temper. He candidly referred the whole business to the senate, and exhorted them to provide for the public service by some other expedient of a less odious nature. They were divided and perplexed. He insinuated to them that their obstinacy would oblige him to *propose* a general land-tax and capitation. They acquiesced in silence. The new imposition on legacies and inheritances was however mitigated by some restrictions. It did not take place unless the object was of a certain value, most probably of fifty or an hundred pieces of gold:[50] nor could it be exacted from the nearest of kin on the father's side.[51] When the rights of nature and property were thus secured, it seemed reasonable

[47] *Pliny's observation that the Indian commodities were sold at Rome at a hundred times their original price, may give us some notion of the produce of the customs, since that original price amounted to more than eight hundred thousand pounds.*

[48] *The ancients were unacquainted with the art of cutting diamonds.*

[49] *Two years afterwards, the reduction of the poor kingdom of Cappadocia gave Tiberius a pretence for diminishing the excise to one half; but the relief was of a very short duration.*

[50] *The sum is only fixed by conjecture.*

[51] *As the Roman law subsisted for many ages, the Cognati, or relations on the mother's side, were not called to the succession. This harsh institution was gradually undermined by humanity, and finally abolished by Justinian.*

that a stranger, or a distant relation, who acquired an unexpected accession of fortune, should cheerfully resign a twentieth part of it for the benefit of the state.

Such a tax, plentiful as it must prove in every wealthy community, was most happily suited to the situation of the Romans, who could frame their arbitrary wills, according to the dictates of reason or caprice, without any restraint from the modern fetters of entails and settlements. From various causes, the partiality of paternal affection often lost its influence over the stern patriots of the commonwealth and the dissolute nobles of the empire; and if the father bequeathed to his son the fourth part of his estate, he removed all ground of legal complaint. But a rich childless old man was a domestic tyrant, and his power increased with his years and infirmities. A servile crowd, in which he frequently reckoned prætors and consuls, courted his smiles, pampered his avarice, applauded his follies, served his passions, and waited with impatience for his death. The arts of attendance and flattery were formed into a most lucrative science; those who professed it acquired a peculiar appellation; and the whole city, according to the lively descriptions of satire, was divided between two parties, the hunters and their game. Yet while so many unjust and extravagant wills were every day dictated by cunning, and subscribed by folly, a few were the result of rational esteem and virtuous gratitude. Cicero, who had so often defended the lives and fortunes of his fellow-citizens, was rewarded with legacies to the amount of an hundred and seventy thousand pounds; nor do the friends of the younger Pliny seem to have been less generous to that amiable orator.[52] Whatever was the motive of the testator, the treasury claimed, without distinction, the twentieth part of his estate; and in the course of two or three generations, the whole property of the subject must have gradually passed through the coffers of the state.

In the first and golden years of the reign of Nero, that prince, from a desire of popularity, and perhaps from a blind impulse of benevolence, conceived a wish of abolishing the oppression of the customs and excise. The wisest senators applauded his magnanimity: but they diverted him from the execution of a design which would have dissolved the strength and resources of the republic. Had it indeed been possible to realize this dream of fancy, such princes as Trajan and the Antonines would surely have embraced with ardour the glorious opportunity of conferring so signal an obligation on mankind. Satisfied, however, with alleviating the

[52] *See his epistles. Every such will gave him an occasion of displaying his reverence to the dead, and his justice to the living. He reconciled both, in his behaviour to a son who had been disinherited by his mother.*

public burden, they attempted not to remove it. The mildness and precision of their laws ascertained the rule and measure of taxation, and protected the subject of every rank against arbitrary interpretations, antiquated claims, and the insolent vexation of the farmers of the revenue. For it is somewhat singular that, in every age, the best and wisest of the Roman governors persevered in this pernicious method of collecting the principal branches at least of the excise and customs.[53]

The sentiments, and indeed the situation, of Caracalla were very different from those of the Antonines. Inattentive, or rather averse, to the welfare of his people, he found himself under the necessity of gratifying the insatiate avarice which he had excited in the army. Of the several impositions introduced by Augustus, the twentieth on inheritances and legacies was the most fruitful as well as the most comprehensive. As its influence was not confined to Rome or Italy, the produce continually increased with the gradual extension of the ROMAN CITY. The new citizens, though charged on equal terms [54] with the payment of new taxes which had not affected them as subjects, derived an ample compensation from the rank they obtained, the privileges they acquired, and the fair prospect of honours and fortune that was thrown open to their ambition. But the favour which implied a distinction was lost in the prodigality of Caracalla, and the reluctant provincials were compelled to assume the vain title and the real obligations of Roman citizens. Nor was the rapacious son of Severus contented with such a measure of taxation as had appeared sufficient to his moderate predecessors. Instead of a twentieth, he exacted a tenth of all legacies and inheritances; and during his reign (for the ancient proportion was restored after his death) he crushed alike every part of the empire under the weight of his iron sceptre.

When all the provincials became liable to the peculiar impositions of Roman citizens, they seemed to acquire a legal exemption from the tributes which they had paid in their former condition of subjects. Such were not the maxims of government adopted by Caracalla and his pretended son. The old as well as the new taxes were, at the same time, levied in the provinces. It was reserved for the virtue of Alexander to relieve them in a great measure from this intolerable grievance, by reducing the tributes to a thirtieth part of the sum exacted at the time of his accession.[55] It is impossible to conjecture the motive that engaged him to spare so trifling a remnant of the public evil; but the noxious weed, which had not been

[53] *The tributes (properly so called) were not farmed; since the good princes often remitted many millions of arrears.*

[54] *The situation of the new citizens is minutely described by Pliny. Trajan published a law very much in their favour.*

[55] *He who paid ten* aurei, *the usual tribute, was charged with no more than the third part of an* aureus, *and proportional pieces of gold were coined by Alexander's order.*

totally eradicated, again sprang up with the most luxuriant growth, and in the succeeding age darkened the Roman world with its deadly shade. In the course of this history, we shall be too often summoned to explain the land-tax, the capitation, and the heavy contributions of corn, wine, oil, and meat, which were exacted from the provinces for the use of the court, the army, and the capital.

As long as Rome and Italy were respected as the centre of government, a national spirit was preserved by the ancient, and insensibly imbibed by the adopted, citizens. The principal commands of the army were filled by men who had received a liberal education, were well instructed in the advantages of laws and letters, and who had risen by equal steps through the regular succession of civil and military honours. To their influence and example we may partly ascribe the modest obedience of the legions during the two first centuries of the Imperial history.

But when the last enclosure of the Roman constitution was trampled down by Caracalla, the separation of possessions gradually succeeded to the distinction of ranks. The more polished citizens of the internal provinces were alone qualified to act as lawyers and magistrates. The rougher trade of arms was abandoned to the peasants and barbarians of the frontiers, who knew no country but their camp, no science but that of war, no civil laws, and scarcely those of military discipline. With bloody hands, savage manners, and desperate resolutions, they sometimes guarded, but much oftener subverted, the throne of the emperors.

VII

THE ELEVATION, AND TYRANNY, OF MAXIMIN · REBELLION
IN AFRICA AND ITALY, UNDER THE AUTHORITY OF THE
SENATE · CIVIL WARS AND SEDITIONS · VIOLENT DEATHS OF
MAXIMIN AND HIS SON, OF MAXIMUS AND BALBINUS, AND
THE THREE GORDIANS · USURPATION AND GAMES OF PHILIP

O F T H E various forms of government which have prevailed in the world, an hereditary monarchy presents the fairest scope for ridicule. Is it possible to relate without an indignant smile, that, on the father's decease, the property of a nation, like that of a drove of oxen, descends to his infant son, as yet unknown to mankind and to himself, and that the bravest warriors and the wisest statesmen, relinquishing their natural right to empire, approach the royal cradle with bended knees and protestations of inviolable fidelity? Satire and declamation may paint these obvious topics in the most dazzling colours, but our more serious thoughts will respect a useful prejudice, that establishes a rule of succession, independent of the passions of mankind; and we shall cheerfully acquiesce in any expedient which deprives the multitude of the dangerous, and indeed the ideal, power of giving themselves a master.

In the cool shade of retirement, we may easily devise imaginary forms of government, in which the sceptre shall be constantly bestowed on the most worthy by the free and incorrupt suffrage of the whole community. Experience overturns these airy fabrics, and teaches us that in a large society the election of a monarch can never devolve to the wisest or to the most numerous part of the people. The army is the only order of men sufficiently united to concur in the same sentiments, and powerful enough to impose them on the rest of their fellow-citizens; but the temper of soldiers, habituated at once to violence and to slavery, renders them very unfit guardians of a legal or even a civil constitution. Justice, humanity, or political wisdom, are qualities they are too little acquainted with in themselves to appreciate them in others. Valour will acquire their esteem, and liberality will purchase their suffrage; but the first of these merits is often lodged in the most savage breasts; the latter can only exert itself at the expense of the public; and both may be turned against the possessor of the throne by the ambition of a rival.

The superior prerogative of birth, when it has obtained the sanction of time and popular opinion, is the plainest and least invidious of all distinctions among mankind. The acknowledged right extinguishes the hopes of faction, and the conscious security disarms the cruelty of the monarch. To the firm establishment of this idea we owe the peaceful succession and mild administration of European monarchies. To the defect of it we must attribute the frequent civil wars, through which an Asiatic despot is obliged to cut his way to the throne of his fathers. Yet, even in the East, the sphere of contention is usually limited to the princes of the reigning house, and, as soon as the more fortunate competitor has removed his brethren, by the sword and the bow-string, he no longer entertains any jealousy of his meaner subjects. But the Roman empire, after the authority of the senate had sunk into contempt, was a vast scene of confusion. The royal, and even noble, families of the provinces had long since been led in triumph before the car of the haughty republicans. The ancient families of Rome had successively fallen beneath the tyranny of the Cæsars; and, whilst those princes were shackled by the forms of a commonwealth, and disappointed by the repeated failure of their posterity,[1] it was impossible that any idea of hereditary succession should have taken root in the minds of their subjects. The right to the throne, which none could claim from birth, every one assumed from merit. The daring hopes of ambition were set loose from the salutary restraints of law and prejudice, and the meanest of mankind might, without folly, entertain a hope of being raised by valour and fortune to a rank in the army, in which a single crime would enable him to wrest the sceptre of the world from his feeble and unpopular master. After the murder of Alexander Severus and the elevation of Maximin, no emperor could think himself safe upon the throne, and every barbarian peasant of the frontier might aspire to that august but dangerous station.

About thirty-two years before that event, the emperor Severus, returning from an Eastern expedition, halted in Thrace, to celebrate, with military games, the birthday of his younger son, Geta. The country flocked in crowds to behold their sovereign, and a

[1] *There had been no example of three successive generations on the throne; only three instances of sons who succeeded their fathers. The marriages of Cæsars (notwithstanding the permission, and the frequent practice, of divorces) were generally unfruitful.*

young barbarian of gigantic stature earnestly solicited, in his rude dialect, that he might be allowed to contend for the prize of wrestling. As the pride of discipline would have been disgraced in the overthrow of a Roman soldier by a Thracian peasant, he was matched with the stoutest followers of the camp, sixteen of whom he successively laid on the ground. His victory was rewarded by some trifling gifts, and a permission to enlist in the troops. The next day the happy barbarian was distinguished above a crowd of recruits, dancing and exulting after the fashion of his country. As soon as he perceived that he had attracted the emperor's notice, he instantly ran up to his horse, and followed him on foot, without the least appearance of fatigue, in a long and rapid career. "Thracian," said Severus, with astonishment, "art thou disposed to wrestle after thy race?" "Most willingly, Sir," replied the unwearied youth, and, almost in a breath, overthrew seven of the strongest soldiers in the army. A gold collar was the prize of his matchless vigour and activity, and he was immediately appointed to serve in the horse-guards who always attended on the person of the sovereign.

Maximin, for that was his name, though born on the territories of the empire, descended from a mixed race of barbarians. His father was a Goth, and his mother of the nation of the Alani. He displayed on every occasion a valour equal to his strength; and his native fierceness was soon tempered or disguised by the knowledge of the world. Under the reign of Severus and his son, he obtained the rank of centurion, with the favour and esteem of both those princes, the former of whom was an excellent judge of merit. Gratitude forbade Maximin to serve under the assassin of Caracalla. Honour taught him to decline the effeminate insults of Elagabalus. On the accession of Alexander he returned to court, and was placed by that prince in a station useful to the service and honourable to himself. The fourth legion, to which he was appointed tribune, soon became, under his care, the best disciplined of the whole army. With the general applause of the soldiers, who bestowed on their favourite hero the names of Ajax and Hercules, he was successively promoted to the first military command,[2] and had not he still retained too much of his savage origin, the emperor might perhaps have given his own sister in marriage to the son of Maximin.

Instead of securing his fidelity, these favours served only to inflame the ambition of the Thracian peasant, who deemed his fortune inadequate to his merit as long as he was constrained to acknowledge a superior. Though a stranger to real wisdom, he

[2] *It should seem that Maximin had the particular command of the Triballian horse, with the general commission of disciplining the recruits of the whole army. His biographer ought to have marked, with more care, his exploits, and the successive steps of his military promotions.*

was not devoid of a selfish cunning, which showed him that the emperor had lost the affection of the army, and taught him to improve their discontent to his own advantage. It is easy for faction and calumny to shed their poison on the administration of the best of princes, and to accuse even their virtues by artfully confounding them with those vices to which they bear the nearest affinity. The troops listened with pleasure to the emissaries of Maximin. They blushed at their own ignominious patience, which, during thirteen years, had supported the vexatious discipline imposed by an effeminate Syrian, the timid slave of his mother and of the senate. It was time, they cried, to cast away that useless phantom of the civil power, and to elect for their prince and general a real soldier, educated in camps, exercised in war, who would assert the glory and distribute among his companions the treasures of the empire. A great army was at that time assembled on the banks of the Rhine, under the command of the emperor himself, who, almost immediately after his return from the Persian war, had been obliged to march against the barbarians of Germany. The important care of training and reviewing the new levies was intrusted to Maximin. One day, as he entered the field of exercise, the troops either from a sudden impulse or a formed conspiracy, saluted him emperor, silenced by their loud acclamations his obstinate refusal, and hastened to consummate their rebellion by the murder of Alexander Severus.

The circumstances of his death are variously related. The writers who suppose that he died in ignorance of the ingratitude and ambition of Maximin affirm that, after taking a frugal repast in the sight of the army, he retired to sleep, and that about the seventh hour of the day a party of his own guards broke into the Imperial tent, and, with many wounds, assassinated their virtuous and unsuspecting prince.[3] If we credit another, and indeed a more probable, account, Maximin was invested with the purple by a numerous detachment, at the distance of several miles from the headquarters, and he trusted for success rather to the secret wishes than to the public declarations of the great army. Alexander had sufficient time to awaken a faint sense of loyalty among his troops; but their reluctant professions of fidelity quickly vanished on the appearance of Maximin, who declared himself the friend and advocate of the military order, and was unanimously acknowledged emperor of the Romans by the applauding legions. The son of Mamæa, betrayed and deserted, withdrew into his tent, desirous at least to con-

[3] I have softened some of the most improbable circumstances of the wretched biographer. From his ill-worded narration, it should seem that, the prince's buffoon having accidentally entered the tent, and awakened the slumbering monarch, the fear of punishment urged him to persuade the disaffected soldiers to commit the murder.

ceal his approaching fate from the insults of the multitude. He was soon followed by a tribune and some centurions, the ministers of death; but instead of receiving with manly resolution the inevitable stroke, his unavailing cries and entreaties disgraced the last moments of his life, and converted into contempt some portion of the just pity which his innocence and misfortunes must inspire. His mother, Mamæa, whose pride and avarice he loudly accused as the cause of his ruin, perished with her son. The most faithful of his friends were sacrificed to the first fury of the soldiers. Others were reserved for the more deliberate cruelty of the usurper, and those who experienced mildest treatment were stripped of their employments and ignominiously driven from the court and army.

The former tyrants Caligula and Nero, Commodus and Caracalla, were all dissolute and unexperienced youths,[4] educated in the purple, and corrupted by the pride of empire, the luxury of Rome, and the perfidious voice of flattery. The cruelty of Maximin was derived from a different source, the fear of contempt. Though he depended on the attachment of the soldiers, who loved him for virtues like their own, he was conscious that his mean and barbarian origin, his savage appearance, and his total ignorance of the arts and institutions of civil life,[5] formed a very unfavourable contrast with the amiable manners of the unhappy Alexander. He remembered that, in his humbler fortune, he had often waited before the doors of the haughty nobles of Rome, and had been denied admittance by the insolence of their slaves. He recollected too the friendship of a few who had relieved his poverty, and assisted his rising hopes. But those who had spurned, and those who had protected, the Thracian, were guilty of the same crime, the knowledge of his original obscurity. For this crime many were put to death; and by the execution of his benefactors Maximin published, in characters of blood, the indelible history of his base ingratitude.[6]

The dark and sanguinary soul of the tyrant was open to every suspicion against those among his subjects who were the most distinguished by their birth or merit. Whenever he was alarmed with the sound of treason, his cruelty was unbounded and unrelenting. A conspiracy against his life was either discovered or imagined, and Magnus, a consular senator, was named as the principal author of it. Without a witness, without a trial, and without an opportunity of defence, Magnus, with four thousand of his supposed accomplices, were put to death. Italy and the whole empire were infested with innumerable spies and informers. On the slightest accusation,

[4] *Caligula, the eldest of the four, was only twenty-five years of age when he ascended the throne; Caracalla was twenty-three, Commodus nineteen, and Nero no more than seventeen.*

[5] *It appears that he was totally ignorant of the Greek language; which, from its universal use in conversation and letters, was an essential part of every liberal education.*

[6] *Herodian has been most unjustly censured for sparing the vices of Maximin.*

the first of the Roman nobles, who had governed provinces, commanded armies, and been adorned with the consular and triumphal ornaments, were chained on the public carriages, and hurried away to the emperor's presence. Confiscation, exile, or simple death, were esteemed uncommon instances of his lenity. Some of the unfortunate sufferers he ordered to be sewed up in the hides of slaughtered animals, others to be exposed to wild beasts, others again to be beaten to death with clubs. During the three years of his reign he disdained to visit either Rome or Italy. His camp, occasionally removed from the banks of the Rhine to those of the Danube, was the seat of his stern despotism, which trampled on every principle of law and justice, and was supported by the avowed power of the sword.[7] No man of noble birth, elegant accomplishments, or knowledge of civil business, was suffered near his person; and the court of a Roman emperor revived the idea of those ancient chiefs of slaves and gladiators, whose savage power had left a deep impression of terror and detestation.[8]

As long as the cruelty of Maximin was confined to the illustrious senators, or even to the bold adventurers who in the court or army expose themselves to the caprice of fortune, the body of the people viewed their sufferings with indifference, or perhaps with pleasure. But the tyrant's avarice, stimulated by the insatiate desires of the soldiers, at length attacked the public property. Every city of the empire was possessed of an independent revenue, destined to purchase corn for the multitude, and to supply the expenses of the games and entertainments. By a single act of authority, the whole mass of wealth was at once confiscated for the use of the Imperial treasury. The temples were stripped of their most valuable offerings of gold and silver, and the statues of gods, heroes, and emperors, were melted down and coined into money. These impious orders could not be executed without tumults and massacres, as in many places the people chose rather to die in the defence of their altars than to behold in the midst of peace their cities exposed to the rapine and cruelty of war. The soldiers themselves, among whom this sacrilegious plunder was distributed, received it with a blush; and, hardened as they were in acts of violence, they dreaded the just reproaches of their friends and relations. Throughout the Roman world a general cry of indignation was heard, imploring vengeance on the common enemy of human kind; and at length, by an act of private oppression, a peaceful and unarmed province was driven into rebellion against him.

[7] *The wife of Maximin, by insinuating wise counsels with female gentleness, sometimes brought back the tyrant to the way of truth and humanity. We may collect from the medals that Paulina was the name of this benevolent empress; and from the title of* Diva *that she died before Maximin.*

[8] *He was compared to Spartacus and Athenio.*

The procurator of Africa was a servant worthy of such a master, who considered the fines and confiscations of the rich as one of the most fruitful branches of the Imperial revenue. An iniquitous sentence had been pronounced against some opulent youths of that country, the execution of which would have stripped them of far the greater part of their patrimony. In this extremity, a resolution that must either complete or prevent their ruin was dictated by despair. A respite of three days, obtained with difficulty from the rapacious treasurer, was employed in collecting from their estates a great number of slaves and peasants blindly devoted to the commands of their lords, and armed with the rustic weapons of clubs and axes. The leaders of the conspiracy, as they were admitted to the audience of the procurator, stabbed him with the daggers concealed under their garments, and, by the assistance of their tumultuary train, seized on the little town of Thysdrus,[9] and erected the standard of rebellion against the sovereign of the Roman empire. They rested their hopes on the hatred of mankind against Maximin, and they judiciously resolved to oppose to that detested tyrant an emperor whose mild virtues had already acquired the love and esteem of the Romans, and whose authority over the province would give weight and stability to the enterprise. Gordianus, their proconsul, and the object of their choice, refused, with unfeigned reluctance, the dangerous honour, and begged with tears that they should suffer him to terminate in peace a long and innocent life, without staining his feeble age with civil blood. Their menaces compelled him to accept the Imperial purple, his only refuge indeed against the jealous cruelty of Maximin; since, according to the reasoning of tyrants, those who have been esteemed worthy of the throne deserve death, and those who deliberate have already rebelled.

The family of Gordianus was one of the most illustrious of the Roman senate. On the father's side he was descended from the Gracchi; on his mother's, from the emperor Trajan. A great estate enabled him to support the dignity of his birth, and in the enjoyment of it he displayed an elegant taste and beneficent disposition. The palace in Rome formerly inhabited by the great Pompey had been, during several generations, in the possession of Gordian's family.[10] It was distinguished by ancient trophies of naval victories, and decorated with the works of modern painting. His villa on the road to Præneste was celebrated for baths of singular beauty and extent, for three stately rooms of an hundred feet in length, and for

[9] *In the fertile territory of Byzacium, one hundred and fifty miles to the south of Carthage. This city was decorated, probably by the Gordians, with the title of colony, and with a fine amphitheatre, which is still in a very perfect state.*

[10] *The celebrated house of Pompey in carinis, was usurped by Marc Antony, and consequently became, after the Triumvir's death, a part of the Imperial domain. The emperor Trajan allowed and even encouraged the rich senators to purchase those magnificent and useless palaces; and it may seem probable, that on this occasion, Pompey's house came into the possession of Gordian's great-grand-father.*

11 *The Claudian, the Nu-midian, the Carystian, and the Synnadian. The colours of Roman marbles have been faintly described and imperfectly distinguished. It appears, however, that the Carystian was a sea green, and that the marble of Synnada was white mixed with oval spots of purple.*

12 *He sometimes gave five hundred pair of Gladiators, never less than one hundred and fifty. He once gave for the use of the Circus one hundred Sicilian, and as many Cappadocian horses. The animals designed for hunting were chiefly bears, boars, bulls, stags, elks, wild asses, &c. Elephants and lions seem to have been appropriated to Imperial magnificence.*

13 *See the original letter, which at once shows Alexander's respect for the authority of the senate, and his esteem for the proconsul appointed by that assembly.*

14 *By each of his concubines, the younger Gordian left three or four children. His literary productions, though less numerous, were by no means contemptible.*

a magnificent portico, supported by two hundred columns of the four most curious and costly sorts of marble.[11] The public shows exhibited at his expense, and in which the people were entertained with many hundreds of wild beasts and gladiators,[12] seem to surpass the fortune of a subject; and, whilst the liberality of other magistrates was confined to a few solemn festivals in Rome, the magnificence of Gordian was repeated, when he was ædile, every month in the year, and extended, during his consulship, to the principal cities of Italy. He was twice elevated to the last-mentioned dignity, by Caracalla and by Alexander; for he possessed the uncommon talent of acquiring the esteem of virtuous princes, without alarming the jealousy of tyrants. His long life was innocently spent in the study of letters and the peaceful honours of Rome; and, till he was named proconsul of Africa by the voice of the senate and the approbation of Alexander,[13] he appears prudently to have declined the command of armies and the government of provinces. As long as that emperor lived, Africa was happy under the administration of his worthy representative; after the barbarous Maximin had usurped the throne, Gordianus alleviated the miseries which he was unable to prevent. When he reluctantly accepted the purple, he was above fourscore years old; a last and valuable remains of the happy age of the Antonines, whose virtues he revived in his own conduct, and celebrated in an elegant poem of thirty books. With the venerable proconsul, his son, who had accompanied him into Africa as his lieutenant, was likewise declared emperor. His manners were less pure, but his character was equally amiable with that of his father. Twenty-two acknowledged concubines, and a library of sixty-two thousand volumes, attested the variety of his inclinations; and from the productions which he left behind him, it appears that both the one and the other were designed for use rather than for ostentation.[14] The Roman people acknowledged in the features of the younger Gordian the resemblance of Scipio Africanus, recollected with pleasure that his mother was the grand-daughter of Antoninus Pius, and rested the public hope on those latent virtues which had hitherto, as they fondly imagined, lain concealed in the luxurious indolence of a private life.

As soon as the Gordians had appeased the first tumult of a popular election they removed their court to Carthage. They were received with the acclamations of the Africans, who honoured their virtues, and who, since the visit of Hadrian, had never beheld the majesty of a Roman emperor. But these vain acclamations neither strengthened nor confirmed the title of the Gordians. They were induced by principle, as well as interest, to solicit the approbation of the senate; and a deputation of the noblest provincials was sent, without delay, to Rome, to relate and justify the conduct of their countrymen, who, having long suffered with patience, were at length resolved to act with vigour. The letters of the new princes were modest and respectful, excusing the necessity which had obliged them to accept the Imperial title, but submitting their election and their fate to the supreme judgment of the senate.

The inclinations of the senate were neither doubtful nor divided. The birth and noble alliances of the Gordians had intimately connected them with the most illustrious houses of Rome. Their fortune had created many dependants in that assembly, their merit had acquired many friends. Their mild administration opened the flattering prospect of the restoration, not only of the civil but even of the republican government. The terror of military violence, which had first obliged the senate to forget the murder of Alexander, and to ratify the election of a barbarian peasant, now produced a contrary effect, and provoked them to assert the injured rights of freedom and humanity. The hatred of Maximin towards the senate was declared and implacable; the tamest submission had not appeased his fury, the most cautious innocence would not remove his suspicions; and even the care of their own safety urged them to share the fortune of an enterprise, of which (if unsuccessful) they were sure to be the first victims. These considerations, and perhaps others of a more private nature, were debated in a previous conference of the consuls and the magistrates. As soon as their resolution was decided, they convoked in the temple of Castor the whole body of the senate, according to an ancient form of secrecy,[15] calculated to awaken their attention and to conceal their decrees. "Conscript fathers," said the consul Syllanus, "the two Gordians, both of consular dignity, the one your proconsul, and the other your lieutenant, have been declared emperors by the general consent of Africa. Let us return thanks," he boldly continued, "to the youth of Thysdrus; let us return thanks to the faithful people of Carthage, our generous deliverers from a horrid monster.—Why do you hear me thus coolly, thus timidly? Why do you cast these anxious looks on each other? why hesitate? Maximin is a public enemy! may his enmity soon expire with him, and may we long enjoy the prudence and felicity of Gordian the father, the valour and constancy of Gordian the son!"[16] The noble ardour of the con-

[15] *Even the servants of the house, the scribes, &c., were excluded, and their office was filled by the senators themselves.*

[16] *This spirited speech seems transcribed from the original registers of the senate.*

sul revived the languid spirit of the senate. By an unanimous decree the election of the Gordians was ratified; Maximin, his son, and his adherents were pronounced enemies of their country, and liberal rewards were offered to whosoever had the courage and good fortune to destroy them.

During the emperor's absence a detachment of the Prætorian guards remained at Rome, to protect, or rather to command, the capital. The præfect Vitalianus had signalized his fidelity to Maximin by the alacrity with which he had obeyed, and even prevented, the cruel mandates of the tyrant. His death alone could rescue the authority of the senate, and the lives of the senators, from a state of danger and suspense. Before their resolves had transpired, a quæstor and some tribunes were commissioned to take his devoted life. They executed the order with equal boldness and success; and, with their bloody daggers in their hands, ran through the streets, proclaiming to the people and the soldiers the news of the happy revolution. The enthusiasm of liberty was seconded by the promise of a large donative in lands and money; the statues of Maximin were thrown down; the capital of the empire acknowledged, with transport, the authority of the two Gordians and the senate; and the example of Rome was followed by the rest of Italy.

A new spirit had arisen in that assembly, whose long patience had been insulted by wanton despotism and military licence. The senate assumed the reins of government, and, with a calm intrepidity, prepared to vindicate by arms the cause of freedom. Among the consular senators recommended by their merit and services to the favour of the emperor Alexander, it was easy to select twenty, not unequal to the command of an army and the conduct of a war. To these was the defence of Italy intrusted. Each was appointed to act in his respective department, authorized to enrol and discipline the Italian youth, and instructed to fortify the ports and highways against the impending invasion of Maximin. A number of deputies, chosen from the most illustrious of the senatorian and equestrian orders, were dispatched at the same time to the governors of the several provinces, earnestly conjuring them to fly to the assistance of their country, and to remind the nations of their ancient ties of friendship with the Roman senate and people. The general respect with which these deputies were received, and the zeal of Italy and the provinces in favour of the senate, sufficiently prove that the subjects of Maximin were reduced to that uncommon distress, in which the body of the people has more to fear from oppression than from resistance. The consciousness of that melancholy truth inspires a degree of persevering fury seldom to be found in those civil wars which are artificially supported for the benefit of a few factious and designing leaders.

For, while the cause of the Gordians was embraced with such diffusive ardour, the Gordians themselves were no more. The feeble court of Carthage was alarmed with the rapid approach of Capelianus, governor of Mauritania, who, with a small band of veterans and a fierce host of barbarians, attacked a faithful but unwarlike province. The younger Gordian sallied out to meet the enemy at the head of a few guards, and a numerous undisciplined multitude, educated in the peaceful luxury of Carthage. His useless valour served only to procure him an honourable death in the field of battle. His aged father, whose reign had not exceeded thirty-six days, put an end to his life on the first news of the defeat. Carthage, destitute of defence, opened her gates to the conqueror, and Africa was exposed to the rapacious cruelty of a slave, obliged to satisfy his unrelenting master with a large account of blood and treasure.[17]

The fate of the Gordians filled Rome with just, but unexpected, terror. The senate, convoked in the temple of Concord, affected to transact the common business of the day; and seemed to decline, with trembling anxiety, the consideration of their own, and the public, danger. A silent consternation prevailed on the assembly, till a senator, of the name and family of Trajan, awakened his brethren from their fatal lethargy. He represented to them that the choice of cautious dilatory measures had been long since out of their power; that Maximin, implacable by nature and exasperated by injuries, was advancing towards Italy, at the head of the military force of the empire; and that their only remaining alternative was either to meet him bravely in the field, or tamely to expect the tortures and ignominious death reserved for unsuccessful rebellion. "We have lost," continued he, "two excellent princes; but, unless we desert ourselves, the hopes of the republic have not perished with the Gordians. Many are the senators whose virtues have deserved, and whose abilities would sustain, the Imperial dignity. Let us elect two emperors, one of whom may conduct the war against the public enemy, whilst his colleague remains at Rome to direct the civil administration. I cheerfully expose myself to the danger and envy of the nomination, and give my vote in favour of Maximus and Balbinus. Ratify my choice, conscript fathers, or appoint, in their place, others more worthy of the empire." The general apprehen-

[17] *Zosimus relates that the two Gordians perished by a tempest in the midst of their navigation. A strange ignorance of history, or a strange abuse of metaphors!*

sion silenced the whispers of jealousy; the merit of the candidates was universally acknowledged; and the house resounded with the sincere acclamations of "Long life and victory to the Emperors Maximus and Balbinus. You are happy in the judgment of the senate; may the republic be happy under your administration!"[18]

The virtues and the reputation of the new emperors justified the most sanguine hopes of the Romans. The various nature of their talents seemed to appropriate to each his peculiar department of peace and war, without leaving room for jealous emulation. Balbinus was an admired orator, a poet of distinguished fame, and a wise magistrate, who had exercised with innocence and applause the civil jurisdiction in almost all the interior provinces of the empire. His birth was noble,[19] his fortune affluent, his manners liberal and affable. In him, the love of pleasure was corrected by a sense of dignity, nor had the habits of ease deprived him of a capacity for business. The mind of Maximus was formed in a rougher mould. By his valour and abilities he had raised himself from the meanest origin to the first employments of the state and army. His victories over the Sarmatians and the Germans, the austerity of his life, and the rigid impartiality of his justice whilst he was præfect of the city, commanded the esteem of a people whose affections were engaged in favour of the more amiable Balbinus. The two colleagues had both been consul (Balbinus had twice enjoyed that honourable office), both had been named among the twenty lieutenants of the senate; and, since the one was sixty and the other seventy-four years old, they had both attained the full maturity of age and experience.

After the senate had conferred on Maximus and Balbinus an equal portion of the consular and tribunitian powers, the title of Fathers of their country, and the joint office of Supreme Pontiff, they ascended to the Capitol to return thanks to the gods, protectors of Rome. The solemn rites of sacrifice were disturbed by a sedition of the people. The licentious multitude neither loved the rigid Maximus, nor did they sufficiently fear the mild and humane Balbinus. Their increasing numbers surrounded the temple of Jupiter; with obstinate clamours they asserted their inherent right of consenting to the election of their sovereign: and demanded, with an apparent moderation, that, besides the two emperors chosen by the senate, a third should be added of the family of the Gordians, as a just return of gratitude to those princes who had sacrificed their lives for the republic. At the head of the city guards and the youth of the equestrian order, Maximus and Balbinus attempted to cut

[18] *The date is confessedly faulty, but the coincidence of the Apollinarian games enables us to correct it.*

[19] *He was descended from Cornelius Balbus, a noble Spaniard, and the adopted son of Theophanes the Greek historian. Balbus obtained the freedom of Rome by the favour of Pompey, and preserved it by the eloquence of Cicero. The friendship of Cæsar (to whom he rendered the most important secret services in the civil war) raised him to the consulship and the pontificate, honours never yet possessed by a stranger. The nephew of this Balbus triumphed over the Garamantes.*

their way through the seditious multitude. The multitude, armed with sticks and stones, drove them back into the Capitol. It is prudent to yield, when the contest, whatever may be the issue of it, must be fatal to both parties. A boy, only thirteen years of age, the grandson of the elder and nephew of the younger Gordian, was produced to the people, invested with the ornaments and title of Cæsar. The tumult was appeased by this easy condescension; and the two emperors, as soon as they had been peaceably acknowledged in Rome, prepared to defend Italy against the common enemy.

Whilst in Rome and Africa revolutions succeeded each other with such amazing rapidity, the mind of Maximin was agitated by the most furious passions. He is said to have received the news of the rebellion of the Gordians, and of the decree of the senate against him, not with the temper of a man, but the rage of a wild beast; which, as it could not discharge itself on the distant senate, threatened the life of his son, of his friends, and of all who ventured to approach his person. The grateful intelligence of the death of the Gordians was quickly followed by the assurance that the senate, laying aside all hopes of pardon or accommodation, had substituted in their room two emperors, with whose merit he could not be unacquainted. Revenge was the only consolation left to Maximin, and revenge could only be obtained by arms. The strength of the legions had been assembled by Alexander from all parts of the empire. Three successful campaigns against the Germans and the Sarmatians had raised their fame, confirmed their discipline, and even increased their numbers, by filling the ranks with the flower of the barbarian youth. The life of Maximin had been spent in war, and the candid severity of history cannot refuse him the valour of a soldier, or even the abilities of an experienced general. It might naturally be expected that a prince of such a character, instead of suffering the rebellion to gain stability by delay, should immediately have marched from the banks of the Danube to those of the Tiber, and that his victorious army, instigated by contempt for the senate, and eager to gather the spoils of Italy, should have burned with impatience to finish the easy and lucrative conquest. Yet, as far as we can trust to the obscure chronology of that period,[20] it appears that the operations of some foreign war deferred the Italian expedition till the ensuing spring. From the prudent conduct of Maximin, we may learn that the savage features of his character have been exaggerated by the pencil of party; that his passions, however impetuous, submitted to the force of reason; and

[20] *The carelessness of the writers of that age leaves us in a singular perplexity. 1. We know that Maximus and Balbinus were killed during the Capitoline games. The authority of Censorinus enables us to fix those games with certainty to the year 238, but leaves us in ignorance of the month or day. 2. The election of Gordian by the senate is fixed, with equal certainty, to the 27th of May; but we are at a loss to discover, whether it was in the same or the preceding year. Tillemont and Muratori, who maintain the two opposite opinions, bring into the field a desultory troop of authorities, conjectures, and probabilities. The one seems to draw out, the other to contract, the series of events, between those periods, more than can be well reconciled to reason and history. Yet it is necessary to choose between them.*

that the barbarian possessed something of the generous spirit of Sylla, who subdued the enemies of Rome before he suffered himself to revenge his private injuries.

When the troops of Maximin, advancing in excellent order, arrived at the foot of the Julian Alps, they were terrified by the silence and desolation that reigned on the frontiers of Italy. The villages and open towns had been abandoned, on their approach, by the inhabitants, the cattle was driven away, the provisions removed or destroyed, the bridges broken down, nor was anything left which could afford either shelter or subsistence to an invader. Such had been the wise orders of the generals of the senate, whose design was to protract the war, to ruin the army of Maximin by the slow operation of famine, and to consume his strength in the sieges of the principal cities of Italy, which they had plentifully stored with men and provisions from the deserted country. Aquileia received and withstood the first shock of the invasion. The streams that issue from the head of the Hadriatic gulf, swelled by the melting of the winter snows,[21] opposed an unexpected obstacle to the arms of Maximin. At length, on a singular bridge, constructed, with art and difficulty, of large hogsheads, he transported his army to the opposite bank, rooted up the beautiful vineyards in the neighbourhood of Aquileia, demolished the suburbs, and employed the timber of the buildings in the engines and towers with which on every side he attacked the city. The walls, fallen to decay during the security of a long peace, had been hastily repaired on this sudden emergency; but the firmest defence of Aquileia consisted in the constancy of the citizens; all ranks of whom, instead of being dismayed, were animated by the extreme danger, and their knowledge of the tyrant's unrelenting temper. Their courage was supported and directed by Crispinus and Menophilus, two of the twenty lieutenants of the senate, who, with a small body of regular troops, had thrown themselves into the besieged place. The army of Maximin was repulsed in repeated attacks, his machines destroyed by showers of artificial fire; and the generous enthusiasm of the Aquileians was exalted into a confidence of success, by the opinion that Belenus, their tutelar deity, combatted in person in the defence of his distressed worshippers.[22]

The emperor Maximus, who had advanced as far as Ravenna to secure that important place, and to hasten the military preparations, beheld the event of the war in the more faithful mirror of reason and policy. He was too sensible that a single town could not resist the persevering efforts of a great army; and he dreaded lest the

[21] Muratori thinks the melting of the snows suits better with the months of June or July than with that of February. The opinion of a man who passed his life between the Alps and the Apennines is undoubtedly of great weight; yet I observe, 1. That the long winter, of which Muratori takes advantage, is to be found only in the Latin version, and not in the Greek text, of Herodian. 2. That the vicissitude of suns and rains, to which the soldiers of Maximin were exposed, denotes the spring rather than the summer. We may observe likewise, that these several streams, as they melted into one, composed the Timavus, so poetically (in every sense of the word) described by Virgil. They are about twelve miles to the east of Aquileia.

[22] The Celtic deity was supposed to be Apollo, and received under that name the thanks of the senate. A temple was likewise built to Venus the Bald, in honour of the women of Aquileia, who had given up their hair to make ropes for the military engines.

enemy, tired with the obstinate resistance of Aquileia, should on a sudden relinquish the fruitless siege and march directly towards Rome. The fate of the empire and the cause of freedom must then be committed to the chance of a battle; and what arms could he oppose to the veteran legions of the Rhine and Danube? Some troops newly levied among the generous but enervated youth of Italy, and a body of German auxiliaries, on whose firmness, in the hour of trial, it was dangerous to depend. In the midst of these just alarms, the stroke of domestic conspiracy punished the crimes of Maximin and delivered Rome and the senate from the calamities that would surely have attended the victory of an enraged barbarian.

The people of Aquileia had scarcely experienced any of the common miseries of a siege; their magazines were plentifully supplied, and several fountains within the walls assured them of an inexhaustible resource of fresh water. The soldiers of Maximin were, on the contrary, exposed to the inclemency of the season, the contagion of disease, and the horrors of famine. The naked country was ruined, the rivers filled with the slain and polluted with blood. A spirit of despair and disaffection began to diffuse itself among the troops; and, as they were cut off from all intelligence, they easily believed that the whole empire had embraced the cause of the senate, and that they were left as devoted victims to perish under the impregnable walls of Aquileia. The fierce temper of the tyrant was exasperated by disappointments, which he imputed to the cowardice of his army; and his wanton and ill-timed cruelty, instead of striking terror, inspired hatred and a just desire of revenge. A party of Prætorian guards, who trembled for their wives and children in the camp of Alba, near Rome, executed the sentence of the senate. Maximin, abandoned by his guards, was slain in his tent, with his son (whom he had associated to the honours of the purple), Anulinus the præfect, and the principal ministers of his tyranny.[23] The sight of their heads, borne on the point of spears, convinced the citizens of Aquileia that the siege was at an end; the gates of the city were thrown open, a liberal market was provided for the hungry troops of Maximin, and the whole army joined in solemn protestations of fidelity to the senate and people of Rome, and to their lawful emperors Maximus and Balbinus. Such was the deserved fate of a brutal savage, destitute, as he has generally been represented, of every sentiment that distinguishes a civilized, or even a human, being. The body was suited to the soul. The stature of Maximin exceeded the measure of eight feet, and circumstances almost

[23] *The duration of Maximin's reign has not been defined with much accuracy, except by Eutropius, who allows him three years and a few days.*

incredible are related of his matchless strength and appetite.[24] Had he lived in a less enlightened age, tradition and poetry might well have described him as one of those monstrous giants, whose supernatural power was constantly exerted for the destruction of mankind.

It is easier to conceive than to describe the universal joy of the Roman world on the fall of the tyrant, the news of which is said to have been carried in four days from Aquileia to Rome. The return of Maximus was a triumphal procession; his colleague and young Gordian went out to meet him, and the three princes made their entry into the capital, attended by the ambassadors of almost all the cities of Italy, saluted with the splendid offerings of gratitude and superstition, and received with the unfeigned acclamations of the senate and people, who persuaded themselves that a golden age would succeed to an age of iron. The conduct of the two emperors corresponded with these expectations. They administered justice in person; and the rigour of the one was tempered by the other's clemency. The oppressive taxes with which Maximin had loaded the rights of inheritance and succession were repealed, or at least moderated. Discipline was revived, and with the advice of the senate many wise laws were enacted by their Imperial ministers, who endeavoured to restore a civil constitution on the ruins of military tyranny. "What reward may we expect for delivering Rome from a monster?" was the question asked by Maximus, in a moment of freedom and confidence. Balbinus answered it without hesitation, "The love of the senate, of the people, and of all mankind." "Alas!" replied his more penetrating colleague, "Alas! I dread the hatred of the soldiers, and the fatal effects of their resentment." His apprehensions were but too well justified by the event.

Whilst Maximus was preparing to defend Italy against the common foe, Balbinus, who remained at Rome, had been engaged in scenes of blood and intestine discord. Distrust and jealousy reigned in the senate; and even in the temples where they assembled every senator carried either open or concealed arms. In the midst of their deliberations, two veterans of the guards, actuated either by curiosity or a sinister motive, audaciously thrust themselves into the house, and advanced by degrees beyond the altar of Victory. Gallicanus, a consular, and Mæcenas, a Prætorian senator, viewed with indignation their insolent intrusion: drawing their daggers, they laid the spies, for such they deemed them, dead at the foot of the altar, and then, advancing to the door of the senate, imprudently exhorted the multitude to massacre the Prætorians as the secret adherents of the tyrant. Those who escaped the first fury of the tumult took refuge in the camp, which they defended with superior advantage against the reiterated attacks of the people, assisted by the numerous bands of gladiators, the property of opulent nobles. The civil war lasted many days, with infinite loss and confusion on both sides. When the pipes were broken that supplied the camp with water, the Prætorians were reduced to intolerable distress; but, in their turn, they made desperate sallies into the city, set fire to a great number of houses, and filled the streets with the blood of the inhabitants. The emperor Balbinus attempted, by ineffectual edicts and precarious truces, to reconcile the factions of Rome. But their animosity, though smothered for a while, burnt with redoubled violence. The soldiers, detesting the senate and the people, despised the weakness of a prince who wanted either the spirit or the power to command the obedience of his subjects.

After the tyrant's death his formidable army had acknowledged, from necessity rather than from choice, the authority of Maximus, who transported himself without delay to the camp before Aquileia. As soon as he had received their oath of fidelity he addressed them in terms full of mildness and moderation; lamented rather than arraigned the wild disorders of the times, and assured the soldiers that, of all their past conduct, the senate would remember only their generous desertion of the tyrant and their voluntary return to their duty. Maximus enforced his exhortations by a liberal donative, purified the camp by a solemn sacrifice of expiation, and then dismissed the legions to their several provinces, impressed, as he hoped, with a lively sense of gratitude and obedience. But nothing could reconcile the haughty spirit of the Prætorians. They attended the emperors on the memorable day of their public entry into Rome; but, amidst the general acclamations, the sullen dejected countenance of the guards sufficiently declared that they considered themselves as the object, rather than the partners, of the triumph. When the whole body was united in their camp, those who had served under Maximin, and those who had remained at Rome, insensibly communicated to each other their complaints and apprehensions. The emperors chosen by the army had perished with ignominy; those elected by the senate were seated on the throne.[25] The long discord between the civil and military powers was decided by a war in which the former had obtained a complete victory. The soldiers must now learn a new doctrine of submission to the senate;

[25] *The observation had been made imprudently enough in the acclamations of the senate, and with regard to the soldiers it carried the appearance of a wanton insult.*

and, whatever clemency was affected by that politic assembly, they dreaded a slow revenge, coloured by the name of discipline, and justified by fair pretences of the public good. But their fate was still in their own hands; and, if they had courage to despise the vain terrors of an impotent republic, it was easy to convince the world that those who were masters of the arms were masters of the authority of the state.

When the senate elected two princes, it is probable that, besides the declared reason of providing for the various emergencies of peace and war, they were actuated by the secret desire of weakening by division the despotism of the supreme magistrate. Their policy was effectual, but it proved fatal both to their emperors and to themselves. The jealousy of power was soon exasperated by the difference of character. Maximus despised Balbinus as a luxurious noble, and was in his turn disdained by his colleague as an obscure soldier. Their silent discord was understood rather than seen; but the mutual consciousness prevented them from uniting in any vigorous measures of defence against their common enemies of the Prætorian camp. The whole city was employed in the Capitoline games, and the emperors were left almost alone in the palace. On a sudden they were alarmed by the approach of a troop of desperate assassins. Ignorant of each other's situation or designs, for they already occupied very distant apartments, afraid to give or to receive assistance, they wasted the important moments in idle debates and fruitless recriminations. The arrival of the guards put an end to the vain strife. They seized on these emperors of the senate, for such they called them with malicious contempt, stripped them of their garments, and dragged them in insolent triumph through the streets of Rome, with a design of inflicting a slow and cruel death on these unfortunate princes. The fear of a rescue from the faithful Germans of the Imperial guards shortened their tortures; and their bodies, mangled with a thousand wounds, were left exposed to the insults or to the pity of the populace.

In the space of a few months six princes had been cut off by the sword. Gordian, who had already received the title of Cæsar, was the only person that occurred to the soldiers as proper to fill the vacant throne. They carried him to the camp and unanimously saluted him Augustus and Emperor. His name was dear to the senate and people; his tender age promised a long impunity of military licence; and the submission of Rome and the provinces to the choice of the Prætorian guards saved the republic, at the expense indeed of its freedom and dignity, from the horrors of a new civil war in the heart of the capital.[26]

As the third Gordian was only nineteen years of age at the time of his death, the history of his life, were it known to us with greater accuracy than it really is, would contain little more than the account of his education and the conduct of the ministers who by turns abused or guided the simplicity of his inexperienced youth. Immediately after his accession he fell into the hands of his mother's eunuchs, that pernicious vermin of the East, who, since the days of Elagabalus, had infested the Roman palace. By the artful conspiracy of these wretches an impenetrable veil was drawn between an innocent prince and his oppressed subjects, the virtuous disposition of Gordian was deceived, and the honours of the empire sold without his knowledge, though in a very public manner, to the most worthless of mankind. We are ignorant by what fortunate accident the emperor escaped from this ignominious slavery, and devolved his confidence on a minister whose wise counsels had no object except the glory of the sovereign and the happiness of the people. It should seem that love and learning introduced Misitheus to the favour of Gordian. The young prince married the daughter of his master of rhetoric, and promoted his father-in-law to the first offices of the empire. Two admirable letters that passed between them are still extant. The minister, with the conscious dignity of virtue, congratulates Gordian that he is delivered from the tyranny of the eunuchs,[27] and still more, that he is sensible of his deliverance. The emperor acknowledges, with an amiable confusion, the errors of his past conduct; and laments, with singular propriety, the misfortune of a monarch from whom a venal tribe of courtiers perpetually labour to conceal the truth.

The life of Misitheus had been spent in the profession of letters, not of arms; yet such was the versatile genius of that great man that, when he was appointed Prætorian præfect, he discharged the military duties of his place with vigour and ability. The Persians had invaded Mesopotamia, and threatened Antioch. By the persuasion of his father-in-law, the young emperor quitted the luxury of Rome, opened, for the last time recorded in history, the temple of Janus, and marched in person into the East. On his approach with a great army, the Persians withdrew their garrisons from the cities which they had already taken, and retired from the Euphrates to the Tigris. Gordian enjoyed the pleasure of announcing to the senate the first success of his arms, which he ascribed with a becoming

[26] Quintus Curtius pays an elegant compliment to the emperor of the day, for having, by his happy accession, extinguished so many firebrands, sheathed so many swords, and put an end to the evils of a divided government. After weighing with attention every word of the passage, I am of opinion that it suits better with the elevation of Gordian than with any other period of the Roman History. In that case, it may serve to decide the age of Quintus Curtius. Those who place him under the first Cæsars argue from the purity of his style, but are embarrassed by the silence of Quintilian in his accurate list of Roman historians.

[27] From some hints in the two letters, I should expect that the eunuchs were not expelled the palace without some degree of gentle violence, and that young Gordian rather approved of, than consented to, their disgrace.

modesty and gratitude to the wisdom of his father and præfect. During the whole expedition, Misitheus watched over the safety and discipline of the army; whilst he prevented their dangerous murmurs by maintaining a regular plenty in the camp, and by establishing ample magazines of vinegar, bacon, straw, barley, and wheat, in all the cities of the frontier.[28] But the prosperity of Gordian expired with Misitheus, who died of a flux, not without very strong suspicions of poison. Philip, his successor in the præfecture, was an Arab by birth, and consequently, in the earlier part of his life, a robber by profession. His rise from so obscure a station to the first dignities of the empire seems to prove that he was a bold and able leader. But his boldness prompted him to aspire to the throne, and his abilities were employed to supplant, not to serve, his indulgent master. The minds of the soldiers were irritated by an artificial scarcity, created by his contrivance in the camp; and the distress of the army was attributed to the youth and incapacity of the prince. It is not in our power to trace the successive steps of the secret conspiracy and open sedition which were at length fatal to Gordian. A sepulchral monument was erected to his memory on the spot[29] where he was killed, near the conflux of the Euphrates with the little river Aboras.[30] The fortunate Philip, raised to the empire by the votes of the soldiers, found a ready obedience from the senate and the provinces.[31]

We cannot forbear transcribing the ingenious, though somewhat fanciful, description, which a celebrated writer of our own times has traced of the military government of the Roman empire. "What in that age was called the Roman empire was only an irregular republic, not unlike the aristocracy[32] of Algiers, where the militia, possessed of the sovereignty, creates and deposes a magistrate, who is styled a Dey. Perhaps, indeed, it may be laid down as a general rule, that a military government is, in some respects, more republican than monarchical. Nor can it be said that the soldiers only partook of the government by their disobedience and rebellions. The speeches made to them by the emperors, were they not at length of the same nature as those formerly pronounced to the people by the consuls and the tribunes? And although the armies had no regular place or forms of assembly, though their debates were short, their action sudden, and their resolves seldom the result of cool reflection, did they not dispose, with absolute sway, of the public fortune? What was the emperor, except the minister of a violent government, elected for the private benefit of the soldiers?

[28] The philosopher Plotinus accompanied the army, prompted by the love of knowledge, and by the hope of penetrating as far as India.

[29] About twenty miles from the little town of Circesium, on the frontier of the two empires.

[30] The inscription (which contained a very singular pun) was erased by the order of Licinius, who claimed some degree of relationship to Philip; but the tumulus or mound of earth which formed the sepulchre, still subsisted in the time of Julian.

[31] Philip, who was a native of Bostra, was about forty years of age.

[32] Can the epithet of Aristocracy be applied, with any propriety, to the government of Algiers? Every military government floats between the extremes of absolute monarchy and wild democracy.

"When the army had elected Philip, who was Prætorian præfect to the third Gordian, the latter demanded that he might remain sole emperor; he was unable to obtain it. He requested that the power might be equally divided between them; the army would not listen to his speech. He consented to be degraded to the rank of Cæsar; the favour was refused him. He desired, at least, he might be appointed Prætorian præfect; his prayer was rejected. Finally, he pleaded for his life. The army, in these several judgments, exercised the supreme magistracy." According to the historian, whose doubtful narrative the president De Montesquieu has adopted, Philip, who, during the whole transaction, had preserved a sullen silence, was inclined to spare the innocent life of his benefactor; till, recollecting that his innocence might excite a dangerous compassion in the Roman world, he commanded, without regard to his suppliant cries, that he should be seized, stript, and led away to instant death. After a moment's pause the inhuman sentence was executed.[33]

On his return from the East to Rome, Philip, desirous of obliterating the memory of his crimes, and of captivating the affections of the people, solemnized the secular games with infinite pomp and magnificence. Since their institution or revival by Augustus,[34] they had been celebrated by Claudius, by Domitian, and by Severus, and were now renewed, the fifth time, on the accomplishment of the full period of a thousand years from the foundation of Rome. Every circumstance of the secular games was skilfully adapted to inspire the superstitious mind with deep and solemn reverence. The long interval between them[35] exceeded the term of human life; and, as none of the spectators had already seen them, none could flatter themselves with the expectation of beholding them a second time. The mystic sacrifices were performed, during three nights, on the banks of the Tiber; and the Campus Martius resounded with music and dances, and was illuminated with innumerable lamps and torches. Slaves and strangers were excluded from any participation in these national ceremonies. A chorus of twenty-seven youths, and as many virgins, of noble families, and whose parents were both alive, implored the propitious gods in favour of the present, and for the hope of the rising generation; requesting, in religious hymns, that, according to the faith of their ancient oracles, they would still maintain the virtue, the felicity, and the empire of the Roman people. The magnificence of Philip's shows and entertainments dazzled the eyes of the multitude. The devout were employed in the rites of superstition, whilst the reflecting few revolved in their

[33] *The Augustan History cannot, in this instance, be reconciled with itself or with probability. How could Philip condemn his predecessor, and yet consecrate his memory? How could he order his public execution, and yet, in his letters to the senate, exculpate himself from the guilt of his death? Philip, though an ambitious usurper, was by no means a mad tyrant.*

[34] *The account of the last supposed celebration, though in an enlightened period of history, was so very doubtful and obscure, that the alternative seems not doubtful. When the popish jubilees, the copy of the secular games, were invented by Boniface VIII., the crafty pope pretended that he only revived an ancient institution.*

[35] *Either of a hundred, or a hundred and ten years. Varro and Livy adopted the former opinion, but the infallible authority of the Sibyl consecrated the latter. The emperors Claudius and Philip, however, did not treat the oracle with implicit respect.*

anxious minds the past history and the future fate of the empire.

Since Romulus, with a small band of shepherds and outlaws, fortified himself on the hills near the Tiber, ten centuries had already elapsed.[36] During the four first ages, the Romans, in the laborious school of poverty, had acquired the virtues of war and government: by the vigorous exertion of those virtues, and by the assistance of fortune, they had obtained, in the course of the three succeeding centuries, an absolute empire over many countries of Europe, Asia, and Africa. The last three hundred years had been consumed in apparent prosperity and internal decline. The nation of soldiers, magistrates, and legislators, who composed the thirty-five tribes of the Roman people, was dissolved into the common mass of mankind, and confounded with the millions of servile provincials, who had received the name, without adopting the spirit, of Romans. A mercenary army, levied among the subjects and barbarians of the frontier, was the only order of men who preserved and abused their independence. By their tumultuary election, a Syrian, a Goth, or an Arab, was exalted to the throne of Rome, and invested with despotic power over the conquests and over the country of the Scipios.

The limits of the Roman empire still extended from the Western Ocean to the Tigris, and from Mount Atlas to the Rhine and the Danube. To the undiscerning eye of the vulgar, Philip appeared a monarch no less powerful than Hadrian or Augustus had formerly been. The form was still the same, but the animating health and vigour were fled. The industry of the people was discouraged and exhausted by a long series of oppression. The discipline of the legions, which alone, after the extinction of every other virtue, had propped the greatness of the state, was corrupted by the ambition, or relaxed by the weakness, of the emperors. The strength of the frontiers, which had always consisted in arms rather than in fortifications, was insensibly undermined; and the fairest provinces were left exposed to the rapaciousness or ambition of the barbarians, who soon discovered the decline of the Roman empire.

[36] *The received calculation of Varro assigns to the foundation of Rome an æra that corresponds with the 754th year before Christ. But so little is the chronology of Rome to be depended on in the more early ages, that Sir Isaac Newton has brought the same event as low as the year 627.*

"*The rise of a city, which swelled into an empire, may deserve, as a singular prodigy, the reflection of a philosophical mind. But the decline of Rome was the natural and inevitable effect of immoderate greatness.*"

A VIEW OF THE ROMAN FORUM

1. Temple of Vespasian
2. Temple of Saturn
3. Arch of Septimius Severus

4. Church of S. Adriano
5. Temple of Antoninus and Faustina
6. Temple of Romulus

VIII

OF THE STATE OF PERSIA AFTER THE RESTORATION OF THE

MONARCHY BY ARTAXERXES · HIS CHARACTER AND MAXIMS

WHENEVER Tacitus indulges himself in those beautiful episodes, in which he relates some domestic transaction of the Germans or Parthians, his principal object is to relieve the attention of the reader from a uniform scene of vice and misery. From the reign of Augustus to the time of Alexander Severus, the enemies of Rome were in her bosom—the tyrants, and the soldiers; and her prosperity had a very distant and feeble interest in the revolutions that might happen beyond the Rhine and the Euphrates. But, when the military order had levelled in wild anarchy the power of the prince, the laws of the senate, and even the discipline of the camp, the barbarians of the North and of the East, who had long hovered on the frontier, boldly attacked the provinces of a declining monarchy. Their vexatious inroads were changed into formidable irruptions, and, after a long vicissitude of mutual calamities, many tribes of the victorious invaders established themselves in the provinces of the Roman empire. To obtain a clearer knowledge of these great events we shall endeavour to form a previous idea of the character, forces, and designs of those nations who avenged the cause of Hannibal and Mithridates.

In the more early ages of the world, whilst the forest that covered Europe afforded a retreat to a few wandering savages, the inhabitants of Asia were already collected into populous cities, and reduced under extensive empires, the seat of the arts, of luxury and of despotism. The Assyrians reigned over the East,[1] till the sceptre of Ninus and Semiramis dropt from the hands of their enervated successors. The Medes and the Babylonians divided their power, and were themselves swallowed up in the monarchy of the Persians, whose arms could not be confined within the narrow limits of Asia. Followed, as it is said, by two millions of *men*, Xerxes, the descendant of Cyrus, invaded Greece. Thirty thousand *soldiers*, under the

[1] *An ancient chronologist observes that the Assyrians, the Medes, the Persians, and the Macedonians, reigned over Asia one thousand nine hundred and ninety-five years, from the accession of Ninus to the defeat of Antiochus by the Romans. As the latter of these great events happened 189 years before Christ, the former may be placed 2184 years before the same æra. The Astronomical Observations, found at Babylon by Alexander, went fifty years higher.*

command of Alexander, the son of Philip, who was intrusted by the Greeks with their glory and revenge, were sufficient to subdue Persia. The princes of the house of Seleucus usurped and lost the Macedonian command over the East. About the same time that, by an ignominious treaty, they resigned to the Romans the country on this side Mount Taurus, they were driven by the Parthians, an obscure horde of Scythian origin, from all the provinces of Upper Asia. The formidable power of the Parthians, which spread from India to the frontiers of Syria, was in its turn subverted by Ardshir, or Artaxerxes; the founder of a new dynasty, which, under the name of Sassanides, governed Persia till the invasion of the Arabs. This great revolution, whose fatal influence was soon experienced by the Romans, happened in the fourth year of Alexander Severus, two hundred and twenty-six years after the Christian æra.[2]

Artaxerxes had served with great reputation in the armies of Artaban, the last king of the Parthians, and it appears that he was driven into exile and rebellion by royal ingratitude, the customary reward for superior merit. His birth was obscure, and the obscurity equally gave room to the aspersions of his enemies, and the flattery of his adherents. If we credit the scandal of the former, Artaxerxes sprang from the illegitimate commerce of a tanner's wife with a common soldier.[3] The latter represents him as descended from a branch of the ancient kings of Persia, though time and misfortune had gradually reduced his ancestors to the humble station of private citizens. As the lineal heir of the monarchy, he asserted his right to the throne, and challenged the noble task of delivering the Persians from the oppression under which they groaned above five centuries since the death of Darius. The Parthians were defeated in three great battles. In the last of these their king Artaban was slain, and the spirit of the nation was for ever broken. The authority of Artaxerxes was solemnly acknowledged in a great assembly held at Balch in Khorasan. Two younger branches of the royal house of Arsaces were confounded among the prostrate satraps. A third, more mindful of ancient grandeur than of present necessity, attempted to retire with a numerous train of vassals, towards their kinsman, the king of Armenia; but this little army of deserters was intercepted and cut off by the vigilance of the conqueror, who boldly assumed the double diadem, and the title of King of Kings, which had been enjoyed by his predecessor. But these pompous titles, instead of gratifying the vanity of the Persian, served only to admonish him of his duty, and to inflame in his soul the ambition

[2] *In the five hundred and thirty-eighth year of the æra of Seleucus. This great event (such is the carelessness of the Orientals) is placed by Eutychius as high as the tenth year of Commodus, and by Moses of Chorene as low as the reign of Philip. Ammianus Marcellinus has so servilely copied his ancient materials, which are indeed very good, that he describes the family of the Arsacides as still seated on the Persian throne in the middle of the fourth century.*

[3] *The tanner's name was Babec; the soldier's, Sassan; from the former Artaxerxes obtained the surname of Babegan; from the latter all his descendants have been styled* Sassanides.

of restoring, in their full splendour, the religion and empire of Cyrus.

I. During the long servitude of Persia under the Macedonian and the Parthian yoke, the nations of Europe and Asia had mutually adopted and corrupted each other's superstitions. The Arsacides, indeed, practised the worship of the Magi; but they disgraced and polluted it with a various mixture of foreign idolatry. The memory of Zoroaster, the ancient prophet and philosopher of the Persians,[4] was still revered in the East; but the obsolete and mysterious language in which the Zendavesta was composed,[5] opened a field of dispute to seventy sects, who variously explained the fundamental doctrines of their religion, and were all equally derided by a crowd of infidels, who rejected the divine mission and miracles of the prophet. To suppress the idolaters, re-unite the schismatics, and confute the unbelievers by the infallible decision of a general council, the pious Artaxerxes summoned the Magi from all parts of his dominions. These priests, who had so long sighed in contempt and obscurity, obeyed the welcome summons; and on the appointed day appeared to the number of about eighty thousand. But as the debates of so tumultuous an assembly could not have been directed by the authority of reason, or influenced by the art of policy, the Persian synod was reduced, by successive operations, to forty thousand, to four thousand, to four hundred, to forty, and at last to seven Magi, the most respected for their learning and piety. One of these, Erdaviraph, a young but holy prelate, received from the hands of his brethren three cups of soporiferous wine. He drank them off, and instantly fell into a long and profound sleep. As soon as he waked, he related to the king and to the believing multitude his journey to Heaven, and his intimate conferences with the Deity. Every doubt was silenced by this supernatural evidence; and the articles of the faith of Zoroaster were fixed with equal authority and precision. A short delineation of that celebrated system will be found useful, not only to display the character of the Persian nation, but to illustrate many of their most important transactions, both in peace and war, with the Roman empire.[6]

The great and fundamental article of the system was the celebrated doctrine of the two principles; a bold and injudicious attempt of Eastern philosophy to reconcile the existence of moral and physical evil with the attributes of a beneficent Creator and Governor of the world. The first and original Being, in whom, or by whom, the universe exists, is denominated in the writings of Zoro-

[4] *Hyde and Prideaux, working up the Persian legends and their own conjectures into a very agreeable story, represent Zoroaster as a contemporary of Darius Hystaspis But it is sufficient to observe that the Greek writers, who lived almost in the same age, agree in placing the æra of Zoroaster many hundred, or even thousand, years before their own time.*

[5] *That ancient idiom was called the* Zend. *The language of the commentary, the* Pehlvi, *though much more modern, has ceased many ages ago to be a living tongue. This fact alone (if it is allowed as authentic) sufficiently warrants the antiquity of those writings, which M. d'Anquetil has brought into Europe, and translated into French.*

[6] *I have principally drawn this account from the Zendavesta of M. d'Anquetil, and the Sadder, subjoined to Dr. Hyde's treatise. It must, however, be confessed, that the studied obscurity*

of a prophet, the figurative style of the East, and the deceitful medium of a French or Latin version, may have betrayed us into error and heresy, in this abridgment of Persian theology.

aster, *Time without bounds;* but it must be confessed that this infinite substance seems rather a metaphysical abstraction of the mind than a real object endowed with self-consciousness, or possessed of moral perfections. From either the blind or the intelligent operation of this infinite Time, which bears but too near an affinity with the Chaos of the Greeks, the two secondary but active principles of the universe were from all eternity produced, Ormusd and Ahriman, each of them possessed of the powers of creation, but each disposed, by his invariable nature, to exercise them with different designs. The principle of good is eternally absorbed in light: the principle of evil eternally buried in darkness. The wise benevolence of Ormusd formed man capable of virtue, and abundantly provided his fair habitation with the materials of happiness. By his vigilant providence, the motion of the planets, the order of the seasons, and the temperate mixture of the elements are preserved. But the malice of Ahriman has long since pierced *Ormusd's egg;* or, in other words, has violated the harmony of his works. Since that fatal eruption, the most minute particles of good and evil are intimately intermingled and agitated together, the rankest poisons spring up amidst the most salutary plants; deluges, earthquakes, and conflagrations attest the conflict of Nature; and the little world of man is perpetually shaken by vice and misfortune. Whilst the rest of human kind are led away captives in the chains of their infernal enemy, the faithful Persian alone reserves his religious adoration for his friend and protector Ormusd, and fights under his banner of light, in the full confidence that he shall, in the last day, share the glory of his triumph. At that decisive period the enlightened wisdom of goodness will render the power of Ormusd superior to the furious malice of his rival. Ahriman and his followers, disarmed and subdued, will sink into their native darkness; and virtue will maintain the eternal peace and harmony of the universe.[7]

[7] *The modern Parsees (and in some degree the Sadder) exalt Ormusd into the first and omnipotent cause, whilst they degrade Ahriman into an inferior but rebellious spirit. Their desire of pleasing the Mahometans may have contributed to refine their theological system.*

[8] *But Dr. Prideaux thinks, with reason, that the use of temples was afterwards permitted in the Magian religion.*

The theology of Zoroaster was darkly comprehended by foreigners, and even by the far greater number of his disciples; but the most careless observers were struck with the philosophic simplicity of the Persian worship. "That people," says Herodotus,[8] "rejects the use of temples, of altars, and of statues, and smiles at the folly of those nations, who imagine that the gods are sprung from, or bear any affinity with, the human nature. The tops of the highest mountains are the places chosen for sacrifices. Hymns and prayers are the principal worship; the Supreme God who fills the wide circle of heaven, is the object to whom they are addressed." Yet, at the same time, in the true spirit of a polytheist, he accuses them of adoring Earth, Water, Fire, the Winds, and the Sun and Moon. But the Persians of every age have denied the charge, and explained the equivocal conduct which might appear to give a colour to it. The elements, and particularly Fire, Light, and the Sun, whom they called Mithra, were the objects of their religious reverence, because they considered them as the purest symbols, the noblest productions, and the most powerful agents of the Divine Power and Nature.[9]

Every mode of religion, to make a deep and lasting impression on the human mind, must exercise our obedience by enjoining practices of devotion, for which we can assign no reason; and must acquire our esteem, by inculcating moral duties analogous to the dictates of our own hearts. The religion of Zoroaster was abundantly provided with the former, and possessed a sufficient portion of the latter. At the age of puberty the faithful Persian was invested with a mysterious girdle, the badge of the divine protection; and from that moment all the actions of his life, even the most indifferent or the most necessary, were sanctified by their peculiar prayers, ejaculations, or genuflexions; the omission of which, under any circumstances, was a grievous sin, not inferior in guilt to the violation of the moral duties. The moral duties, however, of justice, mercy, liberality, &c., were in their turn required of the disciple of Zoroaster, who wished to escape the persecution of Ahriman, and to live with Ormusd in a blissful eternity, where the degree of felicity will be exactly proportioned to the degree of virtue and piety.[10]

But there are some remarkable instances in which Zoroaster lays aside the prophet, assumes the legislator, and discovers a liberal concern for private and public happiness, seldom to be found among the grovelling or visionary schemes of superstition. Fasting and celibacy, the common means of purchasing the divine favour, he condemns with abhorrence, as a criminal rejection of the best gifts of providence. The saint, in the Magian religion, is obliged to beget children, to plant useful trees, to destroy noxious animals, to convey water to the dry lands of Persia, and to work out his salvation by pursuing all the labours of agriculture. We may quote from the Zend Avesta a wise and benevolent maxim, which compensates for many an absurdity. "He who sows the ground with care and diligence acquires a greater stock of religious merit than he could gain by the repetition of ten thousand prayers." In the spring of every year a festival was celebrated, destined to represent the primitive equality, and the present connexion, of mankind. The stately kings

[9] *Notwithstanding all their distinctions and protestations, which seem sincere enough, their tyrants, the Mahometans, have constantly stigmatized them as idolatrous worshippers of the fire.*

[10] *See the Sadder, the smallest part of which consists of moral precepts. The ceremonies enjoined are infinite and trifling. Fifteen genuflections, prayers, &c., were required whenever the devout Persian cut his nails, or as often as he put on the sacred girdle.*

of Persia, exchanging their vain pomp for more genuine greatness, freely mingled with the humblest but most useful of their subjects. On that day the husbandmen were admitted, without distinction, to the table of the king and his satraps. The monarch accepted their petitions, inquired into their grievances, and conversed with them on the most equal terms. "From your labours," was he accustomed to say (and to say with truth, if not with sincerity), "from your labours we receive our subsistence; you derive your tranquillity from our vigilance: since, therefore, we are mutually necessary to each other, let us live together like brothers in concord and love." Such a festival must indeed have degenerated, in a wealthy and despotic empire, into a theatrical representation; but it was at least a comedy well worthy of a royal audience, and which might sometimes imprint a salutary lesson on the mind of a young prince.

Had Zoroaster, in all his institutions, invariably supported this exalted character, his name would deserve a place with those of Numa and Confucius, and his system would be justly entitled to all the applause which it has pleased some of our divines, and even some of our philosophers, to bestow on it. But in that motley composition, dictated by reason and passion, by enthusiasm and by selfish motives, some useful and sublime truths were disgraced by a mixture of the most abject and dangerous superstition. The Magi, or sacerdotal order, were extremely numerous, since, as we have already seen, fourscore thousand of them were convened in a general council. Their forces were multiplied by discipline. A regular hierarchy was diffused through all the provinces of Persia; and the Archimagus, who resided at Balch, was respected as the visible head of the church, and the lawful successor of Zoroaster. The property of the Magi was very considerable. Besides the less invidious possession of a large tract of the most fertile lands of Media,[11] they levied a general tax on the fortunes and the industry of the Persians.[12] "Though your good works," says the interested prophet, "exceed in number the leaves of the trees, the drops of rain, the stars in the heaven, or the sands on the sea-shore, they will all be unprofitable to you, unless they are accepted by the *destour,* or priest. To obtain the acceptation of this guide to salvation, you must faithfully pay him *tithes* of all you possess, of your goods, of your lands, and of your money. If the destour be satisfied, your soul will escape hell tortures; you will secure praise in this world and happiness in the next. For the destours are the teachers of religion; they know all things, and they deliver all men."

[11] *Ammianus informs us (as far as we may credit him) of two curious particulars; 1, that the Magi derived some of their most secret doctrines from the Indian Brachmans; and, 2, that they were a tribe or family, as well as order.*

[12] *The divine institution of tithes exhibits a singular instance of conformity between the law of Zoroaster and that of Moses. Those who cannot otherwise account for it may suppose, if they please, that the Magi of the latter times inserted so useful an interpolation into the writings of their prophet.*

158

These convenient maxims of reverence and implicit faith were doubtless imprinted with care on the tender minds of youth; since the Magi were the masters of education in Persia, and to their hands the children even of the royal family were intrusted. The Persian priests, who were of a speculative genius, preserved and investigated the secrets of Oriental philosophy; and acquired, either by superior knowledge or superior art, the reputation of being well versed in some occult sciences, which have derived their appellation from the Magi.[13] Those of more active dispositions mixed with the world in courts and cities; and it is observed that the administration of Artaxerxes was in a great measure directed by the counsels of the sacerdotal order, whose dignity, either from policy or devotion, that prince restored to its ancient splendour.

The first counsel of the Magi was agreeable to the unsociable genius of their faith,[14] to the practice of ancient kings,[15] and even to the example of their legislator, who had fallen a victim to a religious war excited by his own intolerant zeal. By an edict of Artaxerxes, the exercise of every worship, except that of Zoroaster, was severely prohibited. The temples of the Parthians, and the statues of their deified monarchs, were thrown down with ignominy. The sword of Aristotle (such was the name given by the Orientals to the polytheism and philosophy of the Greeks) was easily broken: the flames of persecution soon reached the more stubborn Jews and Christians;[16] nor did they spare the heretics of their own nation and religion. The majesty of Ormusd, who was jealous of a rival, was seconded by the despotism of Artaxerxes, who could not suffer a rebel; and the schismatics within his vast empire were soon reduced to the inconsiderable number of eighty thousand. This spirit of persecution reflects dishonour on the religion of Zoroaster; but, as it was not productive of any civil commotion, it served to strengthen the new monarchy by uniting all the various inhabitants of Persia in the bands of religious zeal.

II. Artaxerxes, by his valour and conduct, had wrested the sceptre of the East from the ancient royal family of Parthia. There still remained the more difficult task of establishing, throughout the vast extent of Persia, a uniform and vigorous administration. The weak indulgence of the Arsacides had resigned to their sons and brothers the principal provinces and the greatest offices of the kingdom, in the nature of hereditary possessions. The *vitaxæ,* or eighteen most powerful satraps, were permitted to assume the regal title, and the vain pride of the monarch was delighted with a nominal dominion

[13] *Pliny observes that magic held mankind by the triple chain of religion, of physic, and of astronomy.*

[14] *Mr. Hume, in the Natural History of Religion, sagaciously remarks that the most refined and philosophic sects are constantly the most intolerant.*

[15] *Xerxes, by the advice of the Magi, destroyed the temples of Greece.*

[16] *Manes, who suffered an ignominious death, may be deemed a Magian, as well as a Christian, heretic.*

over so many vassal kings. Even tribes of barbarians in their mountains, and the Greek cities of Upper Asia,[17] within their walls, scarcely acknowledged, or seldom obeyed, any superior; and the Parthian empire exhibited, under other names, a lively image of the feudal system [18] which has since prevailed in Europe. But the active victor, at the head of a numerous and disciplined army, visited in person every province of Persia. The defeat of the boldest rebels and the reduction of the strongest fortifications [19] diffused the terror of his arms and prepared the way for the peaceful reception of his authority. An obstinate resistance was fatal to the chiefs; but their followers were treated with lenity.[20] A cheerful submission was rewarded with honours and riches; but the prudent Artaxerxes, suffering no person except himself to assume the title of king, abolished every intermediate power between the throne and the people. His kingdom, nearly equal in extent to modern Persia, was, on every side, bounded by the sea or by great rivers,—by the Euphrates, the Tigris, the Araxes, the Oxus, and the Indus; by the Caspian Sea and the Gulf of Persia.[21] That country was computed to contain, in the last century, five hundred and fifty-four cities, sixty thousand villages, and about forty millions of souls. If we compare the administration of the house of Sassan with that of the house of Sesi, the political influence of the Magian with that of the Mahometan religion, we shall probably infer that the kingdom of Artaxerxes contained at least as great a number of cities, villages, and inhabitants. But it must likewise be confessed that in every age the want of harbours on the sea coast, and the scarcity of fresh water in the inland provinces, have been very unfavourable to the commerce and agriculture of the Persians; who, in the calculation of their numbers, seem to have indulged one of the meanest, though most common, artifices of national vanity.

As soon as the ambitious mind of Artaxerxes had triumphed over the resistance of his vassals, he began to threaten the neighbouring states, who, during the long slumber of his predecessors, had insulted Persia with impunity. He obtained some easy victories over the wild Scythians and the effeminate Indians; but the Romans were an enemy who, by their past injuries and present power, deserved the utmost efforts of his arms. A forty years' tranquillity, the fruit of valour and moderation, had succeeded the victories of Trajan. During the period that elapsed from the accession of Marcus to the reign of Alexander, the Roman and the Parthian empires were twice engaged in war; and, although the whole strength of the

Arsacides contended with a part only of the forces of Rome, the event was most commonly in favour of the latter. Macrinus, indeed, prompted by his precarious situation and pusillanimous temper, purchased a peace at the expense of near two millions of our money; but the generals of Marcus, the emperor Severus, and his son, erected many trophies in Armenia, Mesopotamia, and Assyria. Among their exploits, the imperfect relation of which would have unseasonably interrupted the more important series of domestic revolutions, we shall only mention the repeated calamities of the two great cities of Seleucia and Ctesiphon.

Seleucia, on the western bank of the Tigris, about forty-five miles to the north of ancient Babylon, was the capital of the Macedonian conquests in Upper Asia. Many ages after the fall of their empire, Seleucia retained the genuine characters of a Grecian colony—arts, military virtue, and the love of freedom. The independent republic was governed by a senate of three hundred nobles; the people consisted of six hundred thousand citizens; the walls were strong, and, as long as concord prevailed among the several orders of the state, they viewed with contempt the power of the Parthian: but the madness of faction was sometimes provoked to implore the dangerous aid of the common enemy, who was posted almost at the gates of the colony. The Parthian monarchs, like the Mogul sovereigns of Hindostan, delighted in the pastoral life of their Scythian ancestors; and the Imperial camp was frequently pitched in the plain of Ctesiphon, on the eastern bank of the Tigris, at the distance of only three miles from Seleucia. The innumerable attendants on luxury and despotism resorted to the court, and the little village of Ctesiphon insensibly swelled into a great city.[22] Under the reign of Marcus, the Roman generals penetrated as far as Ctesiphon and Seleucia. They were received as friends by the Greek colony; they attacked as enemies the seat of the Parthian kings; yet both cities experienced the same treatment. The sack and conflagration of Seleucia, with the massacre of three hundred thousand of the inhabitants, tarnished the glory of the Roman triumph.[23] Seleucia, already exhausted by the neighbourhood of a too powerful rival, sunk under the fatal blow; but Ctesiphon, in about thirty-three years, had sufficiently recovered its strength to maintain an obstinate siege against the emperor Severus. The city was, however, taken by assault; the king, who defended it in person, escaped with precipitation; an hundred thousand captives and a rich booty rewarded the fatigues of the Roman soldiers. Notwithstanding these misfortunes, Ctesiphon succeeded

In the time of Alexander, and probably many ages afterwards, it was thinly inhabited by a savage people of Ichthyophagi, or Fishermen, who knew no arts, who acknowledged no master, and who were divided by inhospitable deserts from the rest of the world. In the twelfth century, the little town of Taiz (supposed by M. d'Anville to be the Tesa of Ptolemy) was peopled and enriched by the resort of the Arabian merchants. In the last age the whole country was divided between three princes, one Mahometan and two Idolaters, who maintained their independence.

[22] That most curious traveller, Bernier, who followed the camp of Aurungzebe from Delhi to Cashmir, describes with great accuracy the immense moving city. The guard of cavalry consisted of 35,000 men, that of infantry of 10,000. It was computed that the camp contained 150,000 horses, mules, and elephants; 50,000 camels, 50,000 oxen, and between 300,000 and 400,000 persons. Almost all Delhi followed the court, whose magnificence supported its industry.

[23] *Quadratus attempted to vindicate the Romans by alleging that the citizens of Seleucia had first violated their faith.*

to Babylon and to Seleucia as one of the great capitals of the East. In summer, the monarch of Persia enjoyed at Ecbatana the cool breezes of the mountains of Media; but the mildness of the climate engaged him to prefer Ctesiphon for his winter residence.

From these successful inroads the Romans derived no real or lasting benefit; nor did they attempt to preserve such distant conquests, separated from the provinces of the empire by a large tract of intermediate desert. The reduction of the kingdom of Osrhoene was an acquisition of less splendour indeed, but of a far more solid advantage. That little state occupied the northern and most fertile part of Mesopotamia, between the Euphrates and the Tigris. Edessa, its capital, was situated about twenty miles beyond the former of those rivers, and the inhabitants, since the time of Alexander, were a mixed race of Greeks, Arabs, Syrians, and Armenians.[24] The feeble sovereigns of Osrhoene, placed on the dangerous verge of two contending empires, were attached from inclination to the Parthian cause; but the superior power of Rome exacted from them a reluctant homage, which is still attested by their medals. After the conclusion of the Parthian war under Marcus, it was judged prudent to secure some substantial pledges of their doubtful fidelity. Forts were constructed in several parts of the country, and a Roman garrison was fixed in the strong town of Nisibis. During the troubles that followed the death of Commodus, the princes of Osrhoene attempted to shake off the yoke; but the stern policy of Severus confirmed their dependence, and the perfidy of Caracalla completed the easy conquest. Abgarus, the last king of Edessa, was sent in chains to Rome, his dominions reduced into a province, and his capital dignified with the rank of colony; and thus the Romans, about ten years before the fall of the Parthian monarchy, obtained a firm and permanent establishment beyond the Euphrates.[25]

[24] *The polished citizens of Antioch called those of Edessa mixed barbarians. It was, however, some praise, that, of the three dialects of the Syriac, the purest and most elegant (the Aramæan) was spoken at Edessa.*

[25] *This kingdom, from Osrhoes, who gave a new name to the country, to the last Abgarus, had lasted 353 years.*

[26] *Xenophon, in the preface to the Cyropædia, gives a clear and magnificent idea of the extent of the empire of Cyrus. Herodotus enters into a curious and particular description of the twenty great Satrapies into which the Persian empire was divided by Darius Hystaspis.*

Prudence as well as glory might have justified a war on the side of Artaxerxes, had his views been confined to the defence or the acquisition of a useful frontier. But the ambitious Persian openly avowed a far more extensive design of conquest; and he thought himself able to support his lofty pretensions by the arms of reason as well as by those of power. Cyrus, he alleged, had first subdued, and his successors had for a long time possessed, the whole extent of Asia, as far as the Propontis and the Ægean Sea; the provinces of Caria and Ionia, under their empire, had been governed by Persian satraps; and all Egypt, to the confines of Æthiopia, had acknowledged their sovereignty.[26] Their rights had been suspended, but not destroyed, by a long usurpation; and, as soon as he received the Persian diadem, which birth and successful valour had placed upon his head, the first great duty of his station called upon him to restore the ancient limits and splendour of the monarchy. The Great King, therefore (such was the haughty style of his embassies to the Emperor Alexander), commanded the Romans instantly to depart from all the provinces of his ancestors, and, yielding to the Persians the empire of Asia, to content themselves with the undisturbed possession of Europe. This haughty mandate was delivered by four hundred of the tallest and most beautiful of the Persians; who, by their fine horses, splendid arms, and rich apparel, displayed the pride and greatness of their master. Such an embassy was much less an offer of negotiation than a declaration of war. Both Alexander Severus and Artaxerxes, collecting the military force of the Roman and Persian monarchies, resolved in this important contest to lead their armies in person.

If we credit what should seem the most authentic of all records, an oration, still extant, and delivered by the emperor himself to the senate, we must allow that the victory of Alexander Severus was not inferior to any of those formerly obtained over the Persians by the son of Philip. The army of the Great King consisted of one hundred and twenty thousand horse, clothed in complete armour of steel; of seven hundred elephants, with towers filled with archers on their backs; and of eighteen hundred chariots armed with scythes. This formidable host, the like of which is not to be found in eastern history, and has scarcely been imagined in eastern romance,[27] was discomfited in a great battle, in which the Roman Alexander approved himself an intrepid soldier and a skilful general. The Great King fled before his valour: an immense booty and the conquest of Mesopotamia were the immediate fruits of this signal victory. Such are the circumstances of this ostentatious and improbable relation, dictated, as it too plainly appears, by the vanity of the monarch, adorned by the unblushing servility of his flatterers, and received without contradiction by a distant and obsequious senate. Far from being inclined to believe that the arms of Alexander obtained any memorable advantage over the Persians, we are induced to suspect that all this blaze of imaginary glory was designed to conceal some real disgrace.

Our suspicions are confirmed by the authority of a contemporary historian, who mentions the virtues of Alexander with respect, and his faults with candour. He describes the judicious plan which had

[27] *There were two hundred scythed chariots at the battle of Arbela, in the host of Darius. In the vast army of Tigranes, which was vanquished by Lucullus, seventeen thousand horse only were completely armed. Antiochus brought fifty-four elephants into the field against the Romans: by his frequent wars and negotiations with the princes of India, he had once collected an hundred and fifty of those great animals; but it may be questioned, whether the most powerful monarch of Hindostan ever formed a line of battle of seven hundred elephants. Instead of three or four thousand elephants, which the Great Mogul was supposed to possess, Tavernier discovered, by a more accurate inquiry, that he had only five hundred for his baggage, and eighty or ninety for the service of war. The Greeks have varied with regard to the number which Porus brought into the field; but Quintus Curtius, in this instance judicious and moderate, is contented with eighty-five elephants, distinguished by their size and strength. In Siam, where these animals are the most numerous and the most esteemed, eighteen*

elephants are allowed as a sufficient proportion for each of the nine brigades into which a just army is divided. The whole number, of one hundred and sixty-two elephants of war, may sometimes be doubled.

[28] *Moses of Chorene illustrates this invasion of Media, by asserting that Chosroes, king of Armenia, defeated Artaxerxes, and pursued him to the confines of India. The exploits of Chosroes have been magnified, and he acted as a dependent ally to the Romans.*

been formed for the conduct of the war. Three Roman armies were destined to invade Persia at the same time, and by different roads. But the operations of the campaign, though wisely concerted, were not executed either with ability or success. The first of these armies, as soon as it had entered the marshy plains of Babylon, towards the artificial conflux of the Euphrates and the Tigris, was encompassed by the superior numbers, and destroyed by the arrows, of the enemy. The alliance of Chosroes, king of Armenia,[28] and the long tract of mountainous country, in which the Persian cavalry was of little service, opened a secure entrance into the heart of Media to the second of the Roman armies. These brave troops laid waste the adjacent provinces, and by several successful actions against Artaxerxes gave a faint colour to the emperor's vanity. But the retreat of this victorious army was imprudent, or at least unfortunate. In repassing the mountains, great numbers of soldiers perished by the badness of the roads and the severity of the winter season. It had been resolved that whilst these two great detachments penetrated into the opposite extremes of the Persian dominions, the main body, under the command of Alexander himself, should support their attack by invading the centre of the kingdom. But the unexperienced youth, influenced by his mother's counsels, and perhaps by his own fears, deserted the bravest troops and the fairest prospect of victory; and, after consuming in Mesopotamia an inactive and inglorious summer, he led back to Antioch an army diminished by sickness, and provoked by disappointment. The behaviour of Artaxerxes had been very different. Flying with rapidity from the hills of Media to the marshes of the Euphrates, he had everywhere opposed the invaders in person; and in either fortune had united with the ablest conduct the most undaunted resolution. But in several obstinate engagements against the veteran legions of Rome the Persian monarch had lost the flower of his troops. Even his victories had weakened his power. The favourable opportunities of the absence of Alexander, and of the confusions that followed that emperor's death, presented themselves in vain to his ambition. Instead of expelling the Romans, as he pretended, from the continent of Asia, he found himself unable to wrest from their hands the little province of Mesopotamia.

The reign of Artaxerxes, which from the last defeat of the Parthians lasted only fourteen years, forms a memorable æra in the history of the East, and even in that of Rome. His character seems to have been marked by those bold and commanding features that generally distinguish the princes who conquer, from those who inherit, an empire. Till the last period of the Persian monarchy, his code of laws was respected as the groundwork of their civil and religious policy.[29] Several of his sayings are preserved. One of them in particular discovers a deep insight into the constitution of government. "The authority of the prince," said Artaxerxes, "must be defended by a military force; that force can only be maintained by taxes; all taxes must, at last, fall upon agriculture; and agriculture can never flourish except under the protection of justice and moderation."[30] Artaxerxes bequeathed his new empire, and his ambitious designs against the Romans, to Sapor, a son not unworthy of his great father; but those designs were too extensive for the power of Persia, and served only to involve both nations in a long series of destructive wars and reciprocal calamities.

The Persians, long since civilized and corrupted, were very far from possessing the martial independence, and the intrepid hardiness, both of mind and body, which have rendered the northern barbarians masters of the world. The science of war, that constituted the more rational force of Greece and Rome, as it now does of Europe, never made any considerable progress in the East. Those disciplined evolutions which harmonize and animate a confused multitude were unknown to the Persians. They were equally unskilled in the arts of constructing, besieging, or defending regular fortifications. They trusted more to their numbers than to their courage; more to their courage than to their discipline. The infantry was a half-armed, spiritless crowd of peasants, levied in haste by the allurements of plunder, and as easily dispersed by a victory as by a defeat. The monarch and his nobles transported into the camp the pride and luxury of the seraglio. Their military operations were impeded by a useless train of women, eunuchs, horses, and camels; and in the midst of a successful campaign the Persian host was often separated or destroyed by an unexpected famine.

But the nobles of Persia, in the bosom of luxury and despotism, preserved a strong sense of personal gallantry and national honour. From the age of seven years they were taught to speak truth, to shoot with the bow, and to ride; and it was universally confessed that in the two last of these arts they had made a more than common proficiency.[31] The most distinguished youth were educated under the monarch's eye, practised their exercises in the gate of his palace, and were severely trained up to the habits of temperance and obedience in their long and laborious parties of hunting. In every province

[29] *The great Chosroes Noushirwan sent the code of Artaxerxes to all his satraps, as the invariable rule of their conduct.*

[30] *We may observe that, after an ancient period of fables, and a long interval of darkness, the modern histories of Persia begin to assume an air of truth with the dynasty of the Sassanides.*

[31] *The Persians are still the most skilful horsemen, and their horses the finest, in the East.*

the satrap maintained a like school of military virtue. The Persian nobles (so natural is the idea of feudal tenures) received from the king's bounty lands and houses on the condition of their service in war. They were ready on the first summons to mount on horseback, with a martial and splendid train of followers, and to join the numerous bodies of guards, who were carefully selected from among the most robust slaves and the bravest adventurers of Asia. These armies, both of light and of heavy cavalry, equally formidable by the impetuosity of their charge and the rapidity of their motions, threatened, as an impending cloud, the eastern provinces of the declining empire of Rome.

IX

THE STATE OF GERMANY TILL THE INVASION OF THE BAR-
BARIANS, IN THE TIME OF THE EMPEROR DECIUS · 248 A.D.

THE government and religion of Persia have deserved some notice from their connexion with the decline and fall of the Roman empire. We shall occasionally mention the Scythian or Sarmatian tribes, which, with their arms and horses, their flocks and herds, their wives and families, wandered over the immense plains which spread themselves from the Caspian Sea to the Vistula, from the confines of Persia to those of Germany. But the warlike Germany, who first resisted, then invaded, and at length overturned, the Western monarchy of Rome, will occupy a much more important place in this history, and possess a stronger, and, if we may use the expression, a more domestic, claim to our attention and regard. The most civilized nations of modern Europe issued from the woods of Germany, and in the rude institutions of those barbarians we may still distinguish the original principles of our present laws and manners. In their primitive state of simplicity and independence, the Germans were surveyed by the discerning eye, and delineated by the masterly pencil, of Tacitus, the first of historians who applied the science of philosophy to the study of facts. The expressive conciseness of his descriptions has deserved to exercise the diligence of innumerable antiquarians, and to excite the genius and penetration of the philosophic historians of our own times. The subject, however various and important, has already been so frequently, so ably, and so successfully discussed, that it is now grown familiar to the reader, and difficult to the writer. We shall therefore content ourselves with observing, and indeed with repeating, some of the most important circumstances of climate, of manners, and of institutions, which rendered the wild barbarians of Germany such formidable enemies to the Roman power.

Ancient Germany, excluding from its independent limits the province westward of the Rhine, which had submitted to the Roman yoke, extended itself over a third part of Europe. Almost the whole of modern Germany, Denmark, Norway, Sweden, Finland, Livonia, Prussia, and the greater part of Poland, were peopled by the various tribes of one great nation, whose complexion, manners, and language denoted a common origin, and preserved a striking resemblance. On the west, ancient Germany was divided by the Rhine from the Gallic, and on the south by the Danube from the Illyrian, provinces of the empire. A ridge of hills, rising from the Danube, and called the Carpathian Mountains, covered Germany on the side of Dacia or Hungary. The eastern frontier was faintly marked by the mutual fears of the Germans and the Sarmatians, and was often confounded by the mixture of warring and confederating tribes of the two nations. In the remote darkness of the north the ancients imperfectly descried a frozen ocean that lay beyond the Baltic Sea and beyond the peninsula, or islands,[1] of Scandinavia.

Some ingenious writers have suspected that Europe was much colder formerly than it is at present; and the most ancient descriptions of the climate of Germany tend exceedingly to confirm their theory. The general complaints of intense frost and eternal winter are perhaps little to be regarded, since we have no method of reducing to the accurate standard of the thermometer the feelings or the expressions of an orator born in the happier regions of Greece or Asia. But I shall select two remarkable circumstances of a less equivocal nature. 1. The great rivers which covered the Roman provinces, the Rhine and the Danube, were frequently frozen over, and capable of supporting the most enormous weights. The barbarians, who often chose that severe season for their inroads, transported, without apprehension or danger, their numerous armies, their cavalry, and their heavy waggons, over a vast and solid bridge of ice.[2] Modern ages have not presented an instance of a like phenomenon. 2. The reindeer, that useful animal, from whom the savage of the North derives the best comforts of his dreary life, is of a constitution that supports, and even requires, the most intense cold. He is found on the rock of Spitzberg, within ten degrees of the pole; he seems to delight in the snows of Lapland and Siberia; but at present he cannot subsist, much less multiply, in any country to the south of the Baltic. In the time of Cæsar, the reindeer, as well as the elk and the wild bull, was a native of the Hercynian forest, which then overshadowed a great part of Germany and Poland.[3] The modern improvements sufficiently explain the causes of the diminution of the cold. These immense woods have been gradually cleared, which in-

[1] *The modern philosophers of Sweden seem agreed that the waters of the Baltic gradually sink in a regular proportion, which they have ventured to estimate at half an inch every year. Twenty centuries ago, the flat country of Scandinavia must have been covered by the sea; while the high lands rose above the waters, as so many islands of various forms and dimensions. Such indeed is the notion given us by Mela, Pliny, and Tacitus, of the vast countries round the Baltic.*

[2] *On the banks of the Danube, the wine, when brought to table, was frequently frozen into great lumps,* frusta vini. *The fact is confirmed by a soldier and a philosopher, who had experienced the intense cold of Thrace.*

[3] *The most inquisitive of the Germans were ignorant of its utmost limits, although some of them had travelled in it more than sixty days' journey.*

tercepted from the earth the rays of the sun. The morasses have been drained, and, in proportion as the soil has been cultivated, the air has become more temperate. Canada, at this day, is an exact picture of ancient Germany. Although situate in the same parallel with the finest provinces of France and England, that country experiences the most rigorous cold. The reindeer are very numerous, the ground is covered with deep and lasting snow, and the great river of St. Lawrence is regularly frozen, in a season when the waters of the Seine and the Thames are usually free from ice.

It is difficult to ascertain, and easy to exaggerate, the influence of the climate of ancient Germany over the minds and bodies of the natives. Many writers have supposed, and most have allowed, though, as it should seem, without any adequate proof, that the rigorous cold of the North was favourable to long life and generative vigour, that the women were more fruitful, and the human species more prolific, than in warmer or more temperate climates. We may assert, with greater confidence, that the keen air of Germany formed the large and masculine limbs of the natives, who were, in general, of a more lofty stature than the people of the South, gave them a kind of strength better adapted to violent exertions than to patient labour, and inspired them with constitutional bravery, which is the result of nerves and spirits. The severity of a winter campaign, that chilled the courage of the Roman troops, was scarcely felt by these hardy children of the North,[4] who, in their turn, were unable to resist the summer heats, and dissolved away in languor and sickness under the beams of an Italian sun.[5]

There is not anywhere upon the globe a large tract of country, which we have discovered destitute of inhabitants, or whose first population can be fixed with any degree of historical certainty. And yet, as the most philosophic minds can seldom refrain from investigating the infancy of great nations, our curiosity consumes itself in toilsome and disappointed efforts. When Tacitus considered the purity of the German blood, and the forbidding aspect of the country, he was disposed to pronounce those barbarians *Indigenæ*, or natives of the soil. We may allow with safety, and perhaps with truth, that ancient Germany was not originally peopled by any foreign colonies already formed into a political society;[6] but that the name and nation received their existence from the gradual union of some wandering savages of the Hercynian woods. To assert those savages to have been the spontaneous production of the earth which they inhabited would be a rash inference, thoroughly to be con-

[4] *The Cimbri, by way of amusement, often slid down mountains of snow on their broad shields.*

[5] *The Romans made war in all climates, and by their excellent discipline were in a great measure preserved in health and vigour. It may be remarked that man is the only animal which can live and multiply in every country from the equator to the poles. The hog seems to approach the nearest to our species in that privilege.*

[6] *The emigration of the Gauls followed the course of the Danube, and discharged itself on Greece and Asia. Tacitus could discover only one inconsiderable tribe that retained any traces of a Gallic origin.*

demned by the principles of religion, and unwarranted by reason.

Such rational doubt is but ill suited with the genius of popular vanity. Among the nations who have adopted the Mosaic history of the world, the ark of Noah has been of the same use, as was formerly to the Greeks and Romans the siege of Troy. On a narrow basis of acknowledged truth, an immense but rude superstructure of fable has been erected; and the wild Irishman,[7] as well as the wild Tartar, could point out the individual son of Japhet from whose loins his ancestors were lineally descended. The last century abounded with antiquarians of profound learning and easy faith, who, by the dim light of legends and traditions, of conjectures and etymologies, conducted the great-grandchildren of Noah from the Tower of Babel to the extremities of the globe. Of these judicious critics, one of the most entertaining was Olaus Rudbeck, professor in the university of Upsal.[8] Whatever is celebrated either in history or fable, this zealous patriot ascribes to his country. From Sweden (which formed so considerable a part of ancient Germany) the Greeks themselves derived their alphabetical characters, their astronomy, and their religion. Of that delightful region (for such it appeared to the eyes of a native) the Atlantis of Plato, the country of the Hyperboreans, the gardens of the Hesperides, the Fortunate Islands, and even the Elysian Fields, were all but faint and imperfect transcripts. A clime so profusely favoured by Nature could not long remain desert after the flood. The learned Rudbeck allows the family of Noah a few years to multiply from eight to about twenty thousand persons. He then disperses them into small colonies to replenish the earth, and to propagate the human species. The German or Swedish detachment (which marched, if I am not mistaken, under the command of Askenaz the son of Gomer, the son of Japhet) distinguished itself by a more than common diligence in the prosecution of this great work. The northern hive cast its swarms over the greatest part of Europe, Africa, and Asia; and (to use the author's metaphor) the blood circulated back from the extremities to the heart.

But all this well-laboured system of German antiquities is annihilated by a single fact, too well attested to admit of any doubt, and of too decisive a nature to leave room for any reply. The Germans, in the age of Tacitus, were unacquainted with the use of letters;[9] and the use of letters is the principal circumstance that distinguishes a civilized people from a herd of savages, incapable of knowledge or reflection. Without that artificial help the human memory soon dissipates or corrupts the ideas intrusted to her charge; and the nobler

[7] According to Dr. Keating, the giant Partholanus, who was the son of Seara, the son of Esra, the son of Sru, the son of Framant, the son of Fathaclan, the son of Magog, the son of Japhet, the son of Noah, landed on the coast of Munster, the 14th day of May, in the year of the world one thousand nine hundred and seventy-eight. Though he succeeded in his great enterprise, the loose behaviour of his wife rendered his domestic life very unhappy, and provoked him to such a degree, that he killed — her favourite greyhound. This, as the learned historian very properly observes, was the first instance of female falsehood and infidelity ever known in Ireland.

[8] His work, entitled Atlantica, is uncommonly scarce. Bayle has given two most curious extracts from it.

[9] Tacitus: Literarum secreta viri pariter ac fœminæ ignorant. We may rest contented with this decisive authority, without entering into the obscure disputes concerning the antiquity of the Runic characters. The learned Celsius, a Swede, a scholar and a

faculties of the mind, no longer supplied with models or with materials, gradually forget their powers: the judgment becomes feeble and lethargic, the imagination languid or irregular. Fully to apprehend this important truth, let us attempt, in an improved society, to calculate the immense distance between the man of learning and the *illiterate* peasant. The former, by reading and reflection, multiplies his own experience, and lives in distant ages and remote countries; whilst the latter, rooted to a single spot, and confined to a few years of existence, surpasses but very little his fellow-labourer the ox in the exercise of his mental faculties. The same and even a greater difference will be found between nations than between individuals; and we may safely pronounce, that without some species of writing no people has ever preserved the faithful annals of their history, ever made any considerable progress in the abstract sciences, or ever possessed, in any tolerable degree of perfection, the useful and agreeable arts of life.

Of these arts the ancient Germans were wretchedly destitute. They passed their lives in a state of ignorance and poverty, which it has pleased some declaimers to dignify with the appellation of virtuous simplicity. Modern Germany is said to contain about two thousand three hundred walled towns. In a much wider extent of country the geographer Ptolemy could discover no more than ninety places which he decorates with the name of cities; though, according to our ideas, they would but ill deserve that splendid title. We can only suppose them to have been rude fortifications, constructed in the centre of the woods, and designed to secure the women, children, and cattle, whilst the warriors of the tribe marched out to repel a sudden invasion. But Tacitus asserts, as a well-known fact, that the Germans, in his time, had *no* cities; and that they affected to despise the works of Roman industry as places of confinement rather than of security.[10] Their edifices were not even contiguous, or formed into regular villas;[11] each barbarian fixed his independent dwelling on the spot to which a plain, a wood, or a stream of fresh water, had induced him to give the preference. Neither stone, nor brick, nor tiles, were employed in these slight habitations.[12] They were indeed no more than low huts of a circular figure, built of rough timber, thatched with straw, and pierced at the top to leave a free passage for the smoke. In the most inclement winter, the hardy German was satisfied with a scanty garment made of the skin of some animal. The nations who dwelt towards the North clothed themselves in furs; and the women manufactured for their own use

philosopher, was of opinion that they were nothing more than the Roman letters, with the curves changed into straight lines for the ease of engraving. We may add that the oldest Runic inscriptions are supposed to be of the third century, and the most ancient writer who mentions the Runic characters, is Venantius Fortunatus, who lived towards the end of the sixth century.

[10] *When the Germans commanded the Ubii of Cologne to cast off the Roman yoke, and with their new freedom to resume their ancient manners, they insisted on the immediate demolition of the walls of the colony.*

[11] *The straggling villages of Silesia are several miles in length.*

[12] *One hundred and forty years after Tacitus a few more regular structures were erected near the Rhine and Danube.*

a coarse kind of linen. The game of various sorts with which the forests of Germany were plentifully stocked supplied its inhabitants with food and exercise. Their monstrous herds of cattle, less remarkable indeed for their beauty than for their utility, formed the principal object of their wealth. A small quantity of corn was the only produce exacted from the earth: the use of orchards or artificial meadows was unknown to the Germans; nor can we expect any improvements in agriculture from a people whose property every year experienced a general change by a new division of the arable lands, and who, in that strange operation, avoided disputes by suffering a great part of their territory to lie waste and without tillage.

Gold, silver, and iron were extremely scarce in Germany. Its barbarous inhabitants wanted both skill and patience to investigate those rich veins of silver, which have so liberally rewarded the attention of the princes of Brunswick and Saxony. Sweden, which now supplies Europe with iron, was equally ignorant of its own riches; and the appearance of the arms of the Germans furnished a sufficient proof how little iron they were able to bestow on what they must have deemed the noblest use of that metal. The various transactions of peace and war had introduced some Roman coins (chiefly silver) among the borderers of the Rhine and Danube; but the more distant tribes were absolutely unacquainted with the use of money, carried on their confined traffic by the exchange of commodities, and prized their rude earthen vessels as of equal value with the silver vases, the presents of Rome to their princes and ambassadors. To a mind capable of reflection such leading facts convey more instruction than a tedious detail of subordinate circumstances. The value of money has been settled by general consent to express our wants and our property, as letters were invented to express our ideas; and both these institutions, by giving more active energy to the powers and passions of human nature, have contributed to multiply the objects they were designed to represent. The use of gold and silver is in a great measure factitious; but it would be impossible to enumerate the important and various services which agriculture, and all the arts, have received from iron, when tempered and fashioned by the operation of fire and the dexterous hand of man. Money, in a word, is the most universal incitement, iron the most powerful instrument, of human industry; and it is very difficult to conceive by what means a people, neither actuated by the one nor seconded by the other, could emerge from the grossest barbarism.[13]

If we contemplate a savage nation in any part of the globe, a

[13] *It is said that the Mexicans and Peruvians, without the use of either money or iron, had made a very great progress in the arts. Those arts, and the monuments they produced, have been strangely magnified.*

supine indolence and a carelessness of futurity will be found to constitute their general character. In a civilized state every faculty of man is expanded and exercised; and the great chain of mutual dependence connects and embraces the several members of society. The most numerous portion of it is employed in constant and useful labour. The select few, placed by fortune above that necessity, can, however, fill up their time by the pursuits of interest or glory, by the improvement of their estate or of their understanding, by the duties, the pleasures, and even the follies, of social life. The Germans were not possessed of these varied resources. The care of the house and family, the management of the land and cattle, were delegated to the old and the infirm, to women and slaves. The lazy warrior, destitute of every art that might employ his leisure hours, consumed his days and nights in the animal gratifications of sleep and food. And yet, by a wonderful diversity of nature (according to the remark of a writer who had pierced into its darkest recesses), the same barbarians are by turns the most indolent and the most restless of mankind. They delight in sloth, they detest tranquillity. The languid soul, oppressed with its own weight, anxiously required some new and powerful sensation; and war and danger were the only amusements adequate to its fierce temper. The sound that summoned the German to arms was grateful to his ear. It roused him from his uncomfortable lethargy, gave him an active pursuit, and, by strong exercise of the body, and violent emotions of the mind, restored him to a more lively sense of his existence. In the dull intervals of peace these barbarians were immoderately addicted to deep gaming and excessive drinking; both of which, by different means, the one by inflaming their passions, the other by extinguishing their reason, alike relieved them from the pain of thinking. They gloried in passing whole days and nights at table; and the blood of friends and relations often stained their numerous and drunken assemblies. Their debts of honour (for in that light they have transmitted to us those of play) they discharged with the most romantic fidelity. The desperate gamester, who had staked his person and liberty on a last throw of the dice, patiently submitted to the decision of fortune, and suffered himself to be bound, chastised, and sold into remote slavery, by his weaker but more lucky antagonist.[14]

Strong beer, a liquor extracted with very little art from wheat or barley, and *corrupted* (as it is strongly expressed by Tacitus) into a certain semblance of wine, was sufficient for the gross purposes of German debauchery. But those who had tasted the rich wines of

[14] *The Germans might borrow the* arts of play *from the Romans, but the* passion *is wonderfully inherent in the human species.*

Italy, and afterwards of Gaul, sighed for that more delicious species of intoxication. They attempted not, however (as has since been executed with so much success), to naturalize the vine on the banks of the Rhine and Danube; nor did they endeavour to procure by industry the materials of an advantageous commerce. To solicit by labour what might be ravished by arms was esteemed unworthy of the German spirit. The intemperate thirst of strong liquors often urged the barbarians to invade the provinces on which art or nature had bestowed those much envied presents. The Tuscan who betrayed his country to the Celtic nations attracted them into Italy by the prospect of the rich fruits and delicious wines, the productions of a happier climate. And in the same manner the German auxiliaries, invited into France during the civil wars of the sixteenth century, were allured by the promise of plenteous quarters in the provinces of Champagne and Burgundy. Drunkenness, the most illiberal, but not the most dangerous of *our* vices, was sometimes capable, in a less civilized state of mankind, of occasioning a battle, a war, or a revolution.

The climate of ancient Germany has been mollified, and the soil fertilized, by the labour of ten centuries from the time of Charlemagne. The same extent of ground, which at present maintains, in ease and plenty, a million of husbandmen and artificers, was unable to supply an hundred thousand lazy warriors with the simple necessaries of life.[15] The Germans abandoned their immense forests to the exercise of hunting, employed in pasturage the most considerable part of their lands, bestowed on the small remainder a rude and careless cultivation, and then accused the scantiness and sterility of a country that refused to maintain the multitude of its inhabitants. When the return of famine severely admonished them of the importance of the arts, the national distress was sometimes alleviated by the emigration of a third, perhaps, or a fourth part of their youth. The possession and the enjoyment of property are the pledges which bind a civilized people to an improved country. But the Germans, who carried with them what they most valued, their arms, their cattle, and their women, cheerfully abandoned the vast silence of their woods for the unbounded hopes of plunder and conquest. The innumerable swarms that issued, or seemed to issue, from the great storehouse of nations, were multiplied by the fears of the vanquished and by the credulity of succeeding ages. And from facts thus exaggerated, an opinion was gradually established, and has been supported by writers of distinguished reputation, that, in the age of

[15] *The Helvetian nation, which issued from the country called Switzerland, contained, of every age and sex, 368,000 persons. At present, the number of people in the Pays de Vaud (a small district on the banks of the Leman Lake, much more distinguished for politeness than for industry) amounts to 112,591.*

Cæsar and Tacitus, the inhabitants of the North were far more numerous than they are in our days. A more serious inquiry into the causes of population seems to have convinced modern philosophers of the falsehood, and indeed the impossibility, of the supposition. To the names of Mariana and of Machiavel we can oppose the equal names of Robertson and Hume.

A warlike nation like the Germans, without either cities, letters, arts, or money, found some compensation for this savage state in the enjoyment of liberty. Their poverty secured their freedom, since our desires and our possessions are the strongest fetters of despotism. "Among the Suiones (says Tacitus) riches are held in honour. They are *therefore* subject to an absolute monarch, who instead of intrusting his people with the free use of arms, as is practised in the rest of Germany, commits them to the safe custody, not of a citizen, or even of a freedman, but of a slave. The neighbours of the Suiones, the Sitones, are sunk even below servitude; they obey a woman." [16] In the mention of these exceptions, the great historian sufficiently acknowledges the general theory of government. We are only at a loss to conceive by what means riches and despotism could penetrate into a remote corner of the North, and extinguish the generous flame that blazed with such fierceness on the frontier of the Roman provinces, or how the ancestors of those Danes and Norwegians, so distinguished in later ages by their unconquered spirit, could thus tamely resign the great character of German liberty. [17] Some tribes, however, on the coast of the Baltic, acknowledged the authority of kings, though without relinquishing the rights of men; but in the far greater part of Germany the form of government was a democracy, tempered, indeed, and controlled, not so much by general and positive laws as by the occasional ascendant of birth or valour, of eloquence or superstition.

Civil governments, in their first institutions, are voluntary associations for mutual defence. To obtain the desired end it is absolutely necessary that each individual should conceive himself obliged to submit his private opinion and actions to the judgment of the greater number of his associates. The German tribes were contented with this rude but liberal outline of political society. As soon as a youth, born of free parents, had attained the age of manhood, he was introduced into the general council of his countrymen, solemnly invested with a shield and spear, and adopted as an equal and worthy member of the military commonwealth. The assembly of the warriors of the tribe was convened at stated seasons, or on sud-

[16] *Freinshemius (who dedicated his supplement to Livy, to Christina of Sweden) thinks proper to be very angry with the Roman who expressed so very little reverence for Northern queens.*

[17] *May we not suspect the superstition was the parent of despotism? The descendants of Odin (whose race was not extinct till the year 1060) are said to have reigned in Sweden above a thousand years. The temple of Upsal was the ancient seat of religion and empire. In the year 1153 I find a singular law prohibiting the use and possession of arms to any, except the king's guards. Is it not probable that it was coloured by the pretence of reviving an old institution?*

den emergencies. The trial of public offences, the election of magistrates, and the great business of peace and war, were determined by its independent voice. Sometimes, indeed, these important questions were previously considered and prepared in a more select council of the principal chieftains. The magistrates might deliberate and persuade, the people only could resolve and execute; and the resolutions of the Germans were for the most part hasty and violent. Barbarians accustomed to place their freedom in gratifying the present passion, and their courage in overlooking all future consequences, turned away with indignant contempt from the remonstrances of justice and policy, and it was the practice to signify by a hollow murmur their dislike of such timid councils. But, whenever a more popular orator proposed to vindicate the meanest citizen, from either foreign or domestic injury, whenever he called upon his fellow-countrymen to assert the national honour, or to pursue some enterprise full of danger and glory, a loud clashing of shields and spears expressed the eager applause of the assembly. For the Germans always met in arms, and it was constantly to be dreaded lest an irregular multitude, inflamed with faction and strong liquors, should use those arms to enforce, as well as to declare, their furious resolves. We may recollect how often the diets of Poland have been polluted with blood, and the more numerous party has been compelled to yield to the more violent and seditious.[18]

[18] *Even in* our *ancient parliament, the barons often carried a question not so much by the number of votes as by that of their armed followers.*

A general of the tribe was elected on occasions of danger; and, if the danger was pressing and extensive, several tribes concurred in the choice of the same general. The bravest warrior was named to lead his countrymen into the field, by his example rather than by his commands. But this power, however limited, was still invidious. It expired with the war, and in time of peace, the German tribes acknowledged not any supreme chief. *Princes* were, however, appointed, in the general assembly, to administer justice, or rather to compose differences, in their respective districts. In the choice of these magistrates as much regard was shown to birth as to merit. To each was assigned, by the public, a guard, and a council of an hundred persons, and the first of the princes appears to have enjoyed a pre-eminence of rank and honour which sometimes tempted the Romans to compliment him with the regal title.

The comparative view of the powers of the magistrates, in two remarkable instances, is alone sufficient to represent the whole system of German manners. The disposal of the landed property within their district was absolutely vested in their hands, and they

distributed it every year according to a new division. At the same
time they were not authorized to punish with death, to imprison,
or even to strike a private citizen. A people thus jealous of their persons, and careless of their possessions, must have been totally destitute of industry and the arts, but animated with a high sense of
honour and independence.

The Germans respected only those duties which they imposed on
themselves. The most obscure soldier resisted with disdain the authority of the magistrates. "The noblest youths blushed not to be
numbered among the faithful companions of some renowned chief,
to whom they devoted their arms and service. A noble emulation
prevailed among the companions to obtain the first place in the esteem of their chief; amongst the chiefs, to acquire the greatest number of valiant companions. To be ever surrounded by a band of
select youths was the pride and strength of the chiefs, their ornament in peace, their defence in war. The glory of such distinguished
heroes diffused itself beyond the narrow limits of their own tribe.
Presents and embassies solicited their friendship, and the fame of
their arms often ensured victory to the party which they espoused.
In the hour of danger it was shameful for the chief to be surpassed
in valour by his companions; shameful for the companions not to
equal the valour of their chief. To survive his fall in battle was indelible infamy. To protect his person, and to adorn his glory with
the trophies of their own exploits, were the most sacred of their
duties. The chiefs combated for victory, the companions for the
chief. The noblest warriors, whenever their native country was sunk
in the laziness of peace, maintained their numerous bands in some
distant scene of action, to exercise their restless spirit, and to acquire
renown by voluntary dangers. Gifts worthy of soldiers, the warlike
steed, the bloody and ever victorious lance, were the rewards which
the companions claimed from the liberality of their chief. The rude
plenty of his hospitable board was the only pay that *he* could bestow,
or *they* would accept. War, rapine, and the free-will offerings of his
friends, supplied the materials of this munificence." This institution, however it might accidentally weaken the several republics,
invigorated the general character of the Germans, and even ripened
amongst them all the virtues of which barbarians are susceptible—
the faith and valour, the hospitality and the courtesy, so conspicuous
long afterwards in the ages of chivalry. The honourable gifts, bestowed by the chief on his brave companions, have been supposed,
by an ingenious writer, to contain the first rudiments of the fiefs,

distributed after the conquest of the Roman provinces, by the barbarian lords among their vassals, with a similar duty of homage and military service. These conditions are, however, very repugnant to the maxims of the ancient Germans, who delighted in mutual presents, but without either imposing or accepting the weight of obligations.

"In the days of chivalry, or more properly of romance, all the men were brave, and all the women were chaste"; and, notwithstanding the latter of these virtues is acquired and preserved with much more difficulty than the former, it is ascribed, almost without exception, to the wives of the ancient Germans. Polygamy was not in use, except among the princes, and among them only for the sake of multiplying their alliances. Divorces were prohibited by manners rather than by laws. Adulteries were punished as rare and inexpiable crimes; nor was seduction justified by example and fashion.[19] We may easily discover that Tacitus indulges an honest pleasure in the contrast of barbarian virtue with the dissolute conduct of the Roman ladies: yet there are some striking circumstances that give an air of truth, or at least of probability, to the conjugal faith and chastity of the Germans.

Although the progress of civilization has undoubtedly contributed to assuage the fiercer passions of human nature, it seems to have been less favourable to the virtue of chastity, whose most dangerous enemy is the softness of the mind. The refinements of life corrupt while they polish the intercourse of the sexes. The gross appetite of love becomes most dangerous, when it is elevated, or rather, indeed, disguised, by sentimental passion. The elegance of dress, of motion, and of manners, gives a lustre to beauty, and inflames the senses through the imagination. Luxurious entertainments, midnight dances, and licentious spectacles, present at once temptation and opportunity to female frailty. From such dangers the unpolished wives of the barbarians were secured by poverty, solitude, and the painful cares of a domestic life. The German huts, open on every side to the eye of indiscretion or jealousy, were a better safeguard of conjugal fidelity than the walls, the bolts, and the eunuchs of a Persian haram. To this reason another may be added of a more honourable nature. The Germans treated their women with esteem and confidence, consulted them on every occasion of importance, and fondly believed that in their breasts resided a sanctity and wisdom more than human. Some of these interpreters of fate, such as Velleda, in the Batavian war, governed, in the name

[19] *The adulteress was whipped through the village. Neither wealth nor beauty could inspire compassion, or procure her a second husband.*

of the deity, the fiercest nations of Germany. The rest of the sex, without being adored as goddesses, were respected as the free and equal companions of soldiers; associated even by the marriage ceremony to a life of toil, of danger, and of glory.[20] In their great invasions, the camps of the barbarians were filled with a multitude of women, who remained firm and undaunted amidst the sound of arms, the various forms of destruction, and the honourable wounds of their sons and husbands. Fainting armies of Germans have more than once been driven back upon the enemy by the generous despair of the women, who dreaded death much less than servitude. If the day was irrecoverably lost, they well knew how to deliver themselves and their children, with their own hands, from an insulting victor.[21] Heroines of such a cast may claim our admiration; but they were most assuredly neither lovely nor very susceptible of love. Whilst they affected to emulate the stern virtues of *man,* they must have resigned that attractive softness in which principally consist the charm and weakness of *woman.* Conscious pride taught the German females to suppress every tender emotion that stood in competition with honour, and the first honour of the sex has ever been that of chastity. The sentiments and conduct of these high-spirited matrons may, at once, be considered as a cause, as an effect, and as a proof, of the general character of the nation. Female courage, however it may be raised by fanaticism, or confirmed by habit, can be only a faint and imperfect imitation of the manly valour that distinguishes the age or country in which it may be found.

The religious system of the Germans (if the wild opinions of savages can deserve that name) was dictated by their wants, their fears, and their ignorance.[22] They adored the great visible objects and agents of Nature, the Sun and the Moon, the Fire and the Earth; together with those imaginary deities who were supposed to preside over the most important occupations of human life. They were persuaded that, by some ridiculous arts of divination, they could discover the will of the superior beings, and that human sacrifices were the most precious and acceptable offering to their altars. Some applause has been hastily bestowed on the sublime notion entertained by that people of the Deity whom they neither confined within the walls of a temple, nor represented by any human figure; but when we recollect that the Germans were unskilled in architecture, and totally unacquainted with the art of sculpture, we shall readily assign the true reason of a scruple, which arose not so much from a superiority of reason as from a want of ingenuity. The only

[20] *The marriage present was a yoke of oxen, horses, and arms.*

[21] *Before the wives of the Teutones destroyed themselves and their children, they had offered to surrender, on condition that they should be received as the slaves of the vestal virgins.*

[22] *Tacitus has employed a few lines, and Cluverius one hundred and twenty-four pages, on this obscure subject. The former discovers in Germany the gods of Greece and Rome. The latter is positive that, under the emblems of the sun, the moon, and the fire, his pious ancestors worshipped the Trinity in unity.*

179

temples in Germany were dark and ancient groves, consecrated by the reverence of succeeding generations. Their secret gloom, the imagined residence of an invisible power, by presenting no distinct object of fear or worship, impressed the mind with a still deeper sense of religious horror;[23] and the priests, rude and illiterate as they were, had been taught by experience the use of every artifice that could preserve and fortify impressions so well suited to their own interest.

The same ignorance which renders barbarians incapable of conceiving or embracing the useful restraints of laws exposes them naked and unarmed to the blind terrors of superstition. The German priests, improving this favourable temper of their countrymen, had assumed a jurisdiction even in temporal concerns which the magistrate could not venture to exercise; and the haughty warrior patiently submitted to the lash of correction, when it was inflicted, not by any human power, but by the immediate order of the god of war. The defects of civil policy were sometimes supplied by the interposition of ecclesiastical authority. The latter was constantly exerted to maintain silence and decency in the popular assemblies; and was sometimes extended to a more enlarged concern for the national welfare. A solemn procession was occasionally celebrated in the present countries of Mecklenburgh and Pomerania. The unknown symbol of the *Earth,* covered with a thick veil, was placed on a carriage drawn by cows; and in this manner the goddess, whose common residence was in the isle of Rugen, visited several adjacent tribes of her worshippers. During her progress, the sound of war was hushed, quarrels were suspended, arms laid aside, and the restless Germans had an opportunity of tasting the blessings of peace and harmony. The *truce of God,* so often and so ineffectually proclaimed by the clergy of the eleventh century, was an obvious imitation of this ancient custom.

But the influence of religion was far more powerful to inflame than to moderate the fierce passions of the Germans. Interest and fanaticism often prompted its ministers to sanctify the most daring and the most unjust enterprises, by the approbation of Heaven, and full assurances of success. The consecrated standards, long revered in the groves of superstition, were placed in the front of the battle;[24] and the hostile army was devoted with dire execrations to the gods of war and of thunder. In the faith of soldiers (and such were the Germans) cowardice is the most unpardonable of sins. A brave man was the worthy favourite of their martial deities; the wretch who

[23] *The sacred wood, described with such sublime horror by Lucan, was in the neighbourhood of Marseilles; but there were many of the same kind in Germany.*

[24] *These standards were only the heads of wild beasts.*

had lost his shield was alike banished from the religious and the civil assemblies of his countrymen. Some tribes of the north seem to have embraced the doctrine of transmigration, others imagined a gross paradise of immortal drunkenness. All agreed that a life spent in arms, and a glorious death in battle, were the best preparations for a happy futurity, either in this or in another world.

The immortality so vainly promised by the priests was, in some degree, conferred by the bards. That singular order of men has most deservedly attracted the notice of all who have attempted to investigate the antiquities of the Celts, the Scandinavians, and the Germans. Their genius and character, as well as the reverence paid to that important office, have been sufficiently illustrated. But we cannot so easily express, or even conceive, the enthusiasm of arms and glory which they kindled in the breast of their audience. Among a polished people, a taste for poetry is rather an amusement of the fancy than a passion of the soul. And yet, when in calm retirement we peruse the combats described by Homer or Tasso, we are insensibly seduced by the fiction, and feel a momentary glow of martial ardour. But how faint, how cold is the sensation which a peaceful mind can receive from solitary study! It was in the hour of battle, or in the feast of victory, that the bards celebrated the glory of heroes of ancient days, the ancestors of those warlike chieftains who listened with transport to their artless but animated strains. The view of arms and of danger heightened the effect of the military song; and the passions which it tended to excite, the desire of fame and the contempt of death, were the habitual sentiments of a German mind.[25]

Such was the situation and such were the manners of the ancient Germans. Their climate, their want of learning, of arts, and of laws, their notions of honour, of gallantry, and of religion, their sense of freedom, impatience of peace, and thirst of enterprise, all contributed to form a people of military heroes. And yet we find that, during more than two hundred and fifty years that elapsed from the defeat of Varus to the reign of Decius, these formidable barbarians made few considerable attempts, and not any material impression, on the luxurious and enslaved provinces of the empire. Their progress was checked by their want of arms and discipline, and their fury was diverted by the intestine divisions of ancient Germany.

I. It has been observed, with ingenuity, and not without truth, that the command of iron soon gives a nation the command of gold. But the rude tribes of Germany, alike destitute of both those valu-

[25] *The classical reader may remember the rank of Demodocus in the Phæacian court, and the ardour infused by Tyrtæus into the fainting Spartans. Yet there is little probability that the Greeks and the Germans were the same people. Much learned trifling might be spared, if our antiquarians would condescend to reflect that similar manners will naturally be produced by similar situations.*

able metals, were reduced slowly to acquire, by their unassisted strength, the possession of the one as well as the other. The face of a German army displayed their poverty of iron. Swords and the longer kind of lances they could seldom use. Their *frameæ* (as they called them in their own language) were long spears headed with a sharp but narrow iron point, and which, as occasion required, they either darted from a distance, or pushed in close onset. With this spear and with a shield their cavalry was contented. A multitude of darts, scattered [26] with incredible force, were an additional resource of the infantry. Their military dress, when they wore any, was nothing more than a loose mantle. A variety of colours was the only ornament of their wooden or their osier shields. Few of the chiefs were distinguished by cuirasses, scarce any by helmets. Though the horses of Germany were neither beautiful, swift, nor practised in the skilful evolutions of the Roman manage, several of the nations obtained renown by their cavalry; but, in general, the principal strength of the Germans consisted in their infantry,[27] which was drawn up in several deep columns, according to the distinction of tribes and families. Impatient of fatigue or delay, these half-armed warriors rushed to battle with dissonant shouts and disordered ranks; and sometimes, by the effort of native valour, prevailed over the constrained and more artificial bravery of the Roman mercenaries. But as the barbarians poured forth their whole souls on the first onset, they knew not how to rally or to retire. A repulse was a sure defeat; and a defeat was most commonly total destruction. When we recollect the complete armour of the Roman soldiers, their discipline, exercises, evolutions, fortified camps, and military engines, it appears a just matter of surprise how the naked and unassisted valour of the barbarians could dare to encounter in the field the strength of the legions and the various troops of the auxiliaries, which seconded their operations. The contest was too unequal, till the introduction of luxury had enervated the vigour, and a spirit of disobedience and sedition had relaxed the discipline, of the Roman armies. The introduction of barbarian auxiliaries into those armies was a measure attended with very obvious dangers, as it might gradually instruct the Germans in the arts of war and of policy. Although they were admitted in small numbers and with the strictest precaution, the example of Civilis was proper to convince the Romans that the danger was not imaginary, and that their precautions were not always sufficient. During the civil wars that followed the death of Nero, that artful and intrepid Batavian,

[26] *Missilia spargunt, Tacitus. Either that historian used a vague expression, or he meant that they were thrown at random.*

[27] *It was the principal distinction from the Sarmatians, who generally fought on horseback.*

whom his enemies condescended to compare with Hannibal and Sertorius,[28] formed a great design of freedom and ambition. Eight Batavian cohorts, renowned in the wars of Britain and Italy, repaired to his standard. He introduced an army of Germans into Gaul, prevailed on the powerful cities of Treves and Langres to embrace his cause, defeated the legions, destroyed their fortified camps, and employed against the Romans the military knowledge which he had acquired in their service. When at length, after an obstinate struggle, he yielded to the power of the empire, Civilis secured himself and his country by an honourable treaty. The Batavians still continued to occupy the islands of the Rhine,[29] the allies, not the servants, of the Roman monarchy.

II. The strength of ancient Germany appears formidable when we consider the effects that might have been produced by its united effort. The wide extent of country might very possibly contain a million of warriors, as all who were of an age to bear arms were of a temper to use them. But this fierce multitude, incapable of concerting or executing any plan of national greatness, was agitated by various and often hostile intentions. Germany was divided into more than forty independent states; and even in each state the union of the several tribes was extremely loose and precarious. The barbarians were easily provoked; they knew not how to forgive an injury, much less an insult; their resentments were bloody and implacable. The casual disputes that so frequently happened in their tumultuous parties of hunting or drinking were sufficient to inflame the minds of whole nations; the private feud of any considerable chieftains diffused itself among their followers and allies. To chastise the insolent, or to plunder the defenceless, were alike causes of war. The most formidable states of Germany affected to encompass their territories with a wide frontier of solitude and devastation. The awful distance preserved by their neighbours attested the terror of their arms, and in some measure defended them from the danger of unexpected incursions.

"The Bructeri (it is Tacitus who now speaks) were totally exterminated by the neighbouring tribes,[30] provoked by their insolence, allured by the hopes of spoil, and perhaps inspired by the tutelar deities of the empire. Above sixty thousand barbarians were destroyed, not by the Roman arms, but in our sight, and for our entertainment. May the nations, enemies of Rome, ever preserve this enmity to each other! We have now attained the utmost verge of prosperity, and have nothing left to demand of fortune except the

[28] *Like them, he had lost an eye.*

[29] *It was contained between the two branches of the old Rhine, as they subsisted before the face of the country was changed by art and nature.*

[30] *They are mentioned, however, in the fourth and fifth centuries as a tribe of Franks.*

discord of the barbarians." These sentiments, less worthy of the humanity than of the patriotism of Tacitus, express the invariable maxims of the policy of his countrymen. They deemed it a much safer expedient to divide than to combat the barbarians, from whose defeat they could derive neither honour nor advantage. The money and negotiations of Rome insinuated themselves into the heart of Germany, and every art of seduction was used with dignity to conciliate those nations whom their proximity to the Rhine or Danube might render the most useful friends as well as the most troublesome enemies. Chiefs of renown and power were flattered by the most trifling presents, which they received either as marks of distinction or as the instruments of luxury. In civil dissensions, the weaker faction endeavoured to strengthen its interest by entering into secret connexions with the governors of the frontier provinces. Every quarrel among the Germans was fomented by the intrigues of Rome; and every plan of union and public good was defeated by the stronger bias of private jealousy and interest.[31]

The general conspiracy which terrified the Romans under the reign of Marcus Antoninus comprehended almost all the nations of Germany, and even Sarmatia, from the mouth of the Rhine to that of the Danube.[32] It is impossible for us to determine whether this hasty confederation was formed by necessity, by reason, or by passion; but we may rest assured, that the barbarians were neither allured by the indolence or provoked by the ambition of the Roman monarch. This dangerous invasion required all the firmness and vigilance of Marcus. He fixed generals of ability in the several stations of attack, and assumed in person the conduct of the most important province on the Upper Danube. After a long and doubtful conflict, the spirit of the barbarians was subdued. The Quadi and the Marcomanni,[33] who had taken the lead in the war, were the most severely punished in its catastrophe. They were commanded to retire five miles [34] from their own banks of the Danube, and to deliver up the flower of the youth, who were immediately sent into Britain, a remote island, where they might be secure as hostages and useful as soldiers. On the frequent rebellions of the Quadi and Marcomanni, the irritated emperor resolved to reduce their country into the form of a province. His designs were disappointed by death. This formidable league, however, the only one that appears in the two first centuries of the Imperial history, was entirely dissipated without leaving any traces behind in Germany.

In the course of this introductory chapter, we have confined our-

[31] *Many traces of this policy may be discovered in Tacitus and Dion; and many more may be inferred from the principles of human nature.*

[32] *The emperor Marcus was reduced to sell the rich furniture of the palace, and to enlist slaves and robbers.*

[33] *The Marcomanni, a colony, who, from the banks of the Rhine, occupied Bohemia and Moravia, had once erected a great and formidable monarchy under their king Maroboduus.*

[34] *Mr. Wotton increases the prohibition to ten times the distance. His reasoning is specious but not conclusive. Five miles were sufficient for a fortified barrier.*

Since the fifteenth century, "the temple of Concord and many capital structures" have vanished. "The smallness of their numbers was the sole check on the demands and depredations of the Romans."

Altra Veduta degli avanzi del Pro-
nao del Tempio della Concordia
1 Arco di Settimio Severo   2 S.ª Martina

PORTICO OF THE TEMPLE OF SATURN WITH THE ARCH
OF SEPTIMIUS SEVERUS AND SS. MARTINA E LUCA

selves to the general outlines of the manners of Germany, without attempting to describe or to distinguish the various tribes which filled that great country in the time of Cæsar, of Tacitus, or of Ptolemy. As the ancient, or as new tribes successively present themselves in the series of this history, we shall concisely mention their origin, their situation, and their particular character. Modern nations are fixed and permanent societies, connected among themselves by laws and government, bound to their native soil by arts and agriculture. The German tribes were voluntary and fluctuating associations of soldiers, almost of savages. The same territory often changed its inhabitants in the tide of conquest and emigration. The same communities, uniting in a plan of defence or invasion, bestowed a new title on their new confederacy. The dissolution of an ancient confederacy restored to the independent tribes their peculiar but long forgotten appellation. A victorious state often communicated its own name to a vanquished people. Sometimes crowds of volunteers flocked from all parts to the standard of a favourite leader; his camp became their country, and some circumstance of the enterprise soon gave a common denomination to the mixed multitude. The distinctions of the ferocious invaders were perpetually varied by themselves, and confounded by the astonished subjects of the Roman empire.

Wars and the administration of public affairs are the principal subjects of history; but the number of persons interested in these busy scenes is very different, according to the different condition of mankind. In great monarchies millions of obedient subjects pursue their useful occupations in peace and obscurity. The attention of the writer, as well as of the reader, is solely confined to a court, a capital, a regular army, and the districts which happen to be the occasional scene of military operations. But a state of freedom and barbarism, the season of civil commotions, or the situation of petty republics,[35] raises almost every member of the community into action and consequently into notice. The irregular divisions and the restless motions of the people of Germany dazzle our imagination, and seem to multiply their numbers. The profuse enumeration of kings and warriors, of armies and nations, inclines us to forget that the same objects are continually repeated under a variety of appellations, and that the most splendid appellations have been frequently lavished on the most inconsiderable objects.

[35] *Should we suspect that Athens contained only 21,000 citizens and Sparta no more than 39,000?*

X

F ROM the great secular games celebrated by Philip to the death of the emperor Gallienus, there elapsed twenty years of shame and misfortune. During that calamitous period, every instant of time was marked, every province of the Roman world was afflicted, by barbarous invaders and military tyrants, and the ruined empire seemed to approach the last and fatal moment of its dissolution. The confusion of the times and the scarcity of authentic memorials oppose equal difficulties to the historian, who attempts to preserve a clear and unbroken thread of narration. Surrounded with imperfect fragments, always concise, often obscure, and sometimes contradictory, he is reduced to collect, to compare, and to conjecture: and though he ought never to place his conjectures in the rank of facts, yet the knowledge of human nature, and of the sure operation of its fierce and unrestrained passions, might, on some occasions, supply the want of historical materials.

There is not, for instance, any difficulty in conceiving that the successive murders of so many emperors had loosened all the ties of allegiance between the prince and people; that all the generals of Philip were disposed to imitate the example of their master; and that the caprice of armies, long since habituated to frequent and violent revolutions, might every day raise to the throne the most obscure of their fellow-soldiers. History can only add, that the rebellion against the emperor Philip broke out in the summer of the year two hundred and forty-nine, among the legions of Mæsia, and that a subaltern officer, named Marinus, was the object of their seditious choice. Philip was alarmed. He dreaded lest the treason of the Mæsian army should prove the first spark of a general conflagration. Distracted with the consciousness of his guilt and of his danger, he communicated the intelligence to the senate. A gloomy silence prevailed, the effect of fear, and perhaps of disaffection, till at length Decius, one of the assembly, assuming a spirit worthy of his noble extraction, ventured to discover more intrepidity than the emperor seemed to possess. He treated the whole business with contempt, as a hasty and inconsiderate tumult, and Philip's rival as a phantom of royalty, who in a very few days would be destroyed by the same inconstancy that had created him. The speedy completion of the prophecy inspired Philip with a just esteem for so able a counsellor, and Decius appeared to him the only person capable of restoring peace and discipline to an army whose tumultuous spirit did not immediately subside after the murder of Marinus. Decius,[1] who long resisted his own nomination, seems to have insinuated the danger of presenting a leader of merit to the angry and apprehensive minds of the soldiers; and his prediction was again confirmed by the event. The legions of Mæsia forced their judge to become their accomplice. They left him only the alternative of death or the purple. His subsequent conduct, after that decisive measure, was unavoidable. He conducted or followed his army to the confines of Italy, whither Philip, collecting all his force to repel the formidable competitor whom he had raised up, advanced to meet him. The Imperial troops were superior in number; but the rebels formed an army of veterans, commanded by an able and experienced leader. Philip was either killed in the battle or put to death a few days afterwards at Verona. His son and associate in the empire, was massacred at Rome by the Prætorian guards; and the victorious Decius, with more favourable circumstances than the ambition of that age can usually plead, was universally acknowledged by the senate and provinces. It is reported that, immediately after his reluctant acceptance of the title of Augustus, he had assured Philip by a private message of his innocence and loyalty, solemnly protesting that, on his arrival in Italy, he would resign the Imperial ornaments, and return to the condition of an obedient subject. His professions might be sincere; but, in the situation where fortune had placed him, it was scarcely possible that he could either forgive or be forgiven.

The emperor Decius had employed a few months in the works of peace and the administration of justice, when he was summoned to the banks of the Danube by the invasion of the GOTHS. This is the first considerable occasion in which history mentions that great people, who afterwards broke the Roman power, sacked the Capitol, and reigned in Gaul, Spain, and Italy. So memorable was the part

[1] *His birth at Bubalia, a little village in Pannonia (Victor), seems to contradict, unless it was merely accidental, his supposed descent from the Decii. Six hundred years had bestowed nobility on the Decii; but at the commencement of that period, they were only Plebeians of merit, and among the first who shared the consulship with the haughty Patricians.*

which they acted in the subversion of the Western empire, that the name of GOTHS is frequently but improperly used as a general appellation of rude and warlike barbarism.

In the beginning of the sixth century, and after the conquest of Italy, the Goths, in possession of present greatness, very naturally indulged themselves in the prospect of past and of future glory. They wished to preserve the memory of their ancestors, and to transmit to posterity their own achievements. The principal minister of the court of Ravenna, the learned Cassiodorus, gratified the inclination of the conquerors in a Gothic history, which consisted of twelve books, now reduced to the imperfect abridgment of Jornandes. These writers passed with the most artful conciseness over the misfortunes of the nation, celebrated its successful valour, and adorned the triumph with many Asiatic trophies that more properly belonged to the people of Scythia. On the faith of ancient songs, the uncertain but the only memorials of barbarians, they deduced the first origin of the Goths from the vast island or peninsula of Scandinavia. That extreme country of the North was not unknown to the conquerors of Italy; the ties of ancient consanguinity had been strengthened by recent offices of friendship; and a Scandinavian king had cheerfully abdicated his savage greatness, that he might pass the remainder of his days in the peaceful and polished court of Ravenna. Many vestiges, which cannot be ascribed to the arts of popular vanity, attest the ancient residence of the Goths in the countries beyond the Baltic. From the time of the geographer Ptolemy, the southern part of Sweden seems to have continued in the possession of the less enterprising remnant of the nation, and a large territory is even at present divided into east and west Gothland. During the middle ages (from the ninth to the twelfth century), whilst Christianity was advancing with a slow progress into the North, the Goths and the Swedes composed two distinct and sometimes hostile members of the same monarchy. The latter of these two names has prevailed without extinguishing the former. The Swedes, who might well be satisfied with their own fame in arms, have in every age claimed the kindred glory of the Goths. In a moment of discontent against the court of Rome, Charles the Twelfth insinuated that his victorious troops were not degenerated from their brave ancestors, who had already subdued the mistress of the world.[2]

Till the end of the eleventh century, a celebrated temple subsisted at Upsal, the most considerable town of the Swedes and Goths. It was enriched with the gold which the Scandinavians had acquired

[2] *When the Austrians desired the aid of the court of Rome against Gustavus Adolphus, they always represented that conqueror as the lineal successor of Alaric.*

in their piratical adventures, and sanctified by the uncouth representations of the three principal deities, the god of war, the goddess of generation, and the god of thunder. In the general festival that was solemnized every ninth year, nine animals of every species (without excepting the human) were sacrificed, and their bleeding bodies suspended in the sacred grove adjacent to the temple.[3] The only traces that now subsist of this barbaric superstition are contained in the Edda, a system of mythology, compiled in Iceland about the thirteenth century, and studied by the learned of Denmark and Sweden, as the most valuable remains of their ancient traditions.

Notwithstanding the mysterious obscurity of the Edda, we can easily distinguish two persons confounded under the name of Odin —the god of war, and the great legislator of Scandinavia. The latter, the Mahomet of the North, instituted a religion adapted to the climate and to the people. Numerous tribes on either side of the Baltic were subdued by the invincible valour of Odin, by his persuasive eloquence, and by the fame which he acquired of a most skilful magician. The faith that he had propagated, during a long and prosperous life, he confirmed by a voluntary death. Apprehensive of the ignominious approach of disease and infirmity, he resolved to expire as became a warrior. In a solemn assembly of the Swedes and Goths, he wounded himself in nine mortal places, hastening away (as he asserted with his dying voice) to prepare the feast of heroes in the palace of the god of war.

The native and proper habitation of Odin is distinguished by the appellation of As-gard. The happy resemblance of that name, with As-burg, or As-of, words of a similar signification, has given rise to an historical system of so pleasing a contexture that we could almost wish to persuade ourselves of its truth. It is supposed that Odin was the chief of a tribe of barbarians which dwelt on the banks of the lake Mæotis, till the fall of Mithridates and the arms of Pompey menaced the North with servitude; that Odin, yielding with indignant fury to a power which he was unable to resist, conducted his tribe from the frontiers of the Asiatic Sarmatia into Sweden, with the great design of forming, in that inaccessible retreat of freedom, a religion and a people which, in some remote age, might be subservient to his immortal revenge; when his invincible Goths, armed with martial fanaticism, should issue in swarms from the neighbourhood of the Polar circle, to chastise the oppressors of mankind.[4]

If so many successive generations of Goths were capable of pre-

[3] *The temple of Upsal was destroyed by Ingo King of Sweden, who began his reign in the year 1075, and about four-score years afterwards a Christian cathedral was erected on its ruins.*

[4] *This wonderful expedition of Odin, which, by deducing the enmity of the Goths and Romans from so memorable a cause, might supply the noble groundwork of an Epic Poem, cannot safely be received as authentic history. According to the obvious sense of the Edda, and the interpretation of the most skilful critics, Asgard, instead of denoting a real city of the Asiatic Sarmatia, is the fictitious appellation of the mystic abode of the gods, the Olympus of Scandinavia; from whence the prophet was supposed to descend, when he announced his new religion to the Gothic nations, who were already seated in the southern parts of Sweden.*

[5] If we could yield a firm assent to the navigations of Pytheas of Marseilles, we must allow that the Goths had passed the Baltic at least three hundred years before Christ.

[6] By the German colonies who followed the arms of the Teutonic knights. The conquest and conversion of Prussia were completed by them in the thirteenth century.

[7] Pliny and Procopius agree in this opinion. They lived in distant ages, and possessed different means of investigating the truth.

[8] The Ostro and Visi, the Eastern and Western Goths, obtained those denominations from their original seats in Scandinavia. In all their future marches and settlements they preserved, with their names, the same relative situation. When they first departed from Sweden, the infant colony was contained in three vessels. The third being a heavy sailer lagged behind, and the crew, which afterwards swelled into a nation, received from that circumstance the appellation of Gepidæ or Loiterers.

[9] The Goths probably acquired their iron by the commerce of amber.

serving a faint tradition of their Scandinavian origin, we must not expect, from such unlettered barbarians, any distinct account of the time and circumstances of their emigration. To cross the Baltic was an easy and natural attempt. The inhabitants of Sweden were masters of a sufficient number of large vessels with oars, and the distance is little more than one hundred miles from Carlscroon to the nearest ports of Pomerania and Prussia. Here, at length, we land on firm and historic ground. At least as early as the Christian æra,[5] and as late as the age of the Antonines, the Goths were established towards the mouth of the Vistula, and in that fertile province where the commercial cities of Thorn, Elbing, Königsberg, and Danzig, were long afterwards founded.[6] Westward of the Goths, the numerous tribes of the Vandals were spread along the banks of the Oder, and the sea coast of Pomerania and Mecklenburg. A striking resemblance of manners, complexion, religion, and language, seemed to indicate that the Vandals and the Goths were originally one great people.[7] The latter appear to have been subdivided into Ostrogoths, Visigoths, and Gepidæ.[8] The distinction among the Vandals was more strongly marked by the independent names of Heruli, Burgundians, Lombards, and a variety of other petty states, many of which, in a future age, expanded themselves into powerful monarchies.

In the age of the Antonines the Goths were still seated in Prussia. About the reign of Alexander Severus, the Roman province of Dacia had already experienced their proximity by frequent and destructive inroads. In this interval, therefore, of about seventy years, we must place the second migration of the Goths from the Baltic to the Euxine; but the cause that produced it lies concealed among the various motives which actuate the conduct of unsettled barbarians. Either a pestilence or a famine, a victory or a defeat, an oracle of the gods, or the eloquence of a daring leader, were sufficient to impel the Gothic arms on the milder climates of the south. Besides the influence of a martial religion, the numbers and spirit of the Goths were equal to the most dangerous adventures. The use of round bucklers and short swords rendered them formidable in a close engagement; the manly obedience which they yielded to hereditary kings gave uncommon union and stability to their councils;[9] and the renowned Amala, the hero of that age, and the tenth ancestor of Theodoric, king of Italy, enforced, by the ascendant of personal merit, the prerogative of his birth, which he derived from the *Anses,* or demigods of the Gothic nation.

The fame of a great enterprise excited the bravest warriors from all the Vandalic states of Germany, many of whom are seen a few years afterwards combating under the common standard of the Goths.[10] The first motions of the emigrants carried them to the banks of the Prypec, a river universally conceived by the ancients to be the southern branch of the Borysthenes. The windings of that great stream through the plains of Poland and Russia gave a direction to their line of march, and a constant supply of fresh water and pasturage to their numerous herds of cattle. They followed the unknown course of the river, confident in their valour, and careless of whatever power might oppose their progress. The Bastarnæ and the Venedi were the first who presented themselves; and the flower of their youth, either from choice or compulsion, increased the Gothic army. The Bastarnæ dwelt on the northern side of the Carpathian Mountains; the immense tract of land that separated the Bastarnæ from the savages of Finland was possessed, or rather wasted, by the Venedi: we have some reason to believe that the first of these nations, which distinguished itself in the Macedonian war, and was afterwards divided into the formidable tribes of the Peucini, the Borani, the Carpi, &c., derived its origin from the Germans. With better authority a Sarmatian extraction may be assigned to the Venedi, who rendered themselves so famous in the middle ages.[11] But the confusion of blood and manners on that doubtful frontier often perplexed the most accurate observers.[12] As the Goths advanced near the Euxine Sea, they encountered a purer race of Sarmatians, the Jazyges, the Alani, and the Roxolani; and they were probably the first Germans who saw the mouths of the Borysthenes and of the Tanais. If we inquire into the characteristic marks of the people of Germany and of Sarmatia, we shall discover that those two great portions of human kind were principally distinguished by fixed huts or movable tents, by a close dress or flowing garments, by the marriage of one or of several wives, by a military force consisting, for the most part, either of infantry or cavalry; and, above all, by the use of the Teutonic, or of the Sclavonian language; the last of which has been diffused, by conquest, from the confines of Italy to the neighbourhood of Japan.

The Goths were now in possession of the Ukraine, a country of considerable extent and uncommon fertility, intersected with navigable rivers, which from either side discharge themselves into the Borysthenes; and interspersed with large and lofty forests of oaks. The plenty of game and fish, the innumerable bee-hives, deposited

[10] *The Heruli, and the Uregundi, or Burgundi, are particularly mentioned. The Marcomannic war was partly occasioned by the pressure of barbarous tribes, who fled before the arms of more northern barbarians.*

[11] *The Venedi, the Slavi, and the Antes, were the three great tribes of the same people.*

[12] *Tacitus most assuredly deserves that title, and even his cautious suspense is a proof of his diligent inquiries.*

in the hollow of old trees and in the cavities of rocks, and forming, even in that rude age, a valuable branch of commerce, the size of the cattle, the temperature of the air, the aptness of the soil for every species of grain, and the luxuriancy of the vegetation, all displayed the liberality of Nature, and tempted the industry of man.[13] But the Goths withstood all these temptations, and still adhered to a life of idleness, of poverty, and of rapine.

[13] *Mr. Bell traversed the Ukraine in his journey from Petersburgh to Constantinople. The modern face of the country is a just representation of the ancient, since, in the hands of the Cossacks, it still remains in a state of nature.*

The Scythian hordes, which, towards the east, bordered on the new settlements of the Goths, presented nothing to their arms, except the doubtful chance of an unprofitable victory. But the prospect of the Roman territories was far more alluring; and the fields of Dacia were covered with rich harvests, sown by the hands of an industrious, and exposed to be gathered by those of a warlike, people. It is probable that the conquests of Trajan, maintained by its successors less for any real advantage than for ideal dignity, had contributed to weaken the empire on that side. The new and unsettled province of Dacia was neither strong enough to resist, nor rich enough to satiate, the rapaciousness of the barbarians. As long as the remote banks of the Dniester were considered as the boundary of the Roman power, the fortifications of the Lower Danube were more carelessly guarded, and the inhabitants of Mæsia lived in supine security, fondly conceiving themselves at an inaccessible distance from any barbarian invaders. The irruptions of the Goths, under the reign of Philip, fatally convinced them of their mistake. The king or leader of that fierce nation traversed with contempt the province of Dacia, and passed both the Dniester and the Danube without encountering any opposition capable of retarding his progress. The relaxed discipline of the Roman troops betrayed the most important posts where they were stationed, and the fear of deserved punishment induced great numbers of them to enlist under the Gothic standard. The various multitude of barbarians appeared, at length, under the walls of Marcianopolis, a city built by Trajan in honour of his sister, and at that time the capital of the second Mæsia. The inhabitants consented to ransom their lives and property by the payment of a large sum of money, and the invaders retreated back into their deserts, animated, rather than satisfied, with the first success of their arms against an opulent but feeble country. Intelligence was soon transmitted to the emperor Decius, that Cniva, king of the Goths, had passed the Danube a second time, with more considerable forces; that his numerous detachments scattered devastation over the province of Mæsia, whilst the main body of the army, consisting of seventy thousand Germans and Sarmatians, a force equal to the most daring achievements, required the presence of the Roman monarch, and the exertion of his military power.

Decius found the Goths engaged before Nicopolis, on the Jatrus, one of the many monuments of Trajan's victories.[14] On his approach they raised the siege, but with a design only of marching away to a conquest of greater importance, the siege of Philippopolis, a city of Thrace, founded by the father of Alexander, near the foot of Mount Hæmus. Decius followed them through a difficult country, and by forced marches; but, when he imagined himself at a considerable distance from the rear of the Goths, Cniva turned with rapid fury on his pursuers. The camp of the Romans was surprised and pillaged, and, for the first time, their emperor fled in disorder before a troop of half-armed barbarians. After a long resistance Philippopolis, destitute of succour, was taken by storm. A hundred thousand persons are reported to have been massacred in the sack of that great city. Many prisoners of consequence became a valuable accession to the spoil; and Priscus, a brother of the late emperor Philip, blushed not to assume the purple under the protection of the barbarous enemies of Rome. The time, however, consumed in that tedious siege, enabled Decius to revive the courage, restore the discipline, and recruit the numbers of his troops. He intercepted several parties of Carpi, and other Germans, who were hastening to share the victory of their countrymen, intrusted the passes of the mountains to officers of approved valour and fidelity,[15] repaired and strengthened the fortifications of the Danube, and exerted his utmost vigilance to oppose either the progress or the retreat of the Goths. Encouraged by the return of fortune, he anxiously waited for an opportunity to retrieve, by a great and decisive blow, his own glory, and that of the Roman arms.[16]

At the same time when Decius was struggling with the violence of the tempest, his mind, calm and deliberate amidst the tumult of war, investigated the more general causes that, since the age of the Antonines, had so impetuously urged the decline of the Roman greatness. He soon discovered that it was impossible to replace that greatness on a permanent basis without restoring public virtue, ancient principles and manners, and the oppressed majesty of the laws. To execute this noble but arduous design, he first resolved to revive the obsolete office of censor; an office which, as long as it had subsisted in its pristine integrity, had so much contributed to the perpetuity of the state, till it was usurped and gradually neglected

[14] *The place is still called Nicop. The little stream, on whose banks it stood, falls into the Danube.*

[15] *Claudius (who afterwards reigned with so much glory) was posted in the pass of Thermopylæ with 200 Dardanians, 100 heavy and 160 light horse, 60 Cretan archers, and 1000 well-armed recruits.*

[16] *In the general account of this war, it is easy to discover the opposite prejudices of Jornandes the Gothic and Zosimus the Grecian writer. In carelessness alone they are alike.*

REVIVAL OF THE OFFICE OF CENSOR

[17] *Vespasian and Titus were the last censors. The modesty of Trajan refused an honour which he deserved, and his example became a law to the Antonines.*

by the Cæsars.[17] Conscious that the favour of the sovereign may confer power, but that the esteem of the people can alone bestow authority, he submitted the choice of the censor to the unbiassed voice of the senate. By their unanimous votes, or rather acclamations, Valerian, who was afterwards emperor, and who then served with distinction in the army of Decius, was declared the most worthy of that exalted honour. As soon as the decree of the senate was transmitted to the emperor, he assembled a great council in his camp, and, before the investiture of the censor elect, he apprized him of the difficulty and importance of his great office. "Happy Valerian," said the prince, to his distinguished subject, "happy in the general approbation of the senate and of the Roman republic! Accept the censorship of mankind, and judge of our manners. You will select those who deserve to continue members of the senate; you will restore the equestrian order to its ancient splendour; you will improve the revenue, yet moderate the public burdens. You will distinguish into regular classes the various and infinite multitude of citizens, and accurately review the military strength, the wealth, the virtue, and the resources of Rome. Your decisions shall obtain the force of laws. The army, the palace, the ministers of justice, and the great officers of the empire are all subject to your tribunal. None are exempted, excepting only the ordinary consuls,[18] the præfect of the city, the king of the sacrifices, and (as long as she preserves her chastity inviolate) the eldest of the vestal virgins. Even these few, who may not dread the severity, will anxiously solicit the esteem, of the Roman censor."

[18] *Yet in spite of this exemption Pompey appeared before that tribunal, during his consulship. The occasion indeed was equally singular and honourable.*

A magistrate invested with such extensive powers would have appeared not so much the minister as the colleague of his sovereign. Valerian justly dreaded an elevation so full of envy and of suspicion. He modestly urged the alarming greatness of the trust, his own insufficiency, and the incurable corruption of the times. He artfully insinuated that the office of censor was inseparable from the Imperial dignity, and that the feeble hands of a subject were unequal to the support of such an immense weight of cares and of power. The approaching event of war soon put an end to the prosecution of a project so specious but so impracticable, and, whilst it preserved Valerian from the danger, saved the emperor Decius from the disappointment, which would most probably have attended it. A censor may maintain, he can never restore, the morals of a state. It is impossible for such a magistrate to exert his authority with benefit, or even with effect, unless he is supported by a quick sense of honour and virtue in the minds of the people, by a decent reverence for the public opinion, and by a train of useful prejudices combating on the side of national manners. In a period when these principles are annihilated, the censorial jurisdiction must either sink into empty pageantry, or be converted into a partial instrument of vexatious oppression.[19] It was easier to vanquish the Goths than to eradicate the public vices; yet, even in the first of these enterprises, Decius lost his army and his life.

The Goths were now, on every side, surrounded and pursued by the Roman arms. The flower of their troops had perished in the long siege of Philippopolis, and the exhausted country could no longer afford subsistence for the remaining multitude of licentious barbarians. Reduced to this extremity, the Goths would gladly have purchased, by the surrender of all their booty and prisoners, the permission of an undisturbed retreat. But the emperor, confident of victory, and resolving, by the chastisement of these invaders, to strike a salutary terror into the nations of the North, refused to listen to any terms of accommodation. The high-spirited barbarians preferred death to slavery. An obscure town of Mæsia, called Forum Terebronii, was the scene of the battle. The Gothic army was drawn up in three lines, and, either from choice or accident, the front of the third line was covered by a morass. In the beginning of the action, the son of Decius, a youth of the fairest hopes, and already associated to the honours of the purple, was slain by an arrow, in the sight of his afflicted father; who, summoning all his fortitude, admonished the dismayed troops that the loss of a single soldier was of little importance to the republic. The conflict was terrible; it was the combat of despair against grief and rage. The first line of the Goths at length gave way in disorder; the second, advancing to sustain it, shared its fate; and the third only remained entire, prepared to dispute the passage of the morass, which was imprudently attempted by the presumption of the enemy. "Here the fortune of the day turned, and all things became adverse to the Romans: the place deep with ooze, sinking under those who stood, slippery to such as advanced; their armour heavy, the waters deep; nor could they wield, in that uneasy situation, their weighty javelins. The barbarians, on the contrary, were enured to encounters in the bogs; their persons tall, their spears long, such as could wound at a distance."[20] In this morass the Roman army, after an ineffectual struggle, was irrecoverably lost; nor could the body of the emperor ever be found. Such was the fate of Decius, in the fiftieth year of his age;

[19] *Such as the attempts of Augustus towards a reformation of manners.*

[20] *I have ventured to copy from Tacitus the picture of a similar engagement between a Roman army and a German tribe.*

21 *The Decii were killed before the end of the year two hundred and fifty-one, since the new princes took possession of the consulship on the ensuing calends of January.*

22 *The Augustan History gives them a very honourable place among the small number of good emperors who reigned between Augustus and Diocletian.*

23 *A* Sella, *a* Toga, *and a golden* Patera *of five pounds' weight, were accepted with joy and gratitude by the wealthy king of Egypt.* Quina millia Æris, *a weight of copper in value about eighteen pounds sterling, was the usual present made to foreign ambassadors.*

an accomplished prince, active in war, and affable in peace;[21] who, together with his son, has deserved to be compared, both in life and death, with the brightest examples of ancient virtue.[22]

This fatal blow humbled, for a very little time, the insolence of the legions. They appear to have patiently expected, and submissively obeyed, the decree of the senate which regulated the succession to the throne. From a just regard for the memory of Decius, the Imperial title was conferred on Hostilianus, his only surviving son; but an equal rank, with more effectual power, was granted to Gallus, whose experience and ability seemed equal to the great trust of guardian to the young prince and the distressed empire. The first care of the new emperor was to deliver the Illyrian provinces from the intolerable weight of the victorious Goths. He consented to leave in their hands the rich fruits of their invasion, an immense booty, and, what was still more disgraceful, a great number of prisoners of the highest merit and quality. He plentifully supplied their camp with every conveniency that could assuage their angry spirits, or facilitate their so much wished-for departure; and he even promised to pay them annually a large sum of gold, on condition they should never afterwards infest the Roman territories by their incursions.

In the age of the Scipios, the most opulent kings of the earth, who courted the protection of the victorious commonwealth, were gratified with such trifling presents as could only derive a value from the hand that bestowed them; an ivory chair, a coarse garment of purple, an inconsiderable piece of plate, or a quantity of copper coin.[23] After the wealth of nations had centred in Rome, the emperors displayed their greatness, and even their policy, by the regular exercise of a steady and moderate liberality towards the allies of the state. They relieved the poverty of the barbarians, honoured their merit, and recompensed their fidelity. These voluntary marks of bounty were understood to flow, not from the fears, but merely from the generosity or the gratitude of the Romans; and whilst presents and subsidies were liberally distributed among friends and suppliants, they were sternly refused to such as claimed them as a debt. But this stipulation of an annual payment to a victorious enemy appeared without disguise in the light of an ignominious tribute; the minds of the Romans were not yet accustomed to accept such unequal laws from a tribe of barbarians; and the prince, who by a necessary concession had probably saved his country, became the object of the general contempt and aversion. The death of Hostilianus, though it happened in the midst of a raging pestilence, was interpreted as the personal crime of Gallus; and even the defeat of the late emperor was ascribed by the voice of suspicion to the perfidious counsels of his hated successor. The tranquillity which the empire enjoyed during the first year of his administration served rather to inflame than to appease the public discontent; and, as soon as the apprehensions of war were removed, the infamy of the peace was more deeply and more sensibly felt.

But the Romans were irritated to a still higher degree, when they discovered that they had not even secured their repose, though at the expense of their honour. The dangerous secret of the wealth and weakness of the empire had been revealed to the world. New swarms of barbarians, encouraged by the success, and not conceiving themselves bound by the obligation, of their brethren, spread devastation through the Illyrian provinces, and terror as far as the gates of Rome. The defence of the monarchy, which seemed abandoned by the pusillanimous emperor, was assumed by Æmilianus, governor of Pannonia and Mæsia; who rallied the scattered forces and revived the fainting spirits of the troops. The barbarians were unexpectedly attacked, routed, chased, and pursued beyond the Danube. The victorious leader distributed as a donative the money collected for the tribute, and the acclamations of the soldiers proclaimed him emperor on the field of battle. Gallus, who, careless of the general welfare, indulged himself in the pleasures of Italy, was almost in the same instant informed of the success, of the revolt, and of the rapid approach, of his aspiring lieutenant. He advanced to meet him as far as the plains of Spoleto. When the armies came in sight of each other, the soldiers of Gallus compared the ignominious conduct of their sovereign with the glory of his rival. They admired the valour of Æmilianus; they were attracted by his liberality, for he offered a considerable increase of pay to all deserters. The murder of Gallus, and of his son Volusianus, put an end to the civil war; and the senate gave a legal sanction to the rights of conquest. The letters of Æmilianus to that assembly displayed a mixture of moderation and vanity. He assured them that he should resign to their wisdom the civil administration; and, contenting himself with the quality of their general, would in a short time assert the glory of Rome, and deliver the empire from all the barbarians both of the North and of the East. His pride was flattered by the applause of the senate; and medals are still extant, representing him with the name and attributes of Hercules the Victor, and of Mars the Avenger.

If the new monarch possessed the abilities, he wanted the time, necessary to fulfil these splendid promises. Less than four months intervened between his victory and his fall. He had vanquished Gallus: he sunk under the weight of a competitor more formidable than Gallus. That unfortunate prince had sent Valerian, already distinguished by the honourable title of censor, to bring the legions of Gaul and Germany to his aid. Valerian executed that commission with zeal and fidelity; and, as he arrived too late to save his sovereign, he resolved to revenge him. The troops of Æmilianus, who still lay encamped in the plains of Spoleto, were awed by the sanctity of his character, but much more by the superior strength of his army; and, as they were now become as incapable of personal attachment as they had always been of constitutional principle, they readily imbrued their hands in the blood of a prince who so lately had been the object of their partial choice. The guilt was theirs, but the advantage of it was Valerian's; who obtained the possession of the throne by the means indeed of a civil war, but with a degree of innocence singular in that age of revolutions; since he owed neither gratitude nor allegiance to his predecessor, whom he dethroned.

[24] He was about seventy at the time of his accession, or, as it is more probable, of his death.

[25] In the glorious struggle of the senate against Maximin, Valerian acted a very spirited part.

[26] According to the distinction of Victor, he seems to have received the title of Imperator from the army, and that of Augustus from the senate.

[27] From Victor and from the medals, Tillemont very justly infers that Gallienus was associated to the empire about the month of August of the year 253.

Valerian was about sixty years of age [24] when he was invested with the purple, not by the caprice of the populace or the clamours of the army, but by the unanimous voice of the Roman world. In his gradual ascent through the honours of the state he had deserved the favour of virtuous princes, and had declared himself the enemy of tyrants.[25] His noble birth, his mild but unblemished manners, his learning, prudence, and experience, were revered by the senate and people; and, if mankind (according to the observation of an ancient writer) had been left at liberty to choose a master, their choice would most assuredly have fallen on Valerian.[26] Perhaps the merit of this emperor was inadequate to his reputation; perhaps his abilities, or at least his spirit, were affected by the languor and coldness of old age. The consciousness of his decline engaged him to share the throne with a younger and more active associate:[27] the emergency of the times demanded a general no less than a prince; and the experience of the Roman censor might have directed him where to bestow the Imperial purple, as the reward of military merit. But, instead of making a judicious choice, which would have confirmed his reign and endeared his memory, Valerian, consulting only the dictates of affection or vanity, immediately invested with the supreme honours his son Gallienus, a youth whose effeminate vices had been hitherto concealed by the obscurity of a private station.

The joint government of the father and the son subsisted about seven, and the sole administration of Gallienus continued about eight, years. But the whole period was one uninterrupted series of confusion and calamity. As the Roman empire was at the same time, and on every side, attacked by the blind fury of foreign invaders, and the wild ambition of domestic usurpers, we shall consult order and perspicuity by pursuing not so much the doubtful arrangement of dates as the more natural distribution of subjects. The most dangerous enemies of Rome, during the reigns of Valerian and Gallienus, were,—1. The Franks. 2. The Alemanni. 3. The Goths; and, 4. The Persians. Under these general appellations we may comprehend the adventures of less considerable tribes, whose obscure and uncouth names would only serve to oppress the memory and perplex the attention of the reader.

I. As the posterity of the Franks compose one of the greatest and most enlightened nations of Europe, the powers of learning and ingenuity have been exhausted in the discovery of their unlettered ancestors. To the tales of credulity have succeeded the systems of fancy. Every passage has been sifted, every spot has been surveyed, that might possibly reveal some faint traces of their origin. It has been supposed that Pannonia, that Gaul, that the northern parts of Germany, gave birth to that celebrated colony of warriors. At length the most rational critics, rejecting the fictitious emigrations of ideal conquerors, have acquiesced in a sentiment whose simplicity persuades us of its truth. They suppose that, about the year two hundred and forty,[28] a new confederacy was formed under the name of Franks by the old inhabitants of the Lower Rhine and the Weser. The present circle of Westphalia, the Landgraviate of Hesse, and the duchies of Brunswick and Luneburg, were the ancient seat of the Chauci, who, in their inaccessible morasses, defied the Roman arms; of the Cherusci, proud of the fame of Arminius; of the Catti, formidable by their firm and intrepid infantry; and of several other tribes of inferior power and renown. The love of liberty was the ruling passion of these Germans; the enjoyment of it their best treasure; the word that expressed that enjoyment the most pleasing to their ear. They deserved, they assumed, they maintained the honourable epithet of Franks or Freemen; which concealed, though it did not extinguish, the peculiar names of the several states of the confederacy.[29] Tacit consent and mutual advantage dictated the first laws of the union; it was gradually cemented by habit and experience. The league of the Franks may admit of some comparison with the Hel-

[28] *Most probably under the reign of Gordian.*

[29] *In a subsequent period most of those old names are occasionally mentioned.*

vetic body; in which every canton, retaining its independent sovereignty, consults with its brethren in the common cause, without acknowledging the authority of any supreme head or representative assembly. But the principle of the two confederacies was extremely different. A peace of two hundred years has rewarded the wise and honest policy of the Swiss. An inconstant spirit, the thirst of rapine, and a disregard to the most solemn treaties, disgraced the character of the Franks.

The Romans had long experienced the daring valour of the people of Lower Germany. The union of their strength threatened Gaul with a more formidable invasion, and required the presence of Gallienus, the heir and colleague of Imperial power. Whilst that prince and his infant son Saloninus displayed in the court of Treves the majesty of the empire, its armies were ably conducted by their general Posthumus, who, though he afterwards betrayed the family of Valerian, was ever faithful to the great interest of the monarchy. The treacherous language of panegyrics and medals darkly announces a long series of victories. Trophies and titles attest (if such evidence can attest) the fame of Posthumus, who is repeatedly styled The Conqueror of the Germans, and the Saviour of Gaul.

But a single fact, the only one indeed of which we have any distinct knowledge, erases in a great measure these monuments of vanity and adulation. The Rhine, though dignified with the title of Safeguard of the provinces, was an imperfect barrier against the daring spirit of enterprise with which the Franks were actuated. Their rapid devastations stretched from the river to the foot of the Pyrenees; nor were they stopped by those mountains. Spain, which had never dreaded, was unable to resist, the inroads of the Germans. During twelve years, the greatest part of the reign of Gallienus, that opulent country was the theatre of unequal and destructive hostilities. Tarragona, the flourishing capital of a peaceful province, was sacked and almost destroyed; and so late as the days of Orosius, who wrote in the fifth century, wretched cottages, scattered amidst the ruins of magnificent cities, still recorded the rage of the barbarians.[30]

[30] *In the time of Ausonius (the end of the fourth century) Ilerda or Lerida was in a very ruinous state, which probably was the consequence of this invasion.*

When the exhausted country no longer supplied a variety of plunder, the Franks seized on some vessels in the ports of Spain and transported themselves into Mauritania. The distant province was astonished with the fury of these barbarians, who seemed to fall from a new world, as their name, manners, and complexion were equally unknown on the coast of Africa.

II. In that part of Upper Saxony, beyond the Elbe, which is at present called the Marquisate of Lusace, there existed in ancient times a sacred wood, the awful seat of the superstition of the Suevi. None were permitted to enter the holy precincts without confessing, by their servile bonds and suppliant posture, the immediate presence of the sovereign Deity. Patriotism contributed, as well as devotion, to consecrate the Sonnenwald, or wood of the Semnones. It was universally believed that the nation had received its first existence on that sacred spot. At stated periods the numerous tribes who gloried in the Suevic blood resorted thither by their ambassadors; and the memory of their common extraction was perpetuated by barbaric rights and human sacrifices. The wide extended name of Suevi filled the interior countries of Germany, from the banks of the Oder to those of the Danube. They were distinguished from the other Germans by their peculiar mode of dressing their long hair, which they gathered into a rude knot on the crown of the head; and they delighted in an ornament that showed their ranks more lofty and terrible in the eyes of the enemy. Jealous as the Germans were of military renown, they all confessed the superior valour of the Suevi; and the tribes of the Usipetes and Tencteri, who, with a vast army, encountered the dictator Cæsar, declared that they esteemed it not a disgrace to have fled before a people to whose arms the immortal gods themselves were unequal.

In the reign of the emperor Caracalla, an innumerable swarm of Suevi appeared on the banks of the Main, and in the neighbourhood of the Roman provinces, in quest either of food, of plunder, or of glory. The hasty army of volunteers gradually coalesced into a great and permanent nation, and, as it was composed from so many different tribes, assumed the name of Alemanni, or *Allmen,* to denote at once their various lineage and their common bravery.[31] The latter was soon felt by the Romans in many a hostile inroad. The Alemanni fought chiefly on horseback; but their cavalry was rendered still more formidable by a mixture of light infantry selected from the bravest and most active of the youth, whom frequent exercise had enured to accompany the horsemen in the longest march, the most rapid charge, or the most precipitate retreat.[32]

This warlike people of Germans had been astonished by the immense preparations of Alexander Severus; they were dismayed by the arms of his successor, a barbarian equal in valour and fierceness to themselves. But, still hovering on the frontiers of the empire, they increased the general disorder that ensued after the death of Decius. They inflicted severe wounds on the rich provinces of Gaul:

[31] *This etymology (far different from those which amuse the fancy of the learned) is preserved by Asinius Quadratus, an original historian.*

[32] *The Suevi engaged Cæsar in this manner and the manœuvre deserved the approbation of the conqueror.*

they were the first who removed the veil that covered the feeble majesty of Italy. A numerous body of the Alemanni penetrated across the Danube, and through the Rhætian Alps into the plains of Lombardy, advanced as far as Ravenna, and displayed the victorious banners of barbarians almost in sight of Rome. The insult and the danger rekindled in the senate some sparks of their ancient virtue. Both the emperors were engaged in far distant wars, Valerian in the East, and Gallienus on the Rhine. All the hopes and resources of the Romans were in themselves. In this emergency, the senators resumed the defence of the republic, drew out the Prætorian guards, who had been left to garrison the capital, and filled up their numbers by enlisting into the public service the stoutest and most willing of the Plebeians. The Alemanni, astonished with the sudden appearance of an army more numerous than their own, retired into Germany, laden with spoil; and their retreat was esteemed as a victory by the unwarlike Romans.

When Gallienus received the intelligence that his capital was delivered from the barbarians, he was much less delighted than alarmed with the courage of the senate, since it might one day prompt them to rescue the republic from domestic tyranny, as well as from foreign invasion. His timid ingratitude was published to his subjects in an edict which prohibited the senators from exercising any military employment, and even from approaching the camps of the legions. But his fears were groundless. The rich and luxurious nobles, sinking into their natural character, accepted as a favour this disgraceful exemption from military service; and, as long as they were indulged in the enjoyment of their baths, their theatres, and their villas, they cheerfully resigned the more dangerous cares of empire to the rough hands of peasants and soldiers.

Another invasion of the Alemanni, of a more formidable aspect, but more glorious event, is mentioned by a writer of the Lower Empire. Three hundred thousand of that warlike people are said to have been vanquished, in a battle near Milan, by Gallienus in person, at the head of only ten thousand Romans. We may however, with great probability, ascribe this incredible victory either to the credulity of the historian, or to some exaggerated exploits of one of the emperor's lieutenants. It was by arms of a very different nature that Gallienus endeavoured to protect Italy from the fury of the Germans. He espoused Pipa, the daughter of a king of the Marcomanni, a Suevic tribe, which was often confounded with the Alemanni in their wars and conquests.[33] To the father, as the price

[33] *One of the Victors calls him king of the Marcomanni, the other, of the Germans.*

of his alliance, he granted an ample settlement in Pannonia. The native charms of unpolished beauty seem to have fixed the daughter in the affections of the inconstant emperor, and the bands of policy were more firmly connected by those of love. But the haughty prejudice of Rome still refused the name of marriage to the profane mixture of a citizen and a barbarian; and has stigmatized the German princess with the opprobrious title of concubine of Gallienus.

III. We have already traced the emigration of the Goths from Scandinavia, or at least from Prussia, to the mouth of the Borysthenes, and have followed their victorious arms from the Borysthenes to the Danube. Under the reigns of Valerian and Gallienus the frontier of the last-mentioned river was perpetually infested by the inroads of Germans and Sarmatians; but it was defended by the Romans with more than usual firmness and success. The provinces that were the seat of war recruited the armies of Rome with an inexhaustible supply of hardy soldiers; and more than one of these Illyrian peasants attained the station, and displayed the abilities, of a general. Though flying parties of the barbarians, who incessantly hovered on the banks of the Danube, penetrated sometimes to the confines of Italy and Macedonia, their progress was commonly checked, or their return intercepted, by the Imperial lieutenants. But the great stream of the Gothic hostilities was diverted into a very different channel. The Goths, in their new settlement of the Ukraine, soon became masters of the northern coast of the Euxine: to the south of that inland sea were situated the soft and wealthy provinces of Asia Minor, which possessed all that could attract, and nothing that could resist, a barbarian conqueror.

The banks of the Borysthenes are only sixty miles distant from the narrow entrance [34] of the peninsula of Crim Tartary, known to the ancients under the name of Chersonesus Taurica. On that inhospitable shore, Euripides, embellishing with exquisite art the tales of antiquity, has placed the scene of one of his most affecting tragedies. The bloody sacrifices of Diana, the arrival of Orestes and Pylades, and the triumph of virtue and religion over savage fierceness, serve to represent an historical truth, that the Tauri, the original inhabitants of the peninsula, were in some degree reclaimed from their brutal manners by a gradual intercourse with the Grecian colonies which settled along the maritime coast. The little kingdom of Bosphorus, whose capital was situated on the straits through which the Mæotis communicates itself to the Euxine, was composed of degenerate Greeks and half-civilized barbarians. It subsisted as an in-

[34] *It is about half a league in breadth.*

[35] *The first kings of Bosphorus were the allies of Athens.*

[36] *It was reduced by the arms of Agrippa. The Romans once advanced within three days' march of the Tanais.*

dependent state from the time of the Peloponnesian war,[35] was at last swallowed up by the ambition of Mithridates, and, with the rest of his dominions, sunk under the weight of the Roman arms. From the reign of Augustus,[36] the kings of Bosphorus were the humble, but not useless, allies of the empire. By presents, by arms, and by a slight fortification drawn across the isthmus, they effectually guarded against the roving plunderers of Sarmatia the access of a country which, from its peculiar situation and convenient harbours, commanded the Euxine Sea and Asia Minor. As long as the sceptre was possessed by a lineal succession of kings, they acquitted themselves of their important charge with vigilance and success. Domestic factions, and the fears or private interest of obscure usurpers who seized on the vacant throne, admitted the Goths into the heart of Bosphorus. With the acquisition of a superfluous waste of fertile soil, the conquerors obtained the command of a naval force sufficient to transport their armies to the coast of Asia. The ships used in the navigation of the Euxine were of a very singular construction. They were slight flat-bottomed barks framed of timber only, without the least mixture of iron, and occasionally covered with a shelving roof on the appearance of a tempest. In these floating houses the Goths carelessly trusted themselves to the mercy of an unknown sea, under the conduct of sailors pressed into the service, and whose skill and fidelity were equally suspicious. But the hopes of plunder had banished every idea of danger, and a natural fearlessness of temper supplied in their minds the more rational confidence which is the just result of knowledge and experience. Warriors of such a daring spirit must have often murmured against the cowardice of their guides, who required the strongest assurances of a settled calm before they would venture to embark, and would scarcely ever be tempted to lose sight of the land. Such, at least, is the practice of the modern Turks; and they are probably not inferior in the art of navigation to the ancient inhabitants of Bosphorus.

The fleet of the Goths, leaving the coast of Circassia on the left hand, first appeared before Pityus,[37] the utmost limits of the Roman provinces; a city provided with a convenient port, and fortified with a strong wall. Here they met with a resistance more obstinate than they had reason to expect from the feeble garrison of a distant fortress. They were repulsed; and their disappointment seemed to diminish the terror of the Gothic name. As long as Successianus, an officer of superior rank and merit, defended that frontier, all their efforts were ineffectual; but, as soon as he was removed by Valerian

[37] *Arrian places the frontier garrison at Dioscurias, or Sebastopolis, forty-four miles to the east of Pityus. The garrison of Phasis consisted in his time of only four hundred foot.*

to a more honourable but less important station, they resumed the attack of Pityus; and, by the destruction of that city, obliterated the memory of their former disgrace.

Circling round the eastern extremity of the Euxine Sea, the navigation from Pityus to Trebizond is about three hundred miles. The course of the Goths carried them in sight of the country of Colchis, so famous by the expedition of the Argonauts; and they even attempted, though without success, to pillage a rich temple at the mouth of the river Phasis. Trebizond, celebrated in the retreat of the Ten Thousand as an ancient colony of Greeks, derived its wealth and splendour from the munificence of the emperor Hadrian, who had constructed an artificial port on a coast left destitute by nature of secure harbours. The city was large and populous; a double enclosure of walls seemed to defy the fury of the Goths, and the usual garrison had been strengthened by a reinforcement of ten thousand men. But there are not any advantages capable of supplying the absence of discipline and vigilance. The numerous garrison of Trebizond, dissolved in riot and luxury, disdained to guard their impregnable fortifications. The Goths soon discovered the supine negligence of the besieged, erected a lofty pile of fascines, ascended the walls in the silence of the night, and entered the defenceless city, sword in hand. A general massacre of the people ensued, whilst the affrighted soldiers escaped through the opposite gates of the town. The most holy temples, and the most splendid edifices, were involved in a common destruction. The booty that fell into the hands of the Goths was immense: the wealth of the adjacent countries had been deposited in Trebizond, as in a secure place of refuge. The number of captives was incredible, as the victorious barbarians ranged without opposition through the extensive province of Pontus. The rich spoils of Trebizond filled a great fleet of ships that had been found in the port. The robust youth of the sea coast were chained to the oar; and the Goths, satisfied with the success of their first naval expedition, returned in triumph to their new establishments in the kingdom of Bosphorus.

The second expedition of the Goths was undertaken with greater powers of men and ships; but they steered a different course, and, disdaining the exhausted provinces of Pontus, followed the western coast of the Euxine, passed before the wide mouths of the Borysthenes, the Dniester, and the Danube, and, increasing their fleet by the capture of a great number of fishing barques, they approached the narrow outlet through which the Euxine Sea pours its waters into the Mediterranean, and divides the continents of Europe and Asia. The garrison of Chalcedon was encamped near the temple of Jupiter Urius, on a promontory that commanded the entrance of the strait: and so inconsiderable were the dreaded invasions of the barbarians, that this body of troops surpassed in number the Gothic army. But it was in numbers alone that they surpassed it. They deserted with precipitation their advantageous post, and abandoned the town of Chalcedon, most plentifully stored with arms and money, to the discretion of the conquerors. Whilst they hesitated whether they should prefer the sea or land, Europe or Asia, for the scene of their hostilities, a perfidious fugitive pointed out Nicomedia, once the capital of the kings of Bithynia, as a rich and easy conquest. He guided the march, which was only sixty miles from the camp of Chalcedon, directed the resistless attack, and partook of the booty; for the Goths had learned sufficient policy to reward the traitor whom they detested. Nice, Prusa, Apamæa, Cius, cities that had sometimes rivalled, or imitated, the splendour of Nicomedia, were involved in the same calamity, which, in a few weeks, raged without control through the whole province of Bithynia. Three hundred years of peace, enjoyed by the soft inhabitants of Asia, had abolished the exercise of arms, and removed the apprehension of danger. The ancient walls were suffered to moulder away, and all the revenue of the most opulent cities was reserved for the construction of baths, temples, and theatres.

When the city of Cyzicus withstood the utmost effort of Mithridates,[38] it was distinguished by wise laws, a naval power of two hundred galleys, and three arsenals,—of arms, of military engines, and of corn. It was still the seat of wealth and luxury; but of its ancient strength nothing remained except the situation, in a little island of the Propontis, connected with the continent of Asia only by two bridges. From the recent sack of Prusa, the Goths advanced within eighteen miles of the city, which they had devoted to destruction; but the ruin of Cyzicus was delayed by a fortunate accident. The season was rainy, and the lake Apolloniates, the reservoir of all the springs of Mount Olympus, rose to an uncommon height. The little river of Rhyndacus, which issues from the lake, swelled into a broad and rapid stream and stopped the progress of the Goths. Their retreat to the maritime city of Heraclea, where the fleet had probably been stationed, was attended by a long train of waggons laden with the spoils of Bithynia, and was marked by the flames of Nice and Nicomedia, which they wantonly burnt. Some

[38] *He besieged the place with 400 galleys, 150,000 foot, and a numerous cavalry.*

obscure hints are mentioned of a doubtful combat that secured their retreat. But even a complete victory would have been of little moment, as the approach of the autumnal equinox summoned them to hasten their return. To navigate the Euxine before the month of May, or after that of September, is esteemed by the modern Turks the most unquestionable instance of rashness and folly.

When we are informed that the third fleet, equipped by the Goths in the ports of Bosphorus, consisted of five hundred sail of ships,[39] our ready imagination instantly computes and multiplies the formidable armament; but, as we are assured by the judicious Strabo, that the piratical vessels used by the barbarians of Pontus and the Lesser Scythia, were not capable of containing more than twenty-five or thirty men, we may safely affirm that fifteen thousand warriors at the most embarked in this great expedition. Impatient of the limits of the Euxine, they steered their destructive course from the Cimmerian to the Thracian Bosphorus. When they had almost gained the middle of the Straits, they were suddenly driven back to the entrance of them; till a favourable wind, springing up the next day, carried them in a few hours into the placid sea, or rather lake, of the Propontis. Their landing on the little island of Cyzicus was attended with the ruin of that ancient and noble city. From thence issuing again through the narrow passage of the Hellespont, they pursued their winding navigation amidst the numerous islands scattered over the Archipelago or the Ægean Sea. The assistance of captives and deserters must have been very necessary to pilot their vessels, and to direct their various incursions, as well on the coast of Greece as on that of Asia. At length the Gothic fleet anchored in the port of Piræus, five miles distant from Athens, which had attempted to make some preparations for a vigorous defence. Cleodamus, one of the engineers employed by the emperor's orders to fortify the maritime cities against the Goths, had already begun to repair the ancient walls fallen to decay since the time of Sylla. The efforts of his skill were ineffectual, and the barbarians became masters of the native seat of the muses and the arts. But, while the conquerors abandoned themselves to the licence of plunder and intemperance, their fleet, that lay with a slender guard in the harbour of Piræus, was unexpectedly attacked by the brave Dexippus, who, flying with the engineer Cleodamus from the sack of Athens, collected a hasty band of volunteers, peasants as well as soldiers, and in some measure avenged the calamities of his country.

But this exploit, whatever lustre it might shed on the declining

[39] *Syncellus speaks of this expedition as undertaken by the Heruli.*

age of Athens, served rather to irritate than to subdue the undaunted spirit of the northern invaders. A general conflagration blazed out at the same time in every district of Greece. Thebes and Argos, Corinth and Sparta, which had formerly waged such memorable wars against each other, were now unable to bring an army into the field, or even to defend their ruined fortifications. The rage of war, both by land and by sea, spread from the eastern point of Sunium to the western coast of Epirus. The Goths had already advanced within sight of Italy, when the approach of such imminent danger awakened the indolent Gallienus from his dream of pleasure. The emperor appeared in arms; and his presence seems to have checked the ardour, and to have divided the strength, of the enemy. Naulobatus, a chief of the Heruli, accepted an honourable capitulation, entered with a large body of his countrymen into the service of Rome, and was invested with the ornaments of the consular dignity, which had never before been profaned by the hands of a barbarian.[40] Great numbers of the Goths, disgusted with the perils and hardships of a tedious voyage, broke into Mæsia, with a design of forcing their way over the Danube to their settlements in the Ukraine. The wild attempt would have proved inevitable destruction, if the discord of the Roman generals had not opened to the barbarians the means of an escape.[41] The small remainder of this destroying host returned on board their vessels, and, measuring back their way through the Hellespont and the Bosphorus, ravaged in their passage the shores of Troy, whose fame, immortalized by Homer, will probably survive the memory of the Gothic conquests. As soon as they found themselves in safety within the bason of the Euxine, they landed at Anchialus in Thrace, near the foot of Mount Hæmus, and, after all their toils, indulged themselves in the use of those pleasant and salutary hot baths. What remained of the voyage was a short and easy navigation. Such was the various fate of this third and greatest of their naval enterprises. It may seem difficult to conceive how the original body of fifteen thousand warriors could sustain the losses and divisions of so bold an adventure. But, as their numbers were gradually wasted by the sword, by shipwrecks, and by the influence of a warm climate, they were perpetually renewed by troops of banditti and deserters, who flocked to the standard of plunder, and by a crowd of fugitive slaves, often of German or Sarmatian extraction, who eagerly seized the glorious opportunity of freedom and revenge. In these expeditions the Gothic nation claimed a superior share of honour and danger; but the tribes that

[40] *This body of Heruli was for a long time faithful and famous.*

[41] *Claudius, who commanded on the Danube, thought with propriety and acted with spirit. His colleague was jealous of his fame.*

fought under the Gothic banners are sometimes distinguished and sometimes confounded in the imperfect histories of that age; and, as the barbarian fleets seemed to issue from the mouth of the Tanais, the vague but familiar appellation of Scythians was frequently bestowed on the mixed multitude.

In the general calamities of mankind the death of an individual, however exalted, the ruin of an edifice, however famous, are passed over with careless inattention. Yet we cannot forget that the temple of Diana at Ephesus, after having risen with increasing splendour from seven repeated misfortunes, was finally burnt by the Goths in their third naval invasion. The arts of Greece and the wealth of Asia had conspired to erect that sacred and magnificent structure. It was supported by an hundred and twenty-seven marble columns of the Ionic order; they were the gifts of devout monarchs, and each was sixty feet high. The altar was adorned with the masterly sculptures of Praxiteles, who had, perhaps, selected from the favourite legends of the place the birth of the divine children of Latona, the concealment of Apollo after the slaughter of the Cyclops, and the clemency of Bacchus to the vanquished Amazons. Yet the length of the temple of Ephesus was only four hundred and twenty-five feet, about two thirds the measure of the church of St. Peter's at Rome.[42] In the other dimensions, it was still more inferior to that sublime production of modern architecture. The spreading arms of a Christian cross require a much greater breadth than the oblong temples of the Pagans; and the boldest artists of antiquity would have been startled at the proposal of raising in the air a dome of the size and proportions of the Pantheon. The temple of Diana was, however, admired as one of the wonders of the world. Successive empires, the Persian, the Macedonian, and the Roman, had revered its sanctity, and enriched its splendour.[43] But the rude savages of the Baltic were destitute of a taste for the elegant arts, and they despised the ideal terrors of a foreign superstition.[44]

Another circumstance is related of these invasions, which might deserve our notice were it not justly to be suspected as the fanciful conceit of a recent sophist. We are told that in the sack of Athens the Goths had collected all the libraries, and were on the point of setting fire to this funeral pile of Grecian learning, had not one of their chiefs, of more refined policy than his brethren, dissuaded them from the design, by the profound observation, that as long as the Greeks were addicted to the study of books they would never apply themselves to the exercise of arms. The sagacious counsellor

[42] *The length of St. Peter's is 840 Roman palms, each palm is a very little short of nine English inches.*

[43] *The policy, however, of the Romans induced them to abridge the extent of the sanctuary or asylum, which by successive privileges had spread itself two stadia round the temple.*

[44] *They offered no sacrifices to the Grecians' gods.*

(should the truth of the fact be admitted) reasoned like an ignorant barbarian. In the most polite and powerful nations genius of every kind has displayed itself about the same period; and the age of science has generally been the age of military virtue and success.

IV. The new sovereigns of Persia, Artaxerxes and his son Sapor, had triumphed (as we have already seen) over the house of Arsaces. Of the many princes of that ancient race, Chosroes, king of Armenia, had alone preserved both his life and his independence. He defended himself by the natural strength of his country; by the perpetual resort of fugitives and malcontents; by the alliance of the Romans; and, above all, by his own courage. Invincible in arms, during a thirty years' war, he was assassinated by the emissaries of Sapor, king of Persia. The patriotic satraps of Armenia, who asserted the freedom and dignity of the crown, implored the protection of Rome in favour of Tiridates, the lawful heir. But the son of Chosroes was an infant, the allies were at a distance, and the Persian monarch advanced towards the frontier at the head of an irresistible force. Young Tiridates, the future hope of his country, was saved by the fidelity of a servant, and Armenia continued above twenty-seven years a reluctant province of the great monarchy of Persia. Elated with this easy conquest, and presuming on the distresses or the degeneracy of the Romans, Sapor obliged the strong garrisons of Carrhæ and Nisibis to surrender, and spread devastation and terror on either side of the Euphrates.

The loss of an important frontier, the ruin of a faithful and natural ally, and the rapid success of Sapor's ambition, affected Rome with a deep sense of the insult as well as of the danger. Valerian flattered himself that the vigilance of his lieutenants would sufficiently provide for the safety of the Rhine and of the Danube; but he resolved, notwithstanding his advanced age, to march in person to the defence of the Euphrates. During his progress through Asia Minor, the naval enterprises of the Goths were suspended, and the afflicted province enjoyed a transient and fallacious calm. He passed the Euphrates, encountered the Persian monarch near the walls of Edessa, was vanquished, and taken prisoner by Sapor. The particulars of that great event are darkly and imperfectly represented; yet, by the glimmering light which is afforded us, we may discover a long series of imprudence, of error, and of deserved misfortunes on the side of the Roman emperor. He reposed an implicit confidence in Macrianus, his Prætorian præfect.[45] That worthless minister rendered his master formidable only to the oppressed subjects, and

45 *As Macrianus was an enemy to the Christians, they charged him with being a magician.*

contemptible to the enemies, of Rome. By his weak or wicked counsels the Imperial army was betrayed into a situation where valour and military skill were equally unavailing. The vigorous attempt of the Romans to cut their way through the Persian host was repulsed with great slaughter; and Sapor, who encompassed the camp with superior numbers, patiently waited till the increasing rage of famine and pestilence had ensured his victory. The licentious murmurs of the legions soon accused Valerian as the cause of their calamities; their seditious clamours demanded an instant capitulation. An immense sum of gold was offered to purchase the permission of a disgraceful retreat. But the Persian, conscious of his superiority, refused the money with disdain; and, detaining the deputies, advanced in order of battle to the foot of the Roman rampart, and insisted on a personal conference with the emperor. Valerian was reduced to the necessity of intrusting his life and dignity to the faith of an enemy. The interview ended as it was natural to expect. The emperor was made a prisoner, and his astonished troops laid down their arms. In such a moment of triumph, the pride and policy of Sapor prompted him to fill the vacant throne with a successor entirely dependent on his pleasure. Cyriades, an obscure fugitive of Antioch, stained with every vice, was chosen to dishonour the Roman purple; and the will of the Persian victor could not fail of being ratified by the acclamations, however reluctant, of the captive army.

The Imperial slave was eager to secure the favour of his master by an act of treason to his native country. He conducted Sapor over the Euphrates, and, by the way of Chalcis, to the metropolis of the East. So rapid were the motions of the Persian cavalry, that, if we may credit a very judicious historian,[46] the city of Antioch was surprised when the idle multitude was fondly gazing on the amusements of the theatre. The splendid buildings of Antioch, private as well as public, were either pillaged or destroyed; and the numerous inhabitants were put to the sword or led away into captivity. The tide of devastation was stopped for a moment by the resolution of the high priest of Emesa. Arrayed in his sacerdotal robes he appeared at the head of a great body of fanatic peasants, armed only with slings, and defended his god and his property from the sacrilegious hands of the followers of Zoroaster. But the ruin of Tarsus, and of many other cities, furnishes a melancholy proof that, except in this singular instance, the conquest of Syria and Cilicia scarcely interrupted the progress of the Persian arms. The advantages of the

[46] *The sack of Antioch, anticipated by some historians, is assigned, by the decisive testimony of Ammianus Marcellinus, to the reign of Gallienus.*

narrow passes of Mount Taurus were abandoned, in which an invader whose principal force consisted in his cavalry would have been engaged in a very unequal combat: and Sapor was admitted to form the siege of Cæsarea, the capital of Cappadocia; a city, though of the second rank, which was supposed to contain four hundred thousand inhabitants. Demosthenes commanded in the place, not so much by the commission of the emperor as in the voluntary defence of his country. For a long time he deferred its fate; and, when at last Cæsarea was betrayed by the perfidy of a physician, he cut his way through the Persians, who had been ordered to exert their utmost diligence to take him alive. This heroic chief escaped the power of a foe who might either have honoured or punished his obstinate valour; but many thousands of his fellow-citizens were involved in a general massacre, and Sapor is accused of treating his prisoners with wanton and unrelenting cruelty.[47] Much should undoubtedly be allowed for national animosity, much for humbled pride and impotent revenge; yet, upon the whole, it is certain that the same prince who, in Armenia, had displayed the mild aspect of a legislator, showed himself to the Romans under the stern features of a conqueror. He despaired of making any permanent establishment in the empire, and sought only to leave behind him a wasted desert, whilst he transported into Persia the people and the treasures of the provinces.[48]

At a time when the East trembled at the name of Sapor, he received a present not unworthy of the greatest kings—a long train of camels laden with the most rare and valuable merchandises. The rich offering was accompanied with an epistle, respectful but not servile, from Odenathus, one of the noblest and most opulent senators of Palmyra. "Who is this Odenathus" (said the haughty victor, and he commanded that the presents should be cast into the Euphrates), "that he thus insolently presumes to write to his lord? If he entertains a hope of mitigating his punishment, let him fall prostrate before the foot of our throne, with his hands bound behind his back. Should he hesitate, swift destruction shall be poured on his head, on his whole race, and on his country." The desperate extremity to which the Palmyrenian was reduced called into action all the latent powers of his soul. He met Sapor; but he met him in arms. Infusing his own spirit into a little army collected from the villages of Syria, and the tents of the desert,[49] he hovered round the Persian host, harassed their retreat, carried off part of the treasure, and, what was dearer than any treasure, several of the women of

[47] *Deep valleys were filled up with the slain. Crowds of prisoners were driven to water like beasts, and many perished for want of food.*

[48] *Zosimus asserts that Sapor, had he not preferred spoil to conquest, might have remained master of Asia.*

[49] *He possessed so powerful an interest among the wandering tribes, that Procopius and John Malala style him Prince of the Saracens.*

the Great King; who was at last obliged to repass the Euphrates with some marks of haste and confusion. By this exploit Odenathus laid the foundations of his future fame and fortunes. The majesty of Rome, oppressed by a Persian, was protected by a Syrian or Arab of Palmyra.

The voice of history, which is often little more than the organ of hatred or flattery, reproaches Sapor with a proud abuse of the rights of conquest. We are told that Valerian, in chains, but invested with the Imperial purple, was exposed to the multitude, a constant spectacle of fallen greatness; and that, whenever the Persian monarch mounted on horseback, he placed his foot on the neck of a Roman emperor. Notwithstanding all the remonstrances of his allies, who repeatedly advised him to remember the vicissitude of fortune, to dread the returning power of Rome, and to make his illustrious captive the pledge of peace, not the object of insult, Sapor still remained inflexible. When Valerian sunk under the weight of shame and grief, his skin, stuffed with straw, and formed into the likeness of a human figure, was preserved for ages in the most celebrated temple of Persia; a more real monument of triumph than the fancied trophies of brass and marble so often erected by Roman vanity.[50] The tale is moral and pathetic, but the truth of it may very fairly be called in question. The letters still extant from the princes of the East to Sapor are manifest forgeries;[51] nor is it natural to suppose that a jealous monarch should, even in the person of a rival, thus publicly degrade the majesty of kings. Whatever treatment the unfortunate Valerian might experience in Persia, it is at least certain that the only emperor of Rome who had ever fallen into the hands of the enemy languished away his life in hopeless captivity.

The emperor Gallienus, who had long supported with impatience the censorial severity of his father and colleague, received the intelligence of his misfortunes with secret pleasure, and avowed indifference. "I knew that my father was a mortal," said he, "and, since he has acted as becomes a brave man, I am satisfied." Whilst Rome lamented the fate of her sovereign, the savage coldness of his son was extolled by the servile courtiers as the perfect firmness of a hero and a stoic. It is difficult to paint the light, the various, the inconstant character of Gallienus, which he displayed without constraint as soon as he became sole possessor of the empire. In every art that he attempted his lively genius enabled him to succeed; and, as his genius was destitute of judgment, he attempted every art, except the important ones of war and government. He was a mas-

[50] *The Pagan writers lament, the Christian insult, the misfortunes of Valerian. So little has been preserved of Eastern history before Mahomet, that the modern Persians are totally ignorant of the victory of Sapor, an event so glorious to their nation.*

[51] *One of these epistles is from Artavasdes, king of Armenia: since Armenia was then a province to Persia, the king, the kingdom, and the epistle must be fictitious.*

ter of several curious but useless sciences, a ready orator, an elegant poet, a skilful gardener, an excellent cook, and most contemptible prince. When the great emergencies of the state required his presence and attention, he was engaged in conversation with the philosopher Plotinus,[52] wasting his time in trifling or licentious pleasures, preparing his initiation to the Grecian mysteries, or soliciting a place in the Areopagus of Athens. His profuse magnificence insulted the general poverty; the solemn ridicule of his triumphs impressed a deeper sense of the public disgrace. The repeated intelligence of invasions, defeats, and rebellions, he received with a careless smile; and singling out, with affected contempt, some particular production of the lost province, he carelessly asked, whether Rome must be ruined, unless it was supplied with linen from Egypt, and Arras cloth from Gaul? There were, however, a few short moments in the life of Gallienus when, exasperated by some recent injury, he suddenly appeared the intrepid soldier and the cruel tyrant; till, satiated with blood or fatigued by resistance, he insensibly sunk into the natural mildness and indolence of his character.[53]

At a time when the reins of government were held with so loose a hand, it is not surprising that a crowd of usurpers should start up in every province of the empire, against the son of Valerian. It was probably some ingenious fancy, of comparing the thirty tyrants of Rome with the thirty tyrants of Athens, that induced the writers of the Augustan history to select that celebrated number, which has been gradually received into a popular appellation.[54] But in every light the parallel is idle and defective. What resemblance can we discover between a council of thirty persons, the united oppressors of a single city, and an uncertain list of independent rivals, who rose and fell in irregular succession through the extent of a vast empire? Nor can the number of thirty be completed unless we include in the account the women and children who were honoured with the Imperial title. The reign of Gallienus, distracted as it was, produced only nineteen pretenders to the throne: Cyriades, Macrianus, Balista, Odenathus, and Zenobia in the East; in Gaul and the western provinces, Posthumus, Lollianus, Victorinus and his mother Victoria, Marius, and Tetricus. In Illyricum and the confines of the Danube, Ingenuus, Regillianus and Aureolus; in Pontus,[55] Saturninus; in Isauria, Trebellianus; Piso in Thessaly; Valens in Achaia; Æmilianus in Egypt; and Celsus in Africa. To illustrate the obscure monuments of the life and death of each individual would prove a laborious task, alike barren of instruction and amusement. We

[52] *He was on the point of giving Plotinus a ruined city of Campania to try the experiment of realizing Plato's Republic.*

[53] *This singular character has, I believe, been fairly transmitted to us. The reign of his immediate successor was short and busy, and the historians who wrote before the elevation of the family of Constantine could not have the most remote interest to misrepresent the character of Gallienus.*

[54] *Pollio expresses the most minute anxiety to complete the number.*

[55] *The place of his reign is somewhat doubtful; but there was a tyrant in Pontus, and we are acquainted with the seat of all the others.*

may content ourselves with investigating some general characters, that most strongly mark the condition of the times and the manners of the men, their pretensions, their motives, their fate, and the destructive consequences of their usurpation.

It is sufficiently known that the odious appellation of *Tyrant* was often employed by the ancients to express the illegal seizure of supreme power, without any reference to the abuse of it. Several of the pretenders who raised the standard of rebellion against the emperor Gallienus were shining models of virtue, and almost all possessed a considerable share of vigour and ability. Their merit had recommended them to the favour of Valerian, and gradually promoted them to the most important commands of the empire. The generals who assumed the title of Augustus were either respected by their troops for their able conduct and severe discipline, or admired for valour and success in war, or beloved for frankness and generosity. The field of victory was often the scene of their election; and even the armourer Marius, the most contemptible of all the candidates for the purple, was distinguished however by intrepid courage, matchless strength, and blunt honesty. His mean and recent trade cast, indeed, an air of ridicule on his elevation; but his birth could not be more obscure than was that of the greater part of his rivals, who were born of peasants, and enlisted in the army as private soldiers. In times of confusion every active genius finds the place assigned him by nature; in a general state of war military merit is the road to glory and to greatness. Of the nineteen tyrants Tetricus only was a senator; Piso alone was a noble. The blood of Numa, through twenty-eight successive generations, ran in the veins of Calphurnius Piso, who, by female alliances, claimed a right of exhibiting in his house the images of Crassus and of the great Pompey. His ancestors had been repeatedly dignified with all the honours which the commonwealth could bestow; and, of all the ancient families of Rome, the Calphurnian alone had survived the tyranny of the Cæsars. The personal qualities of Piso added new lustre to his race. The usurper Valens, by whose order he was killed, confessed, with deep remorse, that even an enemy ought to have respected the sanctity of Piso; and, although he died in arms against Gallienus, the senate, with the emperor's generous permission, decreed the triumphal ornaments to the memory of so virtuous a rebel.[56]

The lieutenants of Valerian were grateful to the father, whom they esteemed. They disdained to serve the luxurious indolence of

[56] *The senate, in a moment of enthusiasm, seems to have presumed on the approbation of Gallienus.*

his unworthy son. The throne of the Roman world was unsupported by any principle of loyalty; and treason against such a prince might easily be considered as patriotism to the state. Yet, if we examine with candour the conduct of these usurpers, it will appear that they were much oftener driven into rebellion by their fears than urged to it by their ambition. They dreaded the cruel suspicions of Gallienus: they equally dreaded the capricious violence of their troops. If the dangerous favour of the army had imprudently declared them deserving of the purple, they were marked for sure destruction; and even prudence would counsel them to secure a short enjoyment of the empire, and rather to try the fortune of war than to expect the hand of an executioner. When the clamour of the soldiers invested the reluctant victims with the ensigns of sovereign authority, they sometimes mourned in secret their approaching fate. "You have lost," said Saturninus, on the day of his elevation, "you have lost a useful commander, and you have made a very wretched emperor."

The apprehensions of Saturninus were justified by the repeated experience of revolutions. Of the nineteen tyrants who started up under the reign of Gallienus, there was not one who enjoyed a life of peace, or a natural death. As soon as they were invested with the bloody purple, they inspired their adherents with the same fears and ambition which had occasioned their own revolt. Encompassed with domestic conspiracy, military sedition, and civil war, they trembled on the edge of precipices, in which, after a longer or shorter term of anxiety, they were inevitably lost. These precarious monarchs received, however, such honours as the flattery of their respective armies and provinces could bestow; but their claim, founded on rebellion, could never obtain the sanction of law or history. Italy, Rome, and the senate constantly adhered to the cause of Gallienus, and he alone was considered as the sovereign of the empire. That prince condescended indeed to acknowledge the victorious arms of Odenathus, who deserved the honourable distinction by the respectful conduct which he always maintained towards the son of Valerian. With the general applause of the Romans and the consent of Gallienus, the senate conferred the title of Augustus on the brave Palmyrenian; and seemed to intrust him with the government of the East, which he already possessed, in so independent a manner, that, like a private succession, he bequeathed it to his illustrious widow Zenobia.[57]

The rapid and perpetual transitions from the cottage to the

[57] *The association of the brave Palmyrenian was the most popular act of the whole reign of Gallienus.*

throne, and from the throne to the grave, might have amused an indifferent philosopher, were it possible for a philosopher to remain indifferent amidst the general calamities of human kind. The election of these precarious emperors, their power and their death, were equally destructive to their subjects and adherents. The price of their fatal elevation was instantly discharged to the troops by an immense donative drawn from the bowels of the exhausted people. However virtuous was their character, however pure their intentions, they found themselves reduced to the hard necessity of supporting their usurpation by frequent acts of rapine and cruelty. When they fell, they involved armies and provinces in their fall. There is still extant a most savage mandate from Gallienus to one of his ministers, after the suppression of Ingenuus, who had assumed the purple in Illyricum. "It is not enough," says that soft but inhuman prince, "that you exterminate such as have appeared in arms: the chance of battle might have served me as effectually. The male sex of every age must be extirpated; provided that, in the execution of the children and old men, you can contrive means to save our reputation. Let every one die who has dropt an expression, who has entertained a thought, against me, against *me*, the son of Valerian, the father and brother of so many princes.[58] Remember that Ingenuus was made emperor: tear, kill, hew in pieces. I write to you with my own hand, and would inspire you with my own feelings." Whilst the public forces of the state were dissipated in private quarrels, the defenceless provinces lay exposed to every invader. The bravest usurpers were compelled by the perplexity of their situation to conclude ignominious treaties with the common enemy, to purchase with oppressive tributes the neutrality or services of the barbarians, and to introduce hostile and independent nations into the heart of the Roman monarchy.[59]

Such were the barbarians, and such the tyrants, who, under the reigns of Valerian and Gallienus, dismembered the provinces, and reduced the empire to the lowest pitch of disgrace and ruin, from whence it seemed impossible that it should ever emerge. As far as the barrenness of materials would permit, we have attempted to trace, with order and perspicuity, the general events of that calamitous period. There still remain some particular facts: I. The disorders of Sicily; II. The tumults of Alexandria; and III. The rebellion of the Isaurians—which may serve to reflect a strong light on the horrid picture.

I. Whenever numerous troops of banditti, multiplied by success

[58] *Gallienus had given the titles of Cæsar and Augustus to his son Salonius, slain at Cologne by the usurper Posthumus. A second son of Gallienus succeeded to the name and rank of his elder brother. Valerian, the brother of Gallienus, was also associated to the empire: several other brothers, sisters, nephews, and nieces of the emperor, formed a very numerous royal family.*

[59] *Regillianus had some bands of Roxolani in his service; Posthumus a body of Franks. It was perhaps in the character of auxiliaries that the latter introduced themselves into Spain.*

and impunity, publicly defy, instead of eluding, the justice of their country, we may safely infer that the excessive weakness of the government is felt and abused by the lowest ranks of the community. The situation of Sicily preserved it from the barbarians; nor could the disarmed province have supported an usurper. The sufferings of that once flourishing and still fertile island were inflicted by baser hands. A licentious crowd of slaves and peasants reigned for a while over the plundered country, and renewed the memory of the servile wars of more ancient times. Devastations, of which the husbandman was either the victim or the accomplice, must have ruined the agriculture of Sicily; and as the principal estates were the property of the opulent senators of Rome, who often enclosed within a farm the territory of an old republic, it is not improbable that this private injury might affect the capital more deeply than all the conquests of the Goths or the Persians.

II. The foundation of Alexandria was a noble design, at once conceived and executed by the son of Philip. The beautiful and regular form of that great city, second only to Rome itself, comprehended a circumference of fifteen miles; it was peopled by three hundred thousand free inhabitants, besides at least an equal number of slaves. The lucrative trade of Arabia and India flowed through the port of Alexandria to the capital and provinces of the empire. Idleness was unknown. Some were employed in blowing of glass, others in weaving of linen, others again in manufacturing the papyrus. Either sex, and every age, was engaged in the pursuits of industry, nor did even the blind or the lame want occupations suited to their condition. But the people of Alexandria, a various mixture of nations, united the vanity and inconstancy of the Greeks with the superstition and obstinacy of the Egyptians. The most trifling occasion, a transient scarcity of flesh or lentils, the neglect of an accustomed salutation, a mistake of precedency in the public baths, or even a religious dispute,[60] were at any time sufficient to kindle a sedition among that vast multitude, whose resentments were furious and implacable.[61] After the captivity of Valerian and the indolence of his son had relaxed the authority of the laws, the Alexandrians abandoned themselves to the ungoverned rage of their passions, and their unhappy country was the theatre of a civil war, which continued (with a few short and suspicious truces) above twelve years. All intercourse was cut off between the several quarters of the afflicted city, every street was polluted with blood, every building of strength converted into a citadel; nor did the tumults subside till a

[60] *Such as the sacrilegious murder of a divine cat.*

[61] *This long and terrible sedition was first occasioned by a dispute between a soldier and a townsman about a pair of shoes.*

considerable part of Alexandria was irretrievably ruined. The spacious and magnificent district of Bruchion, with its palaces and musæum, the residence of the kings and philosophers of Egypt, is described above a century afterwards, as already reduced to its present state of a dreary solitude.

III. The obscure rebellion of Trebellianus, who assumed the purple in Isauria, a petty province of Asia Minor, was attended with strange and memorable consequences. The pageant of royalty was soon destroyed by an officer of Gallienus; but his followers, despairing of mercy, resolved to shake off their allegiance, not only to the emperor but to the empire, and suddenly returned to the savage manners from which they had never perfectly been reclaimed. Their craggy rocks, a branch of the wide-extended Taurus, protected their inaccessible retreat. The tillage of some fertile valleys supplied them with necessaries, and a habit of rapine with the luxuries of life. In the heart of the Roman monarchy, the Isaurians long continued a nation of wild barbarians. Succeeding princes, unable to reduce them to obedience either by arms or policy, were compelled to acknowledge their weakness by surrounding the hostile and independent spot with a strong chain of fortifications, which often proved insufficient to restrain the incursions of these domestic foes. The Isaurians, gradually extending their territory to the sea coast, subdued the western and mountainous part of Cilicia, formerly the nest of those daring pirates against whom the republic had once been obliged to exert its utmost force, under the conduct of the great Pompey.

Our habits of thinking so fondly connect the order of the universe with the fate of man, that this gloomy period of history has been decorated with inundations, earthquakes, uncommon meteors, preternatural darkness, and a crowd of prodigies fictitious or exaggerated. But a long and general famine was a calamity of a more serious kind. It was the inevitable consequence of rapine and oppression, which extirpated the produce of the present and the hope of future harvests. Famine is almost always followed by epidemical diseases, the effect of scanty and unwholesome food. Other causes must however have contributed to the furious plague which, from the year two hundred and fifty to the year two hundred and sixty-five, raged without interruption in every province, every city, and almost every family of the Roman empire. During some time five thousand persons died daily in Rome; and many towns that had escaped the hands of the barbarians were entirely depopulated.

We have the knowledge of a very curious circumstance, of some use perhaps in the melancholy calculation of human calamities. An exact register was kept at Alexandria of all the citizens entitled to receive the distribution of corn. It was found that the ancient number of those comprised between the ages of forty and seventy had been equal to the whole sum of claimants, from fourteen to fourscore years of age, who remained alive after the reign of Gallienus.[62] Applying this authentic fact to the most correct tables of mortality, it evidently proves that above half the people of Alexandria had perished; and could we venture to extend the analogy to the other provinces, we might suspect that war, pestilence, and famine, had consumed, in a few years, the moiety of the human species.[63]

[62] *The fact is taken from the Letters of Dionysius, who in the time of those troubles was bishop of Alexandria.*

[63] *In a great number of parishes 11,000 persons were found between fourteen and eighty; 5365 between forty and seventy.*

XI

REIGN OF CLAUDIUS · DEFEAT OF THE GOTHS · VICTORIES,
TRIUMPH, AND DEATH, OF AURELIAN · ZENOBIA'S CHARACTER

NDER the deplorable reigns of Valerian and Gallienus, the empire was oppressed and almost destroyed by the soldiers, the tyrants, and the barbarians. It was saved by a series of great princes, who derived their origin from the martial provinces of Illyricum. Within a period of about thirty years, Claudius, Aurelian, Probus, Diocletian and his colleagues, triumphed over the foreign and domestic enemies of the state, reestablished, with the military discipline, the strength of the frontiers, and deserved the glorious title of Restorers of the Roman world.

The removal of an effeminate tyrant made way for a succession of heroes. The indignation of the people imputed all their calamities to Gallienus, and the far greater part were, indeed, the consequence of his dissolute manners and careless administration. He was even destitute of a sense of honour, which so frequently supplies the absence of public virtue; and, as long as he was permitted to enjoy the possession of Italy, a victory of the barbarians, the loss of a province, or the rebellion of a general, seldom disturbed the tranquil course of his pleasures. At length, a considerable army, stationed on the Upper Danube, invested with the Imperial purple their leader Aureolus; who, disdaining a confined and barren reign over the mountains of Rhætia, passed the Alps, occupied Milan, threatened Rome, and challenged Gallienus to dispute in the field the sovereignty of Italy. The emperor, provoked by the insult, and alarmed by the instant danger, suddenly exerted that latent vigour which sometimes broke through the indolence of his temper. Forcing himself from the luxury of the palace, he appeared in arms at the head of his legions, and advanced beyond the Po to encounter his competitor. The corrupted name of Pontirolo [1] still preserves the memory of a bridge over the Adda, which, during the action, must have proved

[1] Pons Aureoli, *thirteen miles from Bergamo, and thirty-two from Milan. Near this place, in the year 1703, the obstinate battle of Cassano was fought between the French and Austrians.*

an object of the utmost importance to both armies. The Rhætian usurper, after receiving a total defeat and a dangerous wound, retired into Milan. The siege of that great city was immediately formed; the walls were battered with every engine in use among the ancients; and Aureolus, doubtful of his internal strength, and hopeless of foreign succours, already anticipated the fatal consequences of unsuccessful rebellion.

His last resource was an attempt to seduce the loyalty of the besiegers. He scattered libels through their camp, inviting the troops to desert an unworthy master, who sacrificed the public happiness to his luxury, and the lives of his most valuable subjects to the slightest suspicions. The arts of Aureolus diffused fears and discontent among the principal officers of his rival. A conspiracy was formed by Heraclianus, the Prætorian præfect, by Marcian, a general of rank and reputation, and by Cecrops, who commanded a numerous body of Dalmatian guards. The death of Gallienus was resolved, and, notwithstanding their desire of first terminating the siege of Milan, the extreme danger which accompanied every moment's delay obliged them to hasten the execution of their daring purpose. At a late hour of the night, but while the emperor still protracted the pleasures of the table, an alarm was suddenly given that Aureolus, at the head of all his forces, had made a desperate sally from the town; Gallienus, who was never deficient in personal bravery, started from his silken couch, and, without allowing himself time either to put on his armour or to assemble his guards, he mounted on horseback, and rode full speed towards the supposed place of the attack. Encompassed by his declared or concealed enemies, he soon, amidst the nocturnal tumult, received a mortal dart from an uncertain hand. Before he expired, a patriotic sentiment rising in the mind of Gallienus induced him to name a deserving successor, and it was his last request that the Imperial ornaments should be delivered to Claudius, who then commanded a detached army in the neighbourhood of Pavia. The report at least was diligently propagated, and the order cheerfully obeyed by the conspirators, who had already agreed to place Claudius on the throne. On the first news of the emperor's death, the troops expressed some suspicion and resentment, till the one was removed and the other assuaged by a donative of twenty pieces of gold to each soldier. They then ratified the election, and acknowledged the merit, of their new sovereign.

The obscurity which covered the origin of Claudius, though it was afterwards embellished by some flattering fictions,[2] sufficiently betrays the meanness of his birth. We can only discover that he was a native of one of the provinces bordering on the Danube; that his youth was spent in arms, and that his modest valour attracted the favour and confidence of Decius. The senate and people already considered him as an excellent officer, equal to the most important trusts; and censured the inattention of Valerian, who suffered him to remain in the subordinate station of a tribune. But it was not long before that emperor distinguished the merit of Claudius, by declaring him general and chief of the Illyrian frontier, with the command of all the troops in Thrace, Mæsia, Dacia, Pannonia, and Dalmatia, the appointments of the præfect of Egypt, the establishment of the proconsul of Africa, and the sure prospect of the consulship. By his victories over the Goths, he deserved from the senate the honour of a statue and excited the jealous apprehensions of Gallienus. It was impossible that a soldier could esteem so dissolute a sovereign, nor is it easy to conceal a just contempt. Some unguarded expressions which dropped from Claudius were officiously transmitted to the royal ear. The emperor's answer to an officer of confidence describes in very lively colours his own character and that of the times. "There is not anything capable of giving me more serious concern, than the intelligence contained in your last dispatch,[3] that some malicious suggestions have indisposed towards us the mind of our friend and parent Claudius. As you regard your allegiance, use every means to appease his resentment, but conduct your negotiation with secrecy; let it not reach the knowledge of the Dacian troops; they are already provoked, and it might inflame their fury. I myself have sent him some presents: be it your care that he accept them with pleasure. Above all, let him not suspect that I am made acquainted with his imprudence. The fear of my anger might urge him to desperate counsels." The presents which accompanied this humble epistle, in which the monarch solicited a reconciliation with his discontented subject, consisted of a considerable sum of money, a splendid wardrobe, and a valuable service of silver and gold plate. By such arts Gallienus softened the indignation, and dispelled the fears, of his Illyrian general; and during the remainder of that reign the formidable sword of Claudius was always drawn in the cause of a master whom he despised. At last, indeed, he received from the conspirators the bloody purple of Gallienus: but he had been absent from their camps and counsels; and, however he might applaud the deed, we may candidly presume that he was innocent of the knowl-

[2] *Some supposed him, oddly enough, to be a bastard of the younger Gordian. Others took advantage of the province of Dardania, to deduce his origin from Dardanus and the ancient kings of Troy.*

[3] Notoria, *a periodical and official dispatch which the emperors received from the* frumentarii *or agents dispersed through the provinces. Of these we may speak hereafter.*

edge of it. When Claudius ascended the throne, he was about fifty-four years of age.

The siege of Milan was still continued, and Aureolus soon discovered that the success of his artifices had only raised up a more determined adversary. He attempted to negotiate with Claudius a treaty of alliance and partition. "Tell him," replied the intrepid emperor, "that such proposals should have been made to Gallienus; *he,* perhaps, might have listened to them with patience, and accepted a colleague as despicable as himself." This stern refusal, and a last unsuccessful effort, obliged Aureolus to yield the city and himself to the discretion of the conqueror. The judgment of the army pronounced him worthy of death, and Claudius, after a feeble resistance, consented to the execution of the sentence. Nor was the zeal of the senate less ardent in the cause of their new sovereign. They ratified, perhaps with a sincere transport of zeal, the election of Claudius; and, as his predecessor had shown himself the personal enemy of their order, they exercised, under the name of justice, a severe revenge against his friends and family. The senate was permitted to discharge the ungrateful office of punishment, and the emperor reserved for himself the pleasure and merit of obtaining by his intercession a general act of indemnity.[4]

Such ostentatious clemency discovers less of the real character of Claudius than a trifling circumstance in which he seems to have consulted only the dictates of his heart. The frequent rebellions of the provinces had involved almost every person in the guilt of treason, almost every estate in the case of confiscation; and Gallienus often displayed his liberality by distributing among his officers the property of his subjects. On the accession of Claudius, an old woman threw herself at his feet, and complained that a general of the late emperor had obtained an arbitrary grant of her patrimony. This general was Claudius himself, who had not entirely escaped the contagion of the times. The emperor blushed at the reproach, but deserved the confidence which she had reposed in his equity. The confession of his fault was accompanied with immediate and ample restitution.

In the arduous task which Claudius had undertaken, of restoring the empire to its ancient splendour, it was first necessary to revive among his troops a sense of order and obedience. With the authority of a veteran commander, he represented to them that the relaxation of discipline had introduced a long train of disorders, the effects of which were at length experienced by the soldiers themselves; that

[4] *The people loudly prayed for the damnation of Gallienus. The senate decreed that his relations and servants should be thrown down headlong from the Gemonian stairs. An obnoxious officer of the revenue had his eyes torn out whilst under examination.*

a people ruined by oppression, and indolent from despair, could no longer supply a numerous army with the means of luxury, or even of subsistence; that the danger of each individual had increased with the despotism of the military order, since princes who tremble on the throne will guard their safety by the instant sacrifice of every obnoxious subject. The emperor expatiated on the mischiefs of a lawless caprice which the soldiers could only gratify at the expense of their own blood, as their seditious elections had so frequently been followed by civil wars, which consumed the flower of the legions either in the field of battle or in the cruel abuse of victory. He painted in the most lively colours the exhausted state of the treasury, the desolation of the provinces, the disgrace of the Roman name, and the insolent triumph of rapacious barbarians. It was against those barbarians, he declared, that he intended to point the first effort of their arms. Tetricus might reign for a while over the West, and even Zenobia might preserve the dominion of the East. These usurpers were his personal adversaries; nor could he think of indulging any private resentment till he had saved an empire, whose impending ruin would, unless it was timely prevented, crush both the army and the people.

The various nations of Germany and Sarmatia who fought under the Gothic standard had already collected an armament more formidable than any which had yet issued from the Euxine. On the banks of the Dniester, one of the great rivers that discharge themselves into that sea, they constructed a fleet of two thousand, or even of six thousand vessels; numbers which, however incredible they may seem, would have been insufficient to transport their pretended army of three hundred and twenty thousand barbarians. Whatever might be the real strength of the Goths, the vigour and success of the expedition were not adequate to the greatness of the preparations. In their passage through the Bosphorus, the unskilful pilots were overpowered by the violence of the current; and while the multitude of their ships were crowded in a narrow channel, many were dashed against each other, or against the shore. The barbarians made several descents on the coasts both of Europe and Asia; but the open country was already plundered, and they were repulsed with shame and loss from the fortified cities which they assaulted. A spirit of discouragement and division arose in the fleet, and some of their chiefs sailed away towards the islands of Crete and Cyprus; but the main body, pursuing a more steady course, anchored at length near the foot of Mount Athos, and assaulted the city of Thessalonica, the wealthy capital of all the Macedonian provinces. Their attacks, in which they displayed a fierce but artless bravery, were soon interrupted by the rapid approach of Claudius, hastening to a scene of action that deserved the presence of a warlike prince at the head of the remaining powers of the empire. Impatient for battle, the Goths immediately broke up their camp, relinquished the siege of Thessalonica, left their navy at the foot of Mount Athos, traversed the hills of Macedonia, and pressed forwards to engage the last defence of Italy.

We still possess an original letter addressed by Claudius to the senate and people on this memorable occasion. "Conscript fathers," says the emperor, "know that three hundred and twenty thousand Goths have invaded the Roman territory. If I vanquish them, your gratitude will reward my services. Should I fall, remember that I am the successor of Gallienus. The whole republic is fatigued and exhausted. We shall fight after Valerian, after Ingenuus, Regillianus, Lollianus, Posthumus, Celsus, and a thousand others, whom a just contempt for Gallienus provoked into rebellion. We are in want of darts, of spears, and of shields. The strength of the empire, Gaul and Spain, are usurped by Tetricus, and we blush to acknowledge that the archers of the East serve under the banners of Zenobia. Whatever we shall perform will be sufficiently great." The melancholy firmness of this epistle announces a hero careless of his fate, conscious of his danger, but still deriving a well-grounded hope from the resources of his own mind.

The event surpassed his own expectations and those of the world. By the most signal victories he delivered the empire from this host of barbarians, and was distinguished by posterity under the glorious appellation of the Gothic Claudius. The imperfect historians of an irregular war do not enable us to describe the order and circumstances of his exploits; but, if we could be indulged in the illusion, we might distribute into three acts this memorable tragedy. I. The decisive battle was fought near Naissus, a city of Dardania. The legions at first gave way, oppressed by numbers, and dismayed by misfortunes. Their ruin was inevitable, had not the abilities of their emperor prepared a seasonable relief. A large detachment, rising out of the secret and difficult passes of the mountains, which, by his order, they had occupied, suddenly assailed the rear of the victorious Goths. The favourable instant was improved by the activity of Claudius. He revived the courage of his troops, restored their ranks, and pressed the barbarians on every side. Fifty thousand men are reported to have been slain in the battle of Naissus. Several large bodies of barbarians, covering their retreat with a movable fortification of waggons, retired, or rather escaped, from the field of slaughter. II. We may presume that some insurmountable difficulty, the fatigue, perhaps, or the disobedience, of the conquerors, prevented Claudius from completing in one day the destruction of the Goths. The war was diffused over the provinces of Mæsia, Thrace, and Macedonia, and its operations drawn out into a variety of marches, surprises, and tumultuary engagements, as well by sea as by land. When the Romans suffered any loss, it was commonly occasioned by their own cowardice or rashness; but the superior talents of the emperor, his perfect knowledge of the country, and his judicious choice of measures as well as officers, assured on most occasions the success of his arms. The immense booty, the fruit of so many victories, consisted for the greater part of cattle and slaves. A select body of the Gothic youth was received among the Imperial troops; the remainder was sold into servitude; and so considerable was the number of female captives, that every soldier obtained to his share two or three women. A circumstance from which we may conclude that the invaders entertained some designs of settlement as well as of plunder; since even in a naval expedition they were accompanied by their families. III. The loss of their fleet, which was either taken or sunk, had intercepted the retreat of the Goths. A vast circle of Roman posts, distributed with skill, supported with firmness, and gradually closing towards a common centre, forced the barbarians into the most inaccessible parts of Mount Hæmus, where they found a safe refuge, but a very scanty subsistence. During the course of a rigorous winter, in which they were besieged by the emperor's troops, famine and pestilence, desertion and the sword, continually diminished the imprisoned multitude. On the return of spring, nothing appeared in arms except a hardy and desperate band, the remnant of that mighty host which had embarked at the mouth of the Dniester.

The pestilence which swept away such numbers of the barbarians at length proved fatal to their conqueror. After a short but glorious reign of two years, Claudius expired at Sirmium, amidst the tears and acclamations of his subjects. In his last illness, he convened the principal officers of the state and army, and in their presence recommended Aurelian, one of his generals, as the most deserving of the throne, and the best qualified to execute the great design which he himself had been permitted only to undertake. The virtues of

Claudius, his valour, affability, justice, and temperance, his love of fame and of his country, place him in that short list of emperors who added lustre to the Roman purple: Those virtues, however, were celebrated with peculiar zeal and complacency by the courtly writers of the age of Constantine, who was the great-grandson of Crispus, the elder brother of Claudius. The voice of flattery was soon taught to repeat that the gods, who so hastily had snatched Claudius from the earth, rewarded his merit and piety by the perpetual establishment of the empire in his family.

Notwithstanding these oracles, the greatness of the Flavian family (a name which it had pleased them to assume) was deferred above twenty years, and the elevation of Claudius occasioned the immediate ruin of his brother Quintilius, who possessed not sufficient moderation or courage to descend into the private station to which the patriotism of the late emperor had condemned him. Without delay or reflection, he assumed the purple at Aquileia, where he commanded a considerable force; and, though his reign lasted only seventeen days, he had time to obtain the sanction of the senate, and to experience a mutiny of the troops. As soon as he was informed that the great army of the Danube had invested the well-known valour of Aurelian with Imperial power, he sunk under the fame and merit of his rival; and, ordering his veins to be opened, prudently withdrew himself from the unequal contest.

The general design of this work will not permit us minutely to relate the actions of every emperor after he ascended the throne, much less to deduce the various fortunes of his private life. We shall only observe, that the father of Aurelian was a peasant of the territory of Sirmium, who occupied a small farm, the property of Aurelius, a rich senator. His warlike son enlisted in the troops as a common soldier, successively rose to the rank of a centurion, a tribune, the præfect of a legion, the inspector of the camp, the general, or, as it was then called, the duke of a frontier; and at length, during the Gothic war, exercised the important office of commander in chief of the cavalry. In every station he distinguished himself by matchless valour,[5] rigid discipline, and successful conduct. He was invested with the consulship by the emperor Valerian, who styles him, in the pompous language of that age, the deliverer of Illyricum, the restorer of Gaul, and the rival of the Scipios. At the recommendation of Valerian, a senator of the highest rank and merit, Ulpius Crinitus, whose blood was derived from the same source as that of Trajan, adopted the Pannonian peasant, gave him his daugh-

[5] Theoclius affirms that in one day he killed, with his own hand, forty-eight Sarmatians, and in several subsequent engagements nine hundred and fifty. This heroic valour was admired by the soldiers, and celebrated in their rude songs, the burthen of which was mille mille mille occidit.

ter in marriage, and relieved with his ample fortune the honourable poverty which Aurelian had preserved inviolate.

The reign of Aurelian lasted only four years and about nine months; but every instant of that short period was filled by some memorable achievement. He put an end to the Gothic war, chastised the Germans who invaded Italy, recovered Gaul, Spain, and Britain out of the hands of Tetricus, and destroyed the proud monarchy which Zenobia had erected in the East on the ruins of the afflicted empire.

It was the rigid attention of Aurelian even to the minutest articles of discipline which bestowed such uninterrupted success on his arms. His military regulations are contained in a very concise epistle to one of his inferior officers, who is commanded to enforce them, as he wishes to become a tribune, or as he is desirous to live. Gaming, drinking, and the arts of divination were severely prohibited. Aurelian expected that his soldiers should be modest, frugal, and laborious; that their armour should be constantly kept bright, their weapons sharp, their clothing and horses ready for immediate service; that they should live in their quarters with chastity and sobriety, without damaging the corn fields, without stealing even a sheep, a fowl or a bunch of grapes, without exacting from their landlords either salt, or oil, or wood. "The public allowance," continues the emperor, "is sufficient for their support; their wealth should be collected from the spoil of the enemy, not from the tears of the provincials." A single instance will serve to display the rigour, and even cruelty, of Aurelian. One of the soldiers had seduced the wife of his host. The guilty wretch was fastened to two trees forcibly drawn towards each other, and his limbs were torn asunder by their sudden separation. A few such examples impressed a salutary consternation. The punishments of Aurelian were terrible; but he had seldom occasion to punish more than once the same offence. His own conduct gave a sanction to his laws, and the seditious legions dreaded a chief who had learned to obey, and who was worthy to command.

The death of Claudius had revived the fainting spirit of the Goths. The troops which guarded the passes of Mount Hæmus, and the banks of the Danube, had been drawn away by the apprehension of a civil war; and it seems probable that the remaining body of the Goths and Vandalic tribes embraced the favourable opportunity, abandoned their settlements of the Ukraine, traversed the rivers, and swelled with new multitudes the destroying host of their countrymen. Their united numbers were at length encountered by Aurelian, and the bloody and doubtful conflict ended only with the approach of night. Exhausted by so many calamities which they had mutually endured and inflicted during a twenty years' war, the Goths and the Romans consented to a lasting and beneficial treaty. It was earnestly solicited by the barbarians, and cheerfully ratified by the legions, to whose suffrage the prudence of Aurelian referred the decision of that important question. The Gothic nation engaged to supply the armies of Rome with a body of two thousand auxiliaries, consisting entirely of cavalry, and stipulated in return an undisturbed retreat, with a regular market as far as the Danube, provided by the emperor's care, but at their own expense. The treaty was observed with such religious fidelity, that, when a party of five hundred men straggled from the camp in quest of plunder, the king or general of the barbarians commanded that the guilty leader should be apprehended and shot to death with darts, as a victim devoted to the sanctity of their engagements. It is, however, not unlikely that the precaution of Aurelian, who had exacted as hostages the sons and daughters of the Gothic chiefs, contributed something to this pacific temper. The youths he trained in the exercise of arms, and near his own person; to the damsels he gave a liberal and Roman education, and, by bestowing them in marriage on some of his principal officers, gradually introduced between the two nations the closest and most endearing connexions.[6]

Aurelian married one of the Gothic ladies to his general Bonosus, who was able to drink with the Goths and discover their secrets.

But the most important condition of peace was understood rather than expressed in the treaty. Aurelian withdrew the Roman forces from Dacia, and tacitly relinquished that great province to the Goths and Vandals. His manly judgment convinced him of the solid advantages, and taught him to despise the seeming disgrace, of thus contracting the frontiers of the monarchy. The Dacian subjects, removed from those distant possessions which they were unable to cultivate or defend, added strength and populousness to the southern side of the Danube. A fertile territory, which the repetition of barbarous inroads had changed into a desert, was yielded to their industry, and a new province of Dacia still preserved the memory of Trajan's conquests. The old country of that name detained, however, a considerable number of its inhabitants, who dreaded exile more than a Gothic master.[7] These degenerate Romans continued to serve the empire, whose allegiance they had renounced, by introducing among their conquerors the first notions of agriculture, the useful arts, and the conveniences of civilized life. An intercourse of

[7] *The Walachians still preserve many traces of the Latin language, and have boasted in every age of their Roman descent. They are surrounded by, but not mixed with, the barbarians.*

commerce and language was gradually established between the opposite banks of the Danube; and, after Dacia became an independent state, it often proved the firmest barrier of the empire against the invasions of the savages of the North. A sense of interest attached these more settled barbarians to the alliance of Rome, and a permanent interest very frequently ripens into sincere and useful friendship. This various colony, which filled the ancient province and was insensibly blended into one great people, still acknowledged the superior renown and authority of the Gothic tribe, and claimed the fancied honour of a Scandinavian origin. At the same time the lucky though accidental resemblance of the name of Getæ, infused among the credulous Goths a vain persuasion that, in a remote age, their own ancestors, already seated in the Dacian provinces, had received the instructions of Zamolxis, and checked the victorious arms of Sesostris and Darius.[8]

While the vigorous and moderate conduct of Aurelian restored the Illyrian frontier, the nation of the Alemanni violated the conditions of peace, which either Gallienus had purchased, or Claudius had imposed, and, inflamed by their impatient youth, suddenly flew to arms. Forty thousand horse appeared in the field, and the numbers of the infantry doubled those of the cavalry. The first objects of their avarice were a few cities of the Rhætian frontier; but, their hopes soon rising with success, the rapid march of the Alemanni traced a line of devastation from the Danube to the Po.

The emperor was almost at the same time informed of the irruption, and of the retreat, of the barbarians. Collecting an active body of troops, he marched with silence and celerity along the skirts of the Hercynian forest; and the Alemanni, laden with the spoils of Italy, arrived at the Danube, without suspecting that, on the opposite bank, and in an advantageous post, a Roman army lay concealed and prepared to intercept their return. Aurelian indulged the fatal security of the barbarians, and permitted about half their forces to pass the river without disturbance and without precaution. Their situation and astonishment gave him an easy victory; his skilful conduct improved the advantage. Disposing the legions in a semicircular form, he advanced the two horns of the crescent across the Danube, and, wheeling them on a sudden towards the centre, inclosed the rear of the German host. The dismayed barbarians, on whatsoever side they cast their eyes, beheld with despair a wasted country, a deep and rapid stream, a victorious and implacable enemy.

[8] *The Vandals, however, maintained a short independence between the rivers Marisia and Crissia (Maros and Keres) which fell into the Theiss.*

Reduced to this distressed condition, the Alemanni no longer disdained to sue for peace. Aurelian received their ambassadors at the head of his camp, and with every circumstance of martial pomp that could display the greatness and discipline of Rome. The legions stood to their arms in well-ordered ranks and awful silence. The principal commanders, distinguished by the ensigns of their rank, appeared on horseback on either side of the Imperial throne. Behind the throne, the consecrated images of the emperor and his predecessors,[9] the golden eagles, and the various titles of the legions, engraved in letters of gold, were exalted in the air on lofty pikes covered with silver. When Aurelian assumed his seat, his manly grace and majestic figure taught the barbarians to revere the person as well as the purple of their conqueror. The ambassadors fell prostrate on the ground in silence. They were commanded to rise, and permitted to speak. By the assistance of interpreters they extenuated their perfidy, magnified their exploits, expatiated on the vicissitudes of fortune and the advantages of peace, and, with an ill-timed confidence, demanded a large subsidy, as the price of the alliance which they offered to the Romans. The answer of the emperor was stern and imperious. He treated their offer with contempt, and their demand with indignation; reproached the barbarians, that they were as ignorant of the arts of war as of the laws of peace; and finally dismissed them with the choice only of submitting to his unconditioned mercy, or awaiting the utmost severity of his resentment. Aurelian had resigned a distant province to the Goths; but it was dangerous to trust or to pardon these perfidious barbarians, whose formidable power kept Italy itself in perpetual alarms.

Immediately after the conference it should seem that some unexpected emergency required the emperor's presence in Pannonia. He devolved on his lieutenants the care of finishing the destruction of the Alemanni, either by the sword, or by the surer operation of famine. But an active despair has often triumphed over the indolent assurance of success. The barbarians, finding it impossible to traverse the Danube and the Roman camp, broke through the posts in their rear, which were more feebly or less carefully guarded; and with incredible diligence, but by a different road, returned towards the mountains of Italy. Aurelian, who considered the war as totally extinguished, received the mortifying intelligence of the escape of the Alemanni, and of the ravage which they already committed in the territory of Milan. The legions were commanded to follow, with as much expedition as those heavy bodies were capable of exerting,

[9] *The emperor Claudius was certainly of the number; but we are ignorant how far this mark of respect was extended; if to Cæsar and Augustus, it must have produced a very awful spectacle; a long line of the masters of the world.*

the rapid flight of an enemy whose infantry and cavalry moved with almost equal swiftness. A few days afterwards the emperor himself marched to the relief of Italy, at the head of a chosen body of auxiliaries (among whom were the hostages and cavalry of the Vandals), and of all the Prætorian guards who had served in the wars on the Danube.

As the light troops of the Alemanni had spread themselves from the Alps to the Apennine, the incessant vigilance of Aurelian and his officers was exercised in the discovery, the attack, and the pursuit of the numerous detachments. Notwithstanding this desultory war, three considerable battles are mentioned, in which the principal force of both armies was obstinately engaged. The success was various. In the first, fought near Placentia, the Romans received so severe a blow, that, according to the expression of a writer extremely partial to Aurelian, the immediate dissolution of the empire was apprehended. The crafty barbarians, who had lined the woods, suddenly attacked the legions in the dusk of che evening, and, it is most probable, after the fatigue and disorder of a long march. The fury of their charge was irresistible; but at length, after a dreadful slaughter, the patient firmness of the emperor rallied his troops, and restored, in some degree, the honour of his arms. The second battle was fought near Fano in Umbria; on the spot which, five hundred years before, had been fatal to the brother of Hannibal.[10] Thus far the successful Germans had advanced along the Æmilian and Flaminian way, with a design of sacking the defenceless mistress of the world. But Aurelian, who, watchful for the safety of Rome, still hung on their rear, found in this place the decisive moment of giving them a total and irretrievable defeat.[11] The flying remnant of their host was exterminated in a third and last battle near Pavia; and Italy was delivered from the inroads of the Alemanni.

Fear has been the original parent of superstition, and every new calamity urges trembling mortals to deprecate the wrath of their invisible enemies. Though the best hope of the republic was in the valour and conduct of Aurelian, yet such was the public consternation, when the barbarians were hourly expected at the gates of Rome, that, by a decree of the senate, the Sibylline books were consulted. Even the emperor himself, from a motive either of religion or of policy, recommended the salutary measure, chided the tardiness of the senate,[12] and offered to supply whatever expense, whatever animals, whatever captives of any nation, the gods should require. Notwithstanding this liberal offer, it does not appear that any

[10] *The little river or rather torrent of Metaurus, near Fano, has been immortalized, by finding such an historian as Livy, and such a poet as Horace.*

[11] *It is recorded by an inscription found at Pezaro.*

[12] *One should imagine, he said, that you were assembled in a Christian church, not in the temple of all the gods.*

human victims expiated with their blood the sins of the Roman people. The Sibylline books enjoined ceremonies of a more harmless nature, processions of priests in white robes, attended by a chorus of youths and virgins; lustrations of the city and adjacent country; and sacrifices, whose powerful influence disabled the barbarians from passing the mystic ground on which they had been celebrated. However puerile in themselves, these superstitious arts were subservient to the success of the war; and if, in the decisive battle of Fano, the Alemanni fancied they saw an army of spectres combating on the side of Aurelian, he received a real and effectual aid from this imaginary reinforcement.

But, whatever confidence might be placed in ideal ramparts, the experience of the past, and the dread of the future, induced the Romans to construct fortifications of a grosser and more substantial kind. The seven hills of Rome had been surrounded by the successors of Romulus with an ancient wall of more than thirteen miles.[13] The vast inclosure may seem disproportioned to the strength and numbers of the infant state. But it was necessary to secure an ample extent of pasture and arable land against the frequent and sudden incursions of the tribes of Latium, the perpetual enemies of the republic. With the progress of Roman greatness, the city and its inhabitants gradually increased, filled up the vacant space, pierced through the useless walls, covered the field of Mars, and, on every side, followed the public highways in long and beautiful suburbs. The extent of the new walls, erected by Aurelian, and finished in the reign of Probus, was magnified by popular estimation to near fifty; but is reduced by accurate measurement to about twenty-one miles. It was a great but a melancholy labour, since the defence of the capital betrayed the decline of the monarchy. The Romans of a more prosperous age, who trusted to the arms of the legions the safety of the frontier camps, were very far from entertaining a suspicion that it would ever become necessary to fortify the seat of empire against the inroads of the barbarians.

The victory of Claudius over the Goths, and the success of Aurelian against the Alemanni, had already restored to the arms of Rome their ancient superiority over the barbarous nations of the North. To chastise domestic tyrants, and to reunite the dismembered parts of the empire, was a task reserved for the latter of those warlike emperors. Though he was acknowledged by the senate and people, the frontiers of Italy, Africa, Illyricum, and Thrace, confined the limits of his reign. Gaul, Spain, and Britain, Egypt, Syria, and Asia Minor

[13] *To confirm our idea, we may observe that for a long time Mount Cælius was a grove of oaks, and Mount Viminal was overrun with osiers; that in the fourth century, the Aventine was a vacant and solitary retirement; that, till the time of Augustus, the Esquiline was an unwholesome burying ground; and that the numerous inequalities remarked by the ancients in the Quirinal sufficiently prove that it was not covered with buildings. Of the seven hills, the Capitoline and Palatine only, with the adjacent valleys, were the primitive habitations of the Roman people. But this subject would require a dissertation.*

were still possessed by two rebels, who alone, out of so numerous a list, had hitherto escaped the dangers of their situation; and, to complete the ignominy of Rome, these rival thrones had been usurped by women.

A rapid succession of monarchs had arisen and fallen in the provinces of Gaul. The rigid virtues of Posthumus served only to hasten his destruction. After suppressing a competitor, who had assumed the purple at Mentz, he refused to gratify his troops with the plunder of the rebellious city; and, in the seventh year of his reign, became the victim of their disappointed avarice.[14] The death of Victorinus, his friend and associate, was occasioned by a less worthy cause. The shining accomplishments of that prince were stained by a licentious passion, which he indulged in acts of violence, with too little regard to the laws of society, or even to those of love. He was slain at Cologne, by a conspiracy of jealous husbands, whose revenge would have appeared more justifiable, had they spared the innocence of his son. After the murder of so many valiant princes, it is somewhat remarkable that a female for a long time controlled the fierce legions of Gaul, and still more singular that she was the mother of the unfortunate Victorinus. The arts and treasures of Victoria enabled her successfully to place Marius and Tetricus on the throne, and to reign with a manly vigour under the name of those dependent emperors. Money of copper, of silver, and of gold, was coined in her name; she assumed the titles of Augusta and Mother of the Camps: her power ended only with her life; but her life was perhaps shortened by the ingratitude of Tetricus.

When, at the instigation of his ambitious patroness, Tetricus assumed the ensigns of royalty, he was governor of the peaceful province of Aquitaine, an employment suited to his character and education. He reigned four or five years over Gaul, Spain, and Britain, the slave and sovereign of a licentious army, whom he dreaded and by whom he was despised. The valour and fortune of Aurelian at length opened the prospect of a deliverance. He ventured to disclose his melancholy situation, and conjured the emperor to hasten to the relief of his unhappy rival. Had this secret correspondence reached the ears of the soldiers, it would most probably have cost Tetricus his life; nor could he resign the sceptre of the West without committing an act of treason against himself. He affected the appearances of a civil war, led his forces into the field against Aurelian, posted them in the most disadvantageous manner, betrayed his own counsels to the enemy, and with a few chosen friends deserted in the

[14] *His competitor was Lollianus, or Ælianus, if indeed these names mean the same person.*

beginning of the action. The rebel legions, though disordered and dismayed by the unexpected treachery of their chief, defended themselves with a desperate valour, till'they were cut in pieces almost to a man, in this bloody and memorable battle, which was fought near Chalons in Champagne. The retreat of the irregular auxiliaries, Franks and Batavians, whom the conqueror soon compelled or persuaded to repass the Rhine, restored the general tranquillity, and the power of Aurelian was acknowledged from the wall of Antoninus to the columns of Hercules.

As early as the reign of Claudius, the city of Autun, alone and unassisted, had ventured to declare against the legions of Gaul. After a siege of seven months, they stormed and plundered that unfortunate city, already wasted by famine. Lyons, on the contrary, had resisted with obstinate disaffection the arms of Aurelian. We read of the punishment of Lyons,[15] but there is not any mention of the rewards of Autun. Such, indeed, is the policy of civil war; severely to remember injuries, and to forget the most important services. Revenge is profitable, gratitude is expensive.

Aurelian had no sooner secured the person and provinces of Tetricus, than he turned his arms against Zenobia, the celebrated queen of Palmyra and the East. Modern Europe has produced several illustrious women who have sustained with glory the weight of empire; nor is our own age destitute of such distinguished characters. But if we except the doubtful achievements of Semiramis, Zenobia is perhaps the only female whose superior genius broke through the servile indolence imposed on her sex by the climate and manners of Asia. She claimed her descent from the Macedonian kings of Egypt, equalled in beauty her ancestor Cleopatra, and far surpassed that princess in chastity[16] and valour. Zenobia was esteemed the most lovely as well as the most heroic of her sex. She was of dark complexion (for in speaking of a lady these trifles become important). Her teeth were of a pearly whiteness, and her large black eyes sparkled with uncommon fire, tempered by the most attractive sweetness. Her voice was strong and harmonious. Her manly understanding was strengthened and adorned by study. She was not ignorant of the Latin tongue, but possessed in equal perfection the Greek, the Syriac, and the Egyptian languages. She had drawn up for her own use an epitome of oriental history, and familiarly compared the beauties of Homer and Plato under the tuition of the sublime Longinus.

This accomplished woman gave her hand to Odenathus, who

[15] *Autun was not restored till the reign of Diocletian.*

[16] *She never admitted her husband's embraces but for the sake of posterity. If her hopes were baffled, in the ensuing month she reiterated the experiment.*

from a private station raised himself to the dominion of the East. She soon became the friend and companion of a hero. In the intervals of war, Odenathus passionately delighted in the exercise of hunting; he pursued with ardour the wild beasts of the desert, lions, panthers, and bears; and the ardour of Zenobia in that dangerous amusement was not inferior to his own. She had inured her constitution to fatigue, disdained the use of a covered carriage, generally appeared on horseback in a military habit, and sometimes marched several miles on foot at the head of the troops. The success of Odenathus was in a great measure ascribed to her incomparable prudence and fortitude. Their splendid victories over the Great King, whom they twice pursued as far as the gates of Ctesiphon, laid the foundations of their united fame and power. The armies which they commanded, and the provinces which they had saved, acknowledged not any other sovereigns than their invincible chiefs. The senate and people of Rome revered a stranger who had avenged their captive emperor, and even the insensible son of Valerian accepted Odenathus for his legitimate colleague.

After a successful expedition against the Gothic plunderers of Asia, the Palmyrenian prince returned to the city of Emesa in Syria. Invincible in war, he was there cut off by domestic treason, and his favourite amusement of hunting was the cause, or at least the occasion, of his death. His nephew, Mæonius, presumed to dart his javelin before that of his uncle; and, though admonished of his error, repeated the same insolence. As a monarch and as a sportsman, Odenathus was provoked: took away his horse, a mark of ignominy among the barbarians, and chastised the rash youth by a short confinement. The offence was soon forgot, but the punishment was remembered; and Mæonius, with a few daring associates, assassinated his uncle in the midst of a great entertainment. Herod, the son of Odenathus, though not of Zenobia, a young man of a soft and effeminate temper,[17] was killed with his father. But Mæonius obtained only the pleasure of revenge by the bloody deed. He had scarcely time to assume the title of Augustus, before he was sacrificed by Zenobia to the memory of her husband.[18]

With the assistance of her most faithful friends, she immediately filled the vacant throne, and governed with manly counsels Palmyra, Syria, and the East, above five years. By the death of Odenathus, that authority was at an end which the senate had granted him only as a personal distinction; but his martial widow, disdaining both the senate and Gallienus, obliged one of the Roman generals,

[17] *Odenathus and Zenobia often sent him, from the spoils of the enemy, presents of gems and toys, which he received with infinite delight.*

[18] *Some very unjust suspicions have been cast on Zenobia, as if she was accessory to her husband's death.*

who was sent against her, to retreat into Europe, with the loss of his army and his reputation. Instead of the little passions which so frequently perplex a female reign, the steady administration of Zenobia was guided by the most judicious maxims of policy. If it was expedient to pardon, she could calm her resentment; if it was necessary to punish, she could impose silence on the voice of pity. Her strict economy was accused of avarice; yet on every proper occasion she appeared magnificent and liberal. The neighbouring states of Arabia, Armenia, and Persia, dreaded her enmity, and solicited her alliance. To the dominions of Odenathus, which extended from the Euphrates to the frontiers of Bithynia, his widow added the inheritance of her ancestors, the populous and fertile kingdom of Egypt. The emperor Claudius acknowledged her merit, and was content that, while *he* pursued the Gothic war, *she* should assert the dignity of the empire in the East. The conduct, however, of Zenobia was attended with some ambiguity; nor is it unlikely that she had conceived the design of erecting an independent and hostile monarchy. She blended with the popular manners of Roman princes the stately pomp of the courts of Asia, and exacted from her subjects the same adoration that was paid to the successors of Cyrus. She bestowed on her three sons [19] a Latin education, and often showed them to the troops adorned with the Imperial purple. For herself she reserved the diadem, with the splendid but doubtful title of Queen of the East.

When Aurelian passed over into Asia, against an adversary whose sex alone could render her an object of contempt, his presence restored obedience to the province of Bithynia, already shaken by the arms and intrigues of Zenobia. Advancing at the head of his legions, he accepted the submission of Ancyra, and was admitted into Tyana, after an obstinate siege, by the help of a perfidious citizen. The generous though fierce temper of Aurelian abandoned the traitor to the rage of the soldiers: a superstitious reverence induced him to treat with lenity the countrymen of Apollonius the philosopher.[20] Antioch was deserted on his approach, till the emperor, by his salutary edicts, recalled the fugitives, and granted a general pardon to all who, from necessity rather than choice, had been engaged in the service of the Palmyrenian queen. The unexpected mildness of such a conduct reconciled the minds of the Syrians, and, as far as the gates of Emesa, the wishes of the people seconded the terror of his arms.

Zenobia would have ill deserved her reputation, had she indo-

[19] Timolaus, Herennianus, and Vaballathus. It is supposed that the two former were already dead before the war. On the last, Aurelian bestowed a small province of Armenia, with the title of king; several of his medals are still extant.

[20] Vopiscus gives us an authentic letter, and a doubtful vision, of Aurelian. Apollonius of Tyana was born about the same time as Jesus Christ. His life (that of the former) is related in so fabulous a manner by his disciples, that we are at a loss to discover whether he was a sage, an impostor, or a fanatic.

lently permitted the emperor of the West to approach within a hundred miles of her capital. The fate of the East was decided in two great battles; so similar in almost every circumstance that we can scarcely distinguish them from each other, except by observing that the first was fought near Antioch,[21] and the second near Emesa. In both, the queen of Palmyra animated the armies by her presence, and devolved the execution of her orders on Zabdas, who had already signalized his military talents by the conquest of Egypt. The numerous forces of Zenobia consisted for the most part of light archers, and of heavy cavalry clothed in complete steel. The Moorish and Illyrian horse of Aurelian were unable to sustain the ponderous charge of their antagonists. They fled in real or affected disorder, engaged the Palmyrenians in a laborious pursuit, harassed them by a desultory combat, and at length discomfited this impenetrable but unwieldy body of cavalry. The light infantry, in the meantime, when they had exhausted their quivers, remaining without protection against a closer onset, exposed their naked sides to the swords of the legions. Aurelian had chosen these veteran troops, who were usually stationed on the Upper Danube, and whose valour had been severely tried in the Alemannic war. After the defeat of Emesa, Zenobia found it impossible to collect a third army. As far as the frontier of Egypt, the nations subject to her empire had joined the standard of the conqueror, who detached Probus, the bravest of his generals, to possess himself of the Egyptian provinces. Palmyra was the last resource of the widow of Odenathus. She retired within the walls of her capital, made every preparation for a vigorous resistance, and declared, with the intrepidity of a heroine, that the last moment of her reign and of her life should be the same.

Amid the barren deserts of Arabia, a few cultivated spots rise like islands out of the sandy ocean. Even the name of Tadmor, or Palmyra, by its signification in the Syriac as well as in the Latin language, denoted the multitude of palm trees which afforded shade and verdure to that temperate region. The air was pure, and the soil, watered by some invaluable springs, was capable of producing fruits as well as corn. A place possessed of such singular advantages, and situated at a convenient distance,[22] between the Gulf of Persia and the Mediterranean, was soon frequented by the caravans which conveyed to the nations of Europe a considerable part of the rich commodities of India. Palmyra insensibly increased into an opulent and independent city, and, connecting the Roman and the Parthian monarchies by the mutual benefits of commerce, was suffered to ob-

[21] *At a place called Immæ.*

[22] *It was five hundred and thirty-seven miles from Seleucia, and two hundred and three from the nearest coast of Syria, according to the reckoning of Pliny.*

serve an humble neutrality, till at length, after the victories of Trajan, the little republic sunk into the bosom of Rome, and flourished more than one hundred and fifty years in the subordinate though honourable rank of a colony. It was during that peaceful period, if we may judge from a few remaining inscriptions, that the wealthy Palmyrenians constructed those temples, palaces, and porticos of Grecian architecture, whose ruins, scattered over an extent of several miles, have deserved the curiosity of our travellers. The elevation of Odenathus and Zenobia appeared to reflect new ∪plendour on their country, and Palmyra for a while stood forth the rival of Rome: but the competition was fatal, and ages of prosperity were sacrificed to a moment of glory.[23]

In his march over the sandy desert, between Emesa and Palmyra, the Emperor Aurelian was perpetually harassed by the Arabs; nor could he always defend his army, and especially his baggage, from these flying troops of active and daring robbers, who watched the moment of surprise, and eluded the slow pursuit of the legions. The siege of Palmyra was an object far more difficult and important, and the emperor, who with incessant vigour pressed the attacks in person, was himself wounded with a dart. "The Roman people," says Aurelian, in an original letter, "speak with contempt of the war which I am waging against a woman. They are ignorant both of the character and of the power of Zenobia. It is impossible to enumerate her warlike preparations, of stones, of arrows, and of every species of missile weapons. Every part of the walls is provided with two or three *balistæ,* and artificial fires are thrown from her military engines. The fear of punishment has armed her with a desperate courage. Yet still I trust in the protecting deities of Rome, who have hitherto been favourable to all my undertakings." Doubtful, however, of the protection of the gods, and of the event of the siege, Aurelian judged it more prudent to offer terms of an advantageous capitulation: to the queen, a splendid retreat; to the citizens, their ancient privileges. His proposals were obstinately rejected, and the refusal was accompanied with insult.

The firmness of Zenobia was supported by the hope that in a very short time famine would compel the Roman army to repass the desert; and by the reasonable expectation that the kings of the East, and particularly the Persian monarch, would arm in the defence of their most natural ally. But fortune and the perseverance of Aurelian overcame every obstacle. The death of Sapor, which happened about this time, distracted the councils of Persia, and the inconsider-

[23] *Some English travellers from Aleppo* discovered *the ruins of Palmyra, about the end of the last century. Our curiosity has since been gratified in a more splendid manner by Messieurs Wood and Dawkins.*

able succours that attempted to relieve Palmyra, were easily intercepted either by the arms or the liberality of the emperor. From every part of Syria, a regular succession of convoys safely arrived in the camp, which was increased by the return of Probus with his victorious troops from the conquest of Egypt. It was then that Zenobia resolved to fly. She mounted the fleetest of her dromedaries,[24] and had already reached the banks of the Euphrates, about sixty miles from Palmyra, when she was overtaken by the pursuit of Aurelian's light horse, seized, and brought back a captive to the feet of the emperor. Her capital soon afterwards surrendered, and was treated with unexpected lenity. The arms, horses, and camels, with an immense treasure of gold, silver, silk, and precious stones, were all delivered to the conqueror, who, leaving only a garrison of six hundred archers, returned to Emesa, and employed some time in the distribution of rewards and punishments at the end of so memorable a war, which restored to the obedience of Rome those provinces that had renounced their allegiance since the captivity of Valerian.

When the Syrian queen was brought into the presence of Aurelian, he sternly asked her, How she had presumed to rise in arms against the emperors of Rome? The answer of Zenobia was a prudent mixture of respect and firmness. "Because I disdained to consider as Roman emperors an Aureolus or a Gallienus. You alone I acknowledge as my conqueror and my sovereign." But, as female fortitude is commonly artificial, so it is seldom steady or consistent. The courage of Zenobia deserted her in the hour of trial; she trembled at the angry clamours of the soldiers, who called aloud for her immediate execution, forgot the generous despair of Cleopatra, which she had proposed as her model, and ignominiously purchased life by the sacrifice of her fame and her friends. It was to their counsels, which governed the weakness of her sex, that she imputed the guilt of her obstinate resistance; it was on their heads that she directed the vengeance of the cruel Aurelian. The fame of Longinus, who was included among the numerous and perhaps innocent victims of her fear, will survive that of the queen who betrayed, or the tyrant who condemned, him. Genius and learning were incapable of moving a fierce unlettered soldier, but they had served to elevate and harmonize the soul of Longinus. Without uttering a complaint, he calmly followed the executioner, pitying his unhappy mistress, and bestowing comfort on his afflicted friends.

Returning from the conquest of the East, Aurelian had already crossed the Streights which divide Europe from Asia, when he was

[24] *Though the camel is a heavy beast of burden, the dromedary, who is either of the same or of a kindred species, is used by the natives of Asia and Africa, on all occasions which require celerity. The Arabs affirm that he will run over as much ground in one day as their fleetest horses can perform in eight or ten.*

provoked by the intelligence that the Palmyrenians had massacred the governor and garrison which he had left among them, and again erected the standard of revolt. Without a moment's deliberation, he once more turned his face towards Syria. Antioch was alarmed by his rapid approach, and the helpless city of Palmyra felt the irresistible weight of his resentment. We have a letter of Aurelian himself, in which he acknowledges that old men, women, children, and peasants had been involved in that dreadful execution, which should have been confined to armed rebellion; and, although his principal concern seems directed to the re-establishment of a temple of the Sun, he discovers some pity for the remnant of the Palmyrenians, to whom he grants the permission of rebuilding and inhabiting their city. But it is easier to destroy than to restore. The seat of commerce, of arts, and of Zenobia, gradually sunk into an obscure town, a trifling fortress, and at length a miserable village. The present citizens of Palmyra, consisting of thirty or forty families, have erected their mud cottages within the spacious court of a magnificent temple.

Another and a last labour still awaited the indefatigable Aurelian; to suppress a dangerous though obscure rebel, who, during the revolt of Palmyra, had arisen on the banks of the Nile. Firmus, the friend and ally, as he proudly styled himself, of Odenathus and Zenobia, was no more than a wealthy merchant of Egypt. In the course of his trade to India, he had formed very intimate connexions with the Saracens and the Blemmyes, whose situation on either coast of the Red Sea gave them an easy introduction into the Upper Egypt. The Egyptians he inflamed with the hope of freedom, and, at the head of their furious multitude, broke into the city of Alexandria, where he assumed the Imperial purple, coined money, published edicts, and raised an army, which, as he vainly boasted, he was capable of maintaining from the sole profits of his paper trade. Such troops were a feeble defence against the approach of Aurelian; and it seems almost unnecessary to relate that Firmus was routed, taken, tortured, and put to death. Aurelian might now congratulate the senate, the people, and himself, that in little more than three years he had restored universal peace and order to the Roman world.[25]

Since the foundation of Rome, no general had more nobly deserved a triumph than Aurelian; nor was a triumph ever celebrated with superior pride and magnificence. The pomp was opened by twenty elephants, four royal tigers, and above two hundred of the

[25] *As an instance of luxury, it is observed that he had glass windows. He was remarkable for his strength and appetite, his courage and dexterity. From the letter of Aurelian we may justly infer that Firmus was the last of the rebels, and consequently that Tetricus was already suppressed.*

most curious animals from every climate of the North, the East, and the South. They were followed by sixteen hundred gladiators, devoted to the cruel amusement of the amphitheatre. The wealth of Asia, the arms and ensigns of so many conquered nations, and the magnificent plate and wardrobe of the Syrian queen, were disposed in exact symmetry or artful disorder. The ambassadors of the most remote parts of the earth, of Æthiopia, Arabia, Persia, Bactriana, India, and China, all remarkable by their rich or singular dresses, displayed the fame and power of the Roman emperor, who exposed likewise to the public view the presents that he had received, and particularly a great number of crowns of gold, the offerings of grateful cities. The victories of Aurelian were attested by the long train of captives who reluctantly attended his triumph, Goths, Vandals, Sarmatians, Alemanni, Franks, Gauls, Syrians, and Egyptians. Each people was distinguished by its peculiar inscription, and the title of Amazons was bestowed on ten martial heroines of the Gothic nation who had been taken in arms.[26] But every eye, disregarding the crowd of captives, was fixed on the emperor Tetricus and the queen of the East. The former, as well as his son, whom he had created Augustus, was dressed in Gallic trousers,[27] a saffron tunic, and a robe of purple. The beauteous figure of Zenobia was confined by fetters of gold; a slave supported the gold chain which encircled her neck, and she almost fainted under the intolerable weight of jewels. She preceded on foot the magnificent chariot in which she once hoped to enter the gates of Rome. It was followed by two other chariots, still more sumptuous, of Odenathus and of the Persian monarch. The triumphal car of Aurelian (it had formerly been used by a Gothic king) was drawn, on this memorable occasion, either by four stags or by four elephants.[28] The most illustrious of the senate, the people, and the army, closed the solemn procession. Unfeigned joy, wonder and gratitude swelled the acclamations of the multitude; but the satisfaction of the senate was clouded by the appearance of Tetricus; nor could they suppress a rising murmur that the haughty emperor should thus expose to public ignominy the person of a Roman and a magistrate.

But however, in the treatment of his unfortunate rivals, Aurelian might indulge his pride, he behaved towards them with a generous clemency which was seldom exercised by the ancient conquerors. Princes who, without success, had defended their throne or freedom were frequently strangled in prison, as soon as the triumphal pomp ascended the Capitol. These usurpers, whom their defeat had con-

[26] *Among barbarous nations, women have often combated by the side of their husbands. But it is almost impossible that a society of Amazons should ever have existed either in the old or new world.*

[27] *The use of Braccæ, breeches, or trousers, was still considered in Italy as a Gallic and barbarian fashion. The Romans, however, had made great advances towards it. To encircle the legs and thighs with fasciæ, or bands, was understood in the time of Pompey and Horace to be a proof of ill health or effeminacy. In the age of Trajan, the custom was confined to the rich and luxurious. It gradually was adopted by the meanest of the people.*

[28] *Most probably the former: the latter, seen on the medals of Aurelian, only denote an oriental victory.*

victed of the crime of treason, were permitted to spend their lives in affluence and honourable repose. The emperor presented Zenobia with an elegant villa at Tibur, or Tivoli, about twenty miles from the capital; the Syrian queen insensibly sank into a Roman matron, her daughters married into noble families, and her race was not yet extinct in the fifth century. Tetricus and his son were reinstated in their rank and fortunes. They erected on the Cælian hill a magnificent palace, and, as soon as it was finished, invited Aurelian to supper. On his entrance, he was agreeably surprised with a picture which represented their singular history. They were delineated offering to the emperor a civic crown and the sceptre of Gaul, and again receiving at his hands the ornaments of the senatorial dignity. The father was afterwards invested with the government of Lucania, and Aurelian, who soon admitted the abdicated monarch to his friendship and conversation, familiarly asked him, Whether it were not more desirable to administer a province of Italy, than to reign beyond the Alps? The son long continued a respectable member of the senate; nor was there any one of the Roman nobility more esteemed by Aurelian, as well as by his successors.

So long and so various was the pomp of Aurelian's triumph that, although it opened with the dawn of day, the slow majesty of the procession ascended not the Capitol before the ninth hour; and it was already dark when the emperor returned to the palace. The festival was protracted by theatrical representations, the games of the circus, the hunting of wild beasts, combats of gladiators, and naval engagements. Liberal donatives were distributed to the army and people, and several institutions, agreeable or beneficial to the city, contributed to perpetuate the glory of Aurelian. A considerable portion of his oriental spoils was consecrated to the gods of Rome; the Capitol, and every other temple, glittered with the offerings of his ostentatious piety; and the temple of the Sun alone received above fifteen thousand pounds of gold.[29] This last was a magnificent structure, erected by the emperor on the side of the Quirinal hill, and dedicated, soon after the triumph, to that deity whom Aurelian adored as the parent of his life and fortunes. His mother had been an inferior priestess in a chapel of the Sun; a peculiar devotion to the god of Light was a sentiment which the fortunate peasant imbibed in his infancy; and every step of his elevation, every victory of his reign, fortified superstition by gratitude.

The arms of Aurelian had vanquished the foreign and domestic foes of the republic. We are assured that, by his salutary rigour,

[29] *He placed in it the images of Belus and of the Sun, which he had brought from Palmyra. It was dedicated in the fourth year of his reign, but was most assuredly begun immediately on his accession.*

crimes and factions, mischievous arts and pernicious connivance, the luxuriant growth of a feeble and oppressive government, were eradicated throughout the Roman world. But, if we attentively reflect how much swifter is the progress of corruption than its cure, and if we remember that the years abandoned to public disorders exceeded the months allotted to the martial reign of Aurelian, we must confess that a few short intervals of peace were insufficient for the arduous work of reformation. Even his attempt to restore the integrity of the coin was opposed by a formidable insurrection. The emperor's vexation breaks out in one of his private letters: "Surely," says he, "the gods have decreed that my life should be a perpetual warfare. A sedition within the walls has just now given birth to a very serious civil war. The workmen of the mint, at the instigation of Felicissimus, a slave to whom I had intrusted an employment in the finances, have risen in rebellion. They are at length suppressed; but seven thousand of my soldiers have been slain in the contest, of those troops whose ordinary station is in Dacia, and the camps along the Danube." Other writers, who confirm the same fact, add likewise that it happened soon after Aurelian's triumph; that the decisive engagement was fought on the Cælian hill; that the workmen of the mint had adulterated the coin; and that the emperor restored the public credit by delivering out good money in exchange for the bad which the people was commanded to bring into the treasury.

We might content ourselves with relating this extraordinary transaction, but we cannot dissemble how much, in its present form, it appears to us inconsistent and incredible. The debasement of the coin is, indeed, well suited to the administration of Gallienus; nor is it unlikely that the instruments of the corruption might dread the inflexible justice of Aurelian. But the guilt, as well as the profit, must have been confined to a few; nor is it easy to conceive by what arts they could arm a people whom they had injured against a monarch whom they had betrayed. We might naturally expect that such miscreants should have shared the public detestation with the informers and the other ministers of oppression; and that the reformation of the coin should have been an action equally popular with the destruction of those obsolete accounts which, by the emperor's order, were burnt in the forum of Trajan. In an age when the principles of commerce were so imperfectly understood, the most desirable end might perhaps be affected by harsh and injudicious means; but a temporary grievance of such a nature can scarcely excite and support a serious civil war. The repetition and intolerable taxes, imposed either on the land or on the necessaries of life, may at last provoke those who will not, or who cannot, relinquish their country. But the case is far otherwise in every operation which, by whatsoever expedients, restores the just value of money. The transient evil is soon obliterated by the permanent benefit, the loss is divided among multitudes; and, if a few wealthy individuals experience a sensible diminution of treasure, with their riches they at the same time lose the degree of weight and importance which they derived from the possession of them. However Aurelian might choose to disguise the real cause of the insurrection, his reformation of the coin could furnish only a faint pretence to a party already powerful and discontented. Rome, though deprived of freedom, was distracted by faction. The people, towards whom the emperor, himself a plebeian, always expressed a peculiar fondness, lived in perpetual dissension with the senate, the equestrian order, and the Prætorian guards.[30] Nothing less than the firm though secret conspiracy of those orders, of the authority of the first, the wealth of the second, and the arms of the third, could have displayed a strength capable of contending in battle with the veteran legions of the Danube, which, under the conduct of a martial sovereign, had achieved the conquest of the West and of the East.

[30] *It already raged before Aurelian's return from Egypt.*

Whatever was the cause or the object of this rebellion, imputed with so little probability to the workmen of the mint, Aurelian used his victory with unrelenting rigour. He was naturally of a severe disposition. A peasant and a soldier, his nerves yielded not easily to the impressions of sympathy, and he could sustain without emotion the sight of tortures and death. Trained from his earliest youth in the exercise of arms, he set too small a value on the life of a citizen, chastised by military execution the slightest offences, and transferred the stern discipline of the camp into the civil administration of the laws. His love of justice often became a blind and furious passion; and, whenever he deemed his own or the public safety endangered, he disregarded the rules of evidence, and the proportion of punishments. The unprovoked rebellion with which the Romans rewarded his services exasperated his haughty spirit. The noblest families of the capital were involved in the guilt or suspicion of this dark conspiracy. A hasty spirit of revenge urged the bloody prosecution, and it proved fatal to one of the nephews of the emperor. The executioners (if we may use the expression of a contemporary poet) were fatigued, the prisons were crowded, and the unhappy senate lamented the death or absence of its most illustrious members. Nor was the pride of Aurelian less offensive to that assembly than his cruelty. Ignorant or impatient of the restraints of civil institutions, he disdained to hold his power by any other title than that of the sword, and governed by right of conquest an empire which he had saved and subdued.

It was observed by one of the most sagacious of the Roman princes that the talents of his predecessor Aurelian were better suited to the command of an army than to the government of an empire. Conscious of the character in which nature and experience had enabled him to excel, he again took the field a few months after his triumph. It was expedient to exercise the restless temper of the legions in some foreign war, and the Persian monarch, exulting in the shame of Valerian, still braved with impunity the offended majesty of Rome. At the head of an army, less formidable by its numbers than by its discipline and valour, the emperor advanced as far as the Streights which divide Europe from Asia. He there experienced that the most absolute power is a weak defence against the effects of despair. He had threatened one of his secretaries who was accused of extortion; and it was known that he seldom threatened in vain. The last hope which remained for the criminal was to involve some of the principal officers of the army in his danger, or at least in his fears. Artfully counterfeiting his master's hand, he showed them, in a long and bloody list, their own names devoted to death. Without suspecting or examining the fraud, they resolved to secure their lives by the murder of the emperor. On his march, between Byzantium and Heraclea, Aurelian was suddenly attacked by the conspirators, whose stations gave them a right to surround his person; and, after a short resistance, fell by the hand of Mucapor, a general whom he had always loved and trusted. He died regretted by the army, detested by the senate, but universally acknowledged as a warlike and fortunate prince, the useful though severe reformer of a degenerate state.

XII

SUCH was the unhappy condition of the Roman emperors, that, whatever might be their conduct, their fate was commonly the same. A life of pleasure or virtue, of severity or mildness, of indolence or glory, alike led to an untimely grave; and almost every reign is closed by the same disgusting repetition of treason and murder. The death of Aurelian, however, is remarkable by its extraordinary consequences. The legions admired, lamented, and revenged their victorious chief. The artifice of his perfidious secretary was discovered and punished. The deluded conspirators attended the funeral of their injured sovereign, with sincere or well-feigned contrition, and submitted to the unanimous resolution of the military order, which was signified by the following epistle. "The brave and fortunate armies to the senate and people of Rome. The crime of one man, and the error of many, have deprived us of the late emperor Aurelian. May it please you, venerable lords and fathers! to place him in the number of the gods, and to appoint a successor whom your judgment shall declare worthy of the Imperial purple. None of those whose guilt or misfortune have contributed to our loss shall ever reign over us." The Roman senators heard, without surprise, that another emperor had been assassinated in his camp; they secretly rejoiced in the fall of Aurelian; but the modest and dutiful address of the legions, when it was communicated in full assembly by the consul, diffused the most pleasing astonishment. Such honours as fear and perhaps esteem could extort they liberally poured forth on the memory of their deceased sovereign. Such acknowledgments as gratitude could inspire they returned to the faithful armies of the republic, who entertained so just a sense of the legal authority of the senate in the choice of an emperor. Yet, notwithstanding this flattering appeal, the most prudent of the assembly declined exposing their safety and dignity to

"*The contemporaries of Severus, in the enjoyment of the peace and glory of his reign, forgave the cruelties by which it had been introduced. Posterity, who experienced the fatal effect of his maxims and example, justly considered him as the principal author of the decline of the empire.*"

THE COLUMN OF PHOCAS AND THE ARCH OF SEPTIMIUS SEVERUS

1. S. Adriano on the foundations of the Curia or Senate House
2. SS. Martina e Luca
3. SS. Pietro e Paola over the Mamertine Prison
4. Steps to the Capitoline Hill
5. House of the Senators over the ancient Tabularium
6. Church of the Araceli on the foundations of the Temple of Juno Moneta
7. Column of Phocas, dedicated A.D. 608, the last imperial monument erected in the ancient Roman Forum

the caprice of an armed multitude. The strength of the legions was, indeed, a pledge of their sincerity, since those who may command are seldom reduced to the necessity of dissembling; but could it naturally be expected, that a hasty repentance would correct the inveterate habits of fourscore years? Should the soldiers relapse into their accustomed seditions, their insolence might disgrace the majesty of the senate, and prove fatal to the object of its choice. Motives like these dictated a decree by which the election of a new emperor was referred to the suffrage of the military order.

The contention that ensued is one of the best attested, but most improbable, events in the history of mankind. The troops, as if satiated with the exercise of power, again conjured the senate to invest one of its own body with the Imperial purple. The senate still persisted in its refusal; the army in its request. The reciprocal offer was pressed and rejected at least three times, and, whilst the obstinate modesty of either party was resolved to receive a master from the hands of the other, eight months insensibly elapsed; an amazing period of tranquil anarchy, during which the Roman world remained without a sovereign, without an usurper, and without a sedition. The generals and magistrates appointed by Aurelian continued to execute their ordinary functions; and it is observed that a proconsul of Asia was the only considerable person removed from his office in the whole course of the interregnum.

An event somewhat similar, but much less authentic, is supposed to have happened after the death of Romulus, who, in his life and character, bore some affinity with Aurelian. The throne was vacant during twelve months till the election of a Sabine philosopher, and the public peace was guarded in the same manner by the union of the several orders of the state. But, in the time of Numa and Romulus, the arms of the people were controlled by the authority of the Patricians; and the balance of freedom was easily preserved in a small and virtuous community. The decline of the Roman state, far different from its infancy, was attended with every circumstance that could banish from an interregnum the prospect of obedience and harmony: an immense and tumultuous capital, a wide extent of empire, the servile equality of despotism, an army of four hundred thousand mercenaries, and the experience of frequent revolution. Yet, notwithstanding all these temptations, the discipline and memory of Aurelian still restrained the seditious temper of the troops, as well as the fatal ambition of their leaders. The flower of the legions maintained their stations on the banks of the Bosphorus, and the Imperial standard awed the less powerful camps of Rome and of the provinces. A generous though transient enthusiasm seemed to animate the military order; and we may hope that a few real patriots cultivated the returning friendship of the army and the senate, as the only expedient capable of restoring the republic to its ancient beauty and vigour.

On the twenty-fifth of September, near eight months after the murder of Aurelian, the consul convoked an assembly of the senate, and reported the doubtful and dangerous situation of the empire. He slightly insinuated that the precarious loyalty of the soldiers depended on the chance of every hour and of every accident; but he represented, with the most convincing eloquence, the various dangers that might attend any farther delay in the choice of an emperor. Intelligence, he said, was already received that the Germans had passed the Rhine and occupied some of the strongest and most opulent cities of Gaul. The ambition of the Persian king kept the East in perpetual alarms; Egypt, Africa, and Illyricum were exposed to foreign and domestic arms; and the levity of Syria would prefer even a female sceptre to the sanctity of the Roman laws. The consul then, addressing himself to Tacitus, the first of the senators, required his opinion on the important subject of a proper candidate for the vacant throne.

If we can prefer personal merit to accidental greatness, we shall esteem the birth of Tacitus more truly noble than that of kings. He claimed his descent from the philosophic historian whose writings will instruct the last generations of mankind.[1] The senator Tacitus was then seventy-five years of age. The long period of his innocent life was adorned with wealth and honours. He had twice been invested with the consular dignity,[2] and enjoyed with elegance and sobriety his ample patrimony of between two and three millions sterling.[3] The experience of so many princes, whom he had esteemed or endured, from the vain follies of Elagabalus to the useful rigour of Aurelian, taught him to form a just estimate of the duties, the dangers, and the temptations of their sublime station. From the assiduous study of his immortal ancestor he derived the knowledge of the Roman constitution and of human nature.[4] The voice of the people had already named Tacitus as the citizen the most worthy of empire. The ungrateful rumour reached his ears, and induced him to seek the retirement of one of his villas in Campania. He had passed two months in the delightful privacy of Baiæ, when he reluctantly obeyed the summons of the consul to resume his honour-

[1] The only objection to this genealogy is that the historian was named Cornelius, the emperor, Claudius. But under the Lower Empire surnames were extremely various and uncertain.

[2] In the year 273 he was ordinary consul. But he must have been Suffectus many years before, and most probably under Valerian.

[3] Bis millies octingenties. This sum, according to the old standard, was equivalent to eight hundred and forty thousand Roman pounds of silver, each of the value of three pounds sterling. But in the age of Tacitus the coin had lost much of its weight and purity.

[4] After his accession, he gave orders that ten copies of the historian should be annually transcribed and placed in the public libraries. The Roman libraries have long since perished, and the most valuable part of Tacitus was preserved in a single MS. and discovered in a monastery of Westphalia.

able place in the senate, and to assist the republic with his counsels on this important occasion.

He arose to speak, when, from every quarter of the house, he was saluted with the names of Augustus and Emperor. "Tacitus Augustus, the gods preserve thee, we choose thee for our sovereign, to thy care we intrust the republic and the world. Accept the empire from the authority of the senate. It is due to thy rank, to thy conduct, to thy manners." As soon as the tumult of acclamations subsided, Tacitus attempted to decline the dangerous honour, and to express his wonder that they should elect his age and infirmities to succeed the martial vigour of Aurelian. "Are these limbs, conscript fathers! fitted to sustain the weight of armour, or to practise the exercises of the camp? The variety of climates, and the hardships of a military life, would soon oppress a feeble constitution, which subsists only by the most tender management. My exhausted strength scarcely enables me to discharge the duty of a senator; how insufficient would it prove to the arduous labours of war and government! Can you hope that the legions will respect a weak old man, whose days have been spent in the shade of peace and retirement? Can you desire that I should ever find reason to regret the favourable opinion of the senate?"

The reluctance of Tacitus, and it might possibly be sincere, was encountered by the affectionate obstinacy of the senate. Five hundred voices repeated at once, in eloquent confusion, that the greatest of the Roman princes, Numa, Trajan, Hadrian, and the Antonines, had ascended the throne in a very advanced season of life; that the mind, not the body, a sovereign, not a soldier, was the object of their choice; and that they expected from him no more than to guide by his wisdom the valour of the legions. These pressing though tumultuary instances were seconded by a more regular oration of Metius Falconius, the next on the consular bench to Tacitus himself. He reminded the assembly of the evils which Rome had endured from the vices of headstrong and capricious youths, congratulated them on the election of a virtuous and experienced senator, and, with a manly, though perhaps a selfish, freedom, exhorted Tacitus to remember the reasons of his elevation, and to seek a successor, not in his own family, but in the republic. The speech of Falconius was enforced by a general acclamation. The emperor elect submitted to the authority of his country, and received the voluntary homage of his equals. The judgment of the senate was confirmed by the consent of the Roman people, and of the Prætorian guards.

The administration of Tacitus was not unworthy of his life and principles. A grateful servant of the senate, he considered that national council as the author, and himself as the subject, of the laws. He studied to heal the wounds which Imperial pride, civil discord, and military violence had inflicted on the constitution, and to restore, at least, the image of the ancient republic, as it had been preserved by the policy of Augustus, and the virtues of Trajan and the Antonines. It may not be useless to recapitulate some of the most important prerogatives which the senate appeared to have regained by the election of Tacitus. 1. To invest one of their body, under the title of emperor, with the general command of the armies and the government of the frontier provinces. 2. To determine the list, or, as it was then styled, the College of Consuls. They were twelve in number, who, in successive pairs, each during the space of two months, filled the year, and represented the dignity of that ancient office. The authority of the senate in the nomination of the consuls was exercised with such independent freedom that no regard was paid to an irregular request of the emperor in favour of his brother Florianus. "The senate," exclaimed Tacitus, with the honest transport of a patriot, "understand the character of a prince whom they have chosen." 3. To appoint the proconsuls and presidents of the provinces, and to confer on all the magistrates their civil jurisdiction. 4. To receive appeals through the intermediate office of the præfect of the city from all the tribunals of the empire. 5. To give force and validity, by their decrees, to such as they should approve of the emperor's edicts. 6. To these several branches of authority we may add some inspection over the finances, since, even in the stern reign of Aurelian, it was in their power to divert a part of the revenue from the public service.

Circular epistles were sent, without delay, to all the principal cities of the empire, Treves, Milan, Aquileia, Thessalonica, Corinth, Athens, Antioch, Alexandria, and Carthage, to claim their obedience, and to inform them of the happy revolution, which had restored the Roman senate to its ancient dignity. Two of these epistles are still extant. We likewise possess two very singular fragments of the private correspondence of the senators on this occasion. They discover the most excessive joy and the most unbounded hopes. "Cast away your indolence," it is thus that one of the senators addresses his friend, "emerge from your retirements of Baiæ and Puteoli. Give yourself to the city, to the senate. Rome flourishes, the whole republic flourishes. Thanks to the Roman army, to an army truly Roman, at length we have recovered our just authority, the end of all our desires. We hear appeals, we appoint proconsuls, we create emperors: perhaps, too, we may restrain them—to the wise, a word is sufficient." [5] These lofty expectations were, however, soon disappointed; nor, indeed, was it possible that the armies and the provinces should long obey the luxurious and unwarlike nobles of Rome. On the slightest touch, the unsupported fabric of their pride and power fell to the ground. The expiring senate displayed a sudden lustre, blazed for a moment, and was extinguished for ever.

[5] The senators celebrated the happy restoration with hecatombs and public rejoicings.

All that had yet passed at Rome was no more than a theatrical representation, unless it was ratified by the more substantial power of the legions. Leaving the senators to enjoy their dream of freedom and ambition, Tacitus proceeded to the Thracian camp, and was there, by the Prætorian præfect, presented to the assembled troops, as the prince whom they themselves had demanded, and whom the senate had bestowed. As soon as the præfect was silent, the emperor addressed himself to the soldiers with elegance and propriety. He gratified their avarice by a liberal distribution of treasure, under the names of pay and donative. He engaged their esteem by a spirited declaration that, although his age might disable him from the performance of military exploits, his counsels should never be unworthy of a Roman general, the successor of the brave Aurelian.

Whilst the deceased emperor was making preparations for a second expedition into the East, he had negotiated with the Alani, a Scythian people, who pitched their tents in the neighbourhood of the lake Mæotis. Those barbarians, allured by presents and subsidies, had promised to invade Persia with a numerous body of light cavalry. They were faithful to their engagements; but, when they arrived on the Roman frontier, Aurelian was already dead, the design of the Persian war was at least suspended, and the generals, who, during the interregnum, exercised a doubtful authority, were unprepared either to receive or to oppose them. Provoked by such treatment, which they considered as trifling and perfidious, the Alani had recourse to their own valour for their payment and revenge; and, as they moved with the usual swiftness of Tartars, they had soon spread themselves over the provinces of Pontus, Cappadocia, Cilicia, and Galatia. The legions, who from the opposite shores of the Bosphorus could almost distinguish the flames of the cities and villages, impatiently urged their general to lead them against the invaders. The conduct of Tacitus was suitable to his age and station. He convinced the barbarians of the faith, as well as of the power, of the empire. Great numbers of the Alani, appeased by the punctual discharge of the engagements which Aurelian had contracted with them, relinquished their booty and captives, and quietly retreated to their own deserts beyond the Phasis. Against the remainder, who refused peace, the Roman emperor waged, in person, a successful war. Seconded by an army of brave and experienced veterans, in a few weeks he delivered the provinces of Asia from the terror of the Scythian invasion.

But the glory and life of Tacitus were of short duration. Transported, in the depth of winter, from the soft retirement of Campania to the foot of Mount Caucasus, he sunk under the unaccustomed hardships of a military life. The fatigues of the body were aggravated by the cares of the mind. For a while, the angry and selfish passions of the soldiers had been suspended by the enthusiasm of public virtue. They soon broke out with redoubled violence, and raged in the camp, and even in the tent of the aged emperor. His mild and amiable character served only to inspire contempt, and he was incessantly tormented with factions which he could not assuage, and by demands which it was impossible to satisfy. Whatever flattering expectations he had conceived of reconciling the public disorders, Tacitus soon was convinced that the licentiousness of the army disdained the feeble restraint of laws, and his last hour was hastened by anguish and disappointment. It may be doubtful whether the soldiers imbrued their hands in the blood of this innocent prince.[6] It is certain that their insolence was the cause of his death. He expired at Tyana in Cappadocia, after a reign of only six months and about twenty days.[7]

The eyes of Tacitus were scarcely closed before his brother Florianus showed himself unworthy to reign, by the hasty usurpation of the purple, without expecting the approbation of the senate. The reverence for the Roman constitution, which yet influenced the camp and the provinces, was sufficiently strong to dispose them to censure, but not to provoke them to oppose, the precipitate ambition of Florianus. The discontent would have evaporated in idle murmurs, had not the general of the East, the heroic Probus, boldly declared himself the avenger of the senate. The contest, however, was still unequal; nor could the most able leader, at the head of the effeminate troops of Egypt and Syria, encounter, with any hopes of victory, the legions of Europe, whose irresistible strength appeared to support the brother of Tacitus. But the fortune and activity of Probus triumphed over every obstacle. The hardy veterans of his

[6] *Eutropius and Aurelius Victor only say that he died; Victor Junior adds that it was of a fever. Zosimus and Zonaras affirm that he was killed by the soldiers. Vopiscus mentions both accounts, and seems to hesitate. Yet surely these jarring opinions are easily reconciled.*

[7] *According to the two Victors, he reigned exactly two hundred days.*

rival, accustomed to cold climates, sickened and consumed away in the sultry heats of Cilicia, where the summer proved remarkably unwholesome. Their numbers were diminished by frequent desertion, the passes of the mountains were feebly defended; Tarsus opened its gates, and the soldiers of Florianus, when they had permitted him to enjoy the Imperial title about three months, delivered the empire from civil war by the easy sacrifice of a prince whom they despised.

The perpetual revolutions of the throne had so perfectly erased every notion of hereditary right, that the family of an unfortunate emperor was incapable of exciting the jealousy of his successors. The children of Tacitus and Florianus were permitted to descend into a private station, and to mingle with the general mass of the people. Their poverty indeed became an additional safeguard to their innocence. When Tacitus was elected by the senate, he resigned his ample patrimony to the public service, an act of generosity specious in appearance, but which evidently disclosed his intention of transmitting the empire to his descendants. The only consolation of their fallen state was the remembrance of transient greatness, and a distant hope, the child of a flattering prophecy, that, at the end of a thousand years, a monarch of the race of Tacitus should rise, the protector of the senate, the restorer of Rome, and the conqueror of the whole earth.[8]

The peasants of Illyricum, who had already given Claudius and Aurelian to the sinking empire, had an equal right to glory in the elevation of Probus. Above twenty years before, the emperor Valerian, with his usual penetration, had discovered the rising merit of the young soldier, on whom he conferred the rank of tribune long before the age prescribed by the military regulations. The tribune soon justified his choice by a victory over a great body of Sarmatians, in which he saved the life of a near relation of Valerian; and deserved to receive from the emperor's hand the collars, bracelets, spears, and banners, the mural and the civic crown, and all the honourable rewards reserved by ancient Rome for successful valour. The third, and afterwards the tenth, legion were intrusted to the command of Probus, who, in every step of his promotion, showed himself superior to the station which he filled. Africa and Pontus, the Rhine, the Danube, the Euphrates, and the Nile, by turns afforded him the most splendid occasions of displaying his personal prowess and his conduct in war. Aurelian was indebted to him for the conquest of Egypt, and still more indebted for the honest courage with which he often checked the cruelty of his master. Tacitus,

[8] *He was to send judges to the Parthians, Persians, and Sarmatians, a president to Taprobana, and a proconsul to the Roman island (supposed by Casaubon and Salmasius to mean Britain).*

who desired by the abilities of his generals to supply his own deficiency of military talents, named him commander in chief of all the eastern provinces, with five times the usual salary, the promise of the consulship, and the hope of a triumph. When Probus ascended the Imperial throne, he was about forty-four years of age;[9] in the full possession of his fame, of the love of the army, and of a mature vigour of mind and body.

His acknowledged merit, and the success of his arms against Florianus, left him without an enemy or a competitor. Yet, if we may credit his own professions, very far from being desirous of the empire, he had accepted it with the most sincere reluctance. "But it is no longer in my power," says Probus, in a private letter, "to lay down a title so full of envy and of danger. I must continue to personate the character which the soldiers have imposed upon me."[10] His dutiful address to the senate displayed the sentiments, or at least the language, of a Roman patriot: "When you elected one of your order, conscript fathers! to succeed the Emperor Aurelian, you acted in a manner suitable to your justice and wisdom. For you are the legal sovereigns of the world, and the power which you derive from your ancestors will descend to your posterity. Happy would it have been, if Florianus, instead of usurping the purple of his brother, like a private inheritance, had expected what your majesty might determine, either in his favour or in that of any other person. The prudent soldiers have punished his rashness. To me they have offered the title of Augustus. But I submit to your clemency my pretensions and my merits."[11] When this respectful epistle was read by the consul, the senators were unable to disguise their satisfaction that Probus should condescend thus humbly to solicit a sceptre which he already possessed. They celebrated with the warmest gratitude his virtues, his exploits, and above all his moderation. A decree immediately passed, without a dissenting voice, to ratify the election of the eastern armies, and to confer on their chief all the several branches of the Imperial dignity: the names of Cæsar and Augustus, the title of Father of his country, the right of making in the same day three motions in the senate,[12] the office of Pontifex Maximus, the tribunitian power, and the proconsular command; a mode of investiture, which, though it seemed to multiply the authority of the emperor, expressed the constitution of the ancient republic. The reign of Probus corresponded with this fair beginning. The senate was permitted to direct the civil administration of the empire. Their faithful general asserted the honour of the Roman

[9] *According to the Alexandrian Chronicle, he was fifty at the time of his death.*

[10] *The letter was addressed to the Prætorian præfect, whom (on condition of his good behaviour) he promised to continue in his great office.*

[11] *The date of the letter is assuredly faulty.*

[12] *It is odd that the senate should treat Probus less favourably than Marcus Antoninus. That prince had received, even before the death of Pius,* Jus quintae relationis.

arms, and often laid at their feet crowns of gold and barbaric trophies, the fruits of his numerous victories. Yet, whilst he gratified their vanity, he must secretly have despised their indolence and weakness. Though it was every moment in their power to repel the disgraceful edict of Gallienus, the proud successors of the Scipios patiently acquiesced in their exclusion from all military employments. They soon experienced that those who refuse the sword must renounce the sceptre.

The strength of Aurelian had crushed on every side the enemies of Rome. After his death they seemed to revive, with an increase of fury and of numbers. They were again vanquished by the active vigour of Probus, who, in a short reign of about six years, equalled the fame of ancient heroes, and restored peace and order to every province of the Roman world. The dangerous frontier of Rhætia he so firmly secured, that he left it without the suspicion of an enemy. He broke the wandering power of the Sarmatian tribes, and by the terror of his arms compelled those barbarians to relinquish their spoil. The Gothic nation courted the alliance of so warlike an emperor. He attacked the Isaurians in their mountains, besieged and took several of their strongest castles, and flattered himself that he had for ever suppressed a domestic foe, whose independence so deeply wounded the majesty of the empire. The troubles excited by the usurper Firmus in the Upper Egypt had never been perfectly appeased, and the cities of Ptolemais and Coptos, fortified by the alliance of the Blemmyes, still maintained an obscure rebellion. The chastisement of those cities, and of their auxiliaries the savages of the South, is said to have alarmed the court of Persia, and the Great King sued in vain for the friendship of Probus. Most of the exploits which distinguished his reign were achieved by the personal valour and conduct of the emperor, insomuch that the writer of his life expresses some amazement how, in so short a time, a single man could be present in so many distant wars. The remaining actions he intrusted to the care of his lieutenants, the judicious choice of whom forms no inconsiderable part of his glory. Carus, Diocletian, Maximian, Constantius, Galerius, Asclepiodatus, Annibalianus, and a crowd of other chiefs, who afterwards ascended or supported the throne, were trained to arms in the severe school of Aurelian and Probus.

But the most important service which Probus rendered to the republic was the deliverance of Gaul, and the recovery of seventy flourishing cities oppressed by the barbarians of Germany, who, since the death of Aurelian, had ravaged that great province with impunity. Among the various multitude of those fierce invaders we may distinguish, with some degree of clearness, three great armies, or rather nations, successively vanquished by the valour of Probus. He drove back the Franks into their morasses; a descriptive circumstance from whence we may infer that the confederacy known by the manly appellation of *Free* already occupied the flat maritime country, intersected and almost overflown by the stagnating waters of the Rhine, and that several tribes of the Frisians and Batavians had acceded to their alliance. He vanquished the Burgundians, a considerable people of the Vandalic race. They had wandered in quest of booty from the banks of the Oder to those of the Seine. They esteemed themselves sufficiently fortunate to purchase, by the restitution of all their booty, the permission of an undisturbed retreat. They attempted to elude that article of the treaty. Their punishment was immediate and terrible. But of all the invaders of Gaul, the most formidable were the Lygians, a distant people who reigned over a wide domain on the frontiers of Poland and Silesia. In the Lygian nation, the Arii held the first rank by their numbers and fierceness. "The Arii (it is thus that they are described by the energy of Tacitus) study to improve by art and circumstances the innate terrors of their barbarism. Their shields are black, their bodies are painted black. They choose for the combat the darkest hour of the night. Their host advances, covered as it were with a funereal shade; nor do they often find an enemy capable of sustaining so strange and infernal an aspect. Of all our senses, the eyes are the first vanquished in battle." Yet the arms and discipline of the Romans easily discomfited these horrid phantoms. The Lygii were defeated in a general engagement, and Semno, the most renowned of their chiefs, fell alive into the hands of Probus. That prudent emperor, unwilling to reduce a brave people to despair, granted them an honourable capitulation, and permitted them to return in safety to their native country. But the losses which they suffered in the march, the battle, and the retreat, broke the power of the nation: nor is the Lygian name ever repeated in the history either of Germany or of the empire. The deliverance of Gaul is reported to have cost the lives of four hundred thousand of the invaders; a work of labour to the Romans, and of expense to the emperor, who gave a piece of gold for the head of every barbarian. But, as the fame of warriors is built on the destruction of human kind, we may naturally suspect that the sanguinary account was multiplied by the avarice of the soldiers, and accepted without any very severe examination by the liberal vanity of Probus.

Since the expedition of Maximin, the Roman generals had confined their ambition to a defensive war against the nations of Germany, who perpetually pressed on the frontiers of the empire. The more daring Probus pursued his Gallic victories, passed the Rhine, and displayed his invincible eagles on the banks of the Elbe and the Neckar. He was fully convinced that nothing could reconcile the minds of the barbarians to peace, unless they experienced in their own country the calamities of war. Germany, exhausted by the ill success of the last emigration, was astonished by his presence. Nine of the most considerable princes repaired to his camp, and fell prostrate at his feet. Such a treaty was humbly received by the Germans, as it pleased the conqueror to dictate. He exacted a strict restitution of the effects and captives which they had carried away from the provinces; and obliged their own magistrates to punish the more obstinate robbers who presumed to detain any part of the spoil. A considerable tribute of corn, cattle, and horses, the only wealth of barbarians, was reserved for the use of the garrisons which Probus established on the limits of their territory. He even entertained some thoughts of compelling the Germans to relinquish the exercise of arms, and to trust their differences to the justice, their safety to the power, of Rome. To accomplish these salutary ends, the constant residence of an Imperial governor, supported by a numerous army, was indispensably requisite. Probus therefore judged it more expedient to defer the execution of so great a design; which was indeed rather of specious than solid utility. Had Germany been reduced into the state of a province, the Romans, with immense labour and expense, would have acquired only a more extensive boundary to defend against the fiercer and more active barbarians of Scythia.

Instead of reducing the warlike natives of Germany to the condition of subjects, Probus contented himself with the humble expedient of raising a bulwark against their inroads. The country which now forms the circle of Swabia had been left desert in the age of Augustus by the emigration of its ancient inhabitants. The fertility of the soil soon attracted a new colony from the adjacent provinces of Gaul. Crowds of adventurers, of a roving temper and of desperate fortunes, occupied the doubtful possession, and acknowledged, by the payment of tithes, the majesty of the empire. To protect these new subjects, a line of frontier garrisons was gradually extended from the Rhine to the Danube. About the reign of Hadrian, when that mode of defence began to be practised, these garrisons were connected and covered by a strong intrenchment of trees and palisades. In the place of so rude a bulwark, the emperor Probus constructed a stone wall of a considerable height, and strengthened it by towers at convenient distances. From the neighbourhood of Neustadt and Ratisbon on the Danube, it stretched across hills, valleys, rivers, and morasses, as far as Wimpfen on the Neckar, and at length terminated on the banks of the Rhine, after a winding course of near two hundred miles. This important barrier, uniting the two mighty streams that protected the provinces of Europe, seemed to fill up the vacant space through which the barbarians, and particularly the Alemanni, could penetrate with the greatest facility into the heart of the empire. But the experience of the world, from China to Britain, has exposed the vain attempt of fortifying any extensive tract of country. An active enemy, who can select and vary his points of attack, must, in the end, discover some feeble spot or unguarded moment. The strength as well as the attention of the defenders is divided; and such are the blind effects of terror on the firmest troops, that a line broken in a single place is almost instantly deserted. The fate of the wall which Probus erected may confirm the general observation. Within a few years after his death, it was overthrown by the Alemanni. Its scattered ruins, universally ascribed to the power of the Dæmon, now serve only to excite the wonder of the Swabian peasant.

Among the useful conditions of peace, imposed by Probus on the vanquished nations of Germany, was the obligation of supplying the Roman army with sixteen thousand recruits, the bravest and most robust of their youth. The emperor dispersed them through all the provinces, and distributed this dangerous reinforcement in small bands, of fifty or sixty each, among the national troops; judiciously observing that the aid which the republic derived from the barbarians should be felt but not seen.[13] Their aid was now become necessary. The feeble elegance of Italy and the internal provinces could no longer support the weight of arms. The hardy frontier of the Rhine and Danube still produced minds and bodies equal to the labours of the camp; but a perpetual series of wars had gradually diminished their numbers. The infrequency of marriage, and the ruin of agriculture, affected the principles of population, and not only destroyed the strength of the present, but intercepted the hope of future, generations. The wisdom of Probus embraced a great and beneficial plan of replenishing the exhausted frontiers, by new colonies of cap-

[13] *He distributed about fifty or sixty barbarians to a* Numerus, *as it was then called, a corps with whose established number we are not exactly acquainted.*

tive or fugitive barbarians, on whom he bestowed lands, cattle, instruments of husbandry, and every encouragement that might engage them to educate a race of soldiers for the service of the republic. Into Britain, and most probably into Cambridgeshire, he transported a considerable body of Vandals. The impossibility of an escape reconciled them to their situation, and in the subsequent troubles of that island they approved themselves the most faithful servants of the state. Great numbers of Franks and Gepidæ were settled on the banks of the Danube and the Rhine. An hundred thousand Bastarnæ, expelled from their own country, cheerfully accepted an establishment in Thrace, and soon imbibed the manners and sentiments of Roman subjects. But the expectations of Probus were too often disappointed. The impatience and idleness of the barbarians could ill brook the slow labours of agriculture. Their unconquerable love of freedom, rising against despotism, provoked them into hasty rebellions, alike fatal to themselves and to the provinces; nor could these artificial supplies, however repeated by succeeding emperors, restore the important limit of Gaul and Illyricum to its ancient and native vigour.

Of all the barbarians who abandoned their new settlements, and disturbed the public tranquillity, a very small number returned to their own country. For a short season they might wander in arms through the empire; but in the end they were surely destroyed by the power of a warlike emperor. The successful rashness of a party of Franks was attended, however, with such memorable consequences, that it ought not to be passed unnoticed. They had been established by Probus on the sea coast of Pontus, with a view of strengthening that frontier against the inroads of the Alani. A fleet stationed in one of the harbours of the Euxine fell into the hands of the Franks; and they resolved, through unknown seas, to explore their way from the mouth of the Phasis to that of the Rhine. They easily escaped through the Bosphorus and the Hellespont, and, cruising along the Mediterranean, indulged their appetite for revenge and plunder by frequent descents on the unsuspecting shores of Asia, Greece, and Africa. The opulent city of Syracuse, in whose port the navies of Athens and Carthage had formerly been sunk, was sacked by a handful of barbarians, who massacred the greatest part of the trembling inhabitants. From the island of Sicily the Franks proceeded to the columns of Hercules, trusted themselves to the ocean, coasted round Spain and Gaul, and, steering their triumphant course through the British channel, at length finished their surprising voyage by landing in safety on the Batavian or Frisian shores. The example of their success, instructing their countrymen to conceive the advantages, and to despise the dangers, of the sea, pointed out to their enterprising spirit a new road to wealth and glory.

Notwithstanding the vigilance and activity of Probus, it was almost impossible that he could at once contain in obedience every part of his wide-extended dominions. The barbarians, who broke their chains, had seized the favourable opportunity of a domestic war. When the emperor marched to the relief of Gaul, he devolved the command of the East on Saturninus. That general, a man of merit and experience, was driven into rebellion by the absence of his sovereign, the levity of the Alexandrian people, the pressing instances of his friends, and his own fears; but from the moment of his elevation he never entertained a hope of empire, or even of life. "Alas!" he said, "the republic has lost a useful servant, and the rashness of an hour has destroyed the services of many years. You know not," continued he, "the misery of sovereign power: a sword is perpetually suspended over our head. We dread our very guards, we distrust our companions. The choice of action or of repose is no longer in our disposition, nor is there any age, or character, or conduct, that can protect us from the censure of envy. In thus exalting me to the throne, you have doomed me to a life of cares, and to an untimely fate. The only consolation which remains is the assurance

that I shall not fall alone." [11] But, as the former part of his prediction was verified by the victory, so the latter was disappointed by the clemency, of Probus. That amiable prince attempted even to save the unhappy Saturninus from the fury of the soldiers. He had more than once solicited the usurper himself to place some confidence in the mercy of a sovereign who so highly esteemed his character, that he had punished, as a malicious informer, the first who related the improbable news of his defection. Saturninus might, perhaps, have embraced the generous offer, had he not been restrained by the obstinate distrust of his adherents. Their guilt was deeper, and their hopes more sanguine, than those of their experienced leader.

The revolt of Saturninus was scarcely extinguished in the East, before new troubles were excited in the West by the rebellion of Bonosus and Proculus in Gaul. The most distinguished merit of those two officers was their respective prowess, of the one in the combats of Bacchus, of the other in those of Venus; yet neither of them were destitute of courage and capacity, and both sustained, with honour, the august character which the fear of punishment had engaged them to assume, till they sunk at length beneath the superior genius of Probus. He used the victory with his accustomed moderation, and spared the fortunes as well as the lives of their innocent families.[15]

The arms of Probus had now suppressed all the foreign and domestic enemies of the state. His mild but steady administration confirmed the re-establishment of the public tranquillity; nor was there left in the provinces a hostile barbarian, a tyrant, or even a robber, to revive the memory of past disorders. It was time that the emperor should revisit Rome, and celebrate his own glory and the general happiness. The triumph due to the valour of Probus was conducted with a magnificence suitable to his fortune, and the people who had so lately admired the trophies of Aurelian gazed with equal pleasure on those of his heroic successor. We cannot, on this occasion, forget the desperate courage of about fourscore Gladiators, reserved, with near six hundred others, for the inhuman sports of the amphitheatre. Disdaining to shed their blood for the amusement of the populace, they killed their keepers, broke from the place of their confinement, and filled the streets of Rome with blood and confusion. After an obstinate resistance they were overpowered and cut in pieces by the regular forces; but they obtained at least an honourable death, and the satisfaction of a just revenge.

The military discipline which reigned in the camps of Probus was less cruel than that of Aurelian, but it was equally rigid and exact. The latter had punished the irregularities of the soldiers with unrelenting severity, the former prevented them by employing the legions in constant and useful labours. When Probus commanded in Egypt, he executed many considerable works for the splendour and benefit of that rich country. The navigation of the Nile, so important to Rome itself, was improved; and temples, bridges, porticoes, and palaces, were constructed by the hands of the soldiers, who acted by turns as architects, as engineers, and as husbandmen. It was reported of Hannibal that, in order to preserve his troops from the dangerous temptations of idleness, he had obliged them to form large plantations of olive trees along the coast of Africa.[16] From a similar principle, Probus exercised his legions in covering with rich vineyards the hills of Gaul and Pannonia, and two considerable spots are described, which were entirely dug and planted by military labour.[17] One of these, known under the name of Mount Alma, was situated near Sirmium, the country where Probus was born, for which he ever retained a partial affection, and whose gratitude he endeavoured to secure by converting into tillage a large and

[15] *Proculus, who was a native of Albengue on the Genoese coast, armed two thousand of his own slaves. His riches were great, but they were acquired by robbery.*

[16] *The policy of Hannibal, unnoticed by any more ancient writer, is irreconcilable with the history of his life. He left Africa when he was nine years old, returned to it when he was forty-five, and immediately lost his army in the decisive battle of Zama.*

[17] *He revoked the prohibition of Domitian, and granted a general permission of planting vines to the Gauls, the Britons, and the Pannonians.*

unhealthy track of marshy ground. An army thus employed constituted perhaps the most useful, as well as the bravest, portion of the Roman subjects.

But, in the prosecution of a favourite scheme, the best of men, satisfied with the rectitude of their intentions, are subject to forget the bounds of moderation; nor did Probus himself sufficiently consult the patience and disposition of his fierce legionaries. The dangers of the military profession seem only to be compensated by a life of pleasure and idleness; but, if the duties of the soldier are incessantly aggravated by the labours of the peasant, he will at last sink under the intolerable burden, or shake it off with indignation. The imprudence of Probus is said to have inflamed the discontent of his troops. More attentive to the interests of mankind than to those of the army, he expressed the vain hope that, by the establishment of universal peace, he should soon abolish the necessity of a standing and mercenary force. The unguarded expression proved fatal to him. In one of the hottest days of summer, as he severely urged the unwholesome labour of draining the marshes of Sirmium, the soldiers, impatient of fatigue, on a sudden threw down their tools, grasped their arms, and broke out into a furious mutiny. The emperor, conscious of his danger, took refuge in a lofty tower, constructed for the purpose of surveying the progress of the work.[18] The tower was instantly forced, and a thousand swords were plunged at once into the bosom of the unfortunate Probus. The rage of the troops subsided as soon as it had been gratified. They then lamented their fatal rashness, forgot the severity of the emperor whom they had massacred, and hastened to perpetuate, by an honourable monument, the memory of his virtues and victories.

When the legions had indulged their grief and repentance for the death of Probus, their unanimous consent declared Carus, his Prætorian præfect, the most deserving of the Imperial throne. Every circumstance that relates to this prince appears of a mixed and doubtful nature. He gloried in the title of Roman Citizen; and affected to compare the purity of *his* blood with the foreign, and even barbarous, origin of the preceding emperors: yet the most inquisitive of his contemporaries, very far from admitting his claim, have variously deduced his own birth, or that of his parents, from Illyricum, from Gaul, or from Africa.[19] Though a soldier, he had received a learned education; though a senator, he was invested with the first dignity of the army; and, in an age when the civil and military professions began to be irrecoverably separated from each other, they

18 *It seems to have been a movable tower, and cased with iron.*

19 *Yet all this may be conciliated. He was born at Narbonne in Illyricum, confounded by Eutropius with the more famous city of that name in Gaul. His father might be an African, and his mother a noble Roman. Carus himself was educated in the capital.*

were united in the person of Carus. Notwithstanding the severe justice which he exercised against the assassins of Probus, to whose favour and esteem he was highly indebted, he could not escape the suspicion of being accessory to a deed from whence he derived the principal advantage. He enjoyed, at least before his elevation, an acknowledged character of virtue and abilities:[20] but his austere temper insensibly degenerated into moroseness and cruelty; and the imperfect writers of his life almost hesitate whether they shall not rank him in the number of Roman tyrants. When Carus assumed the purple, he was about sixty years of age, and his two sons, Carinus and Numerian, had already attained the season of manhood.

The authority of the senate expired with Probus; nor was the repentance of the soldiers displayed by the same dutiful regard for the civil power which they had testified after the unfortunate death of Aurelian. The election of Carus was decided without expecting the approbation of the senate, and the new emperor contented himself with announcing, in a cold and stately epistle, that he had ascended the vacant throne. A behaviour so very opposite to that of his amiable predecessor afforded no favourable presage of the new reign; and the Romans, deprived of power and freedom, asserted their privilege of licentious murmurs. The voice of congratulation and flattery was not however silent; and we may still peruse, with pleasure and contempt, an eclogue, which was composed on the accession of the emperor Carus. Two shepherds, avoiding the noon-tide heat, retire into the cave of Faunus. On a spreading beech they discover some recent characters. The rural deity had described, in prophetic verses, the felicity promised to the empire under the reign of so great a prince. Faunus hails the approach of that hero, who, receiving on his shoulders the sinking weight of the Roman world, shall extinguish war and faction, and once again restore the innocence and security of the golden age.

It is more than probable that these elegant trifles never reached the ears of a veteran general, who, with the consent of the legions, was preparing to execute the long-suspended design of the Persian war. Before his departure for this distant expedition, Carus conferred on his two sons, Carinus and Numerian, the title of Cæsar; and, investing the former with almost an equal share of the Imperial power, directed the young prince, first to suppress some troubles which had arisen in Gaul, and afterwards to fix the seat of his residence at Rome, and to assume the government of the Western provinces. The safety of Illyricum was confirmed by a memorable defeat

[20] *Probus had requested of the senate an equestrian statue and a marble palace, at the public expense, as a just recompense of the singular merit of Carus.*

of the Sarmatians; sixteen thousand of those barbarians remained on the field of battle, and the number of captives amounted to twenty thousand. The old emperor, animated with the fame and prospect of victory, pursued his march, in the midst of winter, through the countries of Thrace and Asia Minor, and at length, with his younger son, Numerian, arrived on the confines of the Persian monarchy. There, encamping on the summit of a lofty mountain, he pointed out to his troops the opulence and luxury of the enemy whom they were about to invade.

The successor of Artaxerxes, Varanes or Bahram, though he had subdued the Segestans, one of the most warlike nations of Upper Asia, was alarmed at the approach of the Romans and endeavoured to retard their progress by a negotiation of peace. His ambassadors entered the camp about sunset, at the time when the troops were satisfying their hunger with a frugal repast. The Persians expressed their desire of being introduced to the presence of the Roman emperor. They were at length conducted to a soldier, who was seated on the grass. A piece of stale bacon and a few hard peas composed his supper. A coarse woollen garment of purple was the only circumstance that announced his dignity. The conference was conducted with the same disregard of courtly elegance. Carus, taking off a cap which he wore to conceal his baldness, assured the ambassadors that, unless their master acknowledged the superiority of Rome, he would speedily render Persia as naked of trees as his own head was destitute of hair. Notwithstanding some traces of art and preparation, we may discover, in this scene, the manners of Carus, and the severe simplicity which the martial princes, who succeeded Gallienus, had already restored in the Roman camps. The ministers of the Great King trembled and retired.

The threats of Carus were not without effect. He ravaged Mesopotamia, cut in pieces whatever opposed his passage, made himself master of the great cities of Seleucia and Ctesiphon (which seem to have surrendered without resistance), and carried his victorious arms beyond the Tigris. He had seized the favourable moment for an invasion. The Persian councils were distracted by domestic factions, and the greater part of their forces were detained on the frontiers of India. Rome and the East received with transport the news of such important advantages. Flattery and hope painted, in the most lively colours, the fall of Persia, the conquest of Arabia, the submission of Egypt, and a lasting deliverance from the inroads of the Scythian nations. But the reign of Carus was destined to expose the vanity of predictions. They were scarcely uttered before they were contradicted by his death; an event attended with such ambiguous circumstances, that it may best be related in a letter from his own secretary to the præfect of the city. "Carus," says he, "our dearest emperor, was confined by sickness to his bed, when a furious tempest arose in the camp. The darkness which overspread the sky was so thick, that we could no longer distinguish each other; and the incessant flashes of lightning took from us the knowledge of all that passed in the general confusion. Immediately after the most violent clap of thunder, we heard a sudden cry that the emperor was dead; and it soon appeared that his chamberlains, in a rage of grief, had set fire to the royal pavilion, a circumstance which gave rise to the report that Carus was killed by lightning. But, as far as we have been able to investigate the truth, his death was the natural effect of his disorder."

The vacancy of the throne was not productive of any disturbance. The ambition of the aspiring generals was checked by their mutual fears, and young Numerian, with his absent brother Carinus, were unanimously acknowledged as Roman emperors. The public expected that the successor of Carus would pursue his father's footsteps, and, without allowing the Persians to recover from their consternation, would advance sword in hand to the palaces of Susa and Ecbatana. But the legions, however strong in numbers and discipline, were dismayed by the most abject superstition. Notwithstanding all the arts that were practised to disguise the manner of the late emperor's death, it was found impossible to remove the opinion of the multitude, and the power of opinion is irresistible. Places or persons struck with lightning were considered by the ancients with pious horror, as singularly devoted to the wrath of Heaven.[21] An oracle was remembered, which marked the river Tigris as the fatal boundary of the Roman arms. The troops, terrified with the fate of Carus and with their own danger, called aloud on young Numerian to obey the will of the gods, and to lead them away from this inauspicious scene of war. The feeble emperor was unable to subdue their obstinate prejudice, and the Persians wondered at the unexpected retreat of a victorious enemy.

The intelligence of the mysterious fate of the late emperor was soon carried from the frontiers of Persia to Rome; and the senate, as well as the provinces, congratulated the accession of the sons of Carus. These fortunate youths were strangers, however, to that conscious superiority, either of birth or of merit, which can alone render

[21] Places *struck with lightning were surrounded with a wall;* things *were buried with mysterious ceremony.*

the possession of a throne easy; and as it were natural. Born and educated in a private station, the election of their father raised them at once to the rank of princes; and his death, which happened about sixteen months afterwards, left them the unexpected legacy of a vast empire. To sustain with temper this rapid elevation, an uncommon share of virtue and prudence was requisite; and Carinus, the elder of the brothers, was more than commonly deficient in those qualities. In the Gallic war, he discovered some degree of personal courage; but, from the moment of his arrival at Rome, he abandoned himself to the luxury of the capital, and to the abuse of his fortune. He was soft, yet cruel; devoted to pleasure, but destitute of taste; and, though exquisitely susceptible of vanity, indifferent to the public esteem. In the course of a few months, he successively married and divorced nine wives, most of whom he left pregnant; and, notwithstanding this legal inconstancy, found time to indulge such a variety of irregular appetites as brought dishonour on himself and on the noblest houses of Rome. He beheld with inveterate hatred all those who might remember his former obscurity, or censure his present conduct. He banished or put to death the friends and counsellors whom his father had placed about him to guide his inexperienced youth; and he persecuted with the meanest revenge his schoolfellows and companions, who had not sufficiently respected the latent majesty of the emperor. With the senators, Carinus affected a lofty and regal demeanour, frequently declaring that he designed to distribute their estates among the populace of Rome. From the dregs of that populace he selected his favourites, and even his ministers. The palace, and even the Imperial table, was filled with singers, dancers, prostitutes, and all the various retinue of vice and folly. One of his door-keepers [22] he intrusted with the government of the city. In the room of the Prætorian præfect, whom he put to death, Carinus substituted one of the ministers of his looser pleasures. Another who possessed the same, or even a more infamous, title to favour, was invested with the consulship. A confidential secretary, who had acquired uncommon skill in the art of forgery, delivered the indolent emperor, with his own consent, from the irksome duty of signing his name.

When the emperor Carus undertook the Persian war, he was induced, by motives of affection as well as policy, to secure the fortunes of his family by leaving in the hands of his eldest son the armies and provinces of the West. The intelligence which he soon received of the conduct of Carinus filled him with shame and re-

[22] Cancellarius. *This word, so humble in its origin, has, by a singular fortune, risen into the title of the first great office of state in the monarchies of Europe.*

gret; nor had he concealed his resolution of satisfying the republic by a severe act of justice, and of adopting, in the place of an unworthy son, the brave and virtuous Constantius, who at that time was governor of Dalmatia. But the elevation of Constantius was for a while deferred; and, as soon as a father's death had released Carinus from the control of fear or decency, he displayed to the Romans the extravagancies of Elagabalus, aggravated by the cruelty of Domitian.[23]

The only merit of the administration of Carinus that history could record or poetry celebrate was the uncommon splendour with which, in his own and his brother's name, he exhibited the Roman games of the theatre, the circus, and the amphitheatre. More than twenty years afterwards, when the courtiers of Diocletian represented to their frugal sovereign the fame and popularity of his munificent predecessor, he acknowledged that the reign of Carinus had indeed been a reign of pleasure. But this vain prodigality, which the prudence of Diocletian might justly despise, was enjoyed with surprise and transport by the Roman people. The oldest of the citizens, recollecting the spectacles of former days, the triumphal pomp of Probus or Aurelian, and the secular games of the emperor Philip, acknowledged that they were all surpassed by the superior magnificence of Carinus.

The spectacles of Carinus may therefore be best illustrated by the observation of some particulars, which history has condescended to relate concerning those of his predecessors. If we confine ourselves solely to the hunting of wild beasts, however we may censure the vanity of the design or the cruelty of the execution, we are obliged to confess that neither before nor since the time of the Romans so much art and expense have ever been lavished for the amusement of the people. By the order of Probus, a great quantity of large trees, torn up by the roots, were transplanted into the midst of the circus. The spacious and shady forest was immediately filled with a thousand ostriches, a thousand stags, a thousand fallow deer, and a thousand wild boars; and all this variety of game was abandoned to the riotous impetuosity of the multitude. The tragedy of the succeeding day consisted in the massacre of an hundred lions, an equal number of lionesses, two hundred leopards, and three hundred bears. The collection prepared by the younger Gordian for his triumph, and which his successor exhibited in the secular games, was less remarkable by the number than by the singularity of the animals. Twenty zebras[24] displayed their elegant forms and variegated beauty to the

[23] *The reign of Diocletian, indeed, was so long and prosperous that it must have been very unfavourable to the fame of Carinus.*

[24] *They are called* Onagri; *but the number is too inconsiderable for mere wild asses. Cuper has proved that zebras had been seen at Rome. They were brought from some island of the ocean, perhaps Madagascar.*

eyes of the Roman people. Ten elks, and as many camelopards, the loftiest and most harmless creatures that wander over the plains of Sarmatia and Æthiopia, were contrasted with thirty African hyænas, and ten Indian tigers, the most implacable savages of the torrid zone. The unoffending strength with which Nature has endowed the greater quadrupeds was admired in the rhinoceros, the hippopotamus of the Nile,[25] and a majestic troop of thirty-two elephants. While the populace gazed with stupid wonder on the splendid show, the naturalist might indeed observe the figure and properties of so many different species, transported from every part of the ancient world into the amphitheatre of Rome. But this accidental benefit which science might derive from folly is surely insufficient to justify such a wanton abuse of the public riches. There occurs, however, a single instance in the first Punic war, in which the senate wisely connected this amusement of the multitude with the interest of the state. A considerable number of elephants, taken in the defeat of the Carthaginian army, were driven through the circus by a few slaves, armed only with blunt javelins. The useful spectacle served to impress the Roman soldier with a just contempt for those unwieldy animals; and he no longer dreaded to encounter them in the ranks of war.

The hunting or exhibition of wild beasts was conducted with a magnificence suitable to a people who styled themselves the masters of the world; nor was the edifice appropriated to that entertainment less expressive of Roman greatness. Posterity admires, and will long admire, the awful remains of the amphitheatre of Titus, which so well deserved the epithet of Colossal. It was a building of an elliptic figure, five hundred and sixty-four feet in length, and four hundred and sixty-seven in breadth, founded on fourscore arches, and rising, with four successive orders of architecture, to the height of one hundred and forty feet.[26] The outside of the edifice was encrusted with marble, and decorated with statues. The slopes of the vast concave, which formed the inside, were filled and surrounded with sixty or eighty rows of seats, of marble likewise, covered with cushions, and capable of receiving with ease above fourscore thousand spectators.[27] Sixty-four *vomitories* (for by that name the doors were very aptly distinguished) poured forth the immense multitude; and the entrances, passages, and staircases were contrived with such exquisite skill, that each person, whether of the senatorial, the equestrian, or the plebeian order, arrived at his destined place without trouble or confusion. Nothing was omitted which, in any respect, could be sub-

25 Carinus gave an hippopotamus. In the later spectacles, I do not recollect any crocodiles, of which Augustus once exhibited thirty-six.

26 The height was very much exaggerated by the ancients. It reached almost to the heavens, according to Calphurnius, and surpassed the ken of human sight, according to Ammianus Marcellinus. Yet how trifling to the great pyramid of Egypt, which rises five hundred feet perpendicular!

27 According to different copies of Victor, we read seventy-seven thousand, or eighty-seven thousand spectators; but Maffei finds room on the open seats for no more than thirty-four thousand. The remainder were contained in the upper covered galleries.

servient to the convenience and pleasure of the spectators. They were protected from the sun and rain by an ample canopy, occasionally drawn over their heads. The air was continually refreshed by the playing of fountains, and profusely impregnated by the grateful scent of aromatics. In the centre of the edifice, the *arena,* or stage, was strewed with the finest sand, and successively assumed the most different forms. At one moment it seemed to rise out of the earth, like the garden of the Hesperides, and was afterwards broken into the rocks and caverns of Thrace. The subterraneous pipes conveyed an inexhaustible supply of water; and what had just before appeared a level plain, might be suddenly converted into a wide lake, covered with armed vessels, and replenished with the monsters of the deep. In the decoration of these scenes the Roman emperors displayed their wealth and liberality; and we read on various occasions that the whole furniture of the amphitheatre consisted either of silver, or of gold, or of amber. The poet who describes the games of Carinus, in the character of a shepherd attracted to the capital by the fame of their magnificence, affirms that the nets designed as a defence against the wild beasts were of gold wire; that the porticoes were gilded; and that the *belt* or circle which divided the several ranks of spectators from each other was studded with a precious Mosaic of beautiful stones.

In the midst of this glittering pageantry, the emperor Carinus, secure of his fortune, enjoyed the acclamations of the people, the flattery of his courtiers, and the songs of the poets, who, for want of a more essential merit, were reduced to celebrate the divine graces of his person. In the same hour, but at the distance of nine hundred miles from Rome, his brother expired; and a sudden revolution transferred to a stranger the sceptre of the house of Carus.

The sons of Carus never saw each other after their father's death. The arrangements which their new situation required were probably deferred till the return of the younger brother to Rome, where a triumph was decreed to the young emperors, for the glorious success of the Persian war. It is uncertain whether they intended to divide between them the administration or the provinces of the empire; but it is very unlikely that their union would have proved of any long duration. The jealousy of power must have been inflamed by the opposition of characters. In the most corrupt of times, Carinus was unworthy to live: Numerian deserved to reign in a happier period. His affable manners and gentle virtues secured him, as soon as they became known, the regard and affections of the public. He possessed the elegant accomplishments of a poet and orator, which dignify as well as adorn the humblest and the most exalted station. His eloquence, however it was applauded by the senate, was formed not so much on the model of Cicero, as on that of the modern declaimers; but in an age very far from being destitute of poetical merit, he contended for the prize with the most celebrated of his contemporaries, and still remained the friend of his rivals; a circumstance which evinces either the goodness of his heart, or the superiority of his genius.[28] But the talents of Numerian were rather of the contemplative than of the active kind. When his father's elevation reluctantly forced him from the shade of retirement, neither his temper nor his pursuits had qualified him for the command of armies. His constitution was destroyed by the hardships of the Persian war; and he had contracted, from the heat of the climate,[29] such a weakness in his eyes as obliged him, in the course of a long retreat, to confine himself to the solitude and darkness of a tent or litter. The administration of all affairs, civil as well as military, was devolved on Arrius Aper, the Prætorian præfect, who to the power of his important office added the honour of being father-in-law to Numerian. The Imperial pavilion was strictly guarded by his most trusty adherents; and, during many days, Aper delivered to the army the supposed mandates of their invisible sovereign.[30]

It was not till eight months after the death of Carus that the Roman army, returning by slow marches from the banks of the Tigris, arrived on those of the Thracian Bosphorus. The legions halted at Chalcedon in Asia, while the court passed over to Heraclea, on the European side of the Propontis. But a report soon circulated through the camp, at first in secret whispers, and at length in loud clamours, of the emperor's death, and of the presumption of his ambitious minister, who still exercised the sovereign power in the name of a prince who was no more. The impatience of the soldiers could not long support a state of suspense. With rude curiosity they broke into the Imperial tent, and discovered only the corpse of Numerian. The gradual decline of his health might have induced them to believe that his death was natural; but the concealment was interpreted as an evidence of guilt, and the measures which Aper had taken to secure his election became the immediate occasion of his ruin. Yet, even in the transport of their rage and grief, the troops observed a regular proceeding, which proves how firmly discipline had been re-established by the martial successors of Gallienus. A general assembly of the army was appointed to be held at Chalcedon, whither

[28] He won all the crowns from Nemesianus, with whom he vied in didactic poetry. The senate erected a statue to the son of Carus, with a very ambiguous inscription, "To the most powerful of orators."

[29] A more natural cause at least, than that assigned by Vopiscus, incessant weeping for his father's death.

[30] In the Persian war, Aper was suspected of a design to betray Carus.

Aper was transported in chains, as a prisoner and a criminal. A vacant tribunal was erected in the midst of the camp, and the generals and tribunes formed a great military council. They soon announced to the multitude that their choice had fallen on Diocletian, commander of the domestics or body-guards, as the person the most capable of revenging and succeeding their beloved emperor. The future fortunes of the candidate depended on the chance or conduct of the present hour. Conscious that the station which he had filled exposed him to some suspicions, Diocletian ascended the tribunal, and, raising his eyes towards the Sun, made a solemn profession of his own innocence, in the presence of that all-seeing Deity. Then, assuming the tone of a sovereign and a judge, he commanded that Aper should be brought in chains to the foot of the tribunal. "This man," said he, "is the murderer of Numerian"; and, without giving him time to enter on a dangerous justification, drew his sword, and buried it in the breast of the unfortunate præfect. A charge supported by such decisive proof was admitted without contradiction, and the legions, with repeated acclamations, acknowledged the justice and authority of the emperor Diocletian.

Before we enter upon the memorable reign of that prince, it will be proper to punish and dismiss the unworthy brother of Numerian. Carinus possessed arms and treasures sufficient to support his legal title to the empire. But his personal vices overbalanced every advantage of birth and situation. The most faithful servants of the father despised the incapacity, and dreaded the cruel arrogance, of the son. The hearts of the people were engaged in favour of his rival, and even the senate was inclined to prefer an usurper to a tyrant. The arts of Diocletian inflamed the general discontent; and the winter was employed in secret intrigues, and open preparations for a civil war. In the spring the forces of the East and of the West encountered each other in the plains of Margus, a small city of Mæsia, in the neighbourhood of the Danube. The troops, so lately returned from the Persian war, had acquired their glory at the expense of health and numbers, nor were they in a condition to contend with the unexhausted strength of the legions of Europe. Their ranks were broken, and, for a moment, Diocletian despaired of the purple and of life. But the advantage which Carinus had obtained by the valour of his soldiers he quickly lost by the infidelity of his officers. A tribune, whose wife he had seduced, seized the opportunity of revenge, and by a single blow extinguished civil discord in the blood of the adulterer.

XIII

THE REIGN OF DIOCLETIAN AND HIS THREE ASSOCIATES,
MAXIMIAN, GALERIUS, AND CONSTANTIUS · GENERAL RE-ES-
TABLISHMENT OF ORDER AND TRANQUILLITY · THE PERSIAN
WAR, VICTORY, AND TRIUMPH · THE NEW FORM OF ADMINIS-
TRATION · THE ABDICATION OF DIOCLETIAN AND MAXIMIAN

A s t h e reign of Diocletian was more illustrious than that of any of his predecessors, so was his birth more abject and obscure. The claims of merit and of violence had frequently superseded the ideal prerogatives of nobility; but a distinct line of separation was hitherto preserved between the free and the servile part of mankind. The parents of Diocletian had been slaves in the house of Anulinus, a Roman senator; nor was he himself distinguished by any other name than that which he derived from a small town in Dalmatia, from whence his mother deduced her origin.[1] It is, however, probable, that his father obtained the freedom of the family, and that he soon acquired an office of scribe, which was commonly exercised by persons of his condition. Favourable oracles, or rather the consciousness of superior merit, prompted his aspiring son to pursue the profession of arms and the hopes of fortune; and it would be extremely curious to observe the gradation of arts and accidents which enabled him in the end to fulfil those oracles, and to display that merit to the world. Diocletian was successively promoted to the government of Mæsia, the honours of the consulship, and the important command of the guards of the palace. He distinguished his abilities in the Persian war; and, after the death of Numerian, the slave, by the confession and judgment of his rivals, was declared the most worthy of the Imperial throne. The malice of religious zeal, whilst it arraigns the savage fierceness of his colleague Maximian, has affected to cast suspicions on the personal courage of the emperor Diocletian. It would not be easy to persuade us of the cowardice of a soldier of fortune,

[1] *The town seems to have been properly Doclia, from the small tribe of Illyrians; and the original name of the fortunate slave was probably Docles; he first lengthened it to the Grecian harmony of Diocles, and at length to the Roman majesty of Diocletianus. He likewise assumed the Patrician name of Valerius.*

who acquired and preserved the esteem of the legions, as well as the favour of so many warlike princes. Yet even calumny is sagacious enough to discover and to attack the most vulnerable part. The valour of Diocletian was never found inadequate to his duty, or to the occasion; but he appears not to have possessed the daring and generous spirit of a hero, who courts danger and fame, disdains artifice, and boldly challenges the allegiance of his equals. His abilities were useful rather than splendid; a vigorous mind, improved by the experience and study of mankind, dexterity and application in business; a judicious mixture of liberality and economy, of mildness and rigour; profound dissimulation under the disguise of military frankness; steadiness to pursue his ends; flexibility to vary his means; and above all the great art of submitting his own passions, as well as those of others, to the interest of his ambition, and of colouring his ambition with specious pretences of justice and public utility. Like Augustus, Diocletian may be considered as the founder of a new empire. Like the adopted son of Cæsar, he was distinguished as a statesman rather than a warrior; nor did either of those princes employ force, whenever their purpose could be effected by policy.

The victory of Diocletian was remarkable for its singular mildness. A people accustomed to applaud the clemency of the conqueror, if the usual punishments of death, exile and confiscation were inflicted with any degree of temper and equity, beheld with the most pleasing astonishment a civil war, the flames of which were extinguished in the field of battle. Diocletian received into his confidence Aristobulus, the principal minister of the house of Carus, respected the lives, the fortunes, and the dignity of his adversaries, and even continued in their respective stations the greater number of the servants of Carinus. It is not improbable that motives of prudence might assist the humanity of the artful Dalmatian; of these servants many had purchased his favour by secret treachery; in others, he esteemed their grateful fidelity to an unfortunate master. The discerning judgment of Aurelian, of Probus, and of Carus, had filled the several departments of the state and army with officers of approved merit, whose removal would have injured the public service, without promoting the interest of the successor. Such a conduct, however, displayed to the Roman world the fairest prospect of the new reign, and the emperor affected to confirm this favourable prepossession by declaring that, among all the virtues of his predecessors, he was the most ambitious of imitating the humane philosophy of Marcus Antoninus.

The first considerable action of his reign seemed to evince his sincerity as well as his moderation. After the example of Marcus, he gave himself a colleague in the person of Maximian, on whom he bestowed at first the title of Cæsar, and afterwards that of Augustus.[2] But the motives of his conduct, as well as the object of his choice, were of a very different nature from those of his admired predecessor. By investing a luxurious youth with the honours of the purple, Marcus had discharged a debt of private gratitude, at the expense, indeed, of the happiness of the state. By associating a friend and a fellow-soldier to the labours of government, Diocletian, in a time of public danger, provided for the defence both of the East and of the West. Maximian was born a peasant, and, like Aurelian, in the territory of Sirmium. Ignorant of letters,[3] careless of laws, the rusticity of his appearance and manners still betrayed in the most elevated fortune the meanness of his extraction. War was the only art which he professed. In a long course of service, he had distinguished himself on every frontier of the empire; and, though his military talents were formed to obey rather than to command, though, perhaps, he never attained the skill of a consummate general, he was capable, by his valour, constancy, and experience, of executing the most arduous undertakings. Nor were the vices of Maximian less useful to his benefactor. Insensible to pity, and fearless of consequences, he was the ready instrument of every act of cruelty which the policy of that artful prince might at once suggest and disclaim. As soon as a bloody sacrifice had been offered to prudence or to revenge, Diocletian, by his seasonable intercession, saved the remaining few whom he had never designed to punish, gently censured the severity of his stern colleague, and enjoyed the comparison of a golden and an iron age, which was universally applied to their opposite maxims of government. Notwithstanding the difference of their characters, the two emperors maintained, on the throne, that friendship which they had contracted in a private station. The haughty turbulent spirit of Maximian, so fatal afterwards to himself and to the public peace, was accustomed to respect the genius of Diocletian, and confessed the ascendant of reason over brutal violence.[4] From a motive either of pride or superstition, the two emperors assumed the titles, the one of Jovius, the other of Herculius. Whilst the motion of the world (such was the language of their venal orators) was maintained by the all-seeing wisdom of Jupiter, the invincible arm of Hercules purged the earth of monsters and tyrants.

[2] The question of the time when Maximian received the honours of Cæsar and Augustus has divided modern critics, and given occasion to a great deal of learned wrangling. I have followed M. de Tillemont, who has weighed the several reasons and difficulties with his scrupulous accuracy.

[3] In an oration delivered before him, Mamertinus expresses a doubt whether his hero, in imitating the conduct of Hannibal and Scipio, had ever heard of their names. From thence we may fairly infer that Maximian was more desirous of being considered as a soldier, than as a man of letters, and it is in this manner that we can often translate the language of flattery into that of truth.

[4] As among the Panegyrics we find orations pronounced in praise of Maximian, and others which flatter his enemies at his expense, we derive some knowledge from the contrast.

But even the omnipotence of Jovius and Herculius was insufficient to sustain the weight of the public administration. The prudence of Diocletian discovered that the empire, assailed on every side by the barbarians, required on every side the presence of a great army, and of an emperor. With this view he resolved once more to divide his unwieldy power, and, with the inferior title of *Cæsars,* to confer on two generals of approved merit an equal share of the sovereign authority. Galerius, surnamed Armentarius, from his original profession of a herdsman, and Constantius, who from his pale complexion had acquired the denomination of Chlorus, were the two persons invested with the second honours of the Imperial purple. In describing the country, extraction, and manners of Herculius, we have already delineated those of Galerius, who was often, and not improperly, styled the younger Maximian, though in many instances both of virtue and ability he appears to have possessed a manifest superiority over the elder. The birth of Constantius was less obscure than that of his colleagues. Eutropius, his father, was one of the most considerable nobles of Dardania, and his mother was the niece of the emperor Claudius.[5] Although the youth of Constantius had been spent in arms, he was endowed with a mild and amiable disposition, and the popular voice had long since acknowledged him worthy of the rank which he at last attained. To strengthen the bonds of political, by those of domestic, union, each of the emperors assumed the character of a father to one of the Cæsars, Diocletian to Galerius, and Maximian to Constantius; and each, obliging them to repudiate their former wives, bestowed his daughter in marriage on his adopted son.[6] These four princes distributed among themselves the wide extent of the Roman empire. The defence of Gaul, Spain,[7] and Britain, was intrusted to Constantius: Galerius was stationed on the banks of the Danube, as the safeguard of the Illyrian provinces. Italy and Africa were considered as the department of Maximian, and, for his peculiar portion, Diocletian reserved Thrace, Egypt, and the rich countries of Asia. Every one was sovereign within his own jurisdiction; but their united authority extended over the whole monarchy; and each of them was prepared to assist his colleagues with his counsels or presence. The Cæsars, in their exalted rank, revered the majesty of the emperors, and the three younger princes invariably acknowledged, by their gratitude and obedience, the common parent of their fortunes. The suspicious jealousy of power found not any place among them; and the singular happiness of their union has been compared to a

[5] *Julian, the grandson of Constantius, boasts that his family was derived from the warlike Mæsians. The Dardanians dwelt on the edge of Mæsia.*

[6] *Galerius married Valeria, the daughter of Diocletian; if we speak with strictness, Theodora, the wife of Constantius, was daughter only to the wife of Maximian.*

[7] *This division agrees with that of the four præfectures; yet there is some reason to doubt whether Spain was not a province of Maximian.*

chorus of music, whose harmony was regulated and maintained by the skilful hand of the first artist.

This important measure was not carried into execution till about six years after the association of Maximian, and that interval of time had not been destitute of memorable incidents. But we have preferred, for the sake of perspicuity, first to describe the more perfect form of Diocletian's government, and afterwards to relate the actions of his reign, following rather the natural order of the events than the dates of a very doubtful chronology.

The first exploit of Maximian, though it is mentioned in a few words by our imperfect writers, deserves, from its singularity, to be recorded in a history of human manners. He suppressed the peasants of Gaul, who, under the appellation of Bagaudæ,[8] had risen in a general insurrection; very similar to those which in the fourteenth century successively afflicted both France and England. It should seem that very many of those institutions, referred by an easy solution to the feudal system, are derived from the Celtic barbarians. When Cæsar subdued the Gauls, that great nation was already divided into three orders of men; the clergy, the nobility, and the common people. The first governed by superstition, the second by arms, but the third and last was not of any weight or account in their public councils. It was very natural for the Plebeians, oppressed by debt or apprehensive of injuries, to implore the protection of some powerful chief, who acquired over their persons and property the same absolute rights as, among the Greeks and Romans, a master exercised over his slaves.[9] The greatest part of the nation was gradually reduced into a state of servitude; compelled to perpetual labour on the estates of the Gallic nobles, and confined to the soil, either by the real weight of fetters, or by the no less cruel and forcible restraints of the laws. During the long series of troubles which agitated Gaul, from the reign of Gallienus to that of Diocletian, the condition of these servile peasants was peculiarly miserable; and they experienced at once the complicated tyranny of their masters, of the barbarians, of the soldiers, and of the officers of the revenue.

Their patience was at last provoked into despair. On every side they rose in multitudes, armed with rustic weapons, and with irresistible fury. The ploughman became a foot-soldier, the shepherd mounted on horseback, the deserted villages and open towns were abandoned to the flames, and the ravages of the peasants equalled those of the fiercest barbarians. They asserted the natural rights of

[8] *The general name of* Bagaudæ *(in the signification of Rebels) continued till the fifth century in Gaul. Some critics derive it from a Celtic word,* Bagad, *a tumultuous assembly.*

[9] *The Helvetian could arm for his defence a body of ten thousand slaves.*

men, but they asserted those rights with the most savage cruelty. The Gallic nobles, justly dreading their revenge, either took refuge in the fortified cities, or fled from the wild scene of anarchy. The peasants reigned without control; and two of their most daring leaders had the folly and rashness to assume the Imperial ornaments. Their power soon expired at the approach of the legions. The strength of union and discipline obtained an easy victory over a licentious and divided multitude. A severe retaliation was inflicted on the peasants who were found in arms; the affrighted remnant returned to their respective habitations, and their unsuccessful effort for freedom served only to confirm their slavery. So strong and uniform is the current of popular passions that we might almost venture, from very scanty materials, to relate the particulars of this war; but we are not disposed to believe that the principal leaders Ælianus and Amandus were Christians,[10] or to insinuate that the rebellion, as it happened in the time of Luther, was occasioned by the abuse of those benevolent principles of Christianity which inculcate the natural freedom of mankind.

[10] *The fact rests indeed on very slight authority, a life of St. Babolinus, which is probably of the seventh century.*

Maximian had no sooner recovered Gaul from the hands of the peasants, than he lost Britain by the usurpation of Carausius. Ever since the rash but successful enterprise of the Franks under the reign of Probus, their daring countrymen had constructed squadrons of light brigantines, in which they incessantly ravaged the provinces adjacent to the ocean.[11] To repel their desultory incursions, it was found necessary to create a naval power; and the judicious measure was pursued with prudence and vigour. Gessoriacum or Boulogne, in the streights of the British channel, was chosen by the emperor for the station of the Roman fleet; and the command of it was intrusted to Carausius, a Menapian of the meanest origin, but who had long signalized his skill as a pilot, and his valour as a soldier. The integrity of the new admiral corresponded not with his abilities. When the German pirates sailed from their own harbours, he connived at their passage, but he diligently intercepted their return, and appropriated to his own use an ample share of the spoil which they had acquired. The wealth of Carausius was, on this occasion, very justly considered as an evidence of his guilt; and Maximian had already given orders for his death. But the crafty Menapian foresaw and prevented the severity of the emperor. By his liberality he had attached to his fortunes the fleet which he commanded, and secured the barbarians in his interest. From the port of Boulogne he sailed over to Britain, persuaded the legion and the

[11] *Aurelius Victor calls them Germans. Eutropius gives them the name of Saxons. Eutropius lived in the ensuing century, and seems to use the language of his own times.*

[12] *Britain at this time was secure, and slightly guarded.*

[13] *The orator Eumenius wished to exalt the glory of the hero (Constantius), with the importance of the conquest. Notwithstanding our laudable partiality for our native country, it is difficult to conceive that in the beginning of the fourth century England deserved all these commendations. A century and a half before, it hardly paid its own establishment.*

[14] *As a great number of medals of Carausius are still preserved, he is become a very favourite object of antiquarian curiosity, and every circumstance of his life and actions has been investigated with sagacious accuracy. Dr. Stukely in particular has devoted a large volume to the British emperor. I have used his materials, and rejected most of his fanciful conjectures.*

[15] *When Mamertinus pronounced his first Panegyric, the naval preparations of Maximian were completed: and the orator presaged an assured victory. His silence in the second Panegyric might alone inform us that the expedition had not succeeded.*

auxiliaries which guarded that island to embrace his party, and boldly assuming, with the Imperial purple, the title of Augustus, defied the justice and the arms of his injured sovereign.[12]

When Britain was thus dismembered from the empire, its importance was sensibly felt, and its loss sincerely lamented. The Romans celebrated, and perhaps magnified, the extent of that noble island, provided on every side with convenient harbours; the temperature of the climate, and the fertility of the soil, alike adapted for the production of corn or of vines; the valuable minerals with which it abounded; its rich pastures covered with innumerable flocks, and its woods free from wild beasts or venomous serpents. Above all, they regretted the large amount of the revenue of Britain, whilst they confessed that such a province well deserved to become the seat of an independent monarchy.[13] During the space of seven years, it was possessed by Carausius; and fortune continued propitious to a rebellion supported with courage and ability. The British emperor defended the frontiers of his dominions against the Caledonians of the North, invited from the continent a great number of skilful artists, and displayed, on a variety of coins that are still extant, his taste and opulence. Born on the confines of the Franks, he courted the friendship of that formidable people, by the flattering imitation of their dress and manners. The bravest of their youth he enlisted among his land or sea forces; and, in return for their useful alliance, he communicated to the barbarians the dangerous knowledge of military and naval arts. Carausius still preserved the possession of Boulogne and the adjacent country. His fleets rode triumphant in the channel, commanded the mouths of the Seine and of the Rhine, boldly ravaged the coasts of the ocean, and diffused, beyond the Columns of Hercules, the terror of his name. Under his command, Britain, destined in a future age to obtain the empire of the sea, already assumed its natural and respectable station of a maritime power.[14]

By seizing the fleet of Boulogne, Carausius had deprived his master of the means of pursuit and revenge. And, when, after vast expense of time and labour, a new armament was launched into the water,[15] the Imperial troops, unaccustomed to that element, were easily baffled and defeated by the veteran sailors of the usurper. This disappointed effort was soon productive of a treaty of peace. Diocletian and his colleague, who justly dreaded the enterprising spirit of Carausius, resigned to him the sovereignty of Britain, and reluctantly admitted their perfidious servant to a participation of the

THE TEMPLE OF
ANTONINUS & FAUSTINA

"Faustina was represented in her temples, with the attributes of Juno, Venus, and Ceres; and it was decreed that, on the day of their nuptials, the youth of either sex should pay their vows before the altar of their chaste patroness."

THE TEMPLE OF ANTONINUS AND FAUSTINA AND THE
CHURCH OF SAN LORENZO IN MIRANDA DE SPECIALI

Imperial honours.[16] But the adoption of the two Cæsars restored new vigour to the Roman arms; and, while the Rhine was guarded by the presence of Maximian, his brave associate, Constantius, assumed the conduct of the British war. His first enterprise was against the important place of Boulogne. A stupendous mole, raised across the entrance of the harbour, intercepted all hopes of relief. The town surrendered after an obstinate defence; and a considerable part of the naval strength of Carausius fell into the hands of the besiegers. During the three years, which Constantius employed in preparing a fleet adequate to the conquest of Britain, he secured the coast of Gaul, invaded the country of the Franks, and deprived the usurper of the assistance of those powerful allies.

Before the preparations were finished, Constantius received the intelligence of the tyrant's death, and it was considered as a sure presage of the approaching victory. The servants of Carausius imitated the example of treason which he had given. He was murdered by his first minister Allectus, and the assassin succeeded to his power and to his danger. But he possessed not equal abilities either to exercise the one, or to repel the other. He beheld, with anxious terror, the opposite shores of the continent, already filled with arms, with troops, and with vessels; for Constantius had very prudently divided his forces, that he might likewise divide the attention and resistance of the enemy. The attack was at length made by the principal squadron, which, under the command of the præfect Asclepiodotus, an officer of distinguished merit, had been assembled in the mouth of the Seine. So imperfect in those times was the art of navigation that orators have celebrated the daring courage of the Romans, who ventured to set sail with a side-wind, and on a stormy day. The weather proved favourable to their enterprise. Under the cover of a thick fog, they escaped the fleet of Allectus, which had been stationed off the Isle of Wight to receive them, landed in safety on some part of the western coast, and convinced the Britons that a superiority of naval strength will not always protect their country from a foreign invasion. Asclepiodotus had no sooner disembarked the Imperial troops than he set fire to his ships; and, as the expedition proved fortunate, his heroic conduct was universally admired. The usurper had posted himself near London, to expect the formidable attack of Constantius, who commanded in person the fleet of Boulogne; but the descent of a new enemy required his immediate presence in the West. He performed this long march in so precipitate a manner that he encountered the whole force of the

[16] *Aurelius Victor, Eutropius, and the medals inform us of the temporary reconciliation: though I will not presume to insert the identical articles of the treaty.*

præfect with a small body of harassed and disheartened troops. The engagement was soon terminated by the total defeat and death of Allectus; a single battle, as it has often happened, decided the fate of this great island; and, when Constantius landed on the shores of Kent, he found them covered with obedient subjects. Their acclamations were loud and unanimous; and the virtues of the conqueror may induce us to believe that they sincerely rejoiced in a revolution which, after a separation of ten years, restored Britain to the body of the Roman empire.

Britain had none but domestic enemies to dread; and, as long as the governors preserved their fidelity, and the troops their discipline, the incursions of the naked savages of Scotland or Ireland could never materially affect the safety of the province. The peace of the continent, and the defence of the principal rivers which bounded the empire, were objects of far greater difficulty and importance. The policy of Diocletian, which inspired the councils of his associates, provided for the public tranquillity, by encouraging a spirit of dissension among the barbarians, and by strengthening the fortifications of the Roman limit. In the East he fixed a line of camps from Egypt to the Persian dominions, and, for every camp, he instituted an adequate number of stationary troops, commanded by their respective officers, and supplied with every kind of arms, from the new arsenals which he had formed at Antioch, Emesa, and Damascus. Nor was the precaution of the emperor less watchful against the well-known valour of the barbarians of Europe. From the mouth of the Rhine to that of the Danube, the ancient camps, towns, and citadels, were diligently re-established, and, in the most exposed places, new ones were skilfully constructed; the strictest vigilance was introduced among the garrisons of the frontier, and every expedient was practised that could render the long chain of fortifications firm and impenetrable. A barrier so respectable was seldom violated, and the barbarians often turned against each other their disappointed rage. The Goths, the Vandals, the Gepidæ, the Burgundians, the Alemanni, wasted each other's strength by destructive hostilities: and whosoever vanquished, they vanquished the enemies of Rome. The subjects of Diocletian enjoyed the bloody spectacle, and congratulated each other that the mischiefs of civil war were now experienced only by the barbarians.

Notwithstanding the policy of Diocletian, it was impossible to maintain an equal and undisturbed tranquillity during a reign of twenty years, and along a frontier of many hundred miles. Sometimes the barbarians suspended their domestic animosities, and the vigilance of the garrisons sometimes gave a passage to their strength or dexterity. Whenever the provinces were invaded, Diocletian conducted himself with that calm dignity which he always affected or possessed; reserved his presence for such occasions as were worthy of his interposition, never exposed his person or reputation to any unnecessary danger, ensured his success by every means that prudence could suggest, and displayed, with ostentation, the consequences of his victory. In wars of a more difficult nature, and more doubtful event, he employed the rough valour of Maximian, and that faithful soldier was content to ascribe his own victories to the wise counsels and auspicious influence of his benefactor. But, after the adoption of the two Cæsars, the emperors, themselves retiring to a less laborious scene of action, devolved on their adopted sons the defence of the Danube and of the Rhine. The vigilant Galerius was never reduced to the necessity of vanquishing an army of barbarians on the Roman territory. The brave and active Constantius delivered Gaul from a very furious inroad of the Alemanni; and his victories of Langres and Vindonissa appear to have been actions of considerable danger and merit. As he traversed the open country with a feeble guard he was encompassed on a sudden by the superior multitude of the enemy. He retreated with difficulty towards Langres; but, in the general consternation, the citizens refused to open their gates, and the wounded prince was drawn up the wall by the means of a rope. But on the news of his distress the Roman troops hastened from all sides to his relief, and before the evening he had satisfied his honour and revenge by the slaughter of six thousand Alemanni.[17] From the monuments of those times, the obscure traces of several other victories over the barbarians of Sarmatia and Germany might possibly be collected; but the tedious search would not be rewarded either with amusement or with instruction.

The conduct which the emperor Probus had adopted in the disposal of the vanquished was imitated by Diocletian and his associates. The captive barbarians, exchanging death for slavery, were distributed among the provincials, and assigned to those districts (in Gaul, the territories of Amiens, Beauvais, Cambray, Treves, Langres, and Troyes, are particularly specified) which had been depopulated by the calamities of war. They were usefully employed as shepherds and husbandmen, but were denied the exercise of arms, except when it was found expedient to enrol them in the military service. Nor did the emperors refuse the property of lands,

[17] *In the Greek text of Eusebius, we read six thousand, a number which I have preferred to the sixty thousand of Jerome, Orosius, Eutropius, and his Greek translator Pæanius.*

with a less servile tenure, to such of the barbarians as solicited the protection of Rome. They granted a settlement to several colonies of the Carpi, the Bastarnæ, and the Sarmatians; and, by a dangerous indulgence, permitted them in some measure to retain their national manners and independence.[18] Among the provincials, it was a subject of flattering exultation, that the barbarian, so lately an object of terror, now cultivated their lands, drove their cattle to the neighbouring fair, and contributed by his labour to the public plenty. They congratulated their masters on the powerful accession of subjects and soldiers; but they forgot to observe that multitudes of secret enemies, insolent from favour, or desperate from oppression, were introduced into the heart of the empire.

While the Cæsars exercised their valour on the banks of the Rhine and Danube, the presence of the emperors was required on the southern confines of the Roman world. From the Nile to Mount Atlas, Africa was in arms. A confederacy of five Moorish nations issued from their deserts to invade the peaceful provinces. Julian had assumed the purple at Carthage,[19] Achilleus at Alexandria; and even the Blemmyes renewed, or rather continued, their incursions into the Upper Egypt. Scarcely any circumstances have been preserved of the exploits of Maximian in the western parts of Africa; but it appears, by the event, that the progress of his arms was rapid and decisive, that he vanquished the fiercest barbarians of Mauritania, and that he removed them from the mountains, whose inaccessible strength had inspired their inhabitants with a lawless confidence, and habituated them to a life of rapine and violence. Diocletian, on his side, opened the campaign in Egypt by the siege of Alexandria, cut off the aqueducts which conveyed the waters of the Nile into every quarter of that immense city, and, rendering his camp impregnable to the sallies of the besieged multitude, he pushed his reiterated attacks with caution and vigour. After a siege of eight months, Alexandria, wasted by the sword and by fire, implored the clemency of the conqueror; but it experienced the full extent of his severity. Many thousands of the citizens perished in a promiscuous slaughter, and there were few obnoxious persons in Egypt who escaped a sentence either of death or at least of exile. The fate of Busiris and of Coptos was still more melancholy than that of Alexandria; those proud cities, the former distinguished by its antiquity, the latter enriched by the passage of the Indian trade, were utterly destroyed by the arms and by the severe order of Diocletian.[20] The character of the Egyptian nation, insensible to kind-

---

[18] *There was a settlement of the Sarmatians in the neighbourhood of Treves, which seems to have been deserted by those lazy barbarians. There was a town of the Carpi in the Lower Mœsia.*

[19] *After this defeat, Julian stabbed himself with a dagger, and immediately leaped into the flames.*

[20] *Eusebius places their destruction several years sooner, and at a time when Egypt itself was in a state of rebellion against the Romans.*

ness, but extremely susceptible of fear, could alone justify this excessive rigour. The seditions of Alexandria had often affected the tranquillity and subsistence of Rome itself. Since the usurpation of Firmus, the province of Upper Egypt, incessantly relapsing into rebellion, had embraced the alliance of the savages of Æthiopia. The number of the Blemmyes, scattered between the island of Meroe and the Red Sea, was very inconsiderable, their disposition was unwarlike, their weapons rude and inoffensive. Yet in the public disorders these barbarians, whom antiquity, shocked with the deformity of their figure, had almost excluded from the human species, presumed to rank themselves among the enemies of Rome. Such had been the unworthy allies of the Egyptians; and, while the attention of the state was engaged in more serious wars, their vexatious inroads might again harass the repose of the province. With a view of opposing to the Blemmyes a suitable adversary, Diocletian persuaded the Nobatæ, or people of Nubia, to remove from their ancient habitations in the deserts of Libya, and resigned to them an extensive but unprofitable territory, above Syene and the cataracts of the Nile, with the stipulation that they should ever respect and guard the frontier of the empire. The treaty long subsisted; and till the establishment of Christianity introduced stricter notions of religious worship, it was annually ratified by a solemn sacrifice in the isle of Elephantine, in which the Romans, as well as the barbarians, adored the same visible or invisible powers of the universe.

At the same time that Diocletian chastised the past crimes of the Egyptians, he provided for their future safety and happiness by many wise regulations, which were confirmed and enforced under the succeeding reigns.[21] One very remarkable edict, which he published, instead of being condemned as the effect of jealous tyranny deserves to be applauded as an act of prudence and humanity. He caused a diligent inquiry to be made "for all the ancient books which treated of the admirable art of making gold and silver, and without pity committed them to the flames; apprehensive, as we are assured, lest the opulence of the Egyptians should inspire them with confidence to rebel against the empire." But, if Diocletian had been convinced of the reality of that valuable art, far from extinguishing the memory, he would have converted the operation of it to the benefit of the public revenue. It is much more likely that his good sense discovered to him the folly of such magnificent pretensions, and that he was desirous of preserving the reason and fortunes of his subjects from the mischievous pursuit. It may be re-

[21] *He fixed the public allowance of corn for the people of Alexandria, at two millions of medimni; about four hundred thousand quarters.*

marked that these ancient books, so liberally ascribed to Pythagoras, to Solomon, or to Hermes, were the pious frauds of more recent adepts. The Greeks were inattentive either to the use or to the abuse of chymistry. In that immense register where Pliny has deposited the discoveries, the arts, and the errors of mankind, there is not the least mention of the transmutation of metals; and the persecution of Diocletian is the first authentic event in the history of alchymy. The conquest of Egypt by the Arabs diffused that vain science over the globe. Congenial to the avarice of the human heart, it was studied in China as in Europe, with equal eagerness, and with equal success. The darkness of the middle ages ensured a favourable reception to every tale of wonder, and the revival of learning gave new vigour to hope, and suggested more specious arts of deception. Philosophy, with the aid of experience, has at length banished the study of alchymy; and the present age, however desirous of riches, is content to seek them by the humbler means of commerce and industry.

The reduction of Egypt was immediately followed by the Persian war. It was reserved for the reign of Diocletian to vanquish that powerful nation, and to extort a confession from the successors of Artaxerxes, of the superior majesty of the Roman empire.

We have observed, under the reign of Valerian, that Armenia was subdued by the perfidy and the arms of the Persians, and that, after the assassination of Chosroes, his son Tiridates, the infant heir of the monarchy, was saved by the fidelity of his friends, and educated under the protection of the emperors. Tiridates derived from his exile such advantages as he could never have attained on the throne of Armenia; the early knowledge of adversity, of mankind, and of the Roman discipline. He signalized his youth by deeds of valour, and displayed a matchless dexterity, as well as strength, in every martial exercise, and even in the less honourable contests of the Olympian games.[22] Those qualities were more nobly exerted in the defence of his benefactor Licinius.[23] That officer, in the sedition which occasioned the death of Probus, was exposed to the most imminent danger, and the enraged soldiers were forcing their way into his tent, when they were checked by the single arm of the Armenian prince. The gratitude of Tiridates contributed soon afterwards to his restoration. Licinius was in every station the friend and companion of Galerius, and the merit of Galerius, long before he was raised to the dignity of Cæsar, had been known and esteemed by Diocletian. In the third year of that emperor's reign, Tiridates

[22] See the education and strength of Tiridates in the Armenian history of Moses of Chorene. He could seize two wild bulls by the horns, and break them off with his hands.

[23] If we give credit to the younger Victor, who supposes that, in the year 323, Licinius was only sixty years of age, he could scarcely be the same person as the patron of Tiridates; but we know from much better authority (Eusebius) that Licinius was at that time in the last period of old age: sixteen years before, he is represented with grey hairs, and as the contemporary of Galerius. Licinius was probably born about the year 250.

was invested with the kingdom of Armenia. The justice of the measure was not less evident than its expediency. It was time to rescue from the usurpation of the Persian monarch an important territory, which, since the reign of Nero, had been always granted under the protection of the empire to a younger branch of the house of Arsaces.

When Tiridates appeared on the frontiers of Armenia, he was received with an unfeigned transport of joy and loyalty. During twenty-six years, the country had experienced the real and imaginary hardships of a foreign yoke. The Persian monarchs had adorned their new conquest with magnificent buildings; but those monuments had been erected at the expense of the people, and were abhorred as badges of slavery. The apprehension of a revolt had inspired the most rigorous precautions: oppression had been aggravated by insult, and the consciousness of the public hatred had been productive of every measure that could render it still more implacable. We have already remarked the intolerant spirit of the Magian religion. The statues of the deified kings of Armenia, and the sacred images of the sun and moon, were broke in pieces by the zeal of the conqueror; and the perpetual fire of Ormusd was kindled and preserved upon an altar erected on the summit of Mount Bagavan.[24] It was natural that a people exasperated by so many injuries should arm with zeal in the cause of their independence, their religion, and their hereditary sovereign. The torrent bore down every obstacle, and the Persian garrison retreated before its fury. The nobles of Armenia flew to the standard of Tiridates, all alleging their past merit, offering their future service, and soliciting from the new king those honours and rewards from which they had been excluded with disdain under the foreign government. The command of the army was bestowed on Artavasdes, whose father had saved the infancy of Tiridates, and whose family had been massacred for that generous action. The brother of Artavasdes obtained the government of a province. One of the first military dignities was conferred on the satrap Otas, a man of singular temperance and fortitude, who presented to the king his sister and a considerable treasure, both of which, in a sequestered fortress, Otas had preserved from violation. Among the Armenian nobles appeared an ally, whose fortunes are too remarkable to pass unnoticed. His name was Mamgo, his origin was Scythian, and the horde which acknowledged his authority had encamped a very few years before on the skirts of the Chinese empire,[25] which at that time extended

[24] *The statues had been erected by Valarsaces, who reigned in Armenia about 130 years before Christ, and was the first king of the family of Arsaces.*

[25] *In the Armenian history as well as in the Geography China is called Zenia, or Zenastan. It is characterized by the production of silk, by the opulence of the natives, and by their love of peace, above all the other nations of the earth.*

as far as the neighbourhood of Sogdiana.[26] Having incurred the displeasure of his master, Mamgo, with his followers, retired to the banks of the Oxus, and implored the protection of Sapor. The emperor of China claimed the fugitive, and alleged the rights of sovereignty. The Persian monarch pleaded the laws of hospitality, and with some difficulty avoided a war, by the promise that he would banish Mamgo to the uttermost parts of the West; a punishment, as he described it, not less dreadful than death itself. Armenia was chosen for the place of exile, and a large district was assigned to the Scythian horde, on which they might feed their flocks and herds, and remove their encampment from one place to another according to the different seasons of the year. They were employed to repel the invasion of Tiridates; but their leader, after weighing the obligations and injuries which he had received from the Persian monarch, resolved to abandon his party. The Armenian prince, who was well acquainted with the merit as well as power of Mamgo, treated him with distinguished respect; and, by admitting him into his confidence, acquired a brave and faithful servant, who contributed very effectually to his restoration.

For a while, fortune appeared to favour the enterprising valour of Tiridates. He not only expelled the enemies of his family and country from the whole extent of Armenia, but in the prosecution of his revenge he carried his arms, or at least his incursions, into the heart of Assyria. The historian who has preserved the name of Tiridates from oblivion celebrates, with a degree of national enthusiasm, his personal prowess; and, in the true spirit of eastern romance, describes the giants and the elephants that fell beneath his invincible arm. It is from other information that we discover the distracted state of the Persian monarchy, to which the king of Armenia was indebted for some part of his advantages. The throne was disputed by the ambition of contending brothers; and Hormuz, after exerting without success the strength of his own party, had recourse to the dangerous assistance of the barbarians who inhabited the banks of the Caspian Sea.[27] The civil war was, however, soon terminated, either by a victory or by a reconciliation; and Narses, who was universally acknowledged as king of Persia, directed his whole force against the foreign enemy. The contest then became too unequal; nor was the valour of the hero able to withstand the power of the monarch. Tiridates, a second time expelled from the throne of Armenia, once more took refuge in the court of the emperors. Narses soon re-established his authority over the revolted province; and, loudly complaining of the protection afforded by the Romans to rebels and fugitives, aspired to the conquest of the East.

Neither prudence nor honour could permit the emperors to forsake the cause of the Armenian king, and it was resolved to exert the force of the empire in the Persian war. Diocletian, with the calm dignity which he constantly assumed, fixed his own station in the city of Antioch, from whence he prepared and directed the military operations.[28] The conduct of the legions was intrusted to the intrepid valour of Galerius, who, for that important purpose, was removed from the banks of the Danube to those of the Euphrates. The armies soon encountered each other in the plains of Mesopotamia, and two battles were fought with various and doubtful success: but the third engagement was of a more decisive nature; and the Roman army received a total overthrow, which is attributed to the rashness of Galerius, who, with an inconsiderable body of troops, attacked the innumerable host of the Persians. But the consideration of the country that was the scene of action may suggest another reason for his defeat. The same ground, on which Galerius was vanquished, had been rendered memorable by the death of Crassus and the slaughter of ten legions. It was a plain of more than sixty miles, which extended from the hills of Carrhæ to the Euphrates; a smooth and barren surface of sandy desert, without a hillock, without a tree, and without a spring of fresh water. The steady infantry of the Romans, fainting with heat and thirst, could neither hope for victory, if they preserved their ranks, nor break their ranks without exposing themselves to the most imminent danger. In this situation, they were gradually encompassed by the superior numbers, harassed by the rapid evolutions, and destroyed by the arrows, of the barbarian cavalry. The king of Armenia had signalized his valour in the battle, and acquired personal glory by the public misfortune. He was pursued as far as the Euphrates; his horse was wounded, and it appeared impossible for him to escape the victorious enemy. In this extremity, Tiridates embraced the only refuge which he saw before him: he dismounted and plunged into the stream. His armour was heavy, the river very deep, and in those parts at least half a mile in breadth; yet such was his strength and dexterity that he reached in safety the opposite bank. With regard to the Roman general, we are ignorant of the circumstances of his escape; but, when he returned to Antioch, Diocletian received him, not with the tenderness of a friend and colleague, but with the indignation of an offended sov-

[28] *We may readily believe that Lactantius ascribes to cowardice the conduct of Diocletian. Julian, in his oration, says that he remained with all the forces of the empire; a very hyperbolical expression.*

ereign. The haughtiest of men, clothed in his purple, but humbled by the sense of his fault and misfortune, was obliged to follow the emperor's chariot above a mile on foot, and to exhibit before the whole court the spectacle of his disgrace.

As soon as Diocletian had indulged his private resentment, and asserted the majesty of supreme power, he yielded to the submissive entreaties of the Cæsar, and permitted him to retrieve his own honour as well as that of the Roman arms. In the room of the unwarlike troops of Asia, which had most probably served in the first expedition, a second army was drawn from the veterans and new levies of the Illyrian frontier, and a considerable body of Gothic auxiliaries were taken into the Imperial pay. At the head of a chosen army of twenty-five thousand men, Galerius again passed the Euphrates; but, instead of exposing his legions in the open plains of Mesopotamia, he advanced through the mountains of Armenia, where he found the inhabitants devoted to his cause, and the country as favourable to the operations of infantry as it was inconvenient for the motions of cavalry. Adversity had confirmed the Roman discipline, whilst the barbarians, elated by success, were become so negligent and remiss, that, in the moment when they least expected it, they were surprised by the active conduct of Galerius, who, attended only by two horsemen, had, with his own eyes, secretly examined the state and position of their camp. A surprise, especially in the night-time, was for the most part fatal to a Persian army. "Their horses were tied, and generally shackled, to prevent their running away; and, if an alarm happened, a Persian had his housing to fix, his horse to bridle, and his corslet to put on, before he could mount." [29] On this occasion, the impetuous attack of Galerius spread disorder and dismay over the camp of the barbarians. A slight resistance was followed by a dreadful carnage, and, in the general confusion, the wounded monarch (for Narses commanded his armies in person) fled towards the deserts of Media. His sumptuous tents, and those of his satraps, afforded an immense booty to the conqueror; and an incident is mentioned, which proves the rustic but martial ignorance of the legions in the elegant superfluities of life. A bag of shining leather, filled with pearls, fell into the hands of a private soldier; he carefully preserved the bag, but he threw away its contents, judging that whatever was of no use could not possibly be of any value. The principal loss of Narses was of a much more affecting nature. Several of his wives, his sisters, and children, who had attended the army, were made captives in the

[29] *For that reason, the Persian cavalry encamped sixty stadia from the enemy.*

defeat. But, though the character of Galerius had in general very little affinity with that of Alexander, he imitated, after his victory, the amiable behaviour of the Macedonian towards the family of Darius. The wives and children of Narses were protected from violence and rapine, conveyed to a place of safety, and treated with every mark of respect and tenderness that was due, from a generous enemy, to their age, their sex, and their royal dignity.[30]

While the East anxiously expected the decision of this great contest, the emperor Diocletian, having assembled in Syria a strong army of observation, displayed from a distance the resources of the Roman power, and reserved himself for any future emergency of the war. On the intelligence of the victory, he condescended to advance towards the frontier, with a view of moderating, by his presence and counsels, the pride of Galerius. The interview of the Roman princes at Nisibis was accompanied with every expression of respect on one side, and of esteem on the other. It was in that city that they soon afterwards gave audience to the ambassador of the Great King. The power, or at least the spirit, of Narses, had been broken by his last defeat; and he considered an immediate peace as the only means that could stop the progress of the Roman arms. He dispatched Apharban, a servant who possessed his favour and confidence, with a commission to negotiate a treaty, or rather to receive whatever conditions the conqueror should impose. Apharban opened the conference by expressing his master's gratitude for the generous treatment of his family, and by soliciting the liberty of those illustrious captives. He celebrated the valour of Galerius, without degrading the reputation of Narses, and thought it no dishonour to confess the superiority of the victorious Cæsar over a monarch who had surpassed in glory all the princes of his race. Notwithstanding the justice of the Persian cause, he was empowered to submit the present differences to the decision of the emperors themselves; convinced as he was, that, in the midst of prosperity, they would not be unmindful of the vicissitudes of fortune. Apharban concluded his discourse in the style of Eastern allegory, by observing that the Roman and Persian monarchies were the two eyes of the world, which would remain imperfect and mutilated, if either of them should be put out.

"It well becomes the Persians," replied Galerius, with a transport of fury, which seemed to convulse his whole frame, "it well becomes the Persians to expatiate on the vicissitudes of fortune and calmly to read us lectures on the virtues of moderation. Let them

[30] *The Persians confessed the Roman superiority in morals as well as in arms. But this respect and gratitude of enemies is very seldom to be found in their own accounts.*

remember their own *moderation* towards the unhappy Valerian. They vanquished him by fraud, they treated him with indignity. They detained him till the last moment of his life in shameful captivity, and, after his death, they exposed his body to perpetual ignominy." Softening, however, his tone, Galerius insinuated to the ambassador that it had never been the practice of the Romans to trample on a prostrate enemy; and that on this occasion they should consult their own dignity rather than the Persian merit. He dismissed Apharban with a hope that Narses would soon be informed on what conditions he might obtain, from the clemency of the emperors, a lasting peace, and the restoration of his wives and children. In this conference we may discover the fierce passions of Galerius, as well as his deference to the superior wisdom and authority of Diocletian. The ambition of the former grasped at the conquest of the East and had proposed to reduce Persia into the state of a province. The prudence of the latter, who adhered to the moderate policy of Augustus and the Antonines, embraced the favourable opportunity of terminating a successful war by an honourable and advantageous peace.

In pursuance of their promise, the emperors soon afterwards appointed Sicorius Probus, one of their secretaries, to acquaint the Persian court with their final resolution. As the minister of peace, he was received with every mark of politeness and friendship; but, under the pretence of allowing him the necessary repose after so long a journey, the audience of Probus was deferred from day to day; and he attended the slow motions of the king, till at length he was admitted to his presence, near the river Asprudus in Media. The secret motive of Narses, in this delay, had been to collect such a military force as might enable him, though sincerely desirous of peace, to negotiate with the greater weight and dignity. Three persons only assisted at this important conference; the minister Apharban, the præfect of the guards, and an officer who had commanded on the Armenian frontier.[31] The first condition, proposed by the ambassador, is not at present of a very intelligible nature; that the city of Nisibis might be established for the place of mutual exchange, or, as we should formerly have termed it, for the staple of trade between the two empires. There is no difficulty in conceiving the intention of the Roman princes to improve their revenue by some restraints upon commerce; but, as Nisibis was situated within their own dominions, and as they were masters both of the imports and exports, it should seem that such restraints were the objects of an

[31] *He had been governor of Sumium. This province lay to the east of Mount Ararat.*

internal law rather than of a foreign treaty. To render them more effectual, some stipulations were probably required on the side of the king of Persia, which appeared so very repugnant either to his interest or to his dignity, that Narses could not be persuaded to subscribe them. As this was the only article to which he refused his consent, it was no longer insisted on; and the emperors either suffered the trade to flow in its natural channels, or contented themselves with such restrictions as it depended on their own authority to establish.

As soon as this difficulty was removed, a solemn peace was concluded and ratified between the two nations. The conditions of a treaty so glorious to the empire, and so necessary to Persia, may deserve a more peculiar attention, as the history of Rome presents very few transactions of a similar nature; most of her wars having either been terminated by absolute conquest, or waged against barbarians ignorant of the use of letters. I. The Aboras, or, as it is called by Xenophon, the Araxes, was fixed as the boundary between the two monarchies.[32] That river which rose near the Tigris, was increased, a few miles below Nisibis, by the little stream of the Mygdonius, passed under the walls of Singara, and fell into the Euphrates at Circesium, a frontier town, which, by the care of Diocletian, was very strongly fortified. Mesopotamia, the object of so many wars, was ceded to the empire; and the Persians, by this treaty, renounced all pretensions to that great province. II. They relinquished to the Romans five provinces beyond the Tigris. Their situation formed a very useful barrier, and their natural strength was soon improved by art and military skill. Four of these, to the north of the river, were districts of obscure fame and inconsiderable extent: Intiline, Zabdicene, Arzanene, and Moxoene; but, on the east of the Tigris, the empire acquired the large and mountainous territory of Carduene, the ancient seat of the Carduchians, who preserved for many ages their manly freedom in the heart of the despotic monarchies of Asia. The ten thousand Greeks traversed their country, after a painful march, or rather engagement, of seven days; and it is confessed by their leader, in his incomparable relation of the retreat, that they suffered more from the arrows of the Carduchians than from the power of the Great King.[33] Their posterity, the Curds, with very little alteration either of name or manners, acknowledged the nominal sovereignty of the Turkish sultan. III. It is almost needless to observe that Tiridates, the faithful ally of Rome, was restored to the throne of his fathers, and that the

[32] *By an error of the geographer Ptolemy, the position of Singara is removed from the Aboras to the Tigris, which may have produced the mistake of Peter in assigning the latter river for the boundary, instead of the former. The line of the Roman frontier traversed, but never followed, the course of the Tigris.*

[33] *Their bows were three cubits in length, their arrows two; they rolled down stones that were each a waggon load. The Greeks found a great many villages in that rude country.*

rights of the Imperial supremacy were fully asserted and secured. The limits of Armenia were extended as far as the fortress of Sintha in Media, and this increase of dominion was not so much an act of liberality as of justice. Of the provinces already mentioned beyond the Tigris, the four first had been dismembered by the Parthians from the crown of Armenia; and, when the Romans acquired the possession of them, they stipulated, at the expense of the usurpers, an ample compensation, which invested their ally with the extensive and fertile country of Atropatene. Its principal city, in the same situation perhaps as the modern Tauris, was frequently honoured with the residence of Tiridates; and, as it sometimes bore the name of Ecbatana, he imitated, in the buildings and fortifications, the splendid capital of the Medes. IV. The country of Iberia was barren, its inhabitants rude and savage. But they were accustomed to the use of arms, and they separated from the empire barbarians much fiercer and more formidable than themselves. The narrow defiles of Mount Caucasus were in their hands, and it was in their choice either to admit or to exclude the wandering tribes of Sarmatia, whenever a rapacious spirit urged them to penetrate into the richer climates of the South. The nomination of the kings of Iberia, which was resigned by the Persian monarch to the emperors, contributed to the strength and security of the Roman power in Asia. The East enjoyed a profound tranquillity during forty years; and the treaty between the rival monarchies was strictly observed till the death of Tiridates; when a new generation, animated with different views and different passions, succeeded to the government of the world; and the grandson of Narses undertook a long and memorable war against the princes of the house of Constantine.

The arduous work of rescuing the distressed empire from tyrants and barbarians had now been completely achieved by a succession of Illyrian peasants. As soon as Diocletian entered into the twentieth year of his reign, he celebrated that memorable æra, as well as the success of his arms, by the pomp of a Roman triumph. Maximian, the equal partner of his power, was his only companion in the glory of that day. The two Cæsars had fought and conquered, but the merit of their exploits was ascribed, according to the rigour of ancient maxims, to the auspicious influence of their fathers and emperors.[34] The triumph of Diocletian and Maximian was less magnificent, perhaps, than those of Aurelian and Probus, but it was dignified by several circumstances of superior fame and good fortune. Africa and Britain, the Rhine, the Danube, and the Nile, furnished

[34] *At the time of the Vicennalia, Galerius seems to have kept his station on the Danube.*

their respective trophies; but the most distinguished ornament was of a more singular nature, a Persian victory followed by an important conquest. The representations of rivers, mountains, and provinces were carried before the Imperial car. The images of the captive wives, the sisters, and the children of the Great King afforded a new and grateful spectacle to the vanity of the people.[35] In the eyes of posterity this triumph is remarkable by a distinction of a less honourable kind. It was the last that Rome ever beheld. Soon after this period, the emperors ceased to vanquish, and Rome ceased to be the capital of the empire.

The spot on which Rome was founded had been consecrated by ancient ceremonies and imaginary miracles. The presence of some god, or the memory of some hero, seemed to animate every part of the city, and the empire of the world had been promised to the Capitol.[36] The native Romans felt and confessed the power of this agreeable illusion. It was derived from their ancestors, had grown up with their earliest habits of life, and was protected, in some measure, by the opinion of political utility. The form and the seat of government were intimately blended together, nor was it esteemed possible to transport the one without destroying the other.[37] But the sovereignty of the capital was gradually annihilated in the extent of conquest; the provinces rose to the same level, and the vanquished nations acquired the name and privileges, without imbibing the partial affections, of Romans. During a long period, however, the remains of the ancient constitution, and the influence of custom, preserved the dignity of Rome. The emperors, though perhaps of African or Illyrian extraction, respected their adopted country, as the seat of their power, and the centre of their extensive dominions. The emergencies of war very frequently required their presence on the frontiers; but Diocletian and Maximian were the first Roman princes who fixed, in time of peace, their ordinary residence in the provinces; and their conduct, however it might be suggested by private motives, was justified by very specious considerations of policy. The court of the emperor of the West was, for the most part, established at Milan, whose situation, at the foot of the Alps, appeared far more convenient than that of Rome, for the important purpose of watching the motions of the barbarians of Germany. Milan soon assumed the splendour of an Imperial city. The houses are described as numerous and well built; the manners of the people as polished and liberal. A circus, a theatre, a mint, a palace, baths, which bore the name of their founder Maximian; porticoes adorned with statues,

[35] *Eutropius mentions them as a part of the triumph. As the* persons *had been restored to Narses, nothing more than their* images *could be exhibited.*

[36] *Livy gives us a speech of Camillus on that subject, full of eloquence and sensibility, in opposition to a design of removing the seat of government from Rome to the neighbouring city of Veii.*

[37] *Julius Cæsar was reproached with the intention of removing the empire to Ilium or Alexandria. According to the ingenious conjecture of Le Fèvre and Dacier, the third ode of the third book of Horace was intended to divert Augustus from the execution of a similar design.*

and a double circumference of walls, contributed to the beauty of the new capital; nor did it seem oppressed even by the proximity of Rome. To rival the majesty of Rome was the ambition likewise of Diocletian, who employed his leisure, and the wealth of the East, in the embellishment of Nicomedia, a city placed on the verge of Europe and Asia, almost at an equal distance between the Danube and the Euphrates. By the taste of the monarch, and at the expense of the people, Nicomedia acquired, in the space of a few years, a degree of magnificence which might appear to have required the labour of ages, and became inferior only to Rome, Alexandria, and Antioch, in extent or populousness. The life of Diocletian and Maximian was a life of action, and a considerable portion of it was spent in camps, or in their long and frequent marches; but, whenever the public business allowed them any relaxation, they seem to have retired with pleasure to their favourite residences of Nicomedia and Milan. Till Diocletian, in the twentieth year of his reign, celebrated his Roman triumph, it is extremely doubtful whether he ever visited the ancient capital of the empire. Even on that memorable occasion his stay did not exceed two months. Disgusted with the licentious familiarity of the people, he quitted Rome with precipitation thirteen days before it was expected that he should have appeared in the senate, invested with the ensigns of the consular dignity.

The dislike expressed by Diocletian towards Rome and Roman freedom was not the effect of momentary caprice, but the result of the most artful policy. That crafty prince had framed a new system of Imperial government, which was afterwards completed by the family of Constantine, and, as the image of the old constitution was religiously preserved in the senate, he resolved to deprive that order of its small remains of power and consideration. We may recollect, about eight years before the elevation of Diocletian, the transient greatness, and the ambitious hopes, of the Roman senate. As long as that enthusiasm prevailed, many of the nobles imprudently displayed their zeal in the cause of freedom; and, after the successors of Probus had withdrawn their countenance from the republican party, the senators were unable to disguise their impotent resentment. As the sovereign of Italy, Maximian was intrusted with the care of extinguishing this troublesome, rather than dangerous, spirit, and the task was perfectly suited to his cruel temper. The most illustrious members of the senate, whom Diocletian always affected to esteem, were involved, by his colleague, in the accusation of imaginary plots; and the possession of an elegant villa, or a well-cultivated estate, was interpreted as a convincing evidence of guilt. The camp of the Prætorians, which had so long oppressed, began to protect, the majesty of Rome; and as those haughty troops were conscious of the decline of their power, they were naturally disposed to unite their strength with the authority of the senate. By the prudent measures of Diocletian, the numbers of the Prætorians were insensibly reduced, their privileges abolished, and their place supplied by two faithful legions of Illyricum, who, under the new titles of Jovians and Herculians, were appointed to perform the service of the Imperial guards.[38] But the most fatal though secret wound, which the senate received from the hands of Diocletian and Maximian, was inflicted by the inevitable operation of their absence. As long as the emperors resided at Rome, that assembly might be oppressed, but it could scarcely be neglected. The successors of Augustus exercised the power of dictating whatever laws their wisdom or caprice might suggest; but those laws were ratified by the sanction of the senate. The model of ancient freedom was preserved in its deliberations and decrees; and wise princes, who respected the prejudices of the Roman people, were in some measure obliged to assume the language and behaviour suitable to the general and first magistrate of the republic. In the armies and in the provinces, they displayed the dignity of monarchs; and, when they fixed their residence at a distance from the capital, they for ever laid aside the dissimulation which Augustus had recommended to his successors. In the exercise of the legislative as well as of the executive power, the sovereign advised with his ministers, instead of consulting the great council of the nation. The name of the senate was mentioned with honour till the last period of the empire; the vanity of its members was still flattered with honorary distinctions; but the assembly, which had so long been the source, and so long the instrument, of power, was respectfully suffered to sink into oblivion. The senate of Rome, losing all connexion with the Imperial court and the actual constitution, was left a venerable but useless monument of antiquity on the Capitoline hill.

When the Roman princes had lost sight of the senate and of their ancient capital, they easily forgot the origin and nature of their legal power. The civil offices of consul, of proconsul, of censor, and of tribune, by the union of which it had been formed, betrayed to the people its republican extraction. Those modest titles were laid aside; and, if they still distinguished their high station by the appellation of Emperor, or IMPERATOR, that word was understood in a new and

[38] *They were old corps stationed in Illyricum; and, according to the ancient establishment, they each consisted of six thousand men. They had acquired much reputation by the use of the* plumbatæ, *or darts loaded with lead. Each soldier carried five of these, which he darted from a considerable distance, with great strength and dexterity.*

more dignified sense, and no longer denoted the general of the Roman armies, but the sovereign of the Roman world. The name of Emperor, which was at first of a military nature, was associated with another of a more servile kind. The epithet of DOMINUS, or Lord, in its primitive signification, was expressive, not of the authority of a prince over his subjects, or of a commander over his soldiers, but of the despotic power of a master over his domestic slaves.[39] Viewing it in that odious light, it had been rejected with abhorrence by the first Cæsars. Their resistance insensibly became more feeble, and the name less odious; till at length the style of *our Lord and Emperor* was not only bestowed by flattery, but was regularly admitted into the laws and public monuments. Such lofty epithets were sufficient to elate and satisfy the most excessive vanity; and, if the successors of Diocletian still declined the title of King, it seems to have been the effect not so much of their moderation as of their delicacy. Wherever the Latin tongue was in use (and it was the language of government throughout the empire), the Imperial title, as it was peculiar to themselves, conveyed a more respectable idea than the name of king, which they must have shared with an hundred barbarian chieftains; or which, at the best, they could derive only from Romulus or from Tarquin. But the sentiments of the East were very different from those of the West. From the earliest period of history, the sovereigns of Asia had been celebrated in the Greek language by the title of BASILEUS, or King; and since it was considered as the first distinction among men, it was soon employed by the servile provincials of the East in their humble addresses to the Roman throne. Even the attributes, or at least the titles, of the DIVINITY, were usurped by Diocletian and Maximian, who transmitted them to a succession of Christian emperors. Such extravagant compliments, however, soon lose their impiety by losing their meaning; and when the ear is once accustomed to the sound, they are heard with indifference as vague though excessive professions of respect.

From the time of Augustus to that of Diocletian, the Roman princes, conversing in a familiar manner among their fellow-citizens, were saluted only with the same respect that was usually paid to senators and magistrates. Their principal distinction was the Imperial or military robe of purple; whilst the senatorial garment was marked by a broad, and the equestrian by a narrow, band or stripe of the same honourable colour. The pride, or rather the policy, of Diocletian engaged that artful prince to introduce the stately magnificence of the court of Persia. He ventured to assume the diadem,

[39] *Pliny speaks of Dominus with execration, as synonymous to Tyrant, and opposite to Prince. And the same Pliny regularly gives that title (in the tenth book of his epistles) to his friend rather than master, the virtuous Trajan. This strange expression puzzles the commentators who think, and the translators who can write.*

an ornament detested by the Romans as the odious ensign of royalty, and the use of which had been considered as the most desperate act of the madness of Caligula. It was no more than a broad white fillet set with pearls, which encircled the emperor's head. The sumptuous robes of Diocletian and his successors were of silk and gold; and it is remarked, with indignation, that even their shoes were studded with the most precious gems. The access to their sacred person was every day rendered more difficult, by the institution of new forms and ceremonies. The avenues of the palace were strictly guarded by the various *schools,* as they began to be called, of domestic officers. The interior apartments were intrusted to the jealous vigilance of the eunuchs; the increase of whose numbers and influence was the most infallible symptom of the progress of despotism. When a subject was at length admitted to the Imperial presence, he was obliged, whatever might be his rank, to fall prostrate on the ground, and to adore, according to the eastern fashion, the divinity of his lord and master. Diocletian was a man of sense, who, in the course of private as well as public life, had formed a just estimate both of himself and of mankind: nor is it easy to conceive that, in substituting the manners of Persia to those of Rome, he was seriously actuated by so mean a principle as that of vanity. He flattered himself that an ostentation of splendour and luxury would subdue the imagination of the multitude; that the monarch would be less exposed to the rude licence of the people and the soldiers, as his person was secluded from the public view; and that habits of submission would insensibly be productive of sentiments of veneration. Like the modesty affected by Augustus, the state maintained by Diocletian was a theatrical representation; but it must be confessed that, of the two comedies, the former was of a much more liberal and manly character than the latter. It was the aim of the one to disguise, and the object of the other to display, the unbounded power which the emperors possessed over the Roman world.

Ostentation was the first principle of the new system instituted by Diocletian. The second was division. He divided the empire, the provinces, and every branch of the civil as well as military administration. He multiplied the wheels of the machine of government, and rendered its operations less rapid but more secure. Whatever advantages, and whatever defects, might attend these innovations, they must be ascribed in a very great degree to the first inventor; but, as the new frame of policy was gradually improved and completed by succeeding princes, it will be more satisfactory to delay the

[40] *The innovations introduced by Diocletian are chiefly deduced, —1st, from some very strong passages in Lactantius; and 2ndly, from the new and various offices, which, in the Theodosian code, appear* already established in the beginning of the reign of Constantine.

consideration of it till the season of its full maturity and perfection.[40] Reserving, therefore, for the reign of Constantine a more exact picture of the new empire, we shall content ourselves with describing the principal and decisive outline, as it was traced by the hand of Diocletian. He had associated three colleagues in the exercise of the supreme power; and, as he was convinced that the abilities of a single man were inadequate to the public defence, he considered the joint administration of four princes not as a temporary expedient, but as a fundamental law of the constitution. It was his intention that the two elder princes should be distinguished by the use of the diadem, and the title of *Augusti:* that, as affection or esteem might direct their choice, they should regularly call to their assistance two subordinate colleagues; and that the *Cæsars,* rising in their turn to the first rank, should supply an uninterrupted succession of emperors. The empire was divided into four parts. The East and Italy were the most honourable, the Danube and the Rhine the most laborious stations. The former claimed the presence of the *Augusti,* the latter were intrusted to the administration of the *Cæsars.* The strength of the legions was in the hands of the four partners of sovereignty, and the despair of successively vanquishing four formidable rivals might intimidate the ambition of an aspiring general. In their civil government, the emperors were supposed to exercise the undivided power of the monarch, and their edicts, inscribed with their joint names, were received in all the provinces, as promulgated by their mutual councils and authority. Notwithstanding these precautions, the political union of the Roman world was gradually dissolved, and a principle of division was introduced, which, in the course of a few years, occasioned the perpetual separation of the eastern and western empires.

The system of Diocletian was accompanied with another very material disadvantage, which cannot even at present be totally overlooked; a more expensive establishment, and consequently an increase of taxes, and the oppression of the people. Instead of a modest family of slaves and freedmen, such as had contented the simple greatness of Augustus and Trajan, three or four magnificent courts were established in the various parts of the empire, and as many Roman *kings* contended with each other and with the Persian monarch for the vain superiority of pomp and luxury. The number of ministers, of magistrates, of officers, and of servants, who filled the different departments of the state, was multiplied beyond the example of former times; and (if we may borrow the warm expression of a contemporary) "when the proportion of those who received exceeded the proportion of those who contributed, the provinces were oppressed by the weight of tributes." From this period to the extinction of the empire, it would be easy to deduce an uninterrupted series of clamours and complaints. According to his religion and situation, each writer chooses either Diocletian, or Constantine, or Valens, or Theodosius, for the object of his invectives; but they unanimously agree in representing the burden of the public impositions, and particularly the land-tax and capitation, as the intolerable and increasing grievance of their own times. From such a concurrence, an impartial historian, who is obliged to extract truth from satire as well as from panegyric, will be inclined to divide the blame among the princes whom they accuse, and to ascribe their exactions much less to their personal vices than to the uniform system of their administration. The emperor Diocletian was, indeed, the author of that system; but during his reign the growing evil was confined within the bounds of modesty and discretion, and he deserves the reproach of establishing pernicious precedents, rather than of exercising actual oppression. It may be added, that his revenues were managed with prudent economy; and that, after all the current expenses were discharged, there still remained in the Imperial treasury an ample position either for judicious liberality or for any emergency of the state.

It was in the twenty-first year of his reign that Diocletian executed his memorable resolution of abdicating the empire; an action more naturally to have been expected from the elder or the younger Antoninus, than from a prince who had never practised the lessons of philosophy either in the attainment or in the use of supreme power. Diocletian acquired the glory of giving to the world the first example of a resignation, which has not been very frequently imitated by succeeding monarchs. The parallel of Charles the Fifth, however, will naturally offer itself to our mind, not only since the eloquence of a modern historian has rendered that name so familiar to an English reader, but from the very striking resemblance between the characters of the two emperors, whose political abilities were superior to their military genius, and whose specious virtues were much less the effect of nature than of art. The abdication of Charles appears to have been hastened by the vicissitude of fortune; and the disappointment of his favourite schemes urged him to relinquish a power which he found inadequate to his ambition. But the reign of Diocletian had flowed with a tide of uninterrupted success; nor was it till after he had vanquished all his enemies, and accomplished all his designs, that he seems to have entertained any serious thoughts of resigning the empire. Neither Charles nor Diocletian were arrived at a very advanced period of life; since the one was only fifty-five, and the other was no more than fifty-nine, years of age; but the active life of those princes, their wars and journeys, the cares of royalty, and their application to business, had already impaired their constitution, and brought on the infirmities of a premature old age.[41]

41 The particulars of the journey and illness are taken from Lactantius, who may sometimes be admitted as an evidence of public facts, though very seldom of private anecdotes.

Notwithstanding the severity of a very cold and rainy winter, Diocletian left Italy soon after the ceremony of his triumph, and began his progress towards the East round the circuit of the Illyrian provinces. From the inclemency of the weather, and the fatigue of the journey, he soon contracted a slow illness; and, though he made easy marches, and was generally carried in a close litter, his disorder, before he arrived at Nicomedia, about the end of the summer, was become very serious and alarming. During the whole winter he was confined to his palace; his danger inspired a general and unaffected concern; but the people could only judge of the various alterations of his health from the joy or consternation which they discovered in the countenance and behaviour of his attendants. The rumour of his death was for some time universally believed, and it was supposed to be concealed with a view to prevent the troubles that might have happened during the absence of the Cæsar Galerius. At length, however, on the first of March, Diocletian once more appeared in public, but so pale and emaciated that he could scarcely have been recognized by those to whom his person was the most familiar. It was time to put an end to the painful struggle, which he had sustained during more than a year, between the care of his health and that of his dignity. The former required indulgence and relaxation, the latter compelled him to direct, from the bed of sickness, the administration of a great empire. He resolved to pass the remainder of his days in honourable repose, to place his glory beyond the reach of fortune, and relinquish the theatre of the world to his younger and more active associates.[42]

42 Aurelius Victor ascribes the abdication, which had been so variously accounted for, to two causes: 1st, Diocletian's contempt of ambition; and 2ndly, His apprehension of impending troubles. One of the panegyrists mentions the age and infirmities of Diocletian as a very natural reason for his retirement.

The ceremony of his abdication was performed in a spacious plain, about three miles from Nicomedia. The emperor ascended a lofty throne, and in a speech, full of reason and dignity, declared his intention, both to the people and to the soldiers who were assembled on this extraordinary occasion. As soon as he had divested himself of the purple, he withdrew from the gazing multitude, and, traversing the city in a covered chariot, proceeded, without delay, to the favourite retirement which he had chosen in his native country of Dalmatia. On the same day, which was the first of May, Maximian, as it had been previously concerted, made his resignation of the Imperial dignity at Milan. Even in the splendour of the Roman triumph, Diocletian had meditated his design of abdicating the government. As he wished to secure the obedience of Maximian, he exacted from him either a general assurance that he would submit his actions to the authority of his benefactor, or a particular promise that he would descend from the throne, whenever he should receive the advice and the example. This engagement, though it was confirmed by the solemnity of an oath before the altar of the Capitoline Jupiter,[43] would have proved a feeble restraint on the fierce temper of Maximian, whose passion was the love of power, and who neither desired present tranquillity nor future reputation. But he yielded, however reluctantly, to the ascendant which his wiser colleague had acquired over him, and retired, immediately after his abdication, to a villa in Lucania, where it was almost impossible that such an impatient spirit could find any lasting tranquillity.

Diocletian, who, from a servile origin, had raised himself to the throne, passed the nine last years of his life in a private condition. Reason had dictated, and content seems to have accompanied, his retreat, in which he enjoyed for a long time the respect of those princes to whom he had resigned the possession of the world. It is seldom that minds long exercised in business have formed any habits of conversing with themselves, and in the loss of power they principally regret the want of occupation. The amusements of letters and of devotion, which afford so many resources in solitude, were incapable of fixing the attention of Diocletian; but he had preserved, or at least he soon recovered, a taste for the most innocent as well as natural pleasures; and his leisure hours were sufficiently employed in building, planting, and gardening. His answer to Maximian is deservedly celebrated. He was solicited by that restless old man to reassume the reins of government and the Imperial purple. He rejected the temptation with a smile of pity, calmly observing that, if he could show Maximian the cabbages which he had planted with his own hands at Salona, he should no longer be urged to relinquish the enjoyment of happiness for the pursuit of power. In his conversations with his friends, he frequently acknowledged that, of all arts, the most difficult was the art of reigning; and he expressed himself on that favourite topic with a degree of warmth

[43] The oration was pronounced after Maximian had reassumed the purple.

which could be the result only of experience. "How often," was he accustomed to say, "is it the interest of four or five ministers to combine together to deceive their sovereign! Secluded from mankind by his exalted dignity, the truth is concealed from his knowledge; he can see only with their eyes, he hears nothing but their misrepresentations. He confers the most important offices upon vice and weakness, and disgraces the most virtuous and deserving among his subjects. By such infamous arts," added Diocletian, "the best and wisest princes are sold to the venal corruption of their courtiers." A just estimate of greatness, and the assurance of immortal fame, improve our relish for the pleasures of retirement; but the Roman emperor had filled too important a character in the world to enjoy without allay the comforts and security of a private condition. It was impossible that he could remain ignorant of the troubles which afflicted the empire after his abdication. It was impossible that he could be indifferent to their consequences. Fear, sorrow, and discontent sometimes pursued him into the solitude of Salona. His tenderness, or at least his pride, was deeply wounded by the misfortunes of his wife and daughter; and the last moments of Diocletian were embittered by some affronts, which Licinius and Constantine might have spared the father of so many emperors, and the first author of their own fortune. A report, though of a very doubtful nature, has reached our times, that he prudently withdrew himself from their power by a voluntary death.[44]

" The younger Victor slightly mentions the report. But, as Diocletian had disobliged a powerful and successful party, his memory has been loaded with every crime and misfortune. It has been affirmed that he died raving mad, that he was condemned as a criminal by the Roman senate, &c.

Before we dismiss the consideration of the life and character of Diocletian, we may, for a moment, direct our view to the place of his retirement. Salona, a principal city of his native province of Dalmatia, was near two hundred Roman miles (according to the measurement of the public highways) from Aquileia and the confines of Italy, and about two hundred and seventy from Sirmium, the usual residence of the emperors whenever they visited the Illyrian frontier. A miserable village still preserves the name of Salona, but so late as the sixteenth century, the remains of a theatre, and a confused prospect of broken arches and marble columns, continued to attest its ancient splendour. About six or seven miles from the city, Diocletian constructed a magnificent palace, and we may infer from the greatness of the work, how long he had meditated his design of abdicating the empire. The choice of a spot which united all that could contribute either to health or to luxury did not require the partiality of a native. "The soil was dry and fertile, the air is pure and wholesome, and, though extremely hot during the summer months, this country seldom feels those sultry and noxious winds to which the coast of Istria and some parts of Italy are exposed. The views from the palace are no less beautiful than the soil and climate were inviting. Towards the west lies the fertile shore that stretches along the Hadriatic, in which a number of small islands are scattered in such a manner as to give this part of the sea the appearance of a great lake. On the north side lies the bay, which led to the ancient city of Salona, and the country beyond it, appearing in sight, forms a proper contrast to that more extensive prospect of water, which the Hadriatic presents both to the south and to the east. Towards the north, the view is terminated by high and irregular mountains, situated at a proper distance, and, in many places, covered with villages, woods, and vineyards." [45]

Though Constantine, from a very obvious prejudice, affects to mention the palace of Diocletian with contempt, yet one of their successors, who could only see it in a neglected and mutilated state, celebrates its magnificence in terms of the highest admiration. It covered an extent of ground consisting of between nine and ten English acres. The form was quadrangular, flanked with sixteen towers. Two of the sides were near six hundred, and the other two near seven hundred, feet in length. The whole was constructed of a beautiful freestone, extracted from the neighbouring quarries of Trau or Tragutium, and very little inferior to marble itself. Four streets, intersecting each other at right angles, divided the several parts of this great edifice, and the approach to the principal apartment was from a very stately entrance, which is still denominated the Golden Gate. The approach was terminated by a *peristylium* of granite columns, on one side of which we discover the square temple of Æsculapius, on the other the octagon temple of Jupiter. The latter of those deities Diocletian revered as the patron of his fortunes, the former as the protector of his health. By comparing the present remains with the precepts of Vitruvius, the several parts of the building, the baths, bedchamber, the *atrium,* the *basilica,* and the Cyzicene, Corinthian, and Egyptian halls have been described with some degree of precision, or at least of probability. Their forms were various, their proportions just, but they were all attended with two imperfections, very repugnant to our modern notions of taste and conveniency. These stately rooms had neither windows nor chimneys. They were lighted from the top (for the building seems to have consisted of no more than one storey), and they received their heat by the help of pipes that were conveyed along the walls. The

[45] *We may add a circumstance or two from the Abate Fortis; the little stream of the Hyader, mentioned by Lucan, produces most exquisite trout, which a sagacious writer, perhaps a monk, supposes to have been one of the principal reasons that determined Diocletian in the choice of his retirement. The same author observes that a taste for agriculture is reviving at Spalatro; and that an experimental farm has lately been established near the city, by a society of gentlemen.*

range of principal apartments was protected towards the south-west by a portico five hundred and seventeen feet long, which must have formed a very noble and delightful walk, when the beauties of painting and sculpture were added to those of the prospect.

Had this magnificent edifice remained in a solitary country, it would have been exposed to the ravages of time; but it might, perhaps, have escaped the rapacious industry of man. The village of Aspalathus, and, long afterwards, the provincial town of Spalatro, have grown out of its ruins. The Golden Gate now opens into the market place. St. John the Baptist has usurped the honours of Æsculapius; and the temple of Jupiter, under the protection of the Virgin, is converted into the cathedral church. For this account of Diocletian's palace we are principally indebted to an ingenious artist of our own time and country, whom a very liberal curiosity carried into the heart of Dalmatia. But there is room to suspect that the elegance of his designs and engraving has somewhat flattered the objects which it was their purpose to represent. We are informed by a more recent and very judicious traveller that the awful ruins of Spalatro are not less expressive of the decline of the arts than of the greatness of the Roman empire in the time of Diocletian.[46] If such was indeed the state of architecture, we must naturally believe that painting and sculpture had experienced a still more sensible decay. The practice of architecture is directed by a few general and even mechanical rules. But sculpture, and, above all, painting, propose to themselves the imitation not only of the forms of nature, but of the characters and passions of the human soul. In those sublime arts, the dexterity of the hand is of little avail, unless it is animated by fancy and guided by the most correct taste and observation.

It is almost unnecessary to remark that the civil distractions of the empire, the licence of the soldiers, the inroads of the barbarians, and the progress of despotism had proved very unfavourable to genius, and even to learning. The succession of Illyrian princes restored the empire, without restoring the sciences. Their military education was not calculated to inspire them with the love of letters; and even the mind of Diocletian, however active and capacious in business, was totally uninformed by study or speculation. The professions of law and physic are of such common use and certain profit that they will always secure a sufficient number of practitioners endowed with a reasonable degree of abilities and knowledge; but it does not appear that the students in those two faculties appeal to any celebrated masters who have flourished within that period. The voice

[46] *I shall quote the words of the Abate Fortis. "E'bastevolmente nota agli amatori dell' Architettura, e dell' Antichità, l'opera del Signor* ADAMS, *che a donato molto a que' superbi vestigi coll'abituale eleganza del suo toccalapis e del bulino. In generale la rozzezza del scalpello, e'l cattivo gusto del secolo vi gareggiano colla magnificenza del fabricato."*

of poetry was silent. History was reduced to dry and confused abridgments, alike destitute of amusement and instruction. A languid and affected eloquence was still retained in the pay and service of the emperors, who encouraged not any arts except those which contributed to the gratification of their pride or the defence of their power.[47]

The declining age of learning and of mankind is marked, however, by the rise and rapid progress of the new Platonists. The school of Alexandria silenced those of Athens; and the ancient sects enrolled themselves under the banners of the more fashionable teachers, who recommended their system by the novelty of their method and the austerity of their manners. Several of these masters, Ammonious, Plotinus, Amelius, and Porphyry,[48] were men of profound thought and intense application; but, by mistaking the true object of philosophy, their labours contributed much less to improve than to corrupt the human understanding. The knowledge that is suited to our situation and powers, the whole compass of moral, natural, and mathematical science, was neglected by the new Platonists, whilst they exhausted their strength in the verbal disputes of metaphysics, attempted to explore the secrets of the invisible world, and studied to reconcile Aristotle with Plato, on subjects of which both these philosophers were as ignorant as the rest of mankind. Consuming their reason in these deep but unsubstantial meditations, their minds were exposed to illusions of fancy. They flattered themselves that they possessed the secret of disengaging the soul from its corporeal prison; claimed a familiar intercourse with dæmons and spirits; and, by a very singular revolution, converted the study of philosophy into that of magic. The ancient sages had derided the popular superstition; after disguising its extravagance by the thin pretence of allegory, the disciplines of Plotinus and Porphyry became its most zealous defenders. As they agreed with the Christians in a few mysterious points of faith, they attacked the remainder of their theological system with all the fury of civil war. The new Platonists would scarcely deserve a place in the history of science, but in that of the church the mention of them will very frequently occur.

[47] *The orator Eumenius was secretary to the emperors Maximian and Constantius, and Professor of Rhetoric in the College of Autun. His salary was six hundred thousand sesterces, which, according to the lowest computation of that age, must have exceeded three thousand pounds a year. He generously requested the permission of employing it in rebuilding the college.*

[48] *Porphyry died about the time of Diocletian's abdication. The life of his master Plotinus, which he composed, will give us the most complete idea of the genius of the sect, and the manners of its professors.*

XIV

TROUBLES AFTER THE ABDICATION OF DIOCLETIAN · DEATH OF CONSTANTIUS · ELEVATION OF CONSTANTINE AND MAXENTIUS · SIX EMPERORS AT THE SAME TIME · DEATH OF MAXIMIAN AND GALERIUS · VICTORIES OF CONSTANTINE OVER MAXENTIUS AND LICINIUS · REUNION OF THE EMPIRE UNDER AUTHORITY OF CONSTANTINE · HIS LAWS · GENERAL PEACE

T H E balance of power established by Diocletian submitted no longer than while it was sustained by the firm and dexterous hand of the founder. It required such a fortunate mixture of different tempers and abilities as could scarcely be found, or even expected, a second time; two emperors without jealousy, two Cæsars without ambition, and the same general interest invariably pursued by four independent princes. The abdication of Diocletian and Maximian was succeeded by eighteen years of discord and confusion. The empire was afflicted by five civil wars; and the remainder of the time was not so much a state of tranquillity as a suspension of arms between several hostile monarchs, who, viewing each other with an eye of fear and hatred, strove to increase their respective forces at the expense of their subjects.

As soon as Diocletian and Maximian had resigned the purple, their station, according to the rules of the new constitution, was filled by the two Cæsars, Constantius and Galerius, who immediately assumed the title of Augustus.[1] The honours of seniority and precedence were allowed to the former of those princes, and he continued, under a new appellation, to administer his ancient department of Gaul, Spain, and Britain. The government of those ample provinces was sufficient to exercise his talents, and to satisfy his ambition. Clemency, temperance, and moderation distinguished the amiable character of Constantius, and his fortunate subjects had frequently occasion to compare the virtues of their sovereign with the passions of Maximian, and even with the arts of Diocletian. In-

[1] M. de Montesquieu supposes, on the authority of Orosius and Eusebius, that, on this occasion, the empire, for the first time, was really divided into two parts. It is difficult, however, to discover in what respect the plan of Galerius differed from that of Diocletian.

stead of imitating their eastern pride and magnificence, Constantius preserved the modesty of a Roman prince. He declared, with un-affected sincerity, that his most valued treasure was in the hearts of his people, and that, whenever the dignity of the throne or the danger of the state required any extraordinary supply, he could depend with confidence on their gratitude and liberality. The provincials of Gaul, Spain, and Britain, sensible of his worth and of their own happiness, reflected with anxiety on the declining health of the emperor Constantius, and the tender age of his numerous family, the issue of his second marriage with the daughter of Maximian.

The stern temper of Galerius was cast in a very different mould; and, while he commanded the esteem of his subjects, he seldom condescended to solicit their affections. His fame in arms, and, above all, the success of the Persian war, had elated his haughty mind, which was naturally impatient of a superior, or even of an equal. If it were possible to rely on the partial testimony of an injudicious writer, we might ascribe the abdication of Diocletian to the menaces of Galerius, and relate the particulars of a *private* conversation between the two princes, in which the former discovered as much pusillanimity as the latter displayed ingratitude and arrogance. But these obscure anecdotes are sufficiently refuted by an impartial view of the character and conduct of Diocletian. Whatever might otherwise have been his intentions, if he had apprehended any danger from the violence of Galerius, his good sense would have instructed him to prevent the ignominious contest; and, as he had held the sceptre with glory, he would have resigned it without disgrace.

After the elevation of Constantius and Galerius to the rank of *Augusti,* two new *Cæsars* were required to supply their place, and to complete the system of the Imperial government. Diocletian was sincerely desirous of withdrawing himself from the world; he considered Galerius, who had married his daughter, as the firmest support of his family and of the empire; and he consented, without reluctance, that his successor should assume the merit as well as the envy of the important nomination. It was fixed without consulting the interest or inclination of the princes of the West. Each of them had a son who was arrived at the age of manhood, and who might have been deemed the most natural candidates for the vacant honour. But the impotent resentment of Maximian was no longer to be dreaded, and the moderate Constantius, though he might despise the dangers, was humanely apprehensive of the calamities, of civil war. The two persons whom Galerius promoted to the rank of

Cæsar were much better suited to serve the views of his ambition; and their principal recommendation seems to have consisted in the want of merit or personal consequence. The first of these was Daza, or, as he was afterwards called, Maximin, whose mother was the sister of Galerius. The unexperienced youth still betrayed by his manners and language his rustic education, when, to his own astonishment as well as that of the world, he was invested by Diocletian with the purple, exalted to the dignity of Cæsar, and intrusted with the sovereign command of Egypt and Syria. At the same time, Severus, a faithful servant, addicted to pleasure, but not incapable of business, was sent to Milan, to receive from the reluctant hands of Maximian the Cæsarean ornaments, and the possession of Italy and Africa. According to the forms of the constitution, Severus acknowledged the supremacy of the western emperor; but he was absolutely devoted to the commands of his benefactor Galerius, who, reserving to himself the intermediate countries from the confines of Italy to those of Syria, firmly established his power over three-fourths of the monarchy. In the full confidence that the approaching death of Constantius would leave him sole master of the Roman world, we are assured that he had arranged in his mind a long succession of future princes, and that he meditated his own retreat from public life after he should have accomplished a glorious reign of about twenty years.

But, within less than eighteen months, two unexpected revolutions overturned the ambitious schemes of Galerius. The hopes of uniting the western provinces to his empire were disappointed by the elevation of Constantine; whilst Italy and Africa were lost by the successful revolt of Maxentius.

I. The fame of Constantine has rendered posterity attentive to the most minute circumstances of his life and actions. The place of his birth, as well as the condition of his mother Helena, have been the subject not only of literary but of national disputes. Notwithstanding the recent tradition, which assigns for her father a British king, we are obliged to confess that Helena was the daughter of an innkeeper;[2] but at the same time we may defend the legality of her marriage against those who have represented her as the concubine of Constantius. The great Constantine was most probably born at Naissus, in Dacia,[3] and it is not surprising that, in a family and province distinguished only by the profession of arms, the youth should discover very little inclination to improve his mind by the acquisition of knowledge. He was about eighteen years of age when his

[2] This tradition, unknown to the contemporaries of Constantine, was invented in the darkness of monasteries, was embellished by Jeffrey of Monmouth and the writers of the twelfth century, has been defended by our antiquarians of the last age, and is seriously related in the ponderous history of England, compiled by Mr. Carte. He transports, however, the kingdom of Coil, the imaginary father of Helena, from Essex to the wall of Antoninus.

[3] There are three opinions with regard to the place of Constantine's birth. 1. Our English antiquarians were used to dwell with rapture on the words of his panegyrist; "Britannias illic oriendo nobiles fecisti." But this celebrated passage may be referred with as much propriety to the accession as to the nativity of Constantine. 2. Some of the modern Greeks have ascribed the honour of his birth to Drepanum, a town on the gulf of Nicomedia which Constantine dig-

father was promoted to the rank of Cæsar; but that fortunate event was attended with his mother's divorce; and the splendour of an Imperial alliance reduced the son of Helena to a state of disgrace and humiliation. Instead of following Constantius in the West, he remained in the service of Diocletian, signalized his valour in the wars of Egypt and Persia, and gradually rose to the honourable station of a tribune of the first order. The figure of Constantine was tall and majestic; he was dexterous in all his exercises, intrepid in war, affable in peace; in his whole conduct the active spirit of youth was tempered by habitual prudence; and, while his mind was engrossed by ambition, he appeared cold and insensible to the allurements of pleasure. The favour of the people and soldiers, who had named him as a worthy candidate for the rank of Cæsar, served only to exasperate the jealousy of Galerius; and, though prudence might restrain him from exercising any open violence, an absolute monarch is seldom at a loss how to execute a sure and secret revenge.[4] Every hour increased the danger of Constantine and the anxiety of his father, who, by repeated letters, expressed the warmest desire of embracing his son. For some time the policy of Galerius supplied him with delays and excuses, but it was impossible long to refuse so natural a request of his associate, without maintaining his refusal by arms. The permission for the journey was reluctantly granted, and, whatever precautions the emperor might have taken to intercept a return, the consequences of which he, with so much reason, apprehended, they were effectually disappointed by the incredible diligence of Constantine.[5] Leaving the palace of Nicomedia in the night, he travelled post through Bithynia, Thrace, Dacia, Pannonia, Italy, and Gaul, and, amidst the joyful acclamations of the people, reached the port of Boulogne in the very moment when his father was preparing to embark for Britain.

The British expedition, and an easy victory over the barbarians of Caledonia, were the last exploits of the reign of Constantius. He ended his life in the Imperial palace of York, fifteen months after he had assumed the title of Augustus, and almost fourteen years and a half after he had been promoted to the rank of Cæsar. His death was immediately succeeded by the elevation of Constantine. The ideas of inheritance and succession are so very familiar that the generality of mankind consider them as founded, not only in reason, but in nature itself. Our imagination readily transfers the same principles from private property to public dominion: and, whenever a virtuous father leaves behind him a son whose merit seems to justify

nified with the name of Helenopolis, and Justinian adorned with many splendid buildings. It is indeed probable enough that Helena's father kept an inn at Drepanum; and that Constantius might lodge there when he returned from a Persian embassy in the reign of Aurelian. But in the wandering life of a soldier, the place of his marriage, and the place where his children are born, have very little connection with each other. 3. The claim of Naissus is supported by the anonymous writer, published at the end of Ammianus, and who in general copied very good materials; and it is confirmed by Julius Firmicus, who flourished under the reign of Constantine himself.

[4] Galerius, or perhaps his own courage, exposed him to single combat with a Sarmatian and with a monstrous lion.

[5] Zosimus tells a very foolish story, that Constantine caused all the post horses, which he had used, to be hamstrung. Such a bloody execution, without preventing a pursuit, would have scattered suspicions and might have stopped his journey.

the esteem, or even the hopes, of the people, the joint influence of prejudice and of affection operates with irresistible weight. The flower of the western armies had followed Constantius into Britain, and the national troops were reinforced by a numerous body of Alemanni, who obeyed the orders of Crocus, one of their hereditary chieftains.[6] The opinion of their own importance, and the assurance that Britain, Gaul, and Spain would acquiesce in their nomination, were diligently inculcated to the legions by the adherents of Constantine. The soldiers were asked, Whether they could hesitate a moment between the honour of placing at their head the worthy son of their beloved emperor and the ignominy of tamely expecting the arrival of some obscure stranger, on whom it might please the sovereign of Asia to bestow the armies and provinces of the West. It was insinuated to them that gratitude and liberality held a distinguished place among the virtues of Constantine; nor did that artful prince show himself to the troops, till they were prepared to salute him with the names of Augustus and Emperor. The throne was the object of his desires; and, had he been less actuated by ambition, it was his only means of safety. He was well acquainted with the character and sentiments of Galerius, and sufficiently apprized that, if he wished to live, he must determine to reign. The decent and even obstinate resistance which he chose to affect [7] was contrived to justify his usurpation; nor did he yield to the acclamations of the army, till he had provided the proper materials for a letter, which he immediately dispatched to the emperor of the East. Constantine informed him of the melancholy event of his father's death, modestly asserted his natural claim to the succession, and respectfully lamented that the affectionate violence of his troops had not permitted him to solicit the Imperial purple in the regular and constitutional manner. The first emotions of Galerius were those of surprise, disappointment, and rage; and, as he could seldom restrain his passions, he loudly threatened that he would commit to the flames both the letter and the messenger. But his resentment insensibly subsided; and, when he recollected the doubtful chance of war, when he had weighed the character and strength of his adversary, he consented to embrace the honourable accommodation which the prudence of Constantine had left open to him. Without either condemning or ratifying the choice of the British army, Galerius accepted the son of his deceased colleague as the sovereign of the provinces beyond the Alps; but he gave him only the title of Cæsar, and the fourth rank among the Roman princes, whilst he conferred the vacant

[6] *This is perhaps the first instance of a barbarian king who assisted the Roman arms with an independent body of his own subjects. The practice grew familiar, and at last became fatal.*

[7] *His panegyrist Eumenius ventures to affirm, in the presence of Constantine, that he put spurs to his horse, and tried, but in vain, to escape from the hands of his soldiers.*

place of Augustus on his favourite Severus. The apparent harmony of the empire was still preserved, and Constantine, who already possessed the substance, expected, without impatience, an opportunity of obtaining the honours, of supreme power.

The children of Constantius by his second marriage were six in number, three of either sex, and whose Imperial descent might have solicited a preference over the meaner extraction of the son of Helena. But Constantine was in the thirty-second year of his age, in the full vigour both of mind and body, at the time when the eldest of his brothers could not possibly be more than thirteen years old. His claim of superior merit had been allowed and ratified by the dying emperor.[8] In his last moments Constantius bequeathed to his eldest son the care of the safety, as well as greatness, of the family; conjuring him to assume both the authority and the sentiments of a father with regard to the children of Theodora. Their liberal education, advantageous marriages, the secure dignity of their lives, and the first honours of the state with which they were invested, attest the fraternal affection of Constantine; and, as those princes possessed a mild and grateful disposition, they submitted without reluctance to the superiority of his genius and fortune.[9]

II. The ambitious spirit of Galerius was scarcely reconciled to the disappointment of his views upon the Gallic provinces, before the unexpected loss of Italy wounded his pride as well as power in a still more sensible part. The long absence of the emperors had filled Rome with discontent and indignation; and the people gradually discovered that the preference given to Nicomedia and Milan was not to be ascribed to the particular inclination of Diocletian, but to the permanent form of government which he had instituted. It was in vain that, a few months after his abdication, his successors dedicated, under his name, those magnificent baths, whose ruins still supply the ground as well as the materials for so many churches and convents.[10] The tranquillity of those elegant recesses of ease and luxury was disturbed by the impatient murmurs of the Romans; and a report was insensibly circulated that the sums expended in erecting those buildings would soon be required at their hands. About that time the avarice of Galerius, or perhaps the exigencies of the state, had induced him to make a very strict and rigorous inquisition into the property of his subjects for the purpose of a general taxation, both on their lands and on their persons. A very minute survey appears to have been taken of their real estates; and, wherever there was the slightest suspicion of concealment, torture was very freely

8 The choice of Constantine by his dying father, which is warranted by reason, and insinuated by Eumenius, seems to be confirmed by the most unexceptionable authority.

9 Of the three sisters of Constantine, Constantia married the emperor Licinius, Anastasia the Cæsar Bassianus, and Eutropia the consul Nepotianus. The three brothers were, Dalmatius, Julius Constantius, Annibalianus, of whom we shall have occasion to speak hereafter.

10 The six princes are all mentioned, Diocletian and Maximian as the senior Augusti and fathers of the emperors. They jointly dedicate, for the use of their own Romans, this magnificent edifice. The architects have delineated the ruins of these Thermae; and the antiquarians, particularly Donatus and Nardini, have ascertained the ground which they covered. One of the great rooms is now the Carthusian church; and even one of the porter's lodges is sufficient to form another church, which belongs to the Feuillans.

employed to obtain a sincere declaration of their personal wealth. The privileges which had exalted Italy above the rank of the provinces were no longer regarded: and the officers of the revenue already began to number the Roman people, and to settle the proportion of the new taxes. Even when the spirit of freedom had been utterly extinguished, the tamest subjects have sometimes ventured to resist an unprecedented invasion of their property; but on this occasion the injury was aggravated by the insult, and the sense of private interest was quickened by that of national honour. The conquest of Macedonia, as we have already observed, had delivered the Roman people from the weight of personal taxes. Though they had experienced every form of despotism, they had now enjoyed that exemption near five hundred years; nor could they patiently brook the insolence of an Illyrian peasant, who, from his distant residence in Asia, presumed to number Rome among the tributary cities of his empire. The rising fury of the people was encouraged by the authority, or at least the connivance, of the senate; and the feeble remains of the Prætorian guards, who had reason to apprehend their own dissolution, embraced so honourable a pretence, and declared their readiness to draw their swords in the service of their oppressed country. It was the wish, and it soon became the hope, of every citizen, that, after expelling from Italy their foreign tyrants, they should elect a prince who, by the place of his residence, and by his maxims of government, might once more deserve the title of Roman emperor. The name as well as the situation of Maxentius determined in his favour the popular enthusiasm.

Maxentius was the son of the emperor Maximian, and he had married the daughter of Galerius. His birth and alliance seemed to offer him the fairest promise of succeeding to the empire; but his vices and incapacity procured him the same exclusion from the dignity of Cæsar which Constantine had deserved by a dangerous superiority of merit. The policy of Galerius preferred such associates as would never disgrace the choice, nor dispute the commands, of their benefactors. An obscure stranger was therefore raised to the throne of Italy, and the son of the late emperor of the West was left to enjoy the luxury of a private fortune in a villa a few miles distant from the capital. The gloomy passions of his soul, shame, vexation, and rage, were inflamed by envy on the news of Constantine's success; but the hopes of Maxentius revived with the public discontent, and he was easily persuaded to unite his personal injury and pretensions with the cause of the Roman people. Two Prætorian tribunes and a commissary of provisions undertook the management of the conspiracy; and, as every order of men was actuated by the same spirit, the immediate event was neither doubtful or difficult. The præfect of the city and a few magistrates, who maintained their fidelity to Severus, were massacred by the guards; and Maxentius, invested with the Imperial ornaments, was acknowledged by the applauding senate and people as the protector of the Roman freedom and dignity. It is uncertain whether Maximian was previously acquainted with the conspiracy; but, as soon as the standard of rebellion was erected at Rome, the old emperor broke from the retirement where the authority of Diocletian had condemned him to pass a life of melancholy solitude, and concealed his returning ambition under the disguise of paternal tenderness. At the request of his son and of the senate, he condescended to reassume the purple. His ancient dignity, his experience, and his fame in arms added strength as well as reputation to the party of Maxentius.

According to the advice, or rather the orders, of his colleague, the emperor Severus immediately hastened to Rome, in the full confidence that, by his unexpected celerity, he should easily suppress the tumult of an unwarlike populace, commanded by a licentious youth. But he found on his arrival the gates of the city shut against him, the walls filled with men and arms, an experienced general at the head of the rebels, and his own troops without spirit or affection. A large body of Moors deserted to the enemy, allured by the promise of a large donative; and, if it be true that they had been levied by Maximian in his African war, preferring the natural feelings of gratitude to the artificial ties of allegiance. Anulinus, the Prætorian præfect, declared himself in favour of Maxentius, and drew after him the most considerable part of the troops, accustomed to obey his commands. Rome, according to the expression of an orator, recalled her armies, and the unfortunate Severus, destitute of force and of counsel, retired, or rather fled, with precipitation to Ravenna. Here he might for some time have been safe. The fortifications of Ravenna were able to resist the attempts, and the morasses that surrounded the town were sufficient to prevent the approach, of the Italian army. The sea, which Severus commanded with a powerful fleet, secured him an inexhaustible supply of provisions, and gave a free entrance to the legions which, on the return of spring, would advance to his assistance from Illyricum and the East. Maximian, who conducted the siege in person, was soon convinced that he might waste his time and his army in the fruitless enterprise, and that he had nothing to hope either from force or famine. With an art more suitable to the character of Diocletian than to his own, he directed his attack, not so much against the walls of Ravenna as against the mind of Severus. The treachery which he had experienced disposed that unhappy prince to distrust the most sincere of his friends and adherents. The emissaries of Maximian easily persuaded his credulity that a conspiracy was formed to betray the town, and prevailed upon his fears not to expose himself to the discretion of an irritated conqueror, but to accept the faith of an honourable capitulation. He was at first received with humanity, and treated with respect. Maximian conducted the captive emperor to Rome, and gave him the most solemn assurances that he had secured his life by the resignation of the purple. But Severus could obtain only an easy death and an Imperial funeral. When the sentence was signified to him, the manner of executing it was left to his own choice; he preferred the favourite mode of the ancients, that of opening his veins: and, as soon as he expired, his body was carried to the sepulchre which had been constructed for the family of Gallienus.

Though the characters of Constantine and Maxentius had very little affinity with each other, their situation and interest were the same; and prudence seemed to require that they should unite their forces against the common enemy. Notwithstanding the superiority of his age and dignity, the indefatigable Maximian passed the Alps, and, courting a personal interview with the sovereign of Gaul, carried with him his daughter Fausta as the pledge of the new alliance. The marriage was celebrated at Arles with every circumstance of magnificence; and the ancient colleague of Diocletian, who again asserted his claim to the western empire, conferred on his son-in-law and ally the title of Augustus. By consenting to receive that honour from Maximian, Constantine seemed to embrace the cause of Rome and of the senate; but his professions were ambiguous, and his assistance slow and ineffectual. He considered with attention the approaching contest between the masters of Italy and the emperor of the East, and was prepared to consult his own safety or ambition in the event of the war.

The importance of the occasion called for the presence and abilities of Galerius. At the head of a powerful army, collected from Illyricum and the East, he entered Italy, resolved to revenge the death of Severus, and to chastise the rebellious Romans; or, as he expressed his intentions, in the furious language of a barbarian, to extirpate the senate, and to destroy the people by the sword. But the skill of Maximian had concerted a prudent system of defence. The invader found every place hostile, fortified, and inaccessible; and, though he forced his way as far as Narni, within sixty miles of Rome, his dominion in Italy was confined to the narrow limits of his camp. Sensible of the increasing difficulties of his enterprise, the haughty Galerius made the first advances towards a reconciliation, and dispatched two of his most considerable officers to tempt the Roman princes by the offer of a conference and the declaration of his paternal regard for Maxentius, who might obtain much more from his liberality than he could hope from the doubtful chance of war. The offers of Galerius were rejected with firmness, his perfidious friendship refused with contempt, and it was not long before he discovered that, unless he provided for his safety by a timely retreat, he had some reason to apprehend the fate of Severus. The wealth, which the Romans defended against his rapacious tyranny, they freely contributed for his destruction. The name of Maximian, the popular arts of his son, the secret distribution of large sums, and the promise of still more liberal rewards, checked the ardour and corrupted the fidelity of the Illyrian legions; and, when Galerius at length gave the signal of the retreat, it was with some difficulty that he could prevail on his veterans not to desert a banner which had so often conducted them to victory and honour. A contemporary writer assigns two other causes for the failure of the expedition; but they are both of such a nature that a cautious historian will scarcely venture to adopt them. We are told that Galerius, who had formed a very imperfect notion of the greatness of Rome by the cities of the East with which he was acquainted, found his forces inadequate to the siege of that immense capital. But the extent of a city serves only to render it more accessible to the enemy; Rome had long since been accustomed to submit on the approach of a conqueror; nor could the temporary enthusiasm of the people have long contended against the discipline and valour of the legions. We are likewise informed that the legions themselves were struck with horror and remorse, and that those pious sons of the republic refused to violate the sanctity of their venerable parent. But, when we recollect with how much ease in the more ancient civil wars, the zeal of party and the habits of military obedience had converted the native citizens of Rome into her most implacable enemies, we shall be inclined to distrust this extreme delicacy of strangers and barbarians, who had never beheld Italy till they entered it in a hostile manner. Had they not been restrained by motives of a more interested nature, they would probably have answered Galerius in the words of Cæsar's veterans: "If our general wishes to lead us to the banks of the Tiber, we are prepared to trace out his camp. Whatsoever walls he has determined to level with the ground, our hands are ready to work the engines: nor shall we hesitate, should the name of the devoted city be Rome itself." These are indeed the expressions of a poet; but of a poet who has been distinguished, and even censured, for his strict adherence to the truth of history.

The legions of Galerius exhibited a very melancholy proof of their disposition by the ravages which they committed in their retreat. They murdered, they ravished, they plundered, they drove away the flocks and herds of the Italians; they burnt the villages through which they passed, and they endeavoured to destroy the country, which it had not been in their power to subdue. During the whole march Maxentius hung on their rear; but he very prudently declined a general engagement with those brave and desperate veterans. His father had undertaken a second journey into Gaul, with the hope of persuading Constantine, who had assembled an army on the frontier, to join the pursuit and to complete the victory. But the actions of Constantine were guided by reason, and not by resentment. He persisted in the wise resolution of maintaining a balance of power in the divided empire, and he no longer hated Galerius when that aspiring prince had ceased to be an object of terror.

The mind of Galerius was the most susceptible of the sterner passions, but it was not however incapable of a sincere and lasting friendship. Licinius, whose manners as well as character were not unlike his own, seems to have engaged both his affection and esteem. Their intimacy had commenced in the happier period, perhaps, of their youth and obscurity. It had been cemented by the freedom and dangers of a military life; they had advanced, almost by equal steps, through the successive honours of the service; and, as soon as Galerius was invested with the Imperial dignity, he seems to have conceived the design of raising his companion to the same rank with himself. During the short period of his prosperity, he considered the rank of Cæsar as unworthy of the age and merit of Licinius, and rather chose to reserve for him the place of Constantius, and the empire of the West. While the emperor was employed in the Italian war, he intrusted his friend with the defence of the Danube; and immediately after his return from that unfortunate expedition he invested Licinius with the vacant purple of Severus, resigning to his immediate command the provinces of Illyricum.[11] The news of his

[11] M. de Tillemont has proved that Licinius, without passing through the intermediate rank of Cæsar, was declared Augustus, the 11th of November, A.D. 307, after the return of Galerius from Italy.

promotion was no sooner carried into the East, than Maximin, who governed, or rather oppressed, the countries of Egypt and Syria, betrayed his envy and discontent, disdained the inferior name of Cæsar, and, notwithstanding the prayers as well as arguments of Galerius, exacted, almost by violence, the equal title of Augustus.[12] For the first, and indeed for the last, time, the Roman world was administered by six emperors. In the West, Constantine and Maxentius affected to reverence their father Maximian. In the East, Licinius and Maximin honoured with more real consideration their benefactor Galerius. The opposition of interest, and the memory of a recent war, divided the empire into two great hostile powers; but their mutual fears produced an apparent tranquillity, and even a feigned reconciliation, till the deaths of the elder princes, of Maximian, and more particularly of Galerius, gave a new direction to the views and passions of their surviving associates.

When Maximian had reluctantly abdicated the empire, the venal orators of the times applauded his philosophic moderation. When his ambition excited, or at least encouraged, a civil war, they returned thanks to his generous patriotism, and gently censured that love of ease and retirement which had withdrawn him from the public service. But it was impossible that minds like those of Maximian and his son could long possess in harmony an undivided power. Maxentius considered himself as the legal sovereign of Italy, elected by the Roman senate and people; nor would he endure the control of his father, who arrogantly declared that by *his* name and abilities the rash youth had been established on the throne. The cause was solemnly pleaded before the Prætorian guards, and those troops, who dreaded the severity of the old emperor, espoused the party of Maxentius. The life and freedom of Maximian were however respected, and he retired from Italy into Illyricum, affecting to lament his past conduct, and secretly contriving new mischiefs. But Galerius, who was well acquainted with his character, soon obliged him to leave his dominions, and the last refuge of the disappointed Maximian was the court of his son-in-law Constantine. He was received with respect by that artful prince, and with the appearance of filial tenderness by the empress Fausta. That he might remove every suspicion, he resigned the Imperial purple a second time,[13] professing himself at length convinced of the vanity of greatness and ambition. Had he persevered in this resolution, he might have ended his life with less dignity indeed than in his first retirement, yet, however, with comfort and reputation. But the near prospect of

[12] *When Galerius declared Licinius Augustus with himself, he tried to satisfy his younger associates, by inventing from Constantine and* Maximin (*not* Maxentius) *the new title of sons of the Augusti. But, when Maximin acquainted him that he had been saluted Augustus by the army, Galerius was obliged to acknowledge him, as well as Constantine, as equal associates in the Imperial dignity.*

[13] *Yet, after the resignation of the purple, Constantine still continued to Maximian the pomp and honours of the Imperial dignity; and on the public occasions gave the right-hand place to his father-in-law.*

a throne brought back to his remembrance the state from whence he was fallen, and he resolved, by a desperate effort, either to reign or to perish. An incursion of the Franks had summoned Constantine, with a part of his army, to the banks of the Rhine; the remainder of the troops were stationed in the southern provinces of Gaul, which lay exposed to the enterprises of the Italian emperor, and a considerable treasure was deposited in the city of Arles. Maximian either craftily invented, or hastily credited, a vain report of the death of Constantine. Without hesitation he ascended the throne, seized the treasure, and, scattering it with his accustomed profusion among the soldiers, endeavoured to awake in their minds the memory of his ancient dignity and exploits. Before he could establish his authority, or finish the negotiation which he appears to have entered into with his son Maxentius, the celerity of Constantine defeated all his hopes. On the first news of his perfidy and ingratitude, that prince returned by rapid marches from the Rhine to the Saone, embarked on the last-mentioned river at Chalons, and, at Lyons trusting himself to the rapidity of the Rhone, arrived at the gates of Arles, with a military force which it was impossible for Maximian to resist, and which scarcely permitted him to take refuge in the neighbouring city of Marseilles. The narrow neck of land which joined that place to the continent was fortified against the besiegers, whilst the sea was open, either for the escape of Maximian, or for the succours of Maxentius, if the latter should choose to disguise his invasion of Gaul under the honourable pretence of defending a distressed, or, as he might allege, an injured father. Apprehensive of the fatal consequences of delay, Constantine gave orders for an immediate assault; but the scaling ladders were found too short for the height of the walls, and Marseilles might have sustained as long a siege as it formerly did against the arms of Cæsar, if the garrison, conscious either of their fault or of their danger, had not purchased their pardon by delivering up the city and the person of Maximian. A secret but irrevocable sentence of death was pronounced against the usurper; he obtained only the same favour which he had indulged to Severus, and it was published to the world that, oppressed by the remorse of his repeated crimes, he strangled himself with his own hands. After he had lost the assistance, and disdained the moderate counsels, of Diocletian, the second period of his active life was a series of public calamities and personal mortifications, which were terminated, in about three years, by an ignominious death. He deserved his fate; but we should find more reason to applaud the humanity of Constantine, if he had spared an old man, the benefactor of his father, and the father of his wife. During the whole of this melancholy transaction, it appears that Fausta sacrificed the sentiments of nature to her conjugal duties.

The last years of Galerius were less shameful and unfortunate; and, though he had filled with more glory the subordinate station of Cæsar than the superior rank of Augustus, he preserved, till the moment of his death, the first place among the princes of the Roman world. He survived his retreat from Italy about four years; and, wisely relinquishing his views of universal empire, he devoted the remainder of his life to the enjoyment of pleasure, and to the execution of some works of public utility; among which we may distinguish the discharging into the Danube the superfluous waters of the lake Pelso, and the cutting down the immense forests that encompassed it; an operation worthy of a monarch, since it gave an extensive country to the agriculture of his Pannonian subjects.[14] His death was occasioned by a very painful and lingering disorder. His body, swelled by an intemperate course of life to an unwieldy corpulence, was covered with ulcers, and devoured by innumerable swarms of those insects who have given their name to a most loathsome disease; but, as Galerius had offended a very zealous and powerful party among his subjects, his sufferings, instead of exciting their compassion, have been celebrated as the visible effects of divine justice. He had no sooner expired in his palace of Nicomedia, than the two emperors who were indebted for their purple to his favour began to collect their forces, with the intention either of disputing, or of dividing, the dominions which he had left without a master. They were persuaded however to desist from the former design, and to agree in the latter. The provinces of Asia fell to the share of Maximin, and those of Europe augmented the portion of Licinius. The Hellespont and the Thracian Bosphorus formed their mutual boundary, and the banks of those narrow seas, which flowed in the midst of the Roman world, were covered with soldiers, with arms, and with fortifications. The deaths of Maximian and of Galerius reduced the number of emperors to four. The sense of their true interest soon connected Licinius and Constantine; a secret alliance was concluded between Maximin and Maxentius, and their unhappy subjects expected with terror the bloody consequences of their inevitable dissensions, which were no longer restrained by the fear or the respect which they had entertained for Galerius.

Among so many crimes and misfortunes occasioned by the pas-

[14] *But that lake was situated on the Upper Pannonia, near the borders of Noricum; and the province of Valeria (a name which the wife of Galerius gave to the drained country) undoubtedly lay between the Drave and the Danube. I should therefore suspect that Victor has confounded the lake Pelso, with the Volocean marshes, or, as they are now called, the lake Sabaton. It is placed in the heart of Valeria, and its present extent is not less than 12 Hungarian miles (about 70 English) in length, and two in breadth.*

sions of the Roman princes, there is some pleasure in discovering a single action which may be ascribed to their virtue. In the sixth year of his reign, Constantine visited the city of Autun, and generously remitted the arrears of tribute, reducing at the same time the proportion of their assessment, from twenty-five to eighteen thousand heads, subject to the real and personal capitation. Yet even this indulgence affords the most unquestionable proof of the public misery. This tax was so extremely oppressive, either in itself or in the mode of collecting it, that, whilst the revenue was increased by extortion, it was diminished by despair: a considerable part of the territory of Autun was left uncultivated; and great numbers of the provincials rather chose to live as exiles and outlaws than to support the weight of civil society. It is but too probable that the bountiful emperor relieved, by a partial act of liberality, one among the many evils which he had caused by his general maxims of administration. But even those maxims were less the effect of choice than of necessity. And, if we except the death of Maximian, the reign of Constantine in Gaul seems to have been the most innocent and even virtuous period of his life. The provinces were protected by his presence from the inroads of the barbarians, who either dreaded or experienced his active valour. After a signal victory over the Franks and Alemanni, several of their princes were exposed by his order to the wild beasts in the amphitheatre of Treves, and the people seem to have enjoyed the spectacle, without discovering, in such a treatment of royal captives, anything that was repugnant to the laws of nations or of humanity.[15]

[15] *A great number of the French youth were likewise exposed to the same cruel and ignominious death.*

The virtues of Constantine were rendered more illustrious by the vices of Maxentius. Whilst the Gallic provinces enjoyed as much happiness as the condition of the times was capable of receiving, Italy and Africa groaned under the dominion of a tyrant as contemptible as he was odious. The zeal of flattery and faction has indeed too frequently sacrificed the reputation of the vanquished to the glory of their successful rivals; but even those writers who have revealed, with the most freedom and pleasure, the faults of Constantine, unanimously confess that Maxentius was cruel, rapacious, and profligate.[16] He had the good fortune to suppress a slight rebellion in Africa. The governor and a few adherents had been guilty; the province suffered for their crime. The flourishing cities of Cirtha and Carthage, and the whole extent of that fertile country, were wasted by fire and sword. The abuse of victory was followed by the abuse of law and justice. A formidable army of sycophants and

[16] *Julian excludes Maxentius from the banquet of the Cæsars with abhorrence and contempt; and Zosimus accuses him of every kind of cruelty and profligacy.*

delators invaded Africa; the rich and the noble were easily convicted of a connexion with the rebels; and those among them who experienced the emperor's clemency were only punished by the confiscation of their estates. So signal a victory was celebrated by a magnificent triumph, and Maxentius exposed to the eyes of the people the spoils and captives of a Roman province. The state of the capital was no less deserving of compassion than that of Africa. The wealth of Rome supplied an inexhaustible fund for his vain and prodigal expenses, and the ministers of his revenue were skilled in the arts of rapine. It was under his reign that the method of exacting a *free gift* from the senators was first invented; and, as the sum was insensibly increased, the pretences of levying it, a victory, a birth, a marriage, or an Imperial consulship, were proportionably multiplied. Maxentius had imbibed the same implacable aversion to the senate, which had characterized most of the former tyrants of Rome; nor was it possible for his ungrateful temper to forgive the generous fidelity which had raised him to the throne and supported him against all his enemies. The lives of the senators were exposed to his jealous suspicions, the dishonour of their wives and daughters heightened the gratification of his sensual passions.[17] It may be presumed that an Imperial lover was seldom reduced to sigh in vain; but, whenever persuasion proved ineffectual, he had recourse to violence; and there remains *one* memorable example of a noble matron, who preserved her chastity by a voluntary death. The soldiers were the only order of men whom he appeared to respect, or studied to please. He filled Rome and Italy with armed troops, connived at their tumults, suffered them with impunity to plunder, and even to massacre, the defenceless people; and, indulging them in the same licentiousness which their emperor enjoyed, Maxentius often bestowed on his military favourites the splendid villa, or the beautiful wife, of a senator. A prince of such a character, alike incapable of governing either in peace or in war, might purchase the support, but he could never obtain the esteem, of the army. Yet his pride was equal to his other vices. Whilst he passed his indolent life, either within the walls of his palace, or in the neighbouring gardens of Sallust, he was repeatedly heard to declare, that *he alone* was emperor, and that the other princes were no more than his lieutenants, on whom he had devolved the defence of the frontier provinces, that he might enjoy without interruption the elegant luxury of the capital. Rome, which had so long regretted the absence, lamented, during the six years of his reign, the presence, of her sovereign.

[17] *The virtuous matron, who stabbed herself to escape the violence of Maxentius, was a Christian, wife to the præfect of the city, and her name was Sophronia. It still remains a question among the casuists, whether, on such occasions, suicide is justifiable.*

Though Constantine might view the conduct of Maxentius with abhorrence, and the situation of the Romans with compassion, we have no reason to presume that he would have taken up arms to punish the one or to relieve the other. But the tyrant of Italy rashly ventured to provoke a formidable enemy, whose ambition had been hitherto restrained by considerations of prudence, rather than by principles of justice.[18] After the death of Maximian, his titles, according to the established custom, had been erased, and his statues thrown down with ignominy. His son, who had persecuted and deserted him when alive, affected to display the most pious regard for his memory, and gave orders that a similar treatment should be immediately inflicted on all the statues that had been erected in Italy and Africa to the honour of Constantine. That wise prince, who sincerely wished to decline a war, with the difficulty and importance of which he was sufficiently acquainted, at first dissembled the insult, and sought for redress by the milder expedients of negotiation, till he was convinced that the hostile and ambitious designs of the Italian emperor made it necessary for him to arm in his own defence. Maxentius, who openly avowed his pretensions to the whole monarchy of the West, had already prepared a very considerable force to invade the Gallic provinces on the side of Rhætia, and, though he could not expect any assistance from Licinius, he was flattered with the hope that the legions of Illyricum, allured by his presents and promises, would desert the standard of that prince, and unanimously declare themselves his soldiers and subjects. Constantine no longer hesitated. He had deliberated with caution, he acted with vigour. He gave a private audience to the ambassadors, who, in the name of the senate and people, conjured him to deliver Rome from a detested tyrant; and, without regarding the timid remonstrances of his council, he resolved to prevent the enemy, and to carry the war into the heart of Italy.

The enterprise was as full of danger as of glory; and the unsuccessful event of two former invasions was sufficient to inspire the most serious apprehensions. The veteran troops, who revered the name of Maximian, had embraced in both those wars the party of his son, and were now restrained by a sense of honour, as well as of interest, from entertaining an idea of a second desertion. Maxentius, who considered the Prætorian guards as the firmest defence of his throne, had increased them to their ancient establishment; and they composed, including the rest of the Italians who were inlisted into his service, a formidable body of fourscore thousand men. Forty

[18] *After the victory of Constantine, it was universally allowed that the motive of delivering the republic from a detested tyrant would, at any time, have justified his expedition into Italy.*

thousand Moors and Carthaginians had been raised since the reduction of Africa. Even Sicily furnished its proportion of troops; and the army of Maxentius amounted to one hundred and seventy thousand foot and eighteen thousand horse. The wealth of Italy supplied the expenses of the war; and the adjacent provinces were exhausted to form immense magazines of corn and every other kind of provisions. The whole force of Constantine consisted of ninety thousand foot and eight thousand horse;[19] and, as the defence of the Rhine required an extraordinary attention during the absence of the emperor, it was not in his power to employ above half his troops in the Italian expedition, unless he sacrificed the public safety to his private quarrel.[20] At the head of about forty thousand soldiers, he marched to encounter an enemy whose numbers were at least four times superior to his own. But the armies of Rome, placed at a secure distance from danger, were enervated by indulgence and luxury. Habituated to the baths and theatres of Rome, they took the field with reluctance, and were chiefly composed of veterans who had almost forgotten, or of new levies who had never acquired, the use of arms and the practice of war. The hardy legions of Gaul had long defended the frontiers of the empire against the barbarians of the North; and in the performance of that laborious service their valour was exercised and their discipline confirmed. There appeared the same difference between the leaders as between the armies. Caprice or flattery had tempted Maxentius with the hopes of conquest; but these aspiring hopes soon gave way to the habits of pleasure and the consciousness of his inexperience. The intrepid mind of Constantine had been trained from his earliest youth to war, to action, and to military command.

When Hannibal marched from Gaul into Italy, he was obliged, first to discover, and then to open, a way over mountains, and through savage nations, that had never yielded a passage to a regular army.[21] The Alps were then guarded by nature, they are now fortified by art. Citadels, constructed with no less skill than labour and expense, command every avenue into the plain, and on that side render Italy almost inaccessible to the enemies of the king of Sardinia. But in the course of the intermediate period, the generals who have attempted the passage have seldom experienced any difficulty or resistance. In the age of Constantine, the peasants of the mountains were civilized and obedient subjects; the country was plentifully stocked with provisions, and the stupendous highways which the Romans had carried over the Alps opened several communica-

[19] *Zosimus has given us this curious account of the forces on both sides. He makes no mention of any naval armaments, though we are assured that the war was carried on by sea as well as by land; and that the fleet of Constantine took possession of Sardinia, Corsica, and the ports of Italy.*

[20] *It is not surprising that the orator should diminish the numbers with which his sovereign achieved the conquest of Italy; but it appears somewhat singular, that he should esteem the tyrant's army at no more than 100,000 men.*

[21] *The three principal passages of the Alps between Gaul and Italy are those of Mount St. Bernard, Mount Cenis, and Mount Genevre. Tradition, and a resemblance of names (Alpes Penninæ), had assigned the first of these for the march of Hannibal. The Chevalier de Folard and M. d'Anville have led him over Mount Genevre. But, notwithstanding the authority of an experienced officer and a learned geographer, the pretensions of Mount Cenis are supported in a specious, not to say a convincing manner, by M. Grosley.*

tions between Gaul and Italy. Constantine preferred the road of the Cottian Alps, or, as it is now called, of Mount Cenis, and led his troops with such active diligence that he descended into the plain of Piedmont before the court of Maxentius had received any certain intelligence of his departure from the banks of the Rhine. The city of Susa, however, which is situated at the foot of Mount Cenis, was surrounded with walls, and provided with a garrison sufficiently numerous to check the progress of an invader; but the impatience of Constantine's troops disdained the tedious forms of a siege. The same day that they appeared before Susa, they applied fire to the gates and ladders to the walls; and, mounting to the assault amidst a shower of stones and arrows, they entered the place sword in hand, and cut in pieces the greatest part of the garrison. The flames were extinguished by the care of Constantine, and the remains of Susa preserved from total destruction. About forty miles from thence, a more severe contest awaited him. A numerous army of Italians was assembled, under the lieutenants of Maxentius, in the plains of Turin. Its principal strength consisted in a species of heavy cavalry, which the Romans, since the decline of their discipline, had borrowed from the nations of the East. The horses, as well as the men, were clothed in complete armour, the joints of which were artfully adapted to the motions of their bodies. The aspect of this cavalry was formidable, their weight almost irresistible; and, as, on this occasion, their generals had drawn them up in a compact column or wedge, with a sharp point, and with spreading flanks, they flattered themselves that they should easily break and trample down the army of Constantine. They might, perhaps, have succeeded in their design, had not their experienced adversary embraced the same method of defence which in similar circumstances had been practised by Aurelian. The skilful evolutions of Constantine divided and baffled this massy column of cavalry. The troops of Maxentius fled in confusion towards Turin; and, as the gates of the city were shut against them, very few escaped the sword of the victorious pursuers. By this important service Turin deserved to experience the clemency and even favour of the conqueror. He made his entry into the Imperial palace of Milan, and almost all the cities of Italy between the Alps and the Po not only acknowledged the power, but embraced with zeal the party, of Constantine.

From Milan to Rome, the Æmilian and Flaminian highways offered an easy march of about four hundred miles; but, though Constantine was impatient to encounter the tyrant, he prudently directed his operations against another army of Italians, who, by their strength and position, might either oppose his progress, or, in case of a misfortune, might intercept his retreat. Ruricius Pompeianus, a general distinguished by his valour and ability, had under his command the city of Verona, and all the troops that were stationed in the province of Venetia. As soon as he was informed that Constantine was advancing towards him, he detached a large body of cavalry, which was defeated in an engagement near Brescia, and pursued by the Gallic legions as far as the gates of Verona. The necessity, the importance, and the difficulties of the siege of Verona immediately presented themselves to the sagacious mind of Constantine.[22] The city was accessible only by a narrow peninsula towards the west, as the other three sides were surrounded by the Adige, a rapid river which covered the province of Venetia, from whence the besieged derived an inexhaustible supply of men and provisions. It was not without great difficulty, and after several fruitless attempts, that Constantine found means to pass the river, at some distance above the city, and in a place where the torrent was less violent. He then encompassed Verona with strong lines, pushed his attacks with prudent vigour, and repelled a desperate sally of Pompeianus. That intrepid general, when he had used every means of defence that the strength of the place or that of the garrison could afford, secretly escaped from Verona, anxious not for his own but for the public safety. With indefatigable diligence he soon collected an army sufficient either to meet Constantine in the field, or to attack him if he obstinately remained within his lines. The emperor, attentive to the motions, and informed of the approach, of so formidable an enemy, left a part of his legions to continue the operations of the siege, whilst, at the head of those troops on whose valour and fidelity he more particularly depended, he advanced in person to engage the general of Maxentius. The army of Gaul was drawn up in two lines, according to the usual practice of war; but their experienced leader, perceiving that the numbers of the Italians far exceeded his own, suddenly changed his disposition, and, reducing the second, extended the front of his first, line to a just proportion with that of the enemy. Such evolutions, which only veteran troops can execute without confusion in a moment of danger, commonly prove decisive: but, as this engagement began towards the close of the day, and was contested with great obstinacy during the whole night, there was less room for the conduct of the generals than for the courage of the soldiers. The return of light displayed the victory of Constan-

[22] *The Marquis Maffei has examined the siege and battle of Verona with that degree of attention and accuracy which was due to a memorable action that happened in his native country. The fortifications of that city, constructed by Gallienus, were less extensive than the modern walls, and the amphitheatre was not included within their circumference.*

tine, and a field of carnage, covered with many thousands of the vanquished Italians. Their general, Pompeianus, was found among the slain; Verona immediately surrendered at discretion, and the garrison was made prisoners of war.[23] When the officers of the victorious army congratulated their master on this important success, they ventured to add some respectful complaints, of such a nature, however, as the most jealous monarchs will listen to without displeasure. They represented to Constantine that, not contented with performing all the duties of a commander, he had exposed his own person with an excess of valour which almost degenerated into rashness; and they conjured him for the future to pay more regard to the preservation of a life in which the safety of Rome and of the empire was involved.

While Constantine signalized his conduct and valour in the field, the sovereign of Italy appeared insensible of the calamities and danger of a civil war which raged in the heart of his dominions. Pleasure was still the only business of Maxentius. Concealing, or at least attempting to conceal, from the public knowledge the misfortunes of his arms, he indulged himself in vain confidence which deferred the remedies of the approaching evil, without deferring the evil itself. The rapid progress of Constantine [24] was scarcely sufficient to awaken him from this fatal security; he flattered himself that his well-known liberality, and the majesty of the Roman name, which had already delivered him from two invasions, would dissipate with the same facility the rebellious army of Gaul. The officers of experience and ability who had served under the banners of Maximian were at length compelled to inform his effeminate son of the imminent danger to which he was reduced; and, with a freedom that at once surprised and convinced him, to urge the necessity of preventing his ruin by a vigorous exertion of his remaining power. The resources of Maxentius, both of men and money, were still considerable. The Prætorian guards felt how strongly their own interest and safety were connected with his cause; and a third army was soon collected, more numerous than those which had been lost in the battles of Turin and Verona. It was far from the intention of the emperor to lead his troops in person. A stranger to the exercises of war, he trembled at the apprehension of so dangerous a contest; and, as fear is commonly superstitious, he listened with melancholy attention to the rumours of omens and presages which seemed to menace his life and empire. Shame at length supplied the place of courage, and forced him to take the field. He was unable to sustain the

[23] *They wanted chains for so great a multitude of captives; and the whole council was at a loss; but the sagacious conqueror imagined the happy expedient of converting into fetters the swords of the vanquished.*

[24] *The Marquis Maffei has made it extremely probable that Constantine was still at Verona, the 1st of September,* A.D. *312, and that the memorable æra of the Indictions was dated from his conquest of the Cisalpine Gaul.*

contempt of the Roman people. The circus resounded with their indignant clamours, and they tumultuously besieged the gates of the palace, reproaching the pusillanimity of their indolent sovereign, and celebrating the heroic spirit of Constantine. Before Maxentius left Rome, he consulted the Sibylline books. The guardians of these ancient oracles were as well versed in the arts of this world, as they were ignorant of the secrets of fate; and they returned him a very prudent answer, which might adapt itself to the event, and secure their reputation whatever should be the chance of arms.

The celerity of Constantine's march has been compared to the rapid conquest of Italy by the first of the Cæsars; nor is the flattering parallel repugnant to the truth of history, since no more than fifty-eight days elapsed between the surrender of Verona and the final decision of the war. Constantine had always apprehended that the tyrant would obey the dictates of fear, and perhaps of prudence; and that, instead of risking his last hopes in a general engagement, he would shut himself up within the walls of Rome. His ample magazines secured him against the danger of famine; and, as the situation of Constantine admitted not of delay, he might have been reduced to the sad necessity of destroying with fire and sword the Imperial city, the noblest reward of his victory, and the deliverance of which had been the motive, or rather indeed the pretence, of the civil war. It was with equal surprise and pleasure that, on his arrival at a place called Saxa Rubra, about nine miles from Rome,[25] he discovered the army of Maxentius prepared to give him battle. Their long front filled a very spacious plain, and their deep array reached to the banks of the Tiber, which covered their rear, and forbade their retreat. We are informed, and we may believe, that Constantine disposed his troops with consummate skill, and that he chose for himself the post of honour and danger. Distinguished by the splendour of his arms, he charged in person the cavalry of his rival; and his irresistible attack determined the fortune of the day. The cavalry of Maxentius was principally composed either of unwieldy cuirassiers or of light Moors and Numidians. They yielded to the vigour of the Gallic horse, which possessed more activity than the one, more firmness than the other. The defeat of the two wings left the infantry without any protection on its flanks, and the undisciplined Italians fled without reluctance from the standard of a tyrant whom they had always hated, and whom they no longer feared. The Prætorians, conscious that their offences were beyond the reach of mercy, were animated by revenge and despair. Notwithstanding

[25] *Saxa Rubra was in the neighbourhood of the Cremera, a trifling rivulet, illustrated by the valour and glorious death of the three hundred Fabii.*

their repeated efforts, those brave veterans were unable to recover the victory: they obtained, however, an honourable death; and it was observed that their bodies covered the same ground which had been occupied by their ranks. The confusion then became general, and the dismayed troops of Maxentius, pursued by an implacable enemy, rushed by thousands into the deep and rapid stream of the Tiber. The emperor himself attempted to escape back into the city over the Milvian bridge, but the crowds which pressed together through that narrow passage forced him into the river, where he was immediately drowned by the weight of his armour.[26] His body, which had sunk very deep into the mud, was found with some difficulty the next day. The sight of his head, when it was exposed to the eyes of the people, convinced them of their deliverance, and admonished them to receive with acclamations of loyalty and gratitude the fortunate Constantine, who thus achieved by his valour and ability the most splendid enterprise of his life.

In the use of victory, Constantine neither deserved the praise of clemency, nor incurred the censure of immoderate rigour. He inflicted the same treatment to which a defeat would have exposed his own person and family, put to death the two sons of the tyrant, and carefully extirpated his whole race. The most distinguished adherents of Maxentius must have expected to share his fate, as they had shared his prosperity and his crimes: but, when the Roman people loudly demanded a greater number of victims, the conqueror resisted, with firmness and humanity, those servile clamours which were dictated by flattery as well as by resentment. Informers were punished and discouraged; the innocent who had suffered under the late tyranny were recalled from exile, and restored to their estates. A general act of oblivion quieted the minds and settled the property of the people, both in Italy and in Africa. The first time that Constantine honoured the senate with his presence, he recapitulated his own services and exploits in a modest oration, assured that illustrious order of his sincere regard, and promised to re-establish its ancient dignity and privileges. The grateful senate repaid these unmeaning professions by the empty titles of honour, which it was yet in their power to bestow; and, without presuming to ratify the authority of Constantine, they passed a decree to assign him the first rank among the three *Augusti* who governed the Roman world.[27] Games and festivals were instituted to preserve the fame of his victory, and several edifices, raised at the expense of Maxentius, were dedicated to the honour of his successful rival. The triumphal

[26] *A very idle rumour soon prevailed, that Maxentius, who had not taken any precaution for his own retreat, had contrived a very artful snare to destroy the army of the pursuers; but that the wooden bridge, which was to have been loosened on the approach of Constantine, unluckily broke down under the weight of the flying Italians.*

[27] *Maximin, who was confessedly the eldest Cæsar, claimed, with some show of reason, the first rank among the Augusti.*

arch of Constantine still remains a melancholy proof of the decline of the arts, and a singular testimony of the meanest vanity. As it was not possible to find in the capital of the empire a sculptor who was capable of adorning that public monument, the arch of Trajan, without any respect either for his memory or for the rules of propriety, was stripped of its most elegant figures. The difference of times and persons, of actions and characters, was totally disregarded. The Parthian captives appear prostrate at the feet of a prince who never carried his arms beyond the Euphrates; and curious antiquarians can still discover the head of Trajan on the trophies of Constantine. The new ornaments which it was necessary to introduce between the vacancies of ancient sculpture are executed in the rudest and most unskilful manner.

The final abolition of the Prætorian guards was a measure of prudence as well as of revenge. Those haughty troops, whose numbers and privileges had been restored, and even augmented, by Maxentius, were for ever suppressed by Constantine. Their fortified camp was destroyed, and the few Prætorians who had escaped the fury of the sword were dispersed among the legions, and banished to the frontiers of the empire, where they might be serviceable without again becoming dangerous. By suppressing the troops which were usually stationed in Rome, Constantine gave the fatal blow to the dignity of the senate and people, and the disarmed capital was exposed without protection to the insults or neglect of its distant master. We may observe that, in this last effort to preserve their expiring freedom, the Romans, from the apprehension of a tribute, had raised Maxentius to the throne. He exacted that tribute from the senate, under the name of a free gift. They implored the assistance of Constantine. He vanquished the tyrant, and converted the free gift into a perpetual tax. The senators, according to the declaration which was required of their property, were divided into several classes. The most opulent paid annually eight pounds of gold, the next class paid four, the last two, and those whose poverty might have claimed an exemption were assessed, however, at seven pieces of gold. Besides the regular members of the senate, their sons, their descendants, and even their relations, enjoyed the vain privileges, and supported the heavy burdens, of the senatorial order; nor will it any longer excite our surprise that Constantine should be attentive to increase the number of persons who were included under so useful a description. After the defeat of Maxentius, the victorious emperor passed no more than two or three months in Rome, which he visited twice during the remainder of his life, to celebrate the solemn festivals of the tenth and of the twentieth years of his reign. Constantine was almost perpetually in motion, to exercise the legions, or to inspect the state of the provinces. Treves, Milan, Aquileia, Sirmium, Naissus, and Thessalonica were the occasional places of his residence, till he founded A NEW ROME on the confines of Europe and Asia.

Before Constantine marched into Italy, he had secured the friendship, or at least the neutrality, of Licinius, the Illyrian emperor. He had promised his sister Constantia in marriage to that prince; but the celebration of the nuptials was deferred till after the conclusion of the war; and the interview of the two emperors at Milan, which was appointed for that purpose, appeared to cement the union of their families and interests.[28] In the midst of the public festivity they were suddenly obliged to take leave of each other. An inroad of the Franks summoned Constantine to the Rhine, and the hostile approach of the sovereign of Asia demanded the immediate presence of Licinius. Maximin had been the secret ally of Maxentius, and, without being discouraged by his fate, he resolved to try the fortune of a civil war. He moved out of Syria towards the frontiers of Bithynia, in the depth of winter. The season was severe and tempestuous; great numbers of men as well as horses perished in the snow; and, as the roads were broken up by incessant rains, he was obliged to leave behind him a considerable part of the heavy baggage, which was unable to follow the rapidity of his forced marches. By this extraordinary effort of diligence, he arrived with a harassed but formidable army on the banks of the Thracian Bosphorus, before the lieutenants of Licinius were apprized of his hostile intentions. Byzantium surrendered to the power of Maximin, after a siege of eleven days. He was detained some days under the walls of Heraclea; and he had no sooner taken possession of that city than he was alarmed by the intelligence that Licinius had pitched his camp at the distance of only eighteen miles. After a fruitless negotiation, in which the two princes attempted to seduce the fidelity of each other's adherents, they had recourse to arms. The emperor of the East commanded a disciplined and veteran army of above seventy thousand men, and Licinius, who had collected about thirty thousand Illyrians, was at first oppressed by the superiority of numbers. His military skill and the firmness of his troops restored the day, and obtained a decisive victory. The incredible speed which Maximin exerted in his flight is much more celebrated than his prowess

[28] *Zosimus observes that, before the war, the sister of Constantine had been betrothed to Licinius. According to the younger Victor, Diocletian was invited to the nuptials; but, having ventured to plead his age and infirmities, he received a second letter filled with reproaches for his supposed partiality to the cause of Maxentius and Maximin.*

in the battle. Twenty-four hours afterwards he was seen pale, trembling, and without his Imperial ornaments, at Nicomedia, one hundred and sixty miles from the place of his defeat. The wealth of Asia was yet unexhausted; and, though the flower of his veterans had fallen in the late action, he had still power, if he could obtain time, to draw very numerous levies from Syria and Egypt. But he survived his misfortune only three or four months. His death, which happened at Tarsus, was variously ascribed to despair, to poison, and to the divine justice. As Maximin was alike destitute of abilities and of virtue, he was lamented neither by the people nor by the soldiers. The provinces of the East, delivered from the terrors of civil war, cheerfully acknowledged the authority of Licinius.

The vanquished emperor left behind him two children, a boy of about eight, and a girl of about seven, years old. Their inoffensive age might have excited compassion; but the compassion of Licinius was a very feeble resource, nor did it restrain him from *extinguishing* the name and memory of his adversary. The death of Severianus will admit of less excuse, as it was dictated neither by revenge nor by policy. The conqueror had never received any injury from the father of that unhappy youth, and the short and obscure reign of Severus in a distant part of the empire was already forgotten. But the execution of Candidianus was an act of the blackest cruelty and ingratitude. He was the natural son of Galerius, the friend and benefactor of Licinius. The prudent father had judged him too young to sustain the weight of a diadem; but he hoped that, under the protection of princes who were indebted to his favour for the Imperial purple, Candidianus might pass a secure and honourable life. He was now advancing towards the twentieth year of his age, and the royalty of his birth, though unsupported either by merit or ambition, was sufficient to exasperate the jealous mind of Licinius. To these innocent and illustrious victims of his tyranny, we must add the wife and daughter of the emperor Diocletian. When that prince conferred on Galerius the title of Cæsar, he had given him in marriage his daughter Valeria, whose melancholy adventures might furnish a very singular subject for tragedy. She had fulfilled, and even surpassed, the duties of a wife. As she had not any children herself, she condescended to adopt the illegitimate son of her husband, and invariably displayed towards the unhappy Candidianus the tenderness and anxiety of a real mother. After the death of Galerius, her ample possessions provoked the avarice, and her personal attractions excited the desires, of his successor Maximin.

He had a wife still alive; but divorce was permitted by the Roman law, and the fierce passions of the tyrant demanded an immediate gratification. The answer of Valeria was such as became the daughter and widow of emperors; but it was tempered by the prudence which her defenceless condition compelled her to observe. She represented to the persons whom Maximin had employed on this occasion "that, even if honour could permit a woman of her character and dignity to entertain a thought of second nuptials, decency at least must forbid her to listen to his addresses at a time when the ashes of her husband and his benefactor were still warm, and while the sorrows of her mind were still expressed by her mourning garments. She ventured to declare that she could place very little confidence in the professions of a man, whose cruel inconstancy was capable of repudiating a faithful and affectionate wife." On this repulse, the love of Maximin was converted into fury; and, as witnesses and judges were always at his disposal, it was easy for him to cover his fury with an appearance of legal proceedings, and to assault the reputation as well as the happiness of Valeria. Her estates were confiscated, her eunuchs and domestics devoted to the most inhuman tortures, and several innocent and respectable matrons, who were honoured with her friendship, suffered death on a false accusation of adultery. The empress herself, together with her mother Prisca, was condemned to exile; and, as they were ignominiously hurried from place to place before they were confined to a sequestered village in the deserts of Syria, they exposed their shame and distress to the provinces of the East, which, during thirty years, had respected their august dignity. Diocletian made several ineffectual efforts to alleviate the misfortunes of his daughter; and, as the last return that he expected for the Imperial purple, which he had conferred upon Maximin, he entreated that Valeria might· be permitted to share his retirement of Salona, and to close the eyes of her afflicted father. He entreated, but, as he could no longer threaten, his prayers were received with coldness and disdain; and the pride of Maximin was gratified in treating Diocletian as a suppliant, and his daughter as a criminal. The death of Maximin seemed to assure the empresses of a favourable alteration in their fortune. The public disorders relaxed the vigilance of their guard, and they easily found means to escape from the place of their exile, and to repair though with some precaution, and in disguise, to the court of Licinius. His behaviour, in the first days of his reign, and the honourable reception which he gave to young Candidianus, inspired Valeria with a secret satisfaction, both on her own account, and on that of her adopted son. But these grateful prospects were soon succeeded by horror and astonishment; and the bloody executions which stained the palace of Nicomedia sufficiently convinced her that the throne of Maximin was filled by a tyrant more inhuman than himself. Valeria consulted her safety by a hasty flight, and, still accompanied by her mother Prisca, they wandered above fifteen months through the provinces, concealed in the disguise of plebeian habits. They were at length discovered at Thessalonica; and, as the sentence of their death was already pronounced, they were immediately beheaded, and their bodies thrown into the sea. The people gazed on the melancholy spectacle; but their grief and indignation were suppressed by the terrors of a military guard. Such was the unworthy fate of the wife and daughter of Diocletian. We lament their misfortunes, we cannot discover their crimes; and, whatever idea we may justly entertain of the cruelty of Licinius, it remains a matter of surprise that he was not contented with some more secret and decent method of revenge.

The Roman world was now divided between Constantine and Licinius, the former of whom was master of the West, and the latter of the East. It might perhaps have been expected that the conquerors, fatigued with civil war, and connected by a private as well as public alliance, would have renounced, or at least would have suspended, any farther designs of ambition. And yet a year had scarcely elapsed after the death of Maximin, before the victorious emperors turned their arms against each other. The genius, the success, and the aspiring temper of Constantine may seem to mark him out as the aggressor; but the perfidious character of Licinius justifies the most unfavourable suspicions, and by the faint light which history reflects on this transaction we may discover a conspiracy fomented by his arts against the authority of his colleague. Constantine had lately given his sister Anastasia in marriage to Bassianus, a man of a considerable family and fortune, and had elevated his new kinsman to the rank of Cæsar. According to the system of government instituted by Diocletian, Italy, and perhaps Africa, were designed for his department in the empire. But the performance of the promised favour was either attended with so much delay, or accompanied with so many unequal conditions, that the fidelity of Bassianus was alienated rather than secured by the honourable distinction which he had obtained. His nomination had been ratified by the consent of Licinius, and that artful prince, by the means of his emissaries, soon contrived to enter into a secret and dangerous correspondence with the new Cæsar, to irritate his discontents, and to urge him to the rash enterprise of extorting by violence what he might in vain solicit from the justice of Constantine. But the vigilant emperor discovered the conspiracy before it was ripe for execution; and, after solemnly renouncing the alliance of Bassianus, despoiled him of the purple and inflicted the deserved punishment on his treason and ingratitude. The haughty refusal of Licinius, when he was required to deliver up the criminals who had taken refuge in his dominions, confirmed the suspicions already entertained of his perfidy; and the indignities offered at Æmona, on the frontiers of Italy, to the statues of Constantine, became the signal of discord between the two princes.[29]

The first battle was fought near Cibalis, a city of Pannonia, situated on the river Save, about fifty miles above Sirmium.[30] From the inconsiderable forces which in this important contest two such powerful monarchs brought into the field, it may be inferred that the one was suddenly provoked, and that the other was unexpectedly surprised. The emperor of the West had only twenty thousand, and the sovereign of the East no more than five and thirty thousand, men. The inferiority of number was, however, compensated by the advantage of the ground. Constantine had taken post in a defile about half a mile in breadth, between a steep hill and a deep morass; and in that situation he steadily expected and repulsed the first attack of the enemy. He pursued his success, and advanced into the plain. But the veteran legions of Illyricum rallied under the standard of a leader who had been trained to arms in the school of Probus and Diocletian. The missile weapons on both sides were soon exhausted; the two armies, with equal valour, rushed to a closer engagement of swords and spears, and the doubtful contest had already lasted from the dawn of day to a late hour of the evening when the right wing, which Constantine led in person, made a vigorous and decisive charge. The judicious retreat of Licinius saved the remainder of his troops from a total defeat; but, when he computed his loss, which amounted to more than twenty thousand men, he thought it unsafe to pass the night in the presence of an active and victorious enemy. Abandoning his camp and magazines, he marched away with secrecy and diligence at the head of the greatest part of his cavalry, and was soon removed beyond the danger of a pursuit. His diligence preserved his wife, his son, and his treasures, which he had deposited at Sirmium. Licinius passed

[29] *The situation of Æmona, or as it is now called Laybach, in Carniola, may suggest a conjecture. As it lay to the north-east of the Julian Alps, that important territory became a natural object of dispute between the sovereigns of Italy and of Illyricum.*

[30] *Cibalis or Cibalæ (whose name is still preserved in the obscure ruins of Swilei) was situated about fifty miles from Sirmium, the capital of Illyricum, and about one hundred from Taurunum, or Belgrade, and the conflux of the Danube and the Save.*

through that city, and, breaking down the bridge on the Save, hastened to collect a new army in Dacia and Thrace. In his flight he bestowed the precarious title of Cæsar on Valens, his general of the Illyrian frontier.

The plain of Mardia in Thrace was the theatre of a second battle no less obstinate and bloody than the former. The troops on both sides displayed the same valour and discipline; and the victory was once more decided by the superior abilities of Constantine, who directed a body of five thousand men to gain an advantageous height, from whence, during the heat of the action, they attacked the rear of the enemy, and made a very considerable slaughter. The troops of Licinius, however, presenting a double front, still maintained their ground, till the approach of night put an end to the combat, and secured their retreat towards the mountains of Macedonia. The loss of two battles, and of his bravest veterans, reduced the fierce spirit of Licinius to sue for peace. His ambassador, Mistrianus, was admitted to the audience of Constantine; he expatiated on the common topics of moderation and humanity, which are so familiar to the eloquence of the vanquished; represented, in the most insinuating language, that the event of the war was still doubtful, whilst its inevitable calamities were alike pernicious to both the contending parties; and declared that he was authorized to propose a lasting and honourable peace in the name of the *two* emperors his masters. Constantine received the mention of Valens with indignation and contempt. "It was not for such a purpose," he sternly replied, "that we have advanced from the shores of the western ocean in an uninterrupted course of combats and victories, that, after rejecting an ungrateful kinsman, we should accept for our colleague a contemptible slave. The abdication of Valens is the first article of the treaty." It was necessary to accept this humiliating condition, and the unhappy Valens, after a reign of a few days, was deprived of the purple and of his life. As soon as the obstacle was removed, the tranquillity of the Roman world was easily restored. The successive defeats of Licinius had ruined his forces, but they had displayed his courage and abilities. His situation was almost desperate, but the efforts of despair are sometimes formidable; and the good sense of Constantine preferred a great and certain advantage to a third trial of the chance of arms. He consented to leave his rival, or, as he again styled Licinius, his friend and brother, in the possession of Thrace, Asia Minor, Syria, and Egypt; but the provinces of Pannonia, Dalmatia, Dacia, Macedonia, and Greece, were yielded to the western empire, and the dominions of Constantine now extended from the confines of Caledonia to the extremity of Peloponnesus. It was stipulated by the same treaty that three royal youths, the sons of the emperors, should be called to the hopes of the succession. Crispus and the younger Constantine were soon afterwards declared Cæsars in the West, while the younger Licinius was invested with the same dignity in the East. In this double proportion of honours, the conqueror asserted the superiority of his arms and power.

The reconciliation of Constantine and Licinius, though it was embittered by resentment and jealousy, by the remembrance of recent injuries, and by the apprehension of future dangers, maintained, however, above eight years, the tranquillity of the Roman world. As a very regular series of the Imperial laws commences about this period, it would not be difficult to transcribe the civil regulations which employed the leisure of Constantine. But the most important of his institutions are intimately connected with the new system of policy and religion, which was not perfectly established till the last and peaceful years of his reign. There are many of his laws which, as far as they concern the rights and property of individuals, and the practice of the bar, are more properly referred to the private than to the public jurisprudence of the empire; and he published many edicts of so local and temporary a nature, that they would ill deserve the notice of a general history. Two laws, however, may be selected from the crowd; the one, for its importance, the other, for its singularity; the former for its remarkable benevolence, the latter for its excessive severity. 1. The horrid practice, so familiar to the ancients, of exposing or murdering their newborn infants, was become every day more frequent in the provinces, and especially in Italy. It was the effect of distress; and the distress was principally occasioned by the intolerable burden of taxes, and by the vexatious as well as cruel prosecutions of the officers of the revenue against their insolvent debtors. The less opulent or less industrious part of mankind, instead of rejoicing in an increase of family, deemed it an act of paternal tenderness to release their children from the impending miseries of a life which they themselves were unable to support. The humanity of Constantine, moved, perhaps, by some recent and extraordinary instances of despair, engaged him to address an edict to all the cities of Italy, and afterwards of Africa, directing immediate and sufficient relief to be given to those parents who should produce, before the magistrates, the children whom their own poverty would not allow them to educate. But the promise was too liberal, and the provision too vague, to effect any general or permanent benefit. The law, though it may merit some praise, served rather to display than to alleviate the public distress. It still remains an authentic monument to contradict and confound those venal orators, who were too well satisfied with their own situation to discover either vice or misery under the government of a generous sovereign. 2. The laws of Constantine against rapes were dictated with very little indulgence for the most amiable weaknesses of human nature; since the description of that crime was applied not only to the brutal violence which compelled, but even to the gentle seduction which might persuade, an unmarried woman, under the age of twenty-five, to leave the house of her parents. "The successful ravisher was punished with death; and, as if simple death was inadequate to the enormity of his guilt, he was either burnt alive or torn in pieces by wild beasts in the amphitheatre. The virgin's declaration that she had been carried away with her own consent, instead of saving her lover, exposed her to share his fate. The duty of a public prosecution was intrusted to the parents of the guilty or unfortunate maid; and, if the sentiments of Nature prevailed on them to dissemble the injury, and to repair by a subsequent marriage the honour of their family, they were themselves punished by exile and confiscation. The slaves, whether male or female, who were convicted of having been accessory to the rape or seduction, were burned alive, or put to death by the ingenious torture of pouring down their throats a quantity of melted lead. As the crime was of a public kind, the accusation was permitted even to strangers. The commencement of the action was not limited to any term of years, and the consequences of the sentence were extended to the innocent offspring of such an irregular union." But, whenever the offence inspires less horror than the punishment, the rigour of penal law is obliged to give way to the common feelings of mankind. The most odious parts of this edict were softened or repealed in the subsequent reigns; and even Constantine himself very frequently alleviated, by partial acts of mercy, the stern temper of his general institutions. Such, indeed, was the singular humour of that emperor, who showed himself as indulgent, and even remiss, in the execution of his laws, as he was severe, and even cruel, in the enacting of them. It is scarcely possible to observe a more decisive symptom of weakness, either in the character of the prince, or in the constitution of the government.[31]

[31] *Eusebius chooses to affirm that in the reign of his hero the sword of justice hung idle in the hands of the magistrates. Eusebius himself and the Theodosian Code will inform us that this excessive lenity was not owing to the want either of atrocious criminals or of penal laws.*

The civil administration was sometimes interrupted by the military defence of the empire. Crispus, a youth of the most amiable character, who had received with the title of Cæsar the command of the Rhine, distinguished his conduct, as well as valour, in several victories over the Franks and Alemanni; and taught the barbarians of that frontier to dread the eldest son of Constantine, and the grandson of Constantius.[32] The emperor himself had assumed the more difficult and important province of the Danube. The Goths, who in the time of Claudius and Aurelian had felt the weight of the Roman arms, respected the power of the empire, even in the midst of its intestine divisions. But the strength of that warlike nation was now restored by a peace of near fifty years; a new generation had arisen, who no longer remembered the misfortunes of ancient days: the Sarmatians of the lake Mæotis followed the Gothic standard, either as subjects or as allies, and their united force was poured upon the countries of Illyricum. Campona, Margus, and Bononia, appear to have been the scenes of several memorable sieges and battles;[33] and, though Constantine encountered a very obstinate resistance, he prevailed at length in the contest, and the Goths were compelled to purchase an ignominious retreat by restoring the booty and prisoners which they had taken. Nor was this advantage sufficient to satisfy the indignation of the emperor. He resolved to chastise as well as to repulse the insolent barbarians who had dared to invade the territories of Rome. At the head of the legions he passed the Danube, after repairing the bridge which had been constructed by Trajan, penetrated into the strongest recesses of Dacia, and, when he had inflicted a severe revenge, condescended to give peace to the suppliant Goths, on condition that, as often as they were required, they should supply his armies with a body of forty thousand soldiers. Exploits like these were no doubt honourable to Constantine and beneficial to the state; but it may surely be questioned whether they can justify the exaggerated assertion of Eusebius, that ALL SCYTHIA, as far as the extremity of the North, divided as it was into so many names and nations of the most various and savage manners, had been added by his victorious arms to the Roman empire.

In this exalted state of glory it was impossible that Constantine should any longer endure a partner in the empire. Confiding in the superiority of his genius and military power, he determined, without any previous injury, to exert them for the destruction of Licinius, whose advanced age and unpopular vices seemed to offer a very easy conquest. But the old emperor, awakened by the approaching

[32] *The victory of Crispus over the Alemanni is expressed on some medals.*

[33] *It is supposed that the Sarmatian games, celebrated in the month of November, derived their origin from the success of this war.*

danger, deceived the expectations of his friends as well as of his enemies. Calling forth that spirit and those abilities by which he had
deserved the friendship of Galerius and the Imperial purple, he
prepared himself for the contest, collected the forces of the East, and
soon filled the plains of Hadrianople with his troops, and the
Streights of the Hellespont with his fleet. The army consisted of one
hundred and fifty thousand foot, and fifteen thousand horse; and,
as the cavalry was drawn, for the most part, from Phrygia and Cappadocia, we may conceive a more favourable opinion of the beauty
of the horses than of the courage and dexterity of their riders. The
fleet was composed of three hundred and fifty galleys of three ranks
of oars. An hundred and thirty of these were furnished by Egypt,
and the adjacent coast of Africa. An hundred and ten sailed from
the ports of Phœnicia and the isle of Cyprus; and the maritime
countries of Bithynia, Ionia, and Caria were likewise obliged to provide an hundred and ten galleys. The troops of Constantine were
ordered to rendezvous at Thessalonica; they amounted to above an
hundred and twenty thousand horse and foot. Their emperor was
satisfied with their martial appearance, and his army contained
more soldiers, though fewer men, than that of his eastern competitor. The legions of Constantine were levied in the warlike provinces
of Europe; action had confirmed their discipline, victory had elevated their hopes, and there were among them a great number of
veterans, who, after seventeen glorious campaigns under the same
leader, prepared themselves to deserve an honourable dismission by
a last effort of their valour.[34] But the naval preparations of Constantine were in every respect much inferior to those of Licinius. The
maritime cities of Greece sent their respective quotas of men and
ships to the celebrated harbour of Piræus, and their united forces
consisted of no more than two hundred small vessels: a very feeble
armament, if it is compared with those formidable fleets which
were equipped and maintained by the republic of Athens during
the Peloponnesian war.[35] Since Italy was no longer the seat of government, the naval establishments of Misenum and Ravenna had
been gradually neglected; and, as the shipping and mariners of the
empire were supported by commerce rather than by war, it was
natural that they should the most abound in the industrious provinces of Egypt and Asia. It is only surprising that the eastern emperor, who possessed so great a superiority at sea, should have neglected the opportunity of carrying an offensive war into the centre
of his rival's dominions.

[34] *Constantine was very
attentive to the privi-
leges and comforts of
his fellow-veterans
(Conveterani), as he
now began to style them.*

[35] *Whilst the Athenians
maintained the empire
of the sea, their fleet
consisted of three, and
afterwards of four, hun-
dred galleys of three
ranks of oars, all com-
pletely equipped and
ready for immediate
service. The arsenal in
the port of Piræus had
cost the republic a thou-
sand talents, about two
hundred and sixteen
thousand pounds.*

Instead of embracing such an active resolution, which might have changed the whole face of the war, the prudent Licinius expected the approach of his rival in a camp near Hadrianople, which he had fortified with an anxious care that betrayed his apprehension of the event. Constantine directed his march from Thessalonica towards that part of Thrace, till he found himself stopped by the broad and rapid stream of the Hebrus, and discovered the numerous army of Licinius, which filled the steep ascent of the hill, from the river to the city of Hadrianople. Many days were spent in doubtful and distant skirmishes; but at length the obstacles of the passage and of the attack were removed by the intrepid conduct of Constantine. In this place we might relate a wonderful exploit of Constantine, which, though it can scarce be paralleled either in poetry or romance, is celebrated, not by a venal orator devoted to his fortune, but by an historian, the partial enemy of his fame. We are assured that the valiant emperor threw himself into the river Hebrus, accompanied only by *twelve* horsemen, and that, by the effort or terror of his invincible arm, he broke, slaughtered, and put to flight a host of an hundred and fifty thousand men. The credulity of Zosimus prevailed so strongly over his passion that, among the events of the memorable battle of Hadrianople, he seems to have selected and embellished, not the most important, but the most marvellous. The valour and danger of Constantine are attested by a slight wound which he received in the thigh; but it may be discovered even from an imperfect narration, and, perhaps, a corrupted text, that the victory was obtained no less by the conduct of the general than by the courage of the hero; that a body of five thousand archers marched round to occupy a thick wood in the rear of the enemy, whose attention was diverted by the construction of a bridge; and that Licinius, perplexed by so many artful evolutions, was reluctantly drawn from his advantageous post to combat on equal ground in the plain. The contest was no longer equal. His confused multitude of new levies was easily vanquished by the experienced veterans of the West. Thirty-four thousand men are reported to have been slain. The fortified camp of Licinius was taken by assault the evening of the battle; the greater part of the fugitives, who had retired to the mountains, surrendered themselves the next day to the discretion of the conqueror; and his rival, who could no longer keep the field, confined himself within the walls of Byzantium.

The siege of Byzantium, which was immediately undertaken by Constantine, was attended with great labour and uncertainty. In the late civil wars, the fortifications of that place, so justly considered as the key of Europe and Asia, had been repaired and strengthened; and, as long as Licinius remained master of the sea, the garrison was much less exposed to the danger of famine than the army of the besiegers. The naval commanders of Constantinople were summoned to his camp, and received his positive orders to force the passage of the Hellespont, as the fleet of Licinius, instead of seeking and destroying their feeble enemy, continued inactive in those narrow streights where its superiority of numbers was of little use or advantage. Crispus, the emperor's eldest son, was intrusted with the execution of this daring enterprise, which he performed with so much courage and success, that he deserved the esteem, and most probably excited the jealousy, of his father. The engagement lasted two days, and, in the evening of the first, the contending fleets, after a considerable and mutual loss, retired into their respective harbours of Europe and Asia. The second day about noon a strong south wind [36] sprang up, which carried the vessels of Crispus against the enemy; and, as the casual advantage was improved by his skilful intrepidity, he soon obtained a complete victory. An hundred and thirty vessels were destroyed, five thousand men were slain, and Amandus, the admiral of the Asiatic fleet, escaped with the utmost difficulty to the shores of Chalcedon. As soon as the Hellespont was open, a plentiful convoy of provisions flowed into the camp of Constantine, who had already advanced the operations of the siege. He constructed artificial mounds of earth of an equal height with the ramparts of Byzantium. The lofty towers which were erected on that foundation galled the besieged with large stones and darts from the military engines, and the battering rams had shaken the walls in several places. If Licinius persisted much longer in the defence, he exposed himself to be involved in the ruin of the place. Before he was surrounded, he prudently removed his person and treasures to Chalcedon in Asia; and, as he was always desirous of associating companions to the hopes and dangers of his fortune, he now bestowed the title of Cæsar on Martinianus, who exercised one of the most important offices of the empire.

Such were still the resources, and such the abilities, of Licinius, that, after so many successive defeats, he collected in Bithynia a new army of fifty or sixty thousand men, while the activity of Constantine was employed in the siege of Byzantium. The vigilant emperor did not, however, neglect the last struggles of his antagonist. A considerable part of his victorious army was transported over the Bos-

[36] *The current always sets out of the Hellespont; and, when it is assisted by a north wind, no vessel can attempt the passage. A south wind renders the force of the current almost imperceptible.*

phorus in small vessels, and the decisive engagement was fought soon after their landing on the heights of Chrysopolis, or, as it is now called, of Scutari. The troops of Licinius, though they were lately raised, ill armed, and worse disciplined, made head against their conquerors with fruitless but desperate valour, till a total defeat and the slaughter of five and twenty thousand men irretrievably determined the fate of their leader. He retired to Nicomedia, rather with the view of gaining some time for negotiation than with the hope of any effectual defence. Constantia, his wife and the sister of Constantine, interceded with her brother in favour of her husband, and obtained from his policy, rather than from his compassion, a solemn promise, confirmed by an oath, that after the sacrifice of Martinianus, and the resignation of the purple, Licinius himself should be permitted to pass the remainder of his life in peace and affluence. The behaviour of Constantia, and her relation to the contending parties, naturally recalls the remembrance of that virtuous matron who was the sister of Augustus and the wife of Antony. But the temper of mankind was altered, and it was no longer esteemed infamous for a Roman to survive his honour and independence. Licinius solicited and accepted the pardon of his offences, laid himself and his purple at the feet of his *lord* and *master,* was raised from the ground with insulting pity, was admitted the same day to the Imperial banquet, and soon afterwards was sent away to Thessalonica, which had been chosen for the place of his confinement. His confinement was soon terminated by death, and it is doubtful whether a tumult of the soldiers, or a decree of the senate, was suggested as the motive for his execution. According to the rules of tyranny, he was accused of forming a conspiracy, and of holding a treasonable correspondence with the barbarians; but, as he was never convicted, either by his own conduct or by any legal evidence, we may perhaps be allowed, from his weakness, to presume his innocence. The memory of Licinius was branded with infamy, his statues were thrown down, and by a hasty edict, of such mischievous tendency that it was almost immediately corrected, all his laws, and all the judicial proceedings of his reign, were at once abolished. By this victory of Constantine, the Roman world was again united under the authority of one emperor, thirty-seven years after Diocletian had divided his power and provinces with his associate Maximian.

The successive steps of the elevation of Constantine, from his first assuming the purple at York to the resignation of Licinius at

"*After the final destruction of the temple, by the arms of Titus and Hadrian, a ploughshare was drawn over the consecrated ground, as a sign of perpetual interdiction. Sion was deserted. The holy places were polluted with monuments of idolatry; and, either from design or accident, a chapel was dedicated to Venus on the spot which had been sanctified by the death and resurrection of Christ.*"

THE ARCH OF TITUS COMMEMORATING THE DESTRUCTION OF JERUSALEM, LOOKING TOWARD THE PALATINE

Nicomedia, have been related with some minuteness and precision, not only as the events are in themselves both interesting and important, but still more as they contributed to the decline of the empire by the expense of blood and treasure, and by the perpetual increase, as well of the taxes as of the military establishment. The foundation of Constantinople, and the establishment of the Christian religion, were the immediate and memorable consequences of this revolution.

XV

A CANDID but rational inquiry into the progress and establishment of Christianity may be considered as an essential part of the history of the Roman empire. While that great body was invaded by open violence, or undermined by slow decay, a pure and humble religion gently insinuated itself into the minds of men, grew up in silence and obscurity, derived new vigour from opposition, and finally erected the triumphant banner of the cross on the ruins of the Capitol. Nor was the influence of Christianity confined to the period or to the limits of the Roman empire. After a revolution of thirteen or fourteen centuries, that religion is still professed by the nations of Europe, the most distinguished portion of human kind in arts and learning as well as in arms. By the industry and zeal of the Europeans it has been widely diffused to the most distant shores of Asia and Africa; and by the means of their colonies has been firmly established from Canada to Chili, in a world unknown to the ancients.

But this inquiry, however useful or entertaining, is attended with two peculiar difficulties. The scanty and suspicious materials of ecclesiastical history seldom enable us to dispel the dark cloud that hangs over the first age of the church. The great law of impartiality too often obliges us to reveal the imperfections of the uninspired teachers and believers of the gospel; and, to a careless observer, *their* faults may seem to cast a shade on the faith which they professed. But the scandal of the pious Christian, and the fallacious triumph of the Infidel, should cease as soon as they recollect not only *by whom,* but likewise *to whom,* the Divine Revelation was given. The theologian may indulge the pleasing task of describing Religion as she descended from Heaven, arrayed in her native purity. A more melancholy duty is imposed on the historian. He must discover the inevitable mixture of error and corruption which she contracted in a long residence upon earth, among a weak and degenerate race of beings.

Our curiosity is naturally prompted to inquire by what means the Christian faith obtained so remarkable a victory over the established religions of the earth. To this inquiry, an obvious but satisfactory answer may be returned; that it was owing to the convincing evidence of the doctrine itself, and to the ruling providence of its great Author. But, as truth and reason seldom find so favourable a reception in the world, and as the wisdom of Providence frequently condescends to use the passions of the human heart, and the general circumstances of mankind, as instruments to execute its purpose; we may still be permitted, though with becoming submission, to ask not indeed what were the first, but what were the secondary causes of the rapid growth of the Christian church. It will, perhaps, appear that it was most effectually favoured and assisted by the five following causes: I. The inflexible, and, if we may use the expression, the intolerant zeal of the Christians, derived, it is true, from the Jewish religion, but purified from the narrow and unsocial spirit which, instead of inviting, had deterred the Gentiles from embracing the law of Moses. II. The doctrine of a future life, improved by every additional circumstance which could give weight and efficacy to that important truth. III. The miraculous powers ascribed to the primitive church. IV. The pure and austere morals of the Christians. V. The union and discipline of the Christian republic, which gradually formed an independent and increasing state in the heart of the Roman empire.

I. We have already described the religious harmony of the ancient world, and the facility with which the most different and even hostile nations embraced, or at least respected, each other's superstitions. A single people refused to join in the common intercourse of mankind. The Jews, who, under the Assyrian and Persian monarchies, had languished for many ages the most despised portion of their slaves, emerged from obscurity under the successors of Alexander; and, as they multiplied to a surprising degree in the East, and afterwards in the West, they soon excited the curiosity and wonder of other nations. The sullen obstinacy with which they maintained their peculiar rites and unsocial manners seemed to mark them out a distinct species of men, who boldly professed, or who faintly disguised, their implacable hatred to the rest of human kind. Neither the violence of Antiochus, nor the arts of Herod, nor the example of the circumjacent nations, could ever persuade the Jews to associate with the institutions of Moses the elegant mythology of the Greeks.[1] According to the maxims of universal toleration, the Romans protected a superstition which they despised. The polite Augustus condescended to give orders that sacrifices should be offered for his prosperity in the temple of Jerusalem;[2] while the meanest of the posterity of Abraham, who should have paid the same homage to the Jupiter of the Capitol, would have been an object of abhorrence to himself and to his brethren. But the moderation of the conquerors was insufficient to appease the jealous prejudices of their subjects, who were alarmed and scandalized at the ensigns of paganism, which necessarily introduced themselves into a Roman province. The mad attempt of Caligula to place his own statue in the temple of Jerusalem was defeated by the unanimous resolution of a people who dreaded death much less than such an idolatrous profanation.[3] Their attachment to the law of Moses was equal to their detestation of foreign religions. The current of zeal and devotion, as it was contracted into a narrow channel, ran with the strength, and sometimes with the fury, of a torrent.

This inflexible perseverance, which appeared so odious, or so ridiculous, to the ancient world, assumes a more awful character, since Providence has deigned to reveal to us the mysterious history of the chosen people. But the devout, and even scrupulous, attachment to the Mosaic religion, so conspicuous among the Jews who lived under the second temple, becomes still more surprising, if it is compared with the stubborn incredulity of their forefathers. When the law was given in thunder from Mount Sinai; when the tides of the ocean and the course of the planets were suspended for the convenience of the Israelites; and when temporal rewards and punishments were the immediate consequences of their piety or disobedience; they perpetually relapsed into rebellion against the visible majesty of their Divine King, placed the idols of the nations in the sanctuary of Jehovah, and imitated every fantastic ceremony that was practised in the tents of the Arabs or in the cities of Phœnicia.[4] As the protection of Heaven was deservedly withdrawn from the ungrateful race, their faith acquired a proportionable degree of vigour and purity. The contemporaries of Moses and Joshua had beheld, with careless indifference, the most amazing miracles. Under the pressure of every calamity, the belief of those miracles has preserved the Jews of a later period from the universal contagion of idolatry; and, in contradiction to every known principle of the

[1] *A Jewish sect, which indulged themselves in a sort of occasional conformity, derived from Herod, by whose example and authority they had been seduced, the name of Herodians. But their numbers were so inconsiderable, and their duration so short, that Josephus has not thought them worthy of his notice.*

[2] *Augustus left a foundation for a perpetual sacrifice. Yet he approved of the neglect which his grandson Caius expressed towards the temple of Jerusalem.*

[3] *Philo and Josephus gave a very circumstantial, but a very rhetorical, account of this transaction, which exceedingly perplexed the governor of Syria. At the first mention of this idolatrous proposal, King Agrippa fainted away; and did not recover his senses till the third day.*

[4] *For the enumeration of the Syrian and Arabian deities, it may be observed that Milton has comprised, in one hundred and thirty very beautiful lines, the two large and learned syntagmas which Selden had composed on that abstruse subject.*

349

human mind, that singular people seems to have yielded a stronger and more ready assent to the traditions of their remote ancestors than to the evidence of their own senses.[5]

The Jewish religion was admirably fitted for defence, but it was never designed for conquest; and it seems probable that the number of proselytes was never much superior to that of apostates. The divine promises were originally made, and the distinguishing rite of circumcision was enjoined, to a single family. When the posterity of Abraham had multiplied like the sands of the sea, the Deity, from whose mouth they received a system of laws and ceremonies, declared himself the proper and, as it were, the national God of Israel; and, with the most jealous care, separated his favourite people from the rest of mankind. The conquest of the land of Canaan was accompanied with so many wonderful and with so many bloody circumstances that the victorious Jews were left in a state of irreconcilable hostility with all their neighbours. They had been commanded to extirpate some of the most idolatrous tribes; and the execution of the divine will had seldom been retarded by the weakness of humanity. With the other nations they were forbidden to contract any marriages or alliances; and the prohibition of receiving them into the congregation, which, in some cases, was perpetual, almost always extended to the third, to the seventh, or even to the tenth generation. The obligation of preaching to the Gentiles the faith of Moses had never been inculcated as a precept of the law, nor were the Jews inclined to impose it on themselves as a voluntary duty. In the admission of new citizens, that unsocial people was actuated by the selfish vanity of the Greeks, rather than by the generous policy of Rome. The descendants of Abraham were flattered by the opinion that they alone were the heirs of the covenant; and they were apprehensive of diminishing the value of their inheritance, by sharing it too easily with the strangers of the earth. A larger acquaintance with mankind extended their knowledge without correcting their prejudices; and, whenever the God of Israel acquired any new votaries, he was much more indebted to the inconstant humour of polytheism than to the active zeal of his own missionaries. The religion of Moses seems to be instituted for a particular country, as well as for a single nation; and, if a strict obedience had been paid to the order that every male, three times in the year, should present himself before the Lord Jehovah, it would have been impossible that the Jews could ever have spread themselves beyond the narrow limits of the promised land. That obstacle was

---

[5] *"How long will this people provoke me? and how long will it be ere they believe me, for all the signs which I have shown among them?" It would be easy, but it would be unbecoming, to justify the complaint of the Deity, from the whole tenor of the Mosaic history.*

indeed removed by the destruction of the temple of Jerusalem; but the most considerable part of the Jewish religion was involved in its destruction; and the Pagans, who had long wondered at the strange report of an empty sanctuary, were at a loss to discover what could be the object, or what could be the instruments, of a worship which was destitute of temples and of altars, of priests and of sacrifices. Yet even in their fallen state, the Jews, still asserting their lofty and exclusive privileges, shunned, instead of courting, the society of strangers. They still insisted with inflexible rigour on those parts of the law which it was in their power to practise. Their peculiar distinctions of days, of meats, and a variety of trivial though burdensome observances, were so many objects of disgust and aversion for the other nations, to whose habits and prejudices they were diametrically opposite. The painful and even dangerous rite of circumcision was alone capable of repelling a willing proselyte from the door of the synagogue.

Under these circumstances, Christianity offered itself to the world, armed with the strength of the Mosaic law, and delivered from the weight of its fetters. An exclusive zeal for the truth of religion and the unity of God was as carefully inculcated in the new as in the ancient system; and whatever was now revealed to mankind, concerning the nature and designs of the Supreme Being, was fitted to increase their reverence for that mysterious doctrine. The divine authority of Moses and the prophets was admitted, and even established, as the firmest basis of Christianity. From the beginning of the world, an uninterrupted series of predictions had announced and prepared the long expected coming of the Messiah, who, in compliance with the gross apprehensions of the Jews, had been more frequently represented under the character of a King and Conqueror, than under that of a Prophet, a Martyr, and the Son of God. By his expiatory sacrifice, the imperfect sacrifices of the temple were at once consummated and abolished. The ceremonial law, which consisted only of types and figures, was succeeded by a pure and spiritual worship, equally adapted to all climates, as well as to every condition of mankind; and to the initiation of blood was substituted a more harmless initiation of water. The promise of divine favour, instead of being partially confined to the posterity of Abraham, was universally proposed to the freeman and the slave, to the Greek and to the barbarian, to the Jew and to the Gentile. Every privilege that could raise the proselyte from earth to Heaven, that could exalt his devotion, secure his happiness, or even gratify that secret pride which, under the semblance of devotion, insinuates itself into the human heart, was still reserved for the members of the Christian church; but at the same time all mankind was permitted, and even solicited, to accept the glorious distinction, which was not only proffered as a favour, but imposed as an obligation. It became the sacred duty of a new convert to diffuse among his friends and relations the blessing which he had received, and to warn them against a refusal that would be punished as a criminal disobedience to the will of a benevolent but all-powerful deity.

The enfranchisement of the church from the bonds of the synagogue was a work however of some time and of some difficulty. The Jewish converts, who acknowledged Jesus in the character of the Messiah foretold by their ancient oracles, respected him as a prophetic teacher of virtue and religion; but they obstinately adhered to the ceremonies of their ancestors, and were desirous of imposing them on the Gentiles, who continually augmented the number of believers. These Judaizing Christians seem to have argued with some degree of plausibility from the divine origin of the Mosaic law, and from the immutable perfections of its great Author. They affirmed *that,* if the Being, who is the same through all eternity, had designed to abolish those sacred rites which had served to distinguish his chosen people, the repeal of them would have been no less clear and solemn than their first promulgation: *that,* instead of those frequent declarations, which either suppose or assert the perpetuity of the Mosaic religion, it would have been represented as a provisionary scheme intended to last only till the coming of the Messiah, who should instruct mankind in a more perfect mode of faith and of worship: *that* the Messiah himself, and his disciples who conversed with him on earth, instead of authorizing by their example the most minute observance of the Mosaic law, would have published to the world the abolition of those useless and obsolete ceremonies, without suffering Christianity to remain during so many years obscurely confounded among the sects of the Jewish church. Arguments like these appear to have been used in the defence of the expiring cause of the Mosaic law; but the industry of our learned divines has abundantly explained the ambiguous language of the Old Testament, and the ambiguous conduct of the apostolic teachers. It was proper gradually to unfold the system of the Gospel, and to pronounce, with the utmost caution and tenderness, a sentence of condemnation so repugnant to the inclination and prejudices of the believing Jews.

The history of the church of Jerusalem affords a lively proof of the necessity of those precautions, and of the deep impression which the Jewish religion had made on the minds of its sectaries. The first fifteen bishops of Jerusalem were all circumcised Jews; and the congregation over which they presided, united the law of Moses with the doctrine of Christ. It was natural that the primitive tradition of a church which was founded only forty years after the death of Christ, and was governed almost as many years under the immediate inspection of his apostle, should be received as the standard of orthodoxy. The distant churches very frequently appealed to the authority of their venerable Parent, and relieved her distresses by a liberal contribution of alms. But, when numerous and opulent societies were established in the great cities of the empire, in Antioch, Alexandria, Ephesus, Corinth, and Rome, the reverence which Jerusalem had inspired to all the Christian colonies insensibly diminished. The Jewish converts, or, as they were afterwards called, the Nazarenes, who had laid the foundations of the church, soon found themselves overwhelmed by the increasing multitudes that from all the various religions of polytheism inlisted under the banner of Christ; and the Gentiles, who with the approbation of their peculiar apostle had rejected the intolerable weight of Mosaic ceremonies, at length refused to their more scrupulous brethren the same toleration which at first they had humbly solicited for their own practice. The ruin of the temple, of the city, and of the public religion of the Jews, was severely felt by the Nazarenes; as in their manners, though not in their faith, they maintained so intimate a connexion with their impious countrymen, whose misfortunes were attributed by the Pagans to the contempt, and more justly ascribed by the Christians to the wrath, of the Supreme Deity. The Nazarenes retired from the ruins of Jerusalem to the little town of Pella beyond the Jordan, where that ancient church languished above sixty years in solitude and obscurity.[6] They still enjoyed the comfort of making frequent and devout visits to the *Holy City*, and the hope of being one day restored to those seats which both nature and religion taught them to love as well as to revere. But at length, under the reign of Hadrian, the desperate fanaticism of the Jews filled up the measure of their calamities; and the Romans, exasperated by their repeated rebellions, exercised the rights of victory with unusual rigour. The emperor founded, under the name of Ælia Capitolina, a new city on Mount Sion,[7] to which he gave the privileges of a colony; and, denouncing the severest penalties against

[6] *During this occasional absence, the bishop and church of Pella still retained the title of Jerusalem. In the same manner, the Roman pontiffs resided seventy years at Avignon; and the patriarchs of Alexandria have long since transferred their episcopal seat to Cairo.*

[7] *The exile of the Jewish nation from Jerusalem is attested by Aristo of Pella, and is mentioned by several ecclesiastical writers; though some of them too hastily extend this interdiction to the whole country of Palestine.*

any of the Jewish people who should dare to approach its precincts, he fixed a vigilant garrison of a Roman cohort to enforce the execution of his orders. The Nazarenes had only one way left to escape the common proscription, and the force of truth was, on this occasion, assisted by the influence of temporal advantages. They elected Marcus for their bishop, a prelate of the race of the Gentiles, and most probably a native either of Italy or of some of the Latin provinces. At his persuasion, the most considerable part of the congregation renounced the Mosaic law, in the practice of which they had persevered above a century. By this sacrifice of their habits and prejudices they purchased a free admission into the colony of Hadrian, and more firmly cemented their union with the Catholic church.

When the name and honours of the church of Jerusalem had been restored to Mount Sion, the crimes·of heresy and schism were imputed to the obscure remnant of the Nazarenes which refused to accompany their Latin bishop. They still preserved their former habitation of Pella, spread themselves into the villages adjacent to Damascus, and formed an inconsiderable church in the city of Borœa, or, as it is now called, of Aleppo, in Syria.[8] The name of Nazarenes was deemed too honourable for those Christian Jews, and they soon received from the supposed poverty of their understanding, as well as of their condition, the contemptuous epithet of Ebionites.[9] In a few years after the return of the church of Jerusalem, it became a matter of doubt and controversy whether a man who sincerely acknowledged Jesus as the Messiah, but who still continued to observe the law of Moses, could possibly hope for salvation. The humane temper of Justin Martyr inclined him to answer this question in the affirmative; and, though he expressed himself with the most guarded diffidence, he ventured to determine in favour of such an imperfect Christian, if he were content to practise the Mosaic ceremonies, without pretending to assert their general use or necessity. But, when Justin was pressed to declare the sentiment of the church, he confessed that there were very many among the orthodox Christians, who not only excluded their Judaizing brethren from the hope of salvation, but who declined any intercourse with them in the common offices of friendship, hospitality, and social life. The more rigorous opinion prevailed, as it was natural to expect, over the milder; and an external bar of separation was fixed between the disciples of Moses and those of Christ. The unfortunate Ebionites, rejected from one religion as apostates, and from the

[8] *Le Clerc seems to have collected from Eusebius, Jerome, Epiphanius, and other writers, all the principal circumstances that relate to the Nazarenes, or Ebionites. The nature of their opinions soon divided them into a stricter and a milder sect; and there is some reason to conjecture that the family of Jesus Christ remained members, at least, of the latter and more moderate party.*

[9] *Some writers have been pleased to create an Ebion, the imaginary author of their sect and name. But we can more safely rely on the learned Eusebius than on the vehement Tertullian or the credulous Epiphanius.*

other as heretics, found themselves compelled to assume a more decided character; and, although some traces of that obsolete sect may be discovered as late as the fourth century, they insensibly melted away either into the church or the synagogue.[10]

While the orthodox church preserved a just medium between excessive veneration and improper contempt for the law of Moses, the various heretics deviated into equal but opposite extremes of error and extravagance. From the acknowledged truth of the Jewish religion the Ebionites had concluded that it could never be abolished. From its supposed imperfections the Gnostics as hastily inferred that it never was instituted by the wisdom of the Deity. There are some objections against the authority of Moses and the prophets, which too readily present themselves to the sceptical mind; though they can only be derived from our ignorance of remote antiquity, and from our incapacity to form an adequate judgment of the divine œconomy. These objections were eagerly embraced, and as petulantly urged, by the vain science of the Gnostics. As those heretics were, for the most part, averse to the pleasures of sense, they morosely arraigned the polygamy of the patriarchs, the gallantries of David, and the seraglio of Solomon. The conquest of the land of Canaan, and the extirpation of the unsuspecting natives, they were at a loss how to reconcile with the common notions of humanity and justice. But, when they recollected the sanguinary list of murders, of executions, and of massacres, which stain almost every page of the Jewish annals, they acknowledged that the barbarians of Palestine had exercised as much compassion towards their idolatrous enemies as they had ever shown to their friends or countrymen. Passing from the sectaries of the law to the law itself, they asserted that it was impossible that a religion which consisted only of bloody sacrifices and trifling ceremonies, and whose rewards as well as punishments were all of a carnal and temporal nature, could inspire the love of virtue, or restrain the impetuosity of passion. The Mosaic account of the creation and fall of man was treated with profane derision by the Gnostics, who would not listen with patience to the repose of the Deity after six days' labour, to the rib of Adam, the garden of Eden, the trees of life and of knowledge, the speaking serpent, the forbidden fruit, and the condemnation pronounced against human kind for the venial offence of their first progenitors. The God of Israel was impiously represented by the Gnostics as a being liable to passion and to error, capricious in his favour, implacable in his resentment, meanly jealous of his super-

[10] *Of all the systems of Christianity, that of Abyssinia is the only one which still adheres to the Mosaic rites. The eunuch of the queen Candace might suggest some suspicions; but, as we are assured that the Æthiopians were not converted till the fourth century, it is more reasonable to believe that they respected the Sabbath, and distinguished the forbidden meats, in imitation of the Jews, who, in a very early period, were seated on both sides of the Red Sea. Circumcision had been practised by the most ancient Æthiopians, from motives of health and cleanliness, which seem to be explained in the Recherches Philosophiques sur les Américains.*

stitious worship, and confining his partial providence to a single people and to this transitory life. In such a character they could discover none of the features of the wise and omnipotent father of the universe.[11] They allowed that the religion of the Jews was somewhat less criminal than the idolatry of the Gentiles; but it was their fundamental doctrine that the Christ whom they adored as the first and brightest emanation of the Deity appeared upon earth to rescue mankind from their various errors, and to reveal a *new* system of truth and perfection. The most learned of the fathers, by a very singular condescension, have imprudently admitted the sophistry of the Gnostics. Acknowledging that the literal sense is repugnant to every principle of faith as well as reason, they deem themselves secure and invulnerable behind the ample veil of allegory, which they carefully spread over every tender part of the Mosaic dispensation.

It has been remarked, with more ingenuity than truth, that the virgin purity of the church was never violated by schism or heresy before the reign of Trajan or Hadrian, about one hundred years after the death of Christ. We may observe, with much more propriety, that, during that period, the disciples of the Messiah were indulged in a freer latitude both of faith and practice than has ever been allowed in succeeding ages. As the terms of communion were insensibly narrowed, and the spiritual authority of the prevailing party was exercised with increasing severity, many of its most respectable adherents, who were called upon to renounce, were provoked to assert, their private opinions, to pursue the consequences of their mistaken principles, and openly to erect the standard of rebellion against the unity of the church. The Gnostics were distinguished as the most polite, the most learned, and the most wealthy of the Christian name, and that general appellation which expressed a superiority of knowledge was either assumed by their own pride or ironically bestowed by the envy of their adversaries. They were almost without exception of the race of the Gentiles, and their principal founders seem to have been natives of Syria or Egypt, where the warmth of the climate disposes both the mind and the body to indolent and contemplative devotion. The Gnostics blended with the faith of Christ many sublime but obscure tenets which they derived from oriental philosophy, and even from the religion of Zoroaster, concerning the eternity of matter, the existence of two principles, and the mysterious hierarchy of the invisible world. As soon as they launched out into that vast abyss, they delivered them-

[11] *The milder Gnostics considered Jehovah, the Creator, as a Being of a mixed nature between God and the Dæmon. Others confounded him with the evil principle. Consult the second century of the general history of Mosheim, which gives a very distinct, though concise, account of their strange opinions on this subject.*

selves to the guidance of a disordered imagination; and, as the paths of error are various and infinite, the Gnostics were imperceptibly divided into more than fifty particular sects, of whom the most celebrated appear to have been the Basilidians, the Valentinians, the Marcionites, and, in a still later period, the Manichæans. Each of these sects could boast of its bishops and congregations, of its doctors and martyrs, and, instead of the four gospels adopted by the church, the heretics produced a multitude of histories, in which the actions and discourses of Christ and of his apostles were adapted to their respective tenets.[12] The success of the Gnostics was rapid and extensive. They covered Asia and Egypt, established themselves in Rome, and sometimes penetrated into the provinces of the West. For the most part they arose in the second century, flourished during the third, and were suppressed in the fourth or fifth, by the prevalence of more fashionable controversies, and by the superior ascendant of the reigning power. Though they constantly disturbed the peace, and frequently disgraced the name, of religion, they contributed to assist rather than to retard the progress of Christianity. The Gentile converts, whose strongest objections and prejudices were directed against the law of Moses, could find admission into many Christian societies, which required not from their untutored mind any belief of an antecedent revelation. Their faith was insensibly fortified and enlarged, and the church was ultimately benefited by the conquests of its most inveterate enemies.[13]

But, whatever difference of opinion might subsist between the Orthodox, the Ebionites, and the Gnostics, concerning the divinity or the obligation of the Mosaic law, they were all equally animated by the same exclusive zeal and by the same abhorrence for idolatry which had distinguished the Jews from the other nations of the ancient world. The philosopher, who considered the system of polytheism as a composition of human fraud and error, could disguise a smile of contempt under the mask of devotion, without apprehending that either the mockery or the compliance would expose him to the resentment of any invisible, or, as he conceived them, imaginary powers. But the established religions of Paganism were seen by the primitive Christians in a much more odious and formidable light. It was the universal sentiment both of the church and of heretics that the dæmons were the authors, the patrons, and the objects of idolatry. Those rebellious spirits who had been degraded from the rank of angels, and cast down into the infernal pit, were still permitted to roam upon earth, to torment the bodies, and to

[12] *In a very remarkable passage, Origen, that indefatigable writer, who had consumed his life in the study of the scriptures, relies for their authenticity on the inspired authority of the church. It was impossible that the Gnostics could receive our present gospels, many parts of which (particularly in the resurrection of Christ) are directly, and as it might seem designedly, pointed against their favourite tenets. It is therefore somewhat singular that Ignatius should choose to employ a vague and doubtful tradition, instead of quoting the certain testimony of the evangelists.*

[13] *Augustin is a memorable instance of this gradual progress from reason to faith. He was, during several years, engaged in the Manichæan sect.*

seduce the minds, of sinful men. The dæmons soon discovered and abused the natural propensity of the human heart towards devotion, and, artfully withdrawing the adoration of mankind from their Creator, they usurped the place and honours of the Supreme Deity. By the success of their malicious contrivances, they at once gratified their own vanity and revenge, and obtained the only comfort of which they were yet susceptible, the hope of involving the human species in the participation of their guilt and misery. It was confessed, or at least it was imagined, that they had distributed among themselves the most important characters of Polytheism, one dæmon assuming the name and attributes of Jupiter, another of Æsculpius, a third of Venus, and a fourth perhaps of Apollo;[14] and that, by the advantage of their long experience and aerial nature, they were enabled to execute, with sufficient skill and dignity, the parts which they had undertaken. They lurked in the temples, instituted festivals and sacrifices, invented fables, pronounced oracles, and were frequently allowed to perform miracles. The Christians, who, by the interposition of evil spirits, could so readily explain every præternatural appearance, were disposed and even desirous to admit the most extravagant fictions of the Pagan mythology. But the belief of the Christian was accompanied with horror. The most trifling mark of respect to the national worship he considered as a direct homage yielded to the dæmon, and as an act of rebellion against the majesty of God.

In consequence of this opinion, it was the first but arduous duty of a Christian to preserve himself pure and undefiled by the practice of idolatry. The religion of the nations was not merely a speculative doctrine professed in the schools or preached in the temples. The innumerable deities and rites of polytheism were closely interwoven with every circumstance of business or pleasure, of public or of private life; and it seemed impossible to escape the observance of them, without, at the same time, renouncing the commerce of mankind and all the offices and amusements of society.[15] The important transactions of peace and war were prepared or concluded by solemn sacrifices, in which the magistrate, the senator, and the soldier were obliged to preside or to participate.[16] The public spectacles were an essential part of the cheerful devotion of the Pagans, and the gods were supposed to accept, as the most grateful offering, the games that the prince and people celebrated in honour of their peculiar festivals.[17] The Christian, who with pious horror avoided the abomination of the circus or the theatre, found himself encom-

[14] *Tertullian alleges the confession of the Dæmons themselves as often as they were tormented by the Christian exorcists.*

[15] *Tertullian has written a most severe treatise against idolatry, to caution his brethren against the hourly danger of incurring that guilt.*

[16] *The Roman senate was always held in a temple or consecrated place. Before they entered on business, every senator dropped some wine and frankincense on the altar.*

[17] *Tertullian, the severe reformer, shows no more indulgence to a tragedy of Euripides than to a combat of gladiators. The dress of the actors particularly offends him. By the use of the lofty buskin, they impiously strive to add a cubit to their stature.*

passed with infernal snares in every convivial entertainment, as often as his friends, invoking the hospitable deities, poured out libations to each other's happiness.[18] When the bride, struggling with well-affected reluctance, was forced in hymenæal pomp over the threshold of her new habitation, or when the sad procession of the dead slowly moved towards the funeral pile;[19] the Christian, on these interesting occasions, was compelled to desert the persons who were the dearest to him, rather than contract the guilt inherent to those impious ceremonies. Every art and every trade that was in the least concerned in the framing or adorning of idols was polluted by the stain of idolatry; a severe sentence, since it devoted to eternal misery the far greater part of the community, which is employed in the exercise of liberal or mechanic professions. If we cast our eyes over the numerous remains of antiquity, we shall perceive that, besides the immediate representations of the gods and the holy instruments of their worship, the elegant forms and agreeable fictions, consecrated by the imagination of the Greeks, were introduced as the richest ornaments of the houses, the dress, and the furniture, of the Pagans. Even the arts of music and painting, of eloquence and poetry, flowed from the same impure origin. In the style of the fathers, Apollo and the Muses were the organs of the infernal spirit, Homer and Virgil were the most eminent of his servants, and the beautiful mythology which pervades and animates the compositions of their genius is destined to celebrate the glory of the dæmons. Even the common language of Greece and Rome abounded with familiar but impious expressions, which the imprudent Christian might too carelessly utter, or too patiently hear.[20]

The dangerous temptations which on every side lurked in ambush to surprise the unguarded believer assailed him with redoubled violence on the days of solemn festivals. So artfully were they framed and disposed throughout the year that superstition always wore the appearance of pleasure, and often of virtue.[21] Some of the most sacred festivals in the Roman ritual were destined to salute the new calends of January with vows of public and private felicity, to indulge the pious remembrance of the dead and living, to ascertain the inviolable bounds of property, to hail, on the return of spring, the genial powers of fecundity, to perpetuate the two memorable æras of Rome, the foundation of the city and that of the republic, and to restore, during the humane license of the Saturnalia, the primitive equality of mankind. Some idea may be conceived of the abhorrence of the Christians for such impious ceremonies, by the

[18] The ancient practice of concluding the entertainment with libations may be found in every classic.

[19] The ancient funerals (in those of Misenus and Pallas) are no less accurately described by Virgil than they are illustrated by his commentator Servius. The pile itself was an altar, the flames were fed with the blood of victims, and all the assistants were sprinkled with lustral water.

[20] If a Pagan friend (on the occasion perhaps of sneezing) used the familiar expression of "Jupiter bless you," the Christian was obliged to protest against the divinity of Jupiter.

[21] Consult the most laboured work of Ovid, his imperfect Fasti. He finished no more than the first six months of the year. The compilation of Macrobius is called the Saturnalia, but it is only a small part of the first book that bears any relation to the title.

scrupulous delicacy which they displayed on a much less alarming occasion. On days of general festivity, it was the custom of the ancients to adorn their doors with lamps and with branches of laurel, and to crown their heads with a garland of flowers. This innocent and elegant practice might, perhaps, have been tolerated as a mere civil institution. But it most unluckily happened that the doors were under the protection of the household gods, that the laurel was sacred to the lover of Daphne, and that garlands of flowers, though frequently worn as a symbol either of joy or mourning, had been dedicated in their first origin to the service of superstition. The trembling Christians, who were persuaded in this instance to comply with the fashion of their country and the commands of the magistrate, laboured under the most gloomy apprehensions, from the reproaches of their own conscience, the censures of the church, and the denunciations of divine vengeance.[22]

Such was the anxious diligence which was required to guard the chastity of the gospel from the infectious breath of idolatry. The superstitious observances of public or private rites were carelessly practised, from education and habit, by the followers of the established religion. But, as often as they occurred, they afforded the Christians an opportunity of declaring and confirming their zealous opposition. By these frequent protestations, their attachment to the faith was continually fortified, and, in proportion to the increase of zeal, they combated with the more ardour and success in the holy war which they had undertaken against the empire of the dæmons.

II. The writings of Cicero[23] represent, in the most lively colours, the ignorance, the errors, and the uncertainty of the ancient philosophers, with regard to the immortality of the soul. When they are desirous of arming their disciples against the fear of death, they inculcate, as an obvious though melancholy position, that the fatal stroke of our dissolution releases us from the calamities of life, and that those can no longer suffer who no longer exist. Yet there were a few sages of Greece and Rome who had conceived a more exalted, and, in some respects, a juster idea of human nature; though it must be confessed that, in the sublime inquiry, their reason had been often guided by their imagination, and that their imagination had been prompted by their vanity. When they viewed with complacency the extent of their own mental powers, when they exercised the various faculties of memory, of fancy, and of judgment, in the most profound speculations, or the most important labours, and when they reflected on the desire of fame, which transported them

[22] *Tertullian has composed a defence, or rather panegyric, of the rash action of a Christian soldier who, by throwing away his crown of laurel, had exposed himself and his brethren to the most imminent danger. By the mention of the* emperors (*Severus and Caracalla*) *it is evident, notwithstanding the wishes of M. de Tillemont, that Tertullian composed his treatise De Coronâ long before he was engaged in the errors of the Montanists.*

[23] *In particular, the first book of the Tusculan Questions, and the treatise De Senectute, and the Somnium Scipionis contain, in the most beautiful language, everything that Grecian philosophy, or Roman good sense, could possibly suggest on this dark but important object.*

into future ages far beyond the bounds of death and of the grave; they were unwilling to confound themselves with the beasts of the field, or to suppose that a being, for whose dignity they entertained the most sincere admiration, could be limited to a spot of earth and to a few years of duration. With this favourable prepossession, they summoned to their aid the science, or rather the language, of Metaphysics. They soon discovered that, as none of the properties of matter will apply to the operations of the mind, the human soul must consequently be a substance distinct from the body, pure, simple, and spiritual, incapable of dissolution, and susceptible of a much higher degree of virtue and happiness after the release from its corporeal prison. From these spacious and noble principles, the philosophers who trod in the footsteps of Plato deduced a very unjustifiable conclusion, since they asserted, not only the future immortality, but the past eternity of the human soul, which they were too apt to consider as a portion of the infinite and self-existing spirit which pervades and sustains the universe.[24] A doctrine thus removed beyond the senses and the experience of mankind might serve to amuse the leisure of a philosophic mind; or, in the silence of solitude, it might sometimes impart a ray of comfort to desponding virtue; but the faint impression which had been received in the schools was soon obliterated by the commerce and business of active life. We are sufficiently acquainted with the eminent persons who flourished in the age of Cicero, and of the first Cæsars, with their actions, their characters, and their motives, to be assured that their conduct in this life was never regulated by any serious conviction of the rewards or punishments of a future state. At the bar and in the senate of Rome the ablest orators were not apprehensive of giving offence to their hearers by exposing that doctrine as an idle and extravagant opinion, which was rejected with contempt by every man of a liberal education and understanding.

Since, therefore, the most sublime efforts of philosophy can extend no farther than feebly to point out the desire, the hope, or at most the probability, of a future state, there is nothing, except a divine revelation, that can ascertain the existence, and describe the condition, of the invisible country which is destined to receive the souls of men after their separation from the body. But we may perceive several defects inherent to the popular religions of Greece and Rome, which rendered them very unequal to so arduous a task. I. The general system of their mythology was unsupported by any solid proofs; and the wisest among the Pagans had already dis-

[24] *The pre-existence of human souls, so far at least as that doctrine is compatible with religion, was adopted by many of the Greek and Latin fathers.*

claimed its usurped authority. 2. The description of the infernal regions had been abandoned to the fancy of painters and of poets, who peopled them with so many phantoms and monsters, who dispensed their rewards and punishments with so little equity, that a solemn truth, the most congenial to the human heart, was oppressed and disgraced by the absurd mixture of the wildest fictions.[25] 3. The doctrine of a future state was scarcely considered among the devout Polytheists of Greece and Rome as a fundamental article of faith. The providence of the gods, as it related to public communities rather than to private individuals, was principally displayed on the visible theatre of the present world. The petitions which were offered on the altars of Jupiter or Apollo expressed the anxiety of their worshippers for temporal happiness, and their ignorance or indifference concerning a future life. The important truth of the immortality of the soul was inculcated with more diligence as well as success in India, in Assyria, in Egypt, and in Gaul; and, since we cannot attribute such a difference to the superior knowledge of the barbarians, we must ascribe it to the influence of an established priesthood, which employed the motives of virtue as the instrument of ambition.

We might naturally expect that a principle, so essential to religion, would have been revealed in the clearest terms to the chosen people of Palestine, and that it might safely have been intrusted to the hereditary priesthood of Aaron. It is incumbent on us to adore the mysterious dispensations of Providence,[26] when we discover that the doctrine of the immortality of the soul is omitted in the law of Moses; it is darkly insinuated by the prophets, and during the long period which elapsed between the Egyptian and the Babylonian servitudes, the hopes as well as fears of the Jews appear to have been confined within the narrow compass of the present life. After Cyrus had permitted the exiled nation to return into the promised land, and after Ezra had restored the ancient records of their religion, two celebrated sects, the Sadducees and the Pharisees, insensibly arose at Jerusalem.[27] The former, selected from the more opulent and distinguished ranks of society, were strictly attached to the literal sense of the Mosaic law, and they piously rejected the immortality of the soul, as an opinion that received no countenance from the divine book, which they revered as the only rule of their faith. To the authority of scripture the Pharisees added that of tradition, and they accepted, under the name of traditions, several speculative tenets from the philosophy or religion of the eastern nations. The doc-

[25] *The eleventh book of the Odyssey gives a very dreary and incoherent account of the infernal shades. Pindar and Virgil have embellished the picture; but even those poets, though more correct than their great model, are guilty of very strange inconsistencies.*

[26] *The right reverend author of the Divine Legation of Moses assigns a very curious reason for the omission, and most ingeniously retorts it on the unbelievers.*

[27] *According to the most natural interpretation of the words of Josephus, the Sadducees admitted only the Pentateuch; but it has pleased some modern critics to add the prophets to their creed, and to suppose that they contented themselves with rejecting the traditions of the Pharisees.*

trines of fate or predestination, of angels and spirits, and of a future state of rewards and punishments, were in the number of these new articles of belief; and, as the Pharisees, by the austerity of their manners, had drawn into their party the body of the Jewish people, the immortality of the soul became the prevailing sentiment of the synagogue, under the reign of the Asmonæan princes and pontiffs. The temper of the Jews was incapable of contenting itself with such a cold and languid assent as might satisfy the mind of a Polytheist; and, as soon as they admitted the idea of a future state, they embraced it with the zeal which has always formed the characteristic of the nation. Their zeal, however, added nothing to its evidence, or even probability: and it was still necessary that the doctrine of life and immortality, which had been dictated by nature, approved by reason, and received by superstition, should obtain the sanction of divine truth from the authority and example of Christ.

When the promise of eternal happiness was proposed to mankind, on condition of adopting the faith and of observing the precepts of the gospel, it is no wonder that so advantageous an offer should have been accepted by great numbers of every religion, of every rank, and of every province in the Roman empire. The ancient Christians were animated by a contempt for their present existence, and by a just confidence of immortality, of which the doubtful and imperfect faith of modern ages cannot give us any adequate notion. In the primitive church, the influence of truth was very powerfully strengthened by an opinion which, however it may deserve respect for its usefulness and antiquity, has not been found agreeable to experience. It was universally believed that the end of the world and the kingdom of Heaven were at hand. The near approach of this wonderful event had been predicted by the apostles; the tradition of it was preserved by their earliest disciples, and those who understood in their literal sense the discourses of Christ himself were obliged to expect the second and glorious coming of the Son of Man in the clouds, before that generation was totally extinguished, which had beheld his humble condition upon earth, and which might still be witness of the calamities of the Jews under Vespasian or Hadrian. The revolution of seventeen centuries has instructed us not to press too closely the mysterious language of prophecy and revelation; but, as long as, for wise purposes, this error was permitted to subsist in the church, it was productive of the most salutary effects on the faith and practice of Christians, who lived in the awful expectation of that moment when the globe itself, and all the various race of

[28] *This expectation was countenanced by the twenty-fourth chapter of St. Matthew, and by the first epistle of St. Paul to the Thessalonians. Erasmus removes the difficulty by the help of allegory and metaphor; and the learned Grotius ventures to insinuate that, for wise purposes, the pious deception was permitted to take place.*

[29] *This tradition may be traced as high as the author of the Epistle of Barnabas.*

[30] *The primitive church of Antioch computed almost 6000 years from the creation of the world to the birth of Christ. Africanus, Lactantius, and the Greek church, have reduced that number to 5500, and Eusebius has contented himself with 5200 years. These calculations were formed on the Septuagint, which was universally received during the first six centuries. The authority of the Vulgate and of the Hebrew text has determined the moderns, Protestants as well as Catholics, to prefer a period of about 4000 years; though, in the study of profane antiquity, they often find themselves straitened by those narrow limits.*

mankind, should tremble at the appearance of their divine judge.[28]

The ancient and popular doctrine of the Millennium was intimately connected with the second coming of Christ. As the works of the creation had been finished in six days, their duration in their present state, according to a tradition which was attributed to the prophet Elijah, was fixed to six thousand years.[29] By the same analogy it was inferred that this long period of labour and contention, which was now almost elapsed,[30] would be succeeded by a joyful Sabbath of a thousand years; and that Christ, with the triumphant band of the saints and the elect who had escaped death, or who had been miraculously revived, would reign upon earth till the time appointed for the last and general resurrection. So pleasing was this hope to the mind of believers that the *New Jerusalem,* the seat of this blissful kingdom, was quickly adorned with all the gayest colours of the imagination. A felicity consisting only of pure and spiritual pleasure would have appeared too refined for its inhabitants, who were still supposed to possess their human nature and senses. A garden of Eden, with the amusements of the pastoral life, was no longer suited to the advanced state of society, which prevailed under the Roman empire. A city was therefore erected of gold and precious stones, and a supernatural plenty of corn and wine was bestowed on the adjacent territory; in the free enjoyment of whose spontaneous productions the happy and benevolent people was never to be restrained by any jealous laws of exclusive property.[31] The assurance of such a Millennium was carefully inculcated by a succession of fathers from Justin Martyr and Irenæus, who conversed with the immediate disciples of the apostles, down to Lactantius, who was preceptor to the son of Constantine.[32] Though it might not be universally received, it appears to have been the reigning sentiment of the orthodox believers; and it seems so well adapted to the desires and apprehensions of mankind that it must have contributed, in a very considerable degree, to the progress of the Christian faith. But, when the edifice of the church was almost completed, the temporary support was laid aside. The doctrine of Christ's reign upon earth was at first treated as a profound allegory, was considered by degrees as a doubtful and useless opinion, and was at length rejected as the absurd invention of heresy and fanaticism. A mysterious prophecy, which still forms a part of the sacred canon, but which was thought to favour the exploded sentiment, has very narrowly escaped the proscription of the church.[33]

Whilst the happiness and glory of a temporal reign were prom-

[31] Most of these pictures were borrowed from a misinterpretation of Isaiah, Daniel, and the Apocalypse. One of the grossest images may be found in Irenæus, the disciple of Papias, who had seen the apostle St. John.

[32] The testimony of Justin, of his own faith and that of his orthodox brethren, in the doctrine of a Millennium, is delivered in the clearest and most solemn manner. If there is anything like an inconsistency, we may impute it, as we think proper, either to the author or to his transcribers.

[33] In the Council of Laodicea (about the year 360) the Apocalypse was tacitly excluded from the sacred canon, by the same churches of Asia to which it is addressed; and we may learn from the complaint of Sulpicius Severus that their sentence had been ratified by the greater number of Christians of his time. From what causes, then, is the Apocalypse at present so generally received by the Greek, the Roman, and the Protestant churches? The following ones may be assigned. 1. The Greeks were sub-

ised to the disciples of Christ, the most dreadful calamities were denounced against an unbelieving world. The edification of the new Jerusalem was to advance by equal steps with the destruction of the mystic Babylon; and, as long as the emperors who reigned before Constantine persisted in the profession of idolatry, the epithet of Babylon was applied to the city and to the empire of Rome. A regular series was prepared of all the moral and physical evils which can afflict a flourishing nation; intestine discord, and the invasion of the fiercest barbarians from the unknown regions of the North; pestilence and famine, comets and eclipses, earthquakes and inundations. All these were only so many preparatory and alarming signs of the great catastrophe of Rome, when the country of the Scipios and Cæsars should be consumed by a flame from Heaven, and the city of the seven hills, with her palaces, her temples, and her triumphal arches, should be buried in a vast lake of fire and brimstone. It might, however, afford some consolation to Roman vanity, that the period of their empire would be that of the world itself; which, as it had once perished by the element of water, was destined to experience a second and a speedy destruction from the element of fire. In the opinion of a general conflagration, the faith of the Christian very happily coincided with the tradition of the East, the philosophy of the Stoics, and the analogy of Nature; and even the country which, from religious motives, had been chosen for the origin and principal scene of the conflagration, was the best adapted for that purpose by natural and physical causes; by its deep caverns, beds of sulphur, and numerous volcanoes, of which those of Ætna, of Vesuvius, and of Lipari, exhibit a very imperfect representation. The calmest and most intrepid sceptic could not refuse to acknowledge that the destruction of the present system of the world by fire was in itself extremely probable. The Christian, who founded his belief much less on the fallacious arguments of reason than on the authority of tradition and the interpretation of scripture, expected it with terror and confidence, as a certain and approaching event; and, as his mind was perpetually filled with the solemn idea, he considered every disaster that happened to the empire as an infallible symptom of an expiring world.[34]

The condemnation of the wisest and most virtuous of the Pagans, on account of their ignorance or disbelief of the divine truth, seems to offend the reason and the humanity of the present age.[35] But the primitive church, whose faith was of a much firmer consistence, delivered over, without hesitation, to eternal torture the far greater

dued by the authority of an impostor who, in the sixth century, assumed the character of Dionysius the Areopagite. 2. A just apprehension, that the grammarians might become more important than the theologians, engaged the Council of Trent to fix the seal of their infallibility on all the books of Scripture, contained in the Latin Vulgate, in the number of which the Apocalypse was fortunately included. 3. The advantage of turning those mysterious prophecies against the See of Rome inspired the Protestants with uncommon veneration for so useful an ally. See the ingenious and elegant discourses of the present bishop of Lichfield on that unpromising subject.

[34] On this subject every reader of taste will be entertained with the third part of Burnet's Sacred Theory. He blends philosophy, scripture, and tradition, into one magnificent system; in the description of which he displays a strength of fancy not inferior to that of Milton himself.

[35] And yet, whatever may be the language of individuals, it is still the public doctrine of all the

Christian churches; nor can even our own refuse to admit the conclusions which must be drawn from the eighth and the eighteenth of her Articles. The Jansenists, who have so diligently studied the works of the fathers, maintain this sentiment with distinguished zeal; and the learned M. de Tillemont never dismisses a virtuous emperor without pronouncing his damnation. Zuinglius is perhaps the only leader of a party who has ever adopted the milder sentiment, and he gave no less offence to the Lutherans than to the Catholics.

[36] *Justin and Clemens of Alexandria allow that some of the philosophers were instructed by the Logos; confounding its double signification of the human reason and of the Divine Word.*

[37] *In order to ascertain the degree of authority which the zealous African had acquired, it may be sufficient to allege the testimony of Cyprian, the doctor and guide of all the western churches. As often as he applied himself to his daily study of the writings of Tertullian, he was accustomed to say, "Da mihi magistrum; Give me my master."*

part of the human species. A charitable hope might perhaps be indulged in favour of Socrates, or some other sages of antiquity, who had consulted the light of reason before that of the gospel had arisen.[36] But it was unanimously affirmed that those who, since the birth or the death of Christ, had obstinately persisted in the worship of the dæmons, neither deserved, nor could expect, a pardon from the irritated justice of the Deity. These rigid sentiments, which had been unknown to the ancient world, appear to have infused a spirit of bitterness into a system of love and harmony. The ties of blood and friendship were frequently torn asunder by the difference of religious faith; and the Christians, who, in this world, found themselves oppressed by the power of the Pagans, were sometimes seduced by resentment and spiritual pride to delight in the prospect of their future triumph. "You are fond of spectacles," exclaims the stern Tertullian; "expect the greatest of all spectacles, the last and eternal judgment of the universe. How shall I admire, how laugh, how rejoice, how exult, when I behold so many proud monarchs, and fancied gods, groaning in the lowest abyss of darkness; so many magistrates, who persecuted the name of the Lord, liquefying in fiercer fires than they ever kindled against the Christians; so many sage philosophers blushing in red-hot flames, with their deluded scholars; so many celebrated poets trembling before the tribunal, not of Minos, but of Christ; so many tragedians, more tuneful in the expression of their own sufferings; so many dancers——!" But the humanity of the reader will permit me to draw a veil over the rest of this infernal description, which the zealous African pursues in a long variety of affected and unfeeling witticisms.[37]

Doubtless there were many among the primitive Christians of a temper more suitable to the meekness and charity of their profession. There were many who felt a sincere compassion for the danger of their friends and countrymen, and who exerted the most benevolent zeal to save them from the impending destruction. The careless Polytheist, assailed by new and unexpected terrors, against which neither his priests nor his philosophers could afford him any certain protection, was very frequently terrified and subdued by the menace of eternal tortures. His fears might assist the progress of his faith and reason; and, if he could once persuade himself to suspect that the Christian religion might possibly be true, it became an easy task to convince him that it was the safest and most prudent party that he could possibly embrace.

III. The supernatural gifts, which even in this life were ascribed to the Christians above the rest of mankind, must have conduced to their own comfort, and very frequently to the conviction of infidels. Besides the occasional prodigies, which might sometimes be affected by the immediate interposition of the Deity when he suspended the laws of Nature for the service of religion, the Christian church, from the time of the apostles and their first disciples,[38] has claimed an uninterrupted succession of miraculous powers, the gift of tongues, of vision and of prophecy, the power of expelling dæmons, of healing the sick, and of raising the dead. The knowledge of foreign languages was frequently communicated to the contemporaries of Irenæus, though Irenæus himself was left to struggle with the difficulties of a barbarous dialect whilst he preached the gospel to the natives of Gaul. The divine inspiration, whether it was conveyed in the form of a waking or of a sleeping vision, is described as a favour very liberally bestowed on all ranks of the faithful, on women as on elders, on boys as well as upon bishops. When their devout minds were sufficiently prepared by a course of prayer, of fasting, and of vigils, to receive the extraordinary impulse, they were transported out of their senses, and delivered in ecstasy what was inspired, being mere organs of the Holy Spirit, just as a pipe or flute is of him who blows into it. We may add that the design of these visions was, for the most part, either to disclose the future history, or to guide the present administration, of the church. The expulsion of the dæmons from the bodies of those unhappy persons whom they had been permitted to torment was considered as a signal, though ordinary, triumph of religion, and is repeatedly alleged by the ancient apologists as the most convincing evidence of the truth of Christianity. The awful ceremony was usually performed in a public manner, and in the presence of a great number of spectators; the patient was relieved by the power or skill of the exorcist, and the vanquished dæmon was heard to confess that he was one of the fabled gods of antiquity, who had impiously usurped the adoration of mankind. But the miraculous cure of diseases, of the most inveterate or even præternatural kind, can no longer occasion any surprise, when we recollect that in the days of Irenæus, about the end of the second century, the resurrection of the dead was very far from being esteemed an uncommon event; that the miracle was frequently performed on necessary occasions, by great fasting and the joint supplication of the church of the place, and that the persons thus restored to their prayers had lived afterwards among them many years. At such a period, when faith could boast of so many wonder-

[38] *Notwithstanding the evasions of Dr. Middleton, it is impossible to overlook the clear traces of visions and inspiration, which may be found in the apostolic fathers.*

ful victories over death, it seems difficult to account for the scepticism of those philosophers who still rejected and derided the doctrine of the resurrection. A noble Grecian had rested on this important ground the whole controversy, and promised Theophilus,
bishop of Antioch, that, if he could be gratified with the sight of a
single person who had been actually raised from the dead, he would
immediately embrace the Christian religion. It is somewhat remarkable that the prelate of the first eastern church, however anxious for
the conversion of his friend, thought proper to decline this fair and
reasonable challenge.

    The miracles of the primitive church, after obtaining the sanction
of ages, have been lately attacked in a very free and ingenious inquiry;[39] which, though it has met with the most favourable reception from the Public, appears to have excited a general scandal
among the divines of our own as well as of the other Protestant
churches of Europe.[40] Our different sentiments on this subject will
be much less influenced by any particular arguments than by our
habits of study and reflection; and, above all, by the degree of the
evidence which we have accustomed ourselves to require for the
proof of a miraculous event. The duty of an historian does not call
upon him to interpose his private judgment in this nice and important controversy; but he ought not to dissemble the difficulty of
adopting such a theory as may reconcile the interest of religion with
that of reason, of making a proper application of that theory, and of
defining with precision the limits of that happy period, exempt from
error and from deceit, to which we might be disposed to extend the
gift of supernatural powers. From the first of the fathers to the last
of the popes, a succession of bishops, of saints, of martyrs, and of
miracles is continued without interruption, and the progress of
superstition was so gradual and almost imperceptible that we know
not in what particular link we should break the chain of tradition.
Every age bears testimony to the wonderful events by which it was
distinguished, and its testimony appears no less weighty and respectable than that of the preceding generation, till we are insensibly led on to accuse our own inconsistency, if in the eighth or in the
twelfth century we deny to the venerable Bede, or to the holy Bernard, the same degree of confidence which, in the second century,
we had so liberally granted to Justin or to Irenæus.[41] If the truth of
any of those miracles is appreciated by their apparent use and propriety, every age had unbelievers to convince, heretics to confute,
and idolatrous nations to convert; and sufficient motives might al-

[39] Dr. Middleton sent out his Introduction in the year 1747, published his Free Inquiry in 1749, and before his death, which happened in 1750, he had prepared a vin- dication of it against his numerous adversaries.

[40] The university of Ox- ford conferred degrees on his opponents. From the indignation of Mosheim we may dis- cover the sentiments of Lutheran divines.

[41] It may seem somewhat remarkable that Ber- nard of Clairvaux, who records so many miracles of his friend St. Malachi, never takes any notice of his own, which, in their turn, however, are carefully related by his companions and dis- ciples. In the long series of ecclesiastical history, does there exist a single instance of a saint as- serting that he himself possessed the gift of miracles?

ways be produced to justify the interposition of Heaven. And yet, since every friend to revelation is persuaded of the reality, and every reasonable man is convinced of the cessation, of miraculous powers, it is evident that there must have been *some period* in which they were either suddenly or gradually withdrawn from the Christian church. Whatever æra is chosen for that purpose, the death of the apostles, the conversion of the Roman empire, or the extinction of the Arian heresy,[42] the insensibility of the Christians who lived at that time will equally afford a just matter of surprise. They still supported their pretensions after they had lost their power. Credulity performed the office of faith; fanaticism was permitted to assume the language of inspiration, and the effects of accident or contrivance were ascribed to supernatural causes. The recent experience of genuine miracles should have instructed the Christian world in the ways of Providence, and habituated their eye (if we may use a very inadequate expression) to the style of the divine artist. Should the most skilful painter of modern Italy presume to decorate his feeble imitations with the name of Raphael or of Correggio, the insolent fraud would be soon discovered and indignantly rejected.

Whatever opinion may be entertained of the miracles of the primitive church since the time of the apostles, this unresisting softness of temper, so conspicuous among the believers of the second and third centuries, proved of some accidental benefit to the cause of truth and religion. In modern times, a latent, and even involuntary, scepticism adheres to the most pious dispositions. Their admission of supernatural truths is much less an active consent than a cold and passive acquiescence. Accustomed long since to observe and to respect the invariable order of Nature, our reason, or at least our imagination, is not sufficiently prepared to sustain the visible action of the Deity. But, in the first ages of Christianity, the situation of mankind was extremely different. The most curious, or the most credulous, among the Pagans were often persuaded to enter into a society which asserted an actual claim of miraculous powers. The primitive Christians perpetually trod on mystic ground, and their minds were exercised by the habits of believing the most extraordinary events. They felt, or they fancied, that on every side they were incessantly assaulted by dæmons, comforted by visions, instructed by prophecy, and surprisingly delivered from danger, sickness, and from death itself, by the supplications of the church. The real or imaginary prodigies, of which they so frequently conceived themselves to be the objects, the instruments, or the spectators, very hap-

[42] *The conversion of Constantine is the æra which is most usually fixed by Protestants. The more rational divines are unwilling to admit the miracles of the fourth, whilst the more credulous are unwilling to reject those of the fifth century.*

pily disposed them to adopt, with the same ease, but with far greater justice, the authentic wonders of the evangelic history; and thus miracles that exceeded not the measure of their own experience inspired them with the most lively assurance of mysteries which were acknowledged to surpass the limits of their understanding. It is this deep impression of supernatural truths which has been so much celebrated under the name of faith; a state of mind described as the surest pledge of the divine favour and of future felicity, and recommended as the first or perhaps the only merit of a Christian. According to the more rigid doctors, the moral virtues, which may be equally practised by infidels, are destitute of any value or efficacy in the work of our justification.

IV. But the primitive Christian demonstrated his faith by his virtues; and it was very justly supposed that the divine persuasion, which enlightened or subdued the understanding, must, at the same time, purify the heart, and direct the actions, of the believer. The first apologists of Christianity who justify the innocence of their brethren, and the writers of a later period who celebrate the sanctity of their ancestors, display, in the most lively colours, the reformation of manners which was introduced into the world by the preaching of the gospel. As it is my intention to remark only such human causes as were permitted to second the influence of revelation, I shall slightly mention two motives which might naturally render the lives of the primitive Christians much purer and more austere than those of their Pagan contemporaries, or their degenerate successors; repentance for their past sins, and the laudable desire of supporting the reputation of the society in which they were engaged.

It is a very ancient reproach, suggested by the ignorance or the malice of infidelity, that the Christians allured into their party the most atrocious criminals, who, as soon as they were touched by a sense of remorse, were easily persuaded to wash away, in the water of baptism, the guilt of their past conduct, for which the temples of the gods refused to grant them any expiation. But this reproach, when it is cleared from misrepresentation, contributes as much to the honour as it did to the increase of the church. The friends of Christianity may acknowledge without a blush that many of the most eminent saints had been before their baptism the most abandoned sinners. Those persons who in the world had followed, though in an imperfect manner, the dictates of benevolence and propriety, derived such a calm satisfaction from the opinion of their own rectitude, as rendered them much less susceptible of the sudden emotions of shame, of grief, and of terror, which have given birth to so many wonderful conversions. After the example of their Divine Master, the missionaries of the gospel disdained not the society of men, and especially of women, oppressed by the consciousness, and very often by the effects, of their vices. As they emerged from sin and superstition to the glorious hope of immortality, they resolved to devote themselves to a life, not only of virtue, but of penitence. The desire of perfection became the ruling passion of their soul; and it is well known that, while reason embraces a cold mediocrity, our passions hurry us, with rapid violence, over the space which lies between the most opposite extremes.

When the new converts had been enrolled in the number of the faithful and were admitted to the sacraments of the church, they found themselves restrained from relapsing into their past disorders by another consideration of a less spiritual, but of a very innocent and respectable nature. Any particular society that has departed from the great body of the nation or the religion to which it belonged immediately becomes the object of universal as well as invidious observation. In proportion to the smallness of its numbers, the character of the society may be affected by the virtue and vices of the persons who compose it; and every member is engaged to watch with the most vigilant attention over his own behaviour and over that of his brethren, since, as he must expect to incur a part of the common disgrace, he may hope to enjoy a share of the common reputation. When the Christians of Bithynia were brought before the tribunal of the younger Pliny, they assured the proconsul that, far from being engaged in any unlawful conspiracy, they were bound by a solemn obligation to abstain from the commission of those crimes which disturb the private or public peace of society, from theft, robbery, adultery, perjury, and fraud. Near a century afterwards, Tertullian, with an honest pride, could boast that very few Christians had suffered by the hand of the executioner, except on account of their religion. Their serious and sequestered life, averse to the gay luxury of the age, insured them to chastity, temperance, economy, and all the sober and domestic virtues. As the greater number were of some trade or profession, it was incumbent on them, by the strictest integrity and the fairest dealing, to remove the suspicions which the profane are too apt to conceive against the appearances of sanctity. The contempt of the world exercised them in the habits of humility, meekness, and patience. The more they were persecuted, the more closely they adhered to each other. Their mutual charity and unsuspecting confidence has been remarked by infidels, and was too often abused by perfidious friends.[43]

[43] *The philosopher Peregrinus (of whose life and death Lucian has left us so entertaining an account) imposed, for a long time, on the credulous simplicity of the Christians of Asia.*

It is a very honourable circumstance for the morals of the primitive Christians, that even their faults, or rather errors, were derived from an excess of virtue. The bishops and doctors of the church, whose evidence attests, and whose authority might influence, the professions, the principles, and even the practice, of their contemporaries, had studied the scriptures with less skill than devotion, and they often received, in the most literal sense, those rigid precepts of Christ and the apostles to which the prudence of succeeding commentators has applied a looser and more figurative mode of interpretation. Ambitious to exalt the perfection of the gospel above the wisdom of philosophy, the zealous fathers have carried the duties of self-mortification, of purity, and of patience, to a height which it is scarcely possible to attain, and much less to preserve, in our present state of weakness and corruption. A doctrine so extraordinary and so sublime must inevitably command the veneration of the people; but it was ill calculated to obtain the suffrage of those worldly philosophers who, in the conduct of this transitory life, consult only the feelings of nature and the interest of society.

There are two very natural propensities which we may distinguish in the most virtuous and liberal dispositions, the love of pleasure and the love of action. If the former be refined by art and learning, improved by the charms of social intercourse, and corrected by a just regard to economy, to health, and to reputation, it is productive of the greatest part of the happiness of private life. The love of action is a principle of a much stronger and more doubtful nature. It often leads to anger, to ambition, and to revenge; but, when it is guided by the sense of propriety and benevolence, it becomes the parent of every virtue; and, if those virtues are accompanied with equal abilities, a family, a state, or an empire may be indebted for their safety and prosperity to the undaunted courage of a single man. To the love of pleasure we may therefore ascribe most of the agreeable, to the love of action we may attribute most of the useful and respectable qualifications. The character in which both the one and the other should be united and harmonized would seem to constitute the most perfect idea of human nature. The insensible and inactive disposition, which should be supposed alike destitute of both, would be rejected, by the common consent of mankind, as utterly incapable of procuring any happiness to the individual, or any public benefit to the world. But it was not in *this* world that the primitive Christians were desirous of making themselves either agreeable or useful.

The acquisition of knowledge, the exercise of our reason or fancy, and the cheerful flow of unguarded conversation, may employ the leisure of a liberal mind. Such amusements, however, were rejected with abhorrence, or admitted with the utmost caution, by the severity of the fathers, who despised all knowledge that was not useful to salvation, and who considered all levity of discourse as a criminal abuse of the gift of speech. In our present state of existence, the body is so inseparably connected with the soul that it seems to be our interest to taste, with innocence and moderation, the enjoyments of which that faithful companion is susceptible. Very different was the reasoning of our devout predecessors; vainly aspiring to imitate the perfection of angels, they disdained, or they affected to disdain, every earthly and corporeal delight. Some of our senses indeed are necessary for our preservation, others for our subsistence, and others again for our information, and thus far it was impossible to reject the use of them. The first sensation of pleasure was marked as the first moment of their abuse. The unfeeling candidate for Heaven was instructed, not only to resist the grosser allurements of the taste or smell, but even to shut his ears against the profane harmony of sounds, and to view with indifference the most finished productions of human art. Gay apparel, magnificent houses, and elegant furniture were supposed to unite the double guilt of pride and of sensuality: a simple and mortified appearance was more suitable to the Christian who was certain of his sins and doubtful of his salvation. In their censures of luxury, the fathers are extremely minute and circumstantial; and among the various articles which excite their pious indignation, we may enumerate false hair, garments of any colour except white, instruments of music, vases of gold or silver, downy pillows (as Jacob reposed his head on a stone), white bread, foreign wines, public salutations, the use of warm baths, and the practice of shaving the beard, which, according to the expression of Tertullian, is a lie against our own faces, and an impious attempt to improve the works of the Creator. When Christianity was introduced among the rich and the polite, the observation of these singular laws was left, as it would be at present, to the few who were ambitious of superior sanctity. But it is always easy, as well as agreeable, for the inferior ranks of mankind to claim a merit from the contempt of that pomp and pleasure, which fortune has placed beyond their reach. The virtue of the primitive Christians, like that of the first Romans, was very frequently guarded by poverty and ignorance.

The chaste severity of the fathers, in whatever related to the commerce of the two sexes, flowed from the same principle; their abhorrence of every enjoyment which might gratify the sensual, and degrade the spiritual, nature of man. It was their favourite opinion that, if Adam had preserved his obedience to the Creator, he would have lived for ever in a state of virgin purity, and that some harmless mode of vegetation might have peopled paradise with a race of innocent and immortal beings. The use of marriage was permitted only to his fallen posterity, as a necessary expedient to continue the human species, and as a restraint, however imperfect, on the natural licentiousness of desire. The hesitation of the orthodox casuists on this interesting subject betrays the perplexity of men, unwilling to approve an institution which they were compelled to tolerate.[44] The enumeration of the very whimsical laws, which they most circumstantially imposed on the marriage-bed, would force a smile from the young, and a blush from the fair. It was their unanimous sentiment that a first marriage was adequate to all the purposes of nature and of society. The sensual connexion was refined into a resemblance of the mystic union of Christ with his church, and was pronounced to be indissoluble either by divorce or by death. The practice of second nuptials was branded with the name of a legal adultery; and the persons who were guilty of so scandalous an offence against Christian purity were soon excluded from the honours, and even from the alms, of the church. Since desire was imputed as a crime, and marriage was tolerated as a defect, it was consistent with the same principles to consider a state of celibacy as the nearest approach to the divine perfection. It was with the utmost difficulty that ancient Rome could support the institution of six vestals;[45] but the primitive church was filled with a great number of persons of either sex who had devoted themselves to the profession of perpetual chastity. A few of these, among whom we may reckon the learned Origen, judged it the most prudent to disarm the tempter.[46] Some were insensible and some were invincible against the assaults of the flesh. Disdaining an ignominious flight, the virgins of the warm climate of Africa encountered the enemy in the closest engagement; they permitted priests and deacons to share their bed, and gloried amidst the flames in their unsullied purity. But insulted Nature sometimes vindicated her rights, and this new species of martyrdom served only to introduce a new scandal into the

[44] *Some of the Gnostic heretics were more consistent; they rejected the use of marriage.*

[45] *Notwithstanding the honours and rewards which were bestowed on those virgins, it was difficult to procure a sufficient number; nor could the dread of the most horrible death always restrain their incontinence.*

[46] *Before the fame of Origen had excited envy and persecution, this extraordinary action was rather admired than censured. As it was his general practice to allegorize scripture, it seems unfortunate that, in this instance only, he should have adopted the literal sense.*

church.[47] Among the Christian ascetics, however (a name which they soon acquired from their painful exercise), many, as they were less presumptuous, were probably more successful. The loss of sensual pleasure was supplied and compensated by spiritual pride. Even the multitude of Pagans were inclined to estimate the merit of the sacrifice by its apparent difficulty; and it was in the praise of these chaste spouses of Christ that the fathers have poured forth the troubled stream of their eloquence. Such are the early traces of monastic principles and institutions which, in a subsequent age, have counterbalanced all the temporal advantages of Christianity.[48]

The Christians were not less averse to the business than to the pleasures of this world. The defence of our persons and property they knew not how to reconcile with the patient doctrine which enjoined an unlimited forgiveness of past injuries and commanded them to invite the repetition of fresh insults. Their simplicity was offended by the use of oaths, by the pomp of magistracy, and by the active contention of public life, nor could their humane ignorance be convinced that it was lawful on any occasion to shed the blood of our fellow-creatures, either by the sword of justice or by that of war; even though their criminal or hostile attempts should threaten the peace and safety of the whole community.[49] It was acknowledged that, under a less perfect law, the powers of the Jewish constitution had been exercised, with the approbation of Heaven, by inspired prophets and by anointed kings. The Christians felt and confessed that such institutions might be necessary for the present system of the world, and they cheerfully submitted to the authority of their Pagan governors. But, while they inculcated the maxims of passive obedience, they refused to take any active part in the civil administration or the military defence of the empire. Some indulgence might perhaps be allowed to those persons who, before their conversion, were already engaged in such violent and sanguinary occupations; but it was impossible that the Christians, without renouncing a more sacred duty, could assume the character of soldiers, of magistrates, or of princes.[50] This indolent, or even criminal, disregard to the public welfare exposed them to the contempt and reproaches of the Pagans, who very frequently asked, What must be the fate of the empire, attacked on every side by the barbarians, if all mankind should adopt the pusillanimous sentiments of the new sect?[51] To this insulting question the Christian apologists returned obscure and ambiguous answers, as they were unwilling to reveal the secret cause of their security; the expectation that, before the conversion

[47] *Something like this rash attempt was long afterwards imputed to the founder of the order of Fontevrault. Bayle has amused himself and his readers on that very delicate subject.*

[48] *The Ascetics (as early as the second century) made a public profession of mortifying their bodies, and of abstaining from the use of flesh and wine.*

[49] *The same patient principles have been revived since the Reformation by the Socinians, the modern Anabaptists, and the Quakers.*

[50] *Tertullian suggests to them the expedient of deserting; a counsel which, if it had been generally known, was not very proper to conciliate the favour of the emperors towards the Christian sect.*

[51] *As well as we can judge from the mutilated representation of Origen, his adversary, Celsus, had urged his objection with great force and candour.*

of mankind was accomplished, war, government, the Roman empire and the world itself would be no more. It may be observed that, in this instance likewise, the situation of the first Christians coincided very happily with their religious scruples, and that their aversion to an active life contributed rather to excuse them from the service, than to exclude them from the honours, of the state and army.

V. But the human character, however it may be exalted or depressed by a temporary enthusiasm, will return, by degrees, to its proper and natural level, and will resume those passions that seem the most adapted to its present condition. The primitive Christians were dead to the business and pleasures of the world; but their love of action, which could never be entirely extinguished, soon revived, and found a new occupation in the government of the church. A separate society, which attacked the established religion of the empire, was obliged to adopt some form of internal policy, and to appoint a sufficient number of ministers, intrusted not only with the spiritual functions, but even with the temporal direction of the Christian commonwealth. The safety of that society, its honour, its aggrandizement, were productive, even in the most pious minds, of a spirit of patriotism, such as the first of the Romans had felt for the republic, and sometimes, of a similar indifference in the use of whatever means might probably conduce to so desirable an end. The ambition of raising themselves or their friends to the honours and offices of the church was disguised by the laudable intention of devoting to the public benefit the power and consideration which, for that purpose only, it became their duty to solicit. In the exercise of their functions, they were frequently called upon to detect the errors of heresy, or the arts of faction, to oppose the designs of perfidious brethren, to stigmatize their characters with deserved infamy, and to expel them from the bosom of a society whose peace and happiness they had attempted to disturb. The ecclesiastical governors of the Christians were taught to unite the wisdom of the serpent with the innocence of the dove; but, as the former was refined, so the latter was insensibly corrupted, by the habits of government. In the church as well as in the world the persons who were placed in any public station rendered themselves considerable by their eloquence and firmness, by their knowledge of mankind, and by their dexterity in business; and, while they concealed from others, and, perhaps, from themselves, the secret motives of their conduct, they too frequently relapsed into all the turbulent passions of active life, which were tinctured with an additional degree of bitterness and obstinacy from the infusion of spiritual zeal.

The government of the church has often been the subject, as well as the prize, of religious contention. The hostile disputants of Rome, of Paris, of Oxford and of Geneva have alike struggled to reduce the primitive and apostolic model [52] to the respective standards of their own policy. The few who have pursued this inquiry with more candour and impartiality are of opinion [53] that the apostles declined the office of legislation, and rather chose to endure some partial scandals and divisions than to exclude the Christians of a future age from the liberty of varying their forms of ecclesiastical government according to the changes of times and circumstances. The scheme of policy which, under their approbation, was adopted for the use of the first century may be discovered from the practice of Jerusalem, of Ephesus, or of Corinth. The societies which were instituted in the cities of the Roman empire were united only by the ties of faith and charity. Independence and equality formed the basis of their internal constitution. The want of discipline and human learning was supplied by the occasional assistance of the *prophets,* who were called to that function, without distinction of age, of sex, or of natural abilities, and who, as often as they felt the divine impulse, poured forth the effusions of the spirit in the assembly of the faithful. But these extraordinary gifts were frequently abused or misapplied by the prophetic teachers. They displayed them at an improper season, presumptuously disturbed the service of the assembly, and by their pride or mistaken zeal they introduced, particularly into the apostolic church of Corinth, a long and melancholy train of disorders. As the institution of prophets became useless, and even pernicious, their powers were withdrawn and their office abolished. The public functions of religion were solely intrusted to the established ministers of the church, the *bishops* and the *presbyters;* two appellations which, in their first origin, appear to have distinguished the same office and the same order of persons. The name of Presbyter was expressive of their age, or rather of their gravity and wisdom. The title of Bishop denoted their inspection over the faith and manners of the Christians who were committed to their pastoral care. In proportion to the respective numbers of the faithful, a larger or smaller number of these *episcopal presbyters* guided each infant congregation with equal authority and with united councils.

But the most perfect equality of freedom requires the directing hand of a superior magistrate; and the order of public deliberations

[52] *The aristocratical party in France, as well as in England, has strenuously maintained the divine origin of bishops. But the Calvanistical presbyters were impatient of a superior; and the Roman Pontiff refused to acknowledge an equal.*

[53] *In the history of the Christian hierarchy, I have, for the most part, followed the learned and candid Mosheim.*

soon introduces the office of a president, invested at least with the authority of collecting the sentiments, and of executing the resolutions, of the assembly. A regard for the public tranquillity, which would so frequently have been interrupted by annual or by occasional elections, induced the primitive Christians to constitute an honourable and perpetual magistracy, and to choose one of the wisest and most holy among their presbyters to execute, during his life, the duties of their ecclesiastical governor. It was under these circumstances that the lofty title of Bishop began to raise itself above the humble appellation of presbyter; and, while the latter remained the most natural distinction for the members of every Christian senate, the former was appropriated to the dignity of its new president.[54] The advantages of this episcopal form of government, which appears to have been introduced before the end of the first century,[55] were so obvious, and so important for the future greatness, as well as the present peace, of Christianity, that it was adopted without delay by all the societies which were already scattered over the empire, had acquired in a very early period the sanction of antiquity,[56] and is still revered by the most powerful churches, both of the East and of the West, as a primitive and even as a divine establishment.[57] It is needless to observe that the pious and humble presbyters who were first dignified with the episcopal title could not possess, and would probably have rejected, the power and pomp which now encircles the tiara of the Roman pontiff, or the mitre of a German prelate. But we may define, in a few words, the narrow limits of their original jurisdiction, which was chiefly of a spiritual, though in some instances of a temporal, nature. It consisted in the administration of the sacraments and discipline of the church, the superintendency of religious ceremonies, which imperceptibly increased in number and variety, the consecration of ecclesiastical ministers, to whom the bishop assigned their respective functions, the management of the public fund, and the determination of all such differences as the faithful were unwilling to expose before the tribunal of an idolatrous judge. These powers, during a short period, were exercised according to the advice of the presbyteral college, and with the consent and approbation of the assembly of Christians. The primitive bishops were considered only as the first of their equals, and the honourable servants of a free people. Whenever the episcopal chair became vacant by death, a new president was chosen among the presbyters by the suffrage of the whole congregation, every member of which supposed himself of sacred and sacerdotal character.

Such was the mild and equal constitution by which the Christians were governed more than a hundred years after the death of the apostles. Every society formed within itself a separate and independent republic: and, although the most distant of these little states maintained a mutual as well as friendly intercourse of letters and deputations, the Christian world was not yet connected by any supreme authority or legislative assembly. As the numbers of the faithful were gradually multiplied, they discovered the advantages that might result from a closer union of their interest and designs. Towards the end of the second century, the churches of Greece and Asia adopted the useful institutions of provincial synods, and they may justly be supposed to have borrowed the model of a representative council from the celebrated examples of their own country, the Amphictyons, the Achæan league, or the assemblies of the Ionian cities. It was soon established as a custom and as a law that the bishops of the independent churches should meet in the capital of the province at the stated periods of spring and autumn. Their deliberations were assisted by the advice of a few distinguished presbyters, and moderated by the presence of a listening multitude.[58] Their decrees, which were styled Canons, regulated every important controversy of faith and discipline; and it was natural to believe that a liberal effusion of the Holy Spirit would be poured on the united assembly of the delegates of the Christian people. The institution of synods was so well suited to private ambition and to public interest that in the space of a few years it was received throughout the whole empire. A regular correspondence was established between the provincial councils, which mutually communicated and approved their respective proceedings; and the Catholic church soon assumed the form, and acquired the strength, of a great federative republic.

As the legislative authority of the particular churches was insensibly superseded by the use of councils, the bishops obtained by their alliance a much larger share of executive and arbitrary power; and, as soon as they were connected by a sense of their common interest, they were enabled to attack, with united vigour, the original rights of their clergy and people. The prelates of the third century imperceptibly changed the language of exhortation into that of command, scattered the seeds of future usurpations, and supplied, by scripture allegories and declamatory rhetoric, their deficiency of force and of reason. They exalted the unity and power of the church, as it was represented in the EPISCOPAL OFFICE, of which every bishop enjoyed an equal and undivided portion. Princes and magistrates, it was

[58] *This council was composed of eighty-seven bishops from the provinces of Mauritania, Numidia, and Africa; some presbyters and deacons assisted at the assembly; præsente plebis maximâ parte.*

often repeated, might boast an earthly claim to a transitory dominion; it was the episcopal authority alone which was derived from
the Deity, and extended itself over this and over another world. The
bishops were the vicegerents of Christ, the successors of the apostles,
and the mystic substitutes of the high priest of the Mosaic law. Their
exclusive privilege of conferring the sacerdotal character invaded
the freedom both of clerical and of popular elections; and if, in the
administration of the church, they still consulted the judgment of
the presbyters or the inclination of the people, they most carefully
inculcated the merit of such a voluntary condescension. The bishops acknowledged the supreme authority which resided in the assembly of their brethren; but, in the government of his peculiar
diocese, each of them exacted from his *flock* the same implicit
obedience as if that favourite metaphor had been literally just,
and as if the shepherd had been of a more exalted nature than that
of his sheep. This obedience, however, was not imposed without
some efforts on one side, and some resistance on the other. The
democratical part of the constitution was, in many places, very
warmly supported by the zealous or interested opposition of the inferior clergy. But their patriotism received the ignominious epithets
of faction and schism; and the episcopal cause was indebted for its
rapid progress to the labours of many active prelates, who, like
Cyprian of Carthage, could reconcile the arts of the most ambitious
statesman with the Christian virtues which seem adapted to the
character of a saint and martyr.[59]

[59] *If Novatus, Felicissimus, &c., whom the
bishop of Carthage ex-
pelled from his church,
and from Africa, were
not the most detestable
monsters of wickedness,
the zeal of Cyprian must
occasionally have pre-
vailed over his veracity.*

The same causes which at first had destroyed the equality of the
presbyters introduced among the bishops a pre-eminence of rank,
and from thence a superiority of jurisdiction. As often as in the
spring and autumn they met in provincial synod, the difference of
personal merit and reputation was very sensibly felt among the
members of the assembly, and the multitude was governed by the
wisdom and eloquence of the few. But the order of public proceedings required a more regular and less invidious distinction; the
office of perpetual presidents in the councils of each province was
conferred on the bishops of the principal city, and these aspiring
prelates, who soon acquired the lofty titles of Metropolitans and
Primates, secretly prepared themselves to usurp over their episcopal
brethren the same authority which the bishops had so lately assumed above the college of presbyters. Nor was it long before an
emulation of pre-eminence and power prevailed among the metropolitans themselves, each of them affecting to display, in the most

pompous terms, the temporal honours and advantages of the city over which he presided; the numbers and opulence of the Christians who were subject to their pastoral care; the saints and martyrs who had arisen among them, and the purity with which they preserved the tradition of the faith, as it had been transmitted through a series of orthodox bishops from the apostle or the apostolic disciple, to whom the foundation of their church was ascribed.[60] From every cause, either of a civil or of an ecclesiastical nature, it was easy to foresee that Rome must enjoy the respect, and would soon claim the obedience, of the provinces. The society of the faithful bore a just proportion to the capital of the empire; and the Roman church was the greatest, the most numerous, and, in regard to the West, the most ancient of all the Christian establishments, many of which had received their religion from the pious labours of her missionaries. Instead of *one* apostolic founder, the utmost boast of Antioch, of Ephesus, or of Corinth, the banks of the Tiber were supposed to have been honoured with the preaching and martyrdom of the *two* most eminent among the apostles;[61] and the bishops of Rome very prudently claimed the inheritance of whatsoever prerogatives were attributed either to the person or to the office of St. Peter.[62] The bishops of Italy and of the provinces were disposed to allow them a primacy of order and association (such was their very accurate expression) in the Christian aristocracy. But the power of a monarch was rejected with abhorrence, and the aspiring genius of Rome experienced, from the nations of Asia and Africa, a more vigorous resistance to her spiritual, than she had formerly done to her temporal, dominion. The patriotic Cyprian, who ruled with the most absolute sway the church of Carthage and the provincial synods, opposed with resolution and success the ambition of the Roman pontiff, artfully connected his own cause with that of the eastern bishops, and, like Hannibal, sought out new allies in the heart of Asia. If this Punic war was carried on without any effusion of blood, it was owing much less to the moderation than to the weakness of the contending prelates. Invectives and excommunications were *their* only weapons; and these, during the progress of the whole controversy, they hurled against each other with equal fury and devotion. The hard necessity of censuring either a pope, or a saint and martyr, distresses the modern Catholics, whenever they are obliged to relate the particulars of a dispute in which the champions of religion indulged such passions as seem much more adapted to the senate or to the camp.

[60] *Tertullian, in a distinct treatise, has pleaded against the heretics the right of prescription, as it was held by the apostolic churches.*

[61] *The journey of St. Peter to Rome is mentioned by most of the ancients, maintained by all the Catholics, allowed by some Protestants, but has been vigorously attacked by Spanheim. According to Father Hardouin, the monks of the thirteenth century, who composed the Æneid, represented St. Peter under the allegorical character of the Trojan hero.*

[62] *It is in French only that the famous allusion to St. Peter's name is exact. Tu es* Pierre *et sur cette* pierre.—*The same is imperfect in Greek, Latin, Italian, &c., and totally unintelligible in our Teutonic languages.*

The progress of the ecclesiastical authority gave birth to the memorable distinction of the laity and of the clergy, which had been unknown to the Greeks and Romans. The former of these appellations comprehended the body of the Christian people; the latter, according to the signification of the word, was appropriated to the chosen portion that had been set apart for the service of religion; a celebrated order of men which has furnished the most important, though not always the most edifying, subjects for modern history. Their mutual hostilities sometimes disturbed the peace of the infant church, but their zeal and activity were united in the common cause, and the love of power, which (under the most artful disguises) could insinuate itself into the breasts of bishops and martyrs, animated them to increase the number of their subjects, and to enlarge the limits of the Christian empire. They were destitute of any temporal force, and they were for a long time discouraged and oppressed, rather than assisted, by the civil magistrate; but they had acquired, and they employed within their own society, the two most efficacious instruments of government, rewards and punishments; the former derived from the pious liberality, the latter from the devout apprehensions, of the faithful.

I. The community of goods, which had so agreeably amused the imagination of Plato,[63] and which subsisted in some degree among the austere sect of the Essenians, was adopted for a short time in the primitive church. The fervour of the first proselytes prompted them to sell those worldly possessions which they despised, to lay the price of them at the feet of the apostles, and to content themselves with receiving an equal share out of the general distribution. The progress of the Christian religion relaxed, and gradually abolished, this generous institution, which, in hands less pure than those of the apostles, would too soon have been corrupted and abused by the returning selfishness of human nature; and the converts who embraced the new religion were permitted to retain the possession of their patrimony, to receive legacies and inheritances, and to increase their separate property by all the lawful means of trade and industry. Instead of an absolute sacrifice, a moderate proportion was accepted by the ministers of the gospel; and in their weekly or monthly assemblies, every believer, according to the exigency of the occasion, and the measure of his wealth and piety, presented his voluntary offering for the use of the common fund. Nothing, however inconsiderable, was refused; but it was diligently inculcated that, in the article of Tythes, the Mosaic law was still of divine obligation;

63 *The community instituted by Plato is more perfect than that which Sir Thomas More had imagined for his Utopia. The community of women, and that of temporal goods, may be considered as inseparable parts of the same system.*

and that, since the Jews, under a less perfect discipline, had been commanded to pay a tenth part of all that they possessed, it would become the disciples of Christ to distinguish themselves by a superior degree of liberality,[64] and to acquire some merit by resigning a superfluous treasure, which must so soon be annihilated with the world itself.[65] It is almost unnecessary to observe that the revenue of each particular church, which was of so uncertain and fluctuating a nature, must have varied with the poverty or the opulence of the faithful, as they were dispersed in obscure villages, or collected in the great cities of the empire. In the time of the emperor Decius, it was the opinion of the magistrates that the Christians of Rome were possessed of very considerable wealth; that vessels of gold and silver were used in their religious worship; and that many among their proselytes had sold their lands and houses to increase the public riches of the sect, at the expense, indeed, of their unfortunate children, who found themselves beggars, because their parents had been saints.[66] We should listen with distrust to the suspicions of strangers and enemies: on this occasion, however, they receive a very specious and probable colour from the two following circumstances, the only ones that have reached our knowledge, which define any precise sums, or convey any distinct idea. Almost at the same period, the bishop of Carthage, from a society less opulent than that of Rome, collected a hundred thousand sesterces (above eight hundred and fifty pounds sterling), on a sudden call of charity, to redeem the brethren of Numidia, who had been carried away captives by the barbarians of the desert. About an hundred years before the reign of Decius, the Roman church had received in a single donation, the sum of two hundred thousand sesterces from a stranger of Pontus, who had proposed to fix his residence in the capital. These oblations, for the most part, were made in money; nor was the society of Christians either desirous or capable of acquiring, to any considerable degree, the incumbrance of landed property. It had been provided by several laws, which were enacted with the same design as our statutes of mortmain, that no real estates should be given or bequeathed to any corporate body, without either a special privilege or a particular dispensation from the emperor or from the senate; who were seldom disposed to grant them in favour of a sect, at first the object of their contempt, and at last of their fears and jealousy. A transaction, however, is related under the reign of Alexander Severus, which discovers that the restraint was sometimes eluded or suspended, and that the Christians were permitted to claim and to

[64] *The Constitutions introduce this divine precept by declaring that priests are as much above kings, as the soul is above the body. Among the tythable articles, they enumerate corn, wine, oil, and wood.*

[65] *The same opinion which prevailed about the year 1000 was productive of the same effects. Most of the donations express their motive, "appropinquante mundi fine."*

[66] *The subsequent conduct of the deacon Laurence only proves how proper a use was made of the wealth of the Roman church; it was undoubtedly very considerable; but Fra Paolo appears to exaggerate when he supposes that the successors of Commodus were urged to persecute the Christians by their own avarice, or that of their Prætorian præfects.*

[67] *The ground had been public; and was now disputed between the society of Christians and that of butchers.*

possess lands within the limits of Rome itself.[67] The progress of Christianity and the civil confusion of the empire contributed to relax the severity of the laws; and, before the close of the third century, many considerable estates were bestowed on the opulent churches of Rome, Milan, Carthage, Antioch, Alexandria, and the other great cities of Italy and the provinces.

The bishop was the natural steward of the church; the public stock was intrusted to his care, without account or control; the presbyters were confined to their spiritual functions, and the more dependent order of deacons was solely employed in the management and distribution of the ecclesiastical revenue. If we may give credit to the vehement declamations of Cyprian, there were too many among his African brethren who, in the execution of their charge, violated every precept, not only of evangelical perfection, but even of moral virtue. By some of these unfaithful stewards, the riches of the church were lavished in sensual pleasures, by others they were perverted to the purposes of private gain, of fraudulent purchases, and of rapacious usury. But, as long as the contributions of the Christian people were free and unconstrained, the abuse of their confidence could not be very frequent, and the general uses to which their liberality was applied reflected honour on the religious society. A decent portion was reserved for the maintenance of the bishop and his clergy; a sufficient sum was allotted for the expenses of the public worship, of which the feasts of love, the *agapæ,* as they were called, constituted a very pleasing part. The whole remainder was the sacred patrimony of the poor. According to the discretion of the bishop, it was distributed to support widows and orphans, the lame, the sick, and the aged of the community; to comfort strangers and pilgrims, and to alleviate the misfortunes of prisoners and captives, more especially when their sufferings had been occasioned by their firm attachment to the cause of religion. A generous intercourse of charity united the most distant provinces, and the smaller congregations were cheerfully assisted by the alms of their more opulent brethren. Such an institution, which paid less regard to the merit than to the distress of the object, very materially conduced to the progress of Christianity. The Pagans, who were actuated by a sense of humanity, while they derided the doctrines, acknowledged the benevolence, of the new sect.[68] The prospect of immediate relief and of future protection allured into its hospitable bosom many of those unhappy persons whom the neglect of the world would have abandoned to the miseries of want, of sickness, and of old age. There

[68] *Julian seems mortified that the Christian charity maintains not only their own, but likewise the heathen poor.*

is some reason likewise to believe that great numbers of infants who, according to the inhuman practice of the times, had been exposed by their parents were frequently rescued from death, baptized, educated, and maintained by the piety of the Christians, and at the expense of the public treasure.[69]

II. It is the undoubted right of every society to exclude from its communion and benefits such among its members as reject or violate those regulations which have been established by general consent. In the exercise of this power, the censures of the Christian church were chiefly directed against scandalous sinners, and particularly those who were guilty of murder, of fraud, or of incontinence; against the authors, or the followers, of any heretical opinions which had been condemned by the judgment of the episcopal order; and against those unhappy persons who, whether from choice or from compulsion, had polluted themselves after their baptism by any act of idolatrous worship. The consequences of excommunication were of a temporal as well as a spiritual nature. The Christian against whom it was pronounced was deprived of any part in the oblations of the faithful. The ties both of religious and of private friendship were dissolved; he found himself a profane object of abhorrence to the persons whom he the most esteemed, or by whom he had been the most tenderly beloved; and, as far as an expulsion from a respectable society could imprint on his character a mark of disgrace, he was shunned or suspected by the generality of mankind. The situation of these unfortunate exiles was in itself very painful and melancholy; but, as it usually happens, their apprehensions far exceeded their sufferings. The benefits of the Christian communion were those of eternal life, nor could they erase from their minds the awful opinion, that to those ecclesiastical governors by whom they were condemned the Deity had committed the keys of Hell and of Paradise. The heretics, indeed, who might be supported by the consciousness of their intentions, and by the flattering hope that they alone had discovered the true path of salvation, endeavoured to regain, in their separate assemblies, those comforts, temporal as well as spiritual, which they no longer derived from the great society of Christians. But almost all those who had reluctantly yielded to the power of vice or idolatry were sensible of their fallen condition, and anxiously desirous of being restored to the benefits of the Christian communion.

With regard to the treatment of these penitents, two opposite opinions, the one of justice, the other of mercy, divided the primi-

[69] *Such, at least, has been the laudable conduct of more modern missionaries, under the same circumstances. Above three thousand new-born infants are annually exposed in the streets of Pekin.*

tive church. The more rigid and inflexible casuists refused them for ever, and without exception, the meanest place in the holy community, which they had disgraced or deserted, and, leaving them to the remorse of a guilty conscience, indulged them only with a faint ray of hope that the contrition of their life and death might possibly be accepted by the Supreme Being.[70] A milder sentiment was embraced, in practice as well as in theory, by the purest and most respectable of the Christian churches. The gates of reconciliation and of Heaven were seldom shut against the returning penitent; but a severe and solemn form of discipline was instituted, which, while it served to expiate his crime, might powerfully deter the spectators from the imitation of his example. Humbled by a public confession, emaciated by fasting, and clothed in sackcloth, the penitent lay prostrate at the door of the assembly, imploring, with tears, the pardon of his offences, and soliciting the prayers of the faithful.[71] If the fault was of a very heinous nature, whole years of penance were esteemed an inadequate satisfaction to the Divine Justice; and it was always by slow and painful gradations that the sinner, the heretic, or the apostate was re-admitted into the bosom of the church. A sentence of perpetual excommunication was, however, reserved for some crimes of an extraordinary magnitude, and particularly for the inexcusable relapses of those penitents who had already experienced and abused the clemency of their ecclesiastical superiors. According to the circumstances or the number of the guilty, the exercise of the Christian discipline was varied by the discretion of the bishops. The councils of Ancyra and Illiberis were held about the same time, the one in Galatia, the other in Spain; but their respective canons, which are still extant, seem to breathe a very different spirit. The Galatian, who after his baptism had repeatedly sacrificed to idols, might obtain his pardon by a penance of seven years, and, if he had seduced others to imitate his example, only three years more were added to the term of his exile. But the unhappy Spaniard, who had committed the same offence, was deprived of the hope of reconciliation, even in the article of death; and his idolatry was placed at the head of a list of seventeen other crimes, against which a sentence, no less terrible, was pronounced. Among these we may distinguish the inexpiable guilt of calumniating a bishop, a presbyter, or even a deacon.[72]

The well-tempered mixture of liberality and rigour, the judicious dispensation of rewards and punishments, according to the maxims of policy as well as justice, constituted the *human* strength of the

[70] The Montanists and the Novatians, who adhered to this opinion with the greatest rigour and obstinacy, found themselves *at last in the number of excommunicated heretics.*

[71] The admirers of antiquity regret the loss of this public penance.

[72] See in Dupin a short but rational exposition of the canons of those councils, which were assembled in the first moments of tranquillity after the persecution of Diocletian. This persecution had been much less severely felt in Spain than in Galatia; a difference which may, in some measure, account for the contrast of their regulations.

church. The bishops, whose paternal care extended itself to the government of both worlds, were sensible of the importance of these prerogatives, and, covering their ambition with the fair pretence of the love of order, they were jealous of any rival in the exercise of a discipline so necessary to prevent the desertion of those troops which had enlisted themselves under the banner of the cross, and whose numbers every day became more considerable. From the imperious declamations of Cyprian we should naturally conclude that the doctrines of excommunication and penance formed the most essential part of religion; and that it was much less dangerous for the disciples of Christ to neglect the observance of the moral duties than to despise the censures and authority of their bishops. Sometimes we might imagine that we were listening to the voice of Moses, when he commanded the earth to open, and to swallow up, in consuming flames, the rebellious race which refused obedience to the priesthood of Aaron; and we should sometimes suppose that we heard a Roman consul asserting the majesty of the republic, and declaring his inflexible resolution to enforce the rigour of the laws. "If such irregularities are suffered with impunity (it is thus that the bishop of Carthage chides the lenity of his colleague), if such irregularities are suffered, there is an end of EPISCOPAL VIGOUR; an end of the sublime and divine power of governing the church, an end of Christianity itself." Cyprian had renounced those temporal honours which it is probable he would never have obtained; but the acquisition of such absolute command over the consciences and understanding of a congregation, however obscure or despised by the world, is more truly grateful to the pride of the human heart than the possession of the most despotic power imposed by arms and conquest on a reluctant people.

In the course of this important, though perhaps tedious, inquiry, I have attempted to display the secondary causes which so efficaciously assisted the truth of the Christian religion. If among these causes we have discovered any artificial ornaments, any accidental circumstances, or any mixture of error and passion, it cannot appear surprising that mankind should be the most sensibly affected by such motives as were suited to their imperfect nature. It was by the aid of these causes, exclusive zeal, the immediate expectation of another world, the claim of miracles, the practice of rigid virtue, and the constitution of the primitive church, that Christianity spread itself with so much success in the Roman empire. To the first of these the Christians were indebted for their invincible valour, which disdained to capitulate with the enemy whom they were resolved to vanquish. The three succeeding causes supplied their valour with the most formidable arms. The last of these causes united their courage, directed their arms, and gave their efforts that irresistible weight which even a small band of well-trained and intrepid volunteers has so often possessed over an undisciplined multitude, ignorant of the subject, and careless of the event of the war. In the various religions of Polytheism, some wandering fanatics of Egypt and Syria, who addressed themselves to the credulous superstition of the populace, were perhaps the only order of priests [73] that derived their whole support and credit from their sacerdotal profession, and were very deeply affected by a personal concern for the safety or prosperity of their tutelar deities. The ministers of Polytheism, both in Rome and in the provinces, were, for the most part, men of a noble birth, and of an affluent fortune, who received, as an honourable distinction, the care of a celebrated temple, or of a public sacrifice, exhibited, very frequently at their own expense, the sacred games,[74] and with cold indifference performed the ancient rites, according to the laws and fashion of their country. As they were engaged in the ordinary occupations of life, their zeal and devotion were seldom animated by a sense of interest, or by the habits of an ecclesiastical character. Confined to their respective temples and cities, they remained without any connexion of discipline or government; and, whilst they acknowledged the supreme jurisdiction of the senate, of the college of pontiffs, and of the emperor, those civil magistrates contented themselves with the easy task of maintaining, in peace and dignity, the general worship of mankind. We have already seen how various, how loose, and how uncertain were the religious sentiments of Polytheists. They were abandoned, almost without control, to the natural workings of a superstitious fancy. The accidental circumstances of their life and situation determined the object, as well as the degree, of their devotion; and, as long as their adoration was successively prostituted to a thousand deities, it was scarcely possible that their hearts could be susceptible of a very sincere or lively passion for any of them.

When Christianity appeared in the world, even these faint and imperfect impressions had lost much of their original power. Human reason, which, by its unassisted strength, is incapable of perceiving the mysteries of faith, had already obtained an easy triumph over the folly of Paganism; and, when Tertullian or Lactantius employ their labours in exposing its falsehood and extravagance, they

[73] *The arts, the manners, and the vices of the priests of the Syrian goddess are very humorously described by Apuleius, in the eighth book of his Metamorphoses.*

[74] *The office of Asiarch was of this nature, and it is frequently mentioned in Aristides, the Inscriptions, &c. It was annual and elective. None but the vainest citizens could desire the honour; none but the most wealthy could support the expense.*

are obliged to transcribe the eloquence of Cicero or the wit of Lucian. The contagion of these sceptical writings had been diffused far beyond the number of their readers. The fashion of incredulity was communicated from the philosopher to the man of pleasure or business, from the noble to the plebeian, and from the master to the menial slave who waited at his table, and who eagerly listened to the freedom of his conversation. On public occasions the philosophic part of mankind affected to treat with respect and decency the religious institutions of their country; but their secret contempt penetrated through the thin and awkward disguise; and even the people, when they discovered that their deities were rejected and derided by those whose rank or understanding they were accustomed to reverence, were filled with doubts and apprehensions concerning the truth of those doctrines to which they had yielded the most implicit belief. The decline of ancient prejudice exposed a very numerous portion of human kind to the danger of a painful and comfortless situation. A state of scepticism and suspense may amuse a few inquisitive minds. But the practice of superstition is so congenial to the multitude that, if they are forcibly awakened, they still regret the loss of their pleasing vision. Their love of the marvellous and supernatural, their curiosity with regard to future events, and their strong propensity to extend their hopes and fears beyond the limits of the visible world, were the principal causes which favoured the establishment of Polytheism. So urgent on the vulgar is the necessity of believing that the fall of any system of mythology will most probably be succeeded by the introduction of some other mode of superstition. Some deities of a more recent and fashionable cast might soon have occupied the deserted temples of Jupiter and Apollo, if, in the decisive moment, the wisdom of Providence had not interposed a genuine revelation, fitted to inspire the most rational esteem and conviction, whilst, at the same time, it was adorned with all that could attract the curiosity, the wonder, and the veneration of the people. In their actual disposition, as many were almost disengaged from their artificial prejudices, but equally susceptible and desirous of a devout attachment; an object much less deserving would have been sufficient to fill the vacant place in their hearts, and to gratify the uncertain eagerness of their passions. Those who are inclined to pursue this reflection, instead of viewing with astonishment the rapid progress of Christianity, will perhaps be surprised that its success was not still more rapid and still more universal.

It has been observed, with truth as well as propriety, that the conquests of Rome prepared and facilitated those of Christianity. In the second chapter of this work we have attempted to explain in what manner the most civilized provinces of Europe, Asia, and Africa were united under the dominion of one sovereign, and gradually connected by the most intimate ties of laws, of manners, and of language. The Jews of Palestine, who had fondly expected a temporal deliverer, gave so cold a reception to the miracles of the divine prophet that it was found unnecessary to publish, or at least to preserve, any Hebrew gospel.[75] The authentic histories of the actions of Christ were composed in the Greek language, at a considerable distance from Jerusalem, and after the Gentile converts were grown extremely numerous.[76] As soon as those histories were translated into the Latin tongue, they were perfectly intelligible to all the subjects of Rome, excepting only to the peasants of Syria and Egypt, for whose benefit particular versions were afterwards made. The public highways, which had been constructed for the use of the legions, opened an easy passage for the Christian missionaries from Damascus to Corinth, and from Italy to the extremity of Spain or Britain; nor did those spiritual conquerors encounter any of the obstacles which usually retard or prevent the introduction of a foreign religion into a distant country. There is the strongest reason to believe that before the reigns of Diocletian and Constantine, the faith of Christ had been preached in every province, and in all the great cities of the empire; but the foundation of the several congregations, the numbers of the faithful who composed them, and their proportion to the unbelieving multitude, are now buried in obscurity, or disguised by fiction and declamation. Such imperfect circumstances, however, as have reached our knowledge concerning the increase of the Christian name in Asia and Greece, in Egypt, in Italy, and in the West, we shall now proceed to relate, without neglecting the real or imaginary acquisitions which lay beyond the frontiers of the Roman empire.

The rich provinces that extend from the Euphrates to the Ionian sea were the principal theatre on which the apostle of the Gentiles displayed his zeal and piety. The seeds of the gospel, which he had scattered in a fertile soil, were diligently cultivated by his disciples; and it should seem that, during the two first centuries, the most considerable body of Christians was contained within those limits. Among the societies which were instituted in Syria, none were more ancient or more illustrious than those of Damascus, of Berœa or

[75] The modern critics are not disposed to believe what the fathers almost unanimously assert, that St. Matthew composed a Hebrew gospel, of which only the Greek translation is extant. It seems, however, dangerous to reject their testimony.

[76] Under the reigns of Nero and Domitian, and in the cities of Alexandria, Antioch, Rome, and Ephesus.

Aleppo, and of Antioch. The prophetic introduction of the Apocalypse has described and immortalized the seven churches of Asia:—Ephesus, Smyrna, Pergamus, Thyatira,[77] Sardes, Laodicea, and Philadelphia; and their colonies were soon diffused over that populous country. In a very early period, the islands of Cyprus and Crete, the provinces of Thrace and Macedonia, gave a favourable reception to the new religion; and Christian republics were soon founded in the cities of Corinth, of Sparta, and of Athens.[78] The antiquity of the Greek and Asiatic churches allowed a sufficient space of time for their increase and multiplication, and even the swarms of Gnostics and other heretics serve to display the flourishing condition of the orthodox church, since the appellation of heretics has always been applied to the less numerous party. To these domestic testimonies we may add the confession, the complaints, and the apprehensions of the Gentiles themselves. From the writings of Lucian, a philosopher who had studied mankind, and who describes their manners in the most lively colours, we may learn that, under the reign of Commodus, his native country of Pontus was filled with Epicureans and *Christians.*[79] Within fourscore years after the death of Christ,[80] the humane Pliny laments the magnitude of the evil which he vainly attempted to eradicate. In his very curious epistle to the emperor Trajan, he affirms that the temples were almost deserted, that the sacred victims scarcely found any purchasers, and that the superstition had not only infected the cities, but had even spread itself into the villages and the open country of Pontus and Bithynia.

Without descending into a minute scrutiny of the expressions, or of the motives of those writers who either celebrate or lament the progress of Christianity in the East, it may in general be observed that none of them have left us any grounds from whence a just estimate might be formed of the real numbers of the faithful in those provinces. One circumstance, however, has been fortunately preserved, which seems to cast a more distinct light on this obscure but interesting subject. Under the reign of Theodosius, after Christianity had enjoyed, during more than sixty years, the sunshine of Imperial favour, the ancient and illustrious church of Antioch consisted of one hundred thousand persons, three thousand of whom were supported out of the public oblations. The splendour and dignity of the queen of the East, the acknowledged populousness of Cæsarea, Seleucia, and Alexandria, and the destruction of two hundred and fifty thousand souls in the earthquake which afflicted Antioch under the elder Justin,[81] are so many convincing proofs that

[77] *The Alogians disputed the genuineness of the Apocalypse, because the church of Thyatira was not yet founded. Epiphanius, who allows the fact, extricates himself from the difficulty by ingeniously supposing that St. John wrote in the spirit of prophecy.*

[78] *The epistles of Ignatius and Dionysius point out many churches in Asia and Greece. That of Athens seems to have been one of the least flourishing.*

[79] *Christianity, however, must have been very unequally diffused over Pontus; since in the middle of the third century there were no more than seventeen believers in the extensive diocese of Neo-Cæsarea.*

[80] *According to the ancients, Jesus Christ suffered under the consulship of the two Gemini, in the year 29 of our present æra. Pliny was sent into Bithynia (according to Pagi) in the year 110.*

[81] *John Malala draws the same conclusion with regard to the populousness of Antioch.*

the whole number of its inhabitants was not less than half a million, and that the Christians, however multiplied by zeal and power, did not exceed a fifth part of that great city. How different a proportion must we adopt when we compare the persecuted with the triumphant church, the West with the East, remote villages with populous towns, and countries recently converted to the faith with the place where the believers first received the appellation of Christians! It must not, however, be dissembled that, in another passage, Chrysostom, to whom we are indebted for this useful information, computes the multitude of the faithful as even superior to that of the Jews and Pagans. But the solution of this apparent difficulty is easy and obvious. The eloquent preacher draws a parallel between the civil and the ecclesiastical constitution of Antioch; between the list of Christians who had acquired Heaven by baptism and the list of citizens who had a right to share the public liberality. Slaves, strangers, and infants were comprised in the former; they were excluded from the latter.

The extensive commerce of Alexandria, and its proximity to Palestine, gave an easy entrance to the new religion. It was at first embraced by great numbers of the Therapeutæ, or Essenians of the lake Mareotis, a Jewish sect which had abated much of its reverence for the Mosaic ceremonies. The austere life of the Essenians, their fasts and excommunications, the community of goods, the love of celibacy, their zeal for martyrdom, and the warmth though not the purity of their faith, already offered a very lively image of the primitive discipline.[82] It was in the school of Alexandria that the Christian theology appears to have assumed a regular and scientific form; and, when Hadrian visited Egypt, he found a church, composed of Jews and of Greeks, sufficiently important to attract the notice of that inquisitive prince. But the progress of Christianity was for a long time confined within the limits of a single city, which was itself a foreign colony, and, till the close of the second century, the predecessors of Demetrius were the only prelates of the Egyptian church. Three bishops were consecrated by the hands of Demetrius, and the number was increased to twenty by his successor Heraclas.[83] The body of the natives, a people distinguished by a sullen inflexibility of temper, entertained the new doctrine with coldness and reluctance; and even in the time of Origen it was rare to meet with an Egyptian who had surmounted his early prejudices in favour of the sacred animals of his country. As soon, indeed, as Christianity ascended the throne, the zeal of those barbarians obeyed the prevail-

[82] *Basnage has examined, with the most critical accuracy, the curious treatise of Philo which describes the Therapeutæ. By proving that it was composed as early as the time of Augustus, Basnage has demonstrated, in spite of Eusebius and a crowd of modern Catholics, that the Therapeutæ were neither Christians nor monks. It still remains probable that they changed their name, preserved their manners, adopted some new articles of faith, and gradually became the fathers of the Egyptian Ascetics.*

[83] *This curious fact is preserved by the patriarch Eutychius, and its internal evidence would alone be a sufficient answer to all the objections which Bishop Pearnos has urged in the Vindiciæ Ignatianæ.*

ing impulsion; the cities of Egypt were filled with bishops, and the deserts of Thebais swarmed with hermits.

A perpetual stream of strangers and provincials flowed into the capacious bosom of Rome. Whatever was strange or odious, whoever was guilty or suspected, might hope, in the obscurity of that immense capital, to elude the vigilance of the law. In such a various conflux of nations, every teacher, either of truth or of falsehood, every founder, whether of a virtuous or a criminal association, might easily multiply his disciples or accomplices. The Christians of Rome, at the time of the accidental persecution of Nero, are represented by Tacitus as already amounting to a very great multitude, and the language of that great historian is almost similar to the style employed by Livy, when he relates the introduction and the suppression of the rites of Bacchus. After the Bacchanals had awakened the severity of the senate, it was likewise apprehended that a very great multitude, as it were *another people,* had been initiated into those abhorred mysteries. A more careful inquiry soon demonstrated that the offenders did not exceed seven thousand; a number, indeed, sufficiently alarming, when considered as the object of public justice.[84] It is with the same candid allowance that we should interpret the vague expressions of Tacitus, and in a former instance of Pliny, when they exaggerate the crowds of deluded fanatics who had forsaken the established worship of the gods. The church of Rome was undoubtedly the first and most populous of the empire; and we are possessed of an authentic record which attests the state of religion in that city, about the middle of the third century, and after a peace of thirty-eight years. The clergy, at that time, consisted of a bishop, forty-six presbyters, seven deacons, as many sub-deacons, forty-two acolytes, and fifty readers, exorcists, and porters. The number of widows, of the infirm, and of the poor, who were maintained by the oblations of the faithful, amounted to fifteen hundred. From reason, as well as from the analogy of Antioch, we may venture to estimate the Christians of Rome at about fifty thousand. The populousness of that great capital cannot, perhaps, be exactly ascertained; but the most modest calculation will not surely reduce it lower than a million of inhabitants, of whom the Christians might constitute at the most a twentieth part.[85]

The western provincials appeared to have derived the knowledge of Christianity from the same source which had diffused among them the language, the sentiments, and the manners of Rome. In this more important circumstance, Africa, as well as Gaul, was

[84] *Nothing could exceed the horror and consternation of the senate on the discovery of the Bacchanalians, whose depravity is described, and perhaps exaggerated, by Livy.*

[85] *This proportion of the presbyters and of the poor to the rest of the people was originally fixed by Burnet, and is approved by Moyle. They were both unacquainted with the passage of Chrysostom, which converts their conjecture almost into a fact.*

gradually fashioned to the imitation of the capital. Yet, notwithstanding the many favourable occasions which might invite the Roman missionaries to visit their Latin provinces, it was late before they passed either the sea or the Alps;[86] nor can we discover in those great countries any assured traces either of faith or of persecution that ascend higher than the reign of the Antonines.[87] The slow progress of the gospel in the cold climate of Gaul was extremely different from the eagerness with which it seems to have been received on the burning sands of Africa. The African Christians soon formed one of the principal members of the primitive church. The practice introduced into that province of appointing bishops to the most inconsiderable towns, and very frequently to the most obscure villages, contributed to multiply the splendour and importance of their religious societies, which during the course of the third century were animated by the zeal of Tertullian, directed by the abilities of Cyprian, and adorned by the eloquence of Lactantius. But if, on the contrary, we turn our eyes towards Gaul, we must content ourselves with discovering, in the time of Marcus Antoninus, the feeble and united congregations of Lyons and Vienna; and, even as late as the reign of Decius, we are assured that in a few cities only, Arles, Narbonne, Toulouse, Limoges, Clermont, Tours, and Paris, some scattered churches were supported by the devotion of a small number of Christians.[88] Silence is indeed very consistent with devotion, but, as it is seldom compatible with zeal, we may perceive and lament the languid state of Christianity in those provinces which had exchanged the Celtic for the Latin tongue; since they did not, during the three first centuries, give birth to a single ecclesiastical writer. From Gaul, which claimed a just pre-eminence of learning and authority over all the countries on this side of the Alps, the light of the gospel was more faintly reflected on the remote provinces of Spain and Britain; and, if we may credit the vehement assertions of Tertullian, they had already received the first rays of the faith when he addressed his apology to the magistrates of the emperor Severus.[89] But the obscure and imperfect origin of the western churches of Europe has been so negligently recorded that, if we would relate the time and manner of their foundation, we must supply the silence of antiquity by those legends which avarice or superstition long afterwards dictated to the monks in the lazy gloom of their convents.[90] Of these holy romances, that of the apostle St. James can alone, by its single extravagance, deserve to be mentioned. From a peaceful fisherman of the lake of Gennesareth, he

---

[86] *According to the Donatists, whose assertion is confirmed by the tacit acknowledgment of Augustin, Africa was the last of the provinces which received the gospel.*

[87] *It is imagined that the Scyllitan martyrs were the first. One of the adversaries of Apuleius seems to have been a Christian.*

[88] *There is some reason to believe that, in the beginning of the fourth century, the extensive dioceses of Liège, of Treves, and of Cologne composed a single bishopric, which had been very recently founded. See Mémoires de Tillemont.*

[89] *The date of Tertullian's Apology is fixed, in a dissertation of Mosheim, to the year 198.*

[90] *In the fifteenth century, there were few who had either inclination or courage to question, whether Joseph of Arimathea founded the monastery of Glastonbury, and whether Dionysius the Areopagite preferred the residence of Paris to that of Athens.*

was transformed into a valorous knight, who charged at the head of the Spanish chivalry in their battles against the Moors. The gravest historians have celebrated his exploits; the miraculous shrine of Compostella displayed his power; and the sword of a military order, assisted by the terrors of the Inquisition, was sufficient to remove every objection of profane criticism.[91]

The progress of Christianity was not confined to the Roman empire; and, according to the primitive fathers, who interpret facts by prophecy, the new religion within a century after the death of its divine author, had already visited every part of the globe. "There exists not," says Justin Martyr, "a people, whether Greek or barbarian, or any other race of men, by whatsoever appellation or manners they may be distinguished, however ignorant of arts or agriculture, whether they dwell under tents, or wander about in covered waggons, among whom prayers are not offered up in the name of a crucified Jesus to the Father and Creator of all things." But this splendid exaggeration, which even at present it would be extremely difficult to reconcile with the real state of mankind, can be considered only as the rash sally of a devout but careless writer, the measure of whose belief was regulated by that of his wishes. But neither the belief nor the wishes of the fathers can alter the truth of history. It will still remain an undoubted fact, that the barbarians of Scythia and Germany who afterwards subverted the Roman monarchy were involved in the darkness of Paganism; and that even the conversion of Iberia, of Armenia, or of Æthiopia, was not attempted with any degree of success till the sceptre was in the hands of an orthodox emperor.[92] Before that time the various accidents of war and commerce might indeed diffuse an imperfect knowledge of the gospel among the tribes of Caledonia,[93] and among the borderers of the Rhine, the Danube, and the Euphrates.[94] Beyond the last-mentioned river, Edessa was distinguished by a firm and early adherence to the faith.[95] From Edessa the principles of Christianity were easily introduced into the Greek and Syrian cities which obeyed the successors of Artaxerxes; but they do not appear to have made any deep impression on the minds of the Persians, whose religious system, by the labours of a well-disciplined order of priests, had been constructed with much more art and solidity than the uncertain mythology of Greece and Rome.[96]

From this impartial, though imperfect, survey of the progress of Christianity, it may, perhaps, seem probable that the number of its proselytes has been excessively magnified by fear on the one side

[91] *The stupendous metamorphosis was performed in the ninth century.*

[92] *Many, though very confused circumstances, that relate to the conversion of Iberia and Armenia, may be found in Moses of Chorene.*

[93] *According to Tertullian, the Christian faith had penetrated into parts of Britain inaccessible to the Roman arms. About a century afterwards, Ossian, the son of Fingal, is said to have disputed, in his extreme old age, with one of the foreign missionaries, and the dispute is still extant, in verse, and in the Erse language.*

[94] *The Goths, who ravaged Asia in the reign of Gallienus, carried away great numbers of captives; some of whom were Christians, and became missionaries.*

[95] *The legend of Abgarus, fabulous as it is, affords a decisive proof that, many years before Eusebius wrote his history, the greatest part of the inhabitants of Edessa had embraced Christianity. Their rivals, the citizens of Carrhæ, adhered, on the contrary, to the cause of Paganism, as late as the sixth century.*

[96] *According to Bardesanes, there were some Christians in Persia before the end of the second century. In the time of Constantine they composed a flourishing church.*

and by devotion on the other. According to the irreproachable testimony of Origen, the proportion of the faithful was very inconsiderable when compared with the multitude of an unbelieving world; but, as we are left without any distinct information, it is impossible to determine, and it is difficult even to conjecture, the real numbers of the primitive Christians. The most favourable calculation, however, that can be deduced from the examples of Antioch and of Rome will not permit us to imagine that more than a twentieth part of the subjects of the empire had enlisted themselves under the banner of the cross before the important conversion of Constantine. But their habits of faith, of zeal, and of union seemed to multiply their numbers; and the same causes which contributed to their future increase served to render their actual strength more apparent and more formidable.

Such is the constitution of civil society that, whilst a few persons are distinguished by riches, by honours, and by knowledge, the body of the people is condemned to obscurity, ignorance, and poverty. The Christian religion, which addressed itself to the whole human race, must consequently collect a far greater number of proselytes from the lower than from the superior ranks of life. This innocent and natural circumstance has been improved into a very odious imputation, which seems to be less strenuously denied by the apologists than it is urged by the adversaries of the faith; that the new sect of Christians was almost entirely composed of the dregs of the populace, of peasants and mechanics, of boys and women, of beggars and slaves; the last of whom might sometimes introduce the missionaries into the rich and noble families to which they belonged. These obscure teachers (such was the charge of malice and infidelity) are as mute in public as they are loquacious and dogmatical in private. Whilst they cautiously avoid the dangerous encounter of philosophers, they mingle with the rude and illiterate crowd, and insinuate themselves into those minds, whom their age, their sex, or their education has the best disposed to receive the impression of superstitious terrors.

This unfavourable picture, though not devoid of a faint resemblance, betrays, by its dark colouring and distorted features, the pencil of an enemy. As the humble faith of Christ diffused itself through the world, it was embraced by several persons who derived some consequence from the advantages of nature or fortune. Aristides, who presented an eloquent apology to the emperor Hadrian, was an Athenian philosopher. Justin Martyr had sought divine knowledge in the schools of Zeno, of Aristotle, of Pythagoras, and of Plato, before he fortunately was accosted by the old man, or rather the angel, who turned his attention to the study of the Jewish prophets. Clemens of Alexandria had acquired much various reading in the Greek, and Tertullian in the Latin, language. Julius Africanus and Origen possessed a very considerable share of the learning of their times; and, although the style of Cyprian is very different from that of Lactantius, we might almost discover that both those writers had been public teachers of rhetoric. Even the study of philosophy was at length introduced among the Christians, but it was not always productive of the most salutary effects; knowledge was as often the parent of heresy as of devotion, and the description which was designed for the followers of Artemon may, with equal propriety, be applied to the various sects that resisted the successors of the apostles. "They presume to alter the holy scriptures, to abandon the ancient rule of faith, and to form their opinions according to the subtle precepts of logic. The science of the church is neglected for the study of geometry, and they lose sight of Heaven while they are employed in measuring the earth. Euclid is perpetually in their hands. Aristotle and Theophrastus are the objects of their admiration; and they express an uncommon reverence for the works of Galen. Their errors are derived from the abuse of the arts and sciences of the infidels, and they corrupt the simplicity of the Gospel by the refinements of human reason." [97]

Nor can it be affirmed with truth that the advantages of birth and fortune were always separated from the profession of Christianity. Several Roman citizens were brought before the tribunal of Pliny, and he soon discovered that a great number of persons of *every order* of men in Bithynia had deserted the religion of their ancestors. His unsuspected testimony may, in this instance, obtain more credit than the bold challenge of Tertullian, when he addresses himself to the fears as well as to the humanity of the proconsul of Africa, by assuring him that, if he persists in his cruel intentions, he must decimate Carthage, and that he will find among the guilty many persons of his own rank, senators and matrons of noblest extraction, and the friends or relations of his most intimate friends. It appears, however, that about forty years afterwards the emperor Valerian was persuaded of the truth of this assertion, since in one of his rescripts he evidently supposes that senators, Roman knights, and ladies of quality were engaged in the Christian sect. The church still continued to increase its outward splendour as it lost its inter-

[97] *It may be hoped that none, except the heretics, gave occasion to the complaint of Celsus that the Christians were perpetually correcting and altering their Gospels.*

nal purity; and in the reign of Diocletian the palace, the courts of justice, and even the army concealed a multitude of Christians who endeavoured to reconcile the interests of the present with those of a future life.

And yet these exceptions are either too few in number, or too recent in time, entirely to remove the imputation of ignorance and obscurity which has been so arrogantly cast on the first proselytes of Christianity. Instead of employing in our defence the fictions of later ages, it will be more prudent to convert the occasion of scandal into a subject of edification. Our serious thoughts will suggest to us that the apostles themselves were chosen by providence among the fishermen of Galilee, and that, the lower we depress the temporal condition of the first Christians, the more reason we shall find to admire their merit and success. It is incumbent on us diligently to remember that the kingdom of heaven was promised to the poor in spirit, and that minds afflicted by calamity and the contempt of mankind cheerfully listen to the divine promise of future happiness; while, on the contrary, the fortunate are satisfied with the possession of this world; and the wise abuse in doubt and dispute their vain superiority of reason and knowledge.

We stand in need of such reflections to comfort us for the loss of some illustrious characters, which in our eyes might have seemed the most worthy of the heavenly present. The names of Seneca, of the elder and the younger Pliny, of Tacitus, of Plutarch, of Galen, of the slave Epictetus, and of the emperor Marcus Antoninus, adorn the age in which they flourished, and exalt the dignity of human nature. They filled with glory their respective stations, either in active or contemplative life; their excellent understandings were improved by study; Philosophy had purified their minds from the prejudices of the popular superstition; and their days were spent in the pursuit of truth and the practice of virtue. Yet all these sages (it is no less an object of surprise than of concern) overlooked or rejected the perfection of the Christian system. Their language or their silence equally discover their contempt for the growing sect, which in their time had diffused itself over the Roman empire. Those among them who condescend to mention the Christians consider them only as obstinate and perverse enthusiasts, who exacted an implicit submission to their mysterious doctrines, without being able to produce a single argument that could engage the attention of men of sense and learning.[98]

It is at least doubtful whether any of these philosophers perused

[98] *Dr. Lardner, in his first and second volume of Jewish and Christian testimonies, collects and illustrates those of Pliny the younger, of Tacitus, of Galen, of Marcus Antoninus, and perhaps of Epictetus (for it is doubtful whether that philosopher means to speak of the Christians). The new sect is totally unnoticed by Seneca, the elder Pliny, and Plutarch.*

the apologies which the primitive Christians repeatedly published in behalf of themselves and of their religion; but it is much to be lamented that such a cause was not defended by abler advocates. They expose with superfluous wit and eloquence the extravagance of Polytheism. They interest our compassion by displaying the innocence and sufferings of their injured brethren. But, when they would demonstrate the divine origin of Christianity, they insist much more strongly on the predictions which announced, than on the miracles which accompanied, the appearance of the Messiah. Their favourite argument might serve to edify a Christian or to convert a Jew, since both the one and the other acknowledge the authority of those prophecies, and both are obliged, with devout reverence, to search for their sense and their accomplishment. But this mode of persuasion loses much of its weight and influence, when it is addressed to those who neither understand nor respect the Mosaic dispensation and the prophetic style. In the unskilful hands of Justin and of the succeeding apologists, the sublime meaning of the Hebrew oracles evaporates in distant types, affected conceits, and cold allegories; and even their authenticity was rendered suspicious to an unenlightened Gentile by the mixture of pious forgeries, which, under the names of Orpheus, Hermes, and the Sibyls,[99] were obtruded on him as of equal value with the genuine inspirations of Heaven. The adoption of fraud and sophistry in the defence of revelation too often reminds us of the injudicious conduct of those poets who load their *invulnerable* heroes with a useless weight of cumbersome and brittle armour.

But how shall we excuse the supine inattention of the Pagan and philosophic world to those evidences which were presented by the hand of Omnipotence, not to their reason, but to their senses? During the age of Christ, of his apostles, and of their first disciples, the doctrine which they preached was confirmed by innumerable prodigies. The lame walked, the blind saw, the sick were healed, the dead were raised, dæmons were expelled, and the laws of Nature were frequently suspended for the benefit of the church. But the sages of Greece and Rome turned aside from the awful spectacle, and, pursuing the ordinary occupations of life and study, appeared unconscious of any alterations in the moral or physical government of the world. Under the reign of Tiberius, the whole earth,[100] or at least a celebrated province of the Roman empire, was involved in a præternatural darkness of three hours. Even this miraculous event, which ought to have excited the wonder, the curiosity, and the de-

[99] *The Philosophers, who derided the more ancient predictions of the Sibyls, would easily have detected the Jewish and Christian forgeries, which have been so triumphantly quoted by the fathers, from Justin Martyr to Lactantius. When the Sibylline verses had performed their appointed task, they, like the system of the millennium, were quietly laid aside. The Christian Sibyl had unluckily fixed the ruin of Rome for the year 195, A.U.C. 948.*

[100] *The fathers, as they are drawn out in battle array by Dom Calmet seem to cover the whole earth with darkness, in which they are followed by most of the moderns.*

[101] *The celebrated passage of Phlegon is now wisely abandoned. When Tertullian assures the Pagans that the mention of the prodigy is found in Arcanis (not Archivis) vestris, he probably appeals to the Sibylline verses, which relate it exactly in the words of the gospel.*

votion of mankind, passed without notice in an age of science and history.[101] It happened during the lifetime of Seneca and the elder Pliny, who must have experienced the immediate effects, or received the earliest intelligence, of the prodigy. Each of these philosophers, in a laborious work, has recorded all the great phenomena of Nature, earthquakes, meteors, comets, and eclipses, which his indefatigable curiosity could collect. Both the one and the other have omitted to mention the greatest phenomenon to which the mortal eye has been witness since the creation of the globe. A distinct chapter of Pliny is designed for eclipses of an extraordinary nature and unusual duration; but he contents himself with describing the singular defect of light which followed the murder of Cæsar, when, during the greatest part of the year, the orb of the sun appeared pale and without splendour. This season of obscurity, which cannot surely be compared with the præternatural darkness of the Passion, had been already celebrated by most of the poets and historians of that memorable age.

XVI

THE CONDUCT OF THE ROMAN GOVERNMENT TOWARDS THE
CHRISTIANS, FROM REIGN OF NERO TO THAT OF CONSTAN-
TINE · PERSECUTION OF JEWS & CHRISTIANS BY DOMITIAN

I F W E seriously consider the
purity of the Christian religion, the sanctity of its moral precepts,
and the innocent as well as austere lives of the greater number of
those who, during the first ages, embraced the faith of the gospel,
we should naturally suppose that so benevolent a doctrine would
have been received with due reverence, even by the unbelieving
world; that the learned and the polite, however they might deride
the miracles, would have esteemed the virtues of the new sect; and
that the magistrates, instead of persecuting, would have protected
an order of men who yielded the most passive obedience to the laws,
though they declined the active cares of war and government. If,
on the other hand, we recollect the universal toleration of Polytheism, as it was invariably maintained by the faith of the people, the
incredulity of philosophers, and the policy of the Roman senate and
emperors, we are at a loss to discover what new offence the Christians had committed, what new provocation could exasperate the
mild indifference of antiquity, and what new motives could urge
the Roman princes, who beheld, without concern, a thousand forms
of religion subsisting in peace under their gentle sway, to inflict a
severe punishment on any part of their subjects, who had chosen for
themselves a singular, but an inoffensive, mode of faith and worship.

The religious policy of the ancient world seems to have assumed
a more stern and intolerant character, to oppose the progress of
Christianity. About fourscore years after the death of Christ, his
innocent disciples were punished with death, by the sentence of a
proconsul of the most amiable and philosophic character, and, according to the laws of an emperor, distinguished by the wisdom
and justice of his general administration. The apologies which were
repeatedly addressed to the successors of Trajan, are filled with the

most pathetic complaints, that the Christians, who obeyed the dictates, and solicited the liberty, of conscience, were alone, among all the subjects of the Roman empire, excluded from the common benefits of their auspicious government. The deaths of a few eminent martyrs have been recorded with care; and from the time that Christianity was invested with the supreme power, the governors of the church have been no less diligently employed in displaying the cruelty, than in imitating the conduct, of their Pagan adversaries. To separate (if it be possible) a few authentic, as well as interesting, facts, from an undigested mass of fiction and error, and to relate, in a clear and rational manner, the causes, the extent, the duration, and the most important circumstances of the persecutions to which the first Christians were exposed, is the design of the present Chapter.

The sectaries of a persecuted religion, depressed by fear, animated with resentment, and perhaps heated by enthusiasm, are seldom in a proper temper of mind calmly to investigate, or candidly to appreciate, the motives of their enemies, which often escape the impartial and discerning view even of those who are placed at a secure distance from the flames of persecution. A reason has been assigned for the conduct of the emperors towards the primitive Christians, which may appear the more specious and probable as it is drawn from the acknowledged genius of Polytheism. It has already been observed that the religious concord of the world was principally supported by the implicit assent and reverence which the nations of antiquity expressed for their respective traditions and ceremonies. It might therefore be expected that they would unite with indignation against any sect of people which should separate itself from the communion of mankind, and, claiming the exclusive possession of divine knowledge, should disdain every form of worship, except its own, as impious and idolatrous. The rights of toleration were held by mutual indulgence; they were justly forfeited by a refusal of the accustomed tribute. As the payment of this tribute was inflexibly refused by the Jews, and by them alone, the consideration of the treatment which they experienced from the Roman magistrates will serve to explain how far these speculations are justified by facts, and will lead us to discover the true causes of the persecution of Christianity.

Without repeating what has been already mentioned of the reverence of the Roman princes and governors for the temple of Jerusalem, we shall only observe that the destruction of the temple and city was accompanied and followed by every circumstance that could exasperate the minds of the conquerors, and authorize religious persecution by the most specious arguments of political justice and the public safety. From the reign of Nero to that of Antoninus Pius, the Jews discovered a fierce impatience of the dominion of Rome, which repeatedly broke out in the most furious massacres and insurrections. Humanity is shocked at the recital of the horrid cruelties which they committed in the cities of Egypt, of Cyprus, and of Cyrene, where they dwelt in treacherous friendship with the unsuspecting natives;[1] and we are tempted to applaud the severe retaliation which was exercised by the arms of the legions against a race of fanatics, whose dire and credulous superstition seemed to render them the implacable enemies not only of the Roman government, but of human kind.[2] The enthusiasm of the Jews was supported by the opinion that it was unlawful for them to pay taxes to an idolatrous master; and by the flattering promise which they derived from their ancient oracles, that a conquering Messiah would soon arise, destined to break their fetters and to invest the favourites of heaven with the empire of the earth. It was by announcing himself as their long-expected deliverer, and by calling on all the descendants of Abraham to assert the hope of Israel, that the famous Barchochebas collected a formidable army, with which he resisted, during two years, the power of the emperor Hadrian.

Notwithstanding these repeated provocations, the resentment of the Roman princes expired after the victory; nor were their apprehensions continued beyond the period of war and danger. By the general indulgence of Polytheism, and by the mild temper of Antoninus Pius, the Jews were restored to their ancient privileges, and once more obtained the permission of circumcising their children, with the easy restraint that they should never confer on any foreign proselyte that distinguishing mark of the Hebrew race. The numerous remains of that people, though they were still excluded from the precincts of Jerusalem, were permitted to form and to maintain considerable establishments both in Italy and in the provinces, to acquire the freedom of Rome, to enjoy municipal honours, and to obtain, at the same time, an exemption from the burdensome and expensive offices of society. The moderation or the contempt of the Romans gave a legal sanction to the form of ecclesiastical police which was instituted by the vanquished sect. The patriarch, who had fixed his residence at Tiberias, was empowered to appoint his subordinate ministers and apostles, to exercise a domestic jurisdic-

[1] *In Cyrene they massacred 220,000 Greeks; in Cyprus, 240,000; in Egypt, a very great multitude. Many of these unhappy victims were sawed asunder, according to a precedent to which David had given the sanction of his example. The victorious Jews devoured the flesh, licked up the blood, and twisted the entrails like a girdle round their bodies.*

[2] *Without repeating the well-known narratives of Josephus, we may learn from Dion that in Hadrian's war 580,000 Jews were cut off by the sword, besides an infinite number which perished by famine, by disease, and by fire.*

³ *The office of Patriarch was suppressed by Theodosius the younger.*

⁴ *We need only mention the purim, or deliverance of the Jews from the rage of Haman, which, till the reign of Theodosius, was celebrated with insolent triumph and riotous intemperance.*

⁵ *According to the false Josephus, Tsepho, the grandson of Esau, conducted into Italy the army of Æneas, king of Carthage. Another colony of Idumæans, flying from the sword of David, took refuge in the dominions of Romulus. For these, or for other reasons of equal weight, the name of Edom was applied by the Jews to the Roman empire.*

tion, and to receive from his dispersed brethren an annual contribution.³ New synagogues were frequently erected in the principal cities of the empire; and the sabbaths, the fasts, and the festivals, which were either commanded by the Mosaic law or enjoined by the traditions of the Rabbis, were celebrated in the most solemn and public manner.⁴ Such gentle treatment insensibly assuaged the stern temper of the Jews. Awakened from their dream of prophecy and conquest, they assumed the behaviour of peaceable and industrious subjects. Their irreconcilable hatred of mankind, instead of flaming out in acts of blood and violence, evaporated in less dangerous gratifications. They embraced every opportunity of over-reaching the idolaters in trade; and they pronounced secret and ambiguous imprecations against the haughty kingdom of Edom.⁵

Since the Jews, who rejected with abhorrence the deities adored by their sovereign and by their fellow-subjects, enjoyed, however, the free exercise of their unsocial religion; there must have existed some other cause, which exposed the disciples of Christ to those severities from which the posterity of Abraham was exempt. The difference between them is simple and obvious; but, according to the sentiments of antiquity, it was of the highest importance. The Jews were a *nation;* the Christians were a *sect;* and, if it was natural for every community to respect the sacred institutions of their neighbours, it was incumbent on them to persevere in those of their ancestors. The voice of oracles, the precepts of philosophers and the authority of the laws unanimously enforced this national obligation. By their lofty claim of superior sanctity, the Jews might provoke the Polytheists to consider them as an odious and impure race. By disdaining the intercourse of other nations they might deserve their contempt. The laws of Moses might be for the most part frivolous or absurd; yet, since they had been received during many ages by a large society, his followers were justified by the example of mankind; and it was universally acknowledged that they had a right to practise what it would have been criminal in them to neglect. But this principle which protected the Jewish synagogue afforded not any favour or security to the primitive church. By embracing the faith of the Gospel, the Christian incurred the supposed guilt of an unnatural and unpardonable offence. They dissolved the sacred ties of custom and education, violated the religious institutions of their country, and presumptuously despised whatever their fathers had believed as true, or had reverenced as sacred. Nor was this apostacy (if we may use the expression) merely of a partial or local kind;

since the pious deserter who withdrew himself from the temples of Egypt or Syria would equally disdain to seek an asylum in those of Athens or Carthage. Every Christian rejected with contempt the superstitions of his family, his city, and his province. The whole body of Christians unanimously refused to hold any communion with the gods of Rome, of the empire, and of mankind. It was in vain that the oppressed believer asserted the inalienable rights of conscience and private judgment. Though his situation might excite the pity, his arguments could never reach the understanding, either of the philosophic or of the believing part of the Pagan world. To their apprehensions, it was no less a matter of surprise that any individuals should entertain scruples against complying with the established mode of worship, than if they had conceived a sudden abhorrence to the manners, the dress, or the language of their native country.[6]

The surprise of the Pagans was soon succeeded by resentment; and the most pious of men were exposed to the unjust but dangerous imputation of impiety. Malice and prejudice concurred in representing the Christians as a society of atheists, who, by the most daring attack on the religious constitution of the empire, had merited the severest animadversion of the civil magistrate. They had separated themselves (they gloried in the confession) from every mode of superstition which was received in any part of the globe by the various temper of Polytheism; but it was not altogether so evident what deity or what form of worship they had substituted to the gods and temples of antiquity. The pure and sublime idea which they entertained of the Supreme Being escaped the gross conception of the Pagan multitude, who were at a loss to discover a spiritual and solitary God, that was neither represented under any corporeal figure or visible symbol, nor was adored with the accustomed pomp of libations and festivals, of altars and sacrifices. The sages of Greece and Rome, who had elevated their minds to the contemplation of the existence and attributes of the First Cause, were induced, by reason or by vanity, to reserve for themselves and their chosen disciples the privilege of this philosophical devotion.[7] They were far from admitting the prejudices of mankind as the standard of truth; but they considered them as flowing from the original disposition of human nature; and they supposed that any popular mode of faith and worship which presumed to disclaim the assistance of the senses would, in proportion as it receded from superstition, find itself incapable of restraining the wanderings of the fancy and the visions

[6] *From the arguments of Celsus, as they are represented and refuted by Origen, we may clearly discover the distinction that was made between the Jewish people and the Christian sect.*

[7] *It is difficult (says Plato) to attain, and dangerous to publish, the knowledge of the true God.*

405

of fanaticism. The careless glance which men of wit and learning condescended to cast on the Christian revelation served only to confirm their hasty opinion, and to persuade them that the principle, which they might have revered, of the divine unity was defaced by the wild enthusiasm, and annihilated by the airy speculations, of the new sectaries. The author of a celebrated dialogue which has been attributed to Lucian, whilst he affects to treat the mysterious subject of the Trinity in a style of ridicule and contempt, betrays his own ignorance of the weakness of human reason, and of the inscrutable nature of the divine perfections.

It might appear less surprising that the founder of Christianity should not only be revered by his disciples as a sage and a prophet, but that he should be adored as a God. The Polytheists were disposed to adopt every article of faith which seemed to offer any resemblance, however distant or imperfect, with the popular mythology; and the legends of Bacchus, of Hercules, and of Æsculapius had, in some measure, prepared their imagination for the appearance of the Son of God under a human form.[8] But they were astonished that the Christians should abandon the temples of those ancient heroes who, in the infancy of the world, had invented arts, instituted laws, and vanquished the tyrants or monsters who infested the earth; in order to choose, for the exclusive object of their religious worship, an obscure teacher who, in a recent age, and among a barbarous people, had fallen a sacrifice either to the malice of his own countrymen or to the jealousy of the Roman government. The Pagan multitude, reserving their gratitude for temporal benefits alone, rejected the inestimable present of life and immortality which was offered to mankind by Jesus of Nazareth. His mild constancy in the midst of cruel and voluntary sufferings, his universal benevolence, and the sublime simplicity of his actions and character were insufficient, in the opinion of those carnal men, to compensate for the want of fame, of empire, and of success; and, whilst they refused to acknowledge his stupendous triumph over the powers of darkness and of the grave, they misrepresented, or they insulted, the equivocal birth, wandering life, and ignominious death of the divine Author of Christianity.[9]

The personal guilt which every Christian had contracted, in thus preferring his private sentiment to the national religion, was aggravated, in a very high degree, by the number and union of the criminals. It is well known, and has been already observed, that Roman policy viewed with the utmost jealousy and distrust any

[8] According to Justin Martyr, the dæmon, who had gained some imperfect knowledge of the prophecies, purposely contrived this resemblance, which might deter, though by different means, both the people and the philosophers from embracing the faith of Christ.

[9] In the first and second books of Origen, Celsus treats the birth and character of our Saviour with the most impious contempt. The orator Libanius praises Porphyry and Julian for confuting the folly of a sect which styled a dead man of Palestine God, and the Son of God.

association among its subjects; and that the privileges of private corporations, though formed for the most harmless or beneficial purposes, were bestowed with a very sparing hand.[10] The religious assemblies of the Christians, who had separated themselves from the public worship, appeared of a much less innocent nature: they were illegal in their principle and in their consequences might become dangerous; nor were the emperors conscious that they violated the laws of justice, when, for the peace of society, they prohibited those secret and sometimes nocturnal meetings.[11] The pious disobedience of the Christians made their conduct, or perhaps their designs, appear in a much more serious and criminal light; and the Roman princes, who might perhaps have suffered themselves to be disarmed by a ready submission, deeming their honour concerned in the execution of their commands, sometimes attempted by rigorous punishments to subdue this independent spirit, which boldly acknowledged an authority superior to that of the magistrate. The extent and duration of this spiritual conspiracy seemed to render it every day more deserving of his animadversion. We have already seen that the active and successful zeal of the Christians had insensibly diffused them through every province and almost every city of the empire. The new converts seemed to renounce their family and country, that they might connect themselves in an indissoluble band of union with a peculiar society, which everywhere assumed a different character from the rest of mankind. Their gloomy and austere aspect, their abhorrence of the common business and pleasures of life, and their frequent predictions of impending calamities,[12] inspired the Pagans with the apprehension of some danger which would arise from the new sect, the more alarming as it was the more obscure. "Whatever," says Pliny, "may be the principle of their conduct, their inflexible obstinacy appeared deserving of punishment."

The precautions with which the disciples of Christ performed the offices of religion were at first dictated by fear and necessity; but they were continued from choice. By imitating the awful secrecy which reigned in the Eleusinian mysteries, the Christians had flattered themselves that they should render their sacred institutions more respectable in the eyes of the Pagan world. But the event, as it often happens to the operations of subtile policy, deceived their wishes and their expectations. It was concluded that they only concealed what they would have blushed to disclose. Their mistaken prudence afforded an opportunity for malice to invent, and for sus-

[10] *The emperor Trajan refused to incorporate a company of 150 firemen, for the use of the city of Nicomedia. He disliked all associations.*

[11] *The proconsul Pliny had published a general edict against unlawful meetings. The prudence of the Christians suspended their Agapæ; but it was impossible for them to omit the exercise of public worship.*

[12] *As the prophecies of the Antichrist, approaching conflagration, &c., provoked those Pagans whom they did not convert, they were mentioned with caution and reserve; and the Montanists were censured for disclosing too freely the dangerous secret.*

picious credulity to believe, the horrid tales which described the Christians as the most wicked of human kind, who practised in their dark recesses every abomination that a depraved fancy could suggest, and who solicited the favour of their unknown God by the sacrifice of every moral virtue. There were many who pretended to confess or to relate the ceremonies of this abhorred society. It was asserted, "that a new-born infant, entirely covered over with flour, was presented, like some mystic symbol of initiation, to the knife of the proselyte, who unknowingly inflicted many a secret and mortal wound on the innocent victim of his error; that, as soon as the cruel deed was perpetrated, the sectaries drank up the blood, greedily tore asunder the quivering members, and pledged themselves to eternal secrecy, by a mutual consciousness of guilt. It was as confidently affirmed that this inhuman sacrifice was succeeded by a suitable entertainment, in which intemperance served as a provocative to brutal lust; till, at the appointed moment, the lights were suddenly extinguished, shame was banished, nature was forgotten; and, as accident might direct, the darkness of the night was polluted by the incestuous commerce of sisters and brothers, of sons and of mothers."

But the perusal of the ancient apologies was sufficient to remove even the slightest suspicion from the mind of a candid adversary. The Christians, with the intrepid security of innocence, appeal from the voice of rumour to the equity of the magistrates. They acknowledge that, if any proof can be produced of the crimes which calumny has imputed to them, they are worthy of the most severe punishment. They provoke the punishment, and they challenge the proof. At the same time they urge, with equal truth and propriety, that the charge is not less devoid of probability than it is destitute of evidence; they ask whether any one can seriously believe that the pure and holy precepts of the Gospel, which so frequently restrain the use of the most lawful enjoyments, should inculcate the practice of the most abominable crimes; that a large society should resolve to dishonour itself in the eyes of its own members; and that a great number of persons of either sex, and every age and character, insensible to the fear of death or infamy, should consent to violate those principles which nature and education had imprinted most deeply in their minds.[13] Nothing, it should seem, could weaken the force or destroy the effect of so unanswerable a justification, unless it were the injudicious conduct of the apologists themselves, who betrayed the common cause of religion, to gratify their devout

[13] *In the persecution of Lyons, some Gentile slaves were compelled, by the fear of tortures, to accuse their Christian master. The church of Lyons, writing to their brethren of Asia, treat the horrid charge with proper indignation and contempt.*

THE BASILICA
OF CONSTANTINE

"The master of the Roman world, who aspired to erect an eternal monument of the glories of his reign, could employ in the prosecution of that great work the wealth, the labour, and all that yet remained of the genius, of obedient millions."

THE BASILICA OF CONSTANTINE OR MAXENTIUS

hatred to the domestic enemies of the church. It was sometimes faintly insinuated, and sometimes boldly asserted, that the same bloody sacrifices, and the same incestuous festivals, which were so falsely ascribed to the orthodox believers, were in reality celebrated by the Marcionites, by the Carpocratians, and by several other sects of the Gnostics, who, notwithstanding they might deviate into the paths of heresy, were still actuated by the sentiments of men, and still governed by the precepts of Christianity. Accusations of a similar kind were retorted upon the church by the schismatics who had departed from its communion;[14] and it was confessed on all sides that the most scandalous licentiousness of manners prevailed among great numbers of those who affected the name of Christians. A Pagan magistrate, who possessed neither leisure nor abilities to discern the almost imperceptible line which divides the orthodox faith from heretical pravity, might easily have imagined that their mutual animosity had extorted the discovery of their common guilt. It was fortunate for the repose, or at least for the reputation, of the first Christians, that the magistrates sometimes proceeded with more temper and moderation than is usually consistent with religious zeal, and that they reported, as the impartial result of their judicial inquiry, that the sectaries who had deserted the established worship appeared to them sincere in their professions and blameless in their manners; however they might incur, by their absurd and excessive superstition, the censure of the laws.[15]

History, which undertakes to record the transactions of the past, for the instruction of future, ages, would ill deserve that honourable office, if she condescended to plead the cause of tyrants, or to justify the maxims of persecution. It must, however, be acknowledged that the conduct of the emperors who appeared the least favourable to the primitive church is by no means so criminal as that of modern sovereigns who have employed the arm of violence and terror against the religious opinions of any part of their subjects. From their reflections, or even from their own feelings, a Charles V. or a Louis XIV. might have acquired a just knowledge of the rights of conscience, of the obligation of faith, and of the innocence of error. But the princes and magistrates of ancient Rome were strangers to those principles which inspired and authorized the inflexible obstinacy of the Christians in the cause of truth, nor could they themselves discover in their own breasts any motive which would have prompted them to refuse a legal, and as it were a natural, submission to the sacred institutions of their country. The same reason

[14] *When Tertullian became a Montanist, he aspersed the morals of the church which he had so resolutely defended. The 35th canon of the council of Illiberis provides against the scandals which too often polluted the vigils of the church, and disgraced the Christian name in the eyes of unbelievers.*

[15] *Tertullian expatiates on the fair and honourable testimony of Pliny, with much reason, and some declamation.*

which contributes to alleviate the guilt, must have tended to abate the rigour, of their persecutions. As they were actuated, not by the furious zeal of bigots, but by the temperate policy of legislators, contempt must often have relaxed, and humanity must frequently have suspended, the execution of those laws which they enacted against the humble and obscure followers of Christ. From the general view of their character and motives we might naturally conclude: I. That a considerable time elapsed before they considered the new sectaries as an object deserving of the attention of government. II. That, in the conviction of any of their subjects who were accused of so very singular a crime, they proceeded with caution and reluctance. III. That they were moderate in the use of punishments; and IV. That the afflicted church enjoyed many intervals of peace and tranquillity. Notwithstanding the careless indifference which the most copious and the most minute of the Pagan writers have shown to the affairs of the Christians,[16] it may still be in our power to confirm each of these probable suppositions by the evidence of authentic facts.

I. By the wise dispensation of Providence, a mysterious veil was cast over the infancy of the church, which, till the faith of the Christians was matured and their numbers were multiplied, served to protect them not only from the malice, but even from the knowledge, of the Pagan world. The slow and gradual abolition of the Mosaic ceremonies afforded a safe and innocent disguise to the more early proselytes of the Gospel. As they were far the greater part of the race of Abraham, they were distinguished by the peculiar mark of circumcision, offered up their devotions in the temple of Jerusalem till its final destruction, and received both the Law and the Prophets as the genuine inspirations of the Deity. The Gentile converts, who by a spiritual adoption had been associated to the hope of Israel, were likewise confounded under the garb and appearance of Jews,[17] and, as the Polytheists paid less regard to articles of faith than to the external worship, the new sect, which carefully concealed, or faintly announced, its future greatness and ambition, was permitted to shelter itself under the general toleration which was granted to an ancient and celebrated people in the Roman empire. It was not long, perhaps, before the Jews themselves, animated with a fiercer zeal and a more jealous faith, perceived the gradual separation of their Nazarene brethren from the doctrine of the synagogue; and they would gladly have extinguished the dangerous heresy in the blood of its adherents. But the decrees of heaven had

[16] *In the various compilation of the Augustan History (a part of which was composed under the reign of Constantine), there are not six lines which relate to the Christians; nor has the diligence of Xiphilin discovered their name in the large history of Dion Cassius.*

[17] *An obscure passage of Suetonius may seem to offer a proof how strangely the Jews and Christians of Rome were confounded with each other.*

already disarmed their malice; and, though they might sometimes exert the licentious privilege of sedition, they no longer possessed the administration of criminal justice; nor did they find it easy to infuse into the calm breast of a Roman magistrate the rancour of their own zeal and prejudice. The provincial governors declared themselves ready to listen to any accusation that might affect the public safety; but, as soon as they were informed that it was a question not of facts but of words, a dispute relating only to the interpretation of the Jewish laws and prophecies, they deemed it unworthy of the majesty of Rome seriously to discuss the obscure differences which might arise among a barbarous and superstitious people. The innocence of the first Christians was protected by ignorance and contempt; and the tribunal of the Pagan magistrate often proved their most assured refuge against the fury of the synagogue.[18] If, indeed, we were disposed to adopt the traditions of a too credulous antiquity, we might relate the distant peregrinations, the wonderful achievements, and the various deaths, of the twelve apostles; but a more accurate inquiry will induce us to doubt whether any of those persons who had been witnesses to the miracles of Christ were permitted, beyond the limits of Palestine, to seal with their blood the truth of their testimony.[19] From the ordinary term of human life, it may very naturally be presumed that most of them were deceased before the discontent of the Jews broke out into that furious war which was terminated only by the ruin of Jerusalem. During a long period, from the death of Christ to that memorable rebellion, we cannot discover any traces of Roman intolerance, unless they are to be found in the sudden, the transient, but the cruel persecution, which was exercised by Nero against the Christians of the capital, thirty-five years after the former, and only two years before the latter of those great events. The character of the philosophic historian, to whom we are principally indebted for the knowledge of this singular transaction, would alone be sufficient to recommend it to our most attentive consideration.

In the tenth year of the reign of Nero, the capital of the empire was afflicted by a fire which raged beyond the memory or example of former ages. The monuments of Grecian art and of Roman virtue, the trophies of the Punic and Gallic wars, the most holy temples, and the most splendid palaces were involved in one common destruction. Of the fourteen regions or quarters into which Rome was divided, four only subsisted entire, three were levelled with the ground, and the remaining seven, which had experienced the fury

[18] *See in the eighteenth and twenty-fifth chapters of the Acts of the Apostles, the behaviour of Gallio, proconsul of Achaia, and of Festus, procurator of Judæa.*

[19] *In the time of Tertullian and Clemens of Alexandria, the glory of martyrdom was confined to St. Peter, St. Paul, and St. James. It was gradually bestowed on the rest of the apostles, by the more recent Greeks, who prudently selected for the theatre of their preaching and sufferings, some remote country beyond the limits of the Roman empire.*

of the flames, displayed a melancholy prospect of ruin and desolation. The vigilance of government appears not to have neglected any of the precautions which might alleviate the sense of so dreadful a calamity. The Imperial gardens were thrown open to the distressed multitude, temporary buildings were erected for their accommodation, and a plentiful supply of corn and provisions was distributed at a very moderate price.[20] The most generous policy seemed to have dictated the edicts which regulated the disposition of the streets and the construction of private houses; and, as it usually happens in an age of prosperity, the conflagration of Rome, in the course of a few years, produced a new city, more regular and more beautiful than the former. But all the prudence and humanity affected by Nero on this occasion were insufficient to preserve him from the popular suspicion. Every crime might be imputed to the assassin of his wife and mother; nor could the prince who prostituted his person and dignity on the theatre be deemed incapable of the most extravagant folly. The voice of rumour accused the emperor as the incendiary of his own capital; and, as the most incredible stories are the best adapted to the genius of an enraged people, it was gravely reported, and firmly believed, that Nero, enjoying the calamity which he had occasioned, amused himself with singing to his lyre the destruction of ancient Troy.[21] To divert a suspicion which the power of despotism was unable to suppress the emperor resolved to substitute in his own place some fictitious criminals. "With this view (continues Tacitus) he inflicted the most exquisite tortures on those men, who, under the vulgar appellation of Christians, were already branded with deserved infamy. They derived their name and origin from Christ, who, in the reign of Tiberius, had suffered death, by the sentence of the procurator Pontius Pilate.[22] For a while this dire superstition was checked; but it again burst forth, and not only spread itself over Judæa, the first seat of this mischievous sect, but was even introduced into Rome, the common asylum which receives and protects whatever is impure, whatever is atrocious. The confessions of those who were seized, discovered a great multitude of their accomplices, and they were all convicted, not so much for the crime of setting fire to the city, as for their hatred of human kind.[23] They died in torments, and their torments were embittered by insult and derision. Some were nailed on crosses; others sewn up in the skins of wild beasts, and exposed to the fury of dogs; others again, smeared over with combustible materials, were used as torches to illuminate the darkness of the night.

[20] *The price of wheat (probably of the modius) was reduced as low as* terni nummi; *which would be equivalent to about fifteen shillings the English quarter.*

[21] *We may observe, that the rumour is mentioned by Tacitus with a very becoming distrust and hesitation, whilst it is greedily transcribed by Suetonius, and solemnly confirmed by Dion.*

[22] *This testimony is alone sufficient to expose the anachronism of the Jews, who place the birth of Christ near a century sooner. We may learn from Josephus that the procuratorship of Pilate corresponded with the last ten years of Tiberius,* A. D. 27–37. *As to the particular time of the death of Christ, a very early tradition fixed it to the 25th of March,* A.D. 29, *under the consulship of the two Gemini. This date, which is adopted by Pagi, cardinal Noris, and Le Clerc, seems at least as probable as the vulgar æra, which is placed (I know not from what conjectures) four years later.*

[23] Odio humani generis convicti. *These words may either signify the hatred of mankind*

The gardens of Nero were destined for the melancholy spectacle, which was accompanied with a horse race, and honoured with the presence of the emperor, who mingled with the populace in the dress and attitude of a charioteer. The guilt of the Christians deserved, indeed, the most exemplary punishment, but the public abhorrence was changed into commiseration, from the opinion that those unhappy wretches were sacrificed, not so much to the public welfare, as to the cruelty of a jealous tyrant." Those who survey, with a curious eye, the revolutions of mankind may observe that the gardens and circus of Nero on the Vatican, which were polluted with the blood of the first Christians, have been rendered still more famous by the triumph and by the abuse of the persecuted religion. On the same spot, a temple, which far surpasses the ancient glories of the Capitol, has been since erected by the Christian Pontiffs, who, deriving their claim of universal dominion from an humble fisherman of Galilee, have succeeded to the throne of the Cæsars, given laws to the barbarian conquerors of Rome, and extended their spiritual jurisdiction from the coast of the Baltic to the shores of the Pacific Ocean.

But it would be improper to dismiss this account of Nero's persecution, till we have made some observations, that may serve to remove the difficulties with which it is perplexed and to throw some light on the subsequent history of the church.

1. The most sceptical criticism is obliged to respect the truth of this extraordinary fact, and the integrity of this celebrated passage of Tacitus. The former is confirmed by the diligent and accurate Suetonius, who mentions the punishment which Nero inflicted on the Christians, a sect of men who had embraced a new and criminal superstition.[24] The latter may be proved by the consent of the most ancient manuscripts; by the inimitable character of the style of Tacitus; by his reputation, which guarded his text from the interpolations of pious fraud; and by the purport of his narration, which accused the first Christians of the most atrocious crimes, without insinuating that they possessed any miraculous or even magical powers above the rest of mankind.[25] 2. Notwithstanding it is probable that Tacitus was born some years before the fire of Rome, he could derive only from reading and conversation the knowledge of an event which happened during his infancy. Before he gave himself to the Public, he calmly waited till his genius had attained its full maturity, and he was more than forty years of age, when a grateful regard for the memory of the virtuous Agricola extorted

towards the Christians, or the hatred of the Christians towards mankind. I have preferred the latter sense, as the most agreeable to the style of Tacitus, and to the popular error, of which a precept of the Gospel had been, perhaps, the innocent occasion. But as the word convicti does not unite very happily with the rest of the sentence, James Gronovius has preferred the reading of conjuncti, which is authorized by the valuable MS. of Florence.

[24] The epithet of malefica, which some sagacious commentators have translated magical, is considered by the more rational Mosheim as only synonymous to the exitiabilis of Tacitus.

[25] The passage concerning Jesus Christ, which was inserted into the text of Josephus between the time of Origen and that of Eusebius, may furnish an example of no vulgar forgery. The accomplishment of the prophecies, the virtues, miracles and resurrection of Jesus are distinctly related. Josephus acknowledges that he was the Messiah, and hesitates whether he should call him a man.

from him the most early of those historical compositions which will delight and instruct the most distant posterity. After making a trial of his strength in the life of Agricola and the description of Germany, he conceived, and at length executed, a more arduous work; the history of Rome, in thirty books, from the fall of Nero to the accession of Nerva. The administration of Nerva introduced an age of justice and prosperity, which Tacitus had destined for the occupation of his old age; but, when he took a nearer view of his subject, judging, perhaps, that it was a more honourable or a less invidious office to record the vices of past tyrants than to celebrate the virtues of a reigning monarch, he chose rather to relate, under the form of annals, the actions of the four immediate successors of Augustus. To collect, to dispose, and to adorn a series of fourscore years in an immortal work, every sentence of which is pregnant with the deepest observations and the most lively images, was an undertaking sufficient to exercise the genius of Tacitus himself during the greatest part of his life. In the last years of the reign of Trajan, whilst the victorious monarch extended the power of Rome beyond its ancient limits, the historian was describing, in the second and fourth books of his annals, the tyranny of Tiberius; and the emperor Hadrian must have succeeded to the throne, before Tacitus, in the regular prosecution of his work, could relate the fire of the capital and the cruelty of Nero towards the unfortunate Christians. At the distance of sixty years, it was the duty of the annalist to adopt the narratives of contemporaries; but it was natural for the philosopher to indulge himself in the description of the origin, the progress, and the character of the new sect, not so much according to the knowledge or prejudices of the age of Nero, as according to those of the time of Hadrian. 3. Tacitus very frequently trusts to the curiosity or reflection of his readers to supply those intermediate circumstances and ideas which, in his extreme conciseness, he has thought proper to suppress. We may, therefore, presume to imagine some probable cause which could direct the cruelty of Nero against the Christians of Rome, whose obscurity, as well as innocence, should have shielded them from his indignation, and even from his notice. The Jews, who were numerous in the capital, and oppressed in their own country, were a much fitter object for the suspicions of the emperor and of the people; nor did it seem unlikely that a vanquished nation, who already discovered their abhorrence of the Roman yoke, might have recourse to the most atrocious means of gratifying their implacable revenge. But the Jews possessed very powerful advocates in

[26] *The player's name was Aliturus. Through the same channel, Josephus, about two years before, had obtained the pardon and release of some Jewish priests, who were prisoners at Rome.*

414

the palace, and even in the heart of the tyrant; his wife and mistress, the beautiful Poppæa, and a favourite player of the race of Abraham, who had already employed their intercession in behalf of the obnoxious people.[26] In their room it was necessary to offer some other victims, and it might easily be suggested, that, although the genuine followers of Moses were innocent of the fire of Rome, there had arisen among them a new and pernicious sect of GALILÆANS, which was capable of the most horrid crimes. Under the appellation of GALILÆANS, two distinctions of men were confounded, the most opposite to each other in their manners and principles; the disciples who had embraced the faith of Jesus of Nazareth,[27] and the zealots who had followed the standard of Judas the Gaulonite.[28] The former were the friends, and the latter were the enemies, of human kind; and the only resemblance between them consisted in the same inflexible constancy which, in the defence of their cause, rendered them insensible of death and tortures. The followers of Judas, who impelled their countrymen into rebellion, were soon buried under the ruins of Jerusalem; whilst those of Jesus, known by the more celebrated name of Christians, diffused themselves over the Roman empire. How natural was it for Tacitus, in the time of Hadrian, to appropriate to the Christians the guilt and the sufferings which he might, with far greater truth and justice, have attributed to a sect whose odious memory was almost extinguished! 4. Whatever opinion may be entertained of this conjecture (for it is no more than a conjecture), it is evident that the effect, as well as the cause, of Nero's persecution were confined to the walls of Rome; that the religious tenets of the Galilæans, or Christians, were never made a subject of punishment or even of inquiry; and that, as the idea of their sufferings was, for a long time, connected with the idea of cruelty and injustice, the moderation of succeeding princes inclined them to spare a sect, oppressed by a tyrant whose rage had been usually directed against virtue and innocence.

It is somewhat remarkable that the flames of war consumed almost at the same time the temple of Jerusalem and the Capitol of Rome;[29] and it appears no less singular that the tribute which devotion had destined to the former should have been converted by the power of an assaulting victor to restore and adorn the splendour of the latter.[30] The emperors levied a general capitation tax on the Jewish people; and, although the sum assessed on the head of each individual was inconsiderable, the use for which it was designed, and the severity with which it was exacted, were considered as an in-

[27] Dr. Lardner has proved that the name of Galilæans was a very ancient and, perhaps, the primitive appellation of the Christians.

[28] The sons of Judas were crucified in the time of Claudius. His grandson Eleazar, after Jerusalem was taken, defended a strong fortress with 960 of his most desperate followers. When the battering ram had made a breach, they turned their swords against their wives, their children, and at length against their own breasts. They died to the last man.

[29] The Capitol was burnt during the civil war between Vitellius and Vespasian, the 19th of December, A.D. 69. On the 10th of August, A.D. 70, the temple of Jerusalem was destroyed by the hands of the Jews themselves, rather than by those of the Romans.

[30] The new Capitol was dedicated by Domitian. The gilding alone cost 12,000 talents (above two millions and a half). It was the opinion of Martial that, if the emperor had called in his debts, Jupiter himself, even though he had made a general auction of Olympus, would have been unable to pay two shillings in the pound.

tolerable grievance. Since the officers of the revenue extended their unjust claim to many persons who were strangers to the blood or religion of the Jews, it was impossible that the Christians, who had so often sheltered themselves under the shade of the synagogue, should now escape this rapacious persecution. Anxious as they were to avoid the slightest infection of idolatry, their conscience forbade them to contribute to the honour of that dæmon who had assumed the character of the Capitoline Jupiter. As a very numerous, though declining, party among the Christians still adhered to the law of Moses, their efforts to dissemble their Jewish origin were detected by the decisive test of circumcision,[31] nor were the Roman magistrates at leisure to inquire into the difference of their religious tenets. Among the Christians who were brought before the tribunal of the emperor, or, as it seems more probable, before that of the procurator of Judæa, two persons are said to have appeared, distinguished by their extraction, which was more truly noble than that of the greatest monarchs. These were the grandsons of St. Jude the apostle, who himself was the brother of Jesus Christ.[32] Their natural pretensions to the throne of David might perhaps attract the respect of the people, and excite the jealousy of the governor; but the meanness of their garb and the simplicity of their answers soon convinced him that they were neither desirous nor capable of disturbing the peace of the Roman empire. They frankly confessed their royal origin and their near relation to the Messiah; but they disclaimed any temporal views, and professed that his kingdom, which they devoutly expected, was purely of a spiritual and angelic nature. When they were examined concerning their fortune and occupation, they showed their hands hardened with daily labour, and declared that they derived their whole subsistence from the cultivation of a farm near the village of Cocaba, of the extent of about twenty-four English acres, and of the value of nine thousand drachms, or three hundred pounds sterling. The grandsons of St. Jude were dismissed with compassion and contempt.

But, although the obscurity of the house of David might protect them from the suspicions of a tyrant, the present greatness of his own family alarmed the pusillanimous temper of Domitian, which could only be appeased by the blood of those Romans whom he either feared, or hated, or esteemed. Of the two sons of his uncle Flavius Sabinus, the elder was soon convicted of treasonable intentions, and the younger, who bore the name of Flavius Clemens, was indebted for his safety to his want of courage and ability. The em-

[31] *Suetonius had seen an old man of ninety publicly examined before the procurator's tribunal. This is what Martial calls, Mentula tributis damnata.*

[32] *This appellation was at first understood in the most obvious sense, and it was supposed that the brothers of Jesus were the lawful issue of Joseph and of Mary. A devout respect for the virginity of the Mother of God suggested to the Gnostics, and afterwards to the orthodox Greeks, the expedient of bestowing a second wife on Joseph. The Latins (from the time of Jerome) improved on that hint, asserted the perpetual celibacy of Joseph, and justified, by many similar examples, the new interpretation that Jude, as well as Simon and James, who are styled the brothers of Jesus Christ, were only his first cousins.*

peror, for a long time, distinguished so harmless a kinsman by his favour and protection, bestowed on him his own niece Domitilla, adopted the children of that marriage to the hope of the succession, and invested their father with the honours of the consulship. But he had scarcely finished the term of his annual magistracy, when, on a slight pretence, he was condemned and executed; Domitilla was banished to a desolate island on the coast of Campania;[33] and sentences either of death or of confiscation were pronounced against a great number of persons who were involved in the same accusation. The guilt imputed to their charge was that of *Atheism* and *Jewish manners;*[34] a singular association of ideas, which cannot with any propriety be applied except to the Christians, as they were obscurely and imperfectly viewed by the magistrates and by the writers of that period. On the strength of so probable an interpretation, and too eagerly admitting the suspicions of a tyrant as an evidence of their honourable crime, the church has placed both Clemens and Domitilla among its first martyrs, and has branded the cruelty of Domitian with the name of the second persecution. But this persecution (if it deserves that epithet) was of no long duration. A few months after the death of Clemens and the banishment of Domitilla, Stephen, a freedman belonging to the latter, who had enjoyed the favour, but who had not surely embraced the faith, of his mistress, assassinated the emperor in his palace. The memory of Domitian was condemned by the senate; his acts were rescinded; his exiles recalled; and under the gentle administration of Nerva, while the innocent were restored to their rank and fortunes, even the most guilty either obtained pardon or escaped punishment.

II. About ten years afterwards, under the reign of Trajan, the younger Pliny was intrusted by his friend and master with the government of Bithynia, and Pontus. He soon found himself at a loss to determine by what rule of justice or of law he should direct his conduct in the execution of an office the most repugnant to his humanity. Pliny had never assisted at any judicial proceedings against the Christians, with whose name alone he seems to be acquainted; and he was totally uninformed with regard to the nature of their guilt, the method of their conviction, and the degree of their punishment. In this perplexity he had recourse to his usual expedient, of submitting to the wisdom of Trajan an impartial and, in some respects, a favourable account of the new superstition, requesting the emperor that he would condescend to resolve his doubts and to instruct his ignorance. The life of Pliny had been employed in the

[33] *The isle of Pandataria, according to Dion.* **Bruttius Præsens** *banishes her to that of Pontia, which was not far distant from the other. That difference, and a mistake, either of Eusebius or of his transcribers, have given occasion to suppose two Domitillas, the wife and the niece of Clemens.*

[34] *If the Bruttius Præsens, from whom it is probable that he collected this account, was the correspondent of Pliny, we may consider him as a contemporary writer.*

acquisition of learning, and in the business of the world. Since the age of nineteen he had pleaded with distinction in the tribunals of Rome,[35] filled a place in the senate, had been invested with the honours of the consulship, and had formed very numerous connexions with every order of men, both in Italy and in the provinces. From *his* ignorance, therefore, we may derive some useful information. We may assure ourselves that when he accepted the government of Bithynia there were no general laws or decrees of the senate in force against the Christians; that neither Trajan nor any of his virtuous predecessors, whose edicts were received into the civil and criminal jurisprudence, had publicly declared their intentions concerning the new sect; and that, whatever proceedings had been carried on against the Christians, there were none of sufficient weight and authority to establish a precedent for the conduct of a Roman magistrate.

The answer of Trajan, to which the Christians of the succeeding age have frequently appealed, discovers as much regard for justice and humanity as could be reconciled with his mistaken notions of religious policy. Instead of displaying the implacable zeal of an inquisitor, anxious to discover the most minute particles of heresy and exulting in the number of his victims, the emperor expresses much more solicitude to protect the security of the innocent than to prevent the escape of the guilty. He acknowledges the difficulty of fixing any general plan; but he lays down two salutary rules, which often afforded relief and support to the distressed Christians. Though he directs the magistrates to punish such persons as are legally convicted, he prohibits them, with a very humane inconsistency, from making any inquiries concerning the supposed criminals. Nor was the magistrate allowed to proceed on every kind of information. Anonymous charges the emperor rejects, as too repugnant to the equity of his government; and he strictly requires, for the conviction of those to whom the guilt of Christianity is imputed, the positive evidence of a fair and open accuser. It is likewise probable that the persons who assumed so invidious an office were obliged to declare the grounds of their suspicions, to specify (both in respect to time and place) the secret assemblies which their Christian adversary had frequented, and to disclose a great number of circumstances which were concealed with the most vigilant jealousy from the eye of the profane. If they succeeded in their prosecution, they were exposed to the resentment of a considerable and active party, to the censure of the more liberal portion of mankind, and to

[35] *Pliny pleaded his first cause* A.D. *81; the year after the famous eruptions of Mount Vesuvius, in which his uncle lost his life.*

the ignominy which, in every age and country, has attended the character of an informer. If, on the contrary, they failed in their proofs, they incurred the severe, and perhaps capital, penalty which, according to a law published by the emperor Hadrian, was inflicted on those who falsely attributed to their fellow-citizens the crime of Christianity. The violence of personal or superstitious animosity might sometimes prevail over the most natural apprehensions of disgrace and danger; but it cannot surely be imagined that accusations of so unpromising an appearance were either lightly or frequently undertaken by the Pagan subjects of the Roman empire.[36]

The expedient which was employed to elude the prudence of the laws affords a sufficient proof how effectually they disappointed the mischievous designs of private malice or superstitious zeal. In a large and tumultuous assembly, the restraints of fear and shame, so forcible on the minds of individuals, are deprived of the greatest part of their influence. The pious Christian, as he was desirous to obtain or to escape the glory of martyrdom, expected, either with impatience or with terror, the stated returns of the public games and festivals. On those occasions, the inhabitants of the great cities of the empire were collected in the circus of the theatre, where every circumstance of the place, as well as of the ceremony, contributed to kindle their devotion and to extinguish their humanity. Whilst the numerous spectators, crowned with garlands, perfumed with incense, purified with the blood of victims, and surrounded with the altars and statues of their tutelar deities, resigned themselves to the enjoyment of pleasures which they considered as an essential part of their religious worship; they recollected that the Christians alone abhorred the gods of mankind, and by their absence and melancholy on these solemn festivals seemed to insult or to lament the public felicity. If the empire had been afflicted by any recent calamity, by a plague, a famine, or an unsuccessful war; if the Tiber had, or if the Nile had not, risen beyond its banks; if the earth had shaken, or if the temperate order of the seasons had been interrupted, the superstitious Pagans were convinced that the crimes and the impiety of the Christians, who were spared by the excessive lenity of the government, had at length provoked the Divine Justice. It was not among a licentious and exasperated populace that the forms of legal proceedings could be observed; it was not in an amphitheatre, stained with the blood of wild beasts and gladiators, that the voice of compassion could be heard. The impatient clamours of the multitude denounced the Christians as the enemies of

[36] *Eusebius has preserved the edict of Hadrian. He has likewise given us one still more favourable under the name of Antoninus; the authenticity of which is not so universally allowed. The second Apology of Justin contains some curious particulars relative to the accusations of Christians.*

gods and men, doomed them to the severest tortures, and, venturing to accuse by name some of the most distinguished of the new sectaries, required, with irresistible vehemence, that they should be instantly apprehended and cast to the lions.[37] The provincial governors and magistrates who presided in the public spectacles were usually inclined to gratify the inclinations, and to appease the rage, of the people by the sacrifice of a few obnoxious victims. But the wisdom of the emperors protected the church from the danger of these tumultuous clamours and irregular accusations, which they justly censured as repugnant both to the firmness and to the equity of their administration. The edicts of Hadrian and of Antoninus Pius expressly declared that the voice of the multitude should never be admitted as legal evidence to convict or to punish those unfortunate persons who had embraced the enthusiasm of the Christians.[38]

III. Punishment was not the inevitable consequence of conviction, and the Christians, whose guilt was the most clearly proved by the testimony of witnesses, or even by their voluntary confession, still retained in their own power the alternative of life or death. It was not so much the past offence, as the actual resistance, which excited the indignation of the magistrate. He was persuaded that he offered them an easy pardon, since, if they consented to cast a few grains of incense upon the altar, they were dismissed from the tribunal in safety and with applause. It was esteemed the duty of a humane judge to endeavour to reclaim, rather than to punish, those deluded enthusiasts. Varying his tone according to the age, the sex, or the situation of the prisoners, he frequently condescended to set before their eyes every circumstance which could render life more pleasing, or death more terrible; and to solicit, nay, to intreat them, that they would show some compassion to themselves, to their families, and to their friends. If threats and persuasions proved ineffectual, he had often recourse to violence; the scourge and the rack were called in to supply the deficiency of argument, and every art of cruelty was employed to subdue such inflexible and, as it appeared to the Pagans, such criminal obstinacy. The ancient apologists of Christianity have censured, with equal truth and severity, the irregular conduct of their persecutors, who, contrary to every principle of judicial proceeding, admitted the use of torture, in order to obtain not a confession but a denial of the crime which was the object of their inquiry. The monks of succeeding ages, who, in their peaceful solitudes, entertained themselves with diversifying the death and sufferings of the primitive martyrs, have frequently

[37] *The acts of the martyrdom of Polycarp exhibit a lively picture of these tumults, which were usually fomented by the malice of the Jews.*

[38] *These regulations are inserted in the abovementioned edicts of Hadrian and Pius.*

[39] *Jerome, in his Legend of Paul the Hermit, tells a strange story of a young man, who was chained naked on a bed of flowers, and assaulted by a beautiful and wanton courtezan. He quelled the rising temptation by biting off his tongue.*

invented torments of a much more refined and ingenious nature. In particular, it has pleased them to suppose that the zeal of the Roman magistrates, disdaining every consideration of moral virtue or public decency, endeavoured to seduce those whom they were unable to vanquish, and that, by their orders, the most brutal violence was offered to those whom they found it impossible to seduce. It is related that pious females, who were prepared to despise death, were sometimes condemned to a more severe trial, and called upon to determine whether they set a higher value on their religion or on their chastity. The youths to whose licentious embraces they were abandoned received a solemn exhortation from the judge to exert their most strenuous efforts to maintain the honour of Venus against the impious virgin who refused to burn incense on her altars. Their violence, however, was commonly disappointed; and the seasonable interposition of some miraculous power preserved the chaste spouses of Christ from the dishonour even of an involuntary defeat. We should not, indeed, neglect to remark that the more ancient, as well as authentic, memorials of the church are seldom polluted with these extravagant and indecent fictions.[39]

The total disregard of truth and probability in the representation of these primitive martyrdoms was occasioned by a very natural mistake. The ecclesiastical writers of the fourth or fifth centuries ascribed to the magistrates of Rome the same degree of implacable and unrelenting zeal which filled their own breasts against the heretics or the idolaters of their own times. It is not improbable that some of those persons who were raised to the dignities of the empire might have imbibed the prejudices of the populace, and that the cruel disposition of others might occasionally be stimulated by motives of avarice or of personal resentment.[40] But it is certain, and we may appeal to the grateful confessions of the first Christians, that the greatest part of those magistrates who exercised in the provinces the authority of the emperor, or of the senate, and to whose hands alone the jurisdiction of life and death was intrusted, behaved like men of polished manners and liberal educations, who respected the rules of justice, and who were conversant with the precepts of philosophy. They frequently declined the odious task of persecution, dismissed the charge with contempt, or suggested to the accused Christian some legal evasion by which he might elude the severity of the laws.[41] Whenever they were invested with a discretionary power, they used it much less for the oppression than for the relief and benefit of the afflicted church. They were far from condemning

[40] *The conversion of his wife provoked Claudius Herminianus, governor of Cappadocia, to treat the Christians with uncommon severity.*

[41] *Tertullian, in his epistle to the governor of Africa, mentions several remarkable instances of lenity and forbearance which had happened within his knowledge.*

[42] *The mines of Numidia contained nine bishops, with a proportionable number of their clergy and people, to whom Cyprian addressed a pious epistle of praise and comfort.*

[43] *Though we cannot receive with entire confidence either the epistles or the acts of Ignatius (they may be found in the 2nd volume of the Apostolic Fathers), yet we may quote that bishop of Antioch as one of those exemplary martyrs. He was sent in chains to Rome as a public spectacle; and, when he arrived at Troas, he received the pleasing intelligence that the persecution of Antioch was already at an end.*

[44] *Among the martyrs of Lyons, the slave Blandina was distinguished by more exquisite tortures. Of the five martyrs so much celebrated in the acts of Felicitas and Perpetua, two were of a servile, and two others of a very mean, condition.*

[45] *If we recollect that all the Plebeians of Rome were not Christians, and that all the Christians were not saints and martyrs, we may judge with how much safety religious honours can be ascribed to bones or urns indiscriminately taken from the public burial-place. After ten centuries of a very free and open trade, some suspicions have arisen among the more learned Catholics. They now require, as a proof of sanctity and martyrdom, the letters B. M., a vial full of red liquor, supposed to be blood, or the figure of a palm tree. But the two former signs are of little weight, and with regard to the last it is observed by the critics, 1. That the figure, as it is called, of a palm is perhaps a cypress, and perhaps only a stop, the flourish of a comma, used in the monumental inscriptions. 2. That the palm was the symbol of victory among the Pagans. 3. That among the*

all the Christians who were accused before their tribunal, and very far from punishing with death all those who were convicted of an obstinate adherence to the new superstition. Contenting themselves, for the most part, with the milder chastisements of imprisonment, exile, or slavery in the mines,[42] they left the unhappy victims of their justice some reason to hope that a prosperous event, the accession, the marriage, or the triumph of an emperor might speedily restore them, by a general pardon, to their former state. The martyrs, devoted to immediate execution by the Roman magistrates, appear to have been selected from the most opposite extremes. They were either bishops and presbyters, the persons the most distinguished among the Christians by their rank and influence, and whose example might strike terror into the whole sect;[43] or else they were the meanest and most abject among them, particularly those of the servile condition, whose lives were esteemed of little value, and whose sufferings were viewed by the ancients with too careless an indifference.[44] The learned Origen, who, from his experience as well as reading, was intimately acquainted with the history of the Christians, declares, in the most express terms, that the number of martyrs was very inconsiderable. His authority would alone be sufficient to annihilate that formidable army of martyrs whose relics, drawn for the most part from the catacombs of Rome, have replenished so many churches,[45] and whose marvellous achievements have been the subject of so many volumes of holy romance.[46] But the general assertion of Origen may be explained and confirmed by the particular testimony of his friend Dionysius, who, in the immense city of Alexandria, and under the rigorous persecution of Decius, reckons only ten men and seven women who suffered for the profession of the Christian name.

During the same period of persecution, the zealous, the eloquent, the ambitious Cyprian, governed the church, not only of Carthage, but even of Africa. He possessed every quality which could engage the reverence of the faithful or provoke the suspicions and resentment of the Pagan magistrates. His character as well as his station seemed to mark out that holy prelate as the most distinguished object of envy and of danger. The experience, however, of the life of Cyprian is sufficient to prove that our fancy has exaggerated the perilous situation of a Christian bishop; and that the dangers to which he was exposed were less imminent than those which temporal ambition is always prepared to encounter in the pursuit of honours. Four Roman emperors, with their families, their favourites, and their adherents, perished by the sword in the space of ten years, during which the bishop of Carthage guided, by his authority and eloquence, the counsels of the African church. It was only in the third year of his administration that he had reason, during a few months, to apprehend the severe edicts of Decius, the vigilance of the magistrate, and the clamours of the multitude, who loudly demanded that Cyprian, the leader of the Christians, should be thrown to the lions. Prudence suggested the necessity of a temporary retreat, and the voice of prudence was obeyed. He withdrew himself into an obscure solitude, from whence he could maintain a constant correspondence with the clergy and people of Carthage; and, concealing himself till the tempest was past, he preserved his life, without relinquishing either his power or his reputation. His extreme caution did not, however, escape the censure of the more rigid Christians who lamented, or the reproaches of his personal enemies who insulted, a conduct which they considered as a pusillanimous and criminal desertion of the most sacred duty. The propriety of reserving himself for the future exigencies of the church, the example of several holy bishops,[47] and the divine admonitions which, as he declares himself, he frequently received in visions and ecstasies, were the reasons alleged in his justification. But his best apology may be found in the cheerful resolution with which, about eight years afterwards, he suffered death in the cause of religion. The authentic history of his martyrdom has been recorded with unusual candour and impartiality. A short abstract, therefore, of its most important circumstances will convey the clearest information of the spirit, and of the forms, of the Roman persecutions.[48]

When Valerian was consul for the third, and Gallienus for the fourth, time, Paternus, proconsul of Africa, summoned Cyprian to appear in his private council chamber. He there acquainted him with the Imperial mandate which he had just received,[49] that those who had abandoned the Roman religion should immediately return to the practice of the ceremonies of their ancestors. Cyprian replied without hesitation that he was a Christian and a bishop, devoted to the worship of the true and only Deity, to whom he offered up his daily supplications for the safety and prosperity of the two emperors, his lawful sovereigns. With modest confidence he pleaded the privilege of a citizen, in refusing to give any answer to some invidious and, indeed, illegal questions which the proconsul had proposed. A sentence of banishment was pronounced as the penalty of Cyprian's disobedience; and he was conducted, without delay, to

Christians it served as the emblem, not only of martyrdom, but in general of a joyful resurrection.

[46] *As a specimen of these legends, we may be satisfied with 10,000 Christian soldiers crucified in one day, either by Trajan or Hadrian, on Mount Ararat.*

[47] *In particular those of Dionysius of Alexandria and Gregory Thaumaturgus of Neo-Cæsarea.*

[48] *We have an original life of Cyprian by the deacon Pontius, the companion of his exile, and the spectator of his death; and we likewise possess the ancient proconsular act of his martyrdom. These two relations are consistent with each other and with probability; and, what is somewhat remarkable, they are both unsullied by any miraculous circumstances.*

[49] *It should seem that these were circular orders, sent at the same time to all the governors. Dionysius relates the history of his own banishment from Alexandria almost in the same manner. But, as he escaped and survived the persecution, we must account him either more or less fortunate than Cyprian.*

Curubis, a free and maritime city of Zeugitana, in a pleasant situation, a fertile territory, and at the distance of about forty miles from Carthage. The exiled bishop enjoyed the conveniencies of life and the consciousness of virtue. His reputation was diffused over Africa and Italy; an account of his behaviour was published for the edification of the Christian world; and his solitude was frequently interrupted by the letters, the visits, and the congratulations of the faithful. On the arrival of a new proconsul in the province, the fortune of Cyprian appeared for some time to wear a still more favourable aspect. He was recalled from banishment; and, though not yet permitted to return to Carthage, his own gardens in the neighbourhood of the capital were assigned for the place of his residence.[50]

At length, exactly one year [51] after Cyprian was first apprehended, Galerius Maximus, proconsul of Africa, received the Imperial warrant for the execution of the Christian teachers. The bishop of Carthage was sensible that he should be singled out for one of the first victims; and the frailty of nature tempted him to withdraw himself, by a secret flight, from the danger and the honour of martyrdom; but, soon recovering that fortitude which his character required, he returned to his gardens, and patiently expected the ministers of death. Two officers of rank, who were intrusted with that commission, placed Cyprian between them in a chariot; and, as the proconsul was not then at leisure, they conducted him, not to a prison, but to a private house in Carthage, which belonged to one of them. An elegant supper was provided for the entertainment of the bishop, and his Christian friends were permitted for the last time to enjoy his society, whilst the streets were filled with a multitude of the faithful, anxious and alarmed at the approaching fate of their spiritual father.[52] In the morning he appeared before the tribunal of the proconsul, who, after informing himself of the name and situation of Cyprian, commanded him to offer sacrifice, and pressed him to reflect on the consequences of his disobedience. The refusal of Cyprian was firm and decisive; and the magistrate, when he had taken the opinion of his council, pronounced with some reluctance the sentence of death. It was conceived in the following terms: "That Thascius Cyprianus should be immediately beheaded, as the enemy of the gods of Rome, and as the chief and ringleader of a criminal association, which he had seduced into an impious resistance against the laws of the most holy emperors, Valerian and Gallienus." The manner of his execution was the mildest and least painful that could be inflicted on a person convicted of any capital of-

[50] *Upon his conversion, he had sold those gardens for the benefit of the poor. The indulgence of God (most probably the liberality of some Christian friend) restored them to Cyprian.*

[51] *When Cyprian, a twelvemonth before, was sent into exile, he dreamt that he should be put to death the next day. The event made it necessary to explain that word as signifying a year.*

[52] *Pontius acknowledges that Cyprian, with whom he supped, passed the night custodiâ delicatâ. The bishop exercised a last and very proper act of jurisdiction, by directing that the younger females who watched in the street should be removed from the dangers and temptations of a nocturnal crowd.*

fence: nor was the use of torture admitted to obtain from the bishop
of Carthage either the recantation of his principles or the discovery
of his accomplices.

As soon as the sentence was proclaimed, a general cry of "We will
die with him" arose at once among the listening multitude of Christians who waited before the palace gates. The generous effusions of
their zeal and affection were neither serviceable to Cyprian nor dangerous to themselves. He was led away under a guard of tribunes
and centurions, without resistance and without insult, to the place
of his execution, a spacious and level plain near the city, which was
already filled with great numbers of spectators. His faithful presbyters and deacons were permitted to accompany their holy bishop.
They assisted him in laying aside his upper garment, spread linen
on the ground to catch the precious relics of his blood, and received
his orders to bestow five-and-twenty pieces of gold on the executioner. The martyr then covered his face with his hands, and at one
blow his head was separated from his body. His corpse remained
during some hours exposed to the curiosity of the Gentiles; but in
the night it was removed, and transported in a triumphal procession
and with a splendid illumination to the burial-place of the Christians. The funeral of Cyprian was publicly celebrated without receiving any interruption from the Roman magistrates; and those
among the faithful who had performed the last offices to his person
and his memory were secure from the danger of inquiry or of punishment. It is remarkable that of so great a multitude of bishops in
the province of Africa Cyprian was the first who was esteemed
worthy to obtain the crown of martyrdom.

It was in the choice of Cyprian either to die a martyr or to live an
apostate, but on that choice depended the alternative of honour or
infamy. Could we suppose that the bishop of Carthage had employed the profession of the Christian faith only as the instrument of
his avarice or ambition, it was still incumbent on him to support the
character which he had assumed;[53] and, if he possessed the smallest degree of manly fortitude, rather to expose himself to the most
cruel tortures than by a single act to exchange the reputation of a
whole life for the abhorrence of his Christian brethren and the contempt of the Gentile world. But, if the zeal of Cyprian was supported by the sincere conviction of the truth of those doctrines which
he preached, the crown of martyrdom must have appeared to him
as an object of desire rather than of terror. It is not easy to extract
any distinct ideas from the vague though eloquent declamations of

[53] *Whatever opinion we
may entertain of the
character or principles of
Thomas Becket, we must
acknowledge that he suffered death with a constancy not unworthy of
the primitive martyrs.*

the Fathers or to ascertain the degree of immortal glory and happiness which they confidently promised to those who were so fortunate as to shed their blood in the cause of religion.[54] They inculcated with becoming diligence that the fire of martyrdom supplied every defect and expiated every sin; that, while the souls of ordinary Christians were obliged to pass through a slow and painful purification, the triumphant sufferers entered into the immediate fruition of eternal bliss, where, in the society of the patriarchs, the apostles, and the prophets, they reigned with Christ, and acted as his assessors in the universal judgment of mankind. The assurance of a lasting reputation upon earth, a motive so congenial to the vanity of human nature, often served to animate the courage of the martyrs. The honours which Rome or Athens bestowed on those citizens who had fallen in the cause of their country were cold and unmeaning demonstrations of respect, when compared with the ardent gratitude and devotion which the primitive church expressed towards the victorious champions of the faith. The annual commemoration of their virtues and sufferings was observed as a sacred ceremony, and at length terminated in religious worship. Among the Christians who had publicly confessed their religious principles, those who (as it very frequently happened) had been dismissed from the tribunal or the prisons of the Pagan magistrates obtained such honours as were justly due to their imperfect martyrdom and their generous resolution. The most pious females courted the permission of imprinting kisses on the fetters which they had worn and on the wounds which they had received. Their persons were esteemed holy, their decisions were admitted with deference, and they too often abused, by their spiritual pride and licentious manners, the pre-eminence which their zeal and intrepidity had acquired.[55] Distinctions like these, whilst they display the exalted merit, betray the inconsiderable number, of those who suffered and of those who died for the profession of Christianity.

The sober discretion of the present age will more readily censure than admire, but can more easily admire than imitate, the fervour of the first Christians; who, according to the lively expression of Sulpicius Severus, desired martyrdom with more eagerness than his own contemporaries solicited a bishopric. The epistles which Ignatius composed as he was carried in chains through the cities of Asia breathe sentiments the most repugnant to the ordinary feelings of human nature. He earnestly beseeches the Romans that, when he should be exposed in the amphitheatre, they would not, by their

[54] *The learning of Dodwell and the ingenuity of Middleton have left scarcely anything to add concerning the merit, the honours, and the motives of the martyrs.*

[55] *The number of pretended martyrs has been very much multiplied by the custom which was introduced of bestowing that honourable name on confessors.*

kind but unseasonable intercession, deprive him of the crown of glory; and he declares his resolution to provoke and irritate the wild beasts which might be employed as the instruments of his death.[56] Some stories are related of the courage of martyrs who actually performed what Ignatius had intended; who exasperated the fury of the lions, pressed the executioner to hasten his office, cheerfully leaped into the fires which were kindled to consume them, and discovered a sensation of joy and pleasure in the midst of the most exquisite tortures. Several examples have been preserved of a zeal impatient of those restraints which the emperors had provided for the security of the church. The Christians sometimes supplied by their voluntary declaration the want of an accuser, rudely disturbed the public service of Paganism,[57] and, rushing in crowds round the tribunal of the magistrates, called upon them to pronounce and to inflict the sentence of the law. The behaviour of the Christians was too remarkable to escape the notice of the ancient philosophers; but they seem to have considered it with much less admiration than astonishment. Incapable of conceiving the motives which sometimes transported the fortitude of believers beyond the bounds of prudence or reason, they treated such an eagerness to die as the strange result of obstinate despair, of stupid insensibility, or of superstitious frenzy. "Unhappy men!" exclaimed the proconsul Antoninus to the Christians of Asia; "unhappy men! if you are thus weary of your lives, is it so difficult for you to find ropes and precipices?"[58] He was extremely cautious (as it is observed by a learned and pious historian) of punishing men who had found no accusers but themselves, the Imperial laws not having made any provision for so unexpected a case; condemning, therefore, a few as a warning to their brethren, he dismissed the multitude with indignation and contempt. Notwithstanding this real or affected disdain, the intrepid constancy of the faithful was productive of more salutary effects on those minds which nature or grace had disposed for the easy reception of religious truth. On these melancholy occasions, there were many among the Gentiles who pitied, who admired, and who were converted. The generous enthusiasm was communicated from the sufferer to the spectators; and the blood of martyrs, according to a well-known observation, became the seed of the church.

But, although devotion had raised, and eloquence continued to inflame, this fever of the mind, it insensibly gave way to the more natural hopes and fears of the human heart, to the love of life, the apprehension of pain, and the horror of dissolution. The more pru-

[56] *It suited the purpose of Bishop Pearson to justify, by a profusion of examples and authorities, the sentiments of Ignatius.*

[57] *The story of Polyeuctes, on which Corneille has founded a very beautiful tragedy, is one of the most celebrated, though not perhaps the most authentic, instances of this excessive zeal. We should observe that the 60th canon of the council of Illiberis refuses the title of martyrs to those who exposed themselves to death by publicly destroying the idols.*

[58] *The learned are divided between three persons of the same name, who were all proconsuls of Asia. I am inclined to ascribe this story to Antoninus Pius, who was afterwards emperor; and who may have governed Asia under the reign of Trajan.*

dent rulers of the church found themselves obliged to restrain the indiscreet ardour of their followers, and to distrust a constancy which too often abandoned them in the hour of trial. As the lives of the faithful became less mortified and austere, they were every day less ambitious of the honours of martyrdom; and the soldiers of Christ, instead of distinguishing themselves by voluntary deeds of heroism, frequently deserted their post, and fled in confusion before the enemy whom it was their duty to resist. There were three methods, however, of escaping the flames of persecution, which were not attended with an equal degree of guilt: the first, indeed, was generally allowed to be innocent; the second was of a doubtful, or at least of a venial, nature; but the third implied a direct and criminal apostasy from the Christian faith.

I. A modern inquisitor would hear with surprise that, whenever an information was given to a Roman magistrate of any person within his jurisdiction who had embraced the sect of the Christians, the charge was communicated to the party accused, and that a convenient time was allowed him to settle his domestic concerns and to prepare an answer to the crime which was imputed to him.[59] If he entertained any doubt of his own constancy, such a delay afforded him the opportunity of preserving his life and honour by flight, of withdrawing himself into some obscure retirement or some distant province, and of patiently expecting the return of peace and security. A measure so consonant to reason was soon authorized by the advice and example of the most holy prelates, and seems to have been censured by few, except by the Montanists, who deviated into heresy by their strict and obstinate adherence to the rigour of ancient discipline.[60] II. The provincial governors, whose zeal was less prevalent than their avarice, had countenanced the practice of selling certificates (or libels as they were called), which attested that the persons therein mentioned had complied with the laws and sacrificed to the Roman deities. By producing these false declarations, the opulent and timid Christians were enabled to silence the malice of an informer and to reconcile, in some measure, their safety with their religion. A slight penance atoned for this profane dissimulation. III. In every persecution there were great numbers of unworthy Christians who publicly disowned or renounced the faith which they had professed; and who confirmed the sincerity of their abjuration by the legal acts of burning incense or of offering sacrifices. Some of these apostates had yielded on the first menace or exhortation of the magistrate; whilst the patience of others had been sub-

[59] *In the second apology of Justin, there is a particular and very curious instance of this legal delay. The same indulgence was granted to accused Christians in the persecution of Decius; and Cyprian expressly mentions the "Dies negantibus præstitutus."*

[60] *Tertullian considers flight from persecution as an imperfect, but very criminal apostasy, as an impious attempt to elude the will of God, &c. &c. He has written a treatise on this subject, which is filled with the wildest fanaticism and the most incoherent declamation. It is, however, somewhat remarkable that Tertullian did not suffer martyrdom himself.*

dued by the length and repetition of tortures. The affrighted countenances of some betrayed their inward remorse, while others advanced, with confidence and alacrity, to the altars of the gods. But
the disguise which fear had imposed subsisted no longer than the
present danger. As soon as the severity of the persecution was abated,
the doors of the churches were assailed by the returning multitude
of penitents, who detested their idolatrous submission, and who
solicited, with equal ardour, but with various success, their readmis-
sion into the society of Christians.[61]

IV. Notwithstanding the general rules established for the conviction and punishment of the Christians, the fate of those sectaries,
in an extensive and arbitrary government, must still, in a great
measure, have depended on their own behaviour, the circumstances
of the times, and the temper of their supreme as well as subordinate
rulers. Zeal might sometimes provoke, and prudence might sometimes avert or assuage, the superstitious fury of the Pagans. A variety
of motives might dispose the provincial governors either to enforce
or to relax the execution of the laws; and of these motives the most
forcible was their regard not only for the public edicts, but for the
secret intentions of the emperor, a glance from whose eye was sufficient to kindle or to extinguish the flames of persecution. As often
as any occasional severities were exercised in the different parts of
the empire, the primitive Christians lamented and perhaps magnified their own sufferings; but the celebrated number of *ten* persecutions has been determined by the ecclesiastical writers of the fifth
century, who possessed a more distinct view of the prosperous or
adverse fortunes of the church, from the age of Nero to that of Diocletian. The ingenious parallels of the *ten* plagues of Egypt and of
the *ten* horns of the Apocalypse first suggested this calculation to
their minds; and in their application of the faith of prophecy to the
truth of history they were careful to select those reigns which were
indeed the most hostile to the Christian cause.[62] But these transient
persecutions served only to revive the zeal, and to restore the discipline, of the faithful: and the moments of extraordinary rigour
were compensated by much longer intervals of peace and security.
The indifference of some princes and the indulgence of others permitted the Christians to enjoy, though not perhaps a legal, yet an
actual and public, toleration of their religion.

The apology of Tertullian contains two very ancient, very singular, but at the same time very suspicious, instances of Imperial clemency; the edicts published by Tiberius and by Marcus Antoninus,

[61] *It was on this occasion that Cyprian wrote his treatise De Lapsis and many of his epistles. The controversy concerning the treatment of peni-tent apostates does not occur among the Chris-tians of the preceding century. Shall we ascribe this to the superiority of their faith and cour-age or to our less inti-mate knowledge of their history?*

[62] *Sulpicius Severus was the first author of this computation; though he seemed desirous of re-serving the tenth and greatest persecution for the coming of the Anti-christ.*

and designed not only to protect the innocence of the Christians, but even to proclaim those stupendous miracles which had attested the truth of their doctrine. The first of these examples is attended with some difficulties which might perplex the sceptical mind. We are required to believe *that* Pontius Pilate informed the emperor of the unjust sentence of death which he had pronounced against an innocent, and, as it appeared, a divine, person; and that, without acquiring the merit, he exposed himself to the danger, of martyrdom; *that* Tiberius, who avowed his contempt for all religion, immediately conceived the design of placing the Jewish Messiah among the gods of Rome; *that* his servile senate ventured to disobey the commands of their master; *that* Tiberius, instead of resenting their refusal, contented himself with protecting the Christians from the severity of the laws, many years before such laws were enacted, or before the church had assumed any distinct name or existence; and lastly, *that* the memory of this extraordinary transaction was preserved in the most public and authentic records, which escaped the knowledge of the historians of Greece and Rome, and were only visible to the eyes of an African Christian, who composed his apology one hundred and sixty years after the death of Tiberius. The edict of Marcus Antoninus is supposed to have been the effect of his devotion and gratitude for the miraculous deliverance which he had obtained in the Marcomannic war. The distress of the legions, the seasonable tempest of rain and hail, of thunder and lightning, and the dismay and defeat of the barbarians, have been celebrated by the eloquence of several Pagan writers. If there were any Christians in that army, it was natural that they should ascribe some merit to the fervent prayers which, in the moment of danger, they had offered up for their own and the public safety. But we are still assured by monuments of brass and marble, by the Imperial medals, and by the Antonine column, that neither the prince nor the people entertained any sense of this signal obligation, since they unanimously attribute their deliverance to the providence of Jupiter and to the interposition of Mercury. During the whole course of his reign, Marcus despised the Christians as a philosopher, and punished them as a sovereign.

By a singular fatality, the hardships which they had endured under the government of a virtuous prince immediately ceased on the accession of a tyrant, and, as none except themselves had experienced the injustice of Marcus, so they alone were protected by the lenity of Commodus. The celebrated Marcia, the most favoured of his concubines, and who at length contrived the murder of her Imperial lover, entertained a singular affection for the oppressed church; and, though it was impossible that she could reconcile the practice of vice with the precepts of the Gospel, she might hope to atone for the frailties of her sex and profession, by declaring herself the patroness of the Christians. Under the gracious protection of Marcia, they passed in safety the thirteen years of a cruel tyranny; and, when the empire was established in the house of Severus, they formed a domestic but more honourable connexion with the new court. The emperor was persuaded that, in a dangerous sickness, he had derived some benefit, either spiritual or physical, from the holy oil with which one of his slaves had anointed him. He always treated with peculiar distinction several persons of both sexes who had embraced the new religion. The nurse as well as the preceptor of Caracalla were Christians; and, if that young prince ever betrayed a sentiment of humanity, it was occasioned by an incident which, however trifling, bore some relation to the cause of Christianity. Under the reign of Severus, the fury of the populace was checked; the rigour of ancient laws was for some time suspended; and the provincial governors were satisfied with receiving an annual present from the churches within their jurisdiction, as the price, or as the reward, of their moderation.[63] The controversy concerning the precise time of the celebration of Easter armed the bishops of Asia and Italy against each other, and was considered as the most important business of this period of leisure and tranquillity. Nor was the peace of the church interrupted till the increasing numbers of proselytes seem at length to have attracted the attention, and to have alienated the mind, of Severus. With the design of restraining the progress of Christianity, he published an edict which, though it was designed to affect only the new converts, could not be carried into strict execution without exposing to danger and punishment the most zealous of their teachers and missionaries. In this mitigated persecution, we may still discover the indulgent spirit of Rome and of Polytheism, which so readily admitted every excuse in favour of those who practised the religious ceremonies of their fathers.

But the laws which Severus had enacted soon expired with the authority of that emperor; and the Christians, after this accidental tempest, enjoyed a calm of thirty-eight years. Till this period they had usually held their assemblies in private houses and sequestered places. They were now permitted to erect and consecrate convenient edifices for the purpose of religious worship;[64] to purchase

[63] *The present was made during the feast of the Saturnalia; and it is a matter of serious concern to Tertullian that the faithful should be confounded with the most infamous professions which purchased the connivance of the government.*

[64] *The antiquity of Christian churches is discussed by Tillemont and by Mr. Moyle. The former refers the first construction of them to the peace of Alexander Severus; the latter to the peace of Gallienus.*

lands, even at Rome itself, for the use of the community; and to conduct the elections of their ecclesiastical ministers in so public, but at the same time in so exemplary, a manner as to deserve the respectful attention of the Gentiles.[65] This long repose of the church was accompanied with dignity. The reigns of those princes who derived their extraction from the Asiatic provinces proved the most favourable to the Christians; the eminent persons of the sect, instead of being reduced to implore the protection of a slave or concubine, were admitted into the palace in the honourable characters of priests and philosophers; and their mysterious doctrines, which were already diffused among the people, insensibly attracted the curiosity of their sovereign. When the empress Mammæa passed through Antioch, she expressed a desire of conversing with the celebrated Origen, the fame of whose piety and learning was spread over the East. Origen obeyed so flattering an invitation, and, though he could not expect to succeed in the conversion of an artful and ambitious woman, she listened with pleasure to his eloquent exhortations, and honourably dismissed him to his retirement in Palestine.[66] The sentiments of Mammæa were adopted by her son Alexander, and the philosophic devotion of that emperor was marked by a singular but injudicious regard for the Christian religion. In his domestic chapel he placed the statues of Abraham, of Orpheus, of Apollonius, and of Christ, as an honour justly due to those respectable sages who had instructed mankind in the various modes of addressing their homage to the supreme and universal deity.[67] A purer faith, as well as worship, was openly professed and practised among his household. Bishops, perhaps for the first time, were seen at court; and after the death of Alexander, when the inhuman Maximin discharged his fury on the favourites and servants of his unfortunate benefactor, a great number of Christians, of every rank, and of both sexes, were involved in the promiscuous massacre, which, on their account, has improperly received the name of Persecution.[68]

Notwithstanding the cruel disposition of Maximin, the effects of his resentment against the Christians were of a very local and temporary nature, and the pious Origen, who had been proscribed as a devoted victim, was still reserved to convey the truths of the Gospel to the ear of monarchs. He addressed several edifying letters to the emperor Philip, to his wife, and to his mother; and, as soon as that prince, who was born in the neighbourhood of Palestine, had usurped the Imperial sceptre, the Christians acquired a friend and a protector. The public and even partial favour of Philip towards

[65] The emperor Alexander adopted their method of publicly proposing the names of those persons who were candidates for ordination. It is true that the honour of this practice is likewise attributed to the Jews.

[66] Mammæa was styled a holy and pious woman, both by the Christians and the Pagans. From the former, therefore, it was impossible that she should deserve that honourable epithet.

[67] His design of building a public temple to Christ and the objection which was suggested either to him or in similar circumstances to Hadrian appear to have no other foundation than an improbable report, invented by the Christians and credulously adopted by an historian of the age of Constantine.

[68] It may be presumed that the success of the Christians had exasperated the increasing bigotry of the Pagans. Dion Cassius, who composed his history under the former reign, had most probably intended for the use of his master those counsels of persecution which he ascribes to a better age and to the favourite of Augustus.

the sectaries of the new religion, and his constant reverence for the ministers of the church, gave some colour to the suspicion, which prevailed in his own times, that the emperor himself was become a convert to the faith;[69] and afforded some grounds for a fable which was afterwards invented, that he had been purified by confession and penance from the guilt contracted by the murder of his innocent predecessor. The fall of Philip introduced, with the change of masters, a new system of government, so oppressive to the Christians that their former condition, ever since the time of Domitian, was represented as a state of perfect freedom and security, if compared with the rigorous treatment which they experienced under the short reign of Decius. The virtues of that prince will scarcely allow us to suspect that he was actuated by a mean resentment against the favourites of his predecessor, and it is more reasonable to believe that, in the prosecution of his general design to restore the purity of Roman manners, he was desirous of delivering the empire from what he condemned as a recent and criminal superstition. The bishops of the most considerable cities were removed by exile or death; the vigilance of the magistrates prevented the clergy of Rome during sixteen months from proceeding to a new election; and it was the opinion of the Christians that the emperor would more patiently endure a competitor for the purple than a bishop in the capital.[70] Were it possible to suppose that the penetration of Decius had discovered pride under the disguise of humility, or that he could foresee the temporal dominion which might insensibly arise from the claims of spiritual authority, we might be less surprised that he should consider the successors of St. Peter as the most formidable rivals to those of Augustus.

The administration of Valerian was distinguished by a levity and inconstancy, ill-suited to the gravity of the *Roman Censor*. In the first part of his reign, he surpassed in clemency those princes who had been suspected of an attachment to the Christian faith. In the last three years and a half, listening to the insinuations of a minister addicted to the superstitions of Egypt, he adopted the maxims, and imitated the severity, of his predecessor Decius. The accession of Gallienus, which increased the calamities of the empire, restored peace to the church; and the Christians obtained the free exercise of their religion, by an edict addressed to the bishops and conceived in such terms as seemed to acknowledge their office and public character. The ancient laws, without being formally repealed, were suffered to sink into oblivion; and (excepting only some hostile inten-

[69] *The mention of those princes who were publicly supposed to be Christians, as we find it in an epistle of Dionysius of Alexandria, evidently alludes to Philip and his family, and forms a contemporary evidence that such a report had prevailed; but the Egyptian bishop, who lived at an humble distance from the court of Rome, expresses himself with a becoming diffidence concerning the truth of the fact. The epistles of Origen (which were extant in the time of Eusebius), would most probably decide this curious, rather than important, question.*

[70] *The see of Rome remained vacant from the martyrdom of Fabianus, the 20th of January,* A.D. *250, till the election of Cornelius, the 4th of June,* A.D. *251. Decius had probably left Rome, since he was killed before the end of that year.*

tions which are attributed to the emperor Aurelian) the disciples of Christ passed above forty years in a state of prosperity, far more dangerous to their virtue than the severest trials of persecution.

The story of Paul of Samosata, who filled the metropolitan see of Antioch, while the East was in the hands of Odenathus and Zenobia, may serve to illustrate the condition and character of the times. The wealth of that prelate was a sufficient evidence of his guilt, since it was neither derived from the inheritance of his fathers nor acquired by the arts of honest industry. But Paul considered the service of the church as a very lucrative profession.[71] His ecclesiastical jurisdiction was venal and rapacious; he extorted frequent contributions from the most opulent of the faithful, and converted to his own use a considerable part of the public revenue. By his pride and luxury the Christian religion was rendered odious in the eyes of the Gentiles. His council chamber and his throne, the splendour with which he appeared in public, the suppliant crowd who solicited his attention, the multitude of letters and petitions to which he dictated his answers, and the perpetual hurry of business in which he was involved, were circumstances much better suited to the state of a civil magistrate[72] than to the humility of a primitive bishop. When he harangued his people from the pulpit, Paul affected the figurative style and the theatrical gestures of an Asiatic sophist, while the cathedral resounded with the loudest and most extravagant acclamations in the praise of his divine eloquence. Against those who resisted his power, or refused to flatter his vanity, the prelate of Antioch was arrogant, rigid, and inexorable; but he relaxed the discipline, and lavished the treasures, of the church on his dependent clergy, who were permitted to imitate their master in the gratification of every sensual appetite. For Paul indulged himself very freely in the pleasures of the table, and he had received into the episcopal palace two young and beautiful women, as the constant companions of his leisure moments.[73]

Notwithstanding these scandalous vices, if Paul of Samosata had preserved the purity of the orthodox faith, his reign over the capital of Syria would have ended only with his life; and, had a seasonable persecution intervened, an effort of courage might perhaps have placed him in the rank of saints and martyrs. Some nice and subtle errors, which he imprudently adopted and obstinately maintained, concerning the doctrine of the Trinity, excited the zeal and indignation of the eastern churches.[74] From Egypt to the Euxine sea, the bishops were in arms and in motion. Several councils were held,

[71] Paul was better pleased with the title of Ducenarius, than with that of bishop. The Ducenarius was an Imperial procurator, so called from his salary of two hundred Sestertia, or £1600 a year. Some critics suppose that the bishop of Antioch had actually obtained such an office from Zenobia, while others consider it only as a figurative expression of his pomp and insolence.

[72] Simony was not unknown in those times; and the clergy sometimes bought what they intended to sell. It appears that the bishopric of Carthage was purchased by a wealthy matron, named Lucilla, for her servant Majorinus. The price was 400 Folles. Every Follis contained 125 pieces of silver, and the whole sum may be computed at about £2400.

[73] If we are desirous of extenuating the vices of Paul, we must suspect the assembled bishops of the East of publishing the most malicious calumnies in circular epistles addressed to all the churches of the empire.

confutations were published, excommunications were pronounced, ambiguous explanations were by turns accepted and refused, treaties were concluded and violated, and, at length, Paul of Samosata was degraded from his episcopal character, by the sentence of seventy or eighty bishops, who assembled for that purpose at Antioch, and who, without consulting the rights of the clergy or people, appointed a successor by their own authority. The manifest irregularity of this proceeding increased the numbers of the discontented faction; and as Paul, who was no stranger to the arts of courts, had insinuated himself into the favour of Zenobia, he maintained above four years the possession of the episcopal house and office. The victory of Aurelian changed the face of the East, and the two contending parties, who applied to each other the epithets of schism and heresy, were either commanded or permitted to plead their cause before the tribunal of the conqueror. This public and very singular trial affords a convincing proof that the existence, the property, the privileges, and the internal policy of the Christians were acknowledged, if not by the laws, at least by the magistrates, of the empire. As a Pagan and as a soldier, it could scarcely be expected that Aurelian should enter into the discussion, whether the sentiments of Paul or those of his adversaries were most agreeable to the true standard of the orthodox faith. His determination, however, was founded on the general principles of equity and reason. He considered the bishops of Italy as the most impartial and respectable judges among the Christians, and, as soon as he was informed that they had unanimously approved the sentence of the council, he acquiesced in their opinion, and immediately gave orders that Paul should be compelled to relinquish the temporal possessions belonging to an office of which, in the judgment of his brethren, he had been regularly deprived. But, while we applaud the justice, we should not overlook the policy, of Aurelian; who was desirous of restoring and cementing the dependence of the provinces on the capital by every means which could bind the interest or prejudices of any part of his subjects.

Amidst the frequent revolutions of the empire, the Christians still flourished in peace and prosperity; and, notwithstanding a celebrated æra of martyrs has been deduced from the accession of Diocletian,[75] the new system of policy, introduced and maintained by the wisdom of that prince, continued, during more than eighteen years, to breathe the mildest and most liberal spirit of religious toleration. The mind of Diocletian himself was less adapted in-

[74] *His heresy (like those of Noetus and Sabellius, in the same century) tended to confound the mysterious distinction of the divine persons.*

[75] *The æra of Martyrs, which is still in use among the Copts and the Abyssinians, must be reckoned from the 29th of August, A.D. 284; as the beginning of the Egyptian year was nineteen days earlier than the real accession of Diocletian.*

deed to speculative inquiries than to the active labours of war and government. His prudence rendered him averse to any great innovation, and, though his temper was not very susceptible of zeal or enthusiasm, he always maintained an habitual regard for the ancient deities of the empire. But the leisure of the two empresses, of his wife Prisca and of Valeria his daughter, permitted them to listen with more attention and respect to the truths of Christianity, which in every age has acknowledged its important obligations to female devotion. The principal eunuchs, Lucian and Dorotheus, Gorgonius and Andrew, who attended the person, possessed the favour, and governed the household of Diocletian, protected by their powerful influence the faith which they had embraced. Their example was imitated by many of the most considerable officers of the palace, who, in their respective stations, had the care of the Imperial ornaments, of the robes, of the furniture, of the jewels, and even of the private treasury; and, though it might sometimes be incumbent on them to accompany the emperor when he sacrificed in the temple, they enjoyed, with their wives, their children, and their slaves, the free exercise of the Christian religion. Diocletian and his colleagues frequently conferred the most important offices on those persons who avowed their abhorrence for the worship of the gods, but who had displayed abilities proper for the service of the state. The bishops held an honourable rank in their respective provinces, and were treated with distinction and respect, not only by the people, but by the magistrates themselves. Almost in every city, the ancient churches were found insufficient to contain the increasing multitude of proselytes; and in their place more stately and capacious edifices were erected for the public worship of the faithful. The corruption of manners and principles, so forcibly lamented by Eusebius, may be considered, not only as a consequence, but as a proof, of the liberty which the Christians enjoyed and abused under the reign of Diocletian. Prosperity had relaxed the nerves of discipline. Fraud, envy, and malice prevailed in every congregation. The presbyters aspired to the episcopal office, which every day became an object more worthy of their ambition. The bishops, who contended with each other for ecclesiastical pre-eminence, appeared by their conduct to claim a secular and tyrannical power in the church; and the lively faith which still distinguished the Christians from the Gentiles was shown much less in their lives than in their controversial writings.

Notwithstanding this seeming security, an attentive observer

[16] *We might quote, among a great number of instances, the mysterious worship of Mithras, and the Taurobolia; the latter of which became fashionable in the time of the Antonines. The romance of Apuleius is as full of devotion as of satire.*

might discern some symptoms that threatened the church with a more violent persecution than any which she had yet endured. The zeal and rapid progress of the Christians awakened the Polytheists from their supine indifference in the cause of those deities whom custom and education had taught them to revere. The mutual provocations of a religious war, which had already continued above two hundred years, exasperated the animosity of the contending parties. The Pagans were incensed at the rashness of a recent and obscure sect which presumed to accuse their countrymen of error and to devote their ancestors to eternal misery. The habits of justifying the popular mythology against the invectives of an implacable enemy produced in their minds some sentiments of faith and reverence for a system which they had been accustomed to consider with the most careless levity. The supernatural powers assumed by the church inspired at the same time terror and emulation. The followers of the established religion intrenched themselves behind a similar fortification of prodigies; invented new modes of sacrifice, of expiation, and of initiation;[76] attempted to revive the credit of their expiring oracles;[77] and listened with eager credulity to every impostor who flattered their prejudices by a tale of wonders.[78] Both parties seemed to acknowledge the truth of those miracles which were claimed by their adversaries; and, while they were contented with ascribing them to the arts of magic and to the power of dæmons, they mutually concurred in restoring and establishing the reign of superstition.[79] Philosophy, her most dangerous enemy, was now converted into her most useful ally. The groves of the academy, the gardens of Epicurus, and even the portico of the Stoics, were almost deserted, as so many different schools of scepticism or impiety;[80] and many among the Romans were desirous that the writings of Cicero should be condemned and suppressed by the authority of the senate. The prevailing sect of the new Platonicians judged it prudent to connect themselves with the priests, whom perhaps they despised, against the Christians, whom they had reason to fear. These fashionable philosophers prosecuted the design of extracting allegorical wisdom from the fictions of the Greek poets; instituted mysterious rites of devotion for the use of their chosen disciples; recommended the worship of the ancient gods as the emblems or ministers of the Supreme Deity, and composed against the faith of the Gospel many elaborate treatises,[81] which have since been committed to the flames by the prudence of orthodox emperors.

Although the policy of Diocletian and the humanity of Constan-

[77] *The impostor Alexander very strongly recommended the oracle of Trophonius at Mallos, and those of Apollo at Claros and Miletus. The last of these, whose singular history would furnish a very curious episode, was consulted by Diocletian before he published his edicts of persecution.*

[78] *Besides the ancient stories of Pythagoras and Aristeas, the cures performed at the shrine of Æsculapius and the fables related of Apollonius of Tyana were frequently opposed to the miracles of Christ; though I agree with Dr. Lardner that, when Philostratus composed the life of Apollonius, he had no such intention.*

[79] *It is seriously to be lamented that the Christian fathers, by acknowledging the supernatural or, as they deem it, the infernal part of Paganism, destroy with their own hands the great advantage which we might otherwise derive from the liberal concessions of our adversaries.*

tius inclined them to preserve inviolate the maxims of toleration, it was soon discovered that their two associates Maximian and Galerius entertained the most implacable aversion for the name and religion of the Christians. The minds of those princes had never been enlightened by science; education had never softened their temper. They owed their greatness to their swords, and in their most elevated fortune they still retained their superstitious prejudices of soldiers and peasants. In the general administration of the provinces they obeyed the laws which their benefactor had established; but they frequently found occasions of exercising within their camp and palaces a secret persecution,[82] for which the imprudent zeal of the Christians sometimes offered the most specious pretences. A sentence of death was executed upon Maximilianus, an African youth, who had been produced by his own father before the magistrate as a sufficient and legal recruit, but who obstinately persisted in declaring that his conscience would not permit him to embrace the profession of a soldier.[83] It could scarcely be expected that any government should suffer the action of Marcellus the centurion to pass with impunity. On the day of a public festival, that officer threw away his belt, his arms, and the ensigns of his office, and exclaimed with a loud voice that he would obey none but Jesus Christ the eternal King, and that he renounced for ever the use of carnal weapons and the service of an idolatrous master. The soldiers, as soon as they recovered from their astonishment, secured the person of Marcellus. He was examined in the city of Tingi by the president of that part of Mauritania; and, as he was convicted by his own confession, he was condemned and beheaded for the crime of desertion. Examples of such a nature savour much less of religious persecution than of martial or even civil law: but they served to alienate the mind of the emperors, to justify the severity of Galerius, who dismissed a great number of Christian officers from their employments, and to authorize the opinion that a sect of enthusiasts which avowed principles so repugnant to the public safety must either remain useless, or would soon become dangerous, subjects of the empire.

After the success of the Persian war had raised the hopes and the reputation of Galerius, he passed a winter with Diocletian in the palace of Nicomedia; and the fate of Christianity became the object of their secret consultations.[84] The experienced emperor was still inclined to pursue measures of lenity; and, though he readily consented to exclude the Christians from holding any employments in the household or the army, he urged in the strongest terms the danger as well as cruelty of shedding the blood of those deluded fanatics. Galerius at length extorted from him the permission of summoning a council, composed of a few persons the most distinguished in the civil and military departments of the state. The important question was agitated in their presence, and those ambitious courtiers easily discerned that it was incumbent on them to second, by their eloquence, the importunate violence of the Cæsar. It may be presumed that they insisted on every topic which might interest the pride, the piety, or the fears, of their sovereign in the destruction of Christianity. Perhaps they represented that the glorious work of the deliverance of the empire was left imperfect, as long as an independent people was permitted to subsist and multiply in the heart of the provinces. The Christians (it might speciously be alleged), renouncing the gods and the institutions of Rome, had constituted a distinct republic, which might yet be suppressed before it had acquired any military force; but which was already governed by its own laws and magistrates, was possessed of a public treasure, and was intimately connected in all its parts by the frequent assemblies of the bishops, to whose decrees their numerous and opulent congregations yielded an implicit obedience. Arguments like these may seem to have determined the reluctant mind of Diocletian to embrace a new system of persecution: but, though we may suspect, it is not in our power to relate, the secret intrigues of the palace, the private views and resentments, the jealousy of women or eunuchs, and all those trifling but decisive causes which so often influence the fate of empires and the councils of the wisest monarchs.[85]

The pleasure of the emperors was at length signified to the Christians, who, during the course of this melancholy winter, had expected, with anxiety, the result of so many secret consultations. The twenty-third of February, which coincided with the Roman festival of the Terminalia, was appointed (whether from accident or design) to set bounds to the progress of Christianity. At the earliest dawn of day, the Prætorian præfect,[86] accompanied by several generals, tribunes, and officers of the revenue, repaired to the principal church of Nicomedia, which was situated on an eminence in the most populous and beautiful part of the city. The doors were instantly broken open; they rushed into the sanctuary; and, as they searched in vain for some visible object of worship, they were obliged to content themselves with committing to the flames the volumes of holy scripture. The ministers of Diocletian were fol-

St. Maurice still subsists, a rich monument of the credulity of Sigismund, king of Burgundy.

[83] *The accounts of his martyrdom and of that of Marcellus bear every mark of truth and authenticity.*

[84] *Lactantius (or whoever was the author of this little treatise) was, at that time, an inhabitant of Nicomedia; but it seems difficult to conceive how he could acquire so accurate a knowledge of what passed in the Imperial cabinet.*

[85] *The only circumstance which we can discover is the devotion and jealousy of the mother of Galerius. She is described by Lactantius as Deorum montium cultrix; mulier admodum superstitiosa. She had a great influence over her son, and was offended by the disregard of some of her Christian servants.*

[86] *In our only MS. of Lactantius, we read profectus; but reason and the authority of all the critics allow us, instead of that word, which destroys the sense of the passage, to substitute præfectus.*

lowed by a numerous body of guards and pioneers, who marched in order of battle, and were provided with all the instruments used in the destruction of fortified cities. By their incessant labour, a sacred edifice, which towered above the Imperial palace, and had long excited the indignation and envy of the Gentiles, was in a few hours levelled with the ground.

The next day the general edict of persecution was published; and, though Diocletian, still averse to the effusion of blood, had moderated the fury of Galerius, who proposed that every one refusing to offer sacrifice should immediately be burnt alive, the penalties inflicted on the obstinacy of the Christians might be deemed sufficiently rigorous and effectual. It was enacted that their churches, in all the provinces of the empire, should be demolished to their foundations; and the punishment of death was denounced against all who should presume to hold any secret assemblies for the purpose of religious worship. The philosophers, who now assumed the unworthy office of directing the blind zeal of persecution, had diligently studied the nature and genius of the Christian religion; and, as they were not ignorant that the speculative doctrines of the faith were supposed to be contained in the writings of the prophets, of the evangelists, and of the apostles, they most probably suggested the order that the bishops and presbyters should deliver all their sacred books into the hands of the magistrates; who were commanded, under the severest penalties, to burn them in a public and solemn manner. By the same edict, the property of the church was at once confiscated; and the several parts of which it might consist were either sold to the highest bidder, united to the Imperial domain, bestowed on the cities and corporations, or granted to the solicitations of rapacious courtiers. After taking such effectual measures to abolish the worship, and to dissolve the government of the Christians, it was thought necessary to subject to the most intolerable hardships the condition of those perverse individuals who should still reject the religion of Nature, of Rome, and of their ancestors. Persons of a liberal birth were declared incapable of holding any honours or employments; slaves were for ever deprived of the hopes of freedom, and the whole body of the people were put out of the protection of the law. The judges were authorized to hear and to determine every action that was brought against a Christian. But the Christians were not permitted to complain of any injury which they themselves had suffered; and thus those unfortunate sectaries were exposed to the severity, while they were excluded from the

benefits, of public justice. This new species of martyrdom, so painful and lingering, so obscure and ignominious, was, perhaps, the
most proper to weary the constancy of the faithful; nor can it be
doubted that the passions and interest of mankind were disposed on
this occasion to second the designs of the emperors. But the policy
of a well-ordered government must sometimes have interposed in
behalf of the oppressed Christians; nor was it possible for the Roman princes entirely to remove the apprehension of punishment, or
to connive at every act of fraud and violence, without exposing their
own authority and the rest of their subjects to the most alarming
dangers.[87]

This edict was scarcely exhibited to the public view, in the most
conspicuous place of Nicomedia, before it was torn down by the
hands of a Christian, who expressed, at the same time, by the bitter-
est invectives, his contempt as well as abhorrence for such impious
and tyrannical governors. His offence, according to the mildest
laws, amounted to treason, and deserved death. And, if it be true
that he was a person of rank and education, those circumstances
could serve only to aggravate his guilt. He was burnt, or rather
roasted, by a slow fire; and his executioners, zealous to revenge the
personal insult which had been offered to the emperors, exhausted
every refinement of cruelty, without being able to subdue his patience, or to alter the steady and insulting smile which in his dying
agonies he still preserved in his countenance. The Christians, though
they confessed that his conduct had not been strictly conformable
to the laws of prudence, admired the divine fervour of his zeal; and
the excessive commendations which they lavished on the memory
of their hero and martyr contributed to fix a deep impression of
terror and hatred in the mind of Diocletian.

His fears were soon alarmed by the view of a danger from which
he very narrowly escaped. Within fifteen days the palace of Nicomedia, and even the bed-chamber of Diocletian, were twice in
flames; and, though both times they were extinguished without any
material damage, the singular repetition of the fire was justly considered as an evident proof that it had not been the effect of chance
or negligence. The suspicion naturally fell on the Christians; and it
was suggested, with some degree of probability, that those desperate
fanatics, provoked by their present sufferings and apprehensive of
impending calamities, had entered into a conspiracy with their
faithful brethren, the eunuchs of the palace, against the lives of two
emperors, whom they detested as the irreconcilable enemies of the

[87] *Many ages afterwards, Edward I. practised with great success the same mode of persecution against the clergy of England.*

church of God. Jealousy and resentment prevailed in every breast, but especially in that of Diocletian. A great number of persons, distinguished either by the offices which they had filled or by the favour which they had enjoyed, were thrown into prison. Every mode of torture was put in practice, and the court, as well as city, was polluted with many bloody executions. But, as it was found impossible to extort any discovery of this mysterious transaction, it seems incumbent on us either to presume the innocence, or to admire the resolution, of the sufferers. A few days afterwards Galerius hastily withdrew himself from Nicomedia, declaring that, if he delayed his departure from that devoted palace, he should fall a sacrifice to the rage of the Christians. The ecclesiastical historians, from whom alone we derive a partial and imperfect knowledge of this persecution, are at a loss how to account for the fears and dangers of the emperors. Two of these writers, a Prince and a Rhetorician, were eye-witnesses of the fire of Nicomedia. The one ascribes it to lightning and the divine wrath; the other affirms that it was kindled by the malice of Galerius himself.

As the edict against the Christians was designed for a general law of the whole empire, and as Diocletian and Galerius, though they might not wait for the consent, were assured of the concurrence, of the western princes, it would appear more consonant to our ideas of policy that the governors of all the provinces should have received secret instructions to publish, on one and the same day, this declaration of war within their respective departments. It was at least to be expected that the convenience of the public highways and established posts would have enabled the emperors to transmit their orders with the utmost dispatch from the palace of Nicomedia to the extremities of the Roman world; and that they would not have suffered fifty days to elapse before the edict was published in Syria, and near four months before it was signified to the cities of Africa. This delay may perhaps be imputed to the cautious temper of Diocletian, who had yielded a reluctant consent to the measures of persecution, and who was desirous of trying the experiment under his more immediate eye, before he gave way to the disorders and discontent which it must inevitably occasion in the distant provinces. At first, indeed, the magistrates were restrained from the effusion of blood; but the use of every other severity was permitted and even recommended to their zeal; nor could the Christians, though they cheerfully resigned the ornaments of their churches, resolve to interrupt their religious assemblies or to deliver their sacred books to the flames. The pious obstinacy of Felix, an African bishop, appears to have embarrassed the subordinate ministers of the government. The curator of his city sent him in chains to the proconsul. The proconsul transmitted him to the Prætorian præfect of Italy; and Felix, who disdained even to give an evasive answer, was at length beheaded at Venusia, in Lucania, a place on which the birth of Horace has conferred fame. This precedent, and perhaps some Imperial rescript, which was issued in consequence of it, appeared to authorize the governors of provinces in punishing with death the refusal of the Christians to deliver up their sacred books. There were undoubtedly many persons who embraced this opportunity of obtaining the crown of martyrdom; but there were likewise too many who purchased an ignominious life by discovering and betraying the holy scripture into the hands of infidels. A great number even of bishops and presbyters acquired, by this criminal compliance, the opprobrious epithet of *Traditors;* and their offence was productive of much present scandal, and of much future discord, in the African church.

The copies, as well as the versions, of scripture were already so multiplied in the empire that the most severe inquisition could no longer be attended with any fatal consequences; and even the sacrifice of those volumes which, in every congregation, were preserved for public use required the consent of some treacherous and unworthy Christians. But the ruin of the churches was easily effected by the authority of the government and by the labour of the Pagans. In some provinces, however, the magistrates contented themselves with shutting up the places of religious worship. In others, they more literally complied with the terms of the edict; and, after taking away the doors, the benches, and the pulpit, which they burnt, as it were in a funeral pile, they completely demolished the remainder of the edifice.[88] It is perhaps to this melancholy occasion that we should apply a very remarkable story, which is related with so many circumstances of variety and improbability that it serves rather to excite than to satisfy our curiosity. In a small town in Phrygia, of whose name as well as situation we are left ignorant, it should seem that the magistrates and the body of the people had embraced the Christian faith; and, as some resistance might be apprehended to the execution of the edict, the governor of the province was supported by a numerous detachment of legionaries. On their approach the citizens threw themselves into the church, with the resolution either of defending by arms that sacred edifice or of

[88] *The ancient monuments, published at the end of Optatus, describe, in a very circumstantial manner, the proceedings of the governors in the destruction of churches. They made a minute inventory of the plate, &c. which they found in them. That of the Church of Cirta, in Numidia, is still extant. It consisted of two chalices of gold, and six of silver; six urns, one kettle, seven lamps, all likewise of silver; besides a large quantity of brass utensils, and wearing apparel.*

perishing in its ruins. They indignantly rejected the notice and permission which was given them to retire, till the soldiers, provoked by their obstinate refusal, set fire to the building on all sides, and consumed, by this extraordinary kind of martyrdom, a great number of Phrygians, with their wives and children.[89]

Some slight disturbances, though they were suppressed almost as soon as excited, in Syria and the frontiers of Armenia, afforded the enemies of the church a very plausible occasion to insinuate that those troubles had been secretly fomented by the intrigues of the bishops, who had already forgotten their ostentatious professions of passive and unlimited obedience. The resentment, or the fears, of Diocletian at length transported him beyond the bounds of moderation which he had hitherto preserved, and he declared, in a series of cruel edicts, his intention of abolishing the Christian name. By the first of these edicts, the governors of the provinces were directed to apprehend all persons of the ecclesiastical order; and the prisons, destined for the vilest criminals, were soon filled with a multitude of bishops, presbyters, deacons, readers, and exorcists. By a second edict, the magistrates were commanded to employ every method of severity which might reclaim them from their odious superstition and oblige them to return to the established worship of the gods. This rigorous order was extended by a subsequent edict to the whole body of Christians, who were exposed to a violent and general persecution. Instead of those salutary restraints, which had required the direct and solemn testimony of an accuser, it became the duty as well as the interest of the Imperial officers to discover, to pursue, and to torment the most obnoxious among the faithful. Heavy penalties were denounced against all who should presume to save a proscribed sectary from the just indignation of the gods, and of the emperors. Yet, notwithstanding the severity of this law, the virtuous courage of many of the Pagans, in concealing their friends or relations, affords an honourable proof that the rage of superstition had not extinguished in their minds the sentiments of nature and humanity.

Diocletian had no sooner published his edicts against the Christians than, as if he had been desirous of committing to other hands the work of persecution, he divested himself of the Imperial purple. The character and situation of his colleagues and successors sometimes urged them to enforce, and sometimes inclined them to suspend the execution of these rigorous laws; nor can we acquire a just and distinct idea of this important period of ecclesiastical history,

[89] *Lactantius confines the calamity to the conventiculum, with its congregation. Eusebius extends it to a whole city, and introduces something very like a regular siege. His ancient Latin translator, Rufinus, adds the important circumstance of the permission given to the inhabitants of retiring from thence. As Phrygia reached to the confines of Isauria, it is possible that the restless temper of those independent barbarians may have contributed to this misfortune.*

unless we separately consider the state of Christianity, in the different parts of the empire, during the space of ten years, which elapsed between the first edicts of Diocletian and the final peace of the church.

The mild and humane temper of Constantius was averse to the oppression of any part of his subjects. The principal offices of his palace were exercised by Christians. He loved their persons, esteemed their fidelity, and entertained not any dislike to their religious principles. But, as long as Constantius remained in the subordinate station of Cæsar, it was not in his power openly to reject the edicts of Diocletian or to disobey the commands of Maximian. His authority contributed, however, to alleviate the sufferings which he pitied and abhorred. He consented, with reluctance, to the ruin of the churches; but he ventured to protect the Christians themselves from the fury of the populace and from the rigour of the laws. The provinces of Gaul (under which we may probably include those of Britain) were indebted for the singular tranquillity which they enjoyed to the gentle interposition of their sovereign. But Datianus, the president or governor of Spain, actuated either by zeal or policy, chose rather to execute the public edicts of the emperors than to understand the secret intentions of Constantius; and it can scarcely be doubted that his provincial administration was stained with the blood of a few martyrs.[90] The elevation of Constantius to the supreme and independent dignity of Augustus gave a free scope to the exercise of his virtues, and the shortness of his reign did not prevent him from establishing a system of toleration, of which he left the precept and the example to his son Constantine. His fortunate son, from the first moment of his accession declaring himself the protector of the church, at length deserved the appellation of the first emperor who publicly professed and established the Christian religion. The motives of his conversion, as they may variously be deduced from benevolence, from policy, from conviction, or from remorse; and the progress of the revolution which, under his powerful influence, and that of his sons, rendered Christianity the reigning religion of the Roman empire, will form a very interesting and important chapter in the second volume of this history. At present it may be sufficient to observe that every victory of Constantine was productive of some relief or benefit to the church.

The provinces of Italy and Africa experienced a short but violent persecution. The rigorous edicts of Diocletian were strictly and cheerfully executed by his associate Maximian, who had long hated

[90] *Datianus is mentioned in Gruter's Inscriptions, as having determined the limits between the territories of Pax Julia, and those of Ebora, both cities in the southern part of Lusitania. If we recollect the neighbourhood of those places to Cape St. Vincent, we may suspect that the celebrated deacon and martyr of that name has been inaccurately assigned by Prudentius, &c. to Saragossa, or Valentia. Some critics are of opinion that the department of Constantius, as Cæsar, did not include Spain, which still continued under the immediate jurisdiction of Maximian.*

the Christians, and who delighted in acts of blood and violence. In the autumn of the first year of the persecution, the two emperors met at Rome to celebrate their triumph; several oppressive laws appear to have issued from their secret consultations, and the diligence of the magistrates was animated by the presence of their sovereigns. After Diocletian had divested himself of the purple, Italy and Africa were administered under the name of Severus, and were exposed, without defence, to the implacable resentment of his master Galerius. Among the martyrs of Rome, Adauctus deserves the notice of posterity. He was of a noble family in Italy, and had raised himself, through the successive honours of the palace, to the important office of treasurer of the private demesnes. Adauctus is the more remarkable for being the only person of rank and distinction who appears to have suffered death during the whole course of this general persecution.

The revolt of Maxentius immediately restored peace to the churches of Italy and Africa; and the same tyrant who oppressed every other class of his subjects showed himself just, humane, and even partial, towards the afflicted Christians. He depended on their gratitude and affection, and very naturally presumed that the injuries which they had suffered, and the dangers which they still apprehended from his most inveterate enemy, would secure the fidelity of a party already considerable by their numbers and opulence. Even the conduct of Maxentius towards the bishops of Rome and Carthage may be considered as the proof of his toleration, since it is probable that the most orthodox princes would adopt the same measures with regard to their established clergy. Marcellus, the former of those prelates, had thrown the capital into confusion by the severe penance which he imposed on a great number of Christians, who, during the late persecution, had renounced or dissembled their religion. The rage of faction broke out in frequent and violent seditions; the blood of the faithful was shed by each other's hands; and the exile of Marcellus, whose prudence seems to have been less eminent than his zeal, was found to be the only measure capable of restoring peace to the distracted church of Rome. The behaviour of Mensurius, bishop of Carthage, appears to have been still more reprehensible. A deacon of that city had published a libel against the emperor. The offender took refuge in the episcopal palace; and, though it was somewhat early to advance any claims of ecclesiastical immunities, the bishop refused to deliver him up to the officers of justice. For this treasonable resistance, Mensurius was summoned to court, and, instead of receiving a legal sentence of death or banishment, he was permitted, after a short examination, to return to his diocese. Such was the happy condition of the Christian subjects of Maxentius that, whenever they were desirous of procuring for their own use any bodies of martyrs, they were obliged to purchase them from the most distant provinces of the East. A story is related of Aglae, a Roman lady, descended from a consular family, and possessed of so ample an estate that it required the management of seventy-three stewards. Among these, Boniface was the favourite of his mistress; and, as Aglae mixed love with devotion, it is reported that he was admitted to share her bed. Her fortune enabled her to gratify the pious desire of obtaining some sacred relics from the East. She intrusted Boniface with a considerable sum of gold and a large quantity of aromatics; and her lover, attended by twelve horsemen and three covered chariots, undertook a remote pilgrimage, as far as Tarsus in Cilicia.

The sanguinary temper of Galerius, the first and principal author of the persecution, was formidable to those Christians whom their misfortunes had placed within the limits of his dominions; and it may fairly be presumed that many persons of a middle rank, who were not confined by the chains either of wealth or of poverty, very frequently deserted their native country, and sought a refuge in the milder climate of the West. As long as he commanded only the armies and provinces of Illyricum, he could with difficulty either find or make a considerable number of martyrs, in a warlike country, which had entertained the missionaries of the Gospel with more coldness and reluctance than any other part of the empire.[91] But, when Galerius had obtained the supreme power and the government of the East, he indulged in their fullest extent his zeal and cruelty, not only in the provinces of Thrace and Asia, which acknowledged his immediate jurisdiction, but in those of Syria, Palestine, and Egypt, where Maximin gratified his own inclination by yielding a rigorous obedience to the stern commands of his benefactor.[92] The frequent disappointments of his ambitious views, the experience of six years of persecution, and the salutary reflections which a lingering and painful distemper suggested to the mind of Galerius, at length convinced him that the most violent efforts of despotism are insufficient to extirpate a whole people or to subdue their religious prejudices. Desirous of repairing the mischief that he had occasioned, he published in his own name, and in those of Licinius and Constantine, a general edict, which, after a pompous

[91] *During the four first centuries there exist few traces of either bishops or bishoprics in the western Illyricum. It has been thought probable that the primate of Milan extended his jurisdiction over Sirmium, the capital of that great province.*

[92] *The eighth book of Eusebius, as well as the supplement concerning the martyrs of Palestine, principally relate to the persecution of Galerius and Maximin. The general lamentations with which Lactantius opens the fifth book of his Divine Institutions allude to their cruelty.*

recital of the Imperial titles, proceeded in the following manner:

"Among the important cares which have occupied our mind for the utility and preservation of the empire, it was our intention to correct and re-establish all things according to the ancient laws and public discipline of the Romans. We were particularly desirous of reclaiming, into the way of reason and nature, the deluded Christians, who had renounced the religion and ceremonies instituted by their fathers, and, presumptuously despising the practice of antiquity, had invented extravagant laws and opinions, according to the dictates of their fancy, and had collected a various society from the different provinces of our empire. The edicts which we have published to enforce the worship of the gods, having exposed many of the Christians to danger and distress, many having suffered death, and many more, who still persist in their impious folly, being left destitute of *any* public exercise of religion, we are disposed to extend to those unhappy men the effects of our wonted clemency. We permit them, therefore, freely to profess their private opinions, and to assemble in their conventicles without fear or molestation, provided always that they preserve a due respect to the established laws and government. By another rescript we shall signify our intentions to the judges and magistrates; and we hope that our indulgence will engage the Christians to offer up their prayers to the Deity whom they adore, for our safety and prosperity, for their own, and for that of the republic." It is not usually in the language of edicts and manifestoes that we should search for the real character or the secret motives of princes; but, as these were the words of a dying emperor, his situation, perhaps, may be admitted as a pledge of his sincerity.

When Galerius subscribed this edict of toleration, he was well assured that Licinius would readily comply with the inclinations of his friend and benefactor, and that any measures in favour of the Christians would obtain the approbation of Constantine. But the emperor would not venture to insert in the preamble the name of Maximin, whose consent was of the greatest importance, and who succeeded a few days afterwards to the provinces of Asia. In the first six months, however, of his new reign, Maximin affected to adopt the prudent counsels of his predecessor; and, though he never condescended to secure the tranquillity of the church by a public edict, Sabinus, his Prætorian præfect, addressed a circular letter to all the governors and magistrates of the provinces, expatiating on the Imperial clemency, acknowledging the invincible obstinacy of the Christians, and directing the officers of justice to cease their ineffectual prosecutions and to connive at the secret assemblies of those enthusiasts. In consequence of these orders, great numbers of Christians were released from prison or delivered from the mines. The confessors, singing hymns of triumph, returned into their own countries; and those who had yielded to the violence of the tempest solicited with tears of repentance their re-admission into the bosom of the church.

But this treacherous calm was of short duration; nor could the Christians of the East place any confidence in the character of their sovereign. Cruelty and superstition were the ruling passions of the soul of Maximin. The former suggested the means, the latter pointed out the objects, of persecution. The emperor was devoted to the worship of the gods, to the study of magic, and to the belief of oracles. The prophets or philosophers, whom he revered as the favourites of heaven, were frequently raised to the government of provinces and admitted into his most secret counsels. They easily convinced him that the Christians had been indebted for their victories to their regular discipline, and that the weakness of Polytheism had principally flowed from a want of union and subordination among the ministers of religion. A system of government was therefore instituted, which was evidently copied from the policy of the church. In all the great cities of the empire, the temples were repaired and beautified by the order of Maximin; and the officiating priests of the various deities were subjected to the authority of a superior pontiff, destined to oppose the bishop and to promote the cause of Paganism. These pontiffs acknowledged, in their turn, the supreme jurisdiction of the metropolitans or high priests of the province, who acted as the immediate vicegerents of the emperor himself. A white robe was the ensign of their dignity; and these new prelates were carefully selected from the most noble and opulent families. By the influence of the magistrates and of the sacerdotal order, a great number of dutiful addresses were obtained, particularly from the cities of Nicomedia, Antioch, and Tyre, which artfully represented the well-known intentions of the court as the general sense of the people; solicited the emperor to consult the laws of justice rather than the dictates of his clemency; expressed their abhorrence of the Christians; and humbly prayed that those impious sectaries might at least be excluded from the limits of their respective territories. The answer of Maximin to the address which he obtained from the citizens of Tyre is still extant. He praises their zeal and devotion in terms of the highest satisfaction, descants on the obstinate impiety of the Christians, and betrays, by the readiness with which he consents to their banishment, that he considered himself as receiving, rather than as conferring, an obligation. The priests, as well as the magistrates, were empowered to enforce the execution of his edicts, which were engraved on tables of brass; and, though it was recommended to them to avoid the effusion of blood, the most cruel and ignominious punishments were inflicted on the refractory Christians.

The Asiatic Christians had everything to dread from the severity of a bigoted monarch, who prepared his measures of violence with such deliberate policy. But a few months had scarcely elapsed before the edicts published by the two western emperors obliged Maximin to suspend the prosecution of his designs: the civil war, which he so rashly undertook against Licinius, employed all his attention; and the defeat and death of Maximin soon delivered the church from the last and most implacable of her enemies.[93]

In this general view of the persecution, which was first authorized by the edicts of Diocletian. I have purposely refrained from describing the particular sufferings and deaths of the Christian martyrs. It would have been an easy task, from the history of Eusebius, from the declamations of Lactantius, and from the most ancient acts, to collect a long series of horrid and disgustful pictures, and to fill many pages with racks and scourges, with iron hooks, and red-hot beds, and with all the variety of tortures which fire and steel, savage beasts and more savage executioners, could inflict on the human body. These melancholy scenes might be enlivened by a crowd of visions and miracles destined either to delay the death, to celebrate the triumph, or to discover the relics of those canonized saints who suffered for the name of Christ. But I cannot determine what I ought to transcribe, till I am satisfied how much I ought to believe. The gravest of the ecclesiastical historians, Eusebius himself, indirectly confesses that he has related whatever might redound to the glory, and that he has suppressed all that could tend to the disgrace, of religion.[94] Such an acknowledgment will naturally excite a suspicion that a writer who has so openly violated one of the fundamental laws of history has not paid a very strict regard to the observance of the other; and the suspicion will derive additional credit from the character of Eusebius, which was less tinctured with credulity, and more practised in the arts of courts, than that of almost any of his contemporaries. On some particular occasions, when the magistrates were exasperated by some personal motives of interest or re-

[93] *A few days before his death, he published a very ample edict of toleration, in which he imputes all the severities which the Christians suffered to the judges and governors, who had misunderstood his intentions.*

[94] *Such is the fair deduction from two remarkable passages in Eusebius. The prudence of the historian has exposed his own character to censure and suspicion. It is well known that he himself had been thrown into prison; and it was suggested that he had purchased his deliverance by some dishonourable compliance. The reproach was urged in his lifetime, and even in his presence, at the council of Tyre.*

sentment, when the zeal of the martyrs urged them to forget the rules of prudence, and perhaps of decency, to overturn the altars, to pour out imprecations against the emperors, or to strike the judge as he sat on his tribunal, it may be presumed that every mode of torture, which cruelty could invent or constancy could endure, was exhausted on those devoted victims.[95] Two circumstances, however, have been unwarily mentioned, which insinuate that the general treatment of the Christians who had been apprehended by the officers of justice was less intolerable than it is usually imagined to have been. 1. The confessors who were condemned to work in the mines were permitted, by the humanity or the negligence of their keepers, to build chapels and freely to profess their religion in the midst of those dreary habitations. 2. The bishops were obliged to check and to censure the forward zeal of the Christians, who voluntarily threw themselves into the hands of the magistrates. Some of these were persons oppressed by poverty and debts, who blindly sought to terminate a miserable existence by a glorious death. Others were allured by the hope that a short confinement would expiate the sins of a whole life; and others, again, were actuated by the less honourable motive of deriving a plentiful subsistence, and perhaps a considerable profit, from the alms which the charity of the faithful bestowed on the prisoners.[96] After the church had triumphed over all her enemies, the interest as well as vanity of the captives prompted them to magnify the merit of their respective suffering. A convenient distance of time or place gave an ample scope to the progress of fiction; and the frequent instances which might be alleged of holy martyrs, whose wounds had been instantly healed, whose strength had been renewed, and whose lost members had miraculously been restored, were extremely convenient for the purpose of removing every difficulty and of silencing every objection. The most extravagant legends, as they conduced to the honour of the church, were applauded by the credulous multitude, countenanced by the power of the clergy, and attested by the suspicious evidence of ecclesiastical history.

The vague descriptions of exile and imprisonment, of pain and torture, are so easily exaggerated or softened by the pencil of an artful orator that we are naturally induced to inquire into a fact of a more distinct and stubborn kind; the number of persons who suffered death, in consequence of the edicts published by Diocletian, his associates, and his successors. The recent legendaries record whole armies and cities, which were at once swept away by the un-

[95] *The ancient, and perhaps authentic, account of the sufferings of Tarachus and his companions is filled with strong expressions of resentment and contempt, which could not fail of irritating the magistrate.*

[96] *The controversy with the Donatists has reflected some, though perhaps a partial, light on the history of the African church.*

distinguishing rage of persecution. The more ancient writers content themselves with pouring out a liberal effusion of loose and tragical invectives, without condescending to ascertain the precise number of those persons who were permitted to seal with their blood their belief of the gospel. From the history of Eusebius, it may however be collected that only nine bishops were punished with death; and we are assured, by his particular enumeration of the martyrs of Palestine, that no more than ninety-two Christians were entitled to that honourable appellation.[97] As we are unacquainted with the degree of episcopal zeal and courage which prevailed at that time, it is not in our power to draw any useful inferences from the former of these facts; but the latter may serve to justify a very important and probable conclusion. According to the distribution of Roman provinces, Palestine may be considered as the sixteenth part of the Eastern empire;[98] and since there were some governors who, from a real or affected clemency, had preserved their hands unstained with the blood of the faithful, it is reasonable to believe that the country which had given birth to Christianity produced at least the sixteenth part of the martyrs who suffered death within the dominions of Galerius and Maximin; the whole might consequently amount to about fifteen hundred; a number which, if it is equally divided between the ten years of the persecution, will allow an annual consumption of one hundred and fifty martyrs. Allotting the same proportion to the provinces of Italy, Africa, and perhaps Spain, where, at the end of two or three years, the rigour of the penal laws was either suspended or abolished, the multitude of Christians in the Roman empire on whom a capital punishment was inflicted by a judicial sentence will be reduced to somewhat less than two thousand persons. Since it cannot be doubted that the Christians were more numerous, and their enemies more exasperated, in the time of Diocletian, than they had ever been in any former persecution, this probable and moderate computation may teach us to estimate the number of primitive saints and martyrs who sacrificed their lives for the important purpose of introducing Christianity into the world.

We shall conclude this chapter by a melancholy truth which obtrudes itself on the reluctant mind; that even admitting, without hesitation or inquiry, all that history has recorded, or devotion has feigned, on the subject of martyrdoms, it must still be acknowledged that the Christians, in the course of their intestine dissensions, have inflicted far greater severities on each other than they had ex-

[97] *Eusebius closes his narration by assuring us that these were the martyrdoms inflicted in Palestine during the whole course of the persecution. The fifth chapter of his eighth book, which relates to the province of Thebais in Egypt, may seem to contradict our moderate computation; but it will only lead us to admire the artful management of the historian. Choosing for the scene of the most exquisite cruelty the most remote and sequestered country of the Roman empire, he relates that in Thebais from ten to one hundred persons had frequently suffered martyrdom in the same day. But when he proceeds to mention his own journey into Egypt, his language insensibly becomes more cautious and moderate. Instead of a large, but definite number, he speaks of many Christians, and most artfully selects two ambiguous words, which may signify either what he had seen or what he had heard; either the expectation or the execution of the punishment. Having thus provided a secure evasion, he commits the equivocal passage to his readers and translators; justly conceiving that their piety would induce*

perienced from the zeal of infidels. During the ages of ignorance which followed the subversion of the Roman empire in the West, the bishops of the Imperial city extended their dominion over the laity as well as clergy of the Latin church. The fabric of superstition which they had erected, and which might long have defied the feeble efforts of reason, was at length assaulted by a crowd of daring fanatics, who, from the twelfth to the sixteenth century, assumed the popular character of reformers. The church of Rome defended by violence the empire which she had acquired by fraud; a system of peace and benevolence was soon disgraced by proscriptions, wars, massacres, and the institution of the holy office. And, as the reformers were animated by the love of civil, as well as of religious, freedom, the Catholic princes connected their own interest with that of the clergy, and enforced by fire and the sword the terrors of spiritual censures. In the Netherlands alone, more than one hundred thousand of the subjects of Charles the Fifth are said to have suffered by the hand of the executioner; and this extraordinary number is attested by Grotius, a man of genius and learning, who preserved his moderation amidst the fury of contending sects, and who composed the annals of his own age and country, at a time when the invention of printing had facilitated the means of intelligence and increased the danger of detection. If we are obliged to submit our belief to the authority of Grotius, it must be allowed that the number of Protestants who were executed in a single province and a single reign far exceeded that of the primitive martyrs in the space of three centuries and of the Roman empire. But, if the improbability of the fact itself should prevail over the weight of evidence; if Grotius should be convicted of exaggerating the merit and sufferings of the Reformers;[99] we shall be naturally led to inquire what confidence can be placed in the doubtful and imperfect monuments of ancient credulity; what degree of credit can be assigned to a courtly bishop, and a passionate declaimer, who, under the protection of Constantine, enjoyed the exclusive privilege of recording the persecutions inflicted on the Christians by the vanquished rivals, or disregarded predecessors of their gracious sovereign.

them to prefer the most favourable sense. There was perhaps some malice in the remark of Theodorus Metochita, that all who, like Eusebius, had been conversant with Egyptians delighted in an obscure and intricate style.

[98] *When Palestine was divided into three, the præfecture of the East contained forty-eight provinces. As the ancient distinctions of nations were long since abolished, the Romans distributed the provinces according to a general proportion of their extent and opulence.*

[99] *Fra Paolo reduces the number of Belgic martyrs to 50,000. In learning and moderation, Fra Paolo was not inferior to Grotius. The priority of time gives some advantage to the evidence of the former, which he loses on the other hand by the distance of Venice from the Netherlands.*

XVII

THE unfortunate Licinius was the last rival who opposed the greatness, and the last captive who adorned the triumph, of Constantine. After a tranquil and prosperous reign, the conqueror bequeathed to his family the inheritance of the Roman empire: a new capital, a new policy, and a new religion; and the innovations which he established have been embraced and consecrated by succeeding generations. The age of the great Constantine and his sons is filled with important events; but the historian must be oppressed by their number and variety, unless he diligently separates from each other the scenes which are connected only by the order of time. He will describe the political institutions that gave strength and stability to the empire, before he proceeds to relate the wars and revolutions which hastened its decline. He will adopt the division, unknown to the ancients, of civil and ecclesiastical affairs: the victory of the Christians and their intestine discord will supply copious and distinct materials both for edification and for scandal.

After the defeat and abdication of Licinius, his victorious rival proceeded to lay the foundations of a city destined to reign in future times the mistress of the East, and to survive the empire and religion of Constantine. The motives, whether of pride or of policy, which first induced Diocletian to withdraw himself from the ancient seat of government, had acquired additional weight by the example of his successors and the habits of forty years. Rome was insensibly confounded with the dependent kingdoms which had once acknowledged her supremacy; and the country of the Cæsars was viewed with cold indifference by a martial prince, born in the neighbourhood of the Danube, educated in the courts and armies of Asia, and invested with the purple by the legions of Britain. The Italians, who had received Constantine as their deliverer, submissively obeyed the edicts which he sometimes condescended to address to the senate and people of Rome; but they were seldom honoured with the presence of their new sovereign. During the vigour of his age, Constantine, according to the various exigencies of peace and war, moved with slow dignity, or with active diligence, along the frontiers of his extensive dominions; and was always prepared to take the field either against a foreign or a domestic enemy. But, as he gradually reached the summit of prosperity and the decline of life, he began to meditate the design of fixing in a more permanent station the strength as well as majesty of the throne. In the choice of an advantageous situation, he preferred the confines of Europe and Asia; to curb, with a powerful arm, the barbarians who dwelt between the Danube and the Tanais; to watch with an eye of jealousy the conduct of the Persian monarch, who indignantly supported the yoke of an ignominious treaty. With these views Diocletian had selected and embellished the residence of Nicomedia: but the memory of Diocletian was justly abhorred by the protector of the church; and Constantine was not insensible to the ambition of founding a city which might perpetuate the glory of his own name. During the late operations of the war against Licinius, he had sufficient opportunity to contemplate, both as a soldier and as a statesman, the incomparable position of Byzantium; and to observe how strongly it was guarded by nature against an hostile attack, whilst it was accessible on every side to the benefits of commercial intercourse. Many ages before Constantine, one of the most judicious historians of antiquity [1] had described the advantages of a situation, from whence a feeble colony of Greeks derived the command of the sea and the honours of a flourishing and independent republic.[2]

If we survey Byzantium in the extent which it acquired with the august name of Constantinople, the figure of the Imperial city may be represented under that of an unequal triangle. The obtuse point, which advances towards the east and the shores of Asia, meets and repels the waves of the Thracian Bosphorus. The northern side of the city is bounded by the harbour; and the southern is washed by the Propontis, or sea of Marmara. The basis of the triangle is opposed to the west, and terminates the continent of Europe. But the admirable form and division of the circumjacent land and water cannot, without a more ample explanation, be clearly or sufficiently understood.

The winding channel through which the waters of the Euxine

[1] *Polybius observes that the peace of the Byzantines was frequently disturbed, and the extent of their territory contracted, by the inroads of the wild Thracians.*

[2] *The navigator Byzas, who was styled the son of Neptune, founded the city 656 years before the Christian æra. His followers were drawn from Argos and Megara. Byzantium was afterwards rebuilt and fortified by the Spartan general Pausanias. With regard to the wars of the Byzantines against Philip, the Gauls, and the kings of Bithynia, we should trust none but the ancient writers who lived before the greatness of the Imperial city had excited a spirit of flattery and fiction.*

[3] *There are very few conjectures so happy as that of Le Clerc, who supposes that the harpies were only locusts. The Syriac or Phœnician name of those insects, their noisy flight, the stench and devastation which they occasion, and the north wind which drives them into the sea, all contribute to form this striking resemblance.*

[4] *The residence of Amycus was in Asia, between the old and the new castles, at a place called Laurus Insana. That of Phineus was in Europe, near the village of Mauromole and the Black Sea.*

[5] *The deception was occasioned by several pointed rocks, alternately covered and abandoned by the waves. At present there are two small islands, one towards either shore: that of Europe is distinguished by the column of Pompey.*

[6] *The ancients computed one hundred and twenty stadia, or fifteen Roman miles. They measured only from the new castles, but they carried the straits as far as the town of Chalcedon.*

[7] *Under the Greek empire these castles were used as state prisons,*

flow with a rapid and incessant course towards the Mediterranean received the appellation of Bosphorus, a name not less celebrated in the history than in the fables of antiquity. A crowd of temples and of votive altars, profusely scattered along its steep and woody banks, attested the unskilfulness, the terrors, and the devotion of the Grecian navigators who, after the example of the Argonauts, explored the dangers of the inhospitable Euxine. On these banks tradition long preserved the memory of the palace of Phineus, infested by the obscene harpies;[3] and of the sylvan reign of Amycus, who defied the son of Leda to the combat of the Cestus.[4] The straits of the Bosphorus are terminated by the Cyanean rocks, which, according to the description of the poets, had once floated on the face of the waters, and were destined by the gods to protect the entrance of the Euxine against the eye of profane curiosity.[5] From the Cyanean rocks to the point and harbour of Byzantium, the winding length of the Bosphorus extends about sixteen miles,[6] and its most ordinary breadth may be computed at about one mile and a half. The *new* castles of Europe and Asia are constructed, on either continent, upon the foundations of two celebrated temples, of Serapis and of Jupiter Urius. The *old* castles, a work of the Greek emperors, command the narrowest part of the channel, in a place where the opposite banks advance within five hundred paces of each other. These fortresses were restored and strengthened by Mahomet the Second, when he meditated the siege of Constantinople:[7] but the Turkish conqueror was most probably ignorant that, near two thousand years before his reign, Darius had chosen the same situation to connect the two continents by a bridge of boats.[8] At a small distance from the old castles we discover the little town of Chrysopolis, or Scutari, which may almost be considered as the Asiatic suburb of Constantinople. The Bosphorus, as it begins to open into the Propontis, passes between Byzantium and Chalcedon. The latter of those cities was built by the Greeks, a few years before the former; and the blindness of its founders, who overlooked the superior advantages of the opposite coast, has been stigmatized by a proverbial expression of contempt.

The harbour of Constantinople, which may be considered as an arm of the Bosphorus, obtained, in a very remote period, the denomination of the *Golden Horn*. The curve which it describes might be compared to the horn of a stag, or, as it should seem, with more propriety, to that of an ox.[9] The epithet of *golden* was expressive of the riches which every wind wafted from the most distant countries into the secure and capacious port of Constantinople. The river Lycus, formed by the conflux of two little streams, pours into the harbour a perpetual supply of fresh water, which serves to cleanse the bottom and to invite the periodical shoals of fish to seek their retreat in that convenient recess. As the vicissitudes of tides are scarcely felt in those seas, the constant depth of the harbour allows goods to be landed on the quays without the assistance of boats; and it has been observed that in many places the largest vessels may rest their prows against the houses, while their sterns are floating in the water. From the mouth of the Lycus to that of the harbour this arm of the Bosphorus is more than seven miles in length. The entrance is about five hundred yards broad, and a strong chain could be occasionally drawn across it, to guard the port and city from the attack of an hostile navy.[10]

Between the Bosphorus and the Hellespont, the shores of Europe and Asia receding on either side inclose the sea of Marmara, which was known to the ancients by the denomination of Propontis. The navigation from the issue of the Bosphorus to the entrance of the Hellespont is about one hundred and twenty miles. Those who steer their westward course through the middle of the Propontis may at once descry the high lands of Thrace and Bithynia, and never lose sight of the lofty summit of Mount Olympus, covered with eternal snows. They leave on the left a deep gulf, at the bottom of which Nicomedia was seated, the imperial residence of Diocletian; and they pass the small islands of Cyzicus and Proconnesus before they cast anchor at Gallipoli; where the sea, which separates Asia from Europe, is again contracted into a narrow channel.

The geographers who, with the most skilful accuracy, have surveyed the form and extent of the Hellespont, assign about sixty miles for the winding course, and about three miles for the ordinary breadth of those celebrated straits.[11] But the narrowest part of the channel is found to the northward of the old Turkish castles between the cities of Sestus and Abydus. It was here that the adventurous Leander braved the passage of the flood for the possession of his mistress. It was here likewise, in a place where the distance between the opposite banks cannot exceed five hundred paces, that Xerxes imposed a stupendous bridge of boats, for the purpose of transporting into Europe an hundred and seventy myriads of barbarians.[12] A sea contracted within such narrow limits may seem but ill to deserve the singular epithet of *broad,* which Homer, as well as Orpheus, has frequently bestowed on the Hellespont. But our ideas of greatness are of a relative nature: the traveller, and espe-

under the tremendous name of Lethe, or towers of oblivion.

[8] *Darius engraved in Greek and Assyrian letters on two marble columns the names of his subject nations, and the amazing numbers of his land and sea forces. The Byzantines afterwards transported these columns into the city, and used them for the altars of their tutelar deities.*

[9] *Most of the antlers are now broke off; or, to speak less figuratively, most of the recesses of the harbour are filled up.*

[10] *The chain was drawn from the Acropolis near the modern Kiosk to the tower of Galata, and was supported at convenient distances by large wooden piles.*

[11] *The stadia employed by Herodotus in the description of the Euxine, the Bosphorus, &c., must undoubtedly be all of the same species; but it seems impossible to reconcile them either with truth or with each other.*

[12] *See the seventh book of Herodotus, who has erected an elegant trophy to his own fame and to that of his country. The review appears to have been made with tolerable accuracy; but the*

vanity, first of the Persians and afterwards of the Greeks, was interested to magnify the armament and the victory. I should much doubt whether the invaders have ever outnumbered the men of any country which they attacked.

[13] *Demetrius of Scepsis wrote sixty books on thirty lines of Homer's Catalogue. The Thirteenth Book of Strabo is sufficient for our curiosity.*

[14] *The disposition of the ships which were drawn upon dry land, and the posts of Ajax and Achilles, are very clearly described by Homer.*

cially the poet, who sailed along the Hellespont, who pursued the windings of the stream, and contemplated the rural scenery, which appeared on every side to terminate the prospect, insensibly lost the remembrance of the sea; and his fancy painted those celebrated straits with all the attributes of a mighty river flowing with a swift current, in the midst of a woody and inland country, and at length, through a wide mouth, discharging itself into the Ægean or Archipelago. Ancient Troy,[13] seated on an eminence at the foot of Mount Ida, overlooked the mouth of the Hellespont, which scarcely received an accession of waters from the tribute of those immortal rivulets Simois and Scamander. The Grecian camp had stretched twelve miles along the shore from the Sigæan to the Rhœtean promontory; and the flanks of the army were guarded by the bravest chiefs who fought under the banners of Agamemnon. The first of those promontories was occupied by Achilles with his invincible Myrmidons, and the dauntless Ajax pitched his tents on the other. After Ajax had fallen a sacrifice to his disappointed pride and to the ingratitude of the Greeks, his sepulchre was erected on the ground where he had defended the navy against the rage of Jove and of Hector; and the citizens of the rising town of Rhœteum celebrated his memory with divine honours.[14] Before Constantine gave a just preference to the situation of Byzantium, he had conceived the design of erecting the seat of empire on this celebrated spot, from whence the Romans derived their fabulous origin. The extensive plain which lies below ancient Troy, towards the Rhœtean promontory and the tomb of Ajax, was first chosen for his new capital; and, though the undertaking was soon relinquished, the stately remains of unfinished walls and towers attracted the notice of all who sailed through the straits of the Hellespont.

We are at present qualified to view the advantageous position of Constantinople; which appears to have been formed by Nature for the centre and capital of a great monarchy. Situated in the forty-first degree of latitude, the Imperial city commanded, from her seven hills, the opposite shores of Europe and Asia; the climate was healthy and temperate, the soil fertile, the harbour secure and capacious; and the approach on the side of the continent was of small extent and easy defence. The Bosphorus and Hellespont may be considered as the two gates of Constantinople; and the prince who possessed those important passages could always shut them against a naval enemy and open them to the fleets of commerce. The preservation of the eastern provinces may, in some degree, be ascribed to the policy of Constantine, as the barbarians of the Euxine, who in the preceding age had poured their armaments into the heart of the Mediterranean, soon desisted from the exercise of piracy, and despaired of forcing this insurmountable barrier. When the gates of the Hellespont and Bosphorus were shut, the capital still enjoyed, within their spacious inclosure, every production which could supply the wants, or gratify the luxury, of its numerous inhabitants. The sea-coast of Thrace and Bithynia, which languish under the weight of Turkish oppression, still exhibits a rich prospect of vineyards, of gardens, and of plentiful harvests; and the Propontis has ever been renowned for an inexhaustible store of the most exquisite fish, that are taken in their stated seasons without skill and almost without labour.[15] But, when the passages of the straits were thrown open for trade, they alternately admitted the natural and artificial riches of the north and south, of the Euxine, and of the Mediterranean. Whatever rude commodities were collected in the forests of Germany and Scythia, as far as the sources of the Tanais and the Borysthenes; whatsoever was manufactured by the skill of Europe or Asia; the corn of Egypt, and the gems and spices of the farthest India, were brought by the varying winds into the port of Constantinople, which, for many ages, attracted the commerce of the ancient world.

The prospect of beauty, of safety, and of wealth, united in a single spot, was sufficient to justify the choice of Constantine. But, as some decent mixture of prodigy and fable has, in every age, been supposed to reflect a becoming majesty on the origin of great cities, the emperor was desirous of ascribing his resolution, not so much to the uncertain counsels of human policy, as to the infallible and eternal decrees of divine wisdom. In one of his laws he has been careful to instruct posterity that, in obedience to the commands of God, he laid the everlasting foundations of Constantinople: and, though he has not condescended to relate in what manner the celestial inspiration was communicated to his mind, the defect of his modest silence has been liberally supplied by the ingenuity of succeeding writers, who describe the nocturnal vision which appeared to the fancy of Constantine, as he slept within the walls of Byzantium. The tutelar genius of the city, a venerable matron sinking under the weight of years and infirmities, was suddenly transformed into a blooming maid, whom his own hands adorned with all the symbols of imperial greatness.[16] The monarch awoke, interpreted the auspicious omen, and obeyed, without hesitation, the will of heaven. The day

[15] *Among a variety of different species, the Pelamides, a sort of Thunnies, were the most celebrated. We may learn from Polybius, Strabo, and Tacitus that the profits of the fishery constituted the principal revenue of Byzantium.*

[16] *The Greeks, Theophanes, Cedrenus, and the author of the Alexandrian Chronicle, confine themselves to vague and general expressions. For a more particular account of the vision, we are obliged to have recourse to such Latin writers as William of Malmesbury.*

[17] *Among other ceremonies, a large hole, which had been dug for that purpose, was filled up with handfuls of earth, which each of the settlers brought from the place of his birth, and thus adopted his new country.*

[18] *The new wall of Theodosius was constructed in the year 413. In 447 it was thrown down by an earthquake, and rebuilt in three months by the diligence of the præfect Cyrus. The suburb of the Blachernæ was first taken into the city in the reign of Heraclius.*

[19] *The measurement is expressed in the Notitia by 14,075 feet. It is reasonable to suppose that these were Greek feet; the proportion of which has been ingeniously determined by M. d'Anville. He compares the 180 feet with the 78 Hashemite cubits which in different writers are assigned for the height of St. Sophia. Each of these cubits was equal to 27 French inches.*

[20] *The accurate Thévenot walked in one hour and three quarters round two of the sides of the triangle, from the Kiosk of the Seraglio to the seven towers. D'Anville examines with care, and receives with confidence, this decisive testimony,*

which gave birth to a city or colony was celebrated by the Romans with such ceremonies as had been ordained by a generous superstition;[17] and, though Constantine might omit some rites which savoured too strongly of their Pagan origin, yet he was anxious to leave a deep impression of hope and respect on the minds of the spectators. On foot, with a lance in his hand, the emperor himself led the solemn procession; and directed the line which was traced as the boundary of the destined capital; till the growing circumference was observed with astonishment by the assistants, who, at length, ventured to observe that he had already exceeded the most ample measure of a great city. "I shall still advance," replied Constantine, "till HE, the invisible guide who marches before me, thinks proper to stop." Without presuming to investigate the nature or motives of this extraordinary conductor, we shall content ourselves with the more humble task of describing the extent and limits of Constantinople.

In the actual state of the city, the palace and gardens of the Seraglio occupy the eastern promontory, the first of the seven hills, and cover about one hundred and fifty acres of our own measure. The seat of Turkish jealousy and despotism is erected on the foundations of a Grecian republic; but it may be supposed that the Byzantines were tempted by the conveniency of the harbour to extend their habitations on that side beyond the modern limits of the Seraglio. The new walls of Constantine stretched from the port to the Propontis across the enlarged breadth of the triangle, at the distance of fifteen stadia from the ancient fortification; and with the city of Byzantium they inclosed five of the seven hills, which, to the eyes of those who approach Constantinople, appear to rise above each other in beautiful order. About a century after the death of the founder, the new building, extending on one side up the harbour, and on the other along the Propontis, already covered the narrow ridge of the sixth, and the broad summit of the seventh, hill. The necessity of protecting those suburbs from the incessant inroads of the barbarians engaged the younger Theodosius to surround his capital with an adequate and permanent enclosure of walls.[18] From the eastern promontory to the golden gate, the extreme length of Constantinople was about three Roman miles;[19] the circumference measured between ten and eleven; and the surface might be computed as equal to about two thousand English acres. It is impossible to justify the vain and credulous exaggerations of modern travellers, who have sometimes stretched the limits of Constantinople over the adjacent villages of the European, and even of the Asiatic, coast.[20] But the suburbs of Pera and Galata, though situate beyond the harbour, may deserve to be considered as a part of the city;[21] and this addition may perhaps authorize the measure of a Byzantine historian, who assigns sixteen Greek (about fourteen Roman) miles for the circumference of his native city.[22] Such an extent may seem not worthy of an imperial residence. Yet Constantinople must yield to Babylon and Thebes,[23] to ancient Rome, to London, and even to Paris.[24]

The master of the Roman world, who aspired to erect an eternal monument of the glories of his reign, could employ in the prosecution of that great work the wealth, the labour, and all that yet remained of the genius, of obedient millions. Some estimate may be formed of the expense bestowed with imperial liberality on the foundation of Constantinople, by the allowance of about two millions five hundred thousand pounds for the construction of the walls, the porticoes, and the aqueducts.[25] The forests that overshadowed the shores of the Euxine, and the celebrated quarries of white marble in the little island of Proconnesus, supplied an inexhaustible stock of materials, ready to be conveyed, by the convenience of a short water-carriage, to the harbour of Byzantium. A multitude of labourers and artificers urged the conclusion of the work with incessant toil: but the impatience of Constantine soon discovered that, in the decline of the arts, the skill as well as numbers of his architects bore a very unequal proportion to the greatness of his designs. The magistrates of the most distant provinces were therefore directed to institute schools, to appoint professors, and by the hopes of rewards and privileges, to engage in the study and practice of architecture a sufficient number of ingenious youths, who had received a liberal education.[26] The buildings of the new city were executed by such artificers as the reign of Constantine could afford; but they were decorated by the hands of the most celebrated masters of the age of Pericles and Alexander. To revive the genius of Phidias and Lysippus surpassed indeed the power of a Roman emperor; but the immortal productions which they had bequeathed to posterity were exposed without defence to the rapacious vanity of a despot. By his commands the cities of Greece and Asia were despoiled of their most valuable ornaments. The trophies of memorable wars, the objects of religious veneration, the most finished statues of the gods and heroes, of the sages and poets, of ancient times, contributed to the splendid triumph of Constantinople; and gave occasion to the

which gives a circumference of ten or twelve miles. The extravagant computation of Tournefort of thirty-four or thirty miles, without including Scutari, is a strange departure from his usual character.

[21] The sycæ, or fig trees, formed the thirteenth region, and were very much embellished by Justinian. It has since borne the names of Pera and Galata. The etymology of the former is obvious; that of the latter is unknown.

[22] One hundred and eleven stadia, which may be translated into modern Greek miles each of seven stadia, or 660, sometimes only 600, French toises.

[23] When the ancient texts which describe the size of Babylon and Thebes are settled, the exaggerations reduced, and the measures ascertained, we find that those famous cities filled the great but not incredible circumference of about twenty-five or thirty miles.

[24] If we divide Constantinople and Paris into equal squares of 50 French toises, the former contains 850, and the latter 1160 of those divisions.

[25] *Six hundred cente-
naries, or sixty thousand
pounds weight of gold.
This sum is taken from
Codinus; but, unless
that contemptible author
had derived his infor-
mation from some purer
sources, he would prob-
ably have been un-
acquainted with so ob-
solete a mode of reck-
oning.*

[26] *This law is dated in
the year 334, and was ad-
dressed to the præfect of
Italy, whose jurisdiction
extended over Africa.
The commentary of
Godefroy on the title
deserves to be consulted.*

[27] *He describes the
statue, or rather bust, of
Homer with a degree of
taste which plainly in-
dicates that Cedrenus
copied the style of a more
fortunate age.*

[28] *The guardians of the
most holy relics would
rejoice if they were able
to produce such a chain
of evidence as may be
alleged on this occasion.
1. The original conse-
cration of the tripod and
pillar in the temple of
Delphi may be proved
from Herodotus and
Pausanias. 2. The Pagan
Zosimus agrees with the
three ecclesiastical his-
torians, Eusebius, Soc-
rates, and Sozomen, that
the sacred ornaments of
the temple of Delphi*

remark of the historian Cedrenus,[27] who observes, with some enthusiasm, that nothing seemed wanting except the souls of the illustrious men whom those admirable monuments were intended to
represent. But it is not in the city of Constantine, nor in the declining period of an empire when the human mind was depressed by
civil and religious slavery, that we should seek for the souls of
Homer and of Demosthenes.

During the siege of Byzantium, the conqueror had pitched his
tent on the commanding eminence of the second hill. To perpetuate
the memory of his success, he chose the same advantageous position
for the principal Forum; which appears to have been of a circular,
or rather elliptical form. The two opposite entrances formed triumphal arches; the porticoes, which inclosed it on every side, were
filled with statues; and the centre of the Forum was occupied by a
lofty column, of which a mutilated fragment is now degraded by
the appellation of the *burnt pillar*. This column was erected on a
pedestal of white marble twenty feet high; and was composed of
ten pieces of porphyry, each of which measured above ten feet in
height and about thirty-three in circumference. On the summit of
the pillar, above one hundred and twenty feet from the ground,
stood the colossal statue of Apollo. It was of bronze, had been
transported either from Athens or from a town of Phrygia, and was
supposed to be the work of Phidias. The artist had represented the
god of day, or, as it was afterwards interpreted, the emperor Constantine himself, with a sceptre in his right hand, the globe of the
world in his left, and a crown of rays glittering on his head. The
Circus, or Hippodrome, was a stately building about four hundred
paces in length and one hundred in breadth. The space between the
two *metæ* or goals was filled with statues and obelisks; and we may
still remark a very singular fragment of antiquity; the bodies of
three serpents, twisted into one pillar of brass. Their triple heads had
once supported the golden tripod which, after the defeat of Xerxes,
was consecrated in the temple of Delphi by the victorious Greeks.[28]
The beauty of the Hippodrome has been long since defaced by
the rude hands of the Turkish conquerors; but, under the similar
appellation of Atmeidan, it still serves as a place of exercise for their
horses. From the throne, whence the emperor viewed the Circen-
sian games, a winding staircase [29] descended to the palace; a magnificent edifice, which scarcely yielded to the residence of Rome itself, and which, together with the dependent courts, gardens, and
porticoes, covered a considerable extent of ground upon the banks of

the Propontis between the Hippodrome and the church of St. Sophia.[30] We might likewise celebrate the baths, which still retained the name of Zeuxippus, after they had been enriched, by the munificence of Constantine, with lofty columns, various marbles, and above threescore statues of bronze.[31] But we should deviate from the design of this history, if we attempted minutely to describe the different buildings or quarters of the city. It may be sufficient to observe that whatever could adorn the dignity of a great capital, or contribute to the benefit or pleasure of its numerous inhabitants, was contained within the walls of Constantinople. A particular description, composed about a century after its foundation, enumerates a capitol or school of learning, a circus, two theatres, eight public, and one hundred and fifty-three private, baths, fifty-two porticoes, five granaries, eight aqueducts or reservoirs of water, four spacious halls for the meetings of the senate or courts of justice, fourteen churches, fourteen palaces, and four thousand three hundred and eighty-eight houses, which, for their size or beauty, deserved to be distinguished from the multitude of plebeian habitations.[32]

The populousness of his favoured city was the next and most serious object of the attention of its founder. In the dark ages which succeeded the translation of the empire, the remote and the immediate consequences of that memorable event were strangely confounded by the vanity of the Greeks and the credulity of the Latins.[33] It was asserted and believed that all the noble families of Rome, the senate, and the equestrian order, with their innumerable attendants, had followed their emperor to the banks of the Propontis; that a spurious race of strangers and plebeians was left to possess the solitude of the ancient capital; and that the lands of Italy, long since converted into gardens, were at once deprived of cultivation and inhabitants. In the course of this history, such exaggerations will be reduced to their just value: yet, since the growth of Constantinople cannot be ascribed to the general increase of mankind and of industry, it must be admitted that this artificial colony was raised at the expense of the ancient cities of the empire. Many opulent senators of Rome, and of the Eastern provinces, were probably invited by Constantine to adopt for their country the fortunate spot which he had chosen for his own residence. The invitations of a master are scarcely to be distinguished from commands; and the liberality of the emperor obtained a ready and cheerful obedience. He bestowed on his favourites the palaces which he had built in the several quarters of the city, assigned them lands and pensions for the support of

were removed to Constantinople by the order of Constantine; and among these the serpentine pillar of the Hippodrome is particularly mentioned. 3. All the European travellers who have visited Constantinople, from Buondelmonte to Pocock, describe it in the same place, and almost in the same manner; the differences between them are occasioned only by the injuries which it has sustained from the Turks. Mahomet the Second broke the underjaw of one of the serpents with a stroke of his battle-axe.

[29] The Latin name Cochlea was adopted by the Greeks, and very frequently occurs in the Byzantine history.

[30] There are three topographical points which indicate the situation of the palace. 1. The staircase, which connected it with the Hippodrome or Atmeidan. 2. A small artificial port on the Propontis, from whence there was an easy ascent, by a flight of marble steps, to the gardens of the palace. 3. The Augusteum was a spacious court, one side of which was occupied by the front of the palace, and another by the church of St. Sophia.

[31] *Zeuxippus was an epithet of Jupiter, and the baths were a part of old Byzantium. The difficulty of assigning their true situation has not been felt by Ducange. History seems to connect them with St. Sophia and the palace; but the original plan, inserted in Banduri, places them on the other side of the city, near the harbour.*

[32] *Rome only reckoned 1780 large houses,* domus; *but the word must have had a more dignified signification. No insulæ are mentioned at Constantinople. The old capital consisted of 424 streets, the new of 322.*

[33] *The modern Greeks have strangely disfigured the antiquities of Constantinople. We might excuse the errors of the Turkish or Arabian writers; but it is somewhat astonishing that the Greeks, who had access to the authentic materials preserved in their own language, should prefer fiction to truth and loose tradition to genuine history. In a single page of Codinus we may detect twelve unpardonable mistakes: the reconciliation of Severus and Niger, the marriage of their son and daughter, the siege of Byzantium*

their dignity,[34] and alienated the demesnes of Pontus and Asia, to grant hereditary estates by the easy tenure of maintaining a house in the capital. But these encouragements and obligations soon became superfluous, and were gradually abolished. Wherever the seat of government is fixed, a considerable part of the public revenue will be expended by the prince himself, by his ministers, by the officers of justice, and by the domestics of the palace. The most wealthy of the provincials will be attracted by the powerful motives of interest and duty, of amusement and curiosity. A third and more numerous class of inhabitants will insensibly be formed, of servants, of artificers, and of merchants, who derive their subsistence from their own labour and from the wants or luxury of the superior ranks. In less than a century, Constantinople disputed with Rome itself the pre-eminence of riches and numbers. New piles of buildings, crowded together with too little regard to health or convenience, scarcely allowed the intervals of narrow streets for the perpetual throng of men, of horses, and of carriages. The allotted space of ground was insufficient to contain the increasing people; and the additional foundations, which, on either side, were advanced into the sea, might alone have composed a very considerable city.

The frequent and regular distributions of wine and oil, of corn or bread, of money or provisions, had almost exempted the poorer citizens of Rome from the necessity of labour. The magnificence of the first Cæsars was in some measure imitated by the founder of Constantinople:[35] but his liberality, however it might excite the applause of the people, has incurred the censure of posterity. A nation of legislators and conquerors might assert their claim to the harvests of Africa, which had been purchased with their blood; and it was artfully contrived by Augustus that, in the enjoyment of plenty, the Romans should lose the memory of freedom. But the prodigality of Constantine could not be excused by any consideration either of public or private interest; and the annual tribute of corn imposed upon Egypt for the benefit of his new capital was applied to feed a lazy and indolent populace, at the expense of the husbandmen of an industrious province. Some other regulations of this emperor are less liable to blame, but they are less deserving of notice. He divided Constantinople into fourteen regions or quarters,[36] dignified the public council with the appellation of Senate,[37] communicated to the citizens the privileges of Italy, and bestowed on the rising city the title of Colony, the first and most favoured daughter of ancient Rome. The venerable parent still maintained the legal and acknowledged supremacy which was due to her age, to her dignity, and to the remembrance of her former greatness.[38]

As Constantine urged the progress of the work with the impatience of a lover, the walls, the porticoes, and the principal edifices, were completed in a few years, or, according to another account, in a few months; but this extraordinary diligence should excite the less admiration, since many of the buildings were finished in so hasty and imperfect a manner that, under the succeeding reign, they were preserved with difficulty from impending ruin. But, while they displayed the vigour and freshness of youth, the founder prepared to celebrate the dedication of his city.[39] The games and largesses which crowned the pomp of this memorable festival may easily be supposed; but there is one circumstance of a more singular and permanent nature, which ought not entirely to be overlooked. As often as the birthday of the city returned, the statue of Constantine, framed, by his order, of gilt wood, and bearing in its right hand a small image of the genius of the place, was erected on a triumphal car. The guards, carrying white tapers, and clothed in their richest apparel, accompanied the solemn procession as it moved through the Hippodrome. When it was opposite to the throne of the reigning emperor, he rose from his seat, and with grateful reverence adored the memory of his predecessor.[40] At the festival of the dedication, an edict, engraved on a column of marble, bestowed the title of SECOND or NEW ROME on the city of Constantine. But the name of Constantinople[41] has prevailed over that honourable epithet; and, after the revolution of fourteen centuries, still perpetuates the fame of its author.[42]

The foundation of a new capital is naturally connected with the establishment of a new form of civil and military administration. The distinct view of the complicated system of policy, introduced by Diocletian, improved by Constantine, and completed by his immediate successors, may not only amuse the fancy by the singular picture of a great empire, but will tend to illustrate the secret and internal causes of its rapid decay. In the pursuit of any remarkable institution, we may be frequently led into the more early or the more recent times of the Roman history; but the proper limits of this inquiry will be included within a period of about one hundred and thirty years, from the accession of Constantine to the publication of the Theodosian Code;[43] from which, as well as from the *Notitia* of the east and west,[44] we derive the most copious and authentic information of the state of the empire. This variety of objects will

by the Macedonians, the invasion of the Gauls, which recalled Severus to Rome, the sixty years which elapsed from his death to the foundation of Constantinople, &c.

[34] *If we could credit Codinus, Constantine built houses for the senators on the exact model of their Roman palaces, and gratified them, as well as himself, with the pleasure of an agreeable surprise; but the whole story is full of fictions and inconsistencies.*

[35] *It appears by Socrates, that the daily allowances of the city consisted of eight myriads of* σίτου, *which we may either translate with Valesius by the words modii of corn or consider as expressive of the number of loaves of bread.*

[36] *The regions of Constantinople are mentioned in the code of Justinian, and particularly described in the Notitia of the younger Theodosius; but, as the four last of them are not included within the wall of Constantine, it may be doubted whether this division of the city should be referred to the founder.*

[37] *The senators of old Rome were styled* Clarissimi. *From the 11th epistle of Julian, it*

should seem that the place of senator was considered as a burthen rather than as an honour; but the Abbé de la Bléterie has shown that this epistle could not relate to Constantinople. Might we not read, instead of the celebrated name of Βυζαντίοις, *the obscure but more probable word* Βισανθήνοις? *Bisanthe or Rhœdestus, now Rhodosto, was a small maritime city of Thrace.*

[38] *Julian celebrates Constantinople as not less superior to all other cities than she was inferior to Rome itself. His learned commentator, Spanheim, justifies this language by several parallel and contemporary instances. Zosimus, as well as Socrates and Sozomen, flourished after the division of the empire between the two sons of Theodosius, which established a perfect equality between the old and the new capital.*

[39] *Cedrenus and Zonaras, faithful to the mode of superstition which prevailed in their own times, assure us that Constantinople was consecrated to the Virgin Mother of God.*

[40] *The earliest and most complete account of this extraordinary ceremony may be found in the*

suspend, for some time, the course of the narrative; but the interruption will be censured only by those readers who are insensible to the importance of laws and manners, while they peruse, with eager curiosity, the transient intrigues of a court, or the accidental event of a battle.

The manly pride of the Romans, content with substantial power, had left to the vanity of the east the forms and ceremonies of ostentatious greatness. But when they lost even the semblance of those virtues which were derived from their ancient freedom, the simplicity of Roman manners was insensibly corrupted by the stately affectation of the courts of Asia. The distinctions of personal merit and influence, so conspicuous in a republic, so feeble and obscure under a monarchy, were abolished by the despotism of the emperors; who substituted in their room a severe subordination of rank and office, from the titled slaves, who were seated on the steps of the throne, to the meanest instruments of arbitrary power. This multitude of abject dependents was interested in the support of the actual government, from the dread of a revolution, which might at once confound their hopes and intercept the reward of their services. In this divine hierarchy (for such it is frequently styled) every rank was marked with the most scrupulous exactness, and its dignity was displayed in a variety of trifling and solemn ceremonies, which it was a study to learn and a sacrilege to neglect.[45] The purity of the Latin language was debased by adopting, in the intercourse of pride and flattery, a profusion of epithets, which Tully would scarcely have understood, and which Augustus would have rejected with indignation. The principal officers of the empire were saluted, even by the sovereign himself, with the deceitful titles of your *Sincerity,* your *Gravity,* your *Excellency,* your *Eminence,* your *sublime* and *wonderful Magnitude,* your *illustrious and magnificent Highness.* The codicils or patents of their office were curiously emblazoned with such emblems as were best adapted to explain its nature and high dignity; the image or portrait of the reigning emperors; a triumphal car; the book of mandates placed on a table, covered with a rich carpet, and illuminated by four tapers; the allegorical figures of the provinces which they governed; or the appellation and standards of the troops whom they commanded. Some of these official ensigns were really exhibited in their hall of audience; others preceded their pompous march whenever they appeared in public; and every circumstance of their demeanour, their dress, their ornaments, and their train, was calculated to inspire a deep reverence

466

for the representatives of supreme majesty. By a philosophic observer, the system of the Roman government might have been mistaken for a splendid theatre, filled with players of every character and degree, who repeated the language, and imitated the passions, of their original model.

All the magistrates of sufficient importance to find a place in the general state of the empire were accurately divided into three classes. 1. The *Illustrious*. 2. The *Spectabiles*, or *Respectable*: And, 3. The *Clarissimi;* whom we may translate by the word *Honourable*. In the times of Roman simplicity, the last-mentioned epithet was used only as a vague expression of deference, till it became at length the peculiar and appropriated title of all who were members of the senate,[46] and consequently of all who, from that venerable body, were selected to govern the provinces. The vanity of those who, from their rank and office, might claim a superior distinction above the rest of the senatorial order was long afterwards indulged with the new appellation of *Respectable;* but the title of *Illustrious* was always reserved to some eminent personages who were obeyed or reverenced by the two subordinate classes. It was communicated only, I. To the consuls and patricians; II. To the Prætorian præfects, with the præfects of Rome and Constantinople; III. To the masters general of the cavalry and the infantry; and, IV. To the seven ministers of the palace, who exercised their *sacred* functions about the person of the emperor.[47] Among those illustrious magistrates who were esteemed co-ordinate with each other, the seniority of appointment gave place to the union of dignities.[48] By the expedient of honorary codicils, the emperors, who were fond of multiplying their favours, might sometimes gratify the vanity, though not the ambition, of impatient courtiers.

I. As long as the Roman consuls were the first magistrates of a free state, they derived their right to power from the choice of the people. As long as the emperors condescended to disguise the servitude which they imposed, the consuls were still elected by the real or apparent suffrage of the senate. From the reign of Diocletian, even these vestiges of liberty were abolished, and the successful candidates who were invested with the annual honours of the consulship affected to deplore the humiliating condition of their predecessors. The Scipios and the Catos had been reduced to solicit the votes of plebeians, to pass through the tedious and expensive forms of a popular election, and to expose their dignity to the shame of a public refusal; while their own happier fate had reserved them for an age

Alexandrian Chronicle, Tillemont, and the other friends of Constantine, who are offended with the air of Paganism which seems unworthy of a Christian Prince, had a right to consider it as doubtful, but they were not authorized to omit the mention of it.

[41] *The name of Constantinople is extant on the medals of Constantine.*

[42] *The lively Fontenelle affects to deride the vanity of human ambition, and seems to triumph in the disappointment of Constantine, whose immortal name is now lost in the vulgar appellation of Istambol, a Turkish corruption of* εἰς τὴν πόλιν. *Yet the original name is still preserved, 1. By the nations of Europe. 2. By the modern Greeks. 3. By the Arabs, whose writings are diffused over the wide extent of their conquests in Asia and Africa. 4. By the more learned Turks, and by the emperor himself in his public mandates.*

[43] *The Theodosian Code was promulgated* A. D. *438.*

[44] *Pancirolus, in his elaborate Commentary, assigns to the Notitia a date almost similar to that of the Theodosian Code:*

but his proofs, or rather conjectures, are extremely feeble. I should be rather inclined to place this useful work between the final division of the empire (A.D. 395), and the successful invasion of Gaul by the Barbarians (A.D. 407).

[45] *The emperor Gratian, after confirming a law of precedency published by Valentinian, the father of his* Divinity, *thus continues: Siquis igitur indebitum sibi locum usurpaverit, nulla se ignoratione defendat; sitque plane sacrilegii reus, qui divina præcepta neglexerit.*

[46] *In the Pandects, which may be referred to the reigns of the Antonines,* Clarissimus *is the ordinary and legal title of a senator.*

[47] *I have not taken any notice of the two inferior ranks,* Perfectissimus *and* Egregius, *which were given to many persons who were not raised to the senatorial dignity.*

[48] *The rules of precedency are ascertained with the most minute accuracy by the emperors and illustrated with equal prolixity by their learned interpreter.*

[49] *Ausonius basely expatiates on this unworthy topic, which is managed*

and government in which the rewards of virtue were assigned by the unerring wisdom of a gracious sovereign.[49] In the epistles which the emperor addressed to the two consuls elect, it was declared that they were created by his sole authority. Their names and portraits, engraved on gilt tablets of ivory, were dispersed over the empire as presents to the provinces, the cities, the magistrates, the senate, and the people. Their solemn inauguration was performed at the place of the Imperial residence; and, during a period of one hundred and twenty years, Rome was constantly deprived of the presence of her ancient magistrates.[50] On the morning of the first of January, the consuls assumed the ensigns of their dignity. Their dress was a robe of purple, embroidered in silk and gold, and sometimes ornamented with costly gems. On this solemn occasion they were attended by the most eminent officers of the state and army, in the habit of senators; and the useless fasces, armed with the once formidable axes, were borne before them by the lictors. The procession moved from the palace to the Forum, or principal square of the city; where the consuls ascended their tribunal, and seated themselves in the curule chairs, which were framed after the fashion of ancient times. They immediately exercised an act of jurisdiction, by the manumission of a slave, who was brought before them for that purpose; and the ceremony was intended to represent the celebrated action of the elder Brutus, the author of liberty and of the consulship, when he admitted among his fellow-citizens the faithful Vindex, who had revealed the conspiracy of the Tarquins. The public festival was continued during several days in all the principal cities; in Rome, from custom; in Constantinople, from imitation; in Carthage, Antioch, and Alexandria, from the love of pleasure and the superfluity of wealth. In the two capitals of the empire the annual games of the theatre, the circus, and the amphitheatre,[51] cost four thousand pounds of gold, (about) one hundred and sixty thousand pounds sterling: and if so heavy an expense surpassed the faculties or the inclination of the magistrates themselves, the sum was supplied from the Imperial treasury. As soon as the consuls had discharged these customary duties, they were at liberty to retire into the shade of private life, and to enjoy, during the remainder of the year, the undisturbed contemplation of their own greatness. They no longer presided in the national councils; they no longer executed the resolutions of peace or war. Their abilities (unless they were employed in more effective offices) were of little moment; and their names served only as the legal date of the year in which they had filled the chair of Marius and of Cicero. Yet it was still felt and acknowledged, in the last period of Roman servitude, that this empty name might be compared, and even preferred, to the possession of substantial power. The title of consul was still the most splendid object of ambition, the noblest reward of virtue and loyalty. The emperors themselves, who disdained the faint shadow of the republic, were conscious that they acquired added splendour and majesty as often as they assumed the annual honours of the consular dignity.[52]

The proudest and most perfect separation which can be found in any age or country between the nobles and the people is perhaps that of the Patricians and the Plebeians, as it was established in the first age of the Roman republic. Wealth and honours, the offices of the state, and the ceremonies of religion, were almost exclusively possessed by the former; who, preserving the purity of their blood with the most insulting jealousy,[53] held their clients in a condition of specious vassalage. But these distinctions, so incompatible with the spirit of a free people, were removed, after a long struggle, by the persevering efforts of the Tribunes. The most active and successful of the Plebeians accumulated wealth, aspired to honours, deserved triumphs, contracted alliances, and, after some generations, assumed the pride of ancient nobility.[54] The Patrician families, on the other hand, whose original number was never recruited till the end of the commonwealth, either failed in the ordinary course of nature, or were extinguished in so many foreign and domestic wars, or, through a want of merit or fortune, insensibly mingled with the mass of the people.[55] Very few remained who could derive their pure and genuine origin from the infancy of the city, or even from that of the republic, when Cæsar and Augustus, Claudius and Vespasian, created from the body of the senate a competent number of new Patrician families, in the hope of perpetuating an order which was still considered as honourable and sacred.[56] But these artificial supplies (in which the reigning house was always included) were rapidly swept away by the rage of tyrants, by frequent revolutions, by the change of manners, and by the intermixture of nations.[57] Little more was left when Constantine ascended the throne than a vague and imperfect tradition that the Patricians had once been the first of the Romans. To form a body of nobles, whose influence may restrain, while it secures, the authority of the monarch, would have been very inconsistent with the character and policy of Constantine; but, had he seriously entertained such a design, it might have exceeded the measure of his power to ratify, by an arbitrary edict, an

by Mamertinus with somewhat more freedom and ingenuity.

[50] From the reign of Carus to the sixth consulship of Honorius, there was an interval of one hundred and twenty years, during which the emperors were always absent from Rome on the first day of January.

[51] Claudian describes, in a lively and fanciful manner, the various games of the circus, the theatre, and the amphitheatre, exhibited by the new consul. The sanguinary combats of gladiators had already been prohibited.

[52] This exalted idea of the consulship is borrowed from an Oration pronounced by Julian in the servile court of Constantius.

[53] Intermarriages between the Patricians and Plebeians were prohibited by the laws of the Twelve Tables; and the uniform operations of human nature may attest that the custom survived the law.

[54] See the animated pictures drawn by Sallust, in the Jugurthine war, of the pride of the nobles, and even of the virtuous Metellus, who was unable to brook the idea that the honour of the

consulship should be bestowed on the obscure merit of his lieutenant Marius. Two hundred years before, the race of the Metelli themselves were confounded among the Plebeians of Rome; and from the etymology of their name of Cæcilius, there is reason to believe that those haughty nobles derived their origin from a sutler.

[55] In the year of Rome 800, very few remained, not only of the old Patrician families, but even of those which had been created by Cæsar and Augustus. The family of Scaurus (a branch of the Patrician Æmilii) was degraded so low that his father, who exercised the trade of a charcoal merchant, left him only ten slaves, and somewhat less than three hundred pounds sterling. The family was saved from oblivion by the merit of the son.

[56] The virtues of Agricola, who was created a Patrician by the emperor Vespasian, reflected honour on that ancient order; but his ancestors had not any claim beyond an equestrian nobility.

[57] This failure would have been almost impossible, if it were true, as

institution which must expect the sanction of time and of opinion. He revived, indeed, the title of PATRICIANS, but he revived it as a personal, not as an hereditary, distinction. They yielded only to the transient superiority of the annual consuls; but they enjoyed the pre-eminence over all the great officers of state, with the most familiar access to the person of the prince. This honourable rank was bestowed on them for life; and, as they were usually favourites and ministers who had grown old in the Imperial court, the true etymology of the word was perverted by ignorance and flattery; and the Patricians of Constantine were reverenced as the adopted *Fathers* of the emperor and the republic.

II. The fortunes of the Prætorian præfects were essentially different from those of the consuls and patricians. The latter saw their ancient greatness evaporate in a vain title. The former, rising by degrees from the most humble condition, were invested with the civil and military administration of the Roman world. From the reign of Severus to that of Diocletian, the guards and the palace, the laws and the finances, the armies and the provinces, were intrusted to their superintending care; and, like the Vizirs of the East, they held with one hand the seal, and with the other the standard, of the empire. The ambition of the præfects, always formidable and sometimes fatal to the masters whom they served, was supported by the strength of the Prætorian bands; but after those haughty troops had been weakened by Diocletian, and finally suppressed by Constantine, the præfects, who survived their fall, were reduced without difficulty to the station of useful and obedient ministers. When they were no longer responsible for the safety of the emperor's person, they resigned the jurisdiction which they had hitherto claimed and exercised over all the departments of the palace. They were deprived by Constantine of all military command, as soon as they had ceased to lead into the field, under their immediate orders, the flower of the Roman troops; and at length, by a singular revolution, the captains of the guard were transformed into the civil magistrates of the provinces. According to the plan of government instituted by Diocletian, the four princes had each their Prætorian præfect; and, after the monarchy was once more united in the person of Constantine, he still continued to create the same number of FOUR PRÆFECTS, and intrusted to their care the same provinces which they already administered. 1. The præfect of the East stretched his ample jurisdiction into the three parts of the globe which were subject to the Romans, from the cataracts of the Nile to the banks of the

Phasis, and from the mountains of Thrace to the frontiers of Persia. 2. The important provinces of Pannonia, Dacia, Macedonia, and Greece, once acknowledged the authority of the præfect of Illyricum. 3. The power of the præfect of Italy was not confined to the country from whence he derived his title; it extended over the additional territory of Rhætia as far as the banks of the Danube, over the dependent islands of the Mediterranean, and over the part of the continent of Africa which lies between the confines of Cyrene and those of Tingitania. 4. The præfect of the Gauls comprehended under that plural denomination the kindred provinces of Britain and Spain, and his authority was obeyed from the wall of Antoninus to the foot of Mount Atlas.

Casaubon compels Aurelius Victor to affirm that Vespasian created at once a thousand Patrician families. But this extravagant number is too much even for the whole senatorial order, unless we should include all the Roman knights who were distinguished by the permission of wearing the laticlave.

After the Prætorian præfects had been dismissed from all military command, the civil functions which they were ordained to exercise over so many subject nations were adequate to the ambition and abilities of the most consummate ministers. To their wisdom was committed the supreme administration of justice and of the finances, the two objects which, in a state of peace, comprehended almost all the respective duties of the sovereign and of the people; of the former, to protect the citizens who are obedient to the laws; of the latter, to contribute the share of their property which is required for the expenses of the state. The coin, the highways, the posts, the granaries, the manufactures, whatever could interest the public prosperity was moderated by the authority of the Prætorian præfects. As the immediate representatives of the Imperial majesty, they were empowered to explain, to enforce, and on some occasions to modify, the general edicts by their discretionary proclamations. They watched over the conduct of the provincial governors, removed the negligent, and inflicted punishments on the guilty. From all the inferior jurisdictions, an appeal in every matter of importance, either civil or criminal, might be brought before the tribunal of the præfect: but *his* sentence was final and absolute; and the emperors themselves refused to admit any complaints against the judgment or the integrity of a magistrate whom they honoured with such unbounded confidence. His appointments were suitable to his dignity;[58] and, if avarice was his ruling passion, he enjoyed frequent opportunities of collecting a rich harvest of fees, of presents, and of perquisites. Though the emperors no longer dreaded the ambition of their præfects, they were attentive to counterbalance the power of this great office by the uncertainty and shortness of its duration.[59]

[58] *When Justinian, in the exhausted condition of the empire, instituted a Prætorian præfect for Africa, he allowed him a salary of one hundred pounds of gold.*

[59] *For this, and the other dignities of the empire, it may be sufficient to refer to the ample commentaries of Pancirolus and Godefroy, who have diligently collected and accurately digested in their proper order all the legal and historical materials.*

From their superior importance and dignity, Rome and Constantinople were alone excepted from the jurisdiction of the Prætorian præfects. The immense size of the city and the experience of the tardy, ineffectual operation of the laws had furnished the policy of Augustus with a specious pretence for introducing a new magistrate, who alone could restrain a servile and turbulent populace by the strong arm of arbitrary power. Valerius Messalla was appointed the first præfect of Rome, that his reputation might countenance so invidious a measure: but, at the end of a few days, that accomplished citizen [60] resigned his office, declaring with a spirit worthy of the friend of Brutus, that he found himself incapable of exercising a power incompatible with public freedom. As the sense of liberty became less exquisite, the advantages of order were more clearly understood; and the præfect, who seemed to have been designed as a terror only to slaves and vagrants, was permitted to extend his civil and criminal jurisdiction over the equestrian and noble families of Rome. The prætors, annually created as the judges of law and equity, could not long dispute the possession of the Forum with a vigorous and permanent magistrate, who was usually admitted into the confidence of the prince. Their courts were deserted, their number, which had once fluctuated between twelve and eighteen, was gradually reduced to two or three, and their important functions were confined to the expensive obligation of exhibiting games for the amusement of the people. After the office of the Roman consuls had been changed into a vain pageant, which was rarely displayed in the capital, the præfects assumed their vacant place in the senate, and were soon acknowledged as the ordinary presidents of that venerable assembly. They received appeals from the distance of one hundred miles; and it was allowed as a principle of jurisprudence, that all municipal authority was derived from them alone. In the discharge of his laborious employment, the governor of Rome was assisted by fifteen officers, some of whom had been originally his equals, or even his superiors. The principal departments were relative to the command of a numerous watch, established as a safeguard against fires, robberies, and nocturnal disorders; the custody and distribution of the public allowance of corn and provisions; the care of the port, of the aqueducts, of the common sewers, and of the navigation and bed of the Tiber; the inspection of the markets, the theatres, and of the private as well as public works. Their vigilance ensured the three principal objects of a regular police, safety, plenty, and cleanliness; and, as a proof of the attention of government to

[60] *The fame of Messalla has been scarcely equal to his merit. In the earliest youth he was recommended by Cicero to the friendship of Brutus. He followed the standard of the republic till it was broken in the fields of Philippi: he then accepted and deserved the favour of the most moderate of the conquerors; and uniformly asserted his freedom and dignity in the court of Augustus. The triumph of Messalla was justified by the conquest of Aquitain. As an orator he disputed the palm of eloquence with Cicero himself. Messalla cultivated every muse, and was the patron of every man of genius. He spent his evenings in philosophic conversation with Horace; assumed his place at table between Delia and Tibullus; and amused his leisure by encouraging the poetical talents of young Ovid.*

THE COLISEUM AND
ARCH OF CONSTANTINE

*"The Flavian amphitheatre was contemplated
with awe and admiration by the pilgrims of the
North; and their rude enthusiasm broke forth in
a sublime proverbial expression, which is recorded
in the eighth century, in the fragments of the
venerable Bede: 'As long as the Coliseum stands,
Rome shall stand. . .'"*

THE COLISEUM AND THE ARCH OF CONSTANTINE

preserve the splendour and ornaments of the capital, a particular inspector was appointed for the statues; the guardian, as it were, of that inanimate people, which, according to the extravagant computation of an old writer, was scarcely inferior in number to the living inhabitants of Rome. About thirty years after the foundation of Constantinople, a similar magistrate was created in that rising metropolis, for the same uses, and with the same powers. A perfect equality was established between the dignity of the *two* municipal, and that of the *four* Prætorian, Præfects.[61]

Those who, in the Imperial hierarchy, were distinguished by the title of *Respectable,* formed an intermediate class between the *illustrious* præfects and the *honourable* magistrates of the provinces. In this class the proconsuls of Asia, Achaia, and Africa claimed a pre-eminence, which was yielded to the remembrance of their ancient dignity; and the appeal from their tribunal to that of the præfects was almost the only mark of their dependence.[62] But the civil government of the empire was distributed into thirteen great DIOCESES, each of which equalled the just measure of a powerful kingdom. The first of these dioceses was subject to the jurisdiction of the *count* of the east; and we may convey some idea of the importance and variety of his functions, by observing that six hundred apparitors, who would be styled at present either secretaries, or clerks, or ushers, or messengers, were employed in his immediate office.[63] The place of *Augustal præfect* of Egypt was no longer filled by a Roman knight; but the name was retained; and the extraordinary powers which the situation of the country and the temper of the inhabitants had once made indispensable were still continued to the governor. The eleven remaining dioceses, of Asiana, Pontica, and Thrace; of Macedonia, Dacia, and Pannonia or Western Illyricum; of Italy and Africa; of Gaul, Spain, and Britain; were governed by twelve *vicars* or *vice-præfects,*[64] whose name sufficiently explains the nature and dependence of their office. It may be added that the lieutenant-generals of the Roman armies, the military counts and dukes, who will be hereafter mentioned, were allowed the rank and title of *Respectable.*

As the spirit of jealousy and ostentation prevailed in the councils of the emperors, they proceeded with anxious diligence to divide the substance, and to multiply the titles of power. The vast countries which the Roman conquerors had united under the same simple form of administration were imperceptibly crumbled into minute fragments; till at length the whole empire was distributed into one hundred and sixteen provinces, each of which supported an expen-

[61] *Besides our usual guides, we may observe that Felix Cantelorius has written a separate treatise, De Præfecto Urbis; and that many curious details concerning the police of Rome and Constantinople are contained in the fourteenth book of the Theodosian Code.*

[62] *Eunapius affirms that the proconsul of Asia was independent of the præfect; which must, however, be understood with some allowance: the jurisdiction of the vice-præfect he most assuredly disclaimed.*

[63] *The proconsul of Africa had four hundred apparitors; and they all received large salaries, either from the treasury or the province.*

[64] *In Italy there was likewise the* Vicar of Rome. *It has been much disputed, whether his jurisdiction measured one hundred miles from the city, or whether it stretched over the ten southern provinces of Italy.*

sive and splendid establishment. Of these, three were governed by *proconsuls*, thirty-seven by *consulars*, five by *correctors*, and seventy-one by *presidents*. The appellations of these magistrates were different; they ranked in successive order, the ensigns of their dignity were curiously varied, and their situation, from accidental circumstances, might be more or less agreeable or advantageous. But they were all (excepting only the proconsuls) alike included in the class of *honourable* persons; and they were alike intrusted, during the pleasure of the prince, and under the authority of the præfects or their deputies, with the administration of justice and the finances in their respective districts. The ponderous volumes of the Codes and Pandects [65] would furnish ample materials for a minute inquiry into the system of provincial government, as in the space of six centuries it was improved by the wisdom of the Roman statesmen and lawyers. It may be sufficient for the historian to select two singular and salutary provisions intended to restrain the abuse of authority. 1. For the preservation of peace and order, the governors of the provinces were armed with the sword of justice. They inflicted corporal punishments, and they exercised, in capital offences, the power of life and death. But they were not authorized to indulge the condemned criminal with the choice of his own execution, or to pronounce a sentence of the mildest and most honourable kind of exile. These prerogatives were reserved to the præfects, who alone could impose the heavy fine of fifty pounds of gold: their vicegerents were confined to the trifling weight of a few ounces.[66] This distinction, which seems to grant the larger, while it denies the smaller, degree of authority, was founded on a very rational motive. The smaller degree was infinitely more liable to abuse. The passions of a provincial magistrate might frequently provoke him into acts of oppression which affected only the freedom or the fortunes of the subject; though, from a principle of prudence, perhaps of humanity, he might still be terrified by the guilt of innocent blood. It may likewise be considered that exile, considerable fines, or the choice of an easy death relate more particularly to the rich and the noble; and the persons the most exposed to the avarice or resentment of a provincial magistrate were thus removed from his obscure persecution to the more august and impartial tribunal of the Prætorian præfect. 2. As it was reasonably apprehended that the integrity of the judge might be biassed, if his interest was concerned or his affections were engaged; the strictest regulations were established to exclude any person, without the special dispensation of the emperor, from the

[65] *Among the works of the celebrated Ulpian, there was one in ten books concerning the office of a proconsul, whose duties in the most essential articles were the same as those of an ordinary governor of a province.*

[66] *The presidents, or consulars, could impose only two ounces; the vice-præfects, three; the proconsuls, count of the east, and præfect of Egypt, six.*

government of the province where he was born; and to prohibit the governor or his son from contracting marriage with a native or an inhabitant; or from purchasing slaves, lands, or houses, within the extent of his jurisdiction. Notwithstanding these rigorous precautions, the emperor Constantine, after a reign of twenty-five years, still deplores the venal and oppressive administration of justice, and expresses the warmest indignation that the audience of the judge, his dispatch of business, his seasonable delays, and his final sentence were publicly sold, either by himself or by the officers of his court. The continuance, and perhaps the impunity, of these crimes is attested by the repetition of important laws and ineffectual menaces.[67]

All the civil magistrates were drawn from the profession of the law. The celebrated Institutes of Justinian are addressed to the youth of his dominions, who had devoted themselves to the study of Roman jurisprudence; and the sovereign condescends to animate their diligence by the assurance that their skill and ability would in time be rewarded by an adequate share in the government of the republic. The rudiments of this lucrative science were taught in all the considerable cities of the east and west; but the most famous school was that of Berytus,[68] on the coast of Phœnicia; which flourished above three centuries from the time of Alexander Severus, the author perhaps of an institution so advantageous to his native country. After a regular course of education, which lasted five years, the students dispersed themselves through the provinces, in search of fortune and honours; nor could they want an inexhaustible supply of business in a great empire, already corrupted by the multiplicity of laws, of arts, and of vices. The court of the Prætorian præfect of the east could alone furnish employment for one hundred and fifty advocates, sixty-four of whom were distinguished by peculiar privileges, and two were annually chosen with a salary of sixty pounds of gold, to defend the causes of the treasury. The first experiment was made of their judicial talents, by appointing them to act occasionally as assessors to the magistrates; from thence they were often raised to preside in the tribunals before which they had pleaded. They obtained the government of a province; and, by the aid of merit, of reputation, or of favour, they ascended, by successive steps, to the *illustrious* dignities of the state.[69] In the practice of the bar, these men had considered reason as the instrument of dispute; they interpreted the laws according to the dictates of private interest; and the same pernicious habits might still adhere to their characters in the public administration of the state. The honour of a liberal pro-

[67] *Zeno enacted that all governors should remain in the province, to answer any accusations, fifty days after the expiration of their power.*

[68] *The splendour of the school of Berytus, which preserved in the east the language and jurisprudence of the Romans, may be computed to have lasted from the third to the middle of the sixth century.*

[69] *As in a former period I have traced the civil and military promotion of Pertinax, I shall here insert the civil honours of Mallius Theodorus. 1. He was distinguished by his eloquence, while he pleaded as an advocate in the court of the Prætorian præfect. 2. He governed one of the provinces of Africa, either as president or consular, and deserved, by his administration, the honour of a brass statue. 3. He was appointed vicar, or vice-præfect, of Macedonia. 4. Quæstor. 5. Count of the sacred largesses. 6. Prætorian præfect of the Gauls; whilst he might yet be represented as a young man. 7. After a retreat, perhaps a disgrace, of many years, which Mallius (confounded by some critics with the poet Manilius) employed in the study*

of the Grecian philosophy, he was named Prætorian præfect of Italy, in the year 397. 8. While he still exercised that great office, he was created, in the year 399, consul for the West; and his name, on account of the infamy of his colleague, the eunuch Eutropius, often stands alone in the Fasti. 9. In the year 408, Mallius was appointed a second time Prætorian præfect of Italy. Even in the venal panegyric of Claudian, we may discover the merit of Mallius Theodorus, who, by a rare felicity, was the intimate friend both of Symmachus and of St. Augustin.

[70] *The lieutenant of Britain was intrusted with the same powers which Cicero, proconsul of Cilicia, had exercised in the name of the senate and people.*

[71] *The Abbé Dubos, who has examined with accuracy the institutions of Augustus and of Constantine, observes that, if Otho had been put to death the day before he executed his conspiracy, Otho would now appear in history as innocent as Corbulo.*

fession has indeed been vindicated by ancient and modern advocates, who have filled the most important stations with pure integrity and consummate wisdom: but in the decline of Roman jurisprudence, the ordinary promotion of lawyers was pregnant with mischief and disgrace. The noble art, which had once been preserved as the sacred inheritance of the patricians, was fallen into the hands of freedmen and plebeians, who, with cunning rather than with skill, exercised a sordid and pernicious trade. Some of them procured admittance into families for the purpose of fomenting differences, of encouraging suits, and of preparing a harvest of gain for themselves or their brethren. Others, recluse in their chambers, maintained the dignity of legal professors by furnishing a rich client with subtleties to confound the plainest truth and with arguments to colour the most unjustifiable pretensions. The splendid and popular class was composed of the advocates, who filled the Forum with the sound of their turgid and loquacious rhetoric. Careless of fame and of justice, they are described, for the most part, as ignorant and rapacious guides, who conducted their clients through a maze of expense, of delay, and of disappointment; from whence, after a tedious series of years, they were at length dismissed, when their patience and fortune were almost exhausted.

III. In the system of policy introduced by Augustus, the governors, those at least of the Imperial provinces, were invested with the full powers of the sovereign himself. Ministers of peace and war, the distribution of rewards and punishments depended on them alone, and they successively appeared on their tribunal in the robes of civil magistracy, and in complete armour at the head of the Roman legions.[70] The influence of the revenue, the authority of law, and the command of a military force concurred to render their power supreme and absolute; and whenever they were tempted to violate their allegiance, the loyal province which they involved in their rebellion was scarcely sensible of any change in its political state. From the time of Commodus to the reign of Constantine, near one hundred governors might be enumerated, who, with various success, erected the standard of revolt; and though the innocent were too often sacrificed, the guilty might be sometimes prevented, by the suspicious cruelty of their master.[71] To secure his throne and the public tranquillity from these formidable servants, Constantine resolved to divide the military from the civil administration; and to establish, as a permanent and professional distinction, a practice which had been adopted only as an occasional expedient. The supreme jurisdiction exercised by the Prætorian præfects over the armies of the empire was transferred to the two *masters general* whom he instituted, the one for the *cavalry,* the other for the *infantry;* and, though each of these *illustrious* officers was more peculiarly responsible for the discipline of those troops which were under his immediate inspection, they both indifferently commanded in the field the several bodies, whether of horse or foot, which were united in the same army. Their number was soon doubled by the division of the east and west; and, as separate generals of the same rank and title were appointed on the four important frontiers of the Rhine, of the Upper and the Lower Danube, and of the Euphrates, the defence of the Roman empire was at length committed to eight masters general of the cavalry and infantry. Under their orders, thirty-five military commanders were stationed in the provinces: three in Britain, six in Gaul, one in Spain, one in Italy, five on the Upper, and four on the Lower Danube; in Asia eight, three in Egypt, and four in Africa. The titles of *counts,* and *dukes,*[12] by which they were properly distinguished, have obtained in modern languages so very different a sense that the use of them may occasion some surprise. But it should be recollected that the second of those appellations is only a corruption of the Latin word which was indiscriminately applied to any military chief. All these provincial generals were therefore *dukes;* but no more than ten among them were dignified with the rank of *counts* or companions, a title of honour, or rather of favour, which had been recently invented in the court of Constantine. A gold belt was the ensign which distinguished the office of the counts and dukes; and besides their pay, they received a liberal allowance, sufficient to maintain one hundred and ninety servants, and one hundred and fifty-eight horses. They were strictly prohibited from interfering in any matter which related to the administration of justice or the revenue; but the command which they exercised over the troops of their department was independent of the authority of the magistrates. About the same time that Constantine gave a legal sanction to the ecclesiastical order, he instituted in the Roman empire the nice balance of the civil and the military powers. The emulation, and sometimes the discord, which reigned between two professions of opposite interests and incompatible manners, was productive of beneficial and of pernicious consequences. It was seldom to be expected that the general and the civil governor of a province should either conspire for the disturbance, or should unite for the service, of their country. While the one delayed to offer

[12] *Though the military counts and dukes are frequently mentioned, both in history and the codes, we must have recourse to the Notitia for the exact knowledge of their number and stations.*

the assistance which the other disdained to solicit, the troops very frequently remained without orders or without supplies; the public safety was betrayed, and the defenceless subjects were left exposed to the fury of the Barbarians. The divided administration which had been formed by Constantine relaxed the vigour of the state, while it secured the tranquillity of the monarch.

The memory of Constantine has been deservedly censured for another innovation, which corrupted military discipline and prepared the ruin of the empire. The nineteen years which preceded his final victory over Licinius had been a period of licence and intestine war. The rivals who contended for the possession of the Roman world had withdrawn the greatest part of their forces from the guard of the general frontier; and the principal cities which formed the boundary of their respective dominions were filled with soldiers, who considered their countrymen as their most implacable enemies. After the use of these internal garrisons had ceased with the civil war, the conqueror wanted either wisdom or firmness to revive the severe discipline of Diocletian, and to suppress a fatal indulgence which habit had endeared and almost confirmed to the military order. From the reign of Constantine, a popular and even legal distinction was admitted between the *Palatines* [13] and the *Borderers;* the troops of the court as they were improperly styled, and the troops of the frontier. The former, elevated by the superiority of their pay and privileges, were permitted, except in the extraordinary emergencies of war, to occupy their tranquil stations in the heart of the provinces. The most flourishing cities were oppressed by the intolerable weight of quarters. The soldiers insensibly forgot the virtues of their profession, and contracted only the vices of civil life. They were either degraded by the industry of mechanic trades, or enervated by the luxury of baths and theatres. They soon became careless of their martial exercises, curious in their diet and apparel; and, while they inspired terror to the subjects of the empire, they trembled at the hostile approach of the Barbarians.[14] The chain of fortifications which Diocletian and his colleagues had extended along the banks of the great rivers was no longer maintained with the same care or defended with the same vigilance. The numbers which still remained under the name of the troops of the frontier might be sufficient for the ordinary defence. But their spirit was degraded by the humiliating reflection that *they* who were exposed to the hardships and dangers of a perpetual warfare were rewarded only with about two-thirds of the pay and emoluments which were

[13] *The distinction between the two classes of Roman troops is very darkly expressed in the historians, the laws, and the* Notitia. *Consult, however, the copious* paratitlon, *or abstract, which Godefroy has drawn up of the seventh book, de Re Militari, of the Theodosian Code.*

[14] *Ammianus observes that they loved downy beds and houses of marble; and that their cups were heavier than their swords.*

lavished on the troops of the court. Even the bands or legions that were raised the nearest to the level of those unworthy favourites were in some measure disgraced by the title of honour which they were allowed to assume. It was in vain that Constantine repeated the most dreadful menaces of fire and sword against the Borderers who should dare to desert their colours, to connive at the inroads of the Barbarians, or to participate in the spoil. The mischiefs which flow from injudicious counsels are seldom removed by the application of partial severities; and, though succeeding princes laboured to restore the strength and numbers of the frontier garrisons, the empire, till the last moment of its dissolution, continued to languish under the mortal wound which had been so rashly or so weakly inflicted by the hand of Constantine.

The same timid policy, of dividing whatever is united, of reducing whatever is eminent, of dreading every active power, and of expecting that the most feeble will prove the most obedient, seems to persuade the institutions of several princes, and particularly those of Constantine. The martial pride of the legions, whose victorious camps had so often been the scene of rebellion, was nourished by the memory of their past exploits and the consciousness of their actual strength. As long as they maintained their ancient establishment of six thousand men, they subsisted, under the reign of Diocletian, each of them singly, a visible and important object in the military history of the Roman empire. A few years afterwards these gigantic bodies were shrunk to a very diminutive size; and, when *seven* legions, with some auxiliaries, defended the city of Amida against the Persians, the total garrison, with the inhabitants of both sexes, and the peasants of the deserted country, did not exceed the number of twenty thousand persons.[75] From this fact, and from similar examples, there is reason to believe that the constitution of the legionary troops, to which they partly owed their valour and discipline, was dissolved by Constantine; and that the bands of Roman infantry, which still assumed the same names and the same honours, consisted only of one thousand or fifteen hundred men. The conspiracy of so many separate detachments, each of which was awed by the sense of its own weakness, could easily be checked; and the successors of Constantine might indulge their love of ostentation, by issuing their orders to one hundred and thirty-two legions, inscribed on the muster-roll of their numerous armies. The remainder of their troops was distributed into several hundred cohorts of infantry, and squadrons of cavalry. Their arms, and titles, and

[75] *Ammianus observes that the desperate sallies of two Gallic legions were like an handful of water thrown on a great conflagration.*

ensigns were calculated to inspire terror, and to display the variety of nations who marched under the Imperial standard. And not a vestige was left of that severe simplicity which, in the ages of freedom and victory, had distinguished the line of battle of a Roman army from the confused host of an Asiatic monarch. A more particular enumeration, drawn from the *Notitia,* might exercise the diligence of an antiquary; but the historian will content himself with observing that the number of permanent stations or garrisons established on the frontiers of the empire amounted to five hundred and eighty-three; and that, under the successors of Constantine, the complete force of the military establishment was computed at six hundred and forty-five thousand soldiers. An effort so prodigious surpassed the wants of a more ancient, and the faculties of a later, period.

In the various states of society, armies are recruited from very different motives. Barbarians are urged by the love of war; the citizens of a free republic may be prompted by a principle of duty; the subjects, or at least the nobles, of a monarchy are animated by a sentiment of honour; but the timid and luxurious inhabitants of a declining empire must be allured into the service by the hopes of profit, or compelled by the dread of punishment. The resources of the Roman treasury were exhausted by the increase of pay, by the repetition of donatives, and by the invention of new emoluments and indulgences, which, in the opinion of the provincial youth, might compensate the hardships and dangers of a military life. Yet, although the stature was lowered,[76] although slaves, at least by a tacit connivance, were indiscriminately received into the ranks, the insurmountable difficulty of procuring a regular and adequate supply of volunteers obliged the emperors to adopt more effectual and coercive methods. The lands bestowed on the veterans, as the free reward of their valour, were henceforward granted under a condition, which contains the first rudiments of the feudal tenures; that their sons, who succeeded to the inheritance, should devote themselves to the profession of arms, as soon as they attained the age of manhood; and their cowardly refusal was punished by the loss of honour, of fortune, or even of life.[77] But, as the annual growth of the sons of the veterans bore a very small proportion to the demands of the service, levies of men were frequently required from the provinces, and every proprietor was obliged either to take up arms, or to procure a substitute, or to purchase his exemption by the payment of a heavy fine. The sum of forty-two pieces of gold, to which it was

[76] *Valentinian fixes the standard at five feet seven inches, about five feet four inches and a half English measure. It had formerly been five feet ten inches, and in the best corps six Roman feet.*

[77] *See the two titles, De Veteranis, and De Filiis Veteranorum, in the seventh book of the Theodosian Code. The age at which their military service was required varied from twenty-five to sixteen. If the sons of the veterans appeared with a horse, they had a right to serve in the cavalry; two horses gave them some valuable privileges.*

reduced, ascertains the exorbitant price of volunteers and the reluctance with which the government admitted of this alternative.[78] Such was the horror for the profession of a soldier which had affected the minds of the degenerate Romans that many of the youth of Italy and the provinces chose to cut off the fingers of their right hand to escape from being pressed into the service; and this strange expedient was so commonly practised as to deserve the severe animadversion of the laws[79] and a peculiar name in the Latin language.[80]

The introduction of Barbarians into the Roman armies became every day more universal, more necessary, and more fatal. The most daring of the Scythians, of the Goths, and of the Germans, who delighted in war, and who found it more profitable to defend than to ravage the provinces, were enrolled, not only in the auxiliaries of their respective nations, but in the legions themselves, and among the most distinguished of the Palatine troops. As they freely mingled with the subjects of the empire, they gradually learned to despise their manners and to imitate their arts. They abjured the implicit reverence which the pride of Rome had exacted from their ignorance, while they acquired the knowledge and possession of those advantages by which alone she supported her declining greatness. The Barbarian soldiers who displayed any military talents were advanced, without exception, to the most important commands; and the names of the tribunes, of the counts and dukes, and of the generals themselves, betray a foreign origin, which they no longer condescended to disguise. They were often entrusted with the conduct of a war against their countrymen; and, though most of them preferred the ties of allegiance to those of blood, they did not always avoid the guilt, or at least the suspicion, of holding a treasonable correspondence with the enemy, of inviting his invasion, or of sparing his retreat. The camps and the palace of the son of Constantine were governed by the powerful faction of the Franks, who preserved the strictest connexion with each other and with their country, and who resented every personal affront as a national indignity. When the tyrant Caligula was suspected of an intention to invest a very extraordinary candidate with the consular robes, the sacrilegious profanation would have scarcely excited less astonishment, if, instead of a horse, the noblest chieftain of Germany or Britain had been the object of his choice. The revolution of three centuries had produced so remarkable a change in the prejudices of the people that, with the public approbation, Constantine showed

[78] *According to the historian Socrates the same emperor Valens sometimes required eighty pieces of gold for a recruit. In the following law it is faintly expressed that slaves shall not be admitted inter optimas lectissimorum militum turmas.*

[79] *The person and property of a Roman knight, who had mutilated his two sons, were sold by public auction by the order of Augustus. The moderation of that artful usurper proves that this example of severity was justified by the spirit of the times. Ammianus makes a distinction between the effeminate Italians and the hardy Gauls. Yet only fifteen years afterwards, Valentinian, in a law addressed to the præfect of Gaul, is obliged to enact that these cowardly deserters shall be burnt alive. Their numbers in Illyricum were so considerable that the province complained of a scarcity of recruits.*

[80] *They were called Murci. Murcidus is found in Plautus and Festus, to denote a lazy and cowardly person, who, according to Arnobius and Augustin, was under the immediate protection of the goddess*

his successors the example of bestowing the honours of the consulship on the Barbarians who, by their merit and services, had deserved to be ranked among the first of the Romans.[81] But as these hardy veterans, who had been educated in the ignorance or contempt of the laws, were incapable of exercising any civil offices, the powers of the human mind were contracted by the irreconcilable separation of talents as well as of professions. The accomplished citizens of the Greek and Roman republics, whose characters could adapt themselves to the bar, the senate, the camp, or the schools, had learned to write, to speak, and to act, with the same spirit, and with equal abilities.

IV. Besides the magistrates and generals, who at a distance from the court diffused their delegated authority over the provinces and armies, the emperor conferred the rank of *Illustrious* on seven of his more immediate servants, to whose fidelity he entrusted his safety, or his counsels, or his treasures. 1. The private apartments of the palace were governed by a favourite eunuch, who, in the language of that age, was styled the *præpositus* or præfect of the sacred bed-chamber. His duty was to attend the emperor in his hours of state, or in those of amusement, and to perform about his person all those menial services which can only derive their splendour from the influence of royalty. Under a prince who deserved to reign, the great chamberlain (for such we may call him) was an useful and humble domestic; but an artful domestic, who improves every occasion of unguarded confidence, will insensibly acquire over a feeble mind that ascendant which harsh wisdom and uncomplying virtue can seldom obtain. The degenerate grandsons of Theodosius, who were invisible to their subjects and contemptible to their enemies, exalted the præfects of their bed-chamber above the heads of all the ministers of the palace; and even his deputy, the first of the splendid train of slaves who waited in the presence, was thought worthy to rank before the *respectable* proconsuls of Greece or Asia. The jurisdiction of the chamberlain was acknowledged by the *counts,* or superintendents, who regulated the two important provinces of the magnificence of the wardrobe and of the luxury of the Imperial table.[82] 2. The principal administration of public affairs was committed to the diligence and abilities of the *master of the offices.*[83] He was the supreme magistrate of the palace, inspected the discipline of the civil and military *schools,* and received appeals from all parts of the empire; in the causes which related to that numerous army of privileged persons who, as the servants of the court, had obtained, for themselves and families, a right to decline the authority of the ordinary judges. The correspondence between the prince and his subjects was managed by the four *scrinia* or offices of this minister of state. The first was appropriated to memorials, the second to epistles, the third to petitions, and the fourth to papers and orders of a miscellaneous kind. Each of these was directed by an inferior *master* of *respectable* dignity, and the whole business was dispatched by an hundred and forty-eight secretaries, chosen for the most part from the profession of the law, on account of the variety of abstracts of reports and references which frequently occurred in the exercise of their several functions. From a condescension, which in former ages would have been esteemed unworthy of the Roman majesty, a particular secretary was allowed for the Greek language; and interpreters were appointed to receive the ambassadors of the Barbarians: but the department of foreign affairs, which constitutes so essential a part of modern policy, seldom diverted the attention of the master of the offices. His mind was more seriously engaged by the general direction of the posts and arsenals of the empire. There were thirty-four cities, fifteen in the east, and nineteen in the west, in which regular companies of workmen were perpetually employed in fabricating defensive armour, offensive weapons of all sorts, and military engines, which were deposited in the arsenals, and occasionally delivered for the service of the troops. 3. In the course of nine centuries, the office of *quæstor* had experienced a very singular revolution. In the infancy of Rome, two inferior magistrates were annually elected by the people, to relieve the consuls from the invidious management of the public treasure;[84] a similar assistant was granted to every proconsul, and to every prætor, who exercised a military or provincial command; with the extent of conquest, the two quæstors were gradually multiplied to the number of four, of eight, of twenty, and, for a short time, perhaps, of forty;[85] and the noblest citizens ambitiously solicited an office which gave them a seat in the senate, and a just hope of obtaining the honours of the republic. Whilst Augustus affected to maintain the freedom of election, he consented to accept the annual privilege of recommending, or rather indeed of nominating, a certain proportion of candidates; and it was his custom to select one of these distinguished youths, to read his orations or epistles in the assemblies of the senate. The practice of Augustus was imitated by succeeding princes; the occasional commission was established as a permanent office; and the favoured quæstor, assuming a new and more illustrious character, alone sur-

of the Antonines, or even of Nero, the origin of a magistrate who cannot be found in history before the reign of Constantine.

[84] *Tacitus says that the first quæstors were elected by the people, sixty-four years after the foundation of the republic; but he is of opinion that they had, long before that period, been annually appointed by the consuls, and even by the kings. But this obscure point of antiquity is contested by other writers.*

[85] *Tacitus seems to consider twenty as the highest number of quæstors; and Dion insinuates that, if the dictator Cæsar once created forty, it was only to facilitate the payment of an immense debt of gratitude. Yet the augmentation which he made of prætors subsisted under the succeeding reigns.*

[86] *The youth and inexperience of the quæstors, who entered on that important office in their twenty-fifth year, engaged Augustus to remove them from the management of the treasury; and, though they were restored by Claudius, they seem to have been finally dismissed by Nero. In the provinces of the Imperial division, the place of the quæstors was more ably supplied by the* procurators; *or, as they were afterwards called,* rationales. *But in the provinces of the senate we may still discover a series of quæstors till the reign of Marcus Antoninus. From Ulpian we may learn that, under the government of the house of Severus, their provincial administration was abolished; and in the subsequent troubles the annual or triennial elections of quæstors must have naturally ceased.*

[87] *The office must have acquired new dignity, which was occasionally executed by the heir-apparent of the empire. Trajan entrusted the same care to Hadrian his quæstor and cousin.*

vived the suppression of his ancient and useless colleagues.[86] As the orations which he composed in the name of the emperor [87] acquired the force, and, at length, the form of absolute edicts, he was considered as the representative of the legislative power, the oracle of the council, and the original source of the civil jurisprudence. He was sometimes invited to take his seat in the supreme judicature of the Imperial consistory, with the Prætorian præfects, and the master of the offices; and he was frequently requested to resolve the doubts of inferior judges; but, as he was not oppressed with a variety of subordinate business, his leisure and talents were employed to cultivate that dignified style of eloquence which, in the corruption of taste and language, still preserves the majesty of the Roman laws. In some respects, the office of the Imperial quæstor may be compared with that of a modern chancellor; but the use of a great seal, which seems to have been adopted by the illiterate Barbarians, was never introduced to attest the public acts of the emperors. 4. The extraordinary title of *count of the sacred largesses* was bestowed on the treasurer-general of the revenue, with the intention perhaps of inculcating that every payment flowed from the voluntary bounty of the monarch. To conceive the almost infinite detail of the annual and daily expense of the civil and military administration in every part of a great empire would exceed the powers of the most vigorous imagination. The actual account employed several hundred persons, distributed into eleven different offices, which were artfully contrived to examine and control their respective operations. The multitude of these agents had a natural tendency to increase; and it was more than once thought expedient to dismiss to their native homes the useless supernumeraries, who, deserting their honest labours, had pressed with too much eagerness into the lucrative profession of the finances. Twenty-nine provincial receivers, of whom eighteen were honoured with the title of count, corresponded with the treasurer; and he extended his jurisdiction over the mines, from whence the precious metals were extracted, over the mints, in which they were converted into the current coin, and over the public treasuries of the most important cities, where they were deposited for the service of the state. The foreign trade of the empire was regulated by this minister, who directed likewise all the linen and woollen manufactures, in which the successive operations of spinning, weaving, and dyeing were executed, chiefly by women of a servile condition, for the use of the palace and army. Twenty-six of these institutions are enumerated in the west, where the arts had been more recently introduced, and a still larger proportion may be allowed for the industrious provinces of the east.[88] 5. Besides the public revenue, which an absolute monarch might levy and expend according to his pleasure, the emperors, in the capacity of opulent citizens, possessed a very extensive property, which was administered by the *count*, or treasurer, *of the private estate*. Some part had perhaps been the ancient demesnes of kings and republics; some accessions might be derived from the families which were successively invested with the purple; but the most considerable portion flowed from the impure source of confiscations and forfeitures. The Imperial estates were scattered through the provinces, from Mauritania to Britain; but the rich and fertile soil of Cappadocia tempted the monarch to acquire in that country his fairest possessions, and either Constantine or his successors embraced the occasion of justifying avarice by religious zeal. They suppressed the rich temple of Comana, where the high priest of the goddess of war supported the dignity of a sovereign prince; and they applied to their private use the consecrated lands, which were inhabited by six thousand subjects or slaves of the deity and her ministers.[89] But these were not the valuable inhabitants; the plains that stretch from the foot of Mount Argæus to the banks of the Sarus bred a generous race of horses, renowned above all others in the ancient world for their majestic shape and incomparable swiftness. These *sacred* animals, destined for the service of the palace and the Imperial games, were protected by the laws from the profanation of a vulgar master.[90] The demesnes of Cappadocia were important enough to require the inspection of a *count*;[91] officers of an inferior rank were stationed in the other parts of the empire; and the deputies of the private, as well as those of the public, treasurer were maintained in the exercise of their independent functions, and encouraged to control the authority of the provincial magistrates. 6, 7. The chosen bands of cavalry and infantry which guarded the person of the emperor, were under the immediate command of the *two counts of the domestics*. The whole number consisted of three thousand five hundred men, divided into seven *schools*, or troops, of five hundred each; and in the east, this honourable service was almost entirely appropriated to the Armenians. Whenever, on public ceremonies, they were drawn up in the courts and porticoes of the palace, their lofty stature, silent order, and splendid arms of silver and gold displayed a martial pomp, not unworthy of the Roman majesty. From the seven schools two companies of horse and foot were selected, of the protectors, whose ad-

[88] *In the departments of the two counts of the treasury, the eastern part of the* Notitia *happens to be very defective. It may be observed that we had a treasury-chest in London, and a gyneceum or manufacture at Winchester. But Britain was not thought worthy either of a mint or of an arsenal. Gaul alone possessed three of the former, and eight of the latter.*

[89] *The other temple of Comana, in Pontus, was a colony from that of Cappadocia. The president Des Brosses conjectures that the deity adored in both Comanas was Beltis, the Venus of the east, the goddess of generation; a very different being indeed from the goddess of war.*

[90] *Godefroy has collected every circumstance of antiquity relative to the Cappadocian horses. One of the finest breeds, the Palmatian, was the forfeiture of a rebel, whose estate lay about sixteen miles from Tyana, near the great road between Constantinople and Antioch.*

[91] *Justinian subjected the province of the count of Cappadocia to the immediate authority of the favourite eunuch who presided over the sacred bed-chamber.*

vantageous station was the hope and reward of the most deserving soldiers. They mounted guard in the interior apartments, and were occasionally dispatched into the provinces to execute with celerity and vigour the orders of their master.[92] The counts of the domestics had succeeded to the office of the Prætorian præfects; like the præfects, they aspired from the service of the palace to the command of armies.

The perpetual intercourse between the court and the provinces was facilitated by the construction of roads and the institution of posts. But these beneficial establishments were accidentally connected with a pernicious and intolerable abuse. Two or three hundred *agents* or messengers were employed, under the jurisdiction of the master of the offices, to announce the names of the annual consuls and the edicts or victories of the emperors. They insensibly assumed the licence of reporting whatever they could observe of the conduct either of magistrates or of private citizens; and were soon considered as the eyes of the monarch, and the scourge of the people. Under the warm influence of a feeble reign, they multiplied to the incredible number of ten thousand, disdained the mild though frequent admonitions of the laws, and exercised in the profitable management of the posts a rapacious and insolent oppression. These official spies, who regularly corresponded with the palace, were encouraged, by favour and reward, anxiously to watch the progress of every treasonable design, from the faint and latent symptoms of disaffection to the actual preparation of an open revolt. Their careless or criminal violation of truth and justice was covered by the consecrated mask of zeal; and they might securely aim their poisoned arrows at the breast either of the guilty or the innocent, who had provoked their resentment or refused to purchase their silence. A faithful subject, of Syria perhaps, or of Britain, was exposed to the danger, or at least to the dread, of being dragged in chains to the court of Milan or Constantinople, to defend his life and fortune against the malicious charge of these privileged informers. The ordinary administration was conducted by those methods which extreme necessity can alone palliate; and the defects of evidence were diligently supplied by the use of torture.

The deceitful and dangerous experiment of the criminal *question,* as it is emphatically styled, was admitted, rather than approved, in the jurisprudence of the Romans. They applied this sanguinary mode of examination only to servile bodies, whose sufferings were seldom weighed by those haughty republicans in the scale of justice

92 *Ammianus Marcellinus, who served so many years, obtained only the rank of a Protector. The first ten among these honourable soldiers were* Clarissimi.

or humanity: but they would never consent to violate the sacred person of a citizen, till they possessed the clearest evidence of his guilt.[93] The annals of tyranny, from the reign of Tiberius to that of Domitian, circumstantially relate the executions of many innocent victims; but, as long as the faintest remembrance was kept alive of the national freedom and honour, the last hours of a Roman were secure from the danger of ignominious torture.[94] The conduct of the provincial magistrates was not, however, regulated by the practice of the city or the strict maxims of the civilians. They found the use of torture established, not only among the slaves of oriental despotism, but among the Macedonians, who obeyed a limited monarch; among the Rhodians, who flourished by the liberty of commerce; and even among the sage Athenians, who had asserted and adorned the dignity of human kind. The acquiescence of the provincials encouraged their governors to acquire, or perhaps to usurp, a discretionary power of employing the rack, to extort from vagrants or plebeian criminals the confession of their guilt, till they insensibly proceeded to confound the distinction of rank and to disregard the privileges of Roman citizens. The apprehensions of the subjects urged them to solicit, and the interest of the sovereign engaged him to grant, a variety of special exemptions, which tacitly allowed, and even authorized, the general use of torture. They protected all persons of illustrious or honourable rank, bishops and their presbyters, professors of the liberal arts, soldiers and their families, municipal officers, and their posterity to the third generation, and all children under the age of puberty. But a fatal maxim was introduced into the new jurisprudence of the empire, that in the case of treason, which included every offence that the subtlety of lawyers could derive from an *hostile intention* towards the prince or republic,[95] all privileges were suspended, and all conditions were reduced to the same ignominious level. As the safety of the emperor was avowedly preferred to every consideration of justice or humanity, the dignity of age and the tenderness of youth were alike exposed to the most cruel tortures; and the terrors of a malicious information, which might select them as the accomplices, or even as the witnesses, perhaps, of an imaginary crime, perpetually hung over the heads of the principal citizens of the Roman world.[96]

These evils, however terrible they may appear, were confined to the smaller number of Roman subjects, whose dangerous situation was in some degree compensated by the enjoyment of those advantages, either of nature or of fortune, which exposed them to the jeal-

[93] *The Pandects contain the sentiments of the most celebrated civilians on the subject of torture. They strictly confine it to slaves; and Ulpian himself is ready to acknowledge that Res est fragillis, et periculosa, et quæ veritatem fallat.*

[94] *In the conspiracy of Piso against Nero, Epicharis (libertina mulier) was the only person tortured; the rest were intacti tormentis. It would be superfluous to add a weaker, and it would be difficult to find a stronger, example.*

[95] *This definition of the sage Ulpian seems to have been adapted to the court of Caracalla rather than to that of Alexander Severus.*

[96] *Arcadius Charisius is the oldest lawyer quoted in the Pandects to justify the universal practice of torture in all cases of treason; but this maxim of tyranny, which is admitted by Ammianus with the most respectful terror, is enforced by several laws of the successors of Constantine.*

ousy of the monarch. The obscure millions of a great empire have much less to dread from the cruelty than from the avarice of their masters; and *their* humble happiness is principally affected by the grievance of excessive taxes, which, gently pressing on the wealthy, descend with accelerated weight on the meaner and more indigent classes of society. An ingenious philosopher has calculated the universal measure of the public impositions by the degrees of freedom and servitude; and ventures to assert that, according to an invariable law of nature, it must always increase with the former, and diminish in a just proportion to the latter. But this reflection, which would tend to alleviate the miseries of despotism, is contradicted at least by the history of the Roman empire; which accuses the same princes of despoiling the senate of its authority and the provinces of their wealth. Without abolishing all the various customs and duties on merchandises, which are imperceptibly discharged by the apparent choice of the purchaser, the policy of Constantine and his successors preferred a simple and direct mode of taxation, more congenial to the spirit of an arbitrary government.

The name and use of the *indictions*,[97] which serve to ascertain the chronology of the middle ages, was derived from the regular practice of the Roman tributes.[98] The emperor subscribed with his own hand, and in purple ink, the solemn edict, or indiction, which was fixed up in the principal city of each diocese during two months previous to the first day of September. And, by a very easy connexion of ideas, the word *indiction* was transferred to the measure of tribute which it prescribed, and to the annual term which it allowed for the payment. This general estimate of the supplies was proportioned to the real and imaginary wants of the state; but, as often as the expense exceeded the revenue, or the revenue fell short of the computation, an additional tax, under the name of *superindiction,* was imposed on the people, and the most valuable attribute of sovereignty was communicated to the Prætorian præfects, who, on some occasions, were permitted to provide for the unforeseen and extraordinary exigencies of the public service. The execution of these laws (which it would be tedious to pursue in their minute and intricate detail) consisted of two distinct operations; the resolving the general imposition into its constituent parts, which were assessed on the provinces, the cities, and the individuals of the Roman world, and the collecting the separate contributions of the individuals, the cities, and the provinces, till the accumulated sums were poured into the Imperial treasuries. But, as the account between the monarch and the subject was perpetually open, and as the renewal

[97] *The cycle of indictions, which may be traced as high as the reign of Constantius, or perhaps of his father Constantine, is still employed by the papal court: but the commencement of the year has been very reasonably altered to the first of January.*

[98] *The first twenty-eight titles of the eleventh book of the Theodosian Code are filled with the circumstantial regulations on the important subject of tributes; but they suppose a clearer knowledge of fundamental principles than it is at present in our power to attain.*

of the demand anticipated the perfect discharge of the preceding obligation, the weighty machine of the finances was moved by the same hands round the circle of its yearly revolution. Whatever was honourable or important in the administration of the revenue was committed to the wisdom of the præfects and their provincial representatives; the lucrative functions were claimed by a crowd of subordinate officers, some of whom depended on the treasurer, others on the governor of the province; and who, in the inevitable conflicts of a perplexed jurisdiction, had frequent opportunities of disputing with each other the spoils of the people. The laborious offices, which could be productive only of envy and reproach, of expense and danger, were imposed on the *Decurions,* who formed the corporations of the cities, and whom the severity of the Imperial laws had condemned to sustain the burthens of civil society.[99] The whole landed property of the empire (without excepting the patrimonial estates of the monarch) was the object of ordinary taxation; and every new purchaser contracted the obligations of the former proprietor. An accurate *census,* or survey, was the only equitable mode of ascertaining the proportion which every citizen should be obliged to contribute for the public service; and from the well-known period of the indictions there is reason to believe that this difficulty and expensive operation was repeated at the regular distance of fifteen years. The lands were measured by surveyors, who were sent into the provinces; their nature, whether arable or pasture, or vineyards or woods, was distinctly reported; and an estimate was made of their common value from the average produce of five years. The numbers of slaves and of cattle constituted an essential part of the report; an oath was administered to the proprietors, which bound them to disclose the true state of their affairs; and their attempts to prevaricate, or elude the intention of the legislator, were severely watched, and punished as a capital crime which included the double guilt of treason and sacrilege. A large portion of the tribute was paid in money; and of the current coin of the empire, gold alone could be legally accepted. The remainder of the taxes, according to the proportions determined by the annual indiction, was furnished in a manner still more direct, and still more oppressive. According to the different nature of lands, their real produce, in the various articles of wine or oil, corn or barley, wood or iron, was transported by the labour or at the expense of the provincials to the Imperial magazines, from whence they were occasionally distributed, for the use of the court, of the army, and of the two capitals, Rome and Constantinople. The commissioners of the revenue were so frequently obliged to make con-

[99] *The title concerning the Decurions is the most ample in the whole Theodosian Code; since it contains not less than one hundred and ninety-two distinct laws to ascertain the duties and privileges of that useful order of citizens.*

siderable purchases that they were strictly prohibited from allowing any compensation or from receiving in money the value of those supplies which were exacted in kind. In the primitive simplicity of small communities, this method may be well adapted to collect the almost voluntary offerings of the people; but it is at once susceptible of the utmost latitude and of the utmost strictness, which in a corrupt and absolute monarchy must introduce a perpetual contest between the power of oppression and the arts of fraud.[100] The agriculture of the Roman provinces was insensibly ruined, and, in the progress of despotism, which tends to disappoint its own purpose, the emperors were obliged to derive some merit from the forgiveness of debts, or the remission of tributes, which their subjects were utterly incapable of paying. According to the new division of Italy, the fertile and happy province of Campania, the scene of the early victories and of the delicious retirements of the citizens of Rome, extended between the sea and the Apennine from the Tiber to the Silarus. Within sixty years after the death of Constantine, and on the evidence of an actual survey, an exemption was granted in favour of three hundred and thirty thousand English acres of desert and uncultivated land; which amounted to one-eighth of the whole surface of the province. As the footsteps of the Barbarians had not yet been seen in Italy, the cause of this amazing desolation, which is recorded in the laws, can be ascribed only to the administration of the Roman emperors.[101]

Either from design or from accident, the mode of assessment seemed to unite the substance of a land-tax with the forms of a capitation.[102] The returns which were sent of every province or district expressed the number of tributary subjects and the amount of the public impositions. The latter of these sums was divided by the former; and the estimate, that such a province contained so many *capita,* or heads of tribute, and that each *head* was rated at such a price, was universally received, not only in the popular, but even in the legal computation. The value of a tributary head must have varied, according to many accidental, or at least fluctuating, circumstances; but some knowledge has been preserved of a very curious fact, the more important, since it relates to one of the richest provinces of the Roman empire, and which now flourishes as the most splendid of the European kingdoms. The rapacious ministers of Constantius had exhausted the wealth of Gaul, by exacting twenty-five pieces of gold for the annual tribute of every head. The humane policy of his successor reduced the capitation to seven pieces. A moderate proportion between these opposite extremes of extravagant oppression and of transient indulgence may therefore be fixed at sixteen pieces of gold, or about nine pounds sterling, the common standard perhaps of the impositions of Gaul.[103] But this calculation, or rather indeed the facts from whence it is deduced, cannot fail of suggesting two difficulties to a thinking mind, who will be at once surprised by the *equality* and by the *enormity* of the capitation. An attempt to explain them may perhaps reflect some light on the interesting subject of the finances of the declining empire.

I. It is obvious that, as long as the immutable constitution of human nature produces and maintains so unequal a division of property, the most numerous part of the community would be deprived of their subsistence by the equal assessment of a tax from which the sovereign would derive a very trifling revenue. Such indeed might be the theory of the Roman capitation; but in the practice, this unjust equality was no longer felt, as the tribute was collected on the principle of a *real,* not of a *personal,* imposition. Several indigent citizens contributed to compose a single *head,* or share of taxation; while the wealthy provincial, in proportion to his fortune, alone represented several of those imaginary beings. In a poetical request, addressed to one of the last and most deserving of the Roman princes who reigned in Gaul, Sidonius Apollinaris personifies his tribute under the figure of a triple monster, the Geryon of the Grecian fables, and entreats the new Hercules that he would most graciously be pleased to save his life by cutting off three of his heads. The fortune of Sidonius far exceeded the customary wealth of a poet; but, if he had pursued the allusion, he must have painted many of the Gallic nobles with the hundred heads of the deadly Hydra spreading over the face of the country and devouring the substance of an hundred families. II. The difficulty of allowing an annual sum of about nine pounds sterling, even for the average of the capitation of Gaul, may be rendered more evident by the comparison of the present state of the same country, as it is now governed by the absolute monarch of an industrious, wealthy, and affectionate people. The taxes of France cannot be magnified, either by fear or by flattery, beyond the annual amount of eighteen millions sterling, which ought perhaps to be shared among four and twenty millions of inhabitants.[104] Seven millions of these, in the capacity of fathers or brothers or husbands, may discharge the obligations of the remaining multitude of women and children; yet the equal proportion of each tributary subject will scarcely rise above fifty shillings of our money, instead of a proportion almost four times as considerable, which was regularly imposed on their Gallic ancestors.

on the Denarius for the proof of the following principles: 1. That the ancient and modern Roman pound, containing 5256 grains of Troy weight, is about one-twelfth lighter than the English pound, which is composed of 5760 of the same grains. 2. That the pound of gold, which had once been divided into forty-eight aurei, was at this time coined into seventy-two smaller pieces of the same denomination. 3. That five of these aurei were the legal tender for a pound of silver, and that consequently the pound of gold was exchanged for fourteen pounds eight ounces of silver according to the Roman, or about thirteen pounds according to the English, weight. 4. That the English pound of silver is coined into sixty-two shillings. From these elements we may compute the Roman pound of gold, the usual method of reckoning large sums, at forty pounds sterling; and we may fix the currency of the aureus at somewhat more than eleven shillings.

[104] *This assertion, however formidable it may seem, is founded on the original registers of births, deaths, and marriages, collected by public*

The reason of this difference may be found, not so much in the relative scarcity or plenty of gold and silver, as in the different state of society in ancient Gaul and in modern France. In a country where personal freedom is the privilege of every subject, the whole mass of taxes, whether they are levied on property or on consumption, may be fairly divided among the whole body of the nation. But the far greater part of the lands of ancient Gaul, as well as of the other provinces of the Roman world, were cultivated by slaves, or by peasants whose dependent condition was a less rigid servitude. In such a state the poor were maintained at the expense of the masters, who enjoyed the fruits of their labour; and, as the rolls of tribute were filled only with the names of those citizens who possessed the means of an honourable, or at least of a decent, subsistence, the comparative smallness of their numbers explains and justifies the high rate of their capitation. The truth of this assertion may be illustrated by the following example: The Ædui, one of the most powerful and civilized tribes or *cities* of Gaul, occupied an extent of territory which now contains above five hundred thousand inhabitants in the two ecclesiastical dioceses of Autun and Nevers:[105] and with the probable accession of those of Châlons and Macon,[106] the population would amount to eight hundred thousand souls. In the time of Constantine, the territory of the Ædui afforded no more than twenty-five thousand *heads* of capitation, of whom seven thousand were discharged by that prince from the intolerable weight of tribute. A just analogy would seem to countenance the opinion of an ingenious historian, that the free and tributary citizens did not surpass the number of half a million; and if, in the ordinary administration of government, their annual payments may be computed at about four millions and a half of our money, it would appear that, although the share of each individual was four times as considerable, a fourth part only of the modern taxes of France was levied on the Imperial province of Gaul. The exactions of Constantius may be calculated at seven millions sterling, which were reduced to two millions by the humanity or the wisdom of Julian.

But this tax or capitation on the proprietors of land would have suffered a rich and numerous class of free citizens to escape. With the view of sharing that species of wealth which is derived from art or labour, and which exists in money or in merchandise, the emperors imposed a distinct and personal tribute on the trading part of their subjects. Some exemptions, very strictly confined both in time and place, were allowed to the proprietors who disposed of the produce of their own estates. Some indulgence was granted to the profession of the liberal arts: but every other branch of commercial industry was affected by the severity of the law. The honourable merchant of Alexandria, who imported the gems and spices of India for the use of the western world; the usurer, who derived from the interest of money a silent and ignominious profit; the ingenious manufacturer, the diligent mechanic, and even the most obscure retailer of a sequestered village, were obliged to admit the officers of the revenue into the partnership of their gain: and the sovereign of the Roman empire, who tolerated the profession, consented to share the infamous salary, of public prostitutes. As this general tax upon industry was collected every fourth year, it was styled the *Lustral Contribution:* and the historian Zosimus laments that the approach of the fatal period was announced by the tears and terrors of the citizens, who were often compelled by the impending scourge to embrace the most abhorred and unnatural methods of procuring the sum at which their property had been assessed. The testimony of Zosimus cannot indeed be justified from the charge of passion and prejudice; but, from the nature of this tribute, it seems reasonable to conclude that it was arbitrary in the distribution, and extremely rigorous in the mode of collecting. The secret wealth of commerce, and the precarious profits of art or labour, are susceptible only of a discretionary valuation, which is seldom disadvantageous to the interest of the treasury; and, as the person of the trader supplies the want of a visible and permanent security, the payment of the imposition, which, in the case of a land-tax, may be obtained by the seizure of property, can rarely be extorted by any other means than those of corporal punishments. The cruel treatment of the insolvent debtors of the state is attested, and was perhaps mitigated, by a very humane edict of Constantine, who, disclaiming the use of racks and of scourges, allots a spacious and airy prison for the place of their confinement.

These general taxes were imposed and levied by the absolute authority of the monarch; but the occasional offerings of the *coronary gold* still retained the name and semblance of popular consent. It was an ancient custom that the allies of the republic, who ascribed their safety or deliverance to the success of the Roman arms; and even the cities of Italy, who admired the virtues of their victorious general; adorned the pomp of his triumph by their voluntary gifts of crowns of gold, which, after the ceremony, were consecrated in the temple of Jupiter, to remain a lasting monument of his glory to future ages. The progress of zeal and flattery soon multiplied the number, and increased the size, of these popular donations; and the

comprehended the adjacent territory of (Noviodunum) *Nevers. The two dioceses of Autun and Nevers are now composed, the former of 610, and the latter of 160, parishes. The registers of births, taken during eleven years, in 476 parishes of the same province of Burgundy, and multiplied by the moderate proportion of 25, may authorize us to assign an average number of 656 persons for each parish, which being again multiplied by the 770 parishes of the dioceses of Nevers and Autun will produce the sum of 505,120 persons for the extent of country which was once possessed by the Ædui.*

[108] *We might derive an additional supply of 301,750 inhabitants from the dioceses of Châlons* (Cabillonum) *and of Macon* (Matisco); *since they contain, the one 200, and the other 260, parishes. This accession of territory might be justified by very specious reasons. 1. Châlons and Macon were undoubtedly within the original jurisdiction of the Ædui. 2. In the* Notitia *of Gaul, they are enumerated not as* Civitates, *but merely as* Castra. *3. They do not appear to have been episcopal seats before the fifth and sixth centuries. Yet there is a passage in*

triumph of Cæsar was enriched with two thousand eight hundred and twenty-two massy crowns, whose weight amounted to twenty thousand four hundred and fourteen pounds of gold. This treasure was immediately melted down by the prudent dictator, who was satisfied that it would be more serviceable to his soldiers than to the gods: his example was imitated by his successors; and the custom was introduced of exchanging these splendid ornaments for the more acceptable present of the current gold coin of the empire.[107] The spontaneous offering was at length exacted as the debt of duty; and, instead of being confined to the occasion of a triumph, it was supposed to be granted by the several cities and provinces of the monarchy as often as the emperor condescended to announce his accession, his consulship, the birth of a son, the creation of a Cæsar, a victory over the Barbarians, or any other real or imaginary event which graced the annals of his reign. The peculiar free gift of the senate of Rome was fixed by custom at sixteen hundred pounds of gold, or about sixty-four thousand pounds sterling. The oppressed subjects celebrated their own felicity, that their sovereign should graciously consent to accept this feeble but voluntary testimony of their loyalty and gratitude.[108]

A people elated by pride, or soured by discontent, are seldom qualified to form a just estimate of their actual situation. The subjects of Constantine were incapable of discerning the decline of genius and manly virtue, which so far degraded them below the dignity of their ancestors; but they could feel and lament the rage of tyranny, the relaxation of discipline, and the increase of taxes. The impartial historian, who acknowledges the justice of their complaints, will observe some favourable circumstances which tended to alleviate the misery of their condition. The threatened tempest of Barbarians, which so soon subverted the foundations of Roman greatness, was still repelled, or suspended, on the frontiers. The arts of luxury and literature were cultivated, and the elegant pleasures of society were enjoyed, by the inhabitants of a considerable portion of the globe. The forms, the pomp, and the expense of the civil administration contributed to restrain the irregular licence of the soldiers; and, although the laws were violated by power or perverted by subtlety, the sage principles of the Roman jurisprudence preserved a sense of order and equity, unknown to the despotic governments of the east. The rights of mankind might derive some protection from religion and philosophy; and the name of freedom, which could no longer alarm, might admonish, the successors of Augustus that they did not reign over a nation of slaves or barbarians.[109]

XVIII

CHARACTER OF CONSTANTINE · GOTHIC WAR · DEATH OF CON-
STANTINE · DIVISION OF THE EMPIRE AMONG HIS THREE
SONS · PERSIAN WAR · TRAGIC DEATHS OF CONSTANTINE THE
YOUNGER AND CONSTANS · USURPATION OF MAGNENTIUS ·
CIVIL WAR · CONQUEST OF ITALY · VICTORY OF CONSTANTIUS

H E character of the prince who removed the seat of empire and introduced such important changes into the civil and religious constitution of his country has fixed the attention, and divided the opinions, of mankind. By the grateful zeal of the Christians, the deliverer of the church has been decorated with every attribute of a hero, and even of a saint; while the discontent of the vanquished party has compared Constantine to the most abhorred of those tyrants, who, by their vice and weakness, dishonoured the Imperial purple. The same passions have in some degree been perpetuated to succeeding generations, and the character of Constantine is considered, even in the present age, as an object either of satire or of panegyric. By the impartial union of those defects which are confessed by his warmest admirers and of those virtues which are acknowledged by his most implacable enemies, we might hope to delineate a just portrait of that extraordinary man, which the truth and candour of history should adopt without a blush. But it would soon appear that the vain attempt to blend such discordant colours, and to reconcile such inconsistent qualities, must produce a figure monstrous rather than human, unless it is viewed in its proper and distinct lights by a careful separation of the different periods of the reign of Constantine.

The person, as well as the mind, of Constantine had been enriched by nature with her choicest endowments. His stature was lofty, his countenance majestic, his deportment graceful; his strength and activity were displayed in every manly exercise, and from his earliest youth to a very advanced season of life, he preserved the vigour of his constitution by a strict adherence to the domestic virtues of chastity and temperance. He delighted in the social inter-

495

course of familiar conversation; and, though he might sometimes indulge his disposition to raillery with less reserve than was required by the severe dignity of his station, the courtesy and liberality of his manners gained the hearts of all who approached him. The sincerity of his friendship has been suspected; yet he showed, on some occasions, that he was not incapable of a warm and lasting attachment. The disadvantage of an illiterate education had not prevented him from forming a just estimate of the value of learning; and the arts and sciences derived some encouragement from the munificent protection of Constantine. In the dispatch of business, his diligence was indefatigable; and the active powers of his mind were almost continually exercised in reading, writing, or meditating, in giving audience to ambassadors, and in examining the complaints of his subjects. Even those who censured the propriety of his measures were compelled to acknowledge that he possessed magnanimity to conceive, and patience to execute, the most arduous designs, without being checked either by the prejudices of education or by the clamours of the multitude. In the field, he infused his own intrepid spirit into the troops, whom he conducted with the talents of a consummate general; and to his abilities, rather than to his fortune, we may ascribe the signal victories which he obtained over the foreign and domestic foes of the republic. He loved glory, as the reward, perhaps as the motive, of his labours. The boundless ambition, which, from the moment of his accepting the purple at York, appears as the ruling passion of his soul, may be justified by the dangers of his own situation, by the character of his rivals, by the consciousness of superior merit, and by the prospect that his success would enable him to restore peace and order to the distracted empire. In his civil wars against Maxentius and Licinius, he had engaged on his side the inclinations of the people, who compared the undissembled vices of those tyrants with the spirit of wisdom and justice which seemed to direct the general tenor of the administration of Constantine.[1]

Had Constantine fallen on the banks of the Tiber, or even in the plains of Hadrianople, such is the character which, with a few exceptions, he might have transmitted to posterity. But the conclusion of his reign (according to the moderate and indeed tender sentence of a writer of the same age) degraded him from the rank which he had acquired among the most deserving of the Roman princes. In the life of Augustus, we behold the tyrant of the republic converted, almost by imperceptible degrees, into the father of his country and

[1] *The virtues of Constantine are collected for the most part from Eutropius and the younger Victor, two sincere pagans, who wrote after the extinction of his family. Even Zosimus and the* emperor *Julian acknowledge his personal courage and military achievements.*

of human kind. In that of Constantine, we may contemplate a hero, who had so long inspired his subjects with love and his enemies with terror, degenerating into a cruel and dissolute monarch, corrupted by his fortune, or raised by conquest above the necessity of dissimulation. The general peace which he maintained during the last fourteen years of his reign was a period of apparent splendour rather than of real prosperity; and the old age of Constantine was disgraced by the opposite yet reconcilable vices of rapaciousness and prodigality. The accumulated treasures found in the palaces of Maxentius and Licinius were lavishly consumed; the various innovations introduced by the conqueror were attended with an increasing expense; the cost of his buildings, his court, and his festivals, required an immediate and plentiful supply; and the oppression of the people was the only fund which could support the magnificence of the sovereign. His unworthy favourites, enriched by the boundless liberality of their master, usurped with impunity the privilege of rapine and corruption. A secret but universal decay was felt in every part of the public administration, and the emperor himself, though he still retained the obedience, gradually lost the esteem, of his subjects. The dress and manners, which, towards the decline of life, he chose to affect, served only to degrade him in the eyes of mankind. The Asiatic pomp, which had been adopted by the pride of Diocletian, assumed an air of softness and effeminacy in the person of Constantine. He is represented with false hair of various colours, laboriously arranged by the skilful artists of the times; a diadem of a new and more expensive fashion; a profusion of gems and pearls, of collars and bracelets, and a variegated flowing robe of silk, most curiously embroidered with flowers of gold. In such apparel, scarcely to be excused by the youth and folly of Elagabalus, we are at a loss to discover the wisdom of an aged monarch and the simplicity of a Roman veteran.[2] A mind thus relaxed by prosperity and indulgence was incapable of rising to that magnanimity which disdains suspicion and dares to forgive. The deaths of Maximian and Licinius may perhaps be justified by the maxims of policy, as they are taught in the schools of tyrants; but an impartial narrative of the executions, or rather murders, which sullied the declining age of Constantine, will suggest to our most candid thoughts the idea of a prince who could sacrifice without reluctance the laws of justice and the feelings of nature to the dictates either of his passions or of his interest.

The same fortune which so invariably followed the standard of

[2] *Julian, in the Cæsars, attempts to ridicule his uncle. His suspicious testimony is confirmed however by the learned Spanheim, with the authority of medals. Eusebius alleges that Constantine dressed for the public, not for himself. Were this admitted, the vainest coxcomb could never want an excuse.*

Constantine seemed to secure the hopes and comforts of his domestic life. Those among his predecessors who had enjoyed the longest and most prosperous reigns, Augustus, Trajan, and Diocletian, had been disappointed of posterity; and the frequent revolutions had never allowed sufficient time for any Imperial family to grow up and multiply under the shade of the purple. But the royalty of the Flavian line, which had been first ennobled by the Gothic Claudius, descended through several generations; and Constantine himself derived from his royal father the hereditary honours which he transmitted to his children. The emperor had been twice married. Minervina, the obscure but lawful object of his youthful attachment,[3] had left him only one son, who was called Crispus. By Fausta, the daughter of Maximian, he had three daughters, and three sons, known by the kindred names of Constantine, Constantius, and Constans. The unambitious brothers of the great Constantine, Julius Constantius, Dalmatius, and Hannibalianus,[4] were permitted to enjoy the most honourable rank, and the most affluent fortune, that could be consistent with a private station. The youngest of the three lived without a name, and died without posterity. His two elder brothers obtained in marriage the daughters of wealthy senators, and propagated new branches of the Imperial race. Gallus and Julian afterwards became the most illustrious of the children of Julius Constantius, the *Patrician*. The two sons of Dalmatius, who had been decorated with the vain title of *censor,* were named Dalmatius and Hannibalianus. The two sisters of the great Constantine, Anastasia and Eutropia, were bestowed on Optatus and Nepotianus, two senators of noble birth and of consular dignity. His third sister, Constantia, was distinguished by her pre-eminence of greatness and of misery. She remained the widow of the vanquished Licinius; and it was by her entreaties that an innocent boy, the offspring of their marriage, preserved for some time, his life, the title of Cæsar, and a precarious hope of the succession. Besides the females and the allies of the Flavian house, ten or twelve males, to whom the language of modern courts would apply the title of princes of the blood, seemed, according to the order of their birth, to be destined either to inherit or to support the throne of Constantine. But in less than thirty years, this numerous and increasing family was reduced to the persons of Constantius and Julian, who alone had survived a series of crimes and calamities, such as the tragic poets have deplored in the devoted lines of Pelops and of Cadmus.

Crispus, the eldest son of Constantine, and the presumptive heir

[3] *Zosimus and Zonaras agree in representing Minervina as the concubine of Constantine: but Ducange has very gallantly rescued her character, by producing a decisive passage from one of the panegyrics.*

[4] *Ducange bestows on him, after Zonaras, the name of Constantine; a name somewhat unlikely, as it was already occupied by the elder brother.*

498

of the empire, is represented by impartial historians as an amiable and accomplished youth. The care of his education, or at least of his studies, was entrusted to Lactantius, the most eloquent of the Christians; a præceptor admirably qualified to form the taste, and to excite the virtues, of his illustrious disciple.[5] At the age of seventeen, Crispus was invested with the title of Cæsar, and the administration of the Gallic provinces, where the inroads of the Germans gave him an early occasion of signalizing his military prowess. In the civil war which broke out soon afterwards, the father and son divided their powers; and this history has already celebrated the valour as well as conduct displayed by the latter in forcing the straits of the Hellespont, so obstinately defended by the superior fleet of Licinius. This naval victory contributed to determine the event of the war; and the names of Constantine and of Crispus were united in the joyful acclamations of their eastern subjects: who loudly proclaimed that the world had been subdued, and was now governed, by an emperor endowed with every virtue; and by his illustrious son, a prince beloved of heaven, and the lively image of his father's perfections. The public favour, which seldom accompanies old age, diffused its lustre over the youth of Crispus. He deserved the esteem, and he engaged the affections of the court, the army, and the people. The experienced merit of a reigning monarch is acknowledged by his subjects with reluctance, and frequently denied with partial and discontented murmurs; while, from the opening virtues of his successor, they fondly conceive the most unbounded hopes of private as well as public felicity.

This dangerous popularity soon excited the attention of Constantine, who, both as a father and as a king, was impatient of an equal. Instead of attempting to secure the allegiance of his son, by the generous ties of confidence and gratitude, he resolved to prevent the mischiefs which might be apprehended from dissatisfied ambition. Crispus soon had reason to complain that, while his infant brother Constantius was sent, with the title of Cæsar, to reign over his peculiar department of the Gallic provinces, *he,* a prince of mature years, who had performed such recent and signal services, instead of being raised to the superior rank of Augustus, was confined almost a prisoner to his father's court; and exposed, without power or defence, to every calumny which the malice of his enemies could suggest. Under such painful circumstances, the royal youth might not always be able to compose his behaviour, or suppress his discontent; and we may be assured that he was encompassed by a train of indis-

[5] *The poverty of Lactantius may be applied either to the praise of the disinterested philosopher or to the shame of the unfeeling patron.*

creet or perfidious followers, who assiduously studied to inflame, and who were perhaps instructed to betray, the unguarded warmth of his resentment. An edict of Constantine, published about this time, manifestly indicates his real or affected suspicions that a secret conspiracy had been formed against his person and government. By all the allurements of honours and rewards, he invites informers of every degree to accuse without exception his magistrates or ministers, his friends or his most intimate favourites, protesting, with a solemn asseveration, that he himself will listen to the charge, that he himself will revenge his injuries; and concluding with a prayer, which discovers some apprehension of danger, that the providence of the Supreme Being may still continue to protect the safety of the emperor and of the empire.

The informers, who complied with so liberal an invitation, were sufficiently versed in the arts of courts to select the friends and adherents of Crispus as the guilty persons; nor is there any reason to distrust the veracity of the emperor, who had promised an ample measure of revenge and punishment. The policy of Constantine maintained, however, the same appearances of regard and confidence towards a son whom he began to consider as his most irreconcilable enemy. Medals were struck with the customary vows for the long and auspicious reign of the young Cæsar; and as the people, who was not admitted into the secrets of the palace, still loved his virtues and respected his dignity, a poet who solicits his recall from exile, adores with equal devotion the majesty of the father and that of the son.[6] The time was now arrived for celebrating the august ceremony of the twentieth year of the reign of Constantine; and the emperor, for that purpose, removed his court from Nicomedia to Rome, where the most splendid preparations had been made for his reception. Every eye and every tongue affected to express their sense of the general happiness, and the veil of ceremony and dissimulation was drawn for a while over the darkest designs of revenge and murder. In the midst of the festival, the unfortunate Crispus was apprehended by order of the emperor, who laid aside the tenderness of a father, without assuming the equity of a judge. The examination was short and private; and, as it was thought decent to conceal the fate of the young prince from the eyes of the Roman people, he was sent under a strong guard to Pola, in Istria, where, soon afterwards, he was put to death, either by the hand of the executioner or by the more gentle operation of poison. The Cæsar Licinius, a youth of amiable manners, was involved in the

[6] *His name was Porphyrius Optatianus.*

ruin of Crispus; and the stern jealousy of Constantine was unmoved by the prayers and tears of his favourite sister, pleading for the life of a son, whose rank was his only crime, and whose loss she did not long survive. The story of these unhappy princes, the nature and evidence of their guilt, the forms of their trial, and the circumstances of their death, were buried in mysterious obscurity; and the courtly bishop, who has celebrated in an elaborate work the virtues and piety of his hero, observes a prudent silence on the subject of these tragic events.[7] Such haughty contempt for the opinion of mankind, whilst it imprints an indelible stain on the memory of Constantine, must remind us of the very different behaviour of one of the greatest monarchs of the present age. The Czar Peter, in the full possession of despotic power, submitted to the judgment of Russia, of Europe, and of posterity, the reasons which had compelled him to subscribe to the condemnation of a criminal, or at least of a degenerate, son.

The innocence of Crispus was so universally acknowledged that the modern Greeks, who adore the memory of their founder, are reduced to palliate the guilt of a parricide, which the common feelings of human nature forbade them to justify. They pretend that, as soon as the afflicted father discovered the falsehood of the accusation by which his credulity had been so fatally misled, he published to the world his repentance and remorse; that he mourned forty days, during which he abstained from the use of the bath and all the ordinary comforts of life; and that, for the lasting instruction of posterity, he erected a golden statue of Crispus, with this memorable inscription: To My Son, whom I unjustly condemned.[8] A tale so moral and so interesting would deserve to be supported by less exceptionable authority; but, if we consult the more ancient and authentic writers, they will inform us that the repentance of Constantine was manifested only in acts of blood and revenge; and that he atoned for the murder of an innocent son, by the execution, perhaps, of a guilty wife. They ascribe the misfortunes of Crispus to the arts of his stepmother Fausta, whose implacable hatred, or whose disappointed love, renewed in the palace of Constantine the ancient tragedy of Hippolytus and of Phædra.[9] Like the daughter of Minos, the daughter of Maximian accused her son-in-law of an incestuous attempt on the chastity of his father's wife; and easily obtained, from the jealousy of the emperor, a sentence of death against a young prince whom she considered with reason as the most formidable rival of her own children. But Helena, the aged mother of Constantine, lamented and revenged the untimely fate of her grand-

[7] *Two hundred and fifty years afterwards, Evagrius deduced from the silence of Eusebius a vain argument against the reality of the fact.*

[8] *In order to prove that the statue was erected by Constantine, and afterwards concealed by the malice of the Arians, Codinus very readily creates two witnesses, Hippolytus and the younger Herodotus, to whose imaginary histories he appeals with unblushing confidence.*

[9] *Zosimus may be considered as our original. The ingenuity of the moderns, assisted by a few hints from the ancients, has illustrated and improved his obscure and imperfect narrative.*

[10] *Zosimus imputes to Constantine the death of two wives: of the innocent Fausta, and of an adulteress who was the mother of his three successors. According to Jerom, three or four years elapsed between the death of Crispus and that of Fausta. The elder Victor is prudently silent.*

[11] *If Fausta was put to death, it is reasonable to believe that the private apartments of the palace were the scene of her execution. The orator Chrysostom indulges his fancy by exposing the naked empress on a desert mountain, to be devoured by wild beasts.*

[12] *Julian seems to call her the mother of Crispus. She might assume that title by adoption. At least, she was not considered as his mortal enemy. Julian compares the fortune of Fausta with that of Parysatis, the Persian queen. A Roman would have more naturally recollected the second Agrippina:—*

*Et moi, qui sur le trône
ai suivi mes ancêtres:
Moi, fille, femme, sœur
et mère de vos maîtres.*

son Crispus; nor was it long before a real or pretended discovery was made, that Fausta herself entertained a criminal connexion with a slave belonging to the Imperial stables.[10] Her condemnation and punishment were the instant consequences of the charge; and the adulteress was suffocated by the steam of a bath, which, for that purpose, had been heated to an extraordinary degree.[11] By some it will perhaps be thought, that the remembrance of a conjugal union of twenty years, and the honour of their common offspring, the destined heirs of the throne, might have softened the obdurate heart of Constantine; and persuaded him to suffer his wife, however guilty she might appear, to expiate her offences in a solitary prison. But it seems a superfluous labour to weigh the propriety, unless we could ascertain the truth, of this singular event; which is attended with some circumstances of doubt and perplexity. Those who have attacked, and those who have defended, the character of Constantine have alike disregarded two very remarkable passages of two orations pronounced under the succeeding reign. The former celebrates the virtues, the beauty, and the fortune of the empress Fausta, the daughter, wife, sister, and mother of so many princes.[12] The latter asserts, in explicit terms, that the mother of the younger Constantine, who was slain three years after his father's death, survived to weep over the fate of her son. Notwithstanding the positive testimony of several writers of the Pagan as well as of the Christian religion, there may still remain some reason to believe, or at least to suspect, that Fausta escaped the blind and suspicious cruelty of her husband. The deaths of a son, and of a nephew, with the execution of a great number of respectable and perhaps innocent friends, who were involved in their fall, may be sufficient, however, to justify the discontent of the Roman people, and to explain the satirical verses affixed to the palace-gate, comparing the splendid and bloody reigns of Constantine and Nero.

By the death of Crispus, the inheritance of the empire seemed to devolve on the three sons of Fausta, who have been already mentioned under the names of Constantine, of Constantius, and of Constans. These young princes were successively invested with the title of Cæsar; and the dates of their promotion may be referred to the tenth, the twentieth, and the thirtieth years of the reign of their father. This conduct, though it tended to multiply the future masters of the Roman world, might be excused by the partiality of paternal affection; but it is not easy to understand the motives of the emperor, when he endangered the safety both of his family and of his people, by the unnecessary elevation of his two nephews, Dalmatius and Hannibalianus. The former was raised, by the title of Cæsar, to an equality with his cousins. In favour of the latter, Constantine invented the new and singular appellation of *Nobilissimus;*[13] to which he annexed the flattering distinction of a robe of purple and gold. But of the whole series of Roman princes in any age of the empire, Hannibalianus alone was distinguished by the title of KING; a name which the subjects of Tiberius would have detested, as the profane and cruel insult of capricious tyranny. The use of such a title, even as it appears under the reign of Constantine, is a strange and unconnected fact, which can scarcely be admitted on the joint authority of Imperial medals and contemporary writers.

The whole empire was deeply interested in the education of these five youths, the acknowledged successors of Constantine. The exercises of the body prepared them for the fatigues of war and the duties of active life. Those who occasionally mention the education or talents of Constantius allow that he excelled in the gymnastic arts of leaping and running; that he was a dexterous archer, a skilful horseman, and a master of all the different weapons used in the service either of the cavalry or of the infantry. The same assiduous cultivation was bestowed, though not perhaps with equal success, to improve the minds of the sons and nephews of Constantine.[14] The most celebrated professors of the Christian faith, of the Grecian philosophy, and of the Roman jurisprudence were invited by the liberality of the emperor, who reserved for himself the important task of instructing the royal youths in the science of government and the knowledge of mankind. But the genius of Constantine himself had been formed by adversity and experience. In the free intercourse of private life, and amidst the dangers of the court of Galerius, he had learned to command his own passions, to encounter those of his equals, and to depend for his present safety and future greatness on the prudence and firmness of his personal conduct. His destined successors had the misfortune of being born and educated in the Imperial purple. Incessantly surrounded with a train of flatterers, they passed their youth in the enjoyment of luxury and the expectation of a throne; nor would the dignity of their rank permit them to descend from that elevated station from whence the various characters of human nature appear to wear a smooth and uniform aspect. The indulgence of Constantine admitted them at a very tender age to share the administration of the empire; and they studied the art of reigning at the expense of the people entrusted to their

[13] *Under the predecessors of Constantine,* Nobilissimus *was a vague epithet rather than a legal and determined* title.

[14] *Constantius studied with laudable diligence; but the dulness of his fancy prevented him from succeeding in the art of poetry, or even of rhetoric.*

care. The younger Constantine was appointed to hold his court in Gaul; and his brother Constantius exchanged that department, the ancient patrimony of their father, for the more opulent, but less martial, countries of the East. Italy, the Western Illyricum, and Africa were accustomed to revere Constans, the third of his sons, as the representative of the great Constantine. He fixed Dalmatius on the Gothic frontier, to which he annexed the government of Thrace, Macedonia, and Greece. The city of Cæsarea was chosen for the residence of Hannibalianus; and the provinces of Pontus, Cappadocia, and the Lesser Armenia were destined to form the extent of his new kingdom. For each of these princes a suitable establishment was provided. A just proportion of guards, of legions, and of auxiliaries was allotted for their respective dignity and defence. The ministers and generals who were placed about their persons were such as Constantine could trust to assist, and even to control, these youthful sovereigns in the exercise of their delegated power. As they advanced in years and experience, the limits of their authority were insensibly enlarged: but the emperor always reserved for himself the title of Augustus; and, while he showed the *Cæsars* to the armies and provinces, he maintained every part of the empire in equal obedience to its supreme head.[15] The tranquillity of the last fourteen years of his reign was scarcely interrupted by the contemptible insurrection of a camel-driver in the island of Cyprus,[16] or by the active part which the policy of Constantine engaged him to assume in the wars of the Goths and Sarmatians.

Among the different branches of the human race, the Sarmatians form a very remarkable shade; as they seem to unite the manners of the Asiatic barbarians with the figure and complexion of the ancient inhabitants of Europe. According to the various accidents of peace and war, of alliance or conquest, the Sarmatians were sometimes confined to the banks of the Tanais; and they sometimes spread themselves over the immense plains which lie between the Vistula and the Volga. The care of their numerous flocks and herds, the pursuit of game, and the exercise of war, or rather of rapine, directed the vagrant motions of the Sarmatians. The moveable camps or cities, the ordinary residence of their wives and children, consisted only of large waggons, drawn by oxen and covered in the form of tents. The military strength of the nation was composed of cavalry; and the custom of their warriors, to lead in their hand one or two spare horses, enabled them to advance and to retreat with a rapid diligence which surprised the security, and eluded the pursuit, of a

[15] *Eusebius, with a design of exalting the authority and glory of Constantine, affirms that he divided the Roman empire as a private citizen might have divided his patrimony. His distribution of the provinces may be collected from Eutropius, the two Victors, and the Valesian fragment.*

[16] *Calocerus, the obscure leader of this rebellion, or rather tumult, was apprehended and burnt alive in the market-place of Tarsus, by the vigilance of Dalmatius.*

[17] *Pausanias, that inquisitive traveller, had carefully examined a Sarmatian cuirass, which was preserved in the temple of Æsculapius at Athens.*

distant enemy. Their poverty of iron prompted their rude industry to invent a sort of cuirass, which was capable of resisting a sword or javelin, though it was formed only of horses' hoofs, cut into thin and polished slices, carefully laid over each other in the manner of scales or feathers, and strongly sewed upon an under-garment of coarse linen.[17] The offensive arms of the Sarmatians were short daggers, long lances, and a weighty bow with a quiver of arrows. They were reduced to the necessity of employing fish bones for the points of their weapons; but the custom of dipping them in a venomous liquor that poisoned the wounds which they inflicted is alone sufficient to prove the most savage manners; since a people impressed with a sense of humanity would have abhorred so cruel a practice, and a nation skilled in the arts of war would have disdained so impotent a resource.[18] Whenever these Barbarians issued from their deserts in quest of prey, their shaggy beards, uncombed locks, the furs with which they were covered from head to foot, and their fierce countenances, which seemed to express the innate cruelty of their minds, inspired the more civilized provincials of Rome with horror and dismay.

The tender Ovid, after a youth spent in the enjoyment of fame and luxury, was condemned to an hopeless exile on the frozen banks of the Danube, where he was exposed, almost without defence, to the fury of these monsters of the desert, with whose stern spirits he feared that his gentle shade might hereafter be confounded. In his pathetic, but sometimes unmanly, lamentations,[19] he describes, in the most lively colours, the dress and manners, the arms and inroads of the Getæ and Sarmatians, who were associated for the purposes of destruction; and from the accounts of history there is some reason to believe that these Sarmatians were the Jazygæ, one of the most numerous and warlike tribes of the nation. The allurements of plenty engaged them to seek a permanent establishment on the frontiers of the empire. Soon after the reign of Augustus, they obliged the Dacians, who subsisted by fishing on the banks of the river Theiss or Tibiscus, to retire into the hilly country, and to abandon to the victorious Sarmatians the fertile plains of the Upper Hungary, which are bounded by the course of the Danube and the semi-circular inclosure of the Carpathian mountains.[20] In this advantageous position, they watched or suspended the moment of attack, as they were provoked by injuries or appeased by presents; they gradually acquired the skill of using more dangerous weapons; and, although the Sarmatians did not illustrate their name by any

[18] See in the *Recherches sur les Américains*, a very curious dissertation on poisoned darts. The venom was commonly extracted from the vegetable reign; but that employed by the Scythians appears to have been drawn from the viper and a mixture of human blood. The use of poisoned arms, which has been spread over both worlds, never preserved a savage tribe from the arms of a disciplined enemy.

[19] The nine books of Poetical Epistles, which Ovid composed during the seven first years of his melancholy exile, possess, besides the merit of elegance, a double value. They exhibit a picture of the human mind under very singular circumstances; and they contain many curious observations, which no Roman, except Ovid, could have an opportunity of making.

[20] The Sarmatians Jazygæ were settled on the banks of the Pathissus or Tibiscus, when Pliny, in the year 79, published his Natural History. In the time of Strabo and Ovid, sixty or seventy years before, they appear to have inhabited beyond the Getæ, along the coast of the Euxine.

memorable exploits, they occasionally assisted their eastern and western neighbors, the Goths and the Germans, with a formidable body of cavalry. They lived under the irregular aristocracy of their chieftains; but, after they had received into their bosom the fugitive Vandals, who yielded to the pressure of the Gothic power, they seem to have chosen a king from that nation, and from the illustrious race of the Astingi, who had formerly dwelt on the shores of the Northern ocean.[21]

This motive of enmity must have inflamed the subjects of contention, which perpetually arise on the confines of warlike and independent nations. The Vandal princes were stimulated by fear and revenge; the Gothic kings aspired to extend their dominion from the Euxine to the frontiers of Germany: and the waters of the Maros, a small river which falls into the Theiss, were stained with the blood of the contending Barbarians. After some experience of the superior strength and number of their adversaries, the Sarmatians implored the protection of the Roman monarch, who beheld with pleasure the discord of the nations, but who was justly alarmed by the progress of the Gothic arms. As soon as Constantine had declared himself in favour of the weaker party, the haughty Araric, king of the Goths, instead of expecting the attack of the legions, boldly passed the Danube, and spread terror and devastation through the province of Mæsia. To oppose the inroad of this destroying host, the aged emperor took the field in person; but on this occasion either his conduct or his fortune betrayed the glory which he had acquired in so many foreign and domestic wars. He had the mortification of seeing his troops fly before an inconsiderable detachment of the Barbarians, who pursued them to the edge of their fortified camp and obliged him to consult his safety by a precipitate and ignominious retreat. The event of a second and more successful action retrieved the honour of the Roman name; and the powers of art and discipline prevailed, after an obstinate contest, over the efforts of irregular valour. The broken army of the Goths abandoned the field of battle, the wasted province, and the passage of the Danube: and, although the eldest of the sons of Constantine was permitted to supply the place of his father, the merit of the victory, which diffused universal joy, was ascribed to the auspicious counsels of the emperor himself.

He contributed at least to improve this advantage, by his negotiations with the free and warlike people of Chersonesus,[22] whose capital, situate on the western coast of the Tauric or Crimæan peninsula,

[21] This hypothesis of a Vandal king reigning over Sarmatian subjects seems necessary to reconcile the Goth Jornandes with the Greek and Latin historians of Constantine. It may be observed that Isidore, who lived in Spain under the dominion of the Goths, gives them for enemies, not the Vandals, but the Sarmatians.

[22] I may stand in need of some apology for having used, without scruple, the authority of Constantine Porphyrogenitus, in all that relates to the wars and negotiations of the Chersonites. I am aware that he was a Greek of the tenth century, and that his accounts of ancient history are frequently confused and fabulous. But on this occasion his narrative is, for the most part, consistent and probable; nor is there much difficulty in conceiving that an emperor might have access to some secret archives, which had escaped the diligence of meaner historians.

still retained some vestiges of a Grecian colony, and was governed by a perpetual magistrate, assisted by a council of senators, emphatically styled the Fathers of the City. The Chersonites were animated against the Goths by the memory of the wars which, in the preceding century, they had maintained with unequal forces against the invaders of their country. They were connected with the Romans by the mutual benefits of commerce; as they were supplied from the provinces of Asia with corn and manufactures, which they purchased with their only productions, salt, wax, and hides. Obedient to the requisition of Constantine, they prepared, under the conduct of their magistrate Diogenes, a considerable army, of which the principal strength consisted in crossbows and military chariots. The speedy march and intrepid attack of the Chersonites, by diverting the attention of the Goths, assisted the operations of the Imperial generals. The Goths, vanquished on every side, were driven into the mountains, where, in the course of a severe campaign, above an hundred thousand were computed to have perished by cold and hunger. Peace was at length granted to their humble supplications; the eldest son of Araric was accepted as the most valuable hostage; and Constantine endeavoured to convince their chiefs, by a liberal distribution of honours and rewards, how far the friendship of the Romans was preferable to their enmity. In the expressions of his gratitude towards the faithful Chersonites, the emperor was still more magnificent. The pride of the nation was gratified by the splendid and almost royal decorations bestowed on their magistrate and his successors. A perpetual exemption from all duties was stipulated for their vessels which traded to the ports of the Black Sea. A regular subsidy was promised, of iron, corn, oil, and of every supply which could be useful either in peace or war. But it was thought that the Sarmatians were sufficiently rewarded by their deliverance from impending ruin; and the emperor, perhaps with too strict an economy, deducted some part of the expenses of the war from the customary gratifications which were allowed to that turbulent nation.

Exasperated by this apparent neglect, the Sarmatians soon forgot, with the levity of Barbarians, the services which they had so lately received and the dangers which still threatened their safety. Their inroads on the territory of the empire provoked the indignation of Constantine to leave them to their fate, and he no longer opposed the ambition of Geberic, a renowned warrior, who had recently ascended the Gothic throne. Wisumar, the Vandal king, whilst alone and unassisted he defended his dominions with undaunted courage, was vanquished and slain in a decisive battle, which swept away the flower of the Sarmatian youth. The remainder of the nation embraced the desperate expedient of arming their slaves, a hardy race of hunters and herdsmen, by whose tumultuary aid they revenged their defeat and expelled the invader from their confines. But they soon discovered that they had exchanged a foreign for a domestic enemy, more dangerous and more implacable. Enraged by their former servitude, elated by their present glory, the slaves, under the name of Limigantes, claimed and usurped the possession of the country which they had saved. Their masters, unable to withstand the ungoverned fury of the populace, preferred the hardships of exile to the tyranny of their servants. Some of the fugitive Sarmatians solicited a less ignominious dependence, under the hostile standard of the Goths. A more numerous band retired beyond the Carpathian mountains, among the Quadi, their German allies, and were easily admitted to share a superfluous waste of uncultivated land. But the far greater part of the distressed nation turned their eyes towards the fruitful provinces of Rome. Imploring the protection and forgiveness of the emperor, they solemnly promised, as subjects in peace and as soldiers in war, the most inviolable fidelity to the empire which should graciously receive them into its bosom. According to the maxims adopted by Probus and his successors, the offers of this Barbarian colony were eagerly accepted; and a competent portion of lands, in the provinces of Pannonia, Thrace, Macedonia, and Italy, were immediately assigned for the habitation and subsistence of three hundred thousand Sarmatians.

By chastising the pride of the Goths, and by accepting the homage of a suppliant nation, Constantine asserted the majesty of the Roman empire; and the ambassadors of Æthiopia, Persia and the most remote countries of India congratulated the peace and prosperity of his government.[23] If he reckoned, among the favours of fortune, the death of his eldest son, of his nephew, and perhaps of his wife, he enjoyed an uninterrupted flow of private as well as public felicity, till the thirtieth year of his reign; a period which none of his predecessors, since Augustus, had been permitted to celebrate. Constantine survived that solemn festival about ten months; and, at the mature age of sixty-four, after a short illness, he ended his memorable life at the palace of Aquyrion, in the suburbs of Nicomedia, whither he had retired for the benefit of the air, and with the hope of recruiting his exhausted strength by the use of the warm baths.

[23] Eusebius remarks three circumstances relative to these Indians. 1. They came from the shores of the eastern ocean; a description which might be applied to the coast of China or Coromandel. 2. They presented shining gems, and unknown animals. 3. They protested their kings had erected statues to represent the supreme majesty of Constantine.

The excessive demonstrations of grief, or at least of mourning, surpassed whatever had been practised on any former occasion. Notwithstanding the claims of the senate and people of ancient Rome, the corpse of the deceased emperor, according to his last request, was transported to the city which was destined to preserve the name and memory of its founder. The body of Constantine, adorned with the vain symbols of greatness, the purple and diadem, was deposited on a golden bed in one of the apartments of the palace, which for that purpose had been splendidly furnished and illuminated. The forms of the court were strictly maintained. Every day, at the appointed hours, the principal officers of the state, the army, and the household, approaching the person of their sovereign with bended knees and a composed countenance, offered their respectful homage as seriously as if he had been still alive. From motives of policy, this theatrical representation was for some time continued; nor could flattery neglect the opportunity of remarking that Constantine alone, by the peculiar indulgence of heaven, had reigned after his death.[24]

But this reign could subsist only in empty pageantry; and it was soon discovered that the will of the most absolute monarch is seldom obeyed, when his subjects have no longer anything to hope from his favour, or to dread from his resentment. The same ministers and generals who bowed with such reverential awe before the inanimate corpse of their deceased sovereign were engaged in secret consultations to exclude his two nephews, Dalmatius and Hannibalianus, from the share which he had assigned them in the succession of the empire. We are too imperfectly acquainted with the court of Constantine to form any judgment of the real motives which influenced the leaders of the conspiracy; unless we should suppose that they were actuated by a spirit of jealousy and revenge against the præfect Ablavius, a proud favourite, who had long directed the counsels and abused the confidence of the late emperor. The arguments by which they solicited the concurrence of the soldiers and people are of a more obvious nature: and they might with decency, as well as truth, insist on the superior rank of the children of Constantine, the danger of multiplying the number of sovereigns, and the impending mischiefs which threatened the republic, from the discord of so many rival princes, who were not connected by the tender sympathy of fraternal affection. The intrigue was conducted with zeal and secrecy, till a loud and unanimous declaration was procured from the troops that they would suffer none except the

[24] *Constantine had prepared for himself a stately tomb in the church of the Holy Apostles. The best, and indeed almost the only, account of the sickness, death, and funeral of Constantine, is contained in the fourth book of his Life, by Eusebius.*

sons of their lamented monarch to reign over the Roman empire. The younger Dalmatius, who was united with his collateral relations by the ties of friendship and interest, is allowed to have inherited a considerable share of the abilities of the great Constantine; but, on this occasion, he does not appear to have concerted any measures for supporting, by arms, the just claims which himself and his royal brother derived from the liberality of their uncle. Astonished and overwhelmed by the tide of popular fury, they seem to have remained, without the power of flight or of resistance, in the hands of their implacable enemies. Their fate was suspended till the arrival of Constantius, the second, and perhaps the most favoured, of the sons of Constantine.

The voice of the dying emperor had recommended the care of his funeral to the piety of Constantius; and that prince, by the vicinity of his eastern station, could easily prevent the diligence of his brothers, who resided in their distant government of Italy and Gaul. As soon as he had taken possession of the palace of Constantinople, his first care was to remove the apprehensions of his kinsmen by a solemn oath, which he pledged for their security. His next employment was to find some specious pretence which might release his conscience from the obligation of an imprudent promise. The arts of fraud were made subservient to the designs of cruelty; and a manifest forgery was attested by a person of the most sacred character. From the hands of the bishop of Nicomedia, Constantius received a fatal scroll affirmed to be the genuine testament of his father; in which the emperor expressed his suspicions that he had been poisoned by his brother; and conjured his sons to revenge his death, and to consult their own safety by the punishment of the guilty. Whatever reasons might have been alleged by these unfortunate princes to defend their life and honour against so incredible an accusation, they were silenced by the furious clamours of the soldiers, who declared themselves at once their enemies, their judges, and their executioners. The spirit, and even the forms, of legal proceedings were repeatedly violated in a promiscuous massacre; which involved the two uncles of Constantius, seven of his cousins, of whom Dalmatius and Hannibalianus were the most illustrious, the patrician Optatus, who had married a sister of the late emperor, and the præfect Ablavius, whose power and riches had inspired him with some hopes of obtaining the purple. If it were necessary to aggravate the horrors of this bloody scene, we might add that Constantius himself had espoused the daughter of his uncle Julius, and that he had bestowed his sister in marriage on his cousin Hannibalianus. These alliances, which the policy of Constantine, regardless of the public [25] prejudice, had formed between the several branches of the Imperial house, served only to convince mankind that these princes were as cold to the endearments of conjugal affection, as they were insensible to the ties of consanguinity and the moving entreaties of youth and innocence. Of so numerous a family Gallus and Julian alone, the two youngest children of Julius Constantius, were saved from the hands of the assassins, till their rage, satiated with slaughter, had in some measure subsided. The emperor Constantius, who, in the absence of his brothers, was the most obnoxious to guilt and reproach, discovered, on some future occasions, a faint and transient remorse for those cruelties, which the perfidious counsels of his ministers and the irresistible violence of the troops had extorted from his unexperienced youth. [26]

The massacre of the Flavian race was succeeded by a new division of the provinces; which was ratified in a personal interview of the three brothers. Constantine, the eldest of the Cæsars, obtained, with a certain pre-eminence of rank, the possession of the new capital, which bore his own name and that of his father. Thrace and the countries of the east were allotted for the patrimony of Constantius; and Constans was acknowledged as the lawful sovereign of Italy, Africa, and the western Illyricum. The armies submitted to their hereditary right; and they condescended, after some delay, to accept from the Roman senate the title of *Augustus*. When they first assumed the reins of government, the eldest of these princes was twenty-one, the second twenty, and the third only seventeen, years of age.

While the martial nations of Europe followed the standards of his brothers, Constantius, at the head of the effeminate troops of Asia, was left to sustain the weight of the Persian war. At the decease of Constantine, the throne of the east was filled by Sapor, son of Hormouz or Hormisdas, the grandson of Narses, who, after the victory of Galerius, had humbly confessed the superiority of the Roman power. Although Sapor was in the thirtieth year of his long reign, he was still in the vigour of youth, as the date of his accession, by a very strange fatality, had preceded that of his birth. The wife of Hormouz remained pregnant at the time of her husband's death; and the uncertainty of the sex, as well as of the event, excited the ambitious hopes of the princes of the house of Sassan. The apprehensions of civil war were at length removed, by the positive assur-

[25] The repeal of the ancient law, and the practice of five hundred years, were insufficient to eradicate the prejudices of the Romans; who still considered the marriages of cousins-german as a species of imperfect incest; and Julian, whose mind was biassed by superstition and resentment, stigmatizes these unnatural alliances between his own cousins. The jurisprudence of the canons has since revived and enforced this prohibition, without being able to introduce it either into the civil or the common law of Europe.

[26] Julian charges his cousin Constantius with the whole guilt of a massacre from which he himself so narrowly escaped. His assertion is confirmed by Athanasius, who, for reasons of a very different nature, was not less an enemy of Constantius. Zosimus joins in the same accusation. But the three abbreviators, Eutropius and the Victors, use very qualifying expressions; "sinente potius quam jubente;" "incertum quo suasore;" "vi militum."

ance of the Magi that the widow of Hormouz had conceived, and would safely produce, a son. Obedient to the voice of superstition, the Persians prepared, without delay, the ceremony of his coronation. A royal bed, on which the queen lay in state, was exhibited in the midst of the palace; the diadem was placed on the spot which might be supposed to conceal the future heir of Artaxerxes, and the prostrate Satraps adored the majesty of their invisible and insensible sovereign.[27] If any credit can be given to this marvellous tale, which seems however to be countenanced by the manners of the people and by the extraordinary duration of his reign, we must admire not only the fortune, but the genius, of Sapor. In the soft sequestered education of a Persian harem, the royal youth could discover the importance of exercising the vigour of his mind and body; and, by his personal merit, deserved a throne, on which he had been seated while he was yet unconscious of the duties and temptations of absolute power. His minority was exposed to the almost inevitable calamities of domestic discord; his capital was surprised and plundered by Thair, a powerful king of Yemen, or Arabia; and the majesty of the royal family was degraded by the captivity of a princess, the sister of the deceased king. But, as soon as Sapor attained the age of manhood, the presumptuous Thair, his nation, and his country fell beneath the first effort of the young warrior; who used his victory with so judicious a mixture of rigour and clemency that he obtained from the fears and gratitude of the Arabs the title of *Dhoulacnaf,* or protector of the nation.

The ambition of the Persian, to whom his enemies ascribe the virtues of a soldier and a statesman, was animated by the desire of revenging the disgrace of his fathers, and of wresting from the hands of the Romans the five provinces beyond the Tigris. The military fame of Constantine, and the real or apparent strength of his government, suspended the attack; and, while the hostile conduct of Sapor provoked the resentment, his artful negotiations amused the patience, of the Imperial court. The death of Constantine was the signal of war,[28] and the actual condition of the Syrian and Armenian frontiers seemed to encourage the Persians by the prospect of a rich spoil and an easy conquest. The example of the massacres of the palace diffused a spirit of licentiousness and sedition among the troops of the east, who were no longer restrained by their habits of obedience to a veteran commander. By the prudence of Constantius, who, from the interview with his brothers in Pannonia, immediately hastened to the banks of the Euphrates, the legions were

[27] *Agathias, who lived in the sixth century, is the author of this story. He derived his information from some extracts of the Persian Chronicles, obtained and translated by the interpreter Sergius, during his embassy at that court.*

[28] *Sextus Rufus, who on this occasion is no contemptible authority, affirms that the Persians sued in vain for peace, and that Constantine was preparing to march against them: yet the superior weight of the testimony of Eusebius obliges us to admit the preliminaries, if not the ratification, of the treaty.*

gradually restored to a sense of duty and discipline; but the season of anarchy had permitted Sapor to form the siege of Nisibis, and to occupy several of the most important fortresses of Mesopotamia.[29] In Armenia, the renowned Tiridates had long enjoyed the peace and glory which he deserved by his valour and fidelity to the cause of Rome. The firm alliance which he maintained with Constantine was productive of spiritual as well as of temporal benefits: by the conversion of Tiridates, the character of a saint was applied to that of a hero, the Christian faith was preached and established from the Euphrates to the shores of the Caspian, and Armenia was attached to the empire by the double ties of policy and of religion. But, as many of the Armenian nobles still refused to abandon the plurality of their gods and of their wives, the public tranquillity was disturbed by a discontented faction, which insulted the feeble age of their sovereign, and impatiently expected the hour of his death. He died at length after a reign of fifty-six years, and the fortune of the Armenian monarchy expired with Tiridates. His lawful heir was driven into exile, the Christian priests were either murdered or expelled from their churches, the barbarous tribes of Albania were solicited to descend from their mountains; and two of the most powerful governors, usurping the ensigns or the powers of royalty, implored the assistance of Sapor, and opened the gates of their cities to the Persian garrisons. The Christian party, under the guidance of the Archbishop of Artaxata, the immediate successor of St. Gregory the Illuminator, had recourse to the piety of Constantius. After the troubles had continued about three years, Antiochus, one of the officers of the household, executed with success the Imperial commission of restoring Chosroes, the son of Tiridates, to the throne of his fathers, of distributing honours and rewards among the faithful servants of the house of Arsaces, and of proclaiming a general amnesty, which was accepted by the greater part of the rebellious Satraps. But the Romans derived more honour than advantage from this revolution. Chosroes was a prince of a puny stature, and a pusillanimous spirit. Unequal to the fatigues of war, averse to the society of mankind, he withdrew from his capital to a retired palace, which he built on the banks of the river Eleutherus, and in the centre of a shady grove; where he consumed his vacant hours in the rural sports of hunting and hawking. To secure this inglorious ease, he submitted to the conditions of peace which Sapor condescended to impose; the payment of an annual tribute, and the restitution of the fertile province of Atropatene, which the courage of Tiridates and

[29] *From some successes gained possibly in the campaign of this year Constantius won the title of Adiabenicus Maximus.*

the victorious arms of Galerius had annexed to the Armenian monarchy.[30]

During the long period of the reign of Constantius, the provinces of the east were afflicted by the calamities of the Persian war. The irregular incursions of the light troops alternately spread terror and devastation beyond the Tigris and beyond the Euphrates, from the gates of Ctesiphon to those of Antioch; and this active service was performed by the Arabs of the desert, who were divided in their interest and affections; some of their independent chiefs being enlisted in the party of Sapor, whilst others had engaged their doubtful fidelity to the emperor.[31] The more grave and important operations of the war were conducted with equal vigour; and the armies of Rome and Persia encountered each other in nine bloody fields, in two of which Constantius himself commanded in person. The event of the day was most commonly adverse to the Romans, but in the battle of Singara their imprudent valour had almost achieved a signal and decisive victory. The stationary troops of Singara retired on the approach of Sapor, who passed the Tigris over three bridges, and occupied near the village of Hilleh an advantageous camp, which, by the labour of his numerous pioneers, he surrounded in one day with a deep ditch and a lofty rampart. His formidable host, when it was drawn out in order of battle, covered the banks of the river, the adjacent heights, and the whole extent of a plain of above twelve miles, which separated the two armies. Both were alike impatient to engage; but the Barbarians, after a slight resistance, fled in disorder; unable to resist, or desirous to weary, the strength of the heavy legions, who, fainting with heat and thirst, pursued them across the plain, and cut in pieces a line of cavalry, clothed in complete armour, which had been posted before the gates of the camp to protect their retreat. Constantius, who was hurried along in the pursuit, attempted, without effect, to restrain the ardour of his troops, by representing to them the dangers of the approaching night and the certainty of completing their success with the return of day. As they depended much more on their own valour than on the experience or the abilities of their chief, they silenced by their clamours his timid remonstrances; and rushing with fury to the charge filled up the ditch, broke down the rampart, and dispersed themselves through the tents, to recruit their exhausted strength and to enjoy the rich harvest of their labours. But the prudent Sapor had watched the moment of victory. His army, of which the greater part, securely posted on the heights, had been spectators of the

[30] The perfect agreement between the vague hints of the contemporary orator and the circumstantial narrative of the national historian gives light to the former and weight to the latter. For the credit of Moses it may be likewise observed that the name of Antiochus is found a few years before in a civil office of inferior dignity.

[31] Ammianus gives a lively description of the wandering and predatory life of the Saracens, who stretched from the confines of Assyria to the cataracts of the Nile. It appears from the adventures of Malchus, which Jerom has related in so entertaining a manner, that the high road between Berœa and Edessa was infested by these robbers.

action, advanced in silence, and under the shadow of the night; and his Persian archers, guided by the illumination of the camp, poured a shower of arrows on a disarmed and licentious crowd. The sincerity of history declares that the Romans were vanquished with a dreadful slaughter, and that the flying remnant of the legions was exposed to the most intolerable hardships. Even the tenderness of panegyric, confessing that the glory of the emperor was sullied by the disobedience of his soldiers, chooses to draw a veil over the circumstances of this melancholy retreat. Yet one of those venal orators, so jealous of the fame of Constantius, relates with amazing coolness an act of such incredible cruelty, as, in the judgment of posterity, must imprint a far deeper stain on the honour of the Imperial name. The son of Sapor, the heir of his crown, had been made a captive in the Persian camp. The unhappy youth, who might have excited the compassion of the most savage enemy, was scourged, tortured, and publicly executed by the inhuman Romans.

Whatever advantages might attend the arms of Sapor in the field, though nine repeated victories diffused among the nations the fame of his valour and conduct, he could not hope to succeed in the execution of his designs, while the fortified towns of Mesopotamia, and, above all, the strong and ancient city of Nisibis, remained in the possession of the Romans. In the space of twelve years, Nisibis, which, since the time of Lucullus, had been deservedly esteemed the bulwark of the east, sustained three memorable sieges against the power of Sapor, and the disappointed monarch, after urging his attacks above sixty, eighty, and an hundred days, was thrice repulsed with loss and ignominy. This large and populous city was situate about two days' journey from the Tigris, in the midst of a pleasant and fertile plain at the foot of Mount Masius. A treble inclosure of brick walls was defended by a deep ditch;[32] and the intrepid assistance of Count Lucilianus and his garrison was seconded by the desperate courage of the people. The citizens of Nisibis were animated by the exhortations of their bishop,[33] enured to arms by the presence of danger, and convinced of the intentions of Sapor to plant a Persian colony in their room and to lead them away into distant and barbarous captivity. The event of the two former sieges elated their confidence, and exasperated the haughty spirit of the Great King, who advanced a third time towards Nisibis, at the head of the united forces of Persia and India. The ordinary machines invented to batter or undermine the walls were rendered ineffectual by the superior skill of the Romans; and many days had vainly elapsed, when Sapor

[32] *Nisibis is now reduced to one hundred and fifty houses; the marshy lands produce rice, and the fertile meadows as far as Mosul and the Tigris, are covered with the ruins of towns and villages.*

[33] *The miracles which Theodoret ascribes to St. James, Bishop of Edessa, were at least performed in a worthy cause, the defence of his country. He appeared on the walls under the figure of the Roman emperor, and sent an army of gnats to sting the trunks of the elephants, and to discomfit the host of the new Senacherib.*

[31] *Though Niebuhr allows a very considerable swell to the Mygdonius, over which he saw a bridge of twelve arches; it is difficult, however, to understand this parallel of a trifling rivulet with a mighty river. There are many circumstances obscure, and almost unintelligible, in the description of these stupendous water-works.*

embraced a resolution, worthy of an eastern monarch, who believed that the elements themselves were subject to his power. At the stated season of the melting of the snows in Armenia, the river Mygdonius, which divides the plain and the city of Nisibis, forms, like the Nile,[34] an inundation over the adjacent country. By the labour of the Persians, the course of the river was stopped below the town, and the waters were confined on every side by solid mounds of earth. On this artificial lake, a fleet of armed vessels, filled with soldiers and with engines which discharged stones of five hundred pounds' weight, advanced in order of battle, and engaged, almost upon a level, the troops which defended the ramparts. The irresistible force of the waters was alternately fatal to the contending parties, till at length a portion of the walls, unable to sustain the accumulated pressure, gave way at once, and exposed an ample breach of one hundred and fifty feet. The Persians were instantly driven to the assault, and the fate of Nisibis depended on the event of the day. The heavy armed cavalry, who led the van of a deep column, were embarrassed in the mud, and great numbers were drowned in the unseen holes which had been filled by the rushing waters. The elephants, made furious by their wounds, increased the disorder, and trampled down thousands of the Persian archers. The Great King, who, from an exalted throne, beheld the misfortunes of his arms, sounded, with reluctant indignation, the signal of the retreat, and suspended for some hours the prosecution of the attack. But the vigilant citizens improved the opportunity of the night; and the return of day discovered a new wall of six feet in height, rising every moment to fill up the interval of the breach. Notwithstanding the disappointment of his hopes, and the loss of more than twenty thousand men, Sapor still pressed the reduction of Nisibis, with an obstinate firmness which could have yielded only to the necessity of defending the eastern provinces of Persia against a formidable invasion of the Massagetæ. Alarmed by this intelligence, he hastily relinquished the siege, and marched with rapid diligence from the banks of the Tigris to those of the Oxus. The danger and difficulties of the Scythian war engaged him soon afterwards to conclude, or at least to observe, a truce with the Roman emperor, which was equally grateful to both princes; as Constantius himself, after the deaths of his two brothers, was involved, by the revolutions of the west, in a civil contest, which required and seemed to exceed the most vigorous exertion of his undivided strength.

After the partition of the empire three years had scarcely elapsed, before the sons of Constantine seemed impatient to convince mankind that they were incapable of contenting themselves with the dominions which they were unqualified to govern. The eldest of those princes soon complained that he was defrauded of his just proportion of the spoils of their murdered kinsmen; and, though he might yield to the superior guilt and merit of Constantius, he exacted from Constans the cession of the African provinces, as an equivalent for the rich countries of Macedonia and Greece, which his brother had acquired by the death of Dalmatius. The want of sincerity which Constantine experienced in a tedious and fruitless negotiation exasperated the fierceness of his temper; and he eagerly listened to those favourites who suggested to him that his honour, as well as his interest, was concerned in the prosecution of the quarrel. At the head of a tumultuary band, suited for rapine rather than for conquest, he suddenly broke into the dominions of Constans, by the way of the Julian Alps, and the country round Aquileia felt the first effects of his resentment. The measures of Constans, who then resided in Dacia, were directed with more prudence and ability. On the news of his brother's invasion, he dispatched a select and disciplined body of his Illyrian troops, proposing to follow them in person with the remainder of his forces. But the conduct of his lieutenants soon terminated the unnatural contest. By the artful appearances of flight, Constantine was betrayed into an ambuscade, which had been concealed in a wood, where the rash youth, with a few attendants, was surprised, surrounded, and slain. His body, after it had been found in the obscure stream of the Alsa, obtained the honours of an Imperial sepulchre; but his provinces transferred their allegiance to the conqueror, who, refusing to admit his elder brother Constantius to any share in these new acquisitions, maintained the undisputed possession of more than two-thirds of the Roman empire.[35]

The fate of Constans himself was delayed about ten years longer, and the revenge of his brother's death was reserved for the more ignoble hand of a domestic traitor. The pernicious tendency of the system introduced by Constantine was displayed in the feeble administration of his sons; who, by their vices and weakness, soon lost the esteem and affections of their people. The pride assumed by Constans, from the unmerited success of his arms, was rendered more contemptible by his want of abilities and application. His fond partiality towards some German captives, distinguished only by the charms of youth, was an object of scandal to the people;[36] and Mag-

[35] *The causes and the events of this civil war are related with much perplexity and contradiction. I have chiefly followed Zonaras, and the younger Victor. The monody pronounced on the death of Constantine, might have been very instructive; but prudence and false taste engaged the orator to involve himself in vague declamation.*

[36] *Had not the depraved tastes of Constans been publicly avowed, the elder Victor, who held a considerable office in his brother's reign, would not have asserted it in positive terms.*

nentius, an ambitious soldier, who was himself of barbarian extraction, was encouraged by the public discontent to assert the honour of the Roman name.[37] The chosen bands of Jovians and Herculians, who acknowledged Magnentius as their leader, maintained the most respectable and important station in the Imperial camp. The friendship of Marcellinus, count of the sacred largesses, supplied with a liberal hand the means of seduction. The soldiers were convinced, by the most specious arguments, that the republic summoned them to break the bonds of hereditary servitude and, by the choice of an active and vigilant prince, to reward the same virtues which had raised the ancestors of the degenerate Constans from a private condition to the throne of the world. As soon as the conspiracy was ripe for execution, Marcellinus, under the pretence of celebrating his son's birthday, gave a splendid entertainment to the *illustrious* and *honourable* persons of the court of Gaul, which then resided in the city of Autun. The intemperance of the feast was artfully protracted till a very late hour of the night; and the unsuspecting guests were tempted to indulge themselves in a dangerous and guilty freedom of conversation. On a sudden the doors were thrown open, and Magnentius, who had retired for a few moments, returned into the apartment, invested with the diadem and purple. The conspirators instantly saluted him with the titles of Augustus and Emperor. The surprise, the terror, the intoxication, the ambitious hopes, and the mutual ignorance of the rest of the assembly, prompted them to join their voices to the general acclamation. The guards hastened to take the oath of fidelity; the gates of the town were shut; and, before the dawn of day, Magnentius became master of the troops and treasure of the palace and city of Autun. By his secrecy and diligence he entertained some hopes of surprising the person of Constans, who was pursuing in the adjacent forest his favourite amusement of hunting, or perhaps some pleasures of a more private and criminal nature. The rapid progress of fame allowed him, however, an instant for flight, though the desertion of his soldiers and subjects deprived him of the power of resistance. Before he could reach a seaport in Spain, where he intended to embark, he was overtaken near Helena,[38] at the foot of the Pyrenees, by a party of light cavalry, whose chief, regardless of the sanctity of a temple, executed his commission by the murder of the son of Constantine.

As soon as the death of Constans had decided this easy but important revolution, the example of the court of Autun was imitated by the provinces of the west. The authority of Magnentius was ac-

[37] *There is reason to believe that Magnentius was born in one of those Barbarian Colonies which Constantius Chlorus had established in Gaul. His behaviour may remind us of the patriot Earl of Leicester, the famous Simon de Montfort, who could persuade the good people of England that he, a Frenchman by birth, had taken arms to deliver them from foreign favourites.*

[38] *This ancient city had once flourished under the name of Illiberis. The munificence of Constantine gave it new splendour, and his mother's name. Helena (it is still called Elne) became the seat of a bishop, who long afterwards transferred his residence to Perpignan, the capital of modern Rousillon.*

knowledged through the whole extent of the two great præfectures of Gaul and Italy; and the usurper prepared, by every act of oppression, to collect a treasure, which might discharge the obligation of an immense donative and supply the expenses of a civil war. The martial countries of Illyricum, from the Danube to the extremity of Greece, had long obeyed the government of Vetranio, an aged general, beloved for the simplicity of his manners, and who had acquired some reputation by his experience and services in war.[39] Attached, by habit, by duty, and by gratitude, to the house of Constantine, he immediately gave the strongest assurances to the only surviving son of his late master that he would expose, with unshaken fidelity, his person and his troops, to inflict a just revenge on the traitors of Gaul. But the legions of Vetranio were seduced rather than provoked by the example of rebellion; their leader soon betrayed a want of firmness, or a want of sincerity; and his ambition derived a specious pretence from the approbation of the princess Constantina. That cruel and aspiring woman, who had obtained from the great Constantine her father the rank of *Augusta,* placed the diadem with her own hands on the head of the Illyrian general; and seemed to expect from his victory the accomplishment of those unbounded hopes of which she had been disappointed by the death of her husband Hannibalianus. Perhaps it was without the consent of Constantina that the new emperor formed a necessary, though dishonourable, alliance with the usurper of the west, whose purple was so recently stained with her brother's blood.

The intelligence of these important events, which so deeply affected the honour and safety of the Imperial house, recalled the arms of Constantius from the inglorious prosecution of the Persian war. He recommended the care of the east to his lieutenants, and afterwards to his cousin Gallus, whom he raised from a prison to a throne; and marched towards Europe, with a mind agitated by the conflict of hope and fear, of grief and indignation. On his arrival at Heraclea in Thrace, the emperor gave audience to the ambassadors of Magnentius and Vetranio. The first author of the conspiracy, Marcellinus, who in some measure had bestowed the purple on his new master, boldly accepted this dangerous commission; and his three colleagues were selected from the illustrious personages of the state and army. These deputies were instructed to soothe the resentment, and to alarm the fears, of Constantius. They were empowered to offer him the friendship and alliance of the western princes, to cement their union by a double marriage; of Constantius with the daughter of Magnentius, and of Magnentius himself

[39] *Eutropius describes Vetranio with more temper, and probably with more truth, than either of the two Victors. Vetranio was born of obscure parents in the wildest parts of Mæsia; and so much had his education been neglected that, after his elevation, he studied the alphabet.*

with the ambitious Constantina; and to acknowledge in the treaty the pre-eminence of rank, which might justly be claimed by the emperor of the east. Should pride and mistaken piety urge him to refuse these equitable conditions, the ambassadors were ordered to expatiate on the inevitable ruin which must attend his rashness, if he ventured to provoke the sovereigns of the west to exert their superior strength and to employ against him that valour, those abilities, and those legions, to which the house of Constantine had been indebted for so many triumphs. Such propositions and such arguments appeared to deserve the most serious attention; the answer of Constantius was deferred till the next day; and, as he had reflected on the importance of justifying a civil war in the opinion of the people, he thus addressed his council, who listened with real or affected credulity: "Last night," said he, "after I retired to rest, the shade of the great Constantine, embracing the corpse of my murdered brother, rose before my eyes; his well-known voice awakened me to revenge, forbade me to despair of the republic, and assured me of the success and immortal glory which would crown the justice of my arms." The authority of such a vision, or rather of the prince who alleged it, silenced every doubt, and excluded all negotiation. The ignominious terms of peace were rejected with disdain. One of the ambassadors of the tyrant was dismissed with the haughty answer of Constantius; his colleagues, as unworthy of the privileges of the law of nations, were put in irons; and the contending powers prepared to wage an implacable war.

Such was the conduct, and such perhaps was the duty, of the brother of Constans towards the perfidious usurper of Gaul. The situation and character of Vetranio admitted of milder measures; and the policy of the eastern emperor was directed to disunite his antagonists, and to separate the forces of Illyricum from the cause of rebellion. It was an easy task to deceive the frankness and simplicity of Vetranio, who, fluctuating some time between the opposite views of honour and interest, displayed to the world the insincerity of his temper, and was insensibly engaged in the snares of an artful negotiation. Constantius acknowledged him as a legitimate and equal colleague in the empire, on condition that he would renounce his disgraceful alliance with Magnentius and appoint a place of interview on the frontiers of their respective provinces, where they might pledge their friendship by mutual vows of fidelity and regulate by common consent the future operations of the civil war. In consequence of this agreement, Vetranio advanced to the city of Sardica,[40] at the head of twenty thousand horse and of a more

[40] *The position of Sardica, near the modern city of Sophia, appears better suited to this interview than the situation of either Naissus or Sirmium, where it is placed by Jerom, Socrates, and Sozomen.*

numerous body of infantry; a power so far superior to the forces of Constantius that the Illyrian emperor appeared to command the life and fortunes of his rival, who, depending on the success of his private negotiations, had seduced the troops, and undermined the throne, of Vetranio. The chiefs, who had secretly embraced the party of Constantius, prepared in his favour a public spectacle, calculated to discover and inflame the passions of the multitude. The united armies were commanded to assemble in a large plain near the city. In the centre, according to the rules of ancient discipline, a military tribunal, or rather scaffold, was erected, from whence the emperors were accustomed, on solemn and important occasions, to harangue the troops. The well-ordered ranks of Romans and Barbarians, with drawn swords or with erected spears, the squadrons of cavalry and the cohorts of infantry, distinguished by the variety of their arms and ensigns, formed an immense circle round the tribunal; and the attentive silence which they preserved was sometimes interrupted by loud bursts of clamour or of applause. In the presence of this formidable assembly, the two emperors were called upon to explain the situation of public affairs: the precedency of rank was yielded to the royal birth of Constantius; and, though he was indifferently skilled in the arts of rhetoric, he acquitted himself, under these difficult circumstances, with firmness, dexterity, and eloquence. The first part of his oration seemed to be pointed only against the tyrant of Gaul; but, while he tragically lamented the cruel murder of Constans, he insinuated that none, except a brother, could claim a right to the succession of his brother. He displayed, with some complacency, the glories of his Imperial race; and recalled to the memory of the troops the valour, the triumphs, the liberality of the great Constantine, to whose sons they had engaged their allegiance by an oath of fidelity, which the ingratitude of his most favoured servants had tempted them to violate. The officers, who surrounded the tribunal and were instructed to act their parts in this extraordinary scene, confessed the irresistible power of reason and eloquence by saluting the emperor Constantius as their lawful sovereign. The contagion of loyalty and repentance was communicated from rank to rank; till the plain of Sardica resounded with the universal acclamation of "Away with these upstart usurpers! Long life and victory to the son of Constantine! Under his banners alone we will fight and conquer." The shout of thousands, their menacing gestures, the fierce clashing of their arms, astonished and subdued the courage of Vetranio, who stood, amidst the defection of his followers, in anxious and silent suspense. Instead of embracing the last refuge of generous despair, he tamely submitted to his fate; and taking the diadem from his head, in view of both armies, fell prostrate at the feet of his conqueror. Constantius used his victory with prudence and moderation; and raising from the ground the aged suppliant, whom he affected to style by the endearing name of Father, he gave him his hand to descend from the throne. The city of Prusa was assigned for the exile or retirement of the abdicated monarch, who lived six years in the enjoyment of ease and affluence. He often expressed his grateful sense of the goodness of Constantius, and, with a very amiable simplicity, advised his benefactor to resign the sceptre of the world, and to seek for content (where alone it could be found) in the peaceful obscurity of a private condition.[41]

The behaviour of Constantius on this memorable occasion was celebrated with some appearance of justice; and his courtiers compared the studied orations which a Pericles or a Demosthenes addressed to the populace of Athens with the victorious eloquence which had persuaded an armed multitude to desert and depose the object of their partial choice. The approaching contest with Magnentius was of a more serious and bloody kind. The tyrant advanced by rapid marches to encounter Constantius, at the head of a numerous army, composed of Gauls and Spaniards, of Franks and Saxons; of those provincials who supplied the strength of the legions, and of those barbarians who were dreaded as the most formidable enemies of the republic. The fertile plains [42] of the Lower Pannonia, between the Drave, the Save, and the Danube, presented a spacious theatre; and the operations of the civil war were protracted during the summer months by the skill or timidity of the combatants. Constantius had declared his intention of deciding the quarrel in the fields of Cibalis, a name that would animate his troops by the remembrance of the victory which, on the same auspicious ground, had been obtained by the arms of his father Constantine. Yet, by the impregnable fortifications with which the emperor encompassed his camp, he appeared to decline, rather than to invite, a general engagement. It was the object of Magnentius to tempt or to compel his adversary to relinquish this advantageous position; and he employed, with that view, the various marches, evolutions, and stratagems, which the knowledge of the art of war could suggest to an experienced officer. He carried by assault the important town of Siscia; made an attack on the city of Sirmium, which lay in the rear of the Imperial camp; attempted to force a passage over the Save into the eastern provinces of Illyricum; and

[41] The younger Victor assigns to his exile the emphatical appellation of "Voluptarium otium." Socrates is the voucher for the correspondence with the emperor, which would seem to prove that Vetranio was, indeed, prope ad stultitiam simplicissimus.

[42] Busbequius traversed the Lower Hungary and Sclavonia at a time when they were reduced almost to a desert by the reciprocal hostilities of the Turks and Christians. Yet he mentions with admiration the unconquerable fertility of the soil; and observes that the height of the grass was sufficient to conceal a loaded waggon from his sight.

cut in pieces a numerous detachment, which he had allured into the narrow passes of Adarne. During the greater part of the summer, the tyrant of Gaul showed himself master of the field. The troops of Constantius were harassed and dispirited; his reputation declined in the eye of the world; and his pride condescended to solicit a treaty of peace, which would have resigned to the assassin of Constans the sovereignty of the provinces beyond the Alps. These offers were enforced by the eloquence of Philip the Imperial ambassador; and the council as well as the army of Magnentius were disposed to accept them. But the haughty usurper, careless of the remonstrances of his friends, gave orders that Philip should be detained as a captive, or at least as a hostage; while he dispatched an officer to reproach Constantius with the weakness of his reign, and to insult him by the promise of a pardon, if he would instantly abdicate the purple. "That he should confide in the justice of his cause and the protection of an avenging Deity," was the only answer which honour permitted the emperor to return. But he was so sensible of the difficulties of his situation that he no longer dared to retaliate the indignity which had been offered to his representative. The negotiation of Philip was not, however, ineffectual, since he determined Sylvanus, the Frank, a general of merit and reputation, to desert with a considerable body of cavalry, a few days before the battle of Mursa.

The city of Mursa, or Essek, celebrated in modern times for a bridge of boats five miles in length over the river Drave and the adjacent morasses,[43] has been always considered as a place of importance in the wars of Hungary. Magnentius, directing his march towards Mursa, set fire to the gates, and, by a sudden assault, had almost scaled the walls of the town. The vigilance of the garrison extinguished the flames; the approach of Constantius left him no time to continue the operations of the siege; and the emperor soon removed the only obstacle that could embarrass his motions, by forcing a body of troops which had taken post in an adjoining amphitheatre. The field of battle round Mursa was a naked and level plain: on this ground the army of Constantius formed, with the Drave on their right; while their left, either from the nature of their disposition or from the superiority of their cavalry, extended far beyond the right flank of Magnentius. The troops on both sides remained under arms in anxious expectation during the greatest part of the morning; and the son of Constantine, after animating his soldiers by an eloquent speech, retired into a church at some distance from the field of battle, and committed to his generals the conduct

[43] *This remarkable bridge, which is flanked with towers, and supported on large wooden piles, was constructed,* A.D. *1566 by Sultan Soliman, to facilitate the march of his armies into Hungary.*

44 *The emperor passed the day in prayer with Valens, the Arian bishop of Mursa, who gained his confidence by announcing the success of the battle. M. de Tillemont very properly remarks the silence of Julian with regard to the personal prowess of Constantius in the battle of Mursa. The silence of flattery is sometimes equal to the most positive and authentic evidence.*

45 *According to Zonaras, Constantius, out of 80,000 men, lost 30,000, and Magnentius lost 24,000 out of 36,000. The other articles of this account seem probable and authentic, but the numbers of the tyrant's army must have been mistaken, either by the author or his transcribers. Magnentius had collected the whole force of the West, Romans and Barbarians, into one formidable body, which cannot fairly be estimated at less than 100,000 men.*

of this decisive day.44 They deserved his confidence by the valour and military skill which they exerted. They wisely began the action upon the left; and, advancing their whole wing of cavalry in an oblique line, they suddenly wheeled it on the right flank of the enemy, which was unprepared to resist the impetuosity of their charge. But the Romans of the West soon rallied, by the habits of discipline; and the Barbarians of Germany supported the renown of their national bravery. The engagement soon became general; was maintained with various and singular turns of fortune; and scarcely ended with the darkness of the night. The signal victory which Constantius obtained is attributed to the arms of his cavalry. His cuirassiers are described as so many massy statues of steel, glittering with their scaly armour, and breaking with their ponderous lances the firm array of the Gallic legions. As soon as the legions gave way, the lighter and more active squadrons of the second line rode sword in hand into the intervals, and completed the disorder. In the meanwhile, the huge bodies of the Germans were exposed almost naked to the dexterity of the oriental archers; and whole troops of those Barbarians were urged by anguish and despair to precipitate themselves into the broad and rapid stream of the Drave. The number of the slain was computed at fifty-four thousand men, and the slaughter of the conquerors was more considerable than that of the vanquished;45 a circumstance which proves the obstinacy of the contest, and justifies the observation of an ancient writer that the forces of the empire were consumed in the fatal battle of Mursa, by the loss of a veteran army, sufficient to defend the frontiers or to add new triumphs to the glory of Rome. Notwithstanding the invectives of a servile orator, there is not the least reason to believe that the tyrant deserted his own standard in the beginning of the engagement. He seems to have displayed the virtues of a general and of a soldier till the day was irrecoverably lost, and his camp in the possession of the enemy. Magnentius then consulted his safety, and, throwing away the Imperial ornaments, escaped with some difficulty from the pursuit of the light horse, who incessantly followed his flight from the banks of the Drave to the foot of the Julian Alps.

The approach of winter supplied the indolence of Constantius with specious reasons for deferring the prosecution of the war till the ensuing spring. Magnentius had fixed his residence in the city of Aquileia, and showed a seeming resolution to dispute the passage of the mountains and morasses which fortified the confines of the Venetian province. The surprisal of a castle in the Alps by the secret march of the Imperialists could scarcely have determined him to relinquish the possession of Italy, if the inclinations of the people had supported the cause of their tyrant. But the memory of the cruelties exercised by his ministers, after the unsuccessful revolt of Nepotian, had left a deep impression of horror and resentment on the minds of the Romans. That rash youth, the son of the princess Eutropia and the nephew of Constantine, had seen with indignation the sceptre of the West usurped by a perfidious barbarian. Arming a desperate troop of slaves and gladiators, he overpowered the feeble guard of the domestic tranquillity of Rome, received the homage of the senate, and, assuming the title of Augustus, precariously reigned during a tumult of twenty-eight days. The march of some regular forces put an end to his ambitious hopes: the rebellion was extinguished in the blood of Nepotian, of his mother Eutropia, and of his adherents; and the proscription was extended to all who had contracted a fatal alliance with the name and family of Constantine. But, as soon as Constantius, after the battle of Mursa, became master of the sea-coast of Dalmatia, a band of noble exiles, who had ventured to equip a fleet in some harbour of the Hadriatic, sought protection and revenge in his victorious camp. By their secret intelligence with their countrymen, Rome and the Italian cities were persuaded to display the banners of Constantius on their walls. The grateful veterans, enriched by the liberality of the father, signalized their gratitude and loyalty to the son. The cavalry, the legions, and the auxiliaries of Italy renewed their oath of allegiance to Constantius; and the usurper, alarmed by the general desertion, was compelled, with the remains of his faithful troops, to retire beyond the Alps into the provinces of Gaul. The detachments, however, which were ordered either to press or to intercept the flight of Magnentius, conducted themselves with the usual imprudence of success; and allowed him, in the plains of Pavia, an opportunity of turning on his pursuers and of gratifying his despair by the carnage of a useless victory.

The pride of Magnentius was reduced, by repeated misfortunes, to sue, and to sue in vain, for peace. He first dispatched a senator, in whose abilities he confided, and afterwards several bishops, whose holy character might obtain a more favourable audience, with the offer of resigning the purple, and the promise of devoting the remainder of his life to the service of the emperor. But Constantius, though he granted fair terms of pardon and reconciliation to all who abandoned the standard of rebellion, avowed his inflexible resolution to inflict a just punishment on the crimes of an assassin, whom he prepared to overwhelm on every side by the effort of his victorious arms. An Imperial fleet acquired the easy possession of Africa and Spain, confirmed the wavering faith of the Moorish nations, and landed a considerable force, which passed the Pyrenees, and advanced towards Lyons, the last and fatal station of Magnentius. The temper of the tyrant, which was never inclined to clemency, was urged by distress to exercise every act of oppression which could extort an immediate supply from the cities of Gaul.[46] Their patience was at length exhausted; and Treves, the seat of Prætorian government, gave the signal of revolt by shutting her gates against Decentius, who had been raised by his brother to the rank either of Cæsar or of Augustus.[47] From Treves, Decentius was obliged to retire to Sens, where he was soon surrounded by an army of Germans, whom the pernicious arts of Constantius had introduced into the civil dissensions of Rome. In the meantime the Imperial troops forced the passages of the Cottian Alps, and in the bloody combat of Mount Seleucus irrevocably fixed the title of Rebels on the party of Magnentius. He was unable to bring another army into the field; the fidelity of his guards was corrupted: and, when he appeared in public to animate them by his exhortations, he was saluted with an unanimous shout of "Long live the emperor Constantius!" The tyrant, who perceived that they were preparing to deserve pardon and rewards by the sacrifice of the most obnoxious criminal, prevented their design by falling on his sword; a death more easy and more honourable than he could hope to obtain from the hands of an enemy, whose revenge would have been coloured with the specious pretence of justice and fraternal piety. The example of suicide was imitated by Decentius, who strangled himself on the news of his brother's death. The author of the conspiracy, Marcellinus, had long since disappeared in the battle of Mursa,[48] and the public tranquillity was confirmed by the execution of the surviving leaders of a guilty and unsuccessful faction. A severe inquisition was extended over all who, either from choice or from compulsion, had been involved in the cause of rebellion. Paul, surnamed Catena, from his superior skill in the judicial exercise of tyranny, was sent to explore the latent remains of the conspiracy in the remote province of Britain. The honest indignation expressed by Martin, vice-præfect of the island, was interpreted as an evidence of his own guilt; and the governor was urged to the necessity of turning against his breast the sword with which he had been provoked to wound the Imperial minister. The most innocent subjects of the West were exposed to exile and confiscation, to death and torture; and, as the timid are always cruel, the mind of Constantius was inaccessible to mercy.

[46] Julian, who inveighs against the cruel effects of the tyrant's despair, mentions the oppressive edicts which were dictated by his necessities, or by his avarice. His subjects were compelled to purchase the Imperial demesnes; a doubtful and dangerous species of property, which, in case of a revolution, might be imputed to them as a treasonable usurpation.

[47] The medals of Magnentius celebrate the victories of the two Augusti, and of the Cæsar. The Cæsar was another brother, named Desiderius.

[48] Julian seems at a loss to determine whether he inflicted on himself the punishment of his crimes, whether he was drowned in the Drave, or whether he was carried by the avenging demons from the field of battle to his destined place of eternal tortures.

XIX

THE divided provinces of the
empire were again united by the victory of Constantius; but, as that
feeble prince was destitute of personal merit, either in peace or war;
as he feared his generals and distrusted his ministers; the triumph
of his arms served only to establish the reign of the *eunuchs* over the
Roman world. Those unhappy beings, the ancient production of
oriental jealousy and despotism, were introduced into Greece and
Rome by the contagion of Asiatic luxury. Their progress was rapid;
and the eunuchs, who, in the time of Augustus, had been abhorred,
as the monstrous retinue of an Egyptian queen, were gradually admitted into the families of matrons, of senators, and of the emperors
themselves. Restrained by the severe edicts of Domitian and Nerva,
cherished by the pride of Diocletian, reduced to an humble station
by the prudence of Constantine,[1] they multiplied in the palace of
his degenerate sons, and insensibly acquired the knowledge, and at
length the direction, of the secret councils of Constantius. The aversion and contempt which mankind has so uniformly entertained
for that imperfect species appears to have degraded their character,
and to have rendered them almost as incapable as they were supposed to be of conceiving any generous sentiment or of performing
any worthy action.[2] But the eunuchs were skilled in the arts of flattery and intrigue; and they alternately governed the mind of Constantius by his fears, his indolence, and his vanity.[3] Whilst he viewed
in a deceitful mirror the fair appearance of public prosperity, he
supinely permitted them to intercept the complaints of the injured
provinces, to accumulate immense treasures by the sale of justice
and of honours; to disgrace the most important dignities by the promotion of those who had purchased at their hands the powers of
oppression,[4] and to gratify their resentment against the few independent spirits who arrogantly refused to solicit the protection of

[1] *There is a passage in the Augustan History in which Lampridius, whilst he praises Alexander Severus and Constantine for restraining the tyranny of the eunuchs, deplores the mischiefs which they occasioned in other reigns.*

[2] *Xenophon has stated the specious reasons which engaged Cyrus to entrust his person to the guard of eunuchs. He had observed in animals that, although the practice of castration might tame their ungovernable fierceness, it did not diminish their strength or spirit; and he per-suaded himself that those who were se-parated from the rest of human kind would be more firmly attached to the person of their bene factor. But a long ex-perience has contra-dicted the judgment of Cyrus. Some particular instances may occur of eunuchs distinguished*

by their fidelity, their valour, and their abilities; but, if we examine the general history of Persia, India, and China, we shall find that the power of the eunuchs has uniformly marked the decline and fall of every dynasty.

[3] *The whole tenor of his impartial history serves to justify the invectives of Mamertinus, of Libanius, and of Julian himself, who have insulted the vices of the court of Constantius.*

[4] *Aurelius Victor censures the negligence of his sovereign in choosing the governors of the provinces and the generals of the army, and concludes his history with a very bold observation, as it is much more dangerous under a feeble reign to attack the ministers than the master himself.*

[5] *Gregory Nazianzen reproaches the apostate with his ingratitude towards Mark, bishop of Arethusa, who had contributed to save his life; and we learn, though from a less respectable authority, that Julian was concealed in the sanctuary of a church.*

[6] *The most authentic account of the education and adventures of Julian is contained in the epistle or manifesto which*

slaves. Of these slaves the most distinguished was the chamberlain Eusebius, who ruled the monarch and the palace with such absolute sway that Constantius, according to the sarcasm of an impartial historian, possessed some credit with his favourite. By his artful suggestions, the emperor was persuaded to subscribe the condemnation of Gallus, and to add a new crime to the long list of unnatural murders which pollute the honour of the house of Constantine.

When the two nephews of Constantine, Gallus and Julian, were saved from the fury of the soldiers, the former was about twelve, and the latter about six, years of age; and, as the eldest was thought to be of a sickly constitution, they obtained with the less difficulty a precarious and dependent life from the affected pity of Constantius, who was sensible that the execution of these helpless orphans would have been esteemed by all mankind an act of the most deliberate cruelty.[5] Different cities of Ionia and Bithynia were assigned for the places of their exile and education; but, as soon as their growing years excited the jealousy of the emperor, he judged it more prudent to secure those unhappy youths in the strong castle of Macellum, near Cæsarea. The treatment which they experienced during a six years' confinement was partly such as they could hope from a careful guardian, and partly such as they might dread from a suspicious tyrant.[6] Their prison was an ancient palace, the residence of the kings of Cappadocia; the situation was pleasant, the buildings stately, the inclosure spacious. They pursued their studies, and practised their exercises, under the tuition of the most skilful masters; and the numerous household, appointed to attend, or rather to guard, the nephews of Constantine, was not unworthy of the dignity of their birth. But they could not disguise themselves that they were deprived of fortune, of freedom, and of safety; secluded from the society of all whom they could trust or esteem; and condemned to pass their melancholy hours in the company of slaves, devoted to the commands of a tyrant, who had already injured them beyond the hope of reconciliation. At length, however, the emergencies of the state compelled the emperor, or rather his eunuchs, to invest Gallus, in the twenty-fifth year of his age, with the title of Cæsar, and to cement this political connexion by his marriage with the princess Constantina. After a formal interview, in which the two princes mutually engaged their faith never to undertake anything to the prejudice of each other, they repaired without delay to their respective stations. Constantius continued his march towards the West, and Gallus fixed his residence at Antioch, from whence, with a delegated authority, he administered the five great dioceses of the eastern præfecture.[7] In this fortunate change, the new Cæsar was not unmindful of his brother Julian, who obtained the honours of his rank, the appearances of liberty, and the restitution of an ample patrimony.[8]

The writers the most indulgent to the memory of Gallus, and even Julian himself, though he wished to cast a veil over the frailties of his brother, are obliged to confess that the Cæsar was incapable of reigning. Transported from a prison to a throne, he possessed neither genius nor application, nor docility to compensate for the want of knowledge and experience. A temper naturally morose and violent, instead of being corrected, was soured, by solitude and adversity; the remembrance of what he had endured disposed him to retaliation rather than to sympathy; and the ungoverned sallies of his rage were often fatal to those who approached his person or were subject to his power.[9] Constantina, his wife, is described, not as a woman, but as one of the infernal furies tormented with an insatiate thirst of human blood.[10] Instead of employing her influence to insinuate the mild counsels of prudence and humanity, she exasperated the fierce passions of her husband; and, as she retained the vanity, though she had renounced the gentleness, of her sex, a pearl necklace was esteemed an equivalent price for the murder of an innocent and virtuous nobleman.[11] The cruelty of Gallus was sometimes displayed in the undissembled violence of popular or military executions; and was sometimes disguised by the abuse of law, and the forms of judicial proceedings. The private houses of Antioch and the places of public resort were besieged by spies and informers; and the Cæsar himself, concealed in a plebeian habit, very frequently condescended to assume that odious character. Every apartment of the palace was adorned with the instruments of death and torture, and a general consternation was diffused through the capital of Syria. The Prince of the East, as if he had been conscious how much he had to fear, and how little he deserved to reign, selected for the objects of his resentment the provincials, accused of some imaginary treason, and his own courtiers, whom with more reason he suspected of incensing, by their secret correspondence, the timid and suspicious mind of Constantius. But he forgot that he was depriving himself of his only support, the affection of the people; whilst he furnished the malice of his enemies with the arms of truth, and afforded the emperor the fairest pretence of exacting the forfeit of his purple, and of his life.

he himself addressed to to the senate and people of Athens. Libanius on the side of the Pagans, and Socrates on that of the Christians, have preserved several interesting circumstances.

[7] *For the promotion of Gallus, see Idatius, Zosimus, and the two Victors. According to Philostorgius, Theophilus, an Arian bishop, was the witness, and, as it were, the guarantee, of this solemn engagement. He supported that character with generous firmness; but M. de Tillemont thinks it very improbable that an heretic should have possessed such virtue.*

[8] *Julian was at first permitted to pursue his studies at Constantinople, but the reputation which he acquired soon excited the jealousy of Constantius; and the young prince was advised to withdraw himself to the less conspicuous scenes of Bithynia and Ionia.*

[9] *I shall copy the words of Eutropius, who wrote his abridgment about fifteen years after the death of Gallus, when there was no longer any motive either to flatter or to depreciate his character. "Multis incivilibus gestis Gallus Cæsar . . . vir naturâ ferox et ad*

As long as the civil war suspended the fate of the Roman world, Constantius dissembled his knowledge of the weak and cruel administration to which his choice had subjected the East; and the discovery of some assassins, secretly dispatched to Antioch by the tyrant of Gaul, was employed to convince the public, that the emperor and the Cæsar were united by the same interest and pursued by the same enemies.[12] But, when the victory was decided in favour of Constantius, his dependent colleague became less useful and less formidable. Every circumstance of his conduct was severely and suspiciously examined, and it was privately resolved either to deprive Gallus of the purple or at least to remove him from the indolent luxury of Asia to the hardships and dangers of a German war. The death of Theophilus, consular of the province of Syria, who in a time of scarcity had been massacred by the people of Antioch with the connivance, and almost at the instigation, of Gallus, was justly resented, not only as an act of wanton cruelty, but as a dangerous insult on the supreme majesty of Constantius. Two ministers of illustrious rank, Domitian, the oriental præfect, and Montius, quæstor of the palace, were empowered by a special commission to visit and reform the state of the East. They were instructed to behave towards Gallus with moderation and respect, and, by the gentlest arts of persuasion, to engage him to comply with the invitation of his brother and colleague. The rashness of the præfect disappointed these prudent measures, and hastened his own ruin as well as that of his enemy. On his arrival at Antioch, Domitian passed disdainfully before the gates of the palace, and, alleging a slight pretence of indisposition, continued several days in sullen retirement to prepare an inflammatory memorial, which he transmitted to the Imperial court. Yielding at length to the pressing solicitations of Gallus, the præfect condescended to take his seat in council; but his first step was to signify a concise and haughty mandate, importing that the Cæsar should immediately repair to Italy, and threatening that he himself would punish his delay or hesitation by suspending the usual allowance of his household. The nephew and daughter of Constantine, who could ill brook the insolence of a subject, expressed their resentment by instantly delivering Domitian to the custody of a guard. The quarrel still admitted of some terms of accommodation. They were rendered impracticable by the imprudent behaviour of Montius, a statesman whose art and experience were frequently betrayed by the levity of his disposition.[13] The quæstor reproached Gallus in haughty language that a prince who was

tyrannidem pronior, si suo jure imperare licuisset."

[10] *The sincerity of Ammianus would not suffer him to misrepresent facts or characters, but his love of ambitious ornaments frequently betrayed him into an unnatural vehemence of expression.*

[11] *His name was Clematius of Alexandria, and his only crime was a refusal to gratify the desires of his mother-in-law; who solicited his death, because she had been disappointed of his love.*

[12] *The assassins had seduced a great number of legionaries; but their designs were discovered and revealed by an old woman in whose cottage they lodged.*

[13] *In the present text of Ammianus, we read, Asper quidem sed ad lenitatem propensior; which forms a sentence of contradictory nonsense. With the aid of an old manuscript Valesius has rectified the first of these corruptions, and we perceive a ray of light in the substitution of the word wafer. If we*

scarcely authorized to remove a municipal magistrate should presume to imprison a Prætorian præfect; convoked a meeting of the civil and military officers; and required them, in the name of their sovereign, to defend the person and dignity of his representatives. By this rash declaration of war, the impatient temper of Gallus was provoked to embrace the most desperate counsels. He ordered his guards to stand to their arms, assembled the populace of Antioch, and recommended to their zeal the care of his safety and revenge. His commands were too fatally obeyed. They rudely seized the præfect and the quæstor, and, tying their legs together with ropes, they dragged them through the streets of the city, inflicted a thousand insults and a thousand wounds on these unhappy victims, and at last precipitated their mangled and lifeless bodies into the stream of the Orontes.[14]

After such a deed, whatever might have been the designs of Gallus, it was only in a field of battle that he could assert his innocence with any hope of success. But the mind of that prince was formed of an equal mixture of violence and weakness. Instead of assuming the title of Augustus, instead of employing in his defence the troops and treasures of the East, he suffered himself to be deceived by the affected tranquillity of Constantius, who, leaving him the vain pageantry of a court, imperceptibly recalled the veteran legions from the provinces of Asia. But, as it still appeared dangerous to arrest Gallus in his capital, the slow and the safer arts of dissimulation were practised with success. The frequent and pressing epistles of Constantius were filled with professions of confidence and friendship; exhorting the Cæsar to discharge the duties of his high station, to relieve his colleague from a part of the public cares, and to assist the West by his presence, his counsels and his arms. After so many reciprocal injuries, Gallus had reason to fear and to distrust. But he had neglected the opportunities of flight and of resistance; he was seduced by the flattering assurances of the tribune Scudilo, who, under the semblance of a rough soldier, disguised the most artful insinuation; and he depended on the credit of his wife Constantina, till the unseasonable death of that princess completed the ruin in which he had been involved by her impetuous passions.[15]

After a long delay, the reluctant Cæsar set forwards on his journey to the Imperial court. From Antioch to Hadrianople, he traversed the wide extent of his dominions with a numerous and stately train; and, as he laboured to conceal his apprehensions from the world, and perhaps from himself, he entertained the people of Con-

[14] *Instead of being obliged to collect scattered and imperfect hints from various sources, we now enter into the full stream of the history of Ammianus, and need only refer to the seventh and ninth chapters of his fourteenth book. Philostorgius, however, though partial to Gallus, should not be entirely overlooked.*

venture to change lenitatem *into* levitatem, *this alteration of a single letter will render the whole passage clear and consistent.*

[15] *She had preceded her husband; but died of a fever on the road, at a little place in Bithynia, called Cœnum Gallicanum.*

stantinople with an exhibition of the games of the circus. The progress of the journey might, however, have warned him of the impending danger. In all the principal cities he was met by ministers of confidence, commissioned to seize the offices of government, to observe his motions, and to prevent the hasty sallies of his despair. The persons dispatched to secure the provinces which he left behind passed him with cold salutations or affected disdain; and the troops, whose station lay along the public road, were studiously removed on his approach, lest they might be tempted to offer their swords for the service of a civil war.[16] After Gallus had been permitted to repose himself a few days at Hadrianople he received a mandate, expressed in the most haughty and absolute style, that his splendid retinue should halt in that city, while the Cæsar himself, with only ten post-carriages, should hasten to the Imperial residence at Milan. In this rapid journey, the profound respect which was due to the brother and colleague of Constantius was insensibly changed into rude familiarity; and Gallus, who discovered in the countenances of the attendants that they already considered themselves as his guards, and might soon be employed as his executioners, began to accuse his fatal rashness, and to recollect with terror and remorse the conduct by which he had provoked his fate. The dissimulation which had hitherto been preserved, was laid aside at Poetovio in Pannonia. He was conducted to a palace in the suburbs, where the general Barbatio, with a select band of soldiers, who could neither be moved by pity nor corrupted by rewards, expected the arrival of his illustrious victim. In the close of the evening he was arrested, ignominiously stripped of the ensigns of Cæsar, and hurried away to Pola in Istria, a sequestered prison which had been so recently polluted with royal blood. The horror which he felt was soon increased by the appearance of his implacable enemy the eunuch Eusebius, who, with the assistance of a notary and a tribune, proceeded to interrogate him concerning the administration of the East. The Cæsar sunk under the weight of shame and guilt, confessed all the criminal actions, and all the treasonable designs, with which he was charged; and, by imputing them to the advice of his wife, exasperated the indignation of Constantius, who reviewed with partial prejudice the minutes of the examination. The emperor was easily convinced that his own safety was incompatible with the life of his cousin: the sentence of death was signed, dispatched, and executed; and the nephew of Constantine, with his hands tied behind his back, was beheaded in prison like the vilest malefactor.[17] Those who are inclined to pal-

[16] *The Thebæan legions, which were then quartered at Hadrianople, sent a deputation to Gallus, with a tender of their services. The Notitia mentions three several legions which bore the name of Thebæan. The zeal of M. de Voltaire, to destroy a despicable though celebrated legend, has tempted him on the slightest grounds to deny the existence of a Thebæan legion in the Roman armies.*

[17] *Julian complains that his brother was put to death without a trial; attempts to justify, or at least to excuse, the cruel revenge which he had inflicted on his enemies; but seems at last to acknowledge that he might justly have been deprived of the purple.*

liate the cruelties of Constantius assert that he soon relented and endeavoured to recall the bloody mandate: but that the second messenger entrusted with the reprieve was detained by the eunuchs, who dreaded the unforgiving temper of Gallus, and were desirous of reuniting to *their* empire the wealthy provinces of the East.

Besides the reigning emperor, Julian alone survived, of all the numerous posterity of Constantius Chlorus. The misfortune of his royal birth involved him in the disgrace of Gallus. From his retirement in the happy country of Ionia, he was conveyed under a strong guard to the court of Milan; where he languished above seven months, in the continual apprehension of suffering the same ignominious death which was daily inflicted, almost before his eyes, on the friends and adherents of his persecuted family. His looks, his gestures, his silence, were scrutinized with malignant curiosity, and he was perpetually assaulted by enemies whom he had never offended, and by arts to which he was a stranger.[18] But, in the school of adversity, Julian insensibly acquired the virtues of firmness and discretion. He defended his honour, as well as his life, against the ensnaring subtleties of the eunuchs, who endeavoured to extort some declaration of his sentiments; and, whilst he cautiously suppressed his grief and resentment, he nobly disdained to flatter the tyrant by any seeming approbation of his brother's murder. Julian most devoutly ascribes his miraculous deliverance to the protection of the gods, who had exempted his innocence from the sentence of destruction pronounced by their justice against the impious house of Constantine.[19] As the most effectual instrument of their providence, he gratefully acknowledges the steady and generous friendship of the empress Eusebia,[20] a woman of beauty and merit, who, by the ascendant which she had gained over the mind of her husband, counterbalanced, in some measure, the powerful conspiracy of the eunuchs. By the intercession of his patroness, Julian was admitted into the Imperial presence; he pleaded his cause with a decent freedom, he was heard with favour; and, notwithstanding the efforts of his enemies, who urged the danger of sparing an avenger of the blood of Gallus, the milder sentiment of Eusebia prevailed in the council. But the effects of a second interview were dreaded by the eunuchs; and Julian was advised to withdraw for a while into the neighbourhood of Milan, till the emperor thought proper to assign the city of Athens for the place of his honourable exile. As he had discovered from his earliest youth a propensity, or rather passion, for the language, the manners, the learning, and the religion of the

[18] Julian himself, in his epistle to the Athenians, draws a very lively and just picture of his own danger, and of his sentiments. He shows, however, a tendency to exaggerate his sufferings, by insinuating, though in obscure terms, that they lasted above a year; a period which cannot be reconciled with the truth of chronology.

[19] Julian has worked the crimes and misfortunes of the family of Constantine into an allegorical fable, which is happily conceived and agreeably related. It forms the conclusion of the seventh Oration, from whence it has been detached and translated by the Abbé de la Bléterie.

[20] She was a native of Thessalonica in Macedonia, of a noble family, and the daughter as well as sister of consuls. Her marriage with the emperor may be placed in the year 352. In a divided age the historians of all parties agree in her praises.

Greeks, he obeyed with pleasure an order so agreeable to his wishes. Far from the tumult of arms and the treachery of courts, he spent six months amidst the groves of the academy, in a free intercourse with the philosophers of the age, who studied to cultivate the genius, to encourage the vanity, and to inflame the devotion, of their royal pupil. Their labours were not unsuccessful; and Julian inviolably preserved for Athens that tender regard which seldom fails to arise in a liberal mind from the recollection of the place where it has discovered and exercised its growing powers. The gentleness and affability of manners, which his temper suggested and his situation imposed, insensibly engaged the affections of the strangers, as well as citizens, with whom he conversed. Some of his fellow-students might perhaps examine his behaviour with an eye of prejudice and aversion; but Julian established, in the schools of Athens, a general prepossession in favour of his virtues and talents, which was soon diffused over the Roman world.[21]

21 *Libanius and Gregory Nazianzen have exhausted the arts as well as the powers of their eloquence, to represent Julian as the first of heroes, or the worst of tyrants. Gregory was his fellow-student at Athens; and the symptoms, which he so tragically describes, of the future wickedness of the apostate amount only to some bodily imperfections and to some peculiarities in his speech and manner. He protests, however, that he then foresaw and foretold the calamities of the church and state.*

Whilst his hours were passed in studious retirement, the empress, resolute to achieve the generous design which she had undertaken, was not unmindful of the care of his fortune. The death of the late Cæsar had left Constantius invested with the sole command, and oppressed by the accumulated weight, of a mighty empire. Before the wounds of civil discord could be healed, the provinces of Gaul were overwhelmed by a deluge of Barbarians. The Sarmatians no longer respected the barrier of the Danube. The impunity of rapine had increased the boldness and numbers of the wild Isaurians: those robbers descended from their craggy mountains to ravage the adjacent country, and had even presumed, though without success, to besiege the important city of Seleucia, which was defended by a garrison of three Roman legions. Above all, the Persian monarch, elated by victory, again threatened the peace of Asia, and the presence of the emperor was indispensably required both in the West and in the East. For the first time, Constantius sincerely acknowledged that his single strength was unequal to such an extent of care and of dominion. Insensible to the voice of flattery, which assured him that his all-powerful virtue and celestial fortune would still continue to triumph over every obstacle, he listened with complacency to the advice of Eusebia, which gratified his indolence, without offending his suspicious pride. As she perceived that the remembrance of Gallus dwelt on the emperor's mind, she artfully turned his attention to the opposite characters of the two brothers, which from their infancy had been compared to those of Domitian and of

Titus. She accustomed her husband to consider Julian as a youth of a mild unambitious disposition, whose allegiance and gratitude might be secured by the gift of the purple, and who was qualified to fill, with honour, a subordinate station, without aspiring to dispute the commands, or to shade the glories, of his sovereign and benefactor. After an obstinate, though secret, struggle, the opposition of the favourite eunuchs submitted to the ascendancy of the empress; and it was resolved that Julian, after celebrating his nuptials with Helena, sister of Constantius, should be appointed, with the title of Cæsar, to reign over the countries beyond the Alps.

Although the order which recalled him to court was probably accompanied by some intimation of his approaching greatness, he appeals to the people of Athens to witness his tears of undissembled sorrow, when he was reluctantly torn away from his beloved retirement. He trembled for his life, for his fame, and even for his virtue; and his sole confidence was derived from the persuasion that Minerva inspired all his actions, and that he was protected by an invisible guard of angels, whom for that purpose she had borrowed from the Sun and Moon. He approached with horror the palace of Milan; nor could the ingenuous youth conceal his indignation, when he found himself accosted with false and servile respect by the assassins of his family. Eusebia, rejoicing in the success of her benevolent schemes, embraced him with the tenderness of a sister; and endeavoured, by the most soothing caresses, to dispel his terrors and reconcile him to his fortune. But the ceremony of shaving his beard, and his awkward demeanour, when he first exchanged the cloak of a Greek philosopher for the military habit of a Roman prince, amused, during a few days, the levity of the Imperial court.[22]

The emperors of the age of Constantine no longer deigned to consult with the senate in the choice of a colleague; but they were anxious that their nomination should be ratified by the consent of the army. On this solemn occasion, the guards, with the other troops whose stations were in the neighbourhood of Milan, appeared under arms; and Constantius ascended his lofty tribunal, holding by the hand his cousin Julian, who entered the same day into the twenty-fifth year of his age. In a studied speech, conceived and delivered with dignity, the emperor represented the various dangers which threatened the prosperity of the republic, the necessity of naming a Cæsar for the administration of the West, and his own intention, if it was agreeable to their wishes, of rewarding with the honours of the purple the promising virtues of the nephew of Constantine.

[22] *Julian himself relates, with some humour, the circumstances of his own metamorphosis, his downcast looks, and his perplexity at being thus suddenly transported into a new world, where every object appeared strange and hostile.*

The approbation of the soldiers was testified by a respectful mur-mur: they gazed on the manly countenance of Julian, and observed with pleasure that the fire which sparkled in his eyes was tempered by a modest blush, on being thus exposed, for the first time, to the public view of mankind. As soon as the ceremony of his investiture had been performed, Constantius addressed him with the tone of authority which his superior age and station permitted him to as-sume; and, exhorting the new Cæsar to deserve, by heroic deeds, that sacred and immortal name, the emperor gave his colleague the strongest assurances of a friendship which should never be im-paired by time, nor interrupted by their separation into the most distant climates. As soon as the speech was ended, the troops, as a token of applause, clashed their shields against their knees; while the officers who surrounded the tribunal expressed, with decent re-serve, their sense of the merits of the representative of Constantius.

The two princes returned to the palace in the same chariot; and, during the slow procession, Julian repeated to himself a verse of his favourite Homer, which he might equally apply to his fortune and to his fears.[23] The four-and-twenty days which the Cæsar spent at Milan after his investiture, and the first months of his Gallic reign, were devoted to a splendid but severe captivity; nor could the ac-quisition of honour compensate for the loss of freedom.[24] His steps were watched, his correspondence was intercepted; and he was obliged, by prudence, to decline the visits of his most intimate friends. Of his former domestics, four only were permitted to at-tend him; two pages, his physician, and his librarian; the last of whom was employed in the care of a valuable collection of books, the gift of the empress, who studied the inclinations as well as the interest of her friend. In the room of these faithful servants, an household was formed, such indeed as became the dignity of a Cæsar; but it was filled with a crowd of slaves, destitute and perhaps incapable of any attachment for their new master, to whom, for the most part, they were either unknown or suspected. His want of ex-perience might require the assistance of a wise council; but the mi-nute instructions which regulated the service of his table, and the distribution of his hours, were adapted to a youth still under the discipline of his preceptors, rather than to the situation of a prince entrusted with the conduct of an important war. If he aspired to de-serve the esteem of his subjects, he was checked by the fear of dis-pleasing his sovereign; and even the fruits of his marriage-bed were blasted by the jealous artifices of Eusebia herself, who, on this occa-

[23] *The word* purple, *which Homer had used as a vague but common epithet for death, was applied by Julian to ex-press, very aptly, the nature and object of his own apprehensions.*

[24] *He represents in the most pathetic terms the distress of his new situ-ation. The provision for his table was, however, so elegant and sumptu-ous that the young phi-losopher rejected it with disdain.*

"The temples and arches afforded a broad and solid basis for the new structures of brick and stone; and we can name the modern turrets that were raised on the triumphal monuments of Cæsar, Titus, and the Antonines."

"'Behold,' says the laureate, 'the relics of Rome, the image of her pristine greatness! Neither time nor the barbarian can boast the merit of this stupendous destruction: it was perpetrated by her own citizens.'"

SUBSTRUCTURE OF THE TEMPLE OF CLAUDIUS AT SS. GIOVANNI E PAOLO
(ERRONEOUSLY CALLED THE CURIA HOSTILIA)

sion alone, seems to have been unmindful of the tenderness of her sex and the generosity of her character. The memory of his father and of his brothers reminded Julian of his own danger, and his apprehensions were increased by the recent and unworthy fate of Sylvanus. In the summer which preceded his own elevation, that general had been chosen to deliver Gaul from the tyranny of the Barbarians; but Sylvanus soon discovered that he had left his most dangerous enemies in the Imperial court. A dexterous informer, countenanced by several of the principal ministers, procured from him some recommendatory letters; and erasing the whole of the contents, except the signature, filled up the vacant parchment with matters of high and treasonable import. By the industry and courage of his friends, the fraud was however detected, and in a great council of the civil and military officers, held in the presence of the emperor himself, the innocence of Sylvanus was publicly acknowledged. But the discovery came too late; the report of the calumny and the hasty seizure of his estate had already provoked the indignant chief to the rebellion of which he was so unjustly accused. He assumed the purple at his headquarters of Cologne, and his active powers appeared to menace Italy with an invasion, and Milan with a siege. In this emergency, Ursicinus, a general of equal rank, regained, by an act of treachery, the favour which he had lost by his eminent services in the East. Exasperated, as he might speciously allege, by injuries of a similar nature, he hastened with a few followers to join the standard, and to betray the confidence, of his too credulous friend. After a reign of only twenty-eight days, Sylvanus was assassinated: the soldiers who, without any criminal intention, had blindly followed the example of their leader, immediately returned to their allegiance; and the flatterers of Constantius celebrated the wisdom and felicity of the monarch who had extinguished a civil war without the hazard of a battle.[25]

The protection of the Rhætian frontier, and the persecution of the Catholic Church, detained Constantius in Italy above eighteen months after the departure of Julian. Before the emperor returned into the East, he indulged his pride and curiosity in a visit to the ancient capital. He proceeded from Milan to Rome along the Æmilian and Flaminian ways; and, as soon as he approached within forty miles of the city, the march of a prince who had never vanquished a foreign enemy assumed the appearance of a triumphant procession. His splendid train was composed of all the ministers of luxury; but in a time of profound peace, he was encompassed by the

[25] *Ammianus was perfectly well informed of the conduct and fate of Sylvanus. He himself was one of the few followers who attended Ursicinus in his dangerous enterprise.*

glittering arms of the numerous squadrons of his guards and cuirassiers. Their streaming banners of silk, embossed with gold and shaped in the form of dragons, waved round the person of the emperor. Constantius sat alone in a lofty car resplendent with gold and precious gems; and, except when he bowed his head to pass under the gates of the cities, he affected a stately demeanour of inflexible and, as it might seem, of insensible gravity. The severe discipline of the Persian youth had been introduced by the eunuchs into the Imperial palace; and such were the habits of patience which they had inculcated that, during a slow and sultry march, he was never seen to move his hand towards his face or to turn his eyes either to the right or to the left. He was received by the magistrates and senate of Rome; and the emperor surveyed, with attention, the civil honours of the republic and the consular images of the noble families. The streets were lined with an innumerable multitude. Their repeated acclamations expressed their joy at beholding, after an absence of thirty-two years, the sacred person of their sovereign; and Constantius himself expressed, with some pleasantry, his affected surprise that the human race should thus suddenly be collected on the same spot. The son of Constantine was lodged in the ancient palace of Augustus: he presided in the senate, harangued the people from the tribunal which Cicero had so often ascended, assisted with unusual courtesy at the games of the circus, and accepted the crowns of gold as well as the panegyrics which had been prepared for this ceremony by the deputies of the principal cities. His short visit of thirty days was employed in viewing the monuments of art and power which were scattered over the seven hills and the interjacent valleys. He admired the awful majesty of the Capitol, the vast extent of the baths of Caracalla and Diocletian, the severe simplicity of the Pantheon, the massy greatness of the amphitheatre of Titus, the elegant architecture of the theatre of Pompey and the temple of Peace, and, above all, the stately structure of the Forum and column of Trajan; acknowledging that the voice of fame, so prone to invent and to magnify, had made an inadequate report of the metropolis of the world. The traveller, who has contemplated the ruins of ancient Rome, may conceive some imperfect idea of the sentiments which they must have inspired when they reared their heads in the splendour of unsullied beauty.

The satisfaction which Constantius had received from this journey excited him to the generous emulation of bestowing on the Romans some memorial of his own gratitude and munificence. His first idea was to imitate the equestrian and colossal statue which he had seen in the Forum of Trajan; but, when he had maturely weighed the difficulties of the execution,[26] he chose rather to embellish the capital by the gift of an Egyptian obelisk. In a remote but polished age, which seems to have preceded the invention of alphabetical writing, a great number of these obelisks had been erected, in the cities of Thebes and Heliopolis, by the ancient sovereigns of Egypt, in a just confidence that the simplicity of their form and the hardness of their substance would resist the injuries of time and violence.[27] Several of these extraordinary columns had been transported to Rome by Augustus and his successors, as the most durable monuments of their power and victory; but there remained one obelisk which, from its size or sanctity, escaped for a long time the rapacious vanity of the conquerors. It was designed by Constantine to adorn his new city; and, after being removed by his order from the pedestal where it stood before the Temple of the Sun at Heliopolis, was floated down the Nile to Alexandria. The death of Constantine suspended the execution of his purpose, and this obelisk was destined by his son to the ancient capital of the empire. A vessel of uncommon strength and capaciousness was provided to convey this enormous weight of granite, at least an hundred and fifteen feet in length, from the banks of the Nile to those of the Tiber. The obelisk of Constantius was landed about three miles from the city, and elevated by the efforts of art and labour, in the great Circus of Rome.

The departure of Constantius from Rome was hastened by the alarming intelligence of the distress and danger of the Illyrian provinces. The distractions of civil war, and the irreparable loss which the Roman legions had sustained in the battle of Mursa, exposed those countries, almost without defence, to the light cavalry of the Barbarians; and particularly to the inroads of the Quadi, a fierce and powerful nation, who seem to have exchanged the institutions of Germany for the arms and military arts of their Sarmatian allies. The garrisons of the frontier were insufficient to check their progress; and the indolent monarch was at length compelled to assemble, from the extremities of his dominions, the flower of the Palatine troops, to take the field in person, and to employ a whole campaign, with the preceding autumn and the ensuing spring, in the serious prosecution of the war. The emperor passed the Danube on a bridge of boats, cut in pieces all that encountered his march, penetrated into the heart of the country of the Quadi, and severely retaliated the calamities which they had inflicted on the Roman province. The

[26] *Hormisdas, a fugitive prince of Persia, observed to the emperor that, if he made such a horse, he must think of preparing a similar stable (the Forum of Trajan). Another saying of Hormisdas is recorded, "that one thing only had displeased him, to find that men died at Rome as well as elsewhere." If we adopt this reading of the text of Ammianus (displicuisse instead of placuisse), we may consider it as a reproof of Roman vanity. The contrary sense would be that of a misanthrope.*

[27] *When Germanicus visited the ancient monuments of Thebes, the eldest of the priests explained to him the meaning of these hieroglyphics. But it seems probable that before the useful invention of an alphabet these natural or arbitrary signs were the common characters of the Egyptian nation.*

dismayed Barbarians were soon reduced to sue for peace: they offered the restitution of his captive subjects as an atonement for the past, and the noblest hostages as a pledge of their future conduct. The generous courtesy which was shown to the first among their chieftains who implored the clemency of Constantius encouraged the more timid, or the more obstinate, to imitate their examples; and the Imperial camp was crowded with the princes and ambassadors of the most distant tribes, who occupied the plains of the Lesser Poland, and who might have deemed themselves secure behind the lofty ridge of the Carpathian mountains. While Constantius gave laws to the Barbarians beyond the Danube, he distinguished with specious compassion the Sarmatian exiles who had been expelled from their native country by the rebellion of their slaves, and who formed a very considerable accession to the power of the Quadi. The emperor, embracing a generous but artful system of policy, released the Sarmatians from the bands of this humiliating dependence, and restored them, by a separate treaty, to the dignity of a nation united under the government of a king, the friend and ally of the republic. He declared his resolution of asserting the justice of their cause, and of securing the peace of the provinces by the extirpation, or at least the banishment, of the Limigantes, whose manners were still infected with the vices of their servile origin. The execution of this design was attended with more difficulty than glory. The territory of the Limigantes was protected against the Romans by the Danube, against the hostile Barbarians by the Theiss. The marshy lands which lay between those rivers, and were often covered by their inundations, formed an intricate wilderness, pervious only to the inhabitants, who were acquainted with its secret paths and inaccessible fortresses. On the approach of Constantius, the Limigantes tried the efficacy of prayers, of fraud, and of arms; but he sternly rejected their supplications, defeated their rude stratagems, and repelled with skill and firmness the efforts of their irregular valour. One of their most warlike tribes, established in a small island towards the conflux of the Theiss and the Danube, consented to pass the river with the intention of surprising the emperor during the security of an amicable conference. They soon became the victims of the perfidy which they meditated. Encompassed on every side, trampled down by the cavalry, slaughtered by the swords of the legions, they disdained to ask for mercy; and with an undaunted countenance still grasped their weapons in the agonies of death. After this victory a considerable body of Romans was landed on the

opposite banks of the Danube; the Taifalæ, a Gothic tribe engaged
in the service of the empire, invaded the Limigantes on the side of
the Theiss; and their former masters, the free Sarmatians, animated
by hope and revenge, penetrated through the hilly country into the
heart of their ancient possessions. A general conflagration revealed
the huts of the Barbarians, which were seated in the depth of the
wilderness; and the soldier fought with confidence on marshy
ground, which it was dangerous for him to tread. In this extremity
the bravest of the Limigantes were resolved to die in arms, rather
than to yield: but the milder sentiment, enforced by the authority of
their elders, at length prevailed; and the suppliant crowd, followed
by their wives and children, repaired to the Imperial camp, to learn
their fate from the mouth of the conqueror. After celebrating his
own clemency, which was still inclined to pardon their repeated
crimes and to spare the remnant of a guilty nation, Constantius assigned for the place of their exile a remote country, where they
might enjoy a safe and honourable repose. The Limigantes obeyed
with reluctance: but before they could reach, at least before they
could occupy, their destined habitations, they returned to the banks
of the Danube, exaggerating the hardships of their situation, and
requesting, with fervent professions of fidelity, that the emperor
would grant them an undisturbed settlement within the limits of
the Roman provinces. Instead of consulting his own experience of
their incurable perfidy, Constantius listened to his flatterers, who
were ready to represent the honour and advantage of accepting a
colony of soldiers, at a time when it was much easier to obtain the
pecuniary contributions than the military service of the subjects
of the empire. The Limigantes were permitted to pass the Danube; and the emperor gave audience to the multitude in a large
plain near the modern city of Buda. They surrounded the tribunal,
and seemed to hear with respect an oration full of mildness and
dignity; when one of the Barbarians, casting his shoe into the air,
exclaimed with a loud voice, *Marha! Marha!* a word of defiance,
which was received as the signal of the tumult. They rushed with
fury to seize the person of the emperor; his royal throne and golden
couch were pillaged by these rude hands; but the faithful defence of
his guards, who died at his feet, allowed him a moment to mount a
fleet horse, and to escape from the confusion. The disgrace which
had been incurred by a treacherous surprise was soon retrieved by
the numbers and discipline of the Romans; and the combat was
only terminated by the extinction of the name and nation of the

Limigantes. The free Sarmatians were reinstated in the possession of their ancient seats; and, although Constantius distrusted the levity of their character, he entertained some hopes that a sense of gratitude might influence their future conduct. He had remarked the lofty stature and obsequious demeanour of Zizais, one of the noblest of their chiefs. He conferred on him the title of King; and Zizais proved that he was not unworthy to reign by a sincere and lasting attachment to the interest of his benefactor, who, after this splendid success, received the name of *Sarmaticus* from the acclamations of his victorious army.

While the Roman emperor and the Persian monarch, at the distance of three thousand miles, defended their extreme limits against the Barbarians of the Danube and of the Oxus, their intermediate frontier experienced the vicissitudes of a languid war, and a precarious truce. Two of the eastern ministers of Constantius, the Prætorian præfect Musonian, whose abilities were disgraced by the want of truth and integrity, and Cassian, duke of Mesopotamia, a hardy and veteran soldier, opened a secret negotiation with the satrap Tamsapor. These overtures of peace, translated into the servile and flattering language of Asia, were transmitted to the camp of the Great King; who resolved to signify, by an ambassador, the terms which he was inclined to grant to the suppliant Romans. Narses, whom he invested with that character, was honourably received in his passage through Antioch and Constantinople: he reached Sirmium after a long journey, and, at his first audience, respectfully unfolded the silken veil which covered the haughty epistle of his sovereign. Sapor, King of Kings, and Brother of the Sun and Moon (such were the lofty titles affected by oriental vanity), expressed his satisfaction that his brother, Constantius Cæsar, had been taught wisdom by adversity. As the lawful successor of Darius Hystaspes, Sapor asserted that the river Strymon in Macedonia was the true and ancient boundary of his empire; declaring, however, that, as an evidence of his moderation, he would content himself with the provinces of Armenia and Mesopotamia, which had been fraudulently extorted from his ancestors. He alleged that, without the restitution of these disputed countries, it was impossible to establish any treaty on a solid and permanent basis; and he arrogantly threatened that, if his ambassador returned in vain, he was prepared to take the field in the spring, and to support the justice of his cause by the strength of his invincible arms. Narses, who was endowed with the most polite and amiable manners, endeavoured, as far as was consistent with his duty, to soften the harshness of the message. Both the style and the substance were maturely weighed in the Imperial council, and he was dismissed with the following answer: "Constantius had a right to disclaim the officiousness of his ministers, who had acted without any specific orders from the throne: he was not, however, averse to an equal and honourable treaty; but it was highly indecent, as well as absurd, to propose to the sole and victorious emperor of the Roman world the same conditions of peace which he had indignantly rejected at the time when his power was contracted within the narrow limits of the East: the chance of arms was uncertain; and Sapor should recollect that, if the Romans had sometimes been vanquished in battle, they had almost always been successful in the event of the war." A few days after the departure of Narses, three ambassadors were sent to the court of Sapor, who was already returned from the Scythian expedition to his ordinary residence of Ctesiphon. A count, a notary, and a sophist had been selected for this important commission; and Constantius, who was secretly anxious for the conclusion of the peace, entertained some hopes that the dignity of the first of these ministers, the dexterity of the second, and the rhetoric of the third [28] would persuade the Persian monarch to abate the rigour of his demands. But the progress of their negotiation was opposed and defeated by the hostile arts of Antoninus,[29] a Roman subject of Syria, who had fled from the oppression, and was admitted into the councils of Sapor, and even to the royal table, where, according to the custom of the Persians, the most important business was frequently discussed.[30] The dexterous fugitive promoted his interest by the same conduct which gratified his revenge. He incessantly urged the ambition of his new master to embrace the favourable opportunity when the bravest of the Palatine troops were employed with the emperor in a distant war on the Danube. He pressed Sapor to invade the exhausted and defenceless provinces of the East, with the numerous armies of Persia, now fortified by the alliance and accession of the fiercest Barbarians. The ambassadors of Rome retired without success, and a second embassy of a still more honourable rank was detained in strict confinement, and threatened either with death or exile.

The military historian, who was himself dispatched to observe the army of the Persians, as they were preparing to construct a bridge of boats over the Tigris, beheld from an eminence the plain of Assyria, as far as the edge of the horizon, covered with men, with horses, and with arms. Sapor appeared in the front, conspicuous by

[28] The sophist, or philosopher (in that age these words were almost synonymous), was Eustathius the Cappadocian, the disciple of Jamblichus, and the friend of St. Basil. Eunapius fondly attributes to this philosophic ambassador the glory of enchanting the Barbarian king by the persuasive charms of reason and eloquence.

[29] The decent and respectful behaviour of Antoninus towards the Roman general sets him in a very interesting light: and Ammianus himself speaks of the traitor with some compassion and esteem.

[30] This circumstance, as it is noticed by Ammianus, serves to prove the veracity of Herodotus, and the permanency of the Persian manners. In every age the Persians have been addicted to intemperance, and the wines of Shiraz have triumphed over the law of Mahomet.

the splendour of his purple. On his left hand, the place of honour among the Orientals, Grumbates, king of the Chionites, displayed the stern countenance of an aged and renowned warrior. The monarch had reserved a similar place on his right hand for the king of the Albanians, who led his independent tribes from the shores of the Caspian. The satraps and generals were distributed according to their several ranks, and the whole army, besides the numerous train of oriental luxury, consisted of more than one hundred thousand effective men, inured to fatigue, and selected from the bravest nations of Asia. The Roman deserter, who in some measure guided the councils of Sapor, had prudently advised that, instead of wasting the summer in tedious and difficult sieges, he should march directly to the Euphrates, and press forwards without delay to seize the feeble and wealthy metropolis of Syria. But the Persians were no sooner advanced into the plains of Mesopotamia than they discovered that every precaution had been used which could retard their progress or defeat their design. The inhabitants, with their cattle, were secured in places of strength, the green forage throughout the country was set on fire, the fords of the river were fortified by sharp stakes; military engines were planted on the opposite banks, and a seasonable swell of the waters of the Euphrates deterred the Barbarians from attempting the ordinary passage of the bridge of Thapsacus. Their skilful guide, changing his plan of operations, then conducted the army by a longer circuit, but through a fertile territory, towards the head of the Euphrates, where the infant river is reduced to a shallow and accessible stream. Sapor overlooked, with prudent disdain, the strength of Nisibis; but, as he passed under the walls of Amida, he resolved to try whether the majesty of his presence would not awe the garrison into immediate submission. The sacrilegious insult of a random dart, which glanced against the royal tiara, convinced him of his error; and the indignant monarch listened with impatience to the advice of his ministers, who conjured him not to sacrifice the success of his ambition to the gratification of his resentment. The following day Grumbates advanced towards the gates with a select body of troops, and required the instant surrender of the city as the only atonement which could be accepted for such an act of rashness and insolence. His proposals were answered by a general discharge, and his only son, a beautiful and valiant youth, was pierced through the heart by a javelin, shot from one of the balistæ. The funeral of the prince of the Chionites was celebrated according to the rites of his country; and the grief of his aged father was alleviated by the solemn promise of Sapor that the guilty city of Amida should serve as a funeral pile to expiate the death, and to perpetuate the memory, of his son.

The ancient city of Amid or Amida, which sometimes assumes the provincial appellation of Diarbekir,[31] is advantageously situate in a fertile plain, watered by the natural and artificial channels of the Tigris, of which the least inconsiderable stream bends in a semicircular form round the eastern part of the city. The emperor Constantius had recently conferred on Amida the honour of his own name, and the additional fortifications of strong walls and lofty towers. It was provided with an arsenal of military engines, and the ordinary garrison had been reinforced to the amount of seven legions, when the place was invested by the arms of Sapor. His first and most sanguine hopes depended on the success of a general assault. To the several nations which followed his standard their respective posts were assigned; the south to the Vertæ, the north to the Albanians, the east to the Chionites, inflamed with grief and indignation; the west to the Segestans, the bravest of his warriors, who covered their front with a formidable line of Indian elephants.[32] The Persians, on every side, supported their efforts, and animated their courage; and the monarch himself, careless of his rank and safety, displayed, in the prosecution of the siege, the ardour of a youthful soldier. After an obstinate combat the Barbarians were repulsed; they incessantly returned to the charge; they were again driven back with a dreadful slaughter, and two rebel legions of Gauls, who had been banished into the East, signalized their undisciplined courage by a nocturnal sally into the heart of the Persian camp. In one of the fiercest of these repeated assaults, Amida was betrayed by the treachery of a deserter, who indicated to the Barbarians a secret and neglected staircase, scooped out of the rock that hangs over the stream of the Tigris. Seventy chosen archers of the royal guard ascended in silence to the third story of a lofty tower which commanded the precipice; they elevated on high the Persian banner, the signal of confidence to the assailants and of dismay to the besieged; and, if this devoted band could have maintained their post a few minutes longer, the reduction of the place might have been purchased by the sacrifice of their lives. After Sapor had tried, without success, the efficacy of force and of stratagem, he had recourse to the slower but more certain operations of a regular siege, in the conduct of which he was instructed by the skill of the Roman deserters. The trenches were opened at a convenient distance, and the troops destined for

[31] *Diarbekir, which is styled Amid, or Kara-Amid, in the public writings of the Turks, contains above 16,000 houses, and is the residence of a pasha with three tails. The epithet of Kara is derived from the blackness of the stone which composes the strong and ancient wall of Amida.*

[32] *Of these four nations, the Albanians are too well known to require any description. The Segestans inhabited a large and level country, which still preserves their name, to the south of Khorasan, and the west of Hindostan. Notwithstanding the boasted victory of Bahram, the Segestans, above fourscore years afterwards, appear as an independent nation, the ally of Persia. We are ignorant of the situation of the Vertæ and Chionites, but I am inclined to place them (at least the latter) towards the confines of India and Scythia.*

that service advanced under the portable cover of strong hurdles, to fill up the ditch and undermine the foundations of the walls. Wooden towers were at the same time constructed, and moved forwards on wheels, till the soldiers, who were provided with every species of missile weapons, could engage almost on level ground with the troops who defended the rampart. Every mode of resistance which art could suggest, or courage could execute, was employed in the defence of Amida, and the works of Sapor were more than once destroyed by the fire of the Romans. But the resources of a besieged city may be exhausted. The Persians repaired their losses, and pushed their approaches; a large breach was made by the battering-ram, and the strength of the garrison, wasted by the sword and by disease, yielded to the fury of the assault. The soldiers, the citizens, their wives, their children, all who had not time to escape through the opposite gate, were involved by the conquerors in a promiscuous massacre.

But the ruin of Amida was the safety of the Roman provinces. As soon as the first transports of victory had subsided, Sapor was at leisure to reflect that, to chastise a disobedient city, he had lost the flower of his troops, and the most favourable season for conquest.[33] Thirty thousand of his veterans had fallen under the walls of Amida during the continuance of a siege which lasted seventy-three days; and the disappointed monarch returned to his capital with affected triumph and secret mortification. It was more than probable that the inconstancy of his Barbarian allies was tempted to relinquish a war in which they had encountered such unexpected difficulties; and that the aged king of the Chionites, satiated with revenge, turned away with horror from a scene of action where he had been deprived of the hope of his family and nation. The strength as well as spirit of the army with which Sapor took the field in the ensuing spring was no longer equal to the unbounded views of his ambition. Instead of aspiring to the conquest of the East, he was obliged to content himself with the reduction of two fortified cities of Mesopotamia, Singara and Bezabde; the one situate in the midst of a sandy desert, the other in a small peninsula, surrounded almost on every side by the deep and rapid stream of the Tigris. Five Roman legions, of the diminutive size to which they had been reduced in the age of Constantine, were made prisoners, and sent into remote captivity on the extreme confines of Persia. After dismantling the walls of Singara, the conqueror abandoned that solitary and sequestered place; but he carefully restored the fortifications of Bezabde,

[33] *Ammianus has marked the chronology of this year by three signs, which do not perfectly coincide with each other, or with the series of the history. 1. The corn was ripe when Sapor invaded Mesopotamia; a circumstance which, in the latitude of Aleppo, would naturally refer us to the month of April or May. 2. The progress of Sapor was checked by the overflowing of the Euphrates, which generally happens in July and August. When Sapor had taken Amida, after a siege of seventy-three days, the autumn was far advanced. To reconcile these apparent contradictions, we must allow*

and fixed in that important post a garrison or colony of veterans, *for some delay in the* amply supplied with every means of defence, and animated by high *Persian king, some in-* sentiments of honour and fidelity. Towards the close of the cam- *accuracy in the historian,* paign, the arms of Sapor incurred some disgrace by an unsuccessful *and some disorder in* *the seasons.* enterprise against Virtha, or Tecrit, a strong, or as it was universally esteemed till the age of Tamerlane, an impregnable fortress of the independent Arabs.

The defence of the East against the arms of Sapor required, and would have exercised, the abilities of the most consummate general: and it seemed fortunate for the state that it was the actual province of the brave Ursicinus, who alone deserved the confidence of the soldiers and people. In the hour of danger, Ursicinus was removed from his station by the intrigues of the eunuchs; and the military command of the East was bestowed, by the same influence, on Sa- binian, a wealthy and subtle veteran, who had attained the infirmi- ties, without acquiring the experience, of age. By a second order, which issued from the same jealous and inconstant counsels, Ursici- nus was again dispatched to the frontier of Mesopotamia, and con- demned to sustain the labours of a war, the honours of which had been transferred to his unworthy rival. Sabinian fixed his indolent station under the walls of Edessa; and, while he amused himself with the idle parade of military exercise, and moved to the sound of flutes in the Pyrrhic dance, the public defence was abandoned to the boldness and diligence of the former general of the East. But, when- ever Ursicinus recommended any vigorous plan of operations; when he proposed, at the head of a light and active army, to wheel round the foot of the mountains, to intercept the convoys of the enemy, to harass the wide extent of the Persian lines, and to relieve the distress of Amida; the timid and envious commander alleged that he was restrained by his positive orders from endangering the safety of the troops. Amida was at length taken; its bravest defenders, who had escaped the sword of the Barbarians, died in the Roman camp by the hand of the executioner; and Ursicinus himself, after supporting the disgrace of a partial inquiry, was punished for the misconduct of Sabinian by the loss of his military rank. But Constantius soon experienced the truth of the prediction which honest indignation had extorted from his injured lieutenant, that, as long as such max- ims of government were suffered to prevail, the emperor himself would find it no easy task to defend his eastern dominions from the invasion of a foreign enemy. When he had subdued or pacified the Barbarians of the Danube, Constantius proceeded by slow marches into the East; and, after he had wept over the smoking ruins of Amida, he formed, with a powerful army, the siege of Bezabde. The walls were shaken by the reiterated efforts of the most enormous of the battering-rams: the town was reduced to the last extremity; but it was still defended by the patient and intrepid valour of the garrison, till the approach of the rainy season obliged the emperor to raise the siege, and ingloriously to retreat into his winter quarters at Antioch. The pride of Constantius and the ingenuity of his courtiers were at a loss to discover any materials for panegyric in the events of the Persian war; while the glory of his cousin Julian, to whose military command he had entrusted the provinces of Gaul, was proclaimed to the world in the simple and concise narrative of his exploits.

In the blind fury of civil discord, Constantius had abandoned to the Barbarians of Germany the countries of Gaul, which still acknowledged the authority of his rival. A numerous swarm of Franks and Alemanni were invited to cross the Rhine by presents and promises, by the hopes of spoil, and by a perpetual grant of all the territories which they should be able to subdue. But the emperor, who for a temporary service had thus imprudently provoked the rapacious spirit of the Barbarians, soon discovered and lamented the difficulty of dismissing these formidable allies, after they had tasted the richness of the Roman soil. Regardless of the nice distinction of loyalty and rebellion, these undisciplined robbers treated as their natural enemies all the subjects of the empire, who possessed any property which they were desirous of acquiring. Forty-five flourishing cities, Tongres, Cologne, Treves, Worms, Spires, Strasburg, &c., besides a far greater number of towns and villages, were pillaged, and for the most part reduced to ashes. The Barbarians of Germany, still faithful to the maxims of their ancestors, abhorred the confinement of walls, to which they applied the odious names of prisons and sepulchres; and, fixing their independent habitations on the banks of rivers, the Rhine, the Moselle, and the Meuse, they secured themselves against the danger of a surprise by a rude and hasty fortification of large trees, which were felled and thrown across the roads. The Alemanni were established in the modern countries of Alsace and Lorraine; the Franks occupied the island of the Batavians, together with an extensive district of Brabant, which was then known by the appellation of *Toxandria*,[34] and may deserve to be considered as the original seat of their Gallic monarchy.[35] From the sources to the mouth of the Rhine, the conquests of the

[1] *This name seems to be derived from the Toxandri of Pliny, and very frequently occurs in the histories of the middle age. Toxandria was a country of woods and morasses which extended from the neighbourhood of Tongres to the conflux of the Vahal and the Rhine.*

[35] *The paradox of P. Daniel, that the Franks never obtained any permanent settlement on his side of the Rhine before the time of Clovis, is refuted with much learning and good sense by M. Biet, who has proved, by a chain of evidence, their uninterrupted possession of Toxandria one hundred and thirty years before the accession of Clovis. The Dissertation of M. Biet was crowned by the Academy of Soissons in the year 1736, and seems to have been justly preferred to the discourse of his more celebrated competitor, the Abbé le Bœuf, an antiquarian whose name was happily expressive of his talents.*

Germans extended above forty miles to the west of that river, over a country peopled by colonies of their own name and nation; and the scene of their devastations was three times more extensive than that of their conquests. At a still greater distance the open towns of Gaul were deserted, and the inhabitants of the fortified cities, who trusted to their strength and vigilance, were obliged to content themselves with such supplies of corn as they could raise on the vacant land within the inclosure of their walls. The diminished legions, destitute of pay and provisions, of arms and discipline, trembled at the approach, and even at the name, of the Barbarians.

Under these melancholy circumstances, an unexperienced youth was appointed to save and to govern the provinces of Gaul, or rather, as he expresses it himself, to exhibit the vain image of Imperial greatness. The retired scholastic education of Julian, in which he been more conversant with books than with arms, with the dead than with the living, left him in profound ignorance of the practical arts of war and government; and, when he awkwardly repeated some military exercise which it was necessary for him to learn, he exclaimed with a sigh, "O Plato, Plato, what a task for a philosopher!" Yet even this speculative philosophy, which men of business are too apt to despise, had filled the mind of Julian with the noblest precepts and the most shining examples; had animated him with the love of virtue, the desire of fame, and the contempt of death. The habits of temperance recommended in the schools are still more essential in the severe discipline of a camp. The simple wants of nature regulated the measure of his food and sleep. Rejecting with disdain the delicacies provided for his table, he satisfied his appetite with the coarse and common fare which was allotted to the meanest soldiers. During the rigour of a Gallic winter, he never suffered a fire in his bed-chamber; and after a short and interrupted slumber he frequently rose in the middle of the night from a carpet spread on the floor, to dispatch any urgent business, to visit his rounds, or to steal a few moments for the prosecution of his favourite studies.[36] The precepts of eloquence which he had hitherto practised on fancied topics of declamation were more usefully applied to excite or to assuage the passions of an armed multitude: and, although Julian, from his early habits of conversation and literature, was more familiarly acquainted with the beauties of the Greek language, he had attained a competent knowledge of the Latin tongue.[37] Since Julian was not originally designed for the character of a legislator or a judge, it is probable that the civil juris-

[36] *The private life of Julian in Gaul, and the severe discipline which he embraced, are displayed by Ammianus, who professes to praise, and by Julian himself, who affects to ridicule, a conduct which, in a prince of the house of Constantine, might justly excite the surprise of mankind.*

[37] *Julian, educated in the schools of Greece, always considered the language of the Romans as a foreign and popular dialect, which he might use on necessary occasions.*

prudence of the Romans had not engaged any considerable share of his attention: but he derived from his philosophic studies an inflexible regard for justice, tempered by a disposition to clemency; the knowledge of the general principles of equity and evidence; and the faculty of patiently investigating the most intricate and tedious questions which could be proposed for his discussion. The measures of policy and the operations of war must submit to the various accidents of circumstance and character, and the unpractised student will often be perplexed in the application of the most perfect theory. But in the acquisition of this important science, Julian was assisted by the active vigour of his own genius, as well as by the wisdom and experience of Sallust, an officer of rank, who soon conceived a sincere attachment for a prince so worthy of his friendship; and whose incorruptible integrity was adorned by the talent of insinuating the harshest truths without wounding the delicacy of a royal ear.[38]

[38] *We are ignorant of the actual office of this excellent minister, whom Julian afterwards created præfect of Gaul. Sallust was speedily recalled by the jealousy of the emperor; and we may still read a sensible but pedantic discourse in which Julian deplores the loss of so valuable a friend, to whom he acknowledges himself indebted for his reputation.*

Immediately after Julian had received the purple at Milan, he was sent into Gaul, with a feeble retinue of three hundred and sixty soldiers. At Vienna, where he passed a painful and anxious winter, in the hands of those ministers to whom Constantius had entrusted the direction of his conduct, the Cæsar was informed of the siege and deliverance of Autun. That large and ancient city, protected only by a ruined wall and pusillanimous garrison, was saved by the generous resolution of a few veterans, who resumed their arms for the defence of their country. In his march from Autun through the heart of the Gallic provinces, Julian embraced with ardour the earliest opportunity of signalizing his courage. At the head of a small body of archers and heavy cavalry, he preferred the shorter but the more dangerous of two roads; and sometimes eluding, and sometimes resisting, the attacks of the Barbarians, who were masters of the field, he arrived with honour and safety at the camp near Rheims, where the Roman troops had been ordered to assemble. The aspect of their young prince revived the drooping spirit of the soldiers, and they marched from Rheims in search of the enemy, with a confidence which had almost proved fatal to them. The Alemanni, familiarized to the knowledge of the country, secretly collected their scattered forces, and, seizing the opportunity of a dark and rainy day, poured with unexpected fury on the rear-guard of the Romans. Before the inevitable disorder could be remedied two legions were destroyed; and Julian was taught by experience that caution and vigilance are the most important lessons of the art of war. In a second and more successful action, he recovered and established his military fame: but, as the agility of the Barbarians saved them from the pursuit, his victory was neither bloody nor decisive. He advanced, however, to the banks of the Rhine, surveyed the ruins of Cologne, convinced himself of the difficulties of the war, and retreated on the approach of winter, discontented with the court, with his army, and with his own success.[39] The power of the enemy was yet unbroken; and the Cæsar had no sooner separated his troops, and fixed his own quarters at Sens, in the centre of Gaul, than he was surrounded and besieged by a numerous host of Germans. Reduced in this extremity to the resources of his own mind, he displayed a prudent intrepidity which compensated for all the deficiencies of the place and garrison; and the Barbarians, at the end of thirty days, were obliged to retire with disappointed rage.

The conscious pride of Julian, who was indebted only to his sword for this signal deliverance, was embittered by the reflexion that he was abandoned, betrayed, and perhaps devoted to destruction, by those who were bound to assist him by every tie of honour and fidelity. Marcellus, master-general of the cavalry in Gaul, interpreting too strictly the jealous orders of the court, beheld with supine indifference the distress of Julian, and had restrained the troops under his command from marching to the relief of Sens. If the Cæsar had dissembled in silence so dangerous an insult, his person and authority would have been exposed to the contempt of the world; and, if an action so criminal had been suffered to pass with impunity, the emperor would have confirmed the suspicions which received a very specious colour from his past conduct towards the princes of the Flavian family. Marcellus was recalled, and gently dismissed from his office.[40] In his room Severus was appointed general of the cavalry; an experienced soldier, of approved courage and fidelity, who could advise with respect and execute with zeal; and who submitted, without reluctance, to the supreme command which Julian, by the interest of his patroness Eusebia, at length obtained over the armies of Gaul. A very judicious plan of operations was adopted for the approaching campaign. Julian himself, at the head of the remains of the veteran bands, and of some new levies which he had been permitted to form, boldly penetrated into the centre of the German cantonments and carefully re-established the fortifications of Saverne in an advantageous post, which would either check the incursions, or intercept the retreat, of the enemy. At the same time Barbatio, general of the infantry, advanced from Milan with an army of thirty thousand men, and passing the moun-

[39] *Ammianus appears much better satisfied with the success of his first campaign than Julian himself; who very fairly owns that he did nothing of consequence, and that he fled before the enemy.*

[40] *Libanius speaks rather more advantageously of the military talents of Marcellus. And Julian insinuates that he would not have been so easily recalled, unless he had given other reasons of offence to the court.*

tains prepared to throw a bridge over the Rhine, in the neighbourhood of Basil. It was reasonable to expect that the Alemanni, pressed
on either side by the Roman arms, would soon be forced to evacuate
the provinces of Gaul, and to hasten to the defence of their native
country. But the hopes of the campaign were defeated by the incapacity, or the envy, or the secret instructions, of Barbatio; who
acted as if he had been the enemy of the Cæsar and the secret ally
of the Barbarians. The negligence with which he permitted a troop
of pillagers freely to pass, and to return almost before the gates of
his camp, may be imputed to his want of abilities; but the treasonable act of burning a number of boats, and a superfluous stock of
provisions, which would have been of the most essential service to
the army of Gaul, was an evidence of his hostile and criminal intentions. The Germans despised an enemy who appeared destitute
either of power or of inclination to offend them; and the ignominious retreat of Barbatio deprived Julian of the expected support, and
left him to extricate himself from a hazardous situation, where he
could neither remain with safety nor retire with honour.

As soon as they were delivered from the fears of invasion, the
Alemanni prepared to chastise the Roman youth, who presumed to
dispute the possession of that country which they claimed as their
own by the right of conquest and of treaties. They employed three
days and as many nights in transporting over the Rhine their
military powers. The fierce Chnodomar, shaking the ponderous
javelin, which he had victoriously wielded against the brother of
Magnentius, led the van of the Barbarians, and moderated by his experience the martial ardour which his example inspired. He was
followed by six other kings, by ten princes of regal extraction, by a
long train of high-spirited nobles, and by thirty-five thousand of
the bravest warriors of the tribes of Germany. The confidence derived from the view of their own strength was increased by the intelligence which they received from a deserter, that the Cæsar, with
a feeble army of thirteen thousand men, occupied a post about one-
and-twenty miles from their camp of Strasburg. With this inadequate force, Julian resolved to seek and to encounter the Barbarian
host; and the chance of a general action was preferred to the tedious
and uncertain operation of separately engaging the dispersed parties
of the Alemanni. The Romans marched in close order, and in two
columns, the cavalry on the right, the infantry on the left; and the
day was so far spent when they appeared in sight of the enemy, that
Julian was desirous of deferring the battle till the next morning,

and of allowing his troops to recruit their exhausted strength by the necessary refreshments of sleep and food. Yielding, however, with some reluctance to the clamours of the soldiers, and even to the opinion of his council, he exhorted them to justify by their valour the eager impatience, which, in case of a defeat, would be universally branded with the epithets of rashness and presumption. The trumpets sounded, the military shout was heard through the field, and the two armies rushed with equal fury to the charge. The Cæsar, who conducted in person his right wing, depended on the dexterity of his archers, and the weight of his cuirassiers. But his ranks were instantly broken by an irregular mixture of light-horse and of light-infantry, and he had the mortification of beholding the flight of six hundred of his most renowned cuirassiers.[41] The fugitives were stopped and rallied by the presence and authority of Julian, who, careless of his own safety, threw himself before them, and, urging every motive of shame and honour, led them back against the victorious enemy. The conflict between the two lines of infantry was obstinate and bloody. The Germans possessed the superiority of strength and stature, the Romans that of discipline and temper; and, as the Barbarians who served under the standard of the empire united the respective advantages of both parties, their strenuous efforts, guided by a skilful leader, at length determined the event of the day. The Romans lost four tribunes, and two hundred and forty-three soldiers, in this memorable battle of Strasburg, so glorious to the Cæsar,[42] and so salutary to the afflicted provinces of Gaul. Six thousand of the Alemanni were slain in the field, without including those who were drowned in the Rhine or transfixed with darts whilst they attempted to swim across the river.[43] Chnodomar himself was surrounded and taken prisoner, with three of his brave companions, who had devoted themselves to follow in life or death the fate of their chieftain. Julian received him with military pomp in the council of his officers; and, expressing a generous pity for the fallen state, dissembled his inward contempt for the abject humiliation, of his captive. Instead of exhibiting the vanquished king of the Alemanni, as a grateful spectacle to the cities of Gaul, he respectfully laid at the feet of the emperor this splendid trophy of his victory. Chnodomar experienced an honourable treatment: but the impatient Barbarian could not long survive his defeat, his confinement, and his exile.

After Julian had repulsed the Alemanni from the provinces of the Upper Rhine, he turned his arms against the Franks, who were

[41] *After the battle, Julian ventured to revive the rigour of ancient discipline by exposing these fugitives in female apparel to the derision of the whole camp. In the next campaign, these troops nobly retrieved their honour.*

[42] *Julian himself speaks of the battle of Strasburg with the modesty of conscious merit. Zosimus compares it with the victory of Alexander over Darius; and yet we are at a loss to discover any of those strokes of military genius which fix the attention of ages on the conduct and success of a single day.*

[43] *Libanius adds 2000 more to the number of the slain. But these trifling differences disappear before the 60,000 Barbarians whom Zosimus has sacrificed to the glory of his hero. We might attribute this extravagant number to the carelessness of transcribers, if this credulous or partial historian had not swelled the army of 35,000 Alemanni to an innumerable multitude of Barbarians. It is our own fault if this detection does not inspire us with proper distrust on similar occasions.*

seated nearer to the ocean on the confines of Gaul and Germany, and who, from their numbers, and still more from their intrepid valour, had ever been esteemed the most formidable of the Barbarians. Although they were strongly actuated by the allurements of rapine, they professed a disinterested love of war, which they considered as the supreme honour and felicity of human nature; and their minds and bodies were so completely hardened by perpetual action that, according to the lively expression of an orator, the snows of winter were as pleasant to them as the flowers of spring. In the month of December, which followed the battle of Strasburg, Julian attacked a body of six hundred Franks, who had thrown themselves into two castles on the Meuse.⁴⁴ In the midst of that severe season they sustained, with inflexible constancy, a siege of fifty-four days; till at length, exhausted by hunger, and satisfied that the vigilance of the enemy in breaking the ice of the river left them no hopes of escape, the Franks consented, for the first time, to dispense with the ancient law which commanded them to conquer or to die. The Cæsar immediately sent his captives to the court of Constantius, who, accepting them as a valuable present, rejoiced in the opportunity of adding so many heroes to the choicest troops of his domestic guards. The obstinate resistance of this handful of Franks apprized Julian of the difficulties of the expedition which he meditated for the ensuing spring against the whole body of the nation. His rapid diligence surprised and astonished the active Barbarians. Ordering his soldiers to provide themselves with biscuit for twenty days, he suddenly pitched his camp near Tongres, while the enemy still supposed him in his winter quarters of Paris, expecting the slow arrival of his convoys from Aquitain. Without allowing the Franks to unite or to deliberate, he skilfully spread his legions from Cologne to the ocean; and by the terror as well as by the success of his arms soon reduced the suppliant tribes to implore the clemency, and to obey the commands, of their conqueror. The Chamavians submissively retired to their former habitations beyond the Rhine: but the Salians were permitted to possess their new establishment of Toxandria, as the subjects and auxiliaries of the Roman empire. The treaty was ratified by solemn oaths; and perpetual inspectors were appointed to reside among the Franks, with the authority of enforcing the strict observance of the conditions. An incident is related, interesting enough in itself, and by no means repugnant to the character of Julian, who ingeniously contrived both the plot and the catastrophe of the tragedy. When the Chamavians sued

⁴⁴ *The Greek orator, by misapprehending a passage of Julian, has been induced to represent the Franks as consisting of a thousand men; and, as his head was always full of the Peloponnesian war, he compares them to the Lacedæmonians, who were besieged and taken in the island of Sphacteria.*

for peace, he required the son of their king, as the only hostage on whom he could rely. A mournful silence, interrupted by tears and groans, declared the sad perplexity of the Barbarians; and their aged chief lamented in pathetic language that his private loss was now embittered by a sense of the public calamity. While the Chamavians lay prostrate at the foot of his throne, the royal captive, whom they believed to have been slain, unexpectedly appeared before their eyes; and, as soon as the tumult of joy was hushed into attention, the Cæsar addressed the assembly in the following terms: "Behold the son, the prince, whom you wept. You had lost him by your fault. God and the Romans have restored him to you. I shall still preserve and educate the youth, rather as a monument of my own virtue than as a pledge of your sincerity. Should you presume to violate the faith which you have sworn, the arms of the republic will avenge the perfidy, not on the innocent, but on the guilty." The Barbarians withdrew from his presence, impressed with the warmest sentiments of gratitude and admiration.

It was not enough for Julian to have delivered the provinces of Gaul from the Barbarians of Germany. He aspired to emulate the glory of the first and most illustrious of the emperors; after whose example he composed his own commentaries of the Gallic war.[45] Cæsar has related, with conscious pride, the manner in which he *twice* passed the Rhine. Julian could boast that, before he assumed the title of Augustus, he had carried the Roman Eagles beyond that great river in *three* successful expeditions. The consternation of the Germans, after the battle of Strasburg, encouraged him to the first attempt; and the reluctance of the troops soon yielded to the persuasive eloquence of a leader who shared the fatigues and dangers which he imposed on the meanest of the soldiers. The villages on either side of the Main, which were plentifully stored with corn and cattle, felt the ravages of an invading army. The principal houses, constructed with some imitation of Roman elegance, were consumed by the flames; and the Cæsar boldly advanced about ten miles, till his progress was stopped by a dark and impenetrable forest, undermined by subterraneous passages, which threatened, with secret snares and ambush, every step of the assailant. The ground was already covered with snow; and Julian, after repairing an ancient castle which had been erected by Trajan, granted a truce of ten months to the submissive Barbarians. At the expiration of the truce, Julian undertook a second expedition beyond the Rhine, to humble the pride of Surmar and Hortaire, two of the kings of the

[45] *Libanius, the friend of Julian, clearly insinuates that his hero had composed the history of his Gallic campaigns. But Zosimus seems to have derived his information only from the Orations and the Epistles of Julian. The discourse which is addressed to the Athenians contains an accurate, though general, account of the war against the Germans.*

Alemanni, who had been present at the battle of Strasburg. They promised to restore all the Roman captives who yet remained alive; and, as the Cæsar had procured an exact account from the cities and villages of Gaul, of the inhabitants whom they had lost, he detected every attempt to deceive him with a degree of readiness and accuracy which almost established the belief of his supernatural knowledge. His third expedition was still more splendid and important than the two former. The Germans had collected their military powers, and moved along the opposite banks of the river, with a design of destroying the bridge and of preventing the passage of the Romans. But this judicious plan of defence was disconcerted by a skilful diversion. Three hundred light-armed and active soldiers were detached in forty small boats, to fall down the stream in silence, and to land at some distance from the posts of the enemy. They executed their orders with so much boldness and celerity that they had almost surprised the Barbarian chiefs, who returned in the fearless confidence of intoxication from one of their nocturnal festivals. Without repeating the uniform and disgusting tale of slaughter and devastation, it is sufficient to observe that Julian dictated his own conditions of peace to six of the haughtiest kings of the Alemanni, three of whom were permitted to view the severe discipline and martial pomp of a Roman camp. Followed by twenty thousand captives, whom he had rescued from the chains of the Barbarians, the Cæsar repassed the Rhine, after terminating a war, the success of which has been compared to the ancient glories of the Punic and Cimbric victories.

As soon as the valour and conduct of Julian had secured an interval of peace, he applied himself to a work more congenial to his humane and philosophic temper. The cities of Gaul, which had suffered from the inroads of the Barbarians, he diligently repaired; and seven important posts, between Mainz and the mouth of the Rhine, are particularly mentioned, as having been rebuilt and fortified by the order of Julian.[46] The vanquished Germans had submitted to the just but humiliating condition of preparing and conveying the necessary materials. The active zeal of Julian urged the prosecution of the work; and such was the spirit which he had diffused among the troops that the auxiliaries themselves, waving their exemption from any duties of fatigue, contended in the most servile labours with the diligence of the Roman soldiers. It was incumbent on the Cæsar to provide for the subsistence, as well as for the safety, of the inhabitants and of the garrisons. The desertion of the former,

[46] Of these seven posts, four are at present towns of some consequence; Bingen, Andernach, Bonn. and Neuss. The other three, Tricesimæ, Quadriburgium, and Castra Herculis, or Heraclea, no longer subsist; but there is room to believe that, on the ground of Quadriburgium, the Dutch have constructed the fort of Schenk, a name so offensive to the fastidious delicacy of Boileau.

and the mutiny of the latter, must have been the fatal and inevitable consequences of famine. The tillage of the provinces of Gaul had been interrupted by the calamities of war; but the scanty harvests of the continent were supplied, by his paternal care, from the plenty of the adjacent island. Six hundred large barks, framed in the forest of the Ardennes, made several voyages to the coast of Britain; and, returning from thence laden with corn, sailed up the Rhine, and distributed their cargoes to the several towns and fortresses along the banks of the river.[47] The arms of Julian had restored a free and secure navigation, which Constantius had offered to purchase at the expense of his dignity, and of a tributary present of two thousand pounds of silver. The emperor parsimoniously refused to his soldiers the sums which he granted with a lavish and trembling hand to the Barbarians. The dexterity, as well as the firmness, of Julian was put to a severe trial, when he took the field with a discontented army, which had already served two campaigns without receiving any regular pay or any extraordinary donative.[48]

A tender regard for the peace and happiness of his subjects was the ruling principle which directed, or seemed to direct, the administration of Julian. He devoted the leisure of his winter quarters to the offices of civil government, and affected to assume with more pleasure the character of a magistrate than that of a general. Before he took the field, he devolved on the provincial governors most of the public and private causes which had been referred to his tribunal; but, on his return, he carefully revised their proceedings, mitigated the rigour of the law, and pronounced a second judgment on the judges themselves. Superior to the last temptation of virtuous minds, an indiscreet and intemperate zeal for justice, he restrained, with calmness and dignity, the warmth of an advocate who prosecuted, for extortion, the president of the Narbonnese province. "Who will ever be found guilty," exclaimed the vehement Delphidius, "if it be enough to deny?" "And who," replied Julian, "will ever be innocent, if it be sufficient to affirm?" In the general administration of peace and war, the interest of the sovereign is commonly the same as that of his people; but Constantius would have thought himself deeply injured, if the virtues of Julian had defrauded him of any part of the tribute which he extorted from an oppressed and exhausted country. The prince, who was invested with the ensigns of royalty, might sometimes presume to correct the rapacious insolence of the inferior agents, to expose their corrupt arts, and to introduce an equal and easier mode of collection. But

[47] *We may credit Julian himself, who gives a very particular account of the transaction. Zosimus adds two hundred vessels more. If we compute the 600 corn ships of Julian at only seventy tons each, they were capable of exporting 120,000 quarters; and the country which could bear so large an exportation must already have attained an improved state of agriculture.*

[48] *The troops once broke out into a mutiny, immediately before the second passage of the Rhine.*

the management of the finances was more safely entrusted to Florentius, Prætorian præfect of Gaul, an effeminate tyrant, incapable of pity or remorse; and the haughty minister complained of the most decent and gentle opposition, while Julian himself was rather inclined to censure the weakness of his own behaviour. The Cæsar had rejected with abhorrence a mandate for the levy of an extraordinary tax; a new superindiction, which the præfect had offered for his signature; and the faithful picture of the public misery, by which he had been obliged to justify his refusal, offended the court of Constantius. We may enjoy the pleasure of reading the sentiments of Julian, as he expresses them with warmth and freedom in a letter to one of his most intimate friends. After stating his own conduct, he proceeds in the following terms: "Was it possible for the disciple of Plato and Aristotle to act otherwise than I have done? Could I abandon the unhappy subjects entrusted to my care? Was I not called upon to defend them from the repeated injuries of these unfeeling robbers? A tribune who deserts his post is punished with death and deprived of the honours of burial. With what justice could I pronounce *his* sentence, if, in the hour of danger, I myself neglected a duty far more sacred and far more important? God has placed me in this elevated post; his providence will guard and support me. Should I be condemned to suffer, I shall derive comfort from the testimony of a pure and upright conscience. Would to heaven that I still possessed a councillor like Sallust! If they think proper to send me a successor, I shall submit without reluctance; and had much rather improve the short opportunity of doing good than enjoy a long and lasting impunity of evil." The precarious and dependent situation of Julian displayed his virtues and concealed his defects. The young hero who supported, in Gaul, the throne of Constantius was not permitted to reform the vices of the government; but he had courage to alleviate or to pity the distress of the people. Unless he had been able to revive the martial spirit of the Romans, or to introduce the arts of industry and refinement among their savage enemies, he could not entertain any rational hopes of securing the public tranquillity, either by the peace or conquest of Germany. Yet the victories of Julian suspended, for a short time, the inroads of the Barbarians, and delayed the ruin of the Western empire.

His salutary influence restored the cities of Gaul, which had been so long exposed to the evils of civil discord, barbarian war, and domestic tyranny; and the spirit of industry was revived with the hopes of enjoyment. Agriculture, manufactures, and commerce again flourished under the protection of the laws; and the *curiæ*, or civil corporations, were again filled with useful and respectable members: the youth were no longer apprehensive of marriage; and married persons were no longer apprehensive of posterity: the public and private festivals were celebrated with customary pomp; and the frequent and secure intercourse of the provinces displayed the image of national prosperity. A mind like that of Julian must have felt the general happiness of which he was the author; but he viewed with peculiar satisfaction and complacency the city of Paris, the seat of his winter residence, and the object even of his partial affection. That splendid capital, which now embraces an ample territory on either side of the Seine, was originally confined to the small island in the midst of the river, from whence the inhabitants derived a supply of pure and salubrious water. The river bathed the foot of the walls; and the town was accessible only by two wooden bridges. A forest overspread the northern side of the Seine; but on the south, the ground, which now bears the name of the university, was insensibly covered with houses, and adorned with a palace and amphitheatre, baths, an aqueduct, and a field of Mars for the exercise for the Roman troops. The severity of the climate was tempered by the neighbourhood of the ocean; and with some precautions, which experience had taught, the vine and fig-tree were successfully cultivated. But in remarkable winters, the Seine was deeply frozen; and the huge pieces of ice that floated down the stream might be compared, by an Asiatic, to the blocks of white marble which were extracted from the quarries of Phrygia. The licentiousness and corruption of Antioch recalled to the memory of Julian the severe and simple manners of his beloved Lutetia;[49] where the amusements of the theatre were unknown or despised. He indignantly contrasted the effeminate Syrians with the brave and honest simplicity of the Gauls, and almost forgave the intemperance which was the only stain of the Celtic character. If Julian could now revisit the capital of France, he might converse with men of science and genius, capable of understanding and of instructing a disciple of the Greeks; he might excuse the lively and graceful follies of a nation whose martial spirit has never been enervated by the indulgence of luxury; and he must applaud the perfection of that inestimable art which softens and refines and embellishes the intercourse of social life.

[49] *Leucetia, or Lutetia, was the ancient name of the city which, according to the fashion of the fourth century, assumed the territorial appellation of* Parisii.

THE MOTIVES, PROGRESS, AND EFFECTS OF THE CONVERSION
OF CONSTANTINE · LEGAL ESTABLISHMENT AND CONSTITU-
TION OF THE CHRISTIAN OR CATHOLIC CHURCH · THE CLERGY

HE public establishment of Christianity may be considered as one of those important and domestic revolutions which excite the most lively curiosity and afford the most valuable instruction. The victories and the civil policy of Constantine no longer influence the state of Europe; but a considerable portion of the globe still retains the impression which it received from his conversion; and the ecclesiastical institutions of his reign are still connected, by an indissoluble chain, with the opinions, the passions, and the interests of the present generation.

In the consideration of a subject which may be examined with impartiality, but cannot be viewed with indifference, a difficulty immediately arises of a very unexpected nature; that of ascertaining the real and precise date of the conversion of Constantine. The eloquent Lactantius, in the midst of his court, seems impatient [1] to proclaim to the world the glorious example of the sovereign of Gaul; who, in the first moments of his reign, acknowledged and adored the majesty of the true and only God.[2] The learned Eusebius has ascribed the faith of Constantine to the miraculous sign which was displayed in the heavens whilst he meditated and prepared the Italian expedition. The historian Zosimus maliciously asserts that the emperor had imbrued his hands in the blood of his eldest son, before he publicly renounced the gods of Rome and of his ancestors. The perplexity produced by these discordant authorities is derived from the behaviour of Constantine himself. According to the strictness of ecclesiastical language, the first of the *Christian* emperors was unworthy of that name, till the moment of his death; since it was only during his last illness that he received, as a catechumen, the imposition of hands,[3] and was afterwards admitted, by the initiatory rites of baptism, into the number of the faithful.[4] The Christianity of

[1] *The date of the Divine Institutions of Lactantius has been accurately discussed, difficulties have been started, solutions proposed, and an expedient imagined of two original editions: the former published during the persecution of Diocletian, the latter under that of Licinius. For my own part, I am almost convinced that Lactantius dedicated his Institutions to the sovereign of Gaul, at a time when Galerius, Maximin, and even Licinius, persecuted the Christians; that is, between the years 306 and 311.*

[2] *The first and most important of these passages is indeed wanting in twenty-eight manuscripts; but it is found in nineteen. If we weigh the comparative value of those manuscripts, one of 900 years old, in the king of France's*

Constantine must be allowed in a much more vague and qualified sense; and the nicest accuracy is required in tracing the slow and almost imperceptible gradations by which the monarch declared himself the protector, and at length the proselyte, of the church. It was an arduous task to eradicate the habits and prejudices of his education, to acknowledge the divine power of Christ, and to understand that the truth of *his* revelation was incompatible with the worship of the gods. The obstacles which he had probably experienced in his own mind instructed him to proceed with caution in the momentous change of a national religion; and he insensibly discovered his new opinions, as far as he could enforce them with safety and with effect. During the whole course of his reign, the stream of Christianity flowed with a gentle, though accelerated, motion: but its general direction was sometimes checked, and sometimes diverted, by the accidental circumstances of the times, and by the prudence, or possibly by the caprice, of the monarch. His ministers were permitted to signify the intentions of their master in the various language which was best adapted to their respective principles; and he artfully balanced the hopes and fears of his subjects by publishing in the same year two edicts; the first of which enjoined the solemn observance of Sunday,[5] and the second directed the regular consultation of the Aruspices.[6] While this important revolution yet remained in suspense, the Christians and the Pagans watched the conduct of their sovereign with the same anxiety, but with very opposite sentiments. The former were prompted by zeal, as well as vanity, to exaggerate the marks of his favour, and the evidences of his faith. The latter, till their just apprehensions were changed into despair and resentment, attempted to conceal from the world, and from themselves, that the gods of Rome could no longer reckon the emperor in the number of their votaries. The same passions and prejudices have engaged the partial writers of the times to connect the public profession of Christianity with the most glorious or the most ignominious æra of the reign of Constantine.

Whatever symptoms of Christian piety might transpire in the discourses or actions of Constantine, he persevered till he was near forty years of age in the practice of the established religion;[7] and the same conduct, which in the court of Nicomedia might be imputed to his fear, could be ascribed only to the inclination or policy of the sovereign of Gaul. His liberality restored and enriched the temples of the gods: the medals which issued from his Imperial mint are impressed with the figures and attributes of Jupiter and Apollo, of

library, may be alleged in its favour; but the passage is omitted in the correct manuscript of Bologna, which the P. de Montfaucon ascribes to the sixth or seventh century. The taste of most of the editors has felt the genuine style of Lactantius.

[3] *That rite was always used in making a catechumen and Constantine received it for the first time immediately before his baptism and death. From the connexion of these two facts, Valesius has drawn the conclusion, which is reluctantly admitted by Tillemont.*

[4] *The legend of Constantine's baptism at Rome, thirteen years before his death, was invented in the eighth century, as a proper motive for his donation. Such has been the gradual progress of knowledge that a story of which Cardinal Baronius declared himself the unblushing advocate is now feebly supported, even within the verge of the Vatican.*

[5] *Constantine styles the Lord's day dies solis, a name which could not offend the ears of his Pagan subjects.*

[6] *Godefroy, in the character of a commentator, endeavours to excuse Constantine; but the more zealous Baronius censures his profane conduct with truth and asperity.*

[7] *Theodoret seems to insinuate that Helena gave her son a Christian education; but we may be assured, from the superior authority of Eusebius, that she herself was indebted to Constantine for the knowledge of Christianity.*

[8] *See the medals of Constantine in Ducange and Banduri. As few cities had retained the privilege of coining, almost all the medals of that age issued from the mint under the sanction of the Imperial authority.*

[9] *The panegyric of Eumenius, which was pronounced a few months before the Italian war, abounds with the most unexceptional evidence of the Pagan superstition of Constantine, and of his particular veneration for Apollo, or the Sun; to which Julian alludes.*

Mars and Hercules; and his filial piety increased the council of Olympus by the solemn apotheosis of his father Constantius.[8] But the devotion of Constantine was more peculiarly directed to the genius of the Sun, the Apollo of Greek and Roman mythology; and he was pleased to be represented with the symbols of the God of Light and Poetry. The unerring shafts of that deity, the brightness of his eyes, his laurel wreath, immortal beauty, and elegant accomplishments, seem to point him out as the patron of a young hero. The altars of Apollo were crowned with the votive offerings of Constantine; and the credulous multitude were taught to believe that the emperor was permitted to behold with mortal eyes the visible majesty of their tutelar deity, and that, either waking or in a vision, he was blessed with the auspicious omens of a long and victorious reign. The Sun was universally celebrated as the invincible guide and protector of Constantine; and the Pagans might reasonably expect that the insulted god would pursue with unrelenting vengeance the impiety of his ungrateful favourite.[9]

As long as Constantine exercised a limited sovereignty over the provinces of Gaul, his Christian subjects were protected by the authority, and perhaps by the laws, of a prince who wisely left to the gods the care of vindicating their own honour. If we may credit the assertion of Constantine himself, he had been an indignant spectator of the savage cruelties which were inflicted, by the hands of Roman soldiers, on those citizens whose religion was their only crime.[10] In the East and in the West, he had seen the different effects of severity and indulgence; and, as the former was rendered still more odious by the example of Galerius, his implacable enemy, the latter was recommended to his imitation by the authority and advice of a dying father. The son of Constantius immediately suspended or repealed the edicts of persecution, and granted the free exercise of their religious ceremonies to all those who had already professed themselves members of the church. They were soon encouraged to depend on the favour as well as on the justice of their sovereign, who had imbibed a secret and sincere reverence for the name of Christ and for the God of the Christians.

About five months after the conquest of Italy, the emperor made a solemn and authentic declaration of his sentiments, by the celebrated edict of Milan, which restored peace to the Catholic church. In the personal interview of the two western princes, Constantine, by the ascendant of genius and power, obtained the ready concurrence of his colleague Licinius; the union of their names and authority disarmed the fury of Maximin; and, after the death of the tyrant of the East, the edict of Milan was received as a general and fundamental law of the Roman world. The wisdom of the emperors provided for the restitution of all the civil and religious rights of which the Christians had been so unjustly deprived. It was enacted that the places of worship, and public lands, which had been confiscated, should be restored to the church, without dispute, without delay, and without expense: and this severe injunction was accompanied with a gracious promise that, if any of the purchasers had paid a fair and adequate price, they should be indemnified from the Imperial treasury. The salutary regulations which guard the future tranquillity of the faithful are framed on the principles of enlarged and equal toleration; and such an equality must have been interpreted by a recent sect as an advantageous and honourable distinction. The two emperors proclaim to the world that they have granted a free and absolute power to the Christians, and to all others, of following the religion which each individual thinks proper to prefer, to which he has addicted his mind, and which he may deem the best adapted to his own use. They carefully explain every ambiguous word, remove every exception, and exact from the governors of the provinces a strict obedience to the true and simple meaning of an edict which was designed to establish and secure, without any limitation, the claims of religious liberty. They condescend to assign two weighty reasons which have induced them to allow this universal toleration: the humane intention of consulting the peace and happiness of their people; and the pious hope that, by such a conduct, they shall appease and propitiate *the Deity,* whose seat is in heaven. They gratefully acknowledge the many signal proofs which they have received of the divine favour; and they trust that the same Providence will for ever continue to protect the prosperity of the prince and people. From these vague and indefinite expressions of piety, three suppositions may be deduced, of a different, but not of an incompatible, nature. The mind of Constantine might fluctuate between the Pagan and the Christian religions. According to the loose and complying notions of Polytheism, he might acknowledge the God of the Christians as *one* of the *many* deities who composed the hierarchy of heaven. Or perhaps he might embrace the philosophic and pleasing idea that, notwithstanding the variety of names, of rites, and of opinions, all the sects and all the nations of mankind are united in the worship of the common Father and Creator of the universe.

[10] *But it might easily be shown that the Greek translator has improved the sense of the Latin original; and the aged emperor might recollect the persecution of Diocletian with a more lively abhorrence than he had actually felt in the days of his youth and Paganism.*

But the counsels of princes are more frequently influenced by views of temporal advantage than by considerations of abstract and speculative truth. The partial and increasing favour of Constantine may naturally be referred to the esteem which he entertained for the moral character of the Christians; and to a persuasion that the propagation of the gospel would inculcate the practice of private and public virtue. Whatever latitude an absolute monarch may assume in his own conduct, whatever indulgence he may claim for his own passions, it is undoubtedly his interest that all his subjects should respect the natural and civil obligations of society. But the operation of the wisest laws is imperfect and precarious. They seldom inspire virtue, they cannot always restrain vice. Their power is insufficient to prohibit all that they condemn, nor can they always punish the actions which they prohibit. The legislators of antiquity had summoned to their aid the powers of education and of opinion. But every principle which had once maintained the vigour and purity of Rome and Sparta was long since extinguished in a declining and despotic empire. Philosophy still exercised her temperate sway over the human mind, but the cause of virtue derived very feeble support from the influence of the Pagan superstition. Under these discouraging circumstances, a prudent magistrate might observe with pleasure the progress of a religion, which diffused among the people a pure, benevolent, and universal system of ethics, adapted to every duty and every condition of life; recommended as the will and reason of the Supreme Deity, and enforced by the sanction of eternal rewards or punishments. The experience of Greek and Roman history could not inform the world how far the system of national manners might be reformed and improved by the precepts of a divine revelation; and Constantine might listen with some confidence to the flattering, and indeed reasonable, assurances of Lactantius. The eloquent apologist seemed firmly to expect, and almost ventured to promise, *that* the establishment of Christianity would restore the innocence and felicity of the primitive age; *that* the worship of the true God would extinguish war and dissension among those who mutually considered themselves as the children of a common parent; *that* every impure desire, every angry or selfish passion, would be restrained by the knowledge of the gospel; and *that* the magistrates might sheathe the sword of justice among a people who would be universally actuated by the sentiments of truth and piety, of equity and moderation, of harmony and universal love.

The passive and unresisting obedience which bows under the

yoke of authority, or even of oppression, must have appeared, in the eyes of an absolute monarch, the most conspicuous and useful of the evangelic virtues. The primitive Christians derived the institution of civil government, not from the consent of the people, but from the decrees of heaven. The reigning emperor, though he had usurped the sceptre by treason and murder, immediately assumed the sacred character of vicegerent of the Deity. To the Deity alone he was accountable for the abuse of his power; and his subjects were indissolubly bound, by their oath of fidelity, to a tyrant who had violated every law of nature and society. The humble Christians were sent into the world as sheep among wolves; and, since they were not permitted to employ force, even in the defence of their religion, they should be still more criminal if they were tempted to shed the blood of their fellow-creatures in disputing the vain privileges, or the sordid possessions, of this transitory life. Faithful to the doctrine of the apostle who in the reign of Nero had preached the duty of unconditional submission, the Christians of the three first centuries preserved their conscience pure and innocent of the guilt of secret conspiracy or open rebellion. While they experienced the rigour of persecution, they were never provoked either to meet their tyrants in the field or indignantly to withdraw themselves into some remote and sequestered corner of the globe. The Protestants of France, of Germany, and of Britain, who asserted with such intrepid courage their civil and religious freedom, have been insulted by the invidious comparison between the conduct of the primitive and of the reformed Christians. Perhaps, instead of censure, some applause may be due to the superior sense and spirit of our ancestors, who had convinced themselves that religion cannot abolish the unalienable rights of human nature. Perhaps the patience of the primitive church may be ascribed to its weakness, as well as to its virtue. A sect of unwarlike plebeians, without leaders, without arms, without fortifications, must have encountered inevitable destruction in a rash and fruitless resistance to the master of the Roman legions. But the Christians, when they deprecated the wrath of Diocletian, or solicited the favour of Constantine, could allege, with truth and confidence, that they held the principle of passive obedience, and that, in the space of three centuries, their conduct had always been conformable to their principles. They might add that the throne of the emperors would be established on a fixed and permanent basis, if all their subjects, embracing the Christian doctrine, should learn to suffer and to obey.

In the general order of Providence, princes and tyrants are considered as the ministers of Heaven, appointed to rule or to chastise the nations of the earth. But sacred history affords many illustrious examples of the more immediate interposition of the Deity in the government of his chosen people. The sceptre and the sword were committed to the hands of Moses, of Joshua, of Gideon, of David, of the Maccabees; the virtues of those heroes were the motive or the effect of the divine favour, the success of their arms was destined to achieve the deliverance or the triumph of the church. If the judges of Israel were occasional and temporary magistrates, the kings of Judah derived from the royal unction of their great ancestor an hereditary and indefeasible right, which could not be forfeited by their own vices, nor recalled by the caprice of their subjects. The same extraordinary providence, which was no longer confined to the Jewish people, might elect Constantine and his family as the protectors of the Christian world; and the devout Lactantius announces, in a prophetic tone, the future glories of his long and universal reign.[11] Galerius and Maximin, Maxentius and Licinius, were the rivals who shared with the favourite of Heaven the provinces of the empire. The tragic deaths of Galerius and Maximin soon gratified the resentment, and fulfilled the sanguine expectations, of the Christians. The success of Constantine against Maxentius and Licinius removed the two formidable competitors who still opposed the triumph of the second David, and his cause might seem to claim the peculiar interposition of Providence. The character of the Roman tyrant disgraced the purple and human nature; and, though the Christians might enjoy his precarious favour, they were exposed, with the rest of his subjects, to the effects of his wanton and capricious cruelty. The conduct of Licinius soon betrayed the reluctance with which he had consented to the wise and humane regulations of the edict of Milan. The convocation of provincial synods was prohibited in his dominions; his Christian officers were ignominiously dismissed; and, if he avoided the guilt, or rather danger, of a general persecution, his partial oppressions were rendered still more odious by the violation of a solemn and voluntary engagement. While the East, according to the lively expression of Eusebius, was involved in the shades of infernal darkness, the auspicious rays of celestial light warmed and illuminated the provinces of the West. The piety of Constantine was admitted as an unexceptionable proof of the justice of his arms; and his use of victory confirmed the opinion of the Christians, that their hero was inspired, and con-

[11] *Eusebius, in the course of his history, his life, and his oration, repeatedly inculcates the divine right of Constantine to the empire.*

ducted by the Lord of Hosts. The conquest of Italy produced a general edict of toleration: and, as soon as the defeat of Licinius had invested Constantine with the sole dominion of the Roman world, he immediately, by circular letters, exhorted all his subjects to imitate, without delay, the example of their sovereign, and to embrace the divine truth of Christianity.

The assurance that the elevation of Constantine was intimately connected with the designs of Providence instilled into the minds of the Christians two opinions, which, by very different means, assisted the accomplishment of the prophecy. Their warm and active loyalty exhausted in his favour every resource of human industry; and they confidently expected that their strenuous efforts would be seconded by some divine and miraculous aid. The enemies of Constantine have imputed to interested motives the alliance which he insensibly contracted with the Catholic church, and which apparently contributed to the success of his ambition. In the beginning of the fourth century, the Christians still bore a very inadequate proportion to the inhabitants of the empire; but among a degenerate people, who viewed the change of masters with the indifference of slaves, the spirit and union of a religious party might assist the popular leader to whose service, from a principle of conscience, they had devoted their lives and fortunes.[12] The example of his father had instructed Constantine to esteem and to reward the merit of the Christians; and in the distribution of public offices, he had the advantage of strengthening his government, by the choice of ministers or generals in whose fidelity he could repose a just and unreserved confidence. By the influence of these dignified missionaries, the proselytes of the new faith must have multiplied in the court and army; the Barbarians of Germany, who filled the ranks of the legions, were of a careless temper, which acquiesced without resistance in the religion of their commander; and, when they passed the Alps, it may fairly be presumed that a great number of the soldiers had already consecrated their swords to the service of Christ and of Constantine.[13] The habits of mankind, and the interest of religion, gradually abated the horror of war and bloodshed, which had so long prevailed among the Christians; and, in the councils which were assembled under the gracious protection of Constantine, the authority of the bishops was seasonably employed to ratify the obligation of the military oath, and to inflict the penalty of excommunication on those soldiers who threw away their arms during the peace of the church. While Constantine, in his own dominions, increased

[12] *In the beginning of the last century, the Papists of England were only a* thirtieth, *and the Protestants of France only a* fifteenth, *part of the respective nations, to whom their spirit and power were a constant object of apprehension.*

[13] *This careless temper of the Germans appears almost uniformly in the history of the conversion of each of the tribes. The legions of Constantine were recruited with Germans; and the court even of his father had been filled with Christians.*

14 *Eusebius always considers the second civil war against Licinius as a sort of religious crusade. At the invitation of the tyrant, some Christian officers had resumed their zones; or, in other words, had returned to the military service. Their conduct was afterwards censured by the twelfth canon of the council of Nice; if this particular application may be received, instead of the loose and general sense of the Greek interpreters, Balsamon, Zonaras, and Alexis Aristenus.*

15 *The Christian writers, Justin, Minucius Felix, Tertullian, Jerom, and Maximus of Turin, have investigated with tolerable success the figure or likeness of a cross in almost every object of nature or art; in the intersection of the meridian and equator, the human face, a bird flying, a man swimming, a mast and yard, a plough, a standard, &c. &c.*

16 *See Aurelius Victor, who considers this law as one of the examples of Constantine's piety. An edict so honourable to Christianity deserved a place in the Theodosian Code, instead of the indirect mention of it,*

the number and zeal of his faithful adherents, he could depend on the support of a powerful faction in those provinces which were still possessed or usurped by his rivals. A secret disaffection was diffused among the Christian subjects of Maxentius and Licinius; and the resentment which the latter did not attempt to conceal served only to engage them still more deeply in the interest of his competitor. The regular correspondence which connected the bishops of the most distant provinces enabled them freely to communicate their wishes and their designs, and to transmit without danger any useful intelligence, or any pious contributions, which might promote the service of Constantine, who publicly declared that he had taken up arms for the deliverance of the church.[14]

The enthusiasm which inspired the troops, and perhaps the emperor himself, had sharpened their swords, while it satisfied their conscience. They marched to battle with the full assurance that the same God, who had formerly opened a passage to the Israelites through the waters of Jordan, and had thrown down the walls of Jericho at the sound of the trumpets of Joshua, would display his visible majesty and power in the victory of Constantine. The evidence of ecclesiastical history is prepared to affirm that their expectations were justified by the conspicuous miracle to which the conversion of the first Christian emperor has been almost unanimously ascribed. The real or imaginary cause of so important an event deserves and demands the attention of posterity; and I shall endeavour to form a just estimate of the famous vision of Constantine, by a distinct consideration of the *standard,* the *dream,* and the *celestial sign;* by separating the historical, the natural, and the marvellous parts of this extraordinary story, which, in the composition of a specious argument, have been artfully confounded in one splendid and brittle mass.

I. An instrument of the tortures which were inflicted only on slaves and strangers became an object of horror in the eyes of a Roman citizen; and the ideas of guilt, of pain, and of ignominy were closely united with the idea of the cross.[15] The piety rather than the humanity of Constantine soon abolished in his dominions the punishment which the Saviour of mankind had condescended to suffer;[16] but the emperor had already learned to despise the prejudices of his education, and of his people, before he could erect in the midst of Rome his own statue, bearing a cross in its right hand, with an inscription which referred the victory of his arms, and the deliverance of Rome, to the virtue of that salutary sign, the true symbol of force and courage.[17] The same symbol sanctified the arms of the soldiers of Constantine; the cross glittered on their helmets, was engraved on their shields, was interwoven into their banners; and the consecrated emblems which adorned the person of the emperor himself were distinguished only by richer materials and more exquisite workmanship. But the principal standard which displayed the triumph of the cross was styled the *Labarum*,[18] an obscure though celebrated name, which has been vainly derived from almost all the languages of the world. It is described as a long pike intersected by a transversal beam. The silken veil which hung down from the beam was curiously enwrought with the images of the reigning monarch and his children. The summit of the pike supported a crown of gold which inclosed the mysterious monogram, at once expressive of the figure of the cross and the initial letters of the name of Christ.[19] The safety of the labarum was entrusted to fifty guards, of approved valour and fidelity; their station was marked by honours and emoluments; and some fortunate accidents soon introduced an opinion that, as long as the guards of the labarum were engaged in the execution of their office, they were secure and invulnerable amidst the darts of the enemy. In the second civil war Licinius felt and dreaded the power of this consecrated banner, the sight of which, in the distress of battle, animated the soldiers of Constantine with an invincible enthusiasm, and scattered terror and dismay through the ranks of the adverse legions.[20] The Christian emperors, who respected the example of Constantine, displayed in all their military expeditions the standard of the cross; but, when the degenerate successors of Theodosius had ceased to appear in person at the head of their armies, the labarum was deposited as a venerable but useless relic in the palace of Constantinople.[21] Its honours are still preserved on the medals of the Flavian family. Their grateful devotion has placed the monogram of Christ in the midst of the ensigns of Rome. The solemn epithets of, safety of the republic, glory of the army, restoration of public happiness, are equally applied to the religious and military trophies; and there is still extant a medal of the emperor Constantius, where the standard of the labarum is accompanied with these memorable words, BY THIS SIGN THOU SHALT CONQUER.

II. In all occasions of danger or distress, it was the practice of the primitive Christians to fortify their minds and bodies by the sign of the cross, which they used, in all their ecclesiastical rites, in all the daily occurrences of life, as an infallible preservative against every

which seems to result from the comparison of the fifth and eighteenth titles of the ninth book.

[17] *The statue, or at least the cross and inscription, may be ascribed with more probability to the second, or even the third, visit of Constantine to Rome. Immediately after the defeat of Maxentius, the minds of the senate and people were scarcely ripe for this public monument.*

[18] *The derivation and meaning of the word Labarum or Laborum, which is employed by Gregory Nazianzen, Ambrose, Prudentius, &c. still remain totally unknown; in spite of the efforts of the critics, who have ineffectually tortured the Latin, Greek, Spanish, Celtic, Teutonic, Illyric, Armenian, &c. in search of an etymology.*

[19] *Cuper and Baronius have engraved from ancient monuments several specimens of these monograms, which became extremely fashionable in the Christian world.*

[20] *He introduces the Labarum before the Italian expedition; but his narrative seems to indicate that it was never shown at the head of an army, till Constantine, above ten years afterwards, declared himself the enemy of Licinius and the deliverer of the church.*

[21] *Theophanes lived towards the end of the eighth century, almost five hundred years after Constantine. The modern Greeks were not inclined to display in the field the standard of the empire and of Christianity; and, though they depended on every superstitious hope of* defence, the promise of victory *would have appeared too bold a fiction.*

[22] *The learned Jesuit Petavius has collected many similar passages on the virtues of the cross, which in the last age embarrassed our Protestant disputants.*

[23] *It is certain that this historical declamation was composed and published while Licinius, sovereign of the East, still preserved the friendship of Constantine and of the Christians. Every reader of taste must perceive that the style is of a very different and inferior character to that of Lactantius; and*

species of spiritual or temporal evil.[22] The authority of the church might alone have had sufficient weight to justify the devotion of Constantine, who, in the same prudent and gradual progress, acknowledged the truth, and assumed the symbol, of Christianity. But the testimony of a contemporary writer, who in a former treatise has avenged the cause of religion, bestows on the piety of the emperor a more awful and sublime character. He affirms, with the most perfect confidence, that, in the night which preceded the last battle against Maxentius, Constantine was admonished in a dream to inscribe the shields of his soldiers with the *celestial sign of God,* the sacred monogram of the name of Christ; that he executed the commands of heaven; and that his valour and obedience were rewarded by the decisive victory of the Milvian Bridge. Some considerations might perhaps incline a sceptical mind to suspect the judgment or the veracity of the rhetorician, whose pen, either from zeal or interest, was devoted to the cause of the prevailing faction.[23] He appears to have published his deaths of the persecutors at Nicomedia about three years after the Roman victory; but the interval of a thousand miles, and a thousand days, will allow an ample latitude for the invention of declaimers, the credulity of party, and the tacit approbation of the emperor himself; who might listen without indignation to a marvellous tale, which exalted his fame and promoted his designs. In favour of Licinius, who still dissembled his animosity to the Christians, the same author has provided a similar vision, of a form of prayer, which was communicated by an angel, and repeated by the whole army before they engaged the legions of the tyrant Maximin. The frequent repetition of miracles serves to provoke, where it does not subdue, the reason of mankind;[24] but, if the dream of Constantine is separately considered, it may be naturally explained either by the policy or the enthusiasm of the emperor. Whilst his anxiety for the approaching day, which must decide the fate of the empire, was suspended by a short and interrupted slumber, the venerable form of Christ, and the well-known symbol of his religion, might forcibly offer themselves to the active fancy of a prince who reverenced the name, and had perhaps secretly implored the power, of the God of the Christians. As readily might a consummate statesman indulge himself in the use of one of those military stratagems, one of those pious frauds, which Philip and Sertorius had employed with such art and effect.[25] The præternatural origin of dreams was universally admitted by the nations of antiquity, and a considerable part of the Gallic army was already prepared to place their confidence in the salutary sign of the Christian religion. The secret vision of Constantine could be disproved only by the event; and the intrepid hero who had passed the Alps and the Apennine might view with careless despair the consequences of a defeat under the walls of Rome. The senate and people, exulting in their own deliverance from an odious tyrant, acknowledged that the victory of Constantine surpassed the powers of man, without daring to insinuate that it had been obtained by the protection of the *Gods*. The triumphal arch which was erected about three years after the event proclaims, in ambiguous language, that, by the greatness of his own mind and by an *instinct* or impulse of the Divinity, he had saved and avenged the Roman republic. The Pagan orator, who had seized an earlier opportunity of celebrating the virtues of the conqueror, supposes that he alone enjoyed a secret and intimate commerce with the Supreme Being, who delegated the care of mortals to his subordinate deities; and thus assigns a very plausible reason why the subjects of Constantine should not presume to embrace the new religion of their sovereign.

III. The philosopher, who with calm suspicion examines the dreams and omens, the miracles and prodigies, of profane or even of ecclesiastical history, will probably conclude that, if the eyes of the spectators have sometimes been deceived by fraud, the understanding of the readers has much more frequently been insulted by fiction. Every event, or appearance, or accident, which seems to deviate from the ordinary course of nature, has been rashly ascribed to the immediate action of the Deity; and the astonished fancy of the multitude has sometimes given shape and colour, language and motion, to the fleeting but uncommon meteors of the air. Nazarius and Eusebius are the two most celebrated orators who, in studied panegyrics, have laboured to exalt the glory of Constantine. Nine years after the Roman victory, Nazarius[26] describes an army of divine warriors, who seemed to fall from the sky: he marks their beauty, their spirit, their gigantic forms, the stream of light which beamed from their celestial armour, their patience in suffering themselves to be heard, as well as seen, by mortals; and their declaration that they were sent, that they flew, to the assistance of the great Constantine. For the truth of this prodigy, the Pagan orator appeals to the whole Gallic nation, in whose presence he was then speaking; and seems to hope that the ancient apparitions[27] would now obtain credit from this recent and public event. The Christian fable of Eusebius, which in the space of twenty-six years might arise from the original

such indeed is the judgment of Le Clerc and Lardner. Three arguments from the title of the book, and from the names of Donatus and Cæcilius, are produced by the advocates for Lactantius. Each of these proofs is singly weak and defective; but their concurrence has great weight. I have often fluctuated, and shall tamely follow the Colbert MS. in calling the author (whoever he was) Cæcilius.

[24] *There seems to be some reason in the observation of M. de Voltaire, who ascribes to the success of Constantine the superior fame of his Labarum above the angel of Licinius. Yet even this angel is favourably entertained by Pagi, Tillemont, Fleury, &c. who are fond of increasing their stock of miracles.*

[25] *Besides these well-known examples, Tollius has discovered a vision of Antigonus, who assured his troops that he had seen a pentagon (the symbol of safety) with these words, "In this conquer." But Tollius has most inexcusably omitted to produce his authority; and his own character, literary as well as moral, is not free from reproach.*

Without insisting on the silence of Diodorus, Plutarch, Justin, &c. it may be observed that Polyænus, who in a separate chapter has collected nineteen military stratagems of Antigonus, is totally ignorant of this remarkable vision.

[26] *It is unnecessary to name the moderns, whose undistinguishing and ravenous appetite has swallowed even the Pagan bait of Nazarius.*

[27] *The apparitions of Castor and Pollux, particularly to announce the Macedonian victory, are attested by historians and public monuments.*

[28] *The silence of the same Eusebius, in his Ecclesiastical History, is deeply felt by those advocates for the miracle who are not absolutely callous.*

[29] *The narrative of Constantine seems to indicate that he saw the cross in the sky before he passed the Alps against Maxentius. The scene has been fixed by provincial vanity at Treves, Besançon, &c.*

[30] *The pious Tillemont rejects with a sigh the useful Acts of Artemius, a veteran and a martyr, who attests as an eyewitness the vision of Constantine.*

dream, is cast in a much more correct and elegant mould. In one of the marches of Constantine, he is reported to have seen with his own eyes the luminous trophy of the cross, placed above the meridian sun, and inscribed with the following words: BY THIS CONQUER. This amazing object in the sky astonished the whole army, as well as the emperor himself, who was yet undetermined in the choice of a religion; but his astonishment was converted into faith by the vision of the ensuing night. Christ appeared before his eyes; and, displaying the same celestial sign of the cross, he directed Constantine to frame a similar standard, and to march, with an assurance of victory, against Maxentius and all his enemies.[28] The learned bishop of Cæsarea appears to be sensible that the recent discovery of this marvellous anecdote would excite some surprise and distrust among the most pious of his readers. Yet instead of ascertaining the precise circumstances of time and place, which always serve to detect falsehood or establish truth;[29] instead of collecting and recording the evidence of so many living witnesses, who must have been spectators of this stupendous miracle;[30] Eusebius contents himself with alleging a very singular testimony; that of the deceased Constantine, who, many years after the event, in the freedom of conversation, had related to him this extraordinary incident of his own life, and had attested the truth of it by a solemn oath. The prudence and gratitude of the learned prelate forbade him to suspect the veracity of his victorious master; but he plainly intimates that, in a fact of such a nature, he should have refused his assent to any meaner authority. This motive or credibility could not survive the power of the Flavian family; and the celestial sign, which the Infidels might afterwards deride, was disregarded by the Christians of the age which immediately followed the conversion of Constantine.[31] But the Catholic church, both of the East and of the West, has adopted a prodigy, which favours, or seems to favour, the popular worship of the cross. The vision of Constantine maintained an honourable place in the legend of superstition, till the bold and sagacious spirit of criticism presumed to depreciate the triumph, and to arraign the truth of the first Christian emperor.[32]

The protestant and philosophic readers of the present age will incline to believe that, in the account of his own conversion Constantine attested a wilful falsehood by a solemn and deliberate perjury. They may not hesitate to pronounce that, in the choice of a religion, his mind was determined only by a sense of interest; and that (according to the expression of a profane poet) he used the altars of the church as a convenient footstool to the throne of the empire. A conclusion so harsh and so absolute is not, however, warranted by our knowledge of human nature, of Constantine, or of Christianity. In an age of religious fervour, the most artful statesmen are observed to feel some part of the enthusiasm which they inspire; and the most orthodox saints assume the dangerous privilege of defending the cause of truth by the arms of deceit and falsehood. Personal interest is often the standard of our belief, as well as of our practice; and the same motives of temporal advantage which might influence the public conduct and professions of Constantine would insensibly dispose his mind to embrace a religion so propitious to his fame and fortunes. His vanity was gratified by the flattering assurance that *he* had been chosen by Heaven to reign over the earth; success had justified his divine title to the throne, and that title was founded on the truth of the Christian revelation. As real virtue is sometimes excited by undeserved applause, the specious piety of Constantine, if at first it was only specious, might gradually, by the influence of praise, of habit, and of example, be matured into serious faith and fervent devotion. The bishops and teachers of the new sect, whose dress and manners had not qualified them for the residence of a court, were admitted to the Imperial table; they accompanied the monarch in his expeditions; and the ascendant which one of them, an Egyptian or a Spaniard,[33] acquired over his mind was imputed by the Pagans to the effect of magic. Lactantius, who has adorned the precepts of the gospel with the eloquence of Cicero,[34] and Eusebius, who has consecrated the learning and philosophy of the Greeks to the service of religion,[35] were both received into the friendship and familiarity of their sovereign: and those able masters of controversy could patiently watch the soft and yielding moments of persuasion, and dexterously apply the arguments which were the best adapted to his character and understanding. Whatever advantages might be derived from the acquisition of an Imperial proselyte, he was distinguished by the splendour of his purple, rather than by the superiority of wisdom or virtue, from the many thousands of his subjects who had embraced the doctrines of Christianity. Nor can it be deemed incredible that the mind of an unlettered soldier should have yielded to the weight of evidence, which, in a more enlightened age, has satisfied or subdued the reason of a Grotius, a Pascal, or a Locke. In the midst of the incessant labours of his great office, this soldier employed, or affected to employ, the hours of the night in the diligent study of

[31] *The advocates for the vision are unable to produce a single testimony from the Fathers of the fourth and fifth centuries, who, in their voluminous writings, repeatedly celebrate the triumph of the church and of Constantine. As these venerable men had not any dislike to a miracle, we may suspect (and the suspicion is confirmed by the ignorance of Jerom) that they were all unacquainted with the life of Constantine by Eusebius. This tract was recovered by the diligence of those who translated or continued his Ecclesiastical History, and who have represented in various colours the vision of the cross.*

[32] *Godefroy was the first who, in the year 1643, expressed any doubt of a miracle which had been supported with equal zeal by Cardinal Baronius and the Centuriators of Magdeburg. Since that time, many of the Protestant critics have inclined towards doubt and disbelief. The objections are urged, with great force, by M. Chauffepié, and, in the year 1774, a doctor of Sorbonne, the Abbé du Voisin, published an Apology, which deserves the praise of learning and moderation.*

[33] *This favourite was probably the great Osius, bishop of Cordova, who preferred the pastoral care of the whole church to the government of a particular diocese. His character is magnificently, though concisely, expressed by Athanasius. Osius was accused, perhaps unjustly, of retiring from court with a very ample fortune.*

[34] *The Christianity of Lactantius was of a moral rather than of a mysterious cast.*

[35] *Fabricius, with his usual diligence, has collected a list of between three and four hundred authors quoted in the Evangelical Preparation of Eusebius.*

[36] *He chiefly depends on a mysterious acrostic, composed in the sixth age after the Deluge by the Erythræan Sybil, and translated by Cicero into Latin. The initial letters of the thirty-four Greek verses form this prophetic sentence:* JESUS CHRIST, SON OF GOD, SAVIOUR OF THE WORLD.

[37] *In his paraphrase of Virgil, the emperor has frequently assisted and improved the literal sense of the Latin text.*

the Scriptures and the composition of theological discourses; which he afterwards pronounced in the presence of a numerous and applauding audience. In a very long discourse, which is still extant, the royal preacher expatiates on the various proofs of religion; but he dwells with peculiar complacency on the Sybilline verses,[36] and the fourth eclogue of Virgil.[37] Forty years before the birth of Christ, the Mantuan bard, as if inspired by the celestial muse of Isaiah, had celebrated, with all the pomp of oriental metaphor, the return of the Virgin, the fall of the serpent, the approaching birth of a godlike child, the offspring of the great Jupiter, who should expiate the guilt of human kind, and govern the peaceful universe with the virtues of his father; the rise and appearance of an heavenly race, a primitive nation throughout the world; and the gradual restoration of the innocence and felicity of the golden age. The poet was perhaps unconscious of the secret sense and object of these sublime predictions, which have been so unworthily applied to the infant son of a consul or a triumvir:[38] but, if a more splendid, and indeed specious, interpretation of the fourth eclogue contributed to the conversion of the first Christian emperor, Virgil may deserve to be ranked among the most successful missionaries of the gospel.

The awful mysteries of the Christian faith and worship were concealed from the eyes of strangers, and even of catechumens, with an affected secrecy, which served to excite their wonder and curiosity. But the severe rules of discipline which the prudence of the bishops had instituted were relaxed by the same prudence in favour of an Imperial proselyte, whom it was so important to allure, by every gentle condescension, into the pale of the church; and Constantine was permitted, at least by a tacit dispensation, to enjoy *most* of the privileges, before he had contracted *any* of the obligations, of a Christian. Instead of retiring from the congregation when the voice of the deacon dismissed the profane multitude, he prayed with the faithful, disputed with the bishops, preached on the most sublime and intricate subjects of theology, celebrated with sacred rites the vigil of Easter, and publicly declared himself, not only a partaker, but in some measure a priest and hierophant of the Christian mysteries. The pride of Constantine might assume, and his services had deserved, some extraordinary distinction: an ill-timed rigour might have blasted the unripened fruits of his conversion; and, if the doors of the church had been strictly closed against a prince who had deserted the altars of the gods, the master of the empire would have been left destitute of any form of religious worship. In his last visit to Rome, he piously disclaimed and insulted the super-stition of his ancestors by refusing to lead the military procession of the equestrian order and to offer the public vows to the Jupiter of the Capitoline Hill. Many years before his baptism and death, Con-stantine had proclaimed to the world that neither his person nor his image should ever more be seen within the walls of an idolatrous temple; while he distributed through the provinces a variety of medals and pictures, which represented the emperor in an humble and suppliant posture of Christian devotion.

The pride of Constantine, who refused the privileges of a cate-chumen, cannot easily be explained or excused; but the delay of his baptism may be justified by the maxims and the practice of ecclesi-astical antiquity. The sacrament of baptism [39] was regularly admin-istered by the bishop himself, with his assistant clergy, in the cathe-dral church of the diocese, during the fifty days between the solemn festivals of Easter and Pentecost; and this holy term admitted a numerous band of infants and adult persons into the bosom of the church. The discretion of parents often suspended the baptism of their children till they could understand the obligations which they contracted; the severity of ancient bishops exacted from the new converts a novitiate of two or three years; and the catechumens themselves, from different motives of a temporal or a spiritual na-ture, were seldom impatient to assume the character of perfect and initiated Christians. The sacrament of baptism was supposed to con-tain a full and absolute expiation of sin; and the soul was instantly restored to its original purity, and entitled to the promise of eternal salvation. Among the proselytes of Christianity, there were many who judged it imprudent to precipitate a salutary rite, which could not be repeated; to throw away an inestimable privilege, which could never be recovered. By the delay of their baptism, they could venture freely to indulge their passions in the enjoyments of this world, while they still retained in their own hands the means of a sure and easy absolution. [40] The sublime theory of the gospel had made a much fainter impression on the heart than on the under-standing of Constantine himself. He pursued the great object of his ambition through the dark and bloody paths of war and policy; and, after the victory, he abandoned himself, without moderation, to the abuse of his fortune. Instead of asserting his just superiority above the imperfect heroism and profane philosophy of Trajan and the Antonines, the mature age of Constantine forfeited the repu-tation which he had acquired in his youth. As he gradually ad-

[38] *The different claims of an elder and younger son of Pollio, of Julia, of Drusus, of Marcellus, are found to be incom-patible with chronology, history, and the good sense of Virgil.*

[39] *One circumstance may be observed, in which the modern churches have materially departed from the ancient custom. The sacrament of bap-tism (even when it was administered to infants) was immediately fol-lowed by confirmation and the holy commun-ion.*

[40] *The fathers, who cen-sured this criminal delay, could not deny the cer-tain and victorious ef-ficacy even of a deathbed baptism. The ingenious rhetoric of Chrysostom could find only three arguments against these prudent Christians. 1. That we should love and pursue virtue for her own sake, and not merely for the reward. 2. That we may be sur-prised by death without an opportunity of bap-tism. 3. That, although we shall be placed in heaven, we shall only twinkle like little stars, when compared to the suns of righteousness who have run their ap-pointed course with labour, with success, and with glory. I believe that*

this delay of baptism, though attended with the most pernicious consequences, was never condemned by any general or provincial council, or by any public act or declaration of the church. The zeal of the bishops was easily kindled on much slighter occasions.

41 For this disingenuous falsehood he has deserved and experienced the harshest treatment from all the ecclesiastical writers, except Cardinal Baronius, who had occasion to employ the Infidel on a particular service against the Arian Eusebius.

42 The bishop of Cæsarea supposes the salvation of Constantine with the most perfect confidence.

43 The Greeks, the Russians, and, in the darker ages, the Latins themselves have been desirous of placing Constantine in the catalogue of saints.

vanced in the knowledge of truth, he proportionately declined in the practice of virtue; and the same year of his reign in which he convened the council of Nice was polluted by the execution, or rather murder, of his eldest son. This date is alone sufficient to refute the ignorant and malicious suggestions of Zosimus,[41] who affirms that, after the death of Crispus, the remorse of his father accepted from the ministers of Christianity the expiation which he had vainly solicited from the Pagan pontiffs. At the time of the death of Crispus, the emperor could no longer hesitate in the choice of a religion; he could no longer be ignorant that the church was possessed of an infallible remedy, though he chose to defer the application of it, till the approach of death had removed the temptation and danger of a relapse. The bishops, whom he summoned in his last illness to the palace of Nicomedia, were edified by the fervour with which he requested and received the sacrament of baptism, by the solemn protestation that the remainder of his life should be worthy of a disciple of Christ, and by his humble refusal to wear the Imperial purple after he had been clothed in the white garment of a neophyte. The example and reputation of Constantine seemed to countenance the delay of baptism.[42] Future tyrants were encouraged to believe that the innocent blood which they might shed in a long reign would instantly be washed away in the waters of regeneration; and the abuse of religion dangerously undermined the foundations of moral virtue.

The gratitude of the church has exalted the virtues and excused the failings of a generous patron, who seated Christianity on the throne of the Roman world; and the Greeks, who celebrate the festival of the Imperial saint, seldom mention the name of Constantine without adding the title of *equal to the Apostles.*[43] Such a comparison, if it allude to the character of those divine missionaries, must be imputed to the extravagance of impious flattery. But, if the parallel is confined to the extent and number of their evangelic victories, the success of Constantine might perhaps equal that of the Apostles themselves. By the edicts of toleration he removed the temporal disadvantages which had hitherto retarded the progress of Christianity; and its active and numerous ministers received a free permission, a liberal encouragement, to recommend the salutary truths of revelation by every argument which could affect the reason or piety of mankind. The exact balance of the two religions continued but a moment; and the piercing eye of ambition and avarice soon discovered that the profession of Christianity might contribute to the interest of the present, as well as of a future, life.[44] The hopes of wealth and honours, the example of an emperor, his exhortations, his irresistible smiles, diffused conviction among the venal and obsequious crowds which usually fill the apartments of a palace. The cities which signalized a forward zeal by the voluntary destruction of their temples were distinguished by municipal privileges, and rewarded with popular donatives; and the new capital of the East gloried in the singular advantage that Constantinople was never profaned by the worship of idols.[45] As the lower ranks of society are governed by imitation, the conversion of those who possessed any eminence of birth, of power, or of riches, was soon followed by dependent multitudes.[46] The salvation of the common people was purchased at an easy rate, if it be true that, in one year, twelve thousand men were baptized at Rome, besides a proportionable number of women and children; and that a white garment, with twenty pieces of gold, had been promised by the emperor to every convert. The powerful influence of Constantine was not circumscribed by the narrow limits of his life, or of his dominions. The education which he bestowed on his sons and nephews secured to the empire a race of princes whose faith was still more lively and sincere, as they imbibed, in their earliest infancy, the spirit, or at least the doctrine, of Christianity. War and commerce had spread the knowledge of the gospel beyond the confines of the Roman provinces; and the Barbarians, who had disdained an humble and proscribed sect, soon learned to esteem a religion which had been so lately embraced by the greatest monarch and the most civilized nation of the globe. The Goths and Germans who enlisted under the standard of Rome revered the cross which glittered at the head of the legions, and their fierce countrymen received at the same time the lessons of faith and of humanity. The kings of Iberia and Armenia worshipped the God of their protector; and their subjects, who have invariably preserved the name of Christians, soon formed a sacred and perpetual connexion with their Roman brethren. The Christians of Persia were suspected, in time of war, of preferring their religion to their country; but, as long as peace subsisted between the two empires, the persecuting spirit of the Magi was effectually restrained by the interposition of Constantine. The rays of the gospel illuminated the coast of India. The colonies of Jews, who had penetrated into Arabia and Æthiopia, opposed the progress of Christianity; but the labour of the missionaries was in some measure facilitated by a previous knowledge of the Mosaic revela-

[44] *See the third and fourth books of his life. He was accustomed to say that, whether Christ was preached in pretence or in truth, he should still rejoice.*

[45] *M. de Tillemont has defended, with strength and spirit, the virgin purity of Constantinople against some malevolent insinuations of the Pagan Zosimus.*

[46] *The author of the Histoire Politique et Philosophique des deux Indes condemns a law of Constantine, which gave freedom to all the slaves who should embrace Christianity. The emperor did indeed publish a law which restrained the Jews from circumcising, perhaps from keeping, any Christian slaves. But this imperfect exception related only to the Jews; and the great body of slaves, who were the property of Christian or Pagan masters, could not improve their temporal condition by changing their religion. I am ignorant by what guides the Abbé Raynal was deceived; as the total absence of quotations is the unpardonable blemish of his entertaining history.*

tion; and Abyssinia still reveres the memory of Frumentius, who, in the time of Constantine, devoted his life to the conversion of those sequestered regions. Under the reign of his son Constantius, Theophilus,[47] who was himself of Indian extraction, was invested with the double character of ambassador and bishop. He embarked on the Red Sea with two hundred horses of the purest breed of Cappadocia, which were sent by the emperor to the prince of the Sabæans, or Homerites. Theophilus was entrusted with many other useful or curious presents, which might raise the admiration and conciliate the friendship of the Barbarians; and he successfully employed several years in a pastoral visit to the churches of the torrid zone.

[47] *Theophilus had been given in his infancy as a hostage by his countrymen of the isle of Diva, and was educated by the Romans in learning and piety. The Maldives, of which Male, or Diva, may be the capital, are a cluster of 1900 or 2000 minute islands in the Indian ocean.*

The irresistible power of the Roman emperors was displayed in the important and dangerous change of the national religion. The terrors of a military force silenced the faint and unsupported murmurs of the Pagans, and there was reason to expect that the cheerful submission of the Christian clergy, as well as people, would be the result of conscience and gratitude. It was long since established, as a fundamental maxim of the Roman constitution, that every rank of citizens were alike subject to the laws, and that the care of religion was the right as well as duty of the civil magistrate. Constantine and his successors could not easily persuade themselves that they had forfeited, by their conversion, any branch of the Imperial prerogatives, or that they were incapable of giving laws to a religion which they had protected and embraced. The emperors still continued to exercise a supreme jurisdiction over the ecclesiastical order; and the sixteenth book of the Theodosian code represents, under a variety of titles, the authority which they assumed in the government of the Catholic church.

But the distinction of the spiritual and temporal powers, which had never been imposed on the free spirit of Greece and Rome, was introduced and confirmed by the legal establishment of Christianity. The office of supreme pontiff, which, from the time of Numa to that of Augustus, had always been exercised by one of the most eminent of the senators, was at length united to the Imperial dignity. The first magistrate of the state, as often as he was prompted by superstition or policy, performed with his own hands the sacerdotal functions; nor was there any order of priests, either at Rome or in the provinces, who claimed a more sacred character among men, or a more intimate communication with the gods. But in the Christian church, which entrusts the service of the altar to a perpetual succession of consecrated ministers, the monarch, whose spiritual rank is less honourable than that of the meanest deacon, was seated below the rails of the sanctuary, and confounded with the rest of the faithful multitude.[48] The emperor might be saluted as the father of his people, but he owed a filial duty and reverence to the fathers of the church; and the same marks of respect which Constantine had paid to the persons of saints and confessors were soon exacted by the pride of the episcopal order.[49] A secret conflict between the civil and ecclesiastical jurisdictions embarrassed the operations of the Roman government; and a pious emperor was alarmed by the guilt and danger of touching with a profane hand the ark of the covenant. The separation of men into the two orders of the clergy and of the laity was, indeed, familiar to many nations of antiquity; and the priests of India, of Persia, of Assyria, of Judea, of Æthiopia, of Egypt, and of Gaul, derived from a celestial origin the temporal power and possessions which they had acquired. These venerable institutions had gradually assimilated themselves to the manners and government of their respective countries;[50] but the opposition or contempt of the civil power served to cement the discipline of the primitive church. The Christians had been obliged to elect their own magistrates, to raise and distribute a peculiar revenue, and to regulate the internal policy of their republic by a code of laws, which were ratified by the consent of the people and the practice of three hundred years. When Constantine embraced the faith of the Christians, he seemed to contract a perpetual alliance with a distinct and independent society; and the privileges granted or confirmed by that emperor, or by his successors, were accepted, not as the precarious favours of the court, but as the just and unalienable rights of the ecclesiastical order.

The Catholic church was administered by the spiritual and legal jurisdiction of eighteen hundred bishops;[51] of whom one thousand were seated in the Greek, and eight hundred in the Latin, provinces of the empire. The extent and boundaries of their respective dioceses had been variously and accidentally decided by the zeal and success of the first missionaries, by the wishes of the people, and by the propagation of the gospel. Episcopal churches were closely planted along the banks of the Nile, on the sea-coast of Africa, in the proconsular Asia, and through the southern provinces of Italy. The bishops of Gaul and Spain, of Thrace and Pontus, reigned over an ample territory, and delegated their rural suffragans to execute the subordinate duties of the pastoral office. A Christian diocese

[48] *Something of a contrary practice had insensibly prevailed in the church of Constantinople; but the rigid Ambrose commanded Theodosius to retire below the rails, and taught him to know the difference between a king and a priest.*

[49] *At the table of the emperor Maximus, Martin, bishop of Tours, received the cup from an attendant, and gave it to the presbyter his companion, before he allowed the emperor to drink; the empress waited on Martin at table. Yet it may be doubted, whether these extraordinary compliments were paid to the bishop or the saint.*

[50] *Plutarch, in his treatise of Isis and Osiris, informs us that the kings of Egypt, who were not already priests, were initiated, after their election, into the sacerdotal order.*

[51] *The numbers are not ascertained by any ancient writer, or original catalogue; for the partial lists of the eastern churches are comparatively modern. The patient diligence of Charles a S^{to} Paolo, of Luke Holstenius, and of Bingham, has laboriously investigated all the episcopal sees of the Catholic*

church, which was almost commensurate with the Roman empire. The ninth book of the Christian Antiquities is a very accurate map of ecclesiastical geography.

might be spread over a province or reduced to a village; but all the bishops possessed an equal and indelible character: they all derived the same powers and privileges from the apostles, from the people, and from the laws. While the *civil* and *military* professions were separated by the policy of Constantine, a new and perpetual order of *ecclesiastical* ministers, always respectable, sometimes dangerous, was established in the church and state. The important review of their station and attributes may be distributed under the following heads: I. Popular election. II. Ordination of the clergy. III. Property. IV. Civil jurisdiction. V. Spiritual censures. VI. Exercise of public oratory. VII. Privilege of legislative assemblies.

I. The freedom of elections subsisted long after the legal establishment of Christianity; and the subjects of Rome enjoyed in the church the privilege which they had lost in the republic, of choosing the magistrates whom they were bound to obey. As soon as a bishop had closed his eyes, the metropolitan issued a commission to one of his suffragans to administer the vacant see, and prepare, within a limited time, the future election. The right of voting was vested in the inferior clergy, who were best qualified to judge of the merit of the candidates; in the senators or nobles of the city, all those who were distinguished by their rank or property; and finally in the whole body of the people, who, on the appointed day, flocked in multitudes from the most remote parts of the diocese, and sometimes silenced, by their tumultuous acclamations, the voice of reason and the laws of discipline. These acclamations might accidentally fix on the head of the most deserving competitor; of some ancient presbyter, some holy monk, or some layman, conspicuous for his zeal and piety. But the episcopal chair was solicited, especially in the great and opulent cities of the empire, as a temporal rather than as a spiritual dignity. The interested views, the selfish and angry passions, the arts of perfidy and dissimulation, the secret corruption, the open and even bloody violence, which had formerly disgraced the freedom of election in the commonwealth of Greece and Rome, too often influenced the choice of the successors of the apostles. While one of the candidates boasted the honours of his family, a second allured his judges by the delicacies of a plentiful table, and a third, more guilty than his rivals, offered to share the plunder of the church among the accomplices of his sacrilegious hopes.[52] The civil as well as ecclesiastical laws attempted to exclude the populace from this solemn and important transaction. The canons of ancient discipline, by requiring several episcopal qualifi-

[52] *The epistles of Sidonius Apollinaris exhibit some of the scandals of the Gallican church; and Gaul was less polished and less corrupt than the East.*

cations of age, station, &c., restrained in some measure the indis-criminate caprice of the electors. The authority of the provincial bishops, who were assembled in the vacant church to consecrate the choice of the people, was interposed to moderate their passions and to correct their mistakes. The bishops could refuse to ordain an unworthy candidate, and the rage of contending factions some-times accepted their impartial mediation. The submission, or the resistance, of the clergy and people, on various occasions, afforded different precedents, which were insensibly converted into positive laws and provincial customs:[53] but it was everywhere admitted, as a fundamental maxim of religious policy, that no bishop could be imposed on an orthodox church without the consent of its mem-bers. The emperors, as the guardians of the public peace, and as the first citizens of Rome and Constantinople, might effectually de-clare their wishes in the choice of a primate: but those absolute monarchs respected the freedom of ecclesiastical elections; and, while they distributed and resumed the honours of the state and army, they allowed eighteen hundred perpetual magistrates to re-ceive their important offices from the free suffrages of the people. It was agreeable to the dictates of justice, that these magistrates should not desert an honourable station from which they could not be removed; but the wisdom of councils endeavoured, without much success, to enforce the residence, and to prevent the transla-tion, of bishops. The discipline of the West was indeed less relaxed than that of the East; but the same passions which made those regu-lations necessary rendered them ineffectual. The reproaches which angry prelates have so vehemently urged against each other serve only to expose their common guilt and their mutual indiscretion.

II. The bishops alone possessed the faculty of *spiritual* genera-tion; and this extraordinary privilege might compensate, in some degree, for the painful celibacy[54] which was imposed as a virtue, as a duty, and at length as a positive obligation. The religions of an-tiquity, which established a separate order of priests, dedicated a holy race, a tribe or family, to the perpetual service of the gods. Such institutions were founded for possession rather than conquest. The children of the priests enjoyed, with proud and indolent se-curity, their sacred inheritance; and the fiery spirit of enthusiasm was abated by the cares, the pleasures, and the endearments of do-mestic life. But the Christian sanctuary was open to every ambitious candidate who aspired to its heavenly promises or temporal posses-sions. The office of priests, like that of soldiers or magistrates, was

[53] *A compromise was sometimes introduced by law or by consent: either the bishops or the people chose one of the three candidates who had been named by the other party.*

[54] *The celibacy of the clergy during the first five or six centuries is a subject of discipline, and indeed of controversy, which has been very diligently examined.*

[55] The subject of the vocation, ordination, obedience, &c. of the clergy, is laboriously discussed by Thomassin and Bingham. When the brother of St. Jerom was ordained in Cyprus, the deacons forcibly stopped his mouth, lest he should make a solemn protestation which might invalidate the holy rites.

[56] The charter of immunities which the clergy obtained from the Christian emperors is contained in the sixteenth book of the Theodosian code; and is illustrated with tolerable candour by the learned Godefroy, whose mind was balanced by the opposite prejudices of a civilian and a protestant.

[57] Sixty presbyters or priests, one hundred deacons, forty deaconesses, ninety sub-deacons, one hundred and ten readers, twenty-five chanters, and one hundred door-keepers; in all, five hundred and twenty-five. This moderate number was fixed by the emperor, to relieve the distress of the church, which had been involved in debt and usury by the expense of a much higher establishment.

strenuously exercised by those men whose temper and abilities had prompted them to embrace the ecclesiastical profession, or who had been selected by a discerning bishop as the best qualified to promote the glory and interest of the church. The bishops [55] (till the abuse was restrained by the prudence of the laws) might constrain the reluctant, and protect the distressed; and the imposition of hands for ever bestowed some of the most valuable privileges of civil society. The whole body of the Catholic clergy, more numerous perhaps than the legions, was exempted by the emperors from all service, private or public, all municipal offices, and all personal taxes and contributions which pressed on their fellow-citizens with intolerable weight; and the duties of their holy profession were accepted as a full discharge of their obligations to the republic.[56] Each bishop acquired an absolute and indefeasible right to the perpetual obedience of the clerk whom he ordained: the clergy of each episcopal church, with its dependent parishes, formed a regular and permanent society; and the cathedrals of Constantinople [57] and Carthage maintained their peculiar establishment of five hundred ecclesiastical ministers. Their ranks [58] and numbers were insensibly multiplied by the superstition of the times, which introduced into the church the splendid ceremonies of a Jewish or Pagan temple; and a long train of priests, deacons, sub-deacons, acolytes, exorcists, readers, singers, and door-keepers, contributed, in their respective stations, to swell the pomp and harmony of religious worship. The clerical name and privilege were extended to many pious fraternities, who devoutly supported the ecclesiastical throne. Six hundred *parabolani*, or adventurers, visited the sick at Alexandria; eleven hundred *copiatæ*, or gravediggers, buried the dead at Constantinople; and the swarms of monks, who arose from the Nile, overspread and darkened the face of the Christian world.

III. The edict of Milan secured the revenue as well as the peace of the church.[59] The Christians not only recovered the lands and houses of which they had been stripped by the persecuting laws of Diocletian, but they acquired a perfect title to all the possessions which they had hitherto enjoyed by the connivance of the magistrate. As soon as Christianity became the religion of the emperor and the empire, the national clergy might claim a decent and honourable maintenance: and the payment of an annual tax might have delivered the people from the more oppressive tribute which superstition imposes on her votaries. But, as the wants and expenses of the church increased with her prosperity, the ecclesiastical order was still supported and enriched by the voluntary oblations of the faithful. Eight years after the edict of Milan, Constantine granted to all his subjects the free and universal permission of bequeathing their fortunes to the holy Catholic church; and their devout liberality, which during their lives was checked by luxury or avarice, flowed with a profuse stream at the hour of their death. The wealthy Christians were encouraged by the example of their sovereign. An absolute monarch, who is rich without patrimony, may be charitable without merit; and Constantine too easily believed that he should purchase the favour of Heaven, if he maintained the idle at the expense of the industrious, and distributed among the saints the wealth of the republic. The same messenger who carried over to Africa the head of Maxentius might be entrusted with an epistle to Cæcilian, bishop of Carthage. The emperor acquaints him that the treasurers of the province are directed to pay into his hands the sum of three thousand *folles,* or eighteen thousand pounds sterling, and to obey his farther requisitions for the relief of the churches of Africa, Numidia, and Mauritania. The liberality of Constantine increased in a just proportion to his faith, and to his vices. He assigned in each city a regular allowance of corn, to supply the fund of ecclesiastical charity; and the persons of both sexes who embraced the monastic life became the peculiar favourites of their sovereign. The Christian temples of Antioch, Alexandria, Jerusalem, Constantinople, &c. displayed the ostentatious piety of a prince ambitious, in a declining age, to equal the perfect labours of antiquity.[60] The form of these religious edifices was simple and oblong; though they might sometimes swell into the shape of a dome, and sometimes branch into the figure of a cross. The timbers were framed for the most part of cedars of Libanus; the roof was covered with tiles, perhaps of gilt brass; and the walls, the columns, the pavement, were incrusted with variegated marbles. The most precious ornaments of gold and silver, of silk and gems, were profusely dedicated to the service of the altar; and this specious magnificence was supported on the solid and perpetual basis of landed property. In the space of two centuries, from the reign of Constantine to that of Justinian, the eighteen hundred churches of the empire were enriched by the frequent and unalienable gifts of the prince and people. An annual income of six hundred pounds sterling may be reasonably assigned to the bishops, who were placed at an equal distance between riches and poverty,[61] but the standard of their wealth insensibly rose with the dignity and opulence of the

[58] *The number of seven orders has been fixed in the Latin church, exclusive of the episcopal character. But the four inferior ranks, the minor orders, are now reduced to empty and useless titles.*

[59] *The edict of Milan acknowledges, by reciting, that there existed a species of landed property. Such a solemn declaration of the supreme magistrate must have been received in all the tribunals as a maxim of civil law.*

[60] *The bishop of Cæsarea, who studied and gratified the taste of his master, pronounced in public an elaborate description of the church of Jerusalem. It no longer exists, but he has inserted in the Life of Constantine a short account of the architecture and ornaments. He likewise mentions the church of the Holy Apostles at Constantinople.*

[61] *The revenue of the patriarchs, and the most wealthy bishops, is not expressed; the highest annual valuation of a bishopric is stated at thirty, and the lowest at two, pounds of gold; the medium might be taken at sixteen, but these valuations are much below the real value.*

[62] *Every record which comes from the Vatican is justly suspected; yet these rent-rolls have an ancient and authentic colour; and it is at least evident, that, if forged, they were forged in a period when* farms, *not* kingdoms, *were the objects of papal avarice.*

[63] *The legal division of the ecclesiastical revenue does not appear to have been established in the time of Ambrose and Chrysostom. Simplicius and Gelasius, who were bishops of Rome in the latter part of the fifth century, mention it in their pastoral letters as a general law, which was already confirmed by the custom of Italy.*

[64] *From Eusebius and Sozomen we are assured that the episcopal jurisdiction was extended and confirmed by Constantine; but the forgery of a famous edict, which was never fairly inserted in the Theodosian Code, is demonstrated by Godefroy in the most satisfactory manner. It is strange that M. de Montesquieu, who was a lawyer as well as a philosopher, should allege this edict of Constantine without intimating any suspicion.*

cities which they governed. An authentic but imperfect [62] rent-roll specifies some houses, shops, gardens, and farms, which belonged to the three *Basilicæ* of Rome, St. Peter, St. Paul, and St. John Lateran, in the provinces of Italy, Africa, and the East. They produce, besides a reserved rent of oil, linen, paper, aromatics, &c. a clear annual revenue of twenty-two thousand pieces of gold, or twelve thousand pounds sterling. In the age of Constantine and Justinian, the bishops no longer possessed, perhaps they no longer deserved, the unsuspecting confidence of their clergy and people. The ecclesiastical revenues of each diocese were divided into four parts; for the respective uses, of the bishop himself, of his inferior clergy, of the poor, and of the public worship; and the abuse of this sacred trust was strictly and repeatedly checked.[63] The patrimony of the church was still subject to all the public impositions of the state. The clergy of Rome, Alexandria, Thessalonica, &c. might solicit and obtain some partial exemptions; but the premature attempt of the great council of Rimini, which aspired to universal freedom, was successfully resisted by the son of Constantine.

IV. The Latin clergy, who erected their tribunal on the ruins of the civil and common law, have modestly accepted as the gift of Constantine [64] the independent jurisdiction which was the fruit of time, of accident, and of their own industry. But the liberality of the Christian emperors had actually endowed them with some legal prerogatives, which secured and dignified the sacerdotal character.[65] 1. Under a despotic government, the bishops alone enjoyed and asserted the inestimable privilege of being tried only by their *peers;* and even in a capital accusation, a synod of their brethren were the sole judges of their guilt or innocence. Such a tribunal, unless it was inflamed by personal resentment or religious discord, might be favourable, or even partial, to the sacerdotal order: but Constantine was satisfied that secret impunity would be less pernicious than public scandal: and the Nicene council was edified by his public declaration that, if he surprised a bishop in the act of adultery, he should cast his Imperial mantle over the episcopal sinner. 2. The domestic jurisdiction of the bishops was at once a privilege and a restraint of the ecclesiastical order, whose civil causes were decently withdrawn from the cognizance of a secular judge. Their venial offences were not exposed to the shame of a public trial or punishment; and the gentle correction, which the tenderness of youth may endure from its parents or instructors, was inflicted by the temperate severity of the bishops. But, if the clergy were guilty of any crime which could not be sufficiently expiated by their degradation from an honourable and beneficial profession, the Roman magistrate drew the sword of justice without any regard to ecclesiastical immunities. 3. The arbitration of the bishops was ratified by a positive law; and the judges were instructed to execute, without appeal or delay, the episcopal decrees, whose validity had hitherto depended on the consent of the parties. The conversion of the magistrates themselves, and of the whole empire, might gradually remove the fears and scruples of the Christians. But they still resorted to the tribunal of the bishops, whose abilities and integrity they esteemed: and the venerable Austin enjoyed the satisfaction of complaining that his spiritual functions were perpetually interrupted by the invidious labour of deciding the claim or the possession of silver and gold, of lands and cattle. 4. The ancient privilege of sanctuary was transferred to the Christian temples, and extended, by the liberal piety of the younger Theodosius, to the precincts of consecrated ground.[66] The fugitive, and even guilty, suppliants were permitted to implore either the justice or the mercy of the Deity and his ministers. The rash violence of despotism was suspended by the mild interposition of the church; and the lives or fortunes of the most eminent subjects might be protected by the mediation of the bishop.

V. The bishop was the perpetual censor of the morals of his people. The discipline of penance was digested into a system of canonical jurisprudence,[67] which accurately defined the duty of private or public confession, the rules of evidence, the degrees of guilt, and the measure of punishment. It was impossible to execute this spiritual censure, if the Christian pontiff, who punished the obscure sins of the multitude, respected the conspicuous vices and destructive crimes of the magistrate; but it was impossible to arraign the conduct of the magistrate without controlling the administration of civil government. Some considerations of religion, or loyalty, or fear, protected the sacred persons of the emperors from the zeal or resentment of the bishops; but they boldly censured and excommunicated the subordinate tyrants who were not invested with the majesty of the purple. St. Athanasius excommunicated one of the ministers of Egypt; and the interdict which he pronounced, of fire and water, was solemnly transmitted to the churches of Cappadocia.[68] Under the reign of the younger Theodosius, the polite and eloquent Synesius, one of the descendants of Hercules,[69] filled the episcopal seat of Ptolemais, near the ruins of ancient Cyrene, and

[65] *The subject of ecclesiastical jurisdiction has been involved in a mist of passion, of prejudice, and of interest. Two of the fairest books which have fallen into my hands are the Institutes of Canon Law, by the Abbé de Fleury, and the Civil History of Naples, by Giannone. Their moderation was the effect of situation as well as of temper. Fleury was a French ecclesiastic, who respected the authority of the parliaments; Giannone was an Italian lawyer, who dreaded the power of the church. And here let me observe that, as the general propositions which I advance are the result of many particular and imperfect facts, I must either refer the reader to those modern authors who have expressly treated the subject or swell these notes to a disagreeable and disproportioned size.*

[66] *In the works of Fra Paolo there is an excellent discourse on the origin, claims, abuses, and limits of sanctuaries. He justly observes that ancient Greece might perhaps contain fifteen or twenty asyla or sanctuaries; a number which at present may be found in Italy within the walls of a single city.*

[67] *The penitential jurisprudence was continually improved by the canons of the councils. But, as many cases were still left to the discretion of the bishops, they occasionally published, after the example of the Roman Prætor, the rules of discipline which they proposed to observe. Among the canonical epistles of the fourth century, those of Basil the Great were celebrated.*

[68] *Basil, in Baronius, who declares that he purposely relates it, to convince governors that they were not exempt from a sentence of excommunication. In his opinion, even a royal head is not safe from the thunders of the Vatican; and the cardinal shows himself much more consistent than the lawyers and theologians of the Gallican church.*

[69] *The long series of his ancestors, as high as Eurysthenes, the first Doric king of Sparta, and the fifth in lineal descent from Hercules, was inscribed in the public registers of Cyrene, a Lacedæmonian colony. Such a poor and illustrious pedigree of seventeen hundred years, without adding the royal ancestors of Hercules, cannot be equalled in the history of mankind.*

the philosophic bishop supported, with dignity, the character which he had assumed with reluctance.[70] He vanquished the monster of Libya, the president Andronicus, who abused the authority of a venal office, invented new modes of rapine and torture, and aggravated the guilt of oppression by that of sacrilege. After a fruitless attempt to reclaim the haughty magistrate by mild and religious admonition, Synesius proceeds to inflict the last sentence of ecclesiastical justice,[71] which devotes Andronicus, with his associates and their *families*, to the abhorrence of earth and heaven. The impenitent sinners, more cruel than Phalaris or Sennacherib, more destructive than war, pestilence, or a cloud of locusts, are deprived of the name and privileges of Christians, of the participation of the sacraments, and of the hope of Paradise. The bishop exhorts the clergy, the magistrates, and the people, to renounce all society with the enemies of Christ; to exclude them from their houses and tables; and to refuse them the common offices of life and the decent rites of burial. The church of Ptolemais, obscure and contemptible as she may appear, addresses this declaration to all her sister churches of the world; and the profane who reject her decrees will be involved in the guilt and punishment of Andronicus and his impious followers. These spiritual terrors were enforced by a dexterous application to the Byzantine court; the trembling president implored the mercy of the church; and the descendant of Hercules enjoyed the satisfaction of raising a prostrate tyrant from the ground. Such principles and such examples insensibly prepared the triumph of the Roman pontiffs, who have trampled on the necks of kings.

VI. Every popular government has experienced the effects of rude or artificial eloquence. The coldest nature is animated, the firmest reason is moved, by the rapid communication of the prevailing impulse; and each hearer is affected by his own passions, and by those of the surrounding multitude. The ruin of civil liberty had silenced the demagogues of Athens and the tribunes of Rome; the custom of preaching, which seems to constitute a considerable part of Christian devotion, had not been introduced into the temples of antiquity; and the ears of monarchs were never invaded by the harsh sound of popular eloquence, till the pulpits of the empire were filled with sacred orators who possessed some advantages unknown to their profane predecessors.[72] The arguments and rhetoric of the tribune were instantly opposed, with equal arms, by skilful and resolute antagonists; and the cause of truth and reason might derive an accidental support from the conflict of hostile passions. The bishop, or some distinguished presbyter, to whom he cautiously delegated the powers of preaching, harangued, without the danger of interruption or reply, a submissive multitude, whose minds had been prepared and subdued by the awful ceremonies of religion. Such was the strict subordination of the Catholic church that the same concerted sounds might issue at once from an hundred pulpits of Italy or Egypt, if they were *tuned* [73] by the master hand of the Roman or Alexandrian primate. The design of this institution was laudable, but the fruits were not always salutary. The preachers recommended the practice of the social duties; but they exalted the perfection of monastic virtue, which is painful to the individual and useless to mankind. Their charitable exhortations betrayed a secret wish that the clergy might be permitted to manage the wealth of the faithful for the benefit of the poor. The most sublime representations of the attributes and laws of the Deity were sullied by an idle mixture of metaphysical subtleties, puerile rites, and fictitious miracles: and they expatiated, with the most fervent zeal, on the religious merit of hating the adversaries, and obeying the ministers, of the church. When the public peace was distracted by heresy and schism, the sacred orators sounded the trumpet of discord, and perhaps of sedition. The understandings of their congregations were perplexed by mystery, their passions were inflamed by invectives: and they rushed from the Christian temples of Antioch or Alexandria, prepared either to suffer or to inflict martyrdom. The corruption of taste and language is strongly marked in the vehement declamations of the Latin bishops; but the compositions of Gregory and Chrysostom have been compared with the most splendid models of Attic, or at least of Asiatic, eloquence.[74]

VII. The representatives of the Christian republic were regularly assembled in the spring and autumn of each year: and these synods diffused the spirit of ecclesiastical discipline and legislation through the hundred and twenty provinces of the Roman world.[75] The archbishop or metropolitan was empowered, by the laws, to summon the suffragan bishops of his province, to revise their conduct, to vindicate their rights, to declare their faith, and to examine the merit of the candidates who were elected by the clergy and people to supply the vacancies of the episcopal college. The primates of Rome, Alexandria, Antioch, Carthage, and afterwards Constantinople, who exercised a more ample jurisdiction, convened the numerous assembly of their dependent bishops. But the

[70] *Synesius had previously represented his own disqualifications. He loved profane studies and profane sports; he was incapable of supporting a life of celibacy; he disbelieved the resurrection; and he refused to preach fables to the people, unless he might be permitted to philosophize at home. Theophilus, primate of Egypt, who knew his merit, accepted this extraordinary compromise.*

[71] *The sentence of excommunication is expressed in a rhetorical style. The method of involving whole families, though somewhat unjust, was improved into national interdicts.*

[72] *Preaching was considered as the most important office of the bishop; but this function was sometimes entrusted to such presbyters as Chrysostom and Augustin.*

[73] *Queen Elizabeth used this expression, and practised this art, whenever she wished to prepossess the minds of her people in favour of any extraordinary measure of government. The hostile effects of this music were apprehended by her successor, and severely felt by his son. "When pulpit, drum ecclesiastic."*

[74] *Those modest orators acknowledged that, as they were destitute of the gift of miracles, they endeavoured to acquire the arts of eloquence.*

[75] *The council of Nice, in the fourth, fifth, sixth, and seventh canons, has made some fundamental regulations concerning synods, metropolitans, and primates. The Nicene canons have been variously tortured, abused, interpolated, or forged, according to the interest of the clergy. The* Suburbicarian *churches, assigned (by Rufinus) to the bishop of Rome, have been made the subject of vehement controversy.*

[76] *We have only thirty-three or forty-seven episcopal subscriptions: but Ado, a writer indeed of small account, reckons six hundred bishops in the council of Arles.*

convocation of great and extraordinary synods was the prerogative of the emperor alone. Whenever the emergencies of the church required this decisive measure, he dispatched a peremptory summons to the bishops, or the deputies of each province, with an order for the use of post-horses, and a competent allowance for the expenses of their journey. At an early period, when Constantine was the protector, rather than the proselyte, of Christianity, he referred the African controversy to the council of Arles; in which the bishops of York, of Treves, of Milan, and of Carthage, met as friends and brethren, to debate in their native tongue on the common interest of the Latin or Western church.[76] Eleven years afterwards, a more numerous and celebrated assembly was convened at Nice in Bithynia, to extinguish, by their final sentence, the subtle disputes which had arisen in Egypt on the subject of the Trinity. Three hundred and eighteen bishops obeyed the summons of their indulgent master; the ecclesiastics, of every rank and sect and denomination, have been computed at two thousand and forty-eight persons; the Greeks appeared in person; and the consent of the Latins was expressed by the legates of the Roman pontiff. The session, which lasted about two months, was frequently honoured by the presence of the emperor. Leaving his guards at the door, he seated himself (with the permission of the council) on a low stool in the midst of the hall. Constantine listened with patience and spoke with modesty: and, while he influenced the debates, he humbly professed that he was the minister, not the judge, of the successors of the apostles, who had been established as priests and as gods upon earth. Such profound reverence of an absolute monarch towards a feeble and unarmed assembly of his own subjects can only be compared to the respect with which the senate had been treated by the Roman princes, who adopted the policy of Augustus. Within the space of fifty years, a philosophic spectator of the vicissitude of human affairs might have contemplated Tacitus in the senate of Rome, and Constantine in the council of Nice. The fathers of the Capitol and those of the church had alike degenerated from the virtues of their founders; but, as the bishops were more deeply rooted in the public opinion, they sustained their dignity with more decent pride, and sometimes opposed, with a manly spirit, the wishes of their sovereign. The progress of time and superstition erased the memory of the weakness, the passion, the ignorance, which disgraced these ecclesiastical synods; and the Catholic world has unanimously submitted to the *infallible* decrees of the general councils.

XXI

PERSECUTION OF HERESY · THE SCHISM OF THE DONATISTS ·
THE ARIAN CONTROVERSY · ATHANASIUS · DISTRACTED STATE
OF THE CHURCH & EMPIRE UNDER CONSTANTINE & HIS SONS ·
· CHRISTIAN SECTS REVIEWED · TOLERATION OF PAGANISM

THE grateful applause of the clergy has consecrated the memory of a prince who indulged their passions and promoted their interest. Constantine gave them security, wealth, honours, and revenge: and the support of the orthodox faith was considered as the most sacred and important duty of the civil magistrate. The edict of Milan, the great charter of toleration, had confirmed to each individual of the Roman world the privilege of choosing and professing his own religion. But this inestimable privilege was soon violated: with the knowledge of truth, the emperor imbibed the maxims of persecution; and the sects which dissented from the Catholic church were afflicted and oppressed by the triumph of Christianity. Constantine easily believed that the Heretics, who presumed to dispute *his* opinions or to oppose *his* commands, were guilty of the most absurd and criminal obstinacy; and that a seasonable application of moderate severities might save those unhappy men from the danger of an everlasting condemnation. Not a moment was lost in excluding the ministers and teachers of the separated congregations from any share of the rewards and immunities which the emperor had so liberally bestowed on the orthodox clergy. But, as the sectaries might still exist under the cloud of royal disgrace, the conquest of the East was immediately followed by an edict which announced their total destruction. After a preamble filled with passion and reproach, Constantine absolutely prohibits the assemblies of the Heretics, and confiscates their public property to the use either of the revenue or of the Catholic church. The sects against whom the Imperial severity was directed appear to have been the adherents of Paul of Samosata; the Montanists of Phrygia, who maintained an enthusiastic succession of prophecy; the Novatians, who sternly rejected the temporal efficacy of repentance; the Marcionites and Valentinians, under whose leading banners the various Gnostics of Asia and Egypt had insensibly rallied; and perhaps the Manichæans, who had recently imported from Persia a more artful composition of Oriental and Christian theology.[1] The design of extirpating the name, or at least of restraining the progress, of these odious Heretics was prosecuted with vigour and effect. Some of the penal regulations were copied from the edicts of Diocletian; and this method of conversion was applauded by the same bishops who had felt the hand of oppression and had pleaded for the rights of humanity. Two immaterial circumstances may serve, however, to prove that the mind of Constantine was not entirely corrupted by the spirit of zeal and bigotry. Before he condemned the Manichæans and their kindred sects, he resolved to make an accurate inquiry into the nature of their religious principles. As if he distrusted the impartiality of his ecclesiastical counsellors, this delicate commission was entrusted to a civil magistrate, whose learning and moderation he justly esteemed, and of whose venal character he was probably ignorant. The emperor was soon convinced that he had too hastily proscribed the orthodox faith and the exemplary morals of the Novatians, who had dissented from the church in some articles of discipline which were not perhaps essential to salvation. By a particular edict, he exempted them from the general penalties of the law;[2] allowed them to build a church at Constantinople, respected the miracles of their saints, invited their bishop Acesius to the council of Nice, and gently ridiculed the tenets of his sect by a jest, which, from the mouth of a sovereign, must have been received with applause and gratitude.[3]

The complaints and mutual accusations which assailed the throne of Constantine, as soon as the death of Maxentius had submitted Africa to his victorious arms, were ill adapted to edify an imperfect proselyte. He learned with surprise that the provinces of that great country, from the confines of Cyrene to the columns of Hercules, were distracted with religious discord. The source of the division was derived from a double election in the church of Carthage; the second, in rank and opulence, of the ecclesiastical thrones of the West. Cæcilian and Majorinus were the two rival primates of Africa; and the death of the latter soon made room for Donatus, who, by his superior abilities and apparent virtues, was the firmest support of his party. The advantage which Cæcilian might claim from the priority of his ordination was destroyed by the illegal, or

[1] After some examination of the various opinions of Tillemont, Beausobre, Lardner, &c., I am convinced that Manes did not propagate this sect, even in Persia, before the year 270. It is strange that a philosophic and foreign heresy should have penetrated so rapidly into the African provinces; yet I cannot easily reject the edict of Diocletian against the Manichæans, which may be found in Baronius.

[2] As the general law is not inserted in the Theodosian Code, it is probable, that in the year 438 the sects which it had condemned were already extinct.

[3] Sozomen and Socrates have been suspected, but I think without reason, of an attachment to the Novatian doctrine. The emperor said to the bishop, "Acesius, take a ladder, and get up to Heaven by yourself." Most of the Christian sects have, by turns, borrowed the ladder of Acesius.

at least indecent, haste with which it had been performed, without expecting the arrival of the bishops of Numidia. The authority of these bishops, who, to the number of seventy, condemned Cæcilian and consecrated Majorinus, is again weakened by the infamy of some of their personal characters; and by the female intrigues, sacrilegious bargains, and tumultuous proceedings which are imputed to this Numidian council. The bishops of the contending factions maintained, with equal ardour and obstinacy, that their adversaries were degraded, or at least dishonoured, by the odious crime of delivering the Holy Scriptures to the officers of Diocletian. From their mutual reproaches, as well as from the story of this dark transaction, it may justly be inferred that the late persecution had embittered the zeal, without reforming the manners, of the African Christians. That divided church was incapable of affording an impartial judicature; the controversy was solemnly tried in five successive tribunals which were appointed by the emperor; and the whole proceeding, from the first appeal to the final sentence, lasted above three years. A severe inquisition, which was taken by the Prætorian vicar and the proconsul of Africa, the report of two episcopal visitors who had been sent to Carthage, the decrees of the councils of Rome and of Arles, and the supreme judgment of Constantine himself in his sacred consistory, were all favourable to the cause of Cæcilian; and he was unanimously acknowledged by the civil and ecclesiastical powers as the true and lawful primate of Africa. The honours and estates of the church were attributed to *his* suffragan bishops, and it was not without difficulty that Constantine was satisfied with inflicting the punishment of exile on the principal leaders of the Donatist faction. As their cause was examined with attention, perhaps it was determined with justice. Perhaps their complaint was not without foundation, that the credulity of the emperor had been abused by the insidious arts of his favourite Osius. The influence of falsehood and corruption might procure the condemnation of the innocent, or aggravate the sentence of the guilty. Such an act, however, of injustice, if it concluded an importunate dispute, might be numbered among the transient evils of a despotic administration, which are neither felt nor remembered by posterity.

But this incident, so inconsiderable that it scarcely deserves a place in history, was productive of a memorable schism, which afflicted the provinces of Africa above three hundred years, and was extinguished only with Christianity itself. The inflexible zeal of freedom and fanaticism animated the Donatists to refuse obedience to the usurpers whose election they disputed and whose spiritual powers they denied. Excluded from the civil and religious communion of mankind, they boldly excommunicated the rest of mankind, who had embraced the impious party of Cæcilian, and of the Traditors, from whom he derived his pretended ordination. They asserted with confidence, and almost with exultation, that the Apostolical succession was interrupted; that *all* the bishops of Europe and Asia were infected by the contagion of guilt and schism; and that the prerogatives of the Catholic church were confined to the chosen portion of the African believers, who alone had preserved inviolate the integrity of their faith and discipline. This rigid theory was supported by the most uncharitable conduct. Whenever they acquired a proselyte, even from the distant provinces of the East, they carefully repeated the sacred rites of baptism [4] and ordination; as they rejected the validity of those which he had already received from the hands of heretics or schismatics. Bishops, virgins, and even spotless infants were subjected to the disgrace of a public penance, before they could be admitted to the communion of the Donatists. If they obtained possession of a church which had been used by their Catholic adversaries, they purified the unhallowed building with the same jealous care which a temple of idols might have required. They washed the pavement, scraped the walls, burnt the altar, which was commonly of wood, melted the consecrated plate, and cast the Holy Eucharist to the dogs, with every circumstance of ignominy which could provoke and perpetuate the animosity of religious factions. Notwithstanding this irreconcilable aversion, the two parties, who were mixed and separated in all the cities of Africa, had the same language and manners, the same zeal and learning, the same faith and worship. Proscribed by the civil and ecclesiastical powers of the empire, the Donatists still maintained in some provinces, particularly in Numidia, their superior numbers; and four hundred bishops acknowledged the jurisdiction of their primate. But the invincible spirit of the sect sometimes preyed on its own vitals; and the bosom of their schismatical church was torn by intestine divisions. A fourth part of the Donatist bishops followed the independent standard of the Maximianists. The narrow and solitary path which their first leaders had marked out continued to deviate from the great society of mankind. Even the imperceptible sect of the Rogatians could affirm, without a blush, that, when Christ should descend to judge the earth, he

[4] *The councils of Arles, of Nice and of Trent confirmed the wise and moderate practice of the church of Rome. The Donatists, however, had the advantage of maintaining the sentiment of Cyprian, and of a considerable part of the primitive church. Vincentius Lirinensis has explained why the Donatists are eternally burning with the Devil, while St. Cyprian reigns in heaven with Jesus Christ.*

would find his true religion preserved only in a few nameless villages of the Cæsarean Mauritania.

The schism of the Donatists was confined to Africa: the more diffusive mischief of the Trinitarian controversy successively penetrated into every part of the Christian world. The former was an accidental quarrel, occasioned by the abuse of freedom; the latter was a high and mysterious argument, derived from the abuse of philosophy. From the age of Constantine to that of Clovis and Theodoric, the temporal interests both of the Romans and Barbarians were deeply involved in the theological disputes of Arianism. The historian may therefore be permitted respectfully to withdraw the veil of the sanctuary; and to deduce the progress of reason and faith, of error and passion, from the school of Plato to the decline and fall of the empire.

The genius of Plato, informed by his own meditation, or by the traditional knowledge of the priests of Egypt,[5] had ventured to explore the mysterious nature of the Deity. When he had elevated his mind to the sublime contemplation of the first self-existent, necessary cause of the universe, the Athenian sage was incapable of conceiving *how* the simple unity of his essence could admit the infinite variety of distinct and successive ideas which compose the model of the intellectual world; *how* a Being purely incorporeal could execute that perfect model, and mould with a plastic hand the rude and independent chaos. The vain hope of extricating himself from these difficulties, which must ever oppress the feeble powers of the human mind, might induce Plato to consider the divine nature under the threefold modification: of the first cause, the reason or *Logos,* and the soul or spirit of the universe. His poetical imagination sometimes fixed and animated these metaphysical abstractions; the three *archical* or original principles were represented in the Platonic system of three Gods, united with each other by a mysterious and ineffable generation; and the Logos was particularly considered under the more accessible character of the Son of an Eternal Father, and the Creator and Governor of the world. Such appear to have been the secret doctrines which were cautiously whispered in the gardens of the academy; and which, according to the more recent disciples of Plato, could not be perfectly understood, till after an assiduous study of thirty years.

The arms of the Macedonians diffused over Asia and Egypt the language and learning of Greece; and the theological system of Plato was taught with less reserve, and perhaps with some improve-

[5] *The Egyptians might still preserve the traditional creed of the Patriarchs. Josephus has persuaded many of the Christian fathers that Plato derived a part of his knowledge from the Jews; but this vain opinion cannot be reconciled with the obscure state and unsocial manners of the Jewish people, whose scriptures were not accessible to Greek curiosity till more than one hundred years after the death of Plato.*

[6] *The book of the Wisdom of Solomon was received by many of the fathers as the work of that monarch; and, although rejected by the Protestants for want of a Hebrew original, it has obtained, with the rest of the Vulgate, the sanction of the council of Trent.*

[7] *The Platonism of Philo, which was famous to a proverb, is proved beyond a doubt by Le Clerc. Basnage has clearly ascertained that the theological works of Philo were composed before the death, and most probably before the birth, of Christ. In such a time of darkness, the knowledge of Philo is more astonishing than his errors.*

[8] *This notion, till it was abused by the Arians, was freely adopted in the Christian theology. Tertullian has a remarkable and dangerous passage. After contrasting, with indiscreet wit, the nature of God and the actions of Jehovah, he concludes: Scilicet ut hæc de filio Dei non credenda fuisse si non scripta essent; fortasse non credenda de Patre licet scripta.*

ments, in the celebrated school of Alexandria. A numerous colony of Jews had been invited, by the favour of the Ptolemies, to settle in their new capital. While the bulk of the nation practised the legal ceremonies, and pursued the lucrative occupations of commerce, a few Hebrews, of a more liberal spirit, devoted their lives to religious and philosophical contemplation. They cultivated with diligence, and embraced with ardour, the theological system of the Athenian sage. But their national pride would have been mortified by a fair confession of their former poverty: and they boldly marked, as the sacred inheritance of their ancestors, the gold and jewels which they had so lately stolen from their Egyptian masters. One hundred years before the birth of Christ, a philosophical treatise, which manifestly betrays the style and sentiments of the school of Plato, was produced by the Alexandrian Jews, and unanimously received as a genuine and valuable relic of the inspired Wisdom of Solomon.[6] A similar union of the Mosaic faith and the Grecian philosophy distinguishes the works of Philo, which were composed, for the most part, under the reign of Augustus.[7] The material soul of the universe might offend the piety of the Hebrews: but they applied the character of the Logos to the Jehovah of Moses and the patriarchs; and the Son of God was introduced upon earth under a visible, and even human, appearance, to perform those familiar offices which seem incompatible with the nature and attributes of the Universal Cause.[8]

The eloquence of Plato, the name of Solomon, the authority of the school of Alexandria, and the consent of the Jews and Greeks, were insufficient to establish the truth of a mysterious doctrine which might please, but could not satisfy, a rational mind. A prophet or apostle, inspired by the Deity, can alone exercise a lawful dominion over the faith of mankind; and the theology of Plato might have been for ever confounded with the philosophical visions of the Academy, the Porch, and the Lyceum, if the name and divine attributes of the *Logos* had not been confirmed by the celestial pen of the last and most sublime of the Evangelists.[9] The Christian Revelation, which was consummated under the reign of Nerva, disclosed to the world the amazing secret that the Logos, who was with God from the beginning and was God, who had made all things and for whom all things had been made, was incarnate in the person of Jesus of Nazareth; who had been born of a virgin, and suffered death on the cross. Besides the general design of fixing on a perpetual basis the divine honours of Christ, the most ancient and respectable of the ecclesiastical writers have ascribed to the evangelic theologian a particular intention to confute two opposite heresies, which disturbed the peace of the primitive church.[10] I. The faith of the Ebionites, perhaps of the Nazarenes, was gross and imperfect. They revered Jesus as the greatest of the prophets, endowed with supernatural virtue and power. They ascribed to his person and to his future reign all the predictions of the Hebrew oracles which relate to the spiritual and everlasting kingdom of the promised Messiah.[11] Some of them might confess that he was born of a virgin: but they obstinately rejected the preceding existence and divine perfections of the *Logos,* or Son of God, which are so clearly defined in the Gospel of St. John. About fifty years afterwards, the Ebionites, whose errors are mentioned by Justin Martyr with less severity than they seem to deserve, formed a very inconsiderable portion of the Christian name. II. The Gnostics, who were distinguished by the epithet of *Docetes,* deviated into the contrary extreme, and betrayed the human, while they asserted the divine, nature of Christ. Educated in the school of Plato, accustomed to the sublime idea of the *Logos,* they readily conceived that the brightest *Æon,* or *Emanation* of the Deity, might assume the outward shape and visible appearances of a mortal;[12] but they vainly pretended that the imperfections of matter are incompatible with the purity of a celestial substance. While the blood of Christ yet smoked on Mount Calvary, the Docetes invented the impious and extravagant hypothesis that, instead of issuing from the womb of the Virgin, he had descended on the banks of the Jordan in the form of perfect manhood; that he had imposed on the senses of his enemies, and of his disciples; and that the ministers of Pilate had wasted their impotent rage on an airy phantom, who *seemed* to expire on the cross and, after three days, to rise from the dead.

The divine sanction which the Apostle had bestowed on the fundamental principle of the theology of Plato encouraged the learned proselytes of the second and third centuries to admire and study the writings of the Athenian sage, who had thus marvellously anticipated one of the most surprising discoveries of the Christian revelation. The respectable name of Plato was used by the orthodox, and abused by the heretics, as the common support of truth and error: the authority of his skilful commentators, and the science of dialectics, were employed to justify the remote consequences of his opinions, and to supply the discreet silence of the inspired writers. The same subtle and profound questions concerning the nature, the gen-

[9] *The Platonists admired the beginning of the Gospel of St. John, as containing an exact transcript of their own principles. But in the third and fourth centuries, the Platonists of Alexandria might improve their Trinity by the secret study of the Christian theology.*

[10] *The Gospel according to St. John is supposed to have been published about seventy years after the death of Christ.*

[11] *The humble condition and sufferings of Jesus have always been a stumbling block to the Jews. But this objection has obliged the believing Christians to lift up their eyes to a spiritual and everlasting kingdom.*

[12] *The Arians reproached the orthodox party with borrowing their Trinity from the Valentinians and Marcionites.*

eration, the distinction, and the equality of the three divine persons of the mysterious *Triad*, or Trinity,[13] were agitated in the philosophical, and in the Christian, schools of Alexandria. An eager spirit of curiosity urged them to explore the secrets of the abyss; and the pride of the professors and of their disciples was satisfied with the science of words. But the most sagacious of the Christian theologians, the great Athanasius himself, has candidly confessed [14] that, whenever he forced his understanding to meditate on the divinity of the *Logos,* his toilsome and unavailing efforts recoiled on themselves; that the more he thought, the less he comprehended; and the more he wrote, the less capable was he of expressing his thoughts. In every step of the inquiry, we are compelled to feel and acknowledge the immeasurable disproportion between the size of the object and the capacity of the human mind. We may strive to abstract the notions of time, of space, and of matter, which so closely adhere to all the perceptions of our experimental knowledge. But, as soon as we presume to reason of infinite substance, of spiritual generation; as often as we deduce any positive conclusions from a negative idea, we are involved in darkness, perplexity, and inevitable contradiction. As these difficulties arise from the nature of the subject, they oppress, with the same insuperable weight, the philosophic and the theological disputant; but we may observe two essential and peculiar circumstances which discriminated the doctrines of the Catholic church from the opinions of the Platonic school.

I. A chosen society of philosophers, men of a liberal education and curious disposition, might silently meditate, and temperately discuss, in the gardens of Athens or the library of Alexandria, the abstruse questions of metaphysical science. The lofty speculations which neither convinced the understanding, nor agitated the passions, of the Platonists themselves were carelessly overlooked by the idle, the busy, and even the studious part of mankind.[15] But, after the *Logos* had been revealed as the sacred object of the faith, the hope, and the religious worship of the Christians, the mysterious system was embraced by a numerous and increasing multitude in every province of the Roman world. Those persons who, from their age, or sex, or occupations, were the least qualified to judge, who were the least exercised in the habits of abstract reasoning, aspired to contemplate the economy of the Divine Nature; and it is the boast of Tertullian that a Christian mechanic could readily answer such questions as had perplexed the wisest of the Grecian sages. Where the subject lies so far beyond our reach, the difference between the

[13] If Theophilus, bishop of Antioch, was the first who employed the word Triad, Trinity, *that abstract term, which was already familiar to the schools of philosophy, must have been introduced into the theology of the Christians after the middle of the second century.*

[14] *His expressions have an uncommon energy; and, as he was writing to monks, there could not be any occasion for him to affect a rational language.*

[15] *In a treatise which professed to explain the opinions of the ancient philosophers concerning the nature of the gods we might expect to discover the theological Trinity of Plato. But Cicero very honestly confessed that, though he had translated the Timæus, he could never understand that mysterious dialogue.*

highest and the lowest of human understandings may indeed be calculated as infinitely small; yet the degree of weakness may perhaps be measured by the degree of obstinacy and dogmatic confidence. These speculations, instead of being treated as the amusement of a vacant hour, became the most serious business of the present, and the most useful preparation for a future, life. A theology, which it was incumbent to believe, which it was impious to doubt, and which it might be dangerous, and even fatal, to mistake, became the familiar topic of private meditation and popular discourse. The cold indifference of philosophy was inflamed by the fervent spirit of devotion; and even the metaphors of common language suggested the fallacious prejudices of sense and experience. The Christians, who abhorred the gross and impure generation of the Greek mythology, were tempted to argue from the familiar analogy of the filial and paternal relations. The character of *Son* seemed to imply a perpetual subordination to the voluntary author of his existence;[16] but, as the act of generation, in the most spiritual and abstracted sense, must be supposed to transmit the properties of a common nature, they durst not presume to circumscribe the powers of the duration of the Son of an eternal and omnipotent Father. Fourscore years after the death of Christ, the Christians of Bithynia declared before the tribunal of Pliny that they invoked him as a god; and his divine honours have been perpetuated in every age and country by the various sects who assume the name of his disciples. Their tender reverence for the memory of Christ and their horror for the profane worship of any created being would have engaged them to assert the equal and absolute divinity of the *Logos,* if their rapid ascent towards the throne of heaven had not been imperceptibly checked by the apprehension of violating the unity and sole supremacy of the great Father of Christ and of the Universe. The suspense and fluctuation produced in the minds of the Christians by these opposite tendencies may be observed in the writings of the theologians who flourished after the end of the apostolic age and before the origin of the Arian controversy. Their suffrage is claimed, with equal confidence, by the orthodox and by the heretical parties; and the most inquisitive critics have fairly allowed that, if they had the good fortune of possessing the Catholic verity, they have delivered their conceptions in loose, inaccurate, and sometimes contradictory language.

II. The devotion of individuals was the first circumstance which distinguished the Christians from the Platonists; the second was

[16] *Many of the primitive writers have frankly confessed that the Son owed his being to the will of the Father. On the other hand, Athanasius and his followers seem unwilling to grant what they are afraid to deny. The schoolmen extricate themselves from this difficulty by the distinction of a* preceding *and a* concomitant *will.*

the authority of the church. The disciples of philosophy asserted the rights of intellectual freedom, and their respect for the sentiments of their teachers was a liberal and voluntary tribute, which they offered to superior reason. But the Christians formed a numerous and disciplined society; and the jurisdiction of their laws and magistrates was strictly exercised over the minds of the faithful. The loose wanderings of the imagination were gradually confined by creeds and confessions;[17] the freedom of private judgment submitted to the public wisdom of synods; the authority of a theologian was determined by his ecclesiastical rank; and the episcopal successors of the apostles inflicted the censures of the church on those who deviated from the orthodox belief. But in an age of religious controversy every act of oppression adds new force to the elastic vigour of the mind; and the zeal or obstinacy of a spiritual rebel was sometimes stimulated by secret motives of ambition or avarice. A metaphysical argument became the cause or pretence of political contests; the subtleties of the Platonic school were used as the badges of popular factions, and the distance which separated their respective tenets was enlarged or magnified by the acrimony of dispute. As long as the dark heresies of Praxeas and Sabellius laboured to confound the *Father* with the *Son*,[18] the orthodox party might be excused if they adhered more strictly and more earnestly to the *distinction,* than to the *equality,* of the divine persons. But, as soon as the heat of controversy had subsided, and the progress of the Sabellians was no longer an object of terror to the churches of Rome, of Africa, or of Egypt; the tide of theological opinion began to flow with a gentle but steady motion toward the contrary extreme; and the most orthodox doctors allowed themselves the use of the terms and definitions which had been censured in the mouth of the sectaries.[19] After the edict of toleration had restored peace and leisure to the Christians, the Trinitarian controversy was revived in the ancient seat of Platonism, the learned, the opulent, the tumultuous city of Alexandria; and the flame of religious discord was rapidly communicated from the schools to the clergy, the people, the province, and the East. The abstruse question of the eternity of the *Logos* was agitated in ecclesiastical conferences and popular sermons; and the heterodox opinions of Arius[20] were soon made public by his own zeal and by that of his adversaries. His most implacable adversaries have acknowledged the learning and blameless life of that eminent presbyter, who, in a former election, had declared, and perhaps generously declined, his pretensions to the episcopal throne.[21]

[17] *The most ancient creeds were drawn up with the greatest latitude.*

[18] *Praxeas, who came to Rome about the end of the second century, deceived, for some time, the simplicity of the bishop, and was confuted by the pen of the angry Tertullian.*

[19] *Socrates acknowledges that the heresy of Arius proceeded from his strong desire to embrace an opinion the most diametrically opposite to that of Sabellius.*

[20] *The figure and manners of Arius, the character and numbers of his first proselytes, are painted in very lively colours by Epiphanius; and we cannot but regret that he should soon forget the historian, to assume the task of controversy.*

[21] *Yet the credibility of Philostorgius is lessened in the eyes of the orthodox by his Arianism; and in those of rational critics by his passion, his prejudice, and his ignorance.*

His competitor Alexander assumed the office of his judge. The important cause was argued before him; and, if at first he seemed to hesitate, he at length pronounced his final sentence, as an absolute rule of faith. The undaunted presbyter, who presumed to resist the authority of his angry bishop, was separated from the communion of the church. But the pride of Arius was supported by the applause of a numerous party. He reckoned among his immediate followers two bishops of Egypt, seven presbyters, twelve deacons, and (what may appear almost incredible) seven hundred virgins. A large majority of the bishops of Asia appeared to support or favour his cause; and their measures were conducted by Eusebius of Cæsarea, the most learned of the Christian prelates, and by Eusebius of Nicomedia, who had acquired the reputation of a statesman without forfeiting that of a saint. Synods in Palestine and Bithynia were opposed to the synods of Egypt. The attention of the prince and people was attracted by this theological dispute; and the decision, at the end of six years,[22] was referred to the supreme authority of the general council of Nice.

When the mysteries of the Christian faith were dangerously exposed to public debate, it might be observed that the human understanding was capable of forming three distinct, though imperfect, systems concerning the nature of the Divine Trinity; and it was pronounced that none of these systems, in a pure and absolute sense, were exempt from heresy and error. I. According to the first hypothesis, which was maintained by Arius and his disciples, the *Logos* was a dependent and spontaneous production, created from nothing by the will of the Father. The Son, by whom all things were made,[23] had been begotten before all worlds, and the longest of the astronomical periods could be compared only as a fleeting moment to the extent of his duration; yet this duration was not infinite, and there *had* been a time which preceded the ineffable generation of the *Logos*. On this only-begotten Son the Almighty Father had transfused his ample spirit, and impressed the effulgence of his glory. Visible image of invisible perfection, he saw, at an immeasurable distance beneath his feet, the thrones of the brightest archangels: yet he shone only with a reflected light, and, like the sons of the Roman emperors who were invested with the titles of Cæsar or Augustus,[24] he governed the universe in obedience to the will of his Father and Monarch. II. In the second hypothesis, the *Logos* possessed all the inherent, incommunicable perfections which religion and philosophy appropriate to the Supreme God. Three distinct

[22] *The flames of Arianism might burn for some time in secret; but there is reason to believe that they burst out with violence as early as the year 319.*

[23] *As the doctrine of absolute creation from nothing was gradually introduced among the Christians, the dignity of the* workman *very naturally rose with that of the* work.

[24] *This profane and absurd simile is employed by several of the primitive fathers, particularly by Athenagoras, in his Apology to the emperor Marcus and his son; and it is alleged, without censure, by Bull himself.*

and infinite minds or substances, three co-equal and co-eternal be-ings, composed the Divine Essence; and it would have implied con-tradiction that any of them should not have existed or that they should ever cease to exist. The advocates of a system which seemed to establish three independent Deities attempted to preserve the unity of the First Cause, so conspicuous in the design and order of the world, by the perpetual concord of their administration and the essential agreement of their will. A faint resemblance of this unity of action may be discovered in the societies of men, and even of ani-mals. The causes which disturb their harmony proceed only from the imperfection and inequality of their faculties: but the omnipo-tence which is guided by infinite wisdom and goodness cannot fail of choosing the same means for the accomplishment of the same ends. III. Three Beings, who, by the self-derived necessity of their existence, possess all the divine attributes in the most perfect degree; who are eternal in duration, infinite in space, and intimately present to each other and to the whole universe; irresistibly force them-selves on the astonished mind as one and the same Being, who, in the economy of grace, as well as in that of nature, may manifest himself under different forms, and be considered under different aspects. By this hypothesis, a real substantial Trinity is refined into a trinity of names and abstract modifications, that subsist only in the mind which conceives them. The *Logos* is no longer a person, but an attribute; and it is only in a figurative sense that the epithet of Son can be applied to the eternal reason which was with God from the beginning, and by *which,* not by *whom,* all things were made. The incarnation of the *Logos* is reduced to a mere inspira-tion of the Divine Wisdom, which filled the soul, and directed all the actions, of the man Jesus. Thus, after revolving round the theo-logical circle, we are surprised to find that the Sabellian ends where the Ebionite had begun; and that the incomprehensible mystery which excites our adoration eludes our inquiry.[25]

[5] *If the Sabellians were startled at this conclu-sion, they were driven down another precipice into the confession, that the Father was born of a virgin, that he had suf-fered on the cross; and thus deserved the odious epithet of* Patri-passians, *with which they were branded by their adver-saries.*

If the bishops of the council of Nice had been permitted to follow the unbiassed dictates of their conscience, Arius and his associates could scarcely have flattered themselves with the hopes of obtaining a majority of votes, in favour of an hypothesis so directly adverse to the two most popular opinions of the Catholic world. The Arians soon perceived the danger of their situation, and prudently assumed those modest virtues which, in the fury of civil and religious dissen-sions, are seldom practised, or even praised, except by the weaker party. They recommended the exercise of Christian charity and

THE TEMPLE OF VENUS & ROME

"The temple is overthrown, the gold has been pillaged, the wheel of fortune has accomplished her revolution, and the sacred ground is again disfigured with thorns and brambles."

THE TEMPLE OF VENUS AND ROME

moderation; urged the incomprehensible nature of the controversy; disclaimed the use of any terms or definitions which could not be found in the scriptures; and offered, by very liberal concessions, to satisfy their adversaries without renouncing the integrity of their own principles. The victorious faction received all their proposals with haughty suspicion; and anxiously sought for some irreconcilable mark of distinction, the rejection of which might involve the Arians in the guilt and consequences of heresy. A letter was publicly read, and ignominiously torn, in which their patron, Eusebius of Nicomedia, ingenuously confessed that the admission of the HOMOOUSION, or Consubstantial, a word already familiar to the Platonists, was incompatible with the principles of their theological system. The fortunate opportunity was eagerly embraced by the bishops who governed the resolutions of the synod; and, according to the lively expression of Ambrose, they used the sword, which heresy itself had drawn from the scabbard, to cut off the head of the hated monster. The consubstantiality of the Father and the Son was established by the council of Nice, and has been unanimously received as a fundamental article of the Christian faith, by the consent of the Greek, the Latin, the Oriental, and the Protestant churches. But, if the same word had not served to stigmatize the heretics and to unite the Catholics, it would have been inadequate to the purpose of the majority by whom it was introduced into the orthodox creed. This majority was divided into two parties, distinguished by a contrary tendency to the sentiments of the Tritheists and of the Sabellians. But, as those opposite extremes seemed to overthrow the foundations either of natural or revealed religion, they mutually agreed to qualify the rigour of their principles and to disavow the just, but invidious, consequences which might be urged by their antagonists. The interest of the common cause inclined them to join their numbers and to conceal their differences; their animosity was softened by the healing councils of toleration, and their disputes were suspended by the use of the mysterious *Homoousion,* which either party was free to interpret according to their peculiar tenets. The Sabellian sense, which, about fifty years before, had obliged the council of Antioch to prohibit this celebrated term, had endeared it to those theologians who entertained a secret but partial affection for a nominal Trinity. But the more fashionable saints of the Arian times, the intrepid Athanasius, the learned Gregory Nazianzen, and the other pillars of the church, who supported with ability and success the Nicene doctrine, appeared to consider the expression of *substance* as if it had been synonymous with that of *nature;* and they ventured to illustrate their meaning by affirming that three men, as they belong to the same common species, are consubstantial or homoousian to each other. This pure and distinct equality was tempered, on the one hand, by the internal connexion, and spiritual penetration, which indissolubly unites the divine persons; and on the other, by the pre-eminence of the Father, which was acknowledged as far as it is compatible with the independence of the Son.[26] Within these limits the almost invisible and tremulous ball of orthodoxy was allowed securely to vibrate. On either side, beyond this consecrated ground, the heretics and the dæmons lurked in ambush to surprise and devour the unhappy wanderer. But, as the degrees of theological hatred depend on the spirit of the war rather than on the importance of the controversy, the heretics who degraded, were treated with more severity than those who annihilated, the person of the Son. The life of Athanasius was consumed in irreconcilable opposition to the impious *madness* of the Arians;[27] but he defended above twenty years the Sabellianism of Marcellus of Ancyra; and, when at last he was compelled to withdraw himself from his communion, he continued to mention, with an ambiguous smile, the venial errors of his respectable friend.

The authority of a general council, to which the Arians themselves had been compelled to submit, inscribed on the banners of the orthodox party the mysterious characters of the word *Homoousion,* which essentially contributed, notwithstanding some obscure disputes, some nocturnal combats, to maintain and perpetuate the uniformity of faith, or at least of language. The Consubstantialists, who by their success have deserved and obtained the title of Catholics, gloried in the simplicity and steadiness of their own creed, and insulted the repeated variations of their adversaries, who were destitute of any certain rule of faith. The sincerity or the cunning of the Arian chiefs, the fears of the laws or of the people, their reverence for Christ, their hatred of Athanasius, all the causes, human and divine, that influence and disturb the counsels of a theological faction, introduced among the sectaries a spirit of discord and inconstancy, which, in the course of a few years, erected eighteen different models of religion, and avenged the violated dignity of the church. The zealous Hilary,[28] who, from the peculiar hardships of his situation, was inclined to extenuate rather than to aggravate the errors of the Oriental clergy, declares that in the wide extent of the ten provinces of Asia, to which he had been banished, there could be

[26] *The third section of Bull's Defence of the Nicene Faith, which some of his antagonists have called nonsense, and others heresy, is consecrated to the supremacy of the Father.*

[27] *The ordinary appellation with which Athanasius and his followers chose to compliment the Arians was that of Ariomanites.*

[28] *Erasmus, with admirable sense and freedom, has delineated the just character of Hilary. To revise his text, to compose the annals of his life, and to justify his sentiments and conduct, is the province of the Benedictine editors.*

found very few prelates who had preserved the knowledge of the true God. The oppression which he had felt, the disorders of which he was the spectator and the victim, appeased, during a short interval, the angry passions of his soul; and in the following passage, of which I shall transcribe a few lines, the bishop of Poitiers unwarily deviates into the style of a Christian philosopher. "It is a thing," says Hilary, "equally deplorable and dangerous, that there are as many creeds as opinions among men, as many doctrines as inclinations, and as many sources of blasphemy as there are faults among us; because we make creeds arbitrarily, and explain them as arbitrarily. The Homoousion is rejected, and received, and explained away by successive synods. The partial or total resemblance of the Father and of the Son is a subject of dispute for these unhappy times. Every year, nay every moon, we make new creeds to describe invisible mysteries. We repent of what we have done, we defend those who repent, we anathematize those whom we defended. We condemn either the doctrine of others in ourselves or our own in that of others; and, reciprocally tearing one another to pieces, we have been the cause of each other's ruin."

It will not be expected, it would not perhaps be endured, that I should swell this theological digression by a minute examination of the eighteen creeds, the authors of which, for the most part, disclaimed the odious name of their parent Arius. It is amusing enough to delineate the form, and to trace the vegetation, of a singular plant; but the tedious detail of leaves without flowers, and of branches without fruit, would soon exhaust the patience, and disappoint the curiosity, of the laborious student. One question which gradually arose from the Arian controversy may however be noticed, as it served to produce and discriminate the three sects who were united only by their common aversion to the Homoousion of the Nicene synod. 1. If they were asked, whether the Son was *like* unto the Father, the question was resolutely answered in the negative by the heretics who adhered to the principles of Arius, or indeed to those of philosophy; which seem to establish an infinite difference between the Creator and the most excellent of his creatures. This obvious consequence was maintained by Aetius, on whom the zeal of his adversaries bestowed the surname of the Atheist. His restless and aspiring spirit urged him to try almost every profession of human life. He was successively a slave, or at least a husbandman, a travelling tinker, a goldsmith, a physician, a schoolmaster, a theologian, and at last the apostle of a new church, which was propa-

[29] According to the judgment of a man who respected both those sectaries, Aetius had been endowed with a stronger understanding, and Eunomius had acquired more art and learning. The confession and apology of Eunomius is one of the few heretical pieces which have escaped.

[30] Yet, according to the opinion of Estius and Bull, there is one power, that of creation, which God cannot communicate to a creature. Estius, who so accurately defined the limits of Omnipotence, was a Dutchman by birth, and by trade a scholastic divine.

[31] Sabinus had copied the acts; Athanasius and Hilary have explained the divisions of this Arian synod; the other circumstances which are relative to it are carefully collected by Baronius and Tillemont.

[32] In his short apologetical notes (first published by the Benedictines from a MS. of Chartres) he observes, that he used this cautious expression, qui intelligeren et impiam. Philostorgius, who saw those objects through a different medium, is inclined to forget the difference of the important diphthong.

gated by the abilities of his disciple Eunomius.[29] Armed with texts of scripture, and with captious syllogisms from the logic of Aristotle, the subtle Aetius had acquired the fame of an invincible disputant, whom it was impossible either to silence or to convince. Such talents engaged the friendship of the Arian bishops, till they were forced to renounce and even to persecute a dangerous ally, who by the accuracy of his reasoning had prejudiced their cause in the popular opinion and offended the piety of their most devoted followers. 2. The omnipotence of the Creator suggested a specious and respectful solution of the *likeness* of the Father and the Son; and faith might humbly receive what reason could not presume to deny, that the Supreme God might communicate his infinite perfections, and create a being similar only to himself.[30] These Arians were powerfully supported by the weight and abilities of their leaders, who had succeeded to the management of the Eusebian interest, and who occupied the principal thrones of the East. They detested, perhaps with some affectation, the impiety of Aetius; they professed to believe, either without reserve, or according to the scriptures, that the Son was different from all *other* creatures and similar only to the Father. But they denied that he was either of the same or of a similar substance; sometimes boldly justifying their dissent, and sometimes objecting to the use of the word substance, which seems to imply an adequate, or at least a distinct, notion of the nature of the Deity. 3. The sect which asserted the doctrine of a similar substance was the most numerous, at least in the provinces of Asia; and, when the leaders of both parties were assembled in the council of Seleucia,[31] *their* opinion would have prevailed by a majority of one hundred and five to forty-three bishops. The Greek word which was chosen to express this mysterious resemblance bears so close an affinity to the orthodox symbol, that the profane of every age have derided the furious contests which the difference of a single diphthong excited between the Homoousians and the Homoiousians. As it frequently happens that the sounds and characters which approach the nearest to each other accidentally represent the most opposite ideas, the observation would be itself ridiculous, if it were possible to mark any real and sensible distinction between the doctrine of the Semi-Arians, as they were improperly styled, and that of the Catholics themselves. The bishop of Poitiers, who in his Phrygian exile very wisely aimed at a coalition of parties, endeavours to prove that, by a pious and faithful interpretation,[32] the *Homoiousion* may be reduced to a consubstantial sense. Yet he confesses that the word has a dark and suspicious aspect; and, as if darkness were congenial to theological disputes, the Semi-Arians, who advanced to the doors of the church, assailed them with the most unrelenting fury.

The provinces of Egypt and Asia, which cultivated the language and manners of the Greeks, had deeply imbibed the venom of the Arian controversy. The familiar study of the Platonic system, a vain and argumentative disposition, a copious and flexible idiom, supplied the clergy and people of the East with an inexhaustible flow of words and distinctions; and, in the midst of their fierce contentions, they easily forgot the doubt which is recommended by philosophy, and the submission which is enjoined by religion. The inhabitants of the West were of a less inquisitive spirit; their passions were not so forcibly moved by invisible objects; their minds were less frequently exercised by the habits of dispute, and such was the happy ignorance of the Gallican church that Hilary himself, above thirty years after the first general council, was still a stranger to the Nicene creed. The Latins had received the rays of divine knowledge through the dark and doubtful medium of a translation. The poverty and stubbornness of their native tongue was not always capable of affording just equivalents for the Greek terms, for the technical words of the Platonic philosophy, which had been consecrated by the gospel or by the church to express the mysteries of the Christian faith; and a verbal defect might introduce into the Latin theology a long train of error or perplexity.[33] But, as the western provincials had the good fortune of deriving their religion from an orthodox source, they preserved with steadiness the doctrine which they had accepted with docility; and, when the Arian pestilence approached their frontiers, they were supplied with seasonable preservative of the Homoousion, by the paternal care of the Roman pontiff. Their sentiments and their temper were displayed in the memorable synod of Rimini, which surpassed in numbers the council of Nice, since it was composed of above four hundred bishops of Italy, Africa, Spain, Gaul, Britain and Illyricum. From the first debates it appeared that only fourscore prelates adhered to the party, though *they* affected to anathematize the name and memory of Arius. But this inferiority was compensated by the advantages of skill, of experience, and of discipline; and the minority was conducted by Valens and Ursacius, two bishops, of Illyricum, who had spent their lives in the intrigues of courts and councils, and who had been trained under the Eusebian banner in the religious wars of the East. By their arguments and negotiations, they embarrassed, they con-

[33] *The preference which the fourth council of the Lateran at length gave to a* numerical *rather than a* generical *unity was favoured by the Latin language;* τριάς *seems to excite the idea of substance,* trinitas *of qualities.*

founded, they at last deceived, the honest simplicity of the Latin bishops; who suffered the palladium of the faith to be extorted from their hands by fraud and importunity rather than by open violence. The council of Rimini was not allowed to separate, till the members had imprudently subscribed a captious creed, in which some expressions, susceptible of an heretical sense, were inserted in the room of the Homoousion. It was on this occasion that, according to Jerom, the world was surprised to find itself Arian. But the bishops of the Latin provinces had no sooner reached their respective dioceses than they discovered their mistake and repented of their weakness. The ignominious capitulation was rejected with disdain and abhorrence; and the Homoousian standard, which had been shaken but not overthrown, was more firmly replanted in all the churches of the West.

Such was the rise and progress and such were the natural revolutions of those theological disputes which disturbed the peace of Christianity under the reigns of Constantine and of his sons. But, as those princes presumed to extend their despotism over the faith, as well as over the lives and fortunes, of their subjects; the weight of their suffrage sometimes inclined the ecclesiastical balance: and the prerogatives of the King of Heaven were settled, or changed, or modified, in the cabinet of an earthly monarch.

The unhappy spirit of discord which pervaded the provinces of the East interrupted the triumph of Constantine; but the emperor continued for some time to view, with cool and careless indifference, the object of the dispute. As he was yet ignorant of the difficulty of appeasing the quarrels of theologians, he addressed to the contending parties, to Alexander and to Arius, a moderating epistle; which may be ascribed, with far greater reason, to the untutored sense of a soldier and statesman than to the dictates of any of his episcopal counsellors. He attributes the origin of the whole controversy to a trifling and subtle question, concerning an incomprehensible point of the law, which was foolishly asked by the bishop, and imprudently resolved by the presbyter. He laments that the Christian people, who had the same God, the same religion, and the same worship, should be divided by such inconsiderable distinctions; and he seriously recommends to the clergy of Alexandria the example of the Greek philosophers; who could maintain their arguments without losing their temper, and assert their freedom without violating their friendship. The indifference and contempt of the sovereign would have been, perhaps, the most effectual method of silencing the dispute, if the popular current had been less rapid and impetuous, and if Constantine himself, in the midst of faction and fanaticism, could have preserved the calm possession of his own mind. But his ecclesiastical ministers soon contrived to seduce the impartiality of the magistrate, and to awaken the zeal of the proselyte. He was provoked by the insults which had been offered to his statues; he was alarmed by the real, as well as the imaginary, magnitude of the spreading mischief; and he extinguished the hope of peace and toleration, from the moment that he assembled three hundred bishops within the walls of the same palace. The presence of the monarch swelled the importance of the debate; his attention multiplied the arguments; and he exposed his person with a patient intrepidity, which animated the valour of the combatants. Notwithstanding the applause which has been bestowed on the eloquence and sagacity of Constantine, a Roman general, whose religion might be still a subject of doubt, and whose mind had not been enlightened either by study or by inspiration, was indifferently qualified to discuss, in the Greek language, a metaphysical question, or an article of faith. But the credit of his favourite Osius, who appears to have presided in the council of Nice, might dispose the emperor in favour of the orthodox party; and a well-timed insinuation that the same Eusebius of Nicomedia, who now protected the heretic, had lately assisted the tyrant,[34] might exasperate him against their adversaries. The Nicene creed was ratified by Constantine; and his firm declaration that those who resisted the divine judgment of the synod must prepare themselves for an immediate exile annihilated the murmurs of a feeble opposition; which from seventeen, was almost instantly reduced to two, protesting bishops. Eusebius of Cæsarea yielded a reluctant and ambiguous consent to the Homoousion;[35] and the wavering conduct of the Nicomedian Eusebius served only to delay, about three months, his disgrace and exile. The impious Arius was banished into one of the remote provinces of Illyricum; his person and disciples were branded by law with the odious name of Porphyrians; his writings were condemned to the flames: and a capital punishment was denounced against those in whose possession they should be found. The emperor had now imbibed the spirit of controversy, and the angry sarcastic style of his edicts was designed to inspire his subjects with the hatred which he had conceived against the enemies of Christ.

But, as if the conduct of the emperor had been guided by passion instead of principle, three years from the council of Nice were

[34] Theodoret has preserved an epistle from Constantine to the people of Nicomedia, in which the monarch declares himself the public accuser of one of his subjects; he complains of the hostile behaviour of Eusebius during the civil war.

[35] See in Socrates, or rather in Theodoret, an original letter of Eusebius of Cæsarea, in which he attempts to justify his subscribing the Homoousion. The character of Eusebius has always been a problem; but those who have read the second critical epistle of Le Clerc must entertain a very unfavourable opinion of the orthodoxy and sincerity of the bishop of Cæsarea.

scarcely elapsed before he discovered some symptoms of mercy, and even of indulgence, towards the proscribed sect, which was secretly protected by his favourite sister. The exiles were recalled; and Eusebius, who gradually resumed his influence over the mind of Constantine, was restored to the episcopal throne from which he had been ignominiously degraded. Arius himself was treated by the whole court with the respect which would have been due to an innocent and oppressed man. His faith was approved by the synod of Jerusalem; and the emperor seemed impatient to repair his injustice, by issuing an absolute command that he should be solemnly admitted to the communion in the cathedral of Constantinople. On the same day which had been fixed for the triumph of Arius, he expired; and the strange and horrid circumstances of his death might excite a suspicion that the orthodox saints had contributed more efficaciously than by their prayers to deliver the church from the most formidable of her enemies.[36] The three principal leaders of the Catholics, Athanasius of Alexandria, Eustathius of Antioch, and Paul of Constantinople, were deposed on various accusations, by the sentence of numerous councils; and were afterwards banished into distant provinces by the first of the Christian emperors, who, in the last moments of his life, received the rites of baptism from the Arian bishop of Nicomedia. The ecclesiastical government of Constantine cannot be justified from the reproach of levity and weakness. But the credulous monarch, unskilled in the stratagems of theological warfare, might be deceived by the modest and specious professions of the heretics, whose sentiments he never perfectly understood; and, while he protected Arius, and persecuted Athanasius, he still considered the council of Nice as the bulwark of the Christian faith and the peculiar glory of his own reign.

The sons of Constantine must have been admitted from their childhood into the rank of catechumens, but they imitated, in the delay of their baptism, the example of their father. Like him, they presumed to pronounce their judgment on mysteries into which they had never been regularly initiated: and the fate of the Trinitarian controversy depended, in a great measure, on the sentiments of Constantius; who inherited the provinces of the East, and acquired the possession of the whole empire. The Arian presbyter or bishop, who had secreted for his use the testament of the deceased emperor, improved the fortunate occasion which had introduced him to the familiarity of a prince whose public counsels were always swayed by his domestic favourites. The eunuchs and slaves diffused

[36] *We derive the original story from Athanasius, who expresses some reluctance to stigmatize the memory of the dead. He might exaggerate; but the perpetual commerce of Alexandria and Constantinople would have rendered it dangerous to invent. Those who press the literal narrative of the death of Arius (his bowels suddenly burst out in a privy) must make their option between* poison *and* miracle.

the spiritual poison through the palace, and the dangerous infection was communicated, by the female attendants to the guards, and by the empress to her unsuspicious husband. The partiality which Constantius always expressed towards the Eusebian faction was insensibly fortified by the dexterous management of their leaders; and his victory over the tyrant Magnentius increased his inclination, as well as ability, to employ the arms of power in the cause of Arianism. While the two armies were engaged in the plains of Mursa, and the fate of the two rivals depended on the chance of war, the son of Constantine passed the anxious moments in a church of the martyrs, under the walls of the city. His spiritual comforter, Valens, the Arian bishop of the diocese, employed the most artful precautions to obtain such early intelligence as might secure either his favour or his escape. A secret chain of swift and trusty messengers informed him of the vicissitudes of the battle; and, while the courtiers stood trembling round their affrighted master, Valens assured him that the Gallic legions gave way; and insinuated with some presence of mind that the glorious event had been revealed to him by an angel. The grateful emperor ascribed his success to the merits and intercession of the bishop of Mursa, whose faith had deserved the public and miraculous approbation of Heaven. The Arians, who considered as their own the victory of Constantius, preferred his glory to that of his father.[37] Cyril, bishop of Jerusalem, immediately composed the description of a celestial cross encircled with a splendid rainbow; which during the festival of Pentecost, about the third hour of the day, had appeared over the Mount of Olives, to the edification of the devout pilgrims and the people of the holy city.[38] The size of the meteor was gradually magnified; and the Arian historian has ventured to affirm that it was conspicuous to the two armies in the plains of Pannonia; and that the tyrant, who is purposely represented as an idolater, fled before the auspicious sign of orthodox Christianity.

The sentiments of a judicious stranger, who has impartially considered the progress of civil or ecclesiastical discord, are always entitled to our notice: and a short passage of Ammianus, who served in the armies, and studied the character, of Constantius, is perhaps of more value than many pages of theological invectives. "The Christian religion, which, in itself," says that moderate historian, "is plain and simple, *he* confounded by the dotage of superstition. Instead of reconciling the parties by the weight of his authority, he cherished and propagated, by verbal disputes, the differences which

[37] *Cyril expressly observes that in the reign of Constantine the cross had been found in the bowels of the earth; but that it had appeared, in the reign of Constantius, in the midst of the heavens. This opposition evidently proves that Cyril was ignorant of the stupendous miracle to which the conversion of Constantine is attributed; and this ignorance is the more surprising, since it was no more than twelve years after his death that Cyril was consecrated bishop of Jerusalem by the immediate successor of Eusebius of Cæsarea.*

[38] *It is not easy to determine how far the ingenuity of Cyril might be assisted by some natural appearances of a solar halo.*

his vain curiosity had excited. The highways were covered with troops of bishops, galloping from every side to the assemblies, which they call synods; and, while they laboured to reduce the whole sect to their own particular opinions, the public establishment of the posts was almost ruined by their hasty and repeated journies." Our more intimate knowledge of the ecclesiastical transactions of the reign of Constantius would furnish an ample commentary on this remarkable passage; which justifies the rational apprehensions of Athanasius that the restless activity of the clergy, who wandered round the empire in search of the true faith, would excite the contempt and laughter of the unbelieving world. As soon as the emperor was relieved from the terrors of the civil war, he devoted the leisure of his winter quarters at Arles, Milan, Sirmium, and Constantinople, to the amusement or toils of controversy: the sword of the magistrate, and even of the tyrant, was unsheathed, to enforce the reasons of the theologian; and, as he opposed the orthodox faith of Nice, it is readily confessed that his incapacity and ignorance were equal to his presumption. The eunuchs, the women, and the bishops, who governed the vain and feeble mind of the emperor, had inspired him with an insuperable dislike to the Homoousion; but his timid conscience was alarmed by the impiety of Aetius. The guilt of that atheist was aggravated by the suspicious favour of the unfortunate Gallus; and even the deaths of the Imperial ministers who had been massacred at Antioch were imputed to the suggestions of that dangerous sophist. The mind of Constantius, which could neither be moderated by reason nor fixed by faith, was blindly impelled to either side of the dark and empty abyss by his horror of the opposite extreme: he alternately embraced and condemned the sentiments, he successively banished and recalled the leaders, of the Arian and Semi-Arian factions. During the season of public business or festivity, he employed whole days, and even nights, in selecting the words, and weighing the syllables, which composed his fluctuating creeds. The subject of his meditation still pursued and occupied his slumbers; the incoherent dreams of the emperor were received as celestial visions; and he accepted with complacency the lofty title of bishop of bishops, from those ecclesiastics who forgot the interest of their order for the gratification of their passions. The design of establishing an uniformity of doctrine, which had engaged him to convene so many synods in Gaul, Italy, Illyricum, and Asia, was repeatedly baffled by his own levity, by the divisions of the Arians, and by the resistance of the Catholics; and he resolved, as the last and decisive effort, imperiously to dictate the decrees of a general council. The destructive earthquake of Nicomedia, the difficulty of finding a convenient place, and perhaps some secret motives of policy, produced an alteration in the summons. The bishops of the East were directed to meet at Seleucia, in Isauria; while those of the West held their deliberations at Rimini, on the coast of the Hadriatic; and, instead of two or three deputies from each province, the whole episcopal body was ordered to march. The eastern council, after consuming four days in fierce and unavailing debate, separated without any definitive conclusion. The council of the West was protracted till the seventh month. Taurus, the Prætorian præfect, was instructed not to dismiss the prelates till they should all be united in the same opinion; and his efforts were supported by a power of banishing fifteen of the most refractory, and a promise of the consulship if he achieved so difficult an adventure. His prayers and threats, the authority of the sovereign, the sophistry of Valens and Ursacius, the distress of cold and hunger, and the tedious melancholy of a hopeless exile, at length extorted the reluctant consent of the bishops of Rimini. The deputies of the East and of the West attended the emperor in the palace of Constantinople, and he enjoyed the satisfaction of imposing on the world a profession of faith which established the *likeness,* without expressing the *consubstantiality,* of the Son of God. But the triumph of Arianism had been preceded by the removal of the orthodox clergy, whom it was impossible either to intimidate or to corrupt; and the reign of Constantius was disgraced by the unjust and ineffectual persecution of the great Athanasius.

We have seldom an opportunity of observing, either in active or speculative life, what effect may be produced, or what obstacles may be surmounted, by the force of a single mind, when it is inflexibly applied to the pursuit of a single object. The immortal name of Athanasius [39] will never be separated from the Catholic doctrine of the Trinity, to whose defence he consecrated every moment and every faculty of his being. Educated in the family of Alexander, he had vigorously opposed the early progress of the Arian heresy: he exercised the important functions of secretary under the aged prelate; and the fathers of the Nicene council beheld, with surprise and respect, the rising virtues of the young deacon. In a time of public danger, the dull claims of age and of rank are sometimes superseded; and within five months after his return from Nice, the deacon Athanasius was seated on the archiepiscopal throne of

[39] *We may regret that Gregory Nazianzen composed a panegyric instead of a life of Athanasius; but we should enjoy and improve the advantage of drawing our most authentic materials from the rich fund of his own epistles and apologies. I shall not imitate the example of Socrates, who published the first edition of his history without giving himself the trouble to consult the writings of Athanasius. Yet even Socrates, the more curious Sozomen, and the learned Theodoret, connect the life of Athanasius with the series of ecclesiastical history. The diligence of Tillemont and of the Benedictine editors has collected every fact, and examined every difficulty.*

Egypt. He filled that eminent station above forty-six years, and his long administration was spent in a perpetual combat against the powers of Arianism. Five times was Athanasius expelled from his throne; twenty years he passed as an exile or a fugitive; and almost every province of the Roman empire was successively witness to his merit, and his sufferings in the cause of the Homoousion, which he considered as the sole pleasure and business, as the duty, and as the glory, of his life. Amidst the storms of persecution, the archbishop of Alexandria was patient of labour, jealous of fame, careless of safety; and, although his mind was tainted by the contagion of fanaticism, Athanasius displayed a superiority of character and abilities, which would have qualified him, far better than the degenerate sons of Constantine, for the government of a great monarchy. His learning was much less profound and extensive than that of Eusebius of Cæsarea, and his rude eloquence could not be compared with the polished oratory of Gregory or Basil; but, whenever the primate of Egypt was called upon to justify his sentiments or his conduct, his unpremeditated style, either of speaking or writing, was clear, forcible, and persuasive. He has always been revered in the orthodox school, as one of the most accurate masters of the Christian theology; and he was supposed to possess two profane sciences, less adapted to the episcopal character, the knowledge of jurisprudence and that of divination. Some fortunate conjectures of future events, which impartial reasoners might ascribe to the experience and judgment of Athanasius, were attributed by his friends to heavenly inspiration, and imputed by his enemies to infernal magic.

But, as Athanasius was continually engaged with the prejudices and passions of every order of men, from the monk to the emperor, the knowledge of human nature was his first and most important science. He preserved a distinct and unbroken view of a scene which was incessantly shifting; and never failed to improve those decisive moments which are irrecoverably past before they are perceived by a common eye. The archbishop of Alexandria was capable of distinguishing how far he might boldly command, and where he must dexterously insinuate; how long he might contend with power, and when he must withdraw from persecution; and, while he directed the thunders of the church against heresy and rebellion, he could assume, in the bosom of his own party, the flexible and indulgent temper of a prudent leader. The election of Athanasius has not escaped the reproach of irregularity and precipitation;[40] but the pro-

[40] *The irregular ordination of Athanasius was slightly mentioned in the councils which were held against him; but it can scarcely be supposed that the assembly of the bishops of Egypt would solemnly attest a public falsehood.*

priety of his behaviour conciliated the affections both of the clergy and of the people. The Alexandrians were impatient to rise in arms for the defence of an eloquent and liberal pastor. In his distress he always derived support, or at least consolation, from the faithful attachment of his parochial clergy; and the hundred bishops of Egypt adhered, with unshaken zeal, to the cause of Athanasius. In the modest equipage which pride and policy would effect, he frequently performed the episcopal visitation of his provinces, from the mouth of the Nile to the confines of Æthiopia; familiarly conversing with the meanest of the populace, and humbly saluting the saints and hermits of the desert.[41] Nor was it only in ecclesiastical assemblies, among men whose education and manners were similar to his own, that Athanasius displayed the ascendancy of his genius. He appeared with easy and respectful firmness in the courts of princes; and in the various turns of his prosperous and adverse fortune, he never lost the confidence of his friends or the esteem of his enemies.

In his youth, the primate of Egypt resisted the great Constantine, who had repeatedly signified his will that Arius should be restored to the Catholic communion.[42] The emperor respected, and might forgive, this inflexible resolution; and the faction who considered Athanasius as their most formidable enemy were constrained to dissemble their hatred, and silently to prepare an indirect and distant assault. They scattered rumours and suspicions, represented the archbishop as a proud and oppressive tyrant, and boldly accused him of violating the treaty which had been ratified in the Nicene council with the schismatic followers of Meletius.[43] Athanasius had openly disapproved that ignominious peace, and the emperor was disposed to believe that he had abused his ecclesiastical and civil power, to persecute those odious sectaries; that he had sacrilegiously broken a chalice in one of their churches of Mareotis: that he had whipped or imprisoned six of their bishops; and that Arsenius, a seventh bishop of the same party, had been murdered, or at least mutilated, by the cruel hand of the primate.[44] These charges, which affected his honour and his life, were referred by Constantine to his brother Dalmatius the censor, who resided at Antioch; the synods of Cæsarea and Tyre were successively convened; and the bishops of the East were instructed to judge the cause of Athanasius before they proceeded to consecrate the new church of the Resurrection at Jerusalem. The primate might be conscious of his innocence; but he was sensible that the same implacable spirit which had dictated the

[41] *Athanasius himself, who did not disdain to compose the life of his friend Anthony, has carefully observed how often the holy monk deplored and prophesied the mischiefs of the Arian heresy.*

[42] *At first Constantine threatened in speaking, but requested in writing. His letters gradually assumed a menacing tone; but, while he required that the entrance of the church should be open to all, he avoided the odious name of Arius. Athanasius, like a skilful politician, has accurately marked these distinctions, which allowed him some scope for excuse and delay.*

[43] *The Meletians in Egypt, like the Donatists in Africa, were produced by an episcopal quarrel which arose from the persecution. I have not leisure to pursue the obscure controversy, which seems to have been misrepresented by the partiality of Athanasius, and the ignorance of Epiphanius.*

[44] *The treatment of the six bishops is specified by Sozomen; but Athanasius himself, so copious on the subject of Arsenius and the chalice, leaves this grave accusation without a reply.*

accusation would direct the proceeding, and pronounce the sentence. He prudently declined the tribunal of his enemies, despised the summons of the synod of Cæsarea; and, after a long and artful delay, submitted to the peremptory commands of the emperor, who threatened to punish his criminal disobedience if he refused to appear in the council of Tyre.[45] Before Athanasius, at the head of fifty Egyptian prelates, sailed from Alexandria, he had wisely secured the alliance of the Meletians; and Arsenius himself, his imaginary victim and his secret friend, was privately concealed in his train. The synod of Tyre was conducted by Eusebius of Cæsarea with more passion, and with less art, than his learning and experience might promise; his numerous faction repeated the names of homicide and tyrant; and their clamours were encouraged by the seeming patience of Athanasius; who expected the decisive moment to produce Arsenius alive and unhurt in the midst of the assembly. The nature of the other charges did not admit of such clear and satisfactory replies; yet the archbishop was able to prove that, in the village where he was accused of breaking a consecrated chalice, neither church nor altar nor chalice could really exist. The Arians, who had secretly determined the guilt and condemnation of their enemy, attempted, however, to disguise their injustice by the imitation of judicial forms: the synod appointed an episcopal commission of six delegates to collect evidence on the spot; and this measure, which was vigorously opposed by the Egyptian bishops, opened new scenes of violence and perjury. After the return of the deputies from Alexandria, the majority of the council pronounced the final sentence of degradation and exile against the primate of Egypt. The decree, expressed in the fiercest language of malice and revenge, was communicated to the emperor and the Catholic church; and the bishops immediately resumed a mild and devout aspect, such as became their holy pilgrimage to the sepulchre of Christ.

But the injustice of these ecclesiastical judges had not been countenanced by the submission, or even by the presence, of Athanasius. He resolved to make a bold and dangerous experiment, whether the throne was inaccessible to the voice of truth; and, before the final sentence could be pronounced at Tyre, the intrepid primate threw himself into a bark which was ready to hoist sail for the Imperial city. The request of a formal audience might have been opposed or eluded; but Athanasius concealed his arrival, watched the moment of Constantine's return from an adjacent villa, and boldly encountered his angry sovereign as he passed on horseback through the

[45] The emperor, in his epistle of Convocation, seems to prejudge some members of the clergy, and it was more than probable that the synod would apply those reproaches to Athanasius.

[46] In a church dedicated to St. Athanasius this situation would afford a better subject for a picture than most of the stories of miracles and martyrdoms.

principal street of Constantinople. So strange an apparition excited his surprise and indignation; and the guards were ordered to remove the importunate suitor; but his resentment was subdued by involuntary respect; and the haughty spirit of the emperor was awed by the courage and eloquence of a bishop, who implored his justice and awakened his conscience.[46] Constantine listened to the complaints of Athanasius with impartial and even gracious attention; the members of the synod of Tyre were summoned to justify their proceedings; and the arts of the Eusebian faction would have been confounded, if they had not aggravated the guilt of the primate by the dexterous supposition of an unpardonable offence; a criminal design to intercept and detain the corn-fleet of Alexandria, which supplied the subsistence of the new capital.[47] The emperor was satisfied that the peace of Egypt would be secured by the absence of a popular leader; but he refused to fill the vacancy of the archiepiscopal throne; and the sentence which, after a long hesitation, he pronounced was that of a jealous ostracism, rather than of an ignominious exile. In the remote province of Gaul, but in the hospitable court of Treves, Athanasius passed about twenty-eight months. The death of the emperor changed the face of public affairs; and, amidst the general indulgence of a young reign, the primate was restored to his country by an honourable edict of the younger Constantine, who expressed a deep sense of the innocence and merit of his venerable guest.[48]

The death of that prince exposed Athanasius to a second persecution; and the feeble Constantius, the sovereign of the East, soon became the secret accomplice of the Eusebians. Ninety bishops of that sect or faction assembled at Antioch, under the specious pretence of dedicating the cathedral. They composed an ambiguous creed, which is faintly tinged with the colours of Semi-Arianism, and twenty-five canons, which still regulate the discipline of the orthodox Greeks. It was decided, with some appearance of equity, that a bishop, deprived by a synod, should not resume his episcopal functions, till he had been absolved by the judgment of an equal synod; the law was immediately applied to the case of Athanasius, the council of Antioch pronounced, or rather confirmed, his degradation: a stranger, named Gregory, was seated on his throne; and Philagrius,[49] the præfect of Egypt, was instructed to support the new primate with the civil and military powers of the province. Oppressed by the conspiracy of the Asiatic prelates Athanasius withdrew from Alexandria, and passed three[50] years as an exile and a

[47] *Eunapius has related a strange example of the cruelty and credulity of Constantine on a similar occasion. The eloquent Sopater, a Syrian philosopher, enjoyed his friendship, and provoked the resentment of Ablavius, his Prætorian præfect. The corn-fleet was detained for want of a south wind; the people of Constantinople were discontented; and Sopater was beheaded, on a charge that he had bound the winds by the power of magic. Suidas adds that Constantine wished to prove, by this execution, that he had absolutely renounced the superstition of the Gentiles.*

[48] *In his return he saw Constantius twice, at Viminiacum and at Cæsarea in Cappadocia. Tillemont supposes that Constantine introduced him to the meeting of the three royal brothers in Pannonia.*

[49] *This magistrate, so odious to Athanasius, is praised by Gregory Nazianzen. For the credit of human nature, I am always pleased to discover some good qualities in those men whom party has represented as tyrants and monsters.*

[50] *The chronological difficulties which perplex the residence of Athanasius at Rome are strenuously agitated by Valesius and Tillemont. I have followed the simple hypothesis of Valesius, who allows only one journey, after the intrusion of Gregory.*

[51] *If any corruption was used to promote the interest of religion, an advocate of Athanasius might justify or excuse this questionable conduct by the example of Cato and Sidney; the former of whom is* said *to have given, and the latter to have received, a bribe, in the cause of liberty.*

[52] *The Canon which allows appeals to the Roman pontiffs has almost raised the council of Sardica to the dignity of a general council; and its acts have been ignorantly or artfully confounded with those of the Nicene synod.*

[53] *As Athanasius dispersed secret invectives against Constantius (see the Epistle of the Monks), at the same time that he assured him of his profound respect, we might distrust the professions of the archbishop.*

suppliant on the holy threshold of the Vatican. By the assiduous study of the Latin language, he soon qualified himself to negotiate with the western clergy; his decent flattery swayed and directed the haughty Julius: the Roman pontiff was persuaded to consider his appeal as the peculiar interest of the Apostolic see; and his innocence was unanimously declared in a council of fifty bishops of Italy. At the end of three years, the primate was summoned to the court of Milan by the emperor Constans, who, in the indulgence of unlawful pleasures, still professed a lively regard for the orthodox faith. The cause of truth and justice was promoted by the influence of gold,[51] and the ministers of Constans advised their sovereign to require the convocation of an ecclesiastical assembly, which might act as the representative of the Catholic church. Ninety-four bishops of the West, seventy-six bishops of the East, encountered each other at Sardica on the verge of the two empires, but in the dominions of the protector of Athanasius. Their debates soon degenerated into hostile altercations; the Asiatics, apprehensive for their personal safety, retired to Philippopolis in Thrace; and the rival synods reciprocally hurled their spiritual thunders against their enemies, whom they piously condemned as the enemies of the true God. Their decrees were published and ratified in their respective provinces; and Athanasius, who in the West was revered as a saint, was exposed as a criminal to the abhorrence of the East.[52] The council of Sardica reveals the first symptoms of discord and schism between the Greek and Latin churches, which were separated by the accidental difference of faith and the permanent distinction of language.

During the second exile in the West, Athanasius was frequently admitted to the Imperial presence; at Capua, Lodi, Milan, Verona, Padua, Aquileia, and Treves. The bishop of the diocese usually assisted at these interviews; the master of the offices stood before the veil or curtain of the sacred apartment; and the uniform moderation of the primate might be attested by these respectable witnesses, to whose evidence he solemnly appeals.[53] Prudence would undoubtedly suggest the mild and respectful tone that became a subject and a bishop. In these familiar conferences with the sovereign of the West, Athanasius might lament the error of Constantius; but he boldly arraigned the guilt of his eunuchs and his Arian prelates; deplored the distress and danger of the Catholic church; and excited Constans to emulate the zeal and glory of his father. The emperor declared his resolution of employing the troops and treasures of Europe in the orthodox cause; and signified, by a concise and peremptory epistle to his brother Constantius, that, unless he consented to the immediate restoration of Athanasius, he himself, with a fleet and army, would seat the archbishop on the throne of Alexandria.[54] But this religious war, so horrible to nature, was prevented by the timely compliance of Constantius; and the emperor of the East condescended to solicit a reconciliation with a subject whom he had injured. Athanasius waited with decent pride, till he had received three successive epistles full of the strongest assurances of the protection, the favour, and the esteem of his sovereign; who invited him to resume his episcopal seat, and who added the humiliating precaution of engaging his principal ministers to attest the sincerity of his intentions. They were manifested in a still more public manner by the strict orders which were dispatched into Egypt to recall the adherents of Athanasius, to restore their privileges, to proclaim their innocence, and to erase from the public registers the illegal proceedings which had been obtained during the prevalence of the Eusebian faction. After every satisfaction and security had been given, which justice or even delicacy could require, the primate proceeded, by slow journeys, through the provinces of Thrace, Asia, and Syria; and his progress was marked by the abject homage of the Oriental bishops, who excited his contempt without deceiving his penetration.[55] At Antioch he saw the emperor Constantius; sustained, with modest firmness, the embraces and protestations of his master, and eluded the proposal of allowing the Arians a single church at Alexandria, by claiming, in the other cities of the empire, a similar toleration for his own party; a reply which might have appeared just and moderate in the mouth of an independent prince. The entrance of the archbishop into his capital was a triumphal procession; absence and persecution had endeared him to the Alexandrians; his authority, which he exercised with rigour, was more firmly established; and his fame was diffused from Æthiopia to Britain, over the whole extent of the Christian world.

But the subject who has reduced his prince to the necessity of dissembling can never expect a sincere and lasting forgiveness; and the tragic fate of Constans soon deprived Athanasius of a powerful and generous protector. The civil war between the assassin and the only surviving brother of Constans, which afflicted the empire above three years, secured an interval of repose to the Catholic church; and the two contending parties were desirous to conciliate the friendship of a bishop who, by the weight of his personal authority,

[54] *Notwithstanding the discreet silence of Athanasius, and the manifest forgery of a letter inserted by Socrates, these menaces are proved by the unquestionable evidence of Lucifer of Cagliari, and even of Constantius himself.*

[55] *I have always entertained some doubts concerning the retractation of Ursacius and Valens. Their epistles to Julius, bishop of Rome, and to Athanasius himself, are of so different a cast from each other that they cannot both be genuine. The one speaks the language of criminals who confess their guilt and infamy; the other of enemies who solicit on equal terms an honourable reconciliation.*

might determine the fluctuating resolution of an important province. He gave audience to the ambassadors of the tyrant, with whom he was afterwards accused of holding a secret correspondence;[56] and the emperor Constantius repeatedly assured his dearest father, the most revered Athanasius, that, notwithstanding the malicious rumours which were circulated by their common enemies, he had inherited the sentiments, as well as the throne, of his deceased brother. Gratitude and humanity would have disposed the primate of Egypt to deplore the untimely fate of Constans, and to abhor the guilt of Magnentius; but, as he clearly understood that the apprehensions of Constantius were his only safeguard, the fervour of his prayers for the success of the righteous cause might perhaps be somewhat abated. The ruin of Athanasius was no longer contrived by the obscure malice of a few bigoted or angry bishops, who abused the authority of a credulous monarch. The monarch himself avowed the resolution, which he had so long suppressed, of avenging his private injuries;[57] and the first winter after his victory, which he passed at Arles, was employed against an enemy more odious to him than the vanquished tyrant of Gaul.

If the emperor had capriciously decreed the death of the most eminent and virtuous citizen of the republic, the cruel order would have been executed without hesitation, by the ministers of open violence or of specious injustice. The caution, the delay, the difficulty with which he proceeded in the condemnation and punishment of a popular bishop, discovered to the world that the privileges of the church had already revived a sense of order and freedom in the Roman government. The sentence which was pronounced in the synod of Tyre, and subscribed by a large majority of the eastern bishops, had never been expressly repealed; and, as Athanasius had been once degraded from his episcopal dignity by the judgment of his brethren, every subsequent act might be considered as irregular, and even criminal. But the memory of the firm and effectual support which the primate of Egypt had derived from the attachment of the western church engaged Constantius to suspend the execution of the sentence, till he had obtained the concurrence of the Latin bishops. Two years were consumed in ecclesiastical negotiations; and the important cause between the emperor and one of his subjects was solemnly debated, first in the synod of Arles, and afterwards in the great council of Milan,[58] which consisted of above three hundred bishops. Their integrity was gradually undermined by the arguments of the Arians, the dexterity of the eunuchs, and the press-

[56] *Athanasius defends his innocence by pathetic complaints, solemn assertions, and specious arguments. He admits that letters had been forged in his name, but he requests that his own secretaries, and those of the tyrant, may be examined, whether those letters had been written by the former or received by the latter.*

[57] *The emperor declared that he was more desirous to subdue Athanasius than he had been to vanquish Magnentius or Sylvanus.*

[58] *The affairs of the council of Milan are so imperfectly and erroneously related by the Greek writers that we must rejoice in the supply of some letters of Eusebius, extracted by Baronius from the archives of the church of Vercellæ, and of an old life of Dionysius of Milan, published by Bollandus.*

ing solicitations of a prince, who gratified his revenge at the expense of his dignity, and exposed his own passions, whilst he influenced those of the clergy. Corruption, the most infallible symptom of constitutional liberty, was successfully practised: honours, gifts, and immunities were offered and accepted as the price of an episcopal vote;[59] and the condemnation of the Alexandrian primate was artfully represented as the only measure which could restore the peace and union of the Catholic church. The friends of Athanasius were not, however, wanting to their leader, or to their cause. With a manly spirit, which the sanctity of their character rendered less dangerous, they maintained in public debate, and in private conference with the emperor, the eternal obligation of religion and justice. They declared that neither the hope of his favour nor the fear of his displeasure should prevail on them to join in the condemnation of an absent, an innocent, a respectable brother. They affirmed, with apparent reason, that the illegal and obsolete decrees of the council of Tyre had long since been tacitly abolished by the Imperial edicts, the honourable re-establishment of the archbishop of Alexandria, and the silence or recantation of his most clamorous adversaries. They alleged that his innocence had been attested by the unanimous bishops of Egypt, and had been acknowledged, in the councils of Rome and Sardica,[60] by the impartial judgment of the Latin church. They deplored the hard condition of Athanasius, who, after enjoying so many years his seat, his reputation, and the seeming confidence of his sovereign, was again called upon to confute the most groundless and extravagant accusations. Their language was specious; their conduct was honourable: but in this long and obstinate contest, which fixed the eyes of the whole empire on a single bishop, the ecclesiastical factions were prepared to sacrifice truth and justice to the more interesting object of defending, or removing, the intrepid champion of the Nicene faith. The Arians still thought it prudent to disguise, in ambiguous language, their real sentiments and designs: but the orthodox bishops, armed with the favour of the people and the decrees of a general council, insisted on every occasion, and particularly at Milan, that their adversaries should purge themselves from the suspicion of heresy, before they presumed to arraign the conduct of the great Athanasius.

But the voice of reason (if reason was indeed on the side of Athanasius) was silenced by the clamours of a factious or venal majority; and the councils of Arles and Milan were not dissolved, till the archbishop of Alexandria had been solemnly condemned

[59] *The honours, presents, feasts, which seduced so many bishops, are mentioned with indignation by those who were too pure or too proud to accept them. "We combat (says Hilary of Poitiers) against Constantius the antichrist; who strokes the belly instead of scourging the back."*

[60] *More properly by the orthodox part of the council of Sardica. If the bishops of both parties had fairly voted, the division would have been 94 to 76. M. de Tillemont is justly surprised that so small a majority should have proceeded so vigorously against their adversaries, the principal of whom they immediately deposed.*

and deposed by the judgment of the Western, as well as of the Eastern, church. The bishops who had opposed, were required to subscribe, the sentence; and to unite in religious communion with the suspected leaders of the adverse party. A formulary of consent was transmitted by the messengers of state to the absent bishops: and all those who refused to submit their private opinion to the public and inspired wisdom of the councils of Arles and Milan were immediately banished by the emperor, who affected to execute the decrees of the Catholic church. Among those prelates who led the honourable band of confessors and exiles, Liberius of Rome, Osius of Cordova, Paulinus of Treves, Dionysius of Milan, Eusebius of Vercellæ, Lucifer of Cagliari, and Hilary of Poitiers, may deserve to be particularly distinguished. The eminent station of Liberius, who governed the capital of the empire; the personal merit and long experience of the venerable Osius, who was revered as the favourite of the great Constantine, and the father of the Nicene faith; placed those prelates at the head of the Latin church: and their example, either of submission or resistance, would probably be imitated by the episcopal crowd. But the repeated attempts of the emperor to seduce or to intimidate the bishops of Rome and Cordova were for some time ineffectual. The Spaniard declared himself ready to suffer under Constantius, as he had suffered threescore years before under his grandfather Maximian. The Roman, in the presence of his sovereign, asserted the innocence of Athanasius, and his own freedom. When he was banished to Berœa in Thrace, he sent back a large sum which had been offered for the accommodation of his journey; and insulted the court of Milan by the haughty remark that the emperor and his eunuchs might want that gold to pay their soldiers and their bishops. The resolution of Liberius and Osius was at length subdued by the hardships of exile and confinement. The Roman pontiff purchased his return by some criminal compliances; and afterwards expiated his guilt by a seasonable repentance. Persuasion and violence were employed to extort the reluctant signature of the decrepit bishop of Cordova, whose strength was broken, and whose faculties were perhaps impaired, by the weight of an hundred years; and the insolent triumph of the Arians provoked some of the orthodox party to treat with inhuman severity the character, or rather the memory, of an unfortunate old man, to whose former services Christianity itself was so deeply indebted.[61]

The fall of Liberius and Osius reflected a brighter lustre on the

[61] *The life of Osius is collected by Tillemont, who in the most extravagant terms first admires, and then reprobates, the bishop of Cordova. In the midst of their lamentations on his fall, the prudence of Athanasius may be distinguished from the blind and intemperate zeal of Hilary.*

firmness of those bishops who still adhered, with unshaken fidelity, to the cause of Athanasius and religious truth. The ingenious malice of their enemies had deprived them of the benefit of mutual comfort and advice, separated those illustrious exiles into distant provinces, and carefully selected the most inhospitable spots of a great empire.[62] Yet they soon experienced that the deserts of Libya and the most barbarous tracts of Cappadocia were less inhospitable than the residence of those cities in which an Arian bishop could satiate, without restraint, the exquisite rancour of theological hatred. Their consolation was derived from the consciousness of rectitude and independence, from the applause, the visits, the letters, and the liberal alms of their adherents, and from the satisfaction which they soon enjoyed of observing the intestine divisions of the adversaries of the Nicene faith. Such was the nice and capricious taste of the emperor Constantius, and so easily was he offended by the slightest deviation from his imaginary standard of Christian truth, that he persecuted, with equal zeal, those who defended the *consubstantiality,* those who asserted the *similar substance,* and those who denied the *likeness,* of the Son of God. Three bishops, degraded and banished for those adverse opinions, might possibly meet in the same place of exile; and, according to the difference of their temper, might either pity or insult the blind enthusiasm of their antagonists, whose present sufferings would never be compensated by future happiness.

The disgrace and exile of the orthodox bishops of the West were designed as so many preparatory steps to the ruin of Athanasius himself. Six and twenty months had elapsed, during which the Imperial court secretly laboured, by the most insidious arts, to remove him from Alexandria, and to withdraw the allowance which supplied his popular liberality. But, when the primate of Egypt, deserted and proscribed by the Latin church, was left destitute of any foreign support, Constantius dispatched two of his secretaries with a verbal commission to announce and execute the order of his banishment. As the justice of the sentence was publicly avowed by the whole party, the only motive which could restrain Constantius from giving his messengers the sanction of a written mandate must be imputed to his doubt of the event; and to a sense of the danger to which he might expose the second city, and the most fertile province of the empire, if the people should persist in the resolution of defending, by force of arms, the innocence of their spiritual father. Such extreme caution afforded Athanasius a specious pretence re-

[62] *The confessors of the West were successively banished to the deserts of Arabia or Thebais, the lonely places of Mount Taurus, the wildest parts of Phrygia, which were in the possession of the impious Montanists, &c. When the heretic Aetius was too favourably entertained at Mopsuestia in Cilicia, the place of his exile was changed, by the advice of Acacius, to Amblada, a district inhabited by savages and infested by war and pestilence.*

spectfully to dispute the truth of an order, which he could not reconcile either with the equity, or with the former declarations, of his gracious master. The civil powers of Egypt found themselves inadequate to the task of persuading or compelling the primate to abdicate his episcopal throne; and they were obliged to conclude a treaty with the popular leaders of Alexandria, by which it was stipulated that all proceedings and hostilities should be suspended till the emperor's pleasure had been more distinctly ascertained. By this seeming moderation, the Catholics were deceived into a false and fatal security; while the legions of the Upper Egypt and of Libya advanced, by secret orders and hasty marches, to besiege, or rather to surprise, a capital habituated to sedition and inflamed by religious zeal.[63] The position of Alexandria, between the sea and the lake Mareotis, facilitated the approach and landing of the troops; who were introduced into the heart of the city, before any effectual measures could be taken either to shut the gates or to occupy the important posts of defence. At the hour of midnight, twenty-three days after the signature of the treaty, Syrianus, duke of Egypt, at the head of five thousand soldiers, armed and prepared for an assault, unexpectedly invested the church of St. Theonas, where the archbishop, with a party of his clergy and people, performed their nocturnal devotions. The doors of the sacred edifice yielded to the impetuosity of the attack, which was accompanied with every horrid circumstance of tumult and bloodshed; but, as the bodies of the slain and the fragments of military weapons remained the next day an unexceptionable evidence in the possession of the Catholics, the enterprise of Syrianus may be considered as a successful irruption, rather than as an absolute conquest. The other churches of the city were profaned by similar outrages; and, during at least four months, Alexandria was exposed to the insults of a licentious army, stimulated by the ecclesiastics of an hostile faction. Many of the faithful were killed; who may deserve the name of martyrs, if their deaths were neither provoked nor revenged; bishops and presbyters were treated with cruel ignominy; consecrated virgins were stripped naked, scourged, and violated; the houses of wealthy citizens were plundered; and, under the mask of religious zeal, lust, avarice, and private resentment were gratified with impunity, and even with applause. The Pagans of Alexandria, who still formed a numerous and discontented party, were easily persuaded to desert a bishop whom they feared and esteemed. The hopes of some peculiar favours, and the apprehension of being involved in the general penal-

[63] *Athanasius had lately sent for Anthony and some of his chosen monks. They descended from their mountain, announced to the Alexandrians the sanctity of Athanasius, and were honourably conducted by the archbishop as far as the gates of the city.*

ties of rebellion, engaged them to promise their support to the destined successor of Athanasius, the famous George of Cappadocia. The usurper, after receiving the consecration of an Arian synod, was placed on the episcopal throne by the arms of Sebastian, who had been appointed Count of Egypt for the execution of that important design. In the use, as well as in the acquisition, of power, the tyrant George disregarded the laws of religion, of justice, and of humanity; and the same scenes of violence and scandal which had been exhibited in the capital were repeated in more than ninety episcopal cities of Egypt. Encouraged by success, Constantius ventured to approve the conduct of his ministers. By a public and passionate epistle, the emperor congratulates the deliverance of Alexandria from a popular tyrant, who deluded his blind votaries by the magic of his eloquence; expatiates on the virtues and piety of the most reverend George, the elected bishop; and aspires, as the patron and benefactor of the city, to surpass the fame of Alexander himself. But he solemnly declares his unalterable resolution to pursue with fire and sword the seditious adherents of the wicked Athanasius, who, by flying from justice, has confessed his guilt, and escaped the ignominious death which he had so often deserved.[64]

Athanasius had indeed escaped from the most imminent dangers; and the adventures of that extraordinary man deserve and fix our attention. On the memorable night when the church of St. Theonas was invested by the troops of Syrianus, the archbishop, seated on his throne, expected, with calm and intrepid dignity, the approach of death. While the public devotion was interrupted by shouts of rage and cries of terror, he animated his trembling congregation to express their religious confidence, by chanting one of the psalms of David, which celebrates the triumph of the God of Israel over the haughty and impious tyrant of Egypt. The doors were at length burst open; a cloud of arrows was discharged among the people; the soldiers, with drawn swords, rushed forwards into the sanctuary; and the dreadful gleam of their armour was reflected by the holy luminaries which burnt round the altar.[65] Athanasius still rejected the pious importunity of the monks and presbyters, who were attached to his person; and nobly refused to desert his episcopal station, till he had dismissed in safety the last of the congregation. The darkness and tumult of the night favoured the retreat of the archbishop; and, though he was oppressed by the waves of an agitated multitude, though he was thrown to the ground, and left without sense or motion, he still recovered his undaunted cour-

[64] *The emperor, or his Arian secretaries, while they express their resentment, betray their fears and esteem of Athanasius.*

[65] *These minute circumstances are curious, as they are literally transcribed from the protest which was publicly presented three days afterwards by the Catholics of Alexandria.*

age, and eluded the eager search of the soldiers, who were instructed by their Arian guides that the head of Athanasius would be the most acceptable present to the emperor. From that moment the primate of Egypt disappeared from the eyes of his enemies, and remained above six years concealed in impenetrable obscurity.[66]

[66] *The Jansenists have often compared Athanasius and Arnauld, and have expatiated with pleasure on the faith and zeal, the merit and exile, of those celebrated doctors.*

The despotic power of his implacable enemy filled the whole extent of the Roman world; and the exasperated monarch had endeavoured, by a very pressing epistle to the Christian princes of Æthiopia, to exclude Athanasius from the most remote and sequestered regions of the earth. Counts, præfects, tribunes, whole armies, were successively employed to pursue a bishop and a fugitive; the vigilance of the civil and military powers were excited by the Imperial edicts; liberal rewards were promised to the man who should produce Athanasius, either alive or dead; and the most severe penalties were denounced against those who should dare to protect the public enemy. But the deserts of Thebais were now peopled by a race of wild yet submissive fanatics, who preferred the commands of their abbot to the laws of their sovereign. The numerous disciples of Anthony and Pachomius received the fugitive primate as their father, admired the patience and humility with which he conformed to their strictest institutions, collected every word which dropt from his lips as the genuine effusions of inspired wisdom; and persuaded themselves that their prayers, their fasts, and their vigils, were less meritorious than the zeal which they expressed, and the dangers which they braved, in the defence of truth and innocence. The monasteries of Egypt were seated in lonely and desolate places, on the summit of mountains, or in the islands of the Nile; and the sacred horn or trumpet of Tabenne was the well-known signal which assembled several thousand robust and determined monks, who, for the most part, had been the peasants of the adjacent country. When their dark retreats were invaded by a military force, which it was impossible to resist, they silently stretched out their necks to the executioner, and supported their national character that tortures could never wrest from an Egyptian the confession of a secret which he was resolved not to disclose. The archbishop of Alexandria, for whose safety they eagerly devoted their lives, was lost among a uniform and well-disciplined multitude; and on the nearer approach of danger, he was swiftly removed, by their officious hands, from one place of concealment to another, till he reached the formidable deserts, which the gloomy and credulous temper of superstition had peopled with dæmons and savage monsters. The retirement of Athanasius, which ended only with the life of Constantius, was spent, for the most part, in the society of the monks, who faithfully served him as guards, as secretaries, and as messengers; but the importance of maintaining a more intimate connection with the Catholic party tempted him, whenever the diligence of the pursuit was abated, to emerge from the desert, to introduce himself into Alexandria, and to trust his person to the discretion of his friends and adherents. His various adventures might have furnished the subject of a very entertaining romance. He was once secreted in a dry cistern, which he had scarcely left before he was betrayed by the treachery of a female slave;[67] and he was once concealed in a still more extraordinary asylum, the house of a virgin, only twenty years of age, and who was celebrated in the whole city for her exquisite beauty. At the hour of midnight, as she related the story many years afterwards, she was surprised by the appearance of the archbishop in a loose undress, who, advancing with hasty steps, conjured her to afford him the protection which he had been directed by a celestial vision to seek under her hospitable roof. The pious maid accepted and preserved the sacred pledge which was entrusted to her prudence and courage. Without imparting the secret to any one, she instantly conducted Athanasius into her most secret chamber, and watched over his safety with the tenderness of a friend and the assiduity of a servant. As long as the danger continued, she regularly supplied him with books and provisions, washed his feet, managed his correspondence, and dexterously concealed from the eye of suspicion this familiar and solitary intercourse between a saint whose character required the most unblemished chastity and a female whose charms might excite the most dangerous emotions.[68] During the six years of persecution and exile, Athanasius repeated his visits to his fair and faithful companion; and the formal declaration that he *saw* the councils of Rimini and Seleucia forces us to believe that he was secretly present at the time and place of their convocation. The advantage of personally negotiating with his friends, and of observing and improving the divisions of his enemies, might justify, in a prudent statesman, so bold and dangerous an enterprise; and Alexandria was connected by trade and navigation with every seaport of the Mediterranean. From the depth of his inaccessible retreat, the intrepid primate waged an incessant and offensive war against the protector of the Arians; and his seasonable writings, which were diligently circulated and eagerly perused, contributed to unite and animate the orthodox

[67] *This and the following story will be rendered impossible, if we suppose that Athanasius always inhabited the asylum which he accidentally or occasionally had used.*

[68] *Palladius, the original author of this anecdote, had conversed with the damsel, who in her old age still remembered with pleasure so pious and honourable a connexion. I cannot indulge the delicacy of Baronius, Valesius, Tillemont, &c. who almost reject a story so unworthy, as they deem it, of the gravity of ecclesiastical history.*

party. In his public apologies, which he addressed to the emperor himself, he sometimes affected the praise of moderation; whilst at the same time, in secret and vehement invectives, he exposed Constantius as a weak and wicked prince, the executioner of his family, the tyrant of the republic, and the antichrist of the church. In the height of his prosperity, the victorious monarch, who had chastised the rashness of Gallus, and suppressed the revolt of Sylvanus, who had taken the diadem from the head of Vetranio, and vanquished in the field the legions of Magnentius, received from an invisible hand a wound which he could neither heal nor revenge; and the son of Constantine was the first of the Christian princes who experienced the strength of those principles which, in the cause of religion, could resist the most violent exertions of the civil power.[69]

The persecution of Athanasius and of so many respectable bishops, who suffered for the truth of their opinions, or at least for the integrity of their conscience, was a just subject of indignation and discontent to all Christians, except those who were blindly devoted to the Arian faction. The people regretted the loss of their faithful pastors, whose banishment was usually followed by the intrusion of a stranger[70] into the episcopal chair; and loudly complained that the right of election was violated, and that they were condemned to obey a mercenary usurper, whose person was unknown, and whose principles were suspected. The Catholics might prove to the world that they were not involved in the guilt and heresy of their ecclesiastical governor, by publicly testifying their dissent, or by totally separating themselves from his communion. The first of these methods was invented at Antioch, and practised with such success that it was soon diffused over the Christian world. The doxology or sacred hymn, which celebrates the *glory* of the Trinity, is susceptible of very nice, but material, inflexions; and the substance of an orthodox, or an heretical, creed may be expressed by the difference of a disjunctive, or a copulative, particle. Alternate responses, and a more regular psalmody, were introduced into the public service by Flavianus and Diodorus, two devout and active laymen, who were attached to the Nicene faith. Under their conduct, a swarm of monks issued from the adjacent desert, bands of well-disciplined singers were stationed in the cathedral of Antioch, the Glory to the Father, AND the Son, AND the Holy Ghost,[71] was triumphantly chanted by a full chorus of voices; and the Catholics insulted, by the purity of their doctrine, the Arian prelate who had usurped the throne of the venerable Eustathius. The same zeal which inspired their songs prompted the more scrupulous members of the orthodox party to form separate assemblies, which were governed by the presbyters, till the death of their exiled bishop allowed the election and consecration of a new episcopal pastor.[72] The revolutions of the court multiplied the number of pretenders; and the same city was often disputed, under the reign of Constantius, by two, or three, or even four bishops, who exercised their spiritual jurisdiction over their respective followers, and alternately lost and regained the temporal possessions of the church. The abuse of Christianity introduced into the Roman government new causes of tyranny and sedition; the bands of civil society were torn asunder by the fury of religious factions; and the obscure citizen, who might calmly have surveyed the elevation and fall of successive emperors, imagined and experienced that his own life and fortune were connected with the interests of a popular ecclesiastic. The example of the two capitals, Rome and Constantinople, may serve to represent the state of the empire, and the temper of mankind, under the reign of the sons of Constantine.

I. The Roman pontiff, as long as he maintained his station and his principles, was guarded by the warm attachment of a great people; and could reject with scorn the prayers, the menaces, and the oblations of an heretical prince. When the eunuchs had secretly pronounced the exile of Liberius, the well-grounded apprehension of a tumult engaged them to use the utmost precautions in the execution of the sentence. The capital was invested on every side, and the præfect was commanded to seize the person of the bishop, either by stratagem or by open force. The order was obeyed; and Liberius, with the greatest difficulty, at the hour of midnight, was swiftly conveyed beyond the reach of the Roman people, before their consternation was turned into rage. As soon as they were informed of his banishment into Thrace, a general assembly was convened, and the clergy of Rome bound themselves, by a public and solemn oath, never to desert their bishop, never to acknowledge the usurper Felix; who, by the influence of the eunuchs, had been irregularly chosen and consecrated within the walls of a profane palace. At the end of two years, their pious obstinacy subsisted entire and unshaken; and, when Constantius visited Rome, he was assailed by the importunate solicitations of a people, who had preserved, as the last remnant of their ancient freedom, the right of treating their sovereign with familiar insolence. The wives of many of the senators and most honourable citizens, after pressing their husbands to

[72] *After the exile of Eustathius, under the reign of Constantine, the rigid party of the orthodox formed a separation, which afterwards degenerated into a schism, and lasted above fourscore years. In many churches, the Arians and Homoousians, who had renounced each other's communion, continued for some time to join in prayer.*

intercede in favour of Liberius, were advised to undertake a commission, which, in their hands, would be less dangerous and might prove more successful. The emperor received with politeness these female deputies, whose wealth and dignity were displayed in the magnificence of their dress and ornaments: he admired their inflexible resolution of following their beloved pastor to the most distant regions of the earth, and consented that the two bishops, Liberius and Felix, should govern in peace their respective congregations. But the ideas of toleration were so repugnant to the practice, and even to the sentiments, of those times that, when the answer of Constantius was publicly read in the Circus of Rome, so reasonable a project of accommodation was rejected with contempt and ridicule. The eager vehemence which animated the spectators in the decisive moment of a horse-race was now directed towards a different object; and the Circus resounded with the shout of thousands, who repeatedly exclaimed, "One God, One Christ, One Bishop." The zeal of the Roman people in the cause of Liberius was not confined to words alone; and the dangerous and bloody sedition which they excited soon after the departure of Constantius determined that prince to accept the submission of the exiled prelate, and to restore him to the undivided dominion of the capital. After some ineffectual resistance, his rival was expelled from the city by the permission of the emperor, and the power of the opposite faction; the adherents of Felix were inhumanly murdered in the streets, in the public places, in the baths, and even in the churches; and the face of Rome, upon the return of a Christian bishop, renewed the horrid image of the massacres of Marius and the proscriptions of Sylla.

II. Notwithstanding the rapid increase of Christians under the reign of the Flavian family, Rome, Alexandria, and the other great cities of the empire, still contained a strong and powerful faction of Infidels, who envied the prosperity, and who ridiculed, even on their theatres, the theological disputes, of the church. Constantinople alone enjoyed the advantage of being born and educated in the bosom of the faith. The capital of the East had never been polluted by the worship of idols; and the whole body of the people had deeply imbibed the opinions, the virtues, and the passions, which distinguished the Christians of that age from the rest of mankind. After the death of Alexander, the episcopal throne was disputed by Paul and Macedonius. By their zeal and abilities they both deserved the eminent station to which they aspired; and, if the moral character of Macedonius was less exceptionable, his competitor had the advantage of a prior election and a more orthodox doctrine. His firm attachment to the Nicene creed, which has given Paul a place in the calendar among saints and martyrs, exposed him to the resentment of the Arians. In the space of fourteen years he was five times driven from the throne; to which he was more frequently restored by the violence of the people than by the permission of the prince; and the power of Macedonius could be secured only by the death of his rival. The unfortunate Paul was dragged in chains from the sandy deserts of Mesopotamia to the most desolate places of Mount Taurus,[13] confined in a dark and narrow dungeon, left six days without food, and at length strangled, by the order of Philip, one of the principal ministers of the emperor Constantius.[14] The first blood which stained the new capital was spilt in this ecclesiastical contest; and many persons were slain on both sides, in the furious and obstinate seditions of the people. The commission of enforcing a sentence of banishment against Paul had been entrusted to Hermogenes, the master-general of the cavalry; but the execution of it was fatal to himself. The Catholics rose in the defence of their bishop; the palace of Hermogenes was consumed; the first military officer of the empire was dragged by the heels through the streets of Constantinople, and, after he expired, his lifeless corpse was exposed to their wanton insults. The fate of Hermogenes instructed Philip, the Prætorian præfect, to act with more precaution on a similar occasion. In the most gentle and honourable terms, he required the attendance of Paul in the baths of Zeuxippus, which had a private communication with the palace and the sea. A vessel, which lay ready at the garden-stairs, immediately hoisted sail; and, while the people were still ignorant of the meditated sacrilege, their bishop was already embarked on his voyage to Thessalonica. They soon beheld, with surprise and indignation, the gates of the palace thrown open, and the usurper Macedonius seated by the side of the præfect on a lofty chariot, which was surrounded by troops of guards with drawn swords. The military procession advanced towards the cathedral; the Arians and the Catholics eagerly rushed to occupy that important post; and three thousand one hundred and fifty persons lost their lives in the confusion of the tumult. Macedonius, who was supported by a regular force, obtained a decisive victory; but his reign was disturbed by clamour and sedition; and the causes which appeared the least connected with the subject of dispute were sufficient to nourish and to kindle the flame of civil

[13] Cucusus was the last stage of his life and sufferings. The situation of that lonely town, on the confines of Cappadocia, Cilicia, and the Lesser Armenia, has occasioned some geographical perplexity; but we are directed to the true spot by the course of the Roman road from Cæsarea to Anazarbus.

[14] Athanasius affirms, in the most positive terms, that Paul was murdered; and appeals, not only to common fame, but even to the unsuspicious testimony of Philagrius, one of the Arian persecutors. Yet he acknowledges that the heretics attributed to disease the death of the bishop of Constantinople. Athanasius is servilely copied by Socrates; but Sozomen, who discovers a more liberal temper, presumes to insinuate a prudent doubt.

discord. As the chapel in which the body of the great Constantine had been deposited was in a ruinous condition, the bishops transported those venerable remains into the church of St. Acacius. This prudent and even pious measure was represented as a wicked profanation by the whole party which adhered to the Homoousian doctrine. The factions immediately flew to arms, the consecrated ground was used as their field of battle; and one of the ecclesiastical historians has observed, as a real fact, not as a figure of rhetoric, that the well before the church overflowed with a stream of blood, which filled the porticoes and the adjacent courts. The writer who should impute these tumults solely to a religious principle would betray a very imperfect knowledge of human nature; yet it must be confessed that the motive which misled the sincerity of zeal, and the pretence which disguised the licentiousness of passion, suppressed the remorse which, in another cause, would have succeeded to the rage of the Christians of Constantinople.

The cruel and arbitrary disposition of Constantius, which did not always require the provocations of guilt and resistance, was justly exasperated by the tumults of his capital and the criminal behaviour of a faction, which opposed the authority and religion of their sovereign. The ordinary punishments of death, exile, and confiscation were inflicted with partial rigour; and the Greeks still revere the holy memory of two clerks, a reader and a sub-deacon, who were accused of the murder of Hermogenes, and beheaded at the gates of Constantinople. By an edict of Constantius against the Catholics, which has not been judged worthy of a place in the Theodosian code, those who refused to communicate with the Arian bishops, and particularly with Macedonius, were deprived of the immunities of ecclesiastics and of the rights of Christians; they were compelled to relinquish the possession of the churches; and were strictly prohibited from holding their assemblies within the walls of the city. The execution of this unjust law, in the provinces of Thrace and Asia Minor, was committed to the zeal of Macedonius; the civil and military powers were directed to obey his commands; and the cruelties exercised by this Semi-Arian tyrant in the support of the *Homoiousion,* exceeded the commission, and disgraced the reign, of Constantius. The sacraments of the church were administered to the reluctant victims, who denied the vocation, and abhorred the principles, of Macedonius. The rites of baptism were conferred on women and children, who, for that purpose, had been torn from the arms of their friends and parents; the mouths of the communicants were held open, by a wooden engine, while the consecrated bread was forced down their throat; the breasts of tender virgins were either burnt with red-hot egg-shells or inhumanly compressed between sharp and heavy boards.[75] The Novatians of Constantinople and the adjacent country, by their firm attachment to the Homoousian standard, deserved to be confounded with the Catholics themselves. Macedonius was informed that a large district of Paphlagonia was almost entirely inhabited by those sectaries. He resolved either to convert or to extirpate them; and, as he distrusted, on this occasion, the efficacy of an ecclesiastical mission, he commanded a body of four thousand legionaries to march against the rebels, and to reduce the territory of Mantinium under his spiritual dominion. The Novatian peasants, animated by despair and religious fury, boldly encountered the invaders of their country; and, though many of the Paphlagonians were slain, the Roman legions were vanquished by an irregular multitude, armed only with scythes and axes; and, except a few who escaped by an ignominious flight, four thousand soldiers were left dead on the field of battle. The successor of Constantius has expressed, in a concise but lively manner, some of the theological calamities which afflicted the empire, and more especially the East, in the reign of a prince who was the slave of his own passions and of those of his eunuchs. "Many were imprisoned, and persecuted, and driven into exile. Whole troops of those who were styled heretics were massacred, particularly at Cyzicus, and at Samosata. In Paphlagonia, Bithynia, Galatia, and in many other provinces, towns and villages were laid waste and utterly destroyed."

While the flames of the Arian controversy consumed the vitals of the empire, the African provinces were infested by their peculiar enemies the savage fanatics, who, under the name of *Circumcellions,* formed the strength and scandal of the Donatist party. The severe execution of the laws of Constantine had excited a spirit of discontent and resistance; the strenuous efforts of his son Constans to restore the unity of the church exasperated the sentiments of mutual hatred which had first occasioned the separation; and the methods of force and corruption employed by the two Imperial commissioners, Paul and Macarius, furnished the schismatics with a specious contrast between the maxims of the apostles and the conduct of their pretended successors. The peasants who inhabited the villages of Numidia and Mauritania were a ferocious race, who had been imperfectly reduced under the authority of the Roman

[75] *The principal assistants of Macedonius, in the work of persecution, were the two bishops of Nicomedia and Cyzicus, who were esteemed for their virtues, and especially for their charity. I cannot forbear reminding the reader that the difference between the* Homoousion *and* Homoiousion *is almost invisible to the nicest theological eye.*

laws; who were imperfectly converted to the Christian faith; but who were actuated by a blind and furious enthusiasm in the cause of their Donatist teachers. They indignantly supported the exile of their bishops, the demolition of their churches, and the interruption of their secret assemblies. The violence of the officers of justice, who were usually sustained by a military guard, was sometimes repelled with equal violence; and the blood of some popular ecclesiastics, which had been shed in the quarrel, inflamed their rude followers with an eager desire of revenging the death of these holy martyrs. By their own cruelty and rashness, the ministers of persecution sometimes provoked their fate; and the guilt of an accidental tumult precipitated the criminals into despair and rebellion. Driven from their native villages, the Donatist peasants assembled in formidable gangs on the edge of the Gætulian desert; and readily exchanged the habits of labour for a life of idleness and rapine, which was consecrated by the name of religion and faintly condemned by the doctors of the sect. The leaders of the Circumcellions assumed the title of captains of the saints; their principal weapon, as they were indifferently provided with swords and spears, was a huge and weighty club, which they termed an *Israelite;* and the well-known sound of "Praise be to God," which they used as their cry of war, diffused consternation over the unarmed provinces of Africa. At first their depredations were coloured by the plea of necessity; but they soon exceeded the measure of subsistence, indulged without control their intemperance and avarice, burnt the villages which they had pillaged, and reigned the licentious tyrants of the open country. The occupations of husbandry, and the administration of justice, were interrupted; and, as the Circumcellions pretended to restore the primitive equality of mankind and to reform the abuses of civil society, they opened a secure asylum for the slaves and debtors, who flocked in crowds to their holy standard. When they were not resisted, they usually contented themselves with plunder, but the slightest opposition provoked them to acts of violence and murder; and some Catholic priests, who had imprudently signalized their zeal, were tortured by the fanatics with the most refined and wanton barbarity. The spirit of the Circumcellions was not always exerted against their defenceless enemies; they engaged, and sometimes defeated, the troops of the province; and in the bloody action of Bagai, they attacked in the open field, but with unsuccessful valour, an advanced guard of the Imperial cavalry. The Donatists who were taken in arms received, and they soon deserved, the same treatment which might have been shown to the wild beasts of the desert. The captives died, without a murmur, either by the sword, the axe, or the fire; and the measures of retaliation were multiplied in a rapid proportion, which aggravated the horrors of rebellion, and excluded the hope of mutual forgiveness. In the beginning of the present century, the example of the Circumcellions has been renewed in the persecution, the boldness, the crimes, and the enthusiasm of the Camisards; and, if the fanatics of Languedoc surpassed those of Numidia by their military achievements, the Africans maintained their fierce independence with more resolution and perseverance.

Such disorders are the natural effects of religious tyranny; but the rage of the Donatists was inflamed by a frenzy of a very extraordinary kind; and which, if it really prevailed among them in so extravagant a degree, cannot surely be paralleled in any country or in any age. Many of these fanatics were possessed with the horror of life, and the desire of martyrdom; and they deemed it of little moment by what means, or by what hands, they perished, if their conduct was sanctified by the intention of devoting themselves to the glory of the true faith and the hope of eternal happiness.[76] Sometimes they rudely disturbed the festivals and profaned the temples of Paganism, with the design of exciting the most zealous of the idolaters to revenge the insulted honour of their gods. They sometimes forced their way into the courts of justice, and compelled the affrighted judge to give orders for their immediate execution. They frequently stopped travellers on the public highways, and obliged them to inflict the stroke of martyrdom, by the promise of a reward, if they consented, and by the threat of instant death, if they refused to grant so very singular a favour. When they were disappointed of every other resource, they announced the day on which, in the presence of their friends and brethren, they should cast themselves headlong from some lofty rock; and many precipices were shown, which had acquired fame by the number of religious suicides. In the actions of these desperate enthusiasts, who were admired by one party as the martyrs of God, and abhorred by the other as the victims of Satan, an impartial philosopher may discover the influence and the last abuse of that inflexible spirit, which was originally derived from the character and principles of the Jewish nation.

The simple narrative of the intestine divisions, which distracted the peace, and dishonoured the triumph, of the church, will con-

[76] *The Donatist suicides alleged in their justification the example of Razias, which is related in the fourteenth chapter of the second book of the Maccabees.*

firm the remark of a Pagan historian, and justify the complaint of a venerable bishop. The experience of Ammianus had convinced him that the enmity of the Christians towards each other surpassed the fury of savage beasts against man; and Gregory Nazianzen most pathetically laments that the kingdom of heaven was converted, by discord, into the image of chaos, of a nocturnal tempest, and of hell itself. The fierce and partial writers of the times, ascribing *all* virtue to themselves, and imputing *all* guilt to their adversaries, have painted the battle of the angels and dæmons. Our calmer reason will reject such pure and perfect monsters of vice or sanctity, and will impute an equal, or at least an indiscriminate, measure of good and evil to the hostile sectaries, who assumed and bestowed the appellations of orthodox and heretics. They had been educated in the same religion, and the same civil society. Their hopes and fears in the present, or in a future, life were balanced in the same proportion. On either side, the error might be innocent, the faith sincere, the practice meritorious or corrupt. Their passions were excited by similar objects; and they might alternately abuse the favour of the court, or of the people. The metaphysical opinions of the Athanasians and the Arians could not influence their moral character; and they were alike actuated by the intolerant spirit which has been extracted from the pure and simple maxims of the gospel.

A modern writer, who, with a just confidence, has prefixed to his own history the honourable epithets of political and philosophical, accuses the timid prudence of Montesquieu for neglecting to enumerate, among the causes of the decline of the empire, a law of Constantine, by which the exercise of the Pagan worship was absolutely suppressed, and a considerable part of his subjects was left destitute of priests, of temples, and of any public religion. The zeal of the philosophic historian for the rights of mankind has induced him to acquiesce in the ambiguous testimony of those ecclesiastics, who have too lightly ascribed to their favourite hero the *merit* of a general persecution. Instead of alleging this imaginary law, which would have blazed in the front of the Imperial codes, we may safely appeal to the original epistle which Constantine addressed to the followers of the ancient religion; at a time when he no longer disguised his conversion nor dreaded the rivals of his throne. He invites and exhorts, in the most pressing terms, the subjects of the Roman empire to imitate the example of their master; but he declares that those who still refuse to open their

[11] *These acts of authority may be compared with the suppression of the Bacchanals, and the demolition of the temple of Isis, by the magistrates of Pagan Rome.*

[18] *Eusebius and Libanius both mention the pious sacrilege of Constantine, which they viewed in very different lights. The latter expressly declares*

eyes to the celestial light may freely enjoy their temples and their fancied gods. A report that the ceremonies of Paganism were suppressed is formally contradicted by the emperor himself, who wisely assigns, as the principle of his moderation, the invincible force of habit, of prejudice, and of superstition. Without violating the sanctity of his promise, without alarming the fears of the Pagans, the artful monarch advanced, by slow and cautious steps, to undermine the irregular and decayed fabric of Polytheism. The partial acts of severity which he occasionally exercised, though they were secretly prompted by a Christian zeal, were coloured by the fairest pretences of justice and the public good; and, while Constantine designed to ruin the foundations, he seemed to reform the abuses, of the ancient religion. After the example of the wisest of his predecessors, he condemned, under the most rigorous penalties, the occult and impious arts of divination; which excited the vain hopes, and sometimes the criminal attempts, of those who were discontented with their present condition. An ignominious silence was imposed on the oracles, which had been publicly convicted of fraud and falsehood; the effeminate priests of the Nile were abolished; and Constantine discharged the duties of a Roman censor, when he gave orders for the demolition of several temples of Phœnicia, in which every mode of prostitution was devoutly practised in the face of day, and to the honour of Venus.[77] The Imperial city of Constantinople was, in some measure, raised at the expense, and was adorned with the spoils, of the opulent temples of Greece and Asia; the sacred property was confiscated; the statues of gods and heroes were transported, with rude familiarity, among a people who considered them as objects, not of adoration, but of curiosity: the gold and silver were restored to circulation; and the magistrates, the bishops, and the eunuchs, improved the fortunate occasion of gratifying at once their zeal, their avarice, and their resentment. But these depredations were confined to a small part of the Roman world; and the provinces had been long since accustomed to endure the same sacrilegious rapine, from the tyranny of princes and proconsuls, who could not be suspected of any design to subvert the established religion.[78]

The sons of Constantine trod in the footsteps of their father, with more zeal and with less discretion. The pretences of rapine and oppression were insensibly multiplied;[79] every indulgence was shown to the illegal behaviour of the Christians; every doubt was explained to the disadvantage of Paganism; and the demolition of

that "he made use of the sacred money, but made no alteration in the legal worship; the temples indeed were impoverished, but the sacred rites were performed there."

[79] Ammianus speaks of some court eunuchs who were spoliis templorum pasti. Libanius says that the emperor often gave away a temple, like a dog, or a horse, or a slave, or a gold cup: but the devout philosopher takes care to observe that these sacrilegious favourites very seldom prospered.

[80] As I have freely anticipated the use of pagans and paganism, I shall now trace the singular revolutions of those celebrated words. 1. Παγή, in the Doric dialect, so familiar to the Italians, signifies a fountain; and the rural neighbourhood which frequented the same fountain derived the common appellation of pagus and pagans. 2. By an easy extension of the word, pagan and rural became almost synonymous; and the meaner rustics acquired that name, which has been corrupted into peasants in the modern languages of Europe. 3. The amazing increase of the military order introduced the necessity of

a correlative term; and all the people *who were not enlisted in the service of the prince were branded with the contemptuous epithet of pagans. 4. The Christians were the soldiers of Christ; their adversaries, who refused his* sacrament, *or military oath of baptism, might deserve the metaphorical name of pagans: and this popular reproach was introduced as early as the reign of Valentinian (*A.D. *365) into Imperial laws (Cod. Theodos.) and theological writings. 5. Christianity gradually filled the cities of the empire; the old religion, in the time of Prudentius and Orosius, retired and languished in obscure villages; and the word* pagans, *with its new signification, reverted to its primitive origin. 6. Since the worship of Jupiter and his family has expired, the vacant title of pagans has been successively applied to all the idolaters and polytheists of the old and new world. 7. The Latin Christians bestowed it, without scruple, on their mortal enemies the Mahometans; and the purest* unitarians *were branded with the unjust reproach of idolatry and paganism.*

[81] *In the pure language of Ionia and Athens,*

the temples was celebrated as one of the auspicious events of the reign of Constans and Constantius. The name of Constantius is prefixed to a concise law, which might have superseded the necessity of any future prohibitions. "It is our pleasure that in all places, and in all cities, the temples be immediately shut, and carefully guarded, that none may have the power of offending. It is likewise our pleasure that all our subjects should abstain from sacrifices. If any one should be guilty of such an act, let him feel the sword of vengeance, and, after his execution, let his property be confiscated to the public use. We denounce the same penalties against the governors of the provinces, if they neglect to punish the criminals." But there is the strongest reason to believe that this formidable edict was either composed without being published, or was published without being executed. The evidence of facts, and the monuments which are still extant of brass and marble, continue to prove the public exercise of the Pagan worship during the whole reign of the sons of Constantine. In the east, as well as in the west, in cities, as well as in the country, a great number of temples were respected, or at least were spared; and the devout multitude still enjoyed the luxury of sacrifices, of festivals, and of processions, by the permission, or by the connivance, of the civil government. About four years after the supposed date of his bloody edict, Constantius visited the temples of Rome; and the decency of his behaviour is recommended by a Pagan orator as an example worthy of the imitation of succeeding princes. "That emperor," says Symmachus, "suffered the privileges of the vestal virgins to remain inviolate; he bestowed the sacerdotal dignities on the nobles of Rome, granted the customary allowance to defray the expenses of the public rites and sacrifices: and, though he had embraced a different religion, he never attempted to deprive the empire of the sacred worship of antiquity." The senate still presumed to consecrate, by solemn decrees, the *divine* memory of their sovereigns; and Constantine himself was associated, after his death, to those gods whom he had renounced and insulted during his life. The title, the ensigns, the prerogatives of SOVEREIGN PONTIFF, which had been instituted by Numa, and assumed by Augustus, were accepted, without hesitation, by seven Christian emperors; who were invested with a more absolute authority over the religion which they had deserted than over that which they professed.

The divisions of Christianity suspended the ruin of *paganism;*[80]

and the holy war against the infidels was less vigorously prosecuted by princes and bishops who were more immediately alarmed by the guilt and danger of domestic rebellion. The extirpation of *idolatry* [81] might have been justified by the established principles of intolerance: but the hostile sects, which alternately reigned in the Imperial court, were mutually apprehensive of alienating, and perhaps exasperating, the minds of a powerful, though declining, faction. Every motive of authority and fashion, of interest and reason, now militated on the side of Christianity; but two or three generations elapsed before their victorious influence was universally felt. The religion which had so long and so lately been established in the Roman empire was still revered by a numerous people, less attached indeed to speculative opinion than to ancient custom. The honours of the state and army were indifferently bestowed on all the subjects of Constantine and Constantius; and a considerable portion of knowledge and wealth and valour was still engaged in the service of Polytheism. The superstition of the senator and of the peasant, of the poet and the philosopher, was derived from very different causes, but they met with equal devotion in the temples of the gods. Their zeal was insensibly provoked by the insulting triumph of a proscribed sect; and their hopes were revived by the well-grounded confidence that the presumptive heir of the empire, a young and valiant hero, who had delivered Gaul from the arms of the Barbarians, had secretly embraced the religion of his ancestors.

Εἴδωλον *and* Λατρεία *were ancient and familiar words. The former expressed a likeness, an apparition, a representation, an image, created either by fancy or art. The latter denoted any* sort *of* service or slavery. *The Jews of Egypt, who translated the Hebrew scriptures, restrained the use of these words to the religious worship of an image. The peculiar idiom of the Hellenists, or Grecian Jews, has been adopted by the sacred and ecclesiastical writers; and the reproach of* idolatry (Εἰδωλολατρεία) *has stigmatized that visible and abject mode of superstition which some sects of Christianity should not hastily impute to the polytheists of Greece and Rome.*

XXII

JULIAN IS DECLARED EMPEROR BY THE LEGIONS OF GAUL ·
HIS MARCH AND SUCCESS · THE DEATH OF CONSTANTIUS ·
CIVIL ADMINISTRATION OF JULIAN · HIS FINE CHARACTER

W HILE the Romans languished under the tyranny of eunuchs and bishops, the praises of Julian were repeated with transport in every part of the empire, except in the palace of Constantius. The Barbarians of Germany had felt, and still dreaded, the arms of the young Cæsar; his soldiers were the companions of his victory; the grateful provincials enjoyed the blessings of his reign; but the favourites who had opposed his elevation were offended by his virtues; and they justly considered the friend of the people as the enemy of the court. As long as the fame of Julian was doubtful, the buffoons of the palace, who were skilled in the language of satire, tried the efficacy of those arts which they had so often practised with success. They easily discovered that his simplicity was not exempt from affectation: the ridiculous epithets of an hairy savage, of an ape invested with the purple, were applied to the dress and person of the philosophic warrior; and his modest dispatches were stigmatized as the vain and elaborate fictions of a loquacious Greek, a speculative soldier, who had studied the art of war amidst the groves of the academy. The voice of malicious folly was at length silenced by the shouts of victory; the conqueror of the Franks and Alemanni could no longer be painted as an object of contempt; and the monarch himself was meanly ambitious of stealing from his lieutenant the honourable reward of his labours. In the letters crowned with laurel, which, according to ancient custom, were addressed to the provinces, the name of Julian was omitted. "Constantius had made his dispositions in person; *he* had signalized his valour in the foremost ranks; *his* military conduct had secured the victory; and the captive king of the Barbarians was presented to *him* on the field of battle," from which he was at that time distant about forty days' journey.[1] So ex-

[1] *The orator Themistius believed whatever was contained in the Imperial letters which were addressed to the senate of Constantinople. Aurelius Victor, who published his Abridgment in the last year of Constantius, ascribes the German victories to the* wisdom of the emperor, and the fortune of the Cæsar. *Yet the historian, soon afterwards, was indebted to the favour or esteem of Julian for the honour of a brass statue, and the important offices of consular of the second Pannonia, and præfect of the city.*

travagant a fable was incapable, however, of deceiving the public credulity, or even of satisfying the pride of the emperor himself. Secretly conscious that the applause and favour of the Romans accompanied the rising fortunes of Julian, his discontented mind was prepared to receive the subtle poison of those artful sycophants who coloured their mischievous designs with the fairest appearances of truth and candour. Instead of depreciating the merits of Julian, they acknowledged, and even exaggerated, his popular fame, superior talents, and important services. But they darkly insinuated that the virtues of the Cæsar might instantly be converted into the most dangerous crimes, if the inconstant multitude should prefer their inclinations to their duty; or if the general of a victorious army should be tempted from his allegiance by the hopes of revenge and independent greatness. The personal fears of Constantius were interpreted by his council as a laudable anxiety for the public safety; whilst in private, and perhaps in his own breast, he disguised, under the less odious appellation of fear, the sentiments of hatred and envy, which he had secretly conceived for the virtues of Julian.

The apparent tranquillity of Gaul and the imminent danger of the eastern provinces offered a specious pretence for the design which was artfully concerted by the Imperial ministers. They resolved to disarm the Cæsar; to recall those faithful troops who guarded his person and dignity; and to employ in a distant war against the Persian monarch the hardy veterans who had vanquished, on the banks of the Rhine, the fiercest nations of Germany. While Julian used the laborious hours of his winter quarters at Paris in the administration of power, which, in his hands, was the exercise of virtue, he was surprised by the hasty arrival of a tribune and a notary, with positive orders from the emperor, which *they* were directed to execute, and *he* was commanded not to oppose. Constantius signified his pleasure, that four entire legions, the Celtæ, and Petulants, the Heruli, and the Batavians, should be separated from the standard of Julian, under which they had acquired their fame and discipline; that in each of the remaining bands three hundred of the bravest youths should be selected; and that this numerous detachment, the strength of the Gallic army, should instantly begin their march, and exert their utmost diligence to arrive, before the opening of the campaign, on the frontiers of Persia.[2] The Cæsar foresaw, and lamented, the consequences of this fatal mandate. Most of the auxiliaries, who engaged their voluntary service, had stipulated that they should never be obliged to pass the Alps. The

[2] *The minute interval, which may be interposed, between the* hyeme adultâ *and the* primo vere *of Ammianus, instead of allowing a sufficient space for a march of three thousand miles, would render the orders of Constantius as extravagant as they were unjust. The troops of Gaul could not have reached Syria till the end of autumn. The memory of Ammianus must have been inaccurate, and his language incorrect.*

public faith of Rome and the personal honour of Julian had been pledged for the observance of this condition. Such an act of treachery and oppression would destroy the confidence, and excite the resentment, of the independent warriors of Germany, who considered truth as the noblest of their virtues, and freedom as the most valuable of their possessions. The legionaries, who enjoyed the title and privileges of Romans, were enlisted for the general defence of the republic; but those mercenary troops heard with cold indifference the antiquated names of the Republic and of Rome. Attached, either from birth or long habit, to the climate and manners of Gaul, they loved and admired Julian; they despised, and perhaps hated, the emperor; they dreaded the laborious march, the Persian arrows, and the burning deserts of Asia. They claimed as their own the country which they had saved; and excused their want of spirit by pleading the sacred and more immediate duty of protecting their families and friends. The apprehensions of the Gauls were derived from the knowledge of the impending and inevitable danger. As soon as the provinces were exhausted of their military strength, the Germans would violate a treaty which had been imposed on their fears; and, notwithstanding the abilities and valour of Julian, the general of a nominal army, to whom the public calamities would be imputed, must find himself, after a vain resistance, either a prisoner in the camp of the Barbarians or a criminal in the palace of Constantius. If Julian complied with the orders which he had received, he subscribed his own destruction, and that of a people who deserved his affection. But a positive refusal was an act of rebellion and a declaration of war. The inexorable jealousy of the emperor, the peremptory, and perhaps insidious, nature of his commands, left not any room for a fair apology or candid interpretation; and the dependent station of the Cæsar scarcely allowed him to pause or to deliberate. Solitude increased the perplexity of Julian; he could no longer apply to the faithful counsels of Sallust, who had been removed from his office by the judicious malice of the eunuchs: he could not even enforce his representations by the concurrence of the ministers, who would have been afraid or ashamed to approve the ruin of Gaul. The moment had been chosen, when Lupicinus,[3] the general of the cavalry, was dispatched into Britain, to repulse the inroads of the Scots and Picts; and Florentius was occupied at Vienna by the assessment of the tribute. The latter, a crafty and corrupt statesman, declining to assume a responsible part on this dangerous occasion, eluded the pressing and repeated invitations of

[3] *The valour of Lupicinus, and his military skill, are acknowledged by the historian, who, in his affected language, accuses the general of exalting the horns of his pride, bellowing in a tragic tone, and exciting a doubt whether he was more cruel or avaricious. The danger from the Scots and Picts was so serious that Julian himself had some thoughts of passing over into the island.*

Julian, who represented to him that in every important measure, the presence of the præfect was indispensable in the council of the prince. In the meanwhile the Cæsar was oppressed by the rude and importunate solicitations of the Imperial messengers, who presumed to suggest that, if he expected the return of his ministers, he would charge himself with the guilt of the delay, and reserve for them the merit of the execution. Unable to resist, unwilling to comply, Julian expressed, in the most serious terms, his wish, and even his intention, of resigning the purple, which he could not preserve with honour, but which he could not abdicate with safety.

After a painful conflict, Julian was compelled to acknowledge that obedience was the virtue of the most eminent subject, and that the sovereign alone was entitled to judge of the public welfare. He issued the necessary orders for carrying into execution the commands of Constantius; a part of the troops began their march for the Alps; and the detachments from the several garrisons moved towards their respective places of assembly. They advanced with difficulty through the trembling and affrighted crowds of provincials; who attempted to excite their pity by silent despair or loud lamentations; while the wives of the soldiers, holding their infants in their arms, accused the desertion of their husbands, in the mixed language of grief, of tenderness, and of indignation. This scene of general distress afflicted the humanity of the Cæsar; he granted a sufficient number of post-waggons to transport the wives and families of the soldiers,[4] endeavoured to alleviate the hardships which he was constrained to inflict, and increased, by the most laudable arts, his own popularity and the discontent of the exiled troops. The grief of an armed multitude is soon converted into rage; their licentious murmurs, which every hour were communicated from tent to tent with more boldness and effect, prepared their minds for the most daring acts of sedition; and by the connivance of their tribunes, a seasonable libel was secretly dispersed, which painted in lively colours the disgrace of the Cæsar, the oppression of the Gallic army, and the feeble vices of the tyrant of Asia. The servants of Constantius were astonished and alarmed by the progress of this dangerous spirit. They pressed the Cæsar to hasten the departure of the troops: but they imprudently rejected the honest and judicious advice of Julian; who proposed that they should not march through Paris, and suggested the danger and temptation of a last interview.

As soon as the approach of the troops was announced, the Cæsar went out to meet them, and ascended his tribunal, which had been

[4] *He granted them the permission of the* cursus clavularis, *or* clabularis. *These post-waggons are often mentioned in the Code, and were supposed to carry fifteen hundred pounds weight.*

erected in a plain before the gates of the city. After distinguishing the officers and soldiers who by their rank or merit deserved a peculiar attention, Julian addressed himself in a studied oration to the surrounding multitude: he celebrated their exploits with grateful applause: encouraged them to accept, with alacrity, the honour of serving under the eyes of a powerful and liberal monarch; and admonished them that the commands of Augustus required an instant and cheerful obedience. The soldiers, who were apprehensive of offending their general by an indecent clamour, or of belying their sentiments by false and venal acclamations, maintained an obstinate silence, and, after a short pause, were dismissed to their quarters. The principal officers were entertained by the Cæsar, who professed, in the warmest language of friendship, his desire and his inability to reward, according to their deserts, the brave companions of his victories. They retired from the feast, full of grief and perplexity; and lamented the hardship of their fate, which tore them from their beloved general and their native country. The only expedient which could prevent their separation was boldly agitated and approved; the popular resentment was insensibly moulded into a regular conspiracy; their just reasons of complaint were heightened by passion, and their passions were inflamed by wine; as, on the eve of their departure, the troops were indulged in licentious festivity. At the hour of midnight, the impetuous multitude, with swords and bowls and torches in their hands, rushed into the suburbs; encompassed the palace;[5] and, careless of future dangers, pronounced the fatal and irrevocable words, JULIAN AUGUSTUS! The prince, whose anxious suspense was interrupted by their disorderly acclamations, secured the doors against their intrusion; and, as long as it was in his power, secluded his person and dignity from the accidents of a nocturnal tumult. At the dawn of day, the soldiers, whose zeal was irritated by opposition, forcibly entered the palace, seized, with respectful violence, the object of their choice, guarded Julian with drawn swords through the streets of Paris, placed him on the tribunal, and with repeated shouts saluted him as their emperor. Prudence as well as loyalty inculcated the propriety of resisting their treasonable designs and of preparing for his oppressed virtue the excuse of violence. Addressing himself by turns to the multitude and to individuals, he sometimes implored their mercy, and sometimes expressed his indignation; conjured them not to sully the fame of their immortal victories; and ventured to promise that, if they would immediately return to their allegiance, he would

[5] Most probably the palace of the baths (Thermarum), of which a solid and lofty hall still subsists in the rue de la Harpe. The buildings covered a considerable space of the modern quarter of the University; and the gardens, under the Merovingian kings, communicated with the abbey of St. Germain des Prez. By the injuries of time and the Normans, this ancient palace was reduced, in the twelfth century, to a maze of ruins; whose dark recesses were the scene of licentious love.

undertake to obtain from the emperor, not only a free and gracious pardon, but even the revocation of the orders which had excited their resentment. But the soldiers, who were conscious of their guilt, chose rather to depend on the gratitude of Julian than on the clemency of the emperor. Their zeal was insensibly turned into impatience, and their impatience into rage. The inflexible Cæsar sustained, till the third hour of the day, their prayers, their reproaches, and their menaces; nor did he yield, till he had been repeatedly assured that, if he wished to live, he must consent to reign. He was exalted on a shield in the presence, and amidst the unanimous acclamations, of the troops; a rich military collar, which was offered by chance, supplied the want of a diadem;⁶ the ceremony was concluded by the promise of a moderate donative;⁷ and the new emperor, overwhelmed with real or affected grief, retired into the most secret recesses of his apartment.

The grief of Julian could proceed only from his innocence; but his innocence must appear extremely doubtful in the eyes of those who have learned to suspect the motives and the professions of princes. His lively and active mind was susceptible of the various impressions of hope and fear, of gratitude and revenge, of duty and of ambition, of the love of fame and of the fear of reproach. But it is impossible for us to calculate the respective weight and operation of these sentiments; or to ascertain the principles of action, which might escape the observation, while they guided or rather impelled the steps, of Julian himself. The discontent of the troops was produced by the malice of his enemies; their tumult was the natural effect of interest and of passion; and, if Julian had tried to conceal a deep design under the appearances of chance, he must have employed the most consummate artifice without necessity, and probably without success. He solemnly declares, in the presence of Jupiter, of the Sun, of Mars, of Minerva, and of all the other deities, that, till the close of the evening which preceded his elevation, he was utterly ignorant of the designs of the soldiers; and it may seem ungenerous to distrust the honour of a hero and the truth of a philosopher. Yet the superstitious confidence that Constantius was the enemy, and that he himself was the favourite, of the gods, might prompt him to desire, to solicit, and even to hasten the auspicious moment of his reign, which was predestined to restore the ancient religion of mankind. When Julian had received the intelligence of the conspiracy, he resigned himself to a short slumber; and afterwards related to his friends that he had seen the Genius of the em-

⁶ *Even in this tumultuous moment, Julian attended to the forms of superstitious ceremony, and obstinately refused the inauspicious use of a female necklace, or a horse-collar, which the impatient soldiers would have employed in the room of a diadem.*

⁷ *An equal proportion of gold and silver, five pieces of the former, one pound of the latter; the whole amounting to about five pounds ten shillings of our money.*

pire waiting with some impatience at his door, pressing for admittance, and reproaching his want of spirit and ambition. Astonished and perplexed, he addressed his prayers to the great Jupiter; who immediately signified, by a clear and manifest omen, that he should submit to the will of heaven and of the army. The conduct which disclaims the ordinary maxims of reason excites our suspicion and eludes our inquiry. Whenever the spirit of fanaticism, at once so credulous and so crafty, has insinuated itself into a noble mind, it insensibly corrodes the vital principles of virtue and veracity.

To moderate the zeal of his party, to protect the persons of his enemies, to defeat and to despise the secret enterprises which were formed against his life and dignity, were the cares which employed the first days of the reign of the new emperor. Although he was firmly resolved to maintain the station which he had assumed, he was still desirous of saving his country from the calamities of civil war, of declining a contest with the superior forces of Constantine, and of preserving his own character from the reproach of perfidy and ingratitude. Adorned with the ensigns of military and Imperial pomp, Julian showed himself in the field of Mars to the soldiers, who glowed with ardent enthusiasm in the cause of their pupil, their leader, and their friend. He recapitulated their victories, lamented their sufferings, applauded their resolution, animated their hopes, and checked their impetuosity; nor did he dismiss the assembly, till he had obtained a solemn promise from the troops that, if the emperor of the East would subscribe an equitable treaty, they would renounce any views of conquest, and satisfy themselves with the tranquil possession of the Gallic provinces. On this foundation he composed, in his own name, and in that of the army, a specious and moderate epistle, which was delivered to Pentadius, his master of the offices, and to his chamberlain Eutherius; two ambassadors whom he appointed to receive the answer, and observe the dispositions, of Constantius. This epistle is inscribed with the modest appellation of Cæsar; but Julian solicits in a peremptory, though respectful, manner the confirmation of the title of Augustus. He acknowledges the irregularity of his own election, while he justifies, in some measure, the resentment and violence of the troops which had extorted his reluctant consent. He allows the supremacy of his brother Constantius; and engages to send him an annual present of Spanish horses, to recruit his army with a select number of Barbarian youths, and to accept from his choice a Prætorian præfect of approved discretion and fidelity. But he reserves for himself the nomination of his other civil and military officers, with the troops, the revenue, and the sovereignty of the provinces beyond the Alps. He admonishes the emperor to consult the dictates of justice; to distrust the arts of those venal flatterers who subsist only by the discord of princes; and to embrace the offer of a fair and honourable treaty, equally advantageous to the republic and to the house of Constantine. In this negotiation Julian claimed no more than he already possessed. The delegated authority which he had long exercised over the provinces of Gaul, Spain, and Britain was still obeyed under a name more independent and august. The soldiers and the people rejoiced in a revolution which was not stained even with the blood of the guilty. Florentius was a fugitive; Lupicinus a prisoner. The persons who were disaffected to the new government were disarmed and secured; and the vacant offices were distributed, according to the recommendation of merit, by a prince who despised the intrigues of the palace and the clamours of the soldiers.

The negotiations of peace were accompanied and supported by the most vigorous preparations for war. The army, which Julian held in readiness for immediate action, was recruited and augmented by the disorders of the times. The cruel persecution of the faction of Magnentius had filled Gaul with numerous bands of outlaws and robbers. They cheerfully accepted the offer of a general pardon from a prince whom they could trust, submitted to the restraints of military discipline, and retained only their implacable hatred to the person and government of Constantius. As soon as the season of the year permitted Julian to take the field, he appeared at the head of his legions; threw a bridge over the Rhine in the neighbourhood of Cleves; and prepared to chastise the perfidy of the Attuarii, a tribe of Franks, who presumed that they might ravage, with impunity, the frontiers of a divided empire. The difficulty, as well as glory, of this enterprise, consisted in a laborious march; and Julian had conquered, as soon as he could penetrate into, a country which former princes had considered as inaccessible. After he had given peace to the Barbarians, the emperor carefully visited the fortifications along the Rhine from Cleves to Basil; surveyed, with peculiar attention, the territories which he had recovered from the hands of the Alemanni, passed through Besançon,[8] which had severely suffered from their fury, and fixed his headquarters at Vienna for the ensuing winter. The barrier of Gaul was improved and strengthened with additional fortifications; and Julian enter-

[8] *Julian gives a short description of Vesontio, or Besançon; a rocky peninsula almost encircled by the river Doux; once a magnificent city, filled with temples, &c., now reduced to a small town, emerging however from its ruins.*

tained some hopes that the Germans, whom he had so often vanquished, might, in his absence, be restrained by the terror of his name. Vadomair [9] was the only prince of the Alemanni whom he esteemed or feared; and, while the subtle Barbarian affected to observe the faith of treaties, the progress of his arms threatened the state with an unseasonable and dangerous war. The policy of Julian condescended to surprise the prince of the Alemanni by his own arts; and Vadomair who, in the character of a friend, had incautiously accepted an invitation from the Roman governors, was seized in the midst of the entertainment, and sent away prisoner into the heart of Spain. Before the Barbarians were recovered from their amazement, the emperor appeared in arms on the banks of the Rhine, and, once more crossing the river, renewed the deep impressions of terror and respect which had been already made by four preceding expeditions.

The ambassadors of Julian had been instructed to execute, with the utmost diligence, their important commission. But in their passage through Italy and Illyricum, they were detained by the tedious and affected delays of the provincial governors; they were conducted by slow journeys from Constantinople to Cæsarea in Cappadocia; and, when at length they were admitted to the presence of Constantius, they found that he had already conceived, from the dispatches of his own officers, the most unfavourable opinion of the conduct of Julian and of the Gallic army. The letters were heard with impatience; the trembling messengers were dismissed with indignation and contempt; and the looks, the gestures, the furious language of the monarch expressed the disorder of his soul. The domestic connexion, which might have reconciled the brother and the husband of Helena, was recently dissolved by the death of that princess, whose pregnancy had been several times fruitless, and was at last fatal to herself. [10] The empress Eusebia had preserved, to the last moment of her life, the warm and even jealous affection which she had conceived for Julian; and her mild influence might have moderated the resentment of a prince who, since her death, was abandoned to his own passions and to the arts of his eunuchs. But the terror of a foreign invasion obliged him to suspend the punishment of a private enemy; he continued his march towards the confines of Persia, and thought it sufficient to signify the conditions which might entitle Julian and his guilty followers to the clemency of their offended sovereign. He required that the presumptuous Cæsar should expressly renounce the appellation and rank of Augustus, which he

[9] *Vadomair entered into the Roman service, and was promoted from a Barbarian kingdom to the military rank of duke of Phœnicia. He still retained the same artful character: but, under the reign of Valens, he signalized his valour in the Armenian war.*

[10] *Her remains were sent to Rome, and interred near those of her sister Constantina, in the suburb of the Via Nomentana. Libanius has composed a very weak apology to justify his hero from a very absurd charge; of poisoning his wife, and rewarding her physician with his mother's jewels. Elpidius, the Prætorian præfect of the East, to whose evidence the accuser of Julian appeals, is arraigned by Libanius as effeminate and ungrateful; yet the religion of Elpidius is praised by Jerom, and his humanity by Ammianus.*

had accepted from the rebels; that he should descend to his former station of a limited and dependent minister; that he should vest the powers of the state and army in the hands of those officers who were appointed by the Imperial court; and that he should trust his safety to the assurances of pardon, which were announced by Epictetus, a Gallic bishop, and one of the Arian favourites of Constantius. Several months were ineffectually consumed in a treaty which was negotiated at the distance of three thousand miles between Paris and Antioch; and, as soon as Julian perceived that his moderate and respectful behaviour served only to irritate the pride of an implacable adversary, he boldly resolved to commit his life and fortune to the chance of a civil war. He gave a public and military audience to the quæstor Leonas: the haughty epistle of Constantius was read to the attentive multitude; and Julian protested, with the most flattering deference, that he was ready to resign the title of Augustus, if he could obtain the consent of those whom he acknowledged as the authors of his elevation. The faint proposal was impetuously silenced; and the acclamations of "Julian Augustus, continue to reign, by the authority of the army, of the people, of the republic, which you have saved," thundered at once from every part of the field, and terrified the pale ambassador of Constantius. A part of the letter was afterwards read, in which the emperor arraigned the ingratitude of Julian, whom he had invested with the honours of the purple; whom he had educated with so much care and tenderness; whom he had preserved in his infancy, when he was left a helpless orphan; "an orphan!" interrupted Julian, who justified his cause by indulging his passions; "does the assassin of my family reproach me that I was left an orphan? He urges me to revenge those injuries which I have long studied to forget." The assembly was dismissed; and Leonas, who, with some difficulty, had been protected from the popular fury, was sent back to his master, with an epistle, in which Julian expressed, in a strain of the most vehement eloquence, the sentiments of contempt, of hatred, and of resentment, which had been suppressed and embittered by the dissimulation of twenty years. After this message, which might be considered as a signal of irreconcilable war, Julian, who some weeks before had celebrated the Christian festival of the Epiphany, made a public declaration that he committed the care of his safety to the IMMORTAL GODS; and thus publicly renounced the religion, as well as the friendship, of Constantius.

The situation of Julian required a vigorous and immediate resolution. He had discovered from intercepted letters that his adversary, sacrificing the interest of the state to that of the monarch, had again excited the Barbarians to invade the provinces of the West. The position of two magazines, one of them collected on the banks of the lake of Constance, the other formed at the foot of the Cottian Alps, seemed to indicate the march of two armies; and the size of those magazines, each of which consisted of six hundred thousand quarters of wheat, or rather flour,[11] was a threatening evidence of the strength and numbers of the enemy, who prepared to surround him. But the Imperial legions were still in their distant quarters of Asia; the Danube was feebly guarded; and, if Julian could occupy by a sudden incursion the important provinces of Illyricum, he might expect that a people of soldiers would resort to his standard, and that the rich mines of gold and silver would contribute to the expenses of the civil war. He proposed this bold enterprise to the assembly of the soldiers; inspired them with a just confidence in their general and in themselves; and exhorted them to maintain their reputation, of being terrible to the enemy, moderate to their fellow-citizens, and obedient to their officers. His spirited discourse was received with the loudest acclamations, and the same troops which had taken up his arms against Constantius, when he summoned them to leave Gaul, now declared with alacrity, that they would follow Julian to the farthest extremities of Europe or Asia. The oath of fidelity was administered; and the soldiers, clashing their shields, and pointing their drawn swords to their throats, devoted themselves, with horrid imprecations, to the service of a leader whom they celebrated as the deliverer of Gaul and the conqueror of the Germans. This solemn engagement, which seemed to be dictated by affection rather than by duty, was singly opposed by Nebridius, who had been admitted to the office of Prætorian præfect. That faithful minister, alone and unassisted, asserted the rights of Constantius in the midst of an armed and angry multitude, to whose fury he had almost fallen an honourable, but useless, sacrifice. After losing one of his hands by the stroke of a sword, he embraced the knees of the prince whom he had offended. Julian covered the præfect with his Imperial mantle, and, protecting him from the zeal of his followers, dismissed him to his own house, with less respect than was perhaps due to the virtue of an enemy.[12] The high office of Nebridius was bestowed on Sallust; and the provinces of Gaul, which were now delivered from the intolerable oppression of taxes, enjoyed the mild and equitable administration of the

[11] Three hundred myriads or three millions of medimni, a corn-measure familiar to the Athenians, and which contained six Roman modii. Julian explains, like a soldier and a statesman, the danger of his situation, and the necessity and advantages of an offensive war.

[12] He sternly refused his hand to the suppliant præfect, whom he sent into Tuscany. Libanius, with savage fury, insults Nebridius, applauds the soldiers, and almost censures the humanity of Julian.

friend of Julian, who was permitted to practise those virtues which he had instilled into the mind of his pupil.

The hopes of Julian depended much less on the number of his troops than on the celerity of his motions. In the execution of a daring enterprise, he availed himself of every precaution, as far as prudence could suggest; and, where prudence could no longer accompany his steps, he trusted the event to valour and to fortune. In the neighbourhood of Basil he assembled and divided his army. One body, which consisted of ten thousand men, was directed, under the command of Nevitta, general of the cavalry, to advance through the midland parts of Rhætia and Noricum. A similar division of troops, under the orders of Jovius and Jovinus, prepared to follow the oblique course of the highways, through the Alps and the northern confines of Italy. The instructions to the generals were conceived with energy and precision: to hasten their march in close and compact columns, which, according to the disposition of the ground, might readily be changed into any order of battle; to secure themselves against the surprises of the night by strong posts and vigilant guards; to prevent resistance by their unexpected arrival; to elude examination by their sudden departure; to spread the opinion of their strength and the terror of his name; and to join their sovereign under the walls of Sirmium. For himself, Julian had reserved a more difficult and extraordinary part. He selected three thousand brave and active volunteers, resolved, like their leader, to cast behind them every hope of a retreat: at the head of this faithful band, he fearlessly plunged into the recesses of the Marcian or black forest, which conceals the sources of the Danube;[13] and, for many days, the fate of Julian was unknown to the world. The secrecy of his march, his diligence and vigour, surmounted every obstacle; he forced his way over mountains and morasses, occupied the bridges or swam the rivers, pursued his direct course,[14] without reflecting whether he traversed the territory of the Romans or of the Barbarians, and at length emerged, between Ratisbon and Vienna, at the place where he designed to embark his troops on the Danube. By a well-concerted stratagem, he seized a fleet of light brigantines,[15] as it lay at anchor; secured a supply of coarse provisions sufficient to satisfy the indelicate, but voracious, appetite of a Gallic army; and boldly committed himself to the stream of the Danube. The labours of his mariners, who plied their oars with incessant diligence, and the steady continuance of a favourable wind, carried his fleet above seven hundred miles in eleven days; and he had already disem-

[13] *This wood was a part of the great Hercynian forest, which, in the time of Cæsar, stretched away from the country of the Rauraci (Basil) into the boundless regions of the North.*

[14] *Even the saint admires the speed and secrecy of this march. A modern divine might apply to the progress of Julian the lines which were originally designed for another apostate:—*
So eagerly the fiend,
O'er bog, or steep,
* through strait, rough,*
* dense, or rare,*
With head, hands,
* wings, or feet, pursues*
* his way*
And swims, or sinks,
* or wades, or creeps, or*
* flies.*

[15] *In that interval the* Notitia *places two or three fleets, the Lauriacensis (at Lauriacum, or Lorch), the Arlapensis, the Maginensis; and mentions five legions, or cohorts, of Liburnarii, who should be a sort of marines.*

barked his troops at Bononia, only nineteen miles from Sirmium, before his enemies could receive any certain intelligence that he had left the banks of the Rhine. In the course of this long and rapid navigation, the mind of Julian was fixed on the object of his enterprise; and, though he accepted the deputation of some cities, which hastened to claim the merit of an early submission, he passed before the hostile stations, which were placed along the river, without indulging the temptation of signalizing an useless and ill-timed valour. The banks of the Danube were crowded on either side with spectators, who gazed on the military pomp, anticipated the importance of the event, and diffused through the adjacent country the fame of a young hero, who advanced with more than mortal speed at the head of the innumerable forces of the West. Lucilian, who, with the rank of general of the cavalry, commanded the military powers of Illyricum, was alarmed and perplexed by the doubtful reports which he could neither reject nor believe. He had taken some slow and irresolute measures for the purpose of collecting his troops; when he was surprised by Dagalaiphus, an active officer, whom Julian, as soon as he landed at Bononia, had pushed forwards with some light infantry. The captive general, uncertain of his life or death, was hastily thrown upon a horse, and conducted to the presence of Julian; who kindly raised him from the ground, and dispelled the terror and amazement which seemed to stupefy his faculties. But Lucilian had no sooner recovered his spirits than he betrayed his want of discretion, by presuming to admonish his conqueror that he had rashly ventured, with a handful of men, to expose his person in the midst of his enemies. "Reserve for your master Constantius these timid remonstrances," replied Julian, with a smile of contempt; "when I gave you my purple to kiss, I received you not as a counsellor, but as a suppliant." Conscious that success alone could justify his attempt, and that boldness only could command success, he instantly advanced, at the head of three thousand soldiers, to attack the strongest and most populous city of the Illyrian provinces. As he entered the long suburb of Sirmium, he was received by the joyful acclamations of the army and people; who, crowned with flowers, and holding lighted tapers in their hands, conducted their acknowledged sovereign to his Imperial residence. Two days were devoted to the public joy, which was celebrated by the games of the Circus; but, early on the morning of the third day, Julian marched to occupy the narrow pass of Succi, in the defiles of Mount Hæmus; which, almost in the mid-way between Sirmium and Constantinople, separates the provinces of Thrace and Dacia, by an abrupt descent towards the former and a simple declivity on the side of the latter.[16] The defence of this important post was entrusted to the brave Nevitta; who, as well as the generals of the Italian division, successfully executed the plan of the march and junction which their master had so ably conceived.[17]

The homage which Julian obtained, from the fears or the inclination of the people, extended far beyond the immediate effect of his arms. The præfectures of Italy and Illyricum were administered by Taurus and Florentius, who united that important office with the vain honours of the consulship; and, as those magistrates had retired with precipitation to the court of Asia, Julian, who could not always restrain the levity of his temper, stigmatized their flight by adding, in all the Acts of the Year, the epithet of *fugitive* to the names of the two consuls. The provinces which had been deserted by their first magistrates acknowledged the authority of an emperor, who, conciliating the qualities of a soldier with those of a philosopher, was equally admired in the camps of the Danube and in the cities of Greece. From his palace, or, more properly, from his headquarters of Sirmium and Naissus, he distributed to the principal cities of the empire a laboured apology for his own conduct; published the secret dispatches of Constantius; and solicited the judgment of mankind between two competitors, the one of whom had expelled, and the other had invited, the Barbarians.[18] Julian, whose mind was deeply wounded by the reproach of ingratitude, aspired to maintain, by argument as well as by arms, the superior merits of his cause; and to excel, not only in the arts of war, but in those of composition. His epistle to the senate and people of Athens seems to have been dictated by an elegant enthusiasm; which prompted him to submit his actions and his motives to the degenerate Athenians of his own times, with the same humble deference as if he had been pleading, in the days of Aristides, before the tribunal of the Areopagus. His application to the senate of Rome, which was still permitted to bestow the titles of Imperial power, was agreeable to the forms of the expiring republic. An assembly was summoned by Tertullus, præfect of the city; the epistle of Julian was read; and, as he appeared to be master of Italy, his claims were admitted without a dissenting voice. His oblique censure of the innovations of Constantine, and his passionate invective against the vices of Constantius, were heard with less satisfaction; and the senate, as if Julian had been present, unanimously exclaimed, "Respect, we be-

[16] *The description of Ammianus, which might be supported by collateral evidence, ascertains the precise situation of the Angustiæ Succorum, or passes of Succi. M. d'Anville, from the trifling resemblance of names, has placed them between Sardica and Naissus. For my own justification, I am obliged to mention the only error which I have discovered in the maps or writings of that admirable geographer.*

[17] *Whatever circumstances we may borrow elsewhere, Ammianus still supplies the series of the narrative.*

[18] *Julian positively asserts that he intercepted the letters of Constantius to the Barbarians: and Libanius as positively affirms that he read them on his march to the troops and the cities. Yet Ammianus expresses himself with cool and candid hesitation, si famæ solius admittenda est fides. He specifies, however, an intercepted letter from Vadomair to Constantius, which supposes an intimate correspondence between them.*

seech you, the author of your own fortune." An artful expression, which, according to the chance of war, might be differently explained; as a manly reproof of the ingratitude of the usurper, or as a flattering confession that a single act of such benefit to the state ought to atone for all the failings of Constantius.

The intelligence of the march and rapid progress of Julian was speedily transmitted to his rival, who, by the retreat of Sapor, had obtained some respite from the Persian war. Disguising the anguish of his soul under the semblance of contempt, Constantius professed his intention of returning into Europe, and of giving chase to Julian; for he never spoke of this military expedition in any other light than that of a hunting party. In the camp of Hierapolis, in Syria, he communicated this design to his army, slightly mentioned the guilt and rashness of the Cæsar, and ventured to assure them that, if the mutineers of Gaul presumed to meet them in the field, they would be unable to sustain the fire of their eyes and the irresistible weight of their shout of onset. The speech of the emperor was received with military applause, and Theodotus, the president of the council of Hierapolis, requested, with tears of adulation, that *his* city might be adorned with the head of the vanquished rebel. A chosen detachment was dispatched away in post-waggons, to secure, if it were yet possible, the pass of Succi; the recruits, the horses, the arms, and the magazines which had been prepared against Sapor, were appropriated to the service of the civil war; and the domestic victories of Constantius inspired his partisans with the most sanguine assurances of success. The notary Gaudentius had occupied in his name the provinces of Africa; the subsistence of Rome was intercepted; and the distress of Julian was increased by an unexpected event which might have been productive of fatal consequences. Julian had received the submission of two legions and a cohort of archers, who were stationed at Sirmium; but he suspected, with reason, the fidelity of those troops, which had been distinguished by the emperor; and it was thought expedient, under the pretence of the exposed state of the Gallic frontier, to dismiss them from the most important scene of action. They advanced, with reluctance, as far as the confines of Italy; but, as they dreaded the length of the way and the savage fierceness of the Germans, they resolved, by the instigation of one of their tribunes, to halt at Aquileia, and to erect the banners of Constantius on the walls of that impregnable city. The vigilance of Julian perceived at once the extent of the mischief and the necessity of applying an immediate remedy. By his order, Jovinus led back a part of the army into Italy; and the siege of Aquileia was formed with diligence and prosecuted with vigour. But the legionaries, who seemed to have rejected the yoke of discipline, conducted the defence of the place with skill and perseverance; invited the rest of Italy to imitate the example of their courage and loyalty; and threatened the retreat of Julian, if he should be forced to yield to the superior numbers of the arms of the East.

But the humanity of Julian was preserved from the cruel alternative, which he pathetically laments, of destroying or of being himself destroyed: and the seasonable death of Constantius delivered the Roman empire from the calamities of civil war. The approach of winter could not detain the monarch at Antioch; and his favourites durst not oppose his impatient desire of revenge. A slight fever, which was perhaps occasioned by the agitation of his spirits, was increased by the fatigues of the journey; and Constantius was obliged to halt at the little town of Mopsucrene, twelve miles beyond Tarsus, where he expired, after a short illness, in the forty-fifth year of his age, and the twenty-fourth of his reign. His genuine character, which was composed of pride and weakness, of superstition and cruelty, has been fully displayed in the preceding narrative of civil and ecclesiastical events. The long abuse of power rendered him a considerable object in the eyes of his contemporaries; but, as personal merit can alone deserve the notice of posterity, the last of the sons of Constantine may be dismissed from the world with the remark, that he inherited the defects, without the abilities, of his father. Before Constantius expired, he is said to have named Julian for his successor; nor does it seem improbable that his anxious concern for the fate of a young and tender wife, whom he left with child, may have prevailed, in his last moments, over the harsher passions of hatred and revenge. Eusebius, and his guilty associates, made a faint attempt to prolong the reign of the eunuchs by the election of another emperor: but their intrigues were rejected with disdain by an army which now abhorred the thought of civil discord; and two officers of rank were instantly dispatched, to assure Julian that every sword in the empire would be drawn for his service. The military designs of that prince, who had formed three different attacks against Thrace, were prevented by this fortunate event. Without shedding the blood of his fellow-citizens, he escaped the dangers of a doubtful conflict and acquired the advantages of a complete victory. Impatient to visit the place of his birth and the new capital of the empire, he advanced from Naissus through the mountains of Hæmus and the cities of Thrace. When he reached Heraclea, at the distance of sixty miles, all Constantinople was poured forth to receive him; and he made his triumphal entry, amidst the dutiful acclamations of the soldiers, the people, and the senate. An innumerable multitude pressed around him with eager respect; and were perhaps disappointed when they beheld the small stature and simple garb of a hero whose unexperienced youth had vanquished the Barbarians of Germany, and who had now traversed, in a successful career, the whole continent of Europe, from the shores of the Atlantic to those of the Bosphorus. A few days afterwards, when the remains of the deceased emperor were landed in the harbour, the subjects of Julian applauded the real or affected humanity of their sovereign. On foot, without his diadem, and clothed in a mourning habit, he accompanied the funeral as far as the church of the Holy Apostles, where the body was deposited: and, if these marks of respect may be interpreted as a selfish tribute to the birth and dignity of his Imperial kinsman, the tears of Julian professed to the world that he had forgot the injuries, and remembered only the obligations, which he had received from Constantius. As soon as the legions of Aquileia were assured of the death of the emperor, they opened the gates of the city, and, by the sacrifice of their guilty leaders, obtained an easy pardon from the prudence or lenity of Julian; who, in the thirty-second year of his age, acquired the undisputed possession of the Roman empire.[19]

Philosophy had instructed Julian to compare the advantages of action and retirement; but the elevation of his birth and the accidents of his life never allowed him the freedom of choice. He might perhaps sincerely have preferred the groves of the academy and the society of Athens; but he was constrained, at first by the will, and afterwards by the injustice, of Constantius, to expose his person and fame to the dangers of Imperial greatness; and to make himself accountable to the world, and to posterity, for the happiness of millions.[20] Julian recollected with terror the observation of his master Plato, that the government of our flocks and herds is always committed to beings of a superior species; and that the conduct of nations requires and deserves the celestial powers of the Gods or of the Genii. From this principle he justly concluded that the man who presumes to reign should aspire to the perfection of the divine nature; that he should purify his soul from her mortal and terrestrial part; that he should extinguish his appetites, enlighten his un-

[19] The day and year of the birth of Julian are not perfectly ascertained. The day is probably the sixth of November, and the year must be either 331 or 332. I have preferred the earlier date.

[20] Julian himself has expressed these philosophical ideas with much eloquence, and some affectation, in a very elaborate epistle to Themistius. The Abbé de la Bléterie, who has given an elegant translation, is inclined to believe that it was the celebrated Themistius, whose orations are still extant.

derstanding, regulate his passions, and subdue the wild beast which, according to the lively metaphor of Aristotle, seldom fails to ascend the throne of a despot. The throne of Julian, which the death of Constantius fixed on an independent basis, was the seat of reason, of virtue, and perhaps of vanity. He despised the honours, renounced the pleasures, and discharged with incessant diligence the duties, of his exalted station; and there were few among his subjects who would have consented to relieve him from the weight of the diadem, had they been obliged to submit their time and their actions to the rigorous laws which their philosophic emperor imposed on himself. One of his most intimate friends, who had often shared the frugal simplicity of his table, has remarked that his light and sparing diet (which was usually of the vegetable kind) left his mind and body always free and active for the various and important business of an author, a pontiff, a magistrate, a general, and a prince. In one and the same day, he gave audience to several ambassadors, and wrote, or dictated, a great number of letters to his generals, his civil magistrates, his private friends, and the different cities of his dominions. He listened to the memorials which had been received, considered the subject of the petitions, and signified his intentions more rapidly than they could be taken in shorthand by the diligence of his secretaries. He possessed such flexibility of thought, and such firmness of attention, that he could employ his hand to write, his ear to listen, and his voice to dictate; and pursue at once three several trains of ideas without hesitation and without error. While his ministers reposed, the prince flew with agility from one labour to another, and, after a hasty dinner, retired into his library, till the public business, which he had appointed for the evening, summoned him to interrupt the prosecution of his studies. The supper of the emperor was still less substantial than the former meal; his sleep was never clouded by the fumes of indigestion; and, except in the short interval of a marriage, which was the effect of policy rather than love, the chaste Julian never shared his bed with a female companion. He was soon awakened by the entrance of fresh secretaries, who had slept the preceding day; and his servants were obliged to wait alternately, while their indefatigable master allowed himself scarcely any other refreshment than the change of occupations. The predecessors of Julian, his uncle, his brother, and his cousin, indulged their puerile taste for the games of the circus, under the specious pretence of complying with the inclinations of the people; and they frequently remained the greatest part of the day, as idle spectators, and as a part of the splendid spectacle, till the ordinary round of twenty-four races [21] was completely finished. On solemn festivals, Julian, who felt and professed an unfashionable dislike to these frivolous amusements, condescended to appear in the circus; and, after bestowing a careless glance on five or six of the races, he hastily withdrew, with the impatience of a philosopher, who considered every moment as lost that was not devoted to the advantage of the public or the improvement of his own mind.[22] By this avarice of time, he seemed to protract the short duration of his reign; and, if the dates were less securely ascertained, we should refuse to believe that only sixteen months elapsed between the death of Constantius and the departure of his successor for the Persian war. The actions of Julian can only be preserved by the care of the historian; but the portion of his voluminous writings which is still extant remains as a monument of the application, as well as of the genius, of the emperor. The Misopogon, the Cæsars, several of his orations, and his elaborate work against the Christian religion, were composed in the long nights of the two winters, the former of which he passed at Constantinople, and the latter at Antioch.

The reformation of the Imperial court was one of the first and most necessary acts of the government of Julian. Soon after his entrance into the palace of Constantinople, he had occasion for the service of a barber. An officer, magnificently dressed, immediately presented himself. "It is a barber," exclaimed the prince, with affected surprise, "that I want, and not a receiver-general of the finances." He questioned the man concerning the profits of his employment; and was informed that, besides a large salary and some valuable perquisites, he enjoyed a daily allowance for twenty servants and as many horses. A thousand barbers, a thousand cupbearers, a thousand cooks, were distributed in the several offices of luxury; and the number of eunuchs could be compared only with the insects of a summer's day. The monarch who resigned to his subjects the superiority of merit and virtue was distinguished by the oppressive magnificence of his dress, his table, his buildings, and his train. The stately palaces erected by Constantine and his sons were decorated with many coloured marbles and ornaments of massy gold. The most exquisite dainties were procured, to gratify their pride rather than their taste; birds of the most distant climates, fish from the most remote seas, fruits out of their natural season, winter roses, and summer snows. The domestic crowd of the palace surpassed the expense of the legions; yet the smallest part of this

[21] A twenty-fifth race, or missus, *was added, to complete the number of one hundred chariots, four of which, the four colours, started each heat. It appears that they ran five or seven times round the* Meta; *and (from the measure of the Circus Maximus at Rome, the Hippodrome at Constantinople, &c.) it might be about a four-mile course.*

[22] Julius Cæsar had offended the Roman people by reading his dispatches during the actual race. Augustus indulged their taste, or his own, by his constant attention to the important business of the circus, for which he professed the warmest inclination.

costly multitude was subservient to the use, or even to the splendour, of the throne. The monarch was disgraced, and the people was injured, by the creation and sale of an infinite number of obscure, and even titular employments; and the most worthless of mankind might purchase the privilege of being maintained, without the necessity of labour, from the public revenue. The waste of an enormous household, the increase of fees and perquisites, which were soon claimed as a lawful debt, and the bribes which they extorted from those who feared their enmity or solicited their favour, suddenly enriched these haughty menials. They abused their fortune, without considering their past, or their future, condition; and their rapine and venality could be equalled only by the extravagance of their dissipations. Their silken robes were embroidered with gold, their tables were served with delicacy and profusion; the houses which they built for their own use would have covered the farm of an ancient consul; and the most honourable citizens were obliged to dismount from their horses, and respectfully to salute an eunuch whom they met on the public highway. The luxury of the palace excited the contempt and indignation of Julian, who usually slept on the ground, who yielded with reluctance to the indispensable calls of nature, and who placed his vanity, not in emulating, but in despising, the pomp of royalty. By the total extirpation of a mischief which was magnified even beyond its real extent, he was impatient to relieve the distress, and to appease the murmurs, of the people; who support with less uneasiness the weight of taxes, if they are convinced that the fruits of their industry are appropriated to the service of the state. But in the execution of this salutary work Julian is accused of proceeding with too much haste and inconsiderate severity. By a single edict, he reduced the palace of Constantinople to an immense desert, and dismissed with ignominy the whole train of slaves and dependents,[23] without providing any just, or at least benevolent, exceptions, for the age, the services, or the poverty, of the faithful domestics of the Imperial family. Such indeed was the temper of Julian, who seldom recollected the fundamental maxim of Aristotle that true virtue is placed at an equal distance between the opposite vices. The splendid and effeminate dress of the Asiatics, the curls and paint, the collars and bracelets, which had appeared so ridiculous in the person of Constantine, were consistently rejected by his philosophic successor. But with the fopperies, Julian affected to renounce the decencies, of dress; and seemed to value himself for his neglect of the laws of cleanliness. In a satirical performance,

[23] *Yet Julian himself was accused of bestowing whole towns on the eunuchs. Libanius contents himself with a cold but positive denial of the fact, which seems indeed to belong more properly to Constantius. This charge however may allude to some unknown circumstance.*

which was designed for the public eye, the emperor descants with pleasure, and even with pride, on the length of his nails, and the inky blackness of his hands; protests that, although the greatest part of his body was covered with hair, the use of the razor was confined to his head alone; and celebrates, with visible complacency, the shaggy and *populous* beard, which he fondly cherished after the example of the philosophers of Greece. Had Julian consulted the simple dictates of reason, the first magistrate of the Romans would have scorned the affectation of Diogenes as well as that of Darius.

But the work of public reformation would have remained imperfect, if Julian had only corrected the abuses, without punishing the crimes, of his predecessor's reign. "We are now delivered," says he, in a familiar letter to one of his intimate friends, "we are now surprisingly delivered from the voracious jaws of the Hydra. I do not mean to apply that epithet to my brother Constantius. He is no more; may the earth lie light on his head! But his artful and cruel favourites studied to deceive and exasperate a prince whose natural mildness cannot be praised without some efforts of adulation. It is not, however, my intention that even those men should be oppressed: they are accused, and they shall enjoy the benefit of a fair and impartial trial." To conduct this inquiry, Julian named six judges of the highest rank in the state and army; and, as he wished to escape the reproach of condemning his personal enemies, he fixed this extraordinary tribunal at Chalcedon, on the Asiatic side of the Bosphorus; and transferred to the commissioners an absolute power to pronounce and execute their final sentence, without delay and without appeal. The office of president was exercised by the venerable præfect of the East, a *second* Sallust,[24] whose virtues conciliated the esteem of Greek sophists and of Christian bishops. He was assisted by the eloquent Mamertinus, one of the consuls elect, whose merit is loudly celebrated by the doubtful evidence of his own applause. But the civil wisdom of two magistrates was overbalanced by the ferocious violence of four generals, Nevitta, Agilo, Jovinus, and Arbetio. Arbetio, whom the public would have seen with less surprise at the bar than on the bench, was supposed to possess the secret of the commission; the armed and angry leaders of the Jovian and Herculian bands encompassed the tribunal; and the judges were alternately swayed by the laws of justice, and by the clamours of faction.

The chamberlain Eusebius, who had so long abused the favour of

[24] *The two Sallusts, the præfect of Gaul and the præfect of the East, must be carefully distinguished. I have used the surname of* Secundus, *as a convenient epithet. The second Sallust extorted the esteem of the Christians themselves; and Gregory Nazianzen, who condemned his religion, has celebrated his virtues.*

Constantius, expiated, by an ignominious death, the insolence, the corruption, and cruelty of his servile reign. The executions of Paul and Apodemius (the former of whom was burnt alive) were accepted as an inadequate atonement by the widows and orphans of so many hundred Romans, whom those legal tyrants had betrayed and murdered. But Justice herself (if we may use the pathetic expression of Ammianus) appeared to weep over the fate of Ursulus, the treasurer of the empire; and his blood accused the ingratitude of Julian, whose distress had been seasonably relieved by the intrepid liberality of that honest minister. The rage of the soldiers, whom he had provoked by his indiscretion, was the cause and the excuse of his death; and the emperor, deeply wounded by his own reproaches and those of the public, offered some consolation to the family of Ursulus, by the restitution of his confiscated fortunes. Before the end of the year in which they had been adorned with the ensigns of the præfecture and consulship,[25] Taurus and Florentius were reduced to implore the clemency of the inexorable tribunal of Chalcedon. The former was banished to Vercellæ in Italy, and a sentence of death was pronounced against the latter. A wise prince should have rewarded the crime of Taurus: the faithful minister, when he was no longer able to oppose the progress of a rebel, had taken refuge in the court of his benefactor and his lawful sovereign. But the guilt of Florentius justified the severity of the judges; and his escape served to display the magnanimity of Julian; who nobly checked the interested diligence of an informer, and refused to learn what place concealed the wretched fugitive from his just resentment. Some months after the tribunal of Chalcedon had been dissolved, the Prætorian vicegerent of Africa, the notary Gaudentius, and Artemius, duke of Egypt, were executed at Antioch. Artemius had reigned the cruel and corrupt tyrant of a great province; Gaudentius had long practised the arts of calumny against the innocent, the virtuous, and even the person of Julian himself. Yet the circumstances of their trial and condemnation were so unskilfully managed, that these wicked men obtained, in the public opinion, the glory of suffering for the obstinate loyalty with which they had supported the cause of Constantius. The rest of his servants were protected by a general act of oblivion; and they were left to enjoy with impunity the bribes which they had accepted either to defend the oppressed or to oppress the friendless. This measure, which, on the soundest principles of policy, may deserve our approbation, was executed in a manner which seemed to degrade the

[25] *Such respect was still entertained for the venerable names of the commonwealth that the public was surprised and scandalized to hear Taurus summoned as a criminal under the consulship of Taurus. The summons of his colleague Florentius was probably delayed till the commencement of the ensuing year.*

majesty of the throne. Julian was tormented by the importunities of a multitude, particularly of Egyptians, who loudly demanded the gifts which they had imprudently or illegally bestowed; he foresaw the endless prosecution of vexatious suits; and he engaged a promise, which ought always to have been sacred, that, if they would repair to Chalcedon, he would meet them in person, to hear and determine their complaints. But, as soon as they were landed, he issued an absolute order, which prohibited the watermen from transporting any Egyptian to Constantinople; and thus detained his disappointed clients on the Asiatic shore, till, their patience and money being utterly exhausted, they were obliged to return with indignant murmurs to their native country.

The numerous army of spies, of agents, and informers, enlisted by Constantius to secure the repose of one man and to interrupt that of millions, was immediately disbanded by his generous successor. Julian was slow in his suspicions and gentle in his punishments; and his contempt of treason was the result of judgment, of vanity, and of courage. Conscious of superior merit, he was persuaded that few among his subjects would dare to meet him in the field, to attempt his life, or even to seat themselves on his vacant throne. The philosopher could excuse the hasty sallies of discontent; and the hero could despise the ambitious projects which surpassed the fortune or the abilities of the rash conspirators. A citizen of Ancyra had prepared for his own use a purple garment; and this indiscreet action, which, under the reign of Constantius, would have been considered as a capital offence, was reported to Julian by the officious importunity of a private enemy. The monarch, after making some inquiry into the rank and character of his rival, dispatched the informer with a present of a pair of purple slippers, to complete the magnificence of his Imperial habit. A more dangerous conspiracy was formed by ten of the domestic guards, who had resolved to assassinate Julian in the field of exercise near Antioch. Their intemperance revealed their guilt; and they were conducted in chains to the presence of their injured sovereign, who, after a lively representation of the wickedness and folly of their enterprise, instead of a death of torture, which they deserved and expected, pronounced a sentence of exile against the two principal offenders. The only instance in which Julian seemed to depart from his accustomed clemency was the execution of a rash youth, who, with a feeble hand, had aspired to seize the reins of empire. But that youth was the son of Marcellus, the general of cavalry, who in the first campaign of the Gallic war had deserted the standard of the Cæsar and the republic. Without appearing to indulge his personal resentment, Julian might easily confound the crime of the son and of the father: but he was reconciled by the distress of Marcellus, and the liberality of the emperor endeavoured to heal the wound which had been inflicted by the hand of justice.

Julian was not insensible of the advantages of freedom. From his studies he had imbibed the spirit of ancient sages and heroes; his life and fortunes had depended on the caprice of a tyrant; and, when he ascended the throne, his pride was sometimes mortified by the reflection that the slaves who would not dare to censure his defects were not worthy to applaud his virtues. He sincerely abhorred the system of Oriental despotism which Diocletian, Constantine, and the patient habits of fourscore years had established in the empire. A motive of superstition prevented the execution of the design which Julian had frequently meditated, of relieving his head from the weight of a costly diadem: but he absolutely refused the title of *Dominus* or *Lord*,[26] a word which was grown so familiar to the ears of the Romans that they no longer remembered its servile and humiliating origin. The office, or rather the name, of consul, was cherished by a prince who contemplated with reverence the ruins of the republic; and the same behaviour which had been assumed by the prudence of Augustus was adopted by Julian from choice and inclination. On the calends of January, at break of day, the new consuls, Mamertinus and Nevitta, hastened to the palace to salute the emperor. As soon as he was informed of their approach, he leaped from his throne, eagerly advanced to meet them, and compelled the blushing magistrates to receive the demonstrations of his affected humility. From the palace they proceeded to the senate. The emperor, on foot, marched before their litters; and the gazing multitude admired the image of ancient times, or secretly blamed a conduct which, in their eyes, degraded the majesty of the purple.[27] But the behaviour of Julian was uniformly supported. During the games of the Circus, he had, imprudently or designedly, performed the manumission of a slave in the presence of the consul. The moment he was reminded that he had trespassed on the jurisdiction of *another* magistrate, he condemned himself to pay a fine of ten pounds of gold; and embraced this public occasion of declaring to the world that he was subject, like the rest of his fellow-citizens, to the laws, and even to the forms, of the republic. The spirit of his administration, and his regard for the place of his nativity, induced

[26] *As he never abolished, by any public law, the proud appellations of Despot or Dominus, they are still extant on his medals; and the private displeasure which he affected to express only gave a different tone to the servility of the court.*

[27] *The consul Mamertinus celebrates the auspicious day, like an eloquent slave, astonished and intoxicated by the condescension of his master.*

Julian to confer on the senate of Constantinople, the same honours, privileges, and authority, which were still enjoyed by the senate of ancient Rome. A legal fiction was introduced, and gradually established, that one half of the national council had migrated into the East: and the despotic successors of Julian, accepting the title of Senators, acknowledged themselves the members of a respectable body, which was permitted to represent the majesty of the Roman name. From Constantinople, the attention of the monarch was extended to the municipal senates of the provinces. He abolished, by repeated edicts, the unjust and pernicious exemptions which had withdrawn so many idle citizens from the service of their country; and by imposing an equal distribution of public duties he restored the strength, the splendour, or, according to the glowing expression of Libanius, the soul of the expiring cities of his empire. The venerable age of Greece excited the most tender compassion in the mind of Julian; which kindled into rapture when he recollected the gods, the heroes, and the men, superior to heroes and to gods, who had bequeathed to the latest posterity the monuments of their genius or the example of their virtues. He relieved the distress, and restored the beauty, of the cities of Epirus and Peloponnesus. Athens acknowledged him for her benefactor; Argos, for her deliverer. The pride of Corinth, again rising from her ruins with the honours of a Roman colony, exacted a tribute from the adjacent republics, for the purpose of defraying the games of the Isthmus, which were celebrated in the amphitheatre with the hunting of bears and panthers. From this tribute the cities of Elis, of Delphi, and of Argos, which had inherited from their remote ancestors the sacred office of perpetuating the Olympic, the Pythian, and the Nemean games, claimed a just exemption. The immunity of Elis and Delphi was respected by the Corinthians; but the poverty of Argos tempted the insolence of oppression; and the feeble complaints of its deputies were silenced by the decree of a provincial magistrate, who seems to have consulted only the interest of the capital in which he resided. Seven years after this sentence, Julian allowed the cause to be referred to a superior tribunal; and his eloquence was interposed in the defence of a city which had been the royal seat of Agamemnon [28] and had given to Macedonia a race of kings and conquerors.[29]

The laborious administration of military and civil affairs, which were multiplied in proportion to the extent of the empire, exercised the abilities of Julian; but he frequently assumed the two characters of Orator and of Judge, which are almost unknown to the modern

[28] *He reigned in Mycenæ, at the distance of fifty stadia, or six miles, from Argos: but these cities, which alternately flourished, are confounded by the Greek poets.*

[29] *This pedigree from Temenus and Hercules may be suspicious; yet it was allowed, after a strict inquiry by the judges of the Olympic games, at a time when the Macedonian kings were obscure and unpopular in Greece. When the Achæan league declared against Philip, it was thought decent that the deputies of Argos should retire.*

sovereigns of Europe. The arts of persuasion, so diligenly cultivated by the first Cæsars, were neglected by the military ignorance, and Asiatic pride, of their successors; and, if they condescended to harangue the soldiers, whom they feared, they treated with silent disdain the senators, whom they despised. The assemblies of the senate, which Constantius had avoided, were considered by Julian as the place where he could exhibit, with the most propriety, the maxims of a republican and the talents of a rhetorician. He alternately practised, as in a school of declamation, the several modes of praise, of censure, of exhortation; and his friend Libanius has remarked that the study of Homer taught him to imitate the simple, concise style of Menelaus, the copiousness of Nestor, whose words descended like the flakes of a winter's snow, or the pathetic and forcible eloquence of Ulysses. The functions of a judge, which are sometimes incompatible with those of a prince, were exercised by Julian, not only as a duty, but as an amusement: and, although he might have trusted the integrity and discernment of his Prætorian præfects, he often placed himself by their side on the seat of judgment. The acute penetration of his mind was agreeably occupied in detecting and defeating the chicanery of the advocates, who laboured to disguise the truth of facts and to pervert the sense of the laws. He sometimes forgot the gravity of his station, asked indiscreet or unseasonable questions, and betrayed, by the loudness of his voice and the agitation of his body, the earnest vehemence with which he maintained his opinion against the judges, the advocates, and their clients. But his knowledge of his own temper prompted him to encourage, and even to solicit, the reproof of his friends and ministers; and, whenever they ventured to oppose the irregular sallies of his passions, the spectators could observe the shame, as well as the gratitude, of their monarch. The decrees of Julian were almost always founded on the principles of justice; and he had the firmness to resist the two most dangerous temptations which assault the tribunal of a sovereign under the specious forms of compassion and equity. He decided the merits of the cause without weighing the circumstances of the parties; and the poor, whom he wished to relieve, were condemned to satisfy the just demands of a noble and wealthy adversary. He carefully distinguished the judge from the legislator;[30] and, though he meditated a necessary reformation of the Roman jurisprudence, he pronounced sentence according to the strict and literal interpretation of those laws which the magistrates were bound to execute and the subjects to obey.

[30] Of the laws which Julian enacted in a reign of sixteen months, fifty-four have been admitted into the Codes of Theodosius and Justinian.

663

The generality of princes, if they were stripped of their purple and cast naked into the world, would immediately sink to the lowest rank of society, without a hope of emerging from their obscurity. But the personal merit of Julian was, in some measure, independent of his fortune. Whatever had been his choice of life, by the force of intrepid courage, lively wit, and intense application, he would have obtained, or at least he would have deserved, the highest honours of his profession; and Julian might have raised himself to the rank of minister, or general, of the state in which he was born a private citizen. If the jealous caprice of power had disappointed his expectations; if he had prudently declined the paths of greatness, the employment of the same talents in studious solitude would have placed, beyond the reach of kings, his present happiness and his immortal fame. When we inspect, with minute or perhaps malevolent attention, the portrait of Julian, something seems wanting to the grace and perfection of the whole figure. His genius was less powerful and sublime than that of Cæsar; nor did he possess the consummate prudence of Augustus. The virtues of Trajan appear more steady and natural, and the philosophy of Marcus is more simple and consistent. Yet Julian sustained adversity with firmness, and prosperity with moderation. After an interval of one hundred and twenty years from the death of Alexander Severus, the Romans beheld an emperor who made no distinction between his duties and his pleasures; who laboured to relieve the distress, and to revive the spirit, of his subjects; and who endeavoured always to connect authority with merit, and happiness with virtue. Even faction, and religious faction, was constrained to acknowledge the superiority of his genius, in peace as well as in war; and to confess, with a sigh, that the apostate Julian was a lover of his country, and that he deserved the empire of the world.

CRYPT UNDER THE CAPITOLINE HILL

"It was the first act of the Romans, an act of free-dom, to restore the strength, though not the beauty, of the Capitol; to fortify the seat of their arms and counsels; and, as often as they ascended the hill, the coldest minds must have glowed with the remembrance of their ancestors."

CRYPT HOLLOWED UNDER THE CAPITOLINE HILL

XXIII

THE character of Apostate has injured the reputation of Julian; and the enthusiasm which clouded his virtues has exaggerated the real and apparent magnitude of his faults. Our partial ignorance may represent him as a philosophic monarch, who studied to protect, with an equal hand, the religious factions of the empire; and to allay the theological fever which had inflamed the minds of the people from the edicts of Diocletian to the exile of Athanasius. A more accurate view of the character and conduct of Julian will remove his favourable prepossession for a prince who did not escape the general contagion of the times. We enjoy the singular advantage of comparing the pictures which have been delineated by his fondest admirers and his implacable enemies. The actions of Julian are faithfully related by a judicious and candid historian, the impartial spectator of his life and death. The unanimous evidence of his contemporaries is confirmed by the public and private declarations of the emperor himself; and his various writings express the uniform tenor of his religious sentiments, which policy would have prompted him to dissemble rather than to affect. A devout and sincere attachment for the gods of Athens and Rome constituted the ruling passion of Julian; the powers of an enlightened understanding were betrayed and corrupted by the influence of superstitious prejudice; and the phantoms which existed only in the mind of the emperor had a real and pernicious effect on the government of the empire. The vehement zeal of the Christians, who despised the worship, and overturned the altars, of those fabulous deities, engaged their votary in a state of irreconcilable hostility with a very numerous party of his subjects; and he was sometimes tempted, by the desire of victory or the

[1] *The orator, with some eloquence, much enthusiasm, and more vanity, addresses his discourse to heaven and earth, to men and angels, to the living and the dead; and above all, to the great Constantius. He concludes with a bold assurance that he has erected a monument not less durable, and much more portable, than the columns of Hercules.*

[2] *See this long invective, which has been injudiciously divided into two orations in Gregory's Works. It was published by Gregory and his friend Basil about six months after the death of Julian, when his remains had been carried to Tarsus; but while Jovian was still on the throne. I have derived much assistance from a French version and remarks, printed at Lyons 1735.*

shame of a repulse, to violate the laws of prudence, and even of justice. The triumph of the party which he deserted and opposed has fixed a stain of infamy on the name of Julian; and the unsuccessful apostate has been overwhelmed with a torrent of pious invectives, of which the signal was given by the sonorous trumpet [1] of Gregory Nazianzen.[2] The interesting nature of the events which were crowded into the short reign of this active emperor deserves a just and circumstantial narrative. His motives, his counsels, and his actions, as far as they are connected with the history of religion, will be the subject of the present chapter.

The cause of his strange and fatal apostacy may be derived from the early period of his life, when he was left an orphan in the hands of the murderers of his family. The names of Christ and of Constantius, the ideas of slavery and of religion, were soon associated in a youthful imagination, which was susceptible of the most lively impressions. The care of his infancy was entrusted to Eusebius, bishop of Nicomedia,[3] who was related to him on the side of his mother; and, till Julian reached the twentieth year of his age, he received from his Christian preceptors the education, not of a hero, but of a saint. The emperor, less jealous of a heavenly than of an earthly crown, contented himself with the imperfect character of a catechumen, while he bestowed the advantages of baptism [4] on the nephews of Constantine.[5] They were even admitted to the inferior offices of the ecclesiastical order; and Julian publicly read the Holy Scriptures in the church of Nicomedia. The study of religion, which they assiduously cultivated, appeared to produce the fairest fruits of faith and devotion. They prayed, they fasted, they distributed alms to the poor, gifts to the clergy, and oblations to the tombs of the martyrs; and the splendid monument of St. Mamas, at Cæsarea, was erected, or at least was undertaken, by the joint labour of Gallus and Julian.[6] They respectfully conversed with the bishops who were eminent for superior sanctity, and solicited the benediction of the monks and hermits who had introduced into Cappadocia the voluntary hardships of the ascetic life.[7] As the two princes advanced towards the years of manhood, they discovered, in their religious sentiments, the difference of their characters. The dull and obstinate understanding of Gallus embraced, with implicit zeal, the doctrines of Christianity; which never influenced his conduct or moderated his passions. The mild disposition of the younger brother was less repugnant to the precepts of the gospel; and his active curiosity might have been gratified by a theological system

[3] *Julian never expresses any gratitude towards that Arian prelate; but he celebrates his preceptor, the eunuch Mardonius, and describes his mode of education, which inspired his pupil with a passionate admiration for the genius, and perhaps, the religion, of Homer.*

[4] *He laboured to efface that holy mark in the blood, perhaps, of a Taurobolium.*

[5] *Julian himself assures the Alexandrians that he had been a Christian (he must mean a sincere one) till the twentieth year of his age.*

[6] *The share of the work which had been allotted to Gallus was prosecuted with vigour and success; but the earth obstinately rejected and subverted the structures which were imposed by the sacrilegious hand of Julian. Such a partial earthquake, attested by many living spectators, would form one of the clearest miracles in ecclesiastical story.*

[7] *The philosopher ridicules the iron chains, &c. of these solitary fanatics, who had forgot that man is by nature a gentle and social animal. The*

666

which explains the mysterious essence of the Deity and opens the boundless prospect of invisible and future worlds. But the independent spirit of Julian refused to yield the passive and unresisting obedience which was required, in the name of religion, by the haughty ministers of the church. Their speculative opinions were imposed as positive laws, and guarded by the terrors of eternal punishments; but, while they prescribed the rigid formulary of the thoughts, the words, and the actions of the young prince; whilst they silenced his objections and severely checked the freedom of his inquiries, they secretly provoked his impatient genius to disclaim the authority of his ecclesiastical guides. He was educated in the Lesser Asia, amidst the scandals of the Arian controversy.[8] The fierce contests of the eastern bishops, the incessant alterations of their creeds, and the profane motives which appeared to actuate their conduct, insensibly strengthened the prejudice of Julian, that they neither understood nor believed the religion for which they so fiercely contended. Instead of listening to the proofs of Christianity with that favourable attention which adds weight to the most respectable evidence, he heard with suspicion, and disputed with obstinacy and acuteness, the doctrines for which he already entertained an invincible aversion. Whenever the young princes were directed to compose declamations on the subject of the prevailing controversies, Julian always declared himself the advocate of Paganism; under the specious excuse that, in the defence of the weaker cause, his learning and ingenuity might be more advantageously exercised and displayed.

As soon as Gallus was invested with the honours of the purple, Julian was permitted to breathe the air of freedom, of literature, and of Paganism. The crowd of sophists, who were attracted by the taste and liberality of their royal pupil, had formed a strict alliance between the learning and the religion of Greece; and the poems of Homer, instead of being admired as the original productions of human genius, were seriously ascribed to the heavenly inspiration of Apollo and the muses. The deities of Olympus, as they are painted by the immortal bard, imprint themselves on the minds which are the least addicted to superstitious credulity. Our familiar knowledge of their names and characters, their forms and attributes, *seems* to bestow on those airy beings a real and substantial existence; and the pleasing enchantment produces an imperfect and momentary assent of the imagination to those fables which are the most repugnant to our reason and experience. In the age of

Pagan supposes that, because they had renounced the gods, they were possessed and tormented by evil dæmons.

[8] *"You persecute," says Julian, "those heretics who do not mourn the dead man precisely in the way which you approve." He shows himself a tolerable theologian; but he maintains that the Christian Trinity is not derived from the doctrine of Paul, of Jesus, or of Moses.*

Julian every circumstance contributed to prolong and fortify the illusion; the magnificent temples of Greece and Asia; the works of those artists who had expressed, in painting or in sculpture, the divine conceptions of the poet; the pomp of festivals and sacrifices; the successful arts of divination; the popular traditions of oracles and prodigies; and the ancient practice of two thousand years. The weakness of polytheism was, in some measure, excused by the moderation of its claims; and the devotion of the Pagans was not incompatible with the most licentious scepticism.[9] Instead of an indivisible and regular system, which occupies the whole extent of the believing mind, the mythology of the Greeks was composed of a thousand loose and flexible parts, and the servant of the gods was at liberty to define the degree and measure of his religious faith. The creed which Julian adopted for his own use was of the largest dimensions; and, by a strange contradiction, he disdained the salutary yoke of the gospel, whilst he made a voluntary offering of his reason on the altars of Jupiter and Apollo. One of the orations of Julian is consecrated to the honour of Cybele, the mother of the gods, who required from her effeminate priests the bloody sacrifice, so rashly performed by the madness of the Phrygian boy. The pious emperor condescends to relate, without a blush, and without a smile, the voyage of the goddess from the shores of Pergamus to the mouth of the Tiber, and the stupendous miracle, which convinced the senate and people of Rome that the lump of clay which their ambassadors had transported over the seas was endowed with life, and sentiment, and divine power.[10] For the truth of this prodigy, he appeals to the public monuments of the city; and censures, with some acrimony, the sickly and affected taste of those men who impertinently derided the sacred traditions of their ancestors.

But the devout philosopher, who sincerely embraced and warmly encouraged the superstition of the people, reserved for himself the privilege of a liberal interpretation; and silently withdrew from the foot of the altars into the sanctuary of the temple. The extravagance of the Grecian mythology proclaimed with a clear and audible voice that the pious inquirer, instead of being scandalized or satisfied with the literal sense, should diligently explore the occult wisdom which had been disguised, by the prudence of antiquity, under the mask of folly and of fable. The philosophers of the Platonic school, Plotinus, Porphyry, and the divine Iamblichus, were admired as the most skilful masters of this allegorical science which laboured to soften and harmonize the deformed features of Pagan-

[9] A modern philosopher has ingeniously compared the different operation of theism and polytheism, with regard to the doubt or conviction which they produce in the human mind. See Hume's Essays.

[10] The Idæan mother landed in Italy about the end of the second Punic war. The miracle of Claudia, either virgin or matron, who cleared her fame by disgracing the graver modesty of the Roman ladies, is attested by a cloud of witnesses. Their evidence is collected by Drakenborch: but we may observe that Livy slides over the transaction with discreet ambiguity.

ism. Julian himself, who was directed in the mysterious pursuit by Ædesius, the venerable successor of Iamblichus, aspired to the possession of a treasure which he esteemed, if we may credit his solemn asseverations, far above the empire of the world.[11] It was indeed a treasure which derived its value only from opinion; and every artist who flattered himself that he had extracted the precious ore from the surrounding dross claimed an equal right of stamping the name and figure the most agreeable to his peculiar fancy. The fable of Atys and Cybele had been already explained by Porphyry; but his labours served only to animate the pious industry of Julian, who invented and published his own allegory of that ancient and mystic tale. This freedom of interpretation, which might gratify the pride of the Platonists, exposed the vanity of their art. Without a tedious detail, the modern reader could not form a just idea of the strange allusions, the forced etymologies, the solemn trifling, and the impenetrable obscurity of these sages, who professed to reveal the system of the universe. As the traditions of Pagan mythology were variously related, the sacred interpreters were at liberty to select the most convenient circumstances; and, as they translated an arbitrary cypher, they could extract from *any* fable *any* sense which was adapted to their favourite system of religion and philosophy. The lascivious form of a naked Venus was tortured into the discovery of some moral precept or some physical truth: and the castration of Atys explained the revolution of the sun between the tropics or the separation of the human soul from vice and error.[12]

The theological system of Julian appears to have contained the sublime and important principles of natural religion. But, as the faith which is not founded on revelation must remain destitute of any firm assurance, the disciple of Plato imprudently relapsed into the habits of vulgar superstition; and the popular and philosophic notion of the Deity seems to have been confounded in the practice, the writings, and even in the mind of Julian. The pious emperor acknowledged and adored the Eternal Cause of the universe, to whom he ascribed all the perfections of an infinite nature, invisible to the eyes, and inaccessible to the understanding, of feeble mortals. The Supreme God had created, or rather, in the Platonic language, had generated, the gradual succession of dependent spirits, of gods, of dæmons, of heroes, and of men; and every being which derived its existence immediately from the First Cause received the inherent gift of immortality. That so precious an advantage might not be lavished upon unworthy objects, the Creator had entrusted to the

[11] *He swears with the most fervent and enthusiastic devotion; and trembles lest he should betray too much of these holy mysteries, which the profane might deride with an impious sardonic laugh.*

[12] *See the fifth oration of Julian. But all the allegories which ever issued from the Platonic school are not worth the short poem of Catullus on the same extraordinary subject. The transition of Atys from the wildest enthusiasm to sober pathetic complaint, for his irretrievable loss, must inspire a man with pity, an eunuch with despair.*

skill and power of the inferior gods, the office of forming the human body, and of arranging the beautiful harmony of the animal, the vegetable, and the mineral kingdoms. To the conduct of these divine ministers he delegated the temporal government of this lower world; but their imperfect administration is not exempt from discord or error. The earth, and its inhabitants, are divided among them, and the characters of Mars or Minerva, of Mercury or Venus, may be distinctly traced in the laws and manners of their peculiar votaries. As long as our immortal souls are confined in a mortal prison, it is our interest, as well as our duty, to solicit the favour, and to deprecate the wrath, of the powers of heaven; whose pride is gratified by the devotion of mankind; and whose grosser parts may be supposed to derive some nourishment from the fumes of sacrifice.[13] The inferior gods might sometimes condescend to animate the statues, and to inhabit the temples, which were dedicated to their honour. They might occasionally visit the earth, but the heavens were the proper throne and symbol of their glory. The invariable order of the sun, moon, and stars, was hastily admitted by Julian as a proof of their *eternal* duration; and their eternity was a sufficient evidence that they were the workmanship, not of an inferior deity, but of the Omnipotent King. In the system of the Platonists, the visible, was a type of the invisible, world. The celestial bodies, as they were informed by a divine spirit, might be considered as the objects of the most worthy of religious worship. The Sun, whose genial influence pervades and sustains the universe, justly claimed the adoration of mankind, as the bright representative of the Logos, the lively, the rational, the beneficent image of the intellectual Father.

In every age, the absence of genuine inspiration is supplied by the strong illusions of enthusiasm and the mimic arts of imposture. If, in the time of Julian, these arts had been practised only by the Pagan priests, for the support of an expiring cause, some indulgence might perhaps be allowed to the interest and habits of the sacerdotal character. But it may appear a subject of surprise and scandal that the philosophers themselves should have contributed to abuse the superstitious credulity of mankind,[14] and that the Grecian mysteries should have been supported by the magic or theurgy of the modern Platonists. They arrogantly pretended to control the order of nature, to explore the secrets of futurity, to command the service of the inferior dæmons, to enjoy the view and conversation of the superior gods, and, by disengaging the soul from her material bands, to re-

[13] Julian adopts this gross conception, by ascribing it to his favourite Marcus Antoninus. The Stoics and Platonists hesitated between the analogy of bodies and the purity of spirits; yet the gravest philosophers inclined to the whimsical fancy of Aristophanes and Lucian that an unbelieving age might starve the immortal gods.

[14] The sophists of Eunapius perform as many miracles as the saints of the desert; and the only circumstance in their favour is that they are of a less gloomy complexion. Instead of devils with horns and tails, Iamblichus evoked the genii of love, Eros and Anteros, from two adjacent fountains. Two beautiful boys issued from the water, fondly embraced him as their father, and retired at his command.

unite that immortal particle with the Infinite and Divine Spirit.

The devout and fearless curiosity of Julian tempted the philosophers with the hopes of an easy conquest; which, from the situation of their young proselyte, might be productive of the most important consequences. Julian imbibed the first rudiments of the Platonic doctrines from the mouth of Ædesius, who had fixed at Pergamus his wandering and persecuted school. But, as the declining strength of that venerable sage was unequal to the ardour, the diligence, the rapid conception of his pupil, two of his most learned disciples, Chrysanthes and Eusebius, supplied, at his own desire, the place of their aged master. These philosophers seem to have prepared and distributed their respective parts; and they artfully contrived, by dark hints and affected disputes, to excite the impatient hopes of the *aspirant,* till they delivered him into the hands of their associate Maximus, the boldest and most skilful master of the Theurgic science. By his hands Julian was secretly initiated at Ephesus, in the twentieth year of his age. His residence at Athens confirmed this unnatural alliance of philosophy and superstition. He obtained the privilege of a solemn initiation into the mysteries of Eleusis, which, amidst the general decay of the Grecian worship, still retained some vestiges of their primæval sanctity; and such was the zeal of Julian that he afterwards invited the Eleusinian pontiff to the court of Gaul, for the sole purpose of consummating, by mystic rites and sacrifices, the great work of his sanctification. As these ceremonies were performed in the depth of caverns, and in the silence of the night, and as the inviolable secret of the mysteries was preserved by the discretion of the initiated, I shall not presume to describe the horrid sounds and fiery apparitions, which were presented to the senses, or the imagination, of the credulous aspirant,[15] till the visions of comfort and knowledge broke upon him in a blaze of celestial light. In the caverns of Ephesus and Eleusis, the mind of Julian was penetrated with sincere, deep, and unalterable enthusiasm; though he might sometimes exhibit the vicissitudes of pious fraud and hypocrisy, which may be observed, or at least suspected, in the characters of the most conscientious fanatics. From that moment he consecrated his life to the service of the gods; and, while the occupations of war, of government, and of study, seemed to claim the whole measure of his time, a stated portion of the hours of the night was invariably reserved for the exercise of private devotion. The temperance which adorned the severe manners of the soldier and the philosopher was connected with some strict and

[15] *When Julian, in a momentary panic, made the sign of the cross, the dæmons instantly disappeared. Gregory supposes that they were frightened, but the priests declared that they were indignant. The reader, according to the measure of his faith, will determine this profound question.*

frivolous rules of religious abstinence; and it was in honour of Pan or Mercury, of Hecate or Isis, that Julian, on particular days, denied himself the use of some particular food, which might have been offensive to his tutelar deities. By these voluntary fasts, he prepared his senses and his understanding for the frequent and familiar visits with which he was honoured by the celestial powers. Notwithstanding the modest silence of Julian himself, we may learn from his faithful friend, the orator Libanius, that he lived in a perpetual intercourse with the gods and goddesses; that they descended upon earth, to enjoy the conversation of their favourite hero; that they gently interrupted his slumbers, by touching his hand or his hair; that they warned him of every impending danger, and conducted him, by their infallible wisdom, in every action of his life; and that he had acquired such an intimate knowledge of his heavenly guests, as readily to distinguish the voice of Jupiter from that of Minerva, and the form of Apollo from the figure of Hercules.[16] These sleeping or waking visions, the ordinary effects of abstinence and fanaticism, would almost degrade the emperor to the level of an Egyptian monk. But the useless lives of Anthony or Pachomius were consumed in these vain occupations. Julian could break from the dream of superstition to arm himself for battle; and, after vanquishing in the field the enemies of Rome, he calmly retired into his tent, to dictate the wise and salutary laws of an empire, or to indulge his genius in the elegant pursuits of literature and philosophy.

The important secret of the apostacy of Julian was entrusted to the fidelity of the *initiated,* with whom he was united by the sacred ties of friendship and religion.[17] The pleasing rumour was cautiously circulated among the adherents of the ancient worship; and his future greatness became the object of the hopes, the prayers, and the predictions of the Pagans, in every province of the empire. From the zeal and virtues of their royal proselyte, they fondly expected the cure of every evil and the restoration of every blessing; and, instead of disapproving of the ardour of their pious wishes, Julian ingenuously confessed that he was ambitious to attain a situation in which he might be useful to his country and to his religion. But this religion was viewed with an hostile eye by the successor of Constantine, whose capricious passions alternately saved and threatened the life of Julian. The arts of magic and divination were strictly prohibited under a despotic government which condescended to fear them; and, if the Pagans were reluctantly indulged in the exercise of their superstition, the rank of Julian would have excepted him from the

[16] *Julian's modesty confined him to obscure and occasional hints; but Libanius expatiates with pleasure on the fasts and visions of the religious hero.*

[17] *Gallus had some reasons to suspect the secret apostacy of his brother; and in a letter, which may be received as genuine, he exhorts Julian to adhere to the religion of their ancestors; an argument which, as it should seem, was not yet perfectly ripe.*

general toleration. The apostate soon became the presumptive heir of the monarchy, and his death could alone have appeased the just apprehensions of the Christians.[18] But the young prince, who aspired to the glory of a hero rather than of a martyr, consulted his safety by dissembling his religion; and the easy temper of polytheism permitted him to join in the public worship of a sect which he inwardly despised. Libanius has considered the hypocrisy of his friend as a subject, not of censure, but of praise. "As the statues of the gods," says that orator, "which have been defiled with filth, are again placed in a magnificent temple; so the beauty of truth was seated in the mind of Julian, after it had been purified from the errors and follies of his education. His sentiments were changed; but, as it would have been dangerous to have avowed his sentiments, his conduct still continued the same. Very different from the ass in Æsop, who disguised himself with a lion's hide, our lion was obliged to conceal himself under the skin of an ass; and, while he embraced the dictates of reason, to obey the laws of prudence and necessity." The dissimulation of Julian lasted above ten years, from his secret initiation at Ephesus to the beginning of the civil war; when he declared himself at once the implacable enemy of Christ and of Constantius. This state of constraint might contribute to strengthen his devotion; and, as soon as he had satisfied the obligation of assisting, on solemn festivals, at the assemblies of the Christians, Julian returned, with the impatience of a lover, to burn his free and voluntary incense on the domestic chapels of Jupiter and Mercury. But, as every act of dissimulation must be painful to an ingenuous spirit, the profession of Christianity increased the aversion of Julian for a religion which oppressed the freedom of his mind and compelled him to hold a conduct repugnant to the noblest attributes of human nature, sincerity and courage.

The inclination of Julian might prefer the gods of Homer, and of the Scipios, to the new faith which his uncle had established in the Roman empire; and in which he himself had been sanctified by the sacrament of baptism. But, as a philosopher, it was incumbent on him to justify his dissent from Christianity, which was supported by the number of its converts, by the chain of prophecy, the splendour of miracles, and the weight of evidence. The elaborate work, which he composed amidst the preparations of the Persian war, contained the substance of those arguments which he had long revolved in his mind. Some fragments have been transcribed and preserved by his adversary, the vehement Cyril of Alexandria;[19] and

[18] *Gregory, with inhuman zeal, censures Constantius for sparing the infant apostate.*

[19] *About seventy years after the death of Julian, he executed a task which had been feebly attempted by Philip of Side, a prolix and contemptible writer. Even the work of Cyril has not entirely satisfied the most favourable judges: and the Abbé de la Bléterie wishes that some théologien philosophe (a strange centaur) would undertake the refutation of Julian.*

they exhibit a very singular mixture of wit and learning, of sophistry and fanaticism. The elegance of the style, and the rank of the author, recommended his writings to the public attention; and in the impious list of the enemies of Christianity, the celebrated name of Porphyry was effaced by the superior merit or reputation of Julian. The minds of the faithful were either seduced, or scandalized, or alarmed; and the Pagans, who sometimes presumed to engage in the unequal dispute, derived from the popular work of their Imperial missionary an inexhaustible supply of fallacious objections. But in the assiduous prosecution of these theological studies, the emperor of the Romans imbibed the illiberal prejudices and passions of a polemic divine. He contracted an irrevocable obligation to maintain and propagate his religious opinions; and, whilst he secretly applauded the strength and dexterity with which he wielded the weapons of controversy, he was tempted to distrust the sincerity, or to despise the understandings, of his antagonists, who could obstinately resist the force of reason and eloquence.

The Christians, who beheld with horror and indignation the apostacy of Julian, had much more to fear from his power than from his arguments. The Pagans, who were conscious of his fervent zeal, expected, perhaps with impatience, that the flames of persecution should be immediately kindled against the enemies of the gods; and that the ingenious malice of Julian would invent some cruel refinements of death and torture, which had been unknown to the rude and inexperienced fury of his predecessors. But the hopes, as well as the fears, of the religious factions were apparently disappointed by the prudent humanity of a prince who was careful of his own fame, of the public peace, and of the rights of mankind. Instructed by history and reflection, Julian was persuaded that, if the diseases of the body may sometimes be cured by salutary violence, neither steel nor fire can eradicate the erroneous opinions of the mind. The reluctant victim may be dragged to the foot of the altar; but the heart still abhors and disclaims the sacrilegious act of the hand. Religious obstinacy is hardened and exasperated by oppression; and, as soon as the persecution subsides, those who have yielded are restored as penitents, and those who have resisted are honoured as saints and martyrs. If Julian adopted the unsuccessful cruelty of Diocletian and his colleagues, he was sensible that he should stain his memory with the name of tyrant, and add new glories to the Catholic church, which had derived strength and increase from the severity of the Pagan magistrates. Actuated by these motives, and apprehensive of disturbing the repose of an unsettled reign, Julian surprised the world by an edict which was not unworthy of a statesman or a philosopher. He extended to all the inhabitants of the Roman world the benefits of a free and equal toleration; and the only hardship which he inflicted on the Christians was to deprive them of the power of tormenting their fellow-subjects, whom they stigmatized with the odious titles of idolaters and heretics. The Pagans received a gracious permission, or rather an express order, to open ALL their temples;[20] and they were at once delivered from the oppressive laws and arbitrary vexations which they had sustained under the reign of Constantine and of his sons. At the same time, the bishops and clergy who had been banished by the Arian monarch were recalled from exile and restored to their respective churches; the Donatists, the Novatians, the Macedonians, the Eunomians, and those who, with a more prosperous fortune, adhered to the doctrine of the council of Nice. Julian, who understood and derided their theological disputes, invited to the palace the leaders of the hostile sects, that he might enjoy the agreeable spectacle of their furious encounters. The clamour of controversy sometimes provoked the emperor to exclaim, "Hear me! the Franks have heard me, and the Alemanni"; but he soon discovered that he was now engaged with more obstinate and implacable enemies; and, though he exerted the powers of oratory to persuade them to live in concord, or at least in peace, he was perfectly satisfied, before he dismissed them from his presence, that he had nothing to dread from the union of the Christians. The impartial Ammianus has ascribed this affected clemency to the desire of fomenting the intestine divisions of the church; and the insidious design of undermining the foundations of Christianity was inseparably connected with the zeal which Julian professed to restore the ancient religion of the empire.

As soon as he ascended the throne, he assumed, according to the custom of his predecessors, the character of supreme pontiff; not only as the most honourable title of Imperial greatness, but as a sacred and important office, the duties of which he was resolved to execute with pious diligence. As the business of the state prevented the emperor from joining every day in the public devotion of his subjects, he dedicated a domestic chapel to his tutelar deity the Sun; his gardens were filled with statues and altars of the gods; and each apartment of the palace displayed the appearance of a magnificent temple. Every morning he saluted the parent of light with

[20] *In Greece the temples of Minerva were opened by his express command, before the death of Constantius; and Julian declares himself a Pagan in his public manifesto to the Athenians. This unquestionable evidence may correct the hasty assertion of Ammianus, who seems to suppose Constantinople to be the place where he discovered his attachment to the gods.*

a sacrifice; the blood of another victim was shed at the moment when the Sun sunk below the horizon; and the Moon, the Stars, and the Genii of the night, received their respective and seasonable honours from the indefatigable devotion of Julian. On solemn festivals, he regularly visited the temple of the god or goddess to whom the day was peculiarly consecrated, and endeavoured to excite the religion of the magistrates and people by the example of his own zeal. Instead of maintaining the lofty state of a monarch, distinguished by the splendour of his purple, and encompassed by the golden shields of his guards, Julian solicited, with respectful eagerness, the meanest offices which contributed to the worship of the gods. Amidst the sacred but licentious crowd of priests, of inferior ministers, and of female dancers, who were dedicated to the service of the temple, it was the business of the emperor to bring the wood, to blow the fire, to handle the knife, to slaughter the victim, and, thrusting his bloody hand into the bowels of the expiring animal, to draw forth the heart or liver, and to read, with the consummate skill of an haruspex, the imaginary signs of future events. The wisest of the Pagans censured this extravagant superstition which affected to despise the restraints of prudence and decency. Under the reign of a prince who practised the rigid maxims of economy the expense of religious worship consumed a very large portion of the revenue; a constant supply of the scarcest and most beautiful birds was transported from distant climates, to bleed on the altars of the gods; an hundred oxen were frequently sacrificed by Julian on one and the same day; and it soon became a popular jest that, if he should return with conquest from the Persian war, the breed of horned cattle must infallibly be extinguished. Yet this expense may appear inconsiderable, when it is compared with the splendid presents which were offered, either by the hand or by an order of the emperor, to all the celebrated places of devotion in the Roman world; and with the sums allotted to repair and decorate the ancient temples, which had suffered the silent decay of time or the recent injuries of Christian rapine. Encouraged by the example, the exhortations, the liberality, of their pious sovereign, the cities and families resumed the practice of their neglected ceremonies. "Every port of the world," exclaims Libanius with devout transport, "displayed the triumph of religion; and the grateful prospect of flaming altars, bleeding victims, the smoke of incense, and a solemn train of priests and prophets, without fear and without danger. The sound of prayer and of music was heard on the tops of the highest mountains; and the same ox afforded a sacrifice for the gods and a supper for their joyous votaries."

But the genius and power of Julian were unequal to the enterprise of restoring a religion which was destitute of theological principles, of moral precepts, and of ecclesiastical discipline; which rapidly hastened to decay and dissolution, and was not susceptible of any solid or consistent reformation. The jurisdiction of the supreme pontiff, more especially after that office had been united with the Imperial dignity, comprehended the whole extent of the Roman empire. Julian named for his vicars, in the several provinces, the priests and philosophers whom he esteemed the best qualified to co-operate in the execution of his great design; and his pastoral letters, if we may use that name, still represent a very curious sketch of his wishes and intentions. He directs that in every city the sacerdotal order should be composed, without any distinction of birth or fortune, of those persons who were the most conspicuous for their love of the gods and of men. "If they are guilty," continues he, "of any scandalous offence, they should be censured or degraded by the superior pontiff; but, as long as they retain their rank, they are entitled to the respect of the magistrates and people. Their humility may be shown in the plainness of their domestic garb; their dignity, in the pomp of holy vestments. When they are summoned in their turn to officiate before the altar, they ought not, during the appointed number of days, to depart from the precincts of the temple; nor should a single day be suffered to elapse without the prayers and the sacrifice, which they are obliged to offer for the prosperity of the state and of individuals. The exercise of their sacred functions requires an immaculate purity, both of mind and body; and, even when they are dismissed from the temple to the occupations of common life, it is incumbent on them to excel in decency and virtue the rest of their fellow-citizens. The priest of the gods should never be seen in theatres or taverns. His conversation should be chaste, his diet temperate, his friends of honourable reputation; and, if he sometimes visits the Forum or the Palace, he should appear only as the advocate of those who have vainly solicited either justice or mercy. His studies should be suited to the sanctity of his profession. Licentious tales, or comedies, or satires, must be banished from his library; which ought solely to consist of historical and philosophical writings; of history which is founded in truth, and of philosophy which is connected with religion. The impious opinions of the Epicureans and Sceptics deserve his abhorrence and contempt;[21] but he

[21] *The exultation of Julian that these impious sects, and even their writings, are extinguished may be consistent enough with the sacerdotal character: but it is unworthy of a philosopher to wish that any opinions and arguments the most repugnant to his own should be concealed from the knowledge of mankind.*

should diligently study the systems of Pythagoras, of Plato, and of the Stoics, which unanimously teach that there *are* gods; that the world is governed by their providence; that their goodness is the source of every temporal blessing; and that they have prepared for the human soul a future state of reward or punishment." The Imperial pontiff inculcates, in the most persuasive language, the duties of benevolence and hospitality; exhorts his inferior clergy to recommend the universal practice of those virtues; promises to assist their indigence from the public treasury; and declares his resolution of establishing hospitals in every city, where the poor should be received without any invidious distinction of country or of religion. Julian beheld with envy the wise and humane regulations of the church; and he very frankly confesses his intention to deprive the Christians of the applause, as well as advantage, which they had acquired by the exclusive practice of charity and beneficence.[22] The same spirit of imitation might dispose the emperor to adopt several ecclesiastical institutions, the use and importance of which were approved by the success of his enemies. But, if these imaginary plans of reformation had been realized, the forced and imperfect copy would have been less beneficial to Paganism than honourable to Christianity.[23] The Gentiles, who peaceably followed the customs of their ancestors, were rather surprised than pleased with the introduction of foreign manners; and, in the short period of his reign, Julian had frequent occasions to complain of the want of fervour of his own party.[24]

The enthusiasm of Julian prompted him to embrace the friends of Jupiter as his personal friends and brethren; and, though he partially overlooked the merit of Christian constancy, he admired and rewarded the noble perseverance of those Gentiles who had preferred the favour of the gods to that of the emperor.[25] If they cultivated the literature, as well as the religion, of the Greeks, they acquired an additional claim to the friendship of Julian, who ranked the Muses in the number of his tutelar deities. In the religion which he had adopted, piety and learning were almost synonymous; and a crowd of poets, of rhetoricians, and of philosophers, hastened to the Imperial court, to occupy the vacant places of the bishops who had seduced the credulity of Constantius. His successor esteemed the ties of common initiation as far more sacred than those of consanguinity: he chose his favourites among the sages who were deeply skilled in the occult sciences of magic and divination; and every impostor who pretended to reveal the secrets of futurity was

---

[22] *Yet he insinuates that the Christians, under the pretence of charity, inveigled children from their religion and parents, conveyed them on ship-board, and devoted those victims to a life of poverty or servitude in a remote country. Had the charge been proved, it was his duty, not to complain, but to punish.*

[23] *Gregory Nazianzen is facetious, ingenious, and argumentative. He ridicules the folly of such vain imitation; and amuses himself with inquiring, what lessons, moral or theological, could be extracted from the Grecian fables.*

[24] *He accuses one of his pontiffs of a secret confederacy with the Christian bishops and presbyters.*

[25] *He praises the fidelity of Callixene, priestess of Ceres, who had been twice as constant as Penelope, and rewards her with the priesthood of the Phrygian goddess at Pessinus. He applauds the firmness of Sopater of Hierapolis, who had been repeatedly pressed by Constantius and Gallus to apostatize.*

assured of enjoying the present hour in honour and affluence. Among the philosophers, Maximus obtained the most eminent rank in the friendship of his royal disciple, who communicated, with unreserved confidence, his actions, his sentiments, and his religious designs, during the anxious suspense of the civil war. As soon as Julian had taken possession of the palace of Constantinople, he dispatched an honourable and pressing invitation to Maximus; who then resided at Sardes in Lydia, with Chrysanthius, the associate of his art and studies. The prudent and superstitious Chrysanthius refused to undertake a journey which showed itself, according to the rules of divination, with the most threatening and malignant aspect: but his companion, whose fanaticism was of a bolder cast, persisted in his interrogations, till he had extorted from the gods a seeming consent to his own wishes and those of the emperor. The journey of Maximus through the cities of Asia displayed the triumph of philosophic vanity; and the magistrates vied with each other in the honourable reception which they prepared for the friend of their sovereign. Julian was pronouncing an oration before the senate, when he was informed of the arrival of Maximus. The emperor immediately interrupted his discourse, advanced to meet him, and, after a tender embrace, conducted him by the hand into the midst of the assembly; where he publicly acknowledged the benefits which he had derived from the instructions of the philosopher. Maximus, who soon acquired the confidence, and influenced the councils, of Julian, was insensibly corrupted by the temptations of a court. His dress became more splendid, his demeanour more lofty, and he was exposed, under a succeeding reign, to a disgraceful inquiry into the means by which the disciple of Plato had accumulated, in the short duration of his favour, a very scandalous proportion of wealth. Of the other philosophers and sophists, who were invited to the Imperial residence by the choice of Julian or by the success of Maximus, few were able to preserve their innocence or their reputation.[26] The liberal gifts of money, lands, and houses, were insufficient to satiate their rapacious avarice; and the indignation of the people was justly excited by the remembrance of their abject poverty and disinterested professions. The penetration of Julian could not always be deceived: but he was unwilling to despise the characters of those men whose talents deserved his esteem; he desired to escape the double reproach of imprudence and inconstancy; and he was apprehensive of degrading, in the eyes of the profane, the honour of letters and of religion.

[26] *Chrysanthius, who had refused to quit Lydia, was created high-priest of the province. His cautious and temperate use of power secured him after the revolution; and he lived in peace; while Maximus, Priscus, &c., were persecuted by the Christian ministers.*

The favour of Julian was almost equally divided between the Pagans, who had firmly adhered to the worship of their ancestors, and the Christians, who prudently embraced the religion of their sovereign. The acquisition of new proselytes [27] gratified the ruling passions of his soul, superstition and vanity; and he was heard to declare with the enthusiasm of a missionary that, if he could render each individual richer than Midas, and every city greater than Babylon, he should not esteem himself the benefactor of mankind, unless, at the same time, he could reclaim his subjects from their impious revolt against the immortal gods. A prince, who had studied human nature, and who possessed the treasures of the Roman empire, could adapt his arguments, his promises, and his rewards, to every order of Christians; and the merit of a seasonable conversion was allowed to supply the defects of a candidate, or even to expiate the guilt of a criminal. As the army is the most forcible engine of absolute power, Julian applied himself, with peculiar diligence, to corrupt the religion of his troops, without whose hearty concurrence every measure must be dangerous and unsuccessful; and the natural temper of soldiers made this conquest as easy as it was important. The legions of Gaul devoted themselves to the faith, as well as to the fortunes, of their victorious leader; and even before the death of Constantius, he had the satisfaction of announcing to his friends that they assisted with fervent devotion, and voracious appetite, at the sacrifices, which were repeatedly offered in his camp, of whole hecatombs of fat oxen. The armies of the East, which had been trained under the standard of the cross, and of Constantius, required a more artful and expensive mode of persuasion. On the days of solemn and public festivals, the emperor received the homage, and rewarded the merits, of the troops. His throne of state was encircled with the military ensigns of Rome and the republic; the holy name of Christ was erased from the *Laborum;* and the symbols of war, of majesty, and of Pagan superstition, were so dexterously blended, that the faithful subject incurred the guilt of idolatry, when he respectfully saluted the person or image of his sovereign. The soldiers passed successively in review; and each of them, before he received from the hand of Julian a liberal donative, proportioned to his rank and services, was required to cast a few grains of incense into the flame which burnt upon the altar. Some Christian confessors might resist, and others might repent; but the far greater number, allured by the prospect of gold and awed by the presence of the emperor, contracted the criminal engagement; and

[27] *Under the reign of Lewis XIV. his subjects of every rank aspired to the glorious title of Convertisseur, expressive of their zeal and success in making proselytes. The word and the idea are growing obsolete in France; may they never be introduced into England!*

680

their future perseverance in the worship of the gods was enforced by every consideration of duty and of interest. By the frequent repetition of these arts, and at the expense of sums which would have purchased the service of half the nations of Scythia, Julian gradually acquired for his troops the imaginary protection of the gods, and for himself the firm and effectual support of the Roman legions. It is indeed more than probable that the restoration and encouragement of Paganism revealed a multitude of pretended Christians, who, from motives of temporal advantage, had acquiesced in the religion of the former reign; and who afterwards returned, with the same flexibility of conscience, to the faith which was professed by the successors of Julian.

While the devout monarch incessantly laboured to restore and propagate the religion of his ancestors, he embraced the extraordinary design of rebuilding the temple of Jerusalem. In a public epistle to the nation or community of the Jews, dispersed through the provinces, he pities their misfortunes, condemns their oppressors, praises their constancy, declares himself their gracious protector, and expresses a pious hope that, after his return from the Persian war, he may be permitted to pay his grateful vows to the Almighty in his holy city of Jerusalem. The blind superstition and abject slavery of those unfortunate exiles must excite the contempt of a philosophic emperor; but they deserved the friendship of Julian by their implacable hatred of the Christian name. The barren synagogue abhorred and envied the fecundity of the rebellious church: the power of the Jews was not equal to their malice; but their gravest rabbis approved the private murder of an apostate;[28] and their seditious clamours had often awakened the indolence of the Pagan magistrates. Under the reign of Constantine, the Jews became the subjects of their revolted children, nor was it long before they experienced the bitterness of domestic tyranny. The civil immunities which had been granted, or confirmed, by Severus were gradually repealed by the Christian princes; and a rash tumult excited by the Jews of Palestine seemed to justify the lucrative modes of oppression, which were invented by the bishops and eunuchs of the court of Constantius. The Jewish patriarch, who was still permitted to exercise a precarious jurisdiction, held his residence at Tiberias; and the neighbouring cities of Palestine were filled with the remains of a people who fondly adhered to the promised land. But the edict of Hadrian was renewed and enforced; and they viewed from afar the walls of the holy city, which were profaned in their eyes

[28] *The Misnah denounced death against those who abandoned the foundation. Constantine made a law to protect Christian converts from Judaism.*

by the triumph of the cross and the devotion of the Christians.

In the midst of a rocky and barren country, the walls of Jerusalem inclosed the two mountains of Sion and Acra, within an oval figure of about three English miles.[29] Towards the south, the upper town and the fortress of David were erected on the lofty ascent of Mount Sion: on the north side, the buildings of the lower town covered the spacious summit of Mount Acra; and a part of the hill, distinguished by the name of Moriah and levelled by human industry, was crowned with the stately temple of the Jewish nation. After the final destruction of the temple, by the arms of Titus and Hadrian, a ploughshare was drawn over the consecrated ground, as a sign of perpetual interdiction. Sion was deserted; and the vacant space of the lower city was filled with the public and private edifices of the Ælian colony, which spread themselves over the adjacent hill of Calvary. The holy places were polluted with monuments of idolatry; and, either from design or accident, a chapel was dedicated to Venus on the spot which had been sanctified by the death and resurrection of Christ. Almost three hundred years after those stupendous events, the profane chapel of Venus was demolished by the order of Constantine; and the removal of the earth and stones revealed the holy sepulchre to the eyes of mankind. A magnificent church was erected on that mystic ground, by the first Christian emperor; and the effects of his pious munificence were extended to every spot which had been consecrated by the footsteps of patriarchs, of prophets, and of the Son of God.[30]

The passionate desire of contemplating the original monuments of their redemption attracted to Jerusalem a successive crowd of pilgrims, from the shores of the Atlantic ocean and the most distant countries of the East;[31] and their piety was authorized by the example of the empress Helena, who appears to have united the credulity of age with the warm feelings of a recent conversion. Sages and heroes, who have visited the memorable scenes of ancient wisdom or glory, have confessed the inspiration of the genius of the place; and the Christian who knelt before the holy sepulchre ascribed his lively faith and his fervent devotion to the more immediate influence of the divine spirit. The zeal, perhaps the avarice, of the clergy of Jerusalem cherished and multiplied these beneficial visits. They fixed, by unquestionable tradition, the scene of each memorable event. They exhibited the instruments which had been used in the passion of Christ; the nails and the lance that had pierced his hands, his feet, and his side; the crown of thorns that was planted on his

[29] I have consulted a rare and curious treatise of M. d'Anville (sur l'ancienne Jérusalem). The circumference of the ancient city was twenty-seven stadia, or 2550 toises. A plan taken on the spot assigns no more than 1980 for the modern town. The circuit is defined by natural landmarks which cannot be mistaken or removed.

[30] The emperor likewise built churches at Bethlehem, the Mount of Olives, and the oak of Mambre.

[31] The Itinerary from Bourdeaux to Jerusalem was composed in the year 333, for the use of pilgrims; among whom Jerom mentions the Britons and the Indians. The causes of this superstitious fashion are discussed in the learned and judicious preface of Wesseling.

head, the pillar at which he was scourged; and, above all, they showed the cross on which he suffered, and which was dug out of the earth in the reign of those princes who inserted the symbol of Christianity in the banners of the Roman legions.[32] Such miracles as seemed necessary to account for its extraordinary preservation and seasonable discovery were gradually propagated without opposition. The custody of the *true cross,* which on Easter Sunday was solemnly exposed to the people, was entrusted to the bishop of Jerusalem; and he alone might gratify the curious devotion of the pilgrims, by the gift of small pieces, which they enchased in gold or gems, and carried away in triumph to their respective countries. But, as this gainful branch of commerce must soon have been annihilated, it was found convenient to suppose that the marvellous wood possessed a secret power of vegetation; and that its substance, though continually diminished, still remained entire and unimpaired.[33] It might perhaps have been expected that the influence of the place, and the belief of a perpetual miracle, should have produced some salutary effects on the morals as well as on the faith of the people. Yet the most respectable of the ecclesiastical writers have been obliged to confess, not only that the streets of Jerusalem were filled with the incessant tumult of business and pleasure, but that every species of vice, adultery, theft, idolatry, poisoning, murder, was familiar to the inhabitants of the holy city.[34] The wealth and pre-eminence of the church of Jerusalem excited the ambition of Arian, as well as orthodox, candidates; and the virtues of Cyril, who, since his death, has been honoured with the title of Saint, were displayed in the exercise, rather than in the acquisition, of his episcopal dignity.[35]

The vain and ambitious mind of Julian might aspire to restore the ancient glory of the temple of Jerusalem.[36] As the Christians were firmly persuaded that a sentence of everlasting destruction had been pronounced against the whole fabric of the Mosaic law, the Imperial sophist would have converted the success of his undertaking into a specious argument against the faith of the prophecy and the truth of revelation.[37] He was displeased with the spiritual worship of the synagogue; but he approved the institutions of Moses, who had not disdained to adopt many of the rites and ceremonies of Egypt.[38] The local and national deity of the Jews was sincerely adored by a polytheist who desired only to multiply the number of the gods;[39] and such was the appetite of Julian for bloody sacrifice that his emulation might be excited by the piety of Solomon, who had

[32] *Baronius and Tillemont are the historians and champions of the miraculous invention of the cross, under the reign of Constantine. Their oldest witnesses are Paulinus, Sulpicius Severus, Rufinus, Ambrose, and perhaps Cyril of Jerusalem. The silence of Eusebius and the Bourdeaux pilgrim, which satisfies those who think, perplexes those who believe.*

[33] *This multiplication is asserted by Paulinus, who seems to have improved a rhetorical flourish of Cyril into a real fact. The same supernatural privilege must have been communicated to the Virgin's milk, saints' heads, &c. and other relics, which were repeated in so many different churches.*

[34] *The whole epistle, which condemns either the use or the abuse of religious pilgrimage, is painful to the Catholic divines, while it is dear and familiar to our Protestant polemics.*

[35] *He renounced his orthodox ordination, officiated as a deacon, and was reordained by the hands of the Arians. But Cyril afterwards changed with the times, and prudently conformed to the Nicene faith. Tillemont, who*

offered, at the feast of the dedication, twenty-two thousand oxen and one hundred and twenty thousand sheep.⁴⁰ These considerations might influence his designs; but the prospect of an immediate and important advantage would not suffer the impatient monarch to expect the remote and uncertain event of the Persian war. He resolved to erect, without delay, on the commanding eminence of Moriah, a stately temple which might eclipse the splendour of the church of the Resurrection on the adjacent hill of Calvary; to establish an order of priests, whose interested zeal would detect the arts, and resist the ambition, of their Christian rivals; and to invite a numerous colony of Jews, whose stern fanaticism would be always prepared to second, and even to anticipate, the hostile measures of the Pagan government. Among the friends of the emperor (if the names of emperor and of friend are not incompatible) the first place was assigned, by Julian himself, to the virtuous and learned Alypius. The humanity of Alypius was tempered by severe justice and manly fortitude; and, while he exercised his abilities in the civil administration of Britain, he imitated, in his poetical compositions, the harmony and softness of the odes of Sappho. This minister, to whom Julian communicated, without reserve, his most careless levities and his most serious counsels, received an extraordinary commission to restore, in its pristine beauty, the temple of Jerusalem; and the diligence of Alypius required and obtained the strenuous support of the governor of Palestine. At the call of their great deliverer, the Jews, from all the provinces of the empire, assembled on the holy mountain of their fathers; and their insolent triumph alarmed and exasperated the Christian inhabitants of Jerusalem. The desire of rebuilding the temple has, in every age, been the ruling passion of the children of Israel. In this propitious moment the men forget their avarice, and the women their delicacy; spades and pickaxes of silver were provided by the vanity of the rich, and the rubbish was transported in mantles of silk and purple. Every purse was opened in liberal contributions, every hand claimed a share in the pious labour; and the commands of a great monarch were executed by the enthusiasm of a whole people.

Yet, on this occasion, the joint efforts of power and enthusiasm were unsuccessful; and the ground of the Jewish temple, which is now covered by a Mahometan mosque,⁴¹ still continued to exhibit the same edifying spectacle of ruin and desolation. Perhaps the absence and death of the emperor, and the new maxims of a Christian reign, might explain the interruption of an arduous work, which was attempted only in the last six months of the life of Julian.[42] But the Christians entertained a natural and pious expectation that, in this memorable contest, the honour of religion would be vindicated by some signal miracle. An earthquake, a whirlwind, and a fiery eruption, which overturned and scattered the new foundations of the temple, are attested, with some variations, by contemporary and respectable evidence. This public event is described by Ambrose, bishop of Milan, in an epistle to the emperor Theodosius, which must provoke the severe animadversion of the Jews; by the eloquent Chrysostom, who might appeal to the memory of the elder part of his congregation at Antioch; and by Gregory Nazianzen, who published his account of the miracle before the expiration of the same year. The last of these writers has boldly declared that the præternatural event was not disputed by the infidels; and his assertion, strange as it may seem, is confirmed by the unexceptionable testimony of Ammianus Marcellinus. The philosophic soldier, who loved the virtues, without adopting the prejudices, of his master, has recorded, in his judicious and candid history of his own times, the extraordinary obstacles which interrupted the restoration of the temple of Jerusalem. "Whilst Alypius, assisted by the governor of the province, urged with vigour and diligence the execution of the work, horrible balls of fire breaking out near the foundations with frequent and reiterated attacks, rendered the place, from time to time, inaccessible to the scorched and blasted workmen; and, the victorious element continuing in this manner obstinately and resolutely bent, as it were, to drive them to a distance, the undertaking was abandoned." Such authority should satisfy a believing, and must astonish an incredulous, mind. Yet a philosopher may still require the original evidence of impartial and intelligent spectators. At this important crisis, any singular accident of nature would assume the appearance, and produce the effects, of a real prodigy. This glorious deliverance would be speedily improved and magnified by the pious art of the clergy of Jerusalem and the active credulity of the Christian world; and, at the distance of twenty years, a Roman historian, careless of theological disputes, might adorn his work with the specious and splendid miracle.[43]

The restoration of the Jewish temple was secretly connected with the ruin of the Christian church. Julian still continued to maintain the freedom of religious worship, without distinguishing whether this universal toleration proceeded from his justice or his clemency. He affected to pity the unhappy Christians, who were mistaken in

condemns the Christians: for believing and for renouncing the religion of the Jews. Their Deity was a true, but not the only, God.

[40] As the blood and smoke of so many hecatombs might be inconvenient, Lightfoot, the Christian Rabbi, removes them by a miracle. Le Clerc is bold enough to suspect the fidelity of the numbers.

[41] Built by Omar, the second Khalif, who died A.D. 644. This great mosque covers the whole consecrated ground of the Jewish temple, and constitutes almost a square of 760 toises.

[42] Ammianus records the consuls of the year 363, before he proceeds to mention the thoughts of Julian. Warburton has a secret wish to anticipate the design; but he must have understood, from former examples, that the execution of such a work would have demanded many years.

[43] Dr. Lardner, perhaps alone of the Christian critics, presumes to doubt the truth of this famous miracle. The silence of Jerom would lead to a suspicion that the same story, which was celebrated at a distance, might be despised on the spot.

the most important object of their lives; but his pity was degraded by contempt, his contempt was embittered by hatred; and the sentiments of Julian were expressed in a style of sarcastic wit, which inflicts a deep and deadly wound whenever it issues from the mouth of a sovereign. As he was sensible that the Christians gloried in the name of their Redeemer, he countenanced, and perhaps enjoined, the use of the less honourable appellation of GALILÆANS.[44] He declared that, by the folly of the Galilæans, whom he describes as a sect of fanatics, contemptible to men, and odious to the gods, the empire had been reduced to the brink of destruction; and he insinuates in a public edict that a frantic patient might sometimes be cured by salutary violence. An ungenerous distinction was admitted into the mind and counsels of Julian, that, according to the difference of their religious sentiments, one part of his subjects deserved his favour and friendship, while the other was entitled only to the common benefits that his justice could not refuse to an obedient people. According to a principle, pregnant with mischief and oppression, the emperor transferred to the pontiffs of his own religion the management of the liberal allowances from the public revenue which had been granted to the church by the piety of Constantine and his sons. The proud system of clerical honours and immunities, which had been constructed with so much art and labour, was levelled to the ground; the hopes of testamentary donations were intercepted by the rigour of the laws; and the priests of the Christian sect were confounded with the last and most ignominious class of the people. Such of these regulations as appeared necessary to check the ambition and avarice of the ecclesiastics were soon afterwards imitated by the wisdom of an orthodox prince. The peculiar distinctions which policy has bestowed, or superstition has lavished, on the sacerdotal order *must* be confined to those priests who profess the religion of the state. But the will of the legislator was not exempt from prejudice and passion; and it was the object of the insidious policy of Julian to deprive the Christians of all the temporal honours and advantages which rendered them respectable in the eyes of the world.

A just and severe censure has been inflicted on the law which prohibited the Christians from teaching the arts of grammar and rhetoric. The motives alleged by the emperor to justify this partial and oppressive measure might command, during his lifetime, the silence of slaves and the applause of flatterers. Julian abuses the ambiguous meaning of a word which might be indifferently applied to the lan-

[44] And this law was confirmed by the invariable practice of Julian himself. Warburton has justly observed that the Platonists believed in the mysterious virtue of words; and Julian's dislike for the name of Christ might proceed from superstition, as well as from contempt.

guage and the religion of the GREEKS: he contemptuously observes that the men who exalt the merit of implicit faith are unfit to claim or to enjoy the advantages of science; and he vainly contends that, if they refuse to adore the gods of Homer and Demosthenes, they ought to content themselves with expounding Luke and Matthew in the churches of the Galilæans.[45] In all the cities of the Roman world, the education of the youth was entrusted to masters of grammar and rhetoric; who were elected by the magistrates, maintained at the public expense, and distinguished by many lucrative and honourable privileges. The edict of Julian appears to have included the physicians, and professors of all the liberal arts; and the emperor, who reserved to himself the approbation of the candidates, was authorized by the laws to corrupt, or to punish, the religious constancy of the most learned of the Christians. As soon as the resignation of the more obstinate teachers had established the unrivalled dominion of the Pagan sophists, Julian invited the rising generation to resort with freedom to the public schools, in a just confidence that their tender minds would receive the impressions of literature and idolatry. If the greatest part of the Christian youth should be deterred by their own scruples, or by those of their parents, from accepting this dangerous mode of instruction, they must at the same time relinquish the benefits of a liberal education. Julian had reason to expect that, in the space of a few years, the church would relapse into its primæval simplicity, and that the theologians, who possessed an adequate share of the learning and eloquence of the age, would be succeeded by a generation of blind and ignorant fanatics, incapable of defending the truth of their own principles or of exposing the various follies of Polytheism.[46]

It was undoubtedly the wish and the design of Julian to deprive the Christians of the advantages of wealth, of knowledge, and of power; but the injustice of excluding them from all offices of trust and profit seems to have been the result of his general policy rather than the immediate consequence of any positive law. Superior merit might deserve, and obtain, some extraordinary exceptions; but the greater part of the Christian officers were gradually removed from their employments in the state, the army, and the provinces. The hopes of future candidates were extinguished by the declared partiality of a prince who maliciously reminded them that it was unlawful for a Christian to use the sword either of justice or of war; and who studiously guarded the camp and the tribunals with the ensigns of idolatry. The powers of government were en-

[45] *The edict itself, which is still extant among the epistles of Julian, may be compared with the loose invectives of Gregory. Tillemont has collected the seeming differences of ancients and moderns. They may be easily reconciled. The Christians were directly forbid to teach, they were indirectly forbid to learn; since they would not frequent the schools of the Pagans.*

[46] *They had recourse to the expedient of composing books for their own schools. Within a few months Apollinaris produced his Christian imitations of Homer (a sacred history in twenty-four books), Pindar, Euripides, and Menander; and Sozomen is satisfied that they equalled, or excelled, the originals.*

trusted to the Pagans, who professed an ardent zeal for the religion of their ancestors; and, as the choice of the emperor was often directed by the rules of divination, the favourites whom he preferred as the most agreeable to the gods did not always obtain the approbation of mankind. Under the administration of their enemies, the Christians had much to suffer, and more to apprehend. The temper of Julian was averse to cruelty; and the care of his reputation, which was exposed to the eyes of the universe, restrained the philosophic monarch from violating the laws of justice and toleration which he himself had so recently established. But the provincial ministers of his authority were placed in a less conspicuous station. In the exercise of arbitrary power, they consulted the wishes, rather than the commands, of their sovereign; and ventured to exercise a secret and vexatious tyranny against the sectaries, on whom they were not permitted to confer the honours of martyrdom. The emperor, who dissembled as long as possible his knowledge of the injustice that was exercised in his name, expressed his real sense of the conduct of his officers by gentle reproofs and substantial rewards.

The most effectual instrument of oppression with which they were armed was the law that obliged the Christians to make full and ample satisfaction for the temples which they had destroyed under the preceding reign. The zeal of the triumphant church had not always expected the sanction of the public authority; and the bishops, who were secure of impunity, had often marched, at the head of their congregations, to attack and demolish the fortresses of the prince of darkness. The consecrated lands, which had increased the patrimony of the sovereign or of the clergy, were clearly defined, and easily restored. But on these lands, and on the ruins of Pagan superstition, the Christians had frequently erected their own religious edifices: and, as it was necessary to remove the church before the temple could be rebuilt, the justice and piety of the emperor were applauded by one party, while the other deplored and execrated his sacrilegious violence. After the ground was cleared, the restitution of those stately structures which had been levelled with the dust and of the precious ornaments which had been converted to Christian uses swelled into a very large account of damages and debt. The authors of the injury had neither the ability nor the inclination to discharge this accumulated demand: and the impartial wisdom of a legislator would have been displayed in balancing the adverse claims of complaints, by an equitable and temperate arbitration. But the whole empire, and particularly the East, was thrown into confusion by the rash edicts of Julian; and the Pagan magistrates, inflamed by zeal and revenge, abused the rigorous privilege of the Roman law, which substitutes, in the place of his inadequate property, the person of the insolvent debtor. Under the preceding reign, Mark, bishop of Arethusa,[47] had laboured in the conversion of his people with arms more effectual than those of persuasion.[48] The magistrates required the full value of a temple which had been destroyed by his intolerant zeal: but, as they were satisfied of his poverty, they desired only to bend his inflexible spirit to the promise of the slightest compensation. They apprehended the aged prelate, they inhumanly scourged him, they tore his beard; and his naked body, anointed with honey, was suspended in a net between heaven and earth, and exposed to the stings of insects and the rays of a Syrian sun. From this lofty station, Mark still persisted to glory in his crime and to insult the impotent rage of his persecutors. He was at length rescued from their hands, and dismissed to enjoy the honour of his divine triumph. The Arians celebrated the virtue of their pious confessor; the Catholics ambitiously claimed his alliance; and the Pagans, who might be susceptible of shame or remorse, were deterred from the repetition of such unavailing cruelty. Julian spared his life: but, if the bishop of Arethusa had saved the infancy of Julian, posterity will condemn the ingratitude, instead of praising the clemency, of the emperor.

At the distance of five miles from Antioch, the Macedonian kings of Syria had consecrated to Apollo one of the most elegant places of devotion in the Pagan world. A magnificent temple rose in honour of the god of light; and his colossal figure almost filled the capacious sanctuary, which was enriched with gold and gems, and adorned by the skill of the Grecian artists. The deity was represented in a bending attitude, with a golden cup in his hand, pouring out a libation on the earth; as if he supplicated the venerable mother to give to his arms the cold and beauteous DAPHNE: for the spot was ennobled by fiction; and the fancy of the Syrian poets had transported the amorous tale from the banks of the Peneus to those of the Orontes. The ancient rites of Greece were imitated by the royal colony of Antioch. A stream of prophecy, which rivalled the truth and reputation of the Delphic oracle, flowed from the *Castalian* fountain of Daphne.[49] In the adjacent fields a stadium was built by a special privilege,[50] which had been purchased from Elis; the Olympic games were celebrated at the expense of the city; and a revenue of thirty thousand pounds sterling was annually applied to the public

[47] *Restan, or Arethusa, at the equal distance of sixteen miles between Emesa (Hems) and Epiphania (Hamath), was founded, or at least named, by Seleucus Nicator. Its peculiar æra dates from the year of Rome 685 according to the medals of the city. In the decline of the Seleucides, Emesa and Arethusa were usurped by the Arab Sampsiceramus, whose posterity, the vassals of Rome, were not extinguished in the reign of Vespasian.*

[48] *It is surprising that Gregory and Theodoret should suppress a circumstance which, in their eyes, must have enhanced the religious merit of the confessor.*

[49] *Hadrian read the history of his future fortunes on a leaf dipped in the Castalian stream; a trick which, according to the physician Vandale, might be easily performed by chemical preparations. The emperor stopped the source of such dangerous knowledge; which was again opened by the devout curiosity of Julian.*

[50] *It was purchased,* A.D. *44, in the year 92 of the*

æra of Antioch for the term of ninety Olympiads. But the Olympic games of Antioch were not regularly celebrated till the reign of Commodus.

[51] *Fifteen talents of gold, bequeathed by Sosibius, who died in the reign of Augustus. The theatrical merits of the Syrian cities, in the age of Constantine, are compared in the Expositio totius Mundi.*

[52] *Julian discovers his own character with that naïveté, that unconscious simplicity, which always constitutes genuine humour.*

[53] *Babylas is named by Eusebius in the succession of the bishops of Antioch. His triumph over two emperors (the first fabulous, the second historical) is diffusely celebrated by Chrysostom.*

pleasures.[51] The perpetual resort of pilgrims and spectators insensibly formed, in the neighbourhood of the temple, the stately and populous village of Daphne, which emulated the splendour, without acquiring the title, of a provincial city. The temple and the village were deeply bosomed in a thick grove of laurels and cypresses, which reached as far as a circumference of ten miles, and formed in the most sultry summers a cool and impenetrable shade. A thousand streams of the purest water, issuing from every hill, preserved the verdure of the earth and the temperature of the air; the senses were gratified with harmonious sounds and aromatic odours; and the peaceful grove was consecrated to health and joy, to luxury and love. The vigorous youth pursued, like Apollo, the object of his desires; and the blushing maid was warned, by the fate of Daphne, to shun the folly of unseasonable coyness. The soldier and the philosopher wisely avoided the temptation of this sensual paradise; where pleasure, assuming the character of religion, imperceptibly dissolved the firmness of manly virtue. But the groves of Daphne continued for many ages to enjoy the veneration of natives and strangers; the privileges of the holy ground were enlarged by the munificence of succeeding emperors; and every generation added new ornaments to the splendour of the temple.

When Julian, on the day of the annual festival, hastened to adore the Apollo of Daphne, his devotion was raised to the highest pitch of eagerness and impatience. His lively imagination anticipated the grateful pomp of victims, of libations, and of incense; a long procession of youths and virgins, clothed in white robes, the symbol of their innocence; and the tumultuous concourse of an innumerable people. But the zeal of Antioch was diverted, since the reign of Christianity, into a different channel. Instead of hecatombs of fat oxen sacrificed by the tribes of a wealthy city to their tutelar deity, the emperor complains that he found only a single goose, provided at the expense of a priest, the pale and solitary inhabitant of this decayed temple.[52] The altar was deserted, the oracle had been reduced to silence, and the holy ground was profaned by the introduction of Christian and funereal rites. After Babylas [53] (a bishop of Antioch, who died in prison in the persecution of Decius) had rested near a century in his grave, his body, by the order of the Cæsar Gallus, was transported into the midst of the grove of Daphne. A magnificent church was erected over his remains; a portion of the sacred lands was usurped for the maintenance of the clergy, and for the burial of the Christians of Antioch who were ambitious of lying at the feet of their bishop; and the priests of Apollo retired, with their affrighted and indignant votaries. As soon as another revolution seemed to restore the fortune of Paganism, the church of St. Babylas was demolished, and new buildings were added to the mouldering edifice which had been raised by the piety of Syrian kings. But the first and most serious care of Julian was to deliver his oppressed deity from the odious presence of the dead and living Christians who had so effectually suppressed the voice of fraud or enthusiasm.[54] The scene of infection was purified, according to the forms of ancient rituals; the bodies were decently removed; and the ministers of the church were permitted to convey the remains of St. Babylas to their former habitation within the walls of Antioch. The modest behaviour which might have assuaged the jealousy of an hostile government was neglected on this occasion by the zeal of the Christians. The lofty car that transported the relics of Babylas was followed, and accompanied, and received, by an innumerable multitude; who chanted, with thundering acclamations, the Psalms of David the most expressive of their contempt for idols and idolaters. The return of the saint was a triumph; and the triumph was an insult on the religion of the emperor, who exerted his pride to dissemble his resentment. During the night which terminated this indiscreet procession, the temple of Daphne was in flames; the statue of Apollo was consumed; and the walls of the edifice were left a naked and awful monument of ruin. The Christians of Antioch asserted, with religious confidence, that the powerful intercession of St. Babylas had pointed the lightnings of heaven against the devoted roof: but, as Julian was reduced to the alternative of believing either a crime or a miracle, he chose, without hesitation, without evidence, but with some colour of probability, to impute the fire of Daphne to the revenge of the Galilæans.[55] Their offence, had it been sufficiently proved, might have justified the retaliation which was immediately executed by the order of Julian, of shutting the doors, and confiscating the wealth, of the cathedral of Antioch. To discover the criminals who were guilty of the tumult, of the fire, or of secreting the riches of the church, several ecclesiastics were tortured; and a presbyter, of the name of Theodoret, was beheaded by the sentence of the Count of the East. But this hasty act was blamed by the emperor; who lamented, with real or affected concern, that the imprudent zeal of his ministers would tarnish his reign with the disgrace of persecution.

The zeal of the ministers of Julian was instantly checked by the

[54] *Ecclesiastical critics, particularly those who love relics, exult in the confession of Julian and Libanius, that Apollo was disturbed by the vicinity of* one *dead man. Yet Ammianus clears and purifies the whole ground, according to the rites which the Athenians formerly practised in the isle of Delos.*

[55] *Julian rather insinuates than affirms their guilt. Ammianus treats the imputation as* levissimus rumor, *and relates the story with extraordinary candour.*

[56] *Sozomen may be considered as an original, though not impartial, witness. He was a native of Gaza, and had conversed with the confessor Zeno, who, as bishop of Maiuma, lived to the age of an hundred. Philostorgius adds some tragic circumstances, of Christians who were* literally *sacrificed at the altars of the gods, &c.*

[57] *The life and death of George of Cappadocia are described by Ammianus, Gregory Nazianzen, and Epiphanius. The invectives of the two saints might not deserve much credit, unless they were confirmed by the testimony of the cool and impartial infidel.*

[58] *After the massacre of George, the emperor Julian repeatedly sent orders to preserve the library for his own use, and to torture the slaves who might be suspected of secreting any books. He praises the merit of the collection, from whence he had borrowed and transcribed several manuscripts while he pursued his studies in Cappadocia. He could wish indeed that the works of the Galilæans might perish: but he requires an exact account*

frown of their sovereign; but, when the father of his country declares himself the leader of a faction, the licence of popular fury cannot easily be restrained nor consistently punished. Julian, in a public composition, applauds the devotion and loyalty of the holy cities of Syria, whose pious inhabitants had destroyed, at the first signal, the sepulchres of the Galilæans; and faintly complains that they had revenged the injuries of the gods with less moderation than he should have recommended. This imperfect and reluctant confession may appear to confirm the ecclesiastical narratives: that in the cities of Gaza, Ascalon, Cæsarea, Heliopolis, &c. the Pagans abused, without prudence or remorse, the moment of their prosperity; that the unhappy objects of their cruelty were released from torture only by death; that, as their mangled bodies were dragged through the streets, they were pierced (such was the universal rage) by the spits of cooks and the distaffs of enraged women; and that the entrails of Christian priests and virgins, after they had been tasted by those bloody fanatics, were mixed with barley, and contemptuously thrown to the unclean animals of the city.[56] Such scenes of religious madness exhibit the most contemptible and odious picture of human nature; but the massacre of Alexandria attracts still more attention, from the certainty of the fact, the rank of the victims, and the splendour of the capital of Egypt.

George,[57] from his parents or his education surnamed the Cappadocian, was born at Epiphania in Cilicia, in a fuller's shop. From this obscure and servile origin he raised himself by the talents of a parasite: and the patrons, whom he assiduously flattered, procured for their worthless dependent a lucrative commission, or contract, to supply the army with bacon. His employment was mean; he rendered it infamous. He accumulated wealth by the basest arts of fraud and corruption; but his malversations were so notorious that George was compelled to escape from the pursuits of justice. After this disgrace, in which he appears to have saved his fortune at the expense of his honour, he embraced, with real or affected zeal, the profession of Arianism. From the love, or the ostentation, of learning, he collected a valuable library of history, rhetoric, philosophy, and theology;[58] and the choice of the prevailing faction promoted George of Cappadocia to the throne of Athanasius. The entrance of the new archbishop was that of a Barbarian conqueror; and each moment of his reign was polluted by cruelty and avarice. The Catholics of Alexandria and Egypt were abandoned to a tyrant, qualified, by nature and education, to exercise the office of persecution; but he oppressed with an impartial hand the various inhabitants of his extensive diocese. The primate of Egypt assumed the pomp and insolence of his lofty station; but he still betrayed the vices of his base and servile extraction. The merchants of Alexandria were impoverished by the unjust, and almost universal, monopoly, which he acquired, of nitre, salt, paper, funerals, &c.; and the spiritual father of a great people condescended to practise the vile and pernicious arts of an informer. The Alexandrians could never forget nor forgive the tax which he suggested on all the houses of the city; under an obsolete claim that the royal founder had conveyed to his successors, the Ptolemies and the Cæsars, the perpetual property of the soil. The Pagans, who had been flattered with the hopes of freedom and toleration, excited his devout avarice; and the rich temples of Alexandria were either pillaged or insulted by the haughty prelate, who exclaimed, in a loud and threatening tone, "How long will these sepulchres be permitted to stand?" Under the reign of Constantius, he was expelled by the fury, or rather by the justice, of the people; and it was not without a violent struggle that the civil and military powers of the state could restore his authority and gratify his revenge. The messenger who proclaimed at Alexandria the accession of Julian announced the downfall of the archbishop. George, with two of his obsequious ministers, count Diodorus, and Dracontius, master of the mint, were ignominiously dragged in chains to the public prison. At the end of twenty-four days, the prison was forced open by the rage of a superstitious multitude, impatient of the tedious forms of judicial proceedings. The enemies of gods and men expired under their cruel insults; the lifeless bodies of the archbishop and his associates were carried in triumph through the streets on the back of a camel; and the inactivity of the Athanasian party was esteemed a shining example of evangelical patience. The remains of these guilty wretches were thrown into the sea; and the popular leaders of the tumult declared their resolution to disappoint the devotion of the Christians, and to intercept the future honours of these *martyrs,* who had been punished, like their predecessors, by the enemies of their religion.[59] The fears of the Pagans were just, and their precautions ineffectual. The meritorious death of the archbishop obliterated the memory of his life. The rival of Athanasius was dear and sacred to the Arians, and the seeming conversion of those sectaries introduced his worship into the bosom of the Catholic church.[60] The odious stranger, disguising every circumstance of time and place, assumed the mask of a mar-

even of those theological volumes, lest other treatises more valuable should be confounded in their loss.

[59] *Epiphanius proves to the Arians that George was not a martyr.*

[60] *Some Donatists and Priscillianists have in like manner usurped the honours of Catholic saints and martyrs.*

61 *The saints of Cappadocia, Basil and the Gregories, were ignorant of their holy companion. Pope Gelasius* (A. D. 494), *the first Catholic who acknowledges St. George, places him among the martyrs,* "qui Deo magis quam hominibus noti sunt." *He rejects his Acts as the composition of heretics. Some, perhaps not the oldest, of the spurious Acts are still extant; and, through a cloud of fiction, we may yet distinguish the combat which St. George of Cappadocia sustained, in the presence of Queen* Alexandra, *against the* magician Athanasius.

62 *This transformation is not given as absolutely certain, but as* extremely *probable.*

63 *A curious history of the worship of St. George, from the sixth century (when he was already revered in Palestine, in Armenia, at Rome, and at Treves in Gaul), might be extracted from Dr. Heylin and the Bollandists. His fame and popularity in Europe, and especially in England, proceeded from the Crusades.*

tyr, a saint, and a Christian hero;[61] and the infamous George of Cappadocia has been transformed [62] into the renowned St. George of England, the patron of arms, of chivalry, and of the garter.[63]

About the same time that Julian was informed of the tumult of Alexandria, he received intelligence from Edessa that the proud and wealthy faction of the Arians had insulted the weakness of the Valentinians, and committed such disorders as ought not to be suffered with impunity in a well-regulated state. Without expecting the slow forms of justice, the exasperated prince directed his mandate to the magistrates of Edessa, by which he confiscated the whole property of the church: the money was distributed among the soldiers; the lands were added to the domain; and this act of oppression was aggravated by the most ungenerous irony. "I show myself," says Julian, "the true friend of the Galilæans. Their *admirable* law has promised the kingdom of heaven to the poor; and they will advance with more diligence in the paths of virtue and salvation, when they are relieved by my assistance from the load of temporal possessions. Take care," pursued the monarch, in a more serious tone, "take care how you provoke my patience and humanity. If these disorders continue, I will revenge on the magistrates the crimes of the people; and you will have reason to dread, not only confiscation and exile, but fire and the sword." The tumults of Alexandria were doubtless of a more bloody and dangerous nature: but a Christian bishop had fallen by the hands of the Pagans; and the public epistle of Julian affords a very lively proof of the partial spirit of his administration. His reproaches to the citizens of Alexandria are mingled with expressions of esteem and tenderness; and he laments that on this occasion they should have departed from the gentle and generous manners which attested their Grecian extraction. He gravely censures the offence which they had committed against the laws of justice and humanity; but he recapitulates, with visible complacency, the intolerable provocations which they had so long endured from the impious tyranny of George of Cappadocia. Julian admits the principle that a wise and vigorous government should chastise the insolence of the people: yet, in consideration of their founder Alexander and of Serapis their tutelar deity, he grants a free and gracious pardon to the guilty city, for which he again feels the affection of a brother.

After the tumult of Alexandria had subsided, Athanasius, amidst the public acclamations, seated himself on the throne from whence his unworthy competitor had been precipitated; and, as the zeal of the archbishop was tempered with discretion, the exercise of his authority tended not to inflame, but to reconcile, the minds of the people. His pastoral labours were not confined to the narrow limits of Egypt. The state of the Christian world was present to his active and capacious mind; and the age, the merit, the reputation of Athanasius enabled him to assume, in a moment of danger, the office of Ecclesiastical Dictator. Three years were not yet elapsed since the majority of the bishops of the West had ignorantly, or reluctantly, subscribed the Confession of Rimini. They repented, they believed, but they dreaded the unseasonable rigour of their orthodox brethren, and, if their pride was stronger than their faith, they might throw themselves into the arms of the Arians, to escape the indignity of a public penance, which must degrade them to the condition of obscure laymen. At the same time, the domestic differences concerning the union and distinction of the divine persons were agitated with some heat among the Catholic doctors; and the progress of this metaphysical controversy seemed to threaten a public and lasting division of the Greek and Latin churches. By the wisdom of a select synod, to which the name and presence of Athanasius gave the authority of a general council, the bishops who had unwarily deviated into error were admitted to the communion of the church, on the easy condition of subscribing the Nicene Creed; without any formal acknowledgment of their past fault or any minute definition of their scholastic opinions. The advice of the primate of Egypt had already prepared the clergy of Gaul and Spain, of Italy and Greece, for the reception of this salutary measure; and, notwithstanding the opposition of some ardent spirits,[64] the fear of the common enemy promoted the peace and harmony of the Christians.

The skill and diligence of the primate of Egypt had improved the season of tranquillity, before it was interrupted by the hostile edicts of the emperor. Julian, who despised the Christians, honoured Athanasius with his sincere and peculiar hatred. For his sake alone, he introduced an arbitrary distinction, repugnant, at least, to the spirit of his former declarations. He maintained that the Galilæans whom he had recalled from exile were not restored, by that general indulgence, to the possession of their respective churches: and he expressed his astonishment that a criminal, who had been repeatedly condemned by the judgment of the emperors, should dare to insult the majesty of the laws, and insolently usurp the archiepiscopal throne of Alexandria, without expecting the orders of his sov-

[64] *I have not leisure to follow the blind obstinacy of Lucifer of Cagliari. See his adventures in Tillemont; and observe how the colour of the narrative insensibly changes, as the confessor becomes a schismatic.*

ereign. As a punishment for the imaginary offence, he again banished Athanasius from the city: and he was pleased to suppose that this act of justice would be highly agreeable to his pious subjects. The pressing solicitations of the people soon convinced him that the majority of the Alexandrians were Christians; and that the greatest part of the Christians were firmly attached to the cause of their oppressed primate. But the knowledge of their sentiments, instead of persuading him to recall his decree, provoked him to extend to all Egypt the term of the exile of Athanasius. The zeal of the multitude rendered Julian still more inexorable: he was alarmed by the danger of leaving at the head of a tumultuous city a daring and popular leader: and the language of his resentment discovers the opinion which he entertained of the courage and abilities of Athanasius. The execution of the sentence was still delayed, by the caution or negligence of Ecdicius, præfect of Egypt, who was at length awakened from his lethargy by a severe reprimand. "Though you neglect," says Julian, "to write to me on any other subject, at least it is your duty to inform me of your conduct towards Athanasius, the enemy of the gods. My intentions have been long since communicated to you. I swear by the great Serapis that unless, on the calends of December, Athanasius has departed from Alexandria, nay from Egypt, the officers of your government shall pay a fine of one hundred pounds of gold. You know my temper: I am slow to condemn, but I am still slower to forgive." This epistle was enforced by a short postscript, written with the emperor's own hand. "The contempt that is shown for all the gods fills me with grief and indignation. There is nothing that I should see, nothing that I should hear with more pleasure than the expulsion of Athanasius from all Egypt. The abominable wretch! Under my reign, the baptism of several Grecian ladies of the highest rank has been the effect of his persecutions." The death of Athanasius was not *expressly* commanded; but the præfect of Egypt understood that it was safer for him to exceed, than to neglect, the orders of an irritated master. The archbishop prudently retired to the monasteries of the Desert: eluded, with his usual dexterity, the snares of the enemy; and lived to triumph over the ashes of a prince who, in words of formidable import, had declared his wish that the whole venom of the Galilæan school were contained in the single person of Athanasius.[65]

I have endeavoured faithfully to represent the artful system by which Julian proposed to obtain the effects, without incurring the

[65] *The three epistles of Julian which explain his intentions and conduct with regard to Athanasius should be disposed in the following chronological order, twenty-six, ten, six.*

guilt, or reproach, of persecution. But, if the deadly spirit of fanaticism perverted the heart and understanding of a virtuous prince, it must, at the same time, be confessed, that the *real* sufferings of the Christians were inflamed and magnified by human passions and religious enthusiasm. The meekness and resignation which had distinguished the primitive disciples of the gospel was the object of the applause rather than of the imitation of their successors. The Christians, who had now possessed about forty years the civil and ecclesiastical government of the empire, had contracted the insolent vices of prosperity, and the habit of believing that the saints alone were entitled to reign over the earth. As soon as the enmity of Julian deprived the clergy of the privileges which had been conferred by the favour of Constantine, they complained of the most cruel oppression; and the free toleration of idolaters and heretics was a subject of grief and scandal to the orthodox party. The acts of violence, which were no longer countenanced by the magistrates, were still committed by the zeal of the people. At Pessinus, the altar of Cybele was overturned almost in the presence of the emperor; and in the city of Cæsarea in Cappadocia, the temple of Fortune, the sole place of worship which had been left to the Pagans, was destroyed by the rage of a popular tumult. On these occasions, a prince who felt for the honour of the gods was not disposed to interrupt the course of justice; and his mind was still more deeply exasperated, when he found that the fanatics, who had deserved and suffered the punishment of incendiaries, were rewarded with the honours of martyrdom. The Christian subjects of Julian were assured of the hostile designs of their sovereign; and, to their jealous apprehension, every circumstance of his government might afford some grounds of discontent and suspicion. In the ordinary administration of the laws, the Christians, who formed so large a part of the people, must frequently be condemned: but their indulgent brethren, without examining the merits of the cause, presumed their innocence, allowed their claims, and imputed the severity of their judge to the partial malice of religious persecution.[66] These present hardships, intolerable as they might appear, were represented as a slight prelude of the impending calamities. The Christians considered Julian as a cruel and crafty tyrant who suspended the execution of his revenge, till he should return victorious from the Persian war. They expected that, as soon as he had triumphed over the foreign enemies of Rome, he would lay aside the irksome mask of dissimulation; that the amphitheatres would stream with the blood of hermits and

[66] *Julian determined a lawsuit against the new Christian city at Maiuma, the port of Gaza; and his sentence, though it might be imputed to bigotry, was never reversed by his successors.*

bishops; and that the Christians, who still persevered in the profession of the faith, would be deprived of the common benefits of nature and society.[67] Every calumny that could wound the reputation of the Apostate was credulously embraced by the fears and hatred of his adversaries; and their indiscreet clamours provoked the temper of a sovereign whom it was their duty to respect and their interest to flatter. They still protested that prayers and tears were their only weapons against the impious tyrant, whose head they devoted to the justice of offended Heaven. But they insinuated with sullen resolution, that their submission was no longer the effect of weakness; and that, in the imperfect state of human virtue, the patience which is founded on principle may be exhausted by persecution. It is impossible to determine how far the zeal of Julian would have prevailed over his good sense and humanity: but, if we seriously reflect on the strength and spirit of the church, we shall be convinced that, before the emperor could have extinguished the religion of Christ, he must have involved his country in the horrors of a civil war.[68]

[67] *Gregory pretends to speak from the information of Julian's confidants, whom Orosius could not have seen.*

[68] *The resignation of Gregory is truly edifying. Yet, when an officer of Julian attempted to seize the Church of Nazianzus, he would have lost his life, if he had not yielded to the zeal of the bishop and people.*

XXIV

RESIDENCE OF JULIAN AT ANTIOCH · HIS SUCCESSFUL EXPEDI-
TION AGAINST THE PERSIANS · PASSAGE OF THE TIGRIS · THE
RETREAT AND DEATH OF JULIAN · ELECTION OF JOVIAN · HE
SAVES THE ROMAN ARMY BY A DISGRACEFUL PEACE TREATY

THE philosophical fable which Julian composed under the name of the CÆSARS is one of the most agreeable and instructive productions of ancient wit.[1] During the freedom and equality of the days of the Saturnalia, Romulus prepared a feast for the deities of Olympus, who had adopted him as a worthy associate, and for the Roman princes, who had reigned over his martial people and the vanquished nations of the earth. The immortals were placed in just order on their thrones of state, and the table of the Cæsars was spread below the Moon, in the upper region of the air. The tyrants, who would have disgraced the society of gods and men, were thrown headlong, by the inexorable Nemesis, into the Tartarean abyss. The rest of the Cæsars successively advanced to their seats: and, as they passed, the vices, the defects, the blemishes of their respective characters were maliciously noticed by old Silenus, a laughing moralist, who disguised the wisdom of a philosopher under the mask of a Bacchanal.[2] As soon as the feast was ended, the voice of Mercury proclaimed the will of Jupiter, that a celestial crown should be the reward of superior merit. Julius Cæsar, Augustus, Trajan, and Marcus Antoninus were selected as the most illustrious candidates; the effeminate Constantine[3] was not excluded from this honourable competition, and the great Alexander was invited to dispute the prize of glory with the Roman heroes. Each of the candidates was allowed to display the merit of his own exploits; but, in the judgment of the gods, the modest silence of Marcus pleaded more powerfully than the elaborate orations of his haughty rivals. When the judges of this awful contest proceeded to examine the heart and to scrutinize the springs of action, the superiority of the Imperial Stoic appeared still more de-

[1] *Spanheim (in his preface) has most learnedly discussed the etymology, origin, resemblance, and disagreement of the Greek* satyrs, *a dramatic piece, which was acted after the tragedy; and the Latin* satires *(from* satura*), a miscellaneous composition, either in prose or verse. But the Cæsars of Julian are of such an original cast that the critic is perplexed to which class he should ascribe them.*

[2] *This mixed character of Silenus is finely painted in the sixth eclogue of Virgil.*

[3] *Every impartial reader must perceive and condemn the partiality of Julian against his uncle Constantine and the Christian religion. On this occasion, the interpreters are compelled, by a more sacred interest, to renounce their*

allegiance, and to desert the cause of their author.

[4] *Julian was secretly inclined to prefer a Greek to a Roman. But, when he seriously compared a hero with a philosopher, he was sensible that mankind had much greater obligations to Socrates than to Alexander.*

[5] *This island to which the names of Taprobana, Serendib, and Ceylon, have been successively applied manifests how imperfectly the seas and lands to the east of Cape Comorin were known to the Romans. 1. Under the reign of Claudius, a freedman, who farmed the customs of the Red Sea, was accidentally driven by the winds upon this strange and undiscovered coast: he conversed six months with the natives; and the king of Ceylon, who heard, for the first time, of the power and justice of Rome, was persuaded to send an embassy to the emperor. 2. The geographers (and even Ptolemy) have magnified, above fifteen times, the real size of this new world, which they extended as far as the equator and the neighbourhood of China.*

[6] *These embassies had been sent to Constantius. Ammianus, who unwarily deviates into*

cisive and conspicuous.[4] Alexander and Cæsar, Augustus, Trajan, and Constantine, acknowledged with a blush that fame or power or pleasure had been the important object of *their* labours: but the gods themselves beheld, with reverence and love, a virtuous mortal, who had practised on the throne the lessons of philosophy; and who, in a state of human imperfection, had aspired to imitate the moral attributes of the Deity. The value of this agreeable composition (the Cæsars of Julian) is enhanced by the rank of the author. A prince, who delineates with freedom the vices and virtues of his predecessors, subscribes, in every line, the censure or approbation of his own conduct.

In the cool moments of reflection, Julian preferred the useful and benevolent virtues of Antoninus: but his ambitious spirit was inflamed by the glory of Alexander; and he solicited, with equal ardour, the esteem of the wise and the applause of the multitude. In the season of life, when the powers of the mind and body enjoy the most active vigour, the emperor, who was instructed by the experience, and animated by the success, of the German war, resolved to signalize his reign by some more splendid and memorable achievement. The ambassadors of the East, from the continent of India and the isle of Ceylon,[5] had respectfully saluted the Roman purple.[6] The nations of the West esteemed and dreaded the personal virtues of Julian, both in peace and war. He despised the trophies of a Gothic victory and was satisfied that the rapacious Barbarians of the Danube would be restrained from any future violation of the faith of treaties by the terror of his name and the additional fortifications with which he strengthened the Thracian and Illyrian frontiers. The successor of Cyrus and Artaxerxes was the only rival whom he deemed worthy of his arms; and he resolved, by the final conquest of Persia, to chastise the haughty nation which had so long resisted and insulted the majesty of Rome.[7] As soon as the Persian monarch was informed that the throne of Constantius was filled by a prince of a very different character, he condescended to make some artful, or perhaps sincere, overtures towards a negotiation of peace. But the pride of Sapor was astonished by the firmness of Julian; who sternly declared that he would never consent to hold a peaceful conference among the flames and ruins of the cities of Mesopotamia; and who added, with a smile of contempt, that it was needless to treat by ambassadors, as he himself had determined to visit speedily the court of Persia. The impatience of the emperor urged the diligence of the military preparations. The generals were named; a formidable army was destined for this important service; and Julian, marching from Constantinople through the provinces of Asia Minor, arrived at Antioch about eight months after the death of his predecessor. His ardent desire to march into the heart of Persia was checked by the indispensable duty of regulating the state of the empire; by his zeal to revive the worship of the gods; and by the advice of his wisest friends, who represented the necessity of allowing the salutary interval of winter quarters, to restore the exhausted strength of the legions of Gaul and the discipline and spirit of the Eastern troops. Julian was persuaded to fix, till the ensuing spring, his residence at Antioch, among a people maliciously disposed to deride the haste, and to censure the delays, of their sovereign.

If Julian had flattered himself that his personal connexion with the capital of the East would be productive of mutual satisfaction to the prince and people, he made a very false estimate of his own character, and of the manners of Antioch.[8] The warmth of the climate disposed the natives to the most intemperate enjoyment of tranquillity and opulence; and the lively licentiousness of the Greeks was blended with the hereditary softness of the Syrians. Fashion was the only law, pleasure the only pursuit, and the splendour of dress and furniture was the only distinction of the citizens of Antioch. The arts of luxury were honoured; the serious and manly virtues were the subject of ridicule; and the contempt for female modesty and reverent age announced the universal corruption of the capital of the East. The love of spectacles was the taste, or rather passion, of the Syrians: the most skilful artists were procured from the adjacent cities;[9] a considerable share of the revenue was devoted to the public amusements; and the magnificence of the games of the theatre and circus was considered as the happiness, and as the glory, of Antioch. The rustic manners of a prince who disdained such glory, and was insensible of such happiness, soon disgusted the delicacy of his subjects; and the effeminate Orientals could neither imitate nor admire the severe simplicity which Julian always maintained and sometimes affected. The days of festivity, consecrated by ancient custom to the honour of the gods, were the only occasions in which Julian relaxed his philosophic severity; and those festivals were the only days in which the Syrians of Antioch could reject the allurements of pleasure. The majority of the people supported the glory of the Christian name, which had been first invented by their ancestors;[10] they contented themselves with dis-

gross flattery, must have forgotten the length of the way, and the short duration of the reign of Julian.

[7] Alexander reminds his rival Cæsar, who deprecated the fame and merit of an Asiatic victory, that Crassus and Antony had felt the Persian arrows; and that the Romans, in a war of three hundred years, had not yet subdued the single province of Mesopotamia or Assyria.

[8] The satire of Julian and the Homilies of St. Chrysostom exhibit the same picture of Antioch.

[9] Laodicea furnished charioteers; Tyre and Berytus, comedians; Cæsarea, pantomimes; Heliopolis, singers; Gaza, gladiators; Ascalon, wrestlers; and Castabala, rope-dancers.

[10] Χριστὸν δὲ ἀγαπῶντες, ἔχετε πολιοῦχον ἀντι τοῦ Διός. The people of Antioch ingeniously professed their attachment to the Chi (Christ), and the Kappa (Constantius).

obeying the moral precepts, but they were scrupulously attached to the speculative doctrines, of their religion. The church of Antioch was distracted by heresy and schism; but the Arians and the Athanasians, the followers of Meletius and those of Paulinus,[11] were actuated by the same pious hatred of their common adversary.

The strongest prejudice was entertained against the character of an apostate, the enemy and successor of a prince who had engaged the affections of a very numerous sect; and the removal of St. Babylas excited an implacable opposition to the person of Julian. His subjects complained, with superstitious indignation, that famine had pursued the emperor's steps from Constantinople to Antioch; and the discontent of a hungry people was exasperated by the injudicious attempt to relieve their distress. The inclemency of the season had affected the harvests of Syria; and the price of bread,[12] in the markets of Antioch, had naturally risen in proportion to the scarcity of corn. But the fair and reasonable proportion was soon violated by the rapacious arts of monopoly. In this unequal contest, in which the produce of the land is claimed by one party as his exclusive property; is used by another as a lucrative object of trade; and is required by a third for the daily and necessary support of life; all the profits of the intermediate agents are accumulated on the head of the defenceless consumers. The hardships of their situation were exagerated and increased by their own impatience and anxiety; and the apprehension of a scarcity gradually produced the appearances of a famine. When the luxurious citizens of Antioch complained of the high price of poultry and fish, Julian publicly declared that a frugal city ought to be satisfied with a regular supply of wine, oil, and bread; but he acknowledged that it was the duty of a sovereign to provide for the subsistence of his people. With this salutary view, the emperor ventured on a very dangerous and doubtful step, of fixing, by legal authority, the value of corn. He enacted that, in a time of scarcity, it should be sold at a price which had seldom been known in the most plentiful years; and, that his own example might strengthen his laws, he sent into the market four hundred and twenty-two thousand *modii,* or measures, which were drawn by his order from the granaries of Hierapolis, of Chalcis, and even of Egypt. The consequences might have been foreseen, and were soon felt. The Imperial wheat was purchased by the rich merchants; the proprietors of land, or of corn, withheld from the city the accustomed supply; and the small quantities that appeared in the market were secretly sold at an advanced and illegal price. Julian still continued to applaud his own policy, treated the complaints of the people as a vain and ungrateful murmur, and convinced Antioch that he had inherited the obstinacy, though not the cruelty, of his brother Gallus. The remonstrances of the municipal senate served only to exasperate his inflexible mind. He was persuaded, perhaps with truth, that the senators of Antioch who possessed lands, or were concerned in trade, had themselves contributed to the calamities of their country; and he imputed the disrespectful boldness which they assumed to the sense, not of public duty, but of private interest. The whole body, consisting of two hundred of the most noble and wealthy citizens, were sent under a guard from the palace to the prison; and, though they were permitted, before the close of evening, to return to their respective houses, the emperor himself could not obtain the forgiveness which he had so easily granted. The same grievances were still the subject of the same complaints, which were industriously circulated by the wit and levity of the Syrian Greeks. During the licentious days of the Saturnalia, the streets of the city resounded with insolent songs, which derided the laws, the religion, the personal conduct, and even the *beard*, of the emperor; and the spirit of Antioch was manifested by the connivance of the magistrates and the applause of the multitude.[13] The disciple of Socrates was too deeply affected by these popular insults; but the monarch, endowed with quick sensibility, and possessed of absolute power, refused his passions the gratification of revenge. A tyrant might have proscribed, without distinction, the lives and fortunes of the citizens of Antioch; and the unwarlike Syrians must have patiently submitted to the lust, the rapaciousness, and the cruelty of the faithful legions of Gaul. A milder sentence might have deprived the capital of the East of its honours and privileges; and the courtiers, perhaps the subjects, of Julian would have applauded an act of justice which asserted the dignity of the supreme magistrate of the republic.[14] But, instead of abusing, or exerting, the authority of the state to revenge his personal injuries, Julian contented himself with an inoffensive mode of retaliation, which it would be in the power of few princes to employ. He had been insulted by satires and libels; in his turn he composed, under the title of the *Enemy of the Beard,* an ironical confession of his own faults, and a severe satire of the licentious and effeminate manners of Antioch. This Imperial reply was publicly exposed before the gates of the palace; and the Misopogon still remains a singular monument of the resentment, the wit, the humanity, and the indis-

[13] *Libanius, like a skilful advocate, severely censures the folly of the people, who suffered for the crime of a few obscure and drunken wretches.*

[14] *Libanius reminds Antioch of the recent chastisement of Cæsarea: and even Julian insinuates how severely Tarentum had expiated the insult to the Roman ambassadors.*

cretion, of Julian. Though he affected to laugh, he could not forgive.[15] His contempt was expressed, and his revenge might be gratified, by the nomination of a governor worthy only of such subjects: and the emperor, forever renouncing the ungrateful city, proclaimed his resolution to pass the ensuing winter at Tarsus in Cilicia.

Yet Antioch possessed one citizen, whose genius and virtues might atone, in the opinion of Julian, for the vice and folly of his country. The sophist Libanius was born in the capital of the East; he publicly professed the arts of rhetoric and declamation at Nice, Nicomedia, Constantinople, Athens, and, during the remainder of his life, at Antioch. His school was assiduously frequented by the Grecian youth; his disciples, who sometimes exceeded the number of eighty, celebrated their incomparable master; and the jealousy of his rivals, who persecuted him from one city to another, confirmed the favourable opinion which Libanius ostentatiously displayed of his superior merit. The preceptors of Julian had extorted a rash but solemn assurance that he would never attend the lectures of their adversary: the curiosity of the royal youth was checked and inflamed: he secretly procured the writings of this dangerous sophist, and gradually surpassed, in the perfect imitation of his style, the most laborious of his domestic pupils. When Julian ascended the throne, he declared his impatience to embrace and reward the Syrian sophist, who had preserved, in a degenerate age, the Grecian purity of taste, of manners and of religion. The emperor's prepossession was increased and justified by the discreet pride of his favourite. Instead of pressing, with the foremost of the crowd, into the palace of Constantinople, Libanius calmly expected his arrival at Antioch; withdrew from court on the first symptoms of coldness and indifference; required a formal invitation for each visit; and taught his sovereign an important lesson, that he might command the obedience of a subject, but that he must deserve the attachment of a friend. The sophists of every age, despising, or affecting to despise, the accidental distinctions of birth and fortune,[16] reserve their esteem for the superior qualities of the mind, with which they themselves are so plentifully endowed. Julian might disdain the acclamations of a venal court, who adored the Imperial purple; but he was deeply flattered by the praise, the admonition, the freedom, and the envy of an independent philosopher, who refused his favours, loved his person, celebrated his fame, and protected his memory. The voluminous writings of Libanius still exist: for the most part, they are the vain and idle compositions of an orator, who cultivated the science of words; the productions of a recluse student, whose mind, regardless of his contemporaries, was incessantly fixed on the Trojan war and the Athenian commonwealth. Yet the sophist of Antioch sometimes descended from this imaginary elevation; he entertained a various and elaborate correspondence;[17] he praised the virtues of his own times; he boldly arraigned the abuses of public and private life; and he eloquently pleaded the cause of Antioch against the just resentment of Julian and Theodosius. It is the common calamity of old age,[18] to lose whatever might have rendered it desirable; but Libanius experienced the peculiar misfortune of surviving the religion and the sciences to which he had consecrated his genius. The friend of Julian was an indignant spectator of the triumph of Christianity; and his bigotry, which darkened the prospect of the visible world, did not inspire Libanius with any lively hopes of celestial glory and happiness.

The martial impatience of Julian urged him to take the field in the beginning of the spring; and he dismissed, with contempt and reproach, the senate of Antioch, who accompanied the emperor beyond the limits of their own territory, to which he was resolved never to return. After a laborious march of two days,[19] he halted on the third at Berœa, or Aleppo, where he had the mortification of finding a senate almost entirely Christian; who received with cold and formal demonstrations of respect the eloquent sermon of the apostle of Paganism. The son of one of the most illustrious citizens of Berœa, who had embraced, either from interest or conscience, the religion of the emperor, was disinherited by his angry parent. The father and the son were invited to the Imperial table. Julian, placing himself between them, attempted, without success, to inculcate the lesson and example of toleration; supported, with affected calmness, the indiscreet zeal of the aged Christian, who seemed to forget the sentiments of nature and the duty of a subject; and at length turning towards the afflicted youth, "Since you have lost a father," said he, "for my sake, it is incumbent on me to supply his place." The emperor was received in a manner much more agreeable to his wishes at Batnæ, a small town pleasantly seated in a grove of cypresses, about twenty miles from the city of Hierapolis. The solemn rites of sacrifice were decently prepared by the inhabitants of Batnæ, who seemed attached to the worship of their tutelar deities, Apollo and Jupiter; but the serious piety of Julian was offended by the tumult of their applause; and he too clearly discerned that the smoke which arose from their altars was the incense of flat-

[17] Near two thousand of his letters, a mode of composition in which Libanius was thought to excel, are still extant, and already published. The critics may praise their subtle and elegant brevity; yet Dr. Bentley might justly, though quaintly, observe that "you feel, by the emptiness and deadness of them, that you converse with some dreaming pedant, with his elbow on his desk."

[18] His birth is assigned to the year 314. He mentions the seventy-sixth year of his age (A.D. 390), and seems to allude to some events of a still later date.

[19] From Antioch to Litarbe, on the territory of Chalcis, the road, over hills and through morasses, was extremely bad; and the loose stones were cemented only with sand. It is singular enough that the Romans should have neglected the great communication between Antioch and the Euphrates.

tery rather than of devotion. The ancient and magnificent temple, which had sanctified, for so many ages, the city of Hierapolis, no longer subsisted; and the consecrated wealth, which afforded a liberal maintenance to more than three hundred priests, might hasten its downfall. Yet Julian enjoyed the satisfaction of embracing a philosopher and a friend, whose religious firmness had withstood the pressing and repeated solicitations of Constantius and Gallus, as often as those princes lodged at his house, in their passage through Hierapolis. In the hurry of military preparation, and the careless confidence of a familiar correspondence, the zeal of Julian appears to have been lively and uniform. He had now undertaken an important and difficult war; and the anxiety of the event rendered him still more attentive to observe and register the most trifling presages from which, according to the rules of divination, any knowledge of futurity could be derived. He informed Libanius of his progress as far as Hierapolis, by an elegant epistle, which displays the facility of his genius and his tender friendship for the sophist of Antioch.

Hierapolis, situate almost on the banks of the Euphrates, had been appointed for the general rendezvous of the Roman troops, who immediately passed the great river on a bridge of boats, which was previously constructed.[20] If the inclinations of Julian had been similar to those of his predecessor, he might have wasted the active and important season of the year in the circus of Samosata, or in the churches of Edessa. But, as the warlike emperor, instead of Constantius, had chosen Alexander for his model, he advanced without delay to Carrhæ,[21] a very ancient city of Mesopotamia, at the distance of fourscore miles from Hierapolis. The temple of the Moon attracted the devotion of Julian; but the halt of a few days was principally employed in completing the immense preparations of the Persian war. The secret of the expedition had hitherto remained in his own breast; but, as Carrhæ is the point of separation of the two great roads, he could no longer conceal whether it was his design to attack the dominions of Sapor on the side of the Tigris or on that of the Euphrates. The emperor detached an army of thirty thousand men, under the command of his kinsman Procopius, and of Sebastian, who had been duke of Egypt. They were ordered to direct their march towards Nisibis, and to secure the frontier from the desultory incursions of the enemy, before they attempted the passage of the Tigris. Their subsequent operations were left to the discretion of the generals; but Julian expected that, after wasting with fire and sword the fertile districts of Media and Adiabene, they

[20] *There are three passages within a few miles of each other: 1. Zeugma, celebrated by the ancients; 2. Bir, frequented by the moderns; and, 3. the bridge of Menbigz, or Hierapolis, at the distance of four parasangs from the city.*

[21] *Haran, or Carrhæ, was the ancient residence of the Sabæans and of Abraham. See the Index Geographicus of Schultens, a work from which I have obtained much Oriental knowledge concerning the ancient and modern geography of Syria and the adjacent countries.*

might arrive under the walls of Ctesiphon about the same time that he himself, advancing with equal steps along the banks of the Euphrates, should besiege the capital of the Persian monarchy. The success of this well-concerted plan depended, in a great measure, on the powerful and ready assistance of the king of Armenia, who, without exposing the safety of his own dominions, might detach an army of four thousand horse, and twenty thousand foot, to the assistance of the Romans. But the feeble Arsaces Tiranus, king of Armenia, had degenerated still more shamefully than his father Chosroes from the manly virtues of the great Tiridates; and, as the pusillanimous monarch was averse to any enterprise of danger and glory, he could disguise his timid indolence by the more decent excuses of religion and gratitude. He expressed a pious attachment to the memory of Constantius, from whose hands he had received in marriage Olympias, the daughter of the præfect Ablavius; and the alliance of a female who had been educated as the destined wife of the emperor Constans exalted the dignity of a Barbarian king. Tiranus professed the Christian religion; he reigned over a nation of Christians; and he was restrained, by every principle of conscience and interest, from contributing to the victory, which would consummate the ruin of the church. The alienated mind of Tiranus was exasperated by the indiscretion of Julian, who treated the king of Armenia as *his* slave, and as the enemy of the gods. The haughty and threatening style of the Imperial mandates awakened the secret indignation of a prince who, in the humiliating state of dependence, was still conscious of his royal descent from the Arsacides, the lords of the East and the rivals of the Roman power.

The military dispositions of Julian were skilfully contrived to deceive the spies, and to divert the attention, of Sapor. The legions appeared to direct their march towards Nisibis and the Tigris. On a sudden they wheeled to the right; traversed the level and naked plain of Carrhæ; and reached, on the third day, the banks of the Euphrates, where the strong town of Nicephorium, or Callinicum, had been founded by the Macedonian kings. From thence the emperor pursued his march, above ninety miles, along the winding stream of the Euphrates, till, at length, about one month after his departure from Antioch, he discovered the towers of Circesium, the extreme limit of the Roman dominions. The army of Julian, the most numerous that any of the Cæsars had ever led against Persia, consisted of sixty-five thousand effective and well-disciplined soldiers. The veteran bands of cavalry and infantry, of Romans and

Barbarians, had been selected from the different provinces; and a just pre-eminence of loyalty and valour was claimed by the hardy Gauls, who guarded the throne and person of their beloved prince. A formidable body of Scythian auxiliaries had been transported from another climate, and almost from another world, to invade a distant country, of whose name and situation they were ignorant. The love of rapine and war allured to the Imperial standard several tribes of Saracens, or roving Arabs, whose service Julian had commanded, while he sternly refused the payment of the accustomed subsidies. The broad channel of the Euphrates was crowded by a fleet of eleven hundred ships, destined to attend the motions, and to satisfy the wants, of the Roman army. The military strength of the fleet was composed of fifty armed galleys; and these were accompanied by an equal number of flat-bottomed boats, which might occasionally be connected into the form of temporary bridges. The rest of the ships, partly constructed of timber and partly covered with raw hides, were laden with an almost inexhaustible supply of arms and engines, of utensils and provisions. The vigilant humanity of Julian had embarked a very large magazine of vinegar and biscuit for the use of the soldiers, but he prohibited the indulgence of wine; and rigorously stopped a long string of superfluous camels that attempted to follow the rear of the army. The river Chaboras falls into the Euphrates at Circesium; and, as soon as the trumpet gave the signal of march, the Romans passed the little stream which separated two mighty and hostile empires. The custom of ancient discipline required a military oration; and Julian embraced every opportunity of displaying his eloquence. He animated the impatient and attentive legions by the example of the inflexible courage and glorious triumphs of their ancestors. He excited their resentment by a lively picture of the insolence of the Persians; and he exhorted them to imitate his firm resolution, either to extirpate that perfidious nation or to devote his life in the cause of the republic. The eloquence of Julian was enforced by a donative of one hundred and thirty pieces of silver to every soldier; and the bridge of the Chaboras was instantly cut away, to convince the troops that they must place their hopes of safety in the success of their arms. Yet the prudence of the emperor induced him to secure a remote frontier, perpetually exposed to the inroads of the hostile Arabs. A detachment of four thousand men was left at Circesium, which completed, to the number of ten thousand, the regular garrison of that important fortress.

From the moment that the Romans entered the enemy's country, the country of an active and artful enemy, the order of march was disposed in three columns. The strength of the infantry, and consequently of the whole army, was placed in the centre, under the peculiar command of their master-general Victor. On the right, the brave Nevitta led a column of several legions along the banks of the Euphrates, and almost always in sight of the fleet. The left flank of the army was protected by the column of cavalry. Hormisdas and Arinthæus were appointed generals of the horse; and the singular adventures of Hormisdas [22] are not undeserving of our notice. He was a Persian prince, of the royal race of the Sassanides, who, in the troubles of the minority of Sapor, had escaped from prison to the hospitable court of the great Constantine. Hormisdas at first excited the compassion, and at length acquired the esteem, of his new masters; his valour and fidelity raised him to the military honours of the Roman service; and, though a Christian, he might indulge the secret satisfaction of convincing his ungrateful country that an oppressed subject may prove the most dangerous enemy. Such was the disposition of the three principal columns. The front and flanks of the army were covered by Lucillianus with a flying detachment of fifteen hundred light-armed soldiers, whose active vigilance observed the most distant signs, and conveyed the earliest notice, of any hostile approach. Dagalaiphus, and Secundinus duke of Osrhoene, conducted the troops of the rear-guard; the baggage securely proceeded in the intervals of the columns; and the ranks, from a motive either of use or ostentation, were formed in such open order that the whole line of march extended almost ten miles. The ordinary post of Julian was at the head of the centre column; but, as he preferred the duties of a general to the state of a monarch, he rapidly moved, with a small escort of light cavalry, to the front, the rear, the flanks, wherever his presence could animate or protect the march of the Roman army. The country which they traversed from the Chaboras to the cultivated lands of Assyria may be considered as a part of the desert of Arabia, a dry and barren waste, which could never be improved by the most powerful arts of human industry. Julian marched over the same ground which had been trod above seven hundred years before by the footsteps of the younger Cyrus, and which is described by one of the companions of his expedition, the sage and heroic Xenophon. "The country was a plain throughout, as even as the sea, and full of wormwood; and, if any other kind of shrubs or reeds grew there, they had all an aromatic

[22] *The adventures of Hormisdas are related with some mixture of fable. It is almost impossible that he should be the brother (frater germanus) of an* eldest *and* posthumous *child: nor do I recollect that Ammianus ever gives him that title.*

smell; but no trees could be seen. Bustards and ostriches, antelopes and wild asses, appeared to be the only inhabitants of the desert; and the fatigues of the march were alleviated by the amusements of the chase." The loose sand of the desert was frequently raised by the wind into clouds of dust: and a great number of the soldiers of Julian, with their tents, were suddenly thrown to the ground by the violence of an unexpected hurricane.

The sandy plains of Mesopotamia were abandoned to the antelopes and wild asses of the desert; but a variety of populous towns and villages were pleasantly situated on the banks of the Euphrates, and in the islands which are occasionally formed by that river. The city of Annah, or Anatho, the actual residence of an Arabian Emir, is composed of two long streets, which inclose, within a natural fortification, a small island in the midst, and two fruitful spots on either side of the Euphrates. The warlike inhabitants of Anatho showed a disposition to stop the march of a Roman emperor; till they were diverted from such fatal presumption by the mild exhortations of prince Hormisdas and the approaching terrors of the fleet and army. They implored, and experienced, the clemency of Julian, who transplanted the people to an advantageous settlement near Chalcis in Syria, and admitted Pusæus, the governor, to an honourable rank in his service and friendship. But the impregnable fortress of Thilutha could scorn the menace of a siege; and the emperor was obliged to content himself with an insulting promise that, when he had subdued the interior provinces of Persia, Thilutha would no longer refuse to grace the triumph of the conqueror. The inhabitants of the open towns, unable to resist and unwilling to yield, fled with precipitation; and their houses, filled with spoil and provisions, were occupied by the soldiers of Julian, who massacred, without remorse, and without punishment, some defenceless women. During the march, the Surenas, or Persian general, and Malek Rodosaces, the renowned Emir of the tribe of Gassan,[23] incessantly hovered round the army: every straggler was intercepted; every detachment was attacked; and the valiant Hormisdas escaped with some difficulty from their hands. But the Barbarians were finally repulsed; the country became every day less favourable to the operations of cavalry; and, when the Romans arrived at Macepracta, they perceived the ruins of the wall which had been constructed by the ancient kings of Assyria to secure their dominions from the incursions of the Medes. These preliminaries of the expedition of Julian appear to have employed about fifteen days; and

[23] *Famosi nominis latro, says Ammianus; an high encomium for an Arab. The tribe of Gassan had settled on the edge of Syria, and reigned some time in Damascus, under a dynasty of thirty-one kings, or emirs, from the time of Pompey to that of the Khalif Omar. The name of Rodosaces does not appear in the list.*

we may compute near three hundred miles from the fortress of Circesium to the wall of Macepracta.

The fertile province of Assyria, which stretched beyond the Tigris as far as the mountains of Media,[24] extended about four hundred miles from the ancient wall of Macepracta to the territory of Basra, where the united streams of the Euphrates and Tigris discharge themselves into the Persian Gulf.[25] The whole country might have claimed the peculiar name of Mesopotamia; as the two rivers which are never more distant than fifty, approach, between Bagdad and Babylon, within twenty-five, miles of each other. A multitude of artificial canals, dug without much labour in a soft and yielding soil, connected the rivers, and intersected the plain of Assyria. The uses of these artificial canals were various and important. They served to discharge the superfluous waters from one river into the other, at the season of their respective inundations. Subdividing themselves into smaller and smaller branches, they refreshed the dry lands, and supplied the deficiency of rain. They facilitated the intercourse of peace and commerce; and, as the dams could be speedily broke down, they armed the despair of the Assyrians with the means of opposing a sudden deluge to the progress of an invading army. To the soil and climate of Assyria nature had denied some of her choicest gifts, the vine, the olive, and the fig-tree; but the food which supports the life of man, and particularly wheat and barley, were produced with inexhaustible fertility; and the husbandman who committed his seed to the earth was frequently rewarded with an increase of two, or even of three, hundred. The face of the country was interspersed with groves of innumerable palm-trees; and the diligent natives celebrated, either in verse or prose, the three hundred and sixty uses to which the trunk, the branches, the leaves, the juice, and the fruit, were skilfully applied. Several manufacturers, especially those of leather and linen, employed the industry of a numerous people, and afforded valuable materials for foreign trade; which appears, however, to have been conducted by the hands of strangers. Babylon had been converted into a royal park; but near the ruins of the ancient capital new cities had successively arisen, and the populousness of the country was displayed in the multitude of towns and villages, which were built of bricks, dried in the sun, and strongly cemented with bitumen, the natural and peculiar production of the Babylonian soil. While the successors of Cyrus reigned over Asia, the province of Assyria alone maintained, during a third part of the year, the luxurious plenty of the

[24] *Ammianus remarks that the primitive Assyria, which comprehended Ninus (Nineveh) and Arbela, had assumed the more recent and peculiar appellation of Adiabene: and he seems to fix Teredon, Vologesia, and Apollonia, as the extreme cities of the actual province of Assyria.*

[25] *The two rivers unite at Apamea, or Corna (one hundred miles from the Persian Gulf), into the broad stream of the Pasitigris, or Shat-ul-Arab. The Euphrates formerly reached the sea by a separate channel, which was obstructed and diverted by the citizens of Orchoe, about twenty miles to the south-east of modern Basra.*

table and household of the Great King. Four considerable villages were assigned for the subsistence of his Indian dogs; eight hundred stallions and sixteen thousand mares were constantly kept at the expense of the country, for the royal stables; and, as the daily tribute, which was paid to the satrap, amounted to one English bushel of silver, we may compute the annual revenue of Assyria at more than twelve hundred thousand pounds sterling.[26]

The fields of Assyria were devoted by Julian to the calamities of war; and the philosopher retaliated on a guiltless people the acts of rapine and cruelty which had been committed by their haughty master in the Roman provinces. The trembling Assyrians summoned the rivers to their assistance; and completed, with their own hands, the ruin of their country. The roads were rendered impracticable; a flood of waters was poured into the camp; and during several days the troops of Julian were obliged to contend with the most discouraging hardships. But every obstacle was surmounted by the perseverance of the legionaries, who were inured to toil as well as to danger, and who felt themselves animated by the spirit of their leader. The damage was gradually repaired; the waters were restored to their proper channels; whole groves of palm-trees were cut down and placed along the broken parts of the road; and the army passed over the broad and deeper canals on bridges of floating rafts, which were supported by the help of bladders. Two cities of Assyria presumed to resist the arms of a Roman emperor: and they both paid the severe penalty of their rashness. At the distance of fifty miles from the royal residence of Ctesiphon, Perisabor, or Anbar, held the second rank in the province; a city, large, populous, and well fortified, surrounded with a double wall, almost encompassed by a branch of the Euphrates, and defended by the valour of a numerous garrison. The exhortations of Hormisdas were repulsed with contempt; and the ears of the Persian prince were wounded by a just reproach that, unmindful of his royal birth, he conducted an army of strangers against his king and country. The Assyrians maintained their loyalty by a skilful, as well as vigorous, defence; till, the lucky stroke of a battering-ram having opened a large breach by shattering one of the angles of the wall, they hastily retired into the fortifications of the interior citadel. The soldiers of Julian rushed impetuously into the town, and, after the full gratification of every military appetite, Perisabor was reduced to ashes; and the engines which assaulted the citadel were planted on the ruins of the smoking houses. The contest was continued by an in-

[26] *Assyria yielded to the Persian satrap an* artaba *of silver each day. The well-known proportion of weights and measures, the specific gravity of water and silver, and the value of that metal, will afford, after a short process, the annual revenue which I have stated. Yet the Great King received no more than 1000 Euboic, or Tyrian, talents (£252,000) from Assyria. The comparison of two passages in Herodotus reveals an important difference between the* gross, *and the* net, *revenue of Persia; the sums paid by the province, and the gold or silver deposited in the royal treasure. The monarch might annually save three millions six hundred thousand pounds, of the seventeen or eighteen millions raised upon the people.*

cessant and mutual discharge of missile weapons; and the superiority which the Romans might derive from the mechanical powers of their balistæ and catapultæ was counter-balanced by the advantage of the ground on the side of the besieged. But as soon as an *Helepolis* had been constructed, which could engage on equal terms with the loftiest ramparts, the tremendous aspect of a moving turret, that would leave no hope of resistance or of mercy, terrified the defenders of the citadel into an humble submission; and the place was surrendered only two days after Julian first appeared under the walls of Perisabor. Two thousand five hundred persons of both sexes, the feeble remnant of a flourishing people, were permitted to retire: the plentiful magazines of corn, of arms, and of splendid furniture were partly distributed among the troops, and partly reserved for the public service: the useless stores were destroyed by fire or thrown into the stream of the Euphrates; and the fate of Amida was revenged by the total ruin of Perisabor.

The city, or rather fortress, of Maogamalcha, which was defended by sixteen large towers, a deep ditch, and two strong and solid walls of brick and bitumen, appears to have been constructed at the distance of eleven miles, as the safeguard of the capital of Persia. The emperor, apprehensive of leaving such an important fortress in his rear, immediately formed the siege of Maogamalcha; and the Roman army was distributed, for that purpose, into three divisions. Victor, at the head of the cavalry, and of a detachment of heavy-armed foot, was ordered to clear the country as far as the banks of the Tigris and the suburbs of Ctesiphon. The conduct of the attack was assumed by Julian himself, who seemed to place his whole dependence in the military engines which he erected against the walls; while he secretly contrived a more efficacious method of introducing his troops into the heart of the city. Under the direction of Nevitta and Dagalaiphus, the trenches were opened at a considerable distance, and gradually prolonged as far as the edge of the ditch. The ditch was speedily filled with earth; and, by the incessant labour of the troops, a mine was carried under the foundations of the walls, and sustained, at sufficient intervals, by props of timber. Three chosen cohorts, advancing in a single file, silently explored the dark and dangerous passage; till their intrepid leader whispered back the intelligence that he was ready to issue from his confinement into the streets of the hostile city. Julian checked their ardour that he might ensure their success; and immediately diverted the attention of the garrison, by the tumult and clamour of a general assault. The Persians, who from their walls contemptuously beheld the progress of an impotent attack, celebrated, with songs of triumph, the glory of Sapor; and ventured to assure the emperor that he might ascend the starry mansion of Ormusd, before he could hope to take the impregnable city of Maogamalcha. The city was already taken. History has recorded the name of a private soldier, the first who ascended from the mine into a deserted tower. The passage was widened by his companions, who pressed forwards with impatient valour. Fifteen hundred enemies were already in the midst of the city. The astonished garrison abandoned the walls, and their only hope of safety; the gates were instantly burst open; and the revenge of the soldier, unless it were suspended by lust or avarice, was satiated by an undistinguishing massacre. The governor, who had yielded on a promise of mercy, was burnt alive, a few days afterwards, on a charge of having uttered some disrespectful words against the honour of prince Hormisdas. The fortifications were razed to the ground; and not a vestige was left that the city of Maogamalcha had ever existed. The neighbourhood of the capital of Persia was adorned with three stately palaces, laboriously enriched with every production that could gratify the luxury and pride of an Eastern monarch. The pleasant situation of the gardens along the banks of the Tigris was improved, according to the Persian taste, by the symmetry of flowers, fountains, and shady walks: and spacious parks were enclosed for the reception of the bears, lions, and wild boars, which were maintained at a considerable expense for the pleasure of the royal chase. The park-walls were broke down, the savage game was abandoned to the darts of the soldiers, and the palaces of Sapor were reduced to ashes, by the command of the Roman emperor. Julian, on this occasion, showed himself ignorant, or careless, of the laws of civility, which the prudence and refinement of polished ages have established between hostile princes. Yet these wanton ravages need not excite in our breasts any vehement emotions of pity or resentment. A simple, naked statue, finished by the hand of a Grecian artist, is of more genuine value, than all these rude and costly monuments of Barbaric labour: and, if we are more deeply affected by the ruin of a palace than by the conflagration of a cottage, our humanity must have formed a very erroneous estimate of the miseries of human life.

Julian was an object of terror and hatred to the Persians: and the painters of that nation represented the invader of their country under the emblem of a furious lion, who vomited from his mouth a consuming fire. To his friends and soldiers, the philosophic hero appeared in a more amiable light; and his virtues were never more conspicuously displayed than in the last, and most active, period of his life. He practised, without effort, and almost without merit, the habitual qualities of temperance and sobriety. According to the dictates of that artificial wisdom which assumes an absolute dominion over the mind and body, he sternly refused himself the indulgence of the most natural appetites.[27] In the warm climate of Assyria, which solicited a luxurious people to the gratification of every sensual desire, a youthful conqueror preserved his chastity pure and inviolate: nor was Julian ever tempted, even by a motive of curiosity, to visit his female captives of exquisite beauty, who, instead of resisting his power, would have disputed with each other the honour of his embraces. With the same firmness that he resisted the allurements of love, he sustained the hardships of war. When the Romans marched through the flat and flooded country, their sovereign, on foot, at the head of his legions, shared their fatigues, and animated their diligence. In every useful labour, the hand of Julian was prompt and strenuous; and the Imperial purple was wet and dirty, as the coarse garment of the meanest soldier. The two sieges allowed him some remarkable opportunities of signalizing his personal valour, which, in the improved state of the military art, can seldom be exerted by a prudent general. The emperor stood before the citadel of Perisabor, insensible of his extreme danger, and encouraged his troops to burst open the gates of iron, till he was almost overwhelmed under a cloud of missile weapons and huge stones that were directed against his person. As he examined the exterior fortifications of Maogamalcha, two Persians, devoting themselves for their country, suddenly rushed upon him with drawn scimitars: the emperor dexterously received their blows on his uplifted shield; and, with a steady and well-aimed thrust, laid one of his adversaries dead at his feet. The esteem of a prince who possesses the virtues which he approves is the noblest recompense of a deserving subject; and the authority which Julian derived from his personal merit enabled him to revive and enforce the rigour of ancient discipline. He punished with death, or ignominy, the misbehaviour of three troops of horse, who, in a skirmish with the Surenas, had lost their honour, and one of their standards: and he distinguished with *obsidional* crowns the valour of the foremost soldiers who had ascended into the city of Maogamalcha. After the siege of Perisabor, the firmness of the emperor was exercised by the insolent avarice of the army,

[27] *The famous examples of Cyrus, Alexander, and Scipio were acts of justice. Julian's chastity was voluntary, and, in his opinion, meritorious.*

who loudly complained that their services were rewarded by a trifling donative of one hundred pieces of silver. His just indignation was expressed in the grave and manly language of a Roman. "Riches are the object of your desires? those riches are in the hands of the Persians; and the spoils of this fruitful country are proposed as the prize of your valour and discipline. Believe me," added Julian, "the Roman republic, which formerly possessed such immense treasures, is now reduced to want and wretchedness; since our princes have been persuaded, by weak and interested ministers, to purchase with gold the tranquillity of the Barbarians. The revenue is exhausted; the cities are ruined; the provinces are dispeopled. For myself, the only inheritance that I have received from my royal ancestors is a soul incapable of fear; and, as long as I am convinced that every real advantage is seated in the mind, I shall not blush to acknowledge an honourable poverty, which, in the days of ancient virtue, was considered as the glory of Fabricius. That glory, and that virtue, may be your own, if you will listen to the voice of Heaven, and of your leader. But, if you will rashly persist, if you are determined to renew the shameful and mischievous examples of old seditions, proceed.—As it becomes an emperor who has filled the first rank among men, I am prepared to die, standing; and to despise a precarious life, which, every hour, may depend on an accidental fever. If I have been found unworthy of the command, there are now among you (I speak it with pride and pleasure), there are many chiefs, whose merit and experience are equal to the conduct of the most important war. Such has been the temper of my reign that I can retire, without regret, and without apprehension, to the obscurity of a private station." [28] The modest resolution of Julian was answered by the unanimous applause and cheerful obedience of the Romans; who declared their confidence of victory, while they fought under the banners of their heroic prince. Their courage was kindled by his frequent and familiar asseverations (for such wishes were the oaths of Julian), "So may I reduce the Persians under the yoke!" "Thus may I restore the strength and splendour of the republic!" The love of fame was the ardent passion of his soul: but it was not before he trampled on the ruins of Maogamalcha, that he allowed himself to say, "We have now provided some materials for the sophist of Antioch."

The successful valour of Julian had triumphed over all the obstacles that opposed his march to the gates of Ctesiphon. But the reduction, or even the siege, of the capital of Persia was still at a

[28] *I give this speech as original and genuine. Ammianus might hear, could transcribe, and was incapable of inventing, it. I have used some slight freedoms, and conclude with the most forcible sentence.*

distance: nor can the military conduct of the emperor be clearly apprehended without a knowledge of the country which was the theatre of his bold and skilful operations. Twenty miles to the south of Bagdad, and on the eastern bank of the Tigris, the curiosity of travellers has observed some ruins of the palaces of Ctesiphon, which, in the time of Julian, was a great and populous city. The name and glory of the adjacent Seleucia were forever extinguished; and the only remaining quarter of that Greek colony had resumed, with the Assyrian language and manners, the primitive appellation of Coche. Coche was situate on the western side of the Tigris; but it was naturally considered as a suburb of Ctesiphon, with which we may suppose it to have been connected by a permanent bridge of boats. The united parts contributed to form the common epithet of Al Modain, THE CITIES, which the Orientals have bestowed on the winter residence of the Sassanides; and the whole circumference of the Persian capital was strongly fortified by the waters of the river, by lofty walls, and by impracticable morasses. Near the ruins of Seleucia, the camp of Julian was fixed; and secured, by a ditch and rampart, against the sallies of the numerous and enterprising garrison of Coche. In this fruitful and pleasant country, the Romans were plentifully supplied with water and forage; and several forts which might have embarrassed the motions of the army submitted, after some resistance, to the efforts of their valour. The fleet passed from the Euphrates into an artificial derivation of that river, which pours a copious and navigable stream into the Tigris, at a small distance *below* the great city. If they had followed this royal canal, which bore the name of Nahar-Malcha,[29] the intermediate situation of Coche would have separated the fleet and army of Julian; and the rash attempt of steering against the current of the Tigris, and forcing their way through the midst of a hostile capital, must have been attended with the total destruction of the Roman navy. The prudence of the emperor foresaw the danger, and provided the remedy. As he had minutely studied the operations of Trajan in the same country, he soon recollected that his warlike predecessor had dug a new and navigable canal, which, leaving Coche on the right hand, conveyed the waters of the Nahar-Malcha into the river Tigris, at some distance *above* the cities. From the information of the peasants, Julian ascertained the vestiges of this ancient work, which were almost obliterated by design or accident. By the indefatigable labour of the soldiers, a broad and deep channel was speedily prepared for the reception of the Euphrates. A strong dyke was con-

[29] *The royal canal (Nahar-Malcha) might be successively restored, altered, divided, &c.; and these changes may serve to explain the seeming contradictions of antiquity. In the time of Julian, it must have fallen into the Euphrates below Ctesiphon.*

structed to interrupt the ordinary current of the Nahar-Malcha: a flood of waters rushed impetuously into their new bed; and the Roman fleet, steering their triumphant course into the Tigris, derided the vain and ineffectual barriers which the Persians of Ctesiphon had erected to oppose their passage.

As it became necessary to transport the Roman army over the Tigris, another labour presented itself, of less toil, but of more danger, than the preceding expedition. The stream was broad and rapid; the ascent steep and difficult; and the intrenchments, which had been formed on the ridge of the opposite bank, were lined with a numerous army of heavy cuirassiers, dexterous archers, and huge elephants; who (according to the extravagant hyperbole of Libanius) could trample, with the same ease, a field of corn, or a legion of Romans. In the presence of such an enemy, the construction of a bridge was impracticable; and the intrepid prince, who instantly seized the only possible expedient, concealed his design, till the moment of execution, from the knowledge of the Barbarians, of his own troops, and even of his generals themselves. Under the specious pretence of examining the state of the magazines, fourscore vessels were gradually unladen; and a select detachment, apparently destined for some secret expedition, was ordered to stand to their arms on the first signal. Julian disguised the silent anxiety of his own mind with smiles of confidence and joy; and amused the hostile nations with the spectacle of military games, which he insultingly celebrated under the walls of Coche. The day was consecrated to pleasure; but, as soon as the hour of supper was past, the emperor summoned the generals to his tent; and acquainted them that he had fixed that night for the passage of the Tigris. They stood in silent and respectful astonishment; but, when the venerable Sallust assumed the privilege of his age and experience, the rest of the chiefs supported with freedom the weight of his prudent remonstrances. Julian contented himself with observing that conquest and safety depended on the attempt; that, instead of diminishing, the number of their enemies would be increased, by successive reinforcements; and that a longer delay would neither contract the breadth of the stream nor level the height of the bank. The signal was instantly given, and obeyed: the most impatient of the legionaries leaped into five vessels that lay nearest to the bank; and, as they plied their oars with intrepid diligence, they were lost, after a few moments, in the darkness of the night. A flame arose on the opposite side; and Julian, who too clearly understood that his foremost vessels, in attempting to land, had been fired by the enemy, dexterously converted their extreme danger into a presage of victory. "Our fellow-soldiers," he eagerly exclaimed, "are already masters of the bank; see—they make the appointed signal: let us hasten to emulate and assist their courage." The united and rapid motion of a great fleet broke the violence of the current, and they reached the eastern shore of the Tigris with sufficient speed to extinguish the flames and rescue their adventurous companions. The difficulties of a steep and lofty ascent were increased by the weight of armour and the darkness of the night. A shower of stones, darts, and fire was incessantly discharged on the heads of the assailants; who, after an arduous struggle, climbed the bank, and stood victorious upon the ramparts. As soon as they possessed a more equal field, Julian, who, with his light infantry, had led the attack, darted through the ranks a skilful and experienced eye: his bravest soldiers, according to the precepts of Homer, were distributed in the front and rear; and all the trumpets of the Imperial army sounded to battle. The Romans, after sending up a military shout, advanced in measured steps to the animating notes of martial music; launched their formidable javelins; and rushed forwards with drawn swords, to deprive the Barbarians, by a closer onset, of the advantage of their missile weapons. The whole engagement lasted above twelve hours; till the gradual retreat of the Persians was changed into a disorderly flight, of which the shameful example was given by the principal leaders, and the Surenas himself. They were pursued to the gates of Ctesiphon; and the conquerors might have entered the dismayed city, if their general, Victor, who was dangerously wounded with an arrow, had not conjured them to desist from a rash attempt, which must be fatal, if it were not successful. On *their* side, the Romans acknowledged the loss of only seventy-five men; while they affirmed that the Barbarians had left on the field of battle two thousand five hundred, or even six thousand, of their bravest soldiers. The spoil was such as might be expected from the riches and luxury of an Oriental camp; large quantities of silver and gold, splendid arms and trappings, and beds and tables of massy silver. The victorious emperor distributed, as the rewards of valour, some honourable gifts, civic and mural and naval crowns; which he esteemed more precious than the wealth of Asia. A sacrifice was offered to the god of war, but the appearances of the victims threatened the most inauspicious events; and Julian soon discovered, by less ambiguous signs, that he had now reached the term of his prosperity.

On the second day after the battle, the domestic guards, the Jovians and Herculians, and the remaining troops, which composed near two-thirds of the whole army, were securely wafted over the Tigris.[30] While the Persians beheld from the walls of Ctesiphon the desolation of the adjacent country, Julian cast many an anxious look towards the North, in full expectation that, as he himself had victoriously penetrated to the capital of Sapor, the march and junction of his lieutenants, Sebastian and Procopius, would be executed with the same courage and diligence. His expectations were disappointed by the treachery of the Armenian king, who permitted, and most probably directed, the desertion of his auxiliary troops from the camp of the Romans; and by the dissensions of the two generals, who were incapable of forming or executing any plan for the public service. When the emperor had relinquished the hope of this important reinforcement, he condescended to hold a council of war, and approved, after a full debate, the sentiment of those generals who dissuaded the siege of Ctesiphon as a fruitless and pernicious undertaking. It is not easy for us to conceive by what arts of fortification a city thrice besieged and taken by the predecessors of Julian could be rendered impregnable against an army of sixty thousand Romans, commanded by a brave and experienced general, and abundantly supplied with ships, provisions, battering engines, and military stores. But we may rest assured, from the love of glory, and contempt of danger, which formed the character of Julian, that he was not discouraged by any trivial or imaginary obstacles. At the very time when he declined the siege of Ctesiphon, he rejected, with obstinacy and disdain, the most flattering offers of a negotiation of peace. Sapor, who had been so long accustomed to the tardy ostentation of Constantius, was surprised by the intrepid diligence of his successor. As far as the confines of India and Scythia, the satraps of the distant provinces were ordered to assemble their troops, and to march, without delay, to the assistance of their monarch. But their preparations were dilatory, their motions slow; and, before Sapor could lead an army into the field, he received the melancholy intelligence of the devastation of Assyria, the ruin of his palaces, and the slaughter of his bravest troops, who defended the passage of the Tigris. The pride of royalty was humbled in the dust; he took his repasts on the ground; and the disorder of his hair expressed the grief and anxiety of his mind. Perhaps he would not have refused to purchase, with one half of his kingdom, the safety of the remainder: and he would have gladly subscribed himself, in a treaty

[30] *The fleet and army were formed in three divisions, of which the first only had passed during the night. The* πᾶσα δορυφορια, *whom Zosimus transports on the third day, might consist of the protectors, among whom the historian Ammianus, and the future emperor Jovian, actually served,* some schools *of the domestics, and perhaps the Jovians and Herculians, who often did duty as guards.*

of peace, the faithful and dependent ally of the Roman conqueror. Under the pretence of private business, a minister of rank and confidence was secretly dispatched to embrace the knees of Hormisdas, and to request, in the language of a suppliant, that he might be introduced into the presence of the emperor. The Sassanian prince, whether he listened to the voice of pride or humanity, whether he consulted the sentiments of his birth or the duties of his situation, was equally inclined to promote a salutary measure, which would terminate the calamities of Persia, and secure the triumph of Rome. He was astonished by the inflexible firmness of a hero, who remembered, most unfortunately for himself and for his country, that Alexander had uniformly rejected the propositions of Darius. But, as Julian was sensible that the hope of a safe and honourable peace might cool the ardour of his troops, he earnestly requested that Hormisdas would privately dismiss the minister of Sapor and conceal this dangerous temptation from the knowledge of the camp.[31]

The honour, as well as interest, of Julian forbade him to consume his time under the impregnable walls of Ctesiphon; and, as often as he defied the Barbarians, who defended the city, to meet him on the open plain, they prudently replied that, if he desired to exercise his valour, he might seek the army of the Great King. He felt the insult, and he accepted the advice. Instead of confining his servile march to the banks of the Euphrates and Tigris, he resolved to imitate the adventurous spirit of Alexander, and boldly to advance into the inland provinces, till he forced his rival to contend with him, perhaps in the plains of Arbela, for the empire of Asia. The magnanimity of Julian was applauded and betrayed by the arts of a noble Persian, who, in the cause of his country, had generously submitted to act a part full of danger, of falsehood, and of shame.[32] With a train of faithful followers, he deserted to the Imperial camp; exposed, in a specious tale, the injuries which he had sustained; exaggerated the cruelty of Sapor, the discontent of the people, and the weakness of the monarchy; and confidently offered himself as the hostage and guide of the Roman march. The most rational grounds of suspicion were urged, without effect, by the wisdom and experience of Hormisdas; and the credulous Julian, receiving the traitor into his bosom, was persuaded to issue an hasty order, which, in the opinion of mankind, appeared to arraign his prudence, and to endanger his safety. He destroyed, in a single hour, the whole navy, which had been transported above five hundred miles, at so great

[31] *The ecclesiastical historian imputes the refusal of peace to the advice of Maximus. Such advice was unworthy of a philosopher; but the philosopher was likewise a magician, who flattered the hopes and passions of his master.*

[32] *The arts of this new Zopyrus may derive some credit from the testimony of two abbreviators (Sextus Rufus and Victor), and the casual hints of Libanius, and Ammianus. The course of genuine history is interrupted by a most unseasonable chasm in the text of Ammianus.*

expense of toil, of treasure, and of blood. Twelve, or, at the most, twenty-two, small vessels were saved, to accompany, on carriages, the march of the army, and to form occasional bridges for the passage of the rivers. A supply of twenty days' provisions was reserved for the use of the soldiers; and the rest of the magazines, with a fleet of eleven hundred vessels, which rode at anchor in the Tigris, were abandoned to the flames, by the absolute command of the emperor. The Christian bishops, Gregory and Augustin, insult the madness of the apostate, who executed, with his own hands, the sentence of divine justice. Their authority, of less weight, perhaps, in a military question, is confirmed by the cool judgment of an experienced soldier, who was himself spectator of the conflagration, and who could not disapprove the reluctant murmurs of the troops. Yet there are not wanting some specious and perhaps solid reasons, which might justify the resolution of Julian. The navigation of the Euphrates never ascended above Babylon, nor that of the Tigris above Opis. The distance of the last-mentioned city from the Roman camp was not very considerable; and Julian must soon have renounced the vain and impracticable attempt of forcing upwards a great fleet against the stream of a rapid river, which in several places was embarrassed by natural or artificial cataracts. The power of sails or oars was insufficient; it became necessary to tow the ships against the current of the river; the strength of twenty thousand soldiers was exhausted in this tedious and servile labour; and, if the Romans continued to march along the banks of the Tigris, they could only expect to return home without achieving any enterprise worthy of the genius or fortune of their leader. If, on the contrary, it was advisable to advance into the inland country, the destruction of the fleet and magazines was the only measure which could save that valuable prize from the hands of the numerous and active troops which might suddenly be poured from the gates of Ctesiphon. Had the arms of Julian been victorious, we should now admire the conduct, as well as the courage, of a hero, who, by depriving his soldiers of the hopes of a retreat, left them only the alternative of death or conquest.[33]

[33] *Recollect the successful and applauded rashness of Agathocles and Cortez, who burnt their ships on the coasts of Africa and Mexico.*

The cumbersome train of artillery and waggons which retards the operations of a modern army were in a great measure unknown in the camps of the Romans. Yet, in every age, the subsistence of sixty thousand men must have been one of the most important cares of a prudent general; and that subsistence could only be drawn from the enemy's country. Had it been possible for Julian to maintain a bridge of communication on the Tigris, and to preserve the conquered places of Assyria, a desolated province could not afford any large or regular supplies, in a season of the year when the lands were covered by the inundation of the Euphrates,[34] and the unwholesome air was darkened with swarms of innumerable insects.[35] The appearance of the hostile country was far more inviting. The extensive region that lies between the river Tigris and the mountains of Media was filled with villages and towns; and the fertile soil, for the most part, was in a very improved state of cultivation. Julian might expect that a conqueror who possessed the two forcible instruments of persuasion, steel and gold, would easily procure a plentiful subsistence from the fears or the avarice of the natives. But on the approach of the Romans, this rich and smiling prospect was instantly blasted. Wherever they moved, the inhabitants deserted the open villages, and took shelter in the fortified towns; the cattle was driven away; the grass and ripe corn were consumed with fire; and, as soon as the flames had subsided which interrupted the march of Julian, he beheld the melancholy face of a smoking and naked desert. This desperate but effectual method of defence can only be executed by the enthusiasm of a people who prefer their independence to their property; or by the rigour of an arbitrary government, which consults the public safety without submitting to their inclinations the liberty of choice. On the present occasion, the zeal and obedience of the Persians seconded the commands of Sapor; and the emperor was soon reduced to the scanty stock of provisions, which continually wasted in his hands. Before they were entirely consumed, he might still have reached the wealthy and unwarlike cities of Ecbatana or Susa, by the effort of a well directed march;[36] but he was deprived of this last resource by his ignorance of the roads, and by the perfidy of his guides. The Romans wandered several days in the country to the eastward of Bagdad: the Persian deserter, who had artfully led them into the snare, escaped from their resentment; and his followers, as soon as they were put to the torture, confessed the secret of the conspiracy. The visionary conquests of Hyrcania and India, which had so long amused, now tormented, the mind of Julian. Conscious that his own imprudence was the cause of the public distress, he anxiously balanced the hopes of safety or success, without obtaining a satisfactory answer either from gods or men. At length, as the only practicable measure, he embraced the resolution of directing his steps towards the banks of the Tigris, with the design of saving the army by a hasty march to

[34] *The Tigris rises to the south, the Euphrates to the north, of the Armenian mountains. The former overflows in March, the latter in July. These circumstances are well explained in the Geographical Dissertation of Foster, inserted in Spelman's Expedition of Syrus.*

[35] *Ammianus describes, as he had felt, the inconveniency of the flood, the heat, and the insects. The lands of Assyria, oppressed by the Turks, and ravaged by the Curds, or Arabs, yield an increase of ten, fifteen, and twenty-fold, for the seed which is cast into the ground by the wretched and unskilful husbandmen.*

[36] *Isidore of Charax reckons 129 schœni from Seleucia, and Thévenot 128 hours of march from Bagdad, to Ecbatana, or Hamadam. These measures cannot exceed an ordinary parasang, or three Roman miles.*

the confines of Corduene; a fertile and friendly province, which acknowledged the sovereignty of Rome. The desponding troops obeyed the signal of the retreat, only seventy days after they had passed the Chaboras with the sanguine expectation of subverting the throne of Persia.

As long as the Romans seemed to advance into the country, their march was observed and insulted from a distance by several bodies of Persian cavalry; who, showing themselves sometimes in loose, and sometimes in closer, order, faintly skirmished with the advanced guards. These detachments were, however, supported by a much greater force; and the heads of the columns were no sooner pointed towards the Tigris than a cloud of dust arose on the plain. The Romans, who now aspired only to the permission of a safe and speedy retreat, endeavoured to persuade themselves that this formidable appearance was occasioned by a troop of wild asses, or perhaps by the approach of some friendly Arabs. They halted, pitched their tents, fortified their camp, passed the whole night in continual alarms; and discovered, at the dawn of day, that they were surrounded by an army of Persians. This army, which might be considered only as the van of the Barbarians, was soon followed by the main body of cuirassiers, archers, and elephants, commanded by Meranes, a general of rank and reputation. He was accompanied by two of the king's sons, and many of the principal satraps; and fame and expectation exaggerated the strength of the remaining powers, which slowly advanced under the conduct of Sapor himself. As the Romans continued their march, their long array, which was forced to bend, or divide, according to the varieties of the ground, afforded frequent and favourable opportunities to their vigilant enemies. The Persians repeatedly charged with fury; they were repeatedly repulsed with firmness; and the action at Maronga, which almost deserved the name of a battle, was marked by a considerable loss of satraps and elephants, perhaps of equal value in the eyes of their monarch. These splendid advantages were not obtained without an adequate slaughter on the side of the Romans: several officers of distinction were either killed or wounded; and the emperor himself, who, on all occasions of danger, inspired and guided the valour of his troops, was obliged to expose his person and exert his abilities. The weight of offensive and defensive arms, which still constituted the strength and safety of the Romans, disabled them from making any long or effectual pursuit; and, as the horsemen of the East were trained to dart their javelins, and shoot their arrows, at full speed, and in every possible direction, the cavalry of Persia was never more formidable than in the moment of a rapid and disorderly flight. But the most certain and irreparable loss of the Romans was that of time. The hardy veterans, accustomed to the cold climate of Gaul and Germany, fainted under the sultry heat of an Assyrian summer: their vigour was exhausted by the incessant repetition of march and combat; and the progress of the army was suspended by the precautions of a slow and dangerous retreat in the presence of an active enemy. Every day, every hour, as the supply diminished, the value and price of subsistence increased in the Roman camp.[37] Julian, who always contented himself with such food as a hungry soldier would have disdained, distributed for the use of his troops the provisions of the Imperial household, and whatever could be spared from the sumpter-horses of the tribunes and generals. But this feeble relief served only to aggravate the sense of the public distress; and the Romans began to entertain the most gloomy apprehensions that, before they could reach the frontiers of the empire, they should all perish, either by famine or by the sword of the Barbarians.

While Julian struggled with the almost insuperable difficulties of his situation, the silent hours of the night were still devoted to study and contemplation. Whenever he closed his eyes in short and interrupted slumbers, his mind was agitated with painful anxiety; nor can it be thought surprising that the Genius of the empire should once more appear before him, covering with a funeral veil his head and his horn of abundance, and slowly retiring from the Imperial tent. The monarch started from his couch, and stepping forth, to refresh his wearied spirits with the coolness of the midnight air, he beheld a fiery meteor, which shot athwart the sky, and suddenly vanished. Julian was convinced that he had seen the menacing countenance of the god of war;[38] the council which he summoned, of Tuscan haruspices,[39] unanimously pronounced that he should abstain from action: but, on this occasion, necessity. and reason were more prevalent than superstition; and the trumpets sounded at the break of day. The army marched through a hilly country; and the hills had been secretly occupied by the Persians. Julian led the van, with the skill and attention of a consummate general; he was alarmed by the intelligence that his rear was suddenly attacked. The heat of the weather had tempted him to lay aside his cuirass; but he snatched a shield from one of his attendants, and hastened, with a sufficient reinforcement, to the relief of the

[37] *In Mark Antony's retreat, an attic chœnix sold for fifty drachmæ, or, in other words, a pound of flour for twelve or fourteen shillings: barley bread was sold for its weight in silver. It is impossible to peruse the interesting narrative of Plutarch without perceiving that Mark Antony and Julian were pursued by the same enemies and involved in the same distress.*

[38] *Julian had sworn in a passion, nunquam se Marti sacra facturum. Such whimsical quarrels were not uncommon between the gods and their insolent votaries; and even the prudent Augustus, after his fleet had been twice shipwrecked, excluded Neptune from the honours of public processions.*

[39] *They still retained the monopoly of the vain, but lucrative, science which had been invented in Etruria; and professed to derive their knowledge of signs and omens from the ancient books of Tarquitius, a Tuscan sage.*

rear-guard. A similar danger recalled the intrepid prince to the defence of the front; and, as he galloped between the columns, the centre of the left was attacked, and almost overpowered, by a furious charge of the Persian cavalry and elephants. This huge body was soon defeated, by the well-timed evolution of the light infantry, who aimed their weapons, with dexterity and effect, against the backs of the horsemen and the legs of the elephants. The Barbarians fled; and Julian, who was foremost in every danger, animated the pursuit with his voice and gestures. His trembling guards, scattered and oppressed by the disorderly throng of friends and enemies, reminded their fearless sovereign that he was without armour; and conjured him to decline the fall of the impending ruin. As they exclaimed, a cloud of darts and arrows was discharged from the flying squadrons; and a javelin, after razing the skin of his arm, transpierced the ribs, and fixed in the inferior part of the liver. Julian attempted to draw the deadly weapon from his side; but his fingers were cut by the sharpness of the steel, and he fell senseless from his horse. His guards flew to his relief; and the wounded emperor was gently raised from the ground, and conveyed out of the tumult of the battle into an adjacent tent. The report of the melancholy event passed from rank to rank; but the grief of the Romans inspired them with invincible valour and the desire of revenge. The bloody and obstinate conflict was maintained by the two armies, till they were separated by the total darkness of the night. The Persians derived some honour from the advantage which they obtained against the left wing, where Anatolius, master of the offices, was slain, and the præfect Sallust very narrowly escaped. But the event of the day was adverse to the Barbarians. They abandoned the field, their two generals, Meranes and Nohordates,[40] fifty nobles or satraps, and a multitude of their bravest soldiers: and the success of the Romans, if Julian had survived, might have been improved into a decisive and useful victory.

The first words that Julian uttered, after his recovery from the fainting fit into which he had been thrown by loss of blood, were expressive of his martial spirit. He called for his horse and arms, and was impatient to rush into the battle. His remaining strength was exhausted by the painful effort; and the surgeons who examined his wound discovered the symptoms of approaching death. He employed the awful moments with the firm temper of a hero and a sage; the philosophers who had accompanied him in this fatal expedition compared the tent of Julian with the prison of Socrates;

[40] Sapor himself declared to the Romans that it was his practice to comfort the families of his deceased satraps by sending them, as a present, the heads of the guards and officers who had not fallen by their master's side.

and the spectators, whom duty, or friendship, or curiosity, had assembled around his couch, listened with respectful grief to the funeral oration of their dying emperor.[41] "Friends and fellow-soldiers, the seasonable period of my departure is now arrived, and I discharge, with the cheerfulness of a ready debtor, the demands of nature. I have learned from philosophy, how much the soul is more excellent than the body; and that the separation of the nobler substance should be the subject of joy, rather than of affliction. I have learned from religion, that an early death has often been the reward of piety;[42] and I accept, as a favour of the gods, the mortal stroke that secures me from the danger of disgracing a character, which has hitherto been supported by virtue and fortitude. I die without remorse, as I have lived without guilt. I am pleased to reflect on the innocence of my private life; and I can affirm, with confidence, that the supreme authority, that emanation of the Divine Power, has been preserved in my hands pure and immaculate. Detesting the corrupt and destructive maxims of despotism, I have considered the happiness of the people as the end of government. Submitting my actions to the laws of prudence, of justice, and of moderation, I have trusted the event to the care of Providence. Peace was the object of my counsels, as long as peace was consistent with the public welfare; but, when the imperious voice of my country summoned me to arms, I exposed my person to the dangers of war, with the clear foreknowledge (which I had acquired from the art of divination) that I was destined to fall by the sword. I now offer my tribute of gratitude to the Eternal Being, who has not suffered me to perish by the cruelty of a tyrant, by the secret dagger of conspiracy, or by the slow tortures of lingering disease. He has given me, in the midst of an honourable career, a splendid and glorious departure from this world; and I hold it equally absurd, equally base, to solicit, or to decline, the stroke of fate.—Thus much I have attempted to say; but my strength fails me, and I feel the approach of death.—I shall cautiously refrain from any word that may tend to influence your suffrages in the election of an emperor. My choice might be imprudent, or injudicious; and, if it should not be ratified by the consent of the army, it might be fatal to the person whom I should recommend. I shall only, as a good citizen, express my hopes that the Romans may be blessed with the government of a virtuous sovereign." After this discourse, which Julian pronounced in a firm and gentle tone of voice, he distributed, by a military testament,[43] the remains of his private fortune; and,

[41] *The character and situation of Julian might countenance the suspicion that he had previously composed the elaborate oration which Ammianus heard and has transcribed. The version of the Abbé de la Bléterie is faithful and elegant. I have followed him in expressing the Platonic idea of emanations, which is darkly insinuated in the original.*

[42] *Herodotus has displayed that doctrine in an agreeable tale. Yet the Jupiter (in the 16th book of the Iliad) who laments with tears of blood the death of Sarpedon his son had a very imperfect notion of happiness or glory beyond the grave.*

[43] *The soldiers who made their verbal, or nuncupatory, testaments upon actual service (in procinctu) were exempted from the formalities of the Roman law.*

making some inquiry why Anatolius was not present, he understood, from the answer of Sallust, that Anatolius was killed; and bewailed, with amiable inconsistency, the loss of his friend. At the same time he reproved the immoderate grief of the spectators; and conjured them not to disgrace, by unmanly tears, the fate of a prince who in a few moments would be united with heaven, and with the stars.[44] The spectators were silent; and Julian entered into a metaphysical argument with the philosophers Priscus and Maximus, on the nature of the soul. The efforts which he made, of mind as well as body, most probably hastened his death. His wound began to bleed with fresh violence; his respiration was embarrassed by the swelling of the veins: he called for a draught of cold water, and, as soon he had drunk it, expired without pain, about the hour of midnight. Such was the end of that extraordinary man, in the thirty-second year of his age, after a reign of one year and about eight months from the death of Constantius. In his last moments he displayed, perhaps with some ostentation, the love of virtue and of fame which had been the ruling passions of his life.[45]

The triumph of Christianity, and the calamities of the empire, may, in some measure, be ascribed to Julian himself, who had neglected to secure the future execution of his designs by the timely and judicious nomination of an associate and successor. But the royal race of Constantius Chlorus was reduced to his own person; and, if he entertained any serious thoughts of investing with the purple the most worthy among the Romans, he was diverted from his resolution by the difficulty of the choice, the jealousy of power, the fear of ingratitude, and the natural presumption of health, of youth, and of prosperity. His unexpected death left the empire without a master and without an heir, in a state of perplexity and danger, which, in the space of fourscore years, had never been experienced, since the election of Diocletian. In a government which had almost forgotten the distinction of pure and noble blood, the superiority of birth was of little moment; the claims of official rank were accidental and precarious; and the candidates who might aspire to ascend the vacant throne could be supported only by the consciousness of personal merit, or by the hopes of popular favour. But the situation of a famished army, encompassed on all sides by an host of Barbarians, shortened the moments of grief and deliberation. In this scene of terror and distress, the body of the deceased prince, according to his own directions, was decently embalmed; and, at the dawn of day, the generals convened a military senate, at which the commanders

[44] *This union of the human soul with the divine ætherial substance of the universe is the ancient doctrine of Pythagoras and Plato; but it seems to exclude any personal or conscious immortality.*

[45] *The whole relation of the death of Julian is given by Ammianus, an intelligent spectator. Libanius, who turns with horror from the scene, has supplied some circumstances. The calumnies of Gregory, and the legends of more recent saints, may now be silently despised.*

"*The Temple of Peace or the Theatre of Marcellus has been demolished by the slow operation of ages. The theatres of Marcellus and Pompey were occupied, in a great measure, by public and private buildings.*"

THE THEATRE OF MARCELLUS

1. Palace of the Orsini, built into the ancient theatre
2. Cupola of S. Maria in Campitelli

of the legions and the officers, both of cavalry and infantry, were invited to assist. Three or four hours of the night had not passed away without some secret cabals; and, when the election of an emperor was proposed, the spirit of faction began to agitate the assembly. Victor and Arinthæus collected the remains of the court of Constantius; the friends of Julian attached themselves to the Gallic chiefs, Dagalaiphus and Nevitta; and the most fatal consequences might be apprehended from the discord of two factions, so opposite in their character and interest, in their maxims of government, and perhaps in their religious principles. The superior virtues of Sallust could alone reconcile their divisions and unite their suffrages; and the venerable præfect would immediately have been declared the successor of Julian, if he himself, with sincere and modest firmness, had not alleged his age and infirmities, so unequal to the weight of the diadem. The generals, who were surprised and perplexed by his refusal, showed some disposition to adopt the salutary advice of an inferior officer,[46] that they should act as they would have acted in the absence of the emperor; that they should exert their abilities to extricate the army from the present distress; and, if they were fortunate enough to reach the confines of Mesopotamia, they should proceed with united and deliberate counsels in the election of a lawful sovereign. While they debated, a few voices saluted Jovian, who was no more than *first*[47] of the domestics, with the names of Emperor and Augustus. The tumultuary acclamation was instantly repeated by the guards who surrounded the tent, and passed, in a few minutes, to the extremities of the line. The new prince, astonished with his own fortune, was hastily invested with the Imperial ornaments and received an oath of fidelity from the generals whose favour and protection he so lately solicited. The strongest recommendation of Jovian was the merit of his father, Count Varronian, who enjoyed, in honourable retirement, the fruit of his long services. In the obscure freedom of a private station, the son indulged his taste for wine and women; yet he supported, with credit, the character of a Christian and a soldier.[48] Without being conspicuous for any of the ambitious qualifications which excite the admiration and envy of mankind, the comely person of Jovian, his cheerful temper, and familiar wit, had gained the affection of his fellow-soldiers; and the generals of both parties acquiesced in a popular election, which had not been conducted by the arts of their enemies. The pride of this unexpected elevation was moderated by the just apprehension that the same day might terminate the life and reign of the new em-

[46] *Honoratior aliquis miles; perhaps Ammianus himself. The modest and judicious historian describes the scene of the election, at which he was undoubtedly present.*

[47] *The* primus, *or primicerius, enjoyed the dignity of a senator; and, though only a tribune, he ranked with the military dukes. These privileges are perhaps more recent than the time of Jovian.*

[48] *The ecclesiastical historians, Socrates, Sozomen, and Theodoret ascribe to Jovian the merit of a confessor under the preceding reign; and piously suppose that he refused the purple, till the whole army unanimously exclaimed that they were Christians. Ammianus, calmly pursuing his narrative, overthrows the legend by a single sentence. Hostiis pro Joviano extisque inspectis pronuntiatum est, &c.*

peror. The pressing voice of necessity was obeyed without delay; and the first orders issued by Jovian, a few hours after his predecessor had expired, were to prosecute a march which could alone extricate the Romans from their actual distress.[49]

The esteem of an enemy is most sincerely expressed by his fears; and the degree of fear may be accurately measured by the joy with which he celebrates his deliverance. The welcome news of the death of Julian, which a deserter revealed to the camp of Sapor, inspired the desponding monarch with a sudden confidence of victory. He immediately detached the royal cavalry, perhaps the ten thousand *Immortals,*[50] to second and support the pursuit; and discharged the whole weight of his united forces on the rear-guard of the Romans. The rear-guard was thrown into disorder; the renowned legions, which derived their titles from Diocletian and his warlike colleague, were broke and trampled down by the elephants; and three tribunes lost their lives in attempting to stop the flight of their soldiers. The battle was at length restored by the persevering valour of the Romans; the Persians were repulsed with a great slaughter of men and elephants; and the army, after marching and fighting a long summer's day, arrived, in the evening, at Samara on the banks of the Tigris, about one hundred miles above Ctesiphon.[51] On the ensuing day, the Barbarians, instead of harassing the march, attacked the camp, of Jovian which had been seated in a deep and sequestered valley. From the hills, the archers of Persia insulted and annoyed the wearied legionaries; and a body of cavalry, which had penetrated with desperate courage through the Prætorian gate, was cut in pieces, after a doubtful conflict, near the Imperial tent. In the succeeding night, the camp of Carche was protected by the lofty dykes of the river; and the Roman army, though incessantly exposed to the vexatious pursuit of the Saracens, pitched their tents near the city of Dura,[52] four days after the death of Julian. The Tigris was still on their left; their hopes and provisions were almost consumed; and the impatient soldiers, who had fondly persuaded themselves that the frontiers of the empire were not far distant, requested their new sovereign that they might be permitted to hazard the passage of the river. With the assistance of his wisest officers, Jovian endeavoured to check their rashness; by representing that, if they possessed sufficient skill and vigour to stem the torrent of a deep and rapid stream, they would only deliver themselves naked and defenceless to the Barbarians, who had occupied the opposite banks. Yielding at length to their clamorous importuni-

[49] *Ammianus has drawn from the life an impartial portrait of Jovian: to which the younger Victor has added some remarkable strokes. The Abbé de la Bléterie has composed an elaborate history of his short reign; a work remarkably distinguished by elegance of style, critical disquisition, and religious prejudice.*

[50] *Regius equitatus. It appears from Procopius that the Immortals, so famous under Cyrus and his successors, were revived, if we may use that improper word, by the Sassanides.*

[51] *The obscure villages of the inland country are irrecoverably lost; nor can we name the field of battle where Julian fell: but M. d'Anville has demonstrated the precise situation of Sumere, Carche, and Dura, along the banks of the Tigris. In the ninth century, Sumere, or Samara, became, with a slight change of name, the royal residence of the Khalifs of the house of Abbas.*

[52] *Dura was a fortified place in the wars of Antiochus against the rebels of Media and Persia.*

ties, he consented, with reluctance, that five hundred Gauls and Germans, accustomed from their infancy to the waters of the Rhine and Danube, should attempt the bold adventure, which might serve either as an encouragement, or as a warning, for the rest of the army. In the silence of the night, they swam the Tigris, surprised an unguarded post of the enemy, and displayed at the dawn of day the signal of their resolution and fortune. The success of this trial disposed the emperor to listen to the promises of his architects, who proposed to construct a floating bridge of the inflated skins of sheep, oxen, and goats, covered with a floor of earth and fascines.[53] Two important days were spent in the ineffectual labour; and the Romans, who already endured the miseries of famine, cast a look of despair on the Tigris, and upon the Barbarians; whose numbers and obstinacy increased with the distress of the Imperial army.[54]

In this hopeless situation, the fainting spirits of the Romans were revived by the sound of peace. The transient presumption of Sapor had vanished: he observed, with serious concern, that, in the repetition of doubtful combats, he had lost his most faithful and intrepid nobles, his bravest troops, and the greatest part of his train of elephants: and the experienced monarch feared to provoke the resistance of despair, the vicissitudes of fortune, and the unexhausted powers of the Roman empire; which might soon advance to relieve, or to revenge, the successor of Julian. The Surenas himself, accompanied by another satrap, appeared in the camp of Jovian; and declared that the clemency of his sovereign was not averse to signify the conditions on which he would consent to spare and to dismiss the Cæsar with the relics of his captive army. The hopes of safety subdued the firmness of the Romans; the emperor was compelled, by the advice of his council and the cries of the soldiers, to embrace the offer of peace; and the præfect Sallust was immediately sent, with the general Arinthæus, to understand the pleasure of the Great King. The crafty Persian delayed, under various pretences, the conclusion of the agreement; started difficulties, required explanations, suggested expedients, receded from his concessions, increased his demands, and wasted four days in the arts of negotiation, till he had consumed the stock of provisions which yet remained in the camp of the Romans. Had Jovian been capable of executing a bold and prudent measure, he would have continued his march with unremitting diligence; the progress of the treaty would have suspended the attacks of the Barbarians; and, before the expiration of the fourth day, he might have safely reached the

[53] *A similar expedient was proposed to the leaders of the ten thousand, and wisely rejected. It appears from our modern travellers that rafts floating on bladders performed the trade and navigation of the Tigris.*

[54] *The first military acts of the reign of Jovian are related by Ammianus, Libanius, and Zosimus. Though we may distrust the fairness of Libanius, the ocular testimony of Eutropius must incline us to suspect that Ammianus has been too jealous of the honour of the Roman arms.*

fruitful province of Corduene, at the distance only of one hundred miles.[55] The irresolute emperor, instead of breaking through the toils of the enemy, expected his fate with patient resignation; and accepted the humiliating conditions of peace, which it was no longer in his power to refuse. The five provinces beyond the Tigris, which had been ceded by the grandfather of Sapor, were restored to the Persian monarchy. He acquired, by a single article, the impregnable city of Nisibis; which had sustained, in three successive sieges, the effort of his arms. Singara, and the castle of the Moors, one of the strongest places of Mesopotamia, were likewise dismembered from the empire. It was considered as an indulgence, that the inhabitants of those fortresses were permitted to retire with their effects; but the conqueror rigorously insisted that the Romans should for ever abandon the king and kingdom of Armenia. A peace, or rather a long truce, of thirty years was stipulated between the hostile nations; the faith of the treaty was ratified by solemn oaths, and religious ceremonies; and hostages of distinguished rank were reciprocally delivered to secure the performance of the conditions.

The sophist of Antioch, who saw with indignation the sceptre of his hero in the feeble hand of a Christian successor, professes to admire the moderation of Sapor, in contenting himself with so small a portion of the Roman empire. If he had stretched as far as the Euphrates the claims of his ambition, he might have been secure, says Libanius, of not meeting with a refusal. If he had fixed, as the boundary of Persia, the Orontes, the Cydnus, the Sangarius, or even the Thracian Bosphorus, flatterers would not have been wanting in the court of Jovian to convince the timid monarch that his remaining provinces would still afford the most ample gratifications of power and luxury. Without adopting in its full force this malicious insinuation, we must acknowledge that the conclusion of so ignominious a treaty was facilitated by the private ambition of Jovian. The obscure domestic, exalted to the throne by fortune rather than by merit, was impatient to escape from the hands of the Persians; that he might prevent the designs of Procopius, who commanded the army of Mesopotamia, and establish his doubtful reign over the legions and provinces, which were still ignorant of the hasty and tumultuous choice of the camp beyond the Tigris. In the neighbourhood of the same river, at no very considerable distance from the fatal station of Dura,[56] the ten thousand Greeks, without generals, or guides, or provisions, were abandoned, above twelve

[55] It is presumptuous to controvert the opinion of Ammianus, a soldier and a spectator. Yet it is difficult to understand how the mountains of Corduene could extend over the plain of Assyria, as low as the conflux of the Tigris and the great Zab; or how an army of sixty thousand men could march one hundred miles in four days.

[56] The generals were murdered on the banks of the Zabatus, or great Zab, a river of Assyria, 400 feet broad, which falls into the Tigris fourteen hours below Mosul. The error of the Greeks bestowed on the great and lesser Zab the names of the Wolf (Lycus), and the Goat (Capros). They created these animals to attend the Tiger of the East.

hundred miles from their native country, to the resentment of a victorious monarch. The difference of *their* conduct and success depended much more on their character than on their situation. Instead of tamely resigning themselves to the secret deliberations and private views of a single person, the united councils of the Greeks were inspired by the generous enthusiasm of a popular assembly; where the mind of each citizen is filled with the love of glory, the pride of freedom, and the contempt of death. Conscious of their superiority over the Barbarians in arms and discipline, they disdained to yield, they refused to capitulate; every obstacle was surmounted by their patience, courage, and military skill; and the memorable retreat of the ten thousand exposed and insulted the weakness of the Persian monarchy.[57]

As the price of his disgraceful concessions, the emperor might perhaps have stipulated that the camp of the hungry Romans should be plentifully supplied;[58] and that they should be permitted to pass the Tigris on the bridge which was constructed by the hands of the Persians. But, if Jovian presumed to solicit those equitable terms, they were sternly refused by the haughty tyrant of the East; whose clemency had pardoned the invaders of his country. The Saracens sometimes intercepted the stragglers of the march; but the generals and troops of Sapor respected the cessation of arms; and Jovian was suffered to explore the most convenient place for the passage of the river. The small vessels, which had been saved from the conflagration of the fleet, performed the most essential service. They first conveyed the emperor and his favourites; and afterwards transported, in many successive voyages, a great part of the army. But, as every man was anxious for his personal safety, and apprehensive of being left on the hostile shore, the soldiers, who were too impatient to wait the slow returns of the boats, boldly ventured themselves on light hurdles, or inflated skins; and, drawing after them their horses, attempted, with various success, to swim across the river. Many of these daring adventurers were swallowed by the waves; many others, who were carried along by the violence of the stream, fell an easy prey to the avarice, or cruelty, of the wild Arabs: and the loss which the army sustained in the passage of the Tigris was not inferior to the carnage of a day of battle. As soon as the Romans had landed on the western bank, they were delivered from the hostile pursuit of the Barbarians; but, in a laborious march of two hundred miles over the plains of Mesopotamia, they endured the last extremities of thirst and hunger. They were obliged to

[57] *The* Cyropædia *is vague and languid: the* Anabasis *circumstantial and animated. Such is the eternal difference between fiction and truth.*

[58] *According to Rufinus, an immediate supply of provisions was stipulated by the treaty; and Theodoret affirms that the obligation was faithfully discharged by the Persians. Such a fact is probable, but undoubtedly false.*

traverse a sandy desert, which, in the extent of seventy miles, did not afford a single blade of sweet grass, nor a single spring of fresh water; and the rest of the inhospitable waste was untrod by the footsteps either of friends or enemies. Whenever a small measure of flour could be discovered in the camp, twenty pounds weight were greedily purchased with ten pieces of gold: the beasts of burden were slaughtered and devoured; and the desert was strewed with the arms and baggage of the Roman soldiers, whose tattered garments and meagre countenances displayed their past sufferings and actual misery. A small convoy of provisions advanced to meet the army as far as the castle of Ur; and the supply was the more grateful, since it declared the fidelity of Sebastian and Procopius. At Thilsaphata, the emperor most graciously received the generals of Mesopotamia, and the remains of a once flourishing army at length reposed themselves under the walls of Nisibis. The messengers of Jovian had already proclaimed, in the language of flattery, his election, his treaty, and his return; and the new prince had taken the most effectual measures to secure the allegiance of the armies and provinces of Europe; by placing the military command in the hands of those officers who, from motives of interest or inclination, would firmly support the cause of their benefactor.

The friends of Julian had confidently announced the success of his expedition. They entertained a fond persuasion that the temples of the gods would be enriched with the spoils of the East; that Persia would be reduced to the humble state of a tributary province, governed by the laws and magistrates of Rome; that the Barbarians would adopt the dress, and manners, and language, of their conquerors; and that the youth of Ecbatana and Susa would study the art of rhetoric under Grecian masters.[59] The progress of the arms of Julian interrupted his communication with the empire; and, from the moment that he passed the Tigris, his affectionate subjects were ignorant of the fate and fortunes of their prince. Their contemplation of fancied triumphs was disturbed by the melancholy rumour of his death; and they persisted to doubt, after they could no longer deny, the truth of that fatal event.[60] The messengers of Jovian promulgated the specious tale of a prudent and necessary peace: the voice of fame, louder and more sincere, revealed the disgrace of the emperor and the conditions of the ignominious treaty. The minds of the people were filled with astonishment and grief, with indignation and terror, when they were informed that the unworthy successor of Julian relinquished the five provinces which had been

[59] Such were the natural hopes and wishes of a rhetorician.

[60] The people of Carrhæ, a city devoted to Paganism, buried the inauspicious messenger under a pile of stones. Libanius, when he received the fatal intelligence, cast his eye on his sword; but he recollected that Plato had condemned suicide, and that he must live to compose the panegyric of Julian.

acquired by the victory of Galerius; and that he shamefully surrendered to the Barbarians the important city of Nisibis, the firmest bulwark of the provinces of the East.[61] The deep and dangerous question, how far the public faith should be observed, when it becomes incompatible with the public safety, was freely agitated in popular conversation; and some hopes were entertained that the emperor would redeem his pusillanimous behaviour by a splendid act of patriotic perfidy. The inflexible spirit of the Roman senate had always disclaimed the unequal conditions which were extorted from the distress of her captive armies; and, if it were necessary to satisfy the national honour by delivering the guilty general into the hands of the Barbarians, the greatest part of the subjects of Jovian would have cheerfully acquiesced in the precedent of ancient times.[62]

But the emperor, whatever might be the limits of his constitutional authority, was the absolute master of the laws and arms of the state; and the same motives which had forced him to subscribe, now pressed him to execute, the treaty of peace. He was impatient to secure an empire at the expense of a few provinces; and the respectable names of religion and honour concealed the personal fears and ambition of Jovian. Notwithstanding the dutiful solicitations of the inhabitants, decency, as well as prudence, forbade the emperor to lodge in the palace of Nisibis; but, the next morning after his arrival, Bineses, the ambassador of Persia, entered the place, displayed from the citadel the standard of the Great King, and proclaimed, in his name, the cruel alternative of exile or servitude. The principal citizens of Nisibis, who, till that fatal moment, had confided in the protection of their sovereign, threw themselves at his feet. They conjured him not to abandon, or, at least, not to deliver, a faithful colony to the rage of a barbarian tyrant, exasperated by the three successive defeats which he had experienced under the walls of Nisibis. They still possessed arms and courage to repel the invaders of their country; they requested only the permission of using them in their own defence; and, as soon as they had asserted their independence, they should implore the favour of being again admitted into the rank of his subjects. Their arguments, their eloquence, their tears, were ineffectual. Jovian alleged, with some confusion, the sanctity of oaths; and, as the reluctance with which he accepted the present of a crown of gold convinced the citizens of their hopeless condition, the advocate Sylvanus was provoked to exclaim, "O Emperor! may you thus be crowned by all the cities of your dominions!" Jovian, who, in a few weeks, had assumed the

[61] *Ammianus and Eutropius may be admitted as fair and credible witnesses of the public language and opinions. The people of Antioch reviled an ignominious peace, which exposed them to the Persians on a naked and defenceless frontier.*

[62] *The Abbé de la Blèterie, though a severe casuist, has pronounced that Jovian was not bound to execute his promise; since he could not dismember the empire, nor alienate, without their consent, the allegiance of his people. I have never found much delight or instruction in such political metaphysics.*

63 *At Nisibis he per-
formed a* royal *act. A
brave officer, his name-
sake, who had been
thought worthy of the
purple, was dragged
from supper, thrown
into a well, and stoned to
death, without any form
of trial or evidence of
guilt.*

habits of a prince,[63] was displeased with freedom, and offended
with truth: and, as he reasonably supposed that the discontent of the
people might incline them to submit to the Persian government, he
published an edict, under pain of death, that they should leave the
city within the term of three days. Ammianus had delineated in
lively colours the scene of universal despair, which he seems to have
viewed with an eye of compassion. The martial youth had deserted,
with indignant grief, the walls which they had so gloriously defended: the disconsolate mourner dropt a last tear over the tomb
of a son or husband, which must soon be profaned by the rude hand
of a Barbarian master; and the aged citizen kissed the threshold,
and clung to the doors, of the house where he had passed the cheerful and careless hours of infancy. The highways were crowded with
a trembling multitude: the distinctions of rank, and sex, and age,
were lost in the general calamity. Every one strove to bear away
some fragment from the wreck of his fortunes; and, as they could
not command the immediate service of an adequate number of
horses or waggons, they were obliged to leave behind them the
greatest part of their valuable effects. The savage insensibility of
Jovian appears to have aggravated the hardships of these unhappy
fugitives. They were seated, however, in a new-built quarter of
Amida; and that rising city, with the reinforcement of a very considerable colony, soon recovered its former splendour, and became
the capital of Mesopotamia. Similar orders were dispatched by the
emperor for the evacuation of Singara and the castle of the Moors;
and for the restitution of the five provinces beyond the Tigris. Sapor
enjoyed the glory and the fruits of his victory; and this ignominious
peace has justly been considered as a memorable æra in the decline and fall of the Roman empire. The predecessors of Jovian had
sometimes relinquished the dominion of distant and unprofitable
provinces; but, since the foundation of the city, the genius of Rome,
the god Terminus, who guarded the boundaries of the republic,
had never retired before the sword of a victorious enemy.

After Jovian had performed those engagements which the voice
of his people might have tempted him to violate, he hastened away
from the scene of his disgrace, and proceeded with his whole court
to enjoy the luxury of Antioch. Without consulting the dictates of
religious zeal, he was prompted, by humanity and gratitude, to bestow the last honours on the remains of his deceased sovereign;[64]
and Procopius, who sincerely bewailed the loss of his kinsman, was
removed from the command of the army, under the decent pretence

64 *The Abbé de la Blé-
terie handsomely exposes
the brutal bigotry of
Baronius, who would
have thrown Julian to
the dogs, ne cespititiâ
quidem sepulturâ
dignus.*

of conducting the funeral. The corpse of Julian was transported from Nisibis to Tarsus, in a slow march of fifteen days; and, as it passed through the cities of the East, was saluted by the hostile factions, with mournful lamentations and clamorous insults. The Pagans already placed their beloved hero in the rank of those gods whose worship he had restored; while the invectives of the Christians pursued the soul of the apostate to hell, and his body to the grave.[65] One party lamented the approaching ruin of their altars; the other celebrated the marvellous deliverance of the church. The Christians applauded, in lofty and ambiguous strains, the stroke of divine vengeance, which had been so long suspended over the guilty head of Julian. They acknowledged that the death of the tyrant, at the instant he expired beyond the Tigris, was *revealed* to the saints of Egypt, Syria and Cappadocia;[66] and, instead of suffering him to fall by the Persian darts, their indiscretion ascribed the heroic deed to the obscure hand of some mortal or immortal champion of the faith.[67] Such imprudent declarations were eagerly adopted by the malice, or credulity, of their adversaries;[68] who darkly insinuated, or confidently asserted, that the governors of the church had instigated and directed the fanaticism of a domestic assassin. Above sixteen years after the death of Julian, the charge was solemnly and vehemently urged, in a public oration, addressed by Libanius to the emperor Theodosius. His suspicions are unsupported by fact or argument; and we can only esteem the generous zeal of the sophist of Antioch for the cold and neglected ashes of his friend.[69]

It was an ancient custom in the funerals, as well as in the triumphs, of the Romans, that the voice of praise should be corrected by that of satire and ridicule; and that, in the midst of the splendid pageants, which displayed the glory of the living or of the dead, their imperfections should not be concealed from the eyes of the world.[70] This custom was practised in the funeral of Julian. The comedians, who resented his contempt and aversion for the theatre, exhibited, with the applause of a Christian audience, the lively and exaggerated representation of the faults and follies of the deceased emperor. His various character and singular manners afforded an ample scope for pleasantry and ridicule.[71] In the exercise of his uncommon talents, he often descended below the majesty of his rank. Alexander was transformed into Diogenes; the philosopher was degraded into a priest. The purity of his virtue was sullied by excessive vanity: his superstition disturbed the peace, and endangered

[65] *Compare the sophist and the saint (Libanius with Gregory Nazianzen). The Christian orator faintly mutters some exhortations to modesty and forgiveness: but he is well satisfied that the real sufferings of Julian will far exceed the fabulous torments of Ixion or Tantalus.*

[66] *Tillemont has collected these visions. Some saint or angel was observed to be absent in the night on a secret expedition, &c.*

[67] *Sozomen applauds the Greek doctrine of tyrannicide; but the whole passage, which a Jesuit might have translated, is prudently suppressed by the president Cousin.*

[68] *Immediately after the death of Julian, an uncertain rumour was scattered, telo cecidisse Romano. It was carried, by some deserters, to the Persian camp; and the Romans were reproached as the assassins of the emperor by Sapor and his subjects. It was urged, as a decisive proof, that no Persian had appeared to claim the promised reward. But the flying horseman, who darted the fatal javelin, might be ignorant of its effect; or he might be slain in the same action. Ammianus*

737

neither feels nor inspires a suspicion.

[69] *The Orator scatters suspicions, demands an inquiry, and insinuates that proofs might still be obtained. He ascribes the success of the Huns to the criminal neglect of revenging Julian's death.*

[70] *At the funeral of Vespasian, the comedian who personated that frugal emperor anxiously inquired, how much it cost?—Fourscore thousand pounds (centies).—Give me the tenth part of the sum, and throw my body into the Tiber.*

[71] *Gregory compares this supposed ignominy and ridicule to the funeral honours of Constantius, whose body was chaunted over mount Taurus by a choir of angels.*

[72] *The luxuriancy of Quintus Curtius's descriptions has been often censured. Yet it was almost the duty of the historian to describe a river, whose waters had nearly proved fatal to Alexander.*

the safety, of a mighty empire; and his irregular sallies were the less entitled to indulgence, as they appear to be the laborious efforts of art, or even of affectation. The remains of Julian were interred at Tarsus in Cilicia; but his stately tomb which arose in that city, on the banks of the cold and limpid Cydnus,[72] was displeasing to the faithful friends, who loved and revered the memory of that extraordinary man. The philosopher expressed a very reasonable wish that the disciple of Plato might have reposed amidst the groves of the academy: while the soldiers exclaimed in bolder accents that the ashes of Julian should have been mingled with those of Cæsar, in the field of Mars, and among the ancient monuments of Roman virtue. The history of princes does not very frequently renew the example of a similar competition.

XXV

HE death of Julian had left the
public affairs of the empire in a very doubtful and dangerous situation. The Roman army was saved by an inglorious, perhaps a
necessary, treaty;[1] and the first moments of peace were consecrated
by the pious Jovian to restore the domestic tranquillity of the
church and state. The indiscretion of his predecessor, instead of
reconciling, had artfully fomented the religious war; and the balance which he affected to preserve between the hostile factions
served only to perpetuate the contest, by the vicissitudes of hope and
fear, by the rival claims of ancient possession and actual favour.
The Christians had forgotten the spirit of the Gospel; and the
Pagans had imbibed the spirit of the church. In private families, the
sentiments of nature were extinguished by the blind fury of zeal
and revenge; the majesty of the laws was violated or abused; the
cities of the East were stained with blood; and the most implacable enemies of the Romans were in the bosom of their country.
Jovian was educated in the profession of Christianity; and, as he
marched from Nisibis to Antioch, the banner of the Cross, the LA-
BRUM of Constantine, which was again displayed at the head of the
legions, announced to the people the faith of their new emperor. As
soon as he ascended the throne, he transmitted a circular epistle to
all the governors of provinces: in which he confessed the divine
truth, and secured the legal establishment, of the Christian religion.

[1] *The medals of Jovian
adorn him with victories, laurel crowns,
and prostrate captives.
Flattery is a foolish suicide; she destroys herself
with her own hands.*

The insidious edicts of Julian were abolished; the ecclesiastical immunities were restored and enlarged; and Jovian condescended to lament that the distress of the times obliged him to diminish the measure of charitable distributions.[2] The Christians were unanimous in the loud and sincere applause which they bestowed on the pious successor of Julian. But they were still ignorant what creed, or what synod, he would choose for the standard of orthodoxy; and the peace of the church immediately revived those eager disputes which had been suspended during the season of persecution. The episcopal leaders of the contending sects, convinced, from experience, how much their fate would depend on the earliest impressions that were made on the mind of an untutored soldier, hastened to the court of Edessa or Antioch. The highways of the East were crowded with Homoousian, and Arian, and Semi-Arian, and Eunomian bishops, who struggled to outstrip each other in the holy race; the apartments of the palace resounded with their clamours; and the ears of the prince were assaulted, and perhaps astonished, by the singular mixture of metaphysical argument and passionate invective. The moderation of Jovian, who recommended concord and charity and referred the disputants to the sentence of a future council, was interpreted as a symptom of indifference; but his attachment to the Nicene creed was at length discovered and declared by the reverence which he expressed for the *celestial*[3] virtues of the great Athanasius. The intrepid veteran of the faith, at the age of seventy, had issued from his retreat on the first intelligence of the tyrant's death. The acclamations of the people seated him once more on the archiepiscopal throne; and he wisely accepted, or anticipated, the invitation of Jovian. The venerable figure of Athanasius, his calm courage, and insinuating eloquence, sustained the reputation which he had already acquired in the courts of four successive princes.[4] As soon as he had gained the confidence, and secured the faith, of the Christian emperor, he returned in triumph to his diocese, and continued, with mature counsels and undiminished vigour, to direct, ten years longer,[5] the ecclesiastical government of Alexandria, Egypt, and the Catholic church. Before his departure from Antioch, he assured Jovian that his orthodox devotion would be rewarded with a long and peaceful reign. Athanasius had reason to hope that he should be allowed either the merit of a successful prediction or the excuse of a grateful, though ineffectual, prayer.

The slightest force, when it is applied to assist and guide the natural descent of its object, operates with irresistible weight; and Jo-

2 *Jovian restored to the church* τὸν ἀρχαῖον κόσμον; *a forcible and comprehensive expression.*

3 *The word* celestial *faintly expresses the impious and extravagant flattery of the emperor to the archbishop,* τῆς πρὸς τὸν Θεὸν τῶυ ὅλων ὁμοιώσεως. *Gregory Nazianzen celebrates the friendship of Jovian and Athanasius. The primate's journey was advised by the Egyptian monks.*

4 *Athanasius, at the court of Antioch, is agreeably represented by La Bléterie: he translates the singular and original conferences of the emperor, the primate of Egypt, and the Arian deputies. The Abbé is not satisfied with the coarse pleasantry of Jovian; but his partiality for Athanasius assumes, in his eyes, the character of justice.*

5 *The true æra of his death is perplexed with some difficulties. But the date (A.D. 373, May 2) which seems the most consistent with history and reason is ratified by his authentic life.*

vian had the good fortune to embrace the religious opinions which were supported by the spirit of the times and the zeal and numbers of the most powerful sect.[6] Under his reign, Christianity obtained an easy and lasting victory; and, as soon as the smile of royal patronage was withdrawn, the genius of Paganism, which had been fondly raised and cherished by the arts of Julian, sunk irrecoverably in the dust. In many cities, the temples were shut or deserted: the philosophers, who had abused their transient favour, thought it prudent to shave their beards and disguise their profession; and the Christians rejoiced, that they were now in a condition to forgive, or to revenge, the injuries which they had suffered under the preceding reign. The consternation of the Pagan world was dispelled by a wise and gracious edict of toleration; in which Jovian explicitly declared that, although he should severely punish the sacrilegious rites of magic, his subjects might exercise, with freedom and safety the ceremonies of the ancient worship. The memory of this law has been preserved by the orator Themistius, who was deputed by the senate of Constantinople to express their loyal devotion for the new emperor. Themistius expatiates on the clemency of the Divine Nature, the facility of human error, the rights of conscience, and the independence of the mind; and, with some eloquence, inculcates the principles of philosophical toleration; whose aid Superstition herself, in the hour of her distress, is not ashamed to implore. He justly observes that, in the recent changes, both religions had been alternately disgraced by the seeming acquisition of worthless proselytes, of those votaries of the reigning purple who could pass, without a reason and without a blush, from the church to the temple, and from the altars of Jupiter to the sacred table of the Christians.[7]

In the space of seven months, the Roman troops, who were now returned to Antioch, had performed a march of fifteen hundred miles; in which they had endured all the hardships of war, of famine, and of climate. Notwithstanding their services, their fatigues, and the approach of winter, the timid and impatient Jovian allowed only, to the men and horses, a respite of six weeks. The emperor could not sustain the indiscreet and malicious raillery of the people of Antioch. He was impatient to possess the palace of Constantinople, and to prevent the ambition of some competitor, who might occupy the vacant allegiance of Europe. But he soon received the grateful intelligence that his authority was acknowledged from the Thracian Bosphorus to the Atlantic ocean. By the first letters which he dispatched from the camp of Mesopotamia he had delegated the

[6] *Athanasius magnifies the number of the orthodox, who composed the whole world,* παρεξ ὀλίγων τῶν τὰ Ἀρείου φρονούντων. *This assertion was verified in the space of thirty or forty years.*

[7] *The Abbé de la Blèterie judiciously remarks that Sozomen has forgot the general toleration, and Themistius the establishment of the Catholic religion. Each of them turned away from the object which he disliked, and wished to suppress the part of the edict the least honourable, in his opinion, to the emperor Jovian.*

military command of Gaul and Illyricum to Malarich, a brave and faithful officer of the nation of the Franks, and to his father-in-law, Count Lucillian, who had formerly distinguished his courage and conduct in the defence of Nisibis. Malarich had declined an office to which he thought himself unequal; and Lucillian was massacred at Rheims, in an accidental mutiny of the Batavian cohorts. But the moderation of Jovinus, master-general of the cavalry, who forgave the intention of his disgrace, soon appeased the tumult and confirmed the uncertain minds of the soldiers. The oath of fidelity was administered and taken with loyal acclamations; and the deputies of the Western armies saluted their new sovereign as he descended from Mount Taurus to the city of Tyana, in Cappadocia. From Tyana he continued his hasty march to Ancyra, capital of the province of Galatia; where Jovian assumed, with his infant son, the name and ensigns of the consulship.[8] Dadastana,[9] an obscure town, almost at an equal distance between Ancyra and Nice, was marked for the fatal term of his journey and his life. After indulging himself with a plentiful, perhaps an intemperate, supper, he retired to rest; and the next morning the emperor Jovian was found dead in his bed. The cause of this sudden death was variously understood. By some it was ascribed to the consequences of an indigestion, occasioned either by the quantity of the wine, or the quality of the mushrooms, which he had swallowed in the evening. According to others, he was suffocated in his sleep by the vapour of charcoal; which extracted from the walls of the apartment the unwholesome moisture of the fresh plaister. But the want of a regular inquiry into the death of a prince, whose reign and person were soon forgotten, appears to have been the only circumstance which countenanced the malicious whispers of poison and domestic guilt.[10] The body of Jovian was sent to Constantinople, to be interred with his predecessors; and the sad procession was met on the road by his wife Charito, the daughter of Count Lucillian; who still wept the recent death of her father, and was hastening to dry her tears in the embraces of an Imperial husband. Her disappointment and grief were embittered by the anxiety of maternal tenderness. Six weeks before the death of Jovian, his infant son had been placed in the curule chair, adorned with the title of *Nobilissimus,* and the vain ensigns of the consulship. Unconscious of his fortune, the royal youth, who, from his grandfather, assumed the name of Varronian, was reminded only by the jealousy of the government that he was the son of an emperor. Sixteen years afterwards he was still alive, but he had already

[8] *Cujus vagitus, pertinaciter reluctantis, ne in curuli sellâ veheretur ex more, id quod mox accidit protendebat. Augustus and his successors respectfully solicited a dispensation of age for the sons or nephews whom they raised to the consulship. But the curule chair of the first Brutus had never been dishonoured by an infant.*

[9] *The Itinerary of Antoninus fixes Dadastana 125 Roman miles from Nice; 117 from Ancyra. The pilgrim of Bordeaux, by omitting some stages, reduces the whole space from 242 to 181 miles.*

[10] *Ammianus, unmindful of his usual candour and good sense, compares the death of the harmless Jovian to that of the second Africanus, who had excited the fears and resentment of the popular faction.*

been deprived of an eye; and his afflicted mother expected every hour that the innocent victim would be torn from her arms, to appease with his blood the suspicions of the reigning prince.[11]

After the death of Jovian, the throne of the Roman world remained ten days [12] without a master. The ministers and generals still continued to meet in council; to exercise their respective functions; to maintain the public order; and peaceably to conduct the army to the city of Nice in Bithynia, which was chosen for the place of the election.[13] In a solemn assembly of the civil and military powers of the empire, the diadem was again unanimously offered to the præfect Sallust. He enjoyed the glory of a second refusal; and, when the virtues of the father were alleged in favour of his son, the præfect, with the firmness of a disinterested patriot, declared to the electors that the feeble age of the one and the unexperienced youth of the other were equally incapable of the laborious duties of government. Several candidates were proposed, and, after weighing the objections of character or situation, they were successively rejected; but, as soon as the name of Valentinian was pronounced, the merit of that officer united the suffrages of the whole assembly, and obtained the sincere approbation of Sallust himself. Valentinian [14] was the son of Count Gratian, a native of Cibalis, in Pannonia, who, from an obscure condition, had raised himself, by matchless strength and dexterity, to the military commands of Africa and Britain; from which he retired with an ample fortune and suspicious integrity. The rank and services of Gratian contributed, however, to smooth the first steps of the promotion of his son; and afforded him an early opportunity of displaying those solid and useful qualifications which raised his character above the ordinary level of his fellow-soldiers. The person of Valentinian was tall, graceful, and majestic. His manly countenance, deeply marked with the impression of sense and spirit, inspired his friends with awe, and his enemies with fear: and, to second the efforts of his undaunted courage, the son of Gratian had inherited the advantages of a strong and healthy constitution. By the habits of chastity and temperance, which restrain the appetites and invigorate the faculties, Valentinian preserved his own, and the public, esteem. The avocations of a military life had diverted his youth from the elegant pursuits of literature; he was ignorant of the Greek language and the arts of rhetoric; but, as the mind of the orator was never disconcerted by timid perplexity, he was able, as often as the occasion prompted him, to deliver his decided sentiments with bold and ready elocution. The laws of mar-

11 *The Christian orator Chrysostom attempts to comfort a widow by the examples of illustrious misfortunes; and observes that, of nine emperors (including the Cæsar Gallus) who had reigned in his time, only two (Constantine and Constantius) died a natural death. Such vague consolations have never wiped away a single tear.*

12 *Ten days appeared scarcely sufficient for the march and election. But it may be observed: 1. That the generals might command the expeditious use of the public posts for themselves, their attendants, and messengers. 2. That the troops, for the ease of the cities, marched in many divisions; and that the head of the column might arrive at Nice, when the rear halted at Ancyra.*

13 *Philostorgius, who appears to have obtained some curious and authentic intelligence, ascribes the choice of Valentinian to the præfect Sallust, the master-general Arintheus, Dagalaiphus count of the domestics, and the Patrician Datianus, whose pressing recommendations from Ancyra had a weighty influence in the election.*

[14] *Ammianus, and the younger Victor, have furnished the portrait of Valentinian; which naturally precedes and illustrates the history of his reign.*

[15] *At Antioch, where he was obliged to attend the emperor to the temple, he struck a priest, who had presumed to purify him with lustral water. Such public defiance might become Valentinian; but it could leave no room for the unworthy delation of the philosopher Maximus, which supposes some more private offence.*

[16] *A previous exile to Melitene, or Thebais (the first might be possible), is interposed by Sozomen and Philostorgius.*

[17] *Ammianus, in a long, because unseasonable, digression, rashly supposes that he understands an astronomical question of which his readers are ignorant. It is treated with more judgment and propriety by Censorinus and Macrobius. The appellation of* Bissextile, *which marks the inauspicious year, is derived from the* repetition *of the* sixth *day of the calends of March.*

tial discipline were the only laws that he had studied; and he was soon distinguished by the laborious diligence and inflexible severity with which he discharged and enforced the duties of the camp. In the time of Julian he provoked the danger of disgrace by the contempt which he publicly expressed for the reigning religion;[15] and it should seem from his subsequent conduct that the indiscreet and unseasonable freedom of Valentinian was the effect of military spirit rather than of Christian zeal. He was pardoned, however, and still employed by a prince who esteemed his merit;[16] and in the various events of the Persian war he improved the reputation which he had already acquired on the banks of the Rhine. The celerity and success with which he executed an important commission recommended him to the favour of Jovian, and to the honourable command of the second *school,* or company, of Targetteers, of the domestic guards. In the march from Antioch, he had reached his quarters at Ancyra, when he was unexpectedly summoned without guilt, and without intrigue, to assume, in the forty-third year of his age, the absolute government of the Roman empire.

The invitation of the ministers and generals at Nice was of little moment, unless it were confirmed by the voice of the army. The aged Sallust, who had long observed the irregular fluctuations of popular assemblies, proposed, under pain of death, that none of those persons whose rank in the service might excite a party in their favour should appear in public, on the day of the inauguration. Yet such was the prevalence of ancient superstition that a whole day was voluntarily added to this dangerous interval, because it happened to be the intercalation of the Bissextile.[17] At length, when the hour was supposed to be propitious, Valentinian showed himself from a lofty tribunal; the judicious choice was applauded; and the new prince was solemnly invested with the diadem and the purple, amidst the acclamations of the troops, who were disposed in martial order round the tribunal. But, when he stretched forth his hand to address the armed multitude, a busy whisper was accidentally started in the ranks, and insensibly swelled into a loud and imperious clamour, that he should name, without delay, a colleague in the empire. The intrepid calmness of Valentinian obtained silence and commanded respect, and he thus addressed the assembly: "A few minutes since it was in *your* power, fellow-soldiers, to have left me in the obscurity of a private station. Judging, from the testimony of my past life, that I deserved to reign, you have placed me on the throne. It is now *my* duty to consult the safety and interest of the republic. The weight of the universe is undoubtedly too great for the hands of a feeble mortal. I am conscious of the limits of my abilities and the uncertainty of my life; and far from declining, I am anxious to solicit, the assistance of a worthy colleague. But, where discord may be fatal, the choice of a faithful friend requires mature and serious deliberation. That deliberation shall be *my* care. Let *your* conduct be dutiful and consistent. Retire to your quarters; refresh your minds and bodies; and expect the accustomed donative on the accession of a new emperor." [18] The astonished troops, with a mixture of pride, of satisfaction, and of terror, confessed the voice of their master. Their angry clamours subsided into silent reverence; and Valentinian, encompassed with the eagles of the legions and the various banners of the cavalry and infantry, was conducted, in warlike pomp, to the palace of Nice. As he was sensible, however, of the importance of preventing some rash declaration of the soldiers, he consulted the assembly of the chiefs: and their real sentiments were concisely expressed by the generous freedom of Dagalaiphus. "Most excellent prince," said that officer, "if you consider only your family, you have a brother; if you love the republic, look round for the most deserving of the Romans." The emperor, who suppressed his displeasure, without altering his intention, slowly proceeded from Nice to Nicomedia and Constantinople. In one of the suburbs of that capital,[19] thirty days after his own elevation, he bestowed the title of Augustus on his brother Valens; and, as the boldest patriots were convinced that their opposition, without being serviceable to their country, would be fatal to themselves, the declaration of his absolute will was received with silent submission. Valens was now in the thirty-sixth year of his age; but his abilities had never been exercised in any employment, military or civil; and his character had not inspired the world with any sanguine expectations. He possessed, however, one quality, which recommended him to Valentinian, and preserved the domestic peace of the empire: a devout and grateful attachment to his benefactor, whose superiority of genius, as well as of authority, Valens humbly and cheerfully acknowledged in every action of his life.

Before Valentinian divided the provinces, he reformed the administration of the empire. All ranks of subjects, who had been injured or oppressed under the reign of Julian, were invited to support their public accusations. The silence of mankind attested the spotless integrity of the præfect Sallust;[20] and his own pressing solicitations that he might be permitted to retire from the business of

[18] *Valentinian's first speech is full in Ammianus; concise and sententious in Philostorgius.*

[19] *The famous Hebdomon, or field of Mars, was distant from Constantinople either seven stadia or seven miles.*

[20] *Notwithstanding the evidence of Zonaras, Suidas, and the Paschal Chronicle, M. de Tillemont wishes to disbelieve these stories, si avantageuses à un payen.*

the state were rejected by Valentinian with the most honourable expressions of friendship and esteem. But among the favourites of the late emperor there were many who had abused his credulity or superstition, and who could no longer hope to be protected either by favour or justice.[21] The greater part of the ministers of the palace and the governors of the provinces were removed from their respective stations; yet the eminent merit of some officers was distinguished from the obnoxious crowd; and, notwithstanding the opposite clamours of zeal and resentment, the whole proceedings of this delicate inquiry appear to have been conducted with a reasonable share of wisdom and moderation.[22] The festivity of a new reign received a short and suspicious interruption from the sudden illness of the two princes; but, as soon as their health was restored, they left Constantinople in the beginning of the spring. In the castle or palace of Mediana, only three miles from Naissus, they executed the solemn and final division of the Roman empire. Valentinian bestowed on his brother the rich præfecture of the *East*, from the Lower Danube to the confines of Persia; whilst he reserved for his immediate government the warlike præfectures of *Illyricum, Italy* and *Gaul*, from the extremity of Greece to the Caledonian rampart; and from the rampart of Caledonia to the foot of Mount Atlas. The provincial administration remained on its former basis; but a double supply of generals and magistrates was required for two councils and two courts: the division was made with a just regard to their peculiar merit and situation, and seven master-generals were soon created, either of the cavalry or infantry. When this important business had been amicably transacted, Valentinian and Valens embraced for the last time. The emperor of the West established his temporary residence at Milan; and the emperor of the East returned to Constantinople, to assume the dominion of fifty provinces, of whose language he was totally ignorant.

The tranquillity of the East was soon disturbed by rebellion; and the throne of Valens was threatened by the daring attempts of a rival, whose affinity to the Emperor Julian [23] was his sole merit, and had been his only crime. Procopius had been hastily promoted from the obscure station of a tribune and a notary to the joint command of the army of Mesopotamia; the public opinion already named him as the successor of a prince who was destitute of natural heirs; and a vain rumour was propagated by his friends, or his enemies, that Julian, before the altar of the Moon, at Carrhæ, had privately invested Procopius with the Imperial purple.[24] He endeavoured, by his

21 *Eunapius celebrates and exaggerates the sufferings of Maximus, yet he allows that this sophist or magician, the guilty favourite of Julian and the personal enemy of Valentinian, was dismissed on the payment of a small fine.*

22 *The loose assertions of a general disgrace are detected and refuted by Tillemont.*

23 *The uncertain degree of alliance, or consanguinity, is expressed by the words* ᾿ανεψιός, *cognatus, consobrinus. The mother of Procopius might be a sister of Basilina and Count Julian, the mother and uncle of the apostate.*

24 *Ammianus mentions the report with much hesitation: susurravit obscurior fama; nemo enim dicti auctor exstitit verus. It serves, however, to mark that Procopius was a Pagan. Yet his religion does not appear to have promoted, or obstructed, his pretensions.*

dutiful and submissive behaviour, to disarm the jealousy of Jovian; resigned, without a contest, his military command; and retired, with his wife and family, to cultivate the ample patrimony which he possessed in the province of Cappadocia. These useful and innocent occupations were interrupted by the appearance of an officer, with a band of soldiers, who, in the name of his new sovereigns, Valentinian and Valens, was dispatched to conduct the unfortunate Procopius either to a perpetual prison or an ignominious death. His presence of mind procured him a longer respite and a more splendid fate. Without presuming to dispute the royal mandate, he requested the indulgence of a few moments to embrace his weeping family; and, while the vigilance of his guards was relaxed by a plentiful entertainment, he dexterously escaped to the sea-coast of the Euxine, from whence he passed over to the country of Bosphorus. In that sequestered region he remained many months, exposed to the hardships of exile, of solitude, and of want: his melancholy temper brooding over his misfortunes, and his mind agitated by the just apprehension, that, if any accident should discover his name, the faithless Barbarians would violate, without much scruple, the laws of hospitality. In a moment of impatience and despair, Procopius embarked in a merchant vessel, which made sail for Constantinople; and boldly aspired to the rank of a sovereign, because he was not allowed to enjoy the security of a subject. At first he lurked in the village of Bithynia, continually changing his habitation, and his disguise.[25] By degrees he ventured into the capital, trusted his life and fortune to the fidelity of two friends, a senator and an eunuch, and conceived some hopes of success from the intelligence which he obtained of the actual state of public affairs. The body of the people was infected with a spirit of discontent: they regretted the justice and the abilities of Sallust, who had been imprudently dismissed from the præfecture of the East. They despised the character of Valens, which was rude without vigour and feeble without mildness. They dreaded the influence of his father-in-law, the Patrician Petronius, a cruel and rapacious minister, who rigorously exacted all the arrears of tribute that might remain unpaid since the reign of the emperor Aurelian. The circumstances were propitious to the designs of an usurper. The hostile measures of the Persians required the presence of Valens in Syria; from the Danube to the Euphrates the troops were in motion; and the capital was occasionally filled with the soldiers who passed, or repassed, the Thracian Bosphorus. Two cohorts of Gauls were persuaded to lis-

[25] *One of his retreats was a country-house of Eunomius, the heretic. The master was absent, innocent, ignorant; yet he narrowly escaped a sentence of death, and was banished into the remote parts of Mauritania.*

ten to the secret proposals of the conspirators; which were recommended by the promise of a liberal donative; and, as they still revered the memory of Julian, they easily consented to support the hereditary claim of his proscribed kinsman. At the dawn of day they were drawn up near the baths of Anastasia; and Procopius, clothed in a purple garment, more suitable to a player than to a monarch, appeared, as if he rose from the dead, in the midst of Constantinople. The soldiers, who were prepared for his reception, saluted their trembling prince with shouts of joy and vows of fidelity. Their numbers were soon increased by a sturdy band of peasants, collected from the adjacent country; and Procopius, shielded by the arms of his adherents, was successively conducted to the tribunal, the senate, and the palace. During the first moments of his tumultuous reign, he was astonished and terrified by the gloomy silence of the people; who were either ignorant of the cause or apprehensive of the event. But his military strength was superior to any actual resistance: the malcontents flocked to the standard of rebellion; the poor were excited by the hopes, and the rich were intimidated by the fear, of a general pillage; and the obstinate credulity of the multitude was once more deceived by the promised advantages of a revolution. The magistrates were seized; the prisons and arsenals broke open; the gates, and the entrance of the harbour, were diligently occupied; and, in a few hours, Procopius became the absolute, though precarious, master of the Imperial city. The usurper improved this unexpected success with some degree of courage and dexterity. He artfully propagated the rumours and opinions the most favourable to his interest; while he deluded the populace by giving audience to the frequent, but imaginary, ambassadors of distant nations. The large bodies of troops stationed in the cities of Thrace and the fortresses of the Lower Danube were gradually involved in the guilt of rebellion: and the Gothic princes consented to supply the sovereign of Constantinople with the formidable strength of several thousand auxiliaries. His generals passed the Bosphorus, and subdued, without an effort, the unarmed but wealthy provinces of Bithynia and Asia. After an honourable defence, the city and island of Cyzicus yielded to his power; the renowned legions of the Jovians and Herculians embraced the cause of the usurper whom they were ordered to crush; and, as the veterans were continually augmented with new levies, he soon appeared at the head of an army whose valour, as well as numbers, were not unequal to the greatness of the contest. The son[26] of

[26] *The Persian prince escaped with honour and safety, and was afterwards* (A.D. 380) *restored to the same extraordinary office of proconsul of Bithynia. I am ignorant whether the race of Sassan was propagated. I find* (A.D. 514) *a pope Hormisdas; but he was a native of Frusino, in Italy.*

Hormisdas, a youth of spirit and ability, condescended to draw his sword against the lawful emperor of the East; and the Persian prince was immediately invested with the ancient and extraordinary powers of a Roman Proconsul. The alliance of Faustina, the widow of the emperor Constantius, who intrusted herself and her daughter to the hands of the usurper, added dignity and reputation to his cause. The princess Constantia, who was then about five years of age, accompanied in a litter the march of the army. She was shown to the multitude in the arms of her adopted father; and, as often as she passed through the ranks, the tenderness of the soldiers was inflamed into martial fury:[27] they recollected the glories of the house of Constantine, and they declared, with loyal acclamation, that they would shed the last drop of their blood in the defence of the royal infant.

[27] *The infant rebel was afterwards the wife of the Emperor Gratian; but she died young and childless.*

In the meanwhile, Valentinian was alarmed and perplexed by the doubtful intelligence of the revolt of the East. The difficulties of a German war forced him to confine his immediate care to the safety of his own dominions; and, as every channel of communication was stopt or corrupted, he listened, with doubtful anxiety, to the rumours which were industriously spread, that the defeat and death of Valens had left Procopius sole master of the eastern provinces. Valens was not dead: but, on the news of the rebellion, which he received at Cæsarea, he basely despaired of his life and fortune; proposed to negotiate with the usurper, and discovered his secret inclination to abdicate the Imperial purple. The timid monarch was saved from disgrace and ruin by the firmness of his ministers, and their abilities soon decided in his favour the event of the civil war. In a season of tranquillity, Sallust had resigned without a murmur; but, as soon as the public safety was attacked, he ambitiously solicited the pre-eminence of toil and danger; and the restoration of that virtuous minister to the præfecture of the East was the first step which indicated the repentance of Valens and satisfied the minds of the people. The reign of Procopius was apparently supported by powerful armies and obedient provinces. But many of the principal officers, military as well as civil, had been urged, either by motives of duty or interest, to withdraw themselves from the guilty scene; or to watch the moment of betraying and deserting the cause of the usurper. Lupicinus advanced, by hasty marches, to bring the legions of Syria to the aid of Valens. Arintheus, who, in strength, beauty, and valour, excelled all the heroes of the age, attacked with a small troop a superior body of the rebels. When he beheld the faces of the soldiers who had served under his banner, he commanded them, with a loud voice, to seize and deliver up their pretended leader; and such was the ascendant of his genius that this extraordinary order was instantly obeyed.[28] Arbetio, a respectable veteran of the great Constantine, who had been distinguished by the honours of the consulship, was persuaded to leave his retirement, and once more to conduct an army into the field. In the heat of action, calmly taking off his helmet, he showed his grey hairs, and venerable countenance; saluted the soldiers of Procopius by the endearing names of children and companions, and exhorted them, no longer to support the desperate cause of a contemptible tyrant; but to follow their old commander, who had so often led them to honour and victory. In the two engagements of Thyatira[29] and Nacolia, the unfortunate Procopius was deserted by his troops, who were seduced by the instructions and example of their perfidious officers. After wandering some time among the woods and mountains of Phrygia, he was betrayed by his desponding followers, conducted to the Imperial camp, and immediately beheaded. He suffered the ordinary fate of an unsuccessful usurper; but the acts of cruelty which were exercised by the conqueror, under the forms of legal justice, excited the pity and indignation of mankind.[30]

Such indeed are the common and natural fruits of despotism and rebellion. But the inquisition into the crime of magic, which, under the reign of the two brothers, was so rigorously prosecuted both at Rome and Antioch, was interpreted as the fatal symptom either of the displeasure of heaven or of the depravity of mankind.[31] Let us not hesitate to indulge a liberal pride that in the present age the enlightened part of Europe has abolished[32] a cruel and odious prejudice, which reigned in every climate of the globe and adhered to every system of religious opinions.[33] The nations and the sects of the Roman world admitted with equal credulity and similar abhorrence the reality of that infernal art[34] which was able to control the eternal order of the planets and the voluntary operations of the human mind. They dreaded the mysterious power of spells and incantations, of potent herbs, and execrable rites; which could extinguish or recall life, inflame the passions of the soul, blast the works of creation, and extort from the reluctant demons the secrets of futurity. They believed, with the wildest inconsistency, that this preternatural dominion of the air, of earth, and of hell, was exercised, from the vilest motives of malice or gain, by some wrinkled hags and itinerant sorcerers, who passed their obscure lives in pen-

[28] The strength and beauty of Arintheus, the new Hercules, are celebrated by St. Basil, who supposes that God had created him as an inimitable model of the human species. The painters and sculptors could not express his figure: the historians appeared fabulous when they related his exploits.

[29] The same field of battle is placed by Ammianus in Lycia, and by Zosimus at Thyatira, which are at the distance of 150 miles from each other. But Thyatira alluitur Lyco; and the transcribers might easily convert an obscure river into a well-known province.

[30] The adventures, usurpation, and fall of Procopius are related, in a regular series, by Ammianus and Zosimus. They often illustrate, and seldom contradict, each other. Themistius adds some base panegyric; and Eunapius some malicious satire.

[31] Libanius de ulciscend. JULIAN. The sophist deplores the public frenzy, but he does not (after their deaths) impeach the justice of the emperors.

ury and contempt.[35] The arts of magic were equally condemned by the public opinion and by the laws of Rome; but, as they tended to gratify the most imperious passions of the heart of man, they were continually proscribed, and continually practised. An imaginary cause is capable of producing the most serious and mischievous effects. The dark predictions of the death of an emperor, or the success of a conspiracy, were calculated only to stimulate the hopes of ambition and to dissolve the ties of fidelity; and the intentional guilt of magic was aggravated by the actual crimes of treason and sacrilege.[36] Such vain terrors disturbed the peace of society and the happiness of individuals; and the harmless flame which insensibly melted a waxen image might derive a powerful and pernicious energy from the affrighted fancy of the person whom it was maliciously designed to represent. From the infusion of those herbs which were supposed to possess a supernatural influence it was an easy step to the use of more substantial poison; and the folly of mankind sometimes became the instrument, and the mask, of the most atrocious crimes. As soon as the zeal of informers was encouraged by the ministers of Valens and Valentinian, they could not refuse to listen to another charge, too frequently mingled in the scenes of domestic guilt; a charge of a softer and less malignant nature, for which the pious, though excessive, rigour of Constantine had recently decreed the punishment of death. This deadly and incoherent mixture of treason and magic, of poison and adultery, afforded infinite gradations of guilt and innocence, of excuse and aggravation, which in these proceedings appear to have been confounded by the angry or corrupt passions of the judges. They easily discovered that the degree of their industry and discernment was estimated, by the Imperial court, according to the number of executions that were furnished from their respective tribunals. It was not without extreme reluctance that they pronounced a sentence of acquittal; but they eagerly admitted such evidence as was stained with perjury, or procured by torture, to prove the most improbable charges against the most respectable characters. The progress of the inquiry continually opened new subjects of criminal prosecution; the audacious informer, whose falsehood was detected, retired with impunity; but the wretched victim, who discovered his real or pretended accomplices, was seldom permitted to receive the price of his infamy. From the extremity of Italy and Asia, the young and the aged were dragged in chains to the tribunals of Rome and Antioch. Senators, matrons, and philosophers expired in ignominious and

[32] *The French and English lawyers of the present age allow the theory, and deny the practice, of witchcraft. As private reason always prevents or outstrips public wisdom, the president Montesquieu rejects the existence of magic.*

[33] *See Oeuvres de Bayle. The sceptic of Rotterdam exhibits, according to his custom, a strange medley of loose knowledge and lively wit.*

[34] *The pagans distinguished between good and bad magic, the Theurgic and the Goetic. But they could not have defended this obscure distinction against the acute logic of Bayle. In the Jewish and Christian system all demons are infernal spirits, and all commerce with them is idolatry, apostacy, &c., which deserves death and damnation.*

[35] *The Canidia of Horace is a vulgar witch. The Erichtho of Lucan is tedious, disgusting, but sometimes sublime. She chides the delay of the Furies, and threatens, with tremendous obscurity, to pronounce their real names, to reveal the true infernal countenance of Hecate, to invoke the secret powers that lie below hell, &c.*

[36] *The persecution of Antioch was occasioned by a criminal consultation. The twenty-four letters of the alphabet were arranged round a magic tripod; and a dancing ring, which had been placed in the centre, pointed to the first four letters in the name of the future emperor, Θ. E. O. Δ. Theodorus (perhaps with many others who owned the fatal syllables) was executed.*

[37] *The cruel persecution of Rome and Antioch is described, and most probably exaggerated, by Ammianus and Zosimus. The philosopher Maximus, with some justice, was involved in the charge of magic; and young Chrysostom, who had accidentally found one of the proscribed books, gave himself for lost.*

[38] *The younger Victor asserts that he was valde timidus: yet he behaved, as almost every man would do, with decent resolution at the head of an army. The same historian attempts to prove that his anger was harmless. Ammianus observes with more candour and judgment, incidentia crimina ad contemptam vel læsam principis amplitudinem trahens, in sanguinem sæviebat.*

cruel tortures. The soldiers, who were appointed to guard the prisons, declared, with a murmur of pity and indignation, that their numbers were insufficient to oppose the flight or resistance of the multitude of captives. The wealthiest families were ruined by fines and confiscations; the most innocent citizens trembled for their safety; and we may form some notion of the magnitude of the evil from the extravagant assertion of an ancient writer that, in the obnoxious provinces, the prisoners, the exiles, and the fugitives formed the greatest part of the inhabitants.[37]

When Tacitus describes the deaths of the innocent and illustrious Romans, who were sacrificed to the cruelty of the first Cæsars, the art of the historian, or the merit of the sufferers, excite in our breasts the most lively sensations of terror, of admiration, and of pity. The coarse and undistinguishing pencil of Ammianus has delineated his bloody figures with tedious and disgusting accuracy. But, as our attention is no longer engaged by the contrast of freedom and servitude, of recent greatness and of actual misery, we should turn with horror from the frequent executions which disgraced, both at Rome and Antioch, the reign of the two brothers. Valens was of a timid,[38] and Valentinian of a choleric, disposition. An anxious regard to his personal safety was the ruling principle of the administration of Valens. In the condition of a subject, he had kissed, with trembling awe, the hand of the oppressor; and, when he ascended the throne, he reasonably expected that the same fears which had subdued his own mind would secure the patient submission of his people. The favourites of Valens obtained, by the privilege of rapine and confiscation, the wealth which his economy would have refused.[39] They urged, with persuasive eloquence, *that,* in all cases of treason, suspicion is equivalent to proof; *that* the power, supposes the intention, of mischief; *that* the intention is not less criminal than the act; and *that* a subject no longer deserves to live, if his life may threaten the safety, or disturb the repose, of his sovereign. The judgment of Valentinian was sometimes deceived and his confidence abused; but he would have silenced the informers with a contemptuous smile, had they presumed to alarm his fortitude by the sound of danger. They praised his inflexible love of justice; and, in the pursuit of justice, the emperor was easily tempted to consider clemency as a weakness and passion as a virtue. As long as he wrestled with his equals, in the bold competition of an active and ambitious life, Valentinian was seldom injured, and never insulted, with impunity: if his prudence was arraigned, his spirit was applauded;

and the proudest and most powerful generals were apprehensive of provoking the resentment of a fearless soldier. After he became master of the world, he unfortunately forgot that, where no resistance can be made, no courage can be exerted; and, instead of consulting the dictates of reason and magnanimity, he indulged the furious emotions of his temper at a time when they were disgraceful to himself and fatal to the defenceless objects of his displeasure. In the government of his household, or of his empire, slight, or even imaginary, offences, a hasty word, a casual omission, an involuntary delay, were chastised by a sentence of immediate death. The expressions which issued the most readily from the mouth of the emperor of the West were, "Strike off his head"; "Burn him alive"; "Let him be beaten with clubs till he expires";[40] and his most favoured ministers soon understood that, by a rash attempt to dispute, or suspend, the execution of his sanguinary commands, they might involve themselves in the guilt and punishment of disobedience. The repeated gratification of this savage justice hardened the mind of Valentinian against pity and remorse; and the sallies of passion were confirmed by the habits of cruelty.[41] He could behold with calm satisfaction the convulsive agonies of torture and death: he reserved his friendship for those faithful servants whose temper was the most congenial to his own. The merit of Maximin, who had slaughtered the noblest families of Rome, was rewarded with the royal approbation and the præfecture of Gaul. Two fierce and enormous bears, distinguished by the appellations of *Innocence* and *Mica Aurea*, could alone deserve to share the favour of Maximin. The cages of those trusty guards were always placed near the bedchamber of Valentinian, who frequently amused his eyes with the grateful spectacle of seeing them tear and devour the bleeding limbs of the malefactors who were abandoned to their rage. Their diet and exercises were carefully inspected by the Roman emperor; and, when *Innocence* had earned her discharge by a long course of meritorious service, the faithful animal was again restored to the freedom of her native woods.

But in the calmer moments of reflection, when the mind of Valens was not agitated by fear, or that of Valentinian by rage, the tyrant resumed the sentiments, or at least the conduct, of the father of his country. The dispassionate judgment of the Western emperor could clearly perceive, and accurately pursue, his own and the public interest; and the sovereign of the East, who imitated with equal docility the various examples which he received from his

39 *I have transferred the reproach of avarice from Valens to his servants. Avarice more properly belongs to ministers than to kings; in whom that passion is commonly extinguished by absolute possession.*

40 *He sometimes expressed a sentence of death with a tone of pleasantry: "Abi, Comes, et muta ei caput, qui sibi mutari provinciam cupit." A boy, who had slipped too hastily a Spartan hound; an armourer, who had made a polished cuirass that wanted some grains of the legitimate weight, &c., were the victims of his fury.*

41 *The innocents of Milan were an agent and three apparitors, whom Valentinian condemned for signifying a legal summons. Ammianus strangely supposes that all who had been unjustly executed were worshipped as martyrs by the Christians. His impartial silence does not allow us to believe that the great chamberlain Rhodanus was burnt alive for an act of oppression.*

elder brother, was sometimes guided by the wisdom and virtue of the præfect Sallust. Both princes invariably retained, in tl e purple, the chaste and temperate simplicity which had adorned their private life; and, under their reign, the pleasures of the court never cost the people a blush or a sigh. They gradually reformed many of the abuses of the times of Constantius; judiciously adopted and improved the designs of Julian and his successor; and displayed a style and spirit of legislation which might inspire posterity with the most favourable opinion of their character and government. It is not from the master of *Innocence* that we should expect the tender regard for the welfare of his subjects which prompted Valentinian to condemn the exposition of new-born infants; and to establish fourteen skilful physicians, with stipends and privileges, in the fourteen quarters of Rome. The good sense of an illiterate soldier founded an useful and liberal institution for the education of youth, and the support of declining science. It was his intention that the arts of rhetoric and grammar should be taught in the Greek and Latin languages in the metropolis of every province; and as the size and dignity of the school was usually proportioned to the importance of the city, the academies of Rome and Constantinople claimed a just and singular pre-eminence. The fragments of the literary edicts of Valentinian imperfectly represent the school of Constantinople, which was gradually improved by subsequent regulations. That school consisted of thirty-one professors in different branches of learning. One philosopher, and two lawyers; five sophists and ten grammarians for the Greek, and three orators and ten grammarians for the Latin, tongue; besides seven scribes, or, as they were then styled, antiquarians, whose laborious pens supplied the public library with fair and correct copies of the classic writers. The rule of conduct, which was prescribed to the students, is the more curious, as it affords the first outlines of the form and discipline of a modern university. It was required that they should bring proper certificates from the magistrates of their native province. Their names, professions, and places of abode were regularly entered in a public register. The studious youth were severely prohibited from wasting their time in feasts or in the theatre; and the term of their education was limited to the age of twenty. The præfect of the city was empowered to chastise the idle and refractory, by stripes or expulsion; and he was directed to make an annual report to the master of the offices, that the knowledge and abilities of the scholars might be usefully applied to the public service. The institutions of Valentinian contributed to secure the benefits of peace and plenty; and the cities were guarded by the establishment of the *Defensors,* freely elected as the tribunes and advocates of the people, to support their rights and to expose their grievances before the tribunals of the civil magistrates, or even at the foot of the Imperial throne. The finances were diligently administered by two princes, who had been so long accustomed to the rigid economy of a private fortune; but in the receipt and application of the revenue a discerning eye might observe some difference between the government of the East and of the West. Valens was persuaded that royal liberality can be supplied only by public oppression, and his ambition never aspired to secure, by their actual distress, the future strength and prosperity of his people. Instead of increasing the weight of taxes, which, in the space of forty years, had been gradually doubled, he reduced, in the first years of his reign, one-fourth of the tribute of the East.[42] Valentinian appears to have been less attentive and less anxious to relieve the burthens of his people. He might reform the abuses of the fiscal administration; but he exacted, without scruple, a very large share of the private property; as he was convinced that the revenues, which supported the luxury of individuals, would be much more advantageously employed for the defence and improvement of the state. The subjects of the East, who enjoyed the present benefit, applauded the indulgence of their prince. The solid, but less splendid, merit of Valentinian was felt and acknowledged by the subsequent generation.[43]

But the most honourable circumstance of the character of Valentinian is the firm and temperate impartiality which he uniformly preserved in an age of religious contention. His strong sense, unenlightened, but uncorrupted, by study, declined, with respectful indifference, the subtle questions of theological debate. The government of the *Earth* claimed his vigilance and satisfied his ambition; and, while he remembered that he was the disciple of the church, he never forgot that he was the sovereign of the clergy. Under the reign of an apostate, he had signalized his zeal for the honour of Christianity: he allowed to his subjects the privilege which he had assumed for himself; and they might accept, with gratitude and confidence, the general toleration which was granted by a prince addicted to passion, but incapable of fear or of disguise. The Pagans, the Jews, and all the various sects which acknowledged the divine authority of Christ were protected by the laws from arbitrary power or popular insult: nor was any mode of worship prohibited by

[42] *Three lines from Ammianus countenance a whole oration of Themistius, full of adulation, pedantry, and commonplace morality. The eloquent M. Thomas has amused himself with celebrating the virtues and genius of Themistius, who was not unworthy of the age in which he lived.*

[43] *His reformation of costly abuses might entitle him to the praise of: in provinciales admodum parcus, tributorum ubique molliens sarcinas. By some, his frugality was styled avarice.*

Valentinian, except those secret and criminal practices which abused the name of religion for the dark purposes of vice and disorder. The art of magic, as it was more cruelly punished, was more strictly proscribed; but the emperor admitted a formal distinction to protect the ancient methods of divination, which were approved by the senate and exercised by the Tuscan haruspices. He had condemned, with the consent of the most rational Pagans, the licence of nocturnal sacrifices; but he immediately admitted the petition of Prætextatus, proconsul of Achaia, who represented that the life of the Greeks would become dreary and comfortless, if they were deprived of the invaluable blessing of the Eleusinian mysteries. Philosophy alone can boast (and perhaps it is no more than the boast of philosophy), that her gentle hand is able to eradicate from the human mind the latent and deadly principle of fanaticism. But this truce of twelve years, which was enforced by the wise and vigorous government of Valentinian, by suspending the repetition of mutual injuries, contributed to soften the manners, and abate the prejudices, of the religious factions.

The friend of toleration was unfortunately placed at a distance from the scene of the fiercest controversies. As soon as the Christians of the West had extricated themselves from the snares of the creed of Rimini, they happily relapsed into the slumber of orthodoxy; and the small remains of the Arian party that still subsisted at Sirmium or Milan might be considered rather as objects of contempt than of resentment. But in the provinces of the East, from the Euxine to the extremity of Thebais, the strength and numbers of the hostile factions were more equally balanced; and this equality, instead of recommending the counsels of peace, served only to perpetuate the horrors of religious war. The monks and bishops supported their arguments by invectives; and their invectives were sometimes followed by blows. Athanasius still reigned at Alexandria; the thrones of Constantinople and Antioch were occupied by Arian prelates, and every episcopal vacancy was the occasion of a popular tumult. The Homoousians were fortified by the reconciliation of fifty-nine Macedonian, or Semi-Arian, bishops; but their secret reluctance to embrace the divinity of the Holy Ghost clouded the splendour of the triumph: and the declaration of Valens, who, in the first years of his reign, had imitated the impartial conduct of his brother, was an important victory on the side of Arianism. The two brothers had passed their private life in the condition of catechumens; but the piety of Valens prompted him to solicit the sacrament of baptism, before he exposed his person to the dangers of a Gothic war. He naturally addressed himself to Eudoxus,[44] bishop of the Imperial city; and, if the ignorant monarch was instructed by that Arian pastor in the principles of heterodox theology, his misfortune, rather than his guilt, was the inevitable consequence of his erroneous choice. Whatever had been the determination of the emperor, he must have offended a numerous party of his Christian subjects; as the leaders both of the Homoousians and of the Arians believed that, if they were not suffered to reign, they were most cruelly injured and oppressed. After he had taken this decisive step, it was extremely difficult for him to preserve either the virtue or the reputation of impartiality. He never aspired, like Constantius, to the fame of a profound theologian; but, as he had received with simplicity and respect the tenets of Eudoxus, Valens resigned his conscience to the direction of his ecclesiastical guides, and promoted, by the influence of his authority, the reunion of the *Athanasian heretics* to the body of the catholic church. At first, he pitied their blindness; by degrees he was provoked at their obstinacy; and he insensibly hated those sectaries to whom he was an object of hatred.[45] The feeble mind of Valens was always swayed by the persons with whom he familiarly conversed; and the exile or imprisonment of a private citizen is the favour the most readily granted in a despotic court. Such punishments were frequently inflicted on the leaders of the Homoousian party; and the misfortune of fourscore ecclesiastics of Constantinople, who, perhaps accidentally, were burnt on shipboard, was imputed to the cruel and premeditated malice of the emperor and his Arian ministers. In every contest, the catholics (if we may anticipate that name) were obliged to pay the penalty of their own faults, and of those of their adversaries. In every election, the claims of the Arian candidate obtained the preference; and, if they were opposed by the majority of the people, he was usually supported by the authority of the civil magistrate, or even by the terrors of a military force. The enemies of Athanasius attempted to disturb the last years of his venerable age; and his temporary retreat to his father's sepulchre has been celebrated as a fifth exile. But the zeal of a great people who instantly flew to arms, intimidated the præfect; and the archbishop was permitted to end his life in peace and in glory, after a reign of forty-seven years. The death of Athanasius was the signal of the persecution of Egypt; and the Pagan minister of Valens, who forcibly seated the worthless Lucius on the archiepiscopal throne, purchased the favour of the

[44] *Eudoxus was of a mild and timid disposition. When he baptized Valens (A.D. 367), he must have been extremely old; since he had studied theology fifty-five years before, under Lucian, a learned and pious martyr.*

[45] *Gregory Nazianzen insults the persecuting spirit of the Arians, as an infallible symptom of error and heresy.*

reigning party by the blood and sufferings of their Christian brethren. The free toleration of the heathen and Jewish worship was bitterly lamented, as a circumstance which aggravated the misery of the catholics and the guilt of the impious tyrant of the East.[46]

The triumph of the orthodox party has left a deep stain of persecution on the memory of Valens; and the character of a prince who derived his virtues, as well as his vices, from a feeble understanding and a pusillanimous temper scarcely deserves the labour of an apology. Yet candour may discover some reasons to suspect that the ecclesiastical ministers of Valens often exceeded the orders, or even the intentions, of their master; and that the real measure of facts has been very liberally magnified by the vehement declamation and easy credulity of his antagonists.[47] 1. The silence of Valentinian may suggest a probable argument, that the partial severities, which were exercised in the name and provinces of his colleague, amounted only to some obscure and inconsiderable deviations from the established system of religious toleration: and the judicious historian, who has praised the equal temper of the elder brother, has not thought himself obliged to contrast the tranquillity of the West with the cruel persecution of the East.[48] 2. Whatever credit may be allowed to vague and distant reports, the character, or at least the behaviour, of Valens may be most distinctly seen in his personal transactions with the eloquent Basil, archbishop of Cæsarea, who had succeeded Athanasius in the management of the Trinitarian cause.[49] The circumstantial narrative has been composed by the friends and admirers of Basil; and, as soon as we have stripped away a thick coat of rhetoric and miracle, we shall be astonished by the unexpected mildness of the Arian tyrant, who admired the firmness of his character, or was apprehensive, if he employed violence, of a general revolt in the province of Cappadocia. The archbishop, who asserted, with inflexible pride, the truth of his opinions and the dignity of his rank, was left in the free possession of his conscience and his throne. The emperor devoutly assisted at the solemn service of the cathedral; and, instead of a sentence of banishment, subscribed the donation of a valuable estate for the use of an hospital which Basil had lately founded in the neighbourhood of Cæsarea.[50] 3. I am not able to discover that any law (such as Theodosius afterwards enacted against the Arians) was published by Valens against the Athanasian sectaries; and the edict which excited the most violent clamours may not appear so extremely reprehensible. The emperor had observed that several of his subjects, gratifying their lazy

[46] *This sketch of the ecclesiastical government of Valens is drawn from Socrates, Sozomen, Theodoret, and the immense compilations of Tillemont.*

[47] *Dr. Jortin has already conceived and intimated the same suspicion.*

[48] *This reflection is so obvious and forcible that Orosius delays the persecution till after the death of Valentinian. Socrates, on the other hand, supposes that it was appeased by a philosophical oration, which Themistius pronounced in the year 374. Such contradictions diminish the evidence, and reduce the term, of the persecution of Valens.*

[49] *Tillemont, whom I follow and abridge, has extracted the most authentic circumstances from the Panegyrics of the two Gregories: the brother, and the friend, of Basil. The letters of Basil himself do not present the image of a very lively persecution.*

[50] *This noble and charitable foundation (almost a new city) surpassed in merit, if not in greatness, the pyramids, or the walls of Babylon. It was principally intended for the reception of lepers.*

disposition under the pretence of religion, had associated themselves with the monks of Egypt; and he directed the count of the East to drag them from their solitude; and to compel those deserters of society to accept the fair alternative of renouncing their temporal possessions or of discharging the public duties of men and citizens.[51] The ministers of Valens seem to have extended the sense of this penal statute, since they claimed a right of enlisting the young and able-bodied monks in the Imperial armies. A detachment of cavalry and infantry, consisting of three thousand men, marched from Alexandria into the adjacent desert of Nitria, which was peopled by five thousand monks. The soldiers were conducted by Arian priests; and it is reported that a considerable slaughter was made in the monasteries which disobeyed the commands of their sovereign.[52]

The strict regulations which have been framed by the wisdom of modern legislators to restrain the wealth and avarice of the clergy may be originally deduced from the example of the emperor Valentinian. His edict[53] addressed to Damasus, bishop of Rome, was publicly read in the churches of the city. He admonished the ecclesiastics and monks not to frequent the houses of widows and virgins; and menaced their disobedience with the animadversion of the civil judge. The director was no longer permitted to receive any gift, or legacy, or inheritance, from the liberality of his spiritual daughter; every testament contrary to this edict was declared null and void; and the illegal donation was confiscated for the use of the treasury. By a subsequent regulation it should seem that the same provisions were extended to nuns and bishops; and that all persons of the ecclesiastical order were rendered incapable of receiving any testamentary gifts, and strictly confined to the natural and legal rights of inheritance. As the guardian of domestic happiness and virtue, Valentinian applied this severe remedy to the growing evil. In the capital of the empire, the females of noble and opulent houses possessed a very ample share of independent property: and many of those devout females had embraced the doctrines of Christianity, not only with the cold assent of the understanding, but with the warmth of affection, and perhaps with the eagerness of fashion. They sacrificed the pleasures of dress and luxury; and renounced, for the praise of chastity, the soft endearments of conjugal society. Some ecclesiastic, of real or apparent sanctity, was chosen to direct their timorous conscience and to amuse the vacant tenderness of their heart: and the unbounded confidence which they hastily be-

[51] *Godefroy performs the duty of a commentator and advocate. Tillemont supposes a second law to excuse his orthodox friends, who had misrepresented the edict of Valens and suppressed the liberty of choice.*

[52] *The monks of Egypt performed many miracles, which prove the truth of their faith. Right, says Jortin, but what proves the truth of those miracles?*

[53] *Godefroy, after the example of Baronius, impartially collects all that the fathers have said on the subject of this important law; whose spirit was long afterwards revived by the emperor Frederic II., Edward I. of England, and other Christian princes who reigned after the twelfth century.*

stowed was often abused by knaves and enthusiasts; who hastened from the extremities of the East to enjoy, on a splendid theatre, the privileges of the monastic profession. By their contempt of the world, they insensibly acquired its most desirable advantages; the lively attachment, perhaps, of a young and beautiful woman, the delicate plenty of an opulent household, and the respectful homage of the slaves, the freedmen, and the clients of a senatorial family. The immense fortunes of the Roman ladies were gradually consumed in lavish alms and expensive pilgrimages; and the artful monk, who had assigned himself the first or possibly the sole place in the testament of his spiritual daughter, still presumed to declare, with the smooth face of hypocrisy, that *he* was only the instrument of charity and the steward of the poor. The lucrative, but disgraceful, trade [54] which was exercised by the clergy to defraud the expectations of the natural heirs had provoked the indignation of a superstitious age: and two of the most respectable of the Latin fathers very honestly confess that the ignominious edict of Valentinian was just and necessary; and that the Christian priests had deserved to lose a privilege which was still enjoyed by comedians, charioteers, and the ministers of idols. But the wisdom and authority of the legislator are seldom victorious in a contest with the vigilant dexterity of private interest: and Jerom or Ambrose might patiently acquiesce in the justice of an ineffectual or salutary law. If the ecclesiastics were checked in the pursuit of personal emolument, they would exert a more laudable industry to increase the wealth of the church, and dignify their covetousness with the specious names of piety and patriotism.

Damasus, bishop of Rome, who was constrained to stigmatize the avarice of his clergy by the publication of the law of Valentinian, had the good sense or the good fortune to engage in his service the zeal and abilities of the learned Jerom; and the grateful saint has celebrated the merit and purity of a very ambiguous character. [55] But the splendid vices of the church of Rome, under the reign of Valentinian and Damasus, have been curiously observed by the historian Ammianus, who delivers his impartial sense in these expressive words: "The præfecture of Juventius was accompanied with peace and plenty: but the tranquillity of his government was soon disturbed by a bloody sedition of the distracted people. The ardour of Damasus and Ursinus, to seize the episcopal seat, surpassed the ordinary measure of human ambition. They contended with the rage of party; the quarrel was maintained by the wounds

54 *The expressions which I have used are temperate and feeble, if compared with the vehement invectives of Jerom. In his turn, he was reproached with the guilt which he imputed to his brother monks: and the* Sceleratus, *the* Versipellis, *was publicly accused as the lover of the widow Paula. He undoubtedly possessed the affections both of the mother and the daughter; but he declares that he never abused his influence to any selfish or sensual purpose.*

55 *Three words of Jerom,* sanctæ memoriæ Damasus, *wash away all his stains, and blind the devout eyes of Tillemont.*

and death of their followers; and the præfect, unable to resist or to appease the tumult, was constrained, by superior violence, to retire into the suburbs. Damasus prevailed: the well-disputed victory remained on the side of his faction; one hundred and thirty-seven dead bodies [56] were found in the *Basilica* of Sicininus,[57] where the Christians hold their religious assemblies; and it was long before the angry minds of the people resumed their accustomed tranquillity. When I consider the splendour of the capital, I am not astonished that so valuable a prize should inflame the desires of ambitious men, and produce the fiercest and most obstinate contests. The successful candidate is secure that he will be enriched by the offerings of matrons;[58] that, as soon as his dress is composed with becoming care and elegance, he may proceed, in his chariot, through the streets of Rome;[59] and that the sumptuousness of the Imperial table will not equal the profuse and delicate entertainments provided by the taste, and at the expense, of the Roman pontiffs. How much more rationally (continues the honest Pagan) would those pontiffs consult their true happiness, if, instead of alleging the greatness of the city as an excuse for their manners, they would imitate the exemplary life of some provincial bishops, whose temperance and sobriety, whose mean apparel and downcast looks, recommended their pure and modest virtue to the Deity and his true worshippers. The schism of Damasus and Ursinus was extinguished by the exile of the latter; and the wisdom of the præfect Prætextatus [60] restored the tranquillity of the city. Prætextatus was a philosophic Pagan, a man of learning, of taste, and politeness; who disguised a reproach in the form of a jest, when he assured Damasus that, if he could obtain the bishopric of Rome, he himself would immediately embrace the Christian religion. This lively picture of the wealth and luxury of the popes in the fourth century becomes the more curious as it represents the intermediate degree between the humble poverty of the apostolic fisherman and the royal state of a temporal prince whose dominions extend from the confines of Naples to the banks of the Po.

When the suffrage of the generals and of the army committed the sceptre of the Roman empire to the hands of Valentinian, his reputation in arms, his military skill and experience, and his rigid attachment to the forms, as well as spirit, of ancient discipline, were the principal motives of their judicious choice. The eagerness of the troops who pressed him to nominate his colleague was justified by the dangerous situation of public affairs; and Valentinian himself

[56] *Jerom himself is forced to allow, crudelissimæ interfectiones diversi sexus perpetratæ. But an original libel or petition of two presbyters of the adverse party has unaccountably escaped. They affirm that the doors of the Basilica were burnt, and that the roof was untiled; that Damasus marched at the head of his own clergy, gravediggers, charioteers, and hired gladiators; that none of his party were killed, but that one hundred and sixty dead bodies were found. This petition is published by the P. Sirmond, in the first volume of his works.*

[57] *The* Basilica *of Sicininus, or Liberius, is probably the church of Sancta Maria Maggiore, on the Esquiline hill.*

[58] *The enemies of Damasus styled him* Auriscalpius Matronarum, *the ladies' ear-scratcher.*

[59] *Gregory Nazianzen describes the pride and luxury of the prelates who reigned in the imperial cities; their gilt car, fiery steeds, numerous train, &c. The crowd gave way as to a wild beast.*

60 *Ammianus, who makes a fair report of his præfecture, styles him præclaræ indolis gravitatisque senator. A curious inscription records, in two columns, his religious and civil honours. In one line he was Pontiff of the Sun, and of Vesta, Augur, Quindecemvir, Hierophant, &c., &c. In the other, 1. Quæstor candidatus, more probably titular. 2. Prætor. 3. Corrector of Tuscany and Umbria. 4. Consular of Lusitania. 5. Proconsul of Achaia. 6. Præfect of Rome. 7. Prætorian præfect of Italy. 8. Of Illyricum.*

61 *Valesius adds a long and good note on the master of the offices.*

was conscious that the abilities of the most active mind were unequal to the defence of the distant frontiers of an invaded monarchy. As soon as the death of Julian had relieved the Barbarians from the terror of his name, the most sanguine hopes of rapine and conquest excited the nations of the East, and of the North, and of the South. Their inroads were often vexatious, and sometimes formidable; but, during the twelve years of the reign of Valentinian, his firmness and vigilance protected his own dominions; and his powerful genius seemed to inspire and direct the feeble counsels of his brother. Perhaps the method of annals would more forcibly express the urgent and divided cares of the two emperors; but the attention of the reader, likewise, would be distracted by a tedious and desultory narrative. A separate view of the five great theatres of war: I. Germany; II. Britain; III. Africa; IV. The East; and, V. The Danube; will impress a more distinct image of the military state of the empire under the reigns of Valentinian and Valens.

I. The ambassadors of the Alemanni had been offended by the harsh and haughty behaviour of Ursacius, master of the offices;[61] who, by an act of unseasonable parsimony, had diminished the value, as well as the quantity, of the presents to which they were entitled, either from custom or treaty, on the accession of a new emperor. They expressed, and they communicated to their countrymen, their strong sense of the national affront. The irascible minds of the chiefs were exasperated by the suspicion of contempt; and the martial youth crowded to their standard. Before Valentinian could pass the Alps, the villages of Gaul were in flames; before his general Dagalaiphus could encounter the Alemanni, they had secured the captives and the spoil in the forests of Germany. In the beginning of the ensuing year, the military force of the whole nation, in deep and solid columns, broke through the barrier of the Rhine, during the severity of a northern winter. Two Roman counts were defeated and mortally wounded; and the standard of the Heruli and Batavians fell into the hands of the conquerors, who displayed, with insulting shouts and menaces, the trophy of their victory. The standard was recovered; but the Batavians had not redeemed the shame of their disgrace and flight in the eyes of their severe judge. It was the opinion of Valentinian that his soldiers must learn to fear their commander, before they could cease to fear the enemy. The troops were solemnly assembled; and the trembling Batavians were inclosed within the circle of the Imperial army. Valentinian then ascended the tribunal; and, as if he disdained to punish cowardice with death, he inflicted a stain of indelible ignominy on the officers whose misconduct and pusillanimity were found to be the first occasion of the defeat. The Batavians were degraded from their rank, stripped of their arms, and condemned to be sold for slaves to the highest bidder. At this tremendous sentence the troops fell prostrate on the ground, deprecated the indignation of their sovereign, and protested that, if he would indulge them in another trial, they would approve themselves not unworthy of the name of Romans, and of his soldiers. Valentinian, with affected reluctance, yielded to their entreaties: the Batavians resumed their arms, and, with their arms, the invincible resolution of wiping away their disgrace in the blood of the Alemanni.[62] The principal command was declined by Dagalaiphus; and that experienced general, who had represented, perhaps with too much prudence, the extreme difficulties of the undertaking, had the mortification, before the end of the campaign, of seeing his rival Jovinus convert those difficulties into a decisive advantage over the scattered forces of the Barbarians. At the head of a well-disciplined army of cavalry, infantry, and light troops, Jovinus advanced, with cautious and rapid steps, to Scarponna,[63] in the territory of Metz, where he surprised a large division of the Alemanni, before they had time to run to their arms: and flushed his soldiers with the confidence of an easy and bloodless victory. Another division, or rather army, of the enemy, after the cruel and wanton devastation of the adjacent country, reposed themselves on the shady banks of the Moselle. Jovinus, who had viewed the ground with the eyes of a general, made his silent approach through a deep and woody vale, till he could distinctly perceive the indolent security of the Germans. Some were bathing their huge limbs in the river; others were combing their long and flaxen hair; others again were swallowing large draughts of rich and delicious wine. On a sudden they heard the sound of the Roman trumpet; they saw the enemy in their camp. Astonishment produced disorder; disorder was followed by flight and dismay; and the confused multitude of the bravest warriors was pierced by the swords and javelins of the legionaries and auxiliaries. The fugitives escaped to the third and most considerable camp, in the Catalaunian plains, near Châlons in Champagne: the straggling detachments were hastily recalled to their standard; and the Barbarian chiefs, alarmed and admonished by the fate of their companions, prepared to encounter, in a decisive battle, the victorious forces of the lieutenant of Valentinian. The bloody and ob-

[62] *The disgrace of the Batavians is suppressed by the contemporary soldier, from a regard for military honour, which could not affect a Greek rhetorician of the succeeding age.*

[63] *The name of the Moselle, which is not specified by Ammianus, is clearly understood by Moscou.*

stinate conflict lasted a whole summer's day, with equal valour, and with alternate success. The Romans at length prevailed, with the loss of about twelve hundred men. Six thousand of the Alemanni were slain, four thousand were wounded; and the brave Jovinus, after chasing the flying remnant of their host as far as the banks of the Rhine, returned to Paris, to receive the applause of his sovereign and the ensigns of the consulship for the ensuing year.[64] The triumph of the Romans was indeed sullied by their treatment of the captive king, whom they hung on a gibbet without the knowledge of their indignant general. This disgraceful act of cruelty which might be imputed to the fury of the troops, was followed by the deliberate murder of Withicab, the son of Vadomair; a German prince, of a weak and sickly constitution, but of a daring and formidable spirit. The domestic assassin was instigated and protected by the Romans; and the violation of the laws of humanity and justice betrayed their secret apprehension of the weakness of the declining empire. The use of the dagger is seldom adopted in public councils, as long as they retain any confidence in the power of the sword.

While the Alemanni appeared to be humbled by their recent calamities, the pride of Valentinian was mortified by the unexpected surprisal of Moguntiacum, or Mentz, the principal city of the Upper Germany. In the unsuspicious moment of a Christian festival, Rando, a bold and artful chieftain, who had long meditated his attempt, suddenly passed the Rhine; entered the defenceless town, and retired with a multitude of captives of either sex. Valentinian resolved to execute severe vengeance on the whole body of the nation. Count Sebastian, with the bands of Italy and Illyricum, was ordered to invade their country, most probably on the side of Rhætia. The emperor in person, accompanied by his son Gratian, passed the Rhine at the head of a formidable army, which was supported on both flanks by Jovinus and Severus, the two masters-general of the cavalry and infantry of the West. The Alemanni, unable to prevent the devastation of their villages, fixed their camp on a lofty, and almost inaccessible, mountain, in the modern duchy of Wirtemberg, and resolutely expected the approach of the Romans. The life of Valentinian was exposed to imminent danger by the intrepid curiosity with which he persisted to explore some secret and unguarded path. A troop of Barbarians suddenly rose from their ambuscade: and the emperor, who vigorously spurred his horse down a steep and slippery descent, was obliged to leave behind him his armour-bearer, and his helmet, magnificently enriched with gold and precious stones. At the signal of the general assault, the Roman troops encompassed and ascended the mountain of Solicinium on three different sides. Every step which they gained increased their ardour and abated the resistance of the enemy: and, after their united forces had occupied the summit of the hill, they impetuously urged the Barbarians down the northern descent where Count Sebastian was posted to intercept their retreat. After this signal victory, Valentinian returned to his winter-quarters at Treves; where he indulged the public joy by the exhibition of splendid and triumphal games.[65] But the wise monarch, instead of aspiring to the conquest of Germany, confined his attention to the important and laborious defence of the Gallic frontier, against an enemy whose strength was renewed by a stream of daring volunteers, which incessantly flowed from the most distant tribes of the North. The banks of the Rhine, from its source to the straits of the ocean, were closely planted with strong castles and convenient towers; new works, and new arms, were invented by the ingenuity of a prince who was skilled in the mechanical arts; and his numerous levies of Roman and Barbarian youth were severely trained in all the exercises of war. The progress of the work, which was sometimes opposed by modest representations, and sometimes by hostile attempts, secured the tranquillity of Gaul during the nine subsequent years of the administration of Valentinian.

That prudent emperor, who diligently practised the wise maxims of Diocletian, was studious to foment and excite the intestine divisions of the tribes of Germany. About the middle of the fourth century, the countries, perhaps of Lusace and Thuringia, on either side of the Elbe, were occupied by the vague dominion of the BURGUNDIANS; a warlike and numerous people of the Vandal race, whose obscure name insensibly swelled into a powerful kingdom, and has finally settled on a flourishing province. The most remarkable circumstance in the ancient manners of the Burgundians appears to have been the difference of their civil and ecclesiastical constitution. The appellation of *Hendinos* was given to the king or general, and the title of *Sinistus* to the high priest, of the nation. The person of the priest was sacred, and his dignity perpetual; but the temporal government was held by a very precarious tenure. If the events of war accused the courage or conduct of the king, he was immediately deposed; and the injustice of his subjects made him responsible for the fertility of the earth and the regularity of the seasons, which seemed to fall more properly within the sacerdotal department.[66]

[65] *The expedition of Valentinian is related by Ammianus; and celebrated by Ausonius, who foolishly supposes that the Romans were ignorant of the sources of the Danube.*

[66] *I am always apt to suspect historians and travellers of improving extraordinary facts into general laws. Ammianus ascribes a similar custom to Egypt: and the Chinese have imputed it to the Tatsin, or Roman empire.*

The disputed possession of some salt-pits [67] engaged the Alemanni and the Burgundians in frequent contests: the latter were easily tempted by the secret solicitations and liberal offers of the emperor; and their fabulous descent from the Roman soldiers who had formerly been left to garrison the fortresses of Drusus was admitted with mutual credulity, as it was conducive to mutual interest. An army of fourscore thousand Burgundians soon appeared on the banks of the Rhine; and impatiently required the support and subsidies which Valentinian had promised: but they were amused with excuses and delays, till at length, after a fruitless expectation, they were compelled to retire. The arms and fortifications of the Gallic frontier checked the fury of their just resentment; and their massacre of the captives served to embitter the hereditary feud of the Burgundians and the Alemanni. The inconstancy of a wise prince may, perhaps, be explained by some alteration of circumstances; and perhaps it was the original design of Valentinian to intimidate rather than to destroy, as the balance of power would have been equally overturned by the extirpation of either of the German nations. Among the princes of the Alemanni, Macrianus, who, with a Roman name, had assumed the arts of a soldier and a statesman, deserved his hatred and esteem. The emperor himself, with a light and unencumbered band, condescended to pass the Rhine, marched fifty miles into the country, and would infallibly have seized the object of his pursuit, if his judicious measures had not been defeated by the impatience of the troops. Macrianus was afterwards admitted to the honour of a personal conference with the emperor; and the favours which he received fixed him, till the hour of his death, a steady and sincere friend of the republic. [68]

[68] The wars and negotiations relative to the Burgundians and Alemanni are distinctly related by Ammianus Marcellinus. Orosius and the Chronicles of Jerom and Cassiodorius fix some dates and add some circumstances.

[69] At the northern extremity of the peninsula (the Cimbric promontory of Pliny) Ptolemy fixes the remnant of the Cimbri. He fills the interval between the Saxons and the Cimbri with six obscure tribes, who were united, as early as the sixth century, under the national appellation of Danes.

[70] M. d'Anville has marked the extensive limits of the Saxony of Charlemagne.

The land was covered by the fortifications of Valentinian; but the sea-coast of Gaul and Britain was exposed to the depredations of the Saxons. That celebrated name, in which we have a dear and domestic interest, escaped the notice of Tacitus; and in the maps of Ptolemy it faintly marks the narrow neck of the Cimbric peninsula and three small islands towards the mouth of the Elbe. [69] This contracted territory, the present Duchy of Sleswig, or perhaps of Holstein, was incapable of pouring forth the inexhaustible swarms of Saxons who reigned over the ocean, who filled the British island with their language, their laws, and their colonies; and who so long defended the liberty of the North against the arms of Charlemagne. [70] The solution of this difficulty is easily derived from the similar manners and loose constitution of the tribes of Germany; which were blended with each other by the slightest accidents of war or friendship. The situation of the native Saxons disposed them to embrace the hazardous professions of fishermen and pirates; and the success of their first adventures would naturally excite the emulation of their bravest countrymen, who were impatient of the gloomy solitude of their woods and mountains. Every tide might float down the Elbe whole fleets of canoes, filled with hardy and intrepid associates, who aspired to behold the unbounded prospect of the ocean and to taste the wealth and luxury of unknown worlds. It should seem probable, however, that the most numerous auxiliaries of the Saxons were furnished by the nations who dwelt along the shores of the Baltic. They possessed arms and ships, the art of navigation, and the habits of naval war; but the difficulty of issuing through the northern columns of Hercules (which during several months of the year are obstructed with ice) confined their skill and courage within the limits of a spacious lake.[71] The rumour of the successful armaments which sailed from the mouth of the Elbe would soon provoke them to cross the narrow isthmus of Sleswig and to launch their vessels on the great sea. The various troops of pirates and adventurers who fought under the same standard were insensibly united in a permanent society, at first of rapine, and afterwards of government. A military confederation was gradually moulded into a national body, by the gentle operation of marriage and consanguinity; and the adjacent tribes, who solicited the alliance, accepted the name and laws, of the Saxons. If the fact were not established by the most unquestionable evidence, we should appear to abuse the credulity of our readers by the description of the vessels in which the Saxon pirates ventured to sport in the waves of the German Ocean, the British Channel, and the Bay of Biscay. The keel of their large flat-bottomed boats was framed of light timber, but the sides and upper work consisted only of wicker, with a covering of strong hides. In the course of their slow and distant navigations, they must always have been exposed to the danger, and very frequently to the misfortune, of shipwreck; and the naval annals of the Saxons were undoubtedly filled with the accounts of the losses which they sustained on the coasts of Britain and Gaul. But the daring spirit of the pirates braved the perils, both of the sea and of the shore; their skill was confirmed by the habits of enterprise; the meanest of their mariners was alike capable of handling an oar, of rearing a sail, or of conducting a vessel; and the Saxons rejoiced in the appearance of a tempest, which concealed their design, and dispersed the fleets

[71] *The fleet of Drusus had failed in their attempt to pass, or even to approach, the* Sound *(styled, from an obvious resemblance, the columns of Hercules); and the naval enterprise was never resumed. The knowledge which the Romans acquired of the naval powers of the Baltic was obtained by their land journeys in search of amber.*

of the enemy. After they had acquired an accurate knowledge of the maritime provinces of the West, they extended the scene of their depredations, and the most sequestered places had no reason to presume on their security. The Saxon boats drew so little water that they could easily proceed fourscore or an hundred miles up the great rivers; their weight was so inconsiderable that they were transported on waggons from one river to another; and the pirates who had entered the mouth of the Seine or of the Rhine, might descend, with the rapid stream of the Rhone, into the Mediterranean. Under the reign of Valentinian, the maritime provinces of Gaul were afflicted by the Saxons: a military count was stationed for the defence of the sea-coast, or Armorican limit; and that officer, who found his strength, or his abilities, unequal to the task, implored the assistance of Severus, master-general of the infantry. The Saxons, surrounded and out-numbered, were forced to relinquish their spoil, and to yield a select band of their tall and robust youth to serve in the Imperial armies. They stipulated only a safe and honourable retreat: and the condition was readily granted by the Roman general; who meditated an act of perfidy,[72] imprudent as it was inhuman, while a Saxon remained alive, and in arms, to revenge the fate of his countrymen. The premature eagerness of the infantry, who were secretly posted in a deep valley, betrayed the ambuscade; and they would perhaps have fallen the victims of their own treachery, if a large body of cuirassiers, alarmed by the noise of the combat, had not hastily advanced to extricate their companions and to overwhelm the undaunted valour of the Saxons. Some of the prisoners were saved from the edge of the sword, to shed their blood in the amphitheatre; and the orator Symmachus complains that twenty-nine of those desperate savages, by strangling themselves with their own hands, had disappointed the amusement of the public. Yet the polite and philosophic citizens of Rome were impressed with the deepest horror, when they were informed that the Saxons consecrated to the gods the tythe of their *human* spoil; and that they ascertained by lot the objects of the barbarous sacrifice.[73]

II. The fabulous colonies of Egyptians and Trojans, of Scandinavians and Spaniards, which flattered the pride, and amused the credulity, of our rude ancestors, have insensibly vanished in the light of science and philosophy.[74] The present age is satisfied with the simple and rational opinion that the islands of Great Britain and Ireland were gradually peopled from the adjacent continent of Gaul. From the coast of Kent to the extremity of Caithness and

[72] *Ammianus justifies this breach of faith to pirates and robbers; and Orosius more clearly expresses their real guilt; virtute atque agilitate terribiles.*

[73] *Symmachus still presumes to mention the sacred names of Socrates and philosophy. Sidonius, bishop of Clermont, might condemn with less inconsistency the human sacrifices of the Saxons.*

[74] *In the beginning of the last century the learned Cambden was obliged to undermine, with respectful scepticism, the romance of* Brutus *the Trojan, who is now buried in silent oblivion with* Scota, *the daughter of Pharaoh, and her numerous progeny. Yet I am informed that some champions of the* Milesian *colony may still be found among the original natives of Ireland. A people dissatisfied with their present condition grasp at any visions of their past or future glory.*

Ulster, the memory of a Celtic origin was distinctly preserved, in the perpetual resemblance of language, of religion, and of manners: and the peculiar characters of the British tribes might be naturally ascribed to the influence of accidental and local circumstances.[75] The Roman province was reduced to the state of civilized and peaceful servitude: the rights of savage freedom were contracted to the narrow limits of Caledonia. The inhabitants of that northern region were divided, as early as the reign of Constantine, between the two great tribes of the Scots and of the Picts,[76] who have since experienced a very different fortune. The power, and almost the memory, of the Picts have been extinguished by their successful rivals; and the Scots, after maintaining for ages the dignity of an independent kingdom, have multiplied, by an equal and voluntary union, the honours of the English name. The hand of nature had contributed to mark the ancient distinction of the Scots and Picts. The former were the men of the hills, and the latter those of the plain. The eastern coast of Caledonia may be considered as a level and fertile country, which, even in a rude state of tillage, was capable of producing a considerable quantity of corn; and the epithet of *cruitnich*, or wheat-eaters, expressed the contempt, or envy, of the carnivorous highlander. The cultivation of the earth might introduce a more accurate separation of property and the habits of a sedentary life; but the love of arms and rapine was still the ruling passion of the Picts; and their warriors, who stripped themselves for a day of battle, were distinguished, in the eyes of the Romans, by the strange fashion of painting their naked bodies with gaudy colours and fantastic figures. The western part of Caledonia irregularly rises into wild and barren hills, which scarcely repay the toil of the husbandman and are most profitably used for the pasture of cattle. The highlanders were condemned to the occupations of shepherds and hunters; and, as they seldom were fixed to any permanent habitation, they acquired the expressive name of Scots, which, in the Celtic tongue, is said to be equivalent to that of *wanderers* or *vagrants*. The inhabitants of a barren land were urged to seek a fresh supply of food in the waters. The deep lakes and bays which intersect their country are plentifully stored with fish; and they gradually ventured to cast their nets in the waves of the ocean. The vicinity of the Hebrides, so profusely scattered along the western coast of Scotland, tempted their curiosity and improved their skill; and they acquired by slow degrees, the art, or rather the habit, of managing their boats in a tempestuous sea and of steering their noctur-

[75] *Tacitus, or rather his father-in-law Agricola, might remark the German or Spanish complexion of some British tribes. But it was their sober, deliberate opinion: "In universum tamen æstimanti Gallos vicinum solum occupâsse credibile est. Eorum sacra deprehendas ... sermo haud multum diversus." Cæsar had observed their common religion; and in his time the emigration from the Belgic Gaul was a recent, or at least an historical, event. Cambden, the British Strabo, has modestly ascertained our genuine antiquities.*

[76] *In the dark and doubtful paths of Caledonian antiquity, I have chosen for my guides two learned and ingenious Highlanders, whom their birth and education had peculiarly qualified for that office. See Critical Dissertations on the Origin, Antiquities, &c., of the Caledonians, by Dr. John Macpherson, London, 1768; and Introduction to the History of Great Britain and Ireland, by James Macpherson, Esq., London, 1773. Dr. Macpherson was a minister in the Isle of Skye: and it is a circumstance honourable for the present age that a work, replete with*

erudition and criticism, should have been composed in the most remote of the Hebrides.

¹¹ The Irish descent of the Scots has been revived, in the last moments of its decay, and strenuously supported, by the Rev. Mr. Whitaker. Yet he acknowledges, 1. That the Scots of Ammianus Marcellinus (A.D. 340) were already settled in Caledonia; and that the Roman authors do not afford any hints of their emigration from another country. 2. That all the accounts of such emigrations,.which have been asserted, or received, by Irish bards, Scotch historians, or English antiquaries (Buchanan, Cambden, Usher, Stillingfleet, &c.), are totally fabulous. 3. That three of the Irish tribes which are mentioned by Ptolemy (A.D. 150) were of Caledonian extraction. 4. That a younger branch of Caledonian princes, of the house of Fingal, acquired and possessed the monarchy of Ireland. After these concessions, the remaining difference between Mr. Whitaker and his adversaries is minute and obscure. The genuine history which he produces of a Fergus, the cousin of Ossian, who was trans-

nal course by the light of the well-known stars. The two bold headlands of Caledonia almost touch the shores of a spacious island, which obtained, from its luxuriant vegetation, the epithet of *Green;* and has preserved, with a slight alteration, the name of Erin, or Ierne, or Ireland. It is *probable* that in some remote period of antiquity the fertile plains of Ulster received a colony of hungry Scots; and that the strangers of the North, who had dared to encounter the arms of the legions, spread their conquests over the savage and unwarlike natives of a solitary island. It is *certain,* that, in the declining age of the Roman empire, Caledonia, Ireland, and the Isle of Man were inhabited by the Scots, and that the kindred tribes, who were often associated in military enterprise, were deeply affected by the various accidents of their mutual fortunes. They long cherished the lively tradition of their common name and origin; and the missionaries of the Isle of Saints, who diffused the light of Christianity over North Britain, established the vain opinion that their Irish countrymen were the natural as well as spiritual fathers of the Scottish race. The loose and obscure tradition has been preserved by the venerable Bede, who scattered some rays of light over the darkness of the eighth century. On this slight foundation, a huge superstructure of fable was gradually reared, by the bards and the monks; two orders of men who equally abused the privilege of fiction. The Scottish nation, with mistaken pride, adopted their Irish genealogy: and the annals of a long line of imaginary kings have been adorned by the fancy of Boethius and the classic elegance of Buchanan.¹¹

Six years after the death of Constantine, the destructive inroads of the Scots and Picts required the presence of his youngest son, who reigned in the western empire. Constans visited his British dominions; but we may form some estimate of the importance of his achievements by the language of panegyric, which celebrates only his triumph over the elements; or, in other words, the good fortune of a safe and easy passage from the port of Boulogne to the harbour of Sandwich. The calamities which the afflicted provincials continued to experience, from foreign war and domestic tyranny, were aggravated by the feeble and corrupt administration of the eunuchs of Constantius; and the transient relief which they might obtain from the virtues of Julian was soon lost by the absence and death of their benefactor. The sums of gold and silver which had been painfully collected, or liberally transmitted, for the payment of the troops were intercepted by the avarice of the commanders; discharges, or, at least, exemptions, from the military service were publicly sold; the distress of the soldiers, who were injuriously deprived of their legal and scanty subsistence, provoked them to frequent desertion; the nerves of discipline were relaxed, and the highways were infested with robbers. The oppression of the good and the impunity of the wicked equally contributed to diffuse through the island a spirit of discontent and revolt; and every ambitious subject, every desperate exile, might entertain a reasonable hope of subverting the weak and distracted government of Britain. The hostile tribes of the North, who detested the pride and power of the King of the World, suspended their domestic feuds; and the Barbarians of the land and sea, the Scots, the Picts, and the Saxons, spread themselves, with rapid and irresistible fury, from the wall of Antoninus to the shore of Kent. Every production of art and nature, every object of convenience or luxury, which they were incapable of creating by labour or procuring by trade, was accumulated in the rich and fruitful province of Britain.[78] A philosopher may deplore the eternal discord of the human race, but he will confess that the desire of spoil is a more rational provocation than the vanity of conquest. From the age of Constantine to that of the Plantagenets, this rapacious spirit continued to instigate the poor and hardy Caledonians: but the same people, whose generous humanity seems to inspire the songs of Ossian, was disgraced by a savage ignorance of the virtues of peace and of the laws of war. Their southern neighbours have felt, and perhaps exaggerated, the cruel depredations of the Scots and Picts:[79] and a valiant tribe of Caledonia, the Attacotti,[80] the enemies, and afterwards the soldiers, of Valentinian, are accused, by an eye-witness, of delighting in the taste of human flesh. When they hunted the woods for prey, it is said that they attacked the shepherd rather than his flock; and that they curiously selected the most delicate and brawny parts, both of males and females, which they prepared for their horrid repasts. If, in the neighbourhood of the commercial and literary town of Glasgow, a race of canibals has really existed, we may contemplate, in the period of the Scottish history, the opposite extremes of savage and civilized life. Such reflections tend to enlarge the circle of our ideas: and to encourage the pleasing hope that New Zealand may produce, in some future age, the Hume of the Southern Hemisphere.

Every messenger who escaped across the British channel conveyed the most melancholy and alarming tidings to the ears of Valentinian; and the emperor was soon informed that the two mili-

planted (A.D. 320) from Ireland to Caledonia, is built on a conjectural supplement to the Erse poetry, and the feeble evidence of Richard of Cirencester, a monk of the fourteenth century. The lively spirit of the learned and ingenious antiquarian has tempted him to forget the nature of a question, which he so vehemently debates, and so absolutely decides.

[78] The Caledonians praised and coveted the gold, the steeds, the lights, &c., of the stranger.

[79] Lord Lyttleton has circumstantially related, and Sir David Dalrymple has slightly mentioned, a barbarous inroad of the Scots, at a time (A.D. 1137) when law, religion, and society must have softened their primitive manners.

[80] Cambden has restored their true name in the text of Jerom. The bands of Attacotti, which Jerom had seen in Gaul, were afterwards stationed in Italy and Illyricum.

tary commanders of the province had been surprised and cut off by the Barbarians. Severus, count of the domestics, was hastily dispatched, and as suddenly recalled, by the court of Treves. The representations of Jovinus served only to indicate the greatness of the evil; and after a long and serious consultation, the defence, or rather the recovery, of Britain was intrusted to the abilities of the brave Theodosius. The exploits of that general, the father of a line of emperors, have been celebrated, with peculiar complacency, by the writers of the age: but his real merit deserved their applause; and his nomination was received, by the army and province, as a sure presage of approaching victory. He seized the favourable moment of navigation, and securely landed the numerous and veteran bands of the Heruli and Batavians, the Jovians and the Victors. In his march from Sandwich to London, Theodosius defeated several parties of the barbarians, released a multitude of captives, and, after distributing to his soldiers a small portion of the spoil, established the fame of disinterested justice by the restitution of the remainder to the rightful proprietors. The citizens of London, who had almost despaired of their safety, threw open their gates; and, as soon as Theodosius had obtained from the court of Treves the important aid of a military lieutenant and a civil governor, he executed, with wisdom and vigour, the laborious task of the deliverance of Britain. The vagrant soldiers were recalled to their standard; an edict of amnesty dispelled the public apprehensions; and his cheerful example alleviated the rigour of martial discipline. The scattered and desultory warfare of the Barbarians, who infested the land and sea, deprived him of the glory of a signal victory; but the prudent spirit and consummate art of the Roman general were displayed in the operations of two campaigns, which successively rescued every part of the province from the hands of a cruel and rapacious enemy. The splendour of the cities and the security of the fortifications were diligently restored by the paternal care of Theodosius: who with a strong hand confined the trembling Caledonians to the northern angle of the island; and perpetuated, by the name and settlement of the new province of *Valentia,* the glories of the reign of Valentinian. The voice of poetry and panegyric may add, perhaps with some degree of truth, that the unknown regions of Thule were stained with the blood of the Picts; that the oars of Theodosius dashed the waves of the Hyperborean ocean; and that the distant Orkneys were the scene of his naval victory over the Saxon pirates. He left the province with a fair, as well as splendid, reputation: and was immediately promoted to the rank of master-general of the cavalry, by a prince who could applaud without envy the merit of his servants. In the important station of the upper Danube, the conqueror of Britain checked and defeated the armies of the Alemanni before he was chosen to suppress the revolt of Africa.

III. The prince who refuses to be the judge, instructs his people to consider him as the accomplice, of his ministers. The military command of Africa had been long exercised by Count Romanus, and his abilities were not inadequate to his station: but, as sordid interest was the sole motive of his conduct, he acted, on most occasions, as if he had been the enemy of the province and the friend of the Barbarians of the desert. The three flourishing cities of Oea, Leptis, and Sabrata, which, under the name of Tripoli, had long constituted a federal union,[81] were obliged, for the first time, to shut their gates against a hostile invasion; several of their most honourable citizens were surprised and massacred; the villages, and even the suburbs, were pillaged; and the vines and fruit-trees of that rich territory were extirpated by the malicious savages of Gætulia. The unhappy provincials implored the protection of Romanus; but they soon found that their military governor was not less cruel and rapacious than the Barbarians. As they were incapable of furnishing the four thousand camels, and the exorbitant present, which he required before he would march to the assistance of Tripoli, his demand was equivalent to a refusal, and he might justly be accused as the author of the public calamity. In the annual assembly of the three cities, they nominated two deputies, to lay at the feet of Valentinian the customary offering of a gold victory; and to accompany this tribute of duty, rather than of gratitude, with their humble complaint that they were ruined by the enemy and betrayed by their governor. If the severity of Valentinian had been rightly directed, it would have fallen on the guilty head of Romanus. But the count, long exercised in the arts of corruption, had dispatched a swift and trusty messenger to secure the venal friendship of Remigius, master of the offices. The wisdom of the Imperial council was deceived by artifice; and their honest indignation was cooled by delay. At length, when the repetition of complaint had been justified by the repetition of public misfortunes, the notary Palladius was sent from the court of Treves, to examine the state of Africa, and the conduct of Romanus. The rigid impartiality of Palladius was easily disarmed: he was tempted to reserve for himself a part of the public treasure which he brought with him for the payment of

[81] *Ammianus frequently mentions their concilium annuum, legitimum, &c. Leptis and Sabrata are long since ruined; but the city of Oea, the native country of Apuleius, still flourishes under the provincial denomination of Tripoli.*

the troops; and from the moment that he was conscious of his own guilt, he could no longer refuse to attest the innocence and merit of the count. The charge of the Tripolitans was declared to be false and frivolous; and Palladius himself was sent back from Treves to Africa, with a special commission to discover and prosecute the authors of this impious conspiracy against the representatives of the sovereign. His inquiries were managed with so much dexterity and success that he compelled the citizens of Leptis, who had sustained a recent siege of eight days, to contradict the truth of their own decrees and to censure the behaviour of their own deputies. A bloody sentence was pronounced, without hesitation, by the rash and headstrong cruelty of Valentinian. The president of Tripoli, who had presumed to pity the distress of the province, was publicly executed at Utica; four distinguished citizens were put to death as the accomplices of the imaginary fraud; and the tongues of two others were cut out by the express order of the emperor. Romanus, elated by impunity and irritated by resistance, was still continued in the military command; till the Africans were provoked by his avarice to join the rebellious standard of Firmus, the Moor.[82]

His father Nabal was one of the richest and most powerful of the Moorish princes, who acknowledged the supremacy of Rome. But, as he left, either by his wives or concubines, a very numerous posterity, the wealthy inheritance was eagerly disputed; and Zamma, one of his sons, was slain in a domestic quarrel by his brother Firmus. The implacable zeal with which Romanus prosecuted the legal revenge of this murder could be ascribed only to a motive of avarice, or personal hatred: but, on this occasion, his claims were just; his influence was weighty; and Firmus clearly understood that he must either present his neck to the executioner or appeal from the sentence of the Imperial consistory to his sword and to the people.[83] He was received as the deliverer of his country; and, as soon as it appeared that Romanus was formidable only to a submissive province, the tyrant of Africa became the object of universal contempt. The ruin of Cæsarea, which was plundered and burnt by the licentious Barbarians, convinced the refractory cities of the danger of resistance; the power of Firmus was established, at least in the provinces of Mauritania and Numidia; and it seemed to be his only doubt, whether he should assume the diadem of a Moorish king or the purple of a Roman emperor. But the imprudent and unhappy Africans soon discovered that, in this rash insurrection, they had not sufficiently consulted their own strength or the abilities of their

[82] Tillemont has discussed the chronological difficulties of the history of Count Romanus.

[83] The chronology of Ammianus is loose and obscure: and Orosius seems to place the revolt of Firmus after the deaths of Valentinian and Valens. Tillemont endeavours to pick his way. The patient and sure-footed mule of the Alps may be trusted in the most slippery paths.

leader. Before he could procure any certain intelligence that the emperor of the West had fixed the choice of a general, or that a fleet of transports was collected at the mouth of the Rhone, he was suddenly informed that the great Theodosius, with a small band of veterans, had landed near Igilgilis, or Gigeri, on the African coast; and the timid usurper sunk under the ascendant of virtue and military genius. Though Firmus possessed arms and treasures, his despair of victory immediately reduced him to the use of those arts which, in the same country and in a similar situation, had formerly been practised by the crafty Jugurtha. He attempted to deceive, by an apparent submission, the vigilance of the Roman general; to seduce the fidelity of his troops; and to protract the duration of the war, by successively engaging the independent tribes of Africa to espouse his quarrel or to protect his flight. Theodosius imitated the example, and obtained the success, of his predecessor Metellus. When Firmus, in the character of a suppliant, accused his own rashness and humbly solicited the clemency of the emperor, the lieutenant of Valentinian received and dismissed him with a friendly embrace; but he diligently required the useful and substantial pledges of a sincere repentance; nor could he be persuaded, by the assurances of peace, to suspend, for an instant, the operations of an active war. A dark conspiracy was detected by the penetration of Theodosius; and he satisfied, without much reluctance, the public indignation, which he had secretly excited. Several of the guilty accomplices of Firmus were abandoned, according to ancient custom, to the tumult of a military execution; many more, by the amputation of both their hands, continued to exhibit an instructive spectacle of horror; the hatred of the rebels was accompanied with fear; and the fear of the Roman soldiers was mingled with respectful admiration. Amidst the boundless plains of Getulia, and the innumerable valleys of Mount Atlas, it was impossible to prevent the escape of Firmus; and, if the usurper could have tired the patience of his antagonist, he would have secured his person in the depth of some remote solitude, and expected the hopes of a future revolution. He was subdued by the perseverance of Theodosius; who had formed an inflexible determination that the war should end only by the death of the tyrant, and that every nation of Africa which presumed to support his cause should be involved in his ruin. At the head of a small body of troops, which seldom exceeded three thousand five hundred men, the Roman general advanced with a steady prudence, devoid of rashness or of fear, into the heart of a country where he was sometimes attacked by armies of twenty thousand Moors. The boldness of his charge dismayed the irregular Barbarians; they were disconcerted by his seasonable and orderly retreats; they were continually baffled by the unknown resources of the military art; and they felt and confessed the just superiority which was assumed by the leader of a civilized nation. When Theodosius entered the extensive dominions of Igmazen, king of the Isaflenses, the haughty savage required, in words of defiance, his name and the object of his expedition. "I am," replied the stern and disdainful count, "I am the general of Valentinian, the lord of the world; who has sent me hither to pursue and punish a desperate robber. Deliver him instantly into my hands; and be assured that, if thou dost not obey the commands of my invincible sovereign, thou, and the people over whom thou reignest, shall be utterly extirpated." As soon as Igmazen was satisfied that his enemy had strength and resolution to execute the fatal menace, he consented to purchase a necessary peace by the sacrifice of a guilty fugitive. The guards that were placed to secure the person of Firmus deprived him of the hopes of escape; and the Moorish tyrant, after wine had extinguished the sense of danger, disappointed the insulting triumph of the Romans by strangling himself in the night. His dead body, the only present which Igmazen could offer to the conqueror, was carelessly thrown upon a camel; and Theodosius, leading back his victorious troops to Sitifi, was saluted by the warmest acclamations of joy and loyalty.[84]

[84] *The text of this long chapter in Ammianus (fifteen quarto pages) is broken and corrupted, and the narrative is perplexed by the want of chronological and geographical landmarks.*

Africa had been lost by the vices of Romanus; it was restored by the virtues of Theodosius: and our curiosity may be usefully directed to the inquiry of the respective treatment which the two generals received from the Imperial court. The authority of Count Romanus had been suspended by the master-general of the cavalry; and he was committed to safe and honourable custody till the end of the war. His crimes were proved by the most authentic evidence; and the public expected, with some impatience, the decree of severe justice. But the partial and powerful favour of Mellobaudes encouraged him to challenge his legal judges, to obtain repeated delays for the purpose of procuring a crowd of friendly witnesses, and, finally, to cover his guilty conduct by the additional guilt of fraud and forgery. About the same time, the restorer of Britain and Africa, on a vague suspicion that his name and services were superior to the rank of a subject, was ignominiously beheaded at Carthage. Valentinian no longer reigned; and the death of Theodosius, as well as the impunity of Romanus, may justly be imputed to the arts of the ministers who abused the confidence, and deceived the inexperienced youth, of his sons.

If the geographical accuracy of Ammianus had been fortunately bestowed on the British exploits of Theodosius, we should have traced, with eager curiosity, the distinct and domestic footsteps of his march. But the tedious enumeration of the unknown and uninteresting tribes of Africa may be reduced to the general remark that they were all of the swarthy race of the Moors; that they inhabited the back settlements of the Mauritanian and Numidian provinces, the country, as they have since been termed by the Arabs, of dates and of locusts; and that, as the Roman power declined in Africa, the boundary of civilized manners and cultivated land was insensibly contracted. Beyond the utmost limits of the Moors, the vast and inhospitable desert of the South extends above a thousand miles to the banks of the Niger. The ancients, who had a very faint and imperfect knowledge of the great peninsula of Africa, were sometimes tempted to believe that the torrid zone must ever remain destitute of inhabitants:[85] and they sometimes amused their fancy by filling the vacant space with headless men, or rather monsters; with horned and cloven-footed satyrs;[86] with fabulous centaurs;[87] and with human pygmies, who waged a bold and doubtful warfare against the cranes.[88] Carthage would have trembled at the strange intelligence that the countries on either side of the equator were filled with innumerable nations, who differed only in their colour from the ordinary appearance of the human species; and the subjects of the Roman empire might have anxiously expected that the swarms of Barbarians which issued from the North would soon be encountered from the South by new swarms of Barbarians, equally fierce, and equally formidable. These gloomy terrors would indeed have been dispelled by a more intimate acquaintance with the character of their African enemies. The inaction of the negroes does not seem to be the effect either of their virtue or of their pusillanimity. They indulge, like the rest of mankind, their passions and appetites; and the adjacent tribes are engaged in frequent acts of hostility.[89] But their rude ignorance has never invented any effectual weapons of defence or of destruction; they appear incapable of forming any extensive plans of government or conquest; and the obvious inferiority of their mental faculties has been discovered and abused by the nations of the temperate zone. Sixty thousand blacks are annually embarked from the coast of Guinea, never to return to their

[85] *This uninhabitable zone was gradually reduced, by the improvements of ancient geography, from forty-five to twenty-four, or even sixteen, degrees of latitude.*

[86] *If the satyr was the Orang-outang, the great human ape, one of that species might actually be shown alive at Alexandria in the reign of Constantine. Yet some difficulty will still remain about the conversation which St. Anthony held with one of these pious savages in the desert of Thebais.*

[87] *St. Anthony likewise met one of these monsters, whose existence was seriously asserted by the emperor Claudius. The public laughed; but his præfect of Egypt had the address to send an artful preparation, the embalmed corpse of an Hippocentaur, which was preserved almost a century afterwards in the Imperial palace.*

[88] *The fable of the pygmies is as old as Homer. The pygmies of India and Æthiopia were (trispithami) twenty-seven inches high. Every spring their cavalry (mounted on rams and goats) marched in battle array to destroy the cranes' eggs. Their*

houses were built of
mud, feathers, and egg-
shells.

[89] The third and fourth
volumes of the valuable
Histoire des Voyages
describe the present state
of the negroes. The na-
tions of the sea-coast
have been polished by
European commerce,
and those of the inland
country have been im-
proved by Moorish
colonies.

[90] The evidence of Am-
mianus is original and
decisive. Moses of Cho-
rene and Procopius have
been consulted; but those
historians, who con-
found distinct facts, re-
peat the same events,
and introduce strange
stories, must be used
with diffidence and
caution.

[91] Perhaps Artagera, or
Ardis; under whose
walls Gaius, the grand-
son of Augustus, was
wounded. This fortress
was situate above
Amida, near one of the
sources of the Tigris.

[92] Tillemont proves from
chronology that Olympia
must have been the
mother of Para.

native country; but they are embarked in chains: and this constant
emigration, which, in the space of two centuries, might have furnished armies to overrun the globe, accuses the guilt of Europe and
the weakness of Africa.

IV. The ignominious treaty which saved the army of Jovian had
been faithfully executed on the side of the Romans: and, as they had
solemnly renounced the sovereignty and alliance of Armenia and
Iberia, those tributary kingdoms were exposed, without protection,
to the arms of the Persian monarch.[90] Sapor entered the Armenian
territories at the head of a formidable host of cuirassiers, of archers,
and of mercenary foot; but it was the invariable practice of Sapor
to mix war and negotiation, and to consider falsehood and perjury
as the most powerful instruments of regal policy. He affected to
praise the prudent and moderate conduct of the king of Armenia;
and the unsuspicious Tiranus was persuaded, by the repeated assurances of insidious friendship, to deliver his person into the hands
of a faithless and cruel enemy. In the midst of a splendid entertainment, he was bound in chains of silver, as an honour due to the
blood of the Arsacides; and, after a short confinement in the Tower
of Oblivion at Ecbatana, he was released from the miseries of life,
either by his own dagger or by that of an assassin. The kingdom of
Armenia was reduced to the state of a Persian province; the administration was shared between a distinguished satrap and a favourite eunuch; and Sapor marched, without delay, to subdue the
martial spirit of the Iberians. Sauromaces, who reigned in that
country by the permission of the emperors, was expelled by a superior force; and, as an insult on the majesty of Rome, the King of
kings placed a diadem on the head of his abject vassal Aspacuras.
The city of Artogerassa[91] was the only place of Armenia which presumed to resist the effort of his arms. The treasure deposited in that
strong fortress tempted the avarice of Sapor; but the danger of
Olympias, the wife, or widow, of the Armenian king, excited the
public compassion, and animated the desperate valour of her subjects and soldiers. The Persians were surprised and repulsed under
the walls of Artogerassa, by a bold and well-concerted sally of the
besieged. But the forces of Sapor were continually renewed and
increased; the hopeless courage of the garrison was exhausted; the
strength of the walls yielded to the assault; and the proud conqueror, after wasting the rebellious city with fire and sword, led
away captive an unfortunate queen, who, in a more auspicious
hour, had been the destined bride of the son of Constantine.[92] Yet,

if Sapor already triumphed in the easy conquest of two dependent kingdoms, he soon felt that a country is unsubdued, as long as the minds of the people are actuated by an hostile and contumacious spirit. The satraps, whom he was obliged to trust, embraced the first opportunity of regaining the affection of their countrymen and of signalizing their immortal hatred to the Persian name. Since the conversion of the Armenians and Iberians, those nations considered the Christians as the favourites, and the Magians as the adversaries, of the Supreme Being; the influence of the clergy over a superstitious people was uniformly exerted in the cause of Rome; and, as long as the successors of Constantine disputed with those of Artaxerxes the sovereignty of the intermediate provinces, the religious connexion always threw a decisive advantage into the scale of the empire. A numerous and active party acknowledged Para, the son of Tiranus, as the lawful sovereign of Armenia; and his title to the throne was deeply rooted in the hereditary succession of five hundred years. By the unanimous consent of the Iberians, the country was equally divided between the rival princes; and Aspacuras, who owed his diadem to the choice of Sapor, was obliged to declare that his regard for his children, who were detained as hostages by the tyrant, was the only consideration which prevented him from openly renouncing the alliance of Persia. The emperor Valens, who respected the obligations of the treaty, and who was apprehensive of involving the East in a dangerous war, ventured, with slow and cautious measures, to support the Roman party in the kingdoms of Iberia and Armenia. Twelve legions established the authority of Sauromaces on the banks of the Cyrus. The Euphrates was protected by the valour of Arintheus. A powerful army, under the command of Count Trajan, and of Vadomair, king of the Alemanni, fixed their camp on the confines of Armenia. But they were strictly enjoined not to commit the first hostilities, which might be understood as a breach of the treaty: and such was the implicit obedience of the Roman general that they retreated, with exemplary patience, under a shower of Persian arrows, till they had clearly acquired a just title to an honourable and legitimate victory. Yet these appearances of war insensibly subsided in a vain and tedious negotiation. The contending parties supported their claims by mutual reproaches of perfidy and ambition; and it should seem that the original treaty[93] was expressed in very obscure terms, since they were reduced to the necessity of making their inconclusive appeal to the partial testimony of the generals of the two nations

[93] *Ammianus has described the events, without the dates, of the Persian war. Moses of Chorene affords some additional facts; but it is extremely difficult to separate truth from fable.*

who had assisted at the negotiations. The invasion of the Goths and Huns, which soon afterwards shook the foundations of the Roman empire, exposed the provinces of Asia to the arms of Sapor. But the declining age, and perhaps the infirmities, of the monarch suggested new maxims of tranquillity and moderation. His death, which happened in the full maturity of a reign of seventy years, changed in a moment the court and councils of Persia; and their attention was most probably engaged by domestic troubles, and the distant efforts of a Carmanian war.[94] The remembrance of ancient injuries was lost in the enjoyment of peace. The kingdoms of Armenia and Iberia were permitted, by the mutual, though tacit, consent of both empires, to resume their doubtful neutrality. In the first years of the reign of Theodosius, a Persian embassy arrived at Constantinople, to excuse the unjustifiable measures of the former reign; and to offer, as the tribute of friendship, or even of respect, a splendid present of gems, of silk, and of Indian elephants.

In the general picture of the affairs of the East under the reign of Valens, the adventures of Para form one of the most striking and singular objects. The noble youth, by the persuasion of his mother Olympias, had escaped through the Persian host that besieged Artogerassa, and implored the protection of the emperor of the East. By his timid councils, Para was alternately supported, and recalled, and restored, and betrayed. The hopes of the Armenians were sometimes raised by the presence of their natural sovereign; and the ministers of Valens were satisfied that they preserved the integrity of the public faith, if their vassal was not suffered to assume the diadem and title of King. But they soon repented of their own rashness. They were confounded by the reproaches and threats of the Persian monarch. They found reason to distrust the cruel and inconstant temper of Para himself, who sacrificed, to the slightest suspicions, the lives of his most faithful servants; and held a secret and disgraceful correspondence with the assassin of his father and the enemy of his country. Under the specious pretence of consulting with the emperor on the subject of their common interest, Para was persuaded to descend from the mountains of Armenia, where his party was in arms, and to trust his independence and safety to the discretion of a perfidious court. The king of Armenia, for such he appeared in his own eyes and in those of his nation, was received with due honours by the governors of the provinces through which he passed; but, when he arrived at Tarsus in Cilicia, his progress was stopped under various pretences; his motions were watched

[94] *Artaxerxes was the successor and brother (the cousin-german) of the great Sapor; and the guardian of his son Sapor III. The authors of that unequal work have compiled the Sassanian dynasty with erudition and diligence: but it is a preposterous arrangement to divide the Roman and Oriental accounts into two distinct histories.*

with respectful vigilance; and he gradually discovered that he was a prisoner in the hands of the Romans. Para suppressed his indignation, dissembled his fears, and, after secretly preparing his escape, mounted on horseback with three hundred of his faithful followers. The officer stationed at the door of his apartment immediately communicated his flight to the consular of Cilicia, who overtook him in the suburbs, and endeavoured, without success, to dissuade him from prosecuting his rash and dangerous design. A legion was ordered to pursue the royal fugitive; but the pursuit of infantry could not be very alarming to a body of light cavalry; and upon the first cloud of arrows that was discharged into the air they retreated with precipitation to the gates of Tarsus. After an incessant march of two days and two nights, Para and his Armenians reached the banks of the Euphrates; but the passage of the river, which they were obliged to swim, was attended with some delay and some loss. The country was alarmed; and the two roads, which were only separated by an interval of three miles, had been occupied by a thousand archers on horseback, under the command of a count and a tribune. Para must have yielded to superior force, if the accidental arrival of a friendly traveller had not revealed the danger, and the means of escape. A dark and almost impervious path securely conveyed the Armenian troop through the thicket; and Para had left behind him the count and the tribune, while they patiently expected his approach along the public highways. They returned to the Imperial court to excuse their want of diligence or success: and seriously alleged that the king of Armenia, who was a skilful magician, had transformed himself and his followers, and passed before their eyes under a borrowed shape. After his return to his native kingdom, Para still continued to profess himself the friend and ally of the Romans; but the Romans had injured him too deeply ever to forgive, and the secret sentence of his death was signed in the council of Valens. The execution of the bloody deed was committed to the subtle prudence of Count Trajan; and he had the merit of insinuating himself into the confidence of the credulous prince, that he might find an opportunity of stabbing him to the heart. Para was invited to a Roman banquet, which had been prepared with all the pomp and sensuality of the East: the hall resounded with cheerful music, and the company was already heated with wine; when the count retired for an instant, drew his sword, and gave the signal of the murder. A robust and desperate Barbarian instantly rushed on the king of Armenia; and, though he bravely defended his life with the first weapon that chance offered to his hand, the table of the Imperial general was stained with the royal blood of a guest, and an ally. Such were the weak and wicked maxims of the Roman administration, that, to attain a doubtful object of political interest, the laws of nations and the sacred rights of hospitality were inhumanly violated in the face of the world.

V. During a peaceful interval of thirty years, the Romans secured their frontiers, and the Goths extended their dominions. The victories of the great Hermanric,[95] king of the Ostrogoths, and the most noble of the race of the Amali, have been compared, by the enthusiasm of his countrymen, to the exploits of Alexander: with this singular, and almost incredible, difference, that the martial spirit of the Gothic hero, instead of being supported by the vigour of youth, was displayed with glory and success in the extreme period of human life; between the age of fourscore and one hundred and ten years. The independent tribes were persuaded, or compelled, to acknowledge the king of the Ostrogoths as the sovereign of the Gothic nation: the chiefs of the Visigoths, or Thervingi, renounced the royal title, and assumed the more humble appellation of *Judges;* and, among those judges, Athanaric, Fritigern, and Alavivus were the most illustrious, by their personal merit, as well as by their vicinity to the Roman provinces. These domestic conquests, which increased the military power of Hermanric, enlarged his ambitious designs. He invaded the adjacent countries of the North; and twelve considerable nations, whose names and limits cannot be accurately defined, successively yielded to the superiority of the Gothic arms.[96] The Heruli, who inhabited the marshy lands near the lake Mæotis, were renowned for their strength and agility; and the assistance of their light infantry was eagerly solicited, and highly esteemed, in all the wars of the Barbarians. But the active spirit of the Heruli was subdued by the slow and steady perseverance of the Goths; and, after a bloody action, in which the king was slain, the remains of that warlike tribe became an useful accession to the camp of Hermanric. He then marched against the Venedi; unskilled in the use of arms, and formidable only by their numbers, which filled the wide extent of the plains of modern Poland. The victorious Goths, who were not inferior in numbers, prevailed in the contest, by the decisive advantages of exercise and discipline. After the submission of the Venedi, the conqueror advanced, without resistance, as far as the confines of the *Æstii;*[97] an ancient people, whose name is still preserved in the province of Esthonia. Those

[95] *The concise account of the reign and conquests of Hermanric seems to be one of the valuable fragments which Jornandes borrowed from the Gothic histories of Ablavius or Cassiodorius.*

[96] *M. de Buat investigates, with more industry than success, the nations subdued by the arms of Hermanric. He denies the existence of the* Vasinobroncæ, *on account of the immoderate length of their name. Yet the French envoy to Ratisbon, or Dresden, must have traversed the country of the* Mediomatrici.

[97] *The edition of Grotius exhibits the name of* Æstri. *But reason and the Ambrosian MS. have restored the* Æstii, *whose manners and situation are expressed by the pencil of Tacitus.*

distant inhabitants of the Baltic coast were supported by the labours of agriculture, enriched by the trade of amber, and consecrated by the peculiar worship of the Mother of the Gods. But the scarcity of iron obliged the Æstian warriors to content themselves with wooden clubs; and the reduction of that wealthy country is ascribed to the prudence, rather than to the arms, of Hermanric. His dominions, which extended from the Danube to the Baltic, included the native seats, and the recent acquisitions, of the Goths; and he reigned over the greatest part of Germany and Scythia with the authority of a conqueror, and sometimes with the cruelty of a tyrant. But he reigned over a part of the globe incapable of prepetuating and adorning the glory of its heroes. The name of Hermanric is almost buried in oblivion; his exploits are imperfectly known; and the Romans themselves appeared unconscious of the progress of an aspiring power, which threatened the liberty of the North and the peace of the empire.

The Goths had contracted an hereditary attachment for the Imperial house of Constantine, of whose power and liberality they had received so many signal proofs. They respected the public peace; and, if an hostile band sometimes presumed to pass the Roman limit, their irregular conduct was candidly ascribed to the ungovernable spirit of the Barbarian youth. Their contempt for two new and obscure princes, who had been raised to the throne by a popular election, inspired the Goths with bolder hopes; and, while they agitated some design of marching their confederate force under the national standard, they were easily tempted to embrace the party of Procopius, and to foment, by their dangerous aid, the civil discord of the Romans. The public treaty might stipulate no more than ten thousand auxiliaries; but the design was so zealously adopted by the chiefs of the Visigoths that the army which passed the Danube amounted to the number of thirty thousand men.[98] They marched with the proud confidence that their invincible valour would decide the fate of the Roman empire; and the provinces of Thrace groaned under the weight of the Barbarians, who displayed the insolence of masters and the licentiousness of enemies. But the intemperance which gratified their appetites retarded their progress; and, before the Goths could receive any certain intelligence of the defeat and death of Procopius, they perceived, by the hostile state of the country, that the civil and military powers were resumed by his successful rival. A chain of posts and fortifications, skilfully disposed by Valens, or the generals of Valens, resisted their march,

[98] *M. de Buat has curiously ascertained the real number of these auxiliaries. The 3000 of Ammianus, and the 10,000 of Zosimus, were only the first divisions of the Gothic army.*

prevented their retreat, and intercepted their subsistence. The fierceness of the Barbarians was tamed and suspended by hunger; they indignantly threw down their arms at the feet of the conqueror, who offered them food and chains; the numerous captives were distributed in all the cities of the East; and the provincials, who were soon familiarized with their savage appearance, ventured, by degrees, to measure their own strength with these formidable adversaries, whose name had so long been the object of their terror. The king of Scythia (and Hermanric alone could deserve so lofty a title) was grieved and exasperated by this national calamity. His ambassadors loudly complained, at the court of Valens, of the infraction of the ancient and solemn alliance which had so long subsisted between the Romans and the Goths. They alleged that they had fulfilled the duty of allies by assisting the kinsman and successor of the emperor Julian; they required the immediate restitution of the noble captives; and they urged a very singular claim, that the Gothic generals, marching in arms and in hostile array, were entitled to the sacred character and privileges of ambassadors. The decent but peremptory refusal of these extravagant demands was signified to the Barbarians by Victor, master-general of the cavalry; who expressed, with force and dignity, the just complaints of the Emperor of the East.[99] The negotiation was interrupted; and the manly exhortations of Valentinian encouraged his timid brother to vindicate the insulted majesty of the empire.

The splendour and magnitude of this Gothic war are celebrated by a contemporary historian;[100] but the events scarcely deserve the attention of posterity, except as the preliminary steps of the approaching decline and fall of the empire. Instead of leading the nations of Germany and Scythia to the banks of the Danube, or even to the gates of Constantinople, the aged monarch of the Goths resigned to the brave Athanaric the danger and glory of a defensive war, against an enemy who wielded with a feeble hand the powers of a mighty state. A bridge of boats was established upon the Danube; the presence of Valens animated his troops; and his ignorance of the art of war was compensated by personal bravery and a wise deference to the advice of Victor and Arintheus, his masters-general of the cavalry and infantry. The operations of the campaign were conducted by their skill and experience; but they found it impossible to drive the Visigoths from their strong posts in the mountains: and the devastation of the plains obliged the Romans themselves to repass the Danube on the approach of winter. The inces-

[99] *The march and subsequent negotiation are described in the Fragments of Eunapius. The provincials, who afterwards became familiar with the Barbarians, found that their strength was more apparent than real. They were tall of stature; but their legs were clumsy, and their shoulders were narrow.*

[100] *The Greek sophist Eunapius must have considered as one and the same war the whole series of Gothic history till the victories and peace of Theodosius.*

sant rains, which swelled the waters of the river, produced a tacit
suspension of arms, and confined the emperor Valens, during the
whole course of the ensuing summer, to his camp of Marcianopolis.
The third year of the war was more favourable to the Romans and
more pernicious to the Goths. The interruption of trade deprived
the Barbarians of the objects of luxury which they already confounded with the necessaries of life; and the desolation of a very
extensive tract of country threatened them with the horrors of
famine. Athanaric was provoked, or compelled, to risk a battle,
which he lost, in the plains; and the pursuit was rendered more
bloody by the cruel precaution of the victorious generals, who had
promised a large reward for the head of every Goth that was
brought into the Imperial camp. The submission of the Barbarians
appeased the resentment of Valens and his council; the emperor
listened with satisfaction to the flattering and eloquent remon-
strance of the senate of Constantinople, which assumed, for the first
time, a share in the public deliberations; and the same generals,
Victor and Arintheus, who had successfully directed the conduct of
the war, were empowered to regulate the conditions of peace. The
freedom of trade, which the Goths had hitherto enjoyed, was re-
stricted to two cities on the Danube; the rashness of their leaders
was severely punished by the suppression of their pensions and subsidies; and the exception, which was stipulated in favour of Athanaric alone, was more advantageous than honourable to the Judge
of the Visigoths. Athanaric, who, on this occasion, appears to have
consulted his private interest, without expecting the orders of his
sovereign, supported his own dignity, and that of his tribe, in the
personal interview which was proposed by the ministers of Valens.
He persisted in his declaration that it was impossible for him, without incurring the guilt of perjury, ever to set his foot on the territory
of the empire; and it is more than probable that his regard for the
sanctity of an oath was confirmed by the recent and fatal examples
of Roman treachery. The Danube, which separated the dominions
of the two independent nations, was chosen for the scene of the conference. The Emperor of the East and the Judge of the Visigoths,
accompanied by an equal number of armed followers, advanced in
their respective barges to the middle of the stream. After the ratification of the treaty, and the delivery of hostages, Valens returned in
triumph to Constantinople; and the Goths remained in a state of
tranquillity about six years; till they were violently impelled against
the Roman empire by an innumerable host of Scythians, who ap-

[101] *The Gothic war is described by Ammianus, Zosimus, and Themistius. The orator Themistius was sent from the senate of Constantinople to congratulate the victorious emperor; and his servile eloquence compares Valens on the Danube to Achilles in the Scamander. Jornandes forgets a war peculiar to the Visi-Goths, and inglorious to the Gothic name.*

peared to descend from the vast frozen regions of the North.[101]

The Emperor of the West, who had resigned to his brother the command of the Lower Danube, reserved for his immediate care the defence of the Rhætian and Illyrian provinces, which spread so many hundred miles along the greatest of the European rivers. The active policy of Valentinian was continually employed in adding new fortifications to the security of the frontier; but the abuse of this policy provoked the just resentment of the Barbarians. The Quadi complained that the ground for an intended fortress had been marked out on their territories; and their complaints were urged with so much reason and moderation that Equitius, master-general of Illyricum, consented to suspend the prosecution of the work, till he should be more clearly informed of the will of his sovereign. This fair occasion of injuring a rival, and of advancing the fortune of his son, was eagerly embraced by the inhuman Maximin, the præfect, or rather tyrant, of Gaul. The passions of Valentinian were impatient of control; and he credulously listened to the assurances of his favourite that, if the government of Valeria, and the direction of the work, were intrusted to the zeal of his son Marcellinus, the emperor should no longer be importuned with the audacious remonstrances of the Barbarians. The subjects of Rome, and the natives of Germany, were insulted by the arrogance of a young and worthless minister, who considered his rapid elevation as the proof and reward of his superior merit. He affected, however, to receive the modest application of Gabinius, king of the Quadi, with some attention and regard; but this artful civility concealed a dark and bloody design, and the credulous prince was persuaded to accept the pressing invitation of Marcellinus. I am at a loss how to vary the narrative of similar crimes; or how to relate that, in the course of the same year, but in remote parts of the empire, the inhospitable table of two Imperial generals was stained with the royal blood of two guests and allies, inhumanly murdered by their order and in their presence. The fate of Gabinius and of Para was the same: but the cruel death of their sovereign was resented in a very different manner by the servile temper of the Armenians and the free and daring spirit of the Germans. The Quadi were much declined from that formidable power which, in the time of Marcus Antoninus, had spread terror to the gates of Rome. But they still possessed arms and courage; their courage was animated by despair, and they obtained the usual reinforcement of the cavalry of their Sarmatian allies. So improvident was the assassin Marcellinus that he chose the moment when the bravest veterans had been drawn away to suppress the revolt of Firmus; and the whole province was exposed, with a very feeble defence, to the rage of the exasperated Barbarians. They invaded Pannonia in the season of harvest; unmercifully destroyed every object of plunder which they could not easily transport; and either disregarded or demolished the empty fortifications. The princess Constantia, the daughter of the emperor Constantius and the grand-daughter of the great Constantine, very narrowly escaped. That royal maid, who had innocently supported the revolt of Procopius, was now the destined wife of the heir of the Western empire. She traversed the peaceful province with a splendid and unarmed train. Her person was saved from danger, and the republic from disgrace, by the active zeal of Messalla, governor of the provinces. As soon as he was informed that the village, where she stopped only to dine, was almost encompassed by the Barbarians, he hastily placed her in his own chariot, and drove full speed till he reached the gates of Sirmium, which were at the distance of six and twenty miles. Even Sirmium might not have been secure, if the Quadi and Sarmatians had diligently advanced during the general consternation of the magistrates and people. Their delay allowed Probus, the Prætorian præfect, sufficient time to recover his own spirits and to revive the courage of the citizens. He skilfully directed their strenuous efforts to repair and strengthen the decayed fortifications; and procured the seasonable and effectual assistance of a company of archers, to protect the capital of the Illyrian provinces. Disappointed in their attempts against the walls of Sirmium, the indignant Barbarians turned their arms against the master-general of the frontier, to whom they unjustly attributed the murder of their king. Equitius could bring into the field no more than two legions; but they contained the veteran strength of the Mæsian and Pannonian bands. The obstinacy with which they disputed the vain honours of rank and precedency was the cause of their destruction; and, while they acted with separate forces and divided councils, they were surprised and slaughtered by the active vigour of the Sarmatian horse. The success of this invasion provoked the emulation of the bordering tribes; and the province of Mæsia would infallibly have been lost, if young Theodosius, the duke, or military commander, of the frontier, had not signalized, in the defeat of the public enemy, an intrepid genius, worthy of his illustrious father, and of his future greatness.

The mind of Valentinian, who then resided at Treves, was deeply

102 *Ammianus, who ac-
knowledges the merit,
has censured, with be-
coming asperity, the op-
pressive administration,
of Petronius Probus.
When Jerom translated
and continued the
Chronicle of Eusebius,
he expressed the truth,
or at least the public
opinion of his country,
in the following words:
"Probus P. P. Illyrici
iniquissimis tributorum
exactionibus, ante pro-
vincias quas regebat,
quam a Barbaris vas-
tarentur, erasit." The
saint afterwards formed
an intimate and tender
friendship with the
widow of Probus; and
the name of Count
Equitius, with less pro-
priety, but without
much injustice, has been
substituted in the text.*

103 *Julian represents his
friend Iphicles as a man
of virtue and merit, who
had made himself ridi-
culous and unhappy by
adopting the extravagant
dress and manners of the
Cynics.*

104 *Jerom, who exagger-
ates the misfortune of
Valentinian, refuses him
even this last consolation
of revenge.*

affected by the calamities of Illyricum; but the lateness of the season suspended the execution of his designs till the ensuing spring. He marched in person, with a considerable part of the forces of Gaul, from the banks of the Moselle: and to the suppliant ambassadors of the Sarmatians, who met him on the way, he returned a doubtful answer that, as soon as he reached the scene of action, he should examine and pronounce. When he arrived at Sirmium, he gave audience to the deputies of the Illyrian provinces; who loudly congratulated their own felicity under the auspicious government of Probus, his Prætorian præfect.[102] Valentinian, who was flattered by these demonstrations of their loyalty and gratitude, imprudently asked the deputy of Epirus, a Cynic philosopher of intrepid sincerity,[103] whether he was freely sent by the wishes of the province? "With tears and groans am I sent (replied Iphicles) by a reluctant people." The emperor paused: but the impunity of his ministers established the pernicious maxim that they might oppress his subjects without injuring his service. A strict inquiry into their conduct would have relieved the public discontent. The severe condemnation of the murder of Gabinius was the only measure which could restore the confidence of the Germans and vindicate the honour of the Roman name. But the haughty monarch was incapable of the magnanimity which dares to acknowledge a fault. He forgot the provocation, remembered only the injury, and advanced into the country of the Quadi with an insatiate thirst of blood and revenge. The extreme devastation and promiscuous massacre of a savage war were justified, in the eyes of the emperor, and perhaps in those of the world, by the cruel equity of retaliation;[104] and such was the discipline of the Romans, and the consternation of the enemy, that Valentinian repassed the Danube without the loss of a single man. As he had resolved to complete the destruction of the Quadi by a second campaign, he fixed his winter-quarters at Bregetio, on the Danube, near the Hungarian city of Presburg. While the operations of war were suspended by the severity of the weather, the Quadi made an humble attempt to deprecate the wrath of their conqueror; and, at the earnest persuasion of Equitius, their ambassadors were introduced into the Imperial council. They approached the throne with bended bodies and dejected countenances; and, without daring to complain of the murder of their king, they affirmed, with solemn oaths, that the late invasion was the crime of some irregular robbers, which the public council of the nation condemned and abhorred. The answer of the emperor left them but little to hope from his clemency or compassion. He reviled, in the most intemperate language, their baseness, their ingratitude, their insolence.—His eyes, his voice, his colour, his gestures, expressed the violence of his ungoverned fury; and, while his whole frame was agitated with convulsive passion, a large blood-vessel suddenly burst in his body; and Valentinian fell speechless into the arms of his attendants. Their pious care immediately concealed his situation from the crowd; but, in a few minutes, the Emperor of the West expired in an agony of pain, retaining his senses till the last, and struggling, without success, to declare his intentions to the generals and ministers who surrounded the royal couch. Valentinian was about fifty-four years of age; and he wanted only one hundred days to accomplish the twelve years of his reign.

The polygamy of Valentinian is seriously attested by an ecclesiastical historian. "The empress Severa (I relate the fable) admitted into her familiar society the lovely Justina, the daughter of an Italian governor; her admiration of those naked charms which she had often seen in the bath was expressed with such lavish and imprudent praise that the emperor was tempted to introduce a second wife into his bed; and his public edict extended to all the subjects of the empire the same domestic privilege which he had assumed for himself." But we may be assured, from the evidence of reason as well as history, that the two marriages of Valentinian, with Severa, and with Justina, were *successively* contracted; and that he used the ancient permission of divorce, which was still allowed by the laws, though it was condemned by the church. Severa was the mother of Gratian, who seemed to unite every claim which could entitle him to the undoubted succession of the Western empire. He was the eldest son of a monarch, whose glorious reign had confirmed the free and honourable choice of his fellow-soldiers. Before he had attained the ninth year of his age, the royal youth received from the hands of his indulgent father the purple robe and diadem, with the title of Augustus: the election was solemnly ratified by the consent and applause of the armies of Gaul;[105] and the name of Gratian was added to the names of Valentinian and Valens, in all the legal transactions of the Roman government. By his marriage with the grand-daughter of Constantine, the son of Valentinian acquired all the hereditary rights of the Flavian family; which, in a series of three Imperial generations, were sanctified by time, religion, and the reverence of the people. At the death of his father, the royal youth was in the seventeenth year of his age; and his virtues already

[105] *Ammianus describes the form of this military election and* august *investiture. Valentinian does not appear to have consulted, or even informed, the senate of Rome.*

justified the favourable opinion of the army and people. But Gratian resided, without apprehension, in the palace of Treves; whilst, at the distance of many hundred miles, Valentinian suddenly expired in the camp of Bregetio. The passions, which had been so long suppressed by the presence of a master, immediately revived in the Imperial council; and the ambitious design of reigning in the name of an infant, was artfully executed by Mellobaudes and Equitius, who commanded the attachment of the Illyrian and Italian bands. They contrived the most honourable pretences to remove the popular leaders and the troops of Gaul, who might have asserted the claims of the lawful successor; they suggested the necessity of extinguishing the hopes of foreign and domestic enemies by a bold and decisive measure. The empress Justina, who had been left in a palace about one hundred miles from Bregetio, was respectfully invited to appear in the camp, with the son of the deceased emperor. On the sixth day after the death of Valentinian, the infant prince of the same name, who was only four years old, was shewn in the arms of his mother to the legions; and solemnly invested by military acclamation with the titles and ensigns of supreme power. The impending dangers of a civil war were seasonably prevented by the wise and moderate conduct of the emperor Gratian. He cheerfully accepted the choice of the army; declared that he should always consider the son of Justina as a brother, not as a rival; and advised the empress, with her son Valentinian, to fix their residence at Milan, in the fair and peaceful province of Italy; while he assumed the more arduous command of the countries beyond the Alps. Gratian dissembled his resentment till he could safely punish, or disgrace, the authors of the conspiracy; and, though he uniformly behaved with tenderness and regard to his infant colleague, he gradually confounded, in the administration of the Western empire, the office of a guardian with the authority of a sovereign. The government of the Roman world was exercised in the united names of Valens and his two nephews; but the feeble emperor of the East, who succeeded to the rank of his elder brother, never obtained any weight or influence in the councils of the West.[106]

[106] *Tillemont has proved that Gratian reigned in Italy, Africa, and Illyricum. I have endeavored to express his authority over his brother's dominions, as he used it, in an ambiguous style.*

XXVI

MANNERS OF THE PASTORAL NATIONS · PROGRESS OF THE
HUNS, FROM CHINA TO EUROPE · FLIGHT OF THE GOTHS ·
THEY PASS THE DANUBE · GOTHIC WAR · DEFEAT AND DEATH
OF VALENS · GRATIAN INVESTS THEODOSIUS WITH THE EAST-
ERN EMPIRE · HIS CHARACTER AND SUCCESS · PEACE AND SET-
TLEMENT OF GOTHS · DEATH AND FUNERAL OF ATHANARIC

I N T H E second year of the reign
of Valentinian and Valens, on the morning of the twenty-first day
of July, the greatest part of the Roman world was shaken by a violent and destructive earthquake. The impression was communicated to the waters; the shores of the Mediterranean were left dry,
by the sudden retreat of the sea; great quantities of fish were caught
with the hand; large vessels were stranded on the mud; and a curious spectator [1] amused his eye, or rather his fancy, by contemplating
the various appearance of valleys and mountains, which had never,
since the formation of the globe, been exposed to the sun. But the
tide soon returned, with the weight of an immense and irresistible
deluge, which was severely felt on the coast of Sicily, of Dalmatia,
of Greece, and of Egypt; large boats were transported, and lodged
on the roofs of houses, or at the distance of two miles from the
shore; the people, with their habitations, were swept away by the
waters; and the city of Alexandria annually commemorated the
fatal day on which fifty thousand persons had lost their lives in the
inundation. This calamity, the report of which was magnified from
one province to another, astonished and terrified the subjects of
Rome; and their affrighted imagination enlarged the real extent of
a momentary evil. They recollected the preceding earthquakes,
which had subverted the cities of Palestine and Bithynia; they considered these alarming strokes as the prelude only of still more
dreadful calamities, and their fearful vanity was disposed to confound the symptoms of a declining empire and a sinking world. [2]
It was the fashion of the times to attribute every remarkable event

[1] Such is the bad taste of Ammianus that it is not easy to distinguish his facts from his meta-phors. Yet he positively affirms that he saw the rotten carcase of a ship, ad secundum lapidem, at Methone, or Modon, in Peloponnesus.

[2] The earthquakes and inundations are variously described by Libanius, Zosimus, Sozomen, Cedrenus, and Jerom. Epidaurus must have been overwhelmed, had not the prudent citizens placed St. Hilarion, an Egyptian monk, on the beach. He made the sign of the cross; the mountain wave stopped, bowed, and returned.

to the particular will of the Deity; the alterations of nature were connected, by an invisible chain, with the moral and metaphysical opinions of the human mind; and the most sagacious divines could distinguish, according to the colour of their respective prejudices, that the establishment of heresy tended to produce an earthquake, or that a deluge was the inevitable consequence of the progress of sin and error. Without presuming to discuss the truth or propriety of these lofty speculations, the historian may content himself with an observation, which seems to be justified by experience, that man has much more to fear from the passions of his fellow-creatures than from the convulsions of the elements.[3] The mischievous effects of an earthquake or deluge, a hurricane, or the eruption of a volcano, bear a very inconsiderable proportion to the ordinary calamities of war, as they are now moderated by the prudence or humanity of the princes of Europe, who amuse their own leisure, and exercise the courage of their subjects, in the practice of the military art. But the laws and manners of modern nations protect the safety and freedom of the vanquished soldier; and the peaceful citizen has seldom reason to complain that his life, or even his fortune, is exposed to the rage of war. In the disastrous period of the fall of the Roman empire, which may justly be dated from the reign of Valens, the happiness and security of each individual were personally attacked; and the arts and labours of ages were rudely defaced by the Barbarians of Scythia and Germany. The invasion of the Huns precipitated on the provinces of the West the Gothic nation, which advanced, in less than forty years, from the Danube to the Atlantic, and opened a way, by the success of their arms, to the inroads of so many hostile tribes, more savage than themselves. The original principle of motion was concealed in the remote countries of the North; and the curious observation of the pastoral life of the Scythians,[4] or Tartars,[5] will illustrate the latent cause of these destructive emigrations.

The different characters that mark the civilized nations of the globe may be ascribed to the use, and the abuse, of reason; which so variously shapes, and so artificially composes, the manners and opinions of an European or a Chinese. But the operation of instinct is more sure and simple than that of reason: it is much easier to ascertain the appetites of a quadruped than the speculations of a philosopher; and the savage tribes of mankind, as they approach nearer to the condition of animals, preserve a stronger resemblance to themselves and to each other. The uniform stability of their man-

[3] *Dicæarchus, the Peripatetic, composed a formal treatise, to prove this obvious truth; which is not the most honourable to the human species.*

[4] *The original Scythians of Herodotus were confined by the Danube and the Palus Mæotis, within a square of 4000 stadia (400 Roman miles). Diodorus Siculus has marked the gradual progress of the* name *and* nation.

[5] *The* Tartars, *or* Tartars, *were a primitive tribe, the rivals, and at length the subjects, of the Moguls. In the victorious armies of Zingis Khan, and his successors, the Tartars formed the vanguard; and the name, which first reached the ears of foreigners, was applied to the whole nation. In speaking of all, or any, of the northern shepherds of Europe, or Asia, I indifferently use the appellations of* Scythians *or* Tartars.

THE FIRE WALL
FORUM OF AUGUSTUS

"Augustus built in Rome the temple and forum of Mars the Avenger; the Temple of Jupiter Tonans in the capitol; that of Apollo Palatine, with public libraries; the portico and basilica of Caius and Lucius; the porticoes of Livia and Octavia, and the theatre of Marcellus. The example of the sovereign was imitated by his ministers and generals; and his friend Agrippa left behind him the immortal monument of the Pantheon."

THE FIRE WALL OF THE FORUM OF AUGUSTUS

1. Church and Monastery of the Annuziata
2. So-called Arch of Pantani
3. Convent of S. Quirico

ners is the natural consequence of the imperfection of their faculties. Reduced to a similar situation, their wants, their desires, their enjoyments, still continue the same; and the influence of food or climate, which, in a more improved state of society, is suspended or subdued by so many moral causes, most powerfully contributes to form and to maintain the national character of Barbarians. In every age, the immense plains of Scythia or Tartary have been inhabited by vagrant tribes of hunters and shepherds, whose indolence refuses to cultivate the earth, and whose restless spirit disdains the confinement of a sedentary life. In every age, the Scythians and Tartars have been renowned for their invincible courage and rapid conquests. The thrones of Asia have been repeatedly overturned by the shepherds of the North; and their arms have spread terror and devastation over the most fertile and warlike countries of Europe. On this occasion, as well as on many others, the sober historian is forcibly awakened from a pleasing vision; and is compelled, with some reluctance, to confess that the pastoral manners which have been adorned with the fairest attributes of peace and innocence are much better adapted to the fierce and cruel habits of a military life. To illustrate this observation, I shall now proceed to consider a nation of shepherds and of warriors, in the three important articles of, I. Their diet; II. Their habitations; and, III. Their exercises. The narratives of antiquity are justified by the experience of modern times;[6] and the banks of the Borysthenes, of the Volga, or of the Selinga, will indifferently present the same uniform spectacle of similar and native manners.[7]

I. The corn, or even the rice, which constitutes the ordinary and wholesome food of a civilized people, can be obtained only by the patient toil of the husbandman. Some of the happy savages who dwell between the tropics are plentifully nourished by the liberality of nature; but in the climates of the North a nation of shepherds is reduced to their flocks and herds. The skilful practitioners of the medical art will determine (if they are able to determine) how far the temper of the human mind may be affected by the use of animal or of vegetable food; and whether the common association of carnivorous and cruel deserves to be considered in any other light than that of an innocent, perhaps a salutary, prejudice of humanity. Yet, if it be true that the sentiment of compassion is imperceptibly weakened by the sight and practice of domestic cruelty, we may observe that the horrid objects which are disguised by the arts of European refinement are exhibited, in their naked and most disgusting sim-

[6] *The fourth book of Herodotus affords a curious, though imperfect, portrait of the Scythians. Among the moderns, who describe the uniform scene, the Khan of Khowaresm, Abulghazi Bahadur, expresses his native feelings; and his Genealogical History of the Tartars has been copiously illustrated by the French and English editors. Carpin, Ascelin, and Rubruquis represent the Moguls of the fourteenth century. To these guides I have added Gerbillon, and the other Jesuits, who accurately surveyed the Chinese Tartary; and that honest and intelligent traveller, Bell of Antermony.*

[7] *The Uzbeks are the most altered from their primitive manners; 1, by the profession of the Mahometan religion; and, 2, by the possession of the cities and harvests of the great Bucharia.*

plicity, in the tent of a Tartarian shepherd. The ox and the sheep are slaughtered by the same hand from which they were accustomed to receive their daily food; and the bleeding limbs are served, with very little preparation, on the table of their unfeeling murderer. In the military profession, and especially in the conduct of a numerous army, the exclusive use of animal food appears to be productive of the most solid advantages. Corn is a bulky and perishable commodity; and the large magazines, which are indispensably necessary for the subsistence of our troops, must be slowly transported by the labour of men or horses. But the flocks and herds, which accompany the march of the Tartars, afford a sure and increasing supply of flesh and milk; in the far greater part of the uncultivated waste, the vegetation of the grass is quick and luxuriant; and there are few places so extremely barren that the hardy cattle of the North cannot find some tolerable pasture. The supply is multiplied and prolonged by the undistinguishing appetite and patient abstinence of the Tartars. They indifferently feed on the flesh of those animals that have been killed for the table or have died of disease. Horse-flesh, which in every age and country has been proscribed by the civilized nations of Europe and Asia, they devour with peculiar greediness; and this singular taste facilitates the success of their military operations. The active cavalry of Scythia is always followed, in their most distant and rapid incursions, by an adequate number of spare horses, who may be occasionally used, either to redouble the speed, or to satisfy the hunger, of the Barbarians. Many are the resources of courage and poverty. When the forage round a camp of Tartars is almost consumed, they slaughter the greatest part of their cattle, and preserve the flesh either smoked or dried in the sun. On the sudden emergency of a hasty march, they provide themselves with a sufficient quantity of little balls of cheese, or rather of hard curd, which they occasionally dissolve in water; and this unsubstantial diet will support, for many days, the life, and even the spirits, of the patient warrior. But this extraordinary abstinence, which the Stoic would approve and the hermit might envy, is commonly succeeded by the most voracious indulgence of appetite. The wines of a happier climate are the most grateful present, or the most valuable commodity, that can be offered to the Tartars; and the only example of their industry seems to consist in the art of extracting from mares' milk a fermented liquor, which possesses a very strong power of intoxication. Like the animals of prey, the savages, both of the old and new world, experience the alternate vicissitudes of famine and plenty; and their stomach is enured to sustain, without much inconvenience, the opposite extremes of hunger and of intemperance.

II. In the ages of rustic and martial simplicity, a people of soldiers and husbandmen are dispersed over the face of an extensive and cultivated country, and some time must elapse before the warlike youth of Greece or Italy could be assembled under the same standard, either to defend their own confines or to invade the territories of the adjacent tribes. The progress of manufactures and commerce insensibly collects a large multitude within the walls of a city; but these citizens are no longer soldiers; and the arts which adorn and improve the state of civil society corrupt the habits of a military life. The pastoral manners of the Scythians seem to unite the different advantages of simplicity and refinement. The individuals of the same tribe are constantly assembled, but they are assembled in a camp; and the native spirit of these dauntless shepherds is animated by mutual support and emulation. The houses of the Tartars are no more than small tents, of an oval form, which afford a cold and dirty habitation for the promiscuous youth of both sexes. The palaces of the rich consist of wooden huts, of such a size that they may be conveniently fixed on large waggons and drawn by a team perhaps of twenty or thirty oxen. The flocks and herds, after grazing all day in the adjacent pastures, retire, on the approach of night, within the protection of the camp. The necessity of preventing the most mischievous confusion, in such a perpetual concourse of men and animals, must gradually introduce, in the distribution, the order, and the guard of the encampment, the rudiments of the military art. As soon as the forage of a certain district is consumed, the tribe, or rather army, of shepherds makes a regular march to some fresh pastures; and thus acquires, in the ordinary occupations of the pastoral life, the practical knowledge of one of the most important and difficult operations of war. The choice of stations is regulated by the difference of the seasons: in the summer, the Tartars advance towards the North, and pitch their tents on the banks of a river, or, at least, in the neighbourhood of a running stream. But in the winter they return to the South, and shelter their camp behind some convenient eminence, against the winds which are chilled in their passage over the bleak and icy regions of Siberia. These manners are admirably adapted to diffuse, among the wandering tribes, the spirit of emigration and conquest. The connexion between the people and their territory is of so frail a texture that it may be broken by the slightest accident. The camp, and not the soil, is the native country of the genuine Tartar. Within the precincts of that camp, his family, his companions, his property are always included; and in the most distant marches he is still surrounded by the objects which are dear, or valuable, or familiar in his eyes. The thirst of rapine, the fear or the resentment of injury, the impatience of servitude, have, in every age, been sufficient causes to urge the tribes of Scythia boldly to advance into some unknown countries, where they might hope to find a more plentiful subsistence or a less formidable enemy. The revolutions of the North have frequently determined the fate of the South; and, in the conflict of hostile nations, the victor and the vanquished alternately drove and have been driven, from the confines of China to those of Germany.[8] These great emigrations, which have been sometimes executed with almost incredible diligence, were rendered more easy by the peculiar nature of the climate. It is well known that the cold of Tartary is much more severe than in the midst of the temperate zone might reasonably be expected: this uncommon rigour is attributed to the height of the plains, which rise, especially towards the East, more than half a mile above the level of the sea; and to the quantity of saltpetre with which the soil is deeply impregnated.[9] In the winter-season, the broad and rapid rivers, that discharge their waters into the Euxine, the Caspian, or the Icy Sea, are strongly frozen; the fields are covered with a bed of snow; and the fugitive or victorious tribes may securely traverse, with their families, their waggons, and their cattle, the smooth and hard surface of an immense plain.

III. The pastoral life, compared with the labours of agriculture and manufactures, is undoubtedly a life of idleness; and, as the most honourable shepherds of the Tartar race devolve on their captives the domestic management of the cattle, their own leisure is seldom disturbed by any servile and assiduous cares. But this leisure, instead of being devoted to the soft enjoyments of love and harmony, is usefully spent in the violent and sanguinary exercise of the chase. The plains of Tartary are filled with a strong and serviceable breed of horses, which are easily trained for the purposes of war and hunting. The Scythians of every age have been celebrated as bold and skilful riders; and constant practice had seated them so firmly on horseback that they were supposed by strangers to perform the ordinary duties of civil life, to eat, to drink, and even to sleep, without dismounting from their steeds. They excel in the dexterous management of the lance; the long Tartar bow is drawn with a

[8] *These Tartar emigrations have been discovered by M. de Guignes, a skilful and laborious interpreter of the Chinese language; who has thus laid open new and important scenes in the history of mankind.*

[9] *A plain in the Chinese Tartary, only eighty leagues from the great wall, was found by the missionaries to be three thousand geometrical paces above the level of the sea. Montesquieu, who has used, and abused, the relations of travellers, deduces the revolutions of Asia from this important circumstance that heat and cold, weakness and strength, touch each other without any temperate zone.*

nervous arm; and the weighty arrow is directed to its object with unerring aim and irresistible force. These arrows are often pointed against the harmless animals of the desert, which increase and multiply in the absence of their most formidable enemy: the hare, the goat, the roebuck, the fallow-deer, the stag, the elk, and the antelope. The vigour and patience both of the men and horses are continually exercised by the fatigues of the chase; and the plentiful supply of game contributes to the subsistence, and even luxury, of a Tartar camp. But the exploits of the hunters of Scythia are not confined to the destruction of timid or innoxious beasts; they boldly encounter the angry wild boar, when he turns against his pursuers, excite the sluggish courage of the bear, and provoke the fury of the tiger, as he slumbers in the thicket. Where there is danger, there may be glory; and the mode of hunting which opens the fairest field to the exertions of valour may justly be considered as the image and as the school of war. The general hunting-matches, the pride and delight of the Tartar princes, compose an instructive exercise for their numerous cavalry. A circle is drawn, of many miles in circumference, to encompass the game of an extensive district; and the troops that form the circle regularly advance towards a common centre; where the captive animals, surrounded on every side, are abandoned to the darts of the hunters. In this march, which frequently continues many days, the cavalry are obliged to climb the hills, to swim the rivers, and to wind through the valleys, without interrupting the prescribed order of their gradual progress. They acquire the habit of directing their eye, and their steps, to a remote object; of preserving their intervals; of suspending, or accelerating, their pace, according to the motions of the troops on their right and left; and of watching and repeating the signals of their leaders. Their leaders study, in this practical school, the most important lesson of the military art: the prompt and accurate judgment of ground, of distance, and of time. To employ against a human enemy the same patience and valour, the same skill and discipline, is the only alteration which is required in real war; and the amusements of the chase serve as a prelude to the conquest of an empire.[10]

The political society of the ancient Germans has the appearance of a voluntary alliance of independent warriors. The tribes of Scythia, distinguished by the modern appellation of *Hords*, assume the form of a numerous and increasing family; which, in the course of successive generations, has been propagated from the same origi-

[10] *Petit de la Croix represents the full glory and extent of the Mogul chase. The Jesuits Gerbillon and Verbiest followed the emperor Kamhi when he hunted in Tartary. His grandson, Kienlong, who unites the Tartar discipline with the laws and learning of China, describes, as a poet, the pleasures which he had often enjoyed as a sportsman.*

nal stock. The meanest and most ignorant of the Tartars preserve, with conscious pride, the inestimable treasure of their genealogy; and, whatever distinctions of rank may have been introduced by the unequal distribution of pastoral wealth, they mutually respect themselves, and each other, as the descendants of the first founder of the tribe. The custom, which still prevails, of adopting the bravest and most faithful of the captives may countenance the very probable suspicion that this extensive consanguinity is, in a great measure, legal and fictitious. But the useful prejudice, which has obtained the sanction of time and opinion, produces the effects of truth; the haughty Barbarians yield a cheerful and voluntary obedience to the head of their blood; and their chief or *mursa,* as the representative of their great father, exercises the authority of a judge, in peace, and of a leader, in war. In the original state of the pastoral world, each of the *mursas* (if we may continue to use a modern appellation) acted as the independent chief of a large and separate family; and the limits of their peculiar territories were gradually fixed by superior force or mutual consent. But the constant operation of various and permanent causes contributed to unite the vagrant Hords into national communities, under the command of a supreme head. The weak were desirous of support, and the strong were ambitious of dominion; the power, which is the result of union, oppressed and collected the divided forces of the adjacent tribes; and, as the vanquished were freely admitted to share the advantages of victory, the most valiant chiefs hastened to range themselves and their followers under the formidable standard of a confederate nation. The most successful of the Tartar princes assumed the military command, to which he was entitled by the superiority either of merit or of power. He was raised to the throne by the acclamations of his equals; and the title of *Khan* expresses, in the language of the North of Asia, the full extent of the regal dignity. The right of hereditary succession was long confined to the blood of the founder of the monarchy; and at this moment all the Khans, who reign from Crimea to the wall of China, are the lineal descendants of the renowned Zingis.[11] But, as it is the indispensable duty of a Tartar sovereign to lead his warlike subjects into the field, the claims of an infant are often disregarded; and some royal kinsman, distinguished by his age and valour, is intrusted with the sword and sceptre of his predecessor. Two distinct and regular taxes are levied on the tribes, to support the dignity of their national monarch and of their peculiar chief; and each of those con-

[11] *See the second volume of the Genealogical History of the Tartars, and the list of the Khans, at the end of the life of Gengis, or Zingis. Under the reign of Timur, or Tamerlane, one of his subjects, a descendant of Zingis, still bore the regal appellation of Khan; and the conqueror of Asia contented himself with the title of Emir, or Sultan.*

tributions amounts to the tythe both of their property and of their spoil. A Tartar sovereign enjoys the tenth part of the wealth of his people; and, as his own domestic riches of flocks and herds increase in a much larger proportion, he is able plentifully to maintain the rustic splendour of his court, to reward the most deserving, or the more favoured, of his followers, and to obtain, from the gentle influence of corruption, the obedience which might be sometimes refused to the stern mandates of authority. The manners of his subjects, accustomed, like himself, to blood and rapine, might excuse, in their eyes, such partial acts of tyranny as would excite the horror of a civilized people; but the power of a despot has never been acknowledged in the deserts of Scythia. The immediate jurisdiction of the Khan is confined within the limits of his own tribe; and the exercise of his royal prerogative has been moderated by the ancient institution of a national council. The Coroultai, or Diet, of the Tartars was regularly held in the spring and autumn, in the midst of a plain; where the princes of the reigning family and the mursas of the respective tribes may conveniently assemble on horseback, with their martial and numerous trains; and the ambitious monarch, who reviewed the strength, must consult the inclination, of an armed people. The rudiments of a feudal government may be discovered in the constitution of the Scythian or Tartar nations; but the perpetual conflict of these hostile nations has sometimes terminated in the establishment of a powerful and despotic empire. The victor, enriched by the tribute, and fortified by the arms, of dependent kings, has spread his conquests over Europe or Asia; the successful shepherds of the North have submitted to the confinement of arts, of laws, and of cities; and the introduction of luxury, after destroying the freedom of the people, has undermined the foundations of the throne.[12]

The memory of past events cannot long be preserved, in the frequent and remote emigrations of illiterate Barbarians. The modern Tartars are ignorant of the conquests of their ancestors;[13] and our knowledge of the history of the Scythians is derived from their intercourse with the learned and civilized nations of the South, the Greeks, the Persians, and the Chinese. The Greeks, who navigated the Euxine, and planted their colonies along the sea-coast, made the gradual and imperfect discovery of Scythia; from the Danube, and the confines of Thrace, as far as the frozen Mæotis, the seat of eternal winter, and Mount Caucasus, which, in the language of poetry, was described as the utmost boundary of the earth. They

[12] *Montesquieu labours to explain a difference which has not existed between the liberty of the Arabs and the perpetual slavery of the Tartars.*

[13] *Abulghazi Khan, in the two first parts of his Genealogical History, relates the miserable fables and traditions of the Uzbek Tartars concerning the times which preceded the reign of Zingis.*

[14] *In the thirteenth book of the Iliad Jupiter turns away his eyes from the bloody fields of Troy to the plains of Thrace and Scythia. He would not, by changing the prospect, behold a more peaceful or innocent scene.*

[15] *When Darius advanced into the Moldavian desert, between the Danube and the Dneister, the king of the Scythians sent him a mouse, a frog, a bird, and five arrows; a tremendous allegory!*

[16] *The Caspian Sea, and its rivers and adjacent tribes, are laboriously illustrated in the Examen Critique des Historiens d'Alexandre, which compares the true geography and the errors produced by the vanity or ignorance of the Greeks.*

[17] *The original seat of the nation appears to have been in the Northwest of China, in the provinces of Chensi and Chansi. Under the first two dynasties, the principal town was still a moveable camp; the villages were thinly scattered; more land was employed in pasture than in tillage; the exercise of hunting was ordained to clear the country from wild beasts; Petcheli (where Pekin stands)*

celebrated, with simple credulity, the virtues of the pastoral life.[14] They entertained a more rational apprehension of the strength and numbers of the warlike Barbarians, who contemptuously baffled the immense armament of Darius, the son of Hystaspes.[15] The Persian monarchs had extended their western conquests to the banks of the Danube and the limits of European Scythia. The eastern provinces of their empire were exposed to the Scythians of Asia: the wild inhabitants of the plains beyond the Oxus and the Jaxartes, two mighty rivers, which direct their course towards the Caspian Sea. The long and memorable quarrel of Iran and Touran is still the theme of history or romance; the famous, perhaps the fabulous, valour of the Persian heroes, Rustan and Asfendiar, was signalized in the defence of their country against the Afrasiabs of the North; and the invincible spirit of the same Barbarians resisted, on the same ground, the victorious arms of Cyrus and Alexander.[16] In the eyes of the Greeks and Persians, the real geography of Scythia was bounded, on the East, by the mountains of Imaus, or Caf; and their distant prospect of the extreme and inaccessible parts of Asia was clouded by ignorance or perplexed by fiction. But those inaccessible regions are the ancient residence of a powerful and civilized nation,[17] which ascends, by a probable tradition, above forty centuries;[18] and which is able to verify a series of near two thousand years, by the perpetual testimony of accurate and contemporary historians.[19] The annals of China illustrate the state and revolutions of the pastoral tribes, which may still be distinguished by the vague appellation of Scythians, or Tartars; the vassals, the enemies, and sometimes the conquerors, of a great empire; whose policy has uniformly opposed the blind and impetuous valour of the Barbarians of the North. From the mouth of the Danube to the sea of Japan, the whole longitude of Scythia is about one hundred and ten degrees, which, in that parallel, are equal to more than five thousand miles. The latitude of these extensive deserts cannot be so easily or so accurately measured; but, from the fortieth degree, which touches the wall of China, we may securely advance above a thousand miles to the northward, till our progress is stopped by the excessive cold of Siberia. In that dreary climate, instead of the animated picture of a Tartar camp, the smoke which issues from the earth, or rather from the snow, betrays the subterraneous dwellings of the Tongouses and the Samoiedes: the want of horses and oxen is imperfectly supplied by the use of reindeer and of large dogs; and the conquerors of the earth insensibly degenerate into a race of deformed and diminutive savages, who tremble in fear at the sound of arms.

The Huns, who under the reign of Valens threatened the empire of Rome, had been formidable, in a much earlier period, to the empire of China. Their ancient, perhaps their original, seat was an extensive, though dry and barren, tract of country, immediately on the north side of the great wall. Their place is at present occupied by the forty-nine Hords or Banners of the Mongous, a pastoral nation, which consists of about two hundred thousand families. But the valour of the Huns had extended the narrow limits of their dominions; and their rustic chiefs, who assumed the appellation of *Tanjou,* gradually became the conquerors, and the sovereigns, of a formidable empire. Towards the East, their victorious arms were stopped only by the ocean; and the tribes, which are thinly scattered between the Amoor and the extreme peninsula of Corea, adhered with reluctance to the standard of the Huns. On the West, near the head of the Irtish and in the valleys of Imaus, they found a more ample space, and more numerous enemies. One of the lieutenants of the Tanjou subdued in a single expedition twenty-six nations; the Igours,[20] distinguished above the Tartar race by the use of letters, were in the number of his vassals; and by the strange connexion of human events, the flight of one of those vagrant tribes recalled the victorious Parthians from the invasion of Syria. On the side of the North, the ocean was assigned as the limit of the power of the Huns. Without enemies to resist their progress or witnesses to contradict their vanity, they might securely achieve a real, or imaginary, conquest of the frozen regions of Siberia. The *Northern Sea* was fixed as the remote boundary of their empire. But the name of that sea, on whose shores the patriot Sovou embraced the life of a shepherd and an exile,[21] may be transferred, with much more probability, to the Baikal, a capacious basin, above three hundred miles in length, which disdains the modest appellation of a lake,[22] and which actually communicates with the seas of the North, by the long course of the Angara, the Tonguska, and the Jenissea. The submission of so many distant nations might flatter the pride of the Tanjou; but the valour of the Huns could be rewarded only by the enjoyment of the wealth and luxury of the empire of the South. In the third century before the Christian æra, a wall of fifteen hundred miles in length was constructed, to defend the frontiers of China against the inroads of the Huns; but this stupendous work, which holds a conspicuous place in the map of the world, has never contributed to the safety of an unwarlike people. The cavalry of the Tanjou frequently

was a desert, and the southern provinces were peopled with Indian savages. The dynasty of the Han (*before Christ 206*) gave the empire its actual form and extent.

[18] *The æra of the Chinese monarchy has been variously fixed, from 2952 to 2132 years before Christ; and the year 2637 has been chosen for the lawful epoch by the authority of the present emperor. The difference arises from the uncertain duration of the first two dynasties; and the vacant space that lies beyond them as far as the real, or fabulous, times of Fohi, or Hoangti. Sematsien dates his authentic chronology from the year 841: the thirty-six eclipses of Confucius (thirty-one of which have been verified) were observed between the years 722 and 480 before Christ.* The historical period *of China does not ascend above the Greek Olympiads.*

[19] *After several ages of anarchy and despotism, the dynasty of the Han (before Christ 206) was the æra of the revival of learning. The fragments of ancient literature were restored; the characters were improved and fixed, and the future preservation of books was secured by the use-*

consisted of two or three hundred thousand men, formidable by the matchless dexterity with which they managed their bows and their horses; by their hardy patience in supporting the inclemency of the weather; and by the incredible speed of their march, which was sel-dom checked by torrents or precipices, by the deepest rivers or by the most lofty mountains. They spread themselves at once over the face of the country; and their rapid impetuosity surprised, aston-ished, and disconcerted the grave and elaborate tactics of a Chinese army. The emperor Kaoti, a soldier of fortune, whose personal merit had raised him to the throne, marched against the Huns with those veteran troops which had been trained in the civil wars of China. But he was soon surrounded by the Barbarians; and after a siege of seven days, the monarch, hopeless of relief, was reduced to purchase his deliverance by an ignominious capitulation. The suc-cessors of Kaoti, whose lives were dedicated to the arts of peace or the luxury of the palace, submitted to a more permanent disgrace. They too hastily confessed the insufficiency of arms and fortifica-tions. They were too easily convinced that, while the blazing signals announced on every side the approach of the Huns, the Chinese troops, who slept with the helmet on their head and the cuirass on their back, were destroyed by the incessant labour of ineffectual marches. A regular payment of money and silk was stipulated as the condition of a temporary and precarious peace; and the wretched expedient of disguising a real tribute under the names of a gift or a subsidy was practised by the emperors of China, as well as by those of Rome. But there still remained a more disgraceful article of tribute, which violated the sacred feelings of humanity and nature. The hardships of the savage life, which destroy in their infancy the children who are born with a less healthy and robust constitution, introduce a remarkable disproportion between the numbers of the two sexes. The Tartars are an ugly, and even deformed race; and, while they consider their own women as the instruments of domes-tic labour, their desires, or rather their appetites, are directed to the enjoyment of more elegant beauty. A select band of the fairest maidens of China was annually devoted to the rude embraces of the Huns; and the alliance of the haughty Tanjous was secured by their marriage with the genuine, or adopted, daughters of the Im-perial family, which vainly attempted to escape the sacrilegious pol-lution. The situation of these unhappy victims is described in the verses of a Chinese princess, who laments that she had been con-demned by her parents to a distant exile, under a Barbarian husband; who complains that sour milk was her only drink, raw flesh her only food, a tent her only palace; and who expresses, in a strain of pathetic simplicity, the natural wish that she were transformed into a bird, to fly back to her dear country; the object of her tender and perpetual regret.

The conquest of China has been twice achieved by the pastoral tribes of the North: the forces of the Huns were not inferior to those of the Moguls, or of the Mantcheoux; and their ambition might entertain the most sanguine hopes of success. But their pride was humbled, and their progress was checked, by the arms and policy of Vouti, the fifth emperor of the powerful dynasty of the Han. In his long reign of fifty-four years, the Barbarians of the southern provinces submitted to the laws and manners of China; and the ancient limits of the monarchy were enlarged, from the great river of Kiang to the port of Canton. Instead of confining himself to the timid operations of a defensive war, his lieutenants penetrated many hundred miles into the country of the Huns. In those boundless deserts, where it is impossible to form magazines and difficult to transport a sufficient supply of provisions, the armies of Vouti were repeatedly exposed to intolerable hardships: and, of one hundred and forty thousand soldiers, who marched against the Barbarians, thirty thousand only returned in safety to the feet of their master. These losses, however, were compensated by splendid and decisive success. The Chinese generals improved the superiority which they derived from the temper of their arms, their chariots of war, and the service of their Tartar auxiliaries. The camp of the Tanjou was surprised in the midst of sleep and intemperance; and, though the monarch of the Huns bravely cut his way through the ranks of the enemy, he left above fifteen thousand of his subjects on the field of battle. Yet this signal victory, which was preceded and followed by many bloody engagements, contributed much less to the destruction of the power of the Huns than the effectual policy which was employed to detach the tributary nations from their obedience. Intimidated by the arms, or allured by the promises, of Vouti and his successors, the most considerable tribes, both of the East and of the West, disclaimed the authority of the Tanjou. While some acknowledged themselves the allies or vassals of the empire, they all became the implacable enemies of the Huns: and the numbers of that haughty people, as soon as they were reduced to their native strength, might, perhaps, have been contained within the walls of one of the great and populous cities of China.[23] The desertion

[23] *This expression is used in the memorial to the emperor Venti. Without adopting the exaggerations of Marco-Polo and Isaac Vossius, we may rationally allow for Pekin two millions of inhabitants. The cities of the South, which contain the manufactures of China, are still more populous.*

of his subjects, and the perplexity of a civil war, at length compelled the Tanjou himself to renounce the dignity of an independent sovereign and the freedom of a warlike and high-spirited nation. He was received at Sigan, the capital of the monarchy, by the troops, the Mandarins, and the emperor himself, with all the honours that could adorn and disguise the triumph of Chinese vanity. A magnificent palace was prepared for his reception; his place was assigned above all the princes of the royal family; and the patience of the Barbarian king was exhausted by the ceremonies of a banquet, which consisted of eight courses of meat, and of nine solemn pieces of music. But he performed, on his knees, the duty of a respectful homage to the emperor of China; pronounced, in his own name, and in the name of his successors, a perpetual oath of fidelity; and gratefully accepted a seal, which was bestowed as the emblem of his regal dependence. After this humiliating submission, the Tanjous sometimes departed from their allegiance, and seized the favourable moments of war and rapine; but the monarchy of the Huns gradually declined, till it was broken, by civil dissension, into two hostile and separate kingdoms. One of the princes of the nation was urged, by fear and ambition, to retire towards the South with eight hordes, which composed between forty and fifty thousand families. He obtained, with the title of Tanjou, a convenient territory on the verge of the Chinese provinces; and his constant attachment to the service of the empire was secured by weakness and the desire of revenge. From the time of this fatal schism, the Huns of the North continued to languish about fifty years; till they were oppressed on every side by their foreign and domestic enemies. The proud inscription [24] of a column, erected on a lofty mountain, announced to posterity that a Chinese army had marched seven hundred miles into the heart of their country. The Sienpi, a tribe of Oriental Tartars, retaliated the injuries which they had formerly sustained; and the power of the Tanjous, after a reign of thirteen hundred years, was utterly destroyed before the end of the first century of the Christian æra. [25]

The fate of the vanquished Huns was diversified by the various influence of character and situation. [26] Above one hundred thousand persons, the poorest, indeed, and the most pusillanimous of the people, were contented to remain in their native country, to renounce their peculiar name and origin, and to mingle with the victorious nation of the Sienpi. Fifty-eight hords, about two hundred thousand men, ambitious of a more honourable servitude, retired

[24] *This inscription was composed on the spot by Pankou, President of the Tribunal of History. Similar monuments have been discovered in many parts of Tartary.*

[25] *The æra of the Huns is placed, by the Chinese, 1210 years before Christ. But the series of their kings does not commence till the year 230.*

[26] *The various accidents, the downfall, and flight of the Huns are related in the Khan-Mou. The small numbers of each horde may be ascribed to their losses and divisions.*

towards the South; implored the protection of the emperors of China; and were permitted to inhabit, and to guard, the extreme frontiers of the province of Chansi and the territory of Ortous. But the most warlike and powerful tribes of the Huns maintained, in their adverse fortune, the undaunted spirit of their ancestors. The western world was open to their valour; and they resolved, under the conduct of their hereditary chieftains, to discover and subdue some remote country, which was still inaccessible to the arms of the Sienpi and to the laws of China. The course of their emigration soon carried them beyond the mountains of Imaus, and the limits of the Chinese geography, but *we* are able to distinguish the two great divisions of these formidable exiles, which directed their march towards the Oxus, and towards the Volga. The first of these colonies established their dominion in the fruitful and extensive plains of Sogdiana, on the eastern side of the Caspian: where they preserved the name of Huns, with the epithet of Euthalites or Nepthalites. Their manners were softened, and even their features were insensibly improved, by the mildness of the climate and their long residence in a flourishing province [27] which might still retain a faint impression of the arts of Greece.[28] The *white* Huns, a name which they derived from the change of their complexions, soon abandoned the pastoral life of Scythia. Gorgo, which, under the appellation of Carizme, has since enjoyed a temporary splendour, was the residence of the king, who exercised a legal authority over an obedient people. Their luxury was maintained by the labour of the Sogdians; and the only vestige of their ancient barbarism was the custom which obliged all the companions, perhaps to the number of twenty, who had shared the liberality of a wealthy lord, to be buried alive in the same grave. The vicinity of the Huns to the provinces of Persia involved them in frequent and bloody contests with the power of that monarchy. But they respected, in peace, the faith of treaties; in war, the dictates of humanity; and their memorable victory over Peroses, or Firuz, displayed the moderation, as well as the valour, of the Barbarians. The *second* division of their countrymen, the Huns, who gradually advanced towards the North-west, were exercised by the hardships of a colder climate and a more laborious march. Necessity compelled them to exchange the silks of China for the furs of Siberia; the imperfect rudiments of civilized life were obliterated; and the native fierceness of the Huns was exasperated by their intercourse with the savage tribes, who were compared, with some propriety, to the wild beasts of the desert. Their

[27] *Mohammed, Sultan of Carizme, reigned in Sogdiana, when it was invaded (A.D. 1218) by Zingis and his Moguls. The Oriental historians celebrate the populous cities which he ruined, and the fruitful country which he desolated. In the next century, the same provinces of Chorasmia and Mawaralnahr were described by Abulfeda. Their actual misery may be seen in the Genealogical History of the Tartars.*

[28] *Justin has left a short abridgment of the Greek kings of Bactriana. To their industry I should ascribe the new and extraordinary trade, which transported the merchandises of India into Europe, by the Oxus, the Caspian, the Cyrus, the Phasis, and the Euxine. The other ways, both of the land and sea, were possessed by the Seleucides and the Ptolemies.*

29 *In the thirteenth century, the monk Rubru-
quis (who traversed the
immense plain of Kip-
zak, in his journey to the
court of the Great Khan)
observed the remarkable
name of* Hungary, *with
the traces of a common
language and origin.*

30 *This great transmigration of 300,000 Cal-
mucks, or Torgouts,
happened in the year
1771. The original nar-
rative of Kienlong, the
reigning emperor of
China, which was in-
tended for the inscrip-
tion of a column, has
been translated by the
missionaries of Pekin.
The emperor affects the
smooth and specious
language of the Son of
Heaven and the Father
of his People.*

31 *The Kang-Mou as-
cribes to their conquest a
space of 14,000 lis. Ac-
cording to the standard,
200 lis (or more accu-
rately 193) are equal to
one degree of latitude;
and one English mile
consequently exceeds
three miles of China.
But there are strong
reasons to believe that
the ancient* li *scarcely
equalled one-half of the
modern. See the elabo-
rate researches of M.
d'Anville, a geographer
who is not a stranger in
any age, or climate, of
the globe.*

independent spirit soon rejected the hereditary succession of the Tanjous; and, while each hord was governed by its peculiar mursa, their tumultuary council directed the public measures of the whole nation. As late as the thirteenth century, their transient residence on the Eastern banks of the Volga was attested by the name of Great Hungary.[29] In the winter, they descended with their flocks and herds towards the mouth of that mighty river; and their summer excursions reached as high as the latitude of Saratoff, or perhaps the conflux of the Kama. Such at least were the recent limits of the black Calmucks, who remained about a century under the protection of Russia; and who have since returned to their native seats on the frontiers of the Chinese empire. The march and the return of those wandering Tartars, whose united camp consists of fifty thousand tents or families, illustrate the distant emigrations of the ancient Huns.[30]

It is impossible to fill the dark interval of time, which elapsed, after the Huns of the Volga were lost in the eyes of the Chinese, and before they shewed themselves to those of the Romans. There is some reason, however, to apprehend, that the same force which had driven them from their native seats, still continued to impel their march towards the frontiers of Europe. The power of the Sienpi, their implacable enemies, which extended above three thousand miles from East to West,[31] must have gradually oppressed them by the weight and terror of a formidable neighbourhood; and the flight of the tribes of Scythia would inevitably tend to increase the strength, or to contract the territories, of the Huns. The harsh and obscure appellations of those tribes would offend the ear, without informing the understanding, of the reader; but I cannot suppress the very natural suspicion, *that* the Huns of the North derived a considerable reinforcement from the ruin of the dynasty of the South, which, in the course of the third century, submitted to the dominion of China; *that* the bravest warriors marched away in search of their free and adventurous countrymen; *and* that, as they had been divided by prosperity, they were easily reunited by the common hardships of their adverse fortune.[32] The Huns, with their flocks and herds, their wives and children, their dependents and allies, were transported to the West of the Volga, and they boldly advanced to invade the country of the Alani, a pastoral people who occupied, or wasted, an extensive tract of the deserts of Scythia. The plains between the Volga and the Tanais were covered with the tents of the Alani, but their name and manners were diffused over

the wide extent of their conquests; and the painted tribes of the
Agathyrsi and Geloni were confounded among their vassals. Towards the North, they penetrated into the frozen regions of Siberia,
among the savages who were accustomed, in their rage or hunger,
to the taste of human flesh; and their Southern inroads were pushed
as far as the confines of Persia and India. The mixture of Sarmatic
and German blood had contributed to improve the features of the
Alani, to whiten their swarthy complexions, and to tinge their hair
with a yellowish cast, which is seldom found in the Tartar race.
They were less deformed in their persons, less brutish in their manners, than the Huns; but they did not yield to those formidable Barbarians in their martial and independent spirit; in the love of freedom, which rejected even the use of domestic slaves; and in the love
of arms, which considered war and rapine as the pleasure and the
glory of mankind. A naked scymetar, fixed in the ground, was the
only object of their religious worship; the scalps of their enemies
formed the costly trappings of their horses; and they viewed, with
pity and contempt, the pusillanimous warriors, who patiently expected the infirmities of age and the tortures of lingering disease.
On the banks of the Tanais, the military power of the Huns and the
Alani, encountered each other with equal valour, but with unequal
success. The Huns prevailed in the bloody contest: the king of the
Alani was slain; and the remains of the vanquished nation were
dispersed by the ordinary alternative of flight or submission. A colony of exiles found a secure refuge in the mountains of Caucasus,
between the Euxine and the Caspian; where they still preserve their
name and their independence. Another colony advanced, with
more intrepid courage, towards the shores of the Baltic; associated
themselves with the Northern tribes of Germany; and shared the
spoil of the Roman provinces of Gaul and Spain. But the greatest
part of the nation of the Alani embraced the offers of an honourable
and advantageous union; and the Huns, who esteemed the valour
of their less fortunate enemies, proceeded, with an increase of numbers and confidence, to invade the limits of the Gothic empire.

The great Hermanric, whose dominions extended from the Baltic to the Euxine, enjoyed, in the full maturity of age and reputation, the fruit of his victories, when he was alarmed by the formidable
approach of an host of unknown enemies,[33] on whom his barbarous
subjects might, without injustice, bestow the epithet of Barbarians.
The numbers, the strength, the rapid motions, and the implacable
cruelty of the Huns were felt and dreaded and magnified by the

[32] *The subsequent his-
tory of three or four
Hunnic dynasties evi-
dently proves that their
martial spirit was not
impaired by a long resi-
dence in China.*

[33] *As we are possessed of
the authentic history of
the Huns, it would be
impertinent to repeat, or
to refute, the fables,
which misrepresent their
origin and progress, their
passage of the mud or
water of the Mæotis, in
pursuit of an ox or stag.*

astonished Goths; who beheld their fields and villages consumed with flames and deluged with indiscriminate slaughter. To these real terrors they added the surprise and abhorrence which were excited by the shrill voice, the uncouth gestures, and the strange deformity, of the Huns. These savages of Scythia were compared (and the picture had some resemblance) to the animals who walk very awkwardly on two legs; and to the misshapen figures, the *Termini*, which were often placed on the bridges of antiquity. They were distinguished from the rest of the human species by their broad shoulders, flat noses, and small black eyes, deeply buried in the head; and, as they were almost destitute of beards, they never enjoyed either the manly graces of youth or the venerable aspects of age. A fabulous origin was assigned worthy of their form and manners; that the witches of Scythia, who, for their foul and deadly practices, had been driven from society, had copulated in the desert with infernal spirits; and that the Huns were the offspring of this execrable conjunction.[34] The tale, so full of horror and absurdity, was greedily embraced by the credulous hatred of the Goths; but, while it gratified their hatred, it increased their fear; since the posterity of demons and witches might be supposed to inherit some share of the preternatural powers, as well as of the malignant temper, of their parents. Against these enemies, Hermanric prepared to exert the united forces of the Gothic state; but he soon discovered that his vassal tribes, provoked by oppression, were much more inclined to second, than to repel, the invasion of the Huns. One of the chiefs of the Roxolani[35] had formerly deserted the standard of Hermanric, and the cruel tyrant had condemned the innocent wife of the traitor to be torn asunder by wild horses. The brother of that unfortunate woman seized the favourable moment of revenge. The aged king of the Goths languished some time after the dangerous wound which he received from their daggers; but the conduct of the war was retarded by his infirmities, and the public councils of the nation were distracted by a spirit of jealousy and discord. His death, which has been imputed to his own despair, left the reins of government in the hands of Withimer, who, with the doubtful aid of some Scythian mercenaries, maintained the unequal contest against the arms of the Huns and the Alani, till he was defeated and slain in a decisive battle. The Ostrogoths submitted to their fate; and the royal race of the Amali will hereafter be found among the subjects of the haughty Attila. But the person of Witheric, the infant king, was saved by the diligence of Alatheus and Saphrax: two warriors

[34] *This execrable origin, which Jornandes describes with the rancour of a Goth, might be originally derived from a more pleasing fable of the Greeks.*

[35] *The Roxolani may be the fathers of the* Ῥῶς, *the* Russians, *whose residence (A.D. 862) about Novgorod Veliki cannot be very remote from that which the Geographer of Ravenna assigns to the Roxolani (A.D. 886).*

of approved valour and fidelity; who, by cautious marches, conducted the independent remains of the nation of the Ostrogoths towards the Danastus, or Dniester, a considerable river, which now separates the Turkish dominions from the empire of Russia. On the banks of the Dniester the prudent Athanaric, more attentive to his own than to the general safety, had fixed the camp of the Visigoths; with the firm resolution of opposing the victorious Barbarians whom he thought it less advisable to provoke. The ordinary speed of the Huns was checked by the weight of baggage, and the encumbrance of captives; but their military skill deceived, and almost destroyed, the army of Athanaric. While the judge of the Visigoths defended the banks of the Dniester, he was encompassed and attacked by a numerous detachment of cavalry, who, by the light of the moon, had passed the river in a fordable place; and it was not without the utmost efforts of courage and conduct that he was able to effect his retreat towards the hilly country. The undaunted general had already formed a new and judicious plan of defensive war; and the strong lines, which he was preparing to construct between the mountains, the Pruth, and the Danube, would have secured the extensive and fertile territory that bears the modern name of Walachia from the destructive inroads of the Huns.[36] But the hopes and measures of the judge of the Visigoths were soon disappointed by the trembling impatience of his dismayed countrymen; who were persuaded by their fears that the interposition of the Danube was the only barrier that could save them from the rapid pursuit and invincible valour of the Barbarians of Scythia. Under the command of Fritigern and Alavivus,[37] the body of the nation hastily advanced to the banks of the great river, and implored the protection of the Roman emperor of the East. Athanaric himself, still anxious to avoid the guilt of perjury, retired with a band of faithful followers into the mountainous country of Caucaland; which appears to have been guarded, and almost concealed, by the impenetrable forests of Transylvania.[38]

After Valens had terminated the Gothic war with some appearance of glory and success, he made a progress through his dominions of Asia, and at length fixed his residence in the capital of Syria. The five years[39] which he spent at Antioch were employed to watch, from a secure distance, the hostile designs of the Persian monarch; to check the depredations of the Saracens and Isaurians;[40] to enforce, by arguments more prevalent than those of reason and eloquence, the belief of the Arian theology; and to satisfy his anxious suspi-

[36] The text of Ammianus seems to be imperfect or corrupt; but the nature of the ground explains, and almost defines, the Gothic rampart.

[37] M. de Buat has conceived a strange idea that Alavivus was the same person as Ulphilas the Gothic bishop: and that Ulphilas, the grandson of a Cappadocian captive, became a temporal prince of the Goths.

[38] Ammianus and Jornandes describe the subversion of the Gothic empire by the Huns.

[39] The chronology of Ammianus is obscure and imperfect. Tillemont has laboured to clear and settle the Annals of Valens.

[40] The Isaurians, each winter, infested the roads of Asia Minor, as far as the neighbourhood of Constantinople.

cions by the promiscuous execution of the innocent and the guilty. But the attention of the emperor was most seriously engaged by the important intelligence which he received from the civil and military officers who were intrusted with the defence of the Danube. He was informed that the North was agitated by a furious tempest; that the irruption of the Huns, an unknown and monstrous race of savages, had subverted the power of the Goths; and that the suppliant multitudes of that warlike nation, whose pride was now humbled in the dust, covered a space of many miles along the banks of the river. With outstretched arms and pathetic lamentations, they loudly deplored their past misfortunes and their present danger; acknowledged that their only hope of safety was in the clemency of the Roman government; and most solemnly protested that, if the gracious liberality of the emperor would permit them to cultivate the waste·lands of Thrace, they should ever hold themselves bound, by the strongest obligations of duty and gratitude, to obey the laws, and to guard the limits, of the republic. These assurances were confirmed by the ambassadors of the Goths, who impatiently expected, from the mouth of Valens, an answer that must finally determine the fate of their unhappy countrymen. The emperor of the East was no longer guided by the wisdom and authority of his elder brother, whose death happened towards the end of the preceding year: and, as the distressful situation of the Goths required an instant and peremptory decision, he was deprived of the favourite resource of feeble and timid minds; who consider the use of dilatory and ambiguous measures as the most admirable efforts of consummate prudence. As long as the same passions and interests subsist among mankind, the questions of war and peace, of justice and policy, which were debated in the councils of antiquity, will frequently present themselves as the subject of modern deliberation. But the most experienced statesman of Europe has never been summoned to consider the propriety or the danger of admitting or rejecting an innumerable multitude of Barbarians, who are driven by despair and hunger to solicit a settlement on the territories of a civilized nation. When that important proposition, so essentially connected with the public safety, was referred to the ministers of Valens, they were perplexed and divided; but they soon acquiesced in the flattering sentiment which seemed the most favourable to the pride, the indolence, and the avarice of their sovereign. The slaves, who were decorated with the titles of præfects and generals, dissembled or disregarded the terrors of this national emigration, so extremely different from the partial and accidental colonies which had been received on the extreme limits of the empire. But they applauded the liberality of fortune, which had conducted, from the most distant countries of the globe, a numerous and invincible army of strangers, to defend the throne of Valens; who might now add to the royal treasures the immense sums of gold supplied by the provincials to compensate their annual proportion of recruits. The prayers of the Goths were granted, and their service was accepted by the Imperial court: and orders were immediately dispatched to the civil and military governors of the Thracian diocese, to make the necessary preparations for the passage and subsistence of a great people, till a proper and sufficient territory could be allotted for their future residence. The liberality of the emperor was accompanied, however, with two harsh and rigorous conditions, which prudence might justify on the side of the Romans but which distress alone could extort from the indignant Goths. Before they passed the Danube, they were required to deliver their arms; and it was insisted that their children should be taken from them and dispersed through the provinces of Asia, where they might be civilized by the arts of education and serve as hostages to secure the fidelity of their parents.

During this suspense of a doubtful and distant negotiation, the impatient Goths made some rash attempts to pass the Danube, without the permission of the government whose protection they had implored. Their motions were strictly observed by the vigilance of the troops which were stationed along the river, and their foremost detachments were defeated with considerable slaughter; yet such were the timid councils of the reign of Valens that the brave officers who had served their country in the execution of their duty were punished by the loss of their employments and narrowly escaped the loss of their heads. The Imperial mandate was at length received for transporting over the Danube the whole body of the Gothic nation; but the execution of this order was a task of labour and difficulty. The stream of the Danube, which in those parts is above a mile broad, had been swelled by incessant rains; and, in this tumultuous passage, many were swept away and drowned by the rapid violence of the current. A large fleet of vessels, of boats, and of canoes was provided; many days and nights they passed and repassed with indefatigable toil; and the most strenuous diligence was exerted by the officers of Valens that not a single Barbarian, of those who were reserved to subvert the foundations of Rome, should be left on the opposite shore. It was thought expedient that an accurate account should be taken of their numbers; but the persons who were employed soon desisted, with amazement and dismay, from the prosecution of the endless and impracticable task; and the principal historian of the age most seriously affirms that the prodigious armies of Darius and Xerxes, which had so long been considered as the fables of vain and credulous antiquity, were now justified, in the eyes of mankind, by the evidence of fact and experience. A probable testimony has fixed the number of the Gothic warriors at two hundred thousand men; and, if we can venture to add the just proportion of women, of children, and of slaves, the whole mass of people which composed this formidable emigration must have amounted to near a million of persons, of both sexes and of all ages. The children of the Goths, those at least of a distinguished rank, were separated from the multitude. They were conducted, without delay, to the distant seats assigned for their residence and education; and, as the numerous train of hostages or captives passed through the cities, their gay and splendid apparel, their robust and martial figure, excited the surprise and envy of the Provincials. But the stipulation, the most offensive to the Goths and the most important to the Romans, was shamefully eluded. The Barbarians, who considered their arms as the ensigns of honour and the pledges of safety, were disposed to offer a price which the lust or avarice of the Imperial officers was easily tempted to accept. To preserve their arms, the haughty warriors consented, with some reluctance, to prostitute their wives or their daughters; the charms of a beauteous maid, or a comely boy, secured the connivance of the inspectors; who sometimes cast an eye of covetousness on the fringed carpets and linen garments of their new allies,[41] or who sacrificed their duty to the mean consideration of filling their farms with cattle and their houses with slaves. The Goths, with arms in their hands, were permitted to enter the boats; and, when their strength was collected on the other side of the river, the immense camp which was spread over the plains and the hills of the Lower Mæsia assumed a threatening and even hostile aspect. The leaders of the Ostrogoths, Alatheus and Saphrax, the guardians of their infant king, appeared soon afterwards on the Northern banks of the Danube; and immediately dispatched their ambassadors to the court of Antioch, to solicit, with the same professions of allegiance and gratitude, the same favour which had been granted to the suppliant Visigoths. The absolute refusal of Valens suspended their progress, and dis-

[41] *Eunapius and Zosimus curiously specify these articles of Gothic wealth and luxury. Yet it must be presumed that they were the manufactures of the provinces; which the Barbarians had acquired as the spoils of war, or as the gifts or merchandise of peace.*

covered the repentance, the suspicions, and the fears of the Imperial council.

An undisciplined and unsettled nation of Barbarians required the firmest temper and the most dexterous management. The daily subsistence of near a million of extraordinary subjects could be supplied only by constant and skilful diligence, and might continually be interrupted by mistake or accident. The insolence or the indignation of the Goths, if they conceived themselves to be the objects either of fear or of contempt, might urge them to the most desperate extremities; and the fortune of the state seemed to depend on the prudence, as well as the integrity, of the generals of Valens. At this important crisis, the military government of Thrace was exercised by Lupicinus and Maximus, in whose venal minds the slightest hope of private emolument outweighed every consideration of public advantage; and whose guilt was only alleviated by their incapacity of discerning the pernicious effects of their rash and criminal administration. Instead of obeying the orders of their sovereign and satisfying with decent liberality the demands of the Goths, they levied an ungenerous and oppressive tax on the wants of the hungry Barbarians. The vilest food was sold at an extravagant price; and, in the room of wholesome and substantial provisions, the markets were filled with the flesh of dogs, and of unclean animals, who had died of disease. To obtain the valuable acquisition of a pound of bread, the Goths resigned the possession of an expensive, though serviceable, slave; and a small quantity of meat was greedily purchased with ten pounds of a precious, but useless, metal.[42] When their property was exhausted, they continued this necessary traffic by the sale of their sons and daughters; and notwithstanding the love of freedom, which animated every Gothic breast, they submitted to the humiliating maxim that it was better for their children to be maintained in a servile condition than to perish in a state of wretched and helpless independence. The most lively resentment is excited by the tyranny of pretended benefactors, who sternly exact the debt of gratitude which they have cancelled by subsequent injuries: a spirit of discontent insensibly arose in the camp of the Barbarians, who pleaded, without success, the merit of their patient and dutiful behaviour; and loudly complained of the inhospitable treatment which they had received from their new allies. They beheld around them the wealth and plenty of a fertile province, in the midst of which they suffered the intolerable hardships of artificial famine. But the means of relief, and even of revenge, were in their hands;

[42] Decem libras; *the word* silver *must be understood. Jornandes betrays the passions and prejudices of a Goth. The servile Greeks, Eunapius and Zosimus, disguise the Roman oppression and execrate the perfidy of the Barbarians. Ammianus, a patriot historian, slightly, and reluctantly, touches on the odious subject. Jerom, who wrote almost on the spot, is fair, though concise. Per avaritiam Maximi ducis ad rebellionem fame coacti sunt.*

since the rapaciousness of their tyrants had left, to an injured people, the possession and the use of arms. The clamours of a multitude, untaught to disguise their sentiments, announced the first symptoms of resistance, and alarmed the timid and guilty minds of Lupicinus and Maximus. Those crafty ministers, who substituted the cunning of temporary expedients to the wise and salutary counsels of general policy, attempted to remove the Goths from their dangerous station on the frontiers of the empire, and to disperse them in separate quarters of cantonment through the interior provinces. As they were conscious how ill they had deserved the respect, or confidence, of the Barbarians, they diligently collected, from every side, a military force, that might urge the tardy and reluctant march of a people who had not yet renounced the title, or the duties, of Roman subjects. But the generals of Valens, while their attention was solely directed to the discontented Visigoths, imprudently disarmed the ships and fortifications which constituted the defence of the Danube. The fatal oversight was observed and improved by Alatheus and Saphrax, who anxiously watched the favourable moment of escaping from the pursuit of the Huns. By the help of such rafts and vessels as could be hastily procured, the leaders of the Ostrogoths transported, without opposition, their king and their army; and boldly fixed an hostile and independent camp on the territories of the empire.

Under the name of judges, Alavivus and Fritigern were the leaders of the Visigoths in peace and war; and the authority which they derived from their birth was ratified by the free consent of the nation. In a season of tranquillity, their power might have been equal, as well as their rank; but, as soon as their countrymen were exasperated by hunger and oppression, the superior abilities of Fritigern assumed the military command, which he was qualified to exercise for the public welfare. He restrained the impatient spirit of the Visigoths, till the injuries and the insults of their tyrants should justify their resistance in the opinion of mankind; but he was not disposed to sacrifice any solid advantages for the empty praise of justice and moderation. Sensible of the benefits which would result from the union of the Gothic powers under the same standard, he secretly cultivated the friendship of the Ostrogoths; and, while he professed an implicit obedience to the orders of the Roman generals, he proceeded by slow marches towards Marcianopolis, the capital of the Lower Mæsia, about seventy miles from the banks of the Danube. On that fatal spot, the flames of discord and mutual hatred burst forth into a dreadful conflagration. Lupicinus had invited the Gothic chiefs to a splendid entertainment; and their martial train remained under arms at the entrance of the palace. But the gates of the city were strictly guarded; and the Barbarians were sternly excluded from the use of a plentiful market, to which they asserted their equal claim of subjects and allies. Their humble prayers were rejected with insolence and derision; and, as their patience was now exhausted, the townsmen, the soldiers, and the Goths were soon involved in a conflict of passionate altercation and angry reproaches. A blow was imprudently given; a sword was hastily drawn; and the first blood that was spilt in this accidental quarrel became the signal of a long and destructive war. In the midst of noise and brutal intemperance, Lupicinus was informed, by a secret messenger, that many of his soldiers were slain and despoiled of their arms; and, as he was already inflamed by wine and oppressed by sleep, he issued a rash command that their death should be revenged by the massacre of the guards of Fritigern and Alavivus. The clamorous shouts and dying groans apprised Fritigern of his extreme danger; and, as he possessed the calm and intrepid spirit of a hero, he saw that he was lost if he allowed a moment of deliberation to the man who had so deeply injured him. "A trifling dispute," said the Gothic leader, with a firm but gentle tone of voice, "appears to have arisen between the two nations; but it may be productive of the most dangerous consequences, unless the tumult is immediately pacified by the assurance of our safety and the authority of our presence." At these words, Fritigern and his companions drew their swords, opened their passage through the unresisting crowd which filled the palace, the streets, and the gates of Marcianopolis, and, mounting their horses, hastily vanished from the eyes of the astonished Romans. The generals of the Goths were saluted by the fierce and joyful acclamations of the camp; war was instantly resolved, and the resolution was executed without delay; the banners of the nation were displayed according to the custom of their ancestors; and the air resounded with the harsh and mournful music of the Barbarian trumpet. The weak and guilty Lupicinus, who had dared to provoke, who had neglected to destroy, and who still presumed to despise, his formidable enemy, marched against the Goths, at the head of such a military force as could be collected on this sudden emergency. The Barbarians expected his approach about nine miles from Marcianopolis; and on this occasion the talents of the general were found to be of more prevailing efficacy than the weapons and discipline of the troops. The valour of the Goths was so ably directed by the genius of Fritigern that they broke, by a close and vigorous attack, the ranks of the Roman legions. Lupicinus left his arms and standards, his tribunes and his bravest soldiers, on the field of battle; and their useless courage served only to protect the ignominious flight of their leader. "That successful day put an end to the distress of the Barbarians and the security of the Romans: from that day, the Goths, renouncing the precarious condition of strangers and exiles, assumed the character of citizens and masters, claimed an absolute dominion over the possessors of land, and held, in their own right, the northern provinces of the empire, which are bounded by the Danube." Such are the words of the Gothic historian, who celebrates, with rude eloquence, the glory of his countrymen. But the dominion of the Barbarians was exercised only for the purposes of rapine and destruction. As they had been deprived, by the ministers of the emperor, of the common benefits of nature and the fair intercourse of social life, they retaliated the injustice on the subjects of the empire; and the crimes of Lupicinus were expiated by the ruin of the peaceful husbandmen of Thrace, the conflagration of their villages, and the massacre, or captivity, of their innocent families. The report of the Gothic victory was soon diffused over the adjacent country; and, while it filled the minds of the Romans with terror and dismay, their own hasty prudence contributed to increase the forces of Fritigern and the calamities of the province. Some time before the great emigration, a numerous body of Goths, under the command of Suerid and Colias, had been received into the protection and service of the empire. They were encamped under the walls of Hadrianople: but the ministers of Valens were anxious to remove them beyond the Hellespont, at a distance from the dangerous temptation which might so easily be communicated by the neighbourhood, and the success, of their countrymen. The respectful submission with which they yielded to the order of their march might be considered as a proof of their fidelity; and their moderate request of a sufficient allowance of provisions, and of a delay of only two days, was expressed in the most dutiful terms. But the first magistrate of Hadrianople, incensed by some disorders which had been committed at his country-house, refused this indulgence; and arming against them the inhabitants and manufacturers of a populous city, he urged, with hostile threats, their instant departure. The Barbarians stood silent and amazed, till they were exasperated by the insulting clamours, and missile weapons, of the populace: but, when patience or contempt was fatigued, they crushed the undisciplined multitude, inflicted many a shameful wound on the backs of their flying enemies, and despoiled them of the splendid armour,[43] which they were unworthy to bear. The resemblance of their sufferings and their actions soon united this victorious detachment to the nation of the Visigoths; the troops of Colias and Suerid expected the approach of the great Fritigern, ranged themselves under his standard, and signalized their ardour in the siege of Hadrianople. But the resistance of the garrison informed the Barbarians that, in the attack of regular fortifications, the efforts of unskilful courage are seldom effectual. Their general acknowledged his error, raised the siege, declared that "he was at peace with stone walls," and revenged his disappointment on the adjacent country. He accepted, with pleasure, the useful reinforcement of hardy workmen, who laboured in the gold mines of Thrace[44] for the emolument, and under the lash, of an unfeeling master:[45] and these new associates conducted the Barbarians, through the secret paths, to the most sequestered places, which had been chosen to secure the inhabitants, the cattle, and the magazines of corn. With the assistance of such guides, nothing could remain impervious or inaccessible; resistance was fatal; flight was impracticable; and the patient submission of helpless innocence seldom found mercy from the Barbarian conqueror. In the course of these depredations, a great number of the children of the Goths, who had been sold into captivity, were restored to the embraces of their afflicted parents; but these tender interviews, which might have revived and cherished in their minds some sentiments of humanity, tended only to stimulate their native fierceness by the desire of revenge. They listened, with eager attention, to the complaints of their captive children, who had suffered the most cruel indignities from the lustful or angry passions of their masters; and the same cruelties, the same indignities, were severely retaliated on the sons and daughters of the Romans.

The imprudence of Valens and his ministers had introduced into the heart of the empire a nation of enemies; but the Visigoths might even yet have been reconciled, by the manly confession of past errors and the sincere performance of former engagements. These healing and temperate measures seemed to concur with the timorous disposition of the sovereign of the East; but, on this occasion alone, Valens was brave; and his unseasonable bravery was fatal to himself and to his subjects. He declared his intention of marching from

[43] *An Imperial manufacture of shields, &c., was established at Hadrianople; and the populace were headed by the* Fabricenses, *or workmen.*

[44] *These mines were in the country of the Bessi, in the ridge of mountains, the Rhodope, that runs between Philippi and Philippopolis; two Macedonian cities, which derived their name and origin from the father of Alexander. From the mines of Thrace he annually received the value, not the weight, of a thousand talents (£200,000); a revenue which paid the phalanx, and corrupted the orators of Greece.*

[45] *As those unhappy workmen often ran away, Valens had enacted severe laws to drag them from their hiding-places.*

Antioch to Constantinople, to subdue this dangerous rebellion; and, as he was not ignorant of the difficulties of the enterprise, he solicited the assistance of his nephew, the emperor Gratian, who commanded all the forces of the West. The veteran troops were hastily recalled from the defence of Armenia; that important frontier was abandoned to the discretion of Sapor; and the immediate conduct of the Gothic war was intrusted, during the absence of Valens, to his lieutenants Trajan and Profuturus, two generals who indulged themselves in a very false and favourable opinion of their own abilities. On their arrival in Thrace, they were joined by Richomer, count of the domestics; and the auxiliaries of the West, that marched under his banner, were composed of the Gallic legions, reduced indeed by a spirit of desertion to the vain appearances of strength and numbers. In a council of war, which was influenced by pride rather than by reason, it was resolved to seek and to encounter the Barbarians, who lay encamped in the spacious and fertile meadows near the most southern of the six mouths of the Danube.[46] Their camp was surrounded by the usual fortification of waggons;[47] and the Barbarians, secure within the vast circle of the inclosure, enjoyed the fruits of their valour and the spoils of the province. In the midst of riotous intemperance, the watchful Fritigern observed the motions, and penetrated the designs, of the Romans. He perceived that the numbers of the enemy were continually increasing; and, as he understood their intention of attacking his rear as soon as the scarcity of forage should oblige him to remove his camp, he recalled to their standard his predatory detachments which covered the adjacent country. As soon as they descried the flaming beacons,[48] they obeyed, with incredible speed, the signal of their leader; the camp was filled with the martial crowd of Barbarians; their impatient clamours demanded the battle, and their tumultuous zeal was approved and animated by the spirit of their chiefs. The evening was already far advanced; and the two armies prepared themselves for the approaching combat, which was deferred only till the dawn of day. While the trumpets sounded to arms, the undaunted courage of the Goths was confirmed by the mutual obligation of a solemn oath; and, as they advanced to meet the enemy, the rude songs, which celebrated the glory of their forefathers, were mingled with their fierce and dissonant outcries, and opposed to the artificial harmony of the Roman shout. Some military skill was displayed by Fritigern to gain the advantage of a commanding eminence; but the bloody conflict, which began and ended with the light, was

[46] The Itinerary of Antoninus marks the situation of this place about sixty miles north of Tomi, Ovid's exile: and the name of Salices (the willows) expresses the nature of the soil.

[47] This circle of waggons, the Carrago, was the usual fortification of the Barbarians. The practice and the name were preserved by their descendants, as late as the fifteenth century. The Charroy, which surrounded the Ost, is a word familiar to the readers of Froissard or Comines.

[48] Statim ut accensi malleoli. I have used the literal sense of real torches or beacons: but I almost suspect that it is only one of those turgid metaphors, those false ornaments, that perpetually disfigure the style of Ammianus.

maintained, on either side, by the personal and obstinate efforts of strength, valour, and agility. The legions of Armenia supported their fame in arms; but they were oppressed by the irresistible weight of the hostile multitude; the left wing of the Romans was thrown into disorder, and the field was strewed with their mangled carcasses. This partial defeat was balanced, however, by partial success; and when the two armies, at a late hour of the evening, retreated to their respective camps, neither of them could claim the honours, or the effects, of a decisive victory. The real loss was more severely felt by the Romans, in proportion to the smallness of their numbers; but the Goths were so deeply confounded and dismayed by this vigorous, and perhaps unexpected, resistance that they remained seven days within the circle of their fortifications. Such funeral rites as the circumstances of time and place would admit were piously discharged to some officers of distinguished rank; but the indiscriminate vulgar were left unburied on the plain. Their flesh was greedily devoured by the birds of prey, who, in that age, enjoyed very frequent and delicious feasts; and several years afterwards the white and naked bones which covered the wide extent of the fields presented to the eyes of Ammianus a dreadful monument of the battle of Salices.[49]

The progress of the Goths had been checked by the doubtful event of that bloody day; and the Imperial generals, whose army would have been consumed by the repetition of such a contest, embraced the more rational plan of destroying the Barbarians by the wants and pressure of their own multitudes. They prepared to confine the Visigoths in the narrow angle of land between the Danube, the desert of Scythia, and the mountains of Hæmus, till their strength and spirit should be insensibly wasted by the inevitable operation of famine. The design was prosecuted with some conduct and success; the Barbarians had almost exhausted their own magazines, and the harvests of the country; and the diligence of Saturninus, the master-general of the cavalry, was employed to improve the strength, and to contract the extent, of the Roman fortifications. His labours were interrupted by the alarming intelligence that new swarms of Barbarians had passed the unguarded Danube, either to support the cause, or to imitate the example of Fritigern. The just apprehension, that he himself might be surrounded, and overwhelmed, by the arms of hostile and unknown nations, compelled Saturninus to relinquish the siege of the Gothic camp: and the indignant Visigoths, breaking from their confinement, satiated their

[49] *The historian might have viewed these plains either as a soldier or as a traveller. But his modesty has suppressed the adventures of his own life subsequent to the Persian wars of Constantius and Julian. We are ignorant of the time when he quitted the service and retired to Rome, where he appears to have composed his History of his own Times.*

hunger and revenge, by the repeated devastation of the fruitful country, which extends above three hundred miles from the banks of the Danube to the straits of the Hellespont. The sagacious Fritigern had successfully appealed to the passions, as well as to the interest, of his Barbarian allies; and the love of rapine and the hatred of Rome seconded, or even prevented, the eloquence of his ambassadors. He cemented a strict and useful alliance with the great body of his countrymen, who obeyed Alatheus and Saphrax as the guardians of their infant king; the long animosity of rival tribes was suspended by the sense of their common interest; the independent part of the nation was associated under one standard; and the chiefs of the Ostrogoths appear to have yielded to the superior genius of the general of the Visigoths. He obtained the formidable aid of the Taifalæ, whose military renown was disgraced and polluted by the public infamy of their domestic manners. Every youth, on his entrance into the world, was united by the ties of honourable friendship, and brutal love, to some warrior of the tribe; nor could he hope to be released from this unnatural connexion, till he had approved his manhood by slaying, in single combat, a huge bear, or a wild boar of the forest. But the most powerful auxiliaries of the Goths were drawn from the camp of those enemies who had expelled them from their native seats. The loose subordination, and extensive possessions, of the Huns and the Alani delayed the conquests, and distracted the councils, of that victorious people. Several of the hords were allured by the liberal promises of Fritigern; and the rapid cavalry of Scythia added weight and energy to the steady and strenuous efforts of the Gothic infantry. The Sarmatians, who could never forgive the successor of Valentinian, enjoyed and increased the general confusion; and a seasonable irruption of the Alemanni into the provinces of Gaul engaged the attention, and diverted the forces, of the emperor of the West.[50]

[50] *Jerom enumerates the nations, and marks a calamitous period of twenty years. This epistle to Heliodorus was composed in the year 397.*

One of the most dangerous inconveniences of the introduction of the Barbarians into the army and the palace, was sensibly felt in their correspondence with their hostile countrymen, to whom they imprudently, or maliciously, revealed the weakness of the Roman empire. A soldier, of the life-guards of Gratian, was of the nation of the Alemanni, and of the tribe of the Lentienses, who dwelt beyond the lake of Constance. Some domestic business obliged him to request a leave of absence. In a short visit to his family and friends, he was exposed to their curious inquiries; and the vanity of the loquacious soldier tempted him to display his intimate acquaintance with the secrets of the state and the designs of his master. The intelligence that Gratian was preparing to lead the military force of Gaul and of the West to the assistance of his uncle Valens pointed out to the restless spirit of the Alemanni the moment, and the mode, of a successful invasion. The enterprise of some light detachments, who, in the month of February, passed the Rhine upon the ice, was the prelude of a more important war. The boldest hopes of rapine, perhaps of conquest, outweighed the consideration of timid prudence or national faith. Every forest and every village poured forth a band of hardy adventurers; and the great army of the Alemanni, which, on their approach, was estimated at forty thousand men by the fears of the people, was afterwards magnified to the number of seventy thousand by the vain and credulous flattery of the Imperial court. The legions which had been ordered to march into Pannonia were immediately recalled or detained for the defence of Gaul; the military command was divided between Nanienus and Mellobaudes; and the youthful emperor, though he respected the long experience and sober wisdom of the former, was much more inclined to admire and to follow the martial ardour of his colleague; who was allowed to unite the incompatible characters of count of the domestics and of king of the Franks. His rival Priarius, king of the Alemanni, was guided, or rather impelled, by the same headstrong valour; and, as their troops were animated by the spirit of their leaders, they met, they saw, they encountered, each other, near the town of Argentaria, or Colmar,[51] in the plains of Alsace. The glory of the day was justly ascribed to the missile weapons and well-practised evolutions of the Roman soldiers; the Alemanni, who long maintained their ground, were slaughtered with unrelenting fury; five thousand only of the Barbarians escaped to the woods and mountains; and the glorious death of their king on the field of battle saved him from the reproaches of the people, who are always disposed to accuse the justice, or policy, of an unsuccessful war. After this signal victory, which secured the peace of Gaul and asserted the honour of the Roman arms, the emperor Gratian appeared to proceed without delay on his Eastern expedition; but, as he approached the confines of the Alemanni, he suddenly inclined to the left, surprised them by his unexpected passage of the Rhine, and boldly advanced into the heart of their country. The Barbarians opposed to his progress the obstacles of nature and of courage; and still continued to retreat from one hill to another, till they were satisfied, by repeated trials, of the power and per-

[51] *The field of battle, Argentaria or Argentovaria, is accurately fixed by M. d'Anville at twenty-three Gallic leagues, or thirty-four and a half Roman miles, to the south of Strasburg. From its ruins the adjacent town of Colmar has arisen.*

severance of their enemies. Their submission was accepted as a proof, not indeed of their sincere repentance, but of their actual distress; and a select number of their brave and robust youth was exacted from the faithless nation, as the most substantial pledge of their future moderation. The subjects of the empire, who had so often experienced that the Alemanni could neither be subdued by arms nor restrained by treaties, might not promise themselves any solid or lasting tranquillity: but they discovered, in the virtues of their young sovereign, the prospect of a long and auspicious reign. When the legions climbed the mountains, and scaled the fortifications, of the Barbarians, the valour of Gratian was distinguished in the foremost ranks; and the gilt and variegated armour of his guards was pierced and shattered by the blows which they had received in their constant attachment to the person of their sovereign. At the age of nineteen, the son of Valentinian seemed to possess the talents of peace and war; and his personal success against the Alemanni was interpreted as a sure presage of his Gothic triumphs.

While Gratian deserved and enjoyed the applause of his subjects, the emperor Valens, who, at length, had removed his court and army from Antioch, was received by the people of Constantinople as the author of the public calamity. Before he had reposed himself ten days in the capital, he was urged, by the licentious clamours of the Hippodrome, to march against the Barbarians whom he had invited into his dominions: and the citizens, who are always brave at a distance from any real danger, declared, with confidence, that, if they were supplied with arms, *they* alone would undertake to deliver the province from the ravages of an insulting foe. The vain reproaches of an ignorant multitude hastened the downfall of the Roman empire; they provoked the desperate rashness of Valens, who did not find, either in his reputation or in his mind, any motives to support with firmness the public contempt. He was soon persuaded, by the successful achievements of his lieutenants, to despise the power of the Goths, who, by the diligence of Fritigern, were now collected in the neighbourhood of Hadrianople. The march of the Taifalæ had been intercepted by the valiant Frigerid; the king of those licentious Barbarians was slain in battle; and the suppliant captives were sent into distant exile to cultivate the lands of Italy which were assigned for their settlement in the vacant territories of Modena and Parma. The exploits of Sebastian,[52] who was recently engaged in the service of Valens and promoted to the rank of master-general of the infantry, were still more honourable to

[52] *Zosimus expatiates on the desultory exploits of Sebastian, and dispatches, in a few lines, the important battle of Hadrianople. According to the ecclesiastical critics, who hate Sebastian, the praise of Zosimus is disgrace. His prejudice and ignorance undoubtedly render him a very questionable judge of merit.*

himself and useful to the republic. He obtained the permission of selecting three hundred soldiers from each of the legions; and this separate detachment soon acquired the spirit of discipline and the exercise of arms, which were almost forgotten under the reign of Valens. By the vigour and conduct of Sebastian, a large body of the Goths was surprised in their camp: and the immense spoil which was recovered from their hands filled the city of Hadrianople and the adjacent plain. The splendid narratives which the general transmitted of his own exploits alarmed the Imperial court by the appearance of superior merit; and, though he cautiously insisted on the difficulties of the Gothic war, his valour was praised, his advice was rejected; and Valens, who listened with pride and pleasure to the flattering suggestions of the eunuchs of the palace, was impatient to seize the glory of an easy and assured conquest. His army was strengthened by a numerous reinforcement of veterans; and his march from Constantinople to Hadrianople was conducted with so much military skill that he prevented the activity of the Barbarians, who designed to occupy the intermediate defiles and to intercept either the troops themselves or their convoys of provisions. The camp of Valens, which he pitched under the walls of Hadrianople, was fortified, according to the practice of the Romans, with a ditch and rampart; and a most important council was summoned, to decide the fate of the emperor and of the empire. The party of reason and of delay was strenuously maintained by Victor, who had corrected, by the lessons of experience, the native fierceness of the Sarmatian character; while Sebastian, with the flexible and obsequious eloquence of a courtier, represented every precaution and every measure that implied a doubt of immediate victory as unworthy of the courage and majesty of their invincible monarch. The ruin of Valens was precipitated by the deceitful arts of Fritigern and the prudent admonitions of the emperor of the West. The advantages of negotiating in the midst of war were perfectly understood by the general of the Barbarians; and a Christian ecclesiastic was dispatched, as the holy minister of peace, to penetrate, and to perplex, the councils of the enemy. The misfortunes, as well as the provocations, of the Gothic nation were forcibly and truly described by their ambassador; who protested, in the name of Fritigern, that he was still disposed to lay down his arms, or to employ them only in the defence of the empire if he could secure, for his wandering countrymen, a tranquil settlement on the waste lands of Thrace and a sufficient allowance of corn and cattle. But he added, in a whisper of confidential friendship, that the exasperated Barbarians were averse to these reasonable conditions; and that Fritigern was doubtful whether he could accomplish the conclusion of the treaty, unless he found himself supported by the presence and terrors of an Imperial army. About the same time Count Richomer returned from the West, to announce the defeat and submission of the Alemanni; to inform Valens that his nephew advanced by rapid marches at the head of the veteran and victorious legions of Gaul; and to request, in the name of Gratian and of the republic, that every dangerous and decisive measure might be suspended, till the junction of the two emperors should ensure the success of the Gothic war. But the feeble sovereign of the East was actuated only by the fatal illusions of pride and jealousy. He disdained the importunate advice; he rejected the humiliating aid; he secretly compared the ignominious, or at least the inglorious, period of his own reign with the fame of a beardless youth: and Valens rushed into the field, to erect his imaginary trophy, before the diligence of his colleague could usurp any share of the triumphs of the day.

On the ninth of August, a day which has deserved to be marked among the most inauspicious of the Roman Calendar,[53] the emperor Valens, leaving, under a strong guard, his baggage and military treasure, marched from Hadrianople to attack the Goths, who were encamped about twelve miles from the city.[54] By some mistake of the orders, or ignorance of the ground, the right wing, or column of cavalry, arrived in sight of the enemy, whilst the left was still at a considerable distance; the soldiers were compelled, in the sultry heat of summer, to precipitate their pace; and the line of battle was formed with tedious confusion and irregular delay. The Gothic cavalry had been detached to forage in the adjacent country; and Fritigern still continued to practise his customary arts. He dispatched messengers of peace, made proposals, required hostages, and wasted the hours, till the Romans, exposed without shelter to the burning rays of the sun, were exhausted by thirst, hunger, and intolerable fatigue. The emperor was persuaded to send an ambassador to the Gothic camp; the zeal of Richomer, who alone had courage to accept the dangerous commission, was applauded: and the count of the domestics, adorned with the splendid ensigns of his dignity, had proceeded some way in the space between the two armies when he was suddenly recalled by the alarm of battle. The hasty and imprudent attack was made by Bacurius the Iberian, who commanded a body of archers and targetteers; and, as they ad-

[53] *Ammianus almost alone describes the councils and actions which were terminated by the fatal battle of Hadrianople. We might censure the vices of his style, the disorder and perplexity of his narrative; but we must now take leave of this impartial historian, and reproach is silenced by our regret for such an irreparable loss.*

[54] *The difference of the eight miles of Ammianus, and the twelve of Idatius, can only embarrass those critics who suppose a great army to be a mathematical point, without space or dimensions.*

vanced with rashness, they retreated with loss and disgrace. In the same moment, the flying squadrons of Alatheus and Saphrax, whose return was anxiously expected by the general of the Goths, descended like a whirlwind from the hills, swept across the plain, and added new terrors to the tumultuous, but irresistible, charge of the Barbarian host. The event of the battle of Hadrianople, so fatal to Valens and to the empire, may be described in a few words: the Roman cavalry fled; the infantry was abandoned, surrounded, and cut in pieces. The most skilful evolutions, the firmest courage, are scarcely sufficient to extricate a body of foot, encompassed, on an open plain, by superior numbers of horse; but the troops of Valens, oppressed by the weight of the enemy and their own fears, were crowded into a narrow space, where it was impossible for them to extend their ranks, or even to use, with effect, their swords and javelins. In the midst of tumult, of slaughter, and of dismay, the emperor, deserted by his guards and wounded, as it was supposed, with an arrow, sought protection among the Lancearii and the Mattiarii, who still maintained their ground with some appearance of order and firmness. His faithful generals, Trajan and Victor, who perceived his danger, loudly exclaimed that all was lost unless the person of the emperor could be saved. Some troops, animated by their exhortation, advanced to his relief: they found only a bloody spot, covered with a heap of broken arms and mangled bodies, without being able to discover their unfortunate prince, either among the living or the dead. Their search could not indeed be successful, if there is any truth in the circumstances with which some historians have related the death of the emperor. By the care of his attendants, Valens was removed from the field of battle to a neighbouring cottage, where they attempted to dress his wound and to provide for his future safety. But this humble retreat was instantly surrounded by the enemy; they tried to force the door; they were provoked by a discharge of arrows from the roof, till at length, impatient of delay, they set fire to a pile of dry faggots, and consumed the cottage with the Roman emperor and his train. Valens perished in the flames; and a youth, who dropt from the window, alone escaped, to attest the melancholy tale and to inform the Goths of the inestimable prize which they had lost by their own rashness. A great number of brave and distinguished officers perished in the battle of Hadrianople, which equalled in the actual loss, and far surpassed in the fatal consequences, the misfortune which Rome had formerly sustained in the field of Cannæ.[55] Two master-generals of

[55] *According to the grave Polybius, no more than 370 horse and 3000 foot escaped from the field of Cannæ: 10,000 were made prisoners; and the number of the slain amounted to 5630 horse and 70,000 foot. Livy is somewhat less bloody: he slaughters only 2700 horse and 40,000 foot. The Roman army was supposed to consist of 87,200 effective men.*

the cavalry and infantry, two great officers of the palace and thirty-five tribunes were found among the slain; and the death of Sebastian might satisfy the world that he was the victim, as well as the author, of the public calamity. Above two-thirds of the Roman army were destroyed; and the darkness of the night was esteemed a very favourable circumstance, as it served to conceal the flight of the multitude and to protect the more orderly retreat of Victor and Richomer, who alone, amidst the general consternation, maintained the advantage of calm courage and regular discipline.

While the impressions of grief and terror were still recent in the minds of men, the most celebrated rhetorician of the age composed the funeral oration of a vanquished army and of an unpopular prince, whose throne was already occupied by a stranger. "There are not wanting," says the candid Libanius, "those who arraign the prudence of the emperor, or who impute the public misfortune to the want of courage and discipline in the troops. For my own part, I reverence the memory of their former exploits: I reverence the glorious death which they bravely received, standing, and fighting in their ranks: I reverence the field of battle, stained with *their* blood and the blood of the Barbarians. Those honourable marks have been already washed away by the rains; but the lofty monuments of their bones, the bones of generals, of centurions, and of valiant warriors, claim a longer period of duration. The king himself fought and fell in the foremost ranks of the battle. His attendants presented him with the fleetest horses of the Imperial stable, that would soon have carried him beyond the pursuit of the enemy. They vainly pressed him to reserve his important life for the future service of the republic. He still declared that he was unworthy to survive so many of the bravest and most faithful of his subjects; and the monarch was nobly buried under a mountain of the slain. Let none, therefore, presume to ascribe the victory of the Barbarians to the fear, the weakness, or the imprudence, of the Roman troops. The chiefs and the soldiers were animated by the virtue of their ancestors, whom they equalled in discipline and the arts of war. Their generous emulation was supported by the love of glory, which prompted them to contend at the same time with heat and thirst, with fire and the sword; and cheerfully to embrace an honourable death as their refuge against flight and infamy. The indignation of the gods has been the only cause of the success of our enemies." The truth of history may disclaim some parts of this panegyric, which cannot strictly be reconciled with the character of Valens or the circumstances of the battle; but the fairest commendation is due to the eloquence, and still more to the generosity, of the sophist of Antioch.

The pride of the Goths was elated by this memorable victory; but their avarice was disappointed by the mortifying discovery that the richest part of the Imperial spoil had been within the walls of Hadrianople. They hastened to possess the reward of their valour; but they were encountered by the remains of a vanquished army with an intrepid resolution, which was the effect of their despair and the only hope of their safety. The walls of the city and the ramparts of the adjacent camp were lined with military engines, that threw stones of an enormous weight; and astonished the ignorant Barbarians by the noise and velocity, still more than by the real effects, of the discharge. The soldiers, the citizens, the provincials, the domestics of the palace, were united in the danger and in the defence; the furious assault of the Goths was repulsed; their secret arts of treachery and treason were discovered; and, after an obstinate conflict of many hours, they retired to their tents; convinced, by experience, that it would be far more advisable to observe the treaty which their sagacious leader had tacitly stipulated with the fortifications of great and populous cities. After the hasty and impolitic massacre of three hundred deserters, an act of justice extremely useful to the discipline of the Roman armies, the Goths indignantly raised the siege of Hadrianople. The scene of war and tumult was instantly converted into a silent solitude; the multitude suddenly disappeared; the sacred paths of the wood and mountains were marked with the footsteps of the trembling fugitives, who sought a refuge in the distant cities of Illyricum and Macedonia; and the faithful officers of the household and the treasury cautiously proceeded in search of the emperor, of whose death they were still ignorant. The tide of the Gothic inundation rolled from the walls of Hadrianople to the suburbs of Constantinople. The Barbarians were surprised with the splendid appearance of the capital of the East, the height and extent of the walls, the myriads of wealthy and affrighted citizens who crowded the ramparts, and the various prospect of the sea and land. While they gazed with hopeless desire on the inaccessible beauties of Constantinople, a sally was made from one of the gates by a party of Saracens,[56] who had been fortunately engaged in the service of Valens. The cavalry of Scythia was forced to yield to the admirable swiftness and spirit of the Arabian horses; their riders were skilled in the evolutions of irregular war;

[56] *Valens had gained, or rather purchased, the friendship of the Saracens, whose vexatious inroads were felt on the borders of Phœnicia, Palestine, and Egypt. The Christian faith had been lately introduced among a people, reserved, in a future age, to propagate another religion.*

and the Northern Barbarians were astonished, and dismayed, by the inhuman ferocity of the Barbarians of the South. A Gothic soldier was slain by the dagger of an Arab; and the hairy, naked savage, applying his lips to the wound, expressed a horrid delight, while he sucked the blood of his vanquished enemy. The army of the Goths, laden with the spoils of the wealthy suburbs and the adjacent territory, slowly moved from the Bosphorus to the mountains which form the western boundary of Thrace. The important pass of Succi was betrayed by the fear, or the misconduct, of Maurus; and the Barbarians, who no longer had any resistance to apprehend from the scattered and vanquished troops of the East, spread themselves over the face of a fertile and cultivated country, as far as the confines of Italy and the Hadriatic Sea.[57]

The Romans, who so coolly and so concisely mention the acts of *justice* which were exercised by the legions,[58] reserve their compassion and their eloquence for their own sufferings, when the provinces were invaded and desolated by the arms of the successful Barbarians. The simple circumstantial narrative (did such a narrative exist) of the ruin of a single town, of the misfortunes of a single family,[59] might exhibit an interesting and instructive picture of human manners; but the tedious repetition of vague and declamatory complaints would fatigue the attention of the most patient reader. The same censure may be applied, though not perhaps in an equal degree, to the profane and the ecclesiastical writers of this unhappy period; that their minds were inflamed by popular and religious animosity; and that the true size and colour of every object is falsified by the exaggerations of their corrupt eloquence. The vehement Jerom might justly deplore the calamities inflicted by the Goths and their barbarous allies on his native country of Pannonia and the wide extent of the provinces, from the walls of Constantinople to the foot of the Julian Alps; the rapes, the massacres, the conflagrations; and, above all, the profanation of the churches, that were turned into stables, and the contemptuous treatment of the relics of holy martyrs. But the Saint is surely transported beyond the limits of nature and history, when he affirms "that, in those desert countries, nothing was left except the sky and the earth; that, after the destruction of the cities and the extirpation of the human race, the land was overgrown with thick forests and inextricable brambles; and that the universal desolation, announced by the prophet Zephaniah, was accomplished, in the scarcity of the beasts, the birds, and even of the fish." These complaints were pronounced

[57] *The series of events may still be traced in the last pages of Ammianus. Zosimus, whom we are now reduced to cherish, misplaces the sally of the Arabs before the death of Valens. Eunapius praises the fertility of Thrace, Macedonia, &c.*

[58] *Observe with how much indifference Cæsar relates, in the Commentaries of the Gallic war: that he put to death the whole senate of the Veneti, who had yielded to his mercy; that he laboured to extirpate the whole nation of the Eburones; that forty thousand persons were massacred at Bourges by the just revenge of his soldiers, who spared neither age nor sex, &c.*

[59] *Such are the accounts of the sack of Magdeburg, by the ecclesiastic and the fisherman, which Mr. Harte has transcribed, with some apprehension of violating the dignity of history.*

about twenty years after the death of Valens; and the Illyrian provinces, which were constantly exposed to the invasion and passage of the Barbarians, still continued, after a calamitous period of ten centuries, to supply new materials for rapine and destruction. Could it even be supposed that a large tract of country had been left without cultivation and without inhabitants, the consequences might not have been so fatal to the inferior productions of animated nature. The useful and feeble animals, which are nourished by the hand of man, might suffer and perish, if they were deprived of his protection; but the beasts of the forest, his enemies, or his victims, would multiply in the free and undisturbed possession of their solitary domain. The various tribes that people the air, or the waters, are still less connected with the fate of the human species; and it is highly probable that the fish of the Danube would have felt more terror and distress from the approach of a voracious pike than from the hostile inroad of a Gothic army.

Whatever may have been the just measure of the calamities of Europe, there was reason to fear that the same calamities would soon extend to the peaceful countries of Asia. The sons of the Goths had been judiciously distributed through the cities of the East; and the arts of education were employed to polish and subdue the native fierceness of their temper. In the space of about twelve years, their numbers had continually increased; and the children, who, in the first emigration, were sent over the Hellespont, had attained, with rapid growth, the strength and spirit of perfect manhood.[60] It was impossible to conceal from their knowledge the events of the Gothic war; and, as those daring youths had not studied the language of dissimulation, they betrayed their wish, their desire, perhaps their intention, to emulate the glorious example of their fathers. The danger of the times seemed to justify the jealous suspicions of the provincials; and these suspicions were admitted as unquestionable evidence that the Goths of Asia had formed a secret and dangerous conspiracy against the public safety. The death of Valens had left the East without a sovereign; and Julius, who filled the important station of master-general of the troops, with a high reputation of diligence and ability, thought it his duty to consult the senate of Constantinople; which he considered, during the vacancy of the throne, as the representative council of the nation. As soon as he had obtained the discretionary power of acting as he should judge most expedient for the good of the republic, he assembled the principal officers; and privately concerted effectual measures for

[60] *Eunapius foolishly supposes a preternatural growth of the young Goths; that he may introduce Cadmus's armed men, who sprung from the dragon's teeth, &c. Such was the Greek eloquence of the times.*

the execution of his bloody design. An order was immediately promulgated that, on a stated day, the Gothic youth should assemble in the capital cities of their respective provinces; and, as a report was industriously circulated that they were summoned to receive a liberal gift of lands and money, the pleasing hope allayed the fury of their resentment and perhaps suspended the motions of the conspiracy. On the appointed day, the unarmed crowd of the Gothic youth was carefully collected in the square, or Forum; the streets and avenues were occupied by the Roman troops; and the roofs of the houses were covered with archers and slingers. At the same hour, in all the cities of the East, the signal was given of indiscriminate slaughter; and the provinces of Asia were delivered, by the cruel prudence of Julius, from a domestic enemy, who, in a few months, might have carried fire and sword from the Hellespont to the Euphrates.[61] The urgent consideration of the public safety may undoubtedly authorize the violation of every positive law. How far that, or any other, consideration may operate to dissolve the natural obligations of humanity and justice is a doctrine of which I still desire to remain ignorant.

[61] *Ammianus evidently approves this execution, efficacia velox et salutaris, which concludes his work. Zosimus, who is curious and copious, mistakes the date, and labours to find the reason why Julius did not consult the emperor Theodosius, who had not yet ascended the throne of the East.*

The emperor Gratian was far advanced on his march towards the plains of Hadrianople when he was informed, at first by the confused voice of fame, and afterwards by the more accurate reports of Victor and Richomer, that his impatient colleague had been slain in battle, and that two-thirds of the Roman army were exterminated by the sword of the victorious Goths. Whatever resentment the rash and jealous vanity of his uncle might deserve, the resentment of a generous mind is easily subdued by the softer emotions of grief and compassion: and even the sense of pity was soon lost in the serious and alarming consideration of the state of the republic. Gratian was too late to assist, he was too weak to revenge his unfortunate colleague: and the valiant and modest youth felt himself unequal to the support of a sinking world. A formidable tempest of the Barbarians of Germany seemed ready to burst over the provinces of Gaul; and the mind of Gratian was oppressed and distracted by the administration of the Western Empire. In this important crisis, the government of the East and the conduct of the Gothic war required the undivided attention of a hero and a statesman. A subject invested with such ample command would not long have preserved his fidelity to a distant benefactor; and the Imperial council embraced the wise and manly resolution of conferring an obligation rather than of yielding to an insult. It was the wish of Gratian to bestow the purple as the reward of virtue; but, at the age of nineteen, it is not easy for a prince, educated in the supreme rank, to understand the true characters of his ministers and generals. He attempted to weigh, with an impartial hand, their various merits and defects; and, whilst he checked the rash confidence of ambition, he distrusted the cautious wisdom which despaired of the republic. As each moment of delay diminished something of the power and resources of the future sovereign of the East, the situation of the times would not allow a tedious debate. The choice of Gratian was soon declared in favour of an exile, whose father, only three years before, had suffered, under the sanction of *his* authority, an unjust and ignominious death. The great Theodosius, a name celebrated in history and dear to the Catholic church,[62] was summoned to the Imperial court, which had gradually retreated from the confines of Thrace to the more secure station of Sirmium. Five months after the death of Valens, the emperor Gratian produced before the assembled troops *his* colleague and *their* master; who, after a modest, perhaps a sincere, resistance, was compelled to accept, amidst the general acclamations, the diadem, the purple, and the equal title of Augustus. The provinces of Thrace, Asia, and Egypt, over which Valens had reigned, were resigned to the administration of the new emperor; but, as he was specially intrusted with the conduct of the Gothic war, the Illyrian præfecture was dismembered; and the two great dioceses of Dacia and Macedonia were added to the dominions of the Eastern empire.

The same province, and, perhaps, the same city,[63] which had given to the throne the virtues of Trajan and the talents of Hadrian, was the original seat of another family of Spaniards, who, in a less fortunate age, possessed, near fourscore years, the declining empire of Rome.[64] They emerged from the obscurity of municipal honours by the active spirit of the elder Theodosius, a general whose exploits in Britain and Africa have formed one of the most splendid parts of the annals of Valentinian. The son of that general, who likewise bore the name of Theodosius, was educated, by skilful preceptors, in the liberal studies of youth; but he was instructed in the art of war by the tender care and severe discipline of his father.[65] Under the standard of such a leader, young Theodosius sought glory and knowledge, in the most distant scenes of military action; enured his constitution to the difference of seasons and climates; distinguished his valour by sea and land; and observed the various warfare of the Scots, the Saxons, and the Moors. His own merit, and the recommendation of the conqueror of Africa, soon raised him to a separate command; and in the station of Duke of Mæsia, he vanquished

[62] *A life of Theodosius the Great was composed in the last century, to inflame the mind of the young Dauphin with Catholic zeal. The author, Fléchier, afterwards bishop of Nismes, was a celebrated preacher; and his history is adorned, or tainted, with pulpit-eloquence; but he takes his learning from Baronius, and his principles from St. Ambrose and St. Augustin.*

[63] *Italica, founded by Scipio Africanus for his wounded veterans of Italy. The ruins still appear, about a league above Seville, on the opposite bank of the river.*

[64] *I agree with Tillemont in suspecting the royal pedigree, which remained a secret till the promotion of Theodosius. Even after that event the silence of Pacatus outweighs the venal evidence of Themistius, Victor, and Claudian, who connect the family of Theodosius with the blood of Trajan and Hadrian.*

[65] *Pacatus compares, and consequently prefers, the youth of Theodosius to the military education of Alexander, Hannibal, and the second Africanus, who, like him, had served under their fathers.*

[66] *Ammianus mentions this victory of Theodosius Junior Dux Mæsiæ, primâ etiam tum lanugine juvenis, princeps postea perspectissimus. The same fact is attested by Themistius and Zosimus; but Theodoret, who adds some curious circumstances, strangely applies it to the time of the interregnum.*

[67] *Pacatus prefers the rustic life of Theodosius to that of Cincinnatus; the one was the effect of choice, the other of poverty.*

[68] *M. d'Anville has fixed the situation of Caucha, or Coca, in the old province of Gallicia, where Zosimus and Idatius have placed the birth, or patrimony, of Theodosius.*

an army of Sarmatians; saved the province; deserved the love of the soldiers; and provoked the envy of the court.[66] His rising fortunes were soon blasted by the disgrace and execution of his illustrious father; and Theodosius obtained, as a favour, the permission of retiring to a private life in his native province of Spain. He displayed a firm and temperate character in the ease with which he adapted himself to this new situation. His time was almost equally divided between the town and country: the spirit which had animated his public conduct was shewn in the active and affectionate performance of every social duty; and the diligence of the soldier was profitably converted to the improvement of his ample patrimony,[67] which lay between Valladolid and Segovia, in the midst of a fruitful district still famous for a most exquisite breed of sheep.[68] From the innocent but humble labours of his farm Theodosius was transported, in less than four months, to the throne of the Eastern empire; and the whole period of the history of the world will not perhaps afford a similar example of an elevation, at the same time, so pure and so honourable. The princes who peaceably inherit the sceptre of their fathers claim and enjoy a legal right, the more secure as it is absolutely distinct from the merits of their personal characters. The subjects, who, in a monarchy or a popular estate, acquire the possession of supreme power, may have raised themselves, by the superiority either of genius or virtue, above the heads of their equals; but their virtue is seldom exempt from ambition; and the cause of the successful candidate is frequently stained by the guilt of conspiracy or civil war. Even in those governments which allow the reigning monarch to declare a colleague or a successor, his partial choice, which may be influenced by the blindest passions, is often directed to an unworthy object. But the most suspicious malignity cannot ascribe to Theodosius, in his obscure solitude of Caucha, the arts, the desires, or even the hopes, of an ambitious statesman; and the name of the Exile would long since have been forgotten, if his genuine and distinguished virtues had not left a deep impression in the Imperial court. During the season of prosperity, he had been neglected; but, in the public distress, his superior merit was universally felt and acknowledged. What confidence must have been reposed in his integrity, since Gratian could trust that a pious son would forgive, for the sake of the republic, the murder of his father! What expectations must have been formed of his abilities to encourage the hope that a single man could save, and restore, the empire of the East! Theodosius was invested with the purple in the thirty-third year of his age. The vulgar gazed with admiration on the manly beauty of his face, and the graceful majesty of his person, which they were pleased to compare with the pictures and medals of the emperor Trajan; whilst intelligent observers discovered, in the qualities of his heart and understanding, a more important resemblance to the best and greatest of the Roman princes.

It is not without the most sincere regret that I must now take leave of an accurate and faithful guide, who has composed the history of his own times without indulging the prejudices and passions which usually affect the mind of a contemporary. Ammianus Marcellinus, who terminates his useful work with the defeat and death of Valens, recommends the more glorious subject of the ensuing reign to the youthful vigour and eloquence of the rising generation. The rising generation was not disposed to accept his advice or to imitate his example;[69] and, in the study of the reign of Theodosius, we are reduced to illustrate the partial narrative of Zosimus by the obscure hints of fragments and chronicles, by the figurative style of poetry or panegyric, and by the precarious assistance of the ecclesiastical writers who, in the heat of religious faction, are apt to despise the profane virtues of sincerity and moderation. Conscious of these disadvantages, which will continue to involve a considerable portion of the decline and fall of the Roman empire, I shall proceed with doubtful and timorous steps. Yet I may boldly pronounce that the battle of Hadrianople was never revenged by any signal or decisive victory of Theodosius over the Barbarians; and the expressive silence of his venal orators may be confirmed by the observation of the condition and circumstances of the times. The fabric of a mighty state, which has been reared by the labours of successive ages, could not be overturned by the misfortune of a single day, if the fatal power of the imagination did not exaggerate the real measure of the calamity. The loss of forty thousand Romans, who fell in the plains of Hadrianople, might have been soon recruited in the populous provinces of the East, which contained so many millions of inhabitants. The courage of a soldier is found to be the cheapest, and most common, quality of human nature; and sufficient skill to encounter an undisciplined foe might have been speedily taught by the care of the surviving centurions. If the Barbarians were mounted on the horses, and equipped with the armour, of their vanquished enemies, the numerous studs of Cappadocia and Spain would have supplied new squadrons of cavalry; the thirty-four arsenals of the empire were plentifully stored with magazines of offensive and defensive arms; and the wealth of Asia might still have yielded an ample fund for the expenses of the war. But the effects which were

[69] *Ammianus was the last subject of Rome who composed a profane history in the Latin language. The East, in the next century, produced some rhetorical historians, Zosimus, Olympiodorus, Malchus, Candidus, &c.*

produced by the battle of Hadrianople on the minds of the Barbarians, and of the Romans, extended the victory of the former, and the defeat of the latter, far beyond the limits of a single day. A Gothic chief was heard to declare, with insolent moderation, that, for his own part, he was fatigued with slaughter; but that he was astonished how a people who fled before him like a flock of sheep could still presume to dispute the possession of their treasures and provinces. The same terrors which the name of the Huns had spread among the Gothic tribes were inspired, by the formidable name of the Goths, among the subjects and soldiers of the Roman empire. If Theodosius, hastily collecting his scattered forces, had led them into the field to encounter a victorious enemy, his army would have been vanquished by their own fears; and his rashness could not have been excused by the chance of success. But the *great* Theodosius, an epithet which he honourably deserved on this momentous occasion, conducted himself as the firm and faithful guardian of the republic. He fixed his headquarters at Thessalonica, the capital of the Macedonian diocese; from whence he could watch the irregular motions of the Barbarians, and direct the operations of his lieutenants, from the gates of Constantinople to the shores of the Hadriatic. The fortifications and garrisons of the cities were strengthened; and the troops, among whom a sense of order and discipline was revived, were insensibly emboldened by the confidence of their own safety. From these secure stations, they were encouraged to make frequent sallies on the Barbarians, who infested the adjacent country; and, as they were seldom allowed to engage without some decisive superiority either of ground or of numbers, their enterprises were, for the most part, successful; and they were soon convinced, by their own experience, of the possibility of vanquishing their *invincible* enemies. The detachments of these separate garrisons were gradually united into small armies; the same cautious measures were pursued, according to an extensive and well-concerted plan of operations; the events of each day added strength and spirit to the Roman arms; and the artful diligence of the emperor, who circulated the most favourable reports of the success of the war, contributed to subdue the pride of the Barbarians and to animate the hopes and courage of his subjects. If, instead of this faint and imperfect outline, we could accurately represent the counsels and actions of Theodosius, in four successive campaigns, there is reason to believe that his consummate skill would deserve the applause of every military reader. The republic had formerly been saved by the delays of Fabius: and, while the splendid trophies of Scipio in the field of

Zama attract the eyes of posterity, the camps and marches of the Dictator among the hills of Campania may claim a juster proportion of the solid and independent fame which the general is not compelled to share either with fortune or with his troops. Such was likewise the merit of Theodosius; and the infirmities of his body, which most unseasonably languished under a long and dangerous disease, could not oppress the vigour of his mind or divert his attention from the public service.[70]

The deliverance and peace of the Roman provinces was the work of prudence rather than of valour: the prudence of Theodosius was seconded by fortune; and the emperor never failed to seize, and to improve, every favourable circumstance. As long as the superior genius of Fritigern preserved the union, and directed the motions, of the Barbarians, their power was not inadequate to the conquest of a great empire. The death of that hero, the predecessor and master of the renowned Alaric, relieved an impatient multitude from the intolerable yoke of discipline and discretion. The Barbarians, who had been restrained by his authority, abandoned themselves to the dictates of their passions; and their passions were seldom uniform or consistent. An army of conquerors was broken into many disorderly bands of savage robbers; and their blind and irregular fury was not less pernicious to themselves than to their enemies. Their mischievous disposition was shewn in the destruction of every object which they wanted strength to remove or taste to enjoy; and they often consumed, with improvident rage, the harvests or the granaries, which soon afterwards became necessary for their own subsistence. A spirit of discord arose among the independent tribes and nations, which had been united only by the bands of a loose and voluntary alliance. The troops of the Huns and the Alani would naturally upbraid the flight of the Goths who were not disposed to use with moderation the advantages of their fortune; the ancient jealousy of the Ostrogoths and the Visigoths could not long be suspended; and the haughty chiefs still remembered the insults and injuries which they had reciprocally offered, or sustained, while the nation was seated in the countries beyond the Danube. The progress of domestic faction abated the more diffusive sentiment of national animosity; and the officers of Theodosius were instructed to purchase with liberal gifts and promises the retreat, or service, of the discontented party. The acquisition of Modar, a prince of the royal blood of the Amali, gave a bold and faithful champion to the cause of Rome. The illustrious deserter soon obtained the rank of master-general, with an important command; surprised an army of

[70] *Most writers insist on the illness and long repose of Theodosius at Thessalonica: Zosimus, to diminish his glory; Jornandes, to favour the Goths; and the ecclesiastical writers, to introduce his baptism.*

his countrymen who were immersed in wine and sleep; and, after a cruel slaughter of the astonished Goths, returned with an immense spoil, and four thousand waggons, to the Imperial camp.[71] In the hands of a skilful politician, the most different means may be successfully applied to the same ends: and the peace of the empire, which had been forwarded by the divisions, was accomplished by the re-union of the Gothic nation. Athanaric, who had been a patient spectator of these extraordinary events, was at length driven, by the chance of arms, from the dark recesses of the woods of Caucaland. He no longer hesitated to pass the Danube; and a very considerable part of the subjects of Fritigern, who already felt the inconveniences of anarchy, were easily persuaded to acknowledge for their king a Gothic Judge, whose birth they respected and whose abilities they had frequently experienced. But age had chilled the daring spirit of Athanaric; and, instead of leading his people to the field of battle and victory, he wisely listened to the fair proposal of an honourable and advantageous treaty. Theodosius, who was acquainted with the merit and power of his new ally, condescended to meet him at the distance of several miles from Constantinople; and entertained him in the Imperial city, with the confidence of a friend and the magnificence of a monarch. "The Barbarian prince observed, with curious attention, the variety of objects which attracted his notice, and at last broke out into a sincere and passionate exclamation of wonder. I now behold (said he) what I never could believe, the glories of this stupendous capital! and, as he cast his eyes around, he viewed, and he admired, the commanding situation of the city, the strength and beauty of the walls and public edifices, the capacious harbour, crowded with innumerable vessels, the perpetual concourse of distant nations, and the arms and discipline of the troops. Indeed (continued Athanaric), the emperor of the Romans is a god upon earth; and the presumptuous man, who dares to lift his hand against him, is guilty of his own blood." [72] The Gothic king did not long enjoy this splendid and honourable reception; and, as temperance was not the virtue of his nation, it may justly be suspected that his mortal disease was contracted amidst the pleasures of the Imperial banquets. But the policy of Theodosius derived more solid benefit from the death, than he could have expected from the most faithful services, of his ally. The funeral of Athanaric was performed with solemn rites in the capital of the East; a stately monument was erected to his memory; and his whole army, won by the liberal courtesy and decent grief of Theodosius, enlisted under the standard of the Roman empire.[73] The submission of so

[11] *Zosimus styles him a Scythian, a name which the more recent Greeks seem to have appropriated to the Goths.*

[12] *The reader will not be displeased to see the original words of Jornandes or the author whom he transcribed. Regiam urbem ingressus est, miransque, En, inquit, cerno quod sæpe incredulus audiebam, famam videlicet tantæ urbis. Et huc illuc ocolus volvens, nunc situm urbis commeatumque navium, nunc mœnia clara prospectans, miratur; populosque diversarum gentium, quasi fonte in uno e diversis partibus scaturriente undâ, sic quoque militem ordinatum aspiciens. Deus, inquit, est sine dubio terrenus imperator, et quisquis adversus eum manum moverit, ipse sui sanguinis reus existit. Jornandes proceeds to mention his death and funeral.*

[13] *Even Zosimus is compelled to approve the generosity of Theodosius, so honourable to himself, and so beneficial to the public.*

great a body of the Visigoths was productive of the most salutary consequences; and the mixed influence of force, of reason, and of corruption became every day more powerful and more extensive. Each independent chieftain hastened to obtain a separate treaty, from the apprehension that an obstinate delay might expose *him,* alone and unprotected, to the revenge, or justice, of the conqueror. The general, or rather the final, capitulation of the Goths may be dated four years, one month, and twenty-five days, after the defeat and death of the emperor Valens.[74]

The provinces of the Danube had been already relieved from the oppressive weight of the Gruthungi, or Ostrogoths, by the voluntary retreat of Alatheus and Saphrax; whose restless spirit had prompted them to seek new scenes of rapine and glory. Their destructive course was pointed towards the West; but we must be satisfied with a very obscure and imperfect knowledge of their various adventures. The Ostrogoths impelled several of the German tribes on the provinces of Gaul; concluded, and soon violated, a treaty with the emperor Gratian; advanced into the unknown countries of the North; and, after an interval of more than four years, returned, with accumulated force, to the banks of the Lower Danube. Their troops were recruited with the fiercest warriors of Germany and Scythia; and the soldiers, or at least the historians, of the empire no longer recognized the name and countenances of their former enemies. The general, who commanded the military and naval powers of the Thracian frontier, soon perceived that his superiority would be disadvantageous to the public service; and that the Barbarians, awed by the presence of his fleet and legions, would probably defer the passage of the river till the approaching winter. The dexterity of the spies whom he sent into the Gothic camp allured the Barbarians into a fatal snare. They were persuaded that, by a bold attempt, they might surprise, in the silence and darkness of the night, the sleeping army of the Romans; and the whole multitude was hastily embarked in a fleet of three thousand canoes. The bravest of the Ostrogoths led the van; the main body consisted of the remainder of their subjects and soldiers; and the women and children securely followed in the rear. One of the nights without a moon had been selected for the execution of their design; and they had almost reached the southern bank of the Danube, in the firm confidence that they should find an easy landing and an unguarded camp. But the progress of the Barbarians was suddenly stopped by an unexpected obstacle: a triple line of vessels, strongly connected with each other, and which formed an impene-

[74] *The short, but authentic, hints in the* Fasti of Idatius *are stained with contemporary passion. The fourteenth oration of Themistius is a compliment to Peace, and the consul Saturninus* (A.D. 383).

trable chain of two miles and a half along the river. While they struggled to force their way in the unequal conflict, their right rank was overwhelmed by the irresistible attack of a fleet of gallies, which were urged down the stream by the united impulse of oars and of the tide. The weight and velocity of those ships of war broke, and sank, and dispersed, the rude and feeble canoes of the Barbarians; their valour was ineffectual; and Alatheus, the king, or general, of the Ostrogoths, perished with his bravest troops either by the sword of the Romans or in the waves of the Danube. The last division of this unfortunate fleet might regain the opposite shore; but the distress and disorder of the multitude rendered them alike incapable either of action or counsel; and they soon implored the clemency of the victorious enemy. On this occasion, as well as on many others, it is a difficult task to reconcile the passions and prejudices of the writers of the age of Theodosius. The partial and malignant historian who misrepresents every action of his reign affirms that the emperor did not appear in the field of battle till the Barbarians had been vanquished by the valour and conduct of his lieutenant Promotus.[75] The flattering poet, who celebrated, in the court of Honorius, the glory of the father and of the son, ascribes the victory to the personal prowess of Theodosius; and almost insinuates that the King of the Ostrogoths was slain by the hand of the emperor.[76] The truth of history might perhaps be found in a just medium between these extreme and contradictory assertions.

The original treaty, which fixed the settlement of the Goths, ascertained their privileges and stipulated their obligations, would illustrate the history of Theodosius and his successors. The series of their history has imperfectly preserved the spirit and substance of this singular agreement. The ravages of war and tyranny had provided many large tracts of fertile but uncultivated land for the use of those Barbarians who might not disdain the practice of agriculture. A numerous colony of the Visigoths was seated in Thrace; the remains of the Ostrogoths were planted in Phrygia and Lydia; their immediate wants were supplied by a distribution of corn and cattle; and their future industry was encouraged by an exemption from tribute, during a certain term of years. The Barbarians would have deserved to feel the cruel and perfidious policy of the Imperial court, if they had suffered themselves to be dispersed through the provinces. They required, and they obtained, the sole possession of the villages and districts assigned for their residence; they still cherished and propagated their native manners and language; asserted, in the bosom of despotism, the freedom of their domestic govern-

[75] *Zosimus too frequently betrays his poverty of judgment by disgracing the most serious narratives with trifling and incredible circumstances.*

[76] *——Odothæi Regis opima Rettulit—— The opima were the spoils which a Roman general could only win from the king, or general, of the enemy whom he had slain with his own hands; and no more than three such examples are celebrated in the victorious ages of Rome.*

ment; and acknowledged the sovereignty of the emperor, without submitting to the inferior jurisdiction of the laws and magistrates of Rome. The hereditary chiefs of the tribes and families were still permitted to command their followers in peace and war; but the royal dignity was abolished; and the generals of the Goths were appointed and removed at the pleasure of the emperor. An army of forty thousand Goths was maintained for the perpetual service of the empire of the East; and those haughty troops, who assumed the title of *Fœderati,* or allies, were distinguished by their gold collars, liberal pay, and licentious privileges. Their native courage was improved by the use of arms and the knowledge of discipline; and, while the republic was guarded, or threatened, by the doubtful sword of the Barbarians, the last sparks of the military flame were finally extinguished in the minds of the Romans. Theodosius had the address to persuade his allies that the conditions of peace which had been extorted from him by prudence and necessity were the voluntary expressions of his sincere friendship for the Gothic nation.[77] A different mode of vindication or apology was opposed to the complaints of the people; who loudly censured these shameful and dangerous concessions. The calamities of the war were painted in the most lively colours; and the first symptoms of the return of order, of plenty, and security, were diligently exaggerated. The advocates of Theodosius could affirm, with some appearance of truth and reason, that it was impossible to extirpate so many warlike tribes, who were rendered desperate by the loss of their native country; and that the exhausted provinces would be revived by a fresh supply of soldiers and husbandmen. The Barbarians still wore an angry and hostile aspect; but the experience of past times might encourage the hope that they would acquire the habits of industry and obedience; that their manners would be polished by time, education, and the influence of Christianity; and that their prosperity would insensibly blend with the great body of the Roman people.[78]

Notwithstanding these specious arguments and these sanguine expectations, it was apparent to every discerning eye that the Goths would long remain the enemies, and might soon become the conquerors, of the Roman empire. Their rude and insolent behaviour expressed their contempt of the citizens and provincials, whom they insulted with impunity.[79] To the zeal and valour of the Barbarians Theodosius was indebted for the success of his arms; but their assistance was precarious; and they were sometimes seduced by a treacherous and inconstant disposition to abandon his standard at the moment when their service was the most essential. During the

[77] *Amator pacis generisque Gothorum, is the praise bestowed by the Gothic historian, who represents his nation as innocent, peaceable men, slow to anger, and patient of injuries. According to Livy, the Romans conquered the world in their own defence.*

[78] *Themistius composes an elaborate and rational apology, which is not, however, exempt from the puerilities of Greek rhetoric. Orpheus could only charm the wild beasts of Thrace; but Theodosius enchanted the men and women whose predecessors in the same country had torn Orpheus in pieces, &c.*

[79] *Constantinople was deprived, half a day, of the public allowance of bread, to expiate the murder of a Gothic soldier:* κινοῦντες τὸ Σκυθικόν *was the guilt of the people.*

civil war against Maximus, a great number of Gothic deserters retired into the morasses of Macedonia, wasted the adjacent provinces, and obliged the intrepid monarch to expose his person, and exert his power, to suppress the rising flame of rebellion.[80] The public apprehensions were fortified by the strong suspicion that these tumults were not the effect of accidental passion, but the result of deep and premeditated design. It was generally believed that the Goths had signed the treaty of peace with an hostile and insidious spirit; and that their chiefs had previously bound themselves, by a solemn and secret oath, never to keep faith with the Romans; to maintain the fairest shew of loyalty and friendship, and to watch the favourable moment of rapine, of conquest and of revenge. But, as the minds of the Barbarians were not insensible to the power of gratitude, several of the Gothic leaders sincerely devoted themselves to the service of the empire, or, at least, of the emperor; the whole nation was insensibly divided into two opposite factions, and much sophistry was employed in conversation and dispute, to compare the obligations of their first and second engagements. The Goths, who considered themselves as the friends of peace, of justice, and of Rome, were directed by the authority of Fravitta, a valiant and honourable youth, distinguished above the rest of his countrymen by the politeness of his manners, the liberality of his sentiments, and the mild virtues of social life. But the more numerous faction adhered to the fierce and faithless Priulf, who inflamed the passions, and asserted the independence, of his warlike followers. On one of the solemn festivals, when the chiefs of both parties were invited to the Imperial table, they were insensibly heated by wine, till they forgot the usual restraints of discretion and respect; and betrayed, in the presence of Theodosius, the fatal secret of their domestic disputes. The emperor, who had been the reluctant witness of this extraordinary controversy, dissembled his fears and resentment, and soon dismissed the tumultuous assembly. Fravitta, alarmed and exasperated by the insolence of his rival, whose departure from the palace might have been the signal of a civil war, boldly followed him; and, drawing his sword, laid Priulf dead at his feet. Their companions flew to arms; and the faithful champion of Rome would have been oppressed by superior numbers, if he had not been protected by the seasonable interposition of the Imperial guards.[81] Such were the scenes of Barbaric rage which disgraced the palace and table of the Roman emperor; and, as the impatient Goths could only be restrained by the firm character of Theodosius, the public safety seemed to depend on the life and abilities of a single man.

[80] *Zosimus tells a long and ridiculous story of the adventurous prince who roved the country with only five horsemen, of a spy whom they detected, whipped, and killed in an old woman's cottage, &c.*

[81] *Compare Eunapius with Zosimus. The difference of circumstances and names must undoubtedly be applied to the same story. Fravitta, or Travitta, was afterwards consul (A.D. 401), and still continued his faithful service to the eldest son of Theodosius.*

OVERLEAF: THE ROMAN EMPIRE UNDER TRAJAN A.D. 117

HIBERNIA

BRITANNIA

Noviomagus

Colonia Agrippina

Moguntiacum

GALLIA RÆTIA

Marcomann

NORICUM

Burdigala

Tolosa

Aquileia
PANNONIA

ITALIA

Ravenna

ILLYR

Arelate

Narbo

Tarraco

CORSICA

ROMA

HISPANIA

SARDINIA

Capua

Carthago
Nova

Gades

MAURETANIA

Carthago

SICILIA
Syracusæ

NUMIDIA

AFRICA

II: THE ROMAN EMPIRE

UNDER TRAJAN
A.D. 117

Bastarnæ

Sarmatians

COLCHIS

ALBANIA

IBERIA

Artaxata

CIA

ŒSIA

PONTICA

ARMENIA

REGNUM
PARTHORUM

THRACIA

Byzantium

Nicomedia

CAPPADOCIA

ASSYRIA

Edessa   Nisibis

ASIA

CILICIA

MESOPOTAMIA

PAMPHYLIA

Antiochia

Corinthus

ACHÆA.

CYPRUS

SYRIA

Seleucia

Babylon

Cæsarea

AICA

Petra

ARABIA

Alexandria

Memphis

ÆGYPTUS

meek

DANIEL SILVA

A GABRIEL ALLON THRILLER

PORTRAIT OF AN UNKNOWN WOMAN

HarperCollins*Publishers*

HarperCollins*Publishers*
Australia • Brazil • Canada • France • Germany • Holland • India
Italy • Japan • Mexico • New Zealand • Poland • Spain • Sweden
Switzerland • United Kingdom • United States of America

HarperCollins acknowledges the Traditional Custodians
of the land upon which we live and work, and pays respect
to Elders past and present.

First published in the United States of America in 2022
by HarperCollins*Publishers*
First published in Australia in 2022
by HarperCollins*Publishers* Australia Pty Limited
Gadigal Country
Level 13, 201 Elizabeth Street, Sydney NSW 2000
ABN 36 009 913 517
harpercollins.com.au

A catalogue record for this book is available from the National Library of Australia

ISBN 978 1 4607 5555 6 (paperback)
ISBN 978 1 4607 0978 8 (ebook)
ISBN 978 1 4607 8998 8 (audio book)

Cover design by Darren Holt, HarperCollins Design Studio
Cover images: River Seine and Pont au Change by Kryssia Campos/Getty Images;
all other images by shutterstock.com
Author photograph by Marco Grob
Printed and bound in Australia by McPherson's Printing Group

For Burt Bacharach

And, as always, for my wife, Jamie,
and my children, Lily and Nicholas

All that glisters is not gold.

—William Shakespeare, *The Merchant of Venice*

PART ONE

Craquelure

1

Mason's Yard

On any other day, Julian would have tossed it straight into the rubbish bin. Or better yet, he would have fed it into Sarah's professional-grade shredder. During the long, bleak winter of the pandemic, when they had sold but a single painting, she had used the contraption to mercilessly cull the gallery's swollen archives. Julian, who was traumatized by the project, feared that when Sarah had no more needless sales records and shipping documents to destroy, it would be his turn in the machine. He would leave this world as a tiny parallelogram of yellowed paper, carted off to the recycler with the rest of the week's debris. In his next life he would return as an environmentally friendly coffee cup. He supposed, not without some justification, there were worse fates.

The letter had arrived at the gallery on a rainy Friday in late March, addressed to *M. JULIAN ISHERWOOD*. Sarah had nevertheless opened it; a former clandestine officer of the Central Intelligence Agency, she had no qualms about reading other people's mail. Intrigued, she had placed it on Julian's desk along with several inconsequential items from the morning's post, the only sort of correspondence she typically allowed him to see. He read it for the first time while still clad in his dripping mackintosh, his plentiful gray locks in windblown disarray. The time was half past eleven, which in itself was noteworthy. These days Julian rarely set foot in the gallery before noon. It gave him just enough time to make a nuisance of himself before embarking on the three-hour period of his day he reserved for his luncheon.

His first impression of the letter was that its author, a certain Madame Valerie Bérrangar, had the most exquisite handwriting he had seen in ages. It seemed she had noticed the recent story in *Le Monde* concerning the multimillion-pound sale by Isherwood Fine Arts of *Portrait of an Unknown Woman*, oil on canvas, 115 by 92 centimeters, by the Flemish Baroque painter Anthony van Dyck. Apparently, Madame Bérrangar had concerns about the transaction—concerns she wished to discuss with Julian in person, as they were legal and ethical in nature. She would be waiting at Café Ravel in Bordeaux at four o'clock on Monday afternoon. It was her wish that Julian come alone.

"What do you think?" asked Sarah.

"She's obviously mad as a hatter." Julian displayed the handwritten letter, as though it proved his point. "How did it get here? Carrier pigeon?"

"DHL."

"Was there a return address on the waybill?"

"She used the address of a DHL Express in Saint-Macaire. It's about fifty kilometers—"

"I know where Saint-Macaire is," said Julian, and immediately regretted his abrupt tone. "Why do I have this terrible feeling I'm being blackmailed?"

"She doesn't sound like a blackmailer to me."

"That's where you're wrong, petal. All the blackmailers and extortionists I've ever met had impeccable manners."

"Then perhaps we should ring the Met."

"Involve the police? Have you taken leave of your senses?"

"At least show it to Ronnie."

Ronald Sumner-Lloyd was Julian's pricey Berkeley Square attorney. "I have a better idea," he said.

It was then, at 11:36 a.m., with Sarah looking on in disapproval, that Julian dangled the letter over his ancient metal dustbin, a relic of the gallery's glory days, when it was located on stylish New Bond Street—or New Bondstrasse, as it had been known in some quarters of the trade. Try as he might, he couldn't seem to let the damn thing slip from his fingers. Or perhaps, he thought later, it was Madame Bérrangar's letter that had clung to him.

He set it aside, reviewed the remainder of the morning post, returned a few phone calls, and interrogated Sarah on the details of a pending sale. Then, having nothing else to do, he headed off to the Dorchester for lunch. He was accompanied by an employee of a venerable London auction house, female, of course, recently divorced, no children, far too young but not inappropriately so. Julian astonished her with his knowledge of Italian and Dutch Renaissance painters and regaled her with tales of acquisitional derring-do. It was a character he had been playing to modest acclaim for longer than he cared to remember. He was the incomparable Julian Isherwood, Julie to his friends, Juicy Julie to his partners in the occasional crime of drink. He was loyal as the day was long, trusting to a fault, and English to the core. English as high tea and bad teeth, as he was fond of saying. And yet, were it not for the war, he would have been someone else entirely.

Returning to the gallery, he found that Sarah had adhered a fuchsia-colored sticky note to Madame Bérrangar's letter, advising him to reconsider. He read it a second time, slowly. Its tone was as formal as the linenlike stationery upon which it was written. Even Julian had to admit she sounded entirely reasonable and not at all like an extortionist. Surely, he thought, there would be no harm in merely listening to what she had to say. If nothing else, the journey would provide him with a much-needed respite from his crushing workload at the gallery. Besides, the weather forecast for London called for several days of nearly uninterrupted cold and rain. But in the southwest of France, it was springtime already.

5

Among the first actions that Sarah had taken after coming to work at the gallery was to inform Ella, Julian's stunning but useless receptionist, that her services were no longer required. Sarah had never bothered to hire a replacement. She was more than capable, she said, of answering the phone, returning the emails, keeping the appointment book, and buzzing visitors upstairs when they presented themselves at the perpetually locked door in Mason's Yard.

She drew a line, however, at making Julian's travel arrangements, though she consented to peer over his shoulder while he performed the chore himself, if only to make certain he didn't mistakenly book passage on the Orient Express to Istanbul rather than the Eurostar to Paris. From there, it was a scant two hours and fourteen minutes by TGV to Bordeaux. He successfully purchased a first-class ticket and then reserved a junior suite at the InterContinental—for two nights, just to be on the safe side.

The task complete, he repaired to the bar at Wiltons for a drink with Oliver Dimbleby and Roddy Hutchinson, widely regarded as London's most disreputable art dealers. One thing led to another, as was usually the case when Oliver and Roddy were involved, and it was after 2:00 a.m. by the time Julian finally toppled into his bed. He spent Saturday tending to his hangover and devoted much of Sunday to packing a bag. Once he would have thought nothing about hopping on the Concorde with only an attaché case and a pretty girl. But suddenly the preparations for a jaunt across the English Channel required all of his powers of concentration. He supposed it was but another unwanted consequence of growing old, like his alarming absentmindedness, or the strange sounds he emitted, or his seeming inability to cross a room without crashing into something. He kept a list of self-deprecating excuses at the ready to explain his humiliating clumsiness. He had never been the athletic type. It was the bloody lamp's fault. It was the end table that had assaulted *him*.

He slept poorly, as was frequently the case the night before an important journey, and awoke with a nagging sensation that he was about to make yet another in a long series of dreadful mistakes. His spirits lifted, however, as the Eurostar emerged from the Channel Tunnel and surged across the gray-green fields of the Pas-de-Calais toward Paris. He rode the *métro* from the Gare du Nord to the Gare Montparnasse and enjoyed a decent lunch in the buffet car of the TGV as the light beyond his window gradually took on the quality of a Cézanne landscape.

He recalled with startling clarity the instant he had seen it for the first time, this dazzling light of the south. Then, as now, he was riding a train bound from Paris. His father, the German Jewish art dealer Samuel Isakowitz, sat on the opposite side of the compartment. He was reading a day-old newspaper, as though nothing were out of the ordinary. Julian's mother, her hands knotted atop her knees, was staring into space, her face without expression.

Hidden in the luggage above their heads, rolled in protective sheets of paraffin paper, were several paintings. Julian's father had left a few lesser works behind at his gallery on the rue la Boétie, in the elegant Eighth Arrondissement. The bulk of his remaining inventory was already hidden in the château he had rented east of Bordeaux. Julian remained there until the terrible summer of 1942, when a pair of Basque shepherds smuggled him over the Pyrenees to neutral Spain. His parents were arrested in 1943 and deported to the Nazi extermination center at Sobibor, where they were gassed upon arrival.

Bordeaux's Saint-Jean station lay hard against the river Garonne, at the end of the Cours de la Marne. The departure board in the refurbished ticket hall was a modern device—gone was the polite applause of the updates—but the Beaux-Arts exterior, with its two prominent clocks, was as Julian remembered it. So, too, were the honey-colored Louis XV buildings lining the boulevards along which he sped in the back of a taxi. Some of the facades were so bright they seemed to glow with an interior light source. Others were dimmed by grime. It was

7

the porous quality of the local stone, his father had explained. It absorbed soot from the air like a sponge and, like oil paintings, required occasional cleaning.

By some miracle, the hotel hadn't misplaced his reservation. After pressing an overly generous tip into the palm of the immigrant bellman, he hung up his clothes and withdrew to the bathroom to do something about his ragged appearance. It was gone three o'clock when he capitulated. He locked his valuables in the room safe and debated for a moment whether to bring Madame Bérrangar's letter to the café. An inner voice—his father's, he supposed—advised him to leave it behind, concealed within his luggage.

The same voice instructed him to bring along his attaché case, as it would confer upon him a wholly unwarranted patina of authority. He carried it along the Cours de l'Intendance, past a parade of exclusive shops. There were no motorcars, only pedestrians and bicyclists and sleek electric trams that slithered along their steel tracks in near silence. Julian proceeded at an unhurried pace, the attaché case in his right hand, his left lodged in his pocket, along with the card key for his hotel room.

He followed a tram around a corner and onto the rue Vital Carles. Directly before him rose the twin Gothic spires of Bordeaux Cathedral. It was surrounded by the scrubbed paving stones of a broad square. Café Ravel occupied the northwest corner. It was not the sort of place frequented by most Bordelais, but it was centrally located and easily found. Julian supposed that was the reason Madame Bérrangar had chosen it.

The shadow cast by the Hôtel de Ville darkened most of the café's tables, but the one nearest the cathedral was sunlit and unoccupied. Julian sat down and, placing his attaché case at his feet, took stock of the other patrons. With the possible exception of the man sitting three tables to his right, none appeared to be French. The rest were tourists, primarily of the package variety. Julian was the café's sore thumb; in his flannel trousers and gray sport jacket, he looked like a character from an E. M. Forster novel. At least she would have no difficulty spotting him.

He ordered a café crème before coming to his senses and requesting a half bottle of white Bordeaux instead, brutally cold, two glasses. The waiter delivered it as the bells of the cathedral tolled four o'clock. Julian reflexively smoothed the front of his jacket as his eyes searched the square. But at four thirty, as the lengthening shadows crept across his table, Madame Valerie Bérrangar was still nowhere to be found.

———

By the time Julian finished the last of the wine, it was approaching five o'clock. He paid the bill in cash and, taking up his attaché case, moved from table to table like a beggar, repeating Madame Bérrangar's name and receiving only blank stares in return.

The interior of the café was deserted save the man behind the old zinc-topped bar. He had no recollection of anyone named Valerie Bérrangar but suggested Julian leave his name and phone number. "Isherwood," he said when the barman squinted at the spidery lines scrawled on the back of a napkin. "Julian Isherwood. I'm staying at the InterContinental."

Outside, the bells of the cathedral were tolling once more. Julian followed an earthbound pigeon across the paving stones of the square, then turned into the rue Vital Carles. He realized after a moment that he was berating himself for having come all the way to Bordeaux for no reason—and for having permitted this woman, this Madame Bérrangar, to stir up unwanted memories of the past. "How dare she?" he shouted, startling a poor passerby. It was another unsettling development brought about by his advancing years, his recent propensity to say aloud the private thoughts running through his head.

At last the bells fell silent, and the pleasing low murmur of the ancient city returned. An electric tram glided past, sotto voce. Julian, his anger beginning to subside, paused outside a small art gallery and regarded with professional dismay the Impressionist-inspired paintings in the window. He was aware, vaguely, of the sound of an approaching motorbike. It was no scooter, he thought. Not with an engine note like that. It was one of those low-slung beasts ridden by men who wore special wind-resistant costumes.

The gallery's owner appeared in the doorway and invited Julian inside for a closer look at his inventory. Declining, he continued along the street in the direction of his hotel, the attaché case, as usual, in his left hand. The volume of the motorcycle's engine had increased sharply and was a half step higher in register. Suddenly Julian noticed an elderly woman—Madame Bérrangar's doppelgänger, no doubt—pointing at him and shouting something in French he couldn't make out.

Fearing he had once again uttered something inappropriate, he turned in the opposite direction and saw the motorcycle bearing down on him, a gloved hand reaching toward his attaché case. He drew the bag to his chest and pirouetted out of the machine's path, directly into the cold metal of a tall, immovable object. As he lay on the pavement, his head swimming, he saw several faces hovering over him, each wearing an expression of pity. Someone suggested calling an ambulance; someone else, the gendarmes. Humiliated, Julian reached for one of his ready-made excuses. It wasn't his fault, he explained. The bloody lamppost attacked *him*.

2

Venezia

It was Francesco Tiepolo, while standing atop Tintoretto's grave in the church of the Madonna dell'Orto, who had assured Gabriel that one day he would return to Venice. The remark was not idle speculation, as Gabriel discovered a few nights later, during a candlelit dinner with his beautiful young wife on the island of Murano. He offered several considered objections to the scheme, without conviction or success, and in the aftermath of an electrifying conclave in Rome, the deal was concluded. The terms were equitable, everyone was happy. Chiara especially. As far as Gabriel was concerned, nothing else mattered.

Admittedly, it all made a great deal of sense. After all, Gabriel had served his apprenticeship in Venice and had pseudonymously restored many of its greatest masterpieces. Still, the arrangement was not without its potential pitfalls, including the agreed-upon organizational chart of the Tiepolo Restoration Company, the most prominent such enterprise in the city. Under the terms of their arrangement, Francesco would remain at the helm until his retirement, when Chiara, who was Venetian by birth, would assume control. In the meantime she would occupy the position of general manager, with Gabriel serving as the director of the paintings department.

11

Which meant that, for all intents and purposes, he would be working for his wife.

He approved the purchase of a luxurious four-bedroom *piano nobile* overlooking the Grand Canal in San Polo but otherwise left the planning and execution of the pending move in Chiara's capable hands. She oversaw the apartment's renovation and decoration long-distance from Jerusalem while Gabriel served out the remainder of his term at King Saul Boulevard. The final months passed quickly—there always seemed to be one more meeting to attend, one more crisis to avert—and in late autumn he embarked on what a noted columnist at *Haaretz* described as "the long goodbye." The events ranged from cocktail receptions and tribute-laden dinners to a blowout at the King David Hotel attended by espiocrats from around the globe, including the powerful chief of the Jordanian Mukhabarat and his counterparts from Egypt and the United Arab Emirates. Their presence was proof that Gabriel, who had cultivated security partnerships across the Arab world, had left an indelible mark on a region torn by decades of war. For all its problems, the Middle East had changed for the better on his watch.

Reclusive by nature and uncomfortable in crowded settings, he found all the attention unbearable. Indeed, he much preferred the quiet evenings he passed with the members of his senior staff, the men and women with whom he had carried out some of the most storied operations in the history of a storied service. He begged Uzi Navot for forgiveness. He dispensed career and marital advice to Mikhail Abramov and Natalie Mizrahi. He shed tears of laughter while telling uproarious tales about the three years he had spent living underground in Western Europe with the hypochondriacal Eli Lavon. Dina Sarid, archivist of Palestinian and Islamic terrorism, beseeched Gabriel to sit for a series of exit interviews so that she might record his exploits in an unclassified official history. Not surprisingly, he declined. He had no wish to dwell on the past, he told her. Only the future.

Two officers from his senior staff, Yossi Gavish of Research and Yaakov Rossman of Special Ops, were regarded as his most likely successors. But both were overjoyed to learn that Gabriel had chosen Rimona Stern, the chief of Collections, instead. On a blustery Friday afternoon in mid-December, she became the first female director-general in the history of the Office. And Gabriel, after affixing his signature to a stack of documents regarding his modest pension and the dire consequences he would suffer if he ever divulged any of the secrets lodged in his head, officially became the world's most famous retired spy. His ritual disrobing complete, he toured King Saul Boulevard from top to bottom, shaking hands, drying tear-streaked cheeks. He assured his heartbroken troops that they had not seen the last of him, that he intended to keep his hand in the game. No one believed him.

That evening he attended one final gathering, this time on the shore of the Sea of Galilee. Unlike its predecessors, the encounter was at times contentious, though in the end a kind of peace was made. Early the next morning he made a pilgrimage to his son's grave on the Mount of Olives—and to the psychiatric hospital near the old Arab village of Deir Yassin where the child's mother resided in a prison of memory and a body ravaged by fire. With Rimona's blessing, the Allon family flew to Venice aboard the Office's Gulfstream, and at three that afternoon, after a windblown ride across the *laguna* in a gleaming wooden water taxi, they arrived at their new home.

Gabriel headed directly to the large light-filled room he had claimed as his studio and found an antique Italian easel, two halogen work lamps, and an aluminum trolley filled with Winsor & Newton sable-hair brushes, pigment, medium, and solvent. Absent was his old paint-smudged CD player. In its place was a British-made audio system and a pair of floor-standing speakers. His extensive music collection was organized by genre, composer, and artist.

"What do you think?" asked Chiara from the doorway.

"Bach's violin concertos are in the Brahms section. Otherwise, it's absolutely—"

"Amazing, I think."

"How did you possibly manage all this from Jerusalem?"

She waved a hand dismissively.

"Is there any money left?"

"Not much."

"I'll line up a few private commissions after we get settled."

"I'm afraid that's out of the question."

"Why?"

"Because you shall do no work whatsoever until you've had a chance to properly rest and recuperate." She handed him a sheet of paper. "You can start with this."

"A shopping list?"

"There's no food in the house."

"I thought I was supposed to be resting."

"You are." She smiled. "Take your time, darling. Enjoy doing something *normal* for a change."

The closest supermarket was the Carrefour near the Frari church. Gabriel's stress level seemed to subside a notch with each item he placed in his lime-green basket. Returning home, he watched the latest news from the Middle East with only passing interest while Chiara, singing softly to herself, prepared dinner in the apartment's showplace of a kitchen. They finished the last of the Barbaresco upstairs on the roof terrace, huddled closely together against the cold December air. Beneath them, gondolas swayed at their moorings. Along the gentle curve of the Grand Canal, the Rialto Bridge was awash with floodlight.

"And if I were to paint something original?" asked Gabriel. "Would that constitute work?"

"What did you have in mind?"

"A canal scene. Or perhaps a still life."

"Still life? How boring."

"In that case, how about a series of nudes?"

Chiara raised an eyebrow. "I suppose you'll need a model."

"Yes," said Gabriel, tugging at the zipper of her coat. "I suppose I will."

———————

Chiara waited until January before taking up her new position at Tiepolo Restoration. The firm's warehouse was on the mainland, but its business offices were located on the fashionable Calle Larga XXII Marzo in San Marco, a ten-minute commute by vaporetto. Francesco introduced her to the city's artistic elite and dropped cryptic hints that a succession plan had been put in place. Someone leaked the news to *Il Gazzettino*, and in late February a brief article appeared in the newspaper's Cultura section. It referred to Chiara by her maiden name, Zolli, and pointed out that her father was the chief rabbi of Venice's dwindling Jewish community. With the exception of a few nasty reader comments, mainly from the populist far right, the reception was favorable.

The story contained no mention of a spouse or domestic partner, only two children, twins apparently, of indeterminate age and gender. At Chiara's insistence, Irene and Raphael were enrolled in the neighborhood *scuola elementare* rather than one of Venice's many private international schools. Perhaps fittingly, theirs was named for Bernardo Canal, the father of Canaletto. Gabriel deposited them at the entrance at eight o'clock each morning and collected them again at half past three. Along with a daily visit to the Rialto Market, where he fetched the ingredients for the family dinner, the two appointments represented the sum total of his domestic responsibilities.

Forbidden by Chiara to work, or to even set foot in the offices of Tiepolo Restoration, he devised ways of filling his vast reservoir of available time. He read dense books. He listened to his music collection on his new sound system. He painted his nudes—from memory, of course, for his model was no longer available to him. Occasionally she came to the apartment for "lunch," which was the way they referred to the ravenous sessions of midday lovemaking in their glorious bedroom overlooking the Grand Canal.

Mainly, he walked. Not the punishing clifftop hikes of his Cornish exile, but aimless Venetian wanderings conducted in the unhurried manner of a flaneur. If he were so inclined, he would drop in on a painting he had once restored, if only to see how his work had held up. Afterward, he might slip into a bar for a coffee and, if it was cold, a small glass of something stronger to warm his bones. More often than not, one of the other patrons would attempt to engage him in conversation about the weather or the news of the day. Where once he would have spurned their overtures, he now reciprocated, in perfect if slightly accented Italian, with a witticism or keen observation of his own.

One by one, his demons took flight, and the violence of his past, the nights of blood and fire, receded from his thoughts and dreams. He laughed more easily. He allowed his hair to grow. He acquired a new wardrobe of elegant handmade trousers and cashmere jackets befitting a man of his position. Before long he scarcely recognized the figure he glimpsed each morning in the mirror of his dressing room. The transformation, he thought, was nearly complete. He was no longer Israel's avenging angel. He was the director of the paintings department of the Tiepolo Restoration Company. Chiara and Francesco had given him a second chance at life. This time, he vowed, he would not make the same mistakes.

In early March, during a bout of drenching rains, he asked Chiara for permission to begin working. And when she once again denied his request, he ordered a twelve-meter Bavaria C42 yacht and spent the next two weeks preparing a detailed itinerary for a summer sailing trip around the Adriatic and Mediterranean. He presented it to Chiara over a particularly satisfying lunch in the bedroom of their apartment.

"I have to say," she murmured approvingly, "that was one of your better performances."

"It must be all the rest I've been getting."

"Have you?"

"I'm so rested I'm on the verge of becoming bored stiff."

"Then perhaps there's something we can do to make your afternoon a bit more interesting."

"I'm not sure that would be possible."

"How about a drink with an old friend?"

"Depends on the friend."

"Julian rang me at the office as I was leaving. He said he was in Venice and was wondering whether you had a minute or two to spare."

"What did you say to him?"

"That you would meet him for a drink after you were finished having your way with me."

"Surely you left the last bit out."

"I don't believe so, no."

"What time is he expecting me?"

"Three o'clock."

"What about the children?"

"Don't worry, I'll cover for you." She glanced at her wristwatch. "The question is, what shall we do until then?"

"Since you're not wearing any clothing . . ."

"Yes?"

"Why don't you come to my studio and pose for me?"

"I have a better idea."

"What's that?"

Chiara smiled. "Dessert."

3

Harry's Bar

Standing beneath a cascade of scalding water, drained of desire, Gabriel rinsed the last traces of Chiara from his skin. His clothing lay scattered at the foot of their unmade bed, wrinkled, a button ripped from his shirt. He selected clean apparel from his walk-in closet, dressed quickly, and headed downstairs. As luck would have it, a Number 2 was nudging against the pier of the San Tomà stop. He rode it to San Marco and at three o'clock sharp entered the intimate confines of Harry's Bar.

Julian Isherwood was pondering his mobile phone at a corner table, a half-drunk Bellini hovering beneath his lips. When Gabriel joined him, he looked up and frowned, as though annoyed by an unwanted intrusion. Finally his features settled into an expression of recognition, followed by profound approval.

"I guess Chiara wasn't joking about how you two spend your lunch hour."

"This is Italy, Julian. We take at least two hours for lunch."

"You look thirty years younger. What's your secret?"

"Two-hour lunches with Chiara."

Julian's eyes narrowed. "But it's more than that, isn't it? You look as though you've been . . ." His voice trailed off.

"What, Julian?"

"Restored," he answered after a moment. "You've removed the dirty varnish and repaired the damage. It's almost as if none of it ever happened."

"It didn't."

"That's funny, because you bear a vague resemblance to a morose-looking boy who wandered into my gallery about a hundred years ago. Or was it two hundred?"

"That never happened, either. At least not officially," added Gabriel. "I buried your voluminous file in the deepest reaches of Registry on my way out the door of King Saul Boulevard. Your ties to the Office are now formally severed."

"But not to you, I hope."

"I'm afraid you're stuck with me." A waiter delivered two more Bellinis to their table. Gabriel raised his glass in salutation. "So what brings you to Venice?"

"These olives." Julian plucked one from the bowl at the center of the table and with a flourish popped it into his mouth. "They're dangerously good."

He was dressed in one of his Savile Row suits and a blue dress shirt with French cuffs. His gray hair was in need of a trimming, but then it usually was. All things considered, he looked rather well, except for the plaster adhered to his right cheek, perhaps two or three centimeters beneath his eye.

Cautiously Gabriel asked how it got there.

"I had an argument with my razor this morning, and I'm afraid the razor got the better of me." Julian fished another olive from the bowl. "So what do you do with yourself when you're not lunching with your beautiful wife?"

"I spend as much time as possible with my children."

"Are they bored with you yet?"

"They don't appear to be."

"Don't worry, they will be soon."

"Spoken like a lifelong bachelor."

"It has its advantages, you know."

"Name one."

"Give me a minute, I'll think of something." Julian finished his first Bellini and started in on the second. "And what about your work?" he asked.

"I painted three nudes of my wife."

"Poor you. Any good?"

"Not bad, actually."

"Three original Allons would fetch a great deal of money on the open market."

"They're for my eyes only, Julian."

Just then the door opened, and in walked a handsome dark-haired Italian in slim-fitting trousers and a quilted Barbour jacket. He sat down at a nearby table and in the accent of a southerner ordered a Campari and soda.

Julian was contemplating the bowl of olives. "Cleaned anything lately?"

"My entire CD collection."

"I was referring to paintings."

"The Tiepolo Restoration Company was recently awarded a contract by the Culture Ministry to restore Giulia Lama's four evangelists in the church of San Marziale. Chiara says that if I continue to behave myself, she'll let me do the work."

"And how much will the Tiepolo Restoration Company receive in compensation?"

"Don't ask."

"Perhaps I could tempt you with something a bit more lucrative."

"Such as?"

"A lovely Grand Canal scene that you could knock into shape in a week or two while gazing upon the real thing from your studio window."

"Attribution?"

"Northern Italian School."

"How precise," remarked Gabriel.

The "school" attribution was the murkiest designation for the origin of an Old Master painting. In the case of Julian's canal scene, it meant that the work had been produced by *some*one working *some*where in the north of Italy, at some point in the distant past. The designation "by" occupied the opposite end of the spectrum. It declared that the dealer or auction house selling the painting was certain it had been produced by the artist whose name was attached to it. Between them lay a subjective and oftentimes speculative series of categories ranging from the respectable "workshop of" to the ambiguous "after," each designed to whet the appetite of potential buyers while at the same time shielding the seller from legal action.

"Before you turn up your nose at it," said Julian, "you should know that I'll pay you enough to cover the cost of that new sailboat of yours. Two sailboats, in fact."

"It's too much for a painting like that."

"You funneled a great deal of business my way while you were running the Office. It's the least I can do."

"It wouldn't be ethical."

"I'm an art dealer, petal. If I was interested in ethics, I'd be working for Amnesty International."

"Have you run it past your partner?"

"Sarah and I are hardly partners," said Julian. "My name might still be on the door, but these days I am largely underfoot." He smiled. "I suppose I have you to thank for that, too."

It was Gabriel who had arranged for Sarah Bancroft, a veteran covert operative and overeducated art historian, to take over day-to-day control of Isherwood Fine Arts. He had also played a facilitating role in her recent decision to wed. For reasons having to do with her husband's complicated past, the ceremony was a clandestine affair, held at an MI6 safe house in the countryside of Surrey. Julian had been one of the few invited guests in attendance. Gabriel, who was late in arriving from Tel Aviv, had given away the bride.

"So where's this masterpiece of yours?" he asked.

"Under armed guard in London."

"Is there a deadline?"

"Have you another pressing commission?"

"That depends."

"On what?"

"How you answer my next question."

"You want to know what really happened to my face?"

Gabriel nodded. "The truth this time, Julian."

"I was attacked by a lamppost."

"Another one?"

"I'm afraid so."

"Please tell me it was a foggy night in London."

"Actually, it was yesterday afternoon in Bordeaux. I went there at the invitation of a woman named Valerie Bérrangar. She said she wanted to tell me something about a painting I sold not long ago."

"Not the Van Dyck?"

"Yes, that's the one."

"Is there a problem?"

"I wouldn't know. You see, Madame Bérrangar died in an automobile accident on the way to our meeting."

"And the incident involving the lamppost?" asked Gabriel.

"Two men on a motorcycle tried to steal my briefcase as I was walking back to my hotel. At least I think that's what they were doing. For all I know," said Julian, "they were trying to kill me, too."

4

San Marco

In the Piazza San Marco, a string quartet wearily serenaded the day's last customers at Caffè Florian.

"Are they incapable of playing anything other than Vivaldi?" asked Julian.

"What have you got against Vivaldi?"

"I adore him. But how about Corelli for a change of pace? Or Handel, for heaven's sake?"

"Or Anthony van Dyck." Gabriel paused before a shop window in the arcade on the square's southern flank. "The original story in *ARTnews* didn't mention where you found the painting. It didn't identify the buyer, either. The price tag, however, received prominent play."

"Six and a half million pounds." Julian smiled. "Now ask me how much I paid for the bloody thing."

"I was getting to that."

"Three million euros."

"Which means your profit was in excess of one hundred percent."

"But that's how the secondary art market works, petal. Dealers like me search out misattributed, misplaced, or undervalued paintings and bring them to market, hopefully with enough flair and panache to attract one or more deep-pocketed buyers. And don't forget, I had my expenses, too."

"Long lunches at London's finest restaurants?"

"Actually, most of the lunches took place in Paris. You see, I bought the painting from a gallery in the Eighth. The rue la Boétie, of all places."

"Does this gallery have a name?"

"Galerie Georges Fleury."

"Have you done business with him in the past?"

"A great deal. Monsieur Fleury specializes in French paintings from the seventeenth and eighteenth centuries, but he deals in Dutch and Flemish works as well. He has excellent relationships with many of France's oldest and wealthiest families. The ones who live in drafty châteaux crammed with art. He contacts me when he finds something interesting."

"Where did he find *Portrait of an Unknown Woman*?"

"It came from an old private collection. That's all he would say."

"Attribution?"

"Manner of Anthony van Dyck."

"Which covers all *manner* of sins."

"Indeed," agreed Julian. "But Monsieur Fleury thought he saw evidence of the master's hand. He called me for a second opinion."

"And?"

"The instant I laid eyes on it, I got that funny feeling at the back of my neck."

They emerged from the arcade into the fading afternoon light. To their left rose the Campanile. Gabriel led Julian to the right instead, past the ornate facade of the Doge's Palace. On the Ponte della Paglia, they joined a knot of tourists gawking at the Bridge of Sighs.

"Looking for something?" asked Julian.

"You know what they say about old habits."

"I'm afraid that most of mine are bad. You, however, are the most disciplined creature I've ever met."

On the opposite side of the bridge lay the *sestiere* of Castello. They hurried past the souvenir kiosks lining the Riva degli Schiavoni, then followed the passageway to the Campo San Zaccaria, home of the Carabinieri's regional headquarters. Julian had once spent a sleepless night in an interrogation room on the second floor.

"How's your old friend General Ferrari?" he asked. "Still pulling the wings off flies? Or has he managed to find a new hobby?"

General Cesare Ferrari was the commander of the Carabinieri's Division for the Defense of Cultural Patrimony, better known as the Art Squad. It was headquartered in a palazzo in Rome's Piazza di Sant'Ignazio, though three of its officers were stationed full-time in Venice. While not searching for stolen paintings, they kept tabs on the former Israeli spymaster and assassin living quietly in San Polo. It was General Ferrari who had arranged for Gabriel to receive a *permesso di soggiorno*, a permanent Italian residence permit. Consequently, Gabriel tried to stay on his good side, no easy feat.

Adjacent to the Carabinieri headquarters was the church for which the square was named. Among the many monumental works of art adorning the nave was a crucifixion executed by Anthony van Dyck during the six-year period he spent studying and working in Italy. Gabriel stood before it, a hand to his chin, his head tilted slightly to one side.

"You were about to tell me about the painting's provenance."

"It was good enough for me."

"Meaning?"

"It depicted a portrait that had been executed in the late sixteen twenties and had made its way over the centuries from Flanders to France. There were no glaring holes and no red flags."

"Did it require restoration?"

"Monsieur Fleury had it cleaned before he showed it to me. He has his own man. Not your caliber, mind you. But not bad." Julian crossed to the opposite side of the nave and stood before Bellini's majestic *San Zaccaria Altarpiece*. "You did a lovely job with it. Old Giovanni would have approved."

"You think so?"

Julian cast a glance of mild reproach over one shoulder. "Modesty doesn't suit you, my boy. Your restoration of this painting was the talk of the art world."

"It took me longer to clean it than it did for Giovanni to paint it."

"There were extenuating circumstances, as I recall."

"There usually were." Gabriel joined Julian in front of the altarpiece. "I assume that you and Sarah got a second opinion about the attribution after the painting arrived in London."

"Not just a second opinion. A third, a fourth, and a fifth as well. And all of our gold-plated hired guns concluded that the painting was the work of Anthony van Dyck and not a later follower. Within a week we had a bidding war on our hands."

"Who was the lucky winner?"

"Masterpiece Art Ventures. It's an art-based hedge fund run by one of Sarah's old contacts from her days in New York. Someone called Phillip Somerset."

"The name rings a distant bell," said Gabriel.

"Masterpiece Art Ventures buys and sells an enormous number of paintings. Everything from Old Masters to contemporary. Phillip Somerset routinely shows his investors twenty-five-percent annual returns, from which he takes a substantial cut. And he can be quite litigious if he thinks someone has wronged him. Suing people is his favorite pastime."

"Which is why you went running to Bordeaux when you received a rather ambiguous letter from a perfect stranger."

"Actually, it was Sarah who convinced me to go. As for the letter, the men on the motorbike obviously thought it was in my briefcase. That's why they tried to steal it."

"They might have been ordinary thieves, you know. Street crime is one of the few growth industries in France these days."

"They weren't."

"How can you be sure?"

"Because when I got back to the hotel after being discharged from *l'hôpital*, it was quite obvious that my room had been searched." Julian patted the front of his jacket. "Fortunately, they didn't find what they were looking for."

"Searched by whom?"

"Two well-dressed men. They paid the bellman fifty euros to let them into my room."

"How much did the bellman get from you?"

"A hundred," answered Julian. "As you might expect, I passed a rather restless night. When I woke this morning, there was a copy of *Sud Ouest* outside my door. After reading the story about a fatal single-vehicle accident south of Bordeaux, I hastily packed my things and caught the first train to Paris. I was able to make the eleven o'clock flight to Venice."

"Because you were craving the olives at Harry's Bar?"

"Actually, I was wondering—"

"Whether you might prevail upon me to find out what Valerie Bérrangar wanted to tell you about *Portrait of an Unknown Woman* by Anthony van Dyck."

"You *do* have friends in high places in the French government," said Julian. "Which will enable you to conduct an inquiry with absolute discretion and thus reduce the chance of a scandal."

"And if I'm successful?"

"I suppose that depends on the nature of the information. If there is indeed a legal or ethical problem with the sale, I will quietly refund Phillip Somerset's six and a half million quid before he drags me into court and destroys what's left of my once glittering reputation." Julian offered Gabriel Madame Bérrangar's letter. "Not to mention the reputation of your dear friend Sarah Bancroft."

Gabriel hesitated, then accepted the letter. "I'll need the attribution reports from your experts. And photographs of the painting, of course."

Julian produced his smartphone. "Where shall I send them?"

Gabriel recited an address at ProtonMail, the Swiss-based encrypted email service. A moment later, secure mobile phone in hand, he was scrutinizing a high-resolution detail image of the unknown woman's pale cheek.

At length he asked, "Did any of your experts take a close look at the craquelure?"

"Why do you ask?"

"You know that funny feeling you got when you saw this painting for the first time?"

"Of course."

"I just got it, too."

———

Julian had booked a room for the night at the Gritti Palace. Gabriel saw him to the door, then made his way to the Campo Santa Maria del Giglio. There was not a tourist in sight. It was as if a drain had opened, he thought, and washed them out to sea.

On the western side of the square, next to the Hotel Ala, was the entrance to a narrow, darkened *calle*. Gabriel followed it to the vaporetto station and joined three other passengers—a prosperous-looking Scandinavian couple in their late sixties and a world-weary Venetian woman of perhaps forty—waiting beneath the shelter. The Scandinavians were huddled over a map. The Venetian woman was watching a Number 1 crawling up the Grand Canal from the direction of San Marco.

When the vessel nudged against the jetty, the Venetian woman boarded first, followed by the Scandinavians. All three claimed seats in the cabin. Gabriel, as was his habit, stood in the open-air passage behind the pilothouse. There he was able to observe a single late-arriving passenger emerging from the *calle*.

Dark hair. Slim-fitting trousers. A quilted Barbour jacket.

The man from Harry's Bar.

5

___

Canal Grande

He entered the passenger cabin and lowered himself into a blue-green plastic seat in the first row. He was taller than Gabriel remembered, formidably built, in the prime of life. Early thirties, thirty-five at most. The malodorous trail he left in his wake indicated he was a smoker. The slight bulge in the left side of his jacket suggested he was armed.

Fortunately, Gabriel was in possession of a gun as well—a Beretta 92FS 9mm pistol with a walnut grip. He carried it with the full knowledge and consent of General Ferrari and the Carabinieri. Nevertheless, it was his intention to resolve the situation without having to draw the weapon, as an act of violence, even one in self-defense, would likely result in the immediate revocation of his *permesso*, which in turn would endanger his standing at home.

The most obvious course of action was to shed the man as quickly as possible. In a city like Venice, with its labyrinthine streets and gloomy *sotoportegi*, it would not prove difficult. It would, however, deprive Gabriel of the opportunity to determine why the man was following him. It was better to have a quiet word with him in private, he reasoned, than to lose him.

The Palazzo Venier dei Leoni, home of the Peggy Guggenheim Collection, slid right to left through Gabriel's field of vision. The two Scandinavians disembarked at the Accademia; the Venetian woman, at Ca' Rezzonico. San Tomà, Gabriel's stop, was next. He stood stock-still behind the pilothouse as the vaporetto alighted long enough to collect a single passenger.

As the vessel withdrew, he lifted his gaze briefly toward the soaring windows of his new apartment. They were aglow with amber-colored light. His children were doing their schoolwork. His wife was preparing dinner. Doubtless she was troubled over his prolonged absence. He would be home soon, he thought. He had one small matter to attend to first.

The vaporetto crossed the canal to the Sant'Angelo stop, then returned to the San Polo side and docked at San Silvestri. This time Gabriel disembarked and, leaving the platform, entered an unlit *sotoportego*. From behind him came the sound of footsteps—the footsteps of a formidably built man in the prime of life. Perhaps, thought Gabriel, a small measure of violence was called for, after all.

He fell into the easy, unhurried pace of his afternoon sojourns through the city. Even so, he twice had to loiter outside shop windows in order to keep his pursuer in the game. He was no professional surveillance artist; that much was obvious. Nor did he seem to be familiar with the streets of the *sestiere*, a shortcoming that would provide Gabriel with a distinct home-field advantage.

He continued in a northwesterly direction—across the Campo Sant'Aponal, along a succession of slender alleyways, over a hump-backed bridge—until he came to a *corte* bordered on three sides by apartment buildings. He knew with certainty that the dwellings had fallen into a state of disrepair and were unoccupied, which is why he had chosen the courtyard as his destination.

He moved to a darkened corner and listened to his pursuer's

approaching footfalls. A long moment passed before the man blundered into view. He paused in a puddle of moonlight, then, realizing there was no way out, turned to leave.

"Looking for something?" asked Gabriel calmly in Italian.

The man wheeled around and reached reflexively toward the front of his jacket.

"I wouldn't do that if I were you."

The man froze.

"Why are you following me?"

"I'm not."

"You were in Harry's Bar. You were on the Number One. And now you're here." Gabriel stepped from the shadows. "Twice is a coincidence. Third time is the charm."

"I'm looking for a restaurant."

"Tell me the name, and I'll take you there."

"Osteria da Fiore."

"Not even close." Gabriel took another step across the courtyard. "Please reach for your gun again."

"Why?"

"So I won't feel guilty about breaking your nose, your jaw, and several of your ribs."

Wordlessly the young Italian turned to one side, raised his left hand defensively, and bunched his right fist against his hip.

"All right," said Gabriel with a sigh of resignation. "If you insist."

———

The Israeli martial arts discipline known as Krav Maga is characterized by constant aggression, simultaneous offensive and defensive measures, and utter ruthlessness. Speed is prized above all else. Typically contests are short in duration—no more than a few seconds—and decisive in outcome. Once launched, an attack does not cease until the adversary has been completely incapacitated. Permanent injury is commonplace. Death is not out of the question.

No part of the body is off-limits. Indeed, practitioners of Krav Maga are encouraged to focus their attacks on vulnerable, sensitive regions. Gabriel's opening gambit consisted of a vicious kick to his opponent's exposed left kneecap, followed by a crushing downward heel strike on the instep of the left foot. Next he ventured north to the groin and solar plexus before directing several rapid elbows and side-handed blows to the throat, the nose, and the head. At no point did the younger, larger Italian manage to land a punch or kick of his own. Still, Gabriel did not emerge unscathed. His right hand was throbbing painfully, probably from a minor fracture, the Krav Maga equivalent of an own goal.

With the fingers of his left hand, he checked his fallen opponent for evidence of a pulse and respiration. Finding both, he reached inside the front of the man's jacket and confirmed that he was indeed armed—with a Beretta 8000, the standard-issue sidearm for officers of the Carabinieri. Which explained the credentials that Gabriel found in the unconscious man's pocket. They identified him as Capitano Luca Rossetti of the Venice division of Il Nucleo Tutela Patrimonio Artistico.

The Art Squad . . .

Gabriel returned the gun to its holster and the credentials to their pocket, then rang the regional headquarters of the Carabinieri to report an injured man lying in a *corte* near the Campo Sant'Aponal. He did so anonymously, with his phone number concealed, and in perfect *veneziano*. He would deal with General Ferrari in the morning. In the meantime, he had to concoct a plausible cover story to explain his injured hand to Chiara. It came to him as he crossed the Ponte San Polo. It wasn't his fault, he would tell her. The bloody lamppost attacked him.

6

San Polo

Five minutes later, while climbing the staircase toward the door of the apartment, Gabriel encountered the tantalizing fragrance of veal simmering in wine and aromatics. He entered the passcode into the keypad and turned the latch, performing both tasks with his left hand. His right was concealed in the pocket of his jacket. It remained there as he entered the sitting room, where he found Irene stretched upon the carpet, a pencil in her fist, her tiny porcelain brow furrowed.

Gabriel addressed her in Italian. "There's a lovely desk in your room, you know."

"I prefer to work on the floor. It helps me concentrate."

"What sort of work are you doing?"

"Math, silly." She looked up at Gabriel with the eyes of his mother. "Where have you been?"

"I had an appointment."

"With whom?"

"An old friend."

"Does he work for the Office?"

"Wherever did you get an idea like that?"

"Because it seems like all your old *friends* do."

"Not all of them," said Gabriel, and looked at Raphael. The boy was sprawled on the couch, his long-lashed, jade-colored eyes focused with unnerving intensity on the screen of his handheld video console. "What's he playing?"

"Mario."

"Who?"

"It's a computer game."

"Why isn't he doing his schoolwork?"

"He's finished." With the tip of her pencil, Irene pointed toward her brother's notebook. "See for yourself."

Gabriel craned his head to one side and reviewed Raphael's work. Twenty rudimentary equations involving addition and subtraction, all answered correctly on the first attempt.

"Were you good at math when you were little?" asked Irene.

"It didn't interest me much."

"What about Mama?"

"She studied Roman history."

"In Padua?"

"Yes."

"Is that where Raphael and I will go to university?"

"You're rather young to be thinking about that, aren't you?"

Sighing, she licked the tip of her forefinger and turned to a fresh page in her workbook. In the warmth of the kitchen, Gabriel found Chiara removing the cork from a bottle of Brunello di Montalcino. Andrea Bocelli flowed from the Bluetooth speaker on the counter.

"I've always loved that song," said Gabriel.

"I wonder why." Chiara used her phone to lower the volume. "Going somewhere?"

"Sorry?"

"You're still wearing your overcoat."

"I'm a little chilled, that's all." He wandered over to the gleaming stainless-steel Vulcan oven and peered through the window. Inside was the orange casserole dish that Chiara used for preparing osso buco. "What have I done to deserve this?"

"I can think of one or two things. Or three," she added.

"How long until it's ready?"

"It needs another thirty minutes." She poured two glasses of the Brunello. "Leaving you just enough time to tell me about your conversation with Julian."

"We'll talk after dinner, if you don't mind."

"Is there a problem?"

He turned abruptly. "Why do you ask?"

"There usually is one where Julian is concerned." Chiara regarded him carefully for a moment. "And you seem upset about something."

He decided, with no small amount of guilt, that the wisest course of action was to blame his edgy mood on Raphael. "Your son failed to notice my return home because he was hypnotized by that computer game of his."

"I gave him permission."

"Why?"

"Because it took him all of five minutes to finish his math homework. His teachers think he's gifted. They want him to begin working with a specialist."

"He certainly didn't get it from me."

"Nor from me." Chiara offered him a glass of the wine. "There's a package in your studio. It looks as though it might be from your girlfriend Anna Rolfe." She smiled coolly. "Listen to a bit of music and relax. You'll feel better."

"I feel just fine."

Gabriel accepted the wine with his left hand and withdrew to the master bathroom suite, where he subjected the injured extremity to a thorough examination by the light of Chiara's vanity. The sharp pain produced by a gentle probe indicated at least a hairline fracture to the fifth metacarpal. Significant swelling was plainly evident, but as yet there was no visible bruising. At a bare minimum, immediate immobilization and icing were required. Given the circumstances, however, neither was possible, leaving Gabriel no treatment option other than alcohol and pain reliever.

He took down a bottle of ibuprofen from the medicine chest, shook several emerald capsules into his palm, and swallowed them with a mouthful of the Brunello. Repairing to his studio, he found the package. It had been sent to him by the publicity department of Deutsche Grammophon. Inside was a two-CD survey of Mozart's five remarkable violin concertos, notable for the fact that the soloist had recorded the pieces with the same instrument upon which they had been composed.

Gabriel placed the first disc onto the tray of his CD player, tapped the PLAY button, and went to his easel. There he gazed upon a beautiful young woman draped nude across a brocade-covered couch, her melancholy gaze fixed upon the viewer—in this case, the artist who had painted her. *Is there a problem?* No, he thought as his hand throbbed with pain. No problem at all.

———

Gabriel managed to listen to the first two concertos before Chiara summoned him to the dining room. The meal arrayed upon the table looked as though it had been staged for a photo shoot by *Bon Appétit*—the risotto, the platter of roasted vegetables glistening with olive oil, and, of course, the thick veal shanks drenched in a rich sauce of tomato and herbs and wine. As always, they were fork tender, allowing Gabriel to eat with one hand, keeping the other cradled protectively in his lap. The Brunello-and-Advil therapy had worked its magic; he was only vaguely aware of the pain. He was certain, however, it would return with a vengeance the instant the drug wore off, probably sometime around three in the morning.

Chiara's eyes shone with candlelight as she guided the conversation. Diplomatically she raised the subject of Raphael's mathematical prowess, which in turn led to a discussion of how his gifts might be put to good use. Irene, the family environmentalist, suggested that her brother consider pursuing a career as a climate scientist.

"Why?" probed Gabriel.

"Did you read the new UN report about global warming?"

"Did *you*?"

"We talked about it at school. Signora Antonelli says Venice will soon be underwater because the Greenland ice sheet is melting. She says none of it would have happened if the Americans hadn't withdrawn from the Paris Agreement."

"That's debatable."

"She also says it's too late to prevent a significant increase in global temperatures."

"She's right about that."

"Why did the Americans withdraw?"

"The man who was president at the time thought global warming was a hoax."

"Who would believe such a thing?"

"It's a rather common affliction among Americans of the far right. But let's talk about something pleasant, shall we?"

It was Raphael who chose the subject. "What does *woke* mean?"

Gabriel directed his gaze toward his son and, to the best of his ability, answered. "It's a word that emerged from the Black community in the United States. If someone is woke, it means they care about issues involving racial intolerance and societal injustice."

"Are you woke?"

"Evidently."

"I think I'm woke, too."

"I'd keep it to myself, if I were you."

At the conclusion of the meal, the children volunteered to clear away the plates and serving dishes, a feat they accomplished with minimal conflict and no breakage. Chiara poured the last of the wine into their glasses and held hers to the light of the candles.

"Where shall we begin?" she asked. "Your meeting with Julian or the new tattoo on your right hand?"

"It's not a tattoo."

"That's a relief. What is it?"

Gabriel removed his hand from his lap and laid it carefully on the tablecloth.

Chiara winced. "It looks dreadful."

"Yes," said Gabriel gloomily. "But you should see the other guy."

7

San Polo

"Have you tried to hold a paintbrush?"

"I'm not sure I ever will again."

"How bad is the pain?"

"At the moment," said Gabriel, "I can't feel a thing."

He was perched on a stool at the kitchen island, his hand submerged in a bowl of ice and water. It had done nothing to reduce the swelling. If anything, it appeared to be growing worse.

"You really should have it X-rayed," said Chiara.

"And when the orthopedist asks how I broke it?"

"How did you?"

"I assume it was the knifehand strike."

"Where did it land?"

"I'd rather not say."

"Are you sure you didn't kill him?"

"He'll be fine."

"Will he?"

"Eventually."

With a sigh of dismay, Chiara took up Madame Valerie Bérrangar's letter. "What do you suppose she wanted to tell Julian?"

"I can think of several possibilities," said Gabriel. "Starting with the most obvious."

"What's that?"

"The painting was hers."

"If that were the case, why didn't she contact the police?"

"Who's to say she didn't?"

"Surely Julian checked the Art Loss Register before taking it to market?"

"No dealer ever acquires or sells a work of art without first checking to see whether it's been pinched."

"Unless the dealer doesn't want to know whether it's stolen."

"Our Julian is far from perfect," said Gabriel. "But he has never knowingly sold a stolen painting."

"Not even on your behalf?"

"I don't believe so."

Chiara smiled. "Possibility number two?"

"The work was seized from the Bérrangar family during the war and has been missing ever since."

"Do you think Valerie Bérrangar was Jewish?"

"Did I say that?"

Chiara set aside the letter. "Possibility number three?"

"Unlock my phone."

Chiara entered his fourteen-digit hard password. "What am I looking at?"

"A detail image from *Portrait of an Unknown Woman*."

"Is there a problem?"

"What does the craquelure pattern look like to you?"

"Tree bark."

"And what does that tell you?"

"I will defer to your superior knowledge."

"Surface cracks resembling tree bark are typical of Flemish paintings," explained Gabriel. "Van Dyck was a Flemish painter, of course.

But he worked with materials similar to those being used by his contemporaries in Holland."

"So his surface cracks appear more Dutch than Flemish?"

"Correct. If you look at *Lady Elizabeth Thimbelby and Her Sister* on the website of the National Gallery, you'll see what I mean."

"I'll take your word for it," answered Chiara, her thumbnails clicking against the surface of Gabriel's phone.

"What are you looking for?"

"The article in *Sud Ouest*." She dragged the tip of her forefinger down the screen. "Here it is. The accident happened yesterday afternoon on the D10, just north of Saint-Macaire. The gendarmes seem to think she somehow lost control of her car."

"How old was she?"

"Seventy-four."

"Married?"

"Widowed. Apparently, there's a daughter named Juliette Lagarde." Chiara paused. "Perhaps she'll agree to see you."

"I thought I was supposed to be resting."

"You are. But under the circumstances it's probably better if you leave Venice for a few days. With any luck, you'll be airborne before General Ferrari realizes you're gone."

Gabriel removed his hand from the ice water. "What do you think?"

"A splint should suffice. You can pick one up at the pharmacy on your way to the airport. But I would advise you to avoid striking anyone while you're in Bordeaux."

"It wasn't my fault."

"Whose fault was it, darling?"

It was Madame Bérrangar's, he thought. She should have simply telephoned Julian's gallery in London. Instead, she had sent him a letter. And now she was dead.

8

San Polo

Exhausted, Gabriel crawled into bed and, with his hand cradled gently against his chest, fell into a dreamless sleep. The pain roused him at four o'clock. He lay awake for another hour, listening to the barges making their way up the Grand Canal toward the Rialto Market, before padding into the kitchen and pressing the power button on the Lavazza *automatico*.

While waiting for the coffee to brew, he stirred his phone into life and was relieved to discover he had received no overnight correspondence from General Ferrari. A check of *Sud Ouest* confirmed that Valerie Bérrangar, seventy-four years of age, was still dead. There was a small update to the story regarding the arrangements for her funeral. It was scheduled for 10:00 a.m. on Friday, at the Église Saint-Sauveur in Saint-Macaire. Regardless of Madame Bérrangar's religious affiliation at the beginning of her life, thought Gabriel, it appeared as though she had ended it as a Roman Catholic.

He swallowed another dose of ibuprofen with his coffee. Then he showered and dressed and placed a few items of clothing into an overnight bag while Chiara, tangled in Egyptian cotton, slept on in the next room. The children spilled from their beds at half past six and demanded to be fed. Irene fixed Gabriel with an accusatory stare over her customary breakfast of muesli and yogurt.

"Mama says you're going to France."

"Not for long."

"What does that mean?"

"It means that your grandmother will be picking you up at school for the next few days."

"How many days?"

"To be determined."

"We like it when *you* pick us up," declared Raphael.

"That's because I always take you to the *pasticceria* on the way home."

"That's not the only reason."

"I like picking you up, too," said Gabriel. "In fact, it's one of my favorite parts of the day."

"What's your favorite?"

"Next question."

"Why do you have to leave again?" asked Irene.

"A friend needs my help."

"*Another* friend?"

"Same friend, actually."

She inflated her cheeks and stirred the contents of her bowl without appetite. Gabriel knew full well the source of her anxiety. Three times during his tenure as director-general of the Office he had been targeted for assassination. The last attempt had taken place on Inauguration Day in Washington, when he had been shot in the chest by a congresswoman from the American Midwest who believed him to be a member of a blood-drinking, Satan-worshipping cult of pedophiles. The two preceding attempts, though more prosaic, had both taken place in France. For the most part, the children pretended that none of the incidents, though widely publicized, had transpired. Gabriel, who still suffered from the unpleasant aftereffects, was similarly inclined.

"Nothing is going to happen," he assured his daughter.

"You always say that. But something *always* happens."

Having no retort at the ready, Gabriel looked up and saw Chiara standing in the doorway of the kitchen, an expression of mild bemusement on her face.

"She does have a point, you know." Chiara poured herself a cup of coffee and looked at Gabriel's hand. "How does it feel?"

"Good as new."

She gave it a gentle squeeze. "No pain at all?"

He grimaced but said nothing.

"I thought so." She released his hand. "Are you packed?"

"Almost."

"Who's taking Thing One and Thing Two to school?"

"Papa," sang the children in unison.

He returned to the bedroom and unlocked the safe concealed in the walk-in closet. Inside were two false German passports, €20,000 in cash, and his Beretta. He removed one of the passports but left the gun behind, as his arrangement with the Italian authorities did not permit him to carry firearms on airplanes. Besides, if circumstances warranted, he could acquire an untraceable weapon in France with a single phone call, with or without the connivance of his old service.

He deposited the bag in the entrance hall and at 7:45 a.m. followed Chiara and the children down the stairs of the palazzo. Outside in the street, Chiara set off toward the San Tomà vaporetto station. Then she stopped abruptly and kissed Gabriel's lips.

"You *will* be careful in France, won't you?"

"Cross my heart."

"Wrong answer, darling." She placed her palm on the left side of Gabriel's chest and felt the sudden pulse of his phone. "Oh, dear. I wonder who that could be."

9

Bar Dogale

After entrusting Irene and Raphael to Signora Antonelli, their environmentally conscious and reliably democratic socialist teacher, Gabriel made his way through empty streets to the Campo dei Frari. The square remained in morning shadow, but a benevolent sun had established dominion over the red-tile rooftops of the mighty Gothic basilica. At the foot of the bell tower, the second-tallest in Venice, stood eight chrome tables covered in blue, the property of Bar Dogale, one of the better tourist cafés in San Polo.

At one of the tables sat General Ferrari. He had forsaken his blue uniform, with its many medals and insignia, and was wearing a business suit and overcoat instead. The hand he offered in greeting was missing two fingers, the result of a letter bomb he received in 1988 while serving as chief of the Carabinieri's Naples division. Nevertheless, his grip was viselike.

"Something wrong?" he asked as Gabriel sat down.

"Too many years holding a paintbrush."

"Consider yourself lucky. I had to learn how to do almost everything with my left hand. And then, of course, there's this." The general pointed toward his prosthetic right eye. "You, however, appear to

45

have come through your most recent brush with death with scarcely a scratch."

"Hardly."

"How close did we come to losing you in Washington?"

"I flatlined twice. The second time, I was clinically dead for nearly ten minutes."

"Did you happen to see anything?"

"Like what?"

"A brilliant white light? The face of the Almighty?"

"Not that I can recall."

The general seemed disappointed by Gabriel's answer. "I was afraid you were going to say that."

"It doesn't mean that there isn't a life after this one, Cesare. It just means that I have no memory of anything that happened after I lost consciousness."

"Have you given the matter any thought yourself?"

"The existence of God? An afterlife?"

The general nodded.

"The Holocaust robbed my parents of their belief in God. The religion of my childhood home was Zionism."

"You're entirely secular?"

"My faith comes and goes."

"And your wife?"

"She's a rabbi's daughter."

"I have it on the highest authority that the cultural and artistic guardians of Venice are quite smitten with her. It appears the two of you have a bright future here." The general's prosthetic eye contemplated Gabriel sightlessly for a moment. "Which makes your recent behavior all the more difficult to explain."

He entered the passcode into his smartphone and laid it on the tabletop. Gabriel lowered his eyes briefly to the screen. The bruised and swollen face depicted there bore little resemblance to the one he had seen the previous evening.

"His jaw had to be wired shut," said General Ferrari. "For an Italian, a fate worse than death."

"He'd be sitting down to a nice long lunch later today if only he'd identified himself."

"He says you didn't give him much of a chance."

"Why was he following me in the first place?"

"He wasn't," answered Ferrari. "He was following your friend."

"Julian Isherwood? Whatever for?"

"As a result of that unfortunate business in Lake Como a few years ago, Signore Isherwood remains on the Art Squad's watchlist. We keep an eye on him whenever he comes to Italy. Young Rossetti, who was assigned to Venice only last week, drew the short straw."

"He should have walked out of Harry's Bar the minute he saw Julian with me."

"I ordered him to stay."

"Because you wanted to know what we were talking about?"

"I suppose I did."

"That still doesn't explain why he followed me onto the vaporetto."

"I wanted to make certain you arrived home safely. And how did you repay this act of kindness? By beating one of my best young recruits to a pulp in a darkened *corte*."

"It was a misunderstanding."

"Be that as it may, I am left with a most difficult choice."

"What's that?"

"Immediate deportation or a lengthy incarceration. I'm leaning toward the latter."

"And what must I do to avoid this fate?"

"You can start by showing at least a trace of remorse."

"Mea culpa, mea culpa, mea maxima culpa."

"Much better. Now tell me why Signore Isherwood came to Venice. Otherwise," said the general, glancing at his wristwatch, "you're liable to miss your flight."

———

Over a breakfast of *cappuccini* and *cornetti*, Gabriel recounted the story as Julian had told it. Ferrari's artificial eye remained fixed on him throughout, unblinking. His expression betrayed nothing—nothing, thought Gabriel, other than perhaps mild boredom. The general was the leader of the world's largest and most sophisticated art crime unit. He had heard it all before.

"It's not so easily done, you know. Engineering a fatal car accident."

"Unless it was carried out by professionals."

"Have you ever?"

"Killed anyone with a car? Not that I can recall," said Gabriel. "But there's a first time for everything."

The general emitted a parched laugh. "Still, the most logical explanation is that the Bérrangar woman was running late for her appointment with Signore Isherwood and died in a tragic accident."

"What about the two men who tried to steal Julian's briefcase?"

Ferrari shrugged his shoulders. "Thieves."

"And the ones who searched his hotel room?"

"The search," acknowledged the general, "is harder to explain. Therefore, I would advise your friend to tell the French art crime unit everything he knows. It's a division of the Police Nationale called the Central Office for the Fight against Cultural Goods Trafficking."

"Catchy," remarked Gabriel.

"I suppose it sounds better in French."

"Most things do."

"I'd be happy to contact my French counterpart. His name is Jacques Ménard. He dislikes me only a little."

"Signore Isherwood has no wish to involve the police in this matter."

"And why is that?"

"An allergy, I suppose."

"A common affliction among art dealers and collectors. Unless one of their precious paintings goes missing, of course. Then we're suddenly quite popular." The general offered an approximation of a smile. "I assume that you intend to start with the daughter."

"If she'll agree to see me."

"Who could possibly resist the opportunity to meet with the great Gabriel Allon?"

"A woman who is mourning the death of her mother."

"What about the dealer in Paris?"

"Julian swears he's reputable."

"If you like, I can run his name through our database and see if anything turns up."

"I have contacts of my own in the Paris art trade."

"The dirty side of the trade, as I recall." General Ferrari expelled a lungful of air. "Which returns us to the topic of young Capitano Rossetti."

"Perhaps I should speak to him."

"I can assure you, Rossetti has no wish to see you. If the truth be told, he's rather embarrassed by the way things turned out last night. After all, you *are* half his size."

"And twice his age."

"That, too."

Gabriel checked the time.

"Going somewhere?" inquired the general.

"The airport, I hope."

"A Carabinieri patrol boat will collect you at San Tomà at ten o'clock."

"Ten is cutting it rather close, don't you think?"

"A representative from Alitalia will escort you through security and directly onto the plane. And don't worry about Chiara and the children," the general added as he ordered two more *cappuccini*. "We'll keep an eye on them while you're away."

10

Villa Bérrangar

In the Middle Ages, when English kings laid claim to all of France, the picturesque village of Saint-Macaire was designated a *ville royale d'Angleterre*. It seemed that little had changed in the intervening centuries. A medieval tower stood guard over the entrance to the old city, its clockface showing half past five. Next to it was a café called La Belle Lurette. Gabriel handed the waiter twenty euros and asked whether he knew the address of Madame Valerie Bérrangar.

"She was killed in an auto accident on Monday afternoon."

Gabriel wordlessly handed over another banknote.

"Her villa is near Château Malromé. About two kilometers to the east." The waiter slipped the money into the pocket of his apron. "The entrance will be on your left. You can't miss it."

The château stood on a broad hillside north of Saint-Macaire, in the commune of Saint-André-du-Bois. Renowned for the quality of its gravelly clay soil, the forty-hectare property was acquired in the late nineteenth century by Countess Adèle de Toulouse-Lautrec. Her son, a painter and illustrator who often found inspiration in the brothels and cabarets of Paris, had passed his summers there.

East of the château the road was dangerously narrow and lined on both sides with vineyards. With one eye on the instrument panel of his rented sedan, Gabriel drove two kilometers exactly and, as promised, glimpsed a dwelling on the left side of the road. Parked in the forecourt was a Peugeot estate car, metallic blue, Paris registration. Gabriel drew up next to it and switched off the engine. The instant he opened his door, a dog barked ferociously. But of course, he thought, and climbed out.

Warily he approached the entrance of the villa. As he stretched out a hand toward the bell push, the door opened to reveal a woman, dark in dress and demeanor, with the pale skin of someone who assiduously avoided the sun. She looked to be in her early forties, but Gabriel couldn't be sure. An Old Master painting he could reliably date to within a few years. But modern women, with their age-concealing balms and injections, were a mystery to him.

"Madame Lagarde?"

"*Oui*," she answered. "May I help you, monsieur?"

Gabriel introduced himself. Not with a work name, or one he plucked from thin air, but his real name.

"Have we met somewhere before?" asked Juliette Lagarde.

"I rather doubt it."

"But your name is very familiar." Her eyes narrowed. "Your face, too."

"You might have read about me in the newspapers."

"Why?"

"I used to be the chief of the Israeli intelligence service. I worked closely with the French government in the fight against the Islamic State."

"Not *that* Gabriel Allon."

He offered her an apologetic smile. "I'm afraid so."

"What on earth are you doing here?"

"I'd like to ask you a few questions about your mother."

"My mother—"

"Was killed in an accident on Monday afternoon." Gabriel glanced over his shoulder toward the large Belgian shepherd berating him from the forecourt. "Would it be possible for us to talk inside?"

"You're not afraid of dogs, are you?"

"*Non*," said Gabriel. "Only dogs like that."

———————

As it turned out, Juliette Lagarde didn't much care for the dog, either. It belonged to Jean-Luc, the caretaker. He had worked for the Bérrangar family for more than thirty years, looking after the house when they were in Paris, tending to the small vineyard. Juliette's father, a prosperous commercial lawyer, had planted it with his own hands. He had died of a massive heart attack while Juliette was still a student at the Paris-Sorbonne University. Having earned a useless degree in literature, she now worked in the marketing department of one of France's largest fashion houses. Her mother, unnerved by the jihadist terrorist attacks in Paris, had lately been spending most of her time in Saint-André-du-Bois.

"She wasn't an Islamophobe or a follower of the far right, mind you. She just preferred the countryside to the city. I worried about her being alone, but she had friends here. A life of her own."

They were standing in the villa's spacious kitchen, waiting for the water to boil in the electric kettle. The house around them was silent.

"How often did you speak to her?" asked Gabriel.

"Once or twice a week." Juliette Lagarde sighed. "Our relationship had been strained of late."

"May I ask why?"

"We were quarreling over the question of remarriage."

"She was involved with someone?"

"My mother? God, no." Juliette Lagarde held up her left hand. It was absent a wedding ring. "She wanted me to find another husband before it was too late."

"What happened to the first one?"

"I was so busy at work that I failed to notice he was involved in a passionate *cinq à sept* with a young woman from his office."

"I'm sorry."

"Don't be. These things happen. Especially in France." She poured boiling water from the electric kettle into a flowered teapot. "What about you, Monsieur Allon? Are you married?"

"Happily."

"Children?"

"Twins."

"Are they spies, too?"

"They're in elementary school."

Juliette Lagarde took up the tray and led Gabriel along a central corridor, into a sitting room. It was formal, more Paris than Bordeaux. The walls were hung with oil paintings in ornate French antique frames. They were works of high quality but moderate value. Someone had chosen them with care.

Juliette Lagarde placed the tray on a low wooden table and opened the French doors to the chill afternoon air. "Do you know who lived there?" she asked, pointing toward the distant silhouette of Château Malromé.

"A painter whose work I've always admired."

"You're interested in art?"

"You might say that."

She sat down and poured two cups of tea. "Are you always so evasive?"

"Forgive me, Madame Lagarde. But I've only recently traded the secret world for the overt one. I'm not used to talking about myself."

"Try it once."

"I was an art student when I was recruited by Israeli intelligence. I wanted to be a painter, but I became a restorer instead. For many years, I worked in Europe under an assumed identity."

"Your French is excellent."

"My Italian is better." Gabriel accepted a cup of tea and carried it to the fireplace. Photographs in handsome silver frames lined the mantel. One depicted the Bérrangar family in happier times. "You bear a striking resemblance to your mother. But then I'm sure you realize that."

"We were very much alike. Too much, perhaps." A silence fell between them. At length Juliette Lagarde said, "Now that we're properly acquainted, Monsieur Allon, perhaps you can tell me why her death is of any possible interest to a man like you."

"She was on her way to Bordeaux to meet a friend of mine when she had the accident. An art dealer named Julian Isherwood." He handed Juliette Lagarde the letter. "It arrived at his gallery in London last Friday."

She looked down and read.

"Is that your mother's handwriting?"

"Yes, of course. I have boxes and boxes of her letters. She was very old-fashioned. She loathed email and was forever misplacing her mobile phone."

"Do you have any idea what she might have been referring to?"

"The legal and ethical problems concerning your friend's painting?" Juliette Lagarde rose abruptly to her feet. "Yes, Monsieur Allon. I think I might."

———

She led him through a pair of double doors and into an adjoining sitting room. It was smaller than its neighbor, more intimate. It was a room where books were read, thought Gabriel, and letters to London art dealers written. Six Old Master paintings, beautifully framed and illuminated, adorned its walls—including a portrait of a woman, oil on canvas, approximately 115 by 92 centimeters, quite obviously Dutch or Flemish in origin.

"Does it look familiar?" asked Juliette Lagarde.

"Very," said Gabriel, and placed a hand thoughtfully to his chin. "Do you happen to remember where your father purchased it?"

"A small gallery on the rue la Boétie in Paris."

"Galerie Georges Fleury?"

"Yes, that's the one."

"When?"

"It was thirty-four years ago."

"You have a good memory."

"My father gave it to my mother on her fortieth birthday. She always adored this painting."

With his hand still pressed to his chin, Gabriel tilted his head to one side.

"Does she have a name?"

"It's called *Portrait of an Unknown Woman*." Juliette Lagarde paused, then added, "Just like your friend's painting."

"And the attribution?"

"I'd have to check the paperwork in my father's files, but I believe it was a follower of Anthony van Dyck. To be honest, I find the various categories of attribution rather arbitrary."

"So do many art dealers. They generally select the one that will earn them the most money." Gabriel drew his phone, snapped a photograph of the woman's face, and enlarged the image.

"Are you looking for something in particular?"

"The pattern of the surface cracks."

"Is there a problem?"

"No," said Gabriel. "No problem at all."

11

———

Villa Bérrangar

Together they lifted the painting from its hangers and carried it into the next room, where the natural light was more abundant. There Gabriel removed it from its frame and subjected it to a preliminary examination, starting with the image itself—a three-quarter-length portrait of a young woman, late twenties or early thirties, wearing a gown of gold silk trimmed in white lace. The garment was identical to the one worn by the woman in Julian's version of the painting, though the color was less vibrant and the subtle folds and wrinkles in the fabric were less persuasively rendered. The subject's hands were awkwardly arranged, her gaze vacant. The artist, whoever he was, had failed to achieve the lifelike penetration of character for which Anthony van Dyck, among the most sought-after portraitists of his day, was renowned.

Gabriel turned over the painting and examined the back of the canvas. It was consistent with other seventeenth-century Dutch and Flemish paintings he had restored. So, too, was the stretcher. It looked to be the original woodwork, with the addition of two twentieth-century horizontal reinforcements. In short, there was nothing out of the ordinary or suspicious. By all outward appearances, the painting was a copy of the original Van Dyck portrait that Julian had sold to Phillip Somerset, the New York art investor, for the sum of six and a half million pounds.

There was, however, one glaring problem.

Both works had emerged from the same gallery in the Eighth Arrondissement of Paris, thirty-four years apart.

Gabriel propped the Bérrangar family's version of the painting against the coffee table and sat down next to Juliette Lagarde. After a silence she asked, "Who do you suppose she was, our unknown woman?"

"That depends on where she was painted. Van Dyck maintained successful studios in both London and Antwerp and shuttled between them. The London studio was known as the beauty shop. It was a rather well-oiled machine."

"How much of the portraits did he actually paint?"

"Usually, just the head and face. He made no attempt to flatter his subjects by altering their appearance, which made him somewhat controversial. We think he produced about two hundred portraits, but some art historians believe the real number is closer to five hundred. He had so many followers and admirers that authentication can be a tricky business."

"But not for you?"

"Sir Anthony and I are well acquainted."

Juliette Lagarde turned to the painting. "She looks Dutch or Flemish rather than English."

"I agree."

"She was a rich man's wife or daughter?"

"Or mistress," suggested Gabriel. "In fact, she might well have been one of Van Dyck's lovers. He had a lot of them."

"Painters," said Juliette Lagarde with mock disdain, and added tea to Gabriel's cup. "So let's say, for argument's sake, that Anthony van Dyck painted his original portrait of our unknown woman sometime in the sixteen forties."

"Let's," agreed Gabriel.

She nodded toward the frameless canvas. "So who painted that one? And when?"

"If he was a so-called follower of Van Dyck, he was someone who worked in Van Dyck's style but wasn't necessarily a member of his immediate circle."

"A nobody? Is that what you're saying?"

"If this piece is representative of his oeuvre, I doubt he was terribly successful."

"How would he have gone about it?"

"Copying a painting? He might have attempted to do it freehand. But if I were in his shoes, I would have traced Van Dyck's original and then transferred that image to a canvas of the same dimensions."

"How would you have accomplished that in the seventeenth century?"

"I would have started by poking tiny holes along the lines of my tracing. Then I would have laid the paper atop my ground and sprinkled it with charcoal dust, leaving a ghostly but geometrically accurate rendering of Van Dyck's original."

"An underdrawing?"

"Correct."

"And then?"

"I would have prepared my palette and started to paint."

"With the original close at hand?"

"It was probably on a nearby easel."

"So the artist forged it?"

"It would have only been a forgery if he had tried to sell his version as an original Van Dyck."

"Have you ever done it?" asked Juliette Lagarde.

"Copied a painting?"

"No, Monsieur Allon. Forged one."

"I'm an art conservator," said Gabriel with a smile. "There are some critics of our profession who claim that we restorers forge paintings all the time."

The room had turned suddenly cold. Juliette Lagarde closed the French doors and looked on while Gabriel secured the painting to its frame. Together they carried it into the adjoining room and returned it to its place on the wall.

"Which one is better?" asked Juliet Lagarde. "This one or your friend's?"

"I'll let you be the judge." Gabriel held his phone next to the painting. On the screen was a photograph of Julian's version of *Portrait of an Unknown Woman*. "What do you think?"

"I must admit, your friend's is much better. Still, it's rather unsettling to see them side by side like that."

"What's even more troubling," said Gabriel, "is that both paintings passed through the same gallery."

"Is it possible it's a coincidence?"

"I don't believe in them."

"Neither did my mother."

Which is why, thought Gabriel, she was now dead.

He slipped his phone into the breast pocket of his jacket. "Have the gendarmes returned her personal effects?"

"Last night."

"Did anything appear out of the ordinary?"

"Her mobile phone seems to be missing."

"She didn't have it with her when she was driving to Bordeaux?"

"The gendarmes say not."

"You've searched the house?"

"I've looked everywhere. The truth is, she rarely used it. She much preferred her old landline phones." Juliette Lagarde pointed toward the room's elegant antique writing table. "That's the one she used the most."

Gabriel went to the table and switched on the lamp. Stored in the phone's memory he found five incoming calls from Galerie Georges Fleury and three more from a Police Nationale number in central Paris. He also discovered, in Madame Bérrangar's desk calendar, a reminder for an appointment at four in the afternoon, on the last day of her life.

M. Isherwood. Café Ravel.

He turned to Juliette Lagarde. "Have you tried calling her mobile phone recently?"

"Not since this morning. I have a feeling the battery is dead."

"Do you mind if I give it a try?"

Juliette Lagarde recited the number. When Gabriel dialed it, the call went directly to voice mail. He severed the connection and held the unfaltering gaze of the unknown woman, certain for the first time that Valerie Bérrangar had been murdered.

"Did your mother have a computer?"

"Yes, of course. An Apple."

"It's not missing, is it?"

"*Non.* I checked her email this morning."

"Anything interesting?"

"On the same day my mother died in an automobile accident, she received a notification from her insurance agency that they intended to raise her rates. For the life of me, I can't imagine why. She was an excellent driver," said Juliette Lagarde. "Never so much as a parking ticket."

The skies poured with rain during the drive back to Saint-Macaire. Gabriel checked into his hotel, then walked to La Belle Lurette for dinner, a book beneath his arm for company. After placing an order of *poulet rôti* and *pommes frites*, he rang Chiara in Venice. Their phones were Israeli-made Solaris models, the world's most secure. Even so, they chose their words with care.

"I was beginning to get worried about you," she said.

"Sorry. Busy afternoon."

"Productive, I hope."

"Quite."

"She agreed to see you?"

"She made me tea," answered Gabriel. "And then she showed me a painting."

"Attribution?"

"Follower of Anthony van Dyck."

"Subject matter?"

"Portrait of an unknown woman. Late twenties or early thirties. Not terribly pretty."

"What was she wearing?"

"A gown of gold silk trimmed in white lace."

"Sounds like there might be a problem."

"Several, actually. Including the name of the gallery where her father purchased it."

"Do you think her mother was—"

"I do."

"Did you tell her?"

"I didn't see the point."

"What are your plans?"

"I need to go to Paris to have a word with an old friend."

"Do give him my best."

"Don't worry," said Gabriel. "I will."

12

———

Bordeaux—Paris

Gabriel slept poorly, awakened early, and set out for Bordeaux before it was properly light. A kilometer north of the village of Sainte-Croix-du-Mont, his headlamps picked out the gray-white stain of a spent safety flare. The tire marks appeared a few seconds later, two black slashes across the opposing lane.

He eased onto the grassy verge and surveyed his surroundings. On the right side of the road, columns of vines marched down the slope of a steep hill. On the left, nearer the river, there were vineyards as well, but the land was tabletop flat. And largely treeless, observed Gabriel, with the exception of a coppice of white-barked poplar toward which the tire marks led.

He fished an LED torch from the glove box and waited for a cargo truck to pass before climbing out and crossing to the opposite side of the road. He didn't venture much beyond the broken white line at the edge of the tarmac; it wasn't necessary. From his vantage point, the damage was plain to see.

Two of the poplars had been snapped by the force of the collision, and the sodden earth was strewn with cubes of shattered safety glass. Gabriel reckoned that Valerie Bérrangar must have been killed instantly by the force of the impact. Or perhaps she had remained conscious long enough to notice the gloved hand reaching through the broken window. Not to render assistance but to seize her phone. Gabriel dialed the number, hoping he might hear a death rattle from amid the trees, but once again the call went straight to voice mail.

Killing the connection, he turned and examined the parallel tire marks. They crossed the southbound lane at roughly a forty-five-degree angle. Yes, he thought, it was possible that Valerie Bérrangar had been distracted somehow and unwittingly swerved to the left, directly toward the only stand of trees in sight. But the more likely explanation was that her car had been forced off the road by the vehicle behind her.

A car approached from the north, slowed briefly, and continued on toward Sainte-Croix-du-Mont. Two minutes elapsed before another appeared, this time from the south. It was not a busy stretch of road. At three fifteen on a Monday afternoon, it would have been quiet as well. Even so, the associates of the man who had forced Valerie Bérrangar's car into the trees had probably taken steps to contain the traffic in both directions so there would be no witnesses. General Ferrari was right; inducing a fatal accident was not easily done. But the men who murdered Valerie Bérrangar knew what they were doing. After all, thought Gabriel, they were professionals. Of that, he was certain.

He crossed the road and slid behind the wheel of his rental car. The drive to the airport was thirty minutes. His flight to Paris departed promptly at nine, and at half past eleven, having entrusted his bag to the bell staff of the Bristol Hotel, he was walking up the rue de Miromesnil in the Eighth Arrondissement.

At the northern end of the street was a small shop called Antiquités Scientifiques. The sign in the window read OUVERT. The buzzer, when pressed, emitted an inhospitable howl. Several seconds elapsed with no invitation to enter. Finally the deadbolt snapped open with a thud, and Gabriel slipped inside.

———

On the morning of August 22, 1911, Louis Béroud arrived at the Musée du Louvre to resume work on a copy of a portrait of an Italian noblewoman, 77 by 53 centimeters, oil on poplar panel, that hung in the Salon Carré. The Louvre did not discourage the work of artists such as Béroud. In fact, it permitted them to store their paints and easels at the museum overnight. They were forbidden, however, to produce copies with the exact dimensions of the originals, as the European art market was awash with forgeries of Old Master paintings.

Formally attired in a black frock coat and striped trousers, Béroud strode into the Salon Carré that Tuesday morning only to discover that the portrait, Leonardo da Vinci's *Mona Lisa*, had been removed from its protective wood-and-glass case. He was disappointed but not unduly alarmed. Neither, for that matter, was Maximilien Alphonse Paupardin, the guard who kept watch over the Salon Carré and its priceless treasures, usually from atop a stool in the doorway. The Louvre was in the process of photographing its entire inventory of paintings and other objets d'art. Brigadier Paupardin was confident that Mona Lisa was merely having her picture taken.

But later that morning, after visiting the photography studio, a frantic Paupardin informed the Louvre's acting president that the *Mona Lisa* was missing. The gendarmes arrived at one o'clock and immediately sealed the museum. It would remain closed for the next week as the police scoured Paris for clues. Their investigation, such as it was, was a comedy of errors. Among the initial suspects were a brash young Spanish painter named Pablo Picasso and his friend, the poet and writer Guillaume Apollinaire.

Another was Vincenzo Peruggia, the Italian-born carpenter who had helped to construct the *Mona Lisa*'s protective case. But police cleared Peruggia of suspicion after a brief interview conducted in his Paris apartment. Which is where the *Mona Lisa* remained, hidden in a trunk in the bedroom, until 1913, when the humble woodworker attempted to sell the painting to a prominent art dealer in Florence. The dealer took it to the Uffizi Gallery, and Peruggia was promptly arrested. Convicted in an Italian courtroom of the greatest art crime in history, he received a one-year prison sentence but was set free after spending only seven months behind bars.

It was the remarkable tale of the *Mona Lisa*'s theft that inspired a restless Paris shopkeeper named Maurice Durand, in the drab winter of 1985, to steal his first painting—a small still life by Jean-Baptiste-Siméon Chardin that hung in a rarely visited corner of the Musée des Beaux-Arts in Strasbourg. Unlike Vincenzo Peruggia, Durand already had a buyer waiting, a disreputable collector who was in the market for a Chardin and wasn't worried about messy details such as provenance. Durand was well paid, the client was happy, and a lucrative career was born.

Two decades later, a fall through a skylight ended Durand's career as a professional art thief. He now operated solely as a broker in the process known as commissioned theft. Or, as Durand liked to describe it, he managed the acquisition of paintings that were not technically for sale. Working with a stable of Marseilles-based professional thieves, he was the hidden hand behind some of the most spectacular art heists of the twenty-first century. During the summer of 2010 alone, his men stole works by Rembrandt, Picasso, Caravaggio, and Van Gogh. With the exception of the Rembrandt, which hung in the National Gallery of Art in Washington, none of the paintings had resurfaced.

Durand ruled his global empire of art theft from Antiquités Scientifiques, which had been in his family for three generations. Its tastefully lit shelves were lined with antique microscopes, cameras, spectacles, barometers, surveyors, and globes, all meticulously arranged. So, too, was Maurice Durand. He wore a tailored suit, dark blue, and a striped dress shirt. His necktie was the color of gold leaf. His bald head was polished to a high gloss.

"I suppose it's true, after all," he said by way of greeting.

"What's that?" asked Gabriel.

"That men in your line of work never truly retire."

"Or yours, apparently."

Smiling, Durand lifted the lid of a varnished rectangular case. "Perhaps this might be of interest to you. An optician's trial lens kit. Turn of the century. Quite rare."

"Almost as rare as that watercolor you stole from the Musée Matisse a few months back. Or the lovely genre piece by Jan Steen you pinched from the Musée Fabre."

"I had nothing to do with the disappearance of either of those works."

"What about the sale?"

Durand closed the lid, soundlessly. "My associates and I acquired a number of valuable objects for you and your service over the years, including a remarkable terra-cotta hydria by the Amykos Painter. And then, of course, there was the job in Amsterdam. We caused quite a stir with that one, didn't we?"

"Which is why I have refrained from giving your name to the French authorities."

"What about General Cyclops, your friend from the Carabinieri?"

"He remains unaware of your identity. Or the identities of your associates in Marseilles."

"And what must I do to preserve this state of affairs?"

"You must provide me with information."

"About what?"

"Galerie Georges Fleury. It's on the rue—"

"I know where it is, Monsieur Allon."

"Are you in business with him?"

"Georges Fleury? Never. But I did foolishly agree to steal a painting from him once."

"What was it?"

"It was," said Durand, his expression darkening, "a disaster."

13

Rue de Miromesnil

Are you familiar with Pierre-Henri de Valenciennes?"

Gabriel sighed before answering. "Valenciennes was one of the most important landscape artists of the neoclassical period. He was among the earliest proponents of working *en plein air* rather than in a studio." He paused. "Shall I go on?"

"I meant no offense."

"None taken, Maurice."

They had retreated to Durand's cramped rear office. Gabriel was seated in the uncomfortable wooden armchair reserved for visitors; Durand, behind his spotless desk. The light of his antique lamp was reflected in his rimless spectacles, obscuring his watchful brown eyes.

"A number of years ago," he continued, "Galerie Georges Fleury exhibited a stunning landscape said to have been painted by Valenciennes in 1804. It depicted villagers dancing around classical ruins at dusk. Oil on canvas, sixty-six by ninety-eight centimeters. Immaculate condition, as Monsieur Fleury's paintings always are. A collector of considerable expertise and means whom we shall refer to as Monsieur Didier entered into negotiations to purchase the painting. But

67

the talks broke down almost immediately because Monsieur Fleury refused to budge on the price."

"Which was?"

"Let's call it four hundred thousand."

"And how much was Monsieur Didier willing to pay you to steal it for him?"

"The rule of thumb is that a painting retains only ten percent of its value on the black market."

"Forty thousand is rather small beer for you."

"I told him so."

"How much did he offer?"

"Two hundred."

"And you accepted?"

"Unfortunately."

From the cabinet behind his desk Durand removed a bottle of calvados and two antique cut-glass tumblers. Nearly everything in the room was from another age, including the little black-and-white video monitor he used to keep watch on his front door.

He poured two glasses of the brandy and offered one to Gabriel.

"It's a bit early in the day for me."

"Nonsense," said Durand after consulting his wristwatch. "Besides, a little alcohol at midday is good for the blood."

"My blood is just fine, thank you."

"No lingering effects from that unpleasantness in Washington?"

"Only an abiding concern for the future of American democracy." Gabriel reluctantly accepted the brandy. "Who handled the job for you?"

"Your old friend René Monjean."

"Any complications?"

"Not with the robbery itself. The gallery's security system was rather outmoded."

"Surely you didn't take just the one painting."

"Of course not. René grabbed four others to cover our tracks."

"Anything good?"

"Pierre Révoil. Nicolas-André Monsiau." Durand shrugged. "A couple of portraits by Ingres."

"Five pictures is quite a haul. And yet I don't recall reading about the robbery in the newspapers."

"Evidently, Monsieur Fleury never reported it to the police."

"Unusual."

"I thought so."

"But you went ahead with the sale nevertheless."

"What choice did I have?"

"When did things go sideways?"

"About two months after Monsieur Didier took possession of the painting, he demanded a refund."

"Also unusual," said Gabriel. "At least in your line of work."

"Unheard of," murmured Durand.

"Why did he want his money back?"

"He claimed the Valenciennes wasn't a Valenciennes."

"He thought it was a later copy?"

"That's one way of putting it."

"And another?"

"Monsieur Didier was convinced the painting was a modern forgery."

Of course he was, thought Gabriel. A part of him had known it was leading to this from the moment he spotted the incongruous Flemish-style craquelure in the photograph of Julian's painting.

"How did you handle it?"

"I explained to Monsieur Didier that I had fulfilled my end of our arrangement and that he should take his complaints to Galerie Georges Fleury." Durand gave a faint smile over the rim of his glass. "Fortunately, he didn't take my suggestion."

"You returned his money?"

"Half of it," answered Durand. "It turned out to be a wise decision. I've done a great deal of business with him since."

Gabriel raised the glass of calvados to his lips for the first time. "You wouldn't happen to have it lying around, would you?"

"The fake Valenciennes?" Durand shook his head. "I burned it."

"And the four other paintings?"

"I sold them at a steep discount to a dealer in Montreal. They covered René's fee, but barely." He exhaled heavily. "It was a wash."

"All's well that ends well."

"Unless one is a paying customer of Galerie Georges Fleury."

"The phony Valenciennes wasn't a fluke?"

"*Non.* Apparently, selling forgeries is the gallery's business model. Don't get me wrong, Fleury sells plenty of genuine paintings. But that's not where he makes his money." Durand paused. "Or so I have been reliably told."

"By whom?"

"You have your sources, I have mine. And they have assured me that Fleury has been selling worthless fakes for years."

"I have a terrible feeling a friend of mine might have purchased one."

"He's a collector, this friend?"

"A dealer."

"Not Monsieur Isherwood?"

Gabriel hesitated, then nodded slowly.

"Why doesn't he simply return it and demand his money back?"

"He sold the painting to a litigious American."

"Is there any other kind?" Durand eyed a window shopper in the video monitor. "May I ask you one other question, Monsieur Allon?"

"If you insist."

Durand made a face. "What in God's name happened to your hand?"

———

After leaving Maurice Durand's shop, Gabriel walked south on the rue de Miromesnil to the rue la Boétie. He lingered for a moment outside the building at Number 19, then made his way along the elegant, gently curving street to Galerie Georges Fleury. Displayed in its window were three large oil paintings. Two were in the Rococo style. The third, a portrait of a young man by François Gérard, dated from the later period known as Neoclassicism.

Or so it appeared at first glance. But an inspection carried out by a trained professional—an art restorer, for example—might tell a different story. It could not be hurried, this appraisal. The restorer would have to take his time with each work in the gallery, engage in the time-honored tradition of connoisseurship. He might touch the paintings, examine their surfaces with a magnifying glass, even speak a few words to them in the hope they spoke to him. It would be advantageous if the gallery's owner—who was likely engaged in criminal conduct and therefore would be naturally vigilant—were not looking over his shoulder as he was conducting this ritual. Better still if he were distracted by the presence of someone else in the room.

But whom?

This was the question that Gabriel pondered as he made the short walk from the gallery to the Bristol. After checking into his room, he rang Chiara and described his quandary. She replied by immediately forwarding him a list of upcoming performances by the Orchestre de Chambre de Paris.

"Your girlfriend is in town all weekend. Perhaps she has a few minutes tomorrow afternoon to serve as your distraction."

"She's perfect. But are you sure you don't mind?"

"If you spend the weekend in Paris with a woman you were once madly in love with?"

"I was never in love with her."

"Please remind her of that fact the first chance you get."

"Don't worry," said Gabriel before the connection went dead. "I will."

14

Le Bristol Paris

She was staying at the Crillon, in the Leonard Bernstein suite. He was one of the few conductors, she added with a laugh, with whom she had never been romantically linked.

"Are you there now?"

"Actually, I interrupted my rehearsal to take your call. The entire Orchestre de Chambre de Paris is hanging on my every word."

"When will you be back at your hotel?"

"Not until four. But I have press interviews scheduled until six."

"My condolences."

"I plan on misbehaving terribly."

"How about a drink downstairs in Les Ambassadeurs when you're finished?"

"Let's have dinner instead."

"Dinner?"

"It's a meal that most people take in the early evening. Unless one is Spanish, of course. I'll ask the concierge to book us a quiet table for two at the most romantic restaurant in Paris. With any luck, the paparazzi will find us, and a *scandale* will ensue."

Before Gabriel could object, the connection was lost. He briefly considered alerting Chiara to his new dilemma but thought it unwise. Instead, he dialed the number for Valerie Bérrangar's missing phone. Once again the call went straight to her voice mail.

He rang off and scrolled through his contacts until he arrived at the entry for Yuval Gershon. Yuval was the director-general of Unit 8200, Israel's formidable signals intelligence service. Gabriel had not spoken to him—or any of his old colleagues, for that matter—since leaving Israel. It was a momentous step, one that would invite future contact, perhaps unwanted. Still, Gabriel reckoned it was worth the risk. If anyone could locate Madame Bérrangar's phone, it was Yuval and his hackers at the Unit.

He answered instantly, as though he had been anticipating Gabriel's call. Given the Unit's extraordinary capabilities, it was not beyond the realm of possibility.

"You miss me, don't you?"

"Almost as much as the hole in my chest."

"So why are you calling?"

"I have a problem only you can solve."

Yuval exhaled heavily into the phone. "What's the number?"

Gabriel recited it.

"And the problem?"

"The owner was murdered a few days ago. I have a feeling the killers were dumb enough to take her phone. I'd like you to find it for me."

"It won't be a problem if the device is still intact. But if they smashed it to pieces or dropped it into the Seine—"

"Why did you mention the Seine, Yuval?"

"Because you're calling from Paris."

"Bastard."

"I'll send up a flare when I have something. And have fun at dinner tonight."

"How did you know about dinner?"

"Anna Rolfe just sent you a text message. Shall I read it to you?"

"Why not?"

"Your reservation is at eight fifteen."

"Where?"

"She doesn't say. But it must be close to the Bristol, because she's picking you up at eight."

"I never mentioned that I was staying at the Bristol."

"It looks to me as though your room is on the third floor."

"The fourth," said Gabriel. "But who's counting?"

———

The first time Gabriel saw Anna Rolfe, she was standing on a stage in Brussels, delivering an electrifying performance of Tchaikovsky's Violin Concerto in D Major. He left the concert hall that night never imagining they might one day meet. But several years later—after the murder of Anna's father, the immensely wealthy Swiss banker Augustus Rolfe—they were formally introduced. On that occasion, Anna had offered her hand in greeting. Now, as Gabriel joined her in the back of a courtesy Mercedes-Maybach limousine, she threw her arms around his neck and pressed her lips against his cheek.

"Consider yourself my hostage," she said as the car drew away from the hotel. "This time escape is impossible."

"Where are you planning to take me?"

"Back to my suite at the Crillon, of course."

"I was promised dinner."

"A clever ruse on my part." Anna was casually attired in jeans, a cashmere sweater, and a car-length leather coat. Even so, there was no mistaking her for anyone other than the world's most famous violinist. "Did my publicist send you the new CD?"

"It arrived the day before yesterday."

"And?"

"A triumph."

"The reviewer from the *Times* said it displayed a newfound maturity." Anna frowned. "What do you think he meant by that?"

"It's a polite way of saying you're getting older."

"You wouldn't know it from the cover photograph. It's amazing what they can do with the click of a mouse these days. I look younger than Nicola Benedetti."

"You can be sure she idolized you when she was a child."

"I don't want to be anyone's *idol*. I just want to be thirty-three again."

"Whatever for?" Gabriel gazed out his window at the graceful Haussmann buildings lining the rue du Faubourg Saint-Honoré. "Where are we having dinner?"

"It's a surprise."

"I hate them."

"Yes," said Anna distantly. "I remember."

15

———

Chez Janou

The restaurant turned out to be Chez Janou, a bright and crowded bistro on the western fringes of the Marais. A low murmur passed through the dining room as they were escorted to their table. Anna took her time removing her coat and settling onto the red banquette. It was, thought Gabriel, a virtuoso performance.

When the commotion subsided, she leaned across the small wooden table and whispered, "I hope you're not disappointed it isn't more romantic."

"I'm relieved, actually."

"I was only joking, you know."

"Were you?"

"I got over you a long time ago, Gabriel."

"Two husbands ago, in fact."

"That was needlessly vindictive."

"Perhaps," said Gabriel. "But entirely accurate."

Both of Anna's marriages had been brief and unhappy, and both had ended with spectacular divorces. And then there was the string of disastrous affairs, always with rich and famous men. Gabriel had been the exception to Anna's pattern. He had survived her mood swings and episodes of personal recklessness longer than most—six months and fourteen days—and with the exception of a single shattered vase, their parting had been civil. It was true that he had never quite loved her, but he had cared for her a great deal and was pleased that after an interregnum of some twenty years they had renewed their friendship. Anna was a bit like Julian Isherwood. She definitely made life more interesting.

As usual, her perusal of the menu was hurried and her selections decisive. They threw Gabriel onto the defensive, for he had intended to order the same items. His fallback—ratatouille followed by liver and potatoes—produced a sneer of mild rebuke on the famous face of his dinner companion.

"Peasant," she hissed.

The waiter removed the cork from a bottle of Bordeaux and poured a small measure for Gabriel's approval. For all he knew, some of the grapes used to produce the wine had come from the vineyard north of Saint-Macaire where Valerie Bérrangar's life had ended. He sniffed, tasted, and with a nod instructed the waiter to fill their glasses.

"What shall we drink to?" asked Anna.

"Old friends."

"How dreadfully boring." Her lipstick left a smudge on the rim of the glass. She returned it to the tabletop and rotated it slowly between her thumb and forefinger, aware that the eyes of the room were upon her. "Do you ever wonder how our lives would have turned out if you hadn't walked out on me?"

"That's not how I would describe what happened."

"You tossed your meager possessions into a duffel bag and drove away from my villa in Portugal as fast as you could. And I did not receive so much as a single—"

"Please let's not do this again."

"Why not?"

"Because I can't change the past. Besides, if I hadn't left, you would have thrown me out sooner or later."

"Not you, Gabriel. You were a keeper."

"And what would I have done with myself while you were on tour?"

"You could have come with me and kept me out of all the trouble I got into."

"Followed you from city to city while you basked in the adulation of your adoring fans?"

She smiled. "That about sums it up."

"And how would you have explained me? Who would I have been?"

"I always adored Mario Delvecchio."

"Mario was a lie," said Gabriel. "Mario never was."

"But he did the most wonderful things to me in bed." She sighed and drank more of her wine. "You never told me your wife's name."

"It's Chiara."

"What does she look like?"

"A bit like Nicola Benedetti, but prettier."

"She's Italian, I take it."

"Venetian."

"Which would explain why you're living there again."

Gabriel nodded. "She's managing the city's largest restoration company. Eventually, I'll go to work for her."

"Eventually?"

"I'm on administrative leave until further notice."

"Because of what happened in Washington?"

"And other assorted traumas."

"There are worse places to recuperate than Venice."

"Much," agreed Gabriel.

"I think I'll schedule a performance there. A night of Brahms and Tartini at the Scuola Grande di San Rocco. I'll get a suite at that little hotel in San Marco, the Luna Baglioni, and stay there for a month or two. You can come by every afternoon and—"

"Behave, Anna."

"Will you at least introduce me to your family someday?"

"Don't you think that might be a bit awkward?"

"Not at all. In fact, I think your children might enjoy spending time with me. Despite my many faults and failings, all of which have been mercilessly chronicled in the tabloids, most people find me endlessly fascinating."

"Which is why I'd like to borrow you for an hour or two tomorrow."

"What did you have in mind?"

He told her.

"Is it really safe to visit an art gallery in Paris with you?"

"It was a long time ago, Anna."

"Another lifetime," she said. "But why me?"

"I need you to distract the owner while I take a careful look at his inventory."

"Shall I bring along my fiddle and perform a partita or two?"

"That won't be necessary. Just be your usual enchanting self."

"Eye candy?"

"Exactly."

She probed at the skin along her jawline. "I'm a bit old for that, don't you think?"

"You haven't changed a bit since—"

"The morning you walked out on me?" The waiter served their first course and withdrew. Anna lowered her eyes and said, *"Bon appétit."*

16

Rue la Boétie

Gabriel rang the gallery at ten o'clock the following morning and, after a testy exchange with a male receptionist called Bruno, was connected to Monsieur Georges Fleury himself. Not surprisingly, the crooked French art dealer had never heard of anyone named Ludwig Ziegler.

"I advise a single client with a passion for Neoclassical paintings," Gabriel explained in German-accented French. "She happens to be in Paris for the weekend and would like to visit your gallery."

"Galerie Georges Fleury is not a tourist destination, Monsieur Ziegler. If your client wishes to see French paintings, I would suggest a visit to the Louvre instead."

"My client isn't here on holiday. She's performing this weekend at the Philharmonie de Paris."

"Is your client—"

"Yes."

Fleury's tone was suddenly more accommodating. "What time would Madame Rolfe like to stop by?"

"One o'clock this afternoon."

"I'm afraid I've already arranged to see another client at that time."

"Reschedule him. And tell Bruno to take a long lunch. I find him annoying, and so will Madame Rolfe. In case you were wondering, she drinks room-temperature mineral water. *Sans gaz*, with a slice of lemon. Not a wedge, Monsieur Fleury. A slice."

"Any particular brand of water?"

"Anything but Vittel. And no photographs or handshakes. For understandable reasons, Madame Rolfe never shakes hands before a performance."

Gabriel rang off, then dialed Anna's number. Her voice, when at last she answered, was heavy with sleep.

"What time is it?" she groaned.

"A few minutes after ten."

"In the *morning*?"

"Yes, Anna."

Swearing softly, she killed the connection. Madame Rolfe, Gabriel remembered, never rose before noon.

Gabriel left the Bristol at half past twelve and walked beneath a leaden Parisian sky to the Crillon. It was one fifteen when Anna, in jeans and a zippered sweater, finally descended from her suite. Outside, they slid into the back of the Maybach for the short drive to Galerie Georges Fleury.

"Any last instructions?" she asked while appraising her face in the vanity mirror.

"Be charming, but difficult."

"Act naturally? Is that what you're saying?"

Anna glossed her heart-shaped lips as the car turned onto the rue la Boétie. A moment later it stopped outside the gallery. Its owner and namesake was waiting on the pavement like a doorman. His hands remained rigidly at his side as Anna emerged from the back of the limousine.

"Welcome to Galerie Georges Fleury, Madame Rolfe. It is truly an honor to meet you."

Anna acknowledged the art dealer's greeting with a regal nod. Unnerved, he thrust a hand toward Gabriel.

"And you must be Herr Ziegler."

"I must be," said Gabriel evenly.

Fleury regarded him for a moment through a pair of rimless spectacles. "Is it possible we've met somewhere before? At an auction, perhaps?"

"Madame Rolfe and I avoid them." Gabriel glanced at the gallery's heavy glass door. "Shall we go inside? It doesn't take long for her to attract a crowd."

Fleury used a handheld remote to unlock the door. In the vestibule, a bronze life-size bust of a young Greek or Roman man stood atop a plinth of black marble. Next to it was an unoccupied receptionist's desk.

"As you requested, Herr Ziegler, it's just the three of us."

"No hard feelings, I hope."

"None at all." Fleury placed the remote on the desk and escorted them into a high-ceilinged room with a dark wooden floor and walls of garnet red. "My main exhibition room. The better pictures are upstairs. If you wish, we can begin there."

"Madame Rolfe is in no hurry."

"Neither am I."

Dazzled, Fleury led his internationally renowned visitor on a laborious tour of the room's collection while Gabriel conducted an unchaperoned survey of his own. The first work to catch his connoisseur's eye was a large Rococo painting depicting a nude Venus and three young maidens. The inscription at the bottom of the canvas suggested the work had been executed by Nicolas Colombel in 1697. Gabriel doubted that was the case.

He placed a hand to his chin and tilted his head to one side. A moment passed before Fleury noticed his interest in the work and joined him before the canvas.

"I acquired it a few months ago."

"May I ask where?"

"An old private collection here in France."

"Dimensions?"

Fleury smiled. "You tell me, Monsieur Ziegler."

"One hundred and twelve by one hundred and forty-four centimeters." He paused, then added with a disarming smile, "Give or take a centimeter or two."

"Very close."

Only because Gabriel had deliberately misstated the painting's actual dimensions. Any fool could see that the work measured 114 by 148 centimeters.

"It's in remarkable condition," he said.

"I commissioned the restoration after purchasing it."

"May I see the conservator's report?"

"Now?"

"If you wouldn't mind."

When Fleury withdrew, Anna approached the painting. "It's beautiful."

"But too large to transport easily."

"You're not thinking about buying something, are you?"

"Not me," said Gabriel. "But you certainly are."

Before Anna could object, Fleury reappeared, empty-handed. "I'm afraid Bruno must have misfiled it. But if Madame Rolfe is interested in the painting, I can forward you a copy by email."

Gabriel produced his phone. "Would you mind if I photographed her standing next to it?"

"Of course not. In fact, I would be honored."

Anna inched closer to the painting and, turning, adopted the smile she wore when acknowledging the applause of a sold-out concert hall. Gabriel snapped the photograph, then moved to the neighboring painting.

"A follower of Canaletto," declared Fleury.

"A very good one."

"I thought so, too. I acquired it only last week."

"From where?"

"A private collection." The Frenchman treated Anna to a watery smile. "In Switzerland."

Gabriel leaned closer to the canvas. "How certain are you about the attribution?"

"Why do you ask?"

Because the painting, at just 56 by 78 centimeters, was easily transportable. Especially if it were to be removed from its stretcher. "Do you think Bruno mislaid the condition report for this one, too?"

"I'm afraid the painting is already spoken for."

"Is there no way Madame Rolfe can make a competitive bid?"

"I've already accepted the buyer's money."

"Is he a dealer or a collector?"

"Why do you ask?"

"Because if he's a dealer, I'd be interested in taking it off his hands."

"I can't reveal his identity. The terms of the sale are entirely private."

"Not for long," said Gabriel knowingly.

"What do you mean, monsieur?"

"Let's just say I get a funny feeling when I look at this painting." He snapped a photograph of it. "Perhaps you should show us the good pictures now, Monsieur Fleury."

17

Galerie Fleury

Fleury escorted them up a flight of stairs to the second-floor exhibition room. Here the walls were somber gray rather than red, and the paintings, by all appearances, were of a decidedly higher quality. There were several examples of Dutch and Flemish portraiture, including two works executed in the manner of Anthony van Dyck. There was also *A River Scene with Distant Windmills*, oil on canvas, 36 by 58 centimeters, bearing the distinctive initials of the Dutch Golden Age painter Aelbert Cuyp. Gabriel was doubtful the initials were authentic. In fact, after a moment of undisturbed reverie, he reached the conclusion, wholly unsupported by technical analysis, that the painting was a forgery.

"You have a very good eye," said Fleury from the opposite side of the room. He added a slice of lemon to Anna's mineral water and asked, "Something for you, Monsieur Ziegler?"

"The attribution for this painting would be nice."

"It has been firmly assigned by numerous experts to Cuyp himself."

"How do these experts explain the lack of a complete signature? After all, Cuyp generally signed the works he painted with his own hand and placed only his initials on paintings that were produced under his supervision."

"There are exceptions, as you know."

Which was indeed the case, thought Gabriel. "How's the provenance?"

"Lengthy and impeccable."

"Previous owner?"

"A collector of exceptional taste."

"French or Swiss?" asked Gabriel dryly.

"American, actually."

Fleury handed the glass of water to Anna and escorted her from painting to painting, leaving Gabriel free to carry out a second private inspection of the gallery's inventory. Eventually they all three convened before *A River Scene with Distant Windmills*, oil on canvas, 36 by 58 centimeters, by a forger of indisputable talent.

"Do you mind if I touch it?"

"I beg your pardon?"

"The painting," said Gabriel. "I'd like to touch it."

"Carefully," cautioned Fleury.

Gabriel placed the tip of his forefinger gently against the canvas and dragged it over the brushwork. "Did your man handle the cleaning?"

"It came to me in this condition."

"Are there paint losses?"

"Not extensive. But, yes, there is some abrading. Particularly in the sky."

"I assume the condition report contains photographs?"

"Several, monsieur."

Gabriel looked at Anna. "Does Madame Rolfe like it?"

"That depends on the price." She turned to Fleury. "What did you have in mind?"

"A million and a half."

"Come, come," said Gabriel. "Let's be realistic."

"How much would Madame Rolfe be willing to pay for it?"

"Are you asking me to negotiate with myself?"

"Not at all. I am merely offering you the opportunity to name your price."

Gabriel contemplated the worthless painting in silence.

"Well?" asked Fleury.

"Madame Rolfe will give you one million euros and not a euro more."

The art dealer smiled. "Sold."

———————

Downstairs in Fleury's office, Gabriel reviewed the condition report and provenance while Anna, a mobile phone pressed to her ear, transferred the sum of one million euros from her account at Credit Suisse to the gallery's account at Société Générale. The final sale price included the cost of the frame and shipping. Gabriel, however, declined both. Madame Rolfe, he said, did not care for the frame. As for the shipping, he intended to see to it personally.

"I should have the export license in hand by next Wednesday at the latest," said Fleury. "You can pick up the painting then."

"I'm afraid Wednesday won't do."

"Why not?"

"Because Madame Rolfe and I are taking the painting with us."

"*C'est impossible.* There is paperwork to submit and signatures to obtain."

"The paperwork and signatures are your problem. Besides, something tells me you know how to acquire an export license for a painting that has already left the country."

The dealer did not deny the accusation. "What about proper packaging?" he asked.

"Trust me, Monsieur Fleury. I know how to handle a painting."

"The gallery accepts absolutely no liability for any damage once the painting leaves these premises."

"But you *do* guarantee the attribution, along with the accuracy of the condition report and provenance."

"Yes, of course." Fleury handed Gabriel a copy of the certificate of authenticity, which declared the work to be firmly attributed to Aelbert Cuyp. "It says so right here."

The dealer placed the sales agreement before Anna and indicated the line where she should sign her name. After adding his own signature, he photocopied the document and inserted it into an envelope, along with copies of the provenance and condition report. The painting he covered in glassine paper and bubble wrap, which was more protection than it deserved. At three fifteen it was resting on the backseat of the Maybach as it drew to a stop outside the Bristol Hotel.

"I thought I was only supposed to be eye candy," said Anna.

"What's a million euros between friends?"

"A great deal of money."

"It will be back in your account by Monday afternoon at the latest."

"What a pity," she said. "I was hoping you might remain in my debt a little longer."

"And if I were?"

"I would ask you to come to my performance tonight. There's a gala reception afterward. All the beautiful people will be there."

"I thought you hated those things."

"With a passion. But if you were standing at my side, it might be tolerable."

"And how would you explain me, Anna? Who would I be?"

"How about Herr Ludwig Ziegler?" She frowned at the object lying on the seat between them. "The esteemed art adviser who just spent one million euros of my money for a worthless forgery."

Gabriel carried it upstairs to his room and removed the canvas from its stretcher. One hour later it was wedged into the overnight bag he wheeled across the cavernous ticket hall of the Gare du Nord. His journey through passport control proceeded without incident, and at five o'clock he boarded a Eurostar train bound for London. As the banlieues of northern Paris slid past his window, he reflected on the shifting fortunes of his career. Just four months earlier he had been the director-general of one of the world's most formidable intelligence services. Now, he thought, smiling, he had found a new line of work.

Art smuggler.

18

Jermyn Street

Not since the outbreak of the pandemic, when the art world had slipped into something approaching cardiac arrest, had Sarah Bancroft endured such a dreadful week. It began with Julian's calamitous visit to Bordeaux and concluded, late that afternoon, with the collapse of a potential sale—a case of cold feet on the buyer's part and hard-nosed determination on Sarah's not to sell the painting in question, *Adoration of the Magi* by Luca Cambiaso, at a loss. To make matters worse, her new husband had left London on a business trip. Because his trade was espionage, he could not say where he was going or when he might return. For all Sarah knew, it would be Midsummer Day before she laid eyes on him again.

Which explained why, after engaging the gallery's security system and locking the front door, she made straight for Wiltons and settled into her usual corner table at the bar. A perfect three-olive Belvedere martini, Saharan dry, materialized a moment later, delivered by a handsome young waiter in a blue blazer and red necktie. Perhaps, she thought as she raised the glass to her lips, all was not quite as bad as it seemed.

At once there was a burst of uproarious laughter. It was Julian who had provoked it. He was explaining the hideous purple-red bruise on his cheek to Oliver Dimbleby and Jeremy Crabbe, the head of the Old Master department of Bonhams. According to Julian's version of the story, the collision with the lamppost had taken place not in Bordeaux but in Kensington, and was the result of nothing more malicious than a misguided attempt to send a text message while walking.

Mobile phone in hand, Julian reenacted the fictitious incident, much to the delight of the other dealers, curators, and auctioneers lining the bar. For his reward, he was kissed by the crimson lips of the stunning former fashion model who now ran a thriving modern art gallery in King Street. Watching the performance from her corner table, Sarah sipped her martini and whispered, "Bitch."

The kiss was little consolation; Sarah could see that. Julian was mortified by his appearance and distraught over the suspicious death of the woman who had asked him to come to France. So, too, was Sarah. Moreover, she was concerned about the painting she had sold to Phillip Somerset, a man whose acquaintance she had made while working at the Museum of Modern Art in New York. Her old friend Gabriel Allon had agreed to look into the matter. As yet, he had delivered no update on the progress of his investigation.

Amelia March of *ARTnews* detached herself from the bar and approached Sarah's table. She was a slender woman of erect carriage, with short dark hair and the unblinking, too-wide eyes of an Apple emoji. It was Amelia, with Sarah's anonymous help, who had broken the news about *Portrait of an Unknown Woman*. Sarah now regretted having leaked the information. If she had kept her mouth shut, the rediscovery and sale of the painting would have remained shrouded in secrecy. And Madame Valerie Bérrangar, she thought, would still be alive.

"I heard a naughty rumor about you the other day," Amelia announced.

"Only one?" asked Sarah. "I'm disappointed."

She could only imagine the sort of gossip that occasionally reached Amelia's ever-vigilant ears. After all, Sarah was a former covert CIA operative whose husband had worked as a professional assassin before joining the Secret Intelligence Service. She had also served briefly as the art adviser to the crown prince of Saudi Arabia. Indeed, it was Sarah who had convinced His Majesty to plunk down $450 million on Leonardo da Vinci's *Salvator Mundi*, the highest price ever paid at auction for a work of art.

None of which Sarah wished to ever see in print. Therefore, she made no objection when Amelia sat down at her table uninvited. Sarah reckoned it was better to hear the reporter out and, if possible, use the opportunity to make a little mischief of her own. She was in that sort of mood.

"What is it this time?" she asked Amelia.

"I have been reliably told—"

"Oh, for heaven's sake."

"*Very* reliably told," Amelia continued, "that you are planning to move Isherwood Fine Arts from its longtime home in Mason's Yard to, how shall we say, a less secluded location."

"Untrue," declared Sarah.

"You looked at two potential sites in Cork Street last week."

But not for the reason Amelia suspected. It was Sarah's ambition to open a second gallery, one that specialized in contemporary art and would bear her name. She had yet to broach the topic with Julian and was keen that he not read about her plans in *ARTnews*.

"I can't possibly afford Cork Street," she demurred.

"You just sold a newly discovered Van Dyck for six and a half million pounds." Amelia lowered her voice. "Very hush-hush. Secret buyer. Mysterious source."

"Yes," said Sarah. "I think I read about that somewhere."

"I've been very good to you and Julian over the years," said Amelia. "And on numerous occasions, I have refrained from pursuing stories that might well have damaged the gallery's reputation."

"Such as?"

"Your exact role in the reemergence of that Artemisia, for a start."

Sarah sipped her drink but said nothing.

"Well?" probed Amelia.

"Isherwood Fine Arts will never leave Mason's Yard. Is now and ever shall be. World without end. Amen."

"Then why are you looking for a long-term lease in Cork Street?"

Because she wanted to cast a long shadow over the gallery owned by the former fashion model, who at that moment was whispering something into the ear of Simon Mendenhall, the mannequin-like chief auctioneer from Christie's.

"I swear to you," said Sarah, "as a friend and as a woman, that I will tell you when the time is right."

"You'll tell me *first*," insisted Amelia. "And in the meantime, you will give me something juicy."

"Have a quick look over your right shoulder."

Amelia did as Sarah suggested. "The lovely Miss Watson and sleazy Simon Mendenhall?"

"Torrid," said Sarah.

"I thought she was dating that actor."

"She's shagging sleazy Simon on the side."

As if on cue, there was another eruption of laughter from the opposite end of the bar, where Julian had just concluded an encore performance of the alleged incident in Kensington—this time for Nicky Lovegrove, art adviser to the vastly wealthy.

"Is that really how it happened?" asked Amelia.

"No," said Sarah, smiling sadly. "The lamppost attacked *him*."

———

After finishing her drink, Sarah wiped the smudge of lipstick from Julian's cheek and went into Jermyn Street. There were no taxis in sight, so she walked around the corner to Piccadilly and caught one there. As it bore her westward across London, she scrolled through the possibilities on Deliveroo, dithering between Indian and Thai.

She ordered Italian instead and immediately regretted her choice. She had gained five pounds during the pandemic and another five after marrying Christopher. Despite thrice-weekly training runs on the footpaths of Hyde Park, the weight refused to budge.

As the taxi sped past the Royal Albert Hall, Sarah resolved to place herself on yet another diet. But not tonight; she was hungry enough to eat one of her Ferragamo pumps. After dinner, which she would consume while watching something mindless on television, she would crawl into her empty marital bed and remain there for the better part of the weekend, listening to "When Your Lover Has Gone" on repeat. Billie Holiday's classic 1956 recording, of course. When one was truly depressed, no other version would do.

She did her best Lady Day impersonation as the taxi turned into Queen's Gate Terrace and stopped opposite the elegant Georgian house at Number 18. It wasn't all theirs, only the luxurious maisonette on the lower two levels. Sarah was overjoyed to see a light burning downstairs in the kitchen. Environmentally conscious, she was certain she had not left it on by mistake that morning. The most plausible explanation was that her lover was not gone after all.

She paid off the driver and hurried down the steps to the maisonette's lower entrance. There she found the door ajar and the security system disengaged. Inside, lying on the kitchen island, was a canvas that had been removed from its stretcher—a riverscape with distant windmills, somewhere in the neighborhood of 40 by 60 centimeters, bearing what appeared to be the initials of the Dutch Golden Age painter Aelbert Cuyp.

Next to the painting was an envelope from Galerie Georges Fleury in Paris. And next to the envelope was an excellent bottle of Sancerre, from which Gabriel, wincing in pain, was attempting to extract the cork. Sarah closed the door and, laughing in spite of herself, shed her coat. It was, she thought, the perfect end to a perfectly dreadful week.

19

Queen's Gate Terrace

Sarah checked the status of her Deliveroo order and saw it was still open. "Tagliatelle with ragù or veal Milanese?"

"I wouldn't want to impose."

"My husband is away. I could use the company."

"In that case, I'll have the veal."

"Tagliatelle it is." Sarah placed the order, then looked down at the frameless, stretcherless canvas lying on her counter. "I'm sure there's a perfectly reasonable explanation for this. And for that swollen hand of yours as well."

"Where would you like me to begin?"

"Why not the hand?"

"I assaulted a plainclothes Carabinieri officer after meeting with Julian in Venice."

"And the painting?"

"I acquired it this afternoon at Galerie Georges Fleury."

"I can see that." Sarah tapped the envelope. "But how in the world did you pay for it?"

Gabriel removed the sales agreement from the envelope and pointed toward the practiced signature of the buyer.

"That was very generous of her," said Sarah.

"Generosity had nothing to do with it. She expects to be repaid in full."

"By whom?"

"You, of course."

"So the painting is mine? Is that what you're saying?"

"I suppose it is."

"How much did I spend on it?"

"One million euros."

"For that kind of money, I should have got a frame." Sarah tugged at the frayed corner of the canvas. "And a stretcher as well."

"The management of the Bristol Hotel might have found it odd if I had left an antique picture frame behind in my room."

"And the stretcher?"

"It's in a rubbish bin outside the Gare du Nord."

"Of course it is." Sarah sighed. "You should probably put it on a new one first thing in the morning to stabilize the image."

"If I do that, it won't fit in my carry-on luggage."

"Where are you planning to take it?"

"New York," said Gabriel. "And you're coming with me."

"Why?"

"Because that painting is a forgery. And I have a funny feeling the one you sold to Phillip Somerset for six and a half million pounds is a fake as well."

"Oh, hell," said Sarah. "I was afraid you were going to say that."

Gabriel drew his mobile phone and retrieved the photograph of the painting he had seen in Valerie Bérrangar's villa in Saint-André-du-Bois. *Portrait of an Unknown Woman*, oil on canvas, 115 by 92 centimeters, attributed to a follower of the Flemish Baroque painter Anthony van Dyck.

"That would explain the letter she wrote to Julian."

"Only partially."

"Meaning?"

"She called Georges Fleury first."

"Why?"

"She wanted to know whether her version of the painting was a valuable Van Dyck as well."

"And what did Monsieur Fleury tell her?"

"Given my limited experience with him, I can assure you it bore no resemblance to the truth. But whatever he said made her suspicious enough to contact the art crime unit of the Police Nationale."

Sarah swore softly as she pulled the cork from the bottle of Sancerre.

"Don't worry, I'm all but certain the police told Madame Bérrangar that they had no interest in pursuing the matter. Which is why she asked Julian to come to Bordeaux." Gabriel paused. "And why she is now dead."

"Was she—"

"Murdered?" Gabriel nodded. "And her killers took her mobile phone for good measure."

"Who were they?"

"I'm still working on that. I'm quite certain, however, that they were professionals."

Sarah poured two glasses of the wine and handed one to Gabriel. "What kind of art dealer hires professional assassins to kill someone in a dispute over a painting?"

"The kind who's involved in a lucrative criminal enterprise."

Sarah took up Gabriel's phone and enlarged the image. "Is Madame Bérrangar's painting a forgery, too?"

"In my opinion," replied Gabriel, "it is the work of a later follower of Van Dyck. Forty-eight hours ago, I told Valerie Bérrangar's daughter that I thought it was a copy of the painting you sold to Phillip Somerset. But I'm now convinced it's the other way around. Which would explain why the picture doesn't appear in Van Dyck's catalogue raisonné."

"The forger copied the follower?"

"In a manner of speaking, yes. And in the process, he made marked improvements. He's quite amazing. He truly paints like Anthony van Dyck. It's no wonder your five experts were deceived."

"How do you explain the paint losses and retouching that showed up when we examined the painting under ultraviolet light?"

"The forger artificially ages and damages his paintings. Then he restores them using modern pigments and medium in order to make them appear authentic."

Sarah glanced at the canvas lying on the countertop. "This one, too?"

"Absolutely."

Gabriel removed the painting's condition report from the envelope. Attached were three accompanying photographs. The first depicted the canvas in its present state: retouched, with a fresh coat of unsoiled varnish. The second photo, made with ultraviolet light, revealed the paint losses as an archipelago of small black islands. The last photograph presented the painting in its truest state, without retouching or varnish. The losses appeared as white blotches.

"It looks exactly like a four-hundred-year-old painting should look," said Gabriel. "I hate to admit it, but it's possible even I might have been fooled."

"Why weren't you?"

"Because I went into that gallery on the lookout for forgeries. And because I've been around paintings for a hundred years. I know the brushstrokes of the Old Masters like the lines around my eyes."

"With all due respect," replied Sarah, "that isn't good enough to prove the painting is a forgery."

"Which is why we're going to give it to Aiden Gallagher."

Gallagher was the founder of Equus Analytics, a high-tech art research firm that specialized in detecting forgeries. He sold his services to museums, dealers, collectors, auction houses, and, on occasion, to the Art Crime Team of the FBI. It was Aiden Gallagher, a decade earlier, who had proved that one of New York's most successful contemporary art galleries had sold nearly $80 million worth of fake paintings to unsuspecting buyers.

"His lab is in Westport, Connecticut," continued Gabriel. "If the forger made a technical mistake, Gallagher will find it."

"And while we're waiting for the results?"

"You'll arrange for me to have a look at the painting you sold to Phillip Somerset. If, as I suspect, it's a forgery—"

"Julian and I will be the laughingstocks of the art world."

No, thought Gabriel as he reached for his wineglass. If *Portrait of an Unknown Woman* turned out to be a forgery, Isherwood Fine Arts of Mason's Yard, purveyors of museum-quality Italian and Dutch Old Master paintings since 1968, would be ruined.

20

___

Westport

They passed through Heathrow security separately—Gabriel under his real name, with the forged Cuyp crammed into his carry-on—and reunited in the departure lounge. While waiting for the flight to be called, Sarah composed an email to Aiden Gallagher, informing him that Isherwood Fine Arts of London wished to hire Equus Analytics to conduct a technical evaluation of a painting. She did not identify the work in question, though she implied it was a matter of some urgency. She was scheduled to arrive in New York at noon and, barring a traffic disaster, could be in Westport by 3:00 p.m. at the latest. Could she deliver the painting to him then?

On board the plane, Sarah informed the flight attendant that she would require no food or drink during the eight-hour flight across the North Atlantic. Then she closed her eyes and did not open them again until the aircraft thudded onto the runway at John F. Kennedy International Airport. Armed with her American passport and Global Entry card, she glided through the rituals of the arrival process while Gabriel, his status reduced, spent an hour working his way through the maze of stanchions and retractable nylon restraints reserved for unwanted foreigners. His journey ended in a windowless room, where he was briefly questioned by a well-fed Customs and Border Protection officer.

"What brings you back to the United States, Director Allon?"

"Private research."

"Does the Agency know you're in the country?"

"They do now."

"How's your chest feeling?"

"Better than my hand."

"Anything in the bag?"

"A couple of firearms and a dead body."

The officer smiled. "Enjoy your stay."

A blue line directed Gabriel to baggage claim, where Sarah was pondering her mobile phone. "Aiden Gallagher," she said without looking up. "He's wondering whether it could wait until Monday. I told him it couldn't."

Just then her phone pinged with an incoming email.

"Well?"

"He wants a description of the painting."

Gabriel recited the particulars. "*A River Scene with Distant Windmills.* Oil on canvas. Thirty-six by fifty-eight centimeters. Currently attributed to Aelbert Cuyp."

Sarah sent the email. Gallagher's reply arrived two minutes later.

"He'll meet us in Westport at three."

———

Equus Analytics was located in an old redbrick building on Riverside Avenue near the overpass of the Connecticut Turnpike. Gabriel and Sarah arrived a few minutes after two o'clock in the back of an Uber SUV. They picked up coffee from a Dunkin' Donuts up the street and settled onto a bench along the sunlit bank of the Saugatuck. Fat white clouds flew across an otherwise spotless blue sky. Pleasure craft dozed like discarded playthings in their slips at a small marina.

"It almost looks like something Aelbert Cuyp might have painted," remarked Gabriel.

"Westport definitely has its charms. Especially on a day like this."

"Any regrets?"

"About leaving New York?" Sarah shook her head. "I think my story ended rather well, don't you?"

"That depends."

"On what?"

"Whether you're truly happy being married to Christopher."

"Deliriously so. Though I have to admit, my work at the gallery isn't quite as interesting as the jobs I used to do for you." She lifted her face toward the warmth of the sun. "Do you remember our trip to Saint-Barthélemy with Zizi al-Bakari?"

"How could I forget?"

"What about the summer we spent with Ivan and Elena Kharkov in Saint-Tropez? Or the day I shot that Russian assassin in Zurich?" Sarah checked the time on her phone. "It's nearly three. Let's go, shall we? I wouldn't want to keep him waiting."

They set out along Riverside Avenue and arrived at Equus Analytics as a black BMW 7 Series sedan was pulling into the parking lot. The man who emerged from the driver's seat had coal-black hair and blue eyes, and appeared much younger than his fifty-four years.

He extended a hand toward Sarah. "Miss Bancroft, I presume?"

"It's a pleasure to meet you, Dr. Gallagher. Thank you for seeing us on such short notice. And on a Saturday, at that."

"Not at all. Truth be told, I was planning to do a few hours' work before dinner." His accent, though faded, betrayed a Dublin childhood. He looked at Gabriel. "And you are?"

"Johannes Klemp," answered Gabriel, dredging up a name from his tangled past. "I work with Sarah at Isherwood Fine Arts."

"Did anyone ever tell you that you look a great deal like that Israeli who was shot on Inauguration Day? If I'm not mistaken, his name is Gabriel Allon."

"I get that a lot."

"I don't doubt it." Gallagher gave him a knowing smile before turning to Sarah. "That leaves the painting."

She nodded toward Gabriel's overnight bag.

"Ah," said Gallagher. "The plot thickens."

21

Equus

The locks on the outer door were museum grade, as were the security system and the equipment in Gallagher's laboratory. His inventory of high-tech gadgetry included an electron microscope, a shortwave infrared reflectography camera, and a Bruker M6 Jetstream, a sophisticated spatial imaging device. Nevertheless, he began his analysis the old-fashioned way, by examining the painting with the naked eye under visible light.

"It seems to have survived the flight intact, but I'd like to put it on a stretcher as quickly as possible." He cast a reproachful glance in Gabriel's direction. "As long as Herr Klemp has no objections, of course."

"Perhaps you should refer to me by my real name," said Gabriel. "As for the stretcher, a standard fourteen-by-twenty-two should work well. I'd use a five-eighths setback for the canvas."

Gallagher's expression turned quizzical. "Are you a painter, Mr. Allon?"

Gabriel's answer was the same one he had given to Valerie Bérrangar's daughter seventy-two hours earlier, in the commune of Saint-André-du-Bois. Aiden Gallagher was similarly intrigued, though for a different reason.

"It turns out we have a great deal in common."

"I'm sorry to hear that," quipped Gabriel.

"Artistically, I mean. I trained to be a painter at the National College of Art and Design in Dublin before coming to America and enrolling at Columbia."

Where he had earned a PhD in art history and an MA in art conservation. While working on the restoration staff at the Metropolitan Museum of Art, he specialized in provenance research and, later, scientific detection of forgeries. He resigned from the Met in 2005 and founded Equus Analytics. The *Art Newspaper* had recently christened him "a rock star" with no equal in the field. Thus the new BMW 7 Series parked outside his office door.

He directed his gaze toward the painting. "Where was it acquired?"

"Gallery Georges Fleury in Paris," answered Gabriel.

"When?"

"Yesterday afternoon."

Gallagher looked up abruptly. "And you already suspect there's a problem?"

"No," said Gabriel. "I *know* there's a problem. The painting is a forgery."

"And how did you arrive at this conclusion?" asked Gallagher dubiously.

"Instinct."

"I'm afraid instinct isn't good enough, Mr. Allon." Gallagher contemplated the painting again. "How's the provenance?"

"A joke."

"And the condition report?"

"It's a real work of art."

Gabriel fished both documents from his briefcase and laid them on the table. Aiden Gallagher began his review with the provenance and ended with the three photos. The painting in its present form. The painting under ultraviolet light. And the painting with the losses exposed.

"If it's a fake, the forger certainly knew what he was doing." Gallagher doused the overhead lights and examined the painting with an ultraviolet torch. The archipelago of black blotches corresponded with those in the photograph. "So far, so good." He switched on the overhead lights again and looked at Gabriel. "I assume you're familiar with Cuyp's work?"

"Very."

"Then you know his oeuvre has been plagued by confusion and misattribution for hundreds of years. He borrowed heavily from Jan van Goyen, and his followers borrowed heavily from him. One was Abraham van Calraet. Like Cuyp, he was from the Dutch town of Dordrecht. Because they shared the same initials, it can be difficult to tell the work of one from the other."

"Which is why a forger would choose a painter like Cuyp in the first place. Good forgers shrewdly select artists whose work has been subject to misattribution in the past. That way, when a new painting miraculously reemerges from a dusty European collection, the so-called art experts are more inclined to accept it as genuine."

"And if I conclude that the painting is the work of Aelbert Cuyp?"

"I'm confident you won't."

"Are you prepared to wager fifty thousand dollars?"

"Not me." Gabriel pointed at Sarah. "But she will."

"I require twenty-five thousand to begin an investigation. The rest is due upon delivery of my findings."

"How long will it take?" asked Sarah.

"Anywhere from a few weeks to a few months."

"Time is of the essence, Dr. Gallagher."

"When are you planning to return to London?"

"You tell me."

"I can have a preliminary report Monday afternoon. But there's a surcharge for rush jobs."

"How much?"

"Fifty thousand up front," said Gallagher. "Twenty-five thousand on delivery."

———————

After signing the release forms and handing over the check, Gabriel and Sarah hurried along Riverside Avenue to the Metro North station and purchased two tickets to Grand Central.

"The next train is at four twenty-six," said Sarah. "With any luck, we'll be sipping martinis at the Mandarin Oriental by six o'clock."

"I thought you preferred the Four Seasons."

"There was no room at the inn."

"Not even for you?"

"Trust me, I gave the head of reservations a piece of my mind."

"Where do you suppose Phillip Somerset is spending his weekend?"

"Knowing Phillip, he could be anywhere. Besides his town house on East Seventy-Fourth Street, he owns a ski lodge in Aspen, an estate on the East End of Long Island, and a large portion of Lake Placid in the Adirondacks. He flits between them on his Gulfstream."

"Not bad for a former bond trader from Lehman Brothers."

"You've obviously been reading up on him."

"You know me, Sarah. I've never been able to sleep on airplanes." Gabriel gave her a sideways glance. "What's the weather like in Lake Placid this time of year?"

"Miserable."

"What about Aspen?"

"No snow."

"That leaves Manhattan or Long Island."

"I'll call him first thing Monday."

"Get it over with. You'll feel better."

"Unless the Van Dyck turns out to be a forgery." Sarah opened a blank email and added Phillip Somerset's address. "What's the subject?"

"Catching up."

"Nice touch. Keep going."

"Tell him you're in New York unexpectedly. Ask him if he has a few minutes to spare."

"Should I mention the painting?"

"Under no circumstances."

"How should I describe you?"

"You're an art dealer who used to work for the CIA. I'm sure you'll think of something."

She completed the email as the train was drawing into the station. And at half past five, as they were climbing into a taxi outside Grand Central, Phillip Somerset rang her with his answer.

"Lindsay and I are having a few friends to lunch tomorrow at our place on Long Island. You're more than welcome to join us. And bring your friend," he suggested. "I'd love to meet him."

22

North Haven

Sarah declined Phillip's Somerset's offer of a car service and rented a premium European-made sedan instead. They collected it from a garage in Turtle Bay at half past ten the following morning and by noon were speeding through Suffolk County on the Long Island Expressway. To help pass the time, Sarah read aloud the quaint-sounding names of the towns and hamlets as they appeared on the faded green exit signs—first Commack, then Hauppauge, Ronkon-koma, and Patchogue. It was a silly game, she explained to Gabriel, that she had played as a child, when the Bancrofts had passed their summers in East Hampton with other rich Manhattan families like theirs.

"The new crowd is much richer than we were, and they're not ashamed to show it. Grotesque displays of wealth are now de rigueur." She tugged at the sleeve of the dark pantsuit that she had brought from London. "I only wish I'd had time to shop for something more appropriate."

"You look beautiful," said Gabriel, a hand balanced atop the steering wheel.

"But I'm not suitably attired for a weekend gathering at the North Haven estate of Phillip Somerset."

"How should one be dressed?"

"As expensively as possible." Sarah's phone chimed with an incoming text. "Speak of the devil."

"Have we been disinvited?"

"He's checking on our progress."

"Do you suppose he's contacting all his guests, or only you?"

"And just what are you implying?"

"That Phillip Somerset sounded inordinately pleased to hear from you yesterday."

"Our relationship is both personal and professional," admitted Sarah.

"How personal?"

"We were introduced by a mutual friend at MoMA's annual Party in the Garden fundraiser. Phillip was going through a messy divorce at the time. We dated for several months."

"Who ended it?"

"He did, if you must know."

"What on earth was he thinking?"

"I was in my late thirties at the time, and Phillip was looking for someone a bit younger. When he met lovely Lindsay Morgan, a yoga enthusiast and model twelve years my junior, he dropped me like an underperforming stock."

"And yet you remained invested in Masterpiece Art."

"How do you know that?"

"Lucky guess."

"I had already entrusted a small portion of my assets to Phillip before we began dating," said Sarah. "I saw no reason to demand a redemption simply because our relationship went awry."

"How small a portion?"

"Two million dollars."

"I see."

"I thought I made it clear the last time we were in New York that my father left me rather well off."

"You did," said Gabriel. "I only hope that Phillip has looked after your interests."

"My current balance is four point eight million dollars."

"Mazel tov."

"Compared to Phillip's other clients, I'm something of a pauper. He definitely has the Midas touch. That's why so many people in the art world are invested with him. The fund consistently delivers twenty-five-percent annual returns."

"How is that possible?"

"A magical proprietary trading strategy that Phillip guards jealously. Unlike other art funds, Masterpiece doesn't reveal the paintings in its inventory. Its book is entirely opaque. And quite large, apparently. Phillip currently controls one point two billion dollars' worth of art. He buys and sells paintings constantly and earns enormous profits on the churn."

"By churn, you mean volume and speed."

"And arbitrage, of course," replied Sarah. "Masterpiece operates exactly like a hedge fund. It has a million-dollar minimum for new investors, with a five-year lockup. The fee structure is the industry-standard two-and-twenty. A two percent management fee and a twenty percent cut of the profits."

"I suppose the firm is domiciled in the Cayman Islands."

"Aren't they all?" Sarah rolled her eyes. "I must admit, I do enjoy watching my account balance go up and up each year. But a part of me doesn't like to think of paintings as a commodity to be bought and sold like soybeans and oil futures."

"You'll have to get over that if you're going to make it as an art dealer. Most of the paintings purchased at auction will never be seen by the public again. They're locked away in bank vaults or in the Geneva Free Port."

"Or in a climate-controlled warehouse operated by Chelsea Fine Arts Storage. That's where Phillip told me to ship the Van Dyck." Sarah pointed toward the sign for exit 66. "Yaphank."

———

The egg-shaped peninsula known as North Haven protrudes into Peconic Bay between Sag Harbor and Shelter Island. Phillip Somerset's weekend retreat, a thirty-thousand-square-foot acropolis of cedar and glass, stood on the eastern shore. His golden young wife greeted Gabriel and Sarah in the soaring entrance hall, dressed in a sleeveless linen pantsuit belted at her slender waist, her skin so smooth and flawless she looked like a filtered photograph on social media. When Gabriel introduced himself, he received a blank who-are-you stare in return, but Sarah's name Lindsay Somerset recognized instantly.

"You're the art dealer from London who sold my husband the Van Gogh."

"Van Dyck."

"I get them confused."

"It's a common mistake," Sarah assured her.

Lindsay Somerset turned to greet a new arrival, a prime-time television news anchor and his husband. Several more print and broadcast journalists were gathered in the luminous great room along with an assortment of hedge fund managers, painters, art dealers, fashion designers, models, actors, screenwriters, a renowned director of blockbuster motion pictures, an iconic musician who sang about the plight of Long Island's working classes, a progressive congresswoman from the Bronx, and a flock of young assistants from a New York publishing house. Evidently, it was a book party to which they had been invited.

"Carl Bernstein," whispered Sarah. "He was Bob Woodward's partner at the *Washington Post* during the Watergate scandal."

"Unlike you, Sarah, I was alive when Richard Nixon was president. I know who Carl Bernstein is."

"Would you like to meet him? He's right over there." Sarah snatched a glass of champagne from the tray of a passing waiter. "And there's Ina Garten. And that actor whose name I can never remember. The one who just got out of rehab."

"And there's a Rothko," said Gabriel quietly. "And a Basquiat. And a Pollock. And a Lichtenstein, a Diebenkorn, a Hirst, an Adler, a Prince, and a Warhol."

"You should see his town house on East Seventy-Fourth Street. It's like the Whitney in there."

"Not quite," said a baritone voice from behind them. "But you're welcome to visit anytime you like."

The voice belonged to Phillip Somerset. He greeted Sarah first—with a kiss on her cheek and a favorable remark about her appearance—before extending a sun-varnished hand toward Gabriel. He was a tall, physically fit specimen in his mid-fifties, with a boyish head of gray-blond hair and the confident, easy smile that comes naturally to the very rich. Strapped to his wrist was a colossal Richard Mille chronometer, a sporting model worn by wealthy men with pretensions of seamanship. His zippered cashmere sweater was vaguely maritime as well, as were his pale cotton trousers and electric-blue loafers. Indeed, everything about Phillip Somerset suggested that he had just stepped from the deck of a yacht.

Gabriel accepted the proffered hand and introduced himself, first name and last.

Phillip Somerset looked to Sarah for an explanation.

"He's an old friend," she said.

"And I thought I was going to spend the afternoon fending off questions about my trading strategy." Phillip Somerset released Gabriel's hand. "What an unexpected surprise, Mr. Allon. To what do I owe the honor?"

"I was hoping to have a look at a painting."

"Well, you've certainly come to the right place. Is there anything in particular you'd like to see?"

"*Portrait of an Unknown Woman.*"

"By Anthony van Dyck?"

Gabriel smiled. "I certainly hope so."

Phillip Somerset escorted Gabriel and Sarah up a flight of stairs and into a large, light-filled office with outsize computer monitors and a sweeping view of the whitecapped bay. A lengthy silence ensued as he regarded them speculatively from behind the no-man's-land of his half-acre desk. Then he looked directly at Sarah and said, "Perhaps you should tell me what this is all about."

Her answer was precise and lawyerly. "Isherwood Fine Arts has retained Mr. Allon to conduct a discreet inquiry into the circumstances surrounding the rediscovery of *Portrait of an Unknown Woman* and its sale to Masterpiece Art Ventures."

"Why was such an inquiry deemed necessary?"

"Late last week, the gallery received a letter expressing concerns over the transaction. The woman who sent it was killed in an auto accident near Bordeaux a few days later."

"Do the police suspect foul play?"

"No," answered Gabriel. "But I do."

"Why?"

"Her late husband purchased several paintings from the same gallery in Paris where Julian and Sarah acquired *Portrait of an Unknown Woman*. When I paid a visit to the gallery on Friday, I noticed three paintings that appeared to be forgeries. I purchased one of them and turned it over to Equus Analytics."

"Aiden Gallagher is the best in the business. I use him myself."

"He's hoping to have a preliminary report by tomorrow afternoon. But in the meantime—"

"You thought you'd have a look at the Van Dyck."

Gabriel nodded.

"I'd love to show it to you," said Phillip Somerset. "But I'm afraid it's not possible."

"May I ask why not?"

"Masterpiece Art Ventures sold it about three weeks ago. At a considerable profit, I might add."

"To whom?"

"I'm sorry, Mr. Allon. The transaction was private."

"Was there an intermediary?"

"One of the major auction houses."

"Did the house conduct a second review of the attribution?"

"The buyer insisted on one."

"And?"

"*Portrait of an Unknown Woman* was painted by Anthony van Dyck, almost certainly in his studio in Antwerp, sometime in the late sixteen thirties. Which means that, as far as Isherwood Fine Arts and Masterpiece Art Ventures are concerned, the matter is now closed."

"If you don't mind," said Sarah, "I'd like that in writing."

"Send me something tomorrow morning," replied Phillip Somerset. "I'll have a look."

23

Gallery 617

Early the following morning, Sarah rang her man at HSBC in London and instructed him to wire one million euros into the Credit Suisse account of the world's most famous violinist. Then she dialed Ronald Sumner-Lloyd, Julian's Berkeley Square solicitor, and together they drafted a letter shielding Isherwood Fine Arts against any and all future claims related to the sale of *Portrait of an Unknown Woman* by the Flemish Baroque painter Anthony van Dyck. Shortly before 9:00 a.m., she emailed the finished document to Phillip Somerset. He phoned her a few minutes later from his Sikorsky executive helicopter, which was bound from East Hampton to Manhattan.

"The language is rather aggressive, don't you think? Especially the clause regarding confidentiality."

"I have to look after our interests, Phillip. And if your sale goes sideways, I don't ever want to read the words Isherwood Fine Arts in the *New York Times*."

"I thought I made it clear that you have nothing to worry about."

"You also once assured me that you were interested in a long-term relationship."

"You're not still angry over that, are you?"

"I never was," lied Sarah. "Now do me a favor and sign the waiver."

"On one condition."

"What's that?"

"Tell me how you know Gabriel Allon."

"We met when I was working in Washington."

"That was a long time ago."

"Yes," said Sarah. "Lovely Lindsay must have been in elementary school at the time."

"She says you were rude to her."

"She doesn't know the difference between a Van Gogh and a Van Dyck."

"Once upon a time, neither did I," said Phillip before ringing off. "But look at me now."

————————

The document appeared in Sarah's in-box five minutes later, electronically signed and dated. She added her own signature and forwarded it to Julian and Ronnie in London. Then, after confirming two reservations for that evening's seven thirty British Airways flight to Heathrow, she rang Gabriel and told him that Isherwood Fine Arts was now legally and ethically in the clear.

"Which means that Julian and I get to keep our reputations, not to mention our six and a half million pounds. All in all," she said, "a rather fortunate turn of events."

"What are your plans for the rest of the morning?"

"First I'm going to pack my suitcase. Then I'm going to stare at my phone and wait for Aiden Gallagher of Equus Analytics to tell me that you needlessly spent a million euros of my money on *A River Scene with Distant Windmills*."

"How about a nice long walk instead?"

"A much better idea."

It was a perfect spring morning, bright and cloudless, with a mischievous wind blowing from the Hudson. They walked along West Fifty-Ninth Street to Fifth Avenue, then turned uptown.

"Where are you taking me?"

"The Metropolitan Museum of Art."

"Why?"

"Its collection includes several important paintings by Anthony van Dyck." Gabriel smiled. "Real ones."

Sarah rang a friend who worked in the Met's publicity department and requested two complimentary admission tickets. They were waiting at the information desk in the Great Hall. Upstairs, they made their way to Gallery 617, a room dedicated to Baroque portraiture. It contained four works by Van Dyck, including his iconic portrait of Henrietta Maria, wife of King Charles I. Gabriel snapped a photograph of the queen consort's face and showed it to Sarah.

"Craquelure," she said.

"Do you notice anything unusual about it?"

"No."

"Neither do I. It looks exactly like Van Dyck's craquelure should look. But now look at this one." It was the face of the unknown woman, the version that Julian and Sarah had sold to Phillip Somerset. "The craquelure pattern is different."

"It's slight," said Sarah. "But, yes, there's a difference."

"That's because the forger is using a chemical hardening agent to artificially age the painting. It produces four centuries' worth of craquelure in a matter of days. But it's not the right *kind* of craquelure."

"Two separate reviews have declared our *Portrait of an Unknown Woman* to be the work of Anthony van Dyck. Rome has spoken, Gabriel. The case is closed."

"But both reviews were based on expert opinion rather than science."

Sarah sighed in frustration. "Perhaps you're looking at this the wrong way."

"And what would be the right way?"

She gestured toward the portrait of Henrietta Maria. "Maybe that one is fake."

"It isn't."

"Are you sure about that?" Sarah led him into an adjoining gallery. "And what about that landscape over there? Are you absolutely certain that Claude Lorrain painted it? Or are you merely inclined to believe that because it's on display in the Metropolitan Museum of Art?"

"Your point?"

"My point," replied Sarah in a stage whisper, "is that no one really knows whether all the beautiful works of art hanging in the world's great museums are genuine or fakes. Least of all the learned curators and conservators employed by institutions such as this one. It's the dirty little secret they don't like to talk about. Oh, they do their utmost to guarantee the integrity of their collections. But the truth is, they get fooled all the time. By one estimate, at least twenty percent of the paintings in the National Gallery in London are misattributed works or outright forgeries. And I can assure you, the statistics for the private art market are much worse."

"Then perhaps we should do something about it."

"By putting Galerie Georges Fleury out of business?" Sarah shook her head slowly. "Bad idea, Gabriel."

"Why?"

"Because what starts in Paris won't stay in Paris. It will spread through the rest of the art world like a contagion. It will infect the auction houses, the dealers, the collectors, and the ordinary patrons of museums like the Met. No one, not even the most virtuous among us, will be spared its ravages."

"And if Aiden Gallagher tells us that the painting is a forgery?"

"We will pursue restitution quietly and then go our separate ways, never to speak of the matter again. Otherwise, we might shatter the illusion that all that glitters is actually gold."

"Glisters," said Gabriel.

Frowning, Sarah checked the time. "It is now officially afternoon."

They returned to the Mandarin Oriental and settled into the last empty table in the hotel's popular lobby bar. At two fifteen, as they were finishing their lunch, Sarah's phone shivered with an incoming call. It was from Equus Analytics.

"Maybe *you* should answer that," said Sarah.

Gabriel tapped the ACCEPT icon and lifted the device to his ear. "Thank you," he said after a moment. "But that won't be necessary. We're on our way now."

Sarah reclaimed her phone. "*What* won't be necessary?"

"Additional chemical analysis of the pigment."

"Why not?"

"Because Aiden Gallagher discovered several navy-blue polar fleece fibers embedded throughout the painting, including in places that had never been retouched. Since the fabric was invented in Massachusetts in 1979, it's safe to assume that Aelbert Cuyp wasn't wearing a fleece jacket or vest in the mid-seventeenth century. Which means—"

"Georges Fleury owes me a million euros."

Sarah switched their flights, then hurried upstairs to fetch her luggage. They would settle the matter quietly, she thought, and never speak of it again.

24

Galerie Fleury

The navigation application on Sarah's phone estimated the driving time from Columbus Circle to Westport, Connecticut, to be ninety minutes. But Gabriel, behind the wheel of their rented European sedan, managed to cover the distance in a little more than an hour. Aiden Gallagher's flashy BMW 7 Series was parked outside Equus Analytics, and *A River Scene with Distant Windmills*, adhered to a new stretcher, was lying on the examination table in the lab. Next to the painting was a two-page letter declaring the work to be a modern forgery. And next to the letter were three microscope photographs supporting Gallagher's conclusion.

"To be honest, I was a little surprised it was so cut-and-dried. Given the quality of his brushwork, I expected more of him." Gallagher pointed out the dark strands of polar fleece in the photographs. "It's a real amateur's mistake."

"Is there any other possible explanation for the presence of those fibers?" asked Gabriel.

"None whatsoever. That said, you should be prepared for Fleury to take great offense at my findings." Gallagher looked at Sarah. "In my experience, most art dealers become rather indignant when asked to part with a million euros."

"I'm quite confident Monsieur Fleury will see things our way. Especially when he reads your report."

"When are you planning to confront him?"

"We're leaving for Paris tonight. In fact," said Sarah, glancing at her watch, "we need to be on our way."

She made out a check for the final $25,000 of Gallagher's fee while Gabriel removed *A River Scene with Distant Windmills* from its stretcher and folded it into his carry-on bag. Their Air France flight commenced boarding at 6:45 p.m. At half past eight, they were over the East End of Long Island.

"There's North Haven," said Sarah, pointing out her window. "I actually think I can see Phillip's house."

"One wonders how he and Lindsay make do with only thirty thousand square feet."

"You should see the place in the Adirondacks." She lowered her voice. "I spent a long weekend there once."

"Kayaking and hiking?"

"Among other things. Phillip has lots of toys."

"He certainly didn't keep the Van Dyck for long."

"Some people flip houses. Phillip flips paintings."

Sarah accepted a glass of champagne from the flight attendant and insisted that Gabriel take one as well.

"What shall we drink to?" he asked.

"A disaster averted."

"I certainly hope so," said Gabriel, and left his glass untouched.

———

It was a few minutes after nine the following morning when the plane dropped from a cloudless sky and settled onto the runway of Charles de Gaulle Airport. After clearing passport control and customs, Gabriel and Sarah climbed into a taxi and headed for the center of Paris. Their first stop was Brasserie L'Alsace on the Avenue des Champs-Élysées, where, at 10:45 a.m., Gabriel placed his first call to Galerie Georges Fleury. It went unanswered, as did his second. But the third time he tried the number, Bruno the receptionist came on the line. Posing once again as Ludwig Ziegler, art adviser to the renowned Swiss violinist Anna Rolfe, Gabriel demanded to speak to Monsieur Fleury at once.

"I'm sorry, but Monsieur Fleury is with another client."

"It is imperative that I see him immediately."

"May I ask what this is regarding?"

"*A River Scene with Distant Windmills.*"

"Perhaps I can be of help."

"I'm quite certain you can't."

The receptionist placed the call on hold. Two minutes passed before he came back on the line. "Monsieur Fleury will see you at two o'clock," he said, and the connection went dead.

Which left Gabriel and Sarah with three long hours to kill. They drank coffee at Brasserie L'Alsace until noon, then walked up the Champs-Élysées to Fouquet's for an unhurried lunch. Afterward, they crossed to the opposite side of the avenue and, with their luggage in tow, window-shopped their way to the rue la Boétie. It was two o'clock exactly when they arrived at Galerie Georges Fleury. Gabriel stretched his injured right hand toward the intercom, but the automatic lock snapped open before he could place his forefinger atop the call button. He heaved open the glass door and followed Sarah inside.

———

The vestibule was unoccupied save the bronze life-size bust of a young Greek or Roman man perched atop its plinth of black marble. Gabriel called out Fleury's name and, receiving no answer, led Sarah into the ground-floor exhibition room. It was likewise uninhabited. The large Rococo painting depicting a nude Venus and three young maidens was gone, as was the Venetian scene attributed to a follower of Canaletto. No new paintings hung in their place.

"Looks as though Monsieur Fleury is doing a brisk business," said Sarah.

"The missing paintings were both forgeries," answered Gabriel, and headed for Fleury's office. There he found the art dealer seated at his desk, his face tipped toward the ceiling, his mouth open. The wall behind him was spattered with still-damp blood and brain tissue, the result of two recent point-blank gunshot wounds to the center of his forehead. The younger man lying on the floor had also been shot at close range—twice in the chest and at least once in the head. Like Georges Fleury, he was quite obviously dead.

"Dear God," whispered Sarah from the open doorway.

Gabriel made no reply; his phone was ringing. It was Yuval Gershon, calling from his office at Unit 8200 headquarters outside Tel Aviv. He didn't bother with a greeting.

"Someone turned on the dead woman's phone about one thirty local time. We got inside a couple of minutes ago."

"Where is it?"

"The Eighth Arrondissement of Paris. The rue la Boétie."

"I'm in the same location."

"I know," said Yuval. "In fact, it looks to us as though you might be in the same room."

Gabriel rang off and located the number for Valerie Bérrangar's phone in his directory of recent calls. He started to dial, but stopped when his connoisseur's eye fell upon the aluminum-sided Tumi suitcase, 52 by 77 by 28 centimeters, standing in the corner of the cluttered office. It was possible that Monsieur Fleury had been planning to embark on a journey at the time of his death. But the more likely explanation was that the suitcase contained a bomb.

A bomb, thought Gabriel, that would be detonated with a call to Madame Bérrangar's phone.

He did not bother to explain any of this to Sarah. Instead, he seized her arm and pulled her through the exhibition room to the entrance of the gallery. The glass door was locked, and the remote was missing from the receptionist's desk. It was, Gabriel had to admit, a masterpiece of planning and execution. But then he would have expected nothing less. After all, they were professionals.

But even professionals, he thought suddenly, make mistakes. Theirs was the bronze life-size bust of a young Greek or Roman man perched atop its plinth of black marble. Gabriel raised the heavy object above his head and, ignoring the searing pain in his hand, hurled it against the glass door of Galerie Georges Fleury.

PART TWO

Underdrawing

25

Quai des Orfèvres

Perhaps not surprisingly, the French police assumed the worst when, at 2:01 p.m. on an otherwise pleasant spring afternoon, the elegant Eighth Arrondissement of Paris shook with the thunderclap of an explosion. The first units arrived at the scene moments later to find an Old Master art gallery engulfed in flames. Even so, the officers were encouraged by the fact that there appeared to be no large-scale loss of life of the sort associated with jihadist terrorist attacks. Indeed, at first glance, the only casualty appeared to be the life-size bronze bust of a young Greek or Roman man lying on the pavement, surrounded by blue-gray cubes of tempered glass. One veteran detective, after learning of the circumstances by which the weighty objet d'art exited the gallery, would declare it to be the first documented case in the annals of French crime that anyone had broken *out* of an art gallery.

The perpetrators of this most unusual act—a man of late middle age and an attractive fair-haired woman in her early forties—surrendered to police within minutes of the explosion. And at 2:45 p.m., after a series of hasty and incredulous phone calls between senior French intelligence and security officials, they were placed in the back of an unmarked Peugeot and delivered to 36

Quai des Orfèvres, the iconic headquarters of the Police Nationale's criminal division.

There they were separated and relieved of their personal effects. The woman's handbag and luggage contained nothing out of the ordinary, but her companion was in possession of several noteworthy items. They included a false German passport, an Israeli-made Solaris mobile phone, an Italian *permesso di soggiorno*, a painting without a frame or stretcher, documents from Galerie Georges Fleury and Equus Analytics, and a handwritten letter from a certain Valerie Bérrangar to Julian Isherwood, owner and sole proprietor of Isherwood Fine Arts, 7–8 Mason's Yard, St. James's, London.

At half past three, the items were arrayed upon the table of the interrogation room into which the man of late middle age was led. Also present was a sleek creature of about fifty clad in a banker's executive suit. Extending a hand cordially in greeting, he introduced himself as Jacques Ménard, commander of the Central Office for the Fight against Cultural Goods Trafficking. The man smiled as he lowered himself into his seat. It definitely sounded better in French.

———

Jacques Ménard opened the German passport. "Johannes Klemp?"

"A small man with a chip balanced precariously on his insignificant shoulder," said Gabriel. "Much loathed by hoteliers and restaurateurs from Copenhagen to Cairo."

"Do the Germans know you're abusing one of their passports?"

"The way I see it, allowing me to occasionally travel on one of their passports is the least the Germans can do."

Ménard took up the Solaris phone. "Is it as secure as they say?"

"I hope you didn't try to unlock it. I'll go blind reloading my contacts."

Ménard reached for the sales documents from Galerie Georges Fleury. "*The* Anna Rolfe?"

"She was in town last weekend. I borrowed her for a few hours."

"She has a fondness for Aelbert Cuyp?"

"It's not a Cuyp." Gabriel nudged the report from Equus Analytics across the tabletop. "It's a forgery. Which is why I purchased it in the first place."

"You can tell if a painting is a forgery merely by looking at it?"

"Can't you?"

"No," admitted Ménard. "I cannot. But perhaps we should begin here." He indicated the handwritten letter. "With Madame Bérrangar."

"Yes, let's," said Gabriel. "After all, if you had taken her complaint about *Portrait of an Unknown Woman* seriously, she'd still be alive."

"Madame Bérrangar was killed in a single-vehicle traffic accident."

"It wasn't an accident, Ménard. She was murdered."

"How do you know that?"

"Her phone."

"What about it?"

"The bombmaker used it to trigger the detonator."

"Perhaps we should start from the beginning," suggested Ménard.

Yes, agreed Gabriel. Perhaps they should.

Gabriel's account of his investigation into the provenance and authenticity of *Portrait of an Unknown Woman* was chronological in sequence and largely accurate in content. It commenced with Julian's star-crossed visit to Bordeaux and concluded with the destruction of Galerie Georges Fleury and the brutal murder of its owner and his assistant. Absent from Gabriel's briefing was any mention of his visit to a certain antiques shop on the rue de Miromesnil or the assistance he received from Yuval Gershon of Unit 8200. Nor did he divulge the name of the wealthy American art investor who had purchased *Portrait of an Unknown Woman* from Isherwood Fine Arts—only that the painting had since been resold to yet another unidentified buyer and that the matter had been resolved to the satisfaction of all the parties involved.

"Is it a Van Dyck or not?" asked Ménard.

"The auction house that brokered the sale says it is."

"So your investigation was a waste of time? Is that what you're saying?"

"The death of Valerie Bérrangar and the events of this afternoon would suggest otherwise." Gabriel looked down at the forgery. "As would this painting."

"Did you really expect Georges Fleury to return the money based on the findings of a single expert?"

"The expert in question is regarded as the best in the world. I was confident that I could convince Fleury to accept the findings and refund the money."

"You were planning to threaten him?"

"Me? Never."

Ménard smiled in spite of himself. "And you're sure Fleury was dead when you and Madame Bancroft arrived at the gallery?"

"Quite sure," answered Gabriel. "Bruno Gilbert, too."

"In that case, who let you in?"

"The assassin, of course. He unlocked the door using the keyless remote that usually rests on the receptionist's desk. Fortunately, he waited fifteen seconds too long before calling Valerie Bérrangar's phone."

"How do you—"

"It's not important how I know," interjected Gabriel. "All that matters is that you now have the evidence to link her murder to the bombing of the gallery."

"The phone's identification number and SIM card?"

Gabriel nodded.

"Only if they survived the detonation. Still, it was rather reckless on his part, don't you think?"

"Almost as reckless as leaving that bronze bust next to the door. The man who hired him probably thought that I would be suspicious if it wasn't there. After all, I spotted three forgeries within a few minutes of setting foot in that gallery." Gabriel lowered his voice. "Which is why I had to die."

"Because you were a threat to a forgery ring?" asked Ménard skeptically.

"It's not a traditional ring. It's a sophisticated business enterprise that's flooding the art market with high-quality forgeries. And the man who's running it is making enough money to hire professionals to eliminate anyone who threatens him."

Ménard made a show of thought. "An interesting theory, Allon. But you have no proof."

"If you had listened to Valerie Bérrangar, you would have all the proof you need."

"I did listen to her," insisted Ménard. "But Fleury assured me there was nothing wrong with the painting he sold to Monsieur Isherwood, that it was simply a case of two copies of the same portrait."

"And you believed him?"

"Georges Fleury was a respected member of the Paris art community. My unit never received a single complaint about him."

"That's because the fakes he was selling were good enough to fool the best eyes in the art world. Based on what I've seen of the forger's work, he could hold his own among the Old Masters."

"From what I hear, you're not too bad yourself, Allon. One of the world's finest art restorers. At least that's the rumor."

"But I use my talent to heal existing paintings." Gabriel tapped the surface of the forgery. "This man is creating entirely new works that appear as though they were executed by some of the greatest artists who ever lived."

"Do you have any idea who he might be?"

"You're the detective, Ménard. I'm sure you'll be able to find him if you put your mind to it."

"And who are you these days, Allon?"

"I'm the director of the paintings department at the Tiepolo Restoration Company. And I'd like to go home now."

––––––––––

Ménard insisted on keeping the forged painting and the original copies of the documents, including Valerie Bérrangar's letter. Gabriel, who was in no position to make demands of his own, requested only anonymity—for himself and for Isherwood Fine Arts.

The French detective rubbed his jaw noncommittally. "You know how these things go, Allon. Criminal inquiries can be hard to control. But don't worry about the German passport. It will be our little secret."

By then it was approaching eight o'clock. Ménard escorted Gabriel downstairs to the courtyard, where Sarah waited in the backseat of the same unmarked Peugeot. It delivered them to the Gare du Nord in time to make the evening's last Eurostar to London.

"All in all," said Sarah, "a rather disastrous turn of events."

"It could have been worse."

"Much," she agreed. "But why is it that things always explode whenever I'm around you?"

"I just seem to rub certain people the wrong way."

"But not Jacques Ménard?"

"No," said Gabriel. "We got on famously."

"So much for handling the matter quietly. But I suppose that you got exactly what you wanted in the end."

"What's that?"

"A formal investigation by the French police."

"No one will be spared?"

"No one," said Sarah as she closed her eyes. "Not even you."

26

San Polo

For the remainder of that glorious April, as French police and prosecutors sifted through the ruins of Galerie Georges Fleury, the art world looked on in horror and held its collective breath. Those who knew Fleury well were guarded in their comments, in private and especially to the press. And those who had done business with him said little if anything at all. The director of the Musée d'Orsay called it the most unsettled month for the arts in France since the Germans entered Paris in June 1940. Several commentators criticized the remark as insensitive, but few took issue with its sentiment.

Because *l'affaire Fleury* included a bomb and two dead bodies, the serious crimes division of the Police Nationale—the so-called Central Directorate of the Judicial Police—controlled the investigation, with Jacques Ménard's art sleuths reduced to a supporting role. Veteran crime reporters immediately sensed that something was amiss, as their sources at the Quai des Orfèvres seemed incapable of answering even the most basic questions about the probe.

Did the *police judiciaire* have any leads on the bomber's current whereabouts?

If we did, came the terse reply from the Quai des Orfèvres, we would have arrested him by now.

Was it true that Fleury and his assistant were killed before the bomb exploded?

The Quai des Orfèvres was not in a position to say.

Was theft the motive?

The Quai des Orfèvres was pursuing several leads.

Were others involved?

The Quai des Orfèvres had ruled nothing out.

And what about the man of late middle age and the attractive fair-haired woman who were seen smashing their way out of the gallery seconds before the bomb detonated? Here again, the Quai des Orfèvres was at its most elusive. Yes, the police were aware of the eyewitness reports and were looking into them. For now, they would have nothing more to say on the matter, as it was part of an ongoing investigation.

Gradually, the press grew frustrated and sought out greener pastures. The flow of new revelations slowed to a trickle, then dried up entirely. Quietly the inhabitants of the art world breathed a collective sigh of relief. With their reputations and careers intact, they carried on as though nothing had happened.

Such was the case, to a lesser extent, for the man of late middle age. For several days after his return to Venice, he tried to spare his wife the details of his most recent brush with death. He revealed the truth while attempting, with limited success, to accurately reproduce her honey-and-gold-flecked irises on canvas. His task was made more difficult by the late-afternoon light falling across the underside of her left breast.

"You violated every possible rule of tradecraft," she admonished him. "The field officer always controls the environment. And he never allows the target to set the time of a meeting."

"I wasn't debriefing a deep-penetration agent in the backstreets of West Beirut. I was attempting to return a forged painting to a crooked art dealer in the Eighth Arrondissement of Paris."

"Will they try again?"

"To kill me? I can't imagine."

"Why not?"

"Because I've told the French everything I know. What would be the point?"

"What was the point of trying to kill you in the first place?"

"He's afraid of me."

"Who?"

"You really must stop talking." He loaded his brush and placed it against his canvas. "It changes the shape of your eyes when you open your mouth."

She seemed not to hear him. "Your daughter dreamed of your death while you were away. A terrible nightmare. And quite prophetic, as it turns out."

"Why?"

"You were lying on a sidewalk when you died."

"She must have been dreaming of Washington."

"Her dream was different."

"How so?"

"You had no arms or legs."

———————

That evening Gabriel experienced the same dream. It was so vivid he didn't dare close his eyes again for fear of its return. Repairing to his studio, he completed the painting of Chiara in a few fevered hours of uninterrupted work. In the broad light of morning, she declared it the finest piece he had produced in years.

"It reminds me of a Modigliani."

"I'll take that as a compliment."

"You were inspired by him?"

"It's hard not to be."

"Could you paint one?"

"A Modigliani? Yes, of course."

"I like the one that fetched a hundred and seventy million at auction a few years ago."

The painting in question was *Reclining Nude*. Gabriel commenced work on it after dropping the children at school and completed it two days later while listening to Anna Rolfe's new CD. Then he produced a second version of the painting, with a change of perspective and a subtle rearrangement of the woman's pose. He signed it with Modigliani's distinctive signature, in the upper-right corner of the canvas.

"Obviously, your hand suffered no permanent damage," remarked Chiara.

"I painted it with my left."

"It's astonishing. It looks exactly like a Modigliani."

"It *is* a Modigliani. He just didn't paint it."

"Could it fool anyone?"

"Not with a modern canvas and stretcher. But if I found a canvas similar to the type he was using in Montmartre in 1917 and was able to concoct a convincing provenance . . ."

"You could bring it to market as a lost Modigliani?"

"Exactly."

"How much could you get for it?"

"A couple hundred, I'd say."

"Thousand?"

"Million." Gabriel placed a hand reflectively to his chin. "The question is, what should we do with it?"

"Burn it," said Chiara. "And don't ever paint another."

———

Chiara's directive to the contrary, Gabriel hung the two Modiglianis in their bedroom and then retreated once more to his quiet, unhurried life of semiretirement. He dropped the children at school at eight o'clock each morning and collected them again at half past three. He visited the Rialto Market to fetch the ingredients for the family's evening meal. He read dense books and listened to music on his new British sound system. And if he were so inclined, he painted. A Monet one day, a Cézanne the next, a stunning reinterpretation of

Vincent's *Self-Portrait with Bandaged Ear* that, were it not for Gabriel's modern canvas and palette, would have set the art world ablaze.

He followed the news from Paris with mixed emotions. He was relieved that Quai des Orfèvres had seen fit to conceal his role in the affair and that his old friends Sarah Bancroft and Julian Isherwood had suffered no reputational damage. But when three additional weeks passed with no arrests—and no suggestion in the press that Galerie Georges Fleury had been flooding the market with paintings produced by one of the greatest art forgers in history—Gabriel reached the unsettling conclusion that a ministerial thumb had been laid upon the scales of French justice.

The arrival of the Bavaria C42 came as a welcome distraction. Gabriel took it on a pair of test runs in the sheltered waters of the *laguna*. Then, on the first Saturday of May, the Allon family sailed to Trieste for dinner. During their starlit return to Venice, Gabriel revealed that Sarah Bancroft had offered him a minor but lucrative commission. Chiara suggested he execute something original instead. He commenced work on a Picassoesque still life, then buried it beneath a version of Titian's *Portrait of Vincenzo Mosti*. Francesco Tiepolo declared it a masterpiece and advised Gabriel never to produce another.

He disagreed with Francesco's favorable assessment of the work—it was by no means a masterpiece, not by the mighty Titian's standards—so he cut the canvas from its stretcher and burned it. Next morning, after dropping the children at school, he repaired to Bar Dogale to consider how best to squander the remaining hours of his day. While he was consuming *un 'ombra*, a small glass of *vino bianco* taken by Venetians with their breakfast, a shadow fell across his table. It was cast by none other than Luca Rossetti of the Art Squad. His face bore only the faintest trace of the injuries he had suffered some six weeks earlier. He bore a message from Jacques Ménard of the Police Nationale.

"He was wondering whether you were free to come to Paris."

"When?"

"You're booked on the twelve forty Air France flight."

"Today?"

"Do you have something more pressing on your schedule, Allon?"

"That depends on whether Ménard intends to arrest me the minute I step off the plane."

"No such luck."

"In that case, why does he want to see me?"

"He wants to show you something."

"Did he say what it was?"

"No," said Rossetti. "But he said you might want to bring a gun."

27

Musée du Louvre

Jacques Ménard was waiting at the arrival gate at Charles de Gaulle when Gabriel emerged from the jetway, a bag over one shoulder, a 9mm Beretta pressing reassuringly against the base of his spine. After an expedited journey through passport control, they climbed into the back of an unmarked sedan and started toward the center of Paris. Ménard declined to disclose their destination.

"The last time someone surprised me in Paris, it didn't turn out so well."

"Don't worry, Allon. I think you'll actually enjoy this."

They followed the A1 past the Stade de France, then headed west on the boulevard Périphérique, Paris's high-speed ring road. Five minutes later, the Élysée Palace appeared before them.

"You should have warned me," said Gabriel. "I would have worn something appropriate."

Ménard smiled as his driver sped past the presidential palace, then turned left onto the Avenue des Champs-Élysées. Before reaching the Place de la Concorde, they dropped into a tunnel and followed the Quai des Tuileries to the Pont du Carrousel. A right turn would have taken them across the Seine to the Latin Quarter. They turned to the left instead and, after passing beneath an ornate archway, braked to a halt in the immense central courtyard of the world's most famous museum.

"The Louvre?"

"Yes, of course. Where did you think I was taking you?"

"Somewhere a bit more dangerous."

"If it's danger you want," said Ménard, "we've definitely come to the right place."

————

A young woman with the elongated limbs of a Degas dancer greeted Gabriel and Ménard outside I. M. Pei's iconic glass-and-steel pyramid. Wordlessly she escorted them across the immense Cour Napoléon and through a door reserved for museum staff. Two uniformed security guards waited on the other side. Neither seemed to notice when Gabriel set off the magnetometer.

"This way, please," said the woman, and led them along a corridor flooded with fluorescent light. After a walk of perhaps a half kilometer, they arrived at the entrance of the National Center for Research and Restoration, the world's most scientifically advanced facility for the conservation and authentication of art. Its inventory of cutting-edge technology included an electrostatic particle accelerator that allowed researchers to determine the chemical composition of an object without need of a potentially damaging sample.

The woman entered the passcode into the keypad, and Ménard led Gabriel inside. The cathedral-like laboratory was gripped by an air of sudden abandonment.

"I asked the director to close early so we could have a bit of privacy."

"To do what?"

"Look at a painting, Allon. What else?"

It was propped upon a laboratory easel, shrouded in black baize. Ménard removed the cloth to reveal a full-length portrait of a nude Lucretia thrusting a dagger into the center of her chest.

"Lucas Cranach the Elder?" asked Gabriel.

"That's what it says on the placard."

"Where did it come from?"

"Where do you think?"

"Galerie Georges Fleury?"

"I always heard you were good, Allon."

"And where did Monsieur Fleury find it?"

"A very old and prominent French collection," answered Ménard dubiously. "When Fleury showed it to a curator at the Louvre, he said it was probably the work of a later follower of Cranach. The curator had other ideas and brought it here to the center for evaluation. I'm sure you can guess the rest."

"The most advanced facility for the restoration and authentication of paintings in the world declared it to be the work of Lucas Cranach the Elder rather than a later follower."

Ménard nodded. "But wait, it gets better."

"How is that possible?"

"Because the president of the Louvre declared it a national treasure and paid nine and a half million euros to ensure it remain in France permanently."

"And now he's wondering whether it's a Cranach or crap?"

"In so many words." Ménard switched on a standing halogen lamp. "Would you mind having a look at it?"

Gabriel went to the nearest stainless-steel utility cart and after a moment of searching found a professional-grade magnifier. He used it to scrutinize the brushwork and craquelure. Then he stepped away from the painting and placed a hand contemplatively to his chin.

"Well?" asked Ménard.

"It's the best Lucas Cranach the Elder I've ever seen."

"I'm relieved."

"Don't be," said Gabriel.

"Why not?"

"Because Lucas Cranach the Elder didn't paint it."

How many more are there?"

"Three," answered Ménard. "They all emerged from Galerie Georges Fleury with a similar provenance and the same uncertain attribution. And the experts of the National Center for Research and Restoration, after careful evaluation, declared all three to be newly discovered works by the masters themselves."

"Anything good?"

"A Frans Hals, a Gentileschi, and the most delicious Van der Weyden you've ever laid eyes on."

"You're an admirer of Rogier?"

"Who isn't?"

"You'd be surprised."

They were sitting at a table at Café Marly, the Louvre's stylish restaurant. The declining sun had set fire to the glass panels of the pyramid. The light dazzled Gabriel's eyes.

"Are you formally trained?" he asked.

"As an art historian?" Ménard shook his head. "But four of my officers have advanced degrees from the Sorbonne. My background is in fraud and money laundering."

"Heaven knows, there's none of that in the art world."

Smiling, Ménard removed three photographs from a manila envelope—a Frans Hals, a Gentileschi, and an exquisite portrait by Rogier van der Weyden. "They were acquired by the Louvre over a ten-year period. The Van der Weyden and the Cranach were purchased during the tenure of the current president. The Frans Hals and Gentileschi were acquired on his recommendation when he was the director of the paintings department."

"Which means his fingerprints are on all four."

"Evidently, he and Monsieur Fleury were quite close." Lowering his voice, Ménard added, "Close enough so that rumors are swirling."

"Kickbacks?"

Ménard shrugged but said nothing.

"Is there any truth to it?"

"I wouldn't know. You see, the Central Office for the Fight against Cultural Goods Trafficking has been ordered not to investigate the matter."

"What happens if the four paintings turn out to be forgeries?"

"The world's most advanced facility for the conservation and authentication of art has determined that they are genuine. Therefore, absent a videotaped confession on the part of the forger, the Louvre will stand by its findings."

"In that case, why did you ask me to come to Paris?"

Ménard drew another photograph from the envelope and placed it on the table.

28

Café Marly

Nothing about the man depicted in the photograph suggested he belonged anywhere near an Old Master art gallery in the elegant Eighth Arrondissement of Paris. Not the logoless cap pulled low over his brow. Or the wraparound sunglasses covering his eyes. Or the false beard adhered to his face. And certainly not the aluminum-sided Tumi suitcase, 52 by 77 by 28 centimeters, that he was wheeling along the pavements of the rue la Boétie. He was sturdy in manufacture, compact in size, confident in demeanor. An athlete in his day, perhaps a former soldier. He wore a drab overcoat against the cool early-spring weather, and leather gloves—presumably so that he would leave no fingerprints on the handle of the suitcase or in the taxi that was pulling away from the curb.

The time stamp on the photo was 13:39:35. Jacques Ménard handed Gabriel a second image, captured at the same instant. "The first shot came from the camera at the *tabac* across the street. The second one is from the Monoprix a couple of doors down."

"Nothing from your surveillance cameras?"

"This is Paris, Allon. Not London. We have about two thousand cameras in high-traffic tourist areas and around sensitive government buildings. But there are gaps in our coverage. The man in the photograph exploited them."

"Where did he get into the taxi?"

"A little commune east of Paris, in the Seine-en-Marne *département*. My colleagues at the Quai des Orfèvres haven't been able to determine how he got there."

"Did they manage to find the driver?"

"He's an immigrant from the Côte d'Ivoire. He says the customer spoke French like a native and paid the fare in cash."

"He checks out?"

"The driver?" Ménard nodded. "No problem there."

Gabriel lowered his gaze to the second photograph. Same time stamp, slightly different angle. A bit like his reworking of Modigliani's *Reclining Nude*, he thought. "How long did he stay inside?"

Ménard drew two more photographs from the envelope. The first showed the man leaving the gallery at 13:43:34. The second showed him sitting at a table at Brasserie Baroche. It was located about forty meters from the gallery, at the corner of the rue la Boétie and the rue de Ponthieu. The time stamp was 13:59:46. The assassin was looking down at the object in his hand. It was the remote unlocking device he had removed from Bruno Gilbert's desk.

"You and Madame Bancroft approached the gallery from the opposite direction." Ménard produced a photograph of Gabriel and Sarah's arrival, as if to prove his point. "Otherwise, you would have walked right past him."

"Where did he go next?"

"A taxi to the Sixteenth. A nice long walk in the Bois de Boulogne. And then, *poof*, he disappeared."

"Very professional."

"Our explosives experts were quite impressed with his bomb."

"Were they able to identify the phone he used to trigger the detonation?"

"They say not."

"I'm certain that Valerie Bérrangar's phone was inside that gallery."

"My colleagues at the Quai des Orfèvres have their doubts about that. Furthermore, they are inclined to accept the conclusion of the local gendarmerie that Valerie Bérrangar died as the result of an unfortunate road accident."

"I'm glad we cleared that up. What else has the Quai des Orfèvres concluded?"

"That the two men who tried to steal Monsieur Isherwood's attaché case were probably ordinary thieves."

"What about the men who searched his room at the InterContinental?"

"According to the hotel's head of security, they don't exist."

"Did anyone bother to check the internal video?"

"Apparently, it was erased."

"By whom?"

"The Quai des Orfèvres can't say."

"What *can* it say?" asked Gabriel.

Ménard drew a breath before answering. "It is the conclusion of the Quai des Orfèvres that the murder of Georges Fleury and the destruction of his gallery were the result of an embezzlement scheme by Bruno Gilbert and the man with the suitcase."

"Is there a shred of evidence to support this nonsense?"

"A few hours before you and Madame Bancroft arrived at the gallery, someone transferred the entire balance of its accounts at Société Générale to the account of an anonymous shell company in the Channel Islands. The anonymous shell company then transferred it to the account of another anonymous shell company in the Bahamas, which in turn transferred it to the account of another anonymous shell company in the Cayman Islands. And then . . ."

"Poof?"

Ménard nodded.

"How much money are we talking about?"

"Twelve million euros. The Quai des Orfèvres is of the opinion the bomber wanted it all for himself."

"Clean and simple," said Gabriel. "And much more palatable than a scandal involving several million euros' worth of forgeries hanging on the walls of the world's most famous museum."

"Thirty-four million euros, to be exact. All of which had to be raised from outside sources. If it were to become public, the reputation of one of France's most treasured institutions would be severely tarnished."

"And we can't have that," said Gabriel.

"*Non*," agreed Ménard.

"But how do Sarah and I fit into this theory of theirs?"

"You and Madame Bancroft were never there, remember?"

Gabriel displayed the photograph of their arrival at the gallery. "And what happens if this becomes public?"

"Don't worry, Allon. No chance of that."

Gabriel placed the photograph atop the others. "How high does it go?"

"What's that?"

"The cover-up."

"Cover-up is an ugly word, Allon. So *américain*."

"*La conspiration du silence.*"

"Much better."

"The director of the Police Nationale? The prefect?"

"Oh, no," said Ménard. "Much higher than that. The ministers of interior and culture are involved. Perhaps even *le Palais*."

"You disapprove?"

"I am a loyal servant of the French Republic. But I have a conscience as well."

"I'd listen to your conscience."

"You never violated yours?"

"I was an intelligence operative," said Gabriel without elaboration.

"And I am a senior Police Nationale officer who is obligated to follow the orders of my superiors to the letter."

"And if you were to disobey?"

"I would be terminated. *Avec la guillotine.*" Ménard inclined his head toward the west. "*A la Place de la Concorde.*"

"How about a leak to a friendly reporter at *Le Monde*?"

"A leak of what, exactly? A story about a London art dealer who purchased a forged Van Dyck portrait from a Parisian art gallery and then sold it to an American investor?"

"Perhaps the leak could be a bit narrower in scope."

"How narrow?"

"A Cranach, a Hals, a Gentileschi, and the most delicious Van der Weyden you've ever laid eyes on."

"The scandal would be immense." Ménard paused. "And it wouldn't accomplish our shared goal."

"What might that be?" asked Gabriel warily.

"Putting the forger out of business." Ménard nudged the photographs a few millimeters closer to Gabriel. "And while you're at it, you might want to track down the man who tried to kill you and Madame Bancroft."

"How am I supposed to do that?"

Ménard smiled. "You're the former intelligence operative, Allon. I'm sure you'll be able to find him if you put your mind to it."

———

What Jacques Ménard proposed next was *une petite collaboration*, the terms of which he outlined for Gabriel while walking along the footpaths of the Jardin des Tuileries. Theirs was to be an entirely secret relationship, with Ménard playing the role of case officer and Gabriel acting as his informant and asset. It would be up to Ménard, and only Ménard, to determine how best to act upon their findings. If possible, he would resolve the situation quietly, without inflicting undue damage to the reputations of those who had been taken in.

"But if a few eggs need to be broken, well, so be it."

Gabriel made only a single demand in return, that Ménard make no attempt to observe his activities or monitor his movements. The Frenchman readily agreed to avert his eyes. He asked only that Gabriel avoid unnecessary violence, especially within the borders of the Republic.

"What if I'm able to find the man who tried to kill me?"

Ménard pulled his lips into a Gallic expression of indifference. "Do with him what you will. I'm not going to cry over a little spilled blood. Just make certain none of it splashes on me."

With that, the newfound partners went their separate ways— Ménard to the Quai des Orfèvres, Gabriel to the Gare de Lyon. As his train slithered from the station shortly after 5:00 p.m., he made two phone calls, one to his wife in Venice, the other to Sarah. Neither was pleased by his news or by his travel plans, Sarah especially. Nevertheless, after consulting with her husband on a separate line, she reluctantly agreed to Gabriel's request.

"How are you making the crossing?" she asked.

"The morning ferry from Marseilles."

"Peasant," she hissed, and rang off.

29

Ajaccio

At seven fifteen the following evening, Christopher Keller was seated at a waterfront café in the Corsican port of Ajaccio, an empty wineglass on the table before him, a freshly lit Marlboro burning between the first and second fingers of his sledgehammer right hand. He wore a pale gray suit by Richard Anderson of Savile Row, an open-neck white dress shirt, and handmade oxford shoes. His hair was sun-bleached, his skin was taut and dark, his eyes were bright blue. The notch in the center of his thick chin looked as though it had been cleaved with a chisel. His mouth seemed permanently fixed in an ironic half-smile.

His waitress had presumed him to be a European from the mainland and had greeted him accordingly, with apathy bordering on contempt. But when he addressed her in fluent *corsu*, in the dialect of one from the northwestern corner of the island, she warmed to him instantly. They conversed in the Corsican way—about family and foreigners and the damage left by the springtime winds—and when he finished his first glass of rosé, she placed another before him without bothering to ask whether he wanted it.

It had done him no good, the second glass of wine, and neither had the cigarette, the fourth since his arrival at the café. It was a habit he had acquired while living under deep cover in Catholic West Belfast during one of the nastier periods of the Troubles. He now served in a clandestine operations unit of the Secret Intelligence Service sometimes referred to, incorrectly, as the Increment. His visit to Corsica, however, was entirely private in nature. A friend required the assistance of a man for whom Christopher had once worked—a certain Don Anton Orsati, patriarch of one of the island's most notorious families. As the friend's situation involved an attempt to kill Christopher's wife, he was only too happy to oblige him.

Just then the prow of an arriving Corsica Linea ferry nosed into the inner harbor, past the ramparts of the ancient citadel. Christopher slid a twenty-euro banknote beneath the empty wineglass and crossed the Quai de la République to the car park opposite the port's modern terminal. Behind the wheel of his battered Renault hatchback, he watched as the newly arrived passengers came spilling down the steps. Luggage-laden tourists. Returning Corsicans. Mainland French. A man of medium height and build dressed in a well-tailored Italian sport coat and gabardine trousers.

He tossed his overnight bag into the back of the Renault and dropped into the passenger seat. His emerald-green eyes stared with reproach at the cigarette burning in the ashtray.

"Must you?" he asked wearily.

"Yes," said Christopher as he started the engine. "I'm afraid I must."

———————

They crossed the bony ridge of hills north of Ajaccio, then followed the twisting road down to the Golfu di Liscia. The waves somersaulting onto the small crescent beach were unusually large, driven by an approaching *maestral*. It was how the Corsicans referred to the violent, unwelcome wind that blew in winter and springtime from the valleys of the Rhône.

"You arrived in the nick of time," said Christopher, his elbow protruding from the open window. "If you'd waited another day, you would have had the ferry ride from hell."

"It was bad enough as it was."

"Why didn't you fly from Paris?"

Gabriel removed the Beretta from its resting place at the small of his back and laid it on the center console.

"It's good to know that some things don't change." Christopher gave Gabriel a sideways glance. "You need a haircut. Otherwise, you're looking quite well for a man of your advanced age."

"It's the new me."

"What was wrong with the old you?"

"I had a bit of excess baggage I needed to lose."

"You and me both." Christopher turned his head to watch the waves rolling in from the west. "But at this moment, I am suddenly reminded of the man I used to be."

"The director of northern European sales for the Orsati Olive Oil Company?"

"Something like that."

"Does His Holiness know that you're back on the island?"

"We're expected for dinner. As you might imagine, excitement is high."

"Perhaps you should go alone."

"The last person who declined an invitation to dine with Don Anton Orsati is somewhere out there." Christopher gestured toward the waters of the Mediterranean. "In a concrete coffin."

"Has he forgiven me for stealing you away from him?"

"He blames the British. As for forgiveness, Don Orsati is unfamiliar with the word."

"I'm not in a terribly forgiving mood myself," said Gabriel quietly.

"How do you think I feel?"

"Would you like to see a photograph of the man who tried to murder your wife?"

"Not while I'm driving," said Christopher. "I'm liable to kill us both."

———

By the time they reached the town of Porto, the sun was an orange disk balanced atop the dark rim of the sea. Christopher headed inland along a road lined with laricio pine and started the long climb into the mountains. The air smelled of the *macchia*, the dense undergrowth of gorse, briar, rockrose, rosemary, and lavender that covered much of the island's interior. The Corsicans seasoned their foods with the *macchia*, heated their homes with it in winter, and took refuge in it during times of war and vendetta. It had no eyes, went one often-repeated Corsican proverb, but the *macchia* saw everything.

They passed through the hamlets of Chidazzu and Marignana and arrived in the village of the Orsatis a few minutes after ten o'clock. It had been there, or so it was said, since the time of the Vandals, when people from the coasts took to the hills for safety. Beyond it, in a small valley of olive groves that produced the island's finest oil, was the don's sprawling estate. Two heavily armed men stood watch at the entrance. They touched their distinctive Corsican caps respectfully as Christopher turned through the gate.

Several more bodyguards stood like statuary in the floodlit forecourt of the palatial villa. Gabriel left his Beretta in the Renault and followed Christopher up a flight of stone steps to Don Orsati's office. Entering, they found him seated at a large oaken table, before an open leather-bound ledger. As usual, he was wearing a bleached white shirt, loose-fitting cotton trousers, and a pair of dusty leather sandals that looked as though they had been purchased at the local outdoor market. At his elbow was a decorative bottle of Orsati olive oil—olive oil being the legitimate front through which the don laundered the profits of death.

Laboriously he rose to his feet. He was a large man by Corsican standards, well over six feet and broad through the back and shoulders, with coal-black hair, a dense mustache, and the brown-streaked eyes of a canine. They settled first on Christopher, inhospitably. He addressed him in *corsu*.

"I accept your apology."

"For what?"

"The wedding," answered the don. "Never in my life have I been so insulted. And from you of all people."

"My new employers might have found it odd if you had been there."

"How do you explain your eight-million-pound flat in Kensington?"

"It's a maisonette, actually. And it cost me eight and a half."

"All of which you earned working for me." The don frowned. "Did you at least receive my wedding gift?"

"The fifty thousand pounds' worth of Baccarat crystal? I sent you a rather lengthy handwritten note of gratitude."

Don Orsati turned to Gabriel and in French said, "I assume *you* were in attendance."

"Only because they needed someone to give away the bride."

"Is it true she's an American?"

"Barely."

"What does that mean?"

"She spent most of her childhood in England and France."

"Is that supposed to make me feel better?"

"At least she's not Italian," said Gabriel knowingly.

"At the end of many disasters," said Don Orsati, reciting a Corsican proverb, "there is always an Italian. But your lovely wife is definitely the exception to the rule."

"I'm confident you'll feel the same about Sarah."

"She's intelligent?"

"She has a PhD from Harvard."

"Attractive?"

"Stunningly beautiful."

"Is she good to her mother?"

"When they're on speaking terms."

Don Orsati looked at Christopher in horror. "What kind of woman doesn't speak to her mother?"

"They've had their ups and downs."

"I'd like to have a word with her about this as soon as possible."

"We're hoping to spend a week or two on the island this summer."

"He who lives on hope dies on shit."

"How eloquent, Don Orsati."

"Our proverbs," he said gravely, "are sacred and correct."

"And there's one for every occasion."

Don Orsati laid a granite hand gently upon Christopher's cheek. "Only the spoon knows the pot's sorrows."

"Mistakes are made even by priests at the altar."

"Better to have little than nothing."

"But he who has nothing will not eat."

"Shall we?" asked Don Orsati.

"Perhaps we should discuss our mutual friend's problem first," suggested Christopher.

"This business with the art gallery in Paris?"

"Yes."

"Is it true your beautiful American wife was involved?"

"I'm afraid so."

"In that case," said Don Orsati, "you have a problem, too."

30

Villa Orsati

Gabriel laid two photographs on Don Orsati's desk. Same time stamp, slightly different angle. The don contemplated them as though they were Old Master paintings. He was a connoisseur of death and the men who dispensed it for a living.

"Do you recognize him?"

"I'm not sure his own mother would recognize him in that ridiculous disguise." The don glanced up at Christopher. "You would have never been caught dead looking like that."

"Never," he agreed. "One has to maintain certain standards."

Smiling, Don Orsati returned his gaze to the photographs. "Is there anything you can tell me about him?"

"The taxi driver said he spoke French like a native," answered Gabriel.

"The driver would have said the same about Christopher." The don's eyes narrowed. "He looks like a former soldier to me."

"I thought so, too. He certainly seems to know his way around explosive devices."

"Unless someone else built it for him. There are many fine bomb makers in this business of ours." Orsati once again turned to Christopher. "Wouldn't you agree?"

"Not as many as there used to be. But let's not dwell on the past."

"Perhaps we should," said Gabriel. Then he added quietly, "Just for a moment or two."

The don bunched his hands beneath his chin. "Is there something you wish to ask me?"

"There was a similar incident in Paris about twenty years ago. The gallery was owned by a Swiss dealer who was trading in paintings looted by the Nazis during the war. The bomb was delivered by a former British commando who—"

"I remember it well," interjected Don Orsati.

"As do I."

"And now you're wondering whether the man in these photographs works for my organization."

"I suppose I am."

Orsati's expression darkened. "You may rest assured, my old friend, that any man who offered me money to kill you would not leave this island alive."

"It's possible they thought I was someone else."

"With all due respect, I doubt that. For a man of the secret world, you have a rather famous face." Don Orsati looked at Christopher and exhaled heavily. "As for the former British commando, his fair hair, blue eyes, perfect English, and elite military training allowed him to fulfill contracts that were far beyond the skill level of my Corsican-born *taddunaghiu*. Needless to say, my business has suffered as a result of his decision to return home."

"Because you've turned down job offers where the risk of exposure was too high?"

"More than I can count." Orsati tapped the cover of his leather-bound ledger of death. "And my profits have fallen sharply as a result. Oh, don't get me wrong. I still get plenty of criminal and vengeance work. But my higher-profile clients have gone elsewhere."

"Anywhere in particular?"

"An exclusive new organization that offers white-glove concierge service to the sort of men who travel in private aircraft and dress like Christopher."

"Wealthy businessmen?"

"That's the rumor. This organization specializes in accidents and apparent suicides, the sort of thing the Orsati Olive Oil Company never bothered with. It is said that they're quite accomplished when it comes to staging crime scenes, perhaps because they employ several former police officers. They are also rumored to possess certain technical capabilities."

"Phone and computer hacking?"

The don shrugged his heavy shoulders. "This is your area of expertise. Not mine."

"Does this organization have a name?"

"If it does, I am not aware of it." Orsati looked down at the photographs. "The more important question is, who might have retained the services of this organization to kill you?"

"The leader of a sophisticated forgery network."

"Paintings?"

Gabriel nodded.

"He must be making a great deal of money."

"Thirty-four million euros from the Louvre alone."

"Perhaps I'm in the wrong line of work."

"I've often thought the same about myself, Don Orsati."

"What *is* your business these days?" he asked.

"I'm the director of the paintings department at the Tiepolo Restoration Company." Gabriel paused. "Currently on loan to the Police Nationale."

"A complicating factor, to say the least." Orsati made a face. "But please tell me how I can be of assistance to you and your friends from the French police."

"I'd like you to find the man in those photographs."

"And if I can?"

"I'll ask him a simple question."

"The name of the man who hired him to kill you?"

"You know what they say about assassinations, Don Orsati. The important thing is not who fired the shot but who paid for the bullet."

"Who was it who said that?" asked the don, intrigued.

"Eric Ambler."

"Wise words indeed. But in all likelihood, the man who tried to kill you in Paris doesn't know the client's name."

"Perhaps not, but he'll certainly be able to point me in the right direction. If nothing else he can provide valuable information on your competitor." Gabriel lowered his voice. "I would think that would be of interest to you, Don Orsati."

"One hand washes the other, and both hands wash the face."

"A very old Jewish proverb."

The don gave a dismissive wave of his enormous hand. "I'll put these photographs into circulation first thing in the morning. In the meantime, you and Christopher can spend a few days relaxing here on the island."

"Nothing like going on holiday with a man who once tried to kill you."

"If Christopher had actually *tried* to kill you, you would be dead."

"Just like the man who paid for the bullet," remarked Gabriel.

"Did Eric Ambler really say that about assassinations?"

"It's a line from *A Coffin for Dimitrios*."

"Interesting," said the don. "I never knew that Ambler was Corsican."

———

The distinctive scent of the *macchia* rose from the sumptuous feast that awaited them downstairs in Don Orsati's garden. They did not remain there long. Indeed, not five minutes after they sat down, the first knife-edged blast of the *maestral* arrived from the northwest. With the help of the don's bodyguards, they beat a hasty retreat to the dining room, and the meal resumed, though now it was accompanied by the howl and scrape of the much-despised intruder from across the sea.

It was after midnight when Don Orsati finally tossed his napkin onto the table, signaling that the evening had reached its end. Rising, Gabriel thanked the don for his hospitality and asked him to conduct his search with discretion. The don replied that he would use only his most trusted operatives. He was confident of a successful resolution.

"If it is your wish, I'll have my men bring him back here to Corsica. That way you won't have to get your hands dirty."

"It's never bothered me before. Besides," said Gabriel with a glance in Christopher's direction, "I have him."

"Christopher is a respectable English spy now. A man of distinction who resides at one of London's poshest addresses. He couldn't possibly get mixed up in a nasty business like this."

With that, Gabriel and Christopher went into the windblown night and climbed into the Renault. Leaving the estate, they headed eastward into the next valley. Christopher's secluded villa stood at the end of a dirt-and-gravel track lined on both sides by high walls of *macchia*. When the car's headlamps fell upon three ancient olive trees, he lifted his foot from the throttle and leaned anxiously over the steering wheel.

"Surely it's dead by now," said Gabriel.

"We'll know in a minute."

"You didn't ask the don?"

"And spoil an otherwise delightful evening?"

Just then a horned domestic goat, perhaps two hundred and fifty pounds in weight, emerged from the *macchia* and established itself in the center of the track. It had the markings of a palomino and a red beard, and was scarred from old battles. Its eyes shone defiantly in the glare of the headlamps.

"It has to be a different goat."

"No," answered Christopher as he applied the brakes. "Same bloody goat."

"Careful," said Gabriel. "I think it heard you."

The enormous goat, like the three ancient olive trees, belonged to Don Casabianca. It regarded the track as its private property and demanded tribute from those who traveled it. For Christopher, an Englishman with no Corsican blood in his veins, it harbored a particular resentment.

"Perhaps you could have a word with him on my behalf," he suggested.

"Our last conversation didn't go terribly well."

"What did you say to him?"

"It's possible I insulted his ancestry."

"On Corsica? What were you thinking?" Christopher inched the car forward, but the goat lowered its head and stood its ground. A tap of the horn was no more effective. "You won't mention any of this to Sarah, will you?"

"I wouldn't dream of it," vowed Gabriel.

Christopher slipped the car into PARK and exhaled heavily. Then he flung open his door and charged the goat in his bespoke Richard Anderson suit, flailing his arms like a madman. The tactic usually resulted in an immediate capitulation. But on this night, the first night of a *maestral*, the animal fought gamely for a minute or two before finally fleeing into the *macchia*. Fortunately, Gabriel captured the entire confrontation on video, which he immediately dispatched to Sarah in London. All in all, he thought, it was a fine start to their holiday on Corsica.

31

Haute-Corse

The villa had a red tile roof, a large blue swimming pool, and a broad terrace that received the sun in the morning and in the afternoon was shaded by laricio pine. When Gabriel rose the following morning, the granite paving stones were strewn with tree limbs and other assorted flora. In the well-appointed kitchen, he found Christopher, in hiking boots and a waterproof anorak, preparing café au lait on a butane camp stove. A local newscast issued from a battery-powered radio.

"We lost power around three a.m. The winds reached eighty miles per hour last night. They say it's the worst springtime *maestral* in living memory."

"Was there any mention of an incident involving an Englishman and an elderly goat?"

"Not yet. But thanks to you, it's all anyone's talking about in London." Christopher handed Gabriel a bowl of coffee. "Did you manage to get any sleep?"

"Not a wink. You?"

"I'm a combat veteran. I can sleep through anything."

"How long will it last?"

"Three days. Maybe four."

"I guess that rules out windsurfing."

"But not a hike up Monte Rotondo. Care to join me?"

"As tempting as that sounds," said Gabriel, "I think I'll spend the morning in front of a fire with a good book."

He carried his coffee into the comfortably furnished sitting room. Several hundred volumes of fiction and history lined the shelves, and upon the walls hung a modest collection of modern and Impressionist paintings. The most valuable piece was a Provençal landscape by Monet, which Christopher, through an intermediary, had acquired at Christie's in Paris. On that morning, however, Gabriel's eye was caught by the painting hanging next to it—another landscape, this one by Paul Cézanne.

He took down the painting and removed it from the frame. The stretcher appeared similar to those used by Cézanne in the mid-1880s, as did the canvas itself. There was no signature—not unusual, as Cézanne only signed works he considered truly finished—and the varnish was the color of nicotine. Otherwise, the painting appeared to be in good condition.

And yet . . .

Gabriel propped the painting in a rhombus of brilliant morning sunlight streaming through the French doors, then snapped a magnified detail image with his phone. With thumb and forefinger, he enlarged the photograph further and examined the brushwork. His reverie was so complete he failed to notice that Christopher, a gifted surveillance artist, had stolen into the room.

"May I ask what you're doing?"

"Looking for something to read," said Gabriel absently.

Christopher took down Ben McIntyre's biography of Kim Philby. "You might find this more interesting."

"Though somewhat incomplete." Gabriel looked down at the painting again.

"Is there a problem?"

"Where did you purchase it?"

"A gallery in Nice."

"Does the gallery have a name?"

"Galerie Edmond Toussaint."

"Did you seek the opinion of a professional?"

"Monsieur Toussaint gave me a certificate of authentication."

"May I see it? The provenance as well."

Christopher went upstairs to his study. Returning, he handed Gabriel a large business envelope, then slung a nylon rucksack over his powerful right shoulder.

"Last chance."

"Enjoy," said Gabriel as a gust of wind rattled the French doors. "And do give my best to your little caprine friend."

Steeling himself, Christopher went out and climbed into the Renault. A moment later Gabriel heard the blare of a car horn, followed by shouted threats of unspeakable violence. Laughing, he removed the contents of the envelope.

"Idiot," he said after a moment, to no one but himself.

———————

The *maestral* eased around eleven, but by late afternoon it was blowing hard enough to loosen several tiles from Christopher's roof. He returned home at dusk and proudly displayed for Gabriel the 136-kilometer-per-hour wind reading he had taken on Monte Rotondo's northern face. Gabriel reciprocated by disclosing his concerns over the authenticity of the Cézanne, a painting that Christopher had purchased under a false French identity while working as a professional assassin.

"Thus leaving you with no legal recourse. Or moral recourse, for that matter."

"Perhaps one or two of the don's most terrifying men should have a word with Monsieur Toussaint on my behalf."

"Perhaps," countered Gabriel, "you should forget I ever said anything, and let it go."

The wind blew without relent the following day and the day after that as well. Gabriel sheltered in place at the villa while Christopher flung himself against two more mountains—first Renoso, then d'Oro, where his pocket anemometer recorded the winds at 141 kilometers per hour. That evening they dined at Villa Orsati. Over coffee, the don acknowledged that his operatives had no leads on the identity or whereabouts of the man who had carried the bomb into Galerie Georges Fleury. He then chastised Christopher over the tenor and tone of his recent confrontations with Don Casabianca's goat.

"He called me this morning. He's very upset."

"The don or the goat?"

"It's no laughing matter, Christopher."

"How does Don Casabianca even know that things have taken a turn for the worse?"

"The news has spread like wildfire."

"I certainly didn't mention it to anyone."

"It must have been the *macchia*," said Gabriel, and repeated the ancient proverb regarding the ability of the aromatic vegetation to see everything. At this, the don nodded his head solemnly in agreement. It was, he concluded, the only possible explanation.

The wind raged for the remainder of that night, but by dawn it was a memory. Gabriel spent the morning helping Christopher repair the damage to the roof and clear the debris from the terrace and the pool. Then, in late afternoon, he drove into the village. It was a cluster of sandstone-colored cottages huddled around the bell tower of a church, before which lay a dusty square. Several men in newly pressed white shirts were playing a closely fought game of *pétanque*. Once they might have regarded Gabriel with suspicion—or pointed at him in the Corsican way, with their first and fourth fingers, to ward off the effects of the *occhju*, the evil eye. Now they greeted him warmly, as he was known throughout the village as a friend of Don Orsati and the Englishman named Christopher, who, thank goodness, had returned to the island after a prolonged absence.

"Is it true he's married?" asked one of the men.

"That's the rumor."

"Has he killed that goat?" asked another.

"Not yet. But it's only a matter of time."

"Perhaps you can talk some sense into him."

"I've tried. But I'm afraid they've reached the point of no return."

The men insisted that Gabriel join the game, as they were in need of another player. Declining, he repaired to the café in the far corner of the square for a glass of Corsican rosé. As the church bells tolled five o'clock, a young child, a girl of seven or eight, knocked on the door of the crooked little house next to the rectory. It opened a few inches, and a small pale hand appeared, clutching a slip of blue paper. The young girl carried it to the café and placed it on Gabriel's table. She bore an uncanny resemblance to Irene.

"What is your name?" he asked.

"Danielle."

Of course it was, he thought. "Would you like an ice cream?"

The child sat down and pushed the blue slip of paper across the tabletop. "Aren't you going to read it?"

"I don't need to."

"Why not?"

"I know what it says."

"How?"

"I have powers, too."

"Not like hers," said the child.

No, agreed Gabriel. Not like hers.

32

Haute-Corse

The hand the old woman offered Gabriel in greeting was warm and weightless. He held it gently, as though it were a cage bird.

"You've been hiding from me," she said.

"Not from you," he answered. "From the *maestral*."

"I've always liked the wind." Confidingly she added, "It's good for business."

The old woman was a *signadora*. The Corsicans believed that she possessed the power to heal those infected by the *occhju*. Gabriel had once suspected that she was nothing more than a conjurer and a clever teller of fortunes, but that was no longer the case.

She placed her hand against his cheek. "You're burning with fever."

"You always say that."

"That's because you always feel as though you are on fire." Her hand moved to his upper chest. The left side, slightly above his heart. "This is where the madwoman's bullet entered you."

"Did Christopher tell you that?"

"I haven't spoken to Christopher since his return." She lifted the front of Gabriel's dress shirt and examined the scar. "You were dead for several minutes, were you not?"

"Two or three."

She frowned. "Why do you bother trying to lie to me?"

"Because I prefer not to dwell on the fact that I was dead for ten minutes." Gabriel held up the blue slip of paper. "Where did you find that child?"

"Danielle? Why do you ask?"

"She reminds me of someone."

"Your daughter?"

"How is possible that you know what she looks like?"

"Perhaps you're merely seeing what you want to see."

"Don't speak to me in riddles."

"You named the child Irene after your mother. Every time she looks at you, you see your mother's face and the numbers that were written on her arm in the camp named for the trees."

"Someday you're going to have to show me how you do that."

"It is a gift from God." She released the front of his shirt and contemplated him with her bottomless black eyes. The face in which they were set was as white as baker's flour. "You are suffering from the *occhju*. It is as plain as day."

"I must have contracted it from Don Casabianca's goat."

"He is a demon."

"Tell me about it."

"I'm not joking. The animal is possessed. Stay away from it."

The *signadora* drew him into the parlor of her tiny home. On the small circular table was a candle, a shallow plate of water, and a vessel of olive oil. They were the tools of her trade. She lit the candle and sat down in her usual place. Gabriel, after a moment's hesitation, joined her.

"There's no such thing as the evil eye, you know. It's just a superstition that was prevalent among the ancient people of the Mediterranean."

"You are an ancient person of the Mediterranean as well."

"As ancient as it gets," he agreed.

"You were born in the Galilee, not far from the town where Jesus lived. Most of your ancestors were killed by the Romans during the siege of Jerusalem, but a few survived and made their way to Europe." She nudged the vessel of olive oil across the tabletop. "Proceed."

Gabriel returned the vessel to the woman's side of the table. "You first."

"You want me to prove that it's not a trick?"

"Yes."

The old woman dipped her forefinger into the oil. Then she held it over the plate and allowed three drops to fall into the water. They coalesced into a single gobbet.

"Now you."

Gabriel performed the same ritual. This time the oil shattered into a thousand droplets, and soon there was no trace of it.

"*Occhju*," whispered the old woman.

"Magic and misdirection," said Gabriel in reply.

Smiling, she asked, "How's your hand?"

"Which one?"

"The one you injured when you attacked the man who works for the one-eyed creature."

"He shouldn't have followed me."

"Make your peace with him," said the *signadora*. "He will help you find the woman."

"What woman?"

"The Spanish woman."

"I'm looking for a man."

"The one who tried to kill you in the art gallery?"

"Yes."

"Don Orsati hasn't been able to find him. But don't worry, the Spanish woman will lead you to the one you seek. Don Orsati knows of her."

"How?"

"It is not in my power to tell you that."

Without another word, the *signadora* took hold of Gabriel's hand and engaged in the familiar ritual. She recited the words of an ancient Corsican prayer. She wept as the evil passed from his body into hers. She closed her eyes and fell into a deep sleep. When at last she awoke, she instructed Gabriel to repeat the trial of the oil and the water. This time the oil coalesced into a single drop.

"Now you," he said.

The old woman sighed and did as he asked. The oil shattered.

"Just like the door of the art gallery," she said. "Don't worry, the *occhju* won't stay within me for long."

Gabriel laid several banknotes on the table. "Is there anything else you can tell me?"

"Paint four pictures," said the old woman. "And she will come for you."

"Is that all?"

"No," she said. "You didn't contract the *occhju* from Don Casabianca's goat."

————

Upon his return to the villa, Gabriel informed Christopher that Don Orsati's inquiries would bear no fruit and that Don Casabianca's goat was the devil incarnate. Christopher questioned the accuracy of neither assertion, as both had come from the mouth of the *signadora*. He nevertheless advised against telling the don to preemptively break off his search. It was far better, he said, to allow the wheel to spin until the ball had dropped.

"Unless the wheel continues to spin for another week or two."

"Trust me, it won't."

"There's more, I'm afraid."

Gabriel explained the old woman's prophecy regarding the Spanish woman.

"Did she say how the don knows her?"

"She said it wasn't in her power to tell me."

"Or so she claimed. It's her version of 'no comment.'"

"Did you ever run across a Spanish woman when you were working for the don?"

"One or two," said Christopher beneath his breath.

"How should we raise it with him?"

"With the utmost care. His Holiness doesn't like anyone rummaging through his past. Especially the *signadora*."

And so it was that two nights later, while seated beneath a cloud-draped moon in the garden of Villa Orsati, Gabriel feigned incredulity when told that the don's operatives had failed to locate the man who had delivered the expertly constructed bomb to Galerie Fleury. Then, after a moment or two of companionable silence, he cautiously asked Don Orsati whether he had ever encountered a Spanish woman who might have ties to the criminal art world.

The don's brown-streaked eyes narrowed with suspicion. "When did you speak to her?"

"The Spanish woman?"

"The *signadora*."

"I thought the *macchia* sees all."

"Do you want to know about the Spanish woman or not?"

"It was two days ago," admitted Gabriel.

"I suppose she also knew that I wouldn't be able to find the man you're looking for."

"I wanted to tell you, but Christopher said it would be a mistake."

"Did he?" Don Orsati glared at Christopher before turning once more to Gabriel. "Several years ago, perhaps five or six, a woman came to see me. She was from Roussillon, up in the Lubéron. Late thirties, quite composed. One had the impression she was comfortable in the presence of criminals."

"Name?"

"Françoise Vionnet."

"Real?"

Don Orsati nodded.

"What was her story?"

"The man she lived with disappeared one afternoon while walking in the countryside outside Aix-en-Provence. The police found his body a few weeks later near Mont Ventoux. He'd been shot twice in the back of the head."

"Vengeance was required?"

The don nodded.

"I assume you agreed to provide it."

"Money doesn't come from singing, my friend." It was one of the don's most cherished Corsican proverbs and the unofficial slogan of the Orsati Olive Oil Company. "Money is earned by accepting and then fulfilling contracts."

"What was the name on this one?"

"Miranda Álvarez. The Vionnet woman was confident it was an alias. She was able to give us a physical description and a profession, but little else."

"Why don't we start with her appearance."

"Tall, dark hair, very beautiful."

"Age?"

"At the time, she was in her mid-thirties."

"And her profession?"

"She was an art dealer."

"Based where?"

"Maybe Barcelona." The don shrugged his heavy shoulders. "Maybe Madrid."

"That isn't much to go on."

"I've accepted contracts based on less, provided the client agrees to confirm the target's identity once the target is located."

"Thus avoiding needless bloodshed."

"In a business like mine," said Don Orsati, "mistakes are permanent."

"I take it you were never able to find her."

The don shook his head. "Françoise Vionnet begged me to continue looking, but I told her there was no point. I refunded her money, excluding the deposit and the expenses for the search, and we went our separate ways."

"Did she ever tell you why her partner was murdered?"

"Apparently, it was a business dispute."

"He was an art dealer as well?"

"A painter, actually. Not a successful one, mind you. But she spoke highly of his work."

"Do you happen to remember his name?"

"Lucien Marchand."

"And where might Christopher and I find Françoise Vionnet?"

"The Chemin de Joucas in Roussillon. If you like, I can get you the address."

"If it's not too much trouble."

"Not at all."

It was upstairs in his office, said Don Orsati. In his leather-bound ledger of death.

33

Le Lubéron

The next mainland-bound car ferry departed Ajaccio at half past eight the following evening and arrived in Marseilles shortly after dawn. Gabriel and Christopher, having passed the night in adjoining cabins, rolled into the port in a rented Peugeot and made their way to the A7 Autoroute. They headed north through Salon-de-Provence to Cavaillon, then followed a caravan of tour buses into the Lubéron. The honey-colored houses of Gordes, perched on a limestone hilltop overlooking the valley, sparkled in the crystalline morning light.

"That's where Marc Chagall used to live," said Christopher.

"In an old girls' school on the rue de la Fontaine Basse. He and his wife, Bella, were reluctant to leave after the German invasion. They finally fled to the United States in 1941 with the help of the journalist and academic Varian Fry and the Emergency Rescue Committee."

"I was just trying to make conversation."

"Perhaps we should enjoy the scenery instead."

Christopher lit a Marlboro. "Have you given any thought to how you're going to make your approach?"

"To Françoise Vionnet? I thought I'd start with *bonjour* and hope for the best."

"How cunning."

"Maybe I'll tell her I was sent by a mystical Corsican woman who cured me of the *occhju*. Or better yet, I'll say that I'm a friend of the Corsican organized crime figure she hired to kill a Spanish art dealer."

"That should win her over."

"How much do you suppose the don charged her?" asked Gabriel.

"For a job like that? Not much."

"What does that mean?"

"Maybe a hundred thousand."

"How much was the contract on my life?"

"Seven figures."

"I'm flattered. And Anna?"

"You two were part of a package deal."

"Is there a discount for that sort of thing?"

"The don is unfamiliar with that word as well. But it warms my heart that you two have rekindled your relationship after all these years."

"There was no kindling involved. And we don't have a relationship."

"Did you or did you not borrow a million euros from her to buy that fake Cuyp riverscape?"

"The money was repaid three days later."

"By my wife," said Christopher. "As for your approach to the afore-mentioned Françoise, I suggest you fly a false flag. In my experience, respectable residents of the Lubéron don't hand over briefcases filled with cash to someone like His Holiness Don Anton Orsati."

"Are you suggesting that Françoise Vionnet and Lucien Mar-chand, an unknown painter with no established sales record, might have been involved in a criminal enterprise of some sort?"

"I'd bet my Cézanne on it, too."

"You don't own a Cézanne."

They rounded a bend in the road, and the Lubéron Valley revealed itself as a patchwork quilt of vineyards and orchards and fields ablaze with wildflowers. The brick-colored buildings of Roussillon's ancient center occupied a ridge of ocher-rich clay on the southern rim. Christopher approached the village along the narrow Chemin de Joucas and eased onto the grassy verge at the point where the slope of the hill met the valley floor. On one side of the road was newly plowed cropland. On the other, partially hidden from view behind an unkempt wall of vegetation, was a small single-level villa. From somewhere came the muted baritone bark of a large dog.

"But of course," murmured Gabriel.

"Better a canine than a caprine."

"Caprines don't bite."

"Wherever did you get an idea like that?" asked Christopher, and turned into the drive. Instantly a barrel-shaped dog with the jaws of a Rottweiler shot from the front door. Next there appeared a languorous barefoot girl in her early twenties. She wore leggings and a wrinkled cotton pullover. Her light brown hair swung long and loose in the Provençal light.

"She's too young," said Gabriel.

"What about that one?" asked Christopher as an older version of the girl emerged from the villa.

"She looks like a Françoise to me."

"I agree. But how are you going to play it?"

"I'm going to wait for one of them to get that dog under control."

"And then?"

"I thought I'd start with *bonjour* and hope for the best."

"Brilliant," said Christopher.

By the time Gabriel opened his door and extended his hand, he was once again, in aspect and accent, Ludwig Ziegler of Berlin. But this version of Herr Ziegler was not an art adviser with a single famous client. He was a runner—a dealer without a gallery or inventory—who specialized in finding works by undervalued contemporary painters and bringing them to market. He claimed to have heard about

Lucien Marchand through a contact and was intrigued by the terrible story of his disappearance and death. He introduced Christopher as Benjamin Reckless, his London representative.

"Reckless?" asked Françoise Vionnet skeptically.

"It's an old English name," explained Christopher.

"You speak French like a native."

"My mother was French."

In the villa's rustic kitchen, they all four gathered around a pot of tar-black coffee and a pitcher of steamed milk. Françoise Vionnet and the barefoot girl each lit a cigarette from the same packet of Gitanes. They had the same drowsy, heavy-lidded eyes. Beneath the girl's were puffy half-moons of unlined flesh.

"Her name is Chloé," said Françoise Vionnet, as though the girl were incapable of speech. "Her father was a struggling sculptor from Lacoste who walked out on us not long after she was born. Fortunately, Lucien agreed to take us in. We were hardly a traditional family, but we were happy. Chloé was seventeen when Lucien was murdered. His death was very hard on her. He was the only father she ever knew."

The girl yawned and stretched elaborately and then withdrew. A moment later came the sound of a slender female body entering the water of a swimming pool. Frowning, Françoise Vionnet crushed out her cigarette.

"You must excuse my daughter's behavior. I wanted to move to Paris after Lucien's death, but Chloé refused to leave the Lubéron. It was a terrible mistake to raise her here."

"It's very beautiful," said Gabriel in Herr Ziegler's German-accented French.

"*Oui*," said Françoise Vionnet. "The tourists and rich foreigners adore Provence. Especially the English," she added, glancing at Christopher. "But for girls like Chloé who lack a university education or ambition, the Lubéron can be a trap with no escape. She spends her summers waiting tables at a restaurant in the *centre ville* and her winters working at a hotel in Chamonix."

"And you?" asked Gabriel.

She shrugged. "I make do with the modest estate that Lucien was able to leave me."

"You were married?"

"A civil solidarity pact. The French equivalent of a common-law marriage. Chloé and I inherited the villa after Lucien was murdered. And his paintings, of course." She rose suddenly. "Would you like to see some of them?"

"I'd love nothing more."

They filed into the sitting room. Several unframed paintings—Surrealist, Cubist, Abstract Expressionist—hung on the walls. They lacked originality but were competently executed.

"Where was he trained?" asked Gabriel.

"Beaux-Arts de Paris."

"It shows."

"Lucien was an excellent draftsman," said Françoise Vionnet. "But unfortunately he was never terribly successful. He made ends meet painting copies."

"I beg your pardon?"

"Lucien painted copies of Impressionist paintings and sold them in the gift shops of the Lubéron. He also worked for a company that sold hand-painted copies online. He was paid more for those, but not much. Maybe twenty-five euros. He produced them very quickly. He could paint a Monet in fifteen or twenty minutes."

"Do you happen to have one?"

"*Non.* Lucien found the work very embarrassing. Once the paintings were dry, he delivered them to his clients."

Outside, the girl extracted herself from the pool and stretched her body on a chaise longue. Whether she was clothed or not Gabriel could not say, for he was contemplating what was clearly the finest painting in the room. It bore a distinct resemblance to a work called *Les Amoureux aux Coquelicots,* by the French-Russian artist who had lived for a time on the rue de la Fontaine Basse in Gordes. Not an exact copy, more a pastiche. The original was signed in the bottom-right corner. Lucien Marchand's version had no signature at all.

"He was a great admirer of Chagall," said Françoise Vionnet.

"As am I. And if I didn't know better, I would have thought that Chagall painted it himself." Gabriel paused. "Or perhaps that was the point."

"Lucien painted his Chagalls purely for pleasure. That's why there's no signature."

"I'm prepared to make you a generous offer for it."

"I'm afraid it's not for sale, Monsieur Ziegler."

"May I ask why not?"

"Sentimental reasons. It was the last painting Lucien completed."

"Forgive me, Madame Vionnet. But I can't recall the date of his death."

"It was the seventeenth of September."

"Five years ago?"

"*Oui.*"

"That's odd."

"Why, monsieur?"

"Because this painting appears much older than that. In fact, it looks to me as though it was painted in the late nineteen forties."

"Lucien used special techniques to make his paintings appear older than they really were."

Gabriel took down the painting from the wall and turned it over. The canvas was at least a half-century old, as was the stretcher. The upper horizontal bar was stamped with a *6* and an *F*. On the center bar were the remnants of an old adhesive sticker.

"And did Lucien have special techniques for aging his canvases and stretchers as well? Or did he have a ready supplier of worthless old paintings?"

Françoise Vionnet regarded Gabriel calmly with her heavy-lidded eyes. "Get out of my house," she said through gritted teeth. "Or I'll sic the dog on you."

"If that dog comes anywhere near me, I'm going to shoot it. And then I'm going to call the French police and tell them that you and your daughter are living off the money that Lucien Marchand earned forging paintings."

Her full lips curled into a slight smile. Evidently, she didn't frighten easily. "Who are you?"

"You wouldn't believe me if I told you."

She looked at Christopher. "And him?"

"He's anything but reckless."

"What do you want?"

"I want you to help me find the woman who called herself Miranda Álvarez. I'd also like you to give me any additional forgeries you have lying around, along with a complete list of every fake painting Lucien ever sold."

"That's impossible."

"Why?"

"There are far too many."

"Who handled them?"

"Lucien sold most of his forgeries to a dealer in Nice."

"Does the dealer have a name?"

"Edmond Toussaint."

Gabriel looked at Christopher. "I guess that settles that."

34

Roussillon

Why didn't you simply tell me the truth from the beginning, Monsieur Allon?"

"I was afraid you would skip the pleasantries and go straight to the part about setting the dog on me."

"Would you have really shot it?"

"*Non*," replied Gabriel. "Mr. Reckless would have shot it for me."

Françoise Vionnet eyed Christopher down her freshly lit Gitane, then nodded her head slowly in agreement. They had returned to the table in the rustic kitchen, though now it was a chilled bottle of Bandol rosé around which they were gathered.

"How much of the original story was true?" asked Gabriel.

"Most of it."

"Where did the fiction begin?"

"Chloé doesn't spend the winter in Chamonix."

"Where does she go?"

"Saint-Barthélemy."

"Does she work there?"

"Chloé?" She made a face. "Not a day in her life. We have a villa in Lorient."

"Lucien must have painted a lot of twenty-five-euro copies to afford a place like that."

"He never stopped painting them, you know. He needed some form of legitimate income."

"When did the fakes start?"

"A couple of years after Chloé and I moved in."

"It was your idea?"

"More or less."

"Which is it?"

"It was obvious that Lucien's copies were very good," she answered. "One day I asked him whether he thought he could fool anyone. A week later he showed me his first forgery. A reworking of *Place du village* by the French Cubist Georges Valmier."

"What did you do with it?"

She took it to Paris and hung it on the wall of a friend's chic apartment in the Sixth. Then she rang one of the auction houses—which one, she refused to say—and the auction house sent over a so-called expert to have a look at it. The expert asked a couple of questions about the painting's provenance, declared it authentic, and gave Françoise forty thousand euros. She gave two thousand to her chic friend from Paris and the rest to Lucien. They used part of the money to enlarge the villa's swimming pool and renovate the little outbuilding that Lucien used as his atelier. The rest they deposited in a bank account at Credit Suisse in Geneva.

"As for the reworking of *Place du village* by Georges Valmier, it recently sold for nine hundred thousand dollars at auction in New York. Which means the auction house made more in fees and commissions than Lucien was paid for his original painting. Who is the criminal, Monsieur Allon? Did the auction house *really* not realize that it was selling a fake? How is this possible?"

She sold several more forgeries to the same Paris auction house—all lesser-known Cubists and Surrealists, all for five figures—and in the winter of 2004 she sold a Matisse to Galerie Edmond Toussaint.

The dealer purchased a second Matisse from Françoise a few months later, followed in short order by a Gauguin, a Monet, and a Cézanne landscape of Mont Sainte-Victoire. It was then that Toussaint informed Françoise that all five of the paintings she had brought him were forgeries.

"Which is why he had purchased them in the first place," said Gabriel.

"*Oui*. Monsieur Toussaint wanted an exclusive arrangement. No more independent sales through the Paris auction houses or other dealers. He said it was far too risky. He promised to take very good care of Lucien financially."

"Did he?"

"Lucien had no complaints."

"How much money did he earn?"

"Over the lifetime of the deal?" Françoise Vionnet shrugged. "Six or seven million."

"Spare me," said Gabriel.

"Maybe it was in the neighborhood of thirty million."

"Which side of the neighborhood? The north or the south?"

"The north," said Françoise Vionnet. "Definitely the north."

"And Monsieur Toussaint? What was his take?"

"Two hundred million, at least."

"So Lucien got screwed."

"That's what the Spanish woman told him."

"Miranda Álvarez?"

"That's what she called herself."

"Where did you meet with her?"

"Here in Roussillon. She sat in the same chair where you're sitting now."

"She was a dealer?"

"Of some sort. She was quite guarded in how she described herself."

"What did she want?"

"She wanted Lucien to work for her instead of Toussaint."

"How did she know that Lucien was forging paintings?"

"She refused to say. But it was obvious she knew her way around the dirty side of the business. She said Toussaint was selling more forgeries than the art market could absorb, that it was only a matter of time before Lucien and I were arrested. She said she was part of a sophisticated network that knew how to sell forgeries without getting caught. She promised to pay us twice what Toussaint was paying us."

"How did Lucien react?"

"He was intrigued."

"And you?"

"Less so."

"But you agreed to consider her offer?"

"I asked her to come back in three days."

"And when she did?"

"I told her we had a deal. She gave us a million euros in cash and said she would be in touch."

"When did the deal fall apart?"

"After I told Toussaint that we were leaving him."

"How much did he pay you to stay?"

"Two million."

"I assume you banked the million the Spanish woman gave you."

"*Oui*. And six months later Lucien was dead. He was working on another Cézanne when he was killed. The police never found it."

"I don't suppose you told them that Lucien was an art forger or that he had recently received a visit from a mysterious Spanish woman who called herself Miranda Álvarez."

"If I had, I would have implicated myself."

"How did you explain the thirty million at Credit Suisse in Geneva?"

"It was thirty-four million at the time," admitted Françoise Vionnet. "And the police never discovered it."

"What about the villa in Saint-Barthélemy?"

"It's owned by a shell company registered in the Bahamas. Chloé and I keep a low profile here in the Lubéron. But when we go to the island . . ."

"You live well on the proceeds of Lucien's forgeries."

She lit another Gitane but said nothing.

"How many are left?" asked Gabriel.

"Fakes?" She blew a stream of smoke toward the ceiling. "Only the Chagall. The others are all gone."

Gabriel laid his phone on the table. "How many, Françoise?"

———

Outside, Chloé was stretched like a Modigliani nude across the sunbaked paving stones next to the pool. "If only someone would pay her for doing that," said her mother judgmentally. "Chloé would be the richest woman in France."

"You were a front woman for a forger," said Gabriel. "You didn't exactly set a good example."

She led them along a gravel footpath toward Lucien's atelier. It was a small building, ocher in color, with a tile roof. The door was secured with a padlock, as were the wooden shutters.

"Someone tried to break in not long after Lucien was murdered. That's when I got the dog."

She unlocked the door and led Gabriel and Christopher inside. The dank air smelled of canvas and dust and linseed oil. Beneath an overhead skylight stood an ancient studio easel and a cluttered old worktable with shelves and drawers for supplies. The paintings were leaning against the walls, perhaps twenty to a row.

"Is this all of them?" asked Gabriel.

Françoise Vionnet nodded.

"No warehouse or storage unit somewhere?"

"*Non.* Everything is here."

She walked over to the nearest queue of paintings and leafed through them as though they were vinyl record albums. Reluctantly she extracted one and displayed it for Gabriel.

"Fernand Léger."

"You have a good eye, Monsieur Allon."

She moved to the next row. From it she unearthed a pastiche of *Houses at L'Estaque* by Georges Braque. The next row of paintings produced a Picasso and another Léger.

"Surely the police searched this place after the murder," said Gabriel.

"Yes, of course. But fortunately they sent Inspector Clouseau." She removed another painting, a version of *Composition in Blue* by Roger Bissière. "I've always liked this one. Do I really have to give it up?"

"Keep going."

The next painting was a Matisse. It was followed by a Monet, a Cézanne, a Dufy, and, finally, by a second Chagall.

"Is that all of them?"

She nodded.

"Do you know what's going to happen if I find any more?"

Sighing, she produced two additional paintings—a second Matisse and a stunning André Derain. Twelve in all, with an estimated market value of more than €200 million. Gabriel photographed them with his phone, along with the Chagall in the sitting room. Then he removed all thirteen canvases from their stretchers and piled them on the grate. Christopher handed over his gold Dunhill lighter.

"Please don't," said Françoise Vionnet.

"Would you rather I give them to the French police?" Gabriel ignited the lighter and touched the flame to the canvases. "I suppose you'll have to make do with the thirty-four million."

"There's only twenty-five left."

"And you can keep it so long as you never tell anyone that I was here."

Françoise Vionnet saw Gabriel and Christopher to the door and waited until they were nearly inside the Renault before unleashing the dog. They made their escape without resort to violence.

"Tell me something," said Christopher as they sped across the picturesque valley. "When did you realize that you were going to do that Herr Ziegler routine?"

"It came to me while you were needlessly lecturing me about the likelihood that Françoise Vionnet might have been Lucien's front woman."

"I have to say, it was one of your better performances. You did, however, make one serious tactical mistake."

"What's that?"

"You burned the bloody evidence."

"Not all of it."

"The Cézanne?"

"Idiot," murmured Gabriel.

189

35

Le Train Bleu

They jettisoned the rented Peugeot in Marseilles and caught the two o'clock TGV from the Gare Saint-Charles to Paris. An hour before they were due to arrive, Gabriel dialed the number for Antiquités Scientifiques on the rue de Miromesnil. Receiving no answer, he checked the time, then rang a nearby shop that sold antique glassware and figurines. Its proprietor, a woman named Angélique Brossard, seemed slightly out of breath when she picked up the phone. She offered no expression of surprise or evasiveness when Gabriel asked to speak to Maurice Durand. Their longtime *cinq à sept* was one of the worst-kept secrets in the Eighth Arrondissement.

"Enjoying yourself?" asked Gabriel when Durand came on the line.

"I was," answered the Frenchman. "I hope this is important."

"I was wondering whether you might be free for a drink at, say, half past five."

"I believe I'm having open-heart surgery then. Let me check my schedule."

"Meet me at Le Train Bleu."

"If you insist."

The iconic Paris restaurant, with its garish gilded mirrors and painted ceilings, overlooked the ticket hall of the Gare de Lyon.

At five thirty Maurice Durand was seated in a plush royal-blue chair in the lounge area before an open bottle of champagne. Rising, he hesitantly shook Christopher's hand.

"If it isn't my old friend Monsieur Bartholomew. Still caring for widows and orphans, or have you managed to find honest work?" Durand turned to Gabriel. "And what brings you back to Paris, Monsieur Allon? Another bombing in the works?" He smiled. "That's certainly *one* way to put a dirty gallery out of business."

Gabriel sat down and handed Durand his mobile phone. The diminutive Frenchman slipped on a pair of gold half-moon reading glasses and contemplated the screen. "A rather interesting reinterpretation of Braque's *Houses at L'Estaque.*"

"Swipe to the next one."

Durand did as he was told. "Roger Bissière."

"Keep going."

Durand dragged the tip of his forefinger horizontally across the screen and smiled. "I've always had a soft spot for Fernand Léger. He was one of my first."

"How about the next one?"

"My old friend Picasso. Quite a good one, in fact."

"The Chagalls are better. The Monet, the Cézanne, and the two Matisses aren't bad, either."

"Where did you find them?"

"In Roussillon," answered Gabriel. "In the atelier of a failed painter named—"

"Lucien Marchand?"

"You knew him?"

"Lucien and I weren't acquainted, but I knew of his work."

"How?"

"We both did business with the same gallery in Nice."

"Galerie Edmond Toussaint?"

"*Oui.* Quite possibly the dirtiest art gallery in France, if not the Western world. Only a fool would buy a painting there."

Gabriel exchanged a glance with Christopher before returning his gaze to Durand. "I thought you dealt directly with collectors."

"For the most part. But I occasionally filled special orders for Monsieur Toussaint. He did a brisk trade in stolen art, but Lucien Marchand was his golden goose."

"Which is why Toussaint fought so hard to keep Lucien when the front woman from a rival forgery network tried to steal him away."

Durand smiled at Gabriel over the rim of his champagne glass. "You're getting rather good at this, Monsieur Allon. Soon you will no longer require my help."

"Who is she, Maurice?"

"Miranda Álvarez? That depends on whom you ask. Apparently, she's something of a chameleon. They say she lives in a remote village in the Pyrenees. They also say that she and the forger are lovers or perhaps even husband and wife. But this is only a rumor."

"Who are *they*?"

"People who toil in the dirty end of the art trade."

"People like you, you mean?"

Durand was silent.

"Is the forger Spanish, too?"

"That is the assumption. But, again, this is only speculation. Unlike some forgers who crave notoriety, this man is very serious about his privacy. The woman is said to be one of only two people who know his identity."

"And the other?"

"The man who runs the business side of the network. Think of them as an unholy trinity."

"What's the Spanish woman's role?"

"She oversees the delivery of the paintings to the galleries where they are sold. Most are midmarket pieces that quietly generate enormous amounts of cash. But every few months, another so-called lost master magically reappears."

"How many galleries are there?"

"I couldn't say."

"Try."

"One hears rumors about a gallery in Berlin and another in Brussels. One also hears rumors of a recent expansion into Asia and the Middle East."

"One wonders," said Gabriel pointedly, "why you didn't disclose any of this information during our last conversation."

"Perhaps if you had told me that you intended to purchase a painting from Galerie Fleury, I might have been more forthcoming." Durand smiled. *"A River Scene with Distant Windmills.* Definitely *not* by the Dutch Golden Age painter Aelbert Cuyp."

"How do you know about the sale?"

"Fleury was discreet in some matters, less so in others. He boasted of the sale to several of his competitors, despite the fact that he allowed Madame Rolfe's art adviser to remove the painting from France without an export license."

"He had no suspicions about me?"

"Apparently not."

"Then why was I targeted for assassination when I returned to the gallery four days later?"

"Perhaps you should ask the man who delivered the bomb."

Gabriel handed the Frenchman his phone a second time. "Do you recognize him?"

"Fortunately, no."

"I believe he murdered a woman in Bordeaux not long ago."

"The Bérrangar woman?"

Gabriel exhaled heavily. "Is there anything you *don't* know, Maurice?"

"Information is the key to my longevity, Monsieur Allon. And yours, I imagine." Durand looked down at the phone. "How else to explain the fact that you are in possession of this photograph?"

"It was given to me by the head of the Police Nationale's art crime unit."

"Jacques Ménard?"

Gabriel nodded.

"And what exactly is the nature of your relationship?"

"It's a bit like ours."

"Coercive and abusive?"

"Discreet and unofficial."

"Is he aware of our past collaboration?"

"*Non.*"

"I'm relieved." Durand returned the phone. "That said, I think this should be our last meeting for the foreseeable future."

"I'm afraid that's not possible."

"Why not?"

"Because I have an assignment for you."

"The names of those galleries in Berlin and Brussels?"

"If you wouldn't mind."

Durand removed his spectacles and rose. "Tell me something, Monsieur Allon. What happened to those paintings you found in Lucien's workshop?"

"Up in smoke."

"The Picasso?"

"All of them."

"A pity," said Durand with a sigh. "I could have found a good home for them."

At half past ten the following morning, while seated at the Louvre's Café Marly, Gabriel delivered his first report to Jacques Ménard. The briefing was thorough and complete, though evasive when it came to sources and methods. Like Christopher Keller, who occupied a nearby table, Ménard found fault with Gabriel's decision to destroy the forgeries he had discovered in Lucien Marchand's studio in Roussillon. Nevertheless, the French art detective was impressed by the scope of his informant's findings.

"I have to admit, it all makes a great deal of sense." Ménard gestured toward the gleaming glass-and-steel structure in the Cour Napoléon. "The criminal art world is a bit like *la pyramide*. There are tens of thousands of people involved in the illicit market, but it's controlled by a few major players at the top." He paused. "And it's obvious that you're acquainted with at least one or two of them."

"Aren't you?"

"*Oui*. Just not the right ones, apparently. Your ability to gather this much information so quickly is most embarrassing."

"Edmond Toussaint never popped up on your radar?"

Ménard shook his head. "And neither did Lucien Marchand. I don't care what sort of promises you made to the Vionnet woman. I'm going to open a case against her and seize those assets, including the villa in the Lubéron."

"First things first, Ménard."

"I'm afraid nothing has changed," said the Frenchman. "My hands remain tied."

"Then I suppose you'll have to force the issue."

"How?"

"By turning over my findings to one of your European partners."

"Which one?"

"Since we're looking for a Spanish woman who might or might not reside in a remote village in the Pyrenees, I would think the Guardia Civil might be the most logical choice."

"I don't trust them."

"I'm sure they feel the same about you."

"They do."

"How about the British?"

"Scotland Yard dismantled its Art and Antiquities Squad a few years ago. They treat art theft and fraud like any other property or financial crime."

"Then I suppose that leaves the Italians."

"They're the best in the business," conceded Ménard. "But what's the Italian connection?"

"At the moment, there isn't one. But I'm sure General Ferrari and I will think of something."

"He speaks very highly of you, the general."

"As well he should. I helped him crack an antiquities-smuggling ring a few years ago. I also helped him find a missing altarpiece."

"Not the Caravaggio?"

Gabriel nodded.

"The white whale," whispered Ménard. "How did you find it?'

"I hired a gang of French art thieves to steal *Sunflowers* from the Van Gogh Museum in Amsterdam. Then I painted a copy of it in a safe flat overlooking the Pont Marie and sold it for twenty-five million euros to a Syrian named Sam in a warehouse outside Paris." Gabriel lowered his voice. "All without your knowledge."

Jacques Ménard's face turned the color of the tablecloth. "You're not going to steal any paintings this time, are you?"

"*Non.* But I might forge a few."

"How many?"

Gabriel smiled. "Four, I think."

36

Mason's Yard

Lately, it had occurred to Oliver Dimbleby that he was a very lucky man indeed. Yes, his gallery had endured its ups and downs—the Great Recession had been a rather close shave—but somehow the hand of fate had always interceded to save him from ruin. The same was true of his personal life, which was, by universal acclaim, the untidiest in the London art world. Despite his advancing years and ever-increasing girth, Oliver had encountered no shortage of willing partners. He was, after all, a glorified salesman—a man of immense charm and charisma who, as he was fond of saying, could sell sand to a Saudi. He was not, however, a womanizer. Or so he told himself each time he awoke with a strange body on the other side of his bed. Oliver loved women. *All* women. And therein lay the root of his problem.

Tonight he had nothing on his schedule other than a well-deserved drink—and perhaps a few laughs at Julian Isherwood's expense—at Wiltons. To reach his destination he merely had to turn to the left after leaving his gallery and walk one hundred and fourteen paces along the spotless pavements of Bury Street. His journey took him past the premises of a dozen competitors, including the mighty P. & D. Colnaghi & Co., the world's oldest commercial art gallery.

197

Next door was the flagship store of Turnbull & Asser, where Oliver's deficit spending was approaching American levels.

Entering Wiltons, he was pleased to see Sarah Bancroft sitting alone at her usual table. He procured a glass of Pouilly-Fumé at the bar and joined her. The unexpected warmth of her smile nearly stopped his heart.

"Oliver," she purred. "What a pleasant surprise."

"Do you mean that?"

"Why wouldn't I?"

"Because I've always had the distinct impression that you find me repulsive."

"Don't be silly. I positively adore you."

"So there's hope for me yet?"

She raised her left hand and displayed a three-carat diamond ring and accompanying wedding band. "Still married, I'm afraid."

"Any chance of a divorce?"

"Not at the moment."

"In that case," said Oliver with a dramatic sigh, "I suppose I'll have to settle for being your sexual plaything."

"You have plenty of those already. Besides, my husband might not approve."

"Peter Marlowe? The professional assassin?"

"He's a business consultant," said Sarah.

"I think I liked him better when he was a contract killer."

"So did I."

Just then the door swung open and in came Simon Mendenhall and Olivia Watson.

"Did you hear the rumor about those two?" whispered Sarah.

"The one about their torrid affair? Jeremy Crabbe may have mentioned it. Or perhaps it was Nicky Lovegrove. It's on everyone's lips."

"A shame, that."

"I only wish they were saying the same about us." Smiling wolfishly, Oliver drank from his wineglass. "Sell anything lately?"

"A couple of Leonardos and a Giorgione. You?"

"Truth be told, I'm in a bit of a slump."

"Not you, Ollie?"

"Hard to believe, I know."

"How's your cash flow?"

"A bit like a leaky faucet."

"What about the five million I slipped you under the table on the Artemisia deal?"

"Are you referring to the newly discovered painting that I sold for a record price to a Swiss venture capitalist, only to find myself embroiled in a scandal involving the finances of the Russian president?"

"But it was great fun, wasn't it?"

"I enjoyed the five million. The rest of it I could have lived without."

"Fiddlesticks, Oliver. There's nothing you love more than being the center of attention. Especially when beautiful women are involved." Sarah paused. "Spanish women, in particular."

"Wherever did you hear a thing like that?"

"I happen to know that you've been carrying a secret torch for Penélope Cruz for years."

"Nicky," murmured Oliver.

"It was Jeremy who told me."

Oliver regarded Sarah for a moment. "Why do I get the feeling I'm being recruited for something?"

"Perhaps because you are."

"Is it naughty?"

"Extremely."

"In that case," said Oliver, "I'm all ears."

"Not here."

"My place or yours?"

Sarah smiled. "Mine, Ollie."

They slipped out of Wiltons unnoticed and walked along Duke Street to the passageway that led to Mason's Yard. Isherwood Fine Arts was located in the northeast corner of the quadrangle, in three floors of a sagging warehouse once owned by Fortnum & Mason. Parked outside was a silver Bentley Continental. Its gleaming hood was warm to Oliver's touch.

"Isn't this your husband's car?" he asked, but Sarah only smiled and unlocked the gallery's door.

Inside, they climbed a flight of carpeted stairs, then rode the cramped lift to Julian's upper exhibition room. In the half-light Oliver could make out two silhouetted figures. One was contemplating *Baptism of Christ* by Paris Bordone. The other was contemplating Oliver. He wore a dark single-breasted suit, Savile Row, perhaps Richard Anderson. His hair was sun-bleached. His eyes were bright blue.

"Hullo, Oliver," he drawled. Then, almost as an afterthought, he added, "I'm Peter Marlowe."

"The hit man?"

"Former hit man," he said with an ironic smile. "I'm a wildly successful business consultant now. That's why I drive a Bentley and have a wife who looks like Sarah."

"I never laid so much as a finger on her."

"Of course you didn't."

He placed a hand on Oliver's shoulder and guided him toward the Bordone. The man standing before the canvas turned slowly. His green eyes seemed to glow in the faint light.

"Mario Delvecchio!" exclaimed Oliver. "As I live and breathe! Or is it Gabriel Allon? I often can't tell them apart." Receiving no answer, he looked at the man he knew as Peter Marlowe, then at Sarah. At least, he thought that was her name. At that moment he wasn't certain of the ground beneath his feet. "The retired chief of Israeli intelligence, a former hit man, and a beautiful American woman who may or may not have worked for the CIA. What could you possibly want with tubby Oliver Dimbleby?"

It was the retired Israeli spymaster who answered. "Your bottomless reservoir of charm, your ability to talk your way out of almost anything, and your reputation for cutting the occasional corner."

"Me?" Oliver feigned righteous indignation. "I resent the implication. And if it's a dirty dealer you want, Roddy Hutchinson is most definitely your man."

"Roddy lacks your star power. I need someone who can move the needle."

"For what?"

"I'd like you to sell a few paintings for me."

"Anything good?"

"A Titian, a Tintoretto, and a Veronese."

"What's the source?"

"An old European collection."

"And the subject matter?"

"I'll let you know the minute I finish painting them."

The first challenge for any art forger is the acquisition of canvases and stretchers of appropriate age, dimensions, and condition. When executing his copy of Vincent's *Sunflowers*, Gabriel had purchased a third-tier Impressionist streetscape from a small gallery near the Jardin du Luxembourg. He had no need to resort to such methods now. He merely had to ride the lift down to Julian's storerooms, which were crammed with an apocalyptic inventory of what was affectionately known in the trade as dead stock. He selected six minor Venetian School works from the sixteenth century—follower of so-and-so, manner of such-and-such, workshop of what's-his-name— and asked Sarah to express-ship them to his apartment in San Polo.

"Why six instead of only three?"

"I need two spares in the event of a disaster."

"And the other one?"

"I'm planning to leave a Gentileschi with my front man in Florence."

"Silly me," said Sarah. "But how are we going to explain the missing paintings to Julian?"

"With any luck, he won't notice."

Sarah instructed the shippers to arrive no later than nine the following morning and advised Julian to take the day off. Nevertheless, he wandered into Mason's Yard at his usual time, a quarter past twelve, as the crated paintings were being loaded into a Ford Transit van. The tragicomedy that followed included yet another collision with an inanimate object. This time it was Sarah's shredder, into which Julian, in a spasm of self-pity, attempted to insert himself.

Gabriel did not witness the incident, for he was in the back of a taxi bound from Fiumicino Airport toward Rome's Piazza di Sant'Ignazio. Upon arrival he took a table at Le Cave, one of his favorite restaurants in the *centro storico*. It was located a few steps from the ornate yellow-and-white palazzo that served as the headquarters of the Art Squad.

The palazzo's door swung open at half past one, and General Cesare Ferrari emerged in his bemedaled blue-and-gold uniform. He crossed the gray cobbles of the square and without uttering a word of greeting sat down at Gabriel's table. Instantly the waiter delivered a frigid bottle of Frascati and a plate of fried *arancini*.

"Why doesn't that happen when I arrive at restaurants?" asked Gabriel.

"I'm sure it's only the uniform." The general plucked one of the risotto balls from the plate. "Shouldn't you be in Venice with your wife and children?"

"Probably. But I needed to have a word with you first."

"About what?"

"I'm thinking about embarking on a life of crime, and I was wondering whether you would be interested in a piece of the action."

"What sort of misdeed are you contemplating this time?"

"Art forgery."

"Well, you certainly have the talent for it," said the general. "But what would be my end?"

"A high-profile case that will shake the art world to its core and ensure that the generous funding and personnel levels of the Art Squad remain unchanged for years to come."

"Has a crime been committed on Italian soil?"

"Not yet," said Gabriel with a smile. "But soon."

37

———

Bridge of Sighs

Umberto Conti, universally regarded as the greatest art restorer of the twentieth century, had bequeathed to Francesco Tiepolo a magical ring of keys that could open any door in Venice. Over drinks at Harry's Bar, Francesco entrusted them to Gabriel. Late that evening he slipped into the Scuola Grande di San Rocco and spent two hours in solitary communion with some of Tintoretto's greatest works. Then he breached the defenses of the neighboring Frari church and stood transfixed before Titian's magisterial *Assumption of the Virgin*. In the deep silence of the cavernous nave, he recalled the words Umberto had spoken to him when he was a broken, gray-haired boy of twenty-five.

Only a man with a damaged canvas of his own can be a truly great restorer . . .

Umberto would not have approved of his gifted pupil's newest commission. And neither, for that matter, did Francesco. Nevertheless, he agreed to serve as a consultant to the project. He was, after all, one of the world's foremost authorities on the Venetian School painters. If Gabriel could fool Francesco Tiepolo, he could fool anyone.

Francesco likewise agreed to accompany Gabriel during his

nocturnal Venetian wanderings, if only to prevent another mishap like the one involving poor Capitano Rossetti. They stole into churches and *scuole*, roamed the Accademia and the Museo Correr, and even stormed the Doge's Palace. While peering through the stone-barred windows of the Bridge of Sighs, Francesco summarized the difficulty of the task ahead.

"Four different works by four of the greatest painters in history. Only a madman would attempt such a thing."

"If he can do it, so can I."

"The forger?"

Gabriel nodded.

"It's not a competition, you know."

"Of course it is. I have to prove to them that I would be a worthy addition to the network. Otherwise, they won't make a play for me."

"Is that why you allowed yourself to be dragged into this? For the challenge?"

"Wherever did you get the idea that this was going to be a challenge for me?"

"You don't lack for confidence, do you?"

"Neither does he."

"You're all the same, you art forgers. You all have something to prove. He's probably a failed painter who's taking his revenge on the art world by fooling the connoisseurs and the collectors."

"The connoisseurs and collectors," said Gabriel, "haven't seen anything yet."

He spent his days in his studio with his monographs and catalogues raisonnés and photographs from past restorations, including several that he had conducted for Francesco. Together, after much debate, some of it conducted with raised voices, they settled on the subject matter and iconography for the four forgeries. Gabriel produced a series of preparatory sketches, then turned the sketches into four swiftly executed rehearsal paintings. Francesco declared the Gentileschi, a reworking of *Danaë and the Shower of Gold*, to be the finest of the lot, with Veronese's *Susanna in the Bath* a close second. Gabriel agreed with Francesco's assessment of the Gentileschi, though he was fond of his reinterpretation of Tintoretto's *Bacchus, Venus, and Ariadne*. His Titian, a pastiche of *The Lovers*, wasn't bad, either, though he thought the brushwork was a touch tentative.

"How can one *not* be tentative when one is forging a Titian?"

"It's a dead giveaway, Francesco. I have to *become* Titian. Otherwise, we're sunk."

"What are you going to do with that one?"

"Cremation. The others, too."

"Have you taken leave of your senses?"

"Clearly."

Early the following morning, Gabriel uncrated one of the paintings he had pillaged from Julian's storerooms, an early sixteenth-century Venetian School devotional piece of no value and little merit. Even so, he felt a stab of guilt as he scraped the unknown artist's work from the canvas and covered it in gesso and an *imprimatura* of lead white with traces of lampblack and yellow ocher. Next he executed his underdrawing—with a brush, the way *he* would have done it—and meticulously prepared his palette. Lead white, genuine ultramarine, madder lake, burnt sienna, malachite, yellow ocher, red ocher, orpiment, ivory black. Before commencing work, he once again reflected on the shifting fortunes of his career. He was no longer the leader of a powerful intelligence service or even one of the world's finest art restorers.

He was the sun amidst small stars.

He was Titian.

———

For the better part of the next week, Chiara and the children saw little of him. On the rare occasions he emerged from his studio, he was on edge and preoccupied, not at all himself. Only once did he accept an invitation to join Chiara for lunch. His hands left smudges of paint across her breasts and abdomen.

"I feel like I just made love to another man."

"You did."

"Who are you?"

"Come with me. I'll show you."

Wrapped in a bedsheet, Chiara followed him into the studio and stood before the canvas. At length she whispered, "You're a freak."

"Do you like it?"

"It's absolutely—"

"Amazing, I think."

"I see a touch of Giorgione in it."

"That's because I was still under his influence when I painted it in 1510."

"Who will you be next?"

Jacobo Robusti, the artist known as Tintoretto, was a learned and unsmiling man who rarely set foot outside Venice and allowed few visitors to enter his workspace. If there was one consolation, he was among the swiftest painters in the republic. Gabriel completed his version of *Bacchus, Venus, and Ariadne* in half the time it took him to finish *The Lovers.* Chiara nevertheless declared it superior to the Titian in every respect, as did Francesco.

"I'm afraid your wife is right. You truly are a freak."

Next Gabriel assumed the personality and remarkable palette of Paolo Veronese. *Susanna in the Bath* required the largest of the six canvases he had acquired from Isherwood Fine Arts and several additional days to complete—in large part because Gabriel intentionally damaged the work and then restored it. Luca Rossetti visited him three times during the painting's execution. Brush in hand, Gabriel lectured the young Carabinieri officer on the artistic merits and fraudulent pedigrees of his four forged masterpieces. Rossetti in turn briefed Gabriel on the preparations for their forthcoming operation. They included the acquisition of two properties—an isolated villa for the reclusive forger and an apartment in Florence for his front man.

"It's on the south side of the Arno, on the Lungarno Torrigiani. We've loaded it up with paintings and antiquities from the Art Squad's evidence room. It definitely looks like the home of an art dealer."

"And the villa?"

"Your friend the Holy Father called Count Gasparri. It's all arranged."

"How soon can you settle into the apartment and assume your new identity?"

"As soon as you say I'm ready."

"Are you?"

"I know my lines," answered Rossetti. "And I know more about the Venetian School painters than I ever thought possible."

"What was Veronese's name when he was young?" inquired Gabriel.

"Paolo Spezapreda."

"And why was that?"

"His father was a stonecutter. It was traditional for children to be named after their father's occupation."

"Why did he start calling himself Paolo Caliari?"

"His mother was the illegitimate child of a nobleman called Antonio Caliari. Young Paolo thought it was better to be named for a nobleman than a stonecutter."

"Not bad." Gabriel drew his Beretta from the waistband of his trousers. "But will you be able to recite your lines so confidently if someone points one of these at your head?"

"I grew up in Naples," said Rossetti. "Most of my childhood friends are now in the Camorra. I'm not going to fall to pieces if someone starts waving a gun around."

"I heard a rumor that an elderly Venetian School painter gave you a good thrashing the other night in San Polo."

"The elderly painter attacked me without warning."

"That's the way it works in the real world. Criminals don't often announce their intentions before resorting to violence." Gabriel returned the gun to the small of his back and contemplated the towering canvas. "What do you think, Signore Calvi?"

"You have to darken the garments of the two elders. Otherwise, I won't be able to convince Oliver Dimbleby that it was painted in the late sixteenth century."

"Oliver Dimbleby," said Gabriel, "will be the least of your problems."

By the time he commenced work on the Gentileschi, he was so exhausted he could scarcely hold a brush. Fortunately, Chiara agreed to pose for him, as the artist he was attempting to impersonate preferred the Caravaggesque method of painting directly from live models. He gave his Danaë Chiara's body and facial features, but turned his wife's dark hair to gold and her olive skin to luminous alabaster. Most of their sessions necessarily included an intermezzo in the bedroom—a hurried one, for Gabriel's time was limited. The end result of their collaboration was a painting of astonishing beauty and veiled eroticism. It was, they both agreed, the finest of the four works.

Like the other three paintings, it was unmarred by craquelure, a sure sign it was a modern forgery and not the work of an Old Master. The solution was a large professional oven. General Ferrari obtained one from the seized inventory of a Mafia-owned kitchen supplies firm and delivered it to the mainland warehouse of the Tiepolo Restoration Company. After removing the four paintings from their stretchers, Gabriel baked them for three hours at 220 degrees Fahrenheit. Then, with Francesco's help, he dragged the paintings over the edge of a rectangular work table, first vertically, then horizontally. The result was a fine network of Italianate surface cracks.

That evening, alone in his studio, Gabriel covered the paintings with varnish. And in the morning, when the varnish was dry, he photographed them with a tripod-mounted Nikon. He hung the Titian and the Tintoretto in the sitting room of the apartment, surrendered the Gentileschi to General Ferrari, and shipped the Veronese to Sarah Bancroft in London. The photos he emailed directly to Oliver Dimbleby, owner and sole proprietor of Dimbleby Fine Arts of Bury Street, upon whose rounded shoulders the entire venture rested. Shortly before midnight one of the images appeared on the website of *ARTnews*, beneath the byline of Amelia March. Gabriel read the exclusive story to his dark-haired, olive-complected Danaë. She made love to him in a shower of gold.

38

Kurfürstendamm

The article was purportedly based on a single source who wished to remain anonymous. Even this was misleading, as it was Sarah Bancroft who had provided the initial tip and Oliver Dimbleby who had supplied the off-the-record confirmation and the photograph—thus making it, in point of fact, a two-source story.

The work in question was said to be 92 centimeters in height and 74 in width. That much, at least, was accurate. It was not, however, a lost work of the Late Renaissance painter known as Titian, and there had been no quiet sale to a prominent collector who wished to remain unidentified. Truth be told, there was no buyer, prominent or otherwise, and no money had changed hands. As for the painting, it was now hanging in a glorious *piano nobile* overlooking the Grand Canal in Venice, much to the delight of the wife and two young children of the newly minted art forger who had produced it.

The dealers, curators, and auctioneers of the London art world greeted the news with astonishment and no small amount of jealousy. After all, Oliver was still basking in the glow of his last coup. In the salerooms and watering holes of St. James's and Mayfair, questions were raised, usually in conspiratorial whispers. Did this new Titian have a proper provenance, or did it fall off the back of a truck? Was tubby Oliver absolutely certain of the attribution? Did others more learned than he concur? And what exactly was his role in the transaction? Had he actually *sold* the painting to his unnamed buyer? Or had he merely acted as a middleman and pocketed a lucrative commission in the process?

For three interminable days, Oliver refused to either confirm or deny that he handled the work in question. Finally he released a brief corroboratory statement that was scarcely more illuminating than Amelia March's original story. It contained only two new pieces of information, that the painting had emerged from an old European collection and had been examined by no fewer than four leading Venetian School experts. All four agreed, without qualifications or conditions, that the canvas had been executed by Titian himself and not by a member of his workshop or a later follower.

That evening Oliver walked the one hundred and fourteen paces from his gallery to the bar at Wiltons and in keeping with neighborhood tradition promptly ordered six bottles of champagne. Much was made of the fact that it was Taittinger Comtes Blanc de Blanc, the most expensive on the list. Still, all those in attendance would later remark that Oliver seemed subdued for a man who had just pulled off one of the art world's biggest coups in years. He refused to divulge the price the Titian had fetched and feigned deafness when Jeremy Crabbe pressed him for additional details on the painting's provenance. Sometime around eight he pulled Nicky Lovegrove aside for a heart-to-heart, which gave rise to speculation that Oliver's unidentified buyer was one of Nicky's superrich clients. Nicky swore it wasn't so, but Oliver cagily declined comment. Then, after kissing the proffered cheek of Sarah Bancroft, he waddled into Jermyn Street and was gone.

It emerged the following day, in a lengthy article in the *Art Newspaper*, that the unidentified buyer had made a takeaway offer for the Titian after being granted an exclusive viewing at Oliver's gallery. According to the *Independent*, the offer was £25 million.

Niles Dunham, an Old Master specialist from the National Gallery, denied a report that he had authenticated the painting on Oliver's behalf. Curiously, so did every other connoisseur of Italian School painting in the United Kingdom.

But it was the photograph of the painting that raised the most eyebrows, at least among the backbiting world of St. James's. For many years Oliver had utilized the services of the same fine art photographer—the renowned Prudence Cuming of Dover Street. But not, as it turned out, for his newly discovered Titian. Perhaps even more suspicious was his claim that he had taken the photograph himself. All were in agreement that Oliver could handle a tumbler of good whisky, or a shapely backside, but not a camera.

And yet no one, not even the unscrupulous Roddy Hutchinson, suspected Oliver of wrongdoing. Indeed, the general consensus was that he was guilty of nothing more serious than protecting the identity of his source, a common practice among art dealers. The logical conclusion was that it was only a matter of time before another noteworthy picture emerged from the same European collection.

When the inevitable finally happened, it was once again Amelia March of *ARTnews* who broke the story. This time the work in question was *Bacchus, Venus, and Ariadne* by the Venetian painter Tintoretto—deeply private sale, price unavailable upon request. Just ten days later, to absolutely no one's surprise, Dimbleby Fine Arts announced its newest offering: *Susanna in the Bath*, oil on canvas, 194 by 194 centimeters, by Paolo Veronese. The gallery retained Prudence Cuming of Dover Street to make the photograph. The art world swooned.

With the exception, that is, of the powerful director of the Uffizi Gallery in Florence, who found the sudden appearance of three Italian Old Master paintings suspicious, to say the least. He rang General Ferrari of the Art Squad and demanded an immediate investigation.

Surely, he shouted down the line to Rome, the canvases had been smuggled out of Italy in violation of the country's draconian Cultural Heritage Code. The general promised to look into the matter, though his fingers were firmly crossed at the time. Needless to say, he did not inform the director that the paintings in question were all modern fakes and that he himself was operating in league with the forger.

The forger's phantom front man—a collector and occasional dealer who called himself Alessandro Calvi—was currently living in an art-filled apartment within sight of the Uffizi, on the Lungarno Torrigiani. As it happened, General Ferrari had occasion to ring this disreputable character two days later on an unrelated matter. It concerned a piece of information the forger had received from a well-placed informant in Paris, an art thief and antiques dealer named Maurice Durand.

"Galerie Konrad Hassler. It's located on the Kurfürstendamm in Berlin. There's a coffeehouse on the opposite side of the street. Your associate will meet you there tomorrow afternoon at three."

And so it was that the phantom front man, whose real name was Capitano Luca Rossetti, left the luxury apartment on the Arno early the following morning and rode in a taxi to Florence Airport. His tailored Italian suit was new and expensive, as were his handmade shoes and his soft-sided leather attaché case. The watch on his wrist was a Patek Philippe. Like his collection of art and antiquities, it was borrowed from the evidence rooms of the Carabinieri.

Rossetti's travel itinerary included a stopover in Zurich, and it was approaching three o'clock when he arrived at the coffeehouse on the Kurfürstendamm. Gabriel was seated at a table outside, in the dappled shade of a plane tree. He ordered two coffees from the waitress in rapid German before handing a manila envelope to Rossetti.

Inside were two photographs. The first depicted three unframed paintings displayed side by side against the wall of an artist's workshop—a Titian, a Tintoretto, and a Veronese. The second was a high-resolution image of *Danaë and the Shower of Gold*, purportedly by Orazio Gentileschi. Rossetti knew the work well. At present, it was hanging on the wall of the apartment in Florence.

"When is he expecting me?"

"Three thirty. He's under the impression that your name is Giovanni Rinaldi and that you are from Milano."

"How do you want me to play it?"

"I'd like you to present Herr Hassler with a unique opportunity to acquire a lost masterwork. I would also like you to make it clear that you are the source of the three paintings that have resurfaced in London."

"Do I tell him they're forgeries?"

"You won't have to. He'll get the idea when he sees the photos."

"Why am I coming to him?"

"Because you're looking for a second distributor for your merchandise and you've heard rumors that he's less than honest."

"How do you suppose he'll react?"

"He'll either make you an offer or throw you out of his gallery. I'm betting on the latter. Make sure you leave behind the photo of the Gentileschi on your way out the door."

"What happens if he calls the police?"

"Criminals don't call the police, Rossetti. In fact, they do their best to avoid them."

The Carabinieri officer lowered his gaze to the photograph.

"When was he born?" asked Gabriel quietly.

"Fifteen sixty-three."

"What was his name?"

"Orazio Lomi."

"What sort of work did his father do?"

"He was a Florentine goldsmith."

"Who was Gentileschi?"

"An uncle he lived with when he moved to Rome."

"Where did he paint *Danaë and the Shower of Gold*?"

"Probably in Genoa."

"Where did I paint my version?"

"None of your fucking business."

———

Capitano Luca Rossetti left the coffeehouse at 3:27 p.m. and crossed to the opposite side of the elegant tree-lined boulevard. Gabriel tensed as the young Carabinieri officer reached his right hand toward the intercom of Galerie Konrad Hassler. Fifteen seconds elapsed, long enough for the dealer to have a good long look at his visitor. Then Rossetti leaned on the glass door and disappeared from view.

Five minutes later Gabriel's phone shivered with an incoming call. It was General Ferrari.

"Nothing exploded, did it?"

"Not yet."

"Let me know the minute he walks out of there," said the general, and rang off.

Gabriel returned the phone to the tabletop and directed his gaze toward the gallery. By now the introductions had been made and the two men had withdrawn to the dealer's office for a bit of privacy. A photograph had been placed on his desk. Perhaps two. When viewed together, the images made it clear that a talented new forger had stepped onto the stage of the illicit art market. Which was exactly the message that Gabriel wished to send.

Just then his phone pulsed with another call. "What's going on in there?" asked General Ferrari.

"Hold on, I'll run across the road and check."

This time it was Gabriel who killed the connection. Two minutes later the door of the gallery opened, and out stepped Rossetti, followed by a well-dressed man with iron-gray hair and a crimson face. A few final words were exchanged, and fingers were pointed in anger. Then Rossetti ducked into a taxi and was gone, leaving the crimson-faced man alone on the pavement. He looked left and right along the boulevard before returning to the gallery.

Message delivered, thought Gabriel.

He dialed Rossetti's number.

"Looks as though you two really hit it off."

"It went exactly the way you said it would."

"Where's the photograph?"

"It's possible that in my rush to get out of the gallery I might have left it on his desk."

"How long before he sends it to our girl?"

"Not long," said Rossetti.

39

Queen's Gate Terrace

For the remainder of that week, the phone at Dimbleby Fine Arts rang nearly without cease. Cordelia Blake, Oliver's long-suffering receptionist, served as the first line of defense. Those with names she recognized—longtime clients or representatives of prominent museums—she transferred directly to Oliver's line. Those of lesser repute were asked to leave a detailed message and were given no assurance their inquiry would receive a reply. It was Mr. Dimbleby's ambition, Cordelia explained, to find a suitable home for the Veronese. He had no intention of selling the painting to just anyone.

Unbeknownst to Cordelia, Oliver delivered each of her pink message slips to Sarah Bancroft in Mason's Yard, and Sarah in turn forwarded the names and numbers to Gabriel in Venice. By the close of business on that Friday, Dimbleby Fine Arts had received more than two hundred requests to view the forged Veronese—from the directors of the world's greatest museums, from representatives of prominent collectors, and from a multitude of journalists, art dealers, and learned connoisseurs of the Italian Old Masters. With the exception of a curator from the J. Paul Getty Museum in Los Angeles, none of the names on the list was Spanish in origin, and none of the callback numbers began with a Spanish country code. Forty-two women wished to see the painting, all of whom were well-known figures in the art world.

One of the women was a reporter from the London bureau of the *New York Times*. With Gabriel's approval, Oliver allowed her to see the painting the following Monday, and by Wednesday evening her story and accompanying photographs were the talk of the art world. The result was another avalanche of calls to Dimbleby Fine Arts. Twenty-two of the new callers were women. None of their names or callback numbers were Spanish in origin. And none, according to Cordelia Blake, spoke with a Spanish accent.

Gabriel feared the worst, that the forgery network's front woman had no intention of attending the party he had so meticulously planned in her honor. Nevertheless, he instructed Oliver to prepare a schedule for the viewings. They were to last for one week only. The price band would be set at £15 million to £20 million, which would separate the wheat from the chaff. Oliver was to make it clear that he reserved the right not to sell to the highest bidder.

"And make sure you dim the lights in your exhibition room," added Gabriel. "Otherwise, one of your eagle-eyed clients might notice that your newly discovered Veronese is a forgery."

"Not a chance. On the surface, at least, it looks like Veronese painted it in the sixteenth century."

"He did paint it, Oliver. I just happened to be holding the brush at the time."

Gabriel spent Saturday sailing the Adriatic with Chiara and the children, and on Sunday, the day before the viewings were to begin, he flew to London. Upon arrival he headed for Christopher and Sarah's maisonette in Queen's Gate Terrace. There, arrayed on the granite-topped kitchen island, he found a surveillance photograph from Heathrow Airport, a scan of a Spanish passport, and a printout of a guest registration from the Lanesborough Hotel.

Smiling, Sarah handed him a glass of Bollinger Special Cuvée. "Tagliatelle with ragù or veal Milanese?"

————————

She was tall and slender, with the square shoulders of a swimmer, narrow hips, and long legs. The pantsuit she wore was dark and businesslike, but the daring neckline of her white blouse revealed the fine curve of her delicate upturned breasts. Her hair was nearly black and hung long and straight down the center of her back. Even in the unflattering light of Heathrow's Terminal 5, it shone like a newly varnished painting.

Her name, according to the passport, was Magdalena Navarro. She was thirty-nine and a resident of Madrid. She had arrived at Heathrow aboard Iberia Flight 7459 and had dialed Dimbleby Fine Arts at 3:07 p.m. from her room phone at the Lanesborough. The call had bounced automatically to Oliver's mobile. After listening to the message, he had rung Sarah, who had prevailed upon her husband, an officer of Her Majesty's Secret Intelligence Service, to have an off-the-record peek at the Spanish woman's particulars. He had done so with the approval of his director-general.

"It took our brethren at MI5 all of twenty minutes to pull together the file."

"Did they have a look at her recent travel?"

"It seems she's a frequent visitor to France, Belgium, and Germany. She also spends a fair amount of time in Hong Kong and Tokyo."

Christopher ignited a Marlboro and exhaled a cloud of smoke toward the ceiling of his elegantly decorated drawing room. He wore a pair of fitted chinos and a costly cashmere pullover. Sarah was more casually attired, in stretch jeans and a Harvard sweatshirt. She plucked a cigarette from Christopher's packet and quickly lit it before Gabriel could object.

"Any other interesting travel?" he asked.

"She goes to New York about once a month. Apparently, she lived there for a few years in the mid-aughts."

"Credit card?"

"A corporate American Express. The company has a fuzzy Liechtenstein registry. She seems to use it only for foreign travel."

"Which would help to conceal the real location of her home in Spain." Gabriel turned to Sarah. "How did she describe herself in the message?"

"She says she's a broker. But she doesn't have a website or an entry on LinkedIn, and neither Oliver nor Julian has ever heard of her."

"Sounds like she's our girl."

"Yes," agreed Sarah. "The question is, how long do we make her wait?"

"Long enough to create the impression that she is of absolutely no consequence."

"And then?"

"She'll have to convince Oliver to let her see the painting."

"Could be dangerous," said Sarah.

"He'll be fine."

"It's not Oliver I'm worried about."

Gabriel smiled. "All's fair in love and forgery."

40

Dimbleby Fine Arts

The director of the National Gallery arrived at Dimbleby Fine Arts at ten the following morning, accompanied by the infallible Niles Dunham and three other curators who specialized in Italian Old Masters. They sniffed, poked, prodded, kicked the tires, and examined the canvas under ultraviolet light. No one questioned the authenticity of the work, only the provenance.

"An old European collection? It's a bit gossamer, Oliver. That said, I must have it."

"Then I suggest you make me an offer."

"I won't get caught up in a bidding war."

"Of course you will."

"Who's next at bat?"

"The Getty."

"You wouldn't dare."

"I will if the price is right."

"Scoundrel."

"Flattery will get you nowhere."

"See you at Wiltons tonight?"

"Unless I get a better offer."

The delegation from the Getty arrived at eleven. They were young and suntanned and loaded with cash. They made a takeaway offer of £25 million, £5 million above the top end of the estimated price band. Oliver turned them down flat.

"We won't be back," they vowed.

"I have a feeling you will."

"How can you tell?"

"Because I see that look in your eyes."

It was noon when Oliver ushered the Gettys into Bury Street. Cordelia handed him a stack of telephone messages on her way to lunch. He leafed through them quickly before ringing Sarah.

"She's called twice this morning."

"Wonderful news."

"Perhaps we should put her out of her misery."

"Actually, we'd like you to play hard to get a little longer."

"Hard to get isn't my usual modus operandi."

"I've noticed, Ollie."

The afternoon session was a reprise of the morning. The delegation from the Metropolitan Museum of Art was smitten, their counterparts from Boston head over heels. The director of the Art Gallery of Ontario, a Veronese expert himself, was practically speechless.

"How much do you want for it?" he managed to say.

"I've got twenty-five from the Getty."

"They're heathens."

"But rich."

"I might be able to do twenty."

"A novel negotiating tactic."

"Please, Oliver. Don't make me beg."

"Match the Getty's offer, and it's yours."

"Is that a promise?"

"You have my solemn word."

Which is how the first day of viewings ended, with one final untruth. Oliver showed the Ontario delegation out of the gallery and collected the newest telephone messages from Cordelia's desk.

Magdalena Navarro had called at four fifteen.

"She sounded rather annoyed," said Cordelia.

"With good reason."

"Who do you suppose she represents?"

"Someone with enough money to put her up at the Lanesborough."

Cordelia collected her belongings and went out. Alone, Oliver reached for the telephone and dialed Sarah.

"How was your afternoon?" she asked.

"I have a bidding war on my hands for a painting I can't sell. Otherwise, nothing much happened."

"How many times did she call?"

"Only once."

"Perhaps she's losing interest."

"All the more reason I should call her and get it over with."

"Let's discuss it at Wiltons. I feel a martini coming on."

Oliver hung up the phone and engaged in the familiar ritual of putting his gallery to bed for the night. He lowered the internal security screens over the windows. He engaged the alarm. He placed a baize-cloth cover over *Susanna in the Bath*, oil on canvas, 194 by 194 centimeters, by Gabriel Allon.

Outside, Oliver triple-locked his door and set off along Bury Street. It should have been a triumphal march. He was, after all, the toast of the art world, the dealer who had stumbled upon a long-hidden collection of lost masters. Never mind that all of the paintings were forgeries. Oliver assured himself that his actions were in service of a noble cause. If nothing else, it would make for a good story one day.

Crossing Ryder Street, he became conscious of the fact that someone was walking behind him. Someone wearing a pair of well-made pumps, he thought, with stiletto heels. He paused outside the Colnaghi gallery and cast a leftward glance along the pavement.

Tall, slender, expensively attired, lustrous black hair hanging over the front of one shoulder.

Dangerously attractive.

Much to Oliver's surprise, the woman joined him and fixed her wide dark eyes on the Old Master painting displayed in the window. "Bartolomeo Cavarozzi," she said in faintly accented English. "He was an early follower of Caravaggio who spent two years working in Spain, where he was much admired. If I'm not mistaken, he painted this picture after his return to Rome in 1619."

"Who in the world *are* you?" asked Oliver.

The woman turned to him and smiled. "I'm Magdalena Navarro, Mr. Dimbleby. And I've been trying to reach you all day."

———————

Wiltons was overrun with American and Canadian museum curators, all divided into opposing camps. Sarah shook the hand of the Austrian-born director of the Met, then shouldered her way to the bar, where she endured a wait of ten minutes for her martini. The cocktail-party din was so deafening that for a moment she didn't realize her phone was ringing. It was Oliver calling from his mobile.

"Are you in this madhouse somewhere?" she asked.

"Change in plan, I'm afraid. We'll have to do it another time."

"What are you talking about?"

"Yes, tomorrow evening would be fine. Cordelia will call you in the morning and make the arrangements."

And with that, the call went dead.

Sarah quickly dialed Gabriel. "I could be wrong," she said, "but I believe our girl just made her next move."

41

Piccadilly

Where are you taking me?"

"Somewhere I can have you all to myself."

"Not the Lanesborough?"

"No, Mr. Dimbleby." She gave him a look of contrived reproach. "Not on our first date."

They were walking along Piccadilly into the blinding light of the sun. It was one of those perfect early-summer evenings in London, cool and soft, a gentle breeze. The woman's intoxicating scent reminded Oliver of the south of Spain. Orange blossom and jasmine and a hint of manzanilla. Twice the back of her hand brushed against his. Her touch was electric.

She slowed to a stop outside Hide. It was one of London's costliest restaurants, a temple of gastronomic and social excess beloved by Russian billionaires, Emirati princes, and, evidently, beautiful Spanish art criminals.

"I'm not quite posh enough for this place," protested Oliver.

"The art world is at your feet tonight, Mr. Dimbleby. You are, without a doubt, the poshest man in London."

They made quite an entrance—the corpulent, pink-cheeked art dealer and the tall, elegantly dressed woman with shimmering black hair. She led him down a swirling oaken staircase to the dimly lit bar. A secluded candlelit table awaited them.

"I'm impressed," said Oliver.

"My butler at the Lanesborough arranged it."

"Do you stay there often?"

"Only when a certain client of mine is footing the bill."

"A client who's interested in acquiring the Veronese?"

"Let's not rush things, Mr. Dimbleby." She leaned into the warm light of the candle. "We Spaniards like to take our time."

The front of her blouse had fallen open, exposing the inner curve of a pear-shaped breast. "Is it as nice as they say?" blurted Oliver.

"What's that, Mr. Dimbleby?"

"The Lanesborough."

"You've never been?"

"Only the restaurant."

"I have a suite overlooking Hyde Park. The view is quite lovely."

So was Oliver's. He nevertheless forced himself to lower his gaze to the cocktail menu. "What do you recommend?"

"The concoction they call the Currant Affairs is life-changing."

Oliver read the ingredients. "Bruno Paillard champagne with Ketel One vodka, red currant, and guava?"

"Don't mock it until you try it."

"I generally drink my champagne and vodka separately."

"They have an extraordinary sherry selection."

"A much better idea."

She summoned the waiter with a raised eyebrow and ordered a bottle of Cuatro Palmas Amontillado.

"Have you been to Spain, Mr. Dimbleby?"

"Many times."

"Business or pleasure?"

"A little of both."

"I'm from Seville originally," she informed him. "But these days I live mostly in Madrid."

"Your English is quite extraordinary."

"I attended a special art history program at Oxford for a year." She was interrupted by the reappearance of the waiter. After an elaborate presentation of the wine, he poured two glasses and withdrew. She raised hers a fraction of an inch. "Cheers, Mr. Dimbleby. I hope you enjoy it."

"You must call me Oliver."

"I couldn't."

"I insist," he said, and drank some of the wine. "What do you think?"

"It's ambrosia. I only hope that your client is picking up the check."

"He is."

"Does he have a name?"

"Several, in fact."

"He's a spy, your client?"

"He is a member of an aristocratic family. His name is rather cumbersome, to say the least."

"Is he Spanish like you?"

"Perhaps."

Oliver sighed heavily before returning his glass to the tabletop.

"Forgive me, Mr. Dimbleby, but my client is an extremely wealthy man who does not want the world to know the true scale of his art collection. I cannot reveal his identity."

"In that case, perhaps we should discuss yours."

"As I explained to your assistant, I'm a broker."

"How is it that I've never heard of you?"

"I prefer to operate in the shadows." She paused. "As do you, it seems."

"Bury Street is hardly the shadows."

"But you have been, how shall we say, less than forthcoming about the origin of the Veronese. Not to mention the Titian and the Tintoretto."

"You don't know much about the art trade, do you?"

"Actually, I know a great deal, as does my client. He is a sophisticated and shrewd collector. Until he falls in love with a painting, that is. When that happens, money is no object."

"I take it he has a crush on my Veronese?"

"It was love at first sight."

"I already have two bids of twenty-five million."

"My client will match any offer you receive. Pending a thorough examination of the canvas and provenance on my part, of course."

"And if I were to sell it to him? What would he do with it?"

"It would be displayed prominently in one of his many homes."

"Will he agree to lend it for exhibitions?"

"Never."

"I admire your honesty."

She smiled but said nothing.

"How long are you planning to stay in London?"

"I'm scheduled to return to Madrid tomorrow evening."

"A pity."

"Why?"

"Because I might have an opening in my schedule on Wednesday afternoon. Thursday, at the latest."

"How about now instead?"

"Sorry, but my gallery is buttoned up for the night. Besides, it's been a long day, and I'm exhausted."

"A pity," she said playfully. "Because I was hoping you would have dinner with me at the Lanesborough."

"Tempting," said Oliver. "But not on our first date."

———

On the pavements of Piccadilly, Oliver offered the Spanish woman his hand in farewell but received a kiss instead. Not two Iberian air pecks but a single warm and breathy display of affection that landed near his right ear and lingered long after the woman had set off toward Hyde Park Corner and her hotel. The evening was made complete by the seductive final glance she gave him over one shoulder. *Silly boy*, she was saying. *Silly, silly boy.*

He turned in the opposite direction and, feeling slightly inebriated, fished his phone from the breast pocket of his suit jacket. He had received several calls and text messages since he had checked it last, none from Sarah. Curiously, her name and number had vanished from his directory of recent calls. Nor was there any record of a Sarah Bancroft in his contacts. Julian's numbers were likewise missing, as was the entry for Isherwood Fine Arts.

Just then the phone pulsed with an incoming call. Oliver didn't recognize the number. He tapped the ACCEPT icon and raised the device to his ear.

"Your car and driver are waiting for you in Bolton Street," said a male voice, and the connection went dead.

Oliver returned the phone to his pocket and continued on his present easterly heading. Bolton Street was a few paces ahead on the left. He rounded the corner and spotted a silver Bentley Continental idling curbside. Seated behind the wheel was Sarah's husband. Oliver lowered his rotund form into the passenger seat. A moment later they were headed west along Piccadilly.

"Is your name really Peter Marlowe?"

"Why wouldn't it be?"

"Sounds made up."

"So does Oliver Dimbleby." Smiling, he pointed out the tall woman with shimmering black hair walking past the entrance of the Athenaeum. "There's our girl."

"I never laid so much as a finger on her."

"It's probably better not to mix work and play, wouldn't you agree?"

"No," said Oliver as the beautiful Spanish woman disappeared from view. "I most certainly would not."

42

Queen's Gate Terrace

As part of his retirement package from the Office, Gabriel had been given a personal copy of the Israeli cell phone hacking malware known as Proteus. The program's most insidious feature was that it required no blunder on the part of the target—no unwise software update or click of an innocent-looking photograph or advertisement. All Gabriel had to do was enter the target's phone number into the Proteus application on his laptop, and within minutes the device would be under his complete control. He could read the target's emails and text messages, review the target's Internet browsing history and telephone metadata, and monitor the target's physical movements with the GPS location services. Perhaps most important, he could activate the phone's microphone and camera and thus turn the device into a full-time instrument of surveillance.

He had protectively installed Proteus on Oliver Dimbleby's Samsung Galaxy after his recruitment but had allowed the malware to remain dormant until 5:42 that afternoon. With the click of his laptop's trackpad—an action he undertook while drinking tea in Sarah and Christopher's kitchen in Queen's Gate Terrace—he established that his missing operative was at that moment walking westward along Piccadilly, accompanied by a sultry-voiced woman who spoke fluent English with a Spanish accent. Sarah hurried home from Wiltons in time to hear the final minutes of their conversation in the trendy bar of Hive.

"She's a worthy opponent, our Magdalena. And not to be taken lightly."

"All the more reason we need to keep tubby Oliver on a very short leash."

To that end, Gabriel dispatched Christopher to Mayfair to corral his wayward asset. It was approaching seven thirty when they arrived at the maisonette. The after-action debriefing, such as it was, began with an awkward admission on Gabriel's part.

Oliver frowned. "That would explain why Sarah and Julian vanished from my contacts."

"I deleted them as a precautionary measure after you agreed to have drinks with that woman without giving us any warning."

"I'm afraid she didn't leave me much of a choice."

"Why?"

"Because she's nearly six feet tall and shockingly beautiful. What's more, she seems to have left Madrid without packing a brassiere." Oliver looked at Sarah. "I think I'll have that drink now."

"The Currant Affairs or the Tropic Thunder?"

"Whisky, if you have it."

Christopher opened a cabinet and took down a bottle of Johnnie Walker Black Label and a pair of cut-glass tumblers. He filled one of the glasses with two fingers of whisky and sent it across the kitchen island toward Oliver.

"Baccarat," he said approvingly. "Maybe you're a wildly successful business consultant after all." He turned to Gabriel. "Isn't Proteus the software that the Saudi crown prince used to spy on that journalist he murdered?"

"The journalist's name was Omar Nawwaf. And, yes, the Israeli prime minister approved the sale of Proteus to the Saudis over my strenuous objections. In the hands of a repressive government, the malware can be a dangerous weapon of surveillance and blackmail. Imagine how something like this might be used to silence a meddlesome journalist or prodemocracy advocate."

Gabriel clicked the software's PLAY icon.

"Because she's nearly six feet tall and shockingly beautiful. What's more, she seems to have left Madrid without packing a brassiere."

Gabriel paused the recording.

"Dear God," murmured Oliver.

"Or how about this?" Gabriel clicked PLAY again.

"How is it that I've never heard of you?"

"I prefer to operate in the shadows. As do you, it seems."

"Bury Street is hardly the shadows."

Gabriel clicked PAUSE.

"Aren't you going to play the part where I turned down a night of incredible sex in a suite at the Lanesborough?"

"I believe the offer was dinner."

"You need to get out more, Mr. Allon."

He closed the laptop.

"What now?" asked Oliver.

"At some point late tomorrow afternoon, you will invite her to see the painting on Wednesday at six p.m. You will also ask her for the number of her mobile phone. She will no doubt refuse to give it to you."

"And when she arrives at my gallery on Wednesday evening?"

"She won't."

"Why not?"

"Because you're going to call her Wednesday afternoon and reschedule the appointment for eight p.m. on Thursday."

"Why would I do that?"

"To let her know that she is the furthest thing from your mind."

"If only it were true," said Oliver. "But why so late?"

"I don't want Cordelia Blake to be around when you show her the painting." Gabriel lowered his voice. "It might spoil the mood."

"Is she really interested in buying it?"

"Not at all. She just wants to have a look at it before it disappears."

"And if she likes what she sees?"

"After examining the provenance, she will ask you to reveal the identity of the man who sold it to you. You, of course, will refuse, leaving her no choice but to extract the information by some other means."

"Music to my ears."

"It's possible she might try to seduce you," said Gabriel. "But don't be disappointed if she threatens to destroy you instead."

"I can assure you, she won't be the first."

Gabriel tapped a few keys on the laptop. "I just added a new name to your contacts. Alessandro Calvi. Mobile phone number only."

"Who is he?"

"My front man in Florence. Call him at that number in the Spanish woman's presence. Signore Calvi will take care of the rest."

———

The front man, whose real name was Luca Rossetti, left Florence at ten o'clock the following morning and headed south on the E35 Autostrada. The car beneath him was a Maserati Quattroporte sedan. Like the Patek Philippe timepiece on his wrist, it was the property of the Arma dei Carabinieri, Rossetti's employer.

He arrived at his destination, Rome's Fiumicino Airport, at half past one. Another hour elapsed before Gabriel finally emerged from the door of Terminal 3. He tossed his overnight bag in the trunk and dropped into the passenger seat.

"I was starting to get worried about you," said Rossetti as he accelerated away from the curb.

"I spent almost as much time trying to get through passport control as I did flying from London." Gabriel looked around the interior of the luxury automobile. "Nice sled."

"It belonged to a heroin trafficker from the Camorra."

"A childhood friend of yours?"

"I knew his younger brother. They're both down in Palermo now, in Pagliarelli Prison."

Rossetti turned onto the A90, Rome's high-speed orbital motorway, and headed north. He took his eyes off the road long enough to glance at the surveillance photograph that Gabriel had placed in his hand.

"What's her name?"

"According to her passport and credit cards, it's Magdalena Navarro. She made a move on Oliver Dimbleby last night."

"How did he hold up?"

"As well as could be expected." Gabriel reclaimed the photograph. "You're next."

"When?"

"Thursday night. A quick phone call only. I want you to give her a time and a place and then hang up before she can ask any questions."

"What's the time?"

"Nine p.m. on Friday."

"And the place?"

"Beneath the *arcone* in the Piazza della Repubblica. You won't have any difficulty spotting her." Gabriel slipped the photograph into his briefcase. "What year did he go to England?"

"Who?"

"Orazio Gentileschi."

"He traveled from Paris to Rome in 1626."

"Was Artemisia with him?"

"No. Only his three sons."

"When did he return to Italy?"

"He never did. He died in London in 1639."

"Where is he buried?"

Rossetti hesitated.

"The Queen's Chapel of Somerset House." Gabriel frowned. "Does this sled of yours go any faster? I'd like to get to Umbria while it's still light."

Rossetti put his foot to the floor.

"Better," said Gabriel. "You're a criminal now, Signore Calvi. Don't drive like a cop."

43

Villa dei Fiori

The Villa dei Fiori, a thousand-acre estate located between the Tiber and Nera Rivers, had been in the possession of the Gasparri family since the days when Umbria was still ruled by the popes. There was a large and lucrative cattle operation, an equestrian center that bred some of the finest jumpers in all of Italy, and a flock of playful goats kept solely for entertainment value. Its olive groves produced some of Umbria's best oil, and its small vineyard contributed several hundred kilos of grapes each year to the local cooperative. Sunflowers shone in its fields.

The villa itself stood at the end of a dusty drive shaded by towering umbrella pine. In the eleventh century, it had been a monastery. There was still a small chapel and, in the walled interior courtyard, the remains of an oven where the brothers had baked their daily bread. At the base of the house was a large blue swimming pool, and adjacent to the pool was a trellised garden where rosemary and lavender grew along walls of Etruscan stone.

The current Count Gasparri, a faded Roman nobleman with close ties to the Holy See, did not rent Villa dei Fiori or allow friends and relatives to borrow it. Indeed, the last unaccompanied guests of the property had been the morose art restorer from the Vatican

Museums and his beautiful Venetian-born wife, an experience the four-member staff would not soon forget. They were surprised, then, to learn that Count Gasparri had agreed to lend the villa to an unnamed acquaintance for a stay of indeterminate length. Yes, said the count, it was likely his unnamed acquaintance would have guests of his own. No, he would not require the services of the household staff, as he was intensely private by nature and wished not to be disturbed.

Accordingly, two members of the staff—Anna the fabled cook, and Margherita the temperamental housekeeper—departed Villa dei Fiori early on Tuesday morning for a brief and unexpected holiday. Two other employees, however, remained at their posts: Isabella, the ethereal half Swede who ran the equestrian center; and Carlos, the Argentinian cowboy who cared for the cattle and the crops. Both took note of the unmarked blue-black Fiat Ducato van that came bumping up the drive shortly before noon. The two occupants unloaded their cargo with the swiftness of thieves stashing stolen loot. The plunder included two large metal crates of the sort used by touring rock musicians, provisions enough to feed a small army, and, curiously, a professional-grade studio easel and a large blank canvas.

No, thought Isabella. It wasn't possible. Not after all these years.

The van soon departed, and a tense calm returned to the villa. It was shattered at 3:42 p.m. by the appalling roar of a Maserati engine. A moment later the car streaked past the equestrian center in a cloud of powdery dust. Even so, Isabella managed to catch a brief glimpse of the passenger. His most distinguishing feature was the swath of gray hair—like a smudge of ash—at his right temple.

It was a coincidence, Isabella assured herself. It couldn't possibly be the same man.

The Maserati's engine note faded to a dull drone as the sedan sped toward the villa through the twin rows of umbrella pine. It stopped outside the walls of the ancient courtyard, and the man with gray temples emerged. Medium height, noted Isabella with mounting dread. Slender as a cyclist.

He collected an overnight bag from the backseat and spoke a few parting words to the driver. Then he slung the bag over his shoulder—like a soldier, thought Isabella—and walked a few paces across the drive toward the gate of the courtyard. The same forward slump to the shoulders. The same slight outward bend to the legs.

"Dear God," whispered Isabella as the Maserati shot past her in a blur. It was true, after all.

The restorer had returned to Villa dei Fiori.

————

Next morning he settled into his familiar routine. He led himself on a forced march around the property. He went for a vigorous swim in the pool. He leafed through a book about the Flemish Baroque painter Anthony van Dyck while sitting in the shade of the trellised garden. Carlos and Isabella watched over him from afar. His mood, they observed, was much improved. It was as though a great burden had been lifted from his shoulders. Carlos declared that he was a changed man, but Isabella went even further. He was not a changed man, she said. He was a new man entirely.

His work habits, however, were as disciplined as ever. Wednesday's labors before the easel began after a spartan lunch and continued late into the night. In his previous incarnation, he had listened to music while he worked. But now he seemed to be engrossed in a dreadful play on the radio, something that sounded like the output of a butt-dialed mobile phone. The program featured a roguishly charming London art dealer called Oliver and his plucky assistant, Cordelia. Of that much, at least, Isabella was certain. The rest of it was a disjointed hodgepodge of traffic noise, toilet flushes, one-sided phone calls, and bursts of barroom laughter.

The episode that aired Thursday morning featured a conversation between Oliver and Cordelia over a seemingly trivial scheduling matter—a visit to the gallery by a woman called Magdalena Navarro. At the conclusion of the program, the restorer set off on a punishing hike around the estate. And Isabella, in contravention of Count Gasparri's strict instructions, set off toward the now undefended villa. She entered through the kitchen and made her way to the great room, which the restorer had once again converted into an artist's atelier.

The canvas rested on the easel, shimmering with a recent application of oil-based paint. It was a three-quarter-length portrait of a woman wearing a gown of gold silk trimmed in white lace. Isabella, who had studied art history before devoting her life to horses, recognized the style as Van Dyck's. The woman's face was not yet complete, only her hair, which was almost black. Lampblack, thought Isabella, with a magnificent sheen of lead white with touches of lapis lazuli and vermilion.

His pigments and oils were arrayed on a nearby table. Isabella knew better than to touch anything, as he left behind hidden telltales to alert him to intruders. His Winsor & Newton Series 7 sable-hair brush lay on his palette. Like the painting, it was damp. Next to it was a slumbering laptop. The device was connected to a pair of Bose speakers. Better to hear the travails of Oliver and Cordelia, thought Isabella.

She turned to the unfinished painting once more. He had made a remarkable amount of progress in so short a time. But why was he *painting* a painting and not restoring one? And where was his model? The answer, thought Isabella, was that he had no need of one. She remembered the remarkable painting that had flowed from his hand after he had suffered the terrible injury to his eye—*Two Children on a Beach*, in the style of Mary Cassatt. He had finished it in a handful of marathon sessions, with only his memory to guide him.

"What do you think of it so far?" he asked calmly.

Isabella swung round and laid a hand over her heart. Somehow she managed not to scream.

He took a step forward. "What are you doing in here?"

"Count Gasparri asked me to check on you."

"In that case, why did you come when you knew I was out?" He contemplated his pigments and oils. "You didn't touch anything, did you?"

"Of course not. I was just wondering what you were working on."

"Is that all? Or were you also wondering why I returned to this place after all these years?"

"That, too," Isabella conceded.

He took another step forward. "Do you know who I am?"

"Until a moment ago, I thought you were an art restorer who sometimes worked at the Vatican Museums."

"And you no longer believe that to be the case?"

"No," she said after a moment. "I do not."

A silence fell between them.

"Forgive me," said Isabella, and started toward the door.

"Wait," he called out.

She stopped and turned slowly to face him. The greenness of his eyes was unsettling. "Yes, Signore Allon?"

"You never told me what you thought of the painting."

"It's quite extraordinary. But who is she?"

"I'm not sure yet."

"When will you know?"

"Soon, I hope." He took up his palette and brush, and opened the laptop.

"What's it called?" asked Isabella.

"*Portrait of an Unknown Woman.*"

"Not the painting. The program about Oliver and Cordelia."

He looked up suddenly.

"You've been playing it quite loudly. The sound carries well in the countryside."

"I hope it didn't disturb you."

"Not at all," said Isabella, and turned to go.

"Your phone," he said suddenly.

She stopped. "What about it?"

"Please leave it behind. And bring me your laptop and the keys to your car. Tell Carlos to bring me his devices as well. No phone calls or emails until further notice. And no leaving the estate."

241

Isabella switched off her phone and laid it on the table, next to the open laptop. As she slipped from the villa, she heard roguish Oliver tell someone named Nicky that his client would have to increase his offer to £30 million if he wanted the Veronese. Nicky called Oliver a thief, then asked whether he was free for a drink that evening. Oliver said he wasn't.

"What's her name?"

"Magdalena Navarro."

"Spanish?"

"I'm afraid so."

"What does she look like?"

"A bit like Penélope Cruz, but prettier."

44

Dimbleby Fine Arts

It was Sarah Bancroft, from a table at Franco's Italian restaurant in Jermyn Street, who spotted her first—the tall, slender woman with almost black hair, dressed in a shortish skirt and a formfitting white top. She rounded the corner into Bury Street and instantly caught the attention of Simon Mendenhall, who was leaving Christie's after an interminable senior staff meeting. Simon being Simon, he paused to have a look at the woman's backside and was aghast to see her make a beeline for Dimbleby Fine Arts. Simon in turn made a beeline for Wiltons and informed all those present, including the dealer of contemporary art with whom he was rumored to be having a torrid affair, that Oliver's hot streak continued unabated.

At eight o'clock precisely, the raven-haired woman rang the gallery's bell. Oliver waited until she rang it a second time before rising from his Eames desk chair and unlocking the door. Stepping across the threshold, she pressed her lips suggestively against his cheek. During their weeklong game of cat and mouse, Oliver had sidestepped two offers of dinner and a thinly veiled sexual proposition. Only heaven knew what the next few minutes might bring.

He closed the door and locked it tightly. "Would you like a drink?"

"I'd love one."

"Whisky or whisky?"

"Whisky would be perfect."

Oliver led her through the half-light to his office and filled two tumblers with scotch.

"Blue Label," she remarked.

"I keep it for special occasions."

"What are we celebrating?"

"The impending record-shattering sale of *Susanna in the Bath* by Paolo Veronese."

"Where does the bidding stand?"

"As of this evening, I have two firm offers of thirty."

"Museums?"

"One museum," answered Oliver. "One private."

"I have a feeling that both of your bidders are going to be disappointed."

"The museum's offer is final. The collector made a killing during the pandemic and has money to burn."

"So does my client. He's anxious to hear from me."

"Then perhaps we shouldn't keep your client waiting any longer."

They carried their drinks to the gallery's rear exhibition room. The large painting was propped on a pair of baize-covered display easels. The tableau was only faintly visible in the semidarkness.

Oliver reached for the dimmer switch. As Susanna and the two elders emerged from the gloom, the woman raised a hand to her mouth and murmured something in Spanish.

"Translation?" asked Oliver.

"It wouldn't survive." She approached the painting slowly, as though trying not to disturb the three figures. "It's no wonder you have the entire art world at your feet, Mr. Dimbleby. It's a masterwork painted by an artist at the height of his powers."

"I believe those were the very words I used to describe it in the press release."

"Were they?" She reached into her handbag.

"No photographs, please."

She produced a small ultraviolet torch. "Would you mind switching off the lights for a moment?"

Oliver reached for the dimmer again and returned the room to darkness. The woman played the purple-blue beam of the torch over the surface of the painting.

"The losses are rather extensive."

"The *losses*," replied Oliver, "are exactly what one would expect to find in a four-hundred-and-fifty-year-old Venetian School painting."

"Who handled the restoration for you?"

"It came to me in this condition."

"How fortunate," she said, and switched off the ultraviolet torch.

Oliver allowed the darkness to linger for a moment before slowly bringing up the room lights. The woman was now holding a rectangular LED magnifier. She used it to examine the exposed flesh of Susanna's neck and shoulder, followed by the vermilion-colored robe she was clutching to her breasts.

"The brushwork is quite visible," she said. "Not only in the garments but the skin as well."

"Veronese became more overtly painterly in his brushwork later in his career," explained Oliver. "This work reflects the change from his earlier style."

She returned the magnifier to her handbag and stepped away from the painting. A minute passed. Then another.

Oliver cleared his throat gently.

"I heard that," she said.

"I don't mean to rush things, but it's rather late."

"Do you have a moment to show me the provenance?"

Oliver ushered the woman back to his office. There he drew a copy of the provenance from a locked file drawer and laid it on the desk. The woman reviewed it with justifiable skepticism.

"An old European collection?"

"Very old," replied Oliver. "And very private."

The woman pushed the provenance across the desktop. "I must know the identity of the previous owner, Mr. Dimbleby."

"The previous owner, like your client, insists on anonymity."

"Are you in direct contact with him?"

"Her," said Oliver. "And the answer is no. I deal with her representative."

"A lawyer? A dealer?"

"I'm sorry, but I can't reveal the representative's name or characterize his connection to the collection. Especially to a competitor." Oliver lowered his voice. "Even one as attractive as you."

She gave him a coquettish pout. "Is there really nothing I can do to change your mind?"

"I'm afraid not."

The woman sighed. "And if I were to offer you, say, thirty-five million pounds for your Veronese?"

"My answer would be the same."

She tapped the provenance with the tip of her forefinger. "Are none of your other potential buyers concerned about the flimsiness of the painting's chain of ownership?"

"Not at all."

"How can that be?"

"Because it doesn't matter where the painting came from. The work speaks for itself."

"It certainly spoke to me. In fact, it was rather talkative."

"And what did it say?"

She leaned forward across the desk and looked directly into his eyes. "It said that Paolo Veronese didn't paint it."

"Nonsense."

"Is it, Mr. Dimbleby?"

"I have spent the last four days showing that painting to the leading Old Master experts from the world's most respected museums. And not one of them has questioned the authenticity of the work."

"That's because none of those experts know about the man who visited Galerie Konrad Hassler in Berlin a few days after you announced the rediscovery of your so-called Veronese. This man showed Herr Hassler a photograph of the so-called Veronese side by side with the so-called Titian and the so-called Tintoretto. The photograph was taken in the studio of the art forger who painted them."

"That's not possible."

"I'm afraid it is."

"He assured me that the paintings were genuine."

"Signore Rinaldi?"

"Never heard of him," swore Oliver, truthfully.

"That's the name he used when he visited Galerie Hassler. Giovanni Rinaldi."

"I know him by a different name."

"And what name is that?"

Oliver made no reply.

"He deceived you, Mr. Dimbleby. Or perhaps you simply wanted to be deceived. Whatever the case, you are now in a very precarious situation. But don't worry, it will be our little secret." She paused. "For a small fee, of course."

"How small?"

"Half of the final sales price of the Veronese."

Oliver uncharacteristically chose the high road. "I couldn't possibly sell the picture after what you've told me."

"If you withdraw the painting now, you will be forced to return the millions of pounds you accepted for the Titian and the Tintoretto. And then . . ."

"I'll be ruined."

She handed Oliver a sheet of stationery from the Lanesborough. "I would like you to wire fifteen million pounds into that account first thing tomorrow morning. If the money doesn't appear by the close of business, I will telephone that reporter from the *New York Times* and tell her the truth about your so-called Veronese."

"You're a cheap blackmailer."

"And you, Mr. Dimbleby, don't know as much about the art world as you think you do."

He looked down at the account number. "You will receive the money *after* the sale of my Veronese. Which, I might add, is a genuine Veronese and not a fake."

"I insist on immediate payment."

"You can't have it."

"In that case," said the woman, "I will require a security deposit."

"How much?"

"Not money, Mr. Dimbleby. A name."

Oliver hesitated, then said, "Alessandro Calvi."

"And where does Signore Calvi live?"

"Florence."

"Please call Signore Calvi from your mobile phone. I'd like to have a word with him."

It was half past eight when Oliver showed her into Bury Street. She offered him a hand in farewell. And when he refused it, she placed her mouth close to his ear and warned him of the professional humiliation he would suffer if he failed to send her the money as promised.

"Dinner at the Lanesborough?" he asked as she set off toward Jermyn Street.

"Some other time," she said over her shoulder, and was gone.

Inside the gallery, Oliver returned to his office. The scent of orange blossom and jasmine hung in the air. On the desk were two unfinished glasses of Johnnie Walker Blue Label whisky, a fictitious provenance for a fake painting by Paolo Veronese, and a sheet of stationery from the Lanesborough Hotel. Oliver returned the provenance to the file drawer. The sheet of stationery he photographed with his phone.

It rang a moment later. "Bravo!" said the voice at the other end of the connection. "I couldn't have done it better myself."

45

Firenze

General Ferrari arrived at Villa dei Fiori at two the following afternoon. He was accompanied by four tactical officers and two technicians. The tactical officers conducted a site survey of the villa and the grounds while the techs turned the dining room into an op center. The general, in a business suit and open-necked dress shirt, sat in the great room with Gabriel and watched him paint.

"Your girl arrived in Florence shortly before noon."

"How did she manage that?"

"A chartered Dassault Falcon from London City Airport. The Four Seasons sent a car for her. She's there now."

"Doing what?"

"Our surveillance capabilities inside the hotel are limited. But we'll keep an eye on her if she decides to do a bit of sightseeing. And we'll definitely have a couple of teams in the Piazza della Repubblica at nine o'clock."

"If she spots them, we're dead."

"This might come as a surprise to you, my friend, but the Arma dei Carabinieri has done this a time or two. Without your help," the general added. "The minute she purchases that painting, we'll have the grounds to arrest her on numerous art fraud and conspiracy charges.

249

She will be staring down the barrel of a very long sentence in an Italian prison for women. Not a pleasant prospect for a frequent guest of the Lanesborough Hotel in London."

"I don't want her in a prison cell," said Gabriel. "I want her on the opposite side of an interrogation table, telling us everything she knows."

"As do I. But I am obligated under Italian law to provide her with an attorney if she desires one. If I do not, anything she says will be inadmissible at trial."

"What does Italian law say about art restorers taking part in interrogations?"

"Not surprisingly, Italian law is silent on that question. If, however, she were to consent to the restorer's presence, it might be permissible."

Gabriel stepped away from the canvas and appraised his work. "Perhaps the portrait will influence her thinking."

"I wouldn't count on it. In fact, it might be a good idea to put her in handcuffs before you let her see it."

"Please don't," said Gabriel as he loaded his brush. "I wouldn't want to spoil the surprise."

She spent the afternoon at the pool and at 6:00 p.m. headed upstairs to her suite to shower and dress. She chose her clothing with care. Pale blue stretch jeans. A loose-fitting white blouse. Flat-soled suede moccasins. Her face was aglow from the Tuscan sun and required little makeup. Her raven hair she wound into a bun, with a few stray tendrils along her neck. Attractive, she thought as she evaluated her appearance in the mirror, but serious. There would be no flirtation tonight. No fun and games of the sort she had played with the art dealer in London. The man she was meeting in the Piazza della Repubblica could not be seduced or tricked into doing her bidding. She had seen a video of his visit to Galerie Hassler in Berlin. He was young, good-looking, athletically built. A dangerous man, she reckoned. A professional.

Downstairs, she crossed the lobby and stepped through the hotel's unassuming entrance into the Borgo Pinti. The midday crowds had retreated from the city, as had the heat. She stopped for a coffee at Caffè Michelangelo, then walked through the cool twilight to the Piazza della Repubblica. Its dominant architectural feature was the towering triumphal arch on the western flank. She arrived there, as instructed, at nine o'clock exactly. The Piaggio motor scooter drew alongside her a minute later.

She recognized the man at the helm.

Young, good-looking, athletically built.

Wordlessly he moved to the back of the saddle. Magdalena mounted the bike and asked for a destination.

"The Lungarno Torrigiani. It's on the—"

"I know where it is," she said, and executed a flawless U-turn in the narrow street. As she sped toward the river, his strong hands moved over the small of her back, her hips, her crotch, the inside of her thighs, her breasts. There was nothing sexual in his touch. He was merely searching her for a concealed weapon.

He was a professional, she thought. Fortunately, she was a professional, too.

———

The call arrived at Villa dei Fiori at 9:03 p.m. It was from one of the Carabinieri surveillance artists in the Piazza della Repubblica. The woman had appeared at the rendezvous point as instructed. She and Rossetti were now bound for the apartment. General Ferrari quickly relayed the information to Gabriel, who was still at his easel. He carefully wiped the paint from his brush and headed to the makeshift op center to watch the next act. The Oliver Dimbleby show had been a smashing success. Now it was Alessandro Calvi's turn in the spotlight. One mistake, thought Gabriel, and they were dead.

46

Lungarno Torrigiani

The building was the color of burnt sienna, with a balustrade running along the length of the second floor. The apartment was on the third. In the darkened entrance hall, Rossetti relieved the woman of her Hermès Birkin handbag and emptied the contents onto the kitchen counter. Her possessions included an ultraviolet torch, a professional-grade LED magnifier, and a disposable Samsung phone. The device was powered off. The SIM card had been removed.

Rossetti opened her passport. "Is your name really Magdalena Navarro?"

"Is yours really Alessandro Calvi?"

He unsnapped her Cartier wallet and checked the credit cards and the Spanish driver's permit. All bore the name Magdalena Navarro. The cash compartment contained about three thousand euros and a hundred unspent British pounds. In the zippered compartment Rossetti found a few receipts, all from her visit to London. Otherwise, the wallet and bag were unusually free of pocket litter.

He returned her belongings to the bag, leaving a single item on the counter. It was a photograph of *Danaë and the Shower of Gold* by Gabriel Allon. "Where did you get this?" he asked.

"I happened to be in Berlin not long ago and had lunch with an old friend. He told me an interesting story about a recent visitor to his art gallery. Evidently, this visitor tried to sell my friend the painting in that photograph. He said it came from the same private collection as the pictures that have caused such a sensation in London. He showed my friend a photograph of those paintings as well. Three paintings, one photo. My friend found that odd, to say the least."

"The photograph was taken by my restorer."

"In my experience, art restorers make the best forgers. Wouldn't you agree?"

"That sounds like a question a cop would ask."

"I'm not a police officer, Signore Calvi. I am an art broker who connects buyers and sellers and lives off the scraps."

"Lives quite well, from what I hear."

He led her into the apartment's large sitting room. Three tall casement windows, open to the evening air, overlooked the domes and campanili of Florence. The woman, however, had eyes only for the paintings hanging on the walls.

"You have extraordinary taste."

"The apartment doubles as my saleroom."

She pointed out an exquisite terra-cotta Etruscan amphora. "You also deal in antiquities, I see."

"It's a major part of my business. Chinese billionaires love Greek and Etruscan pottery."

She trailed a forefinger along the curve of the vessel. "This piece is quite lovely. But tell me something, Signore Calvi. Is it a forgery like those three paintings you sold to Mr. Dimbleby? Or is it merely looted?"

"The paintings I sold to Dimbleby were examined by the most prominent Italian Old Master experts in London. And no one questioned the attribution."

"That's because your forger is the world's greatest living Old Master painter."

"There's no such thing as a *living* Old Master."

"Of course there is. I should know. You see, I work for one. He, too, can fool the experts. But your forger is far more talented than mine. That Veronese is a masterpiece. I nearly fainted when I saw it."

"I thought you said you were a broker."

"I *am* a broker. But the paintings I represent simply happen to be forgeries."

"So you're a front man? Is that what you're saying?"

"*You* are a front man, Signore Calvi. As you well know, I am in fact a woman."

"Why are you in Florence?"

"Because I'd like to make you and your forger an offer."

"What sort of offer?"

"Show me the Gentileschi," said the woman. "And then I'll explain everything."

———

Rossetti led her into the adjoining room and switched on the lights. She stared at the painting in silence, as though she had been struck mute.

"Shall I bring you the magnifier and ultraviolet torch?" asked Rossetti after a moment.

"That won't be necessary. The painting is . . ."

"Incandescent?"

"Incendiary," whispered the woman. "But also quite dangerous."

"Is that so?"

"Oliver Dimbleby behaved recklessly by bringing those three pictures to market from your so-called old European collection. Already there are whispers in certain corners of the art world that the paintings might be forgeries. And then you compounded the mistake with your conduct at Galerie Hassler. It is only a matter of time before your ruse unravels. And when it does, there will be collateral casualties."

"You?"

She nodded. "The market for museum-quality Old Masters is a small one, Signore Calvi. There are only so many good pictures and so many collectors and museums who are willing to pay millions for them. Two major Old Master forgery rings cannot compete against one another and survive. One will inevitably collapse. And it will take the other one down with it."

"What's the alternative?"

"I am prepared to offer you and your partner the protection of a proven distribution network, one that will guarantee a steady stream of income for many years to come."

"I don't need your network."

"Your behavior in Berlin would suggest otherwise. The painting in the next room is worth thirty million if handled properly. And yet you were willing to let Herr Hassler have it for a mere two million."

"And if I were to entrust it to you?"

"I would sell it in a way that favors long-term security over short-term financial gain."

"I didn't hear a price."

"Five million," said the woman. "But I would insist on meeting with your forger in his studio before payment."

"Ten million," countered Rossetti. "And you will wire the money into my account before meeting with my forger."

"When would such a meeting take place?"

Rossetti pondered his Patek Phillipe wristwatch. "Shortly after midnight, I imagine. Provided, of course, that you have more than three thousand euros hidden in that Cartier wallet of yours."

"Where do you do your banking, Signore Calvi?"

"Banca Monte dei Paschi di Siena."

"I need the account and routing numbers."

"I'll bring you your phone."

She entered the number manually and from memory. The first time she dialed, she received no answer and rang off without leaving a message. The second attempt met with the same result. Call number three, however, found its intended target.

She addressed the person at the other end of the call in excellent English. There was no exchange of pleasantries, only the swift execution of a wire transfer of €10 million to an account at the world's oldest bank. Email confirmation arrived a few minutes after the call was concluded. With her thumb concealing the sender's name, she showed it to Rossetti. Then she carried the phone to the nearest window and hurled it into the black waters of the Arno.

"Where are we going?" she asked.

"A little town in southern Umbria."

"Not by motor scooter, I hope."

The Maserati was parked outside the building. Rossetti behaved himself in town but let it rip when they hit the Autostrada. He waited until they reached Orvieto before informing his forger—with a phone call placed in speaker mode on the car's Bluetooth system—that he was coming to see him on an important matter. His forger expressed disappointment at the intrusion on his privacy, as he was hoping to complete a painting that evening.

"Can't it wait until morning?"

"I'm afraid not. Besides, I have some good news."

"Speaking of news, have you seen the *Times*? Oliver Dimbleby announced that he sold the Veronese to a private collector. Thirty-five million. At least that's the rumor."

And with that, the call went dead.

"He doesn't sound pleased," said the Spanish woman.

"With good reason."

"It wasn't a consignment deal?"

"Straight sale."

"How much did Dimbleby pay you for it?"

"Three million."

"And the new painting?" asked the woman.

"It's a Van Dyck."

"Really? What's the subject matter?"

"I wouldn't want to spoil the surprise," said Rossetti, and put his foot to the floor.

Shortly before midnight Isabella was awakened from a pleasant dream by the frenzied barking of the dogs. Usually, the culprit was one of the wild boars that dwelled in the surrounding woods. But on that evening the source of the commotion was the two men traipsing across the moonlit pasture. They were part of a large all-male party of guests who had arrived that afternoon. Isabella was of the opinion that the *guests* were not guests at all, but were in fact police officers. How else to explain the fact that two of them were now strolling the pasture by moonlight, each armed with a compact submachine gun?

Eventually the dogs fell silent, and Isabella returned to her bed, only to be awakened a second time, at 12:37 a.m. Now the culprit was the wretched Maserati sports car. The same car, she thought, that had delivered the restorer to Villa dei Fiori earlier that week. It shot past her bedroom window in a blur and raced up the tree-lined drive toward the villa. Two figures emerged into the moonlit forecourt. One was an athletically built man, perhaps another police officer. The other was a tall, raven-haired woman.

It was the woman who entered the villa first, with the man a step behind. The shrieking began a few seconds later, a terrible anguished wailing, like the cry of a wounded animal. Surely it had something to do with the painting. *Portrait of an Unknown Woman . . .* Perhaps she had been mistaken, thought Isabella as she covered her ears. Perhaps Signore Allon was the same man after all.

PART THREE

————

Pentimento

47

Villa dei Fiori

She did not surrender without a fight, but then they had not expected she would. Luca Rossetti attempted to subdue her first and was soon the target of a ferocious counterattack, leaving Gabriel no choice but to abandon his defense of the painting and come to his newfound friend's aid. He was joined a few seconds later by two of the tactical officers, who burst into the room with guns drawn like characters in a French farce. Next the techs entered the fray, and Gabriel wisely withdrew to safer ground to observe the end stages of the contest. It was Rossetti, with blood flowing from one nostril, who applied the handcuffs. Gabriel found the metallic crunch of the locking mechanism to be a most satisfying sound.

Only then did General Ferrari step unhurriedly onto the stage. After determining to his satisfaction that the suspect had not been injured, he commenced a review of the evidence against her. It included a €10 million wire transfer to the Banca Monte dei Paschi di Siena as well as the suspect's admission, preserved on video, that she was a key player in an international forgery network. At present, the Carabinieri were attempting to determine the origin of the payment. They were likewise working to identify the last three phone numbers dialed from the disposable Samsung now lying on the bottom of the Arno River. Neither task, said the general, would prove difficult.

But even without the information, he continued, there was sufficient evidence under Italian law to hand the suspect over to a magistrate for an immediate trial. Because she had been caught in flagrante delicto engaging in art fraud and related financial crimes, the outcome of such a proceeding would not be in doubt. She would likely receive a lengthy sentence in one of Italy's prisons for women, which, regrettably, were among Western Europe's worst.

"Upon your release, you will be extradited to France, where you will undoubtedly face charges for your role in the murders of Valerie Bérrangar, Georges Fleury, and Bruno Gilbert. I'm sure Spanish prosecutors will think of something with which to charge you as well. Suffice it to say, you will be an elderly pensioner by the time you are a free woman again. Unless, of course, you accept the lifeline that I am about to offer you."

Under the terms of the deal, the suspect would receive no prison time for her offenses related to the evening's sting operation in Florence. In exchange, she would provide the Carabinieri with the names of the other members of her network, a complete inventory of the forgeries now in circulation, and, of course, the identity of the forger himself. Any attempt at evasion or deception on the suspect's part would result in the withdrawal of the agreement and immediate incarceration. A second offer of immunity would be unlikely.

They had expected a declaration of innocence, but she made none. Nor did she request a lawyer or demand that General Ferrari put his cooperation agreement in writing. Instead, she looked at Gabriel and posed a single question.

"How did you find me, Mr. Allon?"

"I painted four pictures," he replied. "And you walked straight into my arms."

At which point the mêlée resumed. Capitano Luca Rossetti was the only casualty.

She began by clearing up any lingering questions as to the authenticity of her identity. Yes, she assured them, her name was in fact Magdalena Navarro. And, yes, she had been born and raised in the Andalusian city of Seville. Her father was a dealer of Spanish Old Master paintings and antique furniture. His gallery was located near the Plaza Virgen de los Reyes, a few paces from the entrance of the Doña Maria Hotel. It catered to Seville's wealthiest inhabitants, those of noble birth and inherited wealth. The Navarro clan were not members of that rarefied social stratum, but the gallery had given Magdalena a glimpse of the life led by those for whom money was of no concern.

The gallery had also instilled in her a love of art—Spanish art, in particular. She revered Diego Velázquez and Francisco de Goya, but Picasso was her obsession. She imitated his drawings as a young child and at the age of twelve produced a near-perfect copy of *Two Girls Reading*. She began her formal training soon after, at a private art school in Seville, and upon completing her secondary education she entered the Barcelona Academy of Art. Much to the dismay of her classmates, she sold her first canvases while still a student. An important writer from a Barcelona culture magazine predicted that one day Magdalena Navarro would be Spain's most famous female painter.

"When I graduated in 2004, two prominent art galleries offered to show my work. One was in Barcelona, the other in Madrid. Needless to say, they were quite surprised when I turned them down."

They had placed her in a straight-backed chair in the great room's main seating area. Her feet were flat upon the terra-cotta tiles of the floor; her hands were cuffed behind her back. General Ferrari was seated directly opposite, with Rossetti at his side and a tripod-mounted video camera over his shoulder. Gabriel was contemplating the L-shaped tear, 15 by 23 centimeters, in the lower left corner of *Portrait of an Unknown Woman*.

"Why would you do that?" he asked.

"Turn down a chance to show my work at the tender age of twenty-one? Because I had no interest in being the most famous female artist in Spain."

"Spain was too small for a talent like yours?"

"I thought so at the time."

"Where did you go?"

She arrived in New York in the autumn of 2005 and settled into a one-room apartment on Avenue C, in the Alphabet City section of Lower Manhattan. The apartment was soon filled with newly completed paintings, none of which she was able to sell. The money she had brought with her from Spain quickly ran out. Her father sent what he could, but it was never enough.

A year after her arrival in New York, she could no longer afford painting supplies and was facing eviction. She found work waiting tables at El Pote Español in Murray Hill and at Katz's Delicatessen on East Houston Street. Before long she was working sixty hours a week, which left her too exhausted to paint.

Depressed, she started drinking too much and discovered she had a taste for cocaine. She fell into a relationship with her dealer, a handsome Dominican of Spanish descent named Hector Martínez, and was soon acting as a courier and delivery girl in his network. Many of her regular customers were Wall Street traders who were making fortunes selling derivatives and mortgage-backed securities, the complex investment instruments that in three years' time would leave the global economy on the brink of collapse.

"And then, of course, there were the rock musicians, screenwriters, Broadway producers, painters, sculptors, and gallery owners. As strange as it might sound, being a cocaine dealer in New York was a good career move. Anyone who was anyone was using. And everyone knew my name."

The money she earned dealing drugs allowed Magdalena to stop waiting tables and resume painting. She gave one of her canvases to a Chelsea art dealer with a thousand-dollar-a-week cocaine habit. Rather than keep the painting for himself, the dealer sold it to a client for $50,000. He gave half of the proceeds to Magdalena, but refused to divulge the buyer's name.

"Did he tell you why?" asked Gabriel.

"He said the client insisted on anonymity. But he was also concerned I would cut him out of the picture."

"Why would he suspect a thing like that?"

"I was the daughter of an art dealer. I knew how the business worked."

The Chelsea art dealer bought two more canvases from Magdalena and immediately sold both works to the same anonymous client. The dealer then informed Magdalena that the anonymous client was a wealthy investor who admired her work greatly and was interested in becoming her patron.

"But only if I stopped dealing cocaine."

"I assume you agreed."

"I dropped my pager down a sewer on West Twenty-Fifth Street and never made another delivery."

And her new patron, she continued, lived up to his end of the deal. Indeed, during the summer of 2008, he purchased four additional paintings through the auspices of the same Chelsea gallery. Magdalena earned more than $100,000 from the sales. Fearful of losing her patron's financial support, she made no attempt to discover his identity. But on a frigid morning in mid-December, she was awakened by a phone call from a woman claiming to be her patron's secretary.

"She wanted to know whether I was free for dinner that evening. When I said that I was, she said a limousine would collect me at my apartment at four p.m."

"Why so early?"

"My anonymous patron was planning to take me to Le Cirque. He wanted to make certain that I had something appropriate to wear."

The limousine arrived as promised and delivered Magdalena to Bergdorf Goodman, where a personal shopper named Clarissa selected $20,000 worth of clothing and jewelry, including a gold Cartier wristwatch. Then she escorted Magdalena to the store's exclusive hair salon for a cut and blow-dry.

Le Cirque was located a few blocks away, in the Palace Hotel. Magdalena arrived at eight o'clock and was immediately shown to a table in the center of the iconic dining room. In her mind she had sketched an image of her patron as a well-preserved blazer-wearing septuagenarian from Park Avenue. But the man who awaited her was tall and blond and forty-five at most. Rising, he offered Magdalena his hand and at long last introduced himself.

His name, he said, was Phillip Somerset.

48

Villa dei Fiori

Admittedly, it was the last name in the world that Gabriel had expected to come out of Magdalena Navarro's mouth. An experienced interrogator, he offered no expression of surprise or incredulity. Instead, he turned to General Ferrari and Luca Rossetti, to whom the name meant nothing, and recited a redacted version of Phillip Somerset's curriculum vitae. Former bond trader at Lehman Brothers. Founder and chief executive officer of Masterpiece Art Ventures, an art-based hedge fund that routinely returned profits of 25 percent to its investors. It was clear the general suspected there was more to the story. Nevertheless, he permitted Gabriel to resume questioning the suspect. He began by asking Magdalena to describe her evening at what was once Manhattan's most celebrated restaurant.

"The food was awful. And the decor!" She rolled her beautiful dark eyes.

"What about your dinner date?"

"Our conversation was cordial and businesslike. There was nothing romantic about the evening."

"Why the fancy dress and Cartier watch?"

"They were a demonstration of his power to transform my life. The entire evening was a piece of performance art."

"You were impressed by him?"

"Quite the opposite, actually. I thought he was a cross between Jay Gatsby and Bud Fox. He was pretending to be something he wasn't."

"And what was that?"

"A man of extraordinary wealth and sophistication. A Medici-like patron of the arts."

"But Phillip *was* wealthy."

"Not as wealthy as he claimed to be. And he didn't know the first thing about art. Phillip gravitated toward the art world because that's where the money was."

"Why did he gravitate to you?"

"I was young and beautiful and talented, with an exotic name and Hispanic heritage. He said he was going to turn me into a billion-dollar global brand. He promised to make me rich beyond my wildest dreams."

"Was any of it true?"

"Only the part about making me rich."

Phillip acquired Magdalena's paintings almost as quickly as she could finish them and deposited the money in an account at Masterpiece Art Ventures. The balance soon exceeded $2 million. She left her studio apartment in Alphabet City and settled into a brownstone on West Eleventh Street. Phillip retained ownership of the property but allowed her to live there rent-free. He visited often.

"To see your latest paintings?"

"No," she answered. "To see me."

"You were lovers?"

"Love had very little to do with what took place between us, Mr. Allon. It was a bit like our dinner at Le Cirque."

"Awful?"

"Cordial and businesslike."

Occasionally Phillip took her to a Broadway performance or a gallery opening. But for the most part he kept her hidden from view in the brownstone, where she spent her days painting, like Rumpelstiltskin's daughter at her spinning wheel. He assured her that he was arranging a splashy exhibition of her work, one that would turn her into the hottest artist in New York. But when the promised exhibition never materialized, she accused Phillip of deceiving her.

"How did he react?"

"He took me to a loft in Hell's Kitchen, just off Ninth Avenue."

"What was in the loft?"

"Paintings."

"Were any of them genuine?"

"No," said Magdalena. "Not a single one."

————

They were, however, works of breathtaking beauty and quality, executed by a forger of immense talent and technical skill. He had not copied existing paintings. Instead, he had cleverly imitated the style of an Old Master artist to create a picture that could be passed off as newly rediscovered. All of the canvases, stretchers, and frames were appropriate to their period and school, as were the pigments. Which meant that none of the paintings could ever be exposed as forgeries by a scientific evaluation.

"Did Phillip tell you the forger's name that night?"

"Of course not. Phillip has never told me his name."

"You don't really expect us to believe that, do you?"

"Why would he tell me such a thing? Besides, the forger's name wasn't relevant to what Phillip wanted me to do."

"Which was?"

"Sell the paintings, of course."

"But why you?"

"Why *not* me? I was a trained art historian and a former drug dealer who knew how to walk into a room with a quarter-ounce of cocaine and walk out with the money. I was also the daughter of an art dealer from Seville."

"A perfect point of entry for the European market."

"And a perfect place to take a few forged paintings out for a test drive," she added.

"But why would a wildly successful businessman like Phillip Somerset want to get mixed up in art fraud?"

"You tell me, Mr. Allon."

"Because the businessman wasn't so wildly successful after all."

Magdalena nodded in agreement. "Masterpiece Art Ventures was a bust from the beginning. Even when art prices were soaring, Phillip was never able get the trading formula right. He needed some sure bets to show his investors a profit."

"And you agreed to this scheme?"

"Not at first."

"What changed your mind?"

"Another two million dollars in my account at Masterpiece Art Ventures."

Magdalena returned to Seville a month later and took delivery of the first six paintings from New York. The shipping documents described them as Old Master works of minimal value, all produced by later followers or imitators of the masters themselves. But when Magdalena offered them for sale at her father's gallery, she inflated the attributions to "circle of" or "workshop of," which increased the value of the works substantially. Within a few weeks, all six paintings had been snatched up by her father's wealthy Seville clientele. Magdalena gave him a 10 percent cut of the profits and transferred the rest of the money to Masterpiece Art Ventures through an account in Liechtenstein.

"How much?"

"A million and a half." Magdalena shrugged. "Chump change."

After the initial test run, the paintings began arriving from New York at a steady clip. There were too many to sell through the gallery, so Magdalena established herself as a Madrid-based runner. She sold one of the canvases—a biblical scene purportedly by the Venetian painter Andrea Celesti—to Spain's most prominent

Old Master dealer, who in turn sold it to a museum in the American Midwest.

"Where it hangs to this day."

But Phillip soon discovered that it was far easier for Magdalena to simply *sell* the paintings back to Masterpiece Art Ventures—at wildly inflated prices, with no actual money changing hands. He then moved the works in and out of Masterpiece's portfolio through private phantom sales of his own, using an array of corporate shell entities. Each time a painting supposedly changed hands, it increased in value.

"By the end of 2010, Masterpiece Art Ventures claimed to control more than four hundred million dollars' worth of art. But a significant percentage of those paintings were worthless fakes, the value of which had been artificially inflated with fictitious sales."

But Phillip was not content with the scale of the operation, she continued. He wanted to show explosive growth in the value of Masterpiece's portfolio and higher earnings for his investors. Meeting that goal required the introduction of additional paintings to the market. Until then they had limited themselves primarily to middle-tier works, but Phillip was eager to raise the stakes. The current distribution network wouldn't do; he wanted a premier gallery in a major art world hub. Magdalena found such a gallery in Paris, on the rue la Boétie.

"Galerie Georges Fleury."

Magdalena nodded.

"How did you know that Monsieur Fleury would be interested in going into business with you?"

"He acquired a painting from my father once and conveniently forgot to pay for it. Even by the reduced standards of the art world, Monsieur Fleury was an unscrupulous worm."

"How did you play it with him?"

"Straight up."

"He had no qualms about selling forgeries?"

"None whatsoever. But he insisted on subjecting one of our pictures to scientific analysis before agreeing to handle them."

"What did you give him?"

"A Frans Hals portrait. And do you know what Monsieur Fleury did with it?"

"He showed it to the future president of the Louvre. And the future president of the Louvre gave it to the National Center for Research and Restoration, which affirmed its authenticity. And now the forged Frans Hals portrait is part of the Louvre's permanent collection, along with a Gentileschi, a Cranach, and the most delicious little Van der Weyden you've ever laid eyes on."

"Not the outcome Phillip expected. But quite an accomplishment nonetheless."

"How many fakes did the two of you move through Galerie Fleury?"

"Somewhere between two and three hundred."

"How was Fleury compensated?"

"The first sales were consignment deals."

"And after that?"

"Phillip purchased the gallery through an anonymous shell corporation in 2014. For all intents and purposes, Monsieur Fleury was an employee of Masterpiece Art Ventures."

"When did Galerie Hassler in Berlin come under your control?"

"The following year."

"I'm told you have a distribution point in Brussels."

"Galerie Gilles Raymond on the rue de la Concorde."

"Am I missing any?"

"Hong Kong, Tokyo, and Dubai. And all of it flows into the coffers of Masterpiece Art Ventures."

"The greatest scam in the history of the art world," said Gabriel. "And it might well have gone on forever if Phillip hadn't purchased *Portrait of an Unknown Woman* from Isherwood Fine Arts of London."

"It was your friend Sarah Bancroft's fault," said Magdalena. "If she hadn't bragged about the sale to that reporter from *ARTnews*, the Frenchwoman would have never known about it."

Which brought them, at half past two in the morning, to Madame Valerie Bérrangar.

49

Villa dei Fiori

The first time Magdalena heard Valerie Bérrangar's name, she was in her usual suite at the Pierre Hotel in New York. It was a cold and rainy afternoon in mid-March. A frustrated Phillip was lying next to her, annoyed that she had interrupted their lovemaking to take a phone call. It was from Georges Fleury in Paris.

"What were you doing in New York?" asked Gabriel.

"I pop over at least once a month to discuss the sort of things that can't be put in an email or encrypted text."

"Do you and Phillip always end up in bed?"

"That part of our relationship has never changed. Even during his brief infatuation with your friend Sarah Bancroft, Phillip was sleeping with me on the side."

"Does his wife know about the two of you?"

"Lindsay doesn't have a clue. About much of anything."

With General Ferrari's approval, Rossetti had removed the restraints from her wrists. Her long hands were folded atop her right leg, which was crossed over her left. Her dark eyes tracked Gabriel as he slowly paced the perimeter of the room.

"I imagine Monsieur Fleury was rather nervous that afternoon in mid-March," he said.

"Panic stricken. A French policeman named Jacques Ménard had come to the gallery unannounced to question Fleury about *Portrait of an Unknown Woman*. He was afraid the entire house of cards was about to collapse."

"Why did he contact you and not Phillip?"

"I'm in charge of sales and distribution. Phillip owns the galleries, but he keeps the dealers at arm's length. Unless there's a problem, of course."

"Like Valerie Bérrangar?"

"Yes."

"What did Phillip do?"

"He made a phone call."

"To whom?"

"A man who makes his problems go away."

"Does this man have a name?"

"If he does, I'm not aware of it."

"Is he American?"

"I wouldn't know."

"What *do* you know?"

"That he is a former intelligence officer who has a network of skilled professionals at his disposal. They hacked into Madame Bérrangar's mobile phone and laptop, and broke into her villa in Saint-André-du-Bois. That's when they discovered the entry in her desk calendar. And the painting, of course."

"*Portrait of an Unknown Woman*, oil on canvas, one hundred and fifteen by ninety-two centimeters, attributed to a follower of the Flemish Baroque painter Anthony van Dyck."

"It was a dreadful mistake on Fleury's part," said Magdalena. "He should have told me that he had handled the original version of the painting. The truth is, it was so long ago it slipped his mind."

"How did the forger produce his copy?"

"Apparently, he used a photograph he found in an old exhibition catalogue. It was a minor picture produced by a nameless artist working in Van Dyck's style. The forger simply executed a more skillful version of it and, voilà, a lost Van Dyck suddenly reappeared after centuries in hiding."

"At the same Paris gallery where Valerie Bérrangar's husband purchased the original version thirty-four years earlier."

"The scenario wasn't out of the question, but it was suspicious, to say the least. If the French art squad had opened an investigation . . ."

"You would have been arrested. And Phillip Somerset's forgery-and-fraud empire would have unraveled in spectacular fashion."

"With disastrous consequences for the entire art world. Fortunes would have been lost and countless reputations ruined. Emergency measures had to be taken to contain the damage."

"Eliminate Madame Bérrangar," said Gabriel. "And find out what, if anything, she had told Julian Isherwood and his partner, Sarah Bancroft."

"I had nothing to do with the Bérrangar woman's death. It was Phillip who arranged everything."

"A single-car accident on an empty stretch of road." Gabriel paused. "Problem solved."

"Or so it appeared. But less than a week after her death, you and Sarah Bancroft showed up at Phillip's estate on Long Island."

"He told us that he had sold *Portrait of an Unknown Woman*. He also said that a second review of the attribution had determined that the painting was in fact a genuine Van Dyck."

"Neither of which was true."

"But why did he purchase his own forgery in the first place?"

"I explained that to you earlier."

"Explain it again."

"First of all," said Magdalena, "Masterpiece Art Ventures didn't actually pay six and a half million pounds for *Portrait of an Unknown Woman*."

276

"Because Isherwood Fine Arts unwittingly purchased it from Masterpiece Art Ventures for three million euros."

"Correct."

"Nevertheless, Phillip handed over a substantial amount of money for a worthless painting."

"But it was other people's money. And the painting is far from worthless to a man like Phillip. He can use it as collateral to obtain bank loans and then sell it to another art investor for much more than he paid for it."

"And by routing the original sale through Isherwood Fine Arts," added Gabriel, "Phillip gave himself plausible deniability if it was ever discovered to be a forgery. After all, it was Sarah who sold the forgery to *him*. And it was Julian, a well-respected expert in Dutch and Flemish Old Masters, who concluded that the picture was painted by Anthony van Dyck and not by a later follower."

"Julian Isherwood's blessing increased the painting's value significantly."

"Where is it now?"

"Chelsea Fine Arts Storage."

"I suppose Phillip owns that, too."

"Phillip controls the entire physical infrastructure of the network, including Chelsea. And he was afraid that you and Sarah were going to bring it all down."

"What did he do?"

"He made another phone call."

"To whom?"

"Me."

With a small portion of the money that Magdalena had earned working for Phillip Somerset and Masterpiece Art Ventures, she had purchased a luxurious apartment on the Calle de Castelló in the Salamanca district of Madrid. Her circle of friends included artists, writers, musicians, and fashion designers who knew nothing of the true nature of her work. Like most young Spaniards, they usually ate dinner around ten and then headed off to a nightclub. Consequently, Magdalena was still sleeping when Phillip rang her at one o'clock on a Monday afternoon and told her to clean up the mess at Galerie Fleury.

"What sort of cleanup did he have in mind?"

"Destroy the forgeries in the gallery's inventory and, if necessary, return the million euros that you and the violinist paid for *A River Scene with Distant Windmills.*"

"I was right about it being a forgery?"

She nodded. "Evidently, you told Phillip that you had given it to Aiden Gallagher for scientific analysis. Phillip was convinced that Aiden would be able to tell it was a fake."

"Because Aiden is the best in the business."

"The final word," said Magdalena.

"And when you heard the gallery had been bombed?"

"I knew that Phillip had once again misled me." She paused. "And that he had made a dreadful mistake."

For three weeks, she continued, she remained a prisoner of her apartment in Madrid. She followed the news from Paris obsessively, chewed her nails to the quick, painted a Picassoesque self-portrait, and drank far too much. Her suitcases stood in the entrance hall. One of them contained a million euros in cash.

"Where were you planning to go?"

"Marrakesh."

"Leaving your father to face the music for your crimes?"

"My father did nothing wrong."

"I doubt the Spanish police would have seen it that way," said Gabriel. "But please go on."

She instructed the network's remaining galleries to freeze all sales of forged paintings and reduced her telephone-and-text contact with Phillip to a bare minimum. But in late April, he summoned her to New York and told her to open the spigot.

"One of his largest investors had requested a forty-five-million-dollar redemption. The kind of redemption that leaves a mark on the balance sheet. Masterpiece needed to replenish its cash reserves in a hurry."

And so the forgeries flowed into the market, and the money flowed into Phillip's accounts in the Cayman Islands. By June the bombing of Galerie Fleury had receded from the headlines, and the eyes of the art world were on London, where Dimbleby Fine Arts was preparing to exhibit a newly discovered version of *Susanna in the Bath* by Paolo Veronese. The painting had purportedly emerged from the same unidentified European collection that had previously produced a Titian and a Tintoretto. But Magdalena knew what the rest of the art world did not, that all three paintings were forgeries.

"Because the forger's front man," said Gabriel, "made quite a scene at Galerie Hassler in Berlin."

Magdalena looked at Rossetti. "I was suspicious about those paintings even before your front man tried to sell the Gentileschi to Herr Hassler."

"Why?"

"I know a provenance trap when I see one, Mr. Allon. Yours wasn't terribly clever or original. Still, I wasn't surprised by the reaction of the art world. It's the secret of our success."

"What's that?"

"The gullibility of collectors and so-called experts and connoisseurs. The art world desperately wants to believe that there are lost masterpieces just waiting to be rediscovered. Phillip and I make dreams come true." She managed a smile. "As do you, Mr. Allon. Your Veronese took my breath away, but the Gentileschi was to die for."

"You had to have it?"

"No," she answered "I had to have *you.*"

"Because the market for museum-quality Old Masters is small? Because two major Old Master forgery rings cannot compete against one another and survive?"

"And because Phillip's forger is unable to supply enough paintings to meet the demands of my distribution network," said Magdalena. "And because, for all his talent, he cannot hold a candle to you."

"In that case, I accept your offer."

"What offer?"

"To join the team at Masterpiece Art Ventures." Gabriel switched off the video camera. "Let's take a walk, shall we, Magdalena? There are one or two details we need to finalize before you call Phillip and give him the good news."

50

Villa dei Fiori

They made their way down the gentle slope of the drive, beneath the canopy of the umbrella pine. The first brushstrokes of dawn lay over the hills to the east, but overhead the stars shone brightly. The air was cool and still, not a breath of movement. It smelled of orange blossom and jasmine and the cigarette that Magdalena had charmed from Luca Rossetti.

"Where did you learn to paint like that?" she asked.

"In the womb."

"Your mother was an artist?"

"And my grandfather. He was a disciple of Max Beckmann."

"What was his name?"

"Viktor Frankel."

"I know your grandfather's work," said Magdalena. "But good genes alone can't explain talent like yours. If I didn't know better, I would have guessed that you were an apprentice in Titian's workshop."

"It's true that I served my apprenticeship in Venice, but it was with a famous restorer named Umberto Conti."

"And you were no doubt Signore Conti's finest pupil."

"I suppose I have a knack for it."

"Restoring paintings?"

"Not just paintings. People, too. I'm trying to decide whether you're worth the effort." He gave her a sideways glance. "I have a terrible feeling you're beyond repair."

"The damage is self-inflicted, I'm afraid."

"Not all of it. Phillip targeted you for recruitment. He groomed you. Preyed on your vulnerabilities. Got you hooked. I know his techniques. I've used them a time or two myself."

"Are you using them now?"

"A little," he admitted.

She turned away and expelled a slender stream of smoke. "And what if I told you that I willingly stepped into the trap Phillip set for me?"

"Because you wanted the money?"

"It certainly wasn't for the sex."

"How much is there?"

"In addition to the million euros in the suitcase in my apartment?" She lifted her gaze skyward. "I have another four or five scattered around Europe, but the bulk of my money is invested in Masterpiece Art Ventures."

"Current balance?"

"Maybe fifty-five."

"Million?"

"It's a fraction of what I deserve. If it wasn't for me, there wouldn't be a Masterpiece Art Ventures."

"It's not exactly a résumé enhancer, Magdalena."

"How many people can say they built a multibillion-dollar global forgery network?"

"Or brought one down," said Gabriel quietly.

She frowned. "How did you find me, Mr. Allon? The truth, this time."

"Your attempt to recruit Lucien Marchand gave me valuable insight into the way you ran your operation."

Magdalena took a final pull at the cigarette and with a flick of her long forefinger sent the ember arcing into the darkness. "And how is Françoise these days? Still living in Roussillon? Or has she settled permanently in Lucien's villa on Saint-Barthélemy?"

"Why did you try to hire him?"

"Phillip wanted to expand our inventory to include Impressionist and postwar works. His forger wasn't capable of it, so he asked me to find someone who was. I made Lucien a generous offer, which he accepted."

"Along with one million euros in cash."

She made no reply.

"Is that why you had him murdered? A lousy million euros?"

"I'm sales and distribution, Mr. Allon. Phillip deals with problems."

"Why was Lucien a problem?"

"Do I really need to explain that to you?"

"After Lucien and Françoise accepted the money and then reneged on the deal, Phillip was concerned that they posed a threat to you and Masterpiece Art Ventures."

Magdalena nodded. "Françoise is lucky that Phillip didn't have her killed, too. She was the real brains behind that network. Lucien was the brush and Toussaint the cash register, but Françoise was the glue that kept it together." She slowed to a stop before a small shrine to the Virgin Mary, one of several scattered about the estate. "Where in the world are we?"

"The villa was once a monastery. The current owner is quite close to the Vatican."

"As are you. Or so they say." She made the sign of the cross and set off again.

"Are you a believer?" asked Gabriel.

"Like ninety percent of my fellow Spaniards, I no longer attend Mass, and it has been more than twenty years since I last set foot in a confessional. But, yes, Mr. Allon. I remain a believer."

"Do you believe in absolution as well?"

"That depends on how many Hail Marys you intend to make me recite."

"If you help me take down Phillip Somerset," said Gabriel, "your sins will be forgiven."

"All of them?"

"A few years ago, I met a woman who ran a modern art gallery in Saint-Tropez. It was a money-laundering front for her boyfriend's narcotics empire. I got her out of the situation cleanly. Now she's a successful dealer in London."

"Somehow I doubt there's an art gallery in my future," said Magdalena. "But what did you have in mind?"

"A final face-to-face meeting with Phillip in New York next week."

"About the newest member of the team at Masterpiece Art Ventures?"

"Exactly."

"I imagine he's quite anxious to have a look at your Gentileschi."

"Which is why you're going to overnight it to Chelsea Fine Arts Storage."

"I hope your front man is covering the shipping costs."

"I'm afraid it wasn't included in the hammer price."

"I guess ten million euros doesn't go as far as it used to. But how are we going to get the painting through Italian customs?"

"I believe we're covered on that score." Gabriel handed her a mobile phone. "This call is being recorded for quality assurance. If you try to pass a message to him, I'll hand you over to General Ferrari and wave goodbye."

She dialed the number and raised the phone to her ear. "Hello, Lindsay. It's Magdalena. I'm sorry to be calling at such a dreadful hour, but I'm afraid it's rather urgent. I promise not to keep Phillip long."

51

Villa dei Fiori

Rossetti drove Magdalena back to Florence to collect her belongings from the Four Seasons and settle the enormous bill. By noon they had returned to Villa dei Fiori, and Magdalena, in sunglasses and a stunning white two-piece swimsuit, was stretched upon a chaise longue by the pool, a glass of chilled Orvieto wine in her hand. General Ferrari observed her disapprovingly from the shade of the trellised garden.

"Is there anything the staff of the Hotel Carabinieri can do to make her stay more comfortable?" he asked Gabriel.

"What would you have me do? Confine her to her room until we leave for New York?"

"Surely this place has a dungeon. After all, it was built in the eleventh century."

"I believe Count Gasparri converted it into his wine cellar."

Ferrari sighed but said nothing.

"Has the Art Squad never cut a deal with a thief or a fence to get to the next step of the ladder?"

"We do it all the time. And more often than not, the thief or the fence tells us only part of the story." The general paused. "Just like that beautiful creature lying comfortably next to the swimming pool. She's smarter than you realize. And quite dangerous."

"I'm a former intelligence officer, Cesare. I know how to handle an asset."

"She's not an asset, my friend. She is a criminal and a confidence artist who has millions of dollars stashed around the world and access to private airplanes."

"At least she doesn't have tattoos," remarked Gabriel.

"Her one and only redeeming quality. But I assure you, she is not to be trusted."

"I have enough leverage to keep her in line, including her videotaped confession."

"Ah, yes. A tragic tale about a once promising artist who was lured into a life of crime by the evil and manipulative Phillip Somerset. You realize, I hope, that perhaps half of it is true."

"Which half?"

"I haven't a clue. But I find it difficult to believe that she doesn't know the name of the forger."

"It's entirely plausible that Phillip kept it from her."

"Perhaps. But it is also entirely plausible that she was the one who took Phillip to that loft in Hell's Kitchen, and that the forger is now lying in the Umbrian sun with a drink in her hand."

"She doesn't have the training to paint Old Masters."

"So she says. But if I were you, I would revisit the matter."

"I'll boil her in suntan oil after lunch."

"Why don't you let me take her back to Rome instead? She can tell her tragic tale to the FBI legal attaché at the embassy. A prize like Magdalena would do wonders for my standing in Washington. Besides, it's an American problem now. Let the Americans handle it."

"And do you know what the FBI legal attaché will do?" asked Gabriel. "He'll call his superior at FBI headquarters. And his superior will call the assistant director, who will call the director, who will walk across Pennsylvania Avenue to the Justice Department. DOJ will assign the case to the US attorney for the Southern District of New York, and the US attorney will spend months gathering evidence before arresting Phillip and shutting down his company."

"The wheels of justice turn slowly."

"Which is why I'm going to deal with Phillip myself. By the time I'm finished, Masterpiece Art Ventures will be a smoldering ruin. The Feds will have no choice but to immediately make arrests and seize assets."

"A fait accompli?"

Gabriel smiled. "It definitely sounds better in French."

———

General Ferrari and the rest of the Carabinieri team departed Villa dei Fiori at two that afternoon. A unit from the Amelia station kept watch over the gate, but otherwise Gabriel and Magdalena were alone. She slept through the afternoon and insisted on preparing a proper Spanish dinner of tapas and a potato omelet. They ate outside on the villa's terrace, in the cool evening air. Magdalena's personal mobile phone lay between them, flaring with incoming message traffic and silenced phone calls, mainly from her circle of friends in Madrid.

"No man in your life?" asked Gabriel.

"Only Phillip, I'm afraid."

"Are you in love with him?"

"God, no."

"Are you sure about that?"

"Why do you ask?"

"Because it is my intention to leave you alone in his presence for several hours in New York next week. And I want to know whether you intend to live up to our agreement or run away with him."

"Don't worry, Mr. Allon. I'll get you everything you need to take Phillip down."

He asked where the meeting would take place.

"That's up to Phillip," said Magdalena. "Sometimes we meet at Masterpiece's office on East Fifty-Third Street. But usually we get together at the town house on East Seventy-Fourth. It doubles as Masterpiece's gallery. That's where Phillip receives potential investors and buyers."

"How does he handle the sales?"

"He prefers to deal directly with clients to avoid scrutiny and commissions. But if the client insists on an intermediary, he routes the sales through another dealer or one of the auction houses."

"How many other people work for the firm?"

"Three young female art experts and Kenny Vaughan. Kenny used to work with Phillip at Lehman Brothers. He's in it up to his eyeballs."

"What about the women?"

"They think the sun rises and sets on Phillip and that I'm a broker who buys and sells paintings on his behalf in Europe."

"General Ferrari is convinced that you're the forger."

"Me?" She laughed. "A Picasso, maybe. But not an Old Master. I don't have talent like yours."

Gabriel read late into the night and was relieved to find Magdalena still in her bed when he rose the following morning. After loading the *automatico* with Illy and San Benedetto, he unleased Proteus on Phillip's personal smartphone, and within minutes the device was under his control. A scalable map depicted its current location and elevation: the eastern shore of an egg-shaped peninsula, twelve feet above sea level.

Gabriel downloaded Phillip's data onto his laptop and spent the remainder of the morning wandering the digital debris of one of the greatest scam artists in history. It was half past twelve when Magdalena finally appeared. She wandered into the kitchen and emerged a moment later with a bowl of milky coffee. She drank it in silence, her eyes unblinking.

"Not a morning person?" asked Gabriel.

"Opposite of a morning person. A night stalker."

"Is the night stalker ready to do some work?"

"If you insist," she said, and carried her coffee to the pool.

Gabriel followed her outside with the laptop. "What were the first six paintings you sold through your father's gallery?"

"It was a thousand years ago," she groaned.

"The exact amount of time you'll spend in an Italian prison if you don't start talking."

———

She recited the artist, tableau, and dimensions of each work, along with the name of the buyer and the price it had fetched. Next she listed the particulars of more than one hundred paintings that had passed through her brokerage in Madrid during the first year of the scheme. Most of the paintings she had simply sold back to Masterpiece Art Ventures. Phillip had then inflated their value with additional phantom sales before unloading the paintings onto unsuspecting buyers and cashing in on his investment. He also used the works as collateral to secure massive art-backed loans, money he used to acquire legitimate art and pay handsome returns to his investors.

"The loans," said Magdalena, "are the key to everything. Without leverage, Phillip and Kenny Vaughan wouldn't be able to make it work."

"So in addition to selling forged paintings, Phillip is committing bank fraud?"

"On a daily basis."

"Where does he do his banking?"

"Mainly, he deals with Ellis Gray at JPMorgan Chase. But he also has a relationship with Bank of America."

"How much debt is he carrying?"

"I'm not sure even Phillip knows the answer to that."

"Who does?"

"Kenny Vaughan."

The next ground they covered was Magdalena's expansion into bricks-and-mortar retailing, beginning with her partnership with Galerie Georges Fleury of Paris and concluding with the recent acquisition by Masterpiece Art Ventures of galleries in Hong Kong, Tokyo, and Dubai. The total number of forged paintings the network had unleashed on the art market exceeded five hundred, with a paper valuation of more than $1.7 billion—far too many works for Magdalena to recall accurately. She was certain, however, that a significant percentage had passed through Masterpiece's opaque portfolio.

"How many does he currently control?"

"That's impossible to say. Phillip doesn't even reveal the genuine paintings in his possession, let alone the forgeries. His most valuable pictures are in his Manhattan and Long Island homes. The rest are in the warehouse on East Ninety-First Street. It's the equivalent of his trading book."

"Can you get inside?"

"Not without Phillip's approval. But a directory of the warehouse's current contents would tell you everything you need to know."

Over lunch, Gabriel logged into Magdalena's ProtonMail account and forwarded several years' worth of encrypted emails to his own address. Next they reviewed her personal finances, including her account at Masterpiece Art Ventures. Her balance was $56,245,539.

"Don't even think about trying to make a withdrawal," Gabriel warned her.

"My next redemption window isn't until September. I couldn't if I tried."

"I'm sure Phillip would make an exception in your case."

"Actually, he's quite strict when it comes to redemptions. He and Kenny fly rather close to the sun. If a handful of major investors were to simultaneously withdraw their funds, he would have to sell some of his inventory or secure another loan."

"Using a painting as collateral?"

"The art-backed loans," repeated Magdalena, "are the key to every-thing."

Gabriel downloaded Magdalena's account statements, then checked the tracking information for *Danaë and the Shower of Gold*. The painting was currently westbound over the Atlantic. It would spend the night in the air cargo center at Kennedy International and was scheduled to reach its final destination, Chelsea Fine Arts Storage, no later than noon on Monday.

A search of the flights from Rome to New York produced several options. "How do you feel about the ten a.m. Delta into JFK?" asked Gabriel.

"That would require awakening several hours before noon."

"You can sleep on the plane."

"I never sleep on planes." Magdalena reached for the laptop. "Can I pay for your ticket?"

"Phillip might find that suspicious."

"At least let me give you some miles."

"I have plenty."

"How many have you got?"

"The moon and back."

"I've got more." She booked their seats. "That leaves the hotel. Is the Pierre all right?"

"I'm afraid Sarah prefers the Four Seasons."

"Please tell me she's not coming with us."

"I need someone to keep an eye on you when I'm not around."

Magdalena reserved her usual suite at the Pierre and with a child-like frown returned to her chaise longue next to the pool. Her wounds, thought Gabriel, were definitely self-inflicted. Still, she was by no means beyond repair. After all, if a former contract killer like Christopher Keller was salvageable, then surely Magdalena was as well.

For the moment, she was merely a means to an end. All Gabriel required now was a reporter to turn her remarkable story into a weapon that would reduce Masterpiece Art Ventures to rubble. A reporter who was familiar with the worlds of finance and art. Perhaps one who had investigated Masterpiece in the past.

Only a single candidate fit the profile. Fortunately, the number for her cell phone was in Phillip Somerset's contacts. Gabriel dialed it and introduced himself. Not with a work name, or one he plucked from thin air, but his real name.

"Yeah, right," she said, and hung up the phone.

52

Rotten Row

The next call Gabriel placed that afternoon was to Sarah Bancroft. It found her on Rotten Row in Hyde Park, where she was attempting to dislodge the ten pounds that had settled astride her hips. The news from Italy came as a shock, so much so that she asked Gabriel to repeat it, just to make certain she hadn't misunderstood him. It was no less astounding the second time. Masterpiece Art Ventures, the art-based hedge fund where a portion of Sarah's inheritance was invested, was a $1.2 billion fraud propped up by the sale and collateralization of forged paintings. Furthermore, it seemed that Magdalena Navarro, she of the shimmering black hair and elongated body, had been sleeping with Phillip the entire time he had dated Sarah. For that reason alone, she leapt at the chance to travel to New York to take part in his destruction. Even if it meant staying at the Pierre.

"Shall I bring along Mr. Marlowe? I find that he comes in rather handy in situations like these."

"As do I. But I have another job in mind for him."

"Nothing dangerous, I hope."

"I'm afraid so."

Sarah left for New York early the following morning and arrived at JFK at midday. A Nissan Pathfinder awaited her at Hertz. She killed an hour in the cell phone lot and at two fifteen made her way to Terminal 1. Gabriel emerged a moment later, accompanied by the woman whom Sarah had last seen walking along the pavements of Jermyn Street.

Now, as then, she was wearing a shortish skirt and a formfitting white top. Gabriel loaded their bags into the rear storage compartment and slid into the backseat. Magdalena climbed into the passenger seat, bringing with her the scent of orange blossom and jasmine. She crossed one long leg over the other and smiled. Sarah slipped the Nissan into DRIVE and set out for Manhattan.

———

The Pierre Hotel stood at the corner of East Sixty-First Street and Fifth Avenue. Magdalena entered the ornate lobby alone and was received by the hotel's management as though she were returning royalty. Her suite, with its sweeping views of Central Park, was located on the twentieth floor. Gabriel and Sarah had been assigned adjoining rooms on the opposite side of the corridor. Like Magdalena, they checked in pseudonymously and instructed the woman at Reception to block all outside calls.

Upstairs, all three convened in the sitting room of Magdalena's suite. She opened a complimentary bottle of Taittinger champagne while Gabriel connected his laptop to the hotel's Wi-Fi network and logged in to Proteus. It appeared that Phillip had decided to remain in North Haven rather than return to the city. Gabriel increased the volume on the feed from the microphone and heard the clatter of a keyboard. The output from the camera was a rectangle of solid black.

Gabriel handed Magdalena her phone. "Let him know that you've arrived and would like to see him as soon as possible. And remember—"

"This call is being recorded for quality assurance."

Gabriel carried the laptop into the bedroom and closed the heavy internal door. Phillip answered Magdalena's call instantly. "How about one o'clock tomorrow afternoon?" he asked. "We'll have lunch."

"Will Lindsay be joining us?"

"Unfortunately, she's spending the week on the island."

"Lucky you."

"I'll send a car," said Phillip, and the connection went dead.

Gabriel listened to a minute or two of typing before returning to the sitting room. "Now the Gentileschi," he said to Magdalena.

The number for the warehouse was in her contacts. She tapped the screen and lifted the phone to her ear.

"Hello, Anthony. It's Magdalena Navarro calling. Did the painting arrive from Florence as scheduled? . . . Wonderful. Send it to Mr. Somerset's residence tomorrow morning . . . Yes, the town house, please. Place it on the easel in the gallery. And make certain it arrives no later than noon."

Magdalena killed the connection and surrendered her phone to Gabriel.

"Your wallet and passport as well."

She removed them from her Hermès Birkin handbag and handed them over.

"I need to run an errand, which means that you and Sarah will have a chance to get to know one another better. But don't worry," said Gabriel as he stepped into the corridor. "I won't be long."

Sarah chained the door behind him and returned to the sitting room. Magdalena was adding champagne to her glass. At length Sarah asked, "Is it true that Phillip was sleeping with you the entire time he was seeing me?"

"Only when I was in New York."

"Ah, that's a relief."

"If you must know," said Magdalena, "he was only using you."

"For what?"

"Introductions to rich benefactors of the Museum of Modern Art."

"And to think I gave him two million dollars to invest."

"What's your current balance?"

"Four and a half. You?"

"Fifty-six point two."

Sarah smiled without parting her lips. "I guess you were better in bed than I was."

53

Literary Walk

In the spring of 2017, *Vanity Fair* magazine published an investigative profile titled "The Great Somerset." Twelve thousand words in length, the article chronicled its subject's rise from a working-class town in northeastern Pennsylvania to the pinnacle of Wall Street and the art world. No corner of his personal life escaped scrutiny: the instability of his childhood home, his youthful athletic prowess, his brief but meteoric career at Lehman Brothers, his ugly divorce, his peculiar penchant for secrecy. A source described only as a former friend said he had a dark side. An old colleague went further, suggesting he was a sociopath and a malignant narcissist. Both sources agreed that he was hiding something.

The article was written by Evelyn Buchanan, an award-winning reporter whose work for *Vanity Fair* had served as the intellectual property for two Hollywood films and a Netflix limited series. At present, she was seated on a bench along Central Park's Literary Walk. Robert Burns, feather pen in hand, eyes skyward in search of inspiration, loomed over her right shoulder. On the opposite side of the footpath, a sketch artist sat waiting for a subject.

Evelyn Buchanan was waiting, too. Not for a subject but a source. He had called her without warning the previous day—from where he refused to say. No, he had assured her, it was not a practical joke; he was in fact the man he claimed to be. He was coming to New York on an unpublicized visit and wished to meet with her. She was to tell no one that he had been in touch. He promised that she would not be disappointed.

"But national security isn't my beat," Evelyn protested.

"The matter I wish to discuss is related to the financial world and the art market."

"Can you be a bit more specific?"

"The Great Somerset," he said, and rang off.

It was an intriguing clue, all the more so because of the source. He had attended a book party at Phillip's showy North Haven estate that spring. Or so claimed Ina Garten, who insisted he'd had a hot little blonde on his arm. Evelyn, who had attended the same party, had found the prospect laughable. Now she had to admit it was possible after all. How else to explain why a man like Gabriel Allon would be interested in a creep like Phillip Somerset?

Evelyn checked the time. It was one minute before five o'clock. One minute before the world's most famous retired spy had promised to appear. The walkway was crowded with tourists, spandex-clad joggers, and Upper East Side nannies pushing strollers laden with the tycoons of tomorrow. But there was no one who looked as though he might be Gabriel Allon. Indeed, the only possible candidate was a man of medium height and build who was pondering the placard at the foot of the Walter Scott statue.

At the stroke of five o'clock, he crossed the walkway and sat down on Evelyn's bench. "Please go away," she said quietly. "My husband will be back any minute, and he has anger-management issues."

"I thought I made it clear that you were to come alone."

Evelyn turned with a start. Then, regaining her composure, she stared straight ahead. "Who was the blonde?"

"I beg your pardon?"

"The woman you brought to Carl Bernstein's book party."

"She used to work at MoMA. Now she's an art dealer in London. I was helping her with a problem."

"What sort of problem?"

"The Great Somerset."

"You obviously read my article," said Evelyn.

"Several times."

"Why?"

"As you might imagine, the ability to read between the lines is an essential skill for an intelligence officer. Is the information accurate, or is my adversary trying to deceive me? Is my agent overstating his case, or is he playing it too safe? Has my source, for one reason or another, left critical information out of his report?"

"And when you finished reading my story about Phillip?"

"I had the nagging sense that you knew more about him than you shared with your readers."

"Much more," she admitted.

"Why wasn't the material included in the piece?"

"You first, Mr. Allon. Why Phillip Somerset, of all people?"

"Masterpiece Art Ventures is a fraud. And I'd like you to be the one to break the story."

"What have you got for me?"

"A whistleblower."

"An employee of the company?"

"Close enough."

"What does that mean?"

"It means that I'm going to impose some rather strict ground rules in order to protect the whistleblower's identity and to conceal my role in this matter."

"And if I refuse to accept those ground rules?"

"I'll find someone who will. And you and your magazine will be playing catch-up when Masterpiece crashes and burns."

"In that case, I'll listen to what you and your whistleblower have to say." She paused. "But only if you tell me where you got the number for my cell phone."

"I found it in Phillip's contacts."

Evelyn Buchanan smiled. "Ask a silly question."

54

Central Park

"How did you find her?"

"She was arrested in Italy last weekend after purchasing a forged Gentileschi from an undercover Carabinieri officer. I was a consultant to the Italian investigation."

"A consultant?" asked Evelyn dubiously.

"It's possible I might have painted the Gentileschi for them."

"A fake forgery painted by Gabriel Allon? This story is getting better by the minute."

They were moving at an unhurried pace along the footpaths of Central Park. For the moment, Evelyn's notepad was tucked safely into her Chanel handbag. She was a petite woman of perhaps fifty, with short, dark hair and oversize tortoiseshell glasses. They were her trademark, the spectacles, like her razor-sharp prose, acerbic wit, and ruthless competitive streak.

"Where's the painting now?" she asked.

"A warehouse on East Ninety-First Street."

"Chelsea Fine Arts Storage?"

"That's the one."

"I remember when Phillip acquired it. I have to say, it made no sense to me at the time. Why would a tycoon like Phillip Somerset want to own a small-time art services company like Chelsea?"

"Because the tycoon needed the ability to ship and store forged paintings, no questions asked. He's flooded the art market with hundreds of fake paintings, including four that have ended up in the Louvre. But the best part of the story is that—"

"Phillip is using forged paintings as collateral to obtain massive bank loans."

"How did you know?"

"An educated guess." Evelyn smiled. "Did I mention that my husband works for Millennium Management. It's one of the world's largest hedge funds. Before that, he was a prosecutor in the US attorney's office for the Southern District of New York. When I was working on the profile of Phillip, Tom took a hard look at—"

"Your husband is named Tom Buchanan?"

"Do you want to hear the rest of the story or not?"

"Please."

"When Tom analyzed Masterpiece's annual returns, he was quite impressed. Envious, actually."

"Because Masterpiece had outperformed Millennium?"

"Easily. Tom being Tom, he started doing some digging."

"And?"

"He was convinced that Phillip was using borrowed money and money from new investors to pay off his old investors. In short, Tom believes that Phillip Somerset is the Bernie Madoff of the art world."

"He's running a Ponzi scheme?"

"Correct."

"How close did you get to proving it?"

"Not close enough for my editors. But Phillip definitely knew that I was on to him."

"How?"

"He employs a man named Leonard Silk to watch his back. Silk is retired CIA. When he left the Agency, he opened a one-man private security firm here in New York. He called me when I was working on my profile and threatened legal action if the piece alleged wrongdoing of any kind. I also received messages from a man who somehow knew that I liked to take long walks in the park. He warned me to be careful. He said bad things happen to women who walk alone in New York City."

"How subtle."

"Leonard Silk doesn't waste time on subtlety. That's Phillip's department. He was incredibly charming during our interviews. It's no wonder your whistleblower agreed to work for him."

"Actually, she saw through Phillip from the beginning."

"What was the original connection?"

"Drugs. When she couldn't sell any of her paintings here in New York, she earned a living dealing cocaine. Many of her clients were Wall Street types."

"Phillip snorted a mountain of blow back when he was at Lehman Brothers," said Evelyn. "It was just one of the reasons why they fired him. Even by Wall Street standards, he was out of control."

"Your article said he left Lehman on good terms."

"That was the public version of the story, but it isn't true. Phillip was practically frog-marched out of the building, and a do-not-resuscitate order went out on the street. When no one else would hire him, he started a hedge fund called Somerset Asset Management. And when the hedge fund collapsed, he hit upon a novel idea."

"He gravitated to the art world," said Gabriel. "Because that's where the money was."

Evelyn nodded. "Phillip started turning up at gallery openings and museum fundraisers, always with a beautiful woman on his arm and a pocketful of business cards. You have to hand it to him. The art-based hedge fund was an intriguing idea. Prices for blue-chip art were rising faster than equities or any other asset class. How could he possibly go wrong?"

"It never worked. That's why he started loading up his book with forged paintings."

They had arrived at Grand Army Plaza. "You never mentioned your whistleblower's name," said Evelyn.

"Magdalena Navarro."

"Where is she now?"

Gabriel glanced toward the Pierre Hotel. "It's her New York address. She has fifty-six million dollars invested in Masterpiece Art Ventures, all of which she earned selling forgeries for Phillip."

"So she says. But I can't accuse Phillip Somerset of the greatest art fraud in history based solely on the word of a former drug dealer. I need proof that he's knowingly selling forged paintings."

"What if you were able to hear it directly from Phillip's mouth?"

"Do you have a recording?"

"The conversation hasn't happened yet."

"When will it?"

"Tomorrow afternoon at one o'clock."

"What's on the agenda?"

"Me."

———

They threaded their way through the gridlocked traffic along Fifth Avenue and came whirling through the Pierre's revolving door, into the refrigerated cool of the lobby. Upstairs, Gabriel knocked softly on the door of Magdalena's suite. Sarah confirmed his identity before opening the door.

"How's the prisoner?" he asked.

"The prisoner is resting in her room." Sarah offered Evelyn her hand, then turned to Gabriel. "Do we need to clarify the ground rules before we begin?"

"Ms. Buchanan has agreed that your name and the name of your highly regarded gallery in London will not appear in her copy. She will describe you only as an art world insider." Gabriel glanced at Evelyn. "Isn't that correct, Ms. Buchanan?"

"And how will I describe *you*?"

"This story isn't about me. It's about Phillip Somerset and Masterpiece Art Ventures. Any information that I provide is for background purposes only. You may not quote me directly. Nor are you to say where this interview is taking place."

"An undisclosed location?"

"I'll let you choose the words, Ms. Buchanan. I'm not the writer."

"You're just the consultant to the Italian police who painted a fake forgery?"

"Exactly."

"In that case, perhaps it's time for me to meet the prisoner."

Gabriel knocked on the door of the bedroom, and a moment later out stepped Magdalena.

"My goodness," said Evelyn Buchanan. "This story is getting better by the minute."

55

Pierre Hotel

They went through it once from the beginning. And then they went through it a second time, just to make certain of the relevant facts and dates. Magdalena's childhood in Seville. Her formal training as an artist in Barcelona. The years she spent dealing cocaine in New York. Her introduction to Phillip Somerset at Le Cirque. Her role in building and maintaining the most lucrative and sophisticated art-and-financial fraud scheme in history. There were no discrepancies between the version of the story she revealed under interrogation in Umbria and the one she recounted for Evelyn Buchanan of *Vanity Fair*. If anything, thought Gabriel, the Pierre Hotel edition was even more captivating. So, too, was the subject herself. She came across as cosmopolitan and sophisticated and, most important, credible. Never once did she lose her composure, even when the questions turned personal.

"Why would someone with your talent become a drug dealer?"

"At first, I did it because I needed the money. And then I discovered that I enjoyed it."

"You were good at it?"

"Very."

"Are there similarities between selling drugs and forgeries?"

"More than you realize. For some people, art is like a drug. They *have* to have it. Phillip and I simply catered to their addiction."

There was a gaping hole in Magdalena's account—namely, the precise set of circumstances by which she had ended up in Italian custody. Evelyn pressed Gabriel for details, but he refused to budge from his original statement. Magdalena had been arrested after purchasing a forged Gentileschi in Florence. The painting was now in an art storage warehouse on East Ninety-First Street. In the morning it would be moved to the gallery of Phillip Somerset's town house on East Seventy-Fourth Street. And at 1:00 p.m. it would be the subject of a conversation that would provide Evelyn with all the ammunition she needed to expose Masterpiece Art Ventures as a fraud.

"Will Magdalena be wearing a wire?"

"Her phone will be acting as a transmitter. Phillip's phone is also compromised."

"I don't suppose he gave his consent to being hacked."

"I didn't ask for it."

At nine o'clock they took a break for dinner. Sarah arranged for a round of martinis to be sent up from the bar while Magdalena ordered room service from Perrine, the hotel's acclaimed restaurant. At Gabriel's suggestion, Evelyn invited her husband to join them. He arrived as the waiters were rolling the table into the suite. Tom Buchanan was affable and erudite, the very opposite of the wellborn polo player who had lived grandly on the shoreline of East Egg and fretted about the decline of the white race.

Evelyn swore her husband to secrecy, then gave him a detailed briefing on the remarkable story that had landed in her lap earlier that afternoon. Tom Buchanan took out his anger on his Caesar salad.

"Leave it to Phillip Somerset to come up with something like this. Still, one has to admire his ingenuity. He spotted a weakness and cleverly took advantage of it."

"What weakness is that?" asked Gabriel.

"The art market is totally unregulated. Prices are arbitrary, quality control is virtually nonexistent, and most paintings change hands under conditions of total secrecy. All of which makes it the perfect environment for fraud. Phillip took it to the extreme, of course."

"How is it possible that no one noticed?"

"For the same reason no one noticed that mortgage-backed securities and collateralized debt obligations were about to take down the global economy."

"Everyone is making too much money?"

Tom nodded. "And not just Phillip's investors. His bankers, too. And they're all going to suffer enormous losses when Evelyn's story appears. Nevertheless, I approve of your methods. Waiting for the Feds to act isn't an option. That said, I wish you could give my wife an incriminating document or two."

"You mean the inner-office memo in which Phillip spells out his plan to create and maintain the largest art fraud in history?"

"Point taken, Mr. Allon. But what about the documents stored in that warehouse on East Ninety-First Street?"

"Phillip's current inventory?"

"Exactly. If Magdalena can say with absolute certainty that he has forged paintings on his book, it would be devastating."

"Is the former federal prosecutor suggesting that I clandestinely acquire a comprehensive list of paintings contained in that property?"

"I wouldn't dream of it. But if you do, you should definitely give it to my wife."

Gabriel smiled. "Any other advice, counselor?"

"If I were you, I'd think about putting a bit of pressure on Phillip's finances."

"By encouraging a handful of his important investors to take redemptions, you mean?"

"It sounds to me as though you already have a plan in place," said Tom.

"There's a man in London named Nicholas Lovegrove. Nicky's one of the most sought-after art advisers in the world. Several of his clients are invested with Phillip."

"We hedge fund types get very suspicious when investors pull their money. Therefore, it needs to be handled with discretion."

"Don't worry," said Sarah. "We art dealer types are nothing if not discreet."

56

Galerie Watson

The destruction of Masterpiece Art Ventures commenced the following morning at 10:45 a.m. London time—5:45 a.m. in New York—when Christopher Keller presented himself at Galerie Olivia Watson in King Street. The small placard in the window read BY APPOINTMENT ONLY. Christopher hadn't made one, wagering that a surprise attack would prove more successful. He pressed the call button and, wincing, awaited a response.

"Well, well," breathed a sultry female voice. "Look what the cat left on my doorstep. If it isn't my dear friend Mr. Bancroft."

"It's Marlowe, remember? Now open the door."

"Sorry, but I'm all tied up at the moment."

"Untie yourself and let me in."

"I *do* love it when you beg, darling. Hold on, I can't quite seem to reach the button for the damn lock."

Several additional seconds elapsed before the deadbolt thumped and the door yielded to Christopher's touch. Inside, he found Olivia seated at a sleek black writing table in the gallery's main exhibition room. She had arranged herself with care, as though posing for an invisible camera. As usual, her chin was turned slightly to the left, the right side of her face being the one that the photographers and advertisers had preferred. Christopher had never had a favorite. Olivia was a work of art, regardless of the vantage point.

Rising, she stepped from behind the table, crossed one ankle over the other, and placed a hand on her hip. She was clad in a fashionably cut jacket and matching slim-fitting trousers, suitably summer in color and weight.

"Marks and Spencer?" asked Christopher.

"It's a little something that Giorgio threw together for me." She lifted her chin a few degrees and stared at Christopher down the straight lines of her nose. "What brings you to my corner of the neighborhood?"

"A mutual friend needs a favor."

"Which friend is that?"

"The one who cleaned up your dreadful past and allowed you to open a respectable gallery here in St. James's." Christopher paused. "A gallery filled with paintings that were purchased with your boyfriend's drug money."

"Our mutual friend performed a similar service for you, as I recall." Olivia folded her arms. "Does your adorable American wife know what you used to do for a living?"

"My adorable American wife is none of your concern."

"Is it true she used to work for the CIA?"

"Wherever did you hear a thing like that?"

"Neighborhood gossip. There's also a nasty rumor going round that I'm involved in a flaming shag-fest with Simon Mendenhall."

"I thought you were dating a pop star."

"Colin is an actor," said Olivia. "And he's currently starring in the hottest play in the West End."

"Are you two serious?"

"Quite."

"So why are you shagging sleazy Simon on the side?"

"The rumor was started by your wife," said Olivia evenly.

"I find that difficult to believe."

"She also whispers the word *bitch* every time she sees me in Wiltons."

Christopher smiled in spite of himself.

"I'm glad you think it's funny." Olivia scrutinized his clothing. "Who's dressing you these days?"

"Dicky."

"Nice."

"I'll tell him you said so."

"I'd rather you tell your adorable American wife to cease and desist." Olivia shook her head slowly. "Honestly, I can't imagine why she would stoop to something so low."

"She's a bit jealous, that's all."

"If anyone has a right to be jealous, it's me. After all, Sarah's the one who ended up with you."

"Come now, Olivia. You don't really mean that. I was just a comfortable place for you to lay your head while you found your footing here in London. Now you're dating a pop star and your gallery is all the rage."

"All because of our mutual friend?"

Christopher made no reply.

"I thought he retired," said Olivia.

"It's a private matter involving a man named Phillip Somerset."

"*The* Phillip Somerset?"

"Friend of yours?"

"I sat next to Phillip and his wife at Christie's postwar and contemporary evening sale in New York a couple of years ago. The wife did some modeling before she hit the jackpot with Phillip. Laura is her name. Or is it Linda?"

"Lindsay."

"Yes, that's it. She's quite young and unspeakably stupid. Phillip struck me as a real operator. He asked whether I wanted to invest in his fund. I told him I wasn't in his league."

"Wise move on your part."

"Is there a problem?"

"Phillip is a bit like your old boyfriend. Shiny on the outside, dirty underneath. What's more, there's a rumor going around New York that his finances are rather shaky."

"Another rumor?"

"This one happens to be true. Our mutual friend would like you to whisper it into the ear of a prominent London art adviser whose client list includes some of the richest collectors in the world."

"How do you want me to play it?"

"A casual aside over an otherwise pleasant and businesslike lunch."

"When?"

"Today."

She glanced at her watch. "But it's nearly eleven. Surely Nicky has a lunch date already."

"Something tells me he'll break it."

Olivia reached for her mobile. "I'll do it on one condition."

"I'll have a word with her," said Christopher.

"Thank you." Olivia dialed and raised the phone to her ear. "Hello, Nicky. It's Olivia Watson calling. I know it's terribly short notice, but I was wondering whether you happened to be free for lunch today . . . The Wolseley at one? See you then, Nicky."

57

The Wolseley

A nd so it began, with an apparently offhand remark, made over a costly lunch in one of Mayfair's finer dining rooms. The midday clatter of cutlery was such that Nicky leaned forward over his dressed Dorset crab appetizer and asked Olivia to repeat her statement. She did so in a confessional murmur, with the addition of a don't-quote-me-on-this disclaimer. The time was half past one o'clock. Or so claimed Julian Isherwood, who was dining well at a nearby table and noticed the ashen expression wash over Nicky's face. Julian's tubby tablemate didn't see a thing, for he was making a run at young Tessa, the newest addition to the Wolseley's waitstaff.

Nicky pressed Olivia to reveal the name of her source. And when she refused, he begged her pardon and immediately dialed Sterling Dunbar, a wealthy Manhattan real estate developer who bought paintings by the ton, always with Nicky looking over one shoulder. Sterling had been one of the first major investors in Masterpiece Art Ventures.

"Do you know my current balance?" he sniffed.

"I'm sure it's considerably larger than mine."

"A hundred and fifty million, a fivefold increase over my initial investment. Phillip assures me the fund is rock solid. Truth be told, I'm thinking about giving him another hundred."

The reactionary industrialist Max van Egan had parked $250 million at Masterpiece. He told Nicky he wasn't going anywhere. Simon Levinson—of the retailing Levinsons—was also inclined to stay put. But Ainsley Cabot, a collector of exceptional taste but only eight-figure wealth, heeded Nicky's advice. He rang Phillip at 9:15 a.m. Eastern time, as Phillip was stepping from his Sikorsky at the East Thirty-Fourth Street Heliport.

"How much?" he shouted over the whine of the rotors.

"All of it."

"Once you're out, there's no getting back in again. Do you understand me, Ainsley?"

"Spare me the bravado, Phillip, and send me my money."

Buffy Lowell reached Phillip at 9:24 a.m. as he was rolling up Third Avenue in his chauffeured Mercedes. Livingston Ford caught him eight minutes later, as he was crawling crosstown on East Seventy-Second Street. Livingston had $50 million in the fund and wanted out.

"You're going to regret this," warned Phillip.

"That's what my third wife told me, and I've never been happier."

"I'd like you to consider only a partial redemption."

"Are you suggesting there isn't enough cash in the till?"

"The money isn't sitting in an account at Citibank. I'll have to unload several paintings to make you whole."

"In that case, Phillip, I suggest you start unloading."

Which was how a seemingly offhand remark—made forty-five minutes earlier over a costly lunch in London—blew a $100 million hole in Masterpiece Art Ventures. The firm's founder, however, knew nothing of what had transpired. Desperate for information, he conducted a pair of hasty Internet searches—one for his own name, the other for the name of his firm. Neither unearthed anything that would explain why three of his largest investors had suddenly fled his fund. A search of social media likewise produced nothing damaging. Finally, at 9:42 a.m., he tapped the icon for

Telegram, the encrypted cloud-based messaging system, and opened an existing secret chat thread.

I'm bleeding to death, he typed. Find out why.

————

When Phillip Somerset purchased his town house on East Seventy-Fourth Street in 2014, $30 million was considered a great deal of money. He had obtained the loan from his banker at JPMorgan Chase using several forged paintings as collateral, just one of the ways he had waved a magic wand and turned swaths of worthless canvas into gold. Several additional forgeries adorned the interior of the mansion, all to impress prospective investors and confer upon Phillip a patina of extraordinary wealth and sophistication. They were the elite of the art world, his investors. The ones with more money than sense. Phillip was a fraud and a clever forgery himself, but his investors were the fools who had made the elaborate scheme possible. And Magdalena, he thought suddenly. It would have never worked without her.

He entered the mansion's ground-floor foyer and was greeted by Tyler Briggs, his chief of security. Tyler was an Iraq War veteran. He wore a dark suit over a gym-hardened body.

"How was the ride in from the island, Mr. Somerset?"

"Better than the drive from the heliport."

Phillip's phone was ringing again. It was Scooter Eastman, a $20 million investor.

"Any scheduled deliveries today?" asked Tyler.

"A painting is supposed to arrive from the warehouse any minute."

"Clients?"

"Not today. But Ms. Navarro is supposed to drop by around one. Send her up to my office when she arrives."

Phillip dispatched Scooter Eastman's call to his voice mail and mounted the staircase. Soledad and Gustavo Ramírez, the Peruvian couple who ran his household, were waiting on the second-floor landing. Phillip absently returned their greetings while eyeing his phone.

It was Rosamond Pierce. Midnight-blue blood. Ten million invested in Masterpiece Art Ventures.

"I'll be having lunch at home today. Ms. Navarro will be joining me. Seafood Cobb salads, please. One thirty or so."

"Yes, Mr. Somerset," replied the Ramírezes in unison.

Upstairs in his office, he listened to the new voice mails. Scooter Eastman and Rosamond Pierce both wanted out. In the span of thirty minutes, he had lost $135 million in investment money. Redemptions of that scale would threaten the most ethically run hedge fund. For a fund like Masterpiece Art Ventures, they were cataclysmic.

He relayed the news to Kenny Vaughan, the firm's chief investment officer, during their usual ten o'clock video call.

"Are you fucking kidding me?"

"I wish."

"A hundred and thirty-five million is going to hurt, Phillip."

"How long before we start to feel the pain?"

"Livingston Ford, Scooter Eastman, and Rosamond Pierce are all eligible for redemptions this month."

"Eighty million?"

"More like eighty-five."

"How much cash do we have on hand?"

"Fiftyish. Maybe."

"I could dump the Pollock."

"You owe JPMorgan sixty-five against the Pollock. Selling it isn't an option."

"How much do you need to make it work, Kenny?"

"Eighty-five would be nice."

"Be reasonable."

"Is there any chance you can lay your hands on forty?"

Phillip went to the window and watched two men in matching blue coveralls maneuvering a large rectangular crate from the back of a Chelsea Fine Arts Storage delivery truck.

"Yeah, Kenny. I think I might."

58

Pierre Hotel

Evelyn Buchanan arrived at the Pierre at half past twelve. Upstairs in Magdalena's suite, she informed Gabriel that her editors had signed off on an outline of her story. It would appear on *Vanity Fair*'s website immediately upon completion and would be included in the next print edition as well. The magazine's publicity department was putting in place a plan for a social media blitz. The *New York Times*, *Wall Street Journal*, Reuters, Bloomberg News, and CNBC had been alerted that a major story with far-reaching financial implications was forthcoming.

"Which means it will go viral within minutes of appearing on our site. There's no way Phillip will be able to contain the damage. He'll be dead before he knows what hit him."

"How soon can you publish?"

"If today goes as promised, I can have it ready by tonight."

"At the rate Phillip is going, he might not survive that long."

"Redemptions?"

"A hundred and thirty-five million and counting."

"He must be reeling."

"See for yourself."

Gabriel played a recording of Phillip's video call with Kenny Vaughan.

"How much cash do we have on hand?"

"Fiftyish. Maybe."

"I could dump the Pollock."

"You owe JPMorgan sixty-five against the Pollock. Selling it isn't an option."

Gabriel paused the recording.

"Do you realize what you have?" asked Evelyn.

"It gets better."

Gabriel clicked PLAY.

"How much do you need to make it work, Kenny?"

"Eighty-five would be nice."

"Be reasonable."

"Is there any chance you can lay your hands on forty?"

"Yeah, Kenny. I think I might."

Gabriel clicked PAUSE.

"Where is he going to get the money?"

"Unclear. But the timing would suggest he's thinking about putting my Gentileschi into play."

"If he does that—"

"We'll have irrefutable evidence that Phillip is engaged in bank fraud."

Just then the bedroom door opened and Magdalena emerged, wearing white stretch trousers, a loose-fitting blouse, and stiletto-heeled pumps.

Gabriel handed over her phone. "Keep it with you at all times. And whatever you do—"

"Where would I go without a passport, Mr. Allon? Staten Island?"

She dropped the phone into her handbag and went out. Her intoxicating scent lingered in the room after she had gone.

"Does she ever wear a bra?" asked Evelyn.

"Evidently, she forgot to pack one."

Gabriel switched the feed on the Proteus software from Phillip's device to Magdalena's. Then he rang Sarah, who was downstairs in the rented Nissan SUV.

"Don't worry," she said. "I won't let her out of my sight."

Two minutes later Sarah watched as Magdalena emerged from the East Sixty-First Street door of the Pierre and slid into the back of Phillip's waiting Mercedes S-Class limousine. The driver made three consecutive left turns and headed uptown on Madison Avenue. Sarah followed directly behind it—a violation of basic vehicle surveillance techniques, but a necessary one. The traffic was bumper-to-bumper, and Sarah had no backup other than the phone in Magdalena's handbag.

The traffic thinned at East Sixty-Sixth Street, and the Mercedes accelerated. Sarah was forced to run a pair of red lights to keep from losing it, but at East Seventy-Fifth Street she had no choice but to stop. When at last the light changed to green, the Mercedes was nowhere in sight. Two more left turns brought Sarah to the door of Phillip's town house on East Seventy-Fourth Street.

No Mercedes.

No sign of Magdalena.

Sarah drove to the end of the block and found a spot along the curb. Then she snatched up her phone and dialed Gabriel at the Pierre. "Please tell me she's inside that house."

"She's on her way upstairs."

Sarah killed the connection and smiled. Enjoy it while you can, she thought.

Tyler Briggs had instructed Magdalena to proceed directly to Phillip's fourth-floor office. Instead, she had taken a detour to the gallery. The Gentileschi was propped on a display easel. Magdalena snapped a photograph of the work with her mobile phone. Then she took two wide-angle shots that left little doubt as to the painting's current location—a room that had been described in great detail in an unflattering *Vanity Fair* profile written by the woman who was at that moment sitting in Magdalena's suite at the Pierre.

She realized suddenly that Tyler was watching her from the gallery's doorway. He must have spotted her on one of the security cameras. She reacted with the studied calm of a drug dealer.

"Extraordinary, isn't it?"

"If you say so, Ms. Navarro."

"You don't appreciate art, Tyler?"

"To be honest, I don't know much about it."

"Has Mr. Somerset seen it yet?"

"You would have to ask Mr. Somerset. In fact, he's probably wondering where you are."

Magdalena made her way upstairs. The door to Phillip's office was open. He was sitting at his desk with a phone to his ear and a palm pressed to his forehead.

"You're making a big mistake," he snapped, then killed the call.

A frigid silence settled over the room.

"Who's making a mistake?" asked Magdalena.

"Warren Ridgefield. He's one of our investors. Unfortunately, several others are making the same mistake."

"Is there anything I can do to help?"

Phillip took her by the hand and smiled.

59

Upper East Side

Phillip's shower was twice the size of the kitchen in Magdalena's old apartment in Alphabet City, an aquatic wonderland of marble and glass, the shower for the man who had everything. Magdalena could never recall which of the many brushed-chrome handles performed which function. She turned one and was blasted by water cannon on all sides. Frantically she tried another and was caressed by a gentle tropical cascade. She washed herself with Phillip's male-scented soap, dried herself with one of Phillip's monogrammed towels, and then contemplated her nude form in Phillip's gilt-framed mirror. She found the image unappealing and sorely in need of restoration. Portrait of a drug dealer, she thought. Portrait of a thief.

Portrait of an unknown woman . . .

In the master bedroom there was no sign of Phillip other than the stain he had left on the sheet. Their lovemaking had bordered on rape and had been accompanied by the constant tolling and chiming of his mobile phone. Magdalena's was tucked in her Hermès handbag, which lay at the foot of the bed, along with the clothing Phillip had ripped from her body. Aware that others were listening, she had endured his assault in muted silence. Her ravenous lover, however, had been in fine voice.

Dressed, she took up her handbag and went in search of him. She found him downstairs in the gallery, standing before the forged Gentileschi. He was wearing the expression of curatorial refinement he always donned for the benefit of his guileless investors. Phillip Somerset, patron of the arts. To Magdalena he would always be the uncultured philistine whom she had first encountered that night at Le Cirque. Bud Fox with a dash of Jay Gatsby. A forgery, she thought. And quite an obvious one at that.

"How good is it?" he asked finally.

"Better than the version at the Getty."

"Price?"

"All things being equal . . . thirty million."

"I need to unload it."

"I would advise against that, Phillip."

"Why?"

"Because the painting came from the same source as the ones that were sold by Oliver Dimbleby in London. If another picture emerges from the same so-called old European collection, it will raise red flags. The painting needs an entirely new provenance and sufficient time to cool off. We might also want to take the attribution down a notch or two."

"Attributed to Gentileschi?"

"Maybe circle of Gentileschi. Or even a follower."

"I'd be lucky to get a million for it."

"I didn't buy a painting in Florence, Phillip. I bought the greatest art forger in history. He'll pay dividends for years to come. Put the Gentileschi on ice in the warehouse and be patient."

Phillip stared at his phone. "I'm afraid patience is a virtue I can't afford at the moment."

"Who is it now?"

"Harriet Grant."

"What's going on?"

"I haven't a clue."

———————

They ate their seafood Cobb salads at the table in the kitchen, with CNBC playing softly in the background. Magdalena drank Sancerre with hers, but Phillip, parched from his bedroom exertions, guzzled iced tea. His phone lay faceup at his elbow, silenced but aglow with incoming message traffic.

"You never told me his name," he said.

"I'm afraid I can't."

"Why not?"

"Parity, I suppose. You have your forger, and now I have mine."

"But you acquired your forger with ten million dollars of my money."

"You wouldn't have any money if it wasn't for me, Phillip. Besides, I went to a great deal of trouble to find him. I think I'll keep him all to myself."

He laid down his cutlery and eyed her without expression.

"Delvecchio," she said with a sigh. "Mario Delvecchio."

"What's his story?"

"The usual one. A failed painter who takes his revenge on the art world with a palette and a brush. He lives in an isolated villa in southern Umbria. He's extraordinarily well educated and trained. And quite beautiful, I must say. We became lovers during my stay. Unlike you, he's familiar with female pleasure centers."

"Is there something else I can do for you?"

"I'd love some more of this Sancerre."

Phillip signaled Señora Ramírez. "Does your lover have any other finished works lying around?"

"None that I'm inclined to introduce to the market at this time. I've asked him to cool it on the masterpieces for a while and concentrate on mid-level works that I can move under the radar."

"What are we going to do about his partner? This Alessandro Calvi fellow?"

"Now that Mario and I are sleeping together, I think I can convince him to part company with Signore Calvi."

"You're joking, right?"

"You know there's no one but you, Phillip." She patted the back of his hand reassuringly. "The truth is, I'm more worried about he who shall not be named than I am about Signore Calvi."

"Let me worry about him."

"How will he feel about having an Old Master stablemate?"

"I never promised him exclusivity."

Magdalena raised her wineglass to her lips. "Where have I heard that one before?"

Phillip adopted a new expression—caring friend and sexual partner. It was even less authentic than Phillip the intellectual and art world sophisticate. "What's got into you?" he asked.

"Besides you, you mean?" Magdalena laughed quietly at her own witticism. "I suppose I've just been thinking about my future, that's all."

"Your future is assured."

"Is it really?"

"Have you checked your balance lately? You could retire tomorrow and spend the rest of your life lying on a beach in Ibiza."

"And if I did?"

Phillip made no reply; he was staring at his phone again.

"Who is it now?"

"Nicky Lovegrove." He sent the call to voice mail. "Several of his clients are trying to cash out of my fund."

"My money is in that fund. *All* of it."

"Your money is safe."

"You also once assured me that you were going to turn me into a Spanish Damien Hirst. But it was nothing more than a clever ploy on your part to put a little cash in my pocket."

"It wasn't a little cash, as I recall."

"Where are they?" asked Magdalena suddenly.

"The paintings?"

She nodded.

"They're in the warehouse."

"I'd like them back."

"You can't have them."

"Why not?"

"Because they belong to me. And so do you, Magdalena. Never forget that."

His phone flared.

"Not another one."

"No. It's only Lindsay."

Magdalena smiled. "Do give her my best."

———

After speaking briefly to his wife and bidding farewell to his business partner and mistress, Phillip Somerset returned to his office and rang Ellis Gray, head of art-based lending at JPMorgan Chase. Phillip and Ellis had bumped into one another in Sag Harbor over the weekend, rendering foreplay unnecessary. Phillip said he needed a bit of cash. Ellis, who had made millions dealing with Masterpiece Art Ventures, merely asked for the number Phillip had in mind and a description of the painting he intended to use as collateral.

"The number is forty million."

"And the painting?"

Phillip answered.

"A *Gentileschi* Gentileschi?" asked Ellis.

"It's newly discovered. I'm planning to keep it under wraps for a year or two before putting it on the market."

"How's the attribution?"

"Bulletproof."

"And the provenance?"

"On the thin side."

"Where did you purchase it?"

"A Spanish dealer. That's all I can say."

Ellis Gray, who made his living lending money against paintings, was well acquainted with the opacity of the art world. Nevertheless, he was not prepared to fork over $40 million of JPMorgan Chase's money on a picture without a past, even for a client as important and reliable as Phillip Somerset.

"Not without a full scientific evaluation," added Ellis. "Send it to Aiden Gallagher up in Westport. If Aiden says it's kosher, I'll expedite the loan."

Phillip killed the connection. Then he video-called Kenny Vaughan and told him that no emergency infusion of cash was in the offing.

"We might have to consider suspending redemptions."

"We can't. You have to make it work."

"I'll light a few candles and see what I can do."

Phillip dumped Kenny and accepted another call.

It was Allegra Hughes.

Allegra wanted out.

60

Pierre Hotel

Gabriel had made the request of Yuval Gershon early that morning. Yes, he realized it was an imposition and not altogether legal, as he had no official standing. And, no, he could not state with any degree of certainty that it would be the last time. It seemed he had become the first port of call for anyone with a problem, be they adulterous British prime ministers, supreme Roman pontiffs, or London art dealers. His current investigation, as was often the case, had included an attempt on his life. Yuval Gershon, of course, knew this. In fact, were it not for Yuval's timely intercession, the attempt might well have proven successful.

He gave the job to a new kid. It was no matter; in a field like theirs, the new kids were frequently better than the old hands. This one was an artist in the truest sense of the word. He made his first move at ten fifteen Eastern time, and by half past two he owned the place—the place being a Manhattan-based concern called Chelsea Fine Arts Storage.

As instructed, the kid headed straight for the database: insurance records, tax documents, personnel files, a dispatch log with a year's worth of pickups and deliveries, a master list of the paintings stored in a secure, climate-controlled warehouse on East Ninety-

First Street near York Avenue. There were 789 paintings in all. Each entry included the name of the work, the artist, the support, the dimensions, the date of execution, the estimated value, the current owner, and the painting's exact location in the warehouse, by floor and rack number.

Six hundred and fifteen of the paintings were said to be owned directly by Masterpiece Art Ventures—which also happened to own Chelsea Fine Arts Storage. The remaining works were controlled by corporate shell companies with the sort of three-letter uppercase abbreviations beloved by asset concealers and kleptocrats the world over. The most recent arrival was *Danaë and the Shower of Gold*, purportedly by Orazio Gentileschi. The stated value of the work was $30 million, which was approximately $30 million more than what it was actually worth. As yet, the work was uninsured.

The warehouse also contained sixteen canvases by a once promising Spanish artist named Magdalena Navarro. At three fifteen that afternoon—following an incriminating luncheon with one Phillip Somerset, founder and CEO of Masterpiece Art Ventures—she returned to the Pierre Hotel. Upstairs in her suite she immediately surrendered her phone to Gabriel. He gave her a list of 789 paintings, and they went to work.

———

They fell into a predictable if altogether depressing rhythm. Magdalena would cast her eye down the list and call out when she spotted a painting she knew to be a forgery. Then, with Sarah and Evelyn Buchanan taking careful notes, she would recite the date and circumstances by which the work had found its way into the inventory of Masterpiece Art Ventures. The overwhelming majority of the canvases had been acquired through phantom sales conducted within Magdalena's distribution network, which meant no actual money had changed hands. But several had been routed through reputable dealers to provide Phillip with plausible deniability in the event the authenticity of the works was ever called into question.

Notably absent from the directory was Sir Anthony van Dyck's *Portrait of an Unknown Woman*, oil on canvas, 115 by 92 centimeters, which Masterpiece had recently purchased from Isherwood Fine Arts. According to the dispatch logs, the painting was moved to Sotheby's in New York in mid-April.

"A week after the bombing in Paris," Gabriel pointed out.

"Phillip must have unloaded it," replied Magdalena. "Which means some unsuspecting collector is now the proud owner of a worthless painting."

"I'll have a word with Sotheby's tomorrow morning."

"A quiet word," cautioned Sarah.

"Somehow," said Gabriel with a glance at Evelyn, "I don't think that's going to be an option."

By 5:00 p.m. they had twice scoured the list from top to bottom. The final tally was a breathtaking 227 forgeries with a declared valuation of more than $300 million, or 25 percent of Masterpiece's purported assets under management. When combined with the rest of the evidence that Gabriel and Magdalena had acquired in New York—including a recording of an attempt by Phillip Somerset to obtain an art-backed loan from JPMorgan Chase using a forged painting as collateral—it was irrefutable proof that Masterpiece Art Ventures was a criminal enterprise run by one of the greatest financial con artists in history.

At the conclusion of the review, Evelyn rang her editor at *Vanity Fair*'s Fulton Street headquarters and told him to expect her finished draft no later than 9:00 p.m. Then she sat down at her laptop and began to write.

"At some point," she informed Gabriel, "I'll have to ask Phillip for a comment."

Fortunately, they knew how to reach him. According to Proteus, his phone was presently near the corner of Fifth Avenue and East

Seventy-Fourth Street, 134 feet above sea level. There were six missed calls, three new voice mails, and twenty-two unread text messages. The camera was staring at the ceiling. The microphone was listening to nothing at all. The damn thing was just sitting there, thought Gabriel. Like a paperweight with a digital pulse.

61

Sutton Place

Leonard Silk was well acquainted with the dark side of human nature. His clients, all of whom were sufficiently wealthy to afford his services, were a rogues' gallery of fraudsters, schemers, scammers, larcenists, embezzlers, insider traders, philanderers, and sexual deviants of every stripe. Silk never sat in judgment of them, for Silk was not without sin himself. He dwelled in a proverbial house of glass. He did not make a habit of throwing stones.

Silk's fall from grace had occurred in the late 1980s while he was serving in the CIA's station in Bogotá. Recently divorced, his personal finances under duress, he had entered into a lucrative partnership with the Medellín cocaine cartel. Silk had supplied the drug lords with valuable intelligence on DEA and Colombian efforts to penetrate their organization. In return, the drug lords had supplied Silk with money—$20 million in cash, all of it derived from selling cocaine in the country he was sworn to defend.

Somehow Silk managed to extricate himself from the relationship with both his ill-gotten fortune and his life, and retired from the Agency just days before the attacks of 9/11. He used a portion of the funds to purchase a luxury Sutton Place apartment. And in the winter of 2002, while his old colleagues were fighting the opening battle of the global war on terrorism, Silk went into business as a security consultant and private investigator. In a deliberate play on words, he called his one-man firm Integrity Security Solutions.

Silk offered his clients the usual array of advisory services but derived most of his income through illicit activities such as corporate espionage, computer hacking, blackmail, sabotage, and a product he euphemistically referred to as "reputational defense." He was renowned for his ability to make problems go away, or, whenever possible, to prevent problems from arising in the first place. He also possessed the capability, as a last resort, to make "problems" suffer fatal auto accidents or drug overdoses, or vanish without a trace. He had no operatives on his payroll. Instead, he hired freelance professionals as needed. Two recent operations had taken place in France, where Silk was well connected. Both had been carried out at the behest of the same client.

At 9:42 that morning, the client had asked Silk to ascertain why several investors had requested multimillion-dollar redemptions from his art-based hedge fund. With a few phone calls to his network of paid or coerced informants, Silk had discovered a possible explanation. It was not the sort of matter he liked to discuss over the phone, so he summoned his driver and headed uptown. Arriving at the client's residence on East Seventy-Fourth Street, Silk saw two workmen maneuvering a crated painting into the back of a delivery truck. A security man named Tyler Briggs was observing their efforts from the open doorway.

"Where's your boss?" asked Silk.

"Upstairs in his office."

"Is he alone?"

"He is now. He had company earlier."

"Anyone interesting?"

Briggs ushered Silk into the mansion's security control room. The art-filled residence was protected by an array of high-resolution cameras. At present, one was trained on Silk's client. He was sitting at his desk, a phone to his ear. He looked unwell.

Briggs sat down at a computer and wordlessly entered a few keystrokes. A moment later a tall, dark-haired woman appeared on one of the video screens. She was standing before a painting in the gallery. A Gentileschi, thought Silk. Quite stunning, but almost certainly a forgery.

"Why is she photographing it?"

"I didn't ask."

"Where did she go next?"

The security man played the recording.

"That's quite enough," said Silk after a moment.

The image froze.

"Walk upstairs to Mr. Somerset's office and quietly tell him to meet me in the garden."

The security man rose and started toward the door.

"One more thing, Tyler."

"Yes, Mr. Silk?"

"Tell Mr. Somerset to leave his phone behind."

Silk followed a corridor toward the back of the town house—past the wine cellar, the movie theater, and the yoga studio—and emerged into the walled garden. It was shaded by a large tree in midsummer leaf and overlooked on the north and east by elderly apartment buildings. Decorator outdoor furnishings stood forlornly on the spotless stonework. The splashing of the Italianate fountain silenced the rush of afternoon traffic on Fifth Avenue.

Five minutes elapsed before Phillip Somerset finally appeared. As usual, he was nautically attired. They sat down in a pair of low-slung wicker chairs. Silk delivered his findings without preamble or pleasantries. He was a busy man, and Phillip Somerset was in serious trouble.

"How bad is it going to be?"

"My sources haven't been able to uncover anything regarding the content."

"Isn't that exactly the sort of information I pay you for, Leonard?"

"The magazine's publicity department has contacted every business news desk in the city. They wouldn't have done that unless she had something big."

"Is it fatal?"

"Could be."

"And you're sure the story is about me?"

Silk nodded.

"Is the FBI involved?"

"My sources say not."

"So where is it coming from? And why did several of my investors choose today of all days to flee the fund?"

"It's possible that rumors are swirling in the art world about a damaging story in the works. But the more likely explanation is that you are under a coordinated attack by a determined and resourceful adversary."

"Any candidates?"

"Only one."

Silk didn't speak the name; it wasn't necessary. He had opposed targeting a man like Gabriel Allon but had relented when Phillip offered him a payment of $10 million. Silk had given a substantial portion of that money to a French organization known only as the Groupe, the same organization that had handled the Valerie Bérrangar job. He had also supplied the Groupe detailed information regarding Allon's travel plans—specifically, his intention to pay a visit to an art gallery on the rue la Boétie in Paris. Even so, the Israeli and his friend Sarah Bancroft had managed to escape the gallery alive.

"You assured me that Allon was no longer an issue," said Phillip.

"The video of Ms. Navarro's arrival here earlier this afternoon would suggest otherwise."

Phillip frowned. "Is Tyler Briggs on your payroll or mine, Leonard?"

Silk ignored the question. "She took several photographs of the painting that was on display in the gallery. Close-ups and wide shots. Looked to me as though she was trying to establish its location."

Phillip's expression darkened, but he said nothing.

"Did the two of you discuss business after you were finished in the bedroom?"

"In detail," answered Phillip.

"Was your phone with you?"

"Yes, of course."

"Where was hers?"

"I assume it was in her handbag."

"It was probably recording every word you said. You should assume your phone is probably compromised, too."

Phillip swore softly.

"I'm afraid to ask."

"I had two rather candid calls with Kenny Vaughan. I also tried to obtain an art-backed loan from Ellis Gray of JPMorgan Chase."

"Because several of your largest investors just happened to withdraw from your fund on the very day that Ms. Navarro was in your home taking pictures of a painting."

Phillip clambered to his feet.

"Sit down," said Silk calmly. "You're not going anywhere near her."

"You work for *me*, Leonard."

"Which is not something I'd like the FBI to know. Or Gabriel Allon, for that matter. Therefore, you will do exactly what I tell you to do."

Phillip managed a smile. "Did you just threaten me?"

"Only amateurs make threats. And I'm no amateur."

Phillip lowered himself into his chair.

"Where is she staying?" asked Silk.

"Her usual suite at the Pierre."

"I think I'll check in on her. In the meantime, I'd like you to go upstairs and pack a bag."

"Where am I going?"

"To be determined."

"If I leave the country now—"

"Your remaining investors will head for the lifeboats, and your fund will collapse within hours. The question is, do you want to be in New York when that happens? Or would you rather be lying on a beach with Lindsay?"

Phillip gave no answer.

"How much cash is on hand?" asked Silk.

"Not much."

"In that case, now might be a good time for you to settle your bill with Integrity Security Solutions." Silk handed over a phone. "Your outstanding balance is fifteen million."

"Rather steep, don't you think?"

"Now is not the time to quibble over money, Phillip. I'm the only thing standing between you and a cell in the Metropolitan Correctional Center."

Phillip dialed Kenny Vaughn and instructed him to wire $15 million into Silk's account at Oceanic Bank and Trust Ltd. in Nassau. "I know, Kenny. Just do whatever you need to do."

Phillip killed the call and tried to return the phone.

"Keep it," said Silk. "Leave your personal phone on the desk connected to a charger and go to your place on the island. Don't make a move until you hear from me."

62

Pierre Hotel

During the thirteen-block ride from Phillip Somerset's town house to the Pierre Hotel, Leonard Silk made a series of hurried phone calls. The first was to Executive Jet Services at MacArthur Airport on Long Island; the second, to a man who had run guns to the Contras and cocaine for the cartels. Lastly, Silk called an old friend from the Agency named Martin Roth. Marty was a supplier of cyber-and-surveillance specialists and, if circumstances warranted, muscle and firepower. His private security business was based in a warehouse in Greenpoint. Silk was a regular customer.

"When do you need them?" asked Marty.

"Twenty minutes ago."

"The traffic in Midtown is a bitch. And I'm stretched pretty thin as it is."

"Do what you can," said Silk as his Escalade drew to a stop outside the Pierre's Fifth Avenue entrance. "My client will be grateful. And so will I."

Inside, the hostess in the Two E Bar & Lounge greeted Silk by name and showed him to a corner table. A glass of single malt appeared a moment later, followed soon after by Ray Bennett, a retired NYPD detective who now served as the Pierre's director of security. Nothing happened inside the hotel's walls that escaped Bennett's notice, which is why Silk paid him a substantial monthly retainer.

Bennett wasn't alone. There were others like him at every high-end hotel in town, all feeding Silk a steady stream of dirt, most of it accompanied by receipts and security video. Information about the private lives of reporters was a priority. Bennett had once given Silk the means to kill a *New York* magazine exposé about one of his most important clients. Silk had rewarded his asset with a $25,000 bonus, enough to take the financial sting out of his divorce settlement and pay for his kid's tuition at Holy Rosary.

Hotel regulations forbade Bennett to sit down with a customer, so he remained on his feet while Silk made his request. "There's a woman staying in a suite on the twentieth floor. She's acquainted with an important client of mine. The client is concerned she might be in danger."

"What's her name?"

"She checked in under Miranda Álvarez. Her real name is—"

"Magdalena Navarro. She's a regular."

"Have you noticed anything unusual?"

"Unless I'm mistaken, she's only set foot outside the hotel once since she arrived."

"What's she been doing with herself?"

"She had a dinner party last night."

"Really? With whom?"

"Her friends from across the hall. They checked in at the same time. False names. Just like Ms. Navarro."

"I need their real names," said Silk.

"How badly?"

"Ten thousand."

"Twenty."

"Done," said Silk.

———

Ray Bennett returned to his office, closed the door, and sat down at his computer. As director of security, he had unlimited access to guest information, regardless of their demands for privacy. He called Leonard Silk a moment later and read him the names.

"Sarah Bancroft and Gabriel Allon."

Bennett's iPhone pinged with a text message.

"Look at the photograph I just sent you," said Silk.

Bennett enlarged the image.

"Recognize her?"

"She's that reporter from *Vanity Fair*."

"Has she been in Ms. Navarro's suite?"

"I believe she's there now."

"Thanks, Ray. The check's in the mail."

The connection died.

Bennett looked at the two names on his computer screen. One of them was familiar. *Gabriel Allon* . . . Bennett was certain he had seen it before. But where?

Google gave him the answer.

"Shit," he said softly.

———

Outside, Leonard Silk slid into the back of his Escalade and dialed the burner phone he had given to Phillip.

"Did you speak to her?" he asked.

"I couldn't. She's rather busy at the moment."

"Doing what?"

"Telling Evelyn Buchanan everything she knows about Masterpiece Art Ventures. Gabriel Allon and your friend Sarah Bancroft are with her. It's over, Phillip. Your charter leaves MacArthur at ten fifteen. Don't be late."

"Maybe I should take the Gulfstream instead."

"The point of this operation is to get you and Lindsay out of the country without leaving any footprints. When you arrive in Miami, a car will run you down to Key West. By the time the sun rises, you'll be halfway to the Yucatán Peninsula."

"What about you, Leonard?"

"That depends on whether you ever mentioned my name to your friend from Seville."

"Don't worry, she can't implicate you in anything."

Silk heard a chorus of car horns through the phone. "Why aren't you on the chopper yet?"

"Second Avenue is jammed."

"You won't have to worry about traffic where you're going."

Silk hung up the phone and lifted his gaze toward the upper floors of the hotel. *She can't implicate you . . .* Perhaps not, but Silk wasn't prepared to take that chance.

He rang Ray Bennett.

"I have another assignment, if you're interested."

"I'm listening."

Silk explained.

"How much?" asked Bennett.

"Fifty thousand."

"To go up against a man like Gabriel Allon? Get real, Leonard."

"How about seventy-five?"

"A hundred."

"Done," said Silk.

63

North Haven

Alone in the vast, empty house in North Haven, Lindsay Somerset sat in a simple cross-legged pose, her hands resting lightly on her knees. The floor-to-ceiling window before her overlooked the copper waters of Peconic Bay. Ordinarily the panorama filled her with a sense of contentment, but not now. She could find no inner peace, no *shanti*.

Her phone lay on the floor next to her mat, silenced, aglow with an incoming call. She didn't recognize the number, so she tapped DECLINE. Instantly the phone rang a second time, and once again Lindsay terminated the call. After two additional attempts to fend off the intruder, she lifted the device angrily to her ear.

"What the hell do you want?"

"I was hoping to have a word with my wife."

"Sorry, Phillip. I didn't recognize the number. Whose phone are you using?"

"I'll explain when I get there."

"I thought you were staying in the city tonight."

"Change in plan. We're scheduled to land at East Hampton at six forty-five."

"Wonderful news. Shall I make a dinner reservation?"

"I don't think I can face the mob scene tonight. Let's pick up something on the way home."

"Lulu?"

"Perfect."

"Any requests?"

"Surprise me."

"Is something wrong, Phillip? You sound down."

"Rough day. That's all."

Lindsay hung up the phone and, rising, pulled on a pair of Nikes and a Lululemon half-zip hoodie. Then she headed downstairs to the great room. *Rothko, Pollock, Warhol, Basquiat, Lichtenstein, Diebenkorn . . .* Nearly a half-billion dollars' worth of paintings, all controlled by Masterpiece Art Ventures. Phillip had carefully shielded Lindsay from the company's affairs, and her knowledge of how it functioned was limited to the basics. Phillip purchased paintings shrewdly and sold them at an immense profit. He kept a portion of those profits for himself and passed the rest on to his investors. Banks were eager to lend him capital because he never missed a payment and used his inventory as collateral. The loans allowed him to buy still more art, which produced still greater returns for his investors. Most saw the paper valuation of their accounts double in just three years. Few ever withdrew their money. Masterpiece was too sweet a deal.

Lindsay contemplated the Basquiat. She had been at Phillip's side the night he purchased it at Christie's for $75 million. In fact, it was their first real date. Afterward, he had taken her to Bar SixtyFive at the Rainbow Room to celebrate the acquisition with his employees. They were a small team—three ponytailed young women with sensible shoes and Ivy League educations, and a guy named Kenny Vaughan who had worked with Phillip at Lehman Brothers. There was also a tall, beautiful Spanish woman named Magdalena Navarro. Phillip said she worked as a scout and broker for Masterpiece in Europe.

"Are you still sleeping with her?" Lindsay had asked during the drive to Phillip's town house.

"With Magdalena? Not anymore."

Lindsay posed the same question when Phillip proposed marriage—and when he insisted that she sign a prenuptial agreement guaranteeing her a payment of $10 million were they ever to divorce. In neither instance did she believe Phillip's denial. More troubling was her deeply held conviction that her husband and Magdalena remained lovers to this day. The sexual bond they shared was obvious in their every gesture and expression. Lindsay wasn't blind. And she wasn't as dumb as they thought she was.

I'll explain when I get there . . .

The sensation of disharmony returned. Whether it was their marriage or Phillip's business, Lindsay could not say. But something was amiss, off-kilter. She was certain of it.

Outside, she climbed behind the wheel of her white Range Rover and headed up the drive. As she passed the staff cottage, a security guard gave her a perfunctory wave and opened the gate. She turned left into Actors Colony Road, then dialed Lulu Kitchen & Bar in Sag Harbor. She greeted the hostess by name and placed her order: fried calamari, grilled octopus, two Bibb lettuce salads, grilled halibut, and a skirt steak. Phillip's credit card was on file, so there was no discussion of payment or even the size of the bill.

"Is seven fifteen all right, Mrs. Somerset? We're a bit busy tonight."

"Seven would be better."

She followed Route 114 down the length of the peninsula and into downtown Sag Harbor. The airport lay about four miles south of the village, on Daniels Hole Road. Once owned and operated by the town of East Hampton, it was now a fully private airfield that catered to people like the Somersets of North Haven. Phillip's Sikorsky was dropping from the clear evening sky as Lindsay turned through the entrance. The security guard allowed her to drive onto the tarmac, thus sparing Mr. Somerset the indignity of having to walk to the parking lot.

He settled into the passenger seat of the Range Rover while the ground staff loaded two large aluminum-sided Rimowa suitcases into the back. Both bags appeared to be unusually heavy.

"Dumbbells?" asked Lindsay as she kissed Phillip's lips.

"One contains two million dollars in cash. The other is filled with five-hundred-gram gold ingots."

"Why?"

"Because I'm not the man you think I am," said Phillip. "And I'm in trouble."

64

Pierre Hotel

Shortly before taking over day-to-day management of Isherwood Fine Arts, Sarah Bancroft had endured a brutal interrogation at the hands of a senior Russian intelligence officer, during which she was threatened with a deadly radiological toxin. Watching Evelyn Buchanan write her article was only slightly less torturous. Sarah offered guidance where she could, but mainly she kept her head down and tried to stay out of the line of fire, most of which was directed at Gabriel. No, he said time and time again, he had no desire to see his name included in the story. Ground rules were ground rules. There was no going back at the last minute.

"In that case," said Evelyn, "I have a few more questions I'd like to ask Magdalena."

"About what?"

"Oliver Dimbleby."

"Who?"

"Magdalena mentioned his name when she and Phillip were discussing your Gentileschi."

"Did she? I wasn't listening at the time."

"She also implied that all those newly discovered paintings were forgeries."

"That's because they were."

"Who painted them?"

"Who do you think?"

"Why?"

"To lure Magdalena into the open."

"Did anyone actually *buy* them?"

"Goodness, no. That would have been unethical."

"Please tell me the rest of the story."

"Finish the one in front of you, Evelyn. Your editor is expecting your first draft at nine o'clock."

By half past six Sarah could take no more. Rising, she announced her intention to go downstairs for a proper Belvedere martini. Magdalena requested permission to join her.

"Permission denied."

"If I was going to flee, I would have done it this afternoon while I was with Phillip. Besides, we had a deal, Mr. Allon."

She had a point. "One drink only," he said. "And no phone or passport."

"Two drinks," countered Sarah. Then she turned to Magdalena. "I'll meet you at the elevators in five minutes."

"Ten would be better."

Sarah headed to her room to freshen up. Magdalena did the same, leaving Gabriel alone with Evelyn.

"I'd like to ask you a few more questions."

"I'm sure you would," replied Gabriel absently. Then he checked the feed from Phillip Somerset's phone. The device had not moved in more than three hours. Fourteen missed calls, eight new voice mails, thirty-seven unread text messages.

No images.

No audio.

No Phillip.

When it was over, there was near-universal agreement that it was all Christopher's fault. He rang Sarah from London as she was entering her room and kept her on the phone while she stripped off her wrinkled clothing and changed into something more appropriate. Putting her hair and makeup in order proved more of a challenge than she had imagined it would, placing her at the elevators two minutes behind schedule. Arriving, she breathed a sigh of relief. It seemed her new friend from Spain was running late as well.

But when three additional minutes elapsed with no sign of Magdalena, Sarah grew anxious. Her fear of impending disaster worsened when a press of the call button produced a glowing light but no carriage. Frantic, she snatched up the receiver of the house phone, explained her plight to the hotel operator, and was assured she would momentarily be lobby bound.

At last a carriage appeared. It stopped on a half-dozen floors, collecting a menagerie of annoyed hotel guests, before finally reaching the lobby. Sarah made straight for the bar, but Magdalena was nowhere to be found. She asked a waiter whether he had seen a tall, black-haired woman, approximately forty years old, quite beautiful. Unfortunately, said the waiter, he had not.

Sarah received a similar answer from the girl at Reception. And from the dark-suited security man standing nearby. And from the porters and valets at both of the hotel's entrances.

Finally she dialed Gabriel's number. "Please tell me that Magdalena is still upstairs with you."

"She left fifteen minutes ago."

Sarah's shouted obscenity reverberated through the Pierre's grand lobby. She had turned her back on Magdalena. And now she was gone.

65

Midtown

Magdalena had recognized the man who greeted her elevator. She saw him each time she stayed at the Pierre. He was the hotel's head of security. A big guy with an Irish face and an outer boroughs accent. In her previous life, Magdalena would have avoided a man like him. It was obvious the guy was a cop. Retired, sure. But a cop all the same.

On that evening, however, the former police officer whose name Magdalena did not know had presented himself as her guardian. Quietly, his voice calm and assured, he had asked Magdalena whether she was expecting any visitors. And when she replied that she wasn't, he informed her that he had noticed two men loitering outside her suite earlier that afternoon. The same two men, he explained, were now drinking club soda in the lobby bar. It was his considered opinion that both were federal law enforcement agents.

"FBI?"

"Probably. And I think there might be a couple more outside."

"Can you get me out of here?"

"That depends on what you've done."

"I trusted someone I shouldn't have."

"I've done that once or twice myself." He looked her up and down. "Do you need anything from your suite?"

"I can't go back."

"Why not?"

"Because the man I trusted is there now."

With that, he took her by the arm and led her through a doorway. It opened onto a hallway lined with small offices, which in turn gave onto the hotel's loading bay. A black Escalade idled curbside on East Sixty-First Street.

"He's waiting for another guest. It's yours if you want it."

"I don't have any way to pay him."

"I know the driver. I'll take care of it."

The big former cop with an Irish face escorted Magdalena across the sidewalk and opened the rear driver's-side door. Seated in the back was a gray man in a gray suit. The former cop forced Magdalena inside and slammed the door. The Escalade lurched forward and made a left turn onto Fifth Avenue.

The gray man in the gray suit watched Magdalena without expression as she clawed at the door latch. Finally she capitulated and turned to face him. "Who are you?"

"I'm the man who makes Phillip's problems go away," he answered. "And you, Ms. Navarro, are a problem."

———

The driver had a neck like a fire hydrant and stubble-length hair. At the corner of East Fifty-Ninth Street and Park Avenue, Magdalena politely asked him to unlock her door. Receiving no response, she appealed to the gray man in the gray suit, who told her to shut her mouth. Furious, she tried to gouge his eyes from their sockets. Her attack ended when he seized her right wrist and twisted it to the breaking point.

"Are you finished?"

"Yes."

He increased the pain. "Are you sure?"

"I promise."

He reduced the pressure, but only slightly. "Why are you in New York?"

"I was arrested."

"Where?"

"Italy."

"How is Allon involved?"

"He was working with the Italian police."

"I assume you made a deal?"

"Doesn't everyone?"

"What were the terms?"

"He promised me that I wouldn't face charges if I helped him take down Phillip."

"And you fell for this nonsense?"

"He gave me his word."

"He used you, Ms. Navarro. And you can be sure that he was planning to hand you over to the FBI the minute he no longer needed you."

Magdalena tore her wrist from his grasp and retreated to the edge of the seat. They were inching across the intersection of East Fifty-Ninth Street and Third Avenue. On the other side of her blacked-out window was a traffic officer, arm raised. If Magdalena were successful in getting the officer's attention, she might extricate herself from her current circumstances. But she would also set in motion a chain of events that would lead inevitably to her incarceration. It was better, she reasoned, to take her chances with the solver of Phillip's problems.

"How much does Allon know?" he asked.

"Everything."

"And the reporter?"

"More than enough."

"When will the article appear?"

"Later tonight. Masterpiece will be toast by the morning."

"Will the story include my name?"

"How could it? I don't know your name."

"Phillip never whispered it into your ear while you were—"

"Fuck you, you bastard."

The blow came without warning, a lightning-fast backhand. Magdalena tasted blood.

"How chivalrous. There's nothing quite so attractive as a man who strikes a defenseless woman."

His phone rang before he could pose another question. He raised the device to his ear and listened in silence. Finally he said, "Thanks, Marty. Let me know if Allon makes a move." Then he returned the phone to his coat pocket and looked at Magdalena. "Evidently, Evelyn Buchanan's computer is about to have a serious malfunction."

"It won't stop the article."

"Perhaps not. But it will give you and Phillip plenty of time to get out of the country before the FBI issues warrants for your arrest."

"I'm not going anywhere with him."

"The alternative is a shallow grave in the Adirondacks."

Magdalena said nothing.

"Wise choice, Ms. Navarro."

66

Sag Harbor

Lindsay insisted on stopping in downtown Sag Harbor to pick up the food at Lulu. Phillip thought it an act of madness, like the suicide who slips into her wedding gown before swallowing an overdose of sleeping tablets. Now, as he stood at the end of the restaurant's handsome bar awaiting their order, he was relieved to have a moment to himself.

The din of the room was pleasant and midsummer in volume. Phillip's present circumstances notwithstanding, it had been a good day on Wall Street. Money had been made. He shook a few of the better hands, rubbed a couple of important shoulders, and acknowledged the discreet nod of a respected collector who had recently purchased a painting from Masterpiece Art Ventures for $4.5 million. In a few hours' time, the collector would learn that the painting was doubtless a forgery. In an attempt to conceal his embarrassment over being duped, he would assure his closest friends and business associates that he had always known that Phillip Somerset was a con artist and swindler. The collector would likely receive no restitution, as the available assets of Masterpiece Art Ventures would be limited and the line of claimants long. The talented Mr. Somerset would be unable to offer assistance to the authorities, for his whereabouts would be unknown.

Lulu Kitchen & Bar on Main Street in Sag Harbor would be among the last places anyone would recall laying eyes on him.

He felt a hand on his elbow and, turning, found himself gazing into the terrier-like eyes of Edgar Malone. Edgar lived well on the fortune left to him by his grandfather, a substantial portion of which he had unwisely entrusted to Masterpiece Art Ventures.

"I hear you lost several investors today," he announced.

"All of whom profited handsomely from their association with my fund."

"Should I be worried?"

"Do I look worried to you, Edgar?"

"You don't. That said, I'd like to take some of my money off the table."

"Sleep on it. Call me in the morning with your decision."

The hostess informed Phillip that his order was delayed and offered him a glass of complimentary wine as recompense, as he was a valued customer and a prominent member of East End society—at least for a few more hours. He declined the glass of wine but accepted an incoming call to his burner phone.

"Send your helicopter back to Manhattan immediately," said Leonard Silk.

"Why?"

"To pick up the final member of your traveling party."

"Anyone I know?"

"Call your crew," said Silk. "Get that bird back to Manhattan."

———

Five minutes later, bags in hand, Phillip stepped from the restaurant's doorway into the warm evening air. He placed the food in the back of the Range Rover and settled into the passenger seat. Lindsay reversed out of the space without so much as a glance in the rearview mirror. Tires screeched, a horn blared. Phillip supposed it would one day be a part of the lore surrounding his disappearance—

the near-collision on Main Street in Sag Harbor. Much would be made of the fact that Lindsay had been the one behind the wheel.

She jammed the transmission into DRIVE, and the Range Rover shot forward. "Explain how it worked," she demanded.

"There isn't time. Besides, you couldn't possibly understand."

"Because I'm not smart enough?"

Phillip reached for her, but she recoiled. She was driving dangerously fast.

"Tell me!" she screamed.

"In the beginning, it was a way to generate the extra cash that I needed to show a profit to my investors. But as time went on, buying and selling forgeries became my business model. If I had stopped, the fund would have collapsed."

"Because your so-called fund was nothing but a glorified Ponzi scheme?"

"No, Lindsay. It was a real Ponzi scheme. And a very lucrative one at that."

And it would have gone on forever, thought Phillip, if it wasn't for a Frenchwoman named Valerie Bérrangar. She wrote a letter to Julian Isherwood about *Portrait of an Unknown Woman*. And Isherwood asked none other than the great Gabriel Allon to investigate. Phillip might have been able to outwit the FBI, but Allon was a far more formidable adversary—a gifted art restorer who also happened to be a retired intelligence officer. What were the odds? It had been a mistake to let him leave New York alive.

Lindsay ignored the stop sign at the end of Main Street and swerved onto Route 114. Phillip seized his armrest as they flew across the narrow two-lane bridge separating Sag Harbor from North Haven.

"You really need to slow down."

"I thought you have a plane to catch."

"We both do." Phillip released his death grip on the armrest. "It leaves from MacArthur at ten fifteen."

"Bound for where?"

"Miami."

"I know I'm not as smart as you are, Phillip, but I'm fairly certain Miami is part of the United States."

"It's only the first stop."

"And after Miami?"

"A beautiful home overlooking the ocean in Ecuador."

"I thought rich criminals like you and Bobby Axelrod went to Switzerland to avoid arrest."

"Only in the movies, Lindsay. We'll have new identities and plenty of money. No one will ever find us."

She laughed bitterly. "I'm not going anywhere with you, Phillip."

"Do you know what will happen if you stay behind? The minute the fund collapses, the FBI will seize the houses and the paintings and freeze all the bank accounts. You'll be an outcast. Your life will be ruined. And no one will ever believe that you didn't know your husband was a criminal."

"They will if I turn you in."

Phillip unplugged Lindsay's phone from its charger and slipped it into his coat pocket.

"Surely you didn't do this all on your own," she said.

"Kenny Vaughan was the one who made the numbers work."

"What about Magdalena?"

"She ran sales and distribution."

"Where is she now?"

"On her way to the Thirty-Fourth Street Heliport."

Lindsay pressed the accelerator to the floor.

"If you don't slow down," said Phillip, "you're going to kill someone."

"Maybe I'll kill *you*."

"Not if I kill you first, Lindsay."

Pierre Hotel

When Magdalena left her suite on the twentieth floor of the Pierre Hotel for the last time, she was clad in the same dark pantsuit she had been wearing the night she plucked Oliver Dimbleby from the pavements of Bury Street in London. She had her Spanish driver's permit and a single twenty-dollar bill, but no phone or passport. And no handbag, either. It was lying at the foot of her unmade bed, next to a Spanish-language copy of *Love in the Time of Cholera*. It was, in Gabriel's opinion, the clearest evidence of her intent. Of his many female friends and acquaintances, not one would take flight without a purse. Therefore, he was confident that there was some other explanation for Magdalena's sudden disappearance. An explanation that in all likelihood involved Phillip Somerset and Leonard Silk.

Whatever had happened, the hotel's surveillance cameras had been watching. Gabriel rang Yuval Gershon, explained the situation, and asked him to have a look at the recordings. Yuval suggested that Gabriel have a word with hotel security instead.

"I have a terrible feeling hotel security was involved."

"What makes you think that?"

"The elevators mysteriously froze around the time she went missing."

"Describe her."

"Tall, long dark hair, dark pantsuit, no handbag."

"It looks to me as though you're on the nineteenth floor."

"Twentieth, Yuval."

"I'll get back to you when I have something."

Gabriel rang off. Sarah was anxiously pacing the room. Evelyn Buchanan was staring at her laptop with the shocked expression of someone who had just witnessed a murder.

"Is something wrong?" asked Gabriel.

"My article just disappeared from my screen." Evelyn dragged a forefinger across her trackpad. "And my documents folder is empty. All of my work, including my notes and the transcript of my interview with Magdalena, is gone."

Gabriel quickly disconnected his computer from the hotel's Wi-Fi network and instructed Evelyn to do the same. "How long will it take you to retype the piece?"

"It's not a matter of simply retyping it. I have to rewrite it from beginning to end. Five thousand words. Entirely from memory."

"Then I suggest you get started." Gabriel snatched up his phone and looked at Sarah. "Double-lock the door, and don't open it for anyone but me."

He went into the corridor without another word and headed for the elevators. An empty carriage appeared at once. He rode it down to the lobby and left the hotel via the Fifth Avenue entrance.

Outside, the sun had dropped below the trees of Central Park, but the twilight was abundant. Gabriel turned to the left and then made another left onto East Sixtieth Street. As he passed the entrance of the fabled Metropolitan Club, the private playground of New York's financial elite, he spotted two men sitting in a parked Suburban. Both were wearing earpieces. The one behind the wheel noticed Gabriel first. He said something to his partner, who turned his head to have a look at the legend as well.

The legend rounded the corner onto Madison Avenue and walked to East Sixty-First Street. The second team was parked directly opposite the Pierre's delivery entrance. They were three in number—the third member being the hacker who had penetrated the Pierre's Wi-Fi network and sucked the documents off Evelyn's laptop.

Gabriel was tempted to ask the hacker to return the purloined material. Instead, he crossed Fifth Avenue and entered Central Park. There he sat down on a bench and waited for his phone to ring, wondering, not for the first time, how his life had come to this.

———

Though Gabriel did not know it, Magdalena was at that moment pondering the same question. She was seated not on a park bench but in the back of a luxury SUV, next to a man who a few minutes earlier had threatened to kill her if she did not agree to flee the country with the financier whose art-based hedge fund she had exposed as a fraud. She had been given no information regarding their destination, though her lack of a passport suggested that their journey would be unconventional. It would begin, apparently, with a helicopter flight, as they were parked beneath the FDR Drive, near the pale-gray, boxlike terminal of the East Thirty-Fourth Street Heliport.

Magdalena glanced at her wristwatch, the Cartier tank that Clarissa the personal shopper had chosen for her at Bergdorf Goodman that frigid December afternoon in 2008. What a waste, she thought suddenly, these costly trinkets. Art was all that mattered— art and books and music. And family, of course. It had been a mistake to involve her father in Phillip's fraud. Still, she was confident he would not be prosecuted. Art criminals never received the punishment they deserved. It was one of the reasons there was so much art crime.

A second SUV drew up beside them, and Tyler Briggs emerged from the passenger seat. Evidently, Magdalena would have a chaperone on the first leg of her journey into exile, lest she misbehave on board the aircraft and endanger the crew. She was considering one final act of insurrection before leaving Manhattan, a parting gesture to avenge her split and swollen lip.

Her seatmate was looking down at his phone. "Your ride is about to land," he informed her.

"Where am I going?"

"East Hampton."

"In time for dinner, I hope."

"It's only the first stop."

"And then?"

"Somewhere you'll be able to use that Spanish of yours."

"How's yours?"

"Fluent, actually."

"In that case, you won't have any trouble understanding what I'm about to tell you."

Calmly, she recited the crudest, vilest Spanish insult she could bring herself to repeat. The gray man in the gray suit only smiled. "Phillip always said you have quite a mouth on you."

This time it was Magdalena who lashed out without warning. Her blow opened a small cut in the corner of his eye. He wiped away the blood with a linen pocket square.

"Get on the helicopter, Ms. Navarro. Otherwise, there's a shallow grave in your future."

"Yours, too, I imagine."

Tyler Briggs opened Magdalena's door and escorted her to the waiting Sikorsky. Five minutes later they were headed across the East River. Before them stretched the working-class neighborhoods of Queens and the suburbs of Nassau and Suffolk counties. That slender riotous island, thought Magdalena.

She checked her Cartier. It was 7:50 p.m. At least she thought it was. The damn watch kept lousy time.

68

Pierre Hotel

Ray Bennett, the Pierre Hotel's head of security, was roughly the same size as Capitano Luca Rossetti. Well over six feet tall, at least 225 pounds. Most of that weight remained in reasonably good shape for a man of his age, which was mid-fifties. His hair was metallic gray and well groomed, his face was wide and square. It was a face, thought Gabriel, that had been made to take a punch. He asked its owner whether it would be possible for them to have a word in private. Ray Bennett said he preferred to speak in the lobby.

"That would be a mistake on your part, Mr. Bennett."

"And why is that, sir?"

"Because your colleagues will hear what I have to say to you."

Bennett contemplated Gabriel with a pair of all-seeing cop's eyes. "What's this about?"

"A missing guest."

"Name?"

"Not here."

Bennett led Gabriel through a doorway behind Reception and down a corridor to his office. He left the door open. Gabriel closed it soundlessly and turned to face the larger man.

"Where is she?"

"Who?"

Gabriel delivered a lightning-strike blow to Bennett's larynx, then raised a knee to his exposed groin, just to keep things sporting. After all, Gabriel was the smaller and older of the two combatants. A generous point spread was in order.

"You were standing at the elevator when she came downstairs. You told her something that put her mind at ease and escorted her to the delivery entrance. A black Escalade was waiting outside. You forced her into the backseat."

Bennett made no reply. He wasn't capable of one.

"I have a feeling I know who put you up to it, Ray. Nevertheless, I'd like to hear you say his name."

"*S-s-s-s-s-s* . . ."

"Sorry, but I didn't catch that."

"*S-s-s-s-s-s* . . ."

"Leonard Silk? Is that what you're trying to tell me?"

Bennett nodded vigorously.

"How much did he pay you?"

"*H-h-h-h-h* . . ."

"I beg your pardon?"

"*H-h-h-h-h* . . ."

Gabriel patted the front of Bennett's suit jacket and found his phone. It was an iPhone 13 Pro. He waved it before Bennett's face, and he was in. The same New York–based cellular number appeared three times in his RECENTS. One incoming, two outgoing. The last call was approximately an hour earlier, at 6:41 p.m. It was outgoing.

Gabriel showed the number to Ray Bennett. "Is this Silk?"

Bennett nodded.

Gabriel snapped a photograph of the screen with his Solaris. Then he handed Bennett the receiver of his desk phone. "Tell the valet to bring Ms. Bancroft's car to the Fifth Avenue entrance. Not the East Sixty-First Street doorway. Fifth Avenue."

Bennett pressed the speed-dial button and emitted an incomprehensible croak into the mouthpiece.

"Bancroft," said Gabriel slowly. "I know you can do it, Ray."

———————

Upstairs on the twentieth floor, Gabriel forwarded Leonard Silk's phone number to Yuval Gershon before cramming his belongings into his overnight bag. In the room next door, Sarah packed with equal haste. Then she hurried across the hall and stuffed Magdalena's clothing and toiletries into her costly Louis Vuitton carry-on. At the writing desk, Evelyn Buchanan hammered away at her laptop without pause, oblivious, or so it seemed, to the commotion around her.

At 7:40 p.m. the phone in Sarah's room rang. It was the valet calling to say that Ms. Bancroft's car was waiting, as requested, outside the hotel's Fifth Avenue entrance. Evelyn Buchanan shoved her laptop into her bag and followed Gabriel and Sarah into the elevator. Downstairs in the lobby, there was no sign of Ray Bennett. Sarah informed the young woman at Reception that she and Mr. Allon were checking out earlier than expected.

"Is there a problem?" the woman inquired.

"Change in plans," lied Sarah effortlessly, and declined the woman's offer of a printed receipt.

A bellman relieved them of their luggage and loaded it into the Nissan Pathfinder. Evelyn Buchanan crawled into the backseat and immediately removed her laptop. Sarah settled into the passenger seat; Gabriel, behind the wheel. As he sped through the intersection of Fifth Avenue and East Sixtieth Street, he turned his head to the right, hiding his face from the two men sitting in the Suburban outside the Metropolitan Club. They made no attempt to follow them.

"Is kidnapping complimentary at the Pierre?" asked Sarah. "Or is there an extra charge?"

Gabriel laughed quietly.

"Where do you suppose she is?"

"I have a terrible feeling she's about to leave the country, whether she wants to or not."

"With Phillip?"

"Who else?"

"She doesn't have a passport."

"Maybe she won't need one where they're going."

"Phillip keeps his Gulfstream at Teterboro," said Sarah.

"He's too smart to use his own plane. He'll leave on a charter that someone has booked on his behalf." Gabriel paused. "Someone like Leonard Silk."

"Perhaps we should telephone Mr. Silk and ask him where his client is headed."

"I rather doubt that Mr. Silk would prove receptive to our advances."

"In that case," said Sarah, "we should probably contact the FBI."

"Could get ugly."

"For Magdalena?"

"And me."

"Better than the alternative, though."

"The FBI can't arrest Phillip without a warrant. And they can't obtain a warrant based on my say-so alone. They need credible evidence of criminal wrongdoing."

"They'll have it soon enough." Sarah glanced over her shoulder at Evelyn Buchanan, who was typing furiously on her laptop. Then she turned and gazed down the length of Fifth Avenue. "I hope you realize that none of this would have happened if we'd stayed at the Four Seasons."

"Lesson learned."

"And I never got my martini."

"We'll get you a martini after we stop Phillip from fleeing the country."

"I certainly hope so," said Sarah.

Not surprisingly, Ray Bennett chose not to inform Leonard Silk that the number for his personal mobile phone had fallen into the hands of the world's most famous retired spy. Consequently, Silk took no action to protect his device from attack. It came as he was headed uptown on First Avenue—a stealth zero-click invasion carried out by the Israeli-made malware known as Proteus. Like countless other victims before him, including numerous heads of state, Silk was unaware his device had been compromised.

Within minutes the phone was spewing a geyser of valuable information. Of immediate interest to Yuval Gershon were the GPS location data and the call history. On his own initiative, Gershon attacked a second device before calling Gabriel. It was eight fifteen in New York. Gabriel was barreling along Broadway through Lower Manhattan. The two men spoke in Hebrew to ensure that nothing was lost in translation.

"He left the Pierre at six forty-four. By the way, that was the exact time Ray Bennett led your girl out the service door. Something tells me it wasn't a coincidence."

"Where did he go?"

"East Thirty-Fourth Street Heliport. He was there until seven fifty-two."

"Where is he now?"

"Back in his apartment on Sutton Place. Number fourteen, in case you're wondering. Sixteenth floor, if I had to guess."

"Any interesting calls?"

"Executive Jet Services. It's a charter company based at MacArthur Airport on Long Island."

"I know where MacArthur is, Yuval."

"Do you know when Silk made the calls?"

"Maybe you should tell me."

"The first call was at four twenty-three this afternoon. He called again about twenty minutes ago."

"Sounds to me as if someone is planning to take a trip."

"Someone is. Silk called him twice. The last call was around seven o'clock. I lit him up a few minutes ago. There's no data on the phone, which means it's probably a burner. But I was able to get a fix on his location."

"Where is he?"

"The eastern shore of the North Haven Peninsula."

"Twelve feet above sea level?"

"How did you guess?"

"Message me if he so much as twitches."

Gabriel rang off and looked at Sarah.

"What did he say?" she asked.

"He said that we should probably charter a helicopter."

Sarah dialed.

———

The offices of *Vanity Fair* magazine were located on the twenty-fifth floor of One World Trade Center. Gabriel dropped Evelyn Buchanan on West Street near the 9/11 memorial, then followed the Battery Park Underpass to the Downtown Manhattan Heliport. He squeezed the Nissan into an empty space in the small staff parking lot, gave the attendant $500 in cash to keep the vehicle for the night, and led Sarah into the terminal. Their chartered Bell 407 waited at the end of the L-shaped pier. It departed at 9:10 p.m. and raced eastward, into the cooling twilight.

69

North Haven

The Somersets of North Haven were owners of his-and-hers Range Rovers. Phillip's was a fully loaded 2022, black, tan interior. With the help of a security guard, he placed five aluminum-sided suitcases by Rimowa of Madison Avenue into the spacious rear storage compartment. Two of the suitcases contained cash; two, gold ingots. The largest was filled with clothing, toiletries, and a few personal mementos—including a collection of luxury wristwatches valued at $12 million.

Inside the house, Phillip found Lindsay where he had left her, seated at the island in the kitchen, the food properly plated and arrayed before her. She had lit candles, poured wine, touched nothing. The air smelled of lilies and grilled octopus. It turned Phillip's stomach. He checked the display screen of the hardline phone. Lindsay had made no calls during his brief absence.

"Shall I pack a bag for you?" he asked.

She stared silently into an emptiness of Phillip's making. She had not spoken a word since his ill-advised threat of violence. It was Lindsay who had drawn her sword first, but it had been reckless of Phillip to respond in kind. Almost as reckless, he thought, as divulging the name of the country where he planned to take refuge.

"You won't tell them where I am, will you?"

"The first chance I get." She gave him a counterfeit smile. "But not tonight, Phillip. I've decided it would be best if you simply disappeared. That way, I'll never have to look at your face again or, heaven forbid, visit you in prison."

Phillip returned to his office and executed a series of wire transfers, all designed to leave little if no trace of the money's final destination. Taken together, they had the effect of draining every cent from the accounts of Masterpiece Art Ventures. There was nothing left. Nothing but the real estate, the toys, the debt, and the paintings. The genuine works in the company's inventory were worth at least $700 million, but all were leveraged to the hilt. Perhaps Christie's would hold a special evening sale to auction the works off. *The Somerset Collection . . .* It had a certain ring to it, he had to admit.

Rising, he went to his window and for the last time surveyed his realm. The bay. His boat. His manicured garden. His blue swimming pool. He realized suddenly he hadn't used it once all summer.

A green light flared on the multiline desk phone. Phillip snatched up the receiver and heard Lindsay abruptly hang up downstairs. Evidently, she was still entertaining thoughts of turning him in. He switched lines and dialed East Hampton Airport. Mike Knox, the regular evening head of flight operations, answered.

"Your helicopter arrived about twenty minutes ago, Mr. Somerset. The passengers decided to stay on board."

"Any other inbound birds?"

"A Blade, a couple of privates, and a Zip Aviation charter from downtown."

"What's the ETA on the charter?"

"Twenty-five minutes or so."

"Is my helicopter fueled?"

"Finishing now."

"Thanks, Mike. I'm on my way."

Phillip hung up the phone and opened the bottom drawer of his desk. It was where he kept his unregistered firearm.

Not if I kill you first, Lindsay . . .

It would certainly guarantee a clean departure, he thought. But it would also saddle him with eternal infamy. If the truth be told, a part of him was actually looking forward to exile. Keeping the Ponzi scheme up and running all these years had been exhausting; he was sorely in need of a vacation. And now it seemed he would have beautiful Magdalena to keep his bed warm, at least until the storm blew over and it was safe for her to return to Spain.

Or perhaps not, Phillip thought suddenly. Perhaps they would live out their lives together in hiding. He imagined a Ripley-like existence, with Magdalena playing the role of Héloïse Plisson. With the passage of time, he might come to be viewed in a more favorable light—as an alluring figure of mystery, a villain protagonist. Putting a bullet into Lindsay would spoil that. The whole of the Upper East Side would be rooting for his death.

He closed the drawer, deleted his documents and emails, and emptied his digital trash. Downstairs, he returned Lindsay's phone. She stared through him as though he were made of glass. "Leave" was all she said.

The Blade commuter helicopter arrived at East Hampton Airport at ten minutes past nine o'clock. Six passengers, Manhattanites all, spilled onto the tarmac and, after collecting their luggage, traipsed off toward the terminal. Magdalena watched them from the window of the Sikorsky. Tyler Briggs sat in the opposing seat, legs spread, crotch on full display. Magdalena calculated the odds of delivering a debilitating strike and then snatching the phone from his hand. They were reasonable, she reckoned, but retribution would likely be swift and severe. Tyler was ex-military, and Magdalena was already damaged from her skirmishes with the gray eminence. She'd had quite enough excitement for one evening. Better to ask nicely.

"May I borrow your phone for a moment, Tyler?"

"No."

"I just want to check a website."

"The answer is still no."

"Will you please check it for me, please? It's *Vanity Fair*."

"The magazine?"

"Haven't you heard? They're about to publish a story about your boss. By tomorrow morning, the town house will be surrounded by camera crews and reporters. Who knows? If you play your cards right, you might be able to earn a little extra money. But I beg of you, don't sell those naughty videos you've saved on your computer. My poor mother will never get over it."

"Mr. Somerset ordered us to wipe the system this afternoon."

"That was wise of him. Now be a love, Tyler, and check the website for me. It's *Vanity Fair*. I can spell it for you, if that helps."

The phone rang before he could reply. "Yes, Mr. Somerset," he said after a moment. "No, Mr. Somerset. She was no trouble at all . . . Yes, I'll tell her, sir."

He hung up and slipped the phone into his jacket pocket.

"Tell her what?" asked Magdalena.

The security guard pointed toward the black Range Rover speeding across the tarmac. "Mr. Somerset would like a word with you in private before we leave."

———

He braked to a halt a few yards from the Sikorsky's tail and popped the Range Rover's rear door. Magdalena took inventory of the cargo before climbing into the passenger seat. Phillip stared straight ahead, hands gripping the wheel. An unlocked cell phone lay on the center console. It was not his usual device.

At last he turned and looked at her. "What happened to your face?"

"Apparently, I said something that offended the sensibilities of your friend." Magdalena paused. "We were never properly introduced."

"Silk," said Phillip. "Leonard Silk."

"Where did you find him?"

"Smith and Wollensky."

"Chance encounter?"

"There's no such thing where Leonard is concerned."

"What was the occasion?"

"Hamilton Fairchild."

"Buyer?"

Phillip nodded.

"Which painting?"

"*Saint Jerome.*"

"Follower of Caravaggio?"

"Circle of Parmigianino. I dumped it on Hamilton in a private treaty sale arranged by Bonhams."

"I was always fond of that picture," said Magdalena.

"So was Hamilton until he showed it to an art dealer named Patrick Matthiesen. Matthiesen told Hamilton that, in his learned opinion, the painting was the work of, how shall we say, a later imitator."

"I assume Hamilton wanted his money back."

"Naturally."

"And you refused?"

"Of course."

"How did the situation resolve itself?"

"Regrettably, Hamilton and his wife died in a single-engine plane crash off the coast of Maine."

"How many others were there?"

"Fewer than you might imagine. Leonard handled most of them with an envelope filled with naughty photographs or incriminating financial information. And not just buyers. Investors, too. Why do you think Max van Egan still has a quarter-billion in the fund?"

Phillip took up the phone and refreshed the web browser. "How long before the story appears?"

"I'm surprised it hasn't already. When it does, Masterpiece will go up in flames."

"You're as guilty as I am, you know."

"Somehow I don't think your lenders and investors are going to see it that way."

Phillip tossed aside the phone in anger. "Why did you do it?" he asked.

"I was arrested an hour after I purchased the Gentileschi. It was an elaborate sting operation by Gabriel Allon and the Italians. They gave me a choice. I could spend the next several years in an Italian prison, or I could give them your head on a platter."

"You should have asked for a lawyer and kept your mouth shut."

"You wired ten million euros into a Carabinieri-controlled bank account. They would have eventually traced the money back to you, with or without my help."

"I suppose the redemptions were Allon's doing, too. He baited me into committing an act of bank fraud over a compromised phone."

"I told you to put the painting on ice," said Magdalena. "But you wouldn't listen."

"You put a rope around my neck and walked me to the gallows."

"I had no other choice."

"You were a drug dealer when I found you. And this is how you repay me?"

"But they were real drugs, weren't they, Phillip?" Magdalena took a long look over her shoulder. "I don't suppose Lindsay is in one of those suitcases."

"It's just the two of us."

"How romantic. Where are we off to?"

Phillip looked down at the phone; Magdalena, at her Cartier wristwatch.

It was half past nine.

70

Downtown

On the twenty-fifth floor of One World Trade Center, in a conference room overlooking New York Harbor, war had been declared. The combatants were five in number and were broken into three opposing camps. Two were senior editors, two were lawyers, and the last was a reporter with an impeccable track record for accuracy and click-generating copy. The piece under deliberation contained allegations of financial impropriety by a prominent figure in the New York art world. Complicating matters was the fact that the prominent figure's hired henchmen had deleted the only existing draft of the story. Furthermore, it appeared that the prominent figure was at that very moment attempting to flee the country.

Nevertheless, insisted the lawyers, certain legal and editorial standards had to be met. Otherwise, the prominent art world figure, whose name was Phillip Somerset, would have grounds to file a lawsuit, as would his investors.

"Not to mention his lenders at JPMorgan Chase and Bank of America. In short, it has all the makings of a legal clusterfuck for the ages."

"My source is a freelance employee of Masterpiece Art Ventures."

"With a rather dubious personal history."

"I have recordings."

"Provided to you by a former Israeli intelligence officer who was using a highly controversial cell phone hacking malware."

"New York is a one-party consent state. She knew she was being recorded when she met with Phillip."

"But neither Phillip nor Ellis Gray of JPMorgan Chase consented to being recorded. Therefore, their conversation regarding the art-backed loan is inadmissible, as it were."

"What about the paintings in the warehouse?"

"Don't even think about it."

With that, a temporary truce was declared, and work commenced. The reporter wrote, the editors edited, the lawyers lawyered—one paragraph at a time, at a pace more akin to an old-fashioned wire service than a storied cultural-and-current affairs monthly. But such were the exigencies of magazine publishing in the digital age. Even the staid *New Yorker* had been compelled to offer its subscribers daily content. The world had changed, and not necessarily for the better. Phillip Somerset was proof of that.

At half past nine they had a draft in hand. It was limited in scope but devasting in impact. The story appeared on *Vanity Fair*'s website at 9:32 p.m., and within minutes it was trending on social media. In the aftermath, much would be made of its final line. Phillip Somerset, it read, could not be reached for comment.

———

When the first text messages detonated on Lindsay's phone, she assumed they were from Phillip and ignored them. There was a brief pause, followed by a second barrage. Then all hell broke loose.

Reluctantly Lindsay reached for the device and saw a stream of venom and threats, all sent by some of her closest friends. Attached to each of the texts was the same article from *Vanity Fair*. The headline read THE FAKE: INSIDE PHILLIP SOMERSET'S MASTERPIECE OF A PONZI SCHEME. Lindsay clicked on the link. Three paragraphs was all she could take.

She opened her RECENTS, found the number for Phillip's burner, and dialed. The background whir of the Sikorsky's turboshaft engines told her that he had not yet departed East Hampton Airport.

"Have you read the article?" she asked.

"I'm reading it now."

"I can't face this alone."

"What are you saying?"

"Don't leave without me," said Lindsay, and snatched her car keys from the kitchen counter.

———————

The chartered Bell 407 was over the waters of Long Island Sound when Evelyn Buchanan's article popped onto Gabriel's phone. He skimmed it quickly and was relieved to find that neither his name nor Sarah's appeared in the text. Neither, for that matter, did Magdalena's. Her allegations were attributed to an unnamed freelance employee of Masterpiece Art Ventures. There was no mention of her gender or nationality. For the moment, at least, she was in the clear. Phillip Somerset, however, was finished.

Voice calls were prohibited onboard the helicopter, so Gabriel shot a text message to Yuval Gershon and requested an update on Phillip's position. Yuval's reply appeared a minute later. Phillip was still on the tarmac at East Hampton Airport.

"Why hasn't he left yet?" asked Sarah over the drone of the Bell's engines.

"It seems Lindsay has had a change of heart. She called him two minutes ago and told him not to leave until she arrived."

"Perhaps it's time you had that chat with the FBI."

"I'm afraid there's a complicating factor."

"Only one?"

"Magdalena is there, too."

The helicopter remained over Long Island Sound until they reached the old Horton Point Light, where a turn to starboard carried them over the town of Southold and the waters of Peconic Bay. A ferry was crossing the narrow channel separating Shelter Island and North Haven. On the eastern shore of the peninsula, Phillip's now-abandoned estate was ablaze with light.

"It looks as though Lindsay left in a hurry," said Sarah.

They passed over Sag Harbor and commenced their descent toward East Hampton Airport. Directly beneath them, a white Range Rover was headed toward the airfield along Daniels Hole Road. It was Lindsay Somerset, thought Gabriel. And she was definitely in a hurry.

———————

She made the final turn into the airport with deliberate care. Hand-over-hand on the steering wheel, a gentle acceleration mid-arc. Just the way her father had taught her when she was a girl of fourteen. The gate at the edge of the tarmac was open. The guard waved her through. Magdalena stood next to the Sikorsky; Phillip, at the open rear door of his Range Rover. He hoisted an arm in greeting, as though waving from the deck of his sailboat. Lindsay switched off the headlights, put her foot to the floor, and closed her eyes.

PART FOUR

———

Unveiling

71

East Hampton

The call came through on the emergency line of the East Hampton Town Police Department at 9:55 p.m. Sergeant Bruce Logan, a twenty-year veteran of the department and lifelong resident of the East End, braced himself for the worst. It was Mike Knox calling from the airport.

"Helicopter or plane?" asked Logan.

"Actually, it was two Range Rovers."

"Fender bender in the parking lot?"

"Fatality on the tarmac."

"You're shitting me, Mike."

"I wish."

The department's headquarters were located on the southern edge of the airfield, on Wainscott Road, and the first officers arrived at the scene just three minutes after the initial call. They found the victim, a white male in his mid-fifties, lying on the tarmac in a bay of his own blood, his legs nearly severed, surrounded by several hundred carefully packaged five-hundred-gram gold ingots. The driver of the vehicle that had struck the man was an attractive, fit-looking woman in her thirties. She wore leggings, a Lululemon hoodie, and neon-green Nikes. She had no wallet and seemed unable to recall her name. Mike

Knox supplied it for her. The woman was Lindsay Somerset. The dead guy with the nearly severed legs was her husband, a rich investor of some sort who owned a weekend palace in North Haven.

Death was formally declared, an arrest was made, a statement was issued. The news broke at midnight on WINS radio, and by nine the following morning it was all anyone was talking about. The real estate mogul Sterling Dunbar was in the shower when he learned that Lindsay Somerset had run down her scoundrel of a husband; the retailer Simon Levinson, still in his bed. Ellis Gray of JPMorgan Chase, having endured a sleepless night after reading the *Vanity Fair* story, was in his office overlooking Park Avenue. Two hours later he informed senior management that the firm was now on the hook for $436 million in loans issued to Masterpiece Art Ventures—loans that, in all likelihood, had been collateralized with forged paintings. Senior management accepted Gray's resignation, effective immediately.

By midday the FBI had assumed control of the investigation. Agents searched Phillip's homes, sealed his warehouse, and raided his offices on East Fifty-Third Street. The firm's three female art experts were taken to Federal Plaza and questioned at length. All denied any knowledge of financial or art-related impropriety. Kenny Vaughan, Phillip's wingman from his days at Lehman Brothers, was nowhere to be found. Agents seized his computers and printed files and issued a warrant for his arrest.

Phillip's crimes were global in scope, and so was the fallout. Two prominent European dealers—Gilles Raymond of Brussels and Konrad Hassler of Berlin—were arrested and their inventories seized. Dealers in Hong Kong, Tokyo, and Dubai were likewise taken into custody. Under questioning, all admitted that they were part of a far-flung distribution network that had been flooding the art market with high-quality forgeries for years. The French Ministry of Culture grudgingly acknowledged that four of those forgeries had found their way into the permanent collection of the Louvre. The museum's president abruptly resigned, as did the director of the esteemed National Center for Research and Restoration, which had declared all four works to be authentic.

But who was this master forger who had managed to deceive the world's most sophisticated art laboratory? And how many examples of his handiwork were now circulating through the bloodstream of the art world? Evelyn Buchanan, in a follow-up to her original exposé, reported that Phillip's warehouse likely contained more than two hundred forged paintings. Hundreds more, she wrote, had already been foisted upon unsuspecting buyers. When a partial list of those works appeared anonymously on a much-read industry message board, panic swept the art world. Collectors, dealers, curators, and auctioneers—having relied for generations on the pronouncements of connoisseurs—turned to the scientists to help them sort through the wreckage. Aiden Gallagher of Equus Analytics was so inundated with requests for evaluations that he stopped answering his phone and responding to emails. "Mr. Gallagher," wrote an art reporter from the *New York Times*, "is the scandal's only winner."

The losers, of course, were Phillip's well-heeled investors, the ones who had seen hundreds of millions of dollars in paper wealth wiped away in a matter of hours. Their lawsuits, countersuits, and public lamentations earned them little sympathy, especially from art world purists who found the very concept of a fund like Phillip's abhorrent. Great paintings, they declared, were not securities or derivatives to be traded among the superrich. They were objects of beauty and cultural significance that belonged in museums. Not surprisingly, those who made their living buying and selling paintings found such sentiments laughable. Without the rich, they pointed out, there would be no art. And no museums, either.

A federal judge appointed a trustee to sift through Phillip's assets and dole out the proceeds to those he had defrauded. Three hundred and forty-seven investors sought restitution. The largest claim was $254 million by the industrialist Max van Egan. The smallest was

$4.8 million by Sarah Bancroft, a former curator from the Museum of Modern Art who now managed an Old Master gallery in London.

One of Phillip's investors, however, filed no claim at all: Magdalena Navarro, thirty-nine years old, a citizen of Spain who resided in the upscale Salamanca district of Madrid. According to documents seized from the offices of Masterpiece Art Ventures—and to sworn statements given to the FBI by the three cooperating employees of the firm—Navarro was a European-based freelance runner who purchased and sold paintings on Phillip Somerset's behalf. Her last recorded account balance was $56.2 million, a great deal of money to leave lying on the table.

As it turned out, the FBI knew more about Magdalena Navarro than it had revealed in public, which was nothing at all. It knew, for example, that the European art dealers Gilles Raymond and Konrad Hassler had identified her as the link between their galleries and Masterpiece Art Ventures. The Bureau also knew that Navarro had been in New York at the time of the hedge fund's spectacular collapse, having arrived on a Delta Air Lines flight from Rome and departed—less than twelve hours after Phillip Somerset's death—on a flight to London. Interestingly enough, she had been seated next to Gabriel Allon, the legendary former director-general of the Israeli secret intelligence service, on both legs of her journey. The art dealer Sarah Bancroft, who also happened to be a former clandestine CIA officer, had accompanied Allon and Navarro on the flight to Heathrow.

Investigators also established that all three had stayed in separate rooms on the twentieth floor of the Pierre Hotel during their brief visit to New York. And that Magdalena Navarro was likely the source of the exposé in *Vanity Fair*. And that Navarro departed the Pierre Hotel shortly before the article's publication—without luggage or a handbag—and traveled to East Hampton Airport aboard Phillip Somerset's Sikorsky helicopter. And that she subsequently left East Hampton Airport, in the chaotic minutes following Somerset's grisly death, aboard a Bell 407 chartered by Allon and Bancroft. The pilot delivered them to JFK, where they spent the night in the airport Hilton. And by eight the following morning, they were gone.

All of which suggested to the FBI that a friendly chat with Allon was in order. Finding him proved less difficult than they imagined. The FBI's legal attaché in Rome simply rang the offices of the Tiepolo Restoration Company in Venice, and Allon's wife arranged a meeting. It took place in Harry's Bar—which was where, unbeknownst to the legal attaché, Allon's involvement in the affair began. While sipping a Bellini, he told the FBI officer about a private inquiry he had undertaken at the behest of an old friend whom he refused to identify. This private inquiry, he said in conclusion, led him to Magdalena Navarro and, ultimately, Phillip Somerset's $1.2 billion forgery-based Ponzi scheme.

"Where is she now?" asked the FBI man, whose name was Josh Campbell.

"Somewhere in the Pyrenees. Even I don't know where."

"Doing what?"

"Painting, I assume."

"Is she any good?"

"If Phillip hadn't got his hooks into her, she would have been a major artist."

"We'd like to question her."

"I'm sure you would. But as a personal favor to me, I'd like you to let her get on with her life."

"The Bureau isn't in the business of granting personal favors, Allon."

"In that case, you leave me no choice but to call the president directly."

"You wouldn't dare."

"Watch me."

And so Special Agent Josh Campbell returned to Rome empty-handed, but with a fascinating tale to tell. He wrote it up in a lengthy memorandum and fired it simultaneously to Washington and New

York. Those who knew of Allon's past exploits were dubious as to the document's accuracy—and justifiably so. The report made no mention, for example, of a forged portrait by Anthony van Dyck. Or a recently deceased Frenchwoman named Valerie Bérrangar. Or a Parisian antiques dealer and art thief named Maurice Durand. Or the Swiss violinist Anna Rolfe. Or the notorious Corsican crime figure Don Anton Orsati. Or the lecherous but lovable London art dealer Oliver Dimbleby, whose fictitious rediscovery and record-setting sales of three Venetian School masterworks had recently set the art world ablaze.

By the end of July, all three canvases were hanging in the apartment of the forger who had created them, along with two versions of Modigliani's *Reclining Nude*, a Cézanne, a Monet, and a stunning version of Van Gogh's *Self-Portrait with Bandaged Ear*. On the easel in his studio was a painting with an L-shaped tear, 15 by 23 centimeters, in the lower left corner. After repairing the damage and retouching the losses, the forger shipped the work to a small gallery near the Plaza Virgen de los Reyes in Seville. Then, early the next morning, he disappeared.

72

Adriatico

For the first five days of the trip, the *maestral* prevailed. It was not the cold and blustery aggressor that had laid siege to the island of Corsica the previous spring, but a temperate and dependable companion that propelled the Bavaria C42 effortlessly down the length of the Adriatic. With the seas calm and the wind blowing across the stern of his spacious vessel, Gabriel was able to provide Irene and Raphael with a smooth and pleasant introduction to maritime life. No one was more relieved than Chiara, who had prepared herself for six sun-drenched weeks of moaning, groaning, and seasickness.

Their days lacked shape, which was their intention. Most mornings Gabriel awakened early and got under way while Chiara and the children slept in the cabins beneath him. Sometime around noon he would drop his sails and lower the swim platform, and they would enjoy a long lunch at the cockpit table. In the evening they dined in portside restaurants—Italy one night, Croatia or Montenegro the next. Gabriel carried his Beretta whenever they went ashore. Chiara never addressed him by his given name.

When they reached the southern Adriatic port of Bari, they spent the night in a comfortable boutique hotel near the marina, did a large load of laundry, and restocked their stores with food and plenty of local white wine. Late the following morning, when they rounded the heel of Italy, a warm and sultry *jugo* was blowing from the southeast. Gabriel rode it westward across the Ionian and arrived at the Sicilian port of Messina a day earlier than he had anticipated. The Museo Regionale was a short walk along the waterfront from the marina. In Room 10 were two monumental canvases executed by Caravaggio during his nine-month stay in Sicily.

"Is it true he used an actual corpse?" asked Chiara as she pondered *The Raising of Lazarus.*

"Unlikely," answered Gabriel. "But certainly not beyond the realm of possibility."

"It's not one of his better efforts, is it?"

"Much of what you see was painted by studio assistants. The last restoration was about ten years ago. As you can no doubt tell from the quality of the work, I wasn't available at the time."

Chiara gave him a look of reproach. "I think I liked you better before you became a forger."

"Consider yourself lucky that I didn't attempt to forge a Caravaggio. You would have thrown me into the street."

"I have to say, I rather enjoyed my afternoons with Orazio Gentileschi."

"Not as much as he enjoyed his time with Danaë."

"She would love to have lunch alone with you before this trip is over."

"Our cabin is too close to the children's."

"In that case, how about a midnight snack instead?" Smiling, Chiara directed her gaze toward the Caravaggio. "Do you think you could paint one?"

"I'll pretend I didn't hear that."

"And what about your rival? Is he capable of forging a Caravaggio?"

"He produced undetectable Old Master paintings from every school and period. A Caravaggio would be rather easy for him."

"Who do you suppose he is?"

"The last person in the world anyone would ever suspect."

Their midnight snack turned out to be a sumptuous feast several hours in length, and it was nearly ten in the morning by the time they set out for Limpari. Their next stop was a little cove along the Calabrian coast. Then, after an overnight sail that included a snack on the Bavaria's foredeck, they arrived at the Amalfi Coast. From there, they island-hopped their way across the Gulf of Naples—first Capri, then Ischia—before venturing across the Tyrrhenian Sea to Sardinia.

To the north lay Corsica. Gabriel charted a course up the island's western side, into the teeth of a freshening *maestral*. And two days later, on a cool and cloudless Wednesday evening, he guided the Bavaria into Porto's tiny marina. Waiting on the quay, their arms raised in greeting, were Sarah Bancroft and Christopher Keller.

The sun had set by the time they reached the well-guarded home of Don Anton Orsati. Clad in the simple clothing of a Corsican *paesanu*, he greeted Irene and Raphael as though they were blood relatives. Gabriel explained to his children that the large, expansive figure with the dark eyes of a canine was a producer of the island's finest olive oil. Irene, with her peculiar powers of second sight, was clearly dubious.

The don's walled garden was strung with decorative lights and filled with members of his extended clan, including several who worked in the clandestine side of his business. It seemed the arrival of the Allon family after a long and perilous sea voyage was cause for celebration, as was the first visit to the island by Christopher's American wife. Many Corsican proverbs were recited, and a great deal of pale Corsican rosé was drunk. Sarah stared unabashedly at Raphael throughout dinner, entranced by the child's uncanny resemblance to his father. Gabriel, for his part, stared at his wife. She had never looked happier—or more beautiful, he thought.

At the conclusion of the meal, the don invited Gabriel and Christopher upstairs to his office. Lying on the desk was the photograph of the man who had tried to kill Gabriel and Sarah at Galerie Georges Fleury in Paris.

"His name was Rémy Dubois. And you were right," said Orsati. "He had a military background. He spent a couple of years fighting the crazies in Afghanistan, where he became quite familiar with improvised explosives. When he came home, he had trouble getting his life together." The don glanced at Christopher. "Sound familiar?"

"Perhaps you should tell him about Rémy Dubois and leave me out of it."

"The organization for which Dubois worked is known only as the Groupe. The other employees of this organization are all former soldiers and intelligence operatives. Most of their clients are wealthy businessmen. They're very good at what they do. And quite expensive. We found Rémy in Antibes. A nice place near the Plage de Juan les Pins."

"Do I have to ask where he is now?"

"You probably passed over him as you approached Porto."

"How much were you able to get out of him?"

"Chapter and verse. Apparently, the attempt on your life was a rush job."

"Did he happen to mention when he got the order?"

"It was the Sunday before the bombing."

"Sunday evening?"

"Morning, actually. He had to assemble the bomb so quickly that he didn't have time to buy a burner phone to use as the detonator trigger. He used a phone he picked up on another job instead."

"It belonged to a woman named Valerie Bérrangar. Dubois and his associates ran her car off the road south of Bordeaux."

"So he said. He was also involved in the murder of Lucien Marchand." Orsati inclined his head toward an unfinished Cézanne-inspired landscape leaning against the wall. "We found that in his apartment in Antibes."

"Who paid for the bullet?" asked Gabriel.

"An American. Evidently, he was a former CIA officer. Dubois didn't know his name."

"It's Leonard Silk. He lives on Sutton Place in Manhattan." Gabriel paused, then added, "Number fourteen."

"We have friends in New York." Orsati fed the photograph into his shredder. "Good friends, in fact."

"How much?"

"You insult me."

"Money doesn't come from singing," said Gabriel, repeating one of the don's favorite proverbs.

"And dew won't fill the tank," he replied. "But save your money for your children."

"Little children, little worries. Big children, big worries."

"But not tonight, my friend. Tonight we have no worries at all."

Gabriel looked at Christopher and smiled. "We'll see about that."

Downstairs, Gabriel found Raphael and Irene propped against Chiara, their eyes glassy and unfocused. Don Orsati begged them to stay a little longer, but after a final exchange of Corsican proverbs he reluctantly acquiesced to their departure. He could not hide his disappointment, though, over Gabriel's travel plans. The Allon family intended to spend a single night at Christopher's villa, then set out for Venice first thing in the morning.

"Surely you can stay for a week or two."

"The children begin school in mid-September. We'll barely make it home in time as it is."

"To where will you sail next year?" inquired the don.

"The Galápagos, I think."

With that, they said their goodbyes and squeezed into Christopher's battered old Renault hatchback for the drive to the next valley. Gabriel and Chiara sat in back with the children wedged between them. Sarah sat in the passenger seat next to her husband. Despite the gaiety of the evening, her mood was suddenly tense.

"Have you heard from Magdalena?" she asked in the overbright voice of one who feared imminent disaster.

"Magdalena who?" replied Gabriel as the headlamps illuminated the enormous horned goat standing in the center of the track near the three ancient olive trees owned by Don Casabianca.

Christopher applied the brakes, and the car slowed gently to a stop.

"Would you mind awfully if I had a cigarette?" asked Sarah. "I feel one coming on."

"That makes two of us," murmured Gabriel.

Irene and Raphael, somnambulant a moment earlier, were suddenly alert and excited about the prospect of yet another adventure. Christopher sat with his hands upon the wheel, his powerful shoulders slumped, a picture of misery.

His eyes met Gabriel's in the rearview mirror. "I would prefer if your children didn't watch."

"Don't be ridiculous. Why do you think I sailed all the way to Corsica?"

"We've had a rough couple of weeks," explained Sarah. "Last night . . ."

"Last night *what*?" probed Irene.

"I'd rather not say."

Christopher said it for her. "He got a clean shot at me. It was like being hit with a pile driver."

"You must have provoked the poor thing," said Chiara.

"As far as that creature is concerned, my very existence is a provocation."

Christopher tapped the horn and with a cordial movement of his hand invited the goat to step aside. Receiving no response, he lifted his foot from the brake and inched the car forward. The goat lowered his head and drove it into the grille.

"I told you," said Sarah. "He's incorrigible."

"That's no way to talk about Christopher," interjected Gabriel.

"What does incorrigible mean?" asked Raphael.

"Incapable of being corrected. Depraved and inveterate. A hopeless reprobate."

"Reprobate," repeated Irene, and giggled.

Christopher opened his door, igniting the interior dome light. Sarah appeared stricken. "Perhaps we should all check into a hotel. Or better yet, let's spend the night on that beautiful boat of yours."

"Yes, let's," agreed Chiara as the car shuddered with the impact of another blow. Then she looked at Gabriel and said quietly, "Do something, darling."

"My hand is killing me."

"Let me," said Irene.

"Not a chance."

"Don't listen to your father," said Chiara. "Go right ahead, sweetheart."

Gabriel opened his door and looked at his beautiful wife. "If anything happens to her, let it be on your head."

Irene clambered across Gabriel's lap and leapt out of the car. Fearlessly she approached the goat and, stroking his red beard, explained that she and her family were sailing back to Venice tomorrow morning and needed a good night's sleep. The goat clearly found the story implausible. Nevertheless, he withdrew from the track without further contest, and the situation was resolved peaceably.

Irene squeezed into the backseat and rested her head against her father's shoulder as they resumed their progress toward Christopher's villa.

"Reprobate," whispered the child, and laughed hysterically.

73

Bar Dogale

Against all better judgment, Gabriel agreed to remain in Corsica through the weekend. He insisted, however, on spending Sunday night aboard the Bavaria, and by the time Chiara and the children awakened on Monday morning, he had put Ajaccio behind them. With the *maestral* at his back and his spinnaker flying, he reached the southern tip of Sardinia at sunset on Tuesday, and by late Thursday afternoon they were back in Messina.

That evening, while dining at I Ruggeri, one of the city's finer restaurants, Gabriel read with relief that prosecutors in New York's Suffolk County had dropped all charges against Lindsay Somerset in the death of her husband. Locked out of her homes, her bank accounts seized or frozen, she faced an uncertain future. There was speculation in a Long Island weekly that she intended to open a fitness studio in Montauk and settle permanently in the East End. The largely favorable local reaction suggested that Lindsay, with her act of madness at the airport, had emerged from the scandal untarnished by Phillip's fraud.

Three nights later, in Bari, Gabriel read that Kenny Vaughan, Phillip's fugitive chief investment officer, had been found dead of an apparent drug overdose in a New Orleans hotel room. Still unaccounted for was the money that Phillip had drained from the firm's cash reserves during the final hours of his life. According to the *New York Times*, any attempt to sell off the hedge fund's inventory of paintings would likely prove disappointing, as collectors and museums were skittish about acquiring anything Phillip had touched. A team of experts from the Metropolitan Museum of Art had conducted a survey of the warehouse on East Ninety-First Street in an attempt to definitively determine which of the 789 paintings were forgeries and which were authentic. Consensus had proven impossible.

Accompanying the article was a photograph of the last painting Phillip acquired before his death: *Danaë and the Shower of Gold*, purportedly by Orazio Gentileschi. The FBI had determined that it was shipped to New York from the Tuscan city of Florence, doubtless in violation of Italy's strict cultural patrimony laws. Whether it was a forgery or a genuine lost masterpiece the connoisseurs could not say—not without rigorous scientific testing of the sort conducted by Aiden Gallagher of Equus Analytics. Nevertheless, US authorities had acceded to an Italian demand that the painting be returned immediately.

Fittingly enough, it arrived in Italy the same morning that Gabriel, after a moonlit final run up the northern Adriatic, eased the Bavaria into its slip at the Venezia Certosa Marina. Four days later, after watching Chiara board a Number 2 at the San Tomà vaporetto stop, he escorted Irene and Raphael to the Bernardo Canal *scuola elementare* for the start of the fall term. Alone for the first time in many weeks—and having nothing else on his schedule other than a visit to the Rialto Market—he made his way through empty streets to Bar Dogale. Which was where, at a chrome table covered in blue, he found General Cesare Ferrari.

———

The waiter delivered two *cappuccini* and a basket of sugar-dusted, cream-filled *cornetti*. Gabriel drank the coffee but ignored the pastry. "I've been eating nonstop for a month and a half."

"And yet you look as though you haven't gained a kilo."

"I hide it well."

"Like most things." The general was attired in his blue-and-gold Carabinieri finery. Standing upright next to his chair was a shallow portfolio case typically used by art professionals to transport drawings or small paintings. "Somehow you even managed to conceal your involvement in the Somerset affair."

"Not exactly. That FBI agent gave me an earful."

"It is my understanding that the interview was conducted over Bellinis in Harry's Bar."

"You were watching?"

"You don't think we let FBI agents wander around without an escort?"

"I certainly hope not."

"Special Agent Campbell gave me a good going-over as well," said Ferrari. "He was convinced the Art Squad was somehow involved in your shenanigans. I assured him that we were not."

"The swift return of *Danaë and the Shower of Gold* suggests he believed you."

The general sipped his cappuccino. "A rather remarkable development, even by your standards."

"Where is it now?"

"Still at the palazzo," said Ferrari, referring to the Art Squad's Roman headquarters. "But later today it will be taken to the Galleria Borghese for analysis."

"Oh, dear."

"How long will it take them to conclude it's a forgery?"

"According to the *Times*, it passed muster in New York."

"With all due respect, we know a bit more about Gentileschi's work than do the Americans."

"The brushwork and palette are his," said Gabriel. "But the minute they subject the canvas to examination by X-radiography and infra-red reflectography, I'm cooked."

"As well you should be. That painting needs to be exposed as a forgery and destroyed." The general exhaled heavily. "You realize, I hope, that your fictitious sales through Dimbleby Fine Arts of London have added new works to the oeuvres of three of the greatest painters in history."

"As of yet, none of the pictures that Oliver purportedly sold have found their way into the artists' catalogues raisonnés."

"And if they do?"

"I will immediately step forward. Until then, I intend to remain out of the public eye."

"Doing what?"

"I'm going to spend the next month cleaning crumbs and other assorted debris from my boat."

"And then?"

"My wife is considering allowing me to restore a painting."

"For the Tiepolo Restoration Company?"

"Given the perilous state of my bank account, I'm inclined to accept a lucrative private commission first."

The general frowned. "Perhaps you should just forge something instead."

"My brief career as an art forger is now officially over."

"And to think that it was all for naught."

"I brought down the largest forgery network in the history of the art world."

"Without finding the forger himself," the general pointed out.

"I would have if Lindsay Somerset hadn't ruined a perfectly good Range Rover killing her husband."

"Be that as it may, it's a rather unsatisfying conclusion to the story. Wouldn't you agree?"

"The guilty were punished," said Gabriel.

"But the forger remains free."

"Surely the FBI must have some idea who he is by now."

"Young Campbell says not. Clearly, your forger covered his tracks well." General Ferrari reached for the portfolio case and handed it to Gabriel. "But perhaps this might help solve the mystery."

"What is it?"

"A gift from your friend Jacques Ménard in Paris."

Gabriel balanced the case on his knees and popped the latches. Inside was *A River Scene with Distant Windmills*, oil on canvas, 36 by 58 centimeters, purportedly by the Dutch Golden Age painter Aelbert Cuyp. There was also a copy of a report prepared by the Louvre's National Center for Research and Restoration. It stated that the center, after weeks of painstaking scientific analysis, had been unable to render a definitive judgment as to the work's authenticity. On one point, however, it was certain in its findings.

A River Scene with Distant Windmills contained not a single fiber of navy-blue polar fleece fabric.

Gabriel returned the report to the portfolio case and closed the lid.

"Bon voyage," said General Ferrari with a smile.

74

Salamanca

Contrary to the statement that Gabriel made to Special Agent Josh Campbell of the FBI, Magdalena Navarro was not in hiding in a remote village in the Pyrenees. She was holed up in her apartment on the Calle de Castelló in the elegant Salamanca district of Madrid. At half past twelve the following afternoon, Gabriel thumbed the appropriate call button on the building's intercom panel, then turned his back to the camera. Receiving no answer, he pressed the button a second time. At length the speaker crackled into life.

"If you do that again," said a sleep-heavy female voice, "I'm going to come down there and kill you."

"Please don't, Magdalena." Gabriel turned to face the camera. "It's only me."

"My God!" she said, and unlocked the door.

Inside, Gabriel climbed the stairs to her apartment. She was waiting in the open doorway, wearing a gauzy cotton pullover and little else. Her raven hair was a tangled mess. Her hands were stained with paint.

"I hope I'm not intruding on something," said Gabriel.

"Only on my sleep. You should have warned me that you were coming."

"I was afraid you might try to flee the country." He looked down at the two matching Vuitton suitcases standing on the tiled floor of the entrance hall. "Which one has the cash?"

She indicated the bag nearest the door. "It's all the money I have left."

"What happened to the four or five million you had hidden in bank accounts around Europe?"

"I gave it away."

"To whom?"

"The poor and the immigrants, mainly. I also made a rather large donation to my favorite environmental group and another to my old art school in Barcelona. Anonymously, of course."

"Perhaps there's hope for you yet." Gabriel eyed her attire disapprovingly. "But not dressed like that."

Smiling, she padded barefoot down a corridor and reappeared a moment later in stretch jeans and a Real Madrid jersey. In the kitchen she prepared *café con leche*. They drank it at a table overlooking the narrow street. It was lined with luxury apartment buildings, designer clothing boutiques, and trendy bars and restaurants. Magdalena certainly belonged in a place like this, thought Gabriel. It was a pity she hadn't come by it honestly.

"Your skin is the color of Spanish saddle leather," she informed him. "Where have you been?"

"Circumnavigating the globe on my sailboat with my wife and children."

"Did you make any new discoveries?"

"Only the identity of the forger." He looked down at her paint-smudged hands. "I see you're working again."

She nodded. "Late night."

"Anything good?"

"A soon-to-be rediscovered Madonna and child attributed to the circle of Raphael. You?"

"I've turned over a new leaf."

"Not even tempted?"

"To what?"

"Forge a painting or two," said Magdalena. "I would be honored to serve as your front woman. But only if you agree to a fifty-fifty split of the profits."

"Perhaps I was mistaken," said Gabriel. "Perhaps you're a hopeless case, after all."

She smiled and drank her coffee. "I'm not a perfect person, Mr. Allon. But I've turned over a new leaf as well. And in case you're still wondering, I'm not the forger."

"If I thought you were, I would have arrived here with a contingent of Guardia Civil to take you into custody."

"I've been expecting them." She took up her phone and opened the web browser. "Have you read the news from Germany lately? Herr Hassler is now cooperating with federal prosecutors. It's only a matter of time before they request my extradition."

"I prevented a major terrorist attack on the Cologne Cathedral not long ago. If it becomes necessary, I can call in the chit."

"What about the Belgians?"

"Brussels and Antwerp are the organized crime capitals of Europe. I doubt the Belgian police will seek your extradition over a few fake paintings."

"Surely the FBI knows about me."

"And me as well," replied Gabriel. "For the moment, at least, they're inclined to keep our names out of it." He looked up at the unframed painting leaning against the wall. "Yours?"

Magdalena nodded. "It's the one I painted after Phillip and Leonard Silk tried to kill you in Paris. Self-portrait of a front woman."

"It's not half bad."

"My new canvases are much better. I'd love to show them to you, but I'm afraid my studio is filled with half-finished forgeries at the moment."

There were no forgeries, of course—only wildly original works executed by an artist of immense talent and technical skill. Gabriel drifted from canvas to canvas, spellbound.

"What do you think?" asked Magdalena.

"I think Phillip Somerset's greatest crime was depriving the world of your work." Gabriel placed a hand thoughtfully to his chin. "The question is, what should we do with them?"

"We?"

"I would be honored to serve as your front man. I insist, however, on receiving no share of the profits."

"You drive a hard bargain, Mr. Allon. But how do you intend to bring the works to market?"

"With a show at a premier gallery, in a major art world hub. The kind of show that will turn you into a billion-dollar global brand. Anyone who's anyone will be there. And by the end of the night, everyone will know your name."

"For all the right reasons, I hope," said Magdalena. "But where will this show take place?"

"Galerie Olivia Watson in London."

Her face brightened. "Would you really do that for me?"

"On one condition."

"The forger's name?"

He nodded.

"It was me, Mr. Allon. I executed all those undetectable Old Master paintings between shifts at El Pote Español and Katz's Delicatessen." She threw her arms around his neck. "How can I possibly repay you?"

"By allowing me to buy one of your paintings."

"Only if you promise never to sell it for a profit."

"Deal," said Gabriel.

75

Equus

Exactly forty-eight hours later—after yet another transatlantic flight to JFK and a brief stay at a Courtyard Marriott in downtown Stamford, Connecticut—Gabriel slid behind the wheel of a rented American-made sedan and drove into a blinding sunrise to Westport. It was a few minutes after seven when he arrived at Equus Analytics. Aiden Gallagher's flashy BMW 7 Series was nowhere in sight.

Gabriel lowered the portfolio case to the asphalt, drew his Solaris mobile phone, and dialed. Yuval Gershon of Unit 8200 answered instantly. "Ready?" he asked.

"Why else would I be calling?"

Yuval remotely unlocked the door. "Enjoy."

Gabriel slipped the phone into his pocket, picked up the portfolio case, and headed inside.

———

The laboratory was in darkness, the shades tightly drawn. Gabriel switched on his phone's flashlight and directed the beam toward the painting mounted on the Bruker M6 Jetstream spatial imaging device. A portrait of a woman, late twenties or early thirties, wearing a gown of gold silk trimmed in white lace. Any fool could see that the dimensions of the canvas were 115 by 92 centimeters. Gabriel snapped a photograph of the woman's pale cheek. The appearance of the craquelure gave him a funny feeling at the back of his neck.

He placed the portfolio case on an examination table and climbed the stairs to the second floor. There was a single room, identical in size to the lab below. At the end overlooking Riverside Avenue were some twenty wooden shipping crates, each containing a painting awaiting examination by the esteemed Aiden Gallagher. Only one of the crates had been opened, the one that had been used to ship the painting now secured to the Bruker. It had been sent to Equus Analytics by the Old Masters department of Sotheby's in New York.

At the opposite end of the room was an easel, a trolley, and a portable fume extractor. The drawers of the trolley were empty and spotlessly clean. The easel was empty, as well. Gabriel played the beam of the flashlight over the utility tray. Lead white. Charcoal black. Madder lake. Vermilion. Indigo. Green earth. Lapis lazuli. Red and yellow ocher.

Downstairs, he removed the riverscape from the portfolio case and laid it on the examination table. Next to it he placed two reports. One was from France's National Center for Research and Restoration; the other, Equus Analytics. Then he switched off the flashlight and waited. Two hours and twelve minutes later, a car drew up in the parking lot. They would settle the matter quietly, thought Gabriel, and never speak of it again.

———

The museum-grade alarm system emitted eight sharp chirps, and a moment later Aiden Gallagher strode through the door. He wore khaki trousers and a V-neck pullover. He stretched a hand toward the light switch, then hesitated, as though aware of a presence in the laboratory.

Finally the overhead fluorescent panels flickered into life. Aiden Gallagher drew a sharp breath of astonishment and backpedaled. "How did you get in here, Allon?"

"You left the door open. Fortunately, I happened to be in the neighborhood."

Gallagher started to dial a number on his mobile phone.

"I wouldn't, Aiden. You'll only make things worse for yourself."

Gallagher lowered the phone. "Why are you here?"

"You owe my friend Sarah Bancroft seventy-five thousand dollars."

"For what?"

Gabriel lowered his gaze toward *A River Scene with Distant Windmills*. "You assured us that there were polar fleece fibers embedded in the surface paint, ironclad proof that it was a forgery. But a second analysis of the painting has determined that you were incorrect."

"Who conducted this review?"

"The National Center for Research and Restoration."

Gallagher offered Gabriel a half-smile. "Isn't that the same laboratory that mistakenly authenticated those four forgeries that ended up hanging in the Louvre?"

"Theirs was an honest mistake. Yours wasn't. And by the way," added Gabriel, "I knew that Cranach was a forgery the instant I laid eyes on it." He pointed toward the painting attached to the Bruker. "And I certainly don't need a spatial imaging device to tell me that Van Dyck is a forgery as well."

"Based on what I've seen thus far, I'm inclined to accept it as authentic."

"I'm sure you would. But that would be a miscalculation on your part."

"How so?"

"The smarter play is to take all of your forgeries out of circulation, one by one. You'll be the hero of the art world. And you'll get even richer in the process. By my calculation, the paintings upstairs alone will add a million and a half dollars to Equus's bottom line."

"Thanks to the Somerset scandal, my fee is now one hundred thousand for rush jobs. Therefore, those paintings represent two million in new business."

"I didn't hear a denial, Aiden."

"That I'm the forger? I didn't think one was necessary. Your theory is ludicrous."

"You're a trained painter and restorer, and a specialist in provenance research and authentication. Which means you know how to select works that will be accepted by the art world and, more important, how to construct and execute them. But the best part of your scheme is that you were in a unique position to authenticate your own forgeries." Gabriel looked down at *A River Scene with Distant Windmills*. "If only you had authenticated that one, you and Phillip might still be in business." He paused. "And I wouldn't be here now."

"I didn't authenticate that painting, Allon, because it's an obvious forgery."

"Obvious to me, certainly. But not to most connoisseurs. That's why you and Phillip decided that I had to die. You told us that you had found fleece fibers in the painting because it's the most common mistake made by inexperienced forgers. It's also something that could be discovered during, say, a hurried preliminary examination conducted over a weekend. When we collected the painting on Monday afternoon, you asked when we were planning to confront Georges Fleury. And Sarah foolishly answered truthfully."

"Do you realize how insane you sound?"

"I haven't arrived at the good part yet." Gabriel took a step closer to Gallagher. "You are a member of a very small club, Aiden. Its membership is limited to those lucky souls who have tried to kill me or one of my friends and are still walking the face of the earth. So if I were you, I'd stop smiling. Otherwise, I'm liable to lose my temper."

Gallagher regarded Gabriel without expression. "I'm not the man you think I am, Allon."

"I *know* you are."

"Prove it."

"I can't. You and Phillip were too careful. And the condition of your atelier upstairs suggests that you have gone to extraordinary lengths to conceal the evidence of your crimes."

Gallagher indicated the French report. "May I?"

"By all means."

He picked up the document and began to read. After a moment he said, "They weren't able to reach an opinion as to the authenticity." There was a trace of pride in his voice, faint but unmistakable. "Even their foremost expert on Golden Age Dutch painters couldn't rule out the possibility that it's real."

"But you and I both know it isn't. Which is why I'd like to borrow a laboratory knife, please."

Gallagher hesitated. Then he opened a drawer and laid an Olfa AK-1 on the tabletop.

"Perhaps you should do it," suggested Gabriel.

"Be my guest."

Gabriel grasped the high-quality knife by its yellow handle and cleaved two irreparable horizontal gashes through the painting. He was about to inflict a third when Gallagher seized his wrist. The Dubliner's hand was trembling.

"That's quite enough." He relaxed his grip. "There's no need to mutilate the bloody thing."

Gabriel sliced the painting a third time before ripping the swaths of canvas from the stretcher. Then, knife in hand, he approached *Portrait of an Unknown Woman*.

"Don't touch it," said Gallagher evenly.

"Why not?"

"Because that painting is a genuine Van Dyck."

"That painting," said Gabriel, "is one of your forgeries."

"Are you prepared to wager fifteen million dollars?"

"Is that how much Phillip got for it?"

Receiving no answer, Gabriel removed the painting from the Bruker and cut it to ribbons. Looking up, he saw Aiden Gallagher gazing at the ruined painting, his face bloodless with rage.

"Why did you do that?"

"The better question is, why did you paint it? Was it only for the money? Or did you enjoy making fools of people like Julian Isherwood and Sarah Bancroft?" Gabriel laid the laboratory knife on the examination table. "You owe them seventy-five thousand dollars."

"The contract specifically said that the money is nonrefundable."

"In that case, perhaps we can reach a compromise."

"How much did you have in mind?"

Gabriel smiled.

It did not take long to arrive at a figure—hardly surprising, for there was no negotiation involved. Gabriel simply named his price, and Aiden Gallagher, after a moment or two of sputtering remonstration, wrote out the check. The Irishman then requested reimbursement for the Van Dyck. Gabriel laid a five-euro banknote on the examination table and, check in hand, went into the sunlit Connecticut morning.

He took his time driving back to JFK but still managed to arrive four hours before his flight was scheduled to depart. He dined poorly in the food hall, purchased gifts for Chiara and the children in the duty-free shops, and then wandered over to his assigned gate. There he removed the check from the breast pocket of his handmade Italian sport coat—a check for the sum of $10 million, payable to Isherwood Fine Arts.

Included in the final settlement was $75,000 for the fraudulent report from Equus Analytics, $3.4 million for the forged Van Dyck, $1.1 million for the forged Albert Cuyp, $100,000 for the Old Master canvases that Gabriel used for his own forgeries, and $525,000 in assorted expenses such as first-class air travel, five-star hotel rooms, and three-olive Belvedere martinis. And then, of course, there was the $4.8 million that Sarah Bancroft had lost in the collapse of Masterpiece Art Ventures.

All in all, thought Gabriel, it was a rather satisfying end to the story. He rang Chiara in Venice and gave her the good news.

"Reprobate," she said, and laughed hysterically.

Author's Note

Portrait of an Unknown Woman is a work of entertainment and should be read as nothing more. The names, characters, places, and incidents portrayed in the story are the product of the author's imagination or have been used fictitiously. Any resemblance to actual persons, living or dead, businesses, companies, events, or locales is entirely coincidental.

Visitors to the *sestiere* of San Polo will search in vain for the converted palazzo overlooking the Grand Canal where Gabriel Allon, after a long and tumultuous career with Israeli intelligence, has taken up residence with his wife and two young children. The business office of the Tiepolo Restoration Company is likewise impossible to find, for no such enterprise exists. The Andrea Bocelli song playing in the Allon family's kitchen in chapter 6 is "Chiara," from the 2001 album *Cieli di Toscana*. I listened to the CD frequently while writing the first draft of *The Confessor* in 2002 and gave the name to the beautiful daughter of the chief rabbi of Venice, Jacob Zolli. Irene Allon is named for her grandmother, who was one of the early State of Israel's most important artists. Her twin brother is named for the Italian High Renaissance painter Raffaello Sanzio da Urbino, better known as Raphael.

The fictitious Umbrian estate known as Villa dei Fiori appeared for the first time in *Moscow Rules*, a novel I conceived during an extended stay on a similar property. The staff took wonderful care of my family and me, and I repaid their kindness by turning them into minor but important characters in the story. Regrettably, several shopkeepers in the town of Amelia suffered the same fate in the novel's sequel, *The Defector*.

There is indeed a suite named for the conductor Leonard Bernstein at the Hôtel de Crillon in Paris, and Chez Janou is without question one of the city's better bistros. Nevertheless, the Swiss violinist Anna Rolfe could not have sent a low murmur through its brightly lit dining room, because Anna is the product of my imagination. So, too, are Maurice Durand and Georges Fleury, the owners of a disreputable art gallery in the Eighth Arrondissement. The art squad of the Police Nationale is in fact known as the Central Office for the Fight against Cultural Goods Trafficking—it definitely sounds better in French—but its personnel do not work in the historic building located at 36 Quai des Orfèvres.

Thankfully, there is no art-based hedge fund known as Masterpiece Art Ventures, and the crimes of my fictitious Phillip Somerset are entirely my creation. I included the names of real auction houses because, like the names of great painters, they are part of the art world's lexicon. It was not my intention to suggest in any way that companies such as Christie's or Sotheby's knowingly trade in forged paintings. Nor did I wish to leave the impression that the art-based lending units of JPMorgan Chase and Bank of America would accept forged paintings as collateral. Deepest apologies to the head of security at the Pierre for Gabriel's unconscionable behavior during his brief stay. The historic hotel on East Sixty-First Street is one of New York's finest and would never employ the likes of my fictitious Ray Bennett.

The madcap menagerie of London art dealers, museum curators, auctioneers, and journalists who grace the pages of *Portrait of an Unknown Woman* are invented from whole cloth, as are their sometimes questionable personal and professional antics. There is indeed an enchanting art gallery on the northeast corner of Mason's Yard, but it is owned by Patrick Matthiesen, one of the world's most successful and respected Old Master art dealers. A brilliant art historian blessed with an infallible eye, Patrick never would have fallen for a forged Van Dyck, even one as skillfully executed as the painting depicted in the story.

The same cannot be said, however, for many of Patrick's colleagues and competitors. Indeed, in the past quarter century, the multibillion-dollar global business known as the art world has been shaken by a series of high-profile forgery scandals that have raised unsettling questions about the oftentimes subjective process used to determine the origin and authenticity of a painting. Each of the forgery rings utilized some version of the same hackneyed provenance trap—newly rediscovered paintings emerging from a previously unknown collection—and yet each managed to deceive the experts and connoisseurs of the commercial art world with remarkable ease.

John Myatt, a songwriter and part-time art teacher with a knack for mimicking the great painters, was raising two small children alone in a run-down farmhouse in Staffordshire when he made the acquaintance of a clever trickster named John Drewe. Together the two men perpetrated what Scotland Yard described as "the biggest art fraud of the twentieth century." With Myatt supplying the canvases and Drewe the counterfeit provenances, the pair foisted more than 250 forgeries on the art market—for which Drewe pocketed more than £25 million. Many of the forgeries were sold through venerable London auction houses, including several works, purportedly by the French painter Jean Dubuffet, that went under the gavel during a glamorous evening sale at Christie's in King Street. In the audience that night, feeling slightly underdressed, was the forger who had created them. The Dubuffet Foundation, caretaker of the artist's oeuvre, had declared the works to be authentic.

On the other side of the English Channel, two other forgers were simultaneously wreaking havoc on the art world—and making millions in the process. One was Guy Ribes, a gifted painter who could produce a convincing "Chagall" or "Picasso" in a matter of minutes. According to French police and prosecutors, Ribes and a network of crooked dealers likely introduced more than a thousand forged paintings into the art market, most of which remain in circulation. Ribes's German counterpart, Wolfgang Beltracchi, was similarly prolific, sometimes producing as many as ten canvases a month. It was Beltracchi's wife, Helene—not my fictitious Françoise Vionnet—who effortlessly sold a forged "Georges Valmier" to a prominent European auction house after only a brief examination.

Within a few short years, the Beltracchis were selling forgeries through all the major auction houses, all purportedly from the same hitherto unknown collection. In the process, they became fabulously rich. They traveled the world aboard an eighty-foot sailboat, cared for by a crew of five. Their real estate portfolio included a $7 million villa in the German city of Freiburg and a sprawling estate, Domaine des Rivettes, in the French wine country of Languedoc. Among their many victims was the actor and art collector Steve Martin, who purchased a fake Heinrich Campendonk for $860,000 through Galerie Cazeau-Béraudière of Paris in 2004.

One might have assumed that Knoedler & Company, the oldest commercial art gallery in New York, would have been resistant to the virus spreading through the European markets. But in 1995, when an unknown art dealer named Glafira Rosales appeared at the gallery with a "Rothko" wrapped in cardboard, Knoedler president Ann Freedman apparently saw no reason to be suspicious. In the decade that followed, Rosales sold or consigned nearly forty Abstract Expressionist works to Knoedler & Company, including canvases said to have been painted by Jackson Pollock, Lee Krasner, Franz Kline, Robert Motherwell, and Willem de Kooning.

As it turned out, Glafira Rosales was the front woman for an international forgery network that included her Spanish boyfriend, José Carlos Bergantiños Díaz, and his brother. The forger was a Chinese immigrant named Pei-Shen Qian, who worked out of his garage in Queens. According to prosecutors, Bergantiños Diáz discovered Qian selling copies on a street in Lower Manhattan, and recruited him. Qian was paid about $9,000 for each forgery, a tiny fraction of what they fetched at Knoedler. Besieged by lawsuits, the storied gallery closed its doors in November 2011.

With all due respect to the Abstract Expressionists, whom I revere, it is one thing to forge a Motherwell or a Rothko, quite another to execute a convincing Lucas Cranach the Elder. For that reason alone, a French judge sent shockwaves through the art world in March 2016, when she ordered the seizure of *Venus with a Veil*, the star attraction of a successful exhibition at the Caumont Centre d'Art in the southern French city of Aix-en-Provence. An exhaustive 213-page scientific analysis of the painting—the crown jewel of the enormous collection controlled by the prince of Liechtenstein—would later conclude that it could not have come from Cranach's workshop. Among the many red flags cited in the report was the appearance of the craquelure, which was said to be "inconsistent with normal aging." Representatives of His Serene Highness took issue with the findings and demanded the painting's immediate return. At the time of this writing, *Venus* was listed on the official website for the Princely Collections and on display in the Garden Palace in Vienna.

But it was the identity of the painting's previous owner—the French collector-turned-dealer Giuliano Ruffini—that so unnerved the wider art world. Several previously unknown works had recently emerged from Ruffini's inventory, including *Portrait of a Man*, purportedly by the Dutch Golden Age painter Frans Hals. Experts at the Louvre examined the painting in 2008 and declared it *un trésor national* that should never be allowed to leave French soil. Their counterparts at the Mauritshuis in The Hague were similarly rapturous, with one senior curator calling the painting "a very important addition to Hals's oeuvre." No one seemed overly concerned by the thinness of the provenance. The canvas, said the experts, spoke for itself.

For reasons never made clear, the Louvre chose not to acquire the painting, and in 2010 it was purchased by a London art dealer and an art investor for a reported $3 million. Just one year later, the pair sold the portrait to a prominent American collector for more than three times what they had paid for it. The prominent collector, after learning that *Venus* had been seized by the French, wisely subjected his $10 million "Frans Hals" to scientific testing and was told, in no uncertain terms, that it was a fake. Sotheby's quickly agreed to return the prominent American collector's money and sought restitution from the London dealer and the art investor. At which point the lawsuits began to fly.

As many as twenty-five suspect Old Master canvases, with an estimated market value of some $255 million, have emerged from the same collection—including *David with the Head of Goliath*, purportedly by Orazio Gentileschi, which was displayed at the National Gallery in London. It was not the first time the esteemed museum had exhibited a misattributed or fraudulent work. In 2010, the gallery aired its curatorial dirty laundry in a six-room exhibition called "Fakes, Mistakes, and Discoveries." Room 5 featured *An Allegory*. Acquired by the museum in 1874, it was thought to be the work of the Early Renaissance Florentine painter Sandro Botticelli. In truth, it was a pastiche executed by a later follower. More recently, a Swiss art research company utilizing a pioneering form of artificial intelligence determined that *Samson and Delilah*, one of the National Gallery's most prized paintings, was almost certainly *not* the work of Sir Peter Paul Rubens.

The National Gallery purchased the painting in 1980—at Christie's auction house in London—for $5.4 million. At the time, it was the third-highest price ever paid for a work of art. In today's market a sale of that size would hardly be newsworthy, as soaring prices have turned paintings into yet another asset class for the superrich—or, in the words of the late Manhattan art dealer Eugene Thaw, "a commodity like pork bellies or wheat." A. Alfred Taubman, the shopping mall developer and fast-food investor who purchased Sotheby's in 1983, cynically observed that "a precious painting by Degas and a frosted mug of root beer" had much in common, at least when it came to the potential for profit. In April 2002, Taubman was sentenced to a year in prison for his role in the price-fixing scheme with rival Christie's that swindled customers out of more than $100 million.

Increasingly, much of the world's most valuable art resides not in museums or private homes but in darkened, climate-controlled vaults. More than a million paintings are reportedly hidden away in the Geneva Free Port, including at least a thousand works by Pablo Picasso. Many collectors and curators are troubled by the degree to which paintings have become just another investment vehicle. But those who are in the business of buying and selling art for profit are just as likely to disagree. "Paintings," the New York gallery owner David Nash told the *New York Times* in 2016, "are not a public good."

Most change hands under conditions of absolute secrecy, at ever-increasing prices, with little or no oversight. It is little wonder, then, that the art world has been beset by a succession of multimillion-dollar forgery scandals. The problem is doubtless made worse by the apathy of the courts and police. Remarkably, none of the forgers and their accomplices mentioned above received more than a slap on the wrist for their crimes. Front woman Glafira Rosales was sentenced to time served for her role in the Knoedler scandal. John Myatt and Wolfgang Beltracchi, after serving brief prison terms, now make their livings selling "genuine fakes" and other original works online. Beltracchi, during an interview with the CBS News program *60 Minutes*, expressed only one regret— that he had used the inaccurately labeled tube of titanium white paint that had led to his exposure.

The French forger Guy Ribes was likewise able to put his talent to legitimate use. It is Ribes, not actor Michel Bouquet, who mimics the brushstrokes of Auguste-Pierre Renoir in a 2012 film about the final years of the painter's life. Ribes also executed the "Renoirs" used in the film's production—with the assistance of the Musée d'Orsay, which granted him a private viewing of the Renoirs in its possession, including several not on public display. James Ivory lamented the fact that the notorious French art forger had not been available to work on the 1996 motion picture *Surviving Picasso*. Said the legendary director: "It would have been, visually, a different film."

Acknowledgments

I am grateful to my wife, Jamie Gangel, who listened patiently while I worked out the intricate plot and twists of *Portrait of an Unknown Woman* and then skillfully edited the first draft of my typescript. My debt to her is immeasurable, as is my love.

Anthony Scaramucci, founder of the investment firm Skybridge Capital, took time out of his busy schedule to help me create a fraudulent art-based hedge fund propped up by the sale and collateralization of forged paintings. London art dealer Patrick Matthiesen patiently answered each of my questions, as did Maxwell L. Anderson, who has five times served as the director of a North American art museum, including the Whitney Museum of American Art in New York. Not to be outdone, renowned art conservator David Bull—for better or worse, he is known in certain circles as "the real Gabriel Allon"—read my nearly 600-page typescript in its entirety, all while rushing to complete the restoration of a canvas by the Italian Renaissance artist Jacopo Bassano.

Legendary *Vanity Fair* writer-at-large Marie Brenner gave me invaluable insight into her work and the New York art world; and David Friend, the magazine's editor of creative development, shared harrowing stories of past investigations into the affairs of powerful men. I can say with certainty that there is a conference room in *Vanity Fair*'s newsroom on the twenty-fifth floor of One World Trade Center—and that it overlooks New York Harbor.

Otherwise, the chaotic sequence of events depicted in the climax of *Portrait of an Unknown Woman* bears little resemblance to the way *Vanity Fair* reports, edits, and publishes consequential pieces of investigative journalism.

My Los Angeles super-lawyer Michael Gendler was, needless to say, a source of wise counsel. Louis Toscano, my dear friend and long-time editor, made countless improvements to the novel, as did Kathy Crosby, my eagle-eyed personal copy editor. Any typographical errors that slipped through their formidable gauntlet are my responsibility, not theirs.

I consulted more than a hundred newspaper and magazine articles while writing *Portrait of an Unknown Woman*, far too many to cite here. I owe a special debt to the reporters of *Artnet*, *ARTnews*, the *Art Newspaper*, the *Guardian*, and the *New York Times* for their coverage of the most recent Old Master forgery scandal. Five books were especially helpful: Anthony M. Amore, *The Art of the Con: The Most Notorious Fakes, Frauds, and Forgeries in the Art World*; Laney Salisbury and Aly Sujo, *Provenance: How a Con Man and a Forger Rewrote the History of Modern Art*; Noah Charney, *The Art of Forgery: The Minds, Motives and Methods of Master Forgers*; Thomas Hoving, *False Impressions: The Hunt for Big-Time Art Fakes*; and Michael Shnayerson, *Boom: Mad Money, Mega Dealers, and the Rise of Contemporary Art*.

We are blessed with family and friends who fill our lives with love and laughter at critical times during the writing year, especially Jeff Zucker, Phil Griffin, Andrew Lack, Noah Oppenheim, Esther Fein and David Remnick, Elsa Walsh and Bob Woodward, Susan St. James and Dick Ebersol, Jane and Burt Bacharach, Stacey and Henry Winkler, Pete Williams and David Gardner, Virginia Moseley and Tom Nides, Cindi and Mitchell Berger, Donna and Michael Bass, Nancy Dubuc and Michael Kizilbash, Susanna Aaron and Gary Ginsburg, Elena Nachmanoff, Ron Meyer, Andy Lassner, and Peggy Noonan. Also, a heartfelt thanks to the team at HarperCollins, especially

Brian Murray, Jonathan Burnham, Doug Jones, Leah Wasielewski, Sarah Ried, Mark Ferguson, Leslie Cohen, Josh Marwell, Robin Bilardello, Milan Bozic, David Koral, Leah Carlson-Stanisic, Carolyn Robson, Chantal Restivo-Alessi, Frank Albanese, Josh Marwell, and Amy Baker.

Finally, my children, Lily and Nicholas, were a constant source of inspiration and support. Nicholas, now a graduate student at the Security Studies Program at Georgetown University's School of Foreign Service, was once again forced to reside under the same roof as his father as I struggled to complete this, the twenty-fifth novel of my career. And one wonders why neither he nor his twin sister, a successful business consultant, has chosen to pursue a career as a writer.

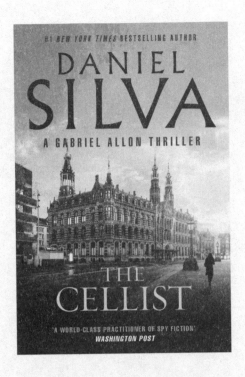

#1 NEW YORK TIMES BESTSELLING AUTHOR

DANIEL
SILVA

A GABRIEL ALLON THRILLER

THE
CELLIST

'A WORLD-CLASS PRACTITIONER OF SPY FICTION'
WASHINGTON POST

The most beautiful music hides the deadliest secrets ...

Once Russia's richest man, Victor Orlov now resides in exile in London, waging a crusade against the kleptocrats in the Kremlin. His mansion is protected by armed bodyguards. Yet somehow, on a rainy summer evening, in the midst of a global pandemic, Russia's vengeful president finally manages to cross Orlov's name off his kill list.

Before him was the receiver from his landline telephone, a half-drunk glass of red wine, and a stack of documents ...

The documents, contaminated with a deadly nerve agent, were delivered by a prominent investigative reporter. And when the reporter vanishes hours after the killing, MI6 concludes she is a Moscow Center assassin who penetrated the billionaire's formidable defenses. But Gabriel Allon believes his friends in British intelligence are dangerously mistaken. His search for the truth will take him to Geneva, where a private intelligence service is plotting an act of violence that will plunge an already divided America into chaos. Only Allon, with the help of a brilliant young woman employed by the world's dirtiest bank, can stop it ...

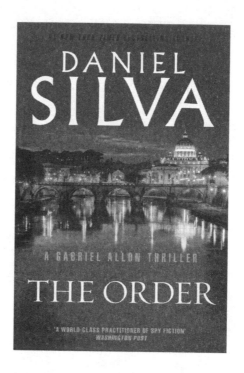

When Pope Paul VII dies suddenly, apparently of a heart attack, legendary spy and art restorer Gabriel Allon is quickly summoned to Rome. The Holy Father's loyal private secretary, Archbishop Luigi Donati, suspects his master was murdered. The Swiss Guard who was standing watch the night of the pope's death is missing. So, too, is the letter the Holy Father was writing during the final hours of his life. A letter that was addressed to an old friend: Gabriel.

While researching in the Vatican Secret Archives, I came upon a most remarkable book ...

The book is a long-suppressed gospel that calls into question the accuracy of the New Testament's depiction of one of the most portentous events in human history. For that reason alone, the Order of St. Helena will stop at nothing to keep it out of Gabriel's hands. A shadowy Catholic society with ties to the European far right, the Order is plotting to seize control of the papacy. And it is only the beginning ...

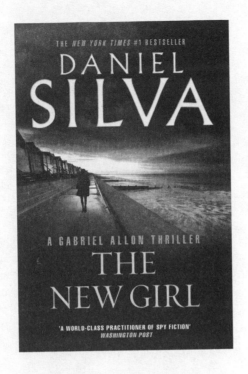

THE *NEW YORK TIMES* #1 BESTSELLER

DANIEL SILVA

A GABRIEL ALLON THRILLER

THE NEW GIRL

'A WORLD-CLASS PRACTITIONER OF SPY FICTION'
WASHINGTON POST

NOW YOU SEE HER.
NOW YOU DON'T.
THE NEW GIRL

A novel of intrigue, betrayal, and revenge.

At an exclusive private school in Switzerland, mystery surrounds the identity of the beautiful girl who arrives each morning and leaves each afternoon in a heavily protected motorcade fit for a head of state. She is said to be the daughter of a wealthy international businessman. She is not.

And when she is brutally kidnapped across the border in the Haute-Savoie region of France, Gabriel Allon, the legendary chief of Israeli intelligence, is thrust into a deadly secret war with an old enemy that will determine the future of the Middle East-and perhaps the world ...

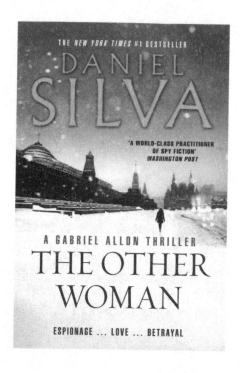

THE *NEW YORK TIMES* #1 BESTSELLER

DANIEL SILVA

'A WORLD-CLASS PRACTITIONER
OF SPY FICTION'
WASHINGTON POST

A GABRIEL ALLON THRILLER

THE OTHER WOMAN

ESPIONAGE ... LOVE ... BETRAYAL

She was his best-kept secret ...

In an isolated village in the mountains of Andalusia, a mysterious Frenchwoman begins work on a dangerous memoir. It is the story of a man she once loved in the Beirut of old, and a child taken from her in treason's name. The woman is the keeper of the Kremlin's most closely guarded secret. Long ago, the KGB inserted a mole into the heart of the West—a mole who stands on the doorstep of ultimate power.

Only one man can unravel the conspiracy: Gabriel Allon, the legendary art restorer and assassin who serves as the chief of Israel's vaunted secret intelligence service. Gabriel has battled the dark forces of the new Russia before, at great personal cost. Now he and the Russians will engage in a final epic showdown, with the fate of the post-war global order hanging in the balance.